THE ESSENTIAL ARTICLES SERIES

Bernard N. Schilling

General Editor

Essential Articles

for the study of
Thomas More

Edited with an Introduction
and Bibliography by
R. S. Sylvester
and
G. P. Marc'hadour

Archon Books   Hamden, Connecticut   1977

Library of Congress Cataloging in Publication Data
Main entry under title:

Essential articles for the study of Thomas More.

   (The Essential articles series)
   Bibliography: p.
   1. More, Thomas, Sir, Saint, 1478-1535--Addresses,
essays, lectures. 2. Christian saints--Great Britain--
Biography--Addresses, essays, lectures. 3. Statesmen--
Great Britain--Biography--Addresses, essays, lectures.
I. Sylvester, Richard Standish. II. Marc'hadour,
Germain.
DA334.M8E85   942.05'2'0924 [B]   76-42303
ISBN 0-208-01554-X

© 1977 Richard S. Sylvester
All rights reserved

First published 1977 as an
Archon Book, an imprint of
The Shoe String Press, Inc.
Hamden, Connecticut 06514

Printed in the United States of America

CONTENTS

CONTENTS

PART IV: GENERAL VIEWS

FOREWORD

Immense resources are now available for literary study in England and America. The contributions to scholarship and criticism are so numerous and often so valuable that the student preparing himself for a career in literary teaching and study may be embarrassed, not to say overwhelmed. Yet from this mass of commentary certain titles have emerged which seem to compel attention. If one offers a seminar in one of the standard areas or periods of English literature, the syllabus will show year after year some items which cannot be omitted, some pieces every serious student should know. And with each new offering of the course, one must face the task of compiling a list of these selections for the seminar's reserve shelf, of searching out and culling the library's holdings, and reserving space for the twenty or thirty or forty volumes the list may demand. As if this were not enough, one must also attempt to repair or replace the volumes whose popularity has had the unfortunate side effects of frequent circulation and the concomitant wear, abuse, and general deterioration.

We propose an alternative to this procedure. We propose to select from the many learned journals, scholarly studies, and critical books the best selections available, the selections which consistently reappear on graduate seminar shelves and on undergraduate honors program reading lists. Let us choose from those articles which time has sanctioned, those too from the best of more recent performances, and let us draw them into a single volume of convenient size. This offers a clear gain in simplicity and usefulness. The articles chosen make up a body of knowledge that cannot fail to be valuable, and they act as models of the kind of contributions to learning which we are training our students to make themselves. And if we can have at hand a concentration of such articles for each of the standard areas, and several individual authors, we may conduct the study of these subjects with greater confidence, knowing more fully the extent and kind of reading we can take for granted. And, while we benefit our classes and students, we can also allow the library to keep the original editions of the articles on its shelves and so fulfill its proper and usual function.

The preceding paragraphs, written some 15 years ago, are still valid. We have reason to believe that our series has fulfilled its declared purposes: that the volumes have been useful to teachers, librarians and graduate students, that they have made a contribution to professional literary study.

From the beginning it was our aim to provide materials at a reasonable cost so that all those interested could afford to purchase them. Many factors in the recent inflationary spiral have required increased prices. However the editors and publishers have continued to make every effort to keep costs at a minimum.

We are pleased now to offer this fine volume, a truly comprehensive selection of the best in modern scholarship and criticism of the great Renaissance figure, Thomas More.

Rochester, N.Y.
June 7, 1976   B.N.S.

The Rev. Edward Surtz, S.J.

INTRODUCTION

When Thomas More, probably about 1505, presented his translation of the *Life of Pico* to a young nun, Joyeuse Lee, he offered his work as a New Year's gift, commenting, as he did so, that "It is, and of long time hath been, a custom in the beginning of the new year, friends to send between presents or gifts, as the witness of their love and friendship, and also signifying that they desire each to other that year a good continuance and prosperous end of that lucky beginning." More's greeting certainly expresses something of the sentiments felt by the editors of this volume, a collection which is dedicated to the memory of a man, the Reverend Edward Surtz, S.J., who did so much to foster "love and friendship" among those, many of them contributors here, who had the pleasure of knowing and working with him on Thomas More and related topics of Renaissance studies. It is equally and no less obviously true that we offer this volume as both a New Year's gift and a birthday present to Thomas More himself, publishing the collection at the beginning of a two-year period (1977–78) that will, on many different occasions, celebrate the five-hundredth anniversary of his birth.[1]

Even without the fortuitousness of a quincentennial, there would have been, in 1977, ample justification for a collection of articles like that presented here. Modern More scholarship can be viewed as beginning with the publication of T. E. Bridgett's biography, *Blessed Thomas More,* in 1891.[2] In the early years of the twentieth century, much of this scholarship was either inspired by or directly connected with the movement which led to More's canonization in 1935. Except for *Utopia,* More studies were centered, until the Second World War, in England, although important contributions, for example the work of Marie Delcourt in Belgium, of Joseph Delcourt in France, and of A. I. Taft in the United States, also came from abroad. A great generation of British scholars, following in Bridgett's footsteps, laid firm foundations for future studies. One singles out here the names of R. W. Chambers, P. E. Hallett, W. E. Campbell, E. V. Hitchcock, W. A. G. Doyle-Davidson, and A. W. Reed; their work culminated in the publication by the Early English Text Society of the sixteenth-century biographies of More and in the two volumes, published in 1927 and 1931, of the Eyre and Spottiswode edition of More's *English Works.*[3]

1. More was born on February 6 or 7, 1477 or 1478. Scholarly opinion now leans toward February 7, 1477 as the best date; for a full discussion, see G. Marc'hadour, *L'Univers de Thomas More* (Paris, Vrin, 1963), pp. 34–41.

2. For publishing data on this and other works cited in what follows, see the appended bibliography.

3. The plates for the third and fourth volumes of this planned eight volume edition were destroyed in an air raid during the war. The series has since been discontinued.

By the 1950s, it was clear that the leading edge of research on Thomas More had passed to America.[4] In 1947, Elizabeth F. Rogers' *The Correspondence of Sir Thomas More,* a work twenty-five years in the making, heralded a period (still continuing, one trusts) that has been tremendously productive for More scholarship and fully expressive of the new transatlantic interest in More. Father Surtz's work on *Utopia* and its backgrounds, J. H. Hexter's "radical" interpretation of More's masterpiece, the many articles by R. J. Schoeck, biographies by Theodore Maynard and Russell Ames, a bilingual edition of the Latin Poems by L. Bradner and C. A. Lynch—all these formed the rising crest of the wave that still flows so strongly to and from the western shores. In 1958, these efforts began to be consolidated as scholars joined together to work on and support the Yale Edition of More's *Complete Works,* a project which has now published eight of its planned sixteen volumes and which aims to finish its task by the mid-1980s. In 1963, the periodical *Moreana* was founded by Germain Marc'hadour, who has served as its executive secretary and editor for the last fourteen years. This journal, with its current comments on the state of More studies, has become as indispensable as the volumes of the Yale Edition for all serious students of Thomas More. Led partly by the example of *Moreana,* continental More scholarship has begun to flourish anew, not only in France, but also in Germany[5] and Italy. More's growing popularity in this century is also witnessed in not-so-far-away Japan where Paul Akio Sawada's *Thomas More Studies* now regularly appears.

In selecting the "essential" articles for this volume, the editors have tried to reflect the rich variety in the scholarship of this century that has begun to turn "the man for all seasons" into a man for all countries and climes.[6] Whether as a layman saint or as a pioneer of socialist thought, as a writer of English prose or as a political and religious martyr, Thomas More seems to speak with a special urgency to this restless age of ours. Some of the essays we have chosen might well be viewed as straightforwardly emphasizing this "popular" side of Thomas More; most of them, however, will be found to present either formidable scholarly research or suggestive, sophisticated criticism. In the best of these pieces, both virtues (learning and interpretive originality) combine happily with each other.

We have had, inevitably, to impose some rather severe restrictions on ourselves and on, as will be seen from the bibliography, the vast amount of material available to us. Chronologically, we begin with an 1892 chapter by Bridgett, not from his biography, but from his lesser known, but no less

4. For a review of this development, see G. Marc'hadour, "Thomas More aux États-Unis," *Études Anglaises,* 9 (1956), 314–22.

5. Here the work of Hubertus Schulte-Herbrüggen, whose *Checklist of Manuscript Materials for the Study of Thomas More* is soon to be published by the Yale University Press, must be singled out for special mention.

6. The editors have been most helpfully assisted in the work of selection by a poll taken among *Moreana* subscribers and by consultation with an editorial committee consisting of Clarence Miller, R. J. Schoeck, C. R. Thompson and J. B. Trapp. The editors, however, willingly assume full responsibility for the final selections.

warmly intimate, *Wit and Wisdom of Thomas More*. Our most recent selection
dates from 1972, an arbitrary time limit that could easily have been extended
to include more recent work.[7] Within this eighty-year period, we have for the
most part avoided reprinting articles or sections of books that remain in print
or are otherwise easily available to anyone with access to a large library. No one
working on More, we felt, would be long without the Introductions to the
volumes of the Yale Edition or would fail to make use of collections like the
recent *St. Thomas More: Action and Contemplation*. For the most part, too,
we have excluded articles already available in more or less "standard" collections. Thus our selection of articles on *Utopia* may seem constricted until one
considers the broad range of essays to be found in the volumes edited by Ligeia
Gallagher, Frank Manuel, and William Nelson. In general, we have tried to
avoid "influence articles," both those which attempt to trace influences upon
More and those which discuss the influence of his works on others. In the
former case, the field is still so embryonic that we found it difficult to evaluate the rather slim efforts already made; in the latter, especially so in the case
of the influence of the *Utopia*, the subject is so vast that it has become almost
a separate discipline.

Within these limits, we have tried not to let anything of major importance
escape us. In one or two instances problems involving excessive reprint fees or
inadequate translations led us to omissions that we would have been happy to
have avoided.[8] We have endeavored to focus on "seminal" articles, essays
which have proven their usefulness to a generation or more of scholars or
which, in our judgment, bid fair to do so in the years to come. The student, if
there be any such, who reads consecutively through this volume, will perhaps
find some of our decisions borne out by the large number of cross references
that occur among the individual articles. We trust that such mutually supporting evidence reflects no pedantic cliquishness but is rather a tribute to the
kinds of value that good scholarship establishes when it comes to know itself
well.

Our authors often disagree with each other, occasionally in matters of fact,
more frequently in shading or emphasis. More's life and works raise many
problems, not all of them, perhaps, open to final answers—at least not until
research has been carried further than it has so far advanced. We have looked,
on the whole, for positive positions, articles which throw new light on More
and his milieu and do so in a sympathetic way. There are some eulogies, to be
sure, none warmer than G. K. Chesterton's brief 1929 address, so startling an
utterance in its day and, so it seems now, a prophecy three quarters fulfilled
in 1976. But we have not eschewed negative views like G. G. Coulton's restive

7. It should also be noted that two articles (those by Michael Anderegg and Hugh
Aveling) have been specifically written for this volume and that several others have been
extensively revised by the authors before re-publication here.

8. We take this opportunity, however, to thank authors, heirs, and publishers for their
admirable generosity in allowing us to reprint, at no cost, the articles upon which they
hold copyright. Specific permissions are acknowledged at the foot of the first page of
each article.

summation of the antipathies of a lifetime. There is material enough here for the reader to come to grips with the eternal debate over the meaning of *Utopia* or to evaluate for himself the issues and principles that were at stake during More's trial. The problem of conscience, as it affected More, looms large in many articles. So too does the much vexed question of religious toleration and More's attitude toward it. A few of the articles might, at first glance, appear to be mere notes,[9] but upon close study they will be found to portray larger matters in a new light.

The collection, as a unit, also provides a kind of anthology of More's writings. This incidental virtue, unappreciated by the editors until the volume was fully assembled, may well serve to introduce many to the charm that early Tudor prose and verse can still have for us today. At the same time, it is an indication of the temptation to quote More which arises for almost anyone who tries to write about him. A number of the essays deal directly with More's style, while several others analyze the artistic structuring that he was able to give to so many of his works. The articles as presented here are divided into four groups and are arranged, within each group, alphabetically by author. Section I offers biographical studies, section II centers on *Utopia;* section III deals with other works, and the final section presents general views of More's life and character. It is our hope that we have furnished enough for a feast, to be enjoyed course by course by each banqueter at his leisure.

R.S.S.
G.M.
Christmas, 1975

---

9. One thinks especially of the two short pieces on *Utopia* by J. Binder and R. J. Schoeck.

BIBLIOGRAPHY AND SHORT TITLES

Systematic scholarship on More being a recent phenomenon, the ordinary student will seldom have to consult ancient lore. Pending the completion of the Yale "Complete Works" Project, two older collections remain indispensable: *The Works of Sir Thomas More in the English Tongue*, London, 1557, cited here as "*EW*," and *Thomae Mori Opera Omnia Latina*, Frankfort and Leipzig, 1689. Erasmus, More's inseparable friend, is also being critically edited: *Opera Omnia Desiderii Erasmi Roterodami* (Amsterdam, 1969 f.), and his major works are being published in English as *The Collected Works of Erasmus* (Toronto, 1974 f.; cited here as "*CWE*"). Meanwhile Latin scholars continue to use Jean Le Clerc's monumental *Des. Erasmi Opera Omnia* (Leiden, 10 vols., 1703–06), an edition designated by the siglum "*LB*" from the initials of Lugdunum Batavorum, the Latin name of Leiden, and the P. S. Allen *Opus Epistolarum Des. Erasmi* (Oxford, 1906–58), often short-titled as *Erasmi Epistolae*, hence the current sigla "*EE*" or "Allen."

The scientific exploration of More's career, essential to an understanding of his personality and of his writings, began in 1830 with the publication of England's *State Papers* by J. S. Brewer, the first year to be covered (1518) being precisely that of More's entry into the King's Council. The companion *Calendar of Letters and Papers, Domestic and Foreign, of the Reign of Henry VIII* appeared in 21 volumes from 1862 to 1910. The research J. Gairdner put into it, as Brewer's first collaborator, led to his voluminous *Lollardy and the Reformation* (1908). Among the pioneer works of the 19th century, born of these newly exhumed documents, and all published in London, one should mention: Frederic Seebohm, *The Oxford Reformers of 1498*, "being a history of the fellow-work of Colet, Erasmus and More" (1867; revised eds. in 1869 and 1887); J. H. Lupton, *A Life of John Colet* (1887, slightly revised in 1909); T. E. Bridgett, *Life of Blessed John Fisher* (1890) and *Life and Writings of Sir Thomas More* (1891), both of which were revised for later editions. More and Fisher were beatified on December 29, 1886; Fisher's *English Works* had been collected by J. E. B. Mayor (EETS, 1876).

Several works of the next two decades: F. M. Nichols and P. S. Allen in editing and translating Erasmus' letters, A. F. Pollard on *Henry VIII* and *Wolsey*, A. D. Innes on *Ten Tudor Statesmen*, provided a firm canvas for projecting the likeness of More. The first large-scale professional study of his English writings fell to the lot of a French philologist, Joseph Delcourt, who was led accidentally (or providentially) to the great Londoner when he started bibliographical work on Erin's bard, the Thomas Moore of *Lalla Rookh*. His *Essai sur la langue de Sir Thomas More d'après ses oeuvres anglaises* (Paris, 1914) included the publication of 22 state letters exchanged between More and Wolsey. The prospect of More's canonization spurred critical interest in his character and in his literary labors, both of which were, by canonical requirement, subjected to close scrutiny. It inspired the grandiose plan of a facsimile edition of the 1557 folio: the two volumes which appeared (in 1927 and 1931) not only rendered that much of his work accessible, but brought together several scholars, one of whom, A. W. Reed, had prepared himself for the task with his important *Early Tudor Drama* (1926). P. E. Hallett, who was Vice-Postulator of the Cause, published several works of More and translated into English (1928) Stapleton's *Vita Mori* (1588). The other Tudor lives of More were published by the Early English Text Society: Harpsfield in 1932, Roper in 1935, Ro:Ba: (delayed by circumstances) in 1950. R. W. Chambers arranged for his *Thomas More* to coincide with the canonization: when he signed the preface (February 6, 1935), it was known that More and Fisher would be sainted in the spring.

Thomas More and His Friends, by E. M. G. Routh (1934), was one of several scholarly monographs which shed welcome oblique light on More. Others were *Thomas Lupset* by J. A. Gee (New Haven, 1928), *Richard Pace,* by J. Wegg (1932), *Cuthbert Tunstal,* by Ch. Sturge (1938), *John Skelton,* by Wm. Nelson (1939), the Tyndale labors of J. F. Mozley and S. L. Greenslade, not to mention books in English by European scholars, like J. Huizinga on Erasmus, H. de Vocht on Cranevelt, Busleiden and the Collegium Trilingue of Louvain, and H. W. Donner on More's own *Utopia.* A peak was reached in 1947 with the publication of the last volume of the Oxford *Erasmi Epistolae;* everyone of the eleven volumes contained precious More material, deliberately omitted by Elizabeth Rogers from her *Correspondence of Sir Thomas More* (cited here as "Rogers"), published in that same year and quoted myriads of times since. With the *Moreana 1478–1945* published in 1946 by F. and M. P. Sullivan, and the Chicago (1953) edition of *The Latin Poems of Thomas More* by L. Bradner and C. A. Lynch (cited here as *B.L.*), taking into account Gee's book on Lupset and the fact that an American, A. I. Taft, had edited More's *Apology* for the EETS (1930), a shift of More scholarship from the Old to the New World became perceptible. England retained its lead in history and biography. E. E. Reynolds' *Saint Thomas More* (1953) was the first step in that author's long series of books on More, Erasmus, and Fisher. That it was superseded by an altogether new life, *The Field Is Won* (Wheathampstead, 1968) dramatically illustrates the spectacular advance made over the course of fifteen years of intensive and often collective research. More's place in the intellectual and spiritual panorama of his day was clarified thanks to comprehensive studies, such as:

Philip Hughes, *The Reformation in England* (Vol. 1, London 1951)
C. S. Lewis, *English Literature in the Sixteenth Century* (Oxford, 1954)
G. R. Elton, *England Under the Tudors* (London, 1955)
E. M. Nugent, ed., *The Thought and Culture of the English Renaissance: an Anthology of Tudor Prose, 1481–1555* (Cambridge, 1956)
David Knowles, *The Religious Orders in England.* Vol. 3: *The Tudor Age* (Cambridge, 1959)

A. B. Emden, *A Biographical Register to the University of Oxford to A.D. 1500*, 3 vols. (Oxford, 1957–59)

J. A. Mason, *Humanism and Poetry in the Early Tudor Period* (London, 1959)

The 1950's were also an active period of examination of More's legal and civic involvements, conducted by the Thomas More Society under the leadership of Richard O'Sullivan.

America's contribution to this broad exploration can be sampled in E. H. Harbison, *The Christian Scholar in the Age of the Reformation* (New York, 1956) and Pearl Hogrefe, *The Sir Thomas More Circle* (Urbana, 1959), while some of its finest scholars, like E. Surtz and J. Hexter, by their analyses of *Utopia*, prepared themselves to edit that book within the Yale Thomas More Project. The Yale venture in its turn fostered a spirit of international coopera- tion and emulation, which resulted in the founding (1962) of the Amici Thomae Mori. The bulletin of that association, *Moreana*, has yielded several articles to this volume. It has published contributions by more than a hundred authors from some twenty countries, including Russia, Mexico, Japan, Egypt and India. No. 40 of the journal, a comprehensive Index to its vols. I–X (1963–73), is available separately and constitutes a guide to everything of importance that appeared in the "world of Thomas More" during that decade.

The Yale Edition of the Works of St. Thomas More

Complete Works Series

1. *English Poems, Life of Pico, Four Last Things.* Ed. R. S. Sylvester.
2. *Richard III.* Ed. R. S. Sylvester. Published 1963; reprinted, 1975. Cited as "*CW 2.*"
3. Part 1: *Lucian Translations.* Ed. Craig R. Thompson (Pennsylvania). Pub- lished 1974. Cited as "*CW 3, Part 1.*"
   Part 2: *Latin Poems*, Ed. L. Bradner, C. A. Lynch and R. P. Oliver.
4. *Utopia.* Ed. E. Surtz and J. H. Hexter. Published 1965; reprinted, 1974. Cited as "*CW 4.*"
5. *Responsio ad Lutherum.* Ed. J. Headley and trans. Sr. Scholastica Mande- ville. Published 1969. In two parts. Cited as "*CW 5.*"
6. *Dialogue Concerning Heresies.* Ed. T. M. C. Lawler, R. Marius, and G. Marc'hadour. In press, 1977.
7. *Supplication of Souls.* Ed. G. Marc'hadour. *Letter Against Frith, Letter to Bugenhagen*, Ed. E. F. Rogers.
8. *Confutation of Tyndale's Answer.* Ed. L. Schuster, R. Marius, J. Lusardi, and R. J. Schoeck. Published 1973. In three parts. Cited as "*CW 8.*"
9. *Apology.* Ed. J. B. Trapp. In press, 1977.
10. *Debellation of Salem and Bizance.* Ed. R. J. Schoeck and R. E. McGugan.
11. *Answer to a Poisoned Book.* Ed. C. Miller.
12. *Dialogue of Comfort.* Ed. L. L. Martz and F. Manley. Published 1976. Cited as "*CW 12.*"

13. *Treatise on the Passion, Treatise on the Blessed Body, Instructions and Prayers.* Ed. G. E. Haupt. Published 1976. Cited as *"CW 13."*
14. *De Tristitia Christi.* Ed. C. Miller. In two parts. Published 1976. Cited as *"CW 14."*
15. *Correspondence.* Ed. E. F. Rogers and H. Schulte Herbrüggen. In three parts.

Selected Works Series (Modern Spelling)

Utopia. Ed. E. Surtz. Published 1964. Hardbound and paperback.
Selected Letters. Ed. E. F. Rogers. Published 1961. Hardbound and paperback. Cited as *"SL."*
Richard III, with Selections from the English and Latin Poems. Ed. R. S. Sylvester. Published 1976. Hardbound and paperback.
A Dialogue of Comfort. Ed. F. Manley. In press, 1977.

Also available:

St. Thomas More: A Preliminary Bibliography. R. W. Gibson and J. Max Patrick. Published, 1961.
Thomas More's Prayer Book. Ed. L. L. Martz and R. S. Sylvester. Published 1969, reprinted 1976.
St. Thomas More: Action and Contemplation, ed. R. S. Sylvester (essays by R. J. Schoeck, L. L. Martz, G. Elton and G. Marc'hadour). Published, 1972.
Two Early Tudor Lives (Cavendish's *Wolsey* and Roper's *More*), ed. R. S. Sylvester and D. P. Harding. Published 1962. Hardbound and paperback.

All volumes are published by the Yale University Press, New Haven, Connecticut.

Modern Works in the English Language

Adams, Robert P., *The Better Part of Valor,* Seattle, 1962.
Bainton, Roland H., *Erasmus of Christendom,* New York, 1969.
Blackburn, E. B., ed., "John More, The legacye of . . . prester Iohn," *Moreana,* 14 (May 1967), 37–98.
Bremond, Henri, *The Blessed Thomas More,* trans. H. Child, London, 1904.
Bridgett, T. E., *Life and Writings of Sir Thomas More,* London, 1891.
Byron, Brian, *Loyalty in the Spirituality of St. Thomas More,* Nieuwkoop, 1972.
Campbell, W. E., *Erasmus, Tyndale and More,* London, 1949.
Chambers, R. W., *Thomas More,* London, 1935.
———, *The Place of Thomas More in English Literature and History,* London, 1937.
Clebsch, W., *England's Earliest Protestants,* New Haven, 1964.
Dickens, A. G., *The English Reformation,* London and New York, 1964.

Donner, H. W., *Introduction to Utopia,* London, 1945.

Egan, Willis J., *The Rule of Faith in More's Controversy with Tyndale,* Los Angeles, 1960.

Encyclopedia Britannica, art., "More," by G. Marc'hadour, Chicago, 1974.

Erasmus, Desiderius, *The Adages of Erasmus,* trans. Margaret M. Phillips, Cambridge, 1964.

————, *The Colloquies of Erasmus,* trans. Craig R. Thompson, Chicago and London, 1965.

————, *Praise of Folly,* trans. H. H. Hudson, Princeton and London, 1941.

————, *Praise of Folly,* trans. Betty Radice, intro. by Peter Levi, London, 1971.

Fisher, John, *The English Works of John Fisher,* ed. J. Mayor, London, 1876 (repr. 1935, and Kraus repr. 1974).

Gairdner, James, *Lollardy and the Reformation in England,* London, 1908.

Gallagher, Ligeia, ed., *More's Utopia and Its Critics,* Chicago, 1964.

Gibson, R. W., and Patrick, J. M., *St. Thomas More: A Preliminary Bibliography of his Works and of Moreana to the Year 1750,* New Haven, 1961. Cited as "Gibson."

Greenslade, S. L., "The Morean Renaissance," *Journal of Eccl. History,* XXIV, 4 (Oct. 1974), 395–403.

Harbison, E. H., *The Christian Scholar in the Age of the Reformation,* New York, 1956.

Harpsfield, Nicholas, *The Life and Death of Sir Thomas More,* ed. E. V. Hitchcock, London, 1932 (and see under Roper).

Heath, Peter, *The English Clergy on the Eve of the Reformation,* London and Toronto, 1969.

Hallett, P. E., Introduction to Thomas More, *History of Passion,* London, 1941, v–xxii.

Hexter, J. H., *More's "Utopia": The Biography of an Idea,* Princeton, 1952.

Hogrefe, Pearl, *The Sir Thomas More Circle,* Urbana, 1959.

Hughes, P. L., and Larkin, J. F., *Tudor Royal Proclamations,* vol. I: 1485–1553, New Haven, 1964.

Huizinga, Johan, *Erasmus and the Age of the Reformation,* New York, 1957.

Innes, A. D., "Sir Thomas More the Idealist," *Leading Figures in English History,* London, 1931.

Janelle, Pierre, *The Catholic Reformation,* London, 1948.

Johnson, Robbin S., *More's Utopia, Ideal and Illusion,* New Haven, 1969.

Knowles, David, *The Religious Orders in England,* vol. 3: The Tudor Age, Cambridge, 1959.

Knox, R. A. (and others), *The Fame of Blessed Thomas More,* London, 1929 and New York, 1933.

Lecler, Joseph, *Toleration and the Reformation,* trans. T. L. Westow, vol. 1, New York, 1960.

Lehmberg, Stanford E., *The Reformation Parliament 1529–1536,* Cambridge, 1970.

Levine, Mortimer, *Tudor England 1485–1603,* Cambridge, 1968.

Lewis, C. S., *English Literature in the Sixteenth Century Excluding Drama*, Oxford, 1954.

Liljegren, S. B., *Studies on the Origin and Early Tradition of English Utopian Fiction*, Uppsala, 1961.

McConica, J. K., *English Humanists and Reformation Politics*, Oxford, 1965.

Mackie, J. D., *The Earlier Tudors 1485–1558*, Oxford, 1952.

Manuel, Frank E., ed., *Utopias and Utopian Thought*, Boston, 1966. A valuable collection of essays.

Mason, H. A., *Humanism and Poetry in the Early Tudor Period*, London, 1959.

Marc'hadour, Germain, *The Bible in the Works of St. Thomas More*, 5 vols., Nieuwkoop, 1969–72.

MORE, Thomas, *The Complete Works of St. Thomas More*, in progress, New Haven, 1963 f. See pp. xix–xx for separate volumes.

———, *The Correspondence of Sir Thomas More*, ed. E. F. Rogers, Princeton, 1947. Cited as "Rogers."

———, *The Latin Epigrams of Thomas More*, ed. L. Bradner and C. A. Lynch, Chicago, 1953. Cited as "*B.L.*"

———, *St. Thomas More: Selected Letters*, ed. E. F. Rogers, New Haven, 1961. Cited as "*SL*."

Morison, Stanley, and Barker, Nicolas, *The Likeness of Thomas More*, London, 1963. A full survey of the iconographical tradition.

Morton, A. L., *The English Utopia*, London, 1952.

Nelson, William, ed., *Twentieth Century Interpretations of Utopia*, Englewood Cliffs, New Jersey, 1968.

New Catholic Encyclopedia, "More," by R. S. Sylvester and R. J. Schoeck, New York, 1967.

O'Sullivan, Richard, ed., *Under God and the Law*, London, 1949.

Patrick, J. Max and Negley, Glenn, eds., *The Quest for Utopia*, New York, 1952.

Reed, A. W., *Early Tudor Drama*, London, 1926.

Reynolds, E. E., *The Trial of St. Thomas More*, London, 1964.

———, *Thomas More and Erasmus*, London, 1965.

———, *Margaret Roper*, London, 1960.

———, *The Field Is Won: The Life and Death of St. Thomas More*, Wheathampstead, 1968.

———, *Saint John Fisher*, Wheathampstead, 1972.

Roper, William, *The Life of Sir Thomas More Knight*, ed. E. V. Hitchcock, London, 1935.

Routh, E. M. G., *Thomas More and his Friends*, London, 1934.

Russell, Lord R. of Killowen, Preface to *Utopia*, ed. P. E. Hallett, London, 1937.

Sawada, Paul A., "Laus Potentiae? H. Oncken and More's *Utopia*," *Moreana*, *15–16* (Nov. 1967), 145–64.

Scarisbrick, John, *Henry VIII*, Berkeley, 1968.

Schoeck, R. J., ed., *Editing Sixteenth-Century Texts*, Toronto, 1966.

Sowards, J. K., "Thomas More, Erasmus and Julius II," *Moreana, 24* (Nov. 1969), 81–99.

Stapleton, Thomas, *The Life of Sir Thomas More,* ed. by E. E. Reynolds, London, 1966.

Surtz, Edward, *The Praise of Pleasure,* Cambridge, Mass., 1957.

————, *The Praise of Wisdom,* Chicago, 1957.

————, *The Works and Days of John Fisher,* Cambridge, Mass., 1967.

Sylvester, R. S., editor, *St. Thomas More: Action and Contemplation,* New Haven, 1972.

Trapp, J. B., "Dame Christian Colet and Thomas More," *Moreana, 15–16* (Nov. 1967), 103–13.

Tucker, Melvin J., "The More-Norfolk Connection," *Moreana, 33* (Feb. 1972), 5–13.

Visser, F. T., *A Syntax of the English Language of St. Thomas More.* A. The Verb., Louvain, 3 vols., 1946–56 (Reprint Kraus, 1963).

PART I: BIOGRAPHICAL STUDIES

THE TRADITION OF EARLY MORE BIOGRAPHY

Michael A. Anderegg

Although Thomas More's lives of Pico della Mirandola and King Richard III have assured him a seminal place in the history of English biography, his indirect contribution as a biographical subject must be considered at least equally crucial to the development of that genre in Tudor and Stuart England. No man, certainly no layman, can have been so frequently written about in the sixteenth and early seventeenth centuries. The seventy years between 1550 and 1620 have given us lives of More by William Roper, Nicholas Harpsfield, Thomas Stapleton, the anonymous "Ro. Ba.," and Cresacre More.[1] To this list should be added the life by More's nephew William Rastell, of which only a fragment remains. We have here ample witness to More's importance at least for his fellow English Catholics. Both seasoned scholars and men not otherwise literary attempted to assess anew the meaning of More's career. The fruit of their labors may appear to the modern reader not so much a series of individualized portraits as a single, composite biography. Each of More's biographers after Roper borrowed directly or indirectly from one or more of his predecessors. Only Roper's *Life* is truly original, and its excellence has long been recognized. Roper's successors nevertheless deserve our attention; they all present slightly different pictures of their subject, and each one contributes not only to our knowledge of More but to the art of biography as well.

The development of the Thomas More "mythos" in these early lives parallels a gradual maturing in the writing of biography in England. From Roper's brief reminiscences to Cresacre More's full-fledged exposition is, technically at least, a long step. On the artistic side, however, the matter must be put somewhat differently. Roper's *Life of More* is not only brilliant in itself, but the main cause of brilliance in the others. Without claiming extraordinary merit for the works of Roper's imitators and disciples, however, we can, by considering the particular point of view and emphasis they bring to bear on their work, isolate and define the nature of their achievement. The following brief treatments of Roper, Harpsfield, Stapleton, Ro. Ba., and Cresacre More are an attempt to outline a tradition, one might almost say a "school," of biographical writing. Cresacre More receives some additional emphasis both because he quite literally synthesizes the work of his predecessors, thereby producing a biography which was, for many years, the standard *Life* of More, and also because he provides, as the lord chancellor's

This article was prepared specifically for publication in this volume.

great-grandson, an important link between Roper's family memoir and the genre of historical biography, of which his own *Life* remains an important early example.

I

William Roper (c. 1498–1578) was the husband of More's eldest daughter Margaret. He resided with his father-in-law, as he tells us, "by the space of xvj yeares and more,"[2] a circumstance which put him in a particularly favored position as a biographer. Unfortunately, Roper did not begin to write his account of More's life until some twenty years after the latter's death. The reason for this, of course, is that the martyr was *persona non grata* in the England of Edward VI. So More had to wait until the reign of the Catholic Queen Mary for a biographer. Meanwhile, "throughe neckligens and long contynuans of tyme" (p. 5), Roper had forgotten a good deal, and his memory played occasional tricks on him. In spite of a few factual inaccuracies, however, Roper's *Life* remains the only biography of More by an eyewitness, and its general reliability has never been seriously questioned.[3]

In one sense, it is perhaps incorrect to refer to Roper's *Life* as a biography. Roper does not attempt to account for all of the events in More's career. Nor does he adhere strictly to chronology. After briefly sketching in his subject's early years, Roper devotes the bulk of the *Life* quite naturally to the period during which he resided in More's household. Primary written documents and secondary materials rarely find their way into his narrative.[4] Furthermore, he shows little concern for More's humanistic activities. Not only is the larger body of More's polemical and devotional writings virtually ignored, but the *Utopia* (perhaps his crowning achievement) is never mentioned. Erasmus is referred to only once and his friendship with More is completely slighted. For these and other reasons, Roper's work should perhaps be considered a memoir rather than a true biography. His sketch of More's personality is built around carefully chosen anecdotes and incidents. What More was, as a human being, becomes of far greater importance than what he did.

The literary virtues of Roper's *Life* have been sensitively dealt with by Richard S. Sylvester and need not be rehearsed in detail here.[5] As Sylvester rightly notes, Roper presents More as an actor on the world's stage, a man of great wit and improvisational ability who ultimately finds himself the star of a tragic drama. Roper accomplishes his portrait by placing More in a series of "scenes" and by giving himself the role of More's somewhat naive and thick-headed dramatic foil. Roper "will cast himself in the fool's part," C. S. Lewis writes, "if the anecdote demands it."[6] In one sense, "foil" is the word that best describes virtually everyone who comes into contact with More. At the same time, however, Roper carefully delineates most of his major characters through vivid description and a sophisticated use of dialogue. The following passage illustrates Roper's technique:

After this, as the duke of Norfolke and Sir Thomas Moore chaunced to falle in familiar talke together, the duke said vnto him: 'By the masse, master Moore, it is perillous stryvinge with princes. And therefore I wold wish you somewhat to inclyne to the kings pleasure; For by god body, master Moore, *Indignatio principis mors est.*'

'Is that all, my Lord?' quoth he. 'Then in good faith is there no more differens betweene your grace and me, but that I shall dye today, and yow tomorowe.' (pp. 71–72)

The picture of More, calm and sure of himself, resigned to accept what fate has to offer, is perfectly balanced by the bluff, gruff, and well-intentioned Norfolk, who is finally unable either to understand or to help his old friend.[7] By similar means, Roper turns the Tower visit (p. 83) of More's second wife Alice into a *tour de force.* Her impatience, her brusqueness, her homely speech ('Tylle valle, Tylle valle') are adroitly juxtaposed to her husband's stoicism and Christian endurance. These anecdotes, though tinged with irony and humor, make a serious point. More's single-minded purpose, his complete devotion to what he believes to be right, cannot be understood even by his friends. If his death is to have any meaning, the reader must supply it himself; Roper does not.

More's life achieves a satisfying consistency in Roper's presentation. We are told that one of More's first public acts as a royal servant is to ask the king for freedom of conscience for Parliament and for himself, and it is for freedom of conscience, among other things, that he dies. More comes to Henry VIII's notice as a direct result of his sagacity in defending the Pope's commercial rights; Henry sends him to the block for continuing to support the Pope's religious rights. More's belief in "right" is absolute: "I assure thee on my faith, that if the parties will at my handes call for iustice, then, al were it my father stood on the one side, and the Divill on the tother, his cause being good, the Divill should haue right" (p. 42). And, near the end of his life, finding himself on one side and most of the English church and nation on the other, he adheres to his position, believing his cause to be good.

Although his clear debt to the medieval saint's life creates a context within which the significance of More's career can be gauged, Roper chooses to dwell throughout on his father-in-law's domestic role. The Thomas More we remember most vividly from his account is the loving father, the indulgent husband, the devoted son. The title of the first printed edition of Roper's *Life* includes a phrase which nicely summarizes the main thrust of the work: "A Mirror of Virtue in Worldly Greatness." And, too, we remember More's wit, the important Renaissance quality that can better be illustrated than defined but that certainly includes everything from mild jesting—the "merry tales" More himself was so fond of relating—to the quickness of mind and temperament he everywhere exhibits in Roper's pages. Here we can see in embryo the Thomas More who would become a jest-book hero to succeeding generations of

Englishmen, including those authors (perhaps Shakespeare among them) of *Sir Thomas More* who tried, apparently without success, to place More on a very literal stage in the last years of the sixteenth century.[8]

Through the power and sincerity of his art, Roper still governs our response to the historical Thomas More to such an extent that modern scholarship and even revisionist history cannot blur the firm outlines of the portrait he drew. Other writers would augment Roper's evocation of his father-in-law, filling in large areas Roper had ignored, some by adding telling details, some by providing unnecessary embellishments and gratuitous flourishes. Scholarship, polemics, and piety would all play a part in expanding and occasionally refining the image of Thomas More Roper had created. But all future biographers would owe to Roper much of the liveliness, credibility, and humanity their versions of Thomas More possessed.

II

Oddly enough, one of Roper's main purposes in writing More's *Life* was to help out his friend Nicholas Harpsfield (1519–1575). Harpsfield (who wrote sometime before 1557) dedicates his *Life of More* to Roper and presents the volume to him as a New Year's gift. In his Epistle Dedicatorie, he claims that he wrote the *Life* at Roper's request and with the aid of materials furnished by him. In fact, he has incorporated most of his predecessor's *Life* nearly verbatim into his own work. But he goes considerably beyond Roper, informing us that he has "not beene altogether negligent. . . . as by the perusing ye shall vnderstand."[9] His contributions include material from a variety of written sources both by and about More, and these are freely intermixed with what he has taken from Roper. Although he often follows his originals quite closely, he resorts to paraphrase pretty much at his convenience. Only occasionally are we given any indication of his source. By thus augmenting Roper's brief memoir, Harpsfield is able to present a rounded and somewhat more complex picture of his subject. Harpsfield's aim also differs from Roper's: where the latter was satisfied with simply portraying the man, the former wishes to portray the martyr, the first layman in England to die for the unity of the Catholic Church. Harpsfield shows, time after time, that he fully appreciated the propaganda value of More's life, and although his work never sinks to the level of a mere anti-Protestant tract he seldom misses an opportunity to strike a telling blow for the faith.

If Harpsfield's biography is something of a paste-pot job, it is also, as R. W. Chambers points out, "the first scholarly biography extant in English."[10] Following a generally chronological structure, Harpsfield skillfully organizes his materials, being careful to "interlace" (to use his own word) his various sources in such a way as not to disturb the logical flow of his narrative. Thus, for example, the letters to Erasmus expressing More's dislike for public life are appropriately sampled at the point where More is about to enter the king's service. Furthermore, Harpsfield throughout exhibits sympathetic knowledge of More's voluminous writings. The passages borrowed from Roper, including the various anecdotes, take on new coloration as they are woven into the fabric of Harpsfield's narrative. While appearing merely to extend and amplify Roper's achievement, Harpsfield provides More's life with his own quite distinct focus and polemical bent.

Harpsfield undertakes his biography primarily to demonstrate that More was "the oddest and notablest man of all Inglande, And that he atchieued such an excellent state of worthines, fame and glory as neuer did (especially laye man) in Inglande before, and muche doubt is there whether anye man shall hereafter" (p. 11). To this end, Harpsfield places great emphasis on More's scholarly accomplishments and quotes liberally from both the Latin and English Works. He refers to the *Utopia* as "the booke that beareth the pricke and price of all his latine bookes of wittie inuention, for prophane matters," and tells us that More also wrote "most elegantly and eloquently the life of kinge Richarde the thirde" (p. 102). But Harpsfield's interest in More's writings transcends purely literary concerns. By spending a disproportionate number of pages discussing the Tyndale controversy, he quickly turns his treatment of this aspect of More's career into a vigorous attack on Protestant heretics. More becomes truly a "Defender of Faith" and his life and work serve as a model for Harpsfield's Catholic readers. This is an aspect of More that Roper had hardly touched upon.

Harpsfield is also quick to point out possible miracles in incidents of More's life which Roper had either ignored or related with little or no comment. We have, for instance, Harpsfield's lively description of Roper's lapse into heresy: "The saide Master William Roper, at what time he maried with mistris Margarete More, was a meruailous zealous Protestant, and so feruent, and withall so well and properly lyked of himselfe and his diuine learning, that he tooke the brydle into the teeth, and ranne forth like a headstronge horse, harde to be plucked backe againe" (p. 84). More prays for his son-in-law's recovery: "And soone after, as he verily beleeued, thorough the great mercy of God, at the deuout prayer of Sir Thomas More, he perceaued his owne ignorance, ouersight, malice and folie, and turned him againe to the Catholic fayth, wherein, God be thanked, he hath hitherto continued" (p. 88). This episode, one feels, is brought in not merely to illustrate a More "miracle," but also as an object lesson which tellingly demonstrates the pernicious influence of Lutheran heresy, a force so pervasive and insidious as to touch even the household of Thomas More. When he recounts Roper's story of how More had foretold the fall of Anne Boleyn, Harpsfield makes certain that the reader does not miss the point: "But that I shall now declare, me thinketh may rather hange vppon some priuate and secrete reuelation and diuine information then any worldly and wise coniecture or foresight" (p. 72). More's rather cryptic comment on the inevitable turning of Dame Fortune's wheel becomes a "miracle" of divine revelation which adds to More's credentials as a saint.

As this last example suggests, Harpsfield's embellishments of Roper function for the most part to point out the significance of a story or anecdote Roper had told without comment. In some instances, the addition is succinct and follows quite logically the story to which it is appended. Harpsfield repeats the story of how Norfolk rebuked More for singing in the choir like a "parishe clarke," for example, but he amplifies More's answer that serving God cannot be dishonorable: "Wherin Sir Thomas More did very godly and deuoutly, and spake very truely and wisely. What would the noble duke haue saide, if he had seene that mightie and noble Emperoure, Charles the great, playing the very same part; or king David, longe before, hopping and dauncing naked before the arke?" (pp. 64–65). By placing More in both the Christian saga of Charlemagne and a biblical context, Harpsfield widens the implications of what had been a simple anecdote without necessarily destroying its basic impact. At other times, however, Harpsfield takes "the brydle into the teeth, and runs forth like a headstronge horse, hard to be plucked back againe." He expands upon Roper's recital of a conversation between More and Cardinal Wolsey in order to blast Wolsey, whom he blames for the events leading to the Reformation. The reference to Wolsey gives him a perfect opportunity to indulge in partisan invective. By emphasizing religious and political issues, Harpsfield allows More to become identified with the Catholic cause to a much greater extent than he had been in Roper. The man is gradually being displaced by the martyr.

Our consideration of Harpsfield's polemical bent should not serve to detract from his talents as biographer. He presents a coherent picture of More's life and accomplishments, and he presents it well. He does not shy away from drawing his own conclusions from his materials (as when he specifically identifies the anecdotes about shrewish wives in More's writings with More's second wife Dame Alice) and his insights are often quite sound. He has a good feel for the dramatic, for creating suspense. After narrating More's life in chronological order he stops his story at just that point where More resigns his chancellorship and turns to More's personal life and his writings, holding off the tragic denouement. In addition, he shows concern for accuracy, correcting Roper's factual errors whenever he is able. His desire to tell the truth can generally be seen to overcome his impulse towards idealization.

Harpsfield's main weakness is verbosity; he is unable to leave well-enough alone. In the words of C. S. Lewis, his "intermittent decorations do not please."[11] Roper had ended his account of More's life with the pointed remark of Charles V to the English ambassador: "We wold rather haue lost the best city of our dominions then haue lost such a worthy councellour" (p. 104). Harpsfield repeats the story and then proceeds to expand upon More's many virtues, his wit, his learning, and his deep religious devotion. He compares More to Socrates. He also compares him to two English Saints, Thomas of Dover and Thomas of Canterbury (perhaps giving a hint to Stapleton). More was, like them, a martyr, but, "speaking it without diminution or derogation of their glorious death, a martyr in a cause that neerer toucheth religion and the whole fayth then doth the death of the other twaine" (p. 214). Harpsfield's conclusion is no doubt anti-climactic, but it fits his didactic purpose. He gives us a portrait of a budding saint, and his observations were not to be lost on those biographers who came after him.

III

Thomas Stapleton (1535–1598), the next biographer of Thomas More, was an important figure in the polemical debates which characterized the Counter-Reformation, and his *Vita* naturally reflects his abiding desire to defend and uphold the Catholic faith.[12] It was first published the year of the Armada and the tone of the work is clearly indicated by its final paragraph:

> May God, the Father of mercies, by the merits of the precious Blood of his beloved Son and through the holy intercession of so many martyrs in England, and especially of Thomas More, deign in his mercy to take pity at length upon the affliction of our nation, which now for twenty-nine years has been suffering dire schism and heretical tyranny, and lead it back from its errors to the bosom of our holy mother, the Catholic Church. To him be all honour and glory for all eternity. Amen.[13]

But Stapleton's *Vita Mori* cannot justly be characterized as merely another polemical treatise. Nor would it be sufficient to consider it a saint's life in any narrow sense. Both Catholic polemics and miraculous or semi-miraculous events play their part in the *Vita*, but Stapleton goes beyond what would be required for either polemics or piety. His is perhaps the only *Life of More* (before Cresacre's synthesis) that aptly and adequately reflects the various sides of its subject. By any standard, Stapleton's biography is a well-researched historical document which utilizes an impressive number of written sources, ancient and contemporary (including Roper and, perhaps, Harpsfield). And he makes excellent use of More's English Works, citing, whenever appropriate, autobiographical passages which are scattered throughout More's writings. Furthermore, Stapleton had access to an important oral tradition. He knew many exiled members of the More circle—John and Margaret Clement, John Harris, Dorothy Colly, John Heywood, and William Rastell, among others—and their reminiscences, albeit hazy after the passage of years, add immeasurably to the feeling of personal involvement Stapleton brings to bear on his work.

Stapleton's scrupulosity in enumerating his sources reflects his stated wish to write "a thoroughly authentic account" (p. xv) of More's career, and the *Vita* as a whole gives the impression of a critical spirit at work. Whatever reservations we may have concerning some of his more pious and semi-miraculous tales (and these are relatively few), there can be little doubt that he wrote at all times what he believed to be true: the reader sees that each supernatural episode has been developed from some genuine and easily explained occurrence.

Stapleton's major purpose in writing More's life is indicated by the form in which the biography was published. The *Vita Mori* constitutes a part of a larger work entitled the *Tres Thomae* (Douai, 1588). The "three Thomases" are the Apostle, Becket, and More. Over half the book, however, is devoted to More; Stapleton canonizes him by association. Furthermore, the inclusion of the Apostle and Becket in a biography of Thomas More heightens the moral and polemical value of the work, for the lives of these earlier saints both complement and set off More's special achievement. Thomas the Apostle was in some ways the most courageous of Christ's disciples.[14] But he was also "doubting Thomas," who could not believe in the Resurrection until he saw the evidence with his own eyes. How great was More's sacrifice, then, who did not see, but whose belief was unshakable even unto death. As for Becket, he, like More, died for opposing an English king who sought illegitimately to grasp ecclesiastical power from the papacy, but his death, however noble, was not, as was More's, a premeditated act of faith.

At the outset of the *Vita Mori*, Stapleton explicitly tells us what induced him to write an account of More's life:

Various motives have led me to write: first the glory of God and my love for the Catholic Church, for his loyalty to which More laid down his life; next, pity for my country in its present deep affliction and distress (More, in his lifetime, was its chief glory and proudest boast); then also the consolation my work will give to right-minded men and the just confusion it will cause to the wicked. (p. XV)

Later in the narrative, he says that he has written this life to portray More "above all as a saint and a glorious martyr for truth and right" (p. 132). In line with this intent, Stapleton makes continual reference to More's piety and virtue. More's asceticism—the hair shirt and the whip—are emphasized; prophetic and semi-miraculous events are reported; frequent parallels are drawn between episodes in More's career and similar episodes in the Lives of the Saints. And as Stapleton approaches More's martyrdom, we get an increasing number of incidents reminiscent of the passion of Christ. For Stapleton, More is above all "the brave soldier of Christ" (p. 148) who died for the "Primacy of the Pope" (p. 190).

We should be careful, however, not to equate Stapleton's stated purpose with his achievement. His scrupulous attempt to record all he could gather concerning More and his activities indicates a broader concern. In contrast to Roper, Stapleton brings More into the larger context of continental humanism and universal Christendom. In Roper's eyes, More appears as an isolated and lonely figure, little understood and even less emulated by those around him. It is salutary, therefore, to see More at one with his European brethren, and to read the opinions of men who clearly saw and understood what More was doing when he took his final walk to Tower Hill. Where Roper ignores the *Utopia*, Stapleton (however inadequately) discusses More's masterpiece and refers to it a good dozen times. Erasmus appears at the very beginning of

Roper's account and is not mentioned again. But Erasmus informs Stapleton's *Life* as an abiding presence, and this in spite of the fact that Stapleton clearly does not approve of him.

Stapleton treats More's scholarly activities as a secondary concern; his hero "was far more zealous to become a saint than a scholar" (p. 8). And Stapleton agrees with More himself that learning without virtue is "a gold ring in the snout of a sow." But he in no way undervalues More's achievement as a humanist scholar. "More's natural bent," he emphasizes, "was entirely to a literary life" (p. 27). Stapleton is, in fact, at pains to demonstrate the importance of More's position in the humanist community: "he was united in the closest bonds of friendship with all those, both at home and abroad, who at that period enjoyed a reputation for eloquence and learning, as will appear in the following chapter" (p. 37). He then gives us a long extract from More's 1518 letter to the University of Oxford which illustrates "how earnest was More in his advocacy and defense of letters" (p. 38). And, although Stapleton finds the fact "astonishing," he nevertheless dutifully records that More "honoured men of learning so highly, solely with an eye to their literary attainments, that even to heretics eminent in literature he did not refuse his favor and his good offices" (p. 58). In short, he finds no real contradiction between More's temporal and his spiritual life: these are inseparable aspects of a single personality. The key words in Stapleton are "virtue" and "learning"; he does not attempt to drive a wedge between them.

Perhaps the gravest distortion in Stapleton's biography, and one which would influence many subsequent commentators, including Cresacre, concerns his treatment of Erasmus. Although Marie Delcourt was wrong in claiming that Stapleton "ne dit pas un mot de son [More's] amitié pour Erasme,"[15] it is true that Stapleton looked upon the famous friendship with some regret: "No one loved Erasmus more than he, and it was a literary friendship," he writes. "In turn Erasmus loved him, and deservedly." But, he quickly adds, "More's friendship for Erasmus . . . honoured Erasmus more than it benefited More." Stapleton then goes on to make a statement for which he probably had no evidence: "as that Protestant heresy increased, for which Erasmus had so widely sown the accursed seed, More's love towards him decreased and grew cool" (p. 36). This remark is followed by the assertion that More attempted to persuade Erasmus to issue (as had Augustine) a book of *Retractations,* in order to purge his youthful writings of errors: "But Erasmus, who was as unlike St Augustine in humility as he was in doctrine, refused and destroyed More's letter so that it should not be inserted in his collected correspondence" (p. 37). Harpsfield tells the same story, and Stapleton may be following him. In any case, proof of this episode is lacking.[16] Whatever the facts, Stapleton's anti-Erasmian bias colors nearly every mention of the Dutch humanist.

Stapleton's prejudice, however unfortunate, is understandable. He was a man of the Counter-Reformation, and when he came to write his biography the religious concerns which had engrossed the earlier generation of humanists

were no longer subject to friendly debate and analysis. The issues were now
clear-cut; the sides were drawn. The fence upon which Erasmus often gave the
appearance of sitting now rose up in a no-man's land of bitter controversy. In
1559, Pope Paul IV had condemned all of Erasmus's works. Catholic apologists like Robert Persons and Edmund Campion attacked Erasmus mercilessly.
In this context, Stapleton's chastisement is relatively mild. Nevertheless, he
sets the tone and creates the attitudes which will be followed by Cresacre
More and others.

Aside from this major distortion, Stapleton's *Life* is, on balance, extremely
fair-minded and quite free from any narrow partisanship. His achievement
remains impressive. Stapleton structures his work thematically, at the same
time maintaining a basic chronological progression. "I have thought it best,"
he tells us, "both to help the reader's memory and to ensure order and method
in the development of the narrative, to divide up my matter into chapters."
The titles of these chapters give a good indication of Stapleton's method:

>   IV. His Wide Learning and Literary Work
>   VII. His Contempt of Honours and Praise
>   X. How he Educated his Children and Grandchildren
>   XIII. His Quick Wit
>   XXI. The Learned and Famous Pay Tribute to Thomas More

and so forth. The portrait that emerges is of a virtuous man, in the classical
sense, who adds to his worldly virtues the (for Stapleton) essential ingredient
of Christian piety and Christian humility. Hence, Stapleton presents a lengthy
comparison of More to Cato the censor as portrayed by Livy. More goes beyond Cato because of his kindness, wit, and good humor. But More is greater
than Cato principally because he is a Christian and not a Stoic. That More was
a layman, and one who achieved so much as a statesman, scholar, lawyer, and
polemicist, at the same time raising a large family, is, for Stapleton, of primary
importance, because More's high standing in the world of affairs makes his
sacrifice that much greater. As an exemplary figure, he stands apart from the
clerics, like Bishop Fisher and the Carthusians, who also died for the faith.

                                        IV

Stapleton and Harpsfield were used as primary sources by the writer known
only as "Ro. Ba.," whose *Lyfe of Syr Thomas More* was probably composed
around 1599. Like Harpsfield before him, Ro. Ba. admits his debt to his predecessors: "the most part of this book is none of my owne; I onely chalenge
the ordering and translating. The most of the rest is Stapletons and Harps-
fields . . ."[17] The major task Ro. Ba. set for himself was combining the more or
less independent accounts of Harpsfield and Stapleton. The kind of book he
is writing is clearly noted in the Epistle Dedicatory (evidently not by Ro. Ba.):
"A sainctes life is a welcome theame to a sainctlike man" (p. 4). And Ro. Ba.
himself tells us that he is writing "the life of the wisest, grauest and most
learned Layman that euer our realme bred, yea, the most innocent, constant

and Sainctlike man that this age hath seene" (p. 13). Although by using the word "sainctlike" Ro. Ba. indicates a desire not to anticipate the judgment of his church, his real attitude towards More is quite unambiguous.

Ro. Ba.'s *Life* is not, like Harpsfield's, chronological; nor is it, like Roper's, simply anecdotal. He is closer to Stapleton because he tends to arrange his materials by topic. Although this is a valid enough approach, it sometimes leads him to unfortunate anticipations. He recounts the story of the weak scaffold, for instance, as one in the series of humorous anecdotes inserted among More's domestic affairs early in the book. Ro. Ba.'s mind, indeed, runs to categories: all of the stories dealing with Dame Alice (including the episode where she visits More in the Tower) and with More's uprightness, etc., are placed in their own particular section. Consciously or unconsciously, Ro. Ba. imitates the favorite method of medieval hagiographers. He can introduce a theme and develop it fully before moving off to something else. In addition, his use of categories enables him to combine his sources with a certain amount of elegance and finesse; he is not content merely to copy his predecessors. At times his changes in wording are minor; elsewhere he alters whole passages. On occasion he strives to heighten the tension or humor of his source, as when he recounts the story (originally in Roper) of how More, through prayer, discovered a method for curing Margaret of the sweating sickness, and adds: "The phisitions misliked this counsaile, yet it pleased god, for her fathers feruent prayer, as we may verily thinke, to restore her to perfect health" (p. 141). Ro. Ba.'s unfounded suggestion that the doctors took affront at More's advice, besides adding a bit of drama to his anecdote, tends to magnify the wonder of More's solution. Occasionally, however, Ro. Ba.'s amplifications of his source manage to dilute the strength of an anecdote. Here is Ro. Ba.'s version of More's response to Norfolk's warning that *indignatio principis mors est*:[18] "'Well, my Lord,' quoth Sir Thomas, 'my account is cast; but is this all? Then is there no more difference between your Grace and me, but that I shall dye today, and you tomorrowe, but what kind of death it skilleth not, My Lord, I say, I feare not to die, because I serue a good maister'" (p. 189). Evidently, Ro. Ba. felt that the original version was too cryptic and needed some elucidation.

Although Ro. Ba.'s biography appears to be mainly a patchwork of other people's material, as was Harpsfield's, he does have some original contributions to make. His main additions are primarily in the form of "merry tales" which tend to reinforce More's reputation as a wit. One of these will have to suffice:

Where fore [he] sought in earnest manner to persuade him that it was true, and said to him, 'Sir, you are but a dead man. It is impossible for you to liue till the afternoone.' Maister More said not a worde, called for an vrinall, and looking on his water, said: 'Maister Pope, for any thinge that I can perceive, this patient is not so sicke but that he may do well, if it be not the king's pleasure he should die. If it were not for that, there is great possibilitie of his good health. Therefore let it suffice that it is the kinges pleasure that I must die. (p. 120)

This story, whether true or not, is certainly not inconsistent with one aspect of More's character as developed by his Tudor biographers.[19]

R. W. Chambers has said of Ro. Ba.'s biography that "in some ways it is the best *Life of More.*"[20] Indeed, if neither Roper's nor Harpsfield's biographies were extant, Ro. Ba.'s work would have to be considered one of the most brilliant of Renaissance prose texts; but clearly, without Harpsfield, and through Harpsfield, Roper, a great part of what is best in Ro. Ba. would not exist. Nevertheless, Ro. Ba. makes his own contributions. His style is lively and picturesque, as in the passage berating the Protestants where he tells us that "Luther, theire great patriarche of Germanie, drunken with the dregges of heresie, belched forth a filthie booke" (p. 62), or where he says that the writing of More's biography "hath wearied painefull Stapleton, grauelled learned Harpsfilde, made silent eloquent Poole" (p. 13). He structures his biography in a logical and attractive fashion and is particularly adept at telling a humorous story. It seems fitting that the last of More's Tudor biographers should exhibit so many of the virtues characteristic of sixteenth-century vernacular prose at its best.

V

Although Cresacre More's *Life of Thomas More* (composed c. 1615–1620; published c. 1626)[21] was, for nearly 250 years, the best known and most frequently read of the biographies of Thomas More, scholars, critics, and historians have not paid it the kind of careful attention they have accorded to the other early English lives of More, particularly those published in our own century by the Early English Text Society. The relative neglect of Cresacre's biography is understandable. Cresacre is not an original writer; the greater part of his material derives either from Roper or Stapleton. His concluding chapter—"Of Sir Thomas More's Books"—is transcribed almost verbatim from Harpsfield. His own additions are relatively modest: a handful of anecdotes, a few facts and observations taken from such sources as Hall's *Chronicle,* Camden's *Remains,* and Stow's *Annals,* together with a distinctive, individual tone. The chancellor's great-grandson was not in a position, as was Harpsfield (who knew Roper and other members of the More circle) to contribute what may be considered genuine "moreana." But even if Cresacre's contribution to Thomas More biography cannot be considered meaningfully apart from the writings of his predecessors, the significance of his work should not be underestimated. His full, well-rounded portrait of More would not be supplanted until T. E. Bridgett's *Life* appeared in 1891. He was successful in welding together the complementary, but nevertheless quite different, views of More presented by Roper and Stapleton. Historically, too, Cresacre's *Life* marks a turning point in English biographical writing, in that it is written at a greater temporal distance from its subject; its fullness of detail, breadth of subject matter, and stylistic virtues make it an important precursor of the better known eighteenth-century experiments in biographical writing.

Historians of the Tudor period, antiquarians, and students of Thomas More from Anthony à Wood and Lord Herbert of Cherbury to Sir James Mackintosh and Lord John Campbell all treated Cresacre's biography as a primary historical source. Few of these writers, of course, relied on Cresacre alone; most of them were familiar with Roper and some had dipped into Stapleton. The extent of Cresacre's debt to his predecessors, however, has seldom been noted. Even W. H. Hutton, in his 1895 biography of Thomas More, could claim that "Cresacre More is not mentioned in [my] notes when he merely repeats Roper or Stapleton,"[22] and then go on to ascribe much to Cresacre that is not his own. One result of this failure to check carefully Cresacre's avowed and unavowed sources, a failure shared by scholars well into the twentieth century, was to give Cresacre the credit (or award him the blame) for originating apocryphal anecdotes and speeches or fathering ideas that, in fact, were carried over from his sources. Thus John Jortin, in his *Life* of Erasmus (1808), testily attacked Cresacre (referring to him as, among other things, "a narrow-minded zealot" and a "wiseacre"[23]) for his negative treatment of Erasmus without, it would appear, being aware that the anti-Erasmian prejudice had been carried over (and somewhat tempered) from Stapleton. And even Marie Delcourt, in an influential article published in 1936,[24] accused Cresacre of inventing speeches which were actually translated from Stapleton's *Tres Thomae*.

The popularity of Cresacre's *Life* among the older historians and biographers can be accounted for partly by the accident of its publishing history,[25] partly because of its length (Roper's brief work seemed, for a long time, an overly subjective sketch), and partly because (unlike Stapleton's *Vita*) it was written in English. In addition, Cresacre, as the great-grandson of Thomas More, was assumed to possess the important heirlooms of private knowledge and family traditions, as well as a natural sympathy with and understanding of his subject. Born into a recusant family and a recusant himself, Cresacre More suffered the penalties and endured the hardships and isolation which were the fruits of those fateful days when his great-grandfather stood nearly alone among English laymen for the preservation of a universal Catholic church. Other readers of Cresacre's biography, less sympathetic to the cause therein espoused, would find in it ample evidence of narrow-mindedness, prejudice, and perfidy. But whether attacked or defended, Cresacre's *Life* was thoroughly combed for anecdotes, jests, and character sketches that could be employed to fill out the bare historical record and to help create what would ultimately become the Thomas More "mythos."

Before discussing his biography in any detail, however, it is necessary to show that Cresacre More (and not his brother Thomas More IV, a secular priest) is indeed the author of the work here ascribed to him, a fact still questioned by a number of scholars. In order to present a convincing argument, Cresacre's own life must briefly be sketched in.

Cresacre More and his older brother Thomas More IV were two of the thirteen children of Thomas More II (1531–1606), the eldest child of the martyr's only son John.[26] Thomas II's adherence to the faith for which his grandfather had died caused him to be persecuted in a variety of ways as a recusant for most of his adult life.[27] He spent four years in the Marshalsea prison, and from 1586 to his death in 1606, hardly a year went by when he was not brought before one court or another and fined for recusancy. He died owing the crown £500 in recusant debts. Of his four sons, only two were still living in 1606. The oldest son, John, died childless around 1600. Henry, a priest, died at the convent of Minims in Nijeon-lès-Paris in 1597. This left Thomas IV and Cresacre, and as Thomas IV freely gave up his inheritance to his younger brother, it was the latter who was destined to marry and carry on the direct male line. Thomas More IV (1565-1625)[28] has long been known to students of recusancy for his involvement in negotiations between the English clergy and Rome. Near the end of his life, he took part in the complex diplomatic arrangements which led to a marriage between Charles I and the French king's daughter, Henrietta Maria.[29] He died at Rome after a brief illness on April 11, 1625, and was buried at San Luigi de' Francesi, the national church of the French community. In his will, dated December 26, 1616, Thomas bequeathes his inheritance to his "dear brother," Christopher Cresacre More.[30]

A clear differentiation between Thomas IV and his brother Cresacre was not fully accomplished until Hunter's edition of the *Life of More* in 1828, and modern research has served primarily to amplify the basic outlines accurately set out in Hunter's *Preface*.[31] Christopher Cresacre More (1572-1649), the youngest of the thirteen children of Thomas II, was born at Barnborough and baptized, as he tells us in his *Preface* to the *Life* (sig. A$_1$), on July 6, 1572, the anniversary of his great-grandfather's martyrdom. His childhood was spent during some of Thomas More II's worst troubles, and Cresacre would never forget the sufferings and humiliations his father experienced.[32] Thomas II intended for his youngest son to follow in the footsteps of his older brothers, Thomas and Henry, and enter the priesthood. But Cresacre was not destined to fulfill his father's ambition. The death of his eldest brother John sometime before 1600 altered the family plans, and Cresacre—the only surviving son not a priest—was called home from the English College at Douai where he was studying theology to marry and keep alive the family name.[33] He married Elizabeth Gage sometime between June 30, 1603 and April 6, 1605. Their first child, Helen, was born on March 25, 1606. Upon his father's death, Cresacre inherited the family estates, together with the family troubles; the penalties suffered by the father now fell upon the son.[34] Cresacre's difficulties were compounded when his young wife died around 1610, an event referred to in an obituary written after the death of Cresacre's younger daughter, Bridget: "her mother died yong, & left her father one son, & two daughters, who for his tendernes to them, would not Marry againe."[35]

In 1617, Cresacre moved to Gobions, in the parish of North Mimms, Hertfordshire, which had been the property of Sir Thomas More's father. For reasons unknown to us, his financial situation seems to have improved, as he was able, in 1620, to contribute money for the establishment of a house of Benedictine nuns at Cambrai. His daughter Helen, who took the religious name of Dame Gertrude, was a founder member of this convent, going over to France with two cousins and six other young women in the summer of 1623.[36] Cresacre accompanied them and saw his daughter established before returning to England soon afterwards.

The following year, Cresacre's relationship to his famous great-grandfather was noted by the printer Bernard Alsop who dedicated his edition of Ralph Robynson's translation of the *Utopia* to him. Alsop seems to have done some genealogical research, for he remarks that "when I looke into your Honourable Pedegree and finde you the vndoubted heire of his Bloud, me thought it was a theft of the worst nature, to giue to another the inheritance of his vertue."[37] Alsop wrote another dedication to Cresacre for his 1639 edition of Thomas More's popular masterpiece.

The presence of his daughter at Cambrai moved Cresacre to visit the continent again in 1625. After passing two or three months with her (he was at Cambrai in April 1625, when his brother died at Rome) he continued to Antwerp and Paris via Douai.[38] He spent Easter, 1626, at Cambrai, on his way to Antwerp, not arriving back in England until November 1627. Upon his return home, he was accompanied by his son Thomas More VI, who had probably been studying abroad, perhaps at St. Omer. Father and son were both arrested at their landing in England for refusing to take the Oath of Allegiance, and taken to be examined before the Privy Council (November 15). After a week, they were released on bond to appear when required. Two years later Thomas VI married and soon thereafter Cresacre's last child, Bridget, entered the Benedictine house at Cambrai. The outbreak of Civil War brought further troubles to Cresacre, and from 1642 to 1646 all of his property was sequestered. He died on a leasehold farm he owned at Chilstone, in the parish of Madley, on March 26, 1649, at the age of 77.

With help from the above outline, we can at least approach a solution to the problem of who wrote *The Life and Death of Sir Thomas Moore*. Actually, the Rev. Joseph Hunter long ago resolved the issue with tact and intelligence. His conclusions, however, have not convinced everyone;[39] in recent years, several students of More have affirmed, with various degrees of conviction, that the *Life* was in fact written (as nearly everyone thought before Hunter) by Thomas More IV, the priest, and then completed and "edited" for publication by his brother, Cresacre.[40] This joint-authorship theory has the virtue of encompassing all of the evidence, no matter how contradictory. But the contradictions cannot be neatly reconciled without great violence to logic.

The discrepancies stem from the *Epistle Dedicatory* and the *Preface to the Reader,* both printed in the first edition. The former ascribes the authorship to Thomas; the latter, with equal certainty, to Cresacre.

The *Epistle Dedicatory,* which appears only in the printed editions, begins: "The author of this Treatise, eldest son by descent, & heire by nature of the family of that worthy Martyr, whose life is described in it..." We go on to discover that the author was a resident of Rome when the marriage contract between Charles I and Henrietta Maria was being negotiated, and that he was "buried in the French church" there. These facts fit in perfectly with what we know of Thomas More IV, secular priest, who died at Rome on April 11, 1625. If we combine this information with the initials M.T.M. (Magister Thomas More?) on the title page, the evidence seems conclusive. Accordingly, the editor of the second (1726) edition, following these hints, and combining them with information supplied by Anthony à Wood, ascribed the work (somewhat inconsistently) to Thomas More, *Esq.* And Thomas More remained the presumed author until Hunter came along to take a fresh view of the evidence.

When we proceed to the *Preface to the Reader,* a different story emerges. The signatory "I" of the *Preface* claims authorship: "so also haue I often had an earnest desire, especially for the spirituall behoofe of my selfe and my Children . . . to giue them a taste, according to my poore abilitie, of some of his most heroicall vertues; professing my self vtterly vnable to sett downe his life in writing, as he deserueth" (sig. A_1). He goes on, in traditional terms, to compare the worthiness of his subject with his own unworthiness as a biographer: "what courage [he continues] can I haue to vndertake a work of so great difficultie as this, who know my selfe a verie puney in comparison of so manie famous men, that haue vndergone this businesse alreadie, finding in the verie beginning of this mine enterprise my small capacitie ouerwhelmed with the plentie and copiousnesse of this subject?" (sig. A_1v). And then, after pointing out the imposing precedents of Thomas Stapleton and William Roper, he adds: "yet for all this I haue now at last ventured to discourse a little of the life and death of this glorious Martyr . . ." (sig. A_2).

Clearly the author of the *Preface* considers himself the author of the entire work. But who is the author of the *Preface?* He gives us several hints, describing himself at one point as "the youngest and meanest of all my familie." And later: "I was the yongest of thirteene children of my father, the last & meanest of fiue sonnes, four of which liued to mens estate . . ." (sig. A_3). We also learn that he was "borne anew and regenerated by the holie Sacrament of Baptisme on the verie same day (though manie yeares after) on which Sr Thomas More entred heauen triumphant, to witt, on the sixt day of Iuly" (sig. A_3). The author also tells us how he came to be the heir of Thomas More:

> And although I knowe myself the vnfittest and vnworthiest of all the foure [sons] to manage this estate, yet they either loathed the world, before the world fawned on them, liuing in voluntarie contempt thereof, and dyed happie soules, in that they chose to be accounted abiect in the sight of men; or else they vtterly cast of all care of earthlie trash, by professing a strayte and religious life . . . (sig. A_3v).

Clearly, the speaker cannot be Thomas More IV, secular priest.

Hunter, faced with this enigma, solved the problem by taking the honor of authorship away from Thomas More and giving it to Cresacre More, whom he for the first time identified as the "yongest of thirteen children" of Thomas More II. Hunter's argument,[41] briefly, is as follows:

I. The *Life* can be shown, from internal evidence, to have been written after 1615, and Thomas More had long been a priest by that date. But the work was clearly written by a layman.

II. There is no evidence, and it seems highly unlikely, that Thomas More had had time to marry and have a family before he became a priest. But the author of the *Life* (in the text proper as well as in the *Preface*) several times mentions his children.

III. There is an obvious conflict between "eldest son" of the *Epistle* and "yongest of thirteen children" of the *Preface.*

IV. The epitaph of Thomas More IV (published in the 1726 ed. of the *Life*) states that the older brother left his inheritance to a younger. And in the *Preface,* the author speaks of himself as the unworthy heir of the family estates.

Hunter then demonstrates that only Cresacre More fits the portrait the author gives of himself in the *Preface.* He concludes his argument triumphantly by citing the following entry from the Register of Barnborough: "1572. Cresacrus More, filius Thomas More ar. fuit baptizatus sexto die Julii (p. xxxiv)." All of the biographical evidence which has come our way since Hunter wrote serves to strengthen and confirm Hunter's identification of Cresacre as, at the very least, the author of the *Preface.*

Nevertheless, to the embarrassing evidence of the title page and *Epistle Dedicatory,* Hunter offered two solutions. The first was simply to suggest that the biography, having been found among the papers of the deceased Thomas More IV by someone ignorant of the true situation, was published with the assumption that he (Thomas) was the author. The other, and for Hunter stronger, argument assumes that Cresacre, either because it gave him the opportunity to strike a personal note with reference to Henrietta Maria, or for private reasons of his own, simply chose to ascribe the work to his brother, forgetting or ignoring the contrary information of the *Preface* and text proper.[42] This latter argument is strengthened by the initials M.C.M.E. subscribed to the dedication. These Hunter deciphers as "Magister Cresacre More Eboracensis." The second argument, in its general outline, is more compelling than the first, but neither, as Hunter was quite aware, can really be proven. In any case, Hunter was satisfied that he had demonstrated his case for Cresacre beyond a reasonable doubt.

Hunter's argument, however, still fails to explain completely the presence of the *Epistle Dedicatory,* and some present-day students of the matter prefer the theory that Thomas More wrote the *Life,* which was then revised and published by his younger brother. This, of course, is a possibility, but not a very strong one. Assuming that all of the personal allusions which point to Cresacre's authorship were added in the process of revision, we must still face up to the simple fact that the *Preface* makes no mention of revision or collaboration: Cresacre is definite in claiming authorship for himself. It should also be pointed out that the *Preface,* but not the *Epistle Dedicatory,* appears in two of the extant manuscripts of the *Life.* If one must choose (as I believe one must) between the dedication and the *Preface,* the former should be rejected.

Without the dedication and the ambiguous title page (both of which were set up in type and printed after the *Preface* and text proper, as the arrangement of signatures suggests)[43] we are left with Cresacre as the undisputed author.

It seems very likely, from what we know of Cresacre's peregrinations on the Continent, that he saw the *Life* through the press, or at least supervised the preliminaries to publication. Thus Hunter's theory that the dedication was written by Cresacre himself, or at his order, seems likely enough. Cresacre's ascription of the *Life* to his deceased older brother can be explained as a simple subterfuge. As a recusant, he must have been well aware of the dangers of publishing such a work which, no matter where it was printed, was clearly meant to be disseminated in England. If, as seems certain, the work was written in the years 1615–1620, and then allowed to circulate in manuscript, the death of Thomas in Rome may have provided Cresacre with the looked-for opportunity to see the book in print. It must not be forgotten that until 1626 there was no English language life of Sir Thomas More in print anywhere.[44] Whatever its numerous sources, both in manuscript and in print, this life would be the first to present a wealth of material heretofore unavailable to the mass of the English reading public. When we add to these factors the marriage of Charles I to Henrietta Maria in May of 1625, the time might indeed have seemed propitious. The new queen was a Catholic, and there was much hope among the recusants that she would be able to influence her husband in their favor. The *Epistle,* then, can be seen as a piece of obfuscation as well as a tactful diplomatic maneuver. Thomas was out of reach of all temporal authority. No one would be likely to notice the inconsistencies between the *Epistle* and the *Preface.* And, in fact, no one did until Hunter came along to edit the text in 1828. The evidence, internal and external, seems to me sufficiently convincing to allow Cresacre his proper place in the history of English biography.

VI

As Hunter pointed out long ago, nearly all of the early More biographies were either written or published at significant moments in the history of English Catholics. Roper and Harpsfield composed their *Lives* during the reign of Queen Mary, at a time when Catholicism seemed to have finally triumphed in England. Stapleton's *Tres Thomae* appeared the year the Armada sailed, when hopes ran high among the exiles that England could be won back to the Catholic fold by the sword of God, if not by reason and persuasion. Ro. Ba. wrote around 1599, near the end of Elizabeth's reign, when there were prospects of a disputed succession. And the *Lives* of both Roper and Cresacre More were published for the first time soon after the marriage of Charles I and Henrietta Maria, a union which appeared to bode well for English Catholics.

What Hunter did not note, however, is that if we are concerned solely with dates of composition, Cresacre in fact stands alone in his spiritual isolation. Writing between 1615 and 1620, he could have held out little hope for the conversion of England. Unlike Roper and Harpsfield, he writes not in triumph, but in defeat; unlike Stapleton and Ro. Ba., his tone is not one of hope, but of resignation. The best that Cresacre and his co-religionists could look forward to, at this point in history, is what Thomas More had long ago feared: "I pray god, ... that some of vs, as highe as we seeme to sitt vppon the mountaynes, treading heretikes vnder our feete like antes, live not the day that we gladly wold wishe to be at a league and composition with them, to let them haue their churches quietly to themselfes, so that they wold be contente to let vs have ours quietly to our selves."[45]

It is this isolation that creates the tone for Cresacre's *Life* as a whole. What comes through most strongly in his biography is a sense of family pride combined with a poignant feeling of *ubi sunt*. With More's martyrdom, as Cresacre sees it, England lost not only a man of incomparable virtue, but a whole way of life as well. More, at least in his early years, lived in and exemplified a golden age, and since his day the world has degenerated. Thus, Cresacre will compare the times of his ancestor with the present in order to show the extent of this degeneration. The strictness of Thomas More's father, for example, kept young Thomas from a whole series of vices "wherein most young men in these our lamentable days plunge themselves too timely, to the vtter ouerthrow as well of learning and future vertue, as their temporal estates" (sig. C_3). The falling off in morals is surpassed only by the tragic fate of religion. When Cresacre repeats Roper's conversation with More, quoted above, he adds: "But yet himself [Roper] found the prediction too true: for he liued vntil the fiueteenth year of Q. Elizabeth's raigne, when he saw religion turned topsie-turuie, and no hope of anie amendment" (sigs. V_3v–V_4). This passage indicates what often happens to Roper's narrative in Cresacre's hands: where More's cryptic prophesies and observations are related either without comment or with seeming incredulity by Roper, Cresacre is always able to point out the justice of More's remarks, and to drive home the moral. When More reveals to Roper his three wishes—universal peace, the end to heresy, a favorable conclusion to the king's matter—Cresacre comments succinctly: "The first he saw in some sorte granted him by his meanes; the other two are this day to be seene, what tragedies they have raised in England and else where" (sig. Bb_2).

Cresacre's deepest regret is reserved for the activities of some of Thomas More's own descendants, just as he finds his greatest comfort in having received some part of his great-grandfather's blessing. Perhaps the last words More wrote, the words which conclude his *English Works,* refer to the children of More's son John: "And our Lorde blisse Thomas and Austen and all that thei shall haue."[46] Thomas was Cresacre's father; Austen, or Augustine, died young. To More's words, Cresacre adds "immediate or mediate; those which they shall haue *vsque ad mille generationes.*"

This hath bene our comfort [he continues], that the tryall thereof hath bene euidently shewed in that *Edward, Thomas, & Bartholomew,* my father's bretheren, being borne after Sir Thomas my great Grandfather's death, and hauing not this blessing so directly, as my father and my vncle *Augustine* had, they haue both degenerated from that religion and those manners, which Sir Thomas More had left as it were a happie *depositum* vnto his Children and famelie (sigs. Yy_4v–Zz_1).

It is both the blessing and the example of Thomas More that have helped to maintain Cresacre and his immediate family in the faith. Cresacre's major purpose in writing a biography of More is, as he tells us, to keep the example of More alive "for the spirituall behoofe of my selfe and my children" (sig. A_1). And Thomas More is not only a spiritual guide; he is an exemplum of virtue and right behavior. Writing of the relationship between the Lord Chancellor and his aged father Sir John, Cresacre cannot decide which of them was more worthy, "yet I iudge the father more happie, that enioyed such an admirable sonne, and wish that my Children may imitate in this kinde their vertuous Anncestours" (sig. C_3v). Cresacre lives with the burden of the past, but it is a burden he carries willingly, passing it on to his descendants as it had been passed on to him.

Cresacre's historical perspective does, however, have its drawbacks. Inevitably, we lose a certain amount of immediacy. Roper's narrative, now related in the third person, declines somewhat both in charm and in power. In Cresacre's version, the various anecdotes and tales no longer have the ring of authenticity they had in Roper; instead, they take on the aura of legend. In Roper's tight context each episode is charged with import and dramatic significance. When these episodes are placed in a larger framework, separated from each other by facts and events of a different nature, their original force dissipates. The third person narrative also affects Roper's personality. As "son Roper" becomes "uncle Roper," the literary persona completely disappears, and Roper the man emerges as someone not nearly so interesting as Roper the narrator. His questions, knowing what we know, seem rather silly, his responses thick-headed. Nevertheless, Roper serves an important function in Cresacre's narrative. He is, for one thing, "family"; he helps to bridge the gap between the saintly More and his great-grandson. In addition he represents, for Cresacre, an unimpeachable authority, a "witness" whose word can be trusted. And, finally, it is Roper's brilliant portrayal of Thomas More's personality that sets the tone for Cresacre's broader portrait, including his original contributions of the More mythos.

Stapleton, too, is modified by Cresacre. Contrary to what seems to be the general opinion, Cresacre's *Life* is not especially prone to emphasizing supernatural or pietistic elements.[47] It is true that he introduces at least two miraculous, or semi-miraculous, incidents on what seems to be his own authority.[48] But, by and large, he tends to tone down the aura of piety that often envelops Stapleton's biography. He includes only a few of Stapleton's many comparisons of More with the older saints. He omits, or modifies, much of what contributes to the *imitatio Christi* atmosphere in Stapleton's account of the events leading up to and including More's execution. It is Stapleton, but not Cresacre, who tells us that More was "more zealous to become a saint than a scholar." And nearly all of Stapleton's Counter-Reformation militancy is missing from Cresacre's account. Cresacre was writing in a different era, and for reasons rather unlike those which motivated Stapleton.

Cresacre builds his biography on a primarily chronological structure, dividing More's life into logically arranged chapters. His two major sources complement each other and at the same time provide both tension and variety to the narrative. From Roper Cresacre borrows the personal elements of More's life; he also adopts Roper's relaxed, anecdotal style. Stapleton contributes both the backbone to Cresacre's narrative line and the public image of Thomas More; here the style is scholarly and (at least ostensibly) objective. In a sense, then, we have two Mores. The first (Roper's) is a private Englishman, oriented by his family duties and responsibilities; pious, witty, human, and humane. Interwoven with this is More the European humanist and Catholic martyr; urbane, wise, caught up in the affairs of the world, competing and clashing with the wits and heretics of the European continent. Cresacre senses a conflict here, but he makes no attempt to resolve it; he simply presents the two Mores side by side and allows the resulting tension to generate by itself. He could not have failed to note that the portrait of More he gives us forms a paradigm for the dilemma of the English Catholic in the seventeenth century, caught between his private, humble duties as an Englishman on the one hand and his allegiance to an international community, a world dangerous and complex, but ancient and eternal, on the other. For the average recusant of Cresacre's time, the major task was to be both a good Englishman and a good Catholic, something that from the government's point of view was impossible to achieve. This, too, had been More's task.

Even though Cresacre's portrait of More is meant to be edifying, it would be wrong, it seems to me, to characterize his biography as a saint's life. Nor, for that matter, can this generic tag be attached to any of the early More biographies. Oddly enough, Roper's life, which contains the smallest amount of supernatural coloration, comes perhaps the closest to being a saint's life in the medieval sense. But the other lives cannot be so characterized. The traditional saint's life can best be defined by its formal simplicity: the narrative line is seldom broken by the introduction of extraneous matter or circumstantial detail. A set pattern is adhered to; certain set scenes are related. Anything that does not exemplify the piety, devotion, courage, and unswerving self-sacrifice of the subject is carefully excluded. "In the common popular biographies," Donald Stauffer notes, "the saints lose their individual characters and tend to merge in a single ideal figure."[49] But the biographers of More —all Renaissance men—were clearly interested in particularity and individuality, two qualities of little or no concern to the medieval hagiographer.[50] Each of these writers—with the partial exception of Roper—aimed to be factual, detailed, and, as much as possible, comprehensive. All of them were concerned with truth, in the narrow as well as the broad sense. The image of More that

emerges from these biographies is of a real man operating in the real world,
with sainthood more or less thrust upon him. For the purposes of edification,
the traditional view of More handed down to and amplified by Cresacre serves
him far better than would that of an ordinary saint's life. It is precisely because of More's actuality, his tangible presence, that he can function so well
as a model to be emulated.

If Cresacre's biography is not, strictly speaking, a saint's life, neither is it
a propaganda tract. As I have noted, he tempers the polemical tone in Stapleton. His *Life* is written for a select, limited, audience. He is not trying to argue
a case, but simply to remind fellow-believers of what they should already
know. His full awareness of being isolated from the larger society, of standing
apart from the prevailing literary and intellectual currents of his time, finds
reflection in the quiet but forceful intensity of his tone and style.

Difficult though it may be to analyze the style of an author whose work
consists primarily of close paraphrase and translation, we can try to isolate
and discuss some elements of Cresacre's prose even if this means considering
only original passages. What emerges as characteristic is a simple and straightforward mode of expression; Cresacre's sentences usually consist of a statement followed by amplifying clauses. He seldom employs careful balance and
antithesis. His sentences are seldom and incidentally periodic. Occasionally,
his syntax will be imprecise, creating slight lapses into logical confusion. At
its best, however, his style resembles Roper's more closely that that of the
major seventeenth-century prose writers. In no way can it be called "man-
nered." Cresacre's aim, and hence his style, is primarily utilitarian. There is
no leisure in his writing for paradox and play; he is not attempting to create
a visionary, transcendent truth. His subject, he would no doubt insist, speaks
for itself and needs no embellishment. What eloquence he achieves is the eloquence of simple, sincere conviction, as in the following passage which comes
immediately after the description of More's acceptance of the Chancellorship:

> Some haue not stucke to say that if Sir Thomas had bene so happie as to
> haue dyed of his naturall death about this time he had bene a very fortu-
> nate man, liuing and dying in all mens fauour in the highest iudgements
> of the world, and prosperous also to his posteritie; for he had left them a
> fayre and great inheritance, especially by the king's gracious guift. But in
> my minde they are carnally wise that affirme this, and no way haue tasted
> of heauenlie wisedome. For the last Scene of this Tragedie is the best and
> not to be wished to haue bene omitted for all the land king *Henry* enioyed,
> though you adde the abbeylands and all, ... (sig. Gg4v).

Here and elsewhere, Cresacre achieves such forthrightness and immediacy
entirely befitting his purpose of pious, calm, and non-controversial edification.

With Cresacre's *Life,* we come full circle in our survey of early More biography. Of these early writers, only Roper and Cresacre More could claim
family relationship, and both men wrote, at least partly, out of a sense of
family duty. Whatever private reason (*secretum meum mibi*) Cresacre might
have had for undertaking the *Life,* it is, finally, his sense of family pride and

responsibility that creates the individual voice which speaks so eloquently in his work. Taking all five biographers together, we can see a clear progression both in their manner of writing biography and in the personality and significance of their subject, Thomas More. What began in Roper as a personal memoir, a tribute to a beloved relative, becomes a public work, a model for the whole body of the Catholic Church. What began as a carefully constructed collection of anecdotes and conversations becomes a relatively thorough exposition of a man's life and work. Roper's stories, as they filter down first to Harpsfield and then to Stapleton, Ro. Ba., and Cresacre More acquire new contexts and different emphases. Although Roper's work contains some elements of a saint's life, these elements are carefully muted; Roper does not commit himself. Harpsfield, in turn, expands upon More's saint-like aspects, and Stapleton and Ro. Ba. make the identification as definite as they can short of canonizing More themselves. At the same time, other sides of the More legend become embroidered. His reputation for wit grows to such an extent that, in Ro. Ba., a quip becomes More's predictable response to any situation. As the portrait of More in these biographies becomes fuller and more rounded, it also tends to solidify, to take on the firm and final shape evident in Cresacre's treatment. In Cresacre's *Life of More,* the continuity of a family tradition merges with the continuity of a literary tradition, and at least part of the humanist achievement to which Thomas More contributed remains in the pious but, in its own way, scholarly, literary act of his great-grandson.

THE MORE FAMILY AND YORKSHIRE

J. C. H. Aveling

Sir Thomas More and most of his descendants were definitely southerners, but the family had a real, if subsidiary and very intermittent, connection with Yorkshire. The tracing of this connection, like all research into the family's history after 1535, is studded with pitfalls and obscurities. Some of these are caused by the all too common natural casualties met with in studying Catholic recusant gentry families: the lack of a surviving family archive, the fact that the scattered surviving family letters (by Thomas More, the secular priest agent; Thomas More S. J., the Jesuit Provincial; Basil and Mary More in 1680–82) are only about business matters; the lack of personal detail in the frequent references to members of the family in administrative records. But the More family was special. The family and its admirers gradually developed a *mystique:* a view that Sir Thomas More was somehow the founder and archetype of English Catholic recusancy, and that his descendants (like medieval 'founder's kin') must therefore be the natural cream of the Catholic community for centuries. This *mystique* bred a special desire to publicise the family history: this comes out in the 1593 composite family portrait, and in Cresacre More's *Life of Sir Thomas More,* and in the pedigrees of the family preserved in Catholic collections. In one way the *mystique* has been an obvious blessing for historians. In another way it has been a curse: the tradition concentrated its attention so much on the major members of the family that it almost ignored, or even made mistakes about, minor members. It usually deliberately ignored members who were thought to have 'let the side down.' Prominent Catholics named More who were distant relations, or sometimes apparently no relation at all, were sometimes farced into the center of the family pedigree. In reality the family's pedigree is still in a state of disarray. An additional reason for this is that the family's moves from county to county made them strangers everywhere. In Yorkshire, for instance, the pedigree was simply not registered when the Heralds conducted their Visitations of the county in 1584, 1612, and 1665–6: the Mores were summoned to court but found to be absentees.[1]

The Yorkshire connection began, to all appearances, quite fortuitously in 1529. Sir Thomas More's approach to the problem of his children's marriages was that common amongst his class. As a high official of State his salary in-cluded windfall perquisites of which the most prized were grants of the 'ward-ship and marriage' of some minor in royal guardianship. Cicely More was married off by her father to one such ward committed to his care. In 1528 he

This article was prepared specifically for this volume.

happened to be Chancellor of the Duchy of Lancaster, and so guardian of the under-age heirs and heiresses of major Duchy tenants; amongst these was Anne Cresacre, a Duchy ward for Yorkshire properties of her father, Edward Cresacre, who died in 1511 leaving her as his only child. By 1529 Sir Thomas had chosen her, taken her into his household at Chelsea, and married her off to his only son, John More. By Court standards, Sir Thomas was not grasping. The Cresacre inheritance was useful, but modest, rated (by 'mean,' or legal, valuation) at £89 a year, not sufficient to qualify its owner for any local government post more exalted than Deputy Lieutenant or head constable. The properties were not a 'lordship' with real manorial rights, but a peasant accumulation of scattered holdings in eight parishes. There were two 'capital messuages,' one in Barnborough ('the Netherhall') and the other in Moseley; there were only a dozen tenants, three of them living in Barnborough. The tenant of two of the properties was apparently Francis Rhodes, a successful London lawyer (later a Judge) who was probably known to the Mores. Anne More was not the squire of Barnborough and she had no lease of its rectory or tithes, which were in other hands.[2]

Why then should so modest an inheritance have tempted Sir Thomas? The Mores were always resolutely *bourgeois,* professional people wedded to the law and the Church as means of subsistence. They had no aspirations or *expertise* for large-scale landownership. Had Sir Thomas conformed to Henry VIII's will, he might well have had a chance to raise his family to large estates and a peerage. But he was well aware that such a course would be foolish, not least because his only son, John More, was a mild, weak person, unlikely to shine at anything legal or practical. It was therefore wiser to collect small properties: his father's Hertfordshire lands (Gubbions and North Mimms with Hatfield), his wife's Essex property (at Low Leyton), a property at South, Kent; the Chelsea house; the Yorkshire property. Such a wide spread of small units with few tenants and relatively little managerial responsibility, and units apparently owned legally by different members of the family and protected by trust deeds and 'life interests' was the best insurance against political ruin or family mismanagement. The bulk of the property lay in the south: the Hertfordshire lands were worth twice the value of the Yorkshire ones. Of the four possible family houses (Gubbions, Low Leyton, Chelsea, and Netherhall, Barnborough) three were within easy, almost commuter, reach of Westminster and the law courts. Barnborough was relatively remote, an occasional holiday-home or refuge for members of the family who were aged or in disgrace. But it was not too remote. It lay beside the great North Road in the very south of Yorkshire, on the edge of an area already sprouting coalpits and iron forges.

Sir Thomas never succeeded in persuading his family to follow his line of dissent from Henry VIII's religious proceedings. His execution brought on them troubles the effects of which were somewhat blunted by his prudent property arrangements and their compliance. The Chelsea House, the Kentish property, and Hertfordshire lands were confiscated by the Crown. In 1543 John More was arrested, ostensibly on suspicion of treason, but secured his release by a full profession of conformity and submission. He died in 1547.

In Edward VI's reign William Rastell, John Clement, and others of Sir Thomas More's circle of relations and friends emigrated to Louvain. But Anne More and her growing family did not follow them: there seems to be no evidence that they did not conform completely to Protestantism.[3]

Late in 1552 Anne's eldest son, Thomas More II, was married to Mary Scrope of Hambleden, Buckinghamshire. Immediately the only help this marriage brought to the Mores was that the Scrope family housed the young couple and even one or two of Thomas' younger brothers at Hambleden. Eventually, though, it seemed likely to be a very profitable match. For the first time the middle class Mores were marrying into the fringes of the aristocracy. Mary Scrope's father, recently dead, had been a younger brother of the 6th Lord Scrope of Bolton Castle, Yorkshire. Hambleden manor house belonged to their cousin, the present Lord. The Scropes were poor relations in rent-free accommodation, but they had powerful relations. One of Mary's brothers was a cleric, an Etonian and Fellow of King's College, Cambridge, undoubtedly, because of his name, bound for high preferment. Another brother was a barrister of Lincoln's Inn and a courtier, soon to marry an important bride, a daughter of Lord Windsor and widow already of the brothers of Lord Sandys and the Marquis of Winchester, the Lord Treasurer. The Scropes' mother was a Rokeby of Mortham, Yorkshire, a family which produced a succession of highly able and successful lawyers. Mary More's uncle was the renowned Dr. John Rokeby. Since 1548 he had been 'Official' of the diocese of York and a leading feed member of the King's Council of the North (and soon to be Vice-President of the North). The patronage of the Marquis of Winchester, Lord Scrope, Lord Windsor, and Dr. Rokeby was soon to gain for various members of the Scrope family of Hambleden advantageous marriages and inheritances in Oxfordshire, Lincolnshire, and Yorkshire. The More family could hope to share in the *largesse.* Moreover the Scrope 'connection' into which they had entered was as yet hardly 'Catholic.'[4]

The accession of Queen Mary and the official restoration of Catholicism in 1554 made relatively little change in the Mores' fortunes. Rastell and the Clements returned to England. The production of Rastell's edition of Sir Thomas More's English works, and of biographies of him by William Roper and Nicholas Harpsfield was very probably meant to promote the authors' claims to high preferment at the hands of the Queen's government. They had some success, but the More family itself received relatively little favour. The Crown was persuaded to regrant to the family the Hertfordshire properties. But the other confiscated lands were not restored, and it was a good many years (possibly even as late as 1607) before the family was able to repossess Gubbions and North Mimms. Thomas More II received no patronage or preferment. Of his younger brothers, Edward was old enough and already literate enough, to have certainly received a university and Inns of Court education. But it seems clear that he also returned home without preferment.[5]

By 1557 the whole family moved from Hambleden (Mrs. Anne More probably came from Low Leyton) up to reside at Barnborough in Yorkshire. The reasons for the move remain obscure. There is no sign of a quarrel with the Scrope family, though it is true that Edward More had just published from Hambleden the first of those literary efforts which conservative minds found scandalous. The Mores were not following the Scropes north. Most of the Scrope family remained permanently in the south and Mary More's brother, Henry Scrope, was not to move from Hambleden to his new properties at Spennithorne and Danby in the remote north of Yorkshire until about 1565.[6] The Mores were not attracted by the house at Barnborough. It must have been unoccupied or leased to tenants for a good many years past. Dr. Pevsner's account of it makes it clear that the old buildings were too small and decrepit and had to be entirely rebuilt by the Mores after 1557.[7] It is unlikely that the family felt much personal or ideological *attrait* for Yorkshire. Anne and Mary More had spent most of their lives in the south. The legal and literary interests of Thomas and Edward More must have focused on Oxford and London. It is true that the flat, southern parts of Yorkshire were not an intellectual desert. Thomas Paynell, who cooperated with William Rastell in editing Sir Thomas More's works, was a pluralist who occasionally visited his rectory at Cottingham near Hull. Percival Creswell, Rastell's law clerk and secretary, was squire of Nunkeeling near Hull, though normally resident in Fleet Street, London. John Clement's student son, Thomas, had obtained from Queen Mary a canonry of York. In fact York Minster had a galaxy of academic talent amongst its new, Marian canons: John Boxall, John Seton, William Taylor, Maurice Clennock. Unfortunately none of these men resided in York. Yorkshire society had strong links with the Westminster legal world and the universities. But these intelligent and ambitious Yorkshiremen whom the Mores must have met in the south only visited their home county occasionally during the legal or academic holidays.[8] At Adwick-le-Street, a village close to Barnborough, resided its curate, Robert Parkyn, a self-educated literary amateur. He received books from his brother, a Cambridge don, and was prominent in a local circle of like-minded clergy, some in parishes and others pensioned ex-religious. Parkyn's MS commonplace books contain transcriptions of a few short devotional writings of Sir Thomas More. The More family must have made his acquaintance between 1557 and his death in 1570. But a few swallows do not make a summer. Yorkshire's intellectual life was thin and straitly dependent on London and the universities. Moreover there is no solid evidence that 'the More circle' functioned after 1535 as a unified group surrounding the More family.[9]

It is quite possible that the Mores moved to Yorkshire for purely material reasons: because the Yorkshire property was now their main source of income; because the Scropes could no longer house them; because, disappointed of patronage and preferment in the south, they decided to try their fortune in Yorkshire. In September 1557 Thomas More's first son was baptised in Barnborough church and Dr. John Rokeby and Mrs. Rokeby consented to be godparents. But as experience was soon to show, Yorkshire gentry society formed a tough, clannish cousinhood unwilling to trust 'foreigners,' and the Scrope-

Rokeby connection did the Mores little good. When Dr. Rokeby died in 1573 he left his choicest silver goblet to Henry Scrope and small bequests to a good many 'cousins,' but nothing to the Mores.[10]

They had not reacted decisively against Edwardine Protestantism: in the 1560s they seem to have showed no sign of reacting against Elizabethan Protestantism. In this they followed the trend of Yorkshire gentry society. Dr. Rokeby conformed and, indeed, remained a pillar of the early Elizabethan Establishment in Yorkshire in Church and State to his death. William Rastell, now a Justice of the Queen's Bench, in 1562 accepted appointment to the *quorum* of the Council of the North in York. It is true that in 1563 he resigned his offices and departed back to Louvain to die: but he had made a considerable initial gesture of conformism. Though Thomas Clement's parents also retired to Louvain, he clung on to the financial emoluments of his York canonry, leasing it in 1561 to Sir William Cecil. It was only in 1564 that he removed to Louvain.[11] Similarly, Thomas Paynell, though in trouble for his religious conservatism, retained his rectory of Cottingham until shortly before his death in 1564. Percival Creswell had died in 1558: his family remained conformist until after 1570. The Scrope-Rokeby cousinhood remained conformist throughout the 1560s. Henry Scrope sat on Exchequer Commissions in Yorkshire and clearly was angling to become a Justice of the Peace.[12] Throughout the county conformism was the order of the day and dissenters extremely few. There was plenty of 'ritual conservatism' (the use of rosaries, the sign of the cross, Catholic devotional books, 'month's minds,' and the like) amongst the usual crowds at Book of Common Prayer services in parish churches. The larger gentry households commonly had perfectly legal manorial 'chapels-of-ease,' served by 'old priests.' Not far from Barnborough such a set-up prevailed, for instance, at Aston (Lord Darcy), Frickley (the Annes), Cawthorne (the Barnebys). Latin Masses were quite possibly said occasionally in such chapels. But all the evidence suggests that this 'domestic ritual Catholicism' was severely limited in scope and declining. Almost never did it provide gentry families with their whole religious diet. Such families crowded obediently on feast days to Protestant services in their parish churches and communicated (very infrequently indeed, as was then the custom) without scruple. Their sons went in large numbers to grammar schools, universities, and Inns of Court where they were bound to attend Protestant sermons and services. The major gentry showed not the slightest hesitation in accepting administrative posts which involved them closely and frequently in enforcing the new religious order and thus, directly and indirectly, conforming to it. The overwhelming majority of the Yorkshire clergy were, like Dr. Rokeby, complete conformists. Even the relatively few of them who lost their benefices for reasons of conscience often practiced, and accepted in others, a considerable degree of occasional conformity.[13]

The More family, some of them permanently and all of them for some years, followed suit. The Netherhall at Barnborough was not a proper manorhouse and had no chapel. It is very unlikely that the family maintained an 'old priest' as chaplain-tutor.[14] They steadily attended services at the church.

In the remoter parts of the county clergy and parishioners not infrequently preserved Catholic church fittings and altars. There was little trace of such practices in Doncaster Deanery and none at Barnborough. The most that could be reasonably charged against the rector to 1578, Robert Salvin, was that he 'mumbled' the English words of the Book of Common Prayer services as if he were reading Latin, and that he occasionally left the church unprovided with Sunday services when he was away on duty as the Earl of Derby's private chaplain.[15]

In 1559 there were two More family marriages at Barnborough. Mrs. Anne More, now 50 years old, remarried to George West of Aughton and Aston, nearby places. Mrs. More's daughter, another Anne More, married George West's son (he was a widower), John West. It seems that Thomas More and his family were now left in possession of the estate and the main part of Netherhall; Mr. and Mrs. West senior lived apart, though in Barnborough (and probably in one wing of the Netherhall); Mr. and Mrs. West junior took over the Aston and Aughton estate and lived there. The weddings seemed, as we shall see, to rouse some resentment amongst the Mores. Above all they seemed to dislike old Mrs. More's decision that the family must forget the hopes roused by the Scrope connection, forget the southern past, and root itself decisively and for good in Yorkshire minor gentry society. There was no doubt that the Wests, and all their previous relations by marriage, were very minor gentry of little 'worship' in Yorkshire society. Their Aston property was small. George West, his son, and his More daughter-in-law and her children always remained conforming Anglicans.[16]

In 1565 Edward More, still a bachelor living idly with his elder brother Thomas' family, was involved in law suits, the surviving cause papers of which cast a welcome (but sometimes obscure) light on the Mores' life at this period. Edward was to be regarded by his family as a black sheep. In his *Life of Sir Thomas More,* his nephew Cresacre wrote of him severely: 'As for mine uncle Edward, who is yet alive, although he were endowed with excellent gifts of nature, as a ready wit, tongue at will, and his pen glib: yet God knows he hath drowned all his talents in self-conceit in no worthy qualities, and besides burieth himself alive in obscurity, in forsaking God, and his mean and base behaviour.' In 1593 Edward's brother, Thomas More II, pointedly had Edward omitted from the composite family portrait. In Catholic legend this judgment on Edward stuck. So, for instance, the MS collection of Catholic gentry pedigrees amassed by the Yorkshireman, Henry Maire, in 1792–5, has under Edward's name the note: 'He degenerated from the Catholic religion.'[17] Edward had wit of a satirical and often (as we shall see) undergraduate kind. As a writer he had facility but was no stylist. There was no apparent reason, except his own idleness, why he should not have made a living at Westminster in the law or administration. It seems that he never had serious conscientious objections to serving the State: even if he had, he could still, like a good many other Catholic lawyers and civil servants, have found ways and means of keeping both his religion and his official career. In 1556–7 he had left his studies (presumably at an Inn of Court) in London for Hambleden and there dashed off for publication *A Lytle and Bryefe Treatyse called the Defence of Women & Especially of English Women, made against 'The Schole House of Women.'* It was dedicated to the secretary of Sir Philip Hoby, a distinguished diplomat of particularly flexible religious opinions. The book was popular enough to run into two or three editions down to 1563. In 1559 Edward was in very serious trouble: he was arrested and indicted, along with Richard Heye yeoman of Derby and Henry Hopwood yeoman of Doncaster, for burgling the house of Alexander Levesey at Arksey in south Yorkshire, assaulting Levesey and stealing plate and other valuables from him. In October 1562 he was out of prison on bail of £66 13s. 4d. and, no doubt by the influence of his relations, secured a pardon. It is likely that the pardon was granted to a plea that the whole episode was a drunken frolic and not a serious robbery. His family now had good reason for trying to keep him with them at Barnborough.[18]

By 1564–5 his boredom boiled over and he embarked on an outrageous series of follies. He 'presented' the rector of Barnborough, Robert Salvin, to the Church authorities for absenteeism from his cure, mumbling the services, committing fornication with the wife of his cousin, Edward Salvin, and striking Edward More in Barnborough church. The Salvins retaliated by accusing Edward More of a great array of crimes: that he habitually quitted the church at the end of Sunday Mattins and before the Holy Communion service (which then usually followed at once if there were communicants), and disturbed the service by horn-blowing in the churchyard and noisy shooting practice with his bow and arrows at the village butts near the church; that he sometimes absented himself from Sunday afternoon Evensong to behave in the same way; that Edward and his younger brother, Bartholomew, often went in for horseplay inside the church, throwing about rushes and straw from the floor, laughing and making indecent jokes, and sewing; that Edward had loudly called his mother, Mrs. West, a whore in church; that he had threatened his stepfather, George West, with his bow in the churchyard and even inside the church, and once ejected him bodily from the More family 'stall' (pew); that Edward carried out a cruel and elaborate jape, pretending to have fornicated in the church porch with a village girl, and then making a violent mock of her and her family. This was not all. Edward was charged with circulating a writing of a very scandalous kind. Lastly, and most seriously, Edward Salvin reported that, in conversation with himself and Thomas More, Edward More had contested a statement by Salvin that the Queen was Supreme Governor of the Church of England.

The cases were of sufficient importance to be passed on to the York Court of High Commission. The Court forthwith put Edward in gaol in York as a punishment for taking offensive weapons into a church. After some months in gaol, he had to endure a series of court hearings. Once more, after careful enquiry, a major Court treated Edward as an irresponsible, naughty child. His remarks about the Supreme Governership were not taken seriously by judges who then normally pursued charges of this kind strictly and punished the guilty severely. The cause papers incidentally show that all the More family were then complete Anglican conformists and not suspected of popery.

Edward's writings were handed back to him, simply with an injunction 'to keep the booke mencioned in the informacion secretly to him selfe and not to let the same go abrode nor yet use the same to the hurte of his owne sowle.' The judges would certainly have confiscated and burned a Catholic book. Edward was reprimanded for his violence and put to do a public penance to be performed at the service of Holy Communion. He was to kneel before his mother and the congregation and express contrition for calling her 'Whore' and for the unpleasant jape at the expense of a servant girl. It is noticeable that he was not required to apologize to George West or to the rector, and there was no suggestion that he had been a non-communicant. The rector was also put to penance to atone for his absenteeism and mumbling: but he was totally acquitted of the charge of fornication.[19]

Study of the York ecclesiastical court books and cause papers of this period shows that Edward More's behaviour was not very unusual. Barnborough was a peasant community. Manners were rude and violent affrays very common. The church, like most country ones, was crowded on Sundays and holy days, stuffy, dirty, and in a bad state of repair. Clergy and congregations had not yet adapted themselves to a new style of Protestant worship. Their religious outlook and habits were the rag-tag and bobtail survivals of the Catholic middle ages, dying fast since they were largely deprived of the multitude of material focuses on which they had relied, shrines, sacramentals, chantries, images, rosaries. People had always 'walked and talked' and transacted business or held 'church ales' in the naves of churches. Churchyards, in spite of centuries of legislation, continued to house dances, rush-bearings and archery tournaments. Confusion of mind about the new religious order of things, and openly expressed cynicism were common. After so many changes of government and official religious policy, people in Yorkshire in the 1560s felt quite unsure whether the Elizabethan order could last: 'rumours' and 'prognostications' abounded at every race-meeting and market-day. We do not even have to take very seriously Edward More's treatment of his mother and stepfather. To judge from George West's will, made in 1572, they were then on very good terms with Thomas and Edward More.[20]

1569–70 saw the faint beginnings in Yorkshire of a wave of Catholic dissent. Dissatisfaction with the religious diet offered in the parish churches produced amongst the gentry a dissenting movement of which the left wing became 'Puritan' and the right wing 'papist.' The division of opinions often cut across families and university colleges. There was something completely spontaneous about the wave. As yet it owed little to the persuasions of existing Roman Catholic worshipping communities having a continuity of full dissent back to before 1558: there were exceedingly few such groups. On the other hand there were, by 1568–72, a handful of very determined 'self-made' Catholic dissenters in Yorkshire, most of whom had converted themselves from Protestantism after long periods of doubt and hesitation. At Broomhall near Sheffield, not very far from Barnborough, lived from 1558 to her death in 1572 the Dowager Countess of Northumberland. Through her niece, Dorothy, Lady Windsor, who lived with her for a time, the Countess was connected with the Scropes. She was a neurotic and difficult character, given to visions and frenzies requiring exorcism. Her large household easily concealed three or four 'old priests.' This in itself was nothing unusual, and did not mean that the Countess and her household were total dissenters. But by 1568 she was sheltering Henry Cumberford, a highly educated academic cleric, who appears to have gone into a state of 'provisional dissent' in 1559–60. By 1568–70, while at Broomhall, after much study of the Bible prophecies, prayer, and visions, Cumberford became very firmly convinced that the Latin liturgy was of God and the Anglican rites of the Devil. So far he was merely inclined to accept the Papacy because it went with the Mass: by 1571 he was saying that he now believed in Rome as firmly as he did in the Mass. His influence on others proved very strong. In 1571 the Earl of Shrewsbury raided Broomhall and arrested Cumberford and various converts he had made amongst the Countess' maids. Cumberford spent the rest of his life in gaol in York and Hull. His tenacious popery deeply impressed all he met, his judges, fellow-prisoners, and people who came to visit him. Archbishop Grindal firmly believed that it was he, almost single-handed, who had recreated Yorkshire popery. Certainly there was a sharp difference between his absolute Catholicism and, say, the 'survivalist' (and ultimately conformist) part-dissent of Anthony Atkinson, Lord Darcy's 'old priest' chaplain at Aston who had shared Edward More's York imprisonment by chance and who was released with him. It is perfectly possible that Mary More took her husband and mother-in-law, Mrs. West, on courtesy visits to Broomhall before 1571, and there met Cumberford.[21]

In 1569 came the revolt of the Northern Earls. The Mores seem to have been totally unaffected by it, as were the great majority of the Yorkshire gentry, Protestant, indifferent or neo-Catholic. In any case, apart from vedettes of rebel horsemen who reached the outskirts of Leeds and Doncaster, the rebels hardly entered south Yorkshire. Mary More's gentry relations took the government side. Lord Scrope was in arms for the government. Henry Scrope, just settling into Danby, was about to become a North Riding Justice of the Peace. As the rebels passed by Danby he made no move to join them. Mary More's nephew, young Christopher Wyvill of Burton Constable, was a rebel but pardoned at the intercession of his relations, Lord Scrope and the Lord President of the North, the Earl of Sussex. Wyvill's father, Mary's brother-in-law, was a government agent. The Rokebys had sat on the fence.[22]

The process by which some members of the More family gradually became Catholic recusants, and its timing, are both obscure. It is clear that, so far from mending his ways after the 1565 court cases, the rector of Barnborough grew slacker with age. Possibly because of his frequent absences from the parish, its churchwardens' presentments at the Archiepiscopal visitations down to 1580 were minimal. No recusants or noncommunicants were named, and the only complaints were about the rector. In December 1570 Edward More brought a suit in the Church courts against the rector for abusing his parishioners ('calling them knaves') and committing adultery with a married woman, Katherine Horsfall. More brought a second suit against a parishioner,

Mr. Thomas Hardwick, for non-communicating. It seems that someone (either the rector or Hardwick) then laid a counter-information to the York High Commissioners against both Edward and his brother Thomas. Both were charged with communicating of late years less frequently than they were required to do by law. In addition, Edward was accused of being the author and distributor of an 'infamous Libell and figure astronomicall . . . a prognostication containing vain tryfles.' The High Commissioners took cognisance of both sets of charges. The rector was found guilty on all counts and penanced. Hardwick was shown 'not often to have communicated' during the last three years, and fined twenty shillings to the poor of Barnborough. Thomas More was found guilty of exactly the same offence and given the same fine. Edward, not unnaturally, had harder treatment, a spell of imprisonment in York Castle for behaving 'indiscretely towardes this courte,' fined twenty shillings for infrequent communicating, and made to enter a bond 'not to make infamous ballades, prognostications and the like.'[23]

It would appear likely therefore that Catholicism had not yet made much inroad into the More family by 1570–1. In 1572 George West died. The same year Mary More's relations, Henry Scrope and Christopher Wyvill made brief incursions into recusancy, but retreated back into conformism when treated sharply by the High Commissioners. By 1575 Henry Scrope achieved his ambition and became a J.P.[24] In 1572 the York authorities, preparing to make a concerted drive against the wave of open or incipient Catholic dissent, carried out a detailed survey of all Yorkshire gentry of sufficient property to qualify them to be Justices. They were marked with symbols to show where they lay in the spectrum of religious opinions, so known open Catholics were not excluded. Thomas More's name does not figure in the list, clearly since he was either thought to be still a 'foreigner' or (more likely) because his income was below the qualifying level.[25]

In 1577 the Archbishop of York answered a questionnaire issued by the Queen's Council to all bishops: he sent to Westminster a list of Yorkshire gentry recusants. Very surprisingly it included the names of old Mrs. Anne West, Thomas More and his wife, all of Barnborough. None of them had yet been presented for full recusancy to either the Archbishop's visitors or the York High Commission.[26] The same year Mrs. West died at Barnborough where her small brass monument can still be seen in the church, with its reference to Sir Thomas More, Chancellor of England. If the Archbishop's information was true, Mrs. West had kept her profession of Catholicism for the very end of her life, and Thomas More and his wife would have to struggle to maintain their new recusancy. The York authorities were now increasingly hard on papists, and Thomas' family was divided in religion. His only surviving sister, Mrs. Anne West junior of Aston, was an Anglican, along with her husband and children. Of his brothers Austin, Bartholomew, and Francis were either dead, or (since they do not figure in the 1593 family portrait) had stayed in Anglicanism. Another brother, Thomas III, had become an Anglican clergyman and married: neither he, nor his wife, nor his three daughters, figure in the 1593 portrait. (Their parents had followed a contemporary custom in giving the same honoured Christian name to two of their sons: the inscriptions on the 1593 portrait show that the family called this son 'Thomas junior.')[27] Edward's religious position was still unclear. Thomas II and his wife Mary had a large brood of ten surviving children. Most of them were still under age, but their education and marriages formed a considerable problem. Two of the older children were already off their hands. The eldest boy, John More III, seems to have been sent up to Trinity College, Oxford in 1574. His residence there inevitably meant some degree of conformity to Anglicanism. But the universities in these years were hotbeds of violent religious discussion, demonstrations, and dissent, Puritan and Catholic. In the event John left Oxford for the English College, Douai in about 1578.[28] By 1581 his second sister, Margaret, had left home to marry John Garford of Heck by Snaith, not far from Barnborough. It is quite likely, though not certain, that Garford was a Catholic. Margaret's elder sister (and the oldest child of the family), Mary, sometime after 1581 made a Catholic marriage to Edward More of Brampton, Oxfordshire. This Edward was no relation to the Barnborough family, but when he entered their circle his name created difficulties for historians.[29]

We do not know when Thomas More II, his wife and children were 'reconciled' sacramentally and canonically with the Roman Catholic Church. In the 1560s the collapse of English society and the Catholic hierarchy away from full, formal connections with Rome had been so complete that the 'new Catholicism' of the 1570s required an immense pastoral task of systematic missionary work by priests with 'faculties' gained abroad to 'reconcile' the many who, for years, had been practising Anglicans, and to deal with the innumerable knotty problems concerning marriages contracted. By 1569 there were reports that a few priests with faculties to reconcile were operating in Yorkshire. The small groups of clerical Catholic exiles in Flanders and Rome had long presumed that they could only wait there for the death of Queen Elizabeth. The spontaneous gestation in England of the 'new Catholic dissent' produced a situation for which they had not bargained. At Louvain and Douai their little academic establishments were flooded out with young immigrants from England proclaiming their new Catholicism. The academics were hustled by circumstances gradually into organizing the English College at Douai, ordaining the newcomers, and sending them in driblets back to England, since they had not the space or resources to keep them in Flanders. By 1574 'seminary priests' were beginning to enter Yorkshire with faculties to reconcile. By 1580–2 they were still few in numbers, and had hardly any organisation. Hence in these years it is often impossible to detect the canonical status of many people presented as papist recusants. Most of them readily dodged back into Anglican practice when under pressure. Households were rarely united in religion, and the most Catholic still regarded some degrees of conformism as inevitable or even right. Consistent and determined Catholic recusancy is, for the historian of these years, no certain proof of 'reconciliation': and occasional conformism is also no proof that the conformists had not been 'reconciled.' The Catholic legend is that the 'seminary priests' normally lived concealed in gentry houses, which were all provided with special 'priests' hiding-holes' constructed with great skill for the occasion. The Netherhall at Barnborough is said today to contain two such 'priests' holes.' The local Catholic legend is that one of them was accidentally discovered and opened early in this century: that it was found to contain vestments, rosaries, etc. which at once crumbled to dust in contact with the air. Such stories are legion, and of the same kind as the legends of underground tunnels connecting monasteries and convents. There certainly were specially-constructed Catholic 'hides' in some country houses. But a great many gentry houses contained secret cupboards and rooms devised to conceal valuables or, in that litigious age, to conceal debtors. The Yorkshire evidence of seminary priests' activities indicates that they normally avoided residence in gentry houses, which often contained Protestants, were natural traps bound to be searched, and the finding of a priest in the house would lead to the arrest of the householders. Hence priests normally travelled in 'circuits,' 'resting' in remote, hired farmhouses. Thomas More II and his family only became recusants very shortly before they quitted Barnborough for the south. By the time they left there were no more than a dozen 'seminary priests' in the county and 'circuits' had not yet been organised. It is therefore very unlikely that any seminary priest resided at Barnborough before 1582. If Latin Masses were celebrated in the Netherhall in those years, it must have happened very occasionally as a priest was passing that way. 'Old' or 'Marian' priests still existed, and a number of them were reconciled and incorporated into the seminary priest organisation by 1590. There is no evidence that the Mores employed one (reconciled or not) at the Netherhall. It seems therefore that, as the family moved over to definite Catholic dissent, they had to make a choice. If they were to have regular access to the Latin Mass and sacraments during the gale of official persecution which was just beginning, it would be very unwise for them to attempt to attract a seminary priest (or provide their own by getting a son ordained at Douai) to live in the Netherhall. Barnborough was only partly their property. Their small household there was never likely to constitute more than a small segment of the village's population. The rest of the villagers never showed any tendency to become Catholics. The old, lax, absentee rector, Robert Salvin, was long dead and gone: later incumbents were of a different stamp, bred to Anglicanism. In fact the Mores' position at Barnborough was far too exposed to the authorities and informers. The alternative was to attach themselves to some fairly nearby 'Catholic strong-point' served regularly by priests. Such places were starting to arise, usually in small areas which had exceptional advantages. Thus, for instance, Margaret Garford and her husband lived in the Snaith area which was a 'peculiar eccesiastical jurisdiction,' a legal island within the diocese of York. The legal formalities required to procure presentments of recusants from the Snaith jurisdiction were so tangled and difficult that the York authorities in practice had only scanty information about recusancy there. In fact there were no real 'Catholic strong-points' within easy riding-distance of Barnborough before 1590: neither Snaith-Carlton (the Stapleton family), nor Frickley-Burghwallis (the Anne family) nor Cawthorne (the Barneby family) as yet could boast regular visits from a seminary priest. There was one final alternative: to leave Barnborough and take refuge, as some Catholics were doing, abroad in Flanders, or, with others, as lodgers in some 'Catholic strong-point' (for instance at Howden-Hemingborough in the East Riding with the Babthorpes), or, with others, to leave the county entirely. Since the Hertfordshire More properties were still not available to them, such a refuge would have to be in Low Leyton. If the Mores delayed a decision, they could expect, when the persecution reached them, imprisonment in York or life as occasional conformists awaiting the day when regular priests' 'circuits' were established. Most of their Yorkshire gentry neighbours of a like mind chose this last course.[30]

In 1580 came simultaneously the full onset of persecution in Yorkshire and the Jesuit 'mission' to the county of Edmund Campion. In 1577 Edward More (of Barnborough) appears to have been serving as a churchwarden of Barnborough parish: that year he served as one of the official sequestrators during an interregnum between incumbents, and had to put in appearances at the York Chancery Court.[31] In the summer of 1580 the York High Commissioners appointed carefully-picked gentry juries of presentment for each area of the county and received their detailed accusations of recusants and noncommunicants. The result of this for Barnborough was that two parishioners were accused, Edward More and Thomas Hawetts. On August 27th Edward appeared before the court in York Minster to answer charges of absenting himself from church and Communion. He had to enter into a bond of £100 to conform and certify the fact to the Commissioners on October 3rd. But a week later, on September 2nd Edward was back again in court 'convented for certain wordes he was presented to have saide against the State, wch. he denyed: though he confessed he gave one John Smith a blowe of the eare for making relation of certain wordes as Smyth affirmed was spoken by More, wch. More denied.' This court session was held at Wakefield. Because of the gravity of the charge, the Commissioners committed Edward to York Castle *'quousque'* (a vague term capable of a number of different expansions, but not explained by the court record.) On September 7th in York Minster the court released Edward, on bond in £40 to reappear on October 3rd for a hearing of the charge. On October 3rd he duly appeared and presented a certificate from the parson and churchwardens of St. Mary's church in Castlegate, York that he had attended their church and communicated. (No doubt this had been done during his brief imprisonment early in September, since St. Mary's was the parish church of York Castle.) The court accepted the certificate, cancelled Edward's bonds, but ordered him to 'attend the court and not depart York without licence.' He had a long and expensive wait. On October 5th Thomas Hawetts of Barnborough appeared in court and was bonded to conform himself, his wife and his family by the following January 17th. Edward was not summoned into court until November 14th. The substance of the 'words against the State' was now revealed: More had 'spoken somethinge againste the booke of common prayer and D. Latymers sermons.'

He was ordered to do penance the following Sunday in Barnborough church by reading a statement saying that the two books were 'good and godly.'[32]

Meanwhile the Commissioners had compelled the extraordinary juries to undertake a second, and far more detailed, survey of 'in anie respect undutifull & disobedient subiectes in matters of religion now established.' The order remarked that the previous presentments had omitted numbers of persons 'notoriously' known to be offenders. However, Edward More remained in court. He had, typically, put in his own accusations against Thomas Parke, the curate of Barnborough, and Leonard Reresby of Thrybergh gent. More's disagreement with Parke was clearly a minor affair, and the Commissioners simply made the two men shake hands and promise friendship. More's accusation against Reresby was that, to the scandal of 'good and godly persons' in Doncaster deanery, Reresby had promised marriage to a lady, bought the licence, and then, for years, postponed the wedding. The court ordered Reresby to marry her forthwith. The case is one of the exceedingly few surviving indications that the Mores had social contacts with the local gentry.[33]

On January 9, 1581 the Commissioners received 'a trewe certificat' of 'disobedient persons' in the West Riding. The Barnborough entries were certified by 'Thomas Jopson, parson, Edward More, Roger Foster churchwardens.' The text ran: 'they do present for not comminge to the churche nor receyvinge the communion, Mr. Thomas More & Mary his wyfe / Henry & Grizacar [Cresacre] his sonns / Marye, Katheren, Grace & Jane his daughters. Also Christofer Cam, An Tourner & Willm. Helaye his servants.' On January 17th Thomas Hawetts of Barnborough presented a certificate of his family's conformity and was dismissed. The records of the High Commission contain a massive amount of material on its dealings with almost all the persons named in the second lot of presentments. But there is no mention whatever of the Mores and their servants: not even a record of the delivery of summonses. Between 1581 and 1619 the York ecclesiastical court books contain one single reference to a recusant at Barnborough: in 1582 the Archbishop's visitors put Alice Boxe on a bond to certify that she had communicated. These facts, and the abundant evidence that Thomas More II and his family resided at Low Leyton in Essex steadily from at least 1582, make it clear that they quitted Yorkshire precipitately, most probably in February or March, 1581. In 1584–5 the Heralds, conducting a Visitation of Yorkshire, reported that Thomas More gent. of Barnborough put in no appearance because he was a recusant in prison.[34]

During these affairs, Edmund Campion S. J. was visiting Yorkshire. He seems to have crossed the southern (Derbyshire) boundary of the county on about January 25, 1581, possibly (though there is no certainty) passed by Otley into Richmondshire and then across for a fortnight's stay at Mount St. John near Thirsk. In mid-March he was guided from the Mount across into Lancashire by a certain 'Mr. More and his wife,' who 'lived near Sheffield,' 'had once been his pupil,' and clearly was conversant with gentry houses in Lancashire. It is not likely that this was Thomas More II. A much more likely candidate was an Edward More (no relative whatever) of Cowley, near Ecclesfield and Sheffield. This Edward came from a north Derbyshire gentry family, and he had bought property at Cowley, a property which was thoroughly searched by pursuivants in 1582 when they were trying to trace Campion's helpers. No effort was made to search Barnborough. Edward More's wife, Elizabeth, came from the Eyre family of Dronfield, Derbyshire. It is quite possible that the Edward More gent., a Yorkshireman and recusant member of Lincoln's Inn in 1577, was this Edward of Cowley, and not, as has sometimes been thought, Edward More of Barnborough.[35]

The later career of the Barnborough Edward More is exceedingly obscure. It seems agreed that the Edward More gent. who appears at Low Leyton with Thomas More II in later years was Thomas' son-in-law, Edward More of Brampton, Oxfordshire. The wayward Edward was buried at Barnborough in 1620. Thomas More II, in his will made in 1606, left £10 each to his brother Edward and 'Anne More daughter of the said Edward Moore.' Some pedigrees of the family credited Edward with a wife named Mary and three children, Thomas and Henry (said to be Jesuits) and Anne (said to have been a Benedictine nun). It is now generally agreed that the two Jesuits were the sons of Edward More of Brampton. It is possible that our Edward's daughter was the Anne More professed a choir nun at the English Benedictine convent at Cambrai in 1625 and said vaguely in the convent register to have been a close relation of Dame Gertrude (Helen) More, a daughter of Cresacre More. If the Barnborough Anne went to Cambrai, she must have been taken in at Low Leyton after her father's death, have become a Catholic, and have been provided with a dowry. There is no trace of Edward More in the Barnborough presentments in York court books down to 1620. If, as seems certain, he remained an Anglican, the absence of references to him would be no proof that he did not reside at the Netherhall for the rest of his life. In June 1592 the York High Commissioners ordered the arrest of 'Edward More gent. of Ripon' (the only trace of the name in the Ripon presentments of the period) for issuing a 'scandalous libel' directed against a clergyman, Richard Shepherd. More was brought to York and put in the custody of the York sheriffs and stayed there for six weeks. He was then brought to court, reprimanded, charged costs amounting to 26s. 8d. and released 'this time.' The case bears all the familiar hallmarks of our Edward More of Barnborough.[36]

From 1581 to 1680 the Mores, now residing at Low Leyton in Essex and Gubbions in Hertfordshire, appear to have had no relations with Yorkshire and Barnborough other than those usual for absentee landlords. The Cecil papers at Hatfield contain a list of recusant gentry dated 1592. Amongst 'recusants at liberty' is 'Thomas More of Barnborough esq.' This was pretty certainly an error by the informer.[37] In 1600 presentments for Burghwallis in south Yorkshire (a home of the recusant Anne family, not far from Barnborough) include 'Thomas More and his woman servant negligent comers to the church: Thomas More, his wife and servant non-communicants.' In 1663–4 William More and his wife were presented as papists at Burghwallis.[38] There is little good reason for connecting these persons with the Low Leyton Mores.

'More' was a confusingly common name in Yorkshire amongst both Catholics and Protestants. In the 1570s and 1580s the rural dean of Doncaster was a Henry More (who, in 1559, as a young priest in York, had refused to subscribe to the Book of Common Prayer and the Elizabethan settlement of religion.) In 1581 one of the chief High Commissioners was a Robert More Esq. In the later sixteenth century there were at least two other More families of gentry recusants in Yorkshire. In the early 17th century a rising family of North Riding lawyers which produced two Clerks of the Peace acquired from the Heralds' College a coat of arms which was that of the Low Leyton and Barnborough Mores with a slight difference. The North Riding Mores became Catholics and, down to the mid-18th century were substantial landowners at Angram and Loftus and maintained a Catholic chaplaincy. They seem to have had no relationship whatever to the Low Leyton Mores. The coat of arms is no proof of relationship, since the Heralds' College sometimes made new grants of arms based on merely imaginary kinships with existing armorial families.[39]

From 1587 Thomas More II of Low Leyton accumulated arrears of court and recusancy fines. In 1599 the Exchequer seized two-thirds of the Hertfordshire and Yorkshire properties as a distraint for debt and leased out the seized parts—most probably to an agent who (as commonly happened) privately sublet them to the Mores. After Thomas More's death in 1606, his son and heir, Christopher Cresacre More, successfully pleaded legal formalities and got the seizure raised. There is reason to believe that he visited Barnborough in the summer of 1619. He certainly asked for, and obtained, that year from the Council at Westminster a recusant's licence to travel for six months to certain named counties, which included Yorkshire. It is noticeable that it is from July 30, 1619 (down to the 1690s) that began the presentments at Barnborough of a recusant gentry family named (variously) Lewling, Lewland. Hence it is quite possible that Cresacre More paid a short visit to Barnborough to see his uncle Edward (who was to die the following year at Barnborough) and inspect the property, and that he installed the Lewling family in the Netherhall. In 1619 they were reported to have been recusants for the past 12 years (not at Barnborough). Perhaps they were tenants of Cresacre's persuaded to move up from Essex or Hertfordshire. It is very unlikely that Cresacre was able to ward off a further seizure of the Yorkshire property. In 1652, during the unsettled years of the Interregnum, the property was threatened with a more severe State occupation. Cresacre's son Thomas More warded off the threat by taking the very anti-Catholic Oath of Abjuration.[40]

The fortunes of the Mores between 1581 and 1680 are not our concern in this article and, indeed, have yet to be worked out in detail. Their part in the affairs of the English Catholic community was in no way remarkable. They were carried along with the stream of the community and their contribution to its life was typical of that of business-like middle-class-gentry families such as the Sheldons of Beoley (with whom they intermarried), the ironmaster Brookes of Shropshire (Cresacre's son Thomas married a Brooke), the Maires and Withams of north Yorkshire and Durham. Dame Gertrude (Helen) More of Cambrai was a 'Bakerist' (disciple of Augustine Baker, the Benedictine spiritual writer) and reproduced his strange spirituality: she was in no way a major spiritual writer. Thomas More, the secular clergy agent in Rome and Madrid, was an important but minor figure in early 17th century clerical disputes and on the opposite side of the fence to his Jesuit cousins, Thomas and Henry More. In an age when antiquarianism and family history were absorbing interests to many educated people, the Mores followed suit. A family committee put together (though it remained in MS) a small *Life of Sir Thomas More,* and Henry More S. J. compiled his very workmanlike history of the Jesuit English Province (also for years only in MS). They were not sufficiently prominent or wealthy to attain to a baronetcy or even knighthood. They generally fought shy of political commitments. It is not easy to make much of Thomas More II's apparent involvement with Robert Persons' secret printing press. The Mores were hardly involved in the Appellant crisis, or in Caroline Court Catholicism. They were neutral during the civil wars and, as we have seen, Thomas More temporarily apostatised in 1652 to avoid heavy recusancy fines. In 1647 Henry More S. J. found himself, as Vice-Provincial of the Jesuits, thrust willy-nilly into signing a joint agreement between all the Catholic groups and the New Model Army, an action for which he was afterwards dismissed and punished by Rome. The lay members of the family did not sign the agreement, most probably because they were not prominent recusant leaders. After 1660 the Mores took no part in the Popish Plot crisis. During the short reign of James II they were preoccupied with the move to Yorkshire and, apart from young Basil More (who appears to have gained a commission from the King and fled abroad to die in Louvain in 1689), they attained no offices of profit (at a time when almost every Catholic gentleman was briefly becoming a Deputy-Lieutenant or Justice of the Peace). Like so many other Catholic families of their kind, they became progressively poorer after 1660. Their symptoms were the common ones: the Hertfordshire and Essex estates were sold off: younger sons were sent wholesale into trade or the law. Basil More seems to have been apprenticed to an Italian Catholic merchant in London in 1659 before he succeeded to the estate: of his sons, William and John became lawyers, Charles a druggist and Augustine a woollen draper. The more fortunate of their kind grew rich on marriages to heiresses: the Mores experimented in this field but seem barely to have broken even.[41]

This economic decline was the real occasion of the family's return to live at Barnborough. It now became their main means of subsistence. The first of the family to return to live in Yorkshire were Basil's sisters, Margaret and Mary More (the Mores who were mission priests before this time appear all to have worked in the south, in Sussex and Essex). They had been professed (probably at Hammersmith convent) sisters of Mary's Ward's Institute. In 1678 they were members of the small community sent to Dolebank near Ripon in Yorkshire to make a foundation. Within a few months, as a result of the 'Yorkshire Plot,' they and their Jesuit chaplain were arrested and put into York Castle. On March 29, 1679 Thomas Yarburgh reported to Sir John Reresby that 'ye 2 Mrs Mores ye Dorteurs' were amongst the small group of

Yorkshire Catholic gentry who had refused to take the Oath of Allegiance and who were therefore in imminent danger of being convicted of *Praemunire*. At the West Riding Quarter Sessions that year the sisters were (rather oddly) convicted of Catholic recusancy as if residents in Barnborough. Later in the year Margaret More died in York Castle and was buried in St. Mary's church, Castlegate (the church in which Edward More had made his formal act of conformity in 1580).[42]

The two sisters' brother, Basil More, his wife Anne (Humble) and three of his daughters arrived at Barnborough in the summer of 1680 for a stay which lasted until at least the spring of 1681. In 1680 they, one woman servant, and Alice Lewling were presented as papists resident in Barnborough. On September 26, 1680 Basil wrote a friendly letter to his Tory Protestant neighbour at Thrybergh, Sir John Reresby, sending with the letter a hound which he had promised Reresby. That December the friendship was closer, and Basil was consulting Reresby on financial problems. (Reresby's archive contains a copy of a letter on money matters from Basil to his cousin, Mr. Francis More 'at Line Street or Crosby Square, London.') On February 23, 1681 Mrs. Anne More wrote to Reresby begging him to send her 'Sir Thomas More's picture.' Soon afterwards she wrote again, complaining that she and her daughters had just been presented for recusancy at Doncaster Quarter Sessions. She appealed to his chivalry and pointed out that the family were not permanent residents at Barnborough but merely passing visitors, 'having come to visit my sister this winter.' (The reference must be to her sister-in-law, Mary More, imprisoned in York Castle.) Mrs. More wished to be 'freed from the inconveniences' attending recusancy conviction. She added: 'I doubt not that one word from you will get us crossed out of the Book of the Clerk of the Peace.' Mrs. More had been pregnant when they arrived in Yorkshire. The Barnborough church register contains a record of the burial of a son in September 1680. Basil More had clearly already left Yorkshire. On September 7, 1682 he wrote from Gubbions, Hertfordshire to Reresby asking whether his influence could spare the family from a militia levy just made on the Barnborough estate.[43]

There is no sign that the More family returned to Yorkshire during the reign of James II (1685–8). Basil More's name does not figure on the list of Catholic gentry promoted to, or proposed for, local government offices in the county, a list which included almost every Yorkshire Catholic of consequence. In 1686, after prolonged legal difficulties over the pardon of prisoners 'in praemunire,' Mary More and her companions were set free from York Castle. They bought a house in Micklegate, York and opened a large school. It seems clear that Mary was the superior of the community down to her death in York in 1699.[44]

The move of Basil More and his family to Barnborough still hung fire. At the Archiepiscopal visitation of 1689 and the West Riding Quarter Sessions round-up of papists in 1691 it was reported that there was only one resident papist at Barnborough, a certain Anne Roe. On the other hand the curate there entered in his church register in 1689 'June 29th Mary More daughter of Thomas and Sarah More baptised,' and in 1691 'November 3rd, Gervas

More son of Thomas More baptised.' Were these illegitimate (or legitimate) children of Basil More's son, Thomas More, who, according to the standard pedigrees, died unmarried in 1696? Were the children really baptised by Anglican rites? A few years later the curate appears to have been willing to falsify entries for the More family, marking as baptised in his church children who were almost certainly baptised elsewhere by a Catholic priest. Such false entries were then made for legal reasons and occurred occasionally: the usual form was to put 'born,' not 'baptised.'[45]

In 1694 Basil's wife died and was buried at Barnborough. This was an indication that the family now had no fixed residence other than Barnborough, but it is no proof that Mrs. More actually died there. Basil himself was buried there in 1702. His eldest son and heir was William More, a lawyer resident in Barnard's Inn in Holborn, London, a bachelor. But a family arrangement appears to have been made whereby the Barnborough estate was vested in his younger brother, Christopher Cresacre More. Christopher had married a Londoner, and had been living in London and then for a time in Hertfordshire. William had prospered and acquired parcels of land in Haldenby and elsewhere in Yorkshire. He was also a partner of his brother-in-law, a Durham Catholic John Forcer, in 'a lease of Lead-work in Kellow, Durham.' When William died in London in 1710 he divided his property between John Forcer, Christopher More of Barnborough, and another brother, Austin More of Whitechapel, London, and asked to be buried in Barnborough church. Meanwhile Christopher More, his wife and family had taken up residence in the Netherhall. Their youngest child was 'baptised' in the church there on September 8, 1703.[46]

To all appearances there now followed 26 years (1703–29) of steady residence of the More family at Barnborough. They were there in 1706 (a presentment), 1710 (William's will), 1715 (a presentment), 1718 (Christopher registered his property as a papist) and 1721 (a mysterious and unidentified More entry in the church register). Of their four surviving children, the one son, Thomas More, married Catherine, the daughter of Peter Gifford of Whiteladies, Staffordshire. This was the first time for many years that the Mores had made a marriage alliance with a Catholic family of real consequence. Catherine's brother, another Peter Gifford, was later to become an Anglican. The young couple received immediately a portion of the Barnborough property (for which they registered by proxy at Wakefield in 1718). But they left England to live cheaply in Ghent. There they no doubt became closely associated with the English Jesuit college and started the Jesuit connection which was to be so strong a feature of their family life.[47] Christopher More's eldest daughter Anne married William Binks, a Catholic gentleman residing in Richmond, Yorkshire. This marriage was not a happy one. Binks was, in 1724, sufficiently prosperous to be able to maintain a Jesuit private chaplain in his house in Richmond. But later he seems to have become impoverished. In 1745 he was living in the Bedern beside York Minster, and he died in Easingwold, Yorkshire in 1748. Of his two children, the son, William Binks, was 'killed in the Indies,' according to the genealogist, Henry Maire. His daughter, Mary

Binks, in 1735 at the tender age of 9, was 'boarded out' on her own in the village of Burghwallis near Barnborough (according to a census of Catholics: Burghwallis Hall was occupied by friends of the Mores, the Anne family.) In 1749 she married a Protestant, John Ullathorne, an Easingwold tradesman. From this marriage derived the famous Benedictine Archbishop Bernard Ullathorne.[48]

Christopher More's youngest daughter, Mary, married a near neighbour, the Catholic Charles Waterton of Walton Hall. Manifestly the Mores were now accepted into the shrinking world of Yorkshire Catholic gentry society. It was customary for the gentry of any consequence to employ private chaplains. But there is no surviving evidence whatever that Christopher More did so. The mission records in Yorkshire of the secular clergy, Jesuits, Benedictines, Franciscans, and Dominicans contain no reference to dealings with the family at Barnborough. Since the mission records are quite full, this seems conclusive evidence that Barnborough had no regularly resident chaplain between 1703 and 1729. How therefore did the family get Mass and the sacraments? There were a number of established missions within reach: a Jesuit mission at Stubbs Walden; another Jesuit mission at Burghwallis (the Annes); Fr. Petre S. J. was at the Waterton house at Walton from 1690 to his death in 1729; there was most likely yet another Jesuit mission in Pontefract. It is very probable that Christopher More arranged with the missioner at Stubbs Walden, Ambrose Iles S. J., the superior of the Yorkshire Jesuits, for a system of regular 'supplies' shared out amongst the neighbouring Jesuit missioners. Such a system was unsatisfactory. The priests were faced with a round trip of at least twenty miles. The roads were foul and blocked in bad weather, and priests notoriously bad horsemen. The Mores were newcomers. There was a contemporary shortage of priests. The existing system of missions and house chaplaincies was extremely uneconomic of manpower and a strain on clerical resources. The Mores' case for having a resident chaplain was most probably weak. There was only a tiny Catholic congregation at Barnborough of the family and a very few household servants. The villagers were solidly Protestant.[49] The Netherhall was small and antiquated. Dr. Pevsner's survey indicates that Christopher More must (perforce) have paid for some small repairs and modernisations: the main rebuilding of the house took place in the nineteenth century long after the Mores' time. On the other hand the family had some claims on Ambrose Iles' consideration. The connection with Sir Thomas More continued to give them a romantic interest. They had in the past produced the Jesuit historian of the English Province, and Christopher's heir was becoming a client of the Jesuits at Ghent. Moreover there is evidence of a sort that the Mores had a special connection with Stubbs Walden. However, the connection may not have been established before 1729. The Mores had a number of relations, some Protestant, some Catholic, who are not included in the official pedigrees of the family. Sylvester Saul of Stubbs Walden Hall married Irene, a daughter of Alexander Nicholson 'of Barkstone' by his wife Irene, daughter of Thomas More of Barnborough.[50]

After the death of Christopher More in 1729, his son Thomas More brought his family to Barnborough. A son of his, Basil (who must have died young) was born there in 1730. But henceforward the family preferred to live in hired lodgings in York, occasionally using Barnborough as a holiday home. Thomas' mother, the widowed Mrs. Catherine More, departed to live with her married daughter, Mrs. Waterton, at Walton. The family were in York in 1732 when their youngest child, Mary, was born, and in 1733 when there was a thorough census of Yorkshire Catholics. They were staying at Barnborough, accompanied by Mr. Walter Gifford, during the census of 1735. Thomas died in 1739 and was buried in Barnborough church. His widow, Catherine, soon returned to her house in Colliergate, York. Old Mrs. More died at Walton in 1744 and was buried at Barnborough. In 1745, the year of the Jacobite invasion scare, the family seem to have been staying at Barnborough. Several Catholic gentry residents in York, friends of the Mores, procured from the Justices special licences to leave the city for brief visits to Barnborough: Thomas Selby Esq. on December 3rd (for 8 days); on February 22, 1746 Selby, with two Catholic manservants or tradesmen, had licences to make an indefinitely long residence there.[51]

York had become a considerable social center for the Yorkshire Catholic gentry. Catholics, though numerically in a tiny minority in a heavily Anglican cathedral city, had an accepted place in society. Their gentry (drawn not only from Yorkshire but all over the north) were not big spenders. They consisted entirely of young married couples awaiting succession to estates, of younger sons living on annuities or rent-charges, of widows and spinsters preferring York society to the isolation of a country dower-house. A considerable number of them (though by no means all) lived in Micklegate, where, at one time or another, almost every second house was occupied by a Catholic family. This grouping centered on the Bar Convent. The Convent ran a 'Young Ladies' boarding school (to which Thomas More's daughters, Biddy and Mally, and probably also Catherine, went 'at any early age'), a 'Poor School,' and received a small number of genteel lady boarders (Lady Hungate, the Duchess of Norfolk) who were given flats in the house for themselves and their servants ('Lady Hungate's barf house made in ye old Hen house, Oct. 1749' as the Procuratrix recorded). The Convent had Jesuit chaplains and tended to act as the focus of prayer-groups of devout laypeople. Down the hill, near the front of the Minster, and hidden discreetly in the backgarden of the priest's house ('Mrs. Holdforth's') in Lop Lane, was the secular clergy chapel. This had a congregation of gentry and tradespeople in the town, and from a strange concentration of Catholic lodgings in 'the Bedern' (the old 'sanctuary' within the jurisdiction of the cathedral Close with its own Justices). For social life there were the Assembly Rooms (with one or two Catholics on the Committee), a theatre in the Minster Close managed by Mr. Keregan, a respectable Irish Catholic with a daughter who became a nun in Paris, the racemeetings on the Knavesmire, and several inns run by Catholics.[52]

It seems clear that Thomas and Catherine More, with their affection for the Jesuits, would find York congenial and the difficulties of securing priestly supplies for Barnborough unbearable. Their two sons both went to the Jesuit school at St. Omer and became Jesuits. Thomas, the elder and heir, came on the English mission in 1752 when he was 30 years old, and spent some years as chaplain with the Watertons (his relations) at Walton, and then at his mother's house in Colliergate, York. In 1769 he became the last Provincial of the English Jesuits before the suppression of the Society. He moved to London, with frequent visits to Walton and York, and died in Bath in 1795. His younger brother, Christopher More S. J., was never employed in Yorkshire, and died at Bath in 1769. Their youngest sister, Mally, went on from the Bar Convent to the Augustinian Canonesses of Bruges, where she was elected Prioress in 1766. She endured the uprooting of the community by war, its exile to England, followed it back to Bruges, and seems to have died there after 1803. She had two older sisters. Biddy (Bridget) More was much-married, first to Peter Metcalfe of Brigg, Lincolnshire, and then to Robert Dalton of Thurnham, Lancashire: she had children by both marriages. The other sister, Catherine More, remained unmarried in York for the rest of her life.

From his father's death in 1739, Thomas More was the legal owner of the Barnborough estate. Though he became a Jesuit, he, by an arrangement which had become quite common in the Society during the eighteenth century, retained his legal ownership. No doubt his regular visits to Yorkshire were partly in order to keep an eye on his property. His mother had a private Jesuit chaplain in her Colliergate house, Peter Maire, from 1741 to 1743 and very possibly on to 1760, when he succeeded to the Bar Convent chaplaincy. From 1765 to his mother's death in 1767, Thomas More S. J. lived with her and his sister Catherine, though he seems to have lodged in a house near the Minster with his married sister, Mrs. Dalton and her husband and children. From 1767 to her death in 1784 the spinster Catherine More continued to live in the Colliergate house, while the Daltons' passed to her nephew, Dr. Robert Dalton, a gentry doctor who rarely practised as a physician. For at least part of this time, Miss More housed yet another Jesuit, Thomas Nixon. This strange arrangement, whereby Catholic gentry retained in their houses private chaplains even when they lived in towns which had easily-accessible public chapels, was no peculiarity of the More family. At one time in the 1740s in Micklegate, York the house adjoining the Bar Convent was occupied by the Meynell family who housed a private Jesuit chaplain; two doors away were the Selby family with another Jesuit, and down the street Lady Haggerston with a third.[53]

At his death in Bath in 1795, Thomas More S. J. disposed of nearly £2000 of the family money. Apart from token sums to his nun sister at Bruges and his Waterton relations, he left the money to the family's sole heir, his sister Mrs. Bridget Dalton. By the terms of a deed of entail, the Barnborough property also went to her and her heirs. Her son, Thomas Metcalfe, had already changed his name to 'More' in expectation of the inheritance, but he had died young in 1794, and left no children. The next heir in the entail was Mrs. Dalton's daughter, through whom the Barnborough property passed eventually to the Catholic Eyston family. The virtual extinction of the More family (at least in its main line: no one has yet attempted to trace the careers and pedigrees of all the numerous younger sons of the family) was in no way remarkable. In the course of the eighteenth century a large proportion of Catholic gentry families suffered a natural extinction or, more commonly, survived through the female line. The change of family was usually covered by the heirs' adoption of the original family's name. Some Catholic families underwent two or even three successive 'transfusions' of this kind.[54]

THOMAS MORE AND THE LEGISLATION OF THE CORPORATION OF LONDON

J. Duncan M. Derrett

The trial of Sir Thomas More, formerly Lord Chancellor and sometime Under-Sheriff of the City of London,[1] continues to command interest, and versions appear in journals, on the stage, and from the B.B.C. These 'popular' reconstructions utilise inferior material, and recent discoveries have antiquated the accounts of the trial which appear in the better-known biographies. In this paper we shall consider one of the arguments which arose in the course of the trial, the meaning of which is quite obscure to the reader. It concerns the legislative capacity of the City of London's legislature, the Common Council, and it is of so interesting a character that it is surprising that London's lawyers, who have always had sympathy for one of the City's greatest citizens, should not have explained it for us before this.

There are only two accounts of the trial which are of any value in the present context. That by the continental well-wisher of More, sent to Paris within ten days of the execution, merely says, "...ac vos soli nullam habetis potestatem statuendi quicquam absque reliquorum Christianorum consensu, quod sit contra unitatem et concordiam religionis Christianae." ("And you have no jurisdiction to enact anything which is contrary to the unity and concord of the Christian faith without the consent of all other Christians.")[2] The argument in general amounted to this, that the Act of Treasons[3] was void, because it was enacted in support of the Act of Supremacy,[4] which was itself void because Parliament had exceeded its legislative competence. There is no doubt but that More believed it was very doubtful, and he argued vigorously accordingly, whether the legislature of any one country could claim omnicompetence in matters which concerned the faith of all Christians. The Supremacy of Parliament, which we now take for granted, was not established until after the sentences against More and his fellow 'martyrs' in 1535. More's case was that in such matters Parliament was a subordinate legislature, and must await the consent of a General Council. This argument was particularly unfortunate at that juncture, and nothing could have been less designed to satisfy the court, which included numerous members of the King's council. We are, however, not concerned here with the law of England on that particular subject. There was indeed a practical precedent which tended to support the prevailing opinion—namely, that the King in Parliament was supreme in matters spiritual

Reprinted with corrections from *The Guildhall Miscellany*, 2, no. 5 (1963), by permission of the author and the publisher.

as well as temporal within his realm—but as it is itself not thoroughly under-stood[5] we shall do well to leave it aside for the present. Thus the *Paris News Letter,* as the source quoted above is called, gives us only the gist of the argument, in keeping with its character as a *précis.*

William Roper's *Life* of More contains a detailed account of the trial. The corresponding passage reads,[6] "... he declared that this Realme, being but one member and smale parte of the Church, might not make a particular lawe disagreable with the generall lawe of Christes vniuersall Catholike Churche, No more then the city of London beinge but one poor member in respecte of the whole realme, might make a lawe against an acte of Parliament to bind the whole realme ..."

It is important to remember that the report which Roper provides is at second hand, and recorded after nearly twenty years.[7] Roper has had to refresh his memory, as we see in other places, by reference to More's own letters: but here they did not help him. What we must suppose is that More argued that Parliament was not competent to legislate so as to bind Englishmen in matters where the only competent legislative body was the General Council; and that it was objected (whether by him or by the court, or by the opposing counsel, we do not know) that there was a possibility of a legislature existing within the bounds of a wider jurisdiction which is nevertheless competent to legislate validly even without the consent of the superior legislature and in matters where the competence of the latter is not doubted. To this he answers that the instance chosen, namely the City of London, is an unfortunate choice, for in fact the legislative capacity of the City does not extend to annulling or abridging Acts of Parliament.

The reason for so construing Roper's words is this: More's arguments were originally reported shortly and tersely, as were the arguments of counsel and judges in the contemporary law reports, such as they were. No attempt was made to reproduce word for word what was said, but rather to give the gist and effect in as crisp a manner as possible. More can hardly have raised the question of the City's legislative powers, which were themselves not beyond debate at that time, without relevance; and the reference to the City is so phrased that it is evidently an exception to another proposition which Roper does not give us. Thus we must insert that proposition, which quite possibly may have come from the other side, or from one of the judges.

So we may paraphrase Roper's account much as follows,

"He declared that his realm, which was only one member of the Church, had no power to pass a special statute repugnant to the general law of the universal Church of Christ. If it were urged that the City of London, a mere corporation within the realm, had legislative competence without the consent of Parliament, this did not conclude the matter, he said, because where an Act of Parliament provided to the contrary no legislation of the City could have any validity, for a repugnant Act of the Common Council was void to the extent of its repugnancy."

Why this reference to the City? In what ways was the relationship between the Common Council and Parliament similar to the alleged relationship between Parliament and the General Council? To understand More's constitutional theories it will be helpful to unravel this question. Fortunately the documentation available is ample enough to make it quite plain.

All corporations had a certain legislative power,[8] and it was in 1535 by no means unusual for cities, boroughs, guilds, and fraternities to legislate for their members, but their by-laws, as these are called, were subject to the control of the royal courts, and might be declared void for want of *vires*, or jurisdiction to legislate so as to 'bind' the persons purported to be bound thereby. The position of London was peculiar. The Acts of Common Council, provided that they were carried for the reformation of an ancient custom, the removal of inconveniences, or the enforcement of customary rights, were not only binding upon citizens of London,[9] but upon all persons whatsoever whose conduct came within the scope of regulation by the Common Council. Thus persons not citizens might be prevented from selling in a particular market, goods to be sold in any market might have to be examined and deposited in a particular place, and the affairs of the various companies might be regulated in such detail, and the regulations might be enforced by fine or imprisonment to such good purpose that those Acts were every bit as important to the tradesman, and indeed any dweller in London, as Acts of Parliament. The special character of legislation by the City lay in the rule that the customs of the City were never extinguished by non-user,[10] and in an equally useful rule, confirmed by several statutes,[11] that the City had power to legislate so as to conserve and amend its customs. The result of this power was that by-laws protected by this very ancient and reiterated statutory privilege would, provided the king's courts admitted their status, bind citizen and non-citizen alike as if they were themselves statutes.[12]

One sees the relevance of this at once. The Church of England, according to the advisers of Henry VIII, had always preserved peculiarities, some of which were recognised by Canon Law, founded upon the 'custom of England'; and this custom, they had been contending, was the foundation of numerous statutes, including some of the famous Reformation statutes of which More himself disapproved. In aid of custom the Church was challenged to show why the King should not legislate even against the Papal supremacy.

The City's legislative powers were often canvassed in the royal courts. A survey of the whole question was undertaken in *Hutchins* (or *Hitchins*) v. *Player*[13] in which Sir Orlando Bridgeman, Chief Justice of the Common Pleas 1660-8, delivered a classic judgment afterwards referred to with great respect, in the course of which the City's legislative powers were vindicated. The Acts of Common Council must be intended *bona fide* to amend customs which are difficult or defective or to apply new remedies to new emergencies.[14] Magna Charta assured to London all her ancient liberties and customs, and the custom of enacting ordinances (as he calls them in certain places in the judgment) is confirmed by Acts of Parliament. In several ways an Act of Common Council resembles an Act of Parliament, in particular the severability of the clauses, each being like a separate Act so that if one be void others will not necessarily be tainted by it.[15] Later the similarity of Acts of the City to Acts of Parliament came under unfavourable comment from the judges,[16] but there is no doubt but that within the extremely broad scope allowed to the City its own laws might differ very considerably from those of the rest of the country, and might be altered without reference to or consent of the rest of the realm. Some of the City's laws affected the succession to property situated within its boundaries wherever the deceased resided, and no one can deny that they were laws of great material importance. In Edward VI's reign a law was passed by the Common Council called "Judd's law" which deprived of his 'orphanage portion' any freeman's child convicted to attempting to cause bodily harm to his parent, etc.[17] This aptly illustrates the City's power of legislation, sheltering under the right to reform ancient customs and so to engraft a new law upon an old, and perhaps virtually obsolete, stock.[18] It goes without saying that the constitution of London, and its legislative power, and the results of its valid legislation, had no necessary connexion with the common law, and that much of the municipal law of London was in derogation from the common law. The debates usually referred to as 'the great *Quo Warranto* case' (1682) centred upon this source of contradiction.[19] A statute of the 33rd year of Henry VIII attempted to curtail elements in the constitution of corporations generally which were inconsistent with common law, and its passage confirms that Parliament was aware of the anomalies as early as that reign.[20]

More curious than the scope of legislation was the right of London, grounded upon her ancient customs, to ignore general statutes.[21] A whole class of statutes was held not to apply to London, though London was not 'ancient demesne.'[22] The customs of London could be set up by citizens against not only the common law but also Acts of Parliament.[23] As Sir Orlando said, general words of statutes did not take away particular customs of London, because the latter are themselves confirmed by several Acts of Parliament.[24] In those days the notion that Parliament could not legislate contrary to the tenor of earlier Acts except by express words (a notion long since exploded)[25] was in vogue, as we see from More's own appeal at his trial to Magna Charta's protection of the Church of England.[26] Sir Orlando instances the statutes of Mortmain which did not take away the custom of London to devise lands in mortmain.[27] All this was clearly held as late as the case of the *Chamberlain of London* in the 32nd and 33rd year of Elizabeth I.[28]

We are now in a position to see what the argument was. More challenged Parliament's power to declare the king head of the Church of England, since this was contrary to the ancient faith and constitution of the Catholic Church which gave pre-eminence to the Pope. Parliament, he argued, could not legislate without the consent of all Christendom expressed in the constitutional way, namely in General Council. It seems to have been objected that the customs of England had from the most ancient times allowed the abridging of the Pope's rights and jurisdiction in England,[29] and the legislative power of Parliament was founded upon this ancient custom, which no higher authority could take away. Moreover the Canon Law recognised variations in custom in the national churches, and indeed from province to province. The nearest parallel from the point of view of an experienced common lawyer was that of

the City of London. Standing upon its ancient customs it could legislate without Parliament's consent, and bind effectively everyone who came within its
scope. A man of Kent trading in London was as much liable to fine in a City
court as a citizen of London, and a man of Cornwall dying leaving lands in
London would be succeeded in respect of those lands by heirs selected according to London law, even though that law might have been varied since he executed his will and without his knowledge, let alone his consent.[30] In this
situation the courts of the realm would recognise the authority of the City,
and the jurists of the western European world (if we assume that their opinions are relevant) would, it was argued, recognise as valid a statute of the
English Parliament in derogation from the Canon Law.[31]

We are now able to understand More's point as Roper reports it. Parliament cannot bind Englishmen by a statute contrary to the Christian faith
upon an analogy with the City of London binding Kentish or Cornish men.
The City cannot enact anything which is *contrary to an express enactment
of Parliament.* In distinction from its special powers of legislation founded
upon its customs, and its rights to ignore certain statutes of general application, there existed no power of positive legislation repugnant to *statute,* as
opposed to *common law.* No Act of the Common Council could enact that,
whereas Parliament had provided such and such, no citizen of London should
obey it, subject to penalty. Only if the ancient custom afforded scope could
such an Act provide that regulations derogating from the common law in one
way should in future derogate from it in another or others, and Parliament
might annul inconvenient Acts of Common Council.[32] The limitation to which
More correctly draws attention is essential to the existence of a corporation
enacting by-laws: any repugnancy must be supported by pre-existing authority, and the national legislature cannot tolerate the existence of an inferior
legislature which purports to nullify, on its own initiative, express legislation
by that superior body. The same, More claimed, was the position with Parliament. Parliament, he argued, was not enacting, in the Act of Supremacy,
something which was established by ancient custom (whatever some might
urge on the subject), but, even if it had purported so to enact, it could not
take advantage of the argument, because there existed express legislation on
the identical subject by a superior legislative body. The General Councils of
the past thousand years, as More is known to have said more than once,[33] had
provided or recognized that the Pope should be the head on earth of the
Catholic Church, and legislation by a national church in derogation from this
was necessarily repugnant and void unless the consent of that head, or of the
supreme legislative body itself, were first obtained. Without the consent of
the head the limb cannot sever itself from the body, and without the consent
of the existing legislative head of the Church, that is to say, the Pope under
the general superintendence of a General Council, England's legislation in the
Act of Supremacy was *ultra vires.* The obvious argument with which to meet
More's point, namely that the acts of the General Councils were not binding
upon Parliament[34] cannot be answered here, since it takes us into the wider
question of the status of the Canon Law in England and the difference be-

tween questions of faith and questions of title, matters beyond the scope of this paper but by no means irrelevant to the general issue: the distinction between spiritual and temporal which seems to us so obvious was, by 1535, hardly beginning to be worked out.

More's professional life had made him very well acquainted with the extent and nature of the customs of London, and of the repugnancy of London laws with the common law. He had himself administered those laws, and had no doubt taken part in the certifying of them at the behest of the royal courts. Whether he himself, or his opponents and judges, drew attention to the alleged analogy between the City and Parliament in this context, it is clear that no one doubted but that he would be excellently placed to see the constitutional value of the comparison. However the alleged parallel arose, More's reply was apt, and convincing. It could be undermined only by showing that the legislation of the superior legislative body, the General Council, did not bind, or must be held not to bind the members of Parliament so as to deprive them severally, or their legislature corporately, of the necessary legislative freedom. The actual behaviour of the English Parliament could be read in more than one way. So far as the City of London was concerned, however, its legislative superior was at its doorstep, and could wield weapons far more terrible than those possessed by Pope or Council. In a conflict between City and Parliament over legislative competence there was no doubt which would win, and though More disposed of the attractive analogy with his accustomed shrewdness and relevance of argument, Parliament stood in no need of such a precedent, and, we might think, might do much better without any reliance upon it. Parliament, unlike the City, would submit to the legislative supremacy of another assembly such as a General Council if it wanted to,[35] and not otherwise.

THE TRIAL OF SIR THOMAS MORE

J. Duncan M. Derrett

Thomas More's trial was a turning-point in English constitutional history. His life, ending as it did, served as an inspiration from the moment of his execution. That an academic man, and a lawyer at that, could *know* the right course, recognize from far off that it would probably lead to his death,[1] and steadily follow it, come what might, is a rare phenomenon. More is wrapped up with England's contribution to the Reformation, and his moment of crisis deserves to be carefully investigated. The entire background of controversy ought ideally to be brought in to illuminate that crisis, but this article will concentrate on the actual trial. It is but poorly represented in the works of historians, including those who specialize in the study of the constitution; and religious and other considerations have bedevilled discussions of the position which More represented and for the truth of which he gave, according to many, his life.[2] The situation is improved by the recent discovery of new materials, publication of which requires the re-examination of the remainder. In particular insufficient attention has been paid to the indictment; the significance of Chapuys's colloquy with the king's servants a little over a year before the trial has been missed; and, most important of all, the relevance of the Affair of Friar Standish, itself poorly handled by constitutional historians, has escaped notice. Since even recent writers make inept comments upon More's situation, in ignorance of a lawyer's technique, and of the actual issues in point of law, this present article will not encumber itself with unnecessary secondary references. One cannot refrain, however, from praising those who preferred to suspend judgment, so long as the story could not be told adequately.

The indictment of More was not published until 1932.[3] William Roper, More's barrister son-in-law,[4] wrote about twenty years after the event, in ignorance of all but the broad features of the trial, and in reliance upon eye-witnesses.[5] The next most authoritative *Life,* that by Nicholas Harpsfield,[6] suffered similarly, but the author incorporated material from the so-called *Paris News Letter,*[7] with the result that one work of art mingled fragments from two other works of art, neither of which was completely authoritative. In fact notes of the indictment were preserved in the papers of Sir John Spelman (or Spilman), one of the judges at More's trial, and a man known to have been keenly interested in the upheavals of the reign.[8] These and the

Reprinted with addenda from *The English Historical Review,* 79 (1964), 449–77, by permission of the author and the publisher.

notes of the somewhat incredulous Lord Herbert, who had access to the indictment,[9] were used by Bishop Burnet.[10] The latter's account of the alleged conversation with Sir Richard Rich is better than Roper's or Harpsfield's. Spelman's notes,[11] though of value as a contemporary record, do not offer much, except by way of emphasising More's insistence on the wording of the statute 26 Hen. VIII, c. 13 (Spelman ignored his motion in arrest of judgment). The publication of the indictment failed, strangely, to elicit a response from biographers and historians: often evidence of the contents of the indictment was preferred to the indictment itself.

Opinion on the Continent was heavily influenced from the first by the account which first obtained currency. This was the *Expositio,* in which Erasmus had a hand.[12] Its relationship to other contemporary documents has already been explained.[13] Cardinal Pole had some scraps of information from an eyewitness,[14] but he used them indifferently and relied upon the *Paris News Letter,* or another version of the original account. This account can now be reconstructed from recent discoveries, and is called below R.[15] The account depicted More as the victim of tyranny, impiety, and unconstitutional innovation. With time the alleged wickedness of Henry VIII and the martyr-like qualities of More became enhanced.[16] The deaths of the Carthusians and Bishop (Cardinal) Fisher added to the horror. Contemporaries on the Continent could not be expected to understand the technicalities of the trial, and were not furnished with information from which they could appraise it. The continental view returned to England in the printed Stapleton,[17] and circulated widely in the manuscripts of Harpsfield's *Life.* Roper, several times published, gives a much more correct picture. More there defends himself as a lawyer, and the trial appears as a genuine conflict between two constitutional theories.

The major sources, *R* and Roper, are quoted (with one exception) *in extenso* below. The footnote references to More's correspondence are needed for two reasons, firstly because Roper evidently refreshed his memory from that correspondence, and secondly because it is useful to see where the trial seems to have caught up points which More had discussed fully previously, and which therefore must have been fully known to the court and to counsel for the Crown when the indictment was being prepared. Yet a note of warning must be sounded: what a man says in discussion, and what he puts forward in his defence on a capital charge need not agree perfectly; and the importance to be attached to the arguments More used cannot be weighed except in the context of the trial as it appears to have proceeded, and in the light of the practice of advocacy, which has changed little since that period. For this very reason More took care that his beloved daughter, Margaret, should make available, if possible, directly or indirectly, the operative and fundamental reasons for the position which he had determined to adopt. From the correspondence we see, in part, how the trial was prepared for by the 'other side.' The counterparts, the (sadly mutilated and incomplete) records in the Public Record Office, which have not been published in their entirety,[18] and which show the king's ministers at work on Fisher's and More's cases, substantiate, so far as they go, More's account of the affair rather remarkably and the discrepancies are at the heart of the matter.

Room for doubt exists here and there. Spelman's notes are admittedly summary; no verbatim report existed; the manuscript progenitor of *R* was written by a foreigner whose estimate of the importance of various parts of his informant's tale differed largely from Roper's and was (it seems certain) coloured by his own views. Roper's account must have suffered from unconscious selection and oversimplification.[19] The order in which arguments were presented is not vouched for. Pole gives an argument which More may not have used.[20] *R* contains remarks which were not true, tested by the indictment itself, and improbable.[21] There are, where they agree, verbal and other differences. Neither explains its deficiencies. Yet, when all is trimmed to accord with common sense, a consistent and intelligible scheme emerges. The motives or causes for the omissions in *R* and Roper (where there are, as is submitted, omissions) would fortunately not be difficult to visualize.

It will be convenient to refer briefly to the Affair of Standish first before passing to the trial of More, and to end with More's own words on the constitutional problem of 'repugnancy,' which was virtually the kernel of the trial, written long before anyone knew that More would have to argue on the issue in his own defence. This passage is important because it places in perspective the arguments which considerations of advocacy required him to urge on his own behalf, and helps us to understand his comments on his situation when the trial was over.

The Affair of Standish

At a time when it was known that, according to canon law, the secular judge might arrest, try, and punish clergy only in a limited scope of cases, a matter of law reaffirmed to some extent by recent papal declaration,[22] Parliament had, in the temporary statute of 1512 (4 H. viii, c. 2), removed the highly controversial 'benefit of clergy' from certain malefactors in all cases where they claimed to be in the 'minor' orders, *i.e.*, below that of sub-deacon. This statute, which was to endure until the next parliament, purported to put an end, for the while, to controversy, so far as the king's courts were concerned. The debate continued, notwithstanding, amongst canon lawyers, whose law was, of course, international.

According to the report of Standish's affair, written, rather from an advocate's point of view than in a judicial spirit, by John Carrell (serjeant-at-law, 1510; king's serjeant, 1514; died 1523) and preserved in the book known as Robert Keilwey's Reports (or Keilwey),[23] Abbot Kedermyster (Kidderminster) of Winchcombe challenged the propriety and validity of the statute during the session of the next parliament when its extension would have arisen for consideration. The propriety of the abbot's own protest, which was given publicity, will be considered later. His main argument was that *all* orders were 'holy,' and he cited a canonical reference in support of his position. The Church, in his view, might censure all members of parliament who passed any such statute. Theologians as well as canonists were consulted by the governmental group and the topic was argued in front of the king's judges and the lay members of the council. There Henry Standish, D.D., argued on

behalf of the statute, the burden of his case being that the customs of England
were in no way contrary in this particular to the law of God and the liberties
of the Church. It would be out of place to enter here into the merits of the
vexed subject of the 'conventing of criminous clerks before the temporal
judge.'[24] The arguments used by Standish were bold and, perhaps in the heat
of controversy, he ventured into the dangerous field where matters of faith
shade off into questions of law. The more audacious of his arguments were
evidently congenial to an anti-clerical approach to the subject, and it is small
wonder that he was himself 'convented' before convocation. The deliberate
steps taken against Standish by convocation, and the formulation of the difference of opinion between the king's advisers and Standish's opponents,
amongst whom Wolsey himself was prominent, are also beyond our present
interest. What is distinctly relevant is that at the final conference, held at
Baynard's Castle (in London) in the presence of the king, his council and the
judges (some of whom participated in More's trial) and, it seemed, of More
himself, a stalemate was achieved in that (i) an approach to Rome to have the
problem resolved by canonists was discouraged; but (ii) whatever the merits
of the governmental case the case of Standish's opponents could be stultified
by the application to each one of them individually of the statutes of *praemunire*. In other words, whether the king in Parliament had the power or not
to legislate contrary to some clerics' view of the law of God, no ecclesiastical
tribunal could punish an individual who supported a statute against canon
law. This practical result was no legal decision, but the care with which the
whole matter was argued, and the authority of the personalities involved, gave
the Affair of Standish, and the law then stated by the judges, a value as a precedent no smaller than an actual decision *inter partes*. Thus, as early as 1515,
long before Cromwell came on the scene, the practical difficulty of impugning an Act of parliament on theological and canonical grounds was notorious.

The Scheme of the Trial

Roper makes it appear that More was tried on indictment for a single
offence against the Act of Treasons,[25] and that More's remarks related to the
evidence led on this point and to the validity of the Act. The *Paris News
Letter* referred to three 'articles,' and this has led to confusion. The indictment solves the problem. The Act of Treasons made it high treason, if after
1 February 1535, any 'do maliciously wish, will or desire by words or writing
or by craft imagine invent practise or attempt ... to deprive them [*i.e.*, the
King, Queen, or their heirs apparent] or any of them of the dignity title or
name of their royal estates ....' The indictment sets out the purport of the
Act of Supremacy, to enforce the objects of which the Act of Treasons was
passed, next the tenor of the Act of Treasons itself, and then a series of
allegations that More *false, proditorie et maliciose* acted in relation to the
king's title of the Supreme Head of the Church of England. The allegations
include acts tending to establish the 'wish, will ... to deprive ...' whilst 'imag-
ining, inventing ...' the same, and distinct allegations of treasonable acts.
Roper's information was incorrect. The allegation of intent contrary to the

Act of Treasons is made at the commencement of the list of 'acts'; it is repeated in connection with the third allegation, and the fourth and last (with
slight variations), and is again repeated in the grand jury's presentment at the
end of the indictment. We have a series of 'acts' each of which would have
sufficed to ground an indictment under the Act.[26] Each act or group of acts
might well be referred to as a 'count' of an indictment. The author of *R* was
thus not substantially inaccurate. There were eight treasonable acts alleged,
an act not necessarily treasonable in itself, and an act of another (Fisher) was
inserted as evidence of the truth of the immediately prior allegation—showing
that modern methods of drafting indictments have improved on the contemporary style. We shall deal hereafter with the four 'counts' into which these
eight acts seem naturally to fall. They may be arranged as under:

1. Refusal on 7 May 1535 to accept the royal suprem-acy of the Church of England.	1st Count
2. Letters written and delivered to a known traitor, *sc.* Fisher. 3. More upheld Fisher in his treasonable attitude, and communicated his own refusal to discuss the issue. 4. He described the Act of Supremacy in hostile terms. 5. He counselled Fisher to answer spontaneously and to avoid expressions which would incriminate More.	2nd Count
6. On 3 of June More refused to break his silence; 7. but, intending to stir up sedition against the King, described the Act of Supremacy as a two-edged sword.	3rd Count
8. On 12 June More in a long conversation with Rich admitted the king might be accepted Head of the Church in England, but denied Parliament's capacity so to declare him and thereby to bind the subject.	4th Count

Though carefully drawn, such an indictment was wide open to argument. The
prosecution must prove the defendant's intent at each stage. The weight lay
entirely upon the allegations of mental disposition, and, although one is held
to intend the natural consequences of one's acts, in this case the only consequence by which the Crown could attempt to show More's intent was the
behaviour of Fisher, which, upon the face of the indictment, was capable of
alternative explanation.

The commission of Oyer and Terminer[27] which sat on 1 July 1535 to hear
this case contained many councillors, particularly prominent amongst whom
were Cromwell, Audley, and Norfolk who had constantly pursued More's
embarrassing behaviour and that of his *ad hoc* comrades, the Carthusians and
Fisher. One might think that Anne Boleyn's father ought to have been dis-
qualified from sitting; also her uncle and brother. All three sat in the court,
which contained most of those named in the commission.[28] By modern standards the presence of Cromwell, Audley, and Norfolk, who supplied information to crown counsel and supervised the preparation of the Crown's case,

would be most objectionable. But in those days it was usual to place great reliance in the jury, and in the learning of the professional judges.

There was a bare majority of lawyers on the bench, all the senior judiciary (including for this purpose the not very learned lord Chancellor Audley) being present with but one exception. There is no evidence that the bench did not perform its proper function of acting as the prisoner's counsel,[29] and the interventions of the duke of Norfolk, the only councillor recorded as having spoken, seem to have been in order even by modern standards. Sir Christopher Hales, the king's 'general attorney,' led for the Crown, Sir Richard Rich, the king's 'general solicitor' with him. Rich, though a principal witness for the Crown, seems not to have been regarded as an improper person to appear on behalf of the Crown. The jury seems to have included a man prejudiced against More,[30] but this, like the constitution of the bench, does not suffice to cast doubts upon the *bona fides* of the trial.

The prisoner had no copy of the indictment, no witnesses, no counsel. This was normal. Courts would assign counsel to a prisoner wishing to raise a point of law against his indictment, but otherwise at that period the accused must plead his own cause.[31] Why were Roper and Rastell, relations of More and members of the Bar, absent? They ultimately achieved eminence in their profession. No doubt they were afraid to assume such a responsibility if it had been offered to them. But fortunately their services were not needed. More dealt with his indictment in a most professional manner, notwithstanding his state of health. The trial was not free from what we call the accidents of litigation; but since the basic issues had been ventilated in print previously, some of them repeatedly, there is no ground for suspicion that More might have been convicted or sentenced hastily or unadvisedly.

The procedure was normal. The accused was arraigned; a return (Venire) was ordered to be made forthwith; the accused was offered the prospect of what would amount to a pardon if he confessed and recanted, and this he refused; he was then required to plead to the indictment. He moved that no count of the indictment disclosed an offence, but for the word 'maliciously,' apparently the essential word of the Act of Treasons. It seems that as the ingredients of the malice had not been alleged it could be urged that the indictment was bad on the face of it. The motion was rejected. More moved that the first three counts disclosed no offence, giving reasons. As to the fourth count he pleaded Not Guilty. The court evidently upheld him on the first three counts, otherwise the Attorney-general would not have dared to abandon, as he plainly did, three-quarters of the Crown's carefully-prepared case. The plea of Not Guilty was entered. Evidence was led for the Crown on the fourth count. More made a speech to the effect that on the evidence led there was no case to answer. The submission was rejected, and the issue, whether More was guilty of high treason under the Act, was delivered to the jury, which returned in a quarter of an hour with the verdict of Guilty. In a motion in arrest of judgment More endeavoured to show that the Act itself was void. The court rejected the motion and sentence was passed. He was offered another opportunity to speak, presumably in order that he might appeal for clemency. His reply, famous for another reason, is of historical interest.

As a privilege in view of his former rank, or of his long association with the king the sentence of drawing and hanging, *etc.*, a multiple sentence for a multiple crime, was commuted to simple beheading, and he was decapitated on Tower Hill on Tuesday 6 July.

The Arraignment, the Offer of Pardon, and Plea to the Indictment

Roper neglects the offer of a pardon. True, the king required his conformity and not his death: but the offer was substantially a formality. More, as his letters show, feared a recantation might have been forced from him by torture. He was concerned to maintain his loyalty to God, which the king himself had promised should come before his loyalty to his sovereign. The offer and response appear in *R*, while Roper supplies the principle behind the plea that followed.

R, para. 1. Thomas Morus . . . ad magistratus ac iudices ordinatos per regem fuit adductus. Quo praesente accusationes in ipsum publice recitatae sunt. Continuo dux Nortfordiae illum huiusmodi verbis allocutus est. Vides, More, te quidem hac ex parte in Regiam Maiestatem graviter deliquisse. Nichilominus tamen de ipsius clementia et benignitate confidimus, si poenitere volueris tuamque hanc temerariam opinionem, cui pertinacissime adhaesisti, in melium commutare, te delicti remissionem facile ab illo consecuturum. Cui Morus: Magnifici viri, maximas vobis gratias habeo, de perquam erga me benevolentia. Verum istud solum Deum Optimum Maximum oro, ut ipsius adiutus ope, in hac mea recta opinione ad mortem usque perseverare valeam. Quantum autem ad accusationes, quibus oneror, attinet, vereor ne vel ingenium vel memoria vel verba ad explicationem sufficiant, cum non solum impediat articulorum prolixitas et magnitudo, verum etiam diuturna in carcere detentio necnon aegritudo debilitasque corporis, quibus nunc sum affectus.

2. Tum iussu magistratus allata est sella, in qua cum resedisset hunc in modum sermonem prosecutus est.

Roper (p. 86, l. 12–p. 87, l. 2): When Sir Thomas Moore was brought from the tower to westminster hall to awneswer the Indictment, and at the kings bench barre before the Iudges thervppon arraigned, he openly told them that he wold vppon that indictment haue abidden in lawe, but that he therby shoulde haue bine driven to confesse of himself the matter indeede, that was the deniall of the kings supremacye, which he protested was vntrue. Wherefore he therto pleaded not giltye; and so reserved vnto himself advantage to be taken of the body of the matter, after verdicte, to avoid that Indictment; And moreouer added that if thos only odious tearmes, 'Maliciously, traiterouslye, and diabolicallye'[32] were put out of the Indictment, he sawe therein nothinge iustlye to charge him.

The right to 'plead over' to the indictment was not yet available in cases of treason to a defendant who 'demurred,' and against whom a verdict was given. More was therefore forced to plead Not Guilty to the fourth count. To the previous three counts, which Roper ignores, he could afford to demur, admitting the facts alleged, and moving that the indictment be quashed *pro tanto*.[33] He would reserve till later his arguments against the sufficiency of the indictment. In fact the motion in arrest of judgment so overshadowed the earlier stages of the trial that Roper almost ignores them.

R invents a first part of the first count, More's alleged obstinate disapproval of the king's 'second' marriage. The reference to Anne in the indictment is very indirect.[34] More may well have referred to the king's 'great matter' during the trial, but hardly at the commencement. A plausible explanation of the mistake is not that the author of R already had points in mind to which his information was made to fit, but that More may have felt obliged to move that the court had no jurisdiction, in view of the notorious connection between the 'marriage' and the controversies in which More and the Council found themselves on opposite sides, and the presence of Anne's close relations on the bench. If he made such an indiscreet motion the court could reasonably have rejected it, since the indictment was not for an offence against Anne and her relatives were not interested in the outcome of the trial.

Further, there is evidence from Pole,[35] supported by a fleeting reference in R,[36] that More submitted that he was, by reason of his imprisonment at all material times, outside the contemplation of the Act of Treasons. Such a far-fetched motion, if submitted, would be likely to be rejected upon the plain construction of the unequivocal words of the statute: his freedom to influence the outside world being apparently not a condition precedent to his coming within its scope. We now come to his motion to quash the first three of our counts.

R, para 2, l. 22 to end: Solum ad praecipuum caput accusationis respondebo. Dicitis me commeruisse poenam quam infligit statutum in postremo Procerum conventu factum, ex quo ego in custodia sum detentus, eo quod malicioso falso ac infido animo laeserim Regiam Maiestatem et nomen et titulos et honorem et dignitatem quae illi in praedicto conventu seu Concilio consensu omnium fuerant attributa, quo ille receptus est post Jesum Christum[37] in supremum caput Ecclesiae Anglicanae; atque ante omnia quod mihi obiicitis me nichil aliud voluisse respondere Secretario Regis et Regiae Maiestatis honorabili Consilio, quando me interrogabat quaenam esset mea de illo decreto sententia, quam (ex quo iam essem mundo mortuus) me huiusmodi rebus non occupare animum, sed tantum meditari de passione Domini Jesu Christi. Ad quod clare respondeo vobis huiusmodi meo silentio me morti adiudicari non licere, quoniam quidem neque vestrum decretum neque quicquid est legum in toto orbe quemquam iure supplicio afficere possunt, nisi quis vel dicto vel facto crimen admiserit, cum silentio nulla poena legibus sit constituta.

3. Tum Regius Procurator suscipiens sermonem, Huiusmodi, inquit, silentium certum aliquod indicium erat, nec obscura significatio malignae alicuius cogitationis contra ipsum decretum, propterea quod singuli subiecti ut fideles suo principi, interrogati sententiam super illo decreto, obligantur aperte et sine dissimulatione respondere, ipsum esse bonum ac sanctum.

4. Tum Morus, At si, inquit, verum est quod ius commune habet, *Qui tacet consentire videtur,* meum istud silentium plus approbavit vestrum statutum quam infirmavit. Quousque vero fidelis quisque tenetur et obligatur respondere, etc., respondeo multo magis ad officium boni viri et fidelis subditi pertinere ut suae conscientiae ac perpetuae saluti consulat et rectae rationis praescriptum sequatur quam ullius alterius rei habeat rationem, propterea quod huiusmodi conscientia, qualis est mea, suo principi nullam praebet offensionem neque seditionem excitat—illud vobis asseverans, nulli mortalium meam conscientiam fuisse apertam.

The indictment alleged[38] that More maliciously kept silence when asked whether he accepted, etc., the king as Supreme Head; refusing a direct answer to the interrogatory, commenting however, 'I wyll not meddyll with any such matters, For I am fully determyned to serue God, and to thynk vppon his passion and my passage out of this worlde.'[39] More submits that silence itself is no crime.[40] In treason an overt act must be proved.[41] The Attorney-General replies that only traitors will hesitate to acknowledge as valid a statute to which the king has assented. More rejoins that a loyal subject, in doubt, will refer to his 'conscience' (*i.e.,* his true and independent opinion),[42] take thought for his spiritual welfare, and follow right reason. The definition of good and faithful subject excludes one who blindly follows a course set by others. By definition the good and faithful subject cannot harbour seditious thoughts. Since the relevant date More had not communicated his own well-known opinion on the supremacy issue. Even if silence were construed as an 'act,' the presumption that 'silence means consent' is with him. The first article is thus bad.

R, para. 5: Quod autem in secunda parte accusor contravenisse decreto et in eius abolitione esse machinatus, scriptis ad Episcopum Roffensem octonis[43] literis quibus illum contra vestrum decretum armaverim: etiam atque etiam optarim illas literas publice fuisse recitatas.[44] Sed quum (sicut vos dicitis) concrematae sunt per eundem Episcopum, ipse vobis ultro ipsarum argumenta commemorabo. In quibusdam tractabantur res familiares sicut nostra vetus consuetudo et amicitia postulabat. Una ex illis responsum habebat ad ipsius epistolam, qua scire desiderabat quonam modo respondissem in carcere cum primo examinarer super dicto decreto. Cui respondi me meam exonerasse conscientiam[45] et rationem esse secutum, idque ut et ipse ageret admonebam. Haec fuit (ita mihi Deus sit propitius) mearum literarum sententia, nec ob illa debeo per decretum vestrum quicquam morte dignum commisisse censeri.

Fisher had been executed as a traitor. Communication with him, counselling him, and the like could be proof of conspiracy, a substitute for an overt act.[46] It was alleged that More instructed Fisher to maintain a treasonable silence, and to comment on the Act of Supremacy in a treasonable fashion, *viz.* that it was like a two-edged sword, etc. The indictment alleged that the letters were burnt,[47] Fisher was dead, the best evidence of their contents therefore must come from the writer. He was not entitled to be heard as a witness, nor to give testimony upon oath; he confirmed, however, with an oath his own account of them. Apparently he said (the indictment is silent on this) that they were 'some eight in all.'[48] The one which related to Fisher's conduct told no more than was a fact, namely that More had disburdened his mind of the subject and would say no more,[49] and advised Fisher to follow common sense in all he did. All this was consistent with an innocent purpose. More's and Fisher's servants were the sources of the allegations in the indictment relating to the correspondence, and More plainly accepted that, in so far as the allegations were factual, they were not wrong in substance. He had already made a number of admissions:[50] but he now submitted that no capital charge could be founded upon those letters.

The indictment further alleges that Fisher did say what More was supposed to have written to him, notwithstanding More's alleged advice to him not to copy his phrases lest they might be suspected of collusion. In *R* this is dealt with along with the third count—a natural synthesis, easily disentangled.

> *R*, para. 6: Quod vero ad tertium articulum attinet, qui continet me quum a senatu examinarer respondisse vestrum decretum simile esse gladio ancipiti, ut qui obtemperaret periclitaretur de salute animae, qui adversaretur amitteret vitam; ac eadem respondisse (sicut dicitis) Episcopum Roffensem, ex quo appareat hoc inter nos de composito agi, utroque eodem modo respondente: ad eam partem accusationis respondeo me non simpliciter sed sub conditione esse locutum, videlicet, si esset aliquod decretum simile gladio ancipiti, quonammodo quisquam hominum sibi possit cavere ne in alterutram aciem incurrat? Porro quid responderit Episcopus Roffensis equidem ignoro, et fieri potest ut eodem modo responderit, sed illud non est factum ex ulla conspiratione sed potius ex ingenii disciplinarumque similitudine processit. Hoc autem pro certissimo creditote me numquam contra decretum vestrum maliciose vel dixisse aut fecisse. Interim tamen fieri potuit ut multa de me ad concitandum mihi odium apud Regiam Maiestatem depravate ac malitiose sint prolata.

It had been supposed that since the reference to the two-edged sword was in fact More's own, and Fisher had used it, More must have used it in correspondence with him.[51] More's answer, by way of motion, to these two counts is here syncopated. More could not admit or deny anything done by Fisher. But for the sake of argument he could admit that Fisher may have used the same phrase: the similarity of their education and approach could sufficiently account for this. More could not deny that he had used the phrase, but moved that the indictment must be bad in that it accused him of using that phrase when its use was equally consistent with an innocent proposition, relevant to hypothetical legislation.

From a letter of More's we gather that at More's interrogation in the Tower, when he refused to commit himself on the Supremacy question, Audley asked him whether he could not be compelled by statute to answer positively whether or not he admitted the Supremacy.[52] A distinguished lawyer could be expected to give a professional answer to such a question. More's objection, to follow his *own* account of it, meant that such a statute might run the risk of being held void by the courts. Such a statute would involve every subject in jeopardy. He would, if it were valid, be forced to swear, which might give him a choice between losing his soul or his life, for if he refused to swear as was expected of him[53] he might come within a statute like the Act of Treasons. Such a statute might be held to be an abuse of the legislative power, which existed so that the king, as father of his people, whether he wielded one sword or two,[54] might protect body and soul alike. The draftsman of the indictment had in front of him an abstract[55] which represented More as saying that the Act *was* a sword with two edges: if one said it were good it was dangerous to the soul; if he said the contrary it was death to the body—no other answer. Could not what there appears as a comment have originated as a hypothetical opinion? More himself adds that Audley rejoined, much as Standish had rejoined against the ecclesiastical party twenty years before, that the ordinaries themselves were armed with the *ex officio* oath, to oblige, for example, alleged heretics to say whether they believed the pope to be Supreme Head of the Church. Wherein lay the difference? More replied that it lay in the fact that that oath could only be used consistently with the Church's received doctrines, and in their defence.[56] Audley's proposition would jeopardize the souls of subjects;[57] and More's opinion was in accord with current doctrines on the interpretation of statutes.[58] Though the councillors were impressed at the time, parliament eventually put Audley's proposition to the test, with apparent success—because, perhaps, More's trial had intervened.[59]

Roper shows that More denied a malicious deprivation of the king's title. From *R* it appears that he denied opposition to the Act of Supremacy. The first three counts evidenced, he submitted, no malicious acts on his part; but they were evidence of malicious misrepresentation of his conduct to the king, a possibility of which we know he had expressed apprehension to the king himself.[60] He craved, therefore, the sympathy of the court. The first three counts were not proceeded with, and the Attorney-General presented the case for the Crown on the fourth count only.

The Fourth Count and Evidence for the Crown

A summary of the conversation between More and Rich as given in the indictment will suffice for our present purpose. Roper's version is slightly more improbable than the original.[61] Rich, after saying that he had no commission or authority to discuss these matters with More, expressed surprise that More could not admit the king to be the Supreme Head. He asked More whether, if it were enacted that he, Rich, were king, and that it should be high treason to deny Rich's kingship, More would not offend if he denied that Rich were king. More, it was said, admitted that he would, but asked in return whether if parliament declared that God should not be God and that it should be treason to deny the validity of the Act, Rich would not offend if he denied that God were God. Rich (it is interesting to note) was made out to have agreed that such an enactment would be void, obviously because, being against reason, it would be beyond parliament's competence as then understood. But, Rich continued, the difference between his, Rich's proposition, and More's was vast. There was an intermediate case: whether More would not offend in denying that parliament had lawfully declared the king to be Head of the Church of England. More was alleged to have answered that there was a difference, in that parliament might dispose of the Crown, which was a temporal and national matter,[62] whereas the headship of the Church was spiritual and international. The subject could not give his consent in parliament to *that*.[63] More denied that the king could be given a 'limping' title, *i.e.,* one true in England and false overseas.

The Act of Supremacy and its ancillary provisions aimed to deny this contention, namely that foreign consent would be required before the king could take a step he judged necessary in performance of his domestic duty. Scholars have been concerned as to whether More really said what is alleged in the indictment. *R* says nothing of this; its author must have feared that More said, more or less, what was alleged. The jury (as we shall see) apparently thought the same. Could he deny the competence of parliament, yet leave its Act intact? Arguments corresponding to these appeared, as the author of *R* knew, in More's own motion in arrest of judgment. But the council did not have so long to wait for More's professional opinion. The indictment, in this very passage, agrees with More's own speech to Audley and Cromwell in the Tower. More's letter to Cromwell is plain enough,[64] and no one contends that that letter was in the remotest degree privileged. These were More's views. Did he utter them to Rich in this very form? Roper tells us that More explained for the jury's benefit what he did say to Rich, and apart from the question about the Pope (which is missing) Roper's account of the crucial sentence is compatible with the official abstract. Fascinatingly that abstract reveals that Rich himself was disappointed with More's 'concelement,' as if his academic answer had avoided the trap—but Cromwell evidently knew better.

> Roper (p. 87, ll. 3–5): And for proof to the Jury that Sir Thomas Moore was guilty of this treason, master Rich was called forth to giue evidence vnto them vppon his oath, as he did.
> *Ibid.* (p. 84, ll. 13–21): ... master Riche, afterwards Lord Riche, then newlye made the kings Solicitor, Sir Richard Sowthwell, and one master Palmer, servaunt to the Secretory, were sent to Sir Thomas Moore into the Tower, to fetche away his bookes from him. And while Sir Richard Southwell and master Palmer were busye in the trussing vppe of his

bookes, master Rich, pretending friendly talk with him, amonge other things, of a sett cours, as it seemed, saide thus vnto him. . . .[65]

Ibid. (p. 87, l. 6–p. 89, l. 2): Against whom thus sworne, Sir Thomas Moore began in this wise to say: 'If I were a man, my lordes, that did not regard an othe, I needed not as it is well knowen, in this place, at this tyme, nor in this case, to stand here as an accused person. And if this othe of yours, master Riche, be true, then pray I that I neuer see god in the face; which I wold not say, were it otherwise, to winne the whole world.' Then recited he to the courte the discourse of all theyr communication in the Tower, according to the truthe, and said: 'In good faithe, master Riche, I am soryer for your periurye then for my own perill. And yow shall vnderstand that neyther I, nor no man else to my knowledge, ever tooke you to be a man of such creditt as in any matter of importuance I, or any other, would at anye tyme vouchsaf to communicate with you. And I, as you knowe, of no small while haue bine acquainted with yow and your conuersacion,[66] who haue knowen you from your youth hitherto; For we longe dwelled both in one parishe together, where, as your self can tell (I am sorry you compell me so to say) you were esteemed very light of your tongue, A greate dicer, and of no comendable fame. And so in your house at the temple, wheare hath bine your cheif bringing vppe, were you likewise accompted.

'Can it therefore seeme likely vnto your honorable Lordshipps that I wold, in so weyghty a cause, so vnadvisedly overshootte my self as to trust master Rich, a man of me alwaies reputed for one of so litle truth, as your lordshipps haue heard, So farre aboue my soueereigne Lord the kinge, or any of his noble Councellours, that I wold vnto him vtter the secreates of my consciens towchinge the kings supremacye, The speciall pointe and only marke at my handes so longe sought for: A thinge which I neuer did, nor neuer wold, after the statute thereof made, reveale either to the kings highnes himself, or to any of his honorable councellours, as it is not vnknowne to your honors, at sundry seuerall times sent from his graces owne person vnto the Tower vnto me for none other purpose? Can this in your iudgments, my lordes, seeme likely to be true?'

More is here preparing the minds of the court for their eventual summing-up, which seems to have been normal practice, if perhaps perfunctory by modern standards,[67] in case he should fail in his motion that there was no case on this evidence to go to the jury. Roper correctly separates these portions of the defence. What looks like an exchange of remarks between More and Rich, or at least a speech by the one to the other was not unusual in the light of contemporary practice. The technique employed corresponds to that used today in cross-examination. He denies the conversation as alleged, giving his own version; he attacks the character of the witness; and submits the gross improbability of the revelation as alleged. Roper, of course, knowing Rich's reputation, has brightened up the middle point, but there is no reason to doubt that More made relevant references to the upstart's character. We note

More's attempt to turn to his advantage the presence on the bench of members of the commission to whom he refused, when in the Tower, to speak his mind plainly.

Not long after this trial it was enacted that two lawful witnesses should be required to support a presentment for treason.[68] Even now Cromwell had qualms about trying a man for treason upon the evidence of a single witness.[69] Perhaps for this reason the prosecution seem to have been ready prepared with two further witnesses, whose presence is hardly explained on the basis that they were to be porters. Roper, wrongly, places their evidence after More's submission that there was no case. All his submissions would have been strengthened by their evidence. After the court had ruled on his submission there could be little point in leading it: hence we are justified in transposing the events as given by Roper.

> Roper, (p. 91, ll. 10–20): Master Rich, seing himself so disproved, and his credit so fowlye defaced, cawsed Sir Richard Southwell and master Palmer, that at the time of their communicacion were in the chamber, to be sworne what wordes had passed betweene them. Wheruppon master Palmer, vppon his deposition, said that he was so buysye about the trussinge vppe of Sr. Thomas Moores bookes in a sack, that he tooke no head to their talke. Sir Richard Southwell likewise, vppon his deposition, said that because he was apointed only to looke vnto the conveyaunce of his bookes, he gaue no eare vnto them.

The unexpected collapse of this evidence[70] could be interpreted in more than one way. The jury saw the witnesses,[71] and had an advantage over us. Perhaps they were alarmed by More's solemn remarks to Rich, and so avoided testifying against him (as Roper seems to have believed); it is equally possible that they listened to the conversation (as Cromwell may well have intended), but doubted at the last minute whether it agreed with the indictment. The jury seem to have thought that they would have testified in support of Rich, but for sympathy for More; concluding from this that More had used those words or words that produced a substantially identical effect. And was More's denial not over-subtle?

The prosecution's case being closed, More submitted that there was no case to go to the jury. There were at least *five* submissions. The last appears, apparently misplaced, in *R*. Roper omits it and gives the other four. He admits that his account of this part of the trial (not the most sensational, after all) is incomplete.[72] A little paraphrasing and supplementation is required to explain what the points were.

> Roper (p. 89, l. 2–p. 91, l. 9): 'And yet, if I had so done indeed, my Lords, as master Rich hath sworne, seing it was spoken but in Familiar secreate talk, nothing affirminge, and only in puttinge of cases without other displeasaunt circumstances, it cannot iustly be taken to be spoken maliciouslye; And where there is no malice, there can be no offence. And ouer this I can never thincke, my lordes, that so many worthye Bishoppes, so many honorable parsonages, and so many other worshippfull, vertuous, wise and

well learned men as att the makinge of that lawe were in the parliament assembled, ever ment to haue any man pvnished by death in whom there coulde be found no malice, taking 'malitia' for 'maleuolentia'; For if 'malicia' be generally taken for 'sinne,' no man is there then that can thereof excuse himself: *Quia si dixerimus quod peccatum non habemus, nosmet ipsos seducimus, et veritas in nobis non est.*[73] And only this word 'maliciously' is in the statute materiall, as this terme 'forcible' is in the statute of forcible entries; By which statute,[74] if a man enter peaceably, and put not his aduersary out forcibly, it is no offence. But if he put him out forcibly, then by that statute it is an offence, and so shall he be punished by this tearme 'forcibly.'

'Besides this, the manifold goodnes of the kings highnes himself, that hath bine so many waies my singuler good Lord and gracious soueraigne, that hath so deerely loved and trusted me, even att my very first cominge into his noble service with the dignity of his honourable pryvy Councell vouchsafing to admit me, and to offices of greate creditt and worshippe most liberally advanced me, and finally with that waighty Roome of his graces highe Chauncelour (the like whereof he neuer did to temporall man before) next to his owne roiall person the highest officer in this noble realme, so farr aboue my merittes or qualities able and meete therefore, of his incomparable benignity honoured and exalted me, by the space of XX[ti] yeares and more shewing his continewall favour towards me, And (vntill at my owne poore suit, it pleased his highness, geving me licens, with his maiesties favour, to bestowe the residue of my life for the provision of my soule in the service of god, of his especiall goodnes thereof to discharg and vnburthen me) most benignly heaped honours continually more and more vppon me: All this his highnes goodnes, I say, so long thus bountifully extended towards me, were in my minde, my Lordes, matter sufficient to convince this sclaunderous surmise by this man so wrongfully imagined against me.'

R, para. 2, ll. 5–21: ...quae habet me, quo magis animi mei contra Regem malevolentiam ostenderem, in contentione de secundo eius matrimonio perpetuo obstetisse Serenissime eius Maiestati, nichil habeo aliud respondere nisi quod antea dixi, videlicet quicquid in ea materia dixi id me urgente conscientia dixisse. Nec enim debebam nec volebam quidem Principem meum celare veritatem. Quod nisi fecissem hostem me illi, non fidelem ministrum exhibuissem.[75] Ob quod peccatum (si tamen peccatum dici debet) adiudicatus sum perpetuis carceribus, quibus iam totis XV mensibus sum detentus, bonis meis praeterea fisco addictis.

The five submissions would appear to be these. (1) The word *maliciose* was deliberately inserted into the Act to meet such a case;[76] the evidence discloses no malicious intent, but rather a professional conversation free from treasonable implications; (2) the meaning of the word is not wide, for that would be out of keeping with the context, but specific;[77] (3) malice is an ingredient in the crime alleged, just as forcible entry in the relevant statute: without proof of force that statute cannot be applied,[78] and here the Act of

Treasons is inapplicable without proof of malice; (4) extraneous events cannot be introduced to raise a presumption of malice—the prosecution must in any case prove the *mens rea*—while, on the contrary, the whole history of More's dealings with the king is consistent only with mutual trust. Finally (5) the presumption, as regards his disposition towards the king, is wholly in his favour, and if it be alleged that he disloyally withheld his assent to the Act of Succession, and that this was a fact in the light of which subsequent evidence might be construed, he was already serving a sentence for this and *nemo debet bis puniri pro uno delicto,* a well-known maxim of our law.

Verdict, Motion in Arrest, and Sentence

The submission was overruled. The jury almost certainly heard an address from Audley, were charged (as *R* rather dramatically narrates for the benefit of continental readers), and returned promptly with a verdict of Guilty. No bullying (as Cromwell had employed before)[79] seems to have been needed. A special verdict was open to them, but they had evidently been directed that it was a simple question of fact: did More speak with Rich as alleged? They found as a fact that he did: they evidently found his explanation beside the point, which is far easier than determining that he was actually lying. The words, even if hypothetical, were spoken.

It was normal practice to await a verdict, and, if it was unfavourable, to attack the indictment on law, alleging that it was 'insufficient' to found a sentence. The heart of More's defence lies in the very complex motion in arrest of judgment. He was not making a parthian shot at a victorious tyrant, but putting the issues of law before this highly competent tribunal. That the court overruled him must be equally understood in its setting. It is incontestable that they were moved by the motion. More's arguments were more numerous and better put than those of his predecessors before that bench, and he must have been exhaustive. Had he succeeded, entirely fresh advice would have been tendered to the king on the manner in which the Reformation should have been forwarded—itself by no means an impossibility, for Henry and his advisers often claimed too much. The suggestion that if the court had accepted More's motion they would all have been traitors within the meaning of the Act of Treasons is nonsense: if the Act had been 'void' they would themselves have been secure.

Audley fumbled with the procedure. Nervousness rather than inexperience probably accounts for his commencing to pass sentence without asking the convicted man whether he had anything to say why sentence should not be passed. The purpose of the *allocutus* was to give the felon convict an opportunity of moving in arrest of judgment on a point of law.[80] More interrupted him, and proceeded. Here *R* and Roper cover much the same ground; each omits two points. It would seem, since all the points are substantial, that we can safely take the one as supplementary, for our purposes, of the other. Since we cannot be sure that all More's points are recorded (we may be sure we have those which contemporaries thought important and persuasive) it is more difficult to be sure of the order in which they were submitted. There is, however, a natural sequence which would be very likely to have been followed by so experienced an advocate before so distinguished a bench: it is hardly to be believed that he would have chosen an irrational or less persuasive order—but there is some room for doubt. An incongruous order of submission could be accounted for if the court interrupted him. Since we are told of interruptions it is likely that we should have been told if he had been so significantly interrupted on other occasions as to be put at a disadvantage, or to be dislodged from a coherent and logical presentation of the case. He had, after all, had years in which to assemble the arguments, and many months in which to rehearse such a speech.

R, para. 8, l. 4 to end: Quando, inquit, morti sum adiudicatus, rectene an secus novit Deus,[81] ad exonerandam meam conscientiam libere vobis super vestro decreto verba faciam, meque totis septem annis affirmo omni studio in cognitione huius argumenti incubuisse nec tamen reperisse apud ullum probatum Ecclesiae doctorem aut posse aut debere quemquam hominum prophanum caput esse ordinis ecclesiastici.

Roper (p. 92, l. 5–p. 93, l. 3): And incontinent vppon their verdicte, the Lord Chauncelour, for that matter cheif Comissioner, begininge to proceede in iudgment against him, Sir Thomas Moore said to him: 'My Lord, when I was toward the Lawe, the manner in such case was to aske the prisoner before Iudgment, why Iudgment should not be geuen agaynste him.' Wherevppon the lord Chauncelour, stayeng his Iudgment, wherein he had partely proceeded, demaunded of him what he was able to say to the contrary. Who then in this sorte moste humbly made awneswer:

'Forasmuch as, my Lorde,' quoth he, 'this Indictment is grounded vppon an acte of parliamente directly repugnant to the lawes of god and his holy churche, the supreeme gouernment of which, or of any parte whereof, may no temporall prince presume by any lawe to take vppon him, as rightfully belonging to the Sea of Roome, a spirituall preheminence by the mouth of our Sauiour hymself, personally present vppon the earth, only to St Peeter and his successors, Byshopps of the same Sea, by speciall prerogative graunted; It is therefore in lawe amongest Christen men insufficient to charge any Christen man.'

More's first point was that the Act of Treasons was repugnant to the law of God, which was fundamental law and immutable. Though continental scholars would go further,[82] More carefully confines the principle to a scriptural authority. Notwithstanding his headship of the laity the king could not be head of the entire Church in England since no canonists of repute had suggested that a layman might be head of the clerical order. More had given great thought to the problem of papal supremacy at various times,[83] and we have here the conclusion he ultimately reached. The head must be of the same nature as the body,[84] otherwise we go against reason, and an unreasonable statute is 'void.' It must have been this submission that provoked the somewhat obvious response, which Roper would place rather later.

R, para. 9: Hic Cancellarius interrupto eius sermone, Num tu, inquit, vis prudentior ac religiosior esse quam omnes Episcopi, tota nobilitas et universus populus regi et regno subiectus?[85]

Roper (p. 94, ll. 11–16): Then was it by the Lorde Chauncelour therunto awneswered, that seinge all the Byshoppes, Vniuersities and best learned of this Realme had to this acte agreed, It was muche mervayled that he alone against them all would so stiffly stick therat, and so vehemently argue there against.

Audley's comment was just. Did More claim that his wisdom and piety exceeded those of the three estates? Ought even a heretic's view of fundamental law to be weighed by a court along with parliament's, as if the judges should judge equally between them? Not only an unwelcome burden, however constitutional theorists might talk, but an unexampled one! Parliament's competence to suppress heresy, for example, might be totally abrogated. More himself denied a fundamental freedom to choose a creed.[86] Whether parliament could solve, for England, disputed points of canon law was open to debate: the continental view, that it could not, was shared by More.[87] He evidently went so far as to contend that the court was competent (as later writers also contended) to consider whether an Act was repugnant to scriptural law (*i.e.*, not a 'human' law, such as a papal rescript), the standard being not of an individual litigant but that of the universal Church.

R, para. 10: Cui Morus, Pro uno Episcopo qui facit vobiscum mihi sunt facile centum, idque ex eorum numero qui relati sunt inter divos. Ac pro uno concilio ac decreto vestro, quod quale sit Deus Optimus Maximus novit,[88] mecum sunt omnia concilia generalia quae intra mille retro annos sunt celebrata. Et pro uno regno mecum sentit regnum Franciae omniaque regna orbis Christiani.

Roper (p. 94, l. 17–p. 95, l. 9): To that Sir Thomas Moore replied, sayenge: 'If the number of Bishoppes and vniuersytyes be so materiall as your lordeshippe seemethe to take it, Then se I litle cause, my lorde, why that thing in my consciens should make any chainge. For I nothing doubte but that, thoughe not in this realme, yeat in Christendome aboute, of these well lerned Bishoppes and vertuous men that are yeat alive they be not the fewer parte that be of my mind therein.[89] But if I should speake of those whiche already be dead, of whom many be nowe holy sainctes in heaven, I am very sure it is the farre greater parte of them that, all the while they lived, thoughte in this case that waye that I thinck nowe.[90] And therefore am I not bounde, my Lord, to conforme my consciens to the Councell of one Realme against the generall Councell of Christendome.'

His answer was threefold. (1) Parliament's competence is to be determined by the law of God as seen by a competent majority, *e.g.*, of a genuine general council. (2) If the individual is bound to follow the legislature, and an academic opinion is bound by resolutions of universities, what weight have they, treated merely as majorities, against general councils upon which laymen were represented, against so many saints who were bishops? The governmental group were certainly obsessed with the principle of majority decision, which Chapuys, about a year before, had handled with some sarcasm and in a rather similar way.[91] (3) More mentioned several countries by name.[92] Their predicaments were similar, particularly that of France. Byzantium was rather an example the other way, though the councillors were very fond of it. Threats to establish national churches were everyday events on the Continent, but no attempt to emulate Henry had been made. The inference to be drawn, More seems to have submitted, was that nothing but their consciousness of fundamental law hindered those countries from taking the ultimate step.

On the first two points no significant comment has survived. The third was tactless in view of the duke of Norfolk's very recent failure to persuade the French to follow Henry's example.[93] Did More intend to urge that the English tribunal should take judicial notice of what was done abroad?

> *R*, para. 11, l. 1–3: Tum dux Nortfordiae interloquens, Nunc, inquit, More, planam facis animi tui obstinatam maliciam.

This has been mistranslated. More's 'malice' had been established by the verdict. Norfolk meant, presumably, to show that More was showing his own determination to hinder the king's policy, hardly proving that the Act of Treasons was invalid. The failure of France and Spain to follow Henry does not prove that Henry's Act was bad. More admitted that it would be improper, if not treasonable, to argue that French decisions invalidated English statutes; but that had not been his point.

> *R*, para. 11, l. 3–end: At Morus, Quod dico, inquit, necessitate cogente dico. Volo enim exonerare conscientiam meam, nec animam degravare. Huius rei Deum, qui est scrutator cordium, testem invoco.

More was obliged by his situation to show the invalidity of the statute; it would be impiety not to do his best in his own defence; and his affection for Henry could not be doubted. He now proceeds. *If* the law of God was held not utterly and *in limine* to invalidate the Act of Supremacy and therefore also the Act of Treasons, further points relating to parliament's legislative capacity lay for consideration. They would be less appropriate where Roper places them, namely after his attack on the royal supremacy and before Audley's interruption.

> Roper (p. 93, l. 11–p. 94, l. 10): So farther shewed he that it was contrary both to the lawes and statutes of our owne Land yeat vnrepealed, As they might evidently perceaue in *Magna charta: Quod ecclesia Anglicana libera sit, et habeat omnia iura sua integra et libertates suas illaesas;*[94] And also contrarye to that sacred oath which the kinges highnes himself and euery other christian prince alwaies with great solemnitye received at their Coronations; Alleaginge moreover that no more might this realme of England refuse obediens to the Sea of Roome then might the child refuse obediens to his owne naturall father. For, as St. Pawle said of the Corinthi-

ans: 'I have regenerated you, my children in Christ,'[95] So might St
Gregorye, Pope of Roome, of whom, by St Austyne, his messenger, we
first receaved the Christian faithe, of vs Englishmen truly saye: 'Yow are
my children, because I haue geuen to you euerlasting salvacion, a farr
higher and better inheritaunce then any carnall father can leaue to his
child, and by regeneration made you my spirituall children in Christe.'

R, para. 12, l. 1–6: Praeterea illudque addo, vestrum decretum perperam
esse factum, quoniam ex professo iurastis numquam quicquam facere
contra Ecclesiam, quae in toto orbe Christiano est sola integra et indivisa.

The two Acts were revolutionary. Papal supremacy, however hindered,
had been left undiminished by previous statutes, and an *implied* repeal of
fundamental statutes securing the liberty of the Church and its constitution
could not, More argued, be relied upon. At this period it was widely believed
that parliament could bind itself, and, for example, that international treaties
limited legislative capacity. The particular oaths of king, nobles, bishops, and
laity limited, it was submitted, the capacity of each estate individually, and
thus of all jointly.[96] The spiritual sonship of the whole realm, to which Henry
himself had drawn attention,[97] was a good argument. If a child destroyed his
father, or a cleric his ordinary, it was petty treason at common law: how
could a professedly treasonable assembly enact an Act of Treasons? *Quod
fieri non debuit factum valet,* provided the *capacity* to act was there: but here
was no legislative capacity at all. And *quae contra ius fiunt debent utique pro
infectis haberi* or so one might well argue.

R, para. 12, ll. 6–10: Ac vos soli nullam habetis potestatem statuendi quicquam absque reliquorum Christianorum consensu, quod sit contra unitatem
et concordiam religionis Christianae.

Roper (p. 93, ll. 4–11): ... he declared that this Realme, being but one
member and smale parte of the Church, might not make a particuler lawe
disagreable with the generall lawe of Christes vniuersall Catholike Churche,
No more then the city of London, being but one poore member in respect
of the whole realme, might make a lawe against an acte of parliament to
bind the whole realme....

No member of a conjoint body could alter its constitution without the
consent of the remainder.[98] Any attempt would be perpetually open to
challenge. While Christians would be bound by a general council a statute
purporting to remove them from 'foreign' jurisdictions must, argues More, be
repugnant to fundamental law and thus inoperative. Apparently the bench
intervened here. What of the City of London (which More knew inside out)?
It was part of the realm, yet could make laws binding its citizens without the
consent of parliament.[99] But, objected More, was it not the case that London
could neither repeal an Act of parliament, nor limit the applicability of such
Acts to citizens of London? The case of London told rather for him than
against him.

More's case ended, Audley faltered. Precedent, we have reason to assert, had helped on the 'maliciously' point in the motion of 'no case.' It had been decided that no one could deny the Supremacy otherwise than maliciously, and that the word was mere surplusage.[100] Acts are not to be construed by reference to the debates in the legislature. But the motion in arrest of judgment raised new issues for judicial determination.

> Roper (p. 95, l. 10–p. 96, l. 2): Nowe when Sir Thomas Moore, for thavoydinge of the Indictment, had taken as many exceptions as he thought meete, and many moe reasons then I can nowe remember alleaged, The Lord Chauncelour, loth to haue the burden of that Iudgmente wholye to depend vppon himself, there openlye asked thadvise of the Lord Fitz James, then Lord Cheif Justice of the kings Bench, and ioyned in Comission with him, whether this indictment were sufficient or not. Who, like a wise man, awneswered: 'My lords all, by St Julian' (that was euer his oath), 'I must needes confes that if thacte of parliament be not vnlawfull, then is not the Indictment in my conscience insufficient.' Wherevppon the Lord Chauncelour said to the rest of the Lordes: 'Loe, my Lordes, loe, you heare what my lord cheif Iustice saith,' and so ymmediately gave he Iudgemente against him.

Fitz James and his brother judges looked at one another for some while.[101] The hedging reply, a veiled question to the other judges, elicited no response. Their discomfort must have been acute. The law of God, so far from being repugnant to the Act, was generally believed to have urgently required its passage.[102] The king's residual powers no one denied; ancient and apparently irrelevant precedents agreed that the church in England might become the Church of England. The judges and More were in no position to agree to differ.

The Final Speech

The defendant on a charge of treason or felony was entitled to all the court's protection, and he was to be given every facility for saving his life. Consequently it was usual to enable him to seek clemency after sentence. More's hope of clemency here was slight, unless it were God's clemency to the nation.

> R, para. 12, l. 10–end, para. 13: Sed non ignoro cur me morti adiudicaveritis. Illa unica causa est quod nolui superioribus annis consentire in secundum Regis matrimonium. Sed tamen magna mihi spes est in clementia ac bonitate divina, quemadmodum Sanctus Paulus legitur persecutus divum Stephanum,[103] qui tamen nunc unanimes in coelo agunt, sic nos omnes quamquam in hac vita dissentiamus, tamen in alia cum perfecta charitate consensuros. Oro itaque Deum Optimum Maximum, ut Regem tueatur, conservet ac salvum faciat ac illi salubre consilium suppeditet.

> Roper (p. 96, ll. 3–16): After whiche ended, the Comissioners yeat further curteouslye offered him, if he had any thinge els to alleage for his defence,

to graunt him favorable audience. Who awneswered: 'More haue I not to say, my Lordes, but that like as the blessed Apostle St Pawle, as we read in thactes of the Apostles, was present, and consented to the death of St Stephen, and kepte their clothes that stoned him to deathe, and yeat be they nowe both twayne holy Sainctes in heaven, and shall continue there frendes for euer, So I verily truste, and shall therefore hartelye pray, that thoughe your lordshippes haue nowe here in earthe bine Judges to my condemnacion, we may yeat hereafter in heaven meerily all meete together, to our euerlasting saluacion.'

The antipathy of Queen Anne may not have influenced the trial: but it would hinder any appeal to the royal clemency. A reprieve would certainly have been reasonable, where the law was so much in doubt. The learning accumulated by then on the subject of fundamental law was unequal to the demands suddenly made upon it. But a reprieve was not to be looked for. Of the divine clemency More has two prayers to offer. The king should be preserved in energy, guided by better principles. A miracle should so adjust the judges' view of the law that they would, when they joined More, be unanimous with him. Their participation was, like Saul's, approving, yet not initiating; like him they believed a transaction of doubtful legality to accord with the needs of the nation: their sincerity was not in doubt. But their vision might be improved, by divine intervention, as in Saul's case. More's prayers were often almost realized in Henry's own reign;[104] perhaps the story is not yet ended.

Conclusion

How More's and his contemporaries' view of fundamental law (a view easily comprehensible in jurisdictions which practice 'judicial review') merged into something more complex, out of which grew our present notion of parliamentary omnicompetence, is a story to be told by legal historians. More's judges and More were not disagreed on the fundamental hypothesis; where they differed was in the interpretation of the law of God. A rule of construction that no positive law could amend or revoke a provision of the law of nature or the law of God—a rule which Henry himself, his parliament and judges accepted[105]—served as a safety-valve, rendering inoperative as much of a statute as might be held to be repugnant. A man indicted under a repugnant provision might well escape sentence. But the only practical test had been the stalemate of Standish's affair. We have seen how instructive this was. The ecclesiastical authorities could not in practice hinder legislation by appeals to canon law or scripture; and where they were powerless, how could a layman, though a common lawyer and a chancery man as well, hope to achieve more? After 1535 observers were entitled to claim that there was virtually nothing a parliament could not do. More had foreseen this situation, and from a striking passage, written before his own danger was imminent, it is possible to infer his opinion on it with some confidence.

His former colleague, Christopher St. German, whose opinions agree remarkably with those of Henry's councillors,[106] followed his survey of the relationship between ecclesiastical and common law in *Doctor and Student* by a series of works frankly devoted to undermining the independence of the ecclesiastical system. He emphasized conflicts of law. He was well-qualified to raise the questions, knowing a good deal of the canon law himself, and parliament, instructed by Cromwell, followed him. He needed to be wary, lest it were suggested that the 'temporalty' in turn had encroached on the spiritual law or its courts. He challenged More to show if this had ever happened, repeating a former challenge of the same character:[107] 'And if master More can shew any lawes, that have ben made by parliament, concernying the spiritualtie, that the parliament had none auctoritie to make, or wher at the spiritualtie or the people have iust cause to complaine: it wyl be well done that he shew them. And verily as me semeth, charitie shulde compell hym to do it, seinge that he is lerned in the lawes of the realme, as he is.' In *Doctor and Student*[108] St. German had actually shown how such a complaint might be made, and indeed there were embarrassing problems outstanding.[109] More hardly anticipated a case where a statute would be entirely repugnant to the traditional view of the law of God, but his reply[110] reveals his attitude to repugnancy, or alleged repugnancy, as a practical issue.

> Veryly, yf I knewe any suche ... But on the tother syde yf I thinke them nought, albeit that in place and tyme convenyent I wold geve myn advice and counsaile to the chaunge, yet to putte out bookes in wrytynge abrode amonge the people agaynste theym, that wolde I neyther do my selfe, nor in the so doynge commende any man that doth. For yf the lawe were such as were so farre agaynste the lawe of god, that it were not possyble to stande wyth mannes salvacyon, than in that case the secret advyse and counsayle may become every man but the open reprofe and redargucyon thereof may not in my mynd well become those that are no more spyrytuall than I. And sure yf the lawes may be kepte and observed without perell of soule, though the chaunge myght be to the better: yet out of tyme and place convenyent to put the defawtes of the lawes abrode amonge the people in wrytynge, and wythout any suretye of the chaunge geve the people occasyon to have the lawes in derysyon, under which they lyve, namely syth he y^t so shall use to do, may sometime missetake the mater and thynke the thyng not good wherof ye change would be worse; y^t way wyll I not as thus advised neither use myself[111] nor advise no frend of myne to do.

He must have been writing in recollection of Abbot Kidderminster. The Abbot's behaviour was possibly within the bounds of propriety, or 'convenience.' The layman's course must be different, and this explains and justifies the different approaches of Bishop Fisher and More himself on the Supremacy and Succession issues. As expressed in 1533 his view was, then, that a statute might be wholly repugnant to fundamental law, but he knew none such. If one came to notice, one might ask was its existence incompatible with the nation's spiritual welfare, or the 'king's conscience?' If it were not he would wait until the issue should arise in practice. If he feared that it were, he would seek to have the matter thrashed out in the council and perhaps in parliament. Only a cleric could denounce the statute in public, provided he did so discreetly. The legislature, and the courts, were the only places where a layman might ventilate such abstruse issues.

In this discussion there is no trace of a doubt but that if parliament decided not to repeal an impugned statute, or the courts held that the statute was not repugnant, More would indeed accept that situation as for practical purposes sound and reliable. One would be under a duty to argue, at the right time and in the right place, but if one's argument failed, the decision stood. Law was law, after all, even if, by standards of eternity, it was wrong. And this attitude is exactly what one would expect of More's career, his training, and his mentality. His conscience was his own affair; it might have been better if the law of England had agreed with it, better for him, and he believed better for the nation; but even if it did not it was still the law. There was no human tribunal to which the issue could go on appeal.

SIR THOMAS MORE AND THE OPPOSITION TO HENRY VIII

G. R. Elton

In considering Thomas More, few historians seem able to forget the end of the story. That More died a victim of Henry VIII, a martyr to his conscience and a defender of the papal supremacy, is, of course, perfectly true, but it is exceedingly rash to suppose that his whole life, or even the last few years of it, was simply a preparation for the tragic outcome.

From about the middle of 1532 More certainly lived in a retirement in which he meant to prepare himself for his death, though not necessarily for one by violence; and from April 1534 he was in the Tower and knew what the end must be. But before that he had spent two and a half years of his life as lord chancellor, the king's highest officer and a leading member of the royal Council, at a time when Henry was manifestly striving for purposes that More detested. How could he justify holding office at all? What line did he take over the politics of those years? This part of his life occupies amazingly little space in the standard accounts.

More's acceptance of the chancellorship has been a stumbling block to his biographers. On Wolsey's fall it was clear to all men in high places that the king's infatuation for Anne Boleyn was about to unleash drastic events, full of danger for the Church and likely to produce bitter clashes between the *regnum* and the *sacerdotium*.[1] More had already made it plain that he thought the Aragon marriage valid and would not be able to support Henry's endeavours to have it annulled. Yet he took office. Bridgett supposed that he did not do so until he had made sure of respect for his scruples of conscience,[2] and even Chambers suggested that he obtained some sort of promise before the appointment.[3] However, according to More himself, the king did not explicitly grant him liberty to dissent on the issue of the Divorce until after he had made him chancellor,[4] and this is also what Roper understood to be the truth.[5] There is no evidence at all that More had such a promise in his pocket when he became chancellor; as far as we know, he entered office aware that he would still be called upon to involve himself in the burning question of the day.

That the decision to accept was not an easy one seems likely. Harpsfield, from whom the tradition of More's reluctance to take the great seal derives, offers no evidence, and Roper gives no hint of it.[6] Since Roper was living in More's household at the time, his silence should perhaps carry more weight

Reprinted, by permission of the author and the publisher, from *Bulletin of the Institute of Historical Research*, 41 (1968), 19–34. An earlier version of this essay appeared in *Moreana*, 15–16 (1967), 285 ff.

than William Rastell's later recollection that More refused, made the king angry, and then was much laboured to; still, the story may be true, being not improbable in itself, though one should be a little more careful of Rastell's fragmentary notes than scholars have been.[7] From More himself we have only the short letter in which he told Erasmus what had happened; this does contain a possible hint that he was submitting to pressure.[8] But, as we shall see, other phrases in the letter are more interesting. Hall knew that the succession to Wolsey caused a good deal of difficulty; long discussions in Council turned on the choice of a layman, and in the end More was appointed.[9] But if there were difficulties it is too simple and hardly necessary to suppose that they were caused by More's inclination to refuse. If the great seal was on no account to go to a spiritual man, as Hall heard, More was the obvious man to choose: a trained lawyer, a man of European reputation and wide experience of affairs, chancellor of the Duchy and for several years one of the king's most intimate councillors. Erasmus understood that even Wolsey, who feared and hated More, regarded him as the only man in the kingdom fit for the office.[10] Yet to appoint at this juncture a man who had already declared his opposition to the Divorce must surely have given Henry pause and troubled the Council. The obviously qualified man was also politically one of the least suitable, whether he wanted the appointment or not.

In the end, the king decided to take the risk, and More decided to submit to the royal pressure. What had either of them in mind? Very likely, as has often enough been suggested, Henry hoped to convert an opponent into a very useful ally; the king had a high opinion of his powers of persuasion and a low one of people's consciences, a subject on which he was something of an expert. As for More, historians have produced various conjectures: he thought he could be useful to the causes he valued;[11] he came in on a wave of Erasmian rejoicing at the prospect of serious reform in the Church;[12] he meant to confine himself to the professional judicial duties of a lord chancellor;[13] he had no choice because, once he had entered the royal service, he was bound to accept whatever was offered.[14] This last is not true; from Erasmus and More himself downward, contemporaries clearly supposed that though actual refusal might be difficult it was not impossible. The third explanation reveals some misunderstanding of what the professional duties of the king's leading officer and councillor were; no Tudor lord chancellor, presiding in Chancery, Star Chamber and House of Lords, and prominent at the Council table, could have thought of confining himself to the hearing of pleas. Incidentally, it is worth notice that except for a few anecdotes of Roper's nothing is so far known about More's much-praised work in the Chancery.

That leaves the first two explanations. Dr. McConica rather overstates his case for an 'Erasmian' domination of Henry VIII's policy in the years after Wolsey's fall; writings are not the same thing as actions, and the things done rather than dreamed of reflect a popular anticlericalism diplomatically exploited by the king's policy much more than they embody a humanist reform programme. But that Erasmus himself was pleased to see his friend in the place of power is true enough, and it would indeed have been odd if More had not expected the office to enable him to exercise some influence on the course of events. It is worth remembering that Chapuys' first reaction to the news of the appointment was to rejoice because this 'upright and learned man' was also reckoned 'a good servant of the Queen' (Catherine).[15] And what did More tell Erasmus? That he would energetically endeavour to fulfil the excessive hopes entertained by the king of his unworthy self, with all the faith and readiness at his disposal.[16] Common form perhaps, or else a hint essentially ironic, in the More manner, in its implications: the king was not the only man to entertain hopes of More.

If More's part in the years 1529–32 is to be understood, two particular problems need to be investigated: his attitude to heresy and his relations with the Reformation Parliament. Between them, they illumine More's own view of the political circumstances of the day—the action these demanded and the way in which they could be exploited.

It is necessary to be very clear about More's reaction to the changes in religion which he saw all around him. No doubt, the more scurrilous stories of his personal ill-treatment of accused heretics have been properly buried,[17] but that is not to make him into a tolerant liberal. Tolerance he would have abominated as treason to God; it was one of his objections to Wolsey that the cardinal had ignored the dangers to the faith.[18] All the evidence goes to show that More hated heresy with a real, even an exceptional, passion. 'Odit ille,' wrote Erasmus in 1532, explaining More to one who did not know him, 'seditiosa dogmata'; of that he had never made any secret.[19] To Hall's parenthetical disgust, he 'leaned much to the spiritual men's part in all causes.'[20] Even the letter in which More told Erasmus of his resignation goes out of its way to lament the spread of the new sects.[21] Rastell recalled, perhaps correctly, that the more energetic pursuit of heretical teaching after 1531 resulted from representations made by More and the bishops.[22] While Dr. McConica's Erasmian humanists were busy bringing out works calling for reform in the Church, More got ever more deeply into his controversy with Tyndale in which he increasingly defended a total orthodoxy. The More of the early 1530s can hardly any longer be called an Erasmian, and Dr. McConica cannot in fact link him with the activities of the 'party' he has tried to document. The More of the *Confutation* may still be able to see, as the author of *Utopia* so clearly did, that not all is well with the old Church, but he is desperately certain that, as things are, reform can lead only to destruction and must be resisted. The only humanist in high places disappointed not only the king's hopes but also those of the Christian humanists.

It would surely have been strange if a man so aware of the pressing dangers of heresy had not used his high office to prevent disaster. Of course, he could not himself try heretics, a matter for the courts Christian; Chambers's argument that no heretics were burned in the diocese of London while More had influence appears to me irrelevant to an assessment of More's actions, and Erasmus was even more off the beam when he praised More for not condemning anyone to death for religion.[23] No lord chancellor [as such] has ever had the opportunity of pronouncing the death sentence on anyone.[24] However, he could arrest men, investigate their opinions, and hold them for trial by the spiritual arm; and this he seems to have done, even by his own admission, to a degree quite unknown among the king's lay councillors before or after. Perhaps a little more credence should be given than has of late been fashionable to the reports which reached Erasmus that More's successor was releasing numbers of 'Lutherans' imprisoned by his predecessor.[25] The numbers varied—forty perhaps, or only twenty—and rumours are not evidence. Yet there is evidence of More's determined persecution of heretics which has been too lightly written off. Thus a London merchant, Thomas Patmer, was in 1531 imprisoned by the bishop of London, and when his servant, John Stanton, tried to raise the matter in Parliament, More (he claimed) intervened to attack him with false accusations as a favourer of heresy.[26] Patmer, no doubt, was no victim of More's; Stanton did not assert anything like that, and if Audley released imprisoned heretics in 1532 Patmer would not appear to have been among them.[27] What matters is that More automatically sprang to the defence of the bishop's action and assumed the petitioner to be a tainted heretic.

There is also the case of John Field whose petition to Audley and the Council was first unearthed and used by Froude.[28] Field claimed to have been detained by More at Chelsea for eighteen days from 7 January 1530, securing his release only after he had bound himself to appear in the Star Chamber on Candlemas next. The outcome of that appearance was more than two years in the Fleet, in conditions of special hardship, without trial or knowledge of why he was held. On Palm Sunday (24 March) 1532 he was 'under our said sovereign's commandment and Sir Thomas More's' transferred to the Marshalsea, the officers of the Fleet having first robbed him of his money—as they said, to obtain their fees. In the Marshalsea he 'fell sick of the house sickness' and on Whit Monday (20 May) was 'carried out on[29] four men's backs' with more loss of money to the keeper there. However, he recovered, which fact came to More's ears. Although More 'went out of his said office of the chancellorship about the time your bedeman was carried out of prison,' he made it his business through the services of the bishops of Winchester and London ('as your bedeman heard say') to persuade the duke of Norfolk to have Field put back in gaol. He was again released in October, on sureties, and for a year had been giving attendance every day of every term, as his bond demanded. Now he asked for his discharge and the restoration of his lost property. As happens so often in the records of this time, nothing else is known of this case.[30] But the ease with which it has been brushed aside will hardly do. The circumstantial detail, the absence of any explicit animus against More (a fallen minister and easy target), the accurate dating of More's resignation, and the care taken to qualify one detail which the petitioner could know only by hearsay, all carry a good deal of conviction.

Against this, it has been urged that More himself answered all such charges when he spoke, in the *Apology,* of accusers who had been investigated by the king's Council and found to be liars.[31] But should More's word be taken without question on points like these? However truthful a man he may have been,

he could surely have been mistaken. Unfortunately there is no evidence except
his work that charges of this kind were after his fall dismissed in the manner
related by him, and what he himself has to say is less straightforward than his
apologists have supposed. He mentions one accuser by name, Thomas Phillips,
and what he offers in his own defence is surely a trifle peculiar. Phillips, he
says, had strongly reminded him of Richard Hunne (some sixteen years earlier),
and because he feared another suicide in the bishop's prison with all the consequences that he remembered from 1514 he had transferred him to the
Tower, not the proper place for suspected heretics.[32] At its best, such action
was irregular and unwise. But, More claims, the king had investigated the
charge and absolved his late chancellor, telling Phillips he had been lucky to
get away with so little. If this is true, it is a case of hard words breaking no
bones: Phillips did well for himself thereafter and is found in 1538 as a gaoler
in the Tower who converted Sir Nicholas Carew on the eve of his execution
by introducing him to the Bible in English.[33] Clearly he was a heretic; clearly
he was troubled by More's personal intervention; clearly he was liberated
after More's departure from the scene. As for Field, the supposition that
More had dealt with his accusation, too, will not do. More does not mention
him by name, and what he has to say about unnamed accusers does not fit
the case. The investigations of this clamour which, he says, resulted in sharp
rebukes for the accusers dealt (according to More's explicit assertion) with
complaints against the bishops and not against himself. But Field said nothing
of bishops and confined his attack to the late lord chancellor. John Foxe may
have collected too many exaggerated stories of More's doings, but he was right
enough in his assessment of the chancellor's share in the seeking out of heresy.

Indeed, it would be quite wrong to 'acquit' More of action against heresy:
he thought it his duty to use his place in the defence of the true religion. If
Field may be trusted—and the weight of probability is in his favour—More
went a very long way in his pursuit of suspects. All this agrees well with his
known beliefs and his frequent bitter words. There is every reason to think
that among the purposes he hoped to fulfil when he accepted office he put
high the protection of the Church against its heretical enemies.

In this, however, he was not at all out of step with the official policy of
those years. At the time, in fact, both king and Commons repeatedly demonstrated their orthodoxy in order to rebut the charge that their actions against
clergy and pope were equal to heresy.[34] More was more zealous and almost
certainly more sincere than most, but as an enemy of heresy he had, during
his years as chancellor, nothing to apprehend from king or Council. Matters
stood differently when it came to the defence of the Church against political
attack, to the cause of the Divorce and the powers of the papacy. On all
these, we know, Thomas More entirely disliked the progress of Henry's policy;
but did he confine his disagreement to the privacy of his own mind or even to
mere expressions of views?

More's recorded official actions in the Parliament, where events took place,
are both few and unexceptionable: not so few as to hide his standing in the
government, but sufficiently unexceptionable to have troubled the hagiogra-

phers. Thus he opened the proceedings of the 1529 session with his notorious attack on Wolsey, and whether one thinks (improbably) that he was here 'preaching to Henry VIII,'[35] or (as is much more likely) 'that he spoke for all who were sympathetic with the need for reform,'[36] it is clear that he was crossing official t's, not official lines. Attacking Wolsey in November 1529 would come well to his successor who had long regarded the cardinal as a major disaster; it would be agreeable to the king who wanted to justify to himself his rejection of a faithful old friend and servant; and it would delight most of the lords assembled to hear the speech. More's next known appearance in Parliament presents greater difficulties. In 1531 it was decided to silence rumour and press the king's views by presenting to both Houses of Parliament the opinions in favour of Henry's case that had been gathered from various universities. The day chosen was 30 March, and the man made responsible was the lord chancellor.[37] He started in the Lords, explaining how untrue it was that the king was seeking his divorce for the love of some woman and not out of a scruple of conscience; then he asked the clerk to read the opinions. Catherine's partisans protested, and Norfolk intervened to the effect that the king had sent the papers for information, not debate. Nevertheless, someone managed to ask More what he himself thought, to which the chancellor allegedly replied only that he had often enough told the king his views. He then led a deputation of peers to the Commons where he repeated the performance. After the reading of the opinions he added: 'Now you of this Common House may report what you have seen and heard, and then all men shall openly perceive that the King hath not attempted this matter of will or pleasure, as some strangers report, but only for the discharge of his conscience and surety of the succession of his realm. This is the cause of our repair hither to you, and now we will depart.' Chapuys heard that the bishops of London and Lincoln (both well known as conservatives) also spoke in the king's defence, and that the Commons received everything in silence.

Roper must be right in saying that More did all this 'at the King's request,' but how true is it that he 'was not showing of what mind himself was therein?'[38] As reported, his words were chosen with care. He did not commit himself on the justice of the king's cause; the only thing he himself supported was the king's claim to be acting for serious reasons of conscience and policy. He may have believed this, as indeed Henry himself believed it. No one could have used his remarks against him. But his omissions must surely have been noted: not a word from him to suggest that the opinions to be read out were in fact the truth. Yet as far as the less subtle were concerned, he had unquestionably associated himself with the king's policy, and while his careful abstention from any expression of personal views may have reassured his friends (and alerted his enemies) it cannot have satisfied More himself. He was in an impossible position, and it is no wonder that rumours about his intention to resign had circulated at the beginning of the session.[39] While he held the highest office in the state he was bound to come into contact with great affairs, in Council and publicly in Parliament, and no gracious concession, sincere or not,[40] to his conscience could insulate him against the conta-

gion. By 1531 he could not really both serve Henry as lord chancellor and
also maintain his conscience clear; and this carefully staged business of 30
March proved it. Thomas More, Catherine's and Chapuys' hope and a determined opponent of the Divorce, had had to take the lead in presenting to the
nation the alleged evidence that the Divorce was just. How did he feel: determined to resign? No doubt, but he stayed another year.

On only one more occasion did More address the Commons, in April 1532,
when he urged them to make a grant for the defence of the northern border.[41]
It is possible that the occasion was not so politically innocent as it appears.
We know that about this time Thomas Temse, burgess for Westbury (Wilts.),
moved for a petition to the king to take back his wife; and James Gairdner
linked this motion with the lord chancellor's request for money.[42] Certainly,
Temse's move was answered by Henry with yet another explanation of the
justice of his case, this time to a Commons' deputation summoned to meet
him. However, Hall, who supplies the only evidence,[43] and who ascribed both
events to the prorogued session that began on 10 April 1532, put More's visit
into the end of 23 Henry VIII and Temse's speech in the beginning of 24
Henry VIII, the dividing date being 21 April. There is no evidence for Gairdner's allegation that Temse touched on Scotland; the troubles he wished to
prevent were, according to Hall, the bastardization of Princess Mary 'and
diverse other inconveniences.' Nevertheless Gairdner may have been right in
linking the two events; as we shall see, the possibility of pre-arrangement even
cannot be excluded. It is just possible that More provided the setting for
Temse's motion. However, it is more certain that at this time the manoeuvres
were going forward which resulted in the Submission of the Clergy and that
in these More played no public part. Whether the king had ever again tried to
involve him publicly in the defence of his proceedings we do not know; at any
rate, More had not allowed himself to be so trapped again. At the end of this
session he did resign, but the circumstances of that resignation and the evidence for his less public activities in his years of office need to be entirely
reassessed.

After More's execution, Thomas Cromwell wrote a long letter to Gregory
da Casale, the man used until 1535 to maintain a tenuous contact with Rome.[44]
In it he explained the reasons for which, he alleged, Fisher and More had died.
This, of course, was a piece of propaganda, and diplomatic propaganda intended for the pope at that; nevertheless, the letter does not deserve the neglect
which More scholars have bestowed upon it.[45] One passage in it, which refers
to a nameless opposition group, must be quoted at length:

And when the public council of the realm, which we call Parliament, was
called to meet at stated times to see to the good order of the realm, they
began everywhere to enquire secretly with busy diligence what matter
should be in hand and what should in that Parliament fall to be done for
the benefit of the commonwealth. And whatever they managed to gather,
by the report of others, from their experience of past usage, and by conjecture, that they at once considered in their policy meetings, arriving at

conclusions very different from what the peace and interest of the realm required.[46]

Having devised such contrary policies, they then buttressed them with much skill of argument, producing a point of view which could easily have deceived the rude people. And when after a bit they realized that the king was getting annoyed at this organizing of opposition, they stepped up their campaign by arranging for select speakers and preachers to spread the arguments that had been worked out. Investigations initiated by the king showed that More and Fisher stood at the heart of this conspiracy.

If Cromwell was telling the truth, he was describing methods of unexpected political maturity. According to his story, the summoning of the Reformation Parliament caused the opponents of the Divorce and defenders of the clergy to form a kind of defence committee which set out to counter everything said and done in Parliament by reasoned arguments designed to meet the exact steps taken, steps of which, since proceedings were secret, they should have been ignorant. What Cromwell called a conspiracy we may more properly call an organized opposition outside Parliament but able to obtain information from within it, sufficiently coherent to prepare counter-efforts to the king's propaganda, and able to arrange for its members to speak publicly against the king's proceedings. The sermons of Peto, for instance, or of Forest might well have resulted from such a concerted programme.[47]

Even if Cromwell was telling the truth, it is still possible that he was unfairly involving More. More's discretion was and is notorious. In the spring of 1531 he even refused to receive a friendly letter from the emperor because such contacts might arouse suspicion, even though he felt that the proofs he had given of his loyalty should have assured his freedom from any such hostility.[48] But what matters is whether this discretion hid inaction or some deeper activity, and even More could not keep the record entirely clear of hints of the true position. In the same breath as he refused Charles V's letter he also told Chapuys that if he were suspected of any contact with the imperial cause he would lose his freedom to speak as frankly in Council as he had hitherto done on all that touched the emperor and his aunt. Chapuys, who had earlier identified both More and the earl of Shrewsbury as friends to Catherine, also thought that the chancellor had gone out of his way to show favour to the emperor and his servants.[49] More stood at any rate close enough to the Aragon faction to open his mouth on occasion, as when he reassured one of the ambassador's men that the emperor's preoccupation with the Turkish danger could not enable the English to take any action: 'there was no order nor power.'[50]

Thus it seems that More not only made no secret of his views but maintained some contact with the centre of intrigue, the emperor's ambassador, and contributed frank opinions in policy debates with king and Council. This is not quite the aloof More of tradition, but such action falls short of what Cromwell later alleged against him. However, there is further evidence which seems to bear Cromwell out in essentials, and in particulars too.

Sir George Throckmorton, a man who in 1536-7 repeatedly ran into political trouble, used one of his confessional statements to tell a fascinating story
which again has been quite unjustly neglected.[51] In 1529 Throckmorton had
been elected knight for the shire of Warwick and, according to his own account, acted in the House as a frequent and persistent opponent of the king's
policy. Now, in 1537, he wished to explain to Henry his 'proud, lewd, and un-
discreet handling of myself to you ward ... since the beginning of your Parliament anno vicesimo primo or thereabouts.' A little before the Parliament
opened, Throckmorton was sent for to Lambeth by Friar Peto, the best known
of Catherine's unswerving supporters. Peto told him what he had allegedly already told the king, both in sermons and in private audience, that since Prince
Arthur's marriage was never consummated (concerning which point he insisted
on believing Catherine's sworn statement) the queen's marriage with Henry
could be dissolved only by death. There could in any case be no marriage with
Anne Boleyn since Henry had 'meddled' with both mother and daughter.
Having thus defined the line of argument, Peto went on to advise Sir George
'if I were in the Parliament House, to stick to that matter as I would have my
soul saved.' Throckmorton took this advice and spoke against all the important acts—Annates, Appeals, Supremacy. He had many conversations with
Fisher about the proposed legislation and the question of the pope's authority,
and Fisher referred him to Nicholas Wilson, another very active supporter of
Catherine, with whom also he had several talks. He went to be confessed by
yet another well known opponent, Father Reynolds, who influenced him in
the same direction: if he did not stick to his opinions he would surely be
damned, 'and also if I did speak or do anything in the Parliament House contrary to my conscience for fear of any earthly power or punishment, I should
stand in a very hard case at the day of judgment.' Reynolds was even more
uncompromising than the others, telling him to speak out even if he was certain that he could not win; Fisher and Wilson had conceded that if he were
sure that his speaking 'could do no good, that then I might hold my peace and
not offend.' Reynolds argued that no one could know 'what comfort I should
be to many men in the House to see me stick in the right way, which should
cause many more to do the same.' Blinded by their pressure and by long habit,
he had ignored many warnings from Cromwell against their influence, till now
of late he had come to see the error of his ways.

Here, then, is proof of an organized opposition group which not only
attempted to counteract the doings of the Reformation Parliament but succeeded in attracting at least one member of the House to itself, instructed
him in parliamentary tactics and the arguments to be used, and used his freedom of speech in the Commons to gain a hearing for the opposition point of
view. This is what Cromwell told Casale had existed since November 1529,
and his letter was written some two years before Throckmorton's confession.
His management of the House included endeavours to talk the opposition
round and break their dependence on this non-parliamentary policy committee, as Throckmorton's reference to the warnings received clearly proves.
Though we know for certain of no other members who took their orders

from the Peto group, it is, of course, possible that Throckmorton was not the only one. Speeches in favour of Queen Catherine were reported on several occasions: they must now all be suspect as somewhat less than spontaneous.[52]

Yet what of More? Throckmorton tied him, too, into the story. Shortly after the opening of the Parliament (and apparently soon after Peto's first approach)[53] More, still chancellor, sent for Sir George to meet him in the Parliament Chamber. The scene is described in detail: More awaited his caller in a little room off the chamber which had an altar or something like it in it on which the chancellor leant throughout the interview. Throckmorton thought he remembered that the bishop of Bath was talking to More when he arrived, but More disengaged himself to speak to Sir George words of great comfort: 'I am very glad to have the good report that goeth of you and that you be so good a catholic man as ye be; if ye do continue in the same way that you began and be not afraid to say your conscience, ye shall deserve great reward of God and thanks of the King's grace at length, and much worship to yourself—or words much like to these.' More's kindness and encouragement sent Throckmorton into ecstasies and greatly encouraged him to seek out the other counsellors already mentioned. There is really no reason to doubt that More spoke to the effect remembered by Throckmorton, but if he did so he must be considered one of the organized group. Peto had picked the right man in a political innocent like Throckmorton who could be threatened with hellfire first and flattered by a kind word from the lord chancellor after, to such good purpose that he maintained opposition in the House for at least five of the Parliament's seven sessions.

Admittedly, More once again practised that care and discretion which distinguish his handling of himself in the tricky situation that his acceptance of the chancellorship had forced upon him. It might be argued that he had just happened to hear about Throckmorton's useful attitude and quite independently wished to offer his commendations; unlike Peto, Fisher, Wilson, and Reynolds he held no long indoctrination sessions with Sir George. But the first is a good deal harder to credit than that More knew of Peto's schemes and helped them along; and as for the second, there was neither reason nor occasion why the lord chancellor should converse at length or frequently with a knight for Warwickshire. What really matters is the remark that support of the catholic cause would in the end earn favour from the king. This shows More well aware that for the present the king's attitude to Throckmorton was likely to be very different, that the present policy was hostile to the catholic cause, and that he himself was involved in trying to change that policy. Throckmorton's testimony supports Cromwell's allegations, and between them they place More firmly with one of the political groups of the time, that organized to oppose the king's Great Matter and to support the cause of Catherine and Rome. There is no doubt that the king and others were well enough aware of More's opinions and heard them expressed; it is another question whether at this early date they knew of his share in the 'conspiracy.' As More told Chapuys in 1531, he wished to retain his usefulness as a proponent of the organization's policy by avoiding all suspicion of contact with the group. Until 1532 he succeeded sufficiently in retaining the king's trust to make his continued stay in office, however distasteful, worth while.

That this is an accurate reconstruction is borne out by the story of his resignation—that moment when the old tie with Henry VIII finally broke and the old love turned to the new hatred that was in the end to bring More to the scaffold. There is no doubt that More resigned; Harpsfield was certainly right to reject the rumours spread by 'adversaries and evil willers' that More had been 'against his will thrust out of the chancellorship.'[54] He had at intervals been pressing for his release, using the friendship of the duke of Norfolk to persuade the king; one wonders just how good a friend he found that devious second-rater.[55] Thus, at least, Roper; but since More in the end resigned quite easily and with assurances of future kindness from Henry, one might ask just how hard he had tried before. In 1532 More pleaded ill health to get free of office,[56] but though no doubt he was at fifty-four no fitter than might be expected in the sixteenth century, he cannot have been really ill, for he was to survive an increasingly rigorous imprisonment with his health unaffected. Erasmus conjectured that 'perhaps he feared the unpopularity of that Divorce against which he had always advised,'[57] and there may be something in this; however, no one even at the time supposed More guilty of promoting that particular piece of policy. It would possibly be more accurate to say that he did not wish any longer to stand by the side of those that advocated the Divorce, whether it was unpopular or not.

This is the usual view, but it will not quite do. Once again it would be wrong to suppose that More had been watching in an inactive despair. The main issue in the spring of 1532 was the attack on the clergy's independence which emerged from the Supplication against the Ordinaries promoted in and by the Commons. There has been some debate about these events. Years ago I suggested that the whole operation was from the first planned by Cromwell: that he took over genuine grievances well ventilated in the Commons in order to compel the clergy's submission to the king's authority. Mr. J. P. Cooper in reply stressed more heavily the Commons' independent concern in these issues, and Dr. M. Kelly has more lately made a good case for supposing that the sequence of events reflects not prearrangement but the playing out of conflicting policies and day-to-day developments.[58] The present reassessment of More's activities in part supports and in part casts doubt on Dr. Kelly's views. For More played his part in this crisis, obscure though that part may once again be. It has long been noted that he resigned on the very day after the Convocation had finally surrendered, and Chapuys knew that in Council More had joined the bishops in opposing the king. Henry was said to be particularly angry with More and Gardiner.[59] Gardiner, of course, who had drafted the tough early replies of Convocation, had throughout stood forth as the champion of clerical liberties. But why More, unless he too had resisted more strenuously than the rest? The Submission was extorted after much public and private struggling in Convocation and Council; if Dr. Kelly is right in thinking that it was 'an unexpected and precipitate development' of May 1532,[60] there is no need to doubt that More, with the bishops, would right to the end have supposed the issue insufficiently settled and could justly have continued argument and opposition for as long as a shadow of hope remained. On the other hand, in the light of the evidence assembled in all the articles cited, it looks as though the anticlericals on the Council, guided by Cromwell, had all along intended to obtain drastic concessions by means of the Supplication. The Submission may have come as a sudden and unwelcome development to More, but that is not to say that his opponents were not looking for something like it from the first.

Thus More resigned, after a last battle in which he had finally jeopardized what remained of the king's favour. The first chapter of Magna Carta was wiped off the book; the liberties of the English Church were destroyed. Surely the whole of More's career as chancellor now hangs together. He had taken office when Wolsey's removal opened some prospect of rational reform, but also at a time when the king's determination to get rid of Catherine showed to all thinking men that Church and clergy were likely to be in much danger. He dreaded heresy with a hatred that in so reasonable and balanced a man strikes one as a trifle abnormal.[61] Thus he hoped to use his office, as best he might, to stand guard over the things in which he believed: the orthodox faith and the liberties of the Church. In so far as he opposed the Divorce, he did so because he thought the king's legal case bad and because he dreaded the larger consequences; it is not easy to see simply a defender of Queen Catherine in the man who 'would not deny to swear to the succession' of Anne Boleyn's issue but could not take the oath tendered in April 1534, because it implied denial of the pope's supremacy.[62] So he employed himself in the detection of heresy, and he lent his aid and authority to that group of dissentients who hoped to organize opposition and seem to have had some success in the House of Commons. At the same time, of course, he tried to apply the brake in the Council and may have been partly responsible for the absence of any clear-cut policy in those years.[63] But he was never either a reckless man or a really subtle politician, and the role he had chosen did not suit him too well. From early in 1531 at the latest, by which time Thomas Cromwell was increasing his influence at Court More realized that he was losing the battle. Nevertheless he stayed at his post; the cause of the Church demanded one last effort from him. The victory of the anticlerical policy in May 1532 and the destruction of the Church's independence in England closed a chapter. His usefulness at an end, his preferred policy irremediably destroyed, More could and must go. Is it any wonder that he now resolved to spend the remainder of his life away from the great affairs and in contemplation of 'the immortality of the life to come?'[64]

One may be sure that More sincerely meant this. Once he had broken with public life he would never in any form engage in it again. And yet, in the circumstances this was an unreal stance. For nearly three years he had been right at the centre of affairs and had not kept silent; as he had told the Lords in 1531, the king knew his views well enough. He had backed a losing policy, and when that policy was lost he had taken himself off out of sight: at least, this is the way in which things must have appeared to Cromwell and the king.

Some suspicion of his relations with known opponents must have existed already, as the later charges concerning the Nun of Kent and Bishop Fisher indicate. What reason had the government to suppose that a man who had actively engaged in such controversial politics would now abandon them altogether? Being the men they were, neither Henry nor Cromwell would have really believed such a turning away to be possible; and even if, knowing their More, they supposed him capable of it,[65] they could well decide that the risk was too great for them to take. Here was a man of stature and ability and European renown who had already done much to discredit their policy both at home and abroad. Left at large, he must have seemed like a time-bomb to them. And so the tragedy was staged: more pressure upon the now inflexible man to accept the new order, the king's increasing hatred, the rigged trial and the condemnation on a charge which rested on perjured evidence. But though the charge was false in fact, it was (as More's speech to his judges showed) true in spirit, and by his part in the events of 1529–32 More had made certain that his conscience could not in the end be left private to himself.

THE ANCESTRY OF SIR THOMAS MORE

Margaret Hastings

"Thomas Morus urbe Londinensi familia non celebri sed honesta natus..."[1] Thus the great chancellor describes his ancestry in the first line of his epitaph. Later, in the Tower, he explained what he meant by the words *honestus* and *celeber*. "Let us now consider," he writes, "*good name, honest estimation,* and *honourable fame*...A *good name* may a man have be he never so poor... *Honest estimation*... belongeth not to any man but him that is taken for one of some countenance and havour [substance], and among his neighbours had in some reputation... In the word of honourable fame folk conceive the renown of great estates, much and far spoken of [*celeber*]."[2] And Erasmus, writing to John Faber in 1532 with a copy of More's epitaph before him, comments as follows: "As for family rank, a matter to which, philosophically, More was indifferent, he was born in London; and to be born and educated in their most famous city implies to Englishmen a considerable degree of superiority. Further, his father had won distinction as a lawyer in a profession held in the highest regard in England, and to which, indeed, many noble English families trace their origin. His son followed in the footsteps of his eminent father so successfully as to surpass him in every kind of honour; though, of course, no one does greater honour to his forbears than a son who eclipses them in this way."[3] These hints are the probable source of the accounts of More's ancestry with which the sixteenth century lives begin.[4] They do not give us much specific help in the solution of the baffling mystery of More's antecedents.

The starting point of a sound solution, as Professor A. W. Reed has pointed out, is the identification of the benefactors mentioned in Sir John More's will. The will was written in February of 1527, the same year that Holbein made the famous sketches for the family portrait.[5] It was proved nearly four years later on December 5, 1530. In it, Sir John directed that two scholars, priests studying in divinity, be found for him, one at Oxford and the other at Cambridge "to pray for my sowle / all my wifes sowles and for the sowles of my Father and mother / kynge Edwarde the fourthe John' Leycester / Johane his dawghter my graunt mother / John' Marchall Thomas Bowes mercers John Clerke grocer / Kateryne Clerke maister Abell More dame Audrey Talbott John Clerke draper Rychard Clowdisley and for the soules of all other that I haue hadd' any goodes of or am charged in conscience to doo eny thinge for / and for all' cristen sowles"[6] /. Professor Reed identified John Marchall,

Reprinted from *The Guildhall Miscellany*, 2, no. 2 (1961), by permission of the author and the publisher.

Thomas Bowes and John Clerke as the former husbands of John More's second, third, and fourth wives respectively, all men of considerable wealth who presumably left their widows with comfortable provision.[7] Richard Clowdisley was a well-known resident of Islington and an associate of John More in the upkeep of the Great North Road. Professor Reed conjectured that John Leycester may have been the bailiff, later sheriff and Mayor of Bristol, whose will was written by a William More scrivener. But this identification was tentative only and did not fully satisfy Professor Reed. He found no mention of a Johanna Leycester as daughter of the Mayor of Bristol.

What I believe to be the true identification of John and Johanna Leycester involves further the identification of John More's father as a William More, baker, not scrivener, of London, not Bristol, and of a later generation than the William More who wrote the will of John Leycester, Mayor of Bristol. It is regrettable that the name More was so common in the fifteenth century and that the Christian names, John, Thomas, and William, seem to have been the popular ones in all the many families.[8]

The clues to a satisfying identification of John and Johanna Leycester, More's ancestors on the distaff side is to be found, I believe, in a series of deeds enrolled in London Husting records, in the Close rolls and in the wills of John Leycester and William More in the records of the Commissary Court of London.

The first set of documents relates to a messuage in the parish of St. Mary Woolchurch Haw in Breadstreet Ward lying in the Poultry between a tenement belonging to St. Augustine's Abbey of Canterbury on the east and tenements belonging to the church of St. John Walbroke on the west. This estate was the subject of two deeds enrolled in Husting records in September 1470. In the first, dated 1 March, 1470, Nicholas Millyngton, esquire, and his wife Johanna, "formerly wife of John Joye, citizen and brewer of London, daughter of John Leycestre, deceased, formerly of London, gentleman," convey the messuage to Thomas Wymark and Robert Walpole, citizens and brewers of London. Johanna is alleged in the deed to have formerly held the estate jointly with William More, citizen of London, now dead, and Johanna, his wife, by gift of John Leycester. And Johanna More, William's widow, is alleged to have surrendered her rights during her widowhood to Johanna Millyngton, formerly Johanna Joye, née Johanna Leycester.[9] By a second deed, dated 16 March, 1470, Thomas Wymark and Robert Walpole convey the estate back to Johanna Millyngton for the term of her life. After her death it is to go to John More, son of William, now dead, but formerly citizen and baker of London, and to John's heirs. Failing heirs of John, it is to go to his brothers and sisters, Abel, William, Nicholas, Katherine, and Alice successively with reversion to the right heirs of Johanna Millyngton.[10] Twenty-nine years later, in 1499, a series of quit-claims enrolled in the records of the hustings court of London indicates that the estate descended according to the intent of the second of the two 1470 deeds to John More and his son, Thomas. By these quit-claims John More, gentleman, Johanna his wife, Richard Staverton and his wife Johanna, and Thomas More, son and heir apparent of John More, release their rights in

the messuage to Nicholas Gybson, chaplain, and Richard Smyth.[11] These quit-
claims are evidently preliminary to a common recovery with single voucher,
because we find recorded on the roll of Pleas of Land in October, 1500, a recovery of the tenement by John More against Gybson and Smyth.[12]

These documents establish quite clearly a connection between Thomas
More, later the martyr chancellor, William, the baker, and John Leycester,
the chancery clerk. This Richard Staverton can be no other than the one who
married Thomas More's eldest sister Johanna.[13] And it will be noted that this
John More, eldest son of William, the baker, has an eldest son, Thomas, and
five younger brothers and sisters, the eldest of them Abel More, whose name
occurs in the list of benefactors of John for whose souls he makes provision
in his will.

A second set of documents, showing a connection between William More,
baker, and the persons mentioned in John More's will relates to a property
called "The Greyhound" in St. Andrew's Parish, Holborn. By a deed dated 10
May 1477, Nicholas Millyngton and his wife Johanna convey this tenement to
a list of feoffees, all but one identified as members of Lincoln's Inn. The two
principal feoffees are John More and Thomas Gay, gentleman.[14] The deed
states that the estate came to Johanna Millyngton, daughter of John Leycester
and formerly wife of John Joye, citizen and brewer, by grant of Thomas
Ryngstone, gentleman, and William More, baker. This estate, "The Greyhound," is the only one of John Leycester's real possessions which is mentioned by name in his will proved in August, 1455. He made provision that
his feoffees in "The Greyhound" in Holborn should make an estate to Johanna
Joye, and to her heirs and assigns forever. The feoffees are not listed but
William More, baker, proves to be one of the executors.

A third set of items illustrating the connection between John Leycester,
Chancery clerk, Johanna, his daughter, William More, baker, and Johanna
More, William's wife, relates to an estate in North Mimms, Herts, and introduces a John More of Cheshunt, who may possibly be Sir John More's grandfather on the paternal side. In 1455, the year of John Leycester's death, in
fact a few weeks before he made his will, John Arnold, citizen of London and
John More of Cheshunt, by a deed entered on the close roll,[15] conveyed to
John Joye, brewer, and Johanna, his wife, "all lands, tenements, and messuages, rents, crofts and services, with woods, meadows, pasturage, pastures,
ways, paths, hedges, hedgerows, ditches, heriots, reliefs, rights of common
and all other rights and appurtenances" which they had held in the vill and
parish of North Mimms jointly with the feoffees by gift of John Leycester,
"one of the clerks of the king's Chancery," John Byron and William More.
After the death of John Joye and Johanna, the tenement is to go to William
More, citizen and baker of London and his wife, Johanna, and their heirs forever. It will be remembered that John More, later Sir John, is alleged to have
held the manor of Gobions or Gubbins in North Mimms in 1500. In fact,
tradition has it that Thomas More wrote the *Utopia* there.[16] This manor, a
century earlier, seems to have been held by John More, citizen and mercer of
London.[17] I have not found it possible to trace a direct line of descent from

this John More to John More, father of the Chancellor. Nor is there proof that the Gubbins estate which John More held in 1500 is the one conveyed by the deed of 1455. But there is certainly evidence of a long association of the More name with North Mimms.[18]

The wills of John Leycester, gentleman of London, and William More, citizen and baker, provide the final threads necessary to establish the connection between the benefactors listed in John More's will and the testators and Johanna Leycester, mentioned by Sir John More in his own will as his "graunt mother." John Leycester, after providing that his body shall be buried in the church of St. Botolph outside Aldrychgate, making the usual money bequest to this same church and its clergy and ten marks to the Friars Minor of London, goes on to make certain bequests in Leicester, evidently his place of origin, and to his family as follows:

> I bequeath to the almshouse called the Bedehouse in Leicester 20s. Item I bequeath to the brothers and sisters of the fraternity of St. John the Baptist in Leicester 20s. Item I bequeath to the poor parishioners of the vills of Buskeby and Thirneby in the county of Leicester one hundred shillings sterling. Item I bequeath for the fabric of the nave of the church of St. Clement Danes outside the bar of the New Temple London 20s. and two new torches to be burned in the same church of St. Clement at the raising of the body of the bishop as long as they shall last. Item I bequeath to John, son of Simon, my brother, 13s. 4d. Item I bequeath to John son of William my brother 20s. Item I bequeath to Ellen, daughter of the same William, my brother, 13s. 4d. Item I bequeath to John, son of John Joye, citizen and brewer of London 13s. 4d. Item I bequeath to Robert, brother of the same John Joye, junior, 13s. 4d. And further, as to the disposition of all of my lands and tenements, rents, services with every and each of all the rights and appurtenances both within the city of London and in the suburbs of the same as well as in the vill and parish of Carshalton (Cressalton) in the county of Surrey or elsewhere in the same county of Surrey, First I will and urgently request that each and every of my feoffees in a certain tenement called the Greyhound in the parish of St. Andrew in Holborn in London shall immediately on my decease make an estate to Johanna, wife of the said John Joye, my eldest daughter, to have and to hold to the said Johanna, my daughter, her heirs and assigns forever of the chief lords of the fee by the service due and accustomed, under this condition, however, that the same Johanna, my daughter, and her heirs and assigns shall find for the ten years following my death a suitable and honest chaplain to celebrate divine services for my soul and the souls of my father and mother, my parents, my friends and benefactors and the souls of all the faithful dead wherever it shall most please my executors to have this chaplain celebrate. And as to all the other lands, tenements, returns and services mentioned above with each and every of their appurtenances, I will that each and every of my feoffees of and in the same, shall make an estate of them to my below-written executors. So that those same execu-

tors may sell in the best way and at the best price they know and can get all the said lands and tenements, returns, services with appurtenances and all the money proceeding from this sale, I will to be disposed and distributed by the said executors for my soul and the souls mentioned above in pious uses and works of charity according to their better discretion. The rest, truly, of all my goods, chattels, credits, in whosoever hands and wheresoever they may be, after my debts and funeral expenses have been paid and my will proved and fulfilled, I give and bequeath wholly to my below-written executors to be disposed and distributed for the celebration of masses for my soul and all the above-recited souls, for the succour of the poor, for repair and re-building of highways and bridges, for providing marriage portions for poor girls of good and honest conversation and for other works of charity to be done for me according to their best discretion and as they themselves, my executors shall deem best to please God and profit my soul's good. As executors, moreover, of this will, I ordain and constitute the said John Joye, senior, William More, baker, and Robert Ellesmere, goldsmith, Citizens of the City of London and I bequeath to each of the same John Joye senior, William More and Robert Ellesmere for his labour in carrying out faithfully the provisions of this will 13s 4d. In witness whereof I attach this my seal to this said will. Dated London, the day and year mentioned above. Witness William Nash, John Betley and others. This will was proved before M. H. S. etc. the 23rd day of August in the year of our lord mentioned above. And it is committed to the administration of the above named executors, on the 3rd day of October in the year of our lord 1456, the executors were dismissed by the below-written acquittance.[19]

It is clear from this will that John Leycester was a man of substance, that he made a good marriage for his daughter, Johanna, and further made careful provision for her and for her heirs. The will of William More, citizen and baker of London (+1467), is a simpler document giving less evidence of wealth and position, but it contributes lively detail concerning family relationships and possessions. It also introduces John More of Much Hadham, brother to William More and therefore uncle to John More, father of the Chancellor, if the whole chain of evidence is accepted. Like John Leycester's will it is written in Latin and reads as follows:

In the name of God, amen, On the first day of the month of August in the year of our Lord, 1467, I, William More, citizen and baker of London, being of whole mind and sound memory; do establish, ordain and make this present will as follows: First, I bequeath and commend my soul to the Holy Trinity my creator and to the holy virgin Mary and all the saints and my body to be buried in the cemetery of St. Dunstan in the West next the south door of the said church. Item I bequeath to the said church of St. Dunstan 6s 8d. Item I bequeath to the vicar of the said church to pray for my soul and for tithes forgotten 6s. 8d. Item I bequeath to John More of

Much Hadham, my brother, my best cloak of murrey furred with marten "pollys" (etc). Item I bequeath to Johanna More, wife of the said John 6s. 8d. Item I bequeath to each of the sons and daughters of the said John, my brother, 6s. 8d. Item I bequeath to Agnes, wife of John More, eldest son of my said brother 6s. 8d. Item I bequeath to the sons and daughters of the said John More, eldest son of my said brother, 13s. 4d. to be divided between them. Item I bequeath to the Carmelite friars in Fleet Street to pray and celebrate for my soul 20s. Item I bequeath to each of my sons and daughters a bed with a coverlet, a copper bowl, a scoop and a basin, a bowl with a cover of silver or gilt. Item I bequeath to my eldest son John my blue cloak furred with marten. Item I bequeath to my son Abell my red coat furred with polecat (fichewys). Item I bequeath the obligation of £87. 16s. 2d. owed me by the lord earl of Northumberland for bread bought of me to be divided between my sons and daughters. Item I bequeath the remainder of the debts owed me after my debts and funeral expenses have been paid and my present will fulfilled to my wife Johanna More and my sons and daughters to be divided in equal portions so that they may distribute part of it for my soul at the discretion of my executors. The remainder of all my goods both movable and immovable not already bequeathed, after my debts and funeral expenses have been paid and my present will fulfilled, I bequeath to my wife Johanna for the term of her life and after the demise of the said Johanna they are to remain to my eldest son John and his heirs. And if it should happen that the said John should die without heirs, then I will that all the said goods both movable and immovable shall remain to my sons and daughters to be divided among them. Moreover I constitute as executors to this testament, my wife, Johanna and my eldest son, John. In witness whereof I have affixed my seal to this present will. Witnesses George Haydyff, vicar of the said St. Dunstan's, Martin Peytewyn, John Sheldon, Nicholas Forest, Robert Byrde, William Kyrkeby and others. Dated the day, year and place indicated above. This will was proved before Master William Wylde, commissary, on the ninth day of September in the said year and the administration of goods committed to the aforementioned executors.[20]

In this collection of documents, the two wills and the various deeds and recoveries, we see the instruments whereby John Leycester, clerk of the Chancery, secured that his City properties and the estate in North Mimms should pass to his great-grandson, Sir John More, who was an infant of four when Leycester died. Sir John had good reason to mention with special gratitude his grandmother, Johanna Leycester. She made one prudent marriage in her father's lifetime, to John Joye, prosperous brewer of London, a second one for her daughter, whom we shall name Johanna II, to William More, baker, also of London. Then with the help of her husband and son-in-law, two of her father's three executors, she saw to the full execution of her father's instructions concerning the property. She outlived both husband and son-in-law, and at William More's death in 1467, with the co-operation of her second husband,

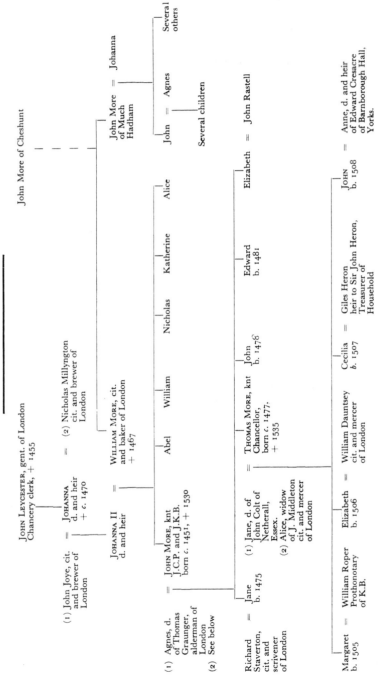

MORE GENEALOGY

John More of Cheshunt

John Leycester, gent. of London
Chancery clerk, + 1455
= (2) Nicholas Millyngton
cit. and brewer of
London

Johanna
d. and heir
+ c. 1470
(1) John Joye, cit.
and brewer of
London

John More
of Much Hadham = Johanna

John = Agnes   Several
others

Several children

Johanna II
d. and heir
=
William More, cit.
and baker of London
+ 1467

Elizabeth = John Rastell

Abel   William   Nicholas   Katherine   Alice

John More, knt
J.C.P. and J.K.B.
born c. 1451, + 1530
(1) Agnes, d.
of Thomas
Graunger,
alderman of
London
(2) See below

John
b. 1478

Edward
b. 1481

Thomas More, knt
Chancellor,
born c. 1477,
+ 1535
(1) Jane, d. of
John Colt of
Netherall,
Essex.
(2) Alice, widow
of J. Middleton
cit. and mercer
of London

Jane
b. 1475
=
Richard
Staverton,
cit. and
scrivener
of London

Elizabeth =
b. 1506

William Dauntsey
cit. and mercer
of London

Cecilia
b. 1507
=
Giles Heron
heir to Sir John Heron,
Treasurer of
Household

John
b. 1508
=
Anne, d. and heir
of Edward Cresacre
of Barnborough Hall,
Yorks.

Margaret =
b. 1505

William Roper
Prothonotary
of K.B.

Nicholas Millyngton, another brewer of London, she made sure that the property was properly safeguarded for young John More, orphaned at sixteen, eldest of six children. The transactions in the case of the North Mimms estate are not so clear as in the case of the London property, but there is at least a strong presumption of a close family connection between John More of Cheshunt and the brothers William and John More of London and Much Hadham respectively. It should be helpful if a continuous line of descent could be traced between John More, citizen and mercer of London, who held an estate in North Mimms in 1397 and John More of Cheshunt, who conveyed an estate in that parish to William More, citizen and baker of London and others in 1455, the year of John Leycester's death. Failing that, we must be satisfied with conjecture.

The entire collection of documents enables us to construct the genealogy for Thomas More as set out on the opposite page; some minor points in it speculative, but most of it reasonably certain, especially as fifteenth-century genealogies go.

There are many other questions one might ask about the early history of the family. Sir John was called to assume the rank of sergeant-at-law in 1503 at the age of fifty-two. Foss argues cogently that he was the younger of the two John Mores of Lincoln's Inn rather than the junior contemporary of the Middle Temple.[21] But, as Egerton Beck has demonstrated,[22] Foss's deductions from the entries in the Lincoln's Inn records that he was a menial in the Inn before his admission are altogether unwarranted. The admissions books show that two John Mores were admitted in the period, the first by "special admission" in 1470 as a reward for past services as butler and steward of the Inn, the second, listed as "John More, junior," without mention of special treatment, in Hilary term, 1474-5.[23] Foss was clearly right in identifying the John More, specially admitted in 1470 with the butler, later steward of the Inn who is mentioned in the Black Books.[24] This man cannot have been the Chancellor's father because at the time of his first mention as steward, in 1464, our John More was only thirteen years old.[25] And at the time of this More's special admission in 1470 the chancellor's father would have been nineteen, scarcely old enough to receive the honor as a reward for long and faithful service. No such problem about age arises with regard to the younger John. He was admitted in 1474-5 when Sir John would have been twenty-three or twenty-four years old. And in 1482 he was elected butler for the Christmas revels, a matter of honor rather than of menial status, as Beck has shown. It is not necessary to assume, as Foss does, that he was the son of the senior More. Nor is it clear that he could not have been the Autumn Reader of 1490 and the Lenten Reader of 1495. Sir John could not have achieved the degree of sergeant-at-law without having been reader for two such terms. If his appointments were rather late in coming and not promptly followed by his call to the degree of sergeant, perhaps it was because he was engaged reader for two such terms. If his appointments were rather late in coming and separated by a longer interval of years than was customary, perhaps it was because he was engaged in a kind of practice which took him seldom to Westminster and so did not give him the kind of reputation which made for recognition by his fellows of the

Inn. He was counsel to the City in matters relating to London Bridge from 1485 until 1517,[26] and he seems also to have been steadily involved in transactions having to do with tenements in the City. If he was, as I hope I have shown above, the orphaned son of William More, citizen and baker of London, and the grandson of Johanna Leycester, successively wife of two prosperous brewers of the City, what could be more natural than that he should have sought and received patronage and business from his London connections?[27] The challenging fact seems to be that, with such a background, he also made connections which enabled him to place his son in Cardinal Morton's household for his early education, that he eventually became a justice of the highest bench in the land and that his son became the founder of a "noble family."

Professor Reed has drawn attention to a further interesting query about Sir John More. That is the reason for his special mention of Edward IV in his will. The heralds' rolls of Henry VIII describe Sir John More's arms as having been granted by Edward. And in 1530, in the midst of a controversy between Garter and Clarenceaux heralds-at-arm, Clarenceaux, having accused Garter of giving arms to "vile persons not able to uphold the honor of nobles," Garter replied that only those "not vyle borne or Rebells myght be admyttyd to be enobled to have armes havynge landes and possessyons of free tenure to the yerlye value of X pounds sterlinge or in movable goods iii c. li. sterlinge," and also the avowance or assurance of some noble person for discharge of honour."[28] Did John More perhaps acquire his arms at the death of his "graunt mother," Johanna Leycester, when he came into the estate left him by his provident great-grandfather, John Leycester, gentleman and clerk of Chancery? And did he perhaps have assurance of avowance from the king himself, perhaps as a reward for some past service? If in Edward IV's reign, he already bore the arms of a gentleman, he cannot at the same time have been a servant in Lincoln's Inn. And those who have read the evidence presented in this paper will, it is hoped, have become convinced that his father was not the butler and steward of the Inn but a substantial citizen and baker of London who supplied the bread for the household of the Earl of Northumberland and had three fur-lined cloaks as well as copper, silver, and gilt vessels to leave to his survivors.

The many unanswered questions about the More ancestors may be answered in time. Meanwhile we have here in the More family an example of how, in Erasmus' words, through practice of a "profession held in the highest regard in England, and to which indeed, many noble families trace their origin," a great man, son of a lawyer, lawyer by profession himself, but humanist and saint by inclination, became the founder of a family's great name and fame. It is a long jump from the sixteen-year-old orphan son of a baker to the martyr chancellor of Henry VIII. If Thomas surpassed his father in every kind of eminence, as no one who has looked at the record would doubt that he did, no man, to quote again from Erasmus' letter to John Faber, "does greater honour to his forbears than a son who eclipses them in this fashion."

APPENDIX A[29]

"Verum quod ad generis claritatem attinet, quam Thomas Morus, ut est ingenio plane philosophico, nec affectavit unquam, nec iactavit: natus est Londini, in qua civitate multo omnium celeberrima natum et educatum esse, apud Anglos nonnulla nobilitatis pars habetur: dein ex patre neutiquam obscuro, iuris Brittanici doctore, cui ordini apud Anglos summa est dignitas, et ex hoc pleraque illius insulae nobilitas fertur originem ducere. Huic ita successit filius, ut parentem per se clarum omni genere decorum obscuravit, tametsi nemo verius illustrat maiores suos, quam qui ad hunc obscurat modum."

(Erasmi Epistolae, X, p. 136, No. 2750.)

APPENDIX B

Will of Sir John More, knight, 1530

P.C.C., Jankyn (24)

IN DEI NOMINE AMEN. This is the last will of me John More knyght one of the Justices of the kynges Benche made the xxvi day of Februarij / the yere of our lorde god $\stackrel{l\ \ c}{MV_{xxvj}}$ and the xviij yere of the reigne of kynge Henry the viij[th] written with my hande beinge in good helthe and hole mynde blyssid be god. Furst I bequethe my soule to allmyghty god and my body to be buryed in the paryshe church of saint Laurance in the olde Jurie in the cyttie of London in the chapel of our Ladye in a tombe there made for me or elleswhere it shall fortune me to deceas' by the discrescion of myn executours' and I bequethe to the vicar of the said churche for my tythes and other thinges negligently forgotton xxs. Allso I will that all my debtes and charges that I owe or am charged into any parsonne duely prouid be shortly and truly paid before all thinges and that doon and my costes of my funerall' reasonably and not to pompiously perfourmed. Then I will that a god and a vertous scoler studyinge in dyuinitie beinge vertous and a preste be founde for me at oxenford duringe the space of vij yeres next after my deceas and an other scoler studyinge in dyuinite beinge vertous and a prest be found for me at Cambryge duringe the space of vij yeres next after my decese euery of the said prestis to take ther sellarye yerely fyue poundes sterlinge or more after the discrescion of myn executours in discharge of my conscience for all thynges / and for to praye for my sowle all my Wifes sowles and for the sowles of my Father and mother kynge Edwarde the fourthe John' Leycester / Johane his dawghter my graunt mother / John' Marchall Thomas Bowes mercers John Clerke grocer / Kateryne Clerke maister Abell More dame Audrey Talbott John Clerke draper Rychard Clowdisley / and for the soules of all other that I haue hadd / any goodes of or am charged in conscience to doo eny thinge for / and for all' cristen sowles / Allso I will that xl li' of mony be bestowid and leid in reparacion makynge

and amendinge of the hight way ledinge from Barnett to' [erasure] bysshiop
hatfelde between potters barre and the belle barre in the Towne of Northmymes / Allso I will that the sum of xl markes whiche I reicyuid of Rycharde
Clowdisley be spent allso in makynge and mendinge of the said wey for the
soule of me and of the same Richard' and all cristen' soules and if it fortune
me to bestowe the said sommes of xl li and xl markes or any of them in my
life then this my will of them and euery of them that it shall fortune me to do
in my liff / be voide of as myche as I shall doo in my life / and the residue to
be truly perfourmed by myne executours accordinge to this my will / Allso I
gyue and bequeth to sir Thomas More knyght my sonne or to John More his
sonne / that there will dwell all the vstilmentes and stuff of houshold being in
my place at Northmymes after the disceas of Alice my wiff she to occupye it
duringe hir life / Allso I bequeth to Johane my doughter one stondinge cupp
of syluer and gylte with a couer / and xij spones of syluer. / Item I bequeth
to Elizabethe my doughter one stondinge cupp' of siluer and gylte with a
couer and a dosyn of sponis of syluer / and to euery of the childern of the
said Elizabeth / v markes / or stuffe of houshold to the valeue of v markes /
Item I bequethe to John' Rastell' hir husbonde / v li / Allso I bequeth to
Richard Staferton sone to my doughter Johane / v li / and to Agnes his suster
Nonne / stuff necessarye for hir to the valewe of / xl s / Also I bequeth to
Margarete Parris Wiff to Fyllip Parris Esquire one stonding cupp' of syluer
and gylte with a couer / Item to William Parrys his sonne / v li / Item I bequethe to Anne Clerke my wiffes doughter one cupp' of syluer and (and)
gylte with a couer / Item I bequethe to Dorothe Chaloner one stonding cupp'
of syluer and gylte with a couer / Item I bequeth to Abell the sonne of Emme
v markes Item I bequeth to Dorathe More xl s the doughter of Cristofer More /
Item I bequeth to Thomas Chaloner and John' Chaloner and to euery of them
xl s / Allso I bequeth to Leonarde Barton v li / Allso I bequethe to euery of
my seruauntes beinge in my seruice at the tyme of my deceas' xx s / Item I
bequeth to Elizabeth Bowers / v li / Item I bequeth to euery of childern of
Sir Thomas More my sonne v li / Allso I will that the sum of xl li be disposed
by myn executours in dedis of charite to pore people / pore maidens mariages
/ pore prysoners / and my pour kynne / after the discrescion of myn executours / Allso I will that an yerely obite be kept for me in the said churche of
Saint Laurance duringe / x / yeres next after my deceas to praye for my soule
and all the soulis aforesaid and all cristen soulis / Allso I bequeth to euery of
the iiij orders of friers to say dirige and masse of requiem by note and one
trentall of masses for my soule and all the soules abouesaid and all christian
soules / And allso I will that a dole be made for me and the soules aforsaid to
pore people of xx markes of syluer to be deuided after the discrescion of myn
executours / The residue of all my goodes after this my will perfourmed / I
gyve to Alice my wiff to hir owne vse for euer and of this my present testament and last will I make and order myn executours Alice my wiffe Sir
Thomas More knyght Cristofer More gentilman and Richard Stauerton the elder
and I bequeth to euery of myn executours for their labour therin / x markes /
Writton with myn owne hand' the daye and yere abouesaid / This witnessith

Walter Marshe mercer / William Southwod' Goldsmythe / Maister William White clerke / wicar of Saint Laurance / Edwarde Byllinge wexchandlour Thomas Daye Tailour / Nicholas Wastlyn Chapellen / John Abbot gentilman / William Ponchon and John Westden et aliorum. PROBATUM fuit suprascriptum testamentum coram domino apud Lambeth quinto die mensis Decembris Anno domini Millimo quigen⁰ xxx⁰ / Juramento Alicie relicte et executricis et domini Thome More militis / et Cristoferi More et Richardi Stauerton executorum in huiusmodi testamento nominatorum / ac approbatum etc. / Et comissa fuit administracio omnium et singulorum bonorum iurum et creditorum dicti defuncti prefate executrici debent et fideli administranda / In persona magistri Johannis Wright literati procuratoris sui etc / Ac de pleno et fideli Inventario etc / Nec non de plano et vero compote reddendo / Ad Sancta dei Euangelia Juratum.[29]

SIR THOMAS MORE: MAKER OF ENGLISH LAW?

Margaret Hastings

Sir Thomas More's fame rests firmly on his *Utopia*, on his other humanist and religious writings and also on his life as reported by his contemporaries, and more particularly on his martyrdom. No one has had much to say about his professional career as a lawyer and judge. To be sure, Holdsworth includes him in his Tagore lecture, *Some Makers of English Law*, but he offers no specific evidence to support the characterization. "Sir Thomas More's beautiful character would have made him an ideal Chancellor at any time," he says. His scrupulousness, and impartiality, his easiness of access, his restraint in granting subpoenas "till he was satisfied that the plaintiff had some real ground of complaint," and his tact in dealing with common law judges justify his recognition as "a maker of English law."[1]

The fact is, however, that More is elusive as a lawyer and judge. His readings at Lincoln's Inn have not been found. He is not quoted in the Yearbooks. The records of the sheriff's court for More's time as under-sheriff have not survived. In the records of the Masters of Requests, it is hard to point to the influence of any one person. Star Chamber records are evidently more promising according to J. A. Guy, who has worked on them in depth for the period of Wolsey's tenure as Chancellor of the Realm.[2] But in Early Chancery Proceedings, it is hard to find what happened to any given case. In fact, the most intriguing document I found when I searched those records (back in 1950) was a petition addressed to Thomas Audeley, sometime in the half year immediately after More's retirement.[3] The petitioner argued that his case had been "examyned (*befor the lady More* at Chelsey)" and had never properly been heard. His complaint was that he had been persuaded by Thomas Campion to enter into an elaborate deception of Campion's wife. The joke turned out to be at *his* expense, cost £92, because he had been foolish enough to sign in the presence of the wife and two independent witnesses acquittances which debarred him from all legal remedy. In all likelihood, the examination before "the lady More at Chelsey," was just one of More's jokes. What better lesson for so foolish a man than to send him to Chelsea to tell his story to Dame Alice, with her "What the good year, my good man?" and here "Tille valles?"

For the Duchy of Lancaster, however, there is a relatively complete and compact set of administrative and judicial records. There is a *Decree and Order Book*[4] for the entire period of More's tenure of the Chancellorship of

This article is based on a paper delivered at the Anglo-American Historical Conference in London, July 1965. Publication here by permission of the author.

the Duchy, that is from the 30th of September, 17 Henry VIII (1525) to the 25th of October, 21 Henry VIII (1529), when he was appointed to the Chancellorship of the realm. There are also two sets of files of case papers containing mainly bills of complaint and pleadings (D.L.1) and the other comprising mainly depositions, interrogatories and examinations of witnesses (D.L.3). The hope is that through a study in depth of these documents, especially the decrees and case papers related to them, one can throw some light on More's performance as a judge, proceeding according to "equity and conscience."

The English humanists had hoped that Henry VIII would be the philosopher king of their Platonic colloquies. Their hopes were frustrated. For Sir Thomas More the nearest approximation to fulfillment was in his Chancellorship of the Duchy. It is not possible to prove that he thought of this office in the terms I have suggested, but it seems likely that he did. The reader may also doubt that he had more power in the lesser office. All I would contend is that he held the higher office only from the brief period from the 25th of October until the 16th of May 1532, when he resigned, having wished to do so a year earlier.[5] In the Duchy of Lancaster he was more nearly an independent ruler, although of only 40,000 people. He was assisted by an able corps of trained servants of the Crown, and, in the Duchy office, was less exposed to extraneous pressures, to royal whims and demands and to the larger forces of change in Europe. He nominated sheriffs and justices in the County Palatine and had in his award also all the lesser offices, subject, of course, to royal approval. As Chancellor of the Duchy, he was the king's lieutenant for the administration of justice, but, instead of having to administer it through King's Council, Star Chamber, Masters of the Requests, and Chancery, he could perform all his judicial duties within the one court beginning in his time to be called regularly the Court of Duchy Chamber. The procedures of the court were more flexible than those of the Chancery. And More was not, as in the Chancellorship of the realm, successor to an overmighty predecessor under necessity of correcting the balance in relation to common law judges. Chancellors of the Duchy (as Sir Robert Somerville shows in his distinguished and monumental book on the history of the Duchy)[6] more often than not, since the Dukes of Lancaster became kings of England, had been laymen.[7] Since 1485 every one of them had been a layman, and all but More's two immediate predecessors (Marny, 1509–1523, Wingfield, 1523–1525) had, like More himself, been trained in one of the Inns of Court.[8] If there ever had been a clash between common law and equity, there is no obvious evidence of it in the Duchy records. In Marny's time, 1509–1523, and probably also in More's, when important decrees were given, the chief common law justices of the Duchy were present and party to the court's decisions.

The Duchy estates stretched across England from Morecambe sands to Mablethorpe, and north and south from Wrynose Pass to Willingden, near Eastbourne. Some subjects and tenants of the Duchy, then, were not resident in the County Palatine, and their resort to the Chancellor and Council for justice on the ground of "right and conscience" came from outside Lancashire. But what reason is there for supposing that More performed his functions in the Duchy in person? Henry, in the Eltham Ordinances of 1526, appointed him among four of his counsellors of whom two were to be in "continual attendance." He specified that they were to be "in the king's dining chamber" every day at ten in the morning, and again at two in the afternoon to "commune or confer upon any cause or matter, but also for hearing and direction of poor men's complaints on matters of justice."[9] Moreover, we know that More was abroad during the early summer of 1527 with Wolsey and again with Tunstal in 1529.

It is a pity that William Heydon, Clerk of the Council, did not continue during More's Chancellorship his own and his father's earlier practice of noting in the margin of the *Decree and Order Book* the names of the members of the court on important court days.[10] There are only two such marginals for More's term of office. On the other hand, there are so many and such various references to "Master Chancellor" or "Master More" that it is clear that he paid regular attention to the court's business.

"Master More," for example, receives bond from sureties for a defendant's future appearance. More becomes impatient with the farmer of a mill for not making repairs which he had undertaken to make, and calls "hastily for the bond," presumably to collect the penalty due the king for non-fulfillment.[11] The serjeant-at-arms appears in the court to answer a petition "by commaundment of Mr. Chauncellor."[12] More writes a letter to an executor demanding the arrearages of the king's rent.[13] He writes hasty marginal notes on the memorandum for a decree in an enclosure case.[14] "Master Chancellor himself" examines witnesses in an important case.[15] He delivers "by his own handes into this courte in the Duchie Chamber at Westminster three bokes of patentes sealed with the Duchie seale belonging to my Lord Marques concernyng the honour of Leicestere ..." to be safely kept in the chest behind the clerks' chair in the Duchy Chamber.[16] In relation to the same matter George Hastings surrenders into More's hands Edward IV's patents appointing William Lord Hastings and his heirs stewards of the honour of Leicester, parcel of the Duchy.[17] Thomas Gerrard delivers into his hands Thomas Parr, claimed as the king's ward.[18] The parties in a suit about a title of inheritance agree to abide his "award, order, and judgement."[19] More, the general attorney, and the receiver-general reason with a petitioner urging him to come to terms with the defendants—unsuccessfully, it seems, because the defendants were discharged without further responsibility.[20] More delivers by his own hand in Westminster the interrogatories, depositions, and examinations of witnesses in a particularly lengthy and difficult case.[21] He writes at the foot of an information "fiat privatum sigillum ..." Thomas More, knight, in a bold and rapid hand.[22] The king's poor tenants of Enfield petition that during his absence in France with Wolsey, defendants against whom they have a suit before the court have brought a counter-suit and have got injunctions to keep them in attendance at Westminster when they should be planting their fields in Enfield. This would not have happened, they think, if More had been present. The implication is that he was normally available.[23]

Many more examples of More's attention to Duchy matters could be given and there is also negative evidence. The usual procedure of the clerk was to note in the lower right-hand corner on the face of the petition what the court ordered in the first instance, usually a sub-poena under privy seal of the Duchy, addressed to one or more defendants. But this was not, like judicial process in the common law courts, a routine matter for clerks to deal with. Sub-poenas were sometimes addressed not to the list of defendants provided by the complaintant but to one or more persons not mentioned at all in the petition. At least once, there is a note that further proceedings in the matter are to be postponed until the coming to Westminster of the auditor for the north parts of the Duchy. And there are several cases where a commission was appointed to make enquiry in the county before any sub-poena at all was issued. That the Chancellor was the person who normally took responsibility for these first responses to petitions is suggested by the fact that, when More's immediate predecessor was absent in Spain, Knyghtley, the general attorney, signed his name above the clerk's note of process—presumably as a warrant in the absence of the Chancellor. I have found few such signatures in More's term of office. It is possible that More sometimes heard petitions elsewhere than in the Chamber at Westminster. Biographers mention his invitation to petitioners in Chancery to come to him at Chelsea.

The Chancellor and Council of the Duchy performed with respect to the Duchy the administrative functions of the royal council with respect to the realm. But the *Decree and Order Book,* in More's time, is primarily a record of judicial matters, mainly process to get defendants into court, appearances, injunctions for further appearance, and interim or final decrees. Only twenty-two of the 358 entries for More's four years relate to purely administrative matters such as the livery of estates, the delivery of royal wards, arrears of rent, and the like.

Before going farther in the attempt to present illustrations of More's work in the court, it might be as well to discuss the procedure of the court, although not in the ample and technical detail in which Chancery procedure is discussed for the Elizabethan Chancery by W. J. Jones.[24] That would be impossible in a short and tentative paper like the present one. But a general outline may help the reader the more readily to follow the discussion of particular cases.

In general, the procedure is like Chancery procedure, but it is less complex because the court has a less complex internal organization than the Chancery. An action began with either a bill or an "information" addressed to the Chancellor. An information was the usual form to use against or by a Duchy officer; the bill or petition the one to use against a private party. The bill stated not only the cause of complaint but also the justification for bringing the case to the Chancellor and Council rather than to the common law courts. The usual reasons given are that no remedy is available at common law, or that the defendant wields such overweening power that "your humble bedesman" would not be able to contend with him at common law, or that certain evidences necessary to prosecution of the suit at common law are not available to the plaintiff because the defendant has possession of them, or that a riot has occurred. The plaintiff concludes his bill with a request to the Chancellor to

grant a "privy seal," that is, a writ (or *sub-poena*) under privy seal to go to
the defendant ordering him to do right to the plaintiff or come into court to
explain why he does not do so. The court then issues a privy seal either to
the defendant as named or to someone who is considered to be responsible
in relation to the substance of the complaint. The striking fact to anyone
coming to the Duchy records from a background of reading the records of the
common law courts is the extraordinary effectiveness of process. Only twenty-
seven of approximately four hundred persons summoned by privy seal failed
to come.[25] In the case of these individuals, the usual entry is that a servant of
the plaintiff or in one entry, a Duchy messenger delivered the writ at a certain
time and place (the church door was a convenient place because of the avail-
ability of witnesses), but that the defendant either resisted or ignored the
writ. In one case, the defendant's servant called the server "Ye horson,"
knocked him down and broke his head in several places.[26] In another, a defendant burned the privy seal.[27] But more often the excuse of illness or debility
was brought in by a servant. In the few cases where no resistance was alleged
and no excuse made, an attachment or command to the sheriff to arrest the
defendant was the next step.

Where the defendant appeared, the usual entry was that he was enjoined
to appear from day to day under penalty of £40 if he did not do so. Sometimes, either because he gave his answer on the day for which he was summoned and sworn and examined on it for "various considerations," often not
made explicit, he was allowed to appear by attorney and/or he was given a
"day over" into the next term to come with "evidences" or witnesses. Sometimes the entry in the *Decree and Order Book* mentions that he took a copy
of the bill. At any rate, according to the evidence in the files of "Pleadings"
(D.L.1) it was at this stage that pleadings occurred. The next step was usually
the appointment of a commission to take depositions and examine witnesses
in the country on the basis of interrogatories prepared by the parties. The
commission was, as a rule, commanded to settle the matter forthwith if possible and to certify its findings at some future date, usually in the next term.
If this move was successful, that presumably ended the case, and there is consequently no decree to be found in the *Decree and Order Book*. If it was not,
the case was carried back to the Chancellor and Council to be dealt with there.
The Chancellor and Council might call up key witnesses and examine them,
and take depositions and then issue a decree based on its findings. But there
are only fifty-six decrees among the three hundred and fifty-eight entries for
More's period of office, and this seems to be a fairly normal ratio. So we are
left with the impression that many cases were settled by commissions locally,
or settled by agreement, or referred to arbitration.

The problem of the researcher in these documents is to find all the material
in the files relating to any important case and to match it up with the entries
in the *Decree and Order Book*. The nineteenth-century calendars of Pleadings
(D.L.1) and of Depositions and Examinations (D.L.3) list separately the
several parts of the same case if they happen to have been found in separate
bundles, where they presumably were filed by the clerks of the sixteenth

century. The calendar also fails to note by cross-reference that as many as five petitions may be based on the same set of facts. In the major cases, there are often counter-suits, and these help to confound the researcher still further.

Altogether over three hundred cases came into the court in More's period of office. By counting as one suits and counter-suits based on the same set of facts, I find a total of three hundred and nine.[28] Of these ninety-seven have to do with rights in land or attached to land. Some fifteen of these involve copy-hold rights and seven involve uses. Sixty-five have to do with violence in the country-side; thirty-five based on alleged riot and forcible entry and thirty on ambush, threats, attempted murder, resistance to arrest, seizure of felon's goods. Twenty-two complaints are of interruption of rights of common. Twenty-one are presented by royal officers or farmers that defendants have refused to pay monies due or have rescued animals taken in distraint. Seventeen are the obverse of this, that is, complaints against royal bailiffs and other officers for monies levied or beasts taken illegally. Fifteen have to do with the killing of the king's deer or poaching in waters held by the king's farmers. Three especially interesting cases have to do with mining rights, one of these with coal mining on Burneley common in Blacburnshire. Other cases are scattered among many categories. Two are prosecutions of jurors for perjury; one involves treasure-trove, and so on. The variety of informations against persons who have intruded on royal rights or failed in obligations to the king is manifold. These suits are brought either directly in the king's name or in the name of some officer of the Duchy.

This general and superficial survey of the categories of cases does give some notion of the variety and scope of More's necessary preoccupations in an equity court. But it does not tell us much about More's place in the history of English law. To be sure of that, we need to know not only what decisions he made but how they fit into a whole sequence of decisions. We need also to know whether More was an innovator so far as procedures of the court were concerned. In a merely exploratory paper like this, it is possible to give a barely tentative answer to the question announced in the title.

Something can be said perhaps about his assiduity in fulfilling his duties in the court. He was appointed on the 30th of September 1525, but there are only three entries in the *Decree and Order Book* for Michaelmas term. A note in the Hilary term following[29] records that Michaelmas term had been adjourned from the Morrow of All Souls to Hilary term following. For Hilary term there are fourteen entries, only one of more than routine nature. For Easter term, there are four decrees, the first in Latin, an unusual phenomenon in a court which did most of its business in a mixture of mainly English, some Latin and some French. Trinity term, 1526, was pushed two weeks deeper into the summer for unexplained reasons. The term began on the 25th of June instead of the 11th. The peak term for decrees is Easter, 1527, just before More went with Wolsey on a mission to France. There were eight. Trinity term, 1528, was adjourned altogether owing to the "sweating sickness" in London. In More's last term, that is, Michaelmas, 1529, he managed to push through seven decrees in spite of his new and overlapping responsibilities as

Chancellor of the realm. Altogether there are fifty-three decrees entered in
the *Decree and Order Book* and three orders. A rather superficial survey of
the draft decrees (D.L.6/1 and 2)[30] and some drafts found in the case papers
shows that not all the decrees were entered in the book.

But there is really little profit in the mere counting of numbers of petitions
and decrees, especially not until I am certain of the final count. As in other
courts, one finds that many cases simply disappear without trace of the outcome. Presumably the defendant or the plaintiff decided to yield rather than
bear the cost of further proceedings, or both parties agreed to a settlement
out of court. In three cases, we have mention of such an agreement.[31] In four
cases, the matter in controversy was referred to arbitration.[32] Many petitions
must have been dismissed on first hearing. Sometimes, as in the case of
Nicholas Ratclyff v. John and Cecily Barton,[33] the court heard lengthy pleadings by counsel but ultimately referred the case for trial at the common law
before the Justices at Lancaster. The papers in this case include summations
by counsel for both parties and the main arguments for or against a hearing
in Duchy Chamber. The dismissal of this case is not enough evidence in itself
to confirm Roper's account of More's restraint in interfering with common
law proceedings, but with others, it is the sort of thing which may help in
time to give clearer delineation to our picture of More as a judge.

One other item, so far as it goes, helps to strengthen the popular picture of
the Chancellor—the man who finished off all the cases pending in the Chancery and looked around for more:

> When More sometime had Chancellor been,
>   No more suits did remain
> The like will never more be seen
>   Till More be there again.[34]

This is the case of Richard Grey, who, having got the king's grant of the farm
of two corn mills and a walk mill in Tutbury (Staffs.), found that the corn
mills were in great decay and that the walk mill had collapsed altogether. He
brought action against the former farmer for his neglect in Michaelmas, 1527,
the term in which his lease was to have taken effect. The defendant appeared
on the day given, that is Hilary quindene, 1528. The court issued a decree by
which the defendant was bonded to pay half the cost of the repairs. The king
was to supply timber, trusses, and piles and to pay one third of the cost. The
new farmer was to pay the fourth part of the cost (sic) and to have an amendment to the terms of his lease in view of the untimely burden.[35] Among the
case papers are two letters from John Burgoyn. He writes to the defendant
and to the receiver general on the 18th of May warning them in friendship
that the Chancellor has received information that the repairs have not yet
been made, and that "Master Chancellor callythe hastily for the sute of the
obligaceion therffor."[36]

The most interesting cases in the court, for me, are those which show Sir
Thomas More, citizen of London, royal servant and humanist, under necessity
of understanding and dealing with changing rural society. To anyone brought

up on More's vivid description of the sheep devouring not only the arable fields but also the poor peasants who cultivate them, it is surprising to find that the main cases involving enclosures in the records arise from enclosing of waste, or from dividing in severalty lands which had formerly been commoned between harvest and seed time. In the first case, villagers lost pasture, turves for fuel, marsh grasses and reeds needed in the home. In the second they lost an important part of the pasture for beasts.

Cases involving enclosures usually appear in the guise of complaints of riot and other acts of violence. The most intricate case of this sort is *Bold v. Gerard*. It is really a complex of cases, five altogether, which have to do with Sir Richard Bold's attempt to enclose for arable a section of the Coptholt, part of a common in the parish of Prescott inter-commoned between the villages of Prescott, Eccleston, Rainhill, and Whiston. Sir Richard charged the Gerard faction with riot and arson, that is of appearing in warlike array to prevent his action and of twice burning the three houses he has built in the enclosed area.[37] In another case, certain tenants of Enfield are at odds with the king's demesne tenants, also of Enfield, for closing off certain fields usually commoned in fallow years and during the intervals between crops.[38] In a third case, the tenants of Barton complain of Sir Walter Griffith and his tenants that he buys up copyhold tenements that fall vacant and closes them against pasturing of animals.[39] More seems to have taken a close interest in all three cases. In *Bold v. Gerard*, a case which began in the king's Council, More had a fair copy made of depositions and examinations taken before that body at the end of Trinity term of leading defendants and witnesses. Michaelmas term in the Duchy council was prorogued that year, More having been appointed only on the 30th of September. More delivered the fair copy to the clerk of the Duchy council in Hilary term.[40] In the Enfield case, which has already been referred to above, one set of tenants complain that the defendants, in a complaint that they had made a riot, took advantage of More's absence to bring a vexatious counter-suit.[41] In the complex cluster of cases between tenants of Barton and Sir Walter Griffith and several tenants of his manor of Whichenor,[42] More issued a preliminary order against the Whichenor tenants pending the findings of a commission appointed for the purpose.

The most significant case for adumbrating the future of Lancashire is the Burneley Mines case.[43] Sir Thomas More evidently thought the case important. He himself examined the chief defendants on their first appearance. The facts appear to be as follows. Early in 1526, the king had granted to Sir Richard Townely, gentleman, a twenty-year lease of the farm of some open-cast mines on Broad Head Moor, near Burneley. Townely had barely begun to exploit his grant when, on the 7th of May, by his report, eighty of the king's tenants of Blackburnshire, came with force and arms, broke down his pit props, indulged in "threats and menaces" and took away coal at their will. In his petition Townely asked the Chancellor and Council to command Sir Richard Tempest, steward of Blackburn hundred, to enjoin the king's tenants from meddling further. More must have acted promptly on this request. Three weeks after the alleged riot, he sent a letter under the Duchy seal to Tempest, and a month later, Tempest reported back that he had summoned the tenants before him and commanded them to dig no more coal for the present. He has also sent the ringleaders among the tenants to appear personally before More to tell him their side of the story. More examined them on the 28th of June.[44] Five days later,[45] the court issued an interim decree. The tenants were to forbear digging coal until the matter should have been fully heard. Meanwhile an "indifferent person" was to dig coal for them, not in Towneley's pits but elsewhere. He was to keep a "score tail" of the quantity delivered to each person and was to be paid for his labor in digging. Then, depending on how the case should be decided, the tenants were to pay him for the value of the coal taken. If they should succeed in proving their right, they were to have coal in the future as fully and freely as heretofore.

In Michaelmas term following, on the 15th of November, the chief defendants appeared again, this time in answer to the sub-poena issued at the time of the original petition. They were again examined, presumably in full court in the presence of the complainant. The four men agreed on all essential parts of their testimony. There had been no assembly, no riot, and no riotous intent. One of them, Sutclyff, had talked to Towneley, the new farmer, before the day of the alleged riot, had asked what his authority was and what he meant to do, and had been told to be on the ground on Monday, 7 May, when all would be explained. Each man had set out separately to the Broad Hedd but one had fallen in with two friends on the way. Within an hour of their arrival at the pits, thirty or more people had gathered, none of them armed except with spades or other digging instruments, and staves such as "they use to go to church there with all, for it was procession day in Gang week." They all admitted that the new farmer had shown them his letters patent from the king under the Duchy Seal, but they denied that anyone at all had used opprobrious or threatening words. Hugh Haverjambe admitted that he had said that they had heard nothing in the patent to prevent them digging coal "after their use and custom."

The court's response was its usual first step. It appointed a commission to investigate on the spot. The commissioners were to hear and, if possible, to settle the matter and to send word of what they had done in Easter term following. At Colne, on the 16th of March they examined, individually or in large groups, eighty witnesses. What they discovered was that about eighty years earlier two men who had a smithy in Bentley Wood had been hunting for "iron stone" on the moor when they stumbled upon open seams of coal. Then Bentley Wood was emparked and they were forced to give up the smithy. They turned to digging coal for their living. James Robert, the most garrulous witness, aged 79, says that neither his father, who told him this tale, nor any other inhabitant had need in times past to get coal for fuel because they had plenty of wood from the forest and turves at their liberty "wiche now be decayed and restrayned from them." It is clear from the testimony that the tenants of Blackburnshire do not really see the difference between digging turves and digging coal. The record of the case ends with an entry in Easter term, 1527, that the commissioners' report, or certificate, was read and "For certeyn consyderacions yt is ordered,"[46] but the record stops abruptly at this point. No order was entered in the book, and we would be left wondering what happened if it were not that, among the case papers, is a long list of names, and after each name, a list of "fothers," presumably of coal. At the bottom, in a rather cramped hand is written "Memorandum, it ys ordered that every of the persones above namyd shall pay to the kynges farmor ii s. iij d. for every fother above expressid." This is signed "Thomas More, knight," in an unmistakable handwriting.[47]

So the tenants lost, but it is hard to see what else could have been the outcome, given the rules that prescription does not run against the king, and that everything below the earth's surface belongs to him anyhow. The interesting fact is that More heard the tenants' point of view before it was more formally presented in full court and that he protected them from a charge of riot when, in fact, nothing more violent had occurred than a great deal of angry talk. You will remember that in Utopia, there are no lawyers, that every man conducts his own case, but that the judge "skillfully weighs each statement and helps untutored minds to defeat the false accusations of the crafty . . ."[48]

For More as a "law-maker" the two instances that I can give you now do not depend on the careful study of a sequence of cases or a knowledge of what More's predecessors and successors did to illustrate this humanist Chancellor's outlook. The first is one in which More seems to have tried to apply in the borough of Preston some of the principles of Utopian election procedures.[49] The second has to do with the Statute of Uses. The Preston case began in Michaelmas, 1527, when James Walton, late Mayor of Preston sent up a petition by hand of the parson of the Church of Preston. It seems that, on 7 October, Walton had summoned a meeting of the borough court for the 10th of the month to elect a new mayor, bailiff, and sergeant. The normal election procedure, he says, was for those who had already served in the town offices to nominate one candidate and for the burgesses at large to nominate the other. Then, on election day, the mayor appointed two priests to act as tellers to record the votes. For this election, the two candidates were William Wall, a former mayor of the town, and Nicholas Banaster, the popular candidate, a man without experience in the borough administration. Two days before the election, Sir Richard Houghton, a "foreign burgess," and a great landowner in the neighbourhood, called a meeting for the middle of the night at the house of one Janet Fydler. There his "mind and plesier" concerning the elections was communicated by two of his servants.

On the day of the election, when all had assembled in the moot hall, Sir Richard rose to demand that his chaplain be appointed as one of the tellers. Not waiting for the Mayor's response, he asked those who favored his proposal to put up their hands and go to one side of the hall. The Mayor indignantly asserted his official authority, called on Houghton not to "intermeddle" and announced that he would refer the whole matter to the Chancellor and Council of the Duchy. Sixty of the more substantial burgesses supported him in this, all of them former office-holders. But he adjourned the meeting and withdrew from the hall, uncomfortably aware that there was a larger number of supporters of Houghton and that the crowd was out of hand. In fear of his life, he says, he fled with 10 of his supporters to an abandoned mill outside the town. There he met one of the justices of the peace of the county. This man, Faryngton, rallied two of the other justices to his support and they demanded and got from Sir Richard a recognisance to keep the peace. Even so, Walton continued to avoid the town until after his term of office had expired. After the expiration of the term, on 3 November, Sir Richard's party held a rump election and chose Houghton's candidates. John Houghton, Sir Richard's brother, took the chair in place of the missing mayor; John Powell, "although a Welshman born," took over the duties of clerk, and one of Sir Richard's household servants was the chief tally-keeper.

This is James Walton's account of the matter. John Powell also came before the court, without summons, in the same term. He said that the burgesses had intended to make their own complaint to the court and to give him good and sufficient letters under the common seal to speak on their behalf, but that they had been prevented by Walton's having one of the three keys to the chest in which the seal was kept and his refusing to surrender it. Powell's account of the election differs from Walton's only in the construction put upon the acts of the participants. Walton's candidate for mayor was a notorious stirrer-up of quarrels and law-suits he says. The burgesses had appealed to Sir Richard as "a man of worship" resident near the town who would have the power to help them get a free election. The midnight meeting in Janet Fydler's house was held to plan the overthrow of a pernicious faction. The rump election was held out of necessity—because Walton's terms had expired and no new mayor had been elected. He himself had served as clerk on the insistence of the burgesses and "of his own gentleness," as he had done many times for James Walton when he was Mayor.

It is evident that More saw in this crisis a chance to apply to sixteenth-century England some Utopian principles about the election of magistrates. An interim government of the town was appointed by the Chancellor and Council, the leading partisans on both sides were bound over to keep the peace in relation to one another and the townspeople, and "two discrete, honest burgesses" of the town were to come to the court with all such "patents, grauntes, alowaunces, constitucions, and ordenances as they have in writyng concernyng the liberties, usages, and customes" of the town and authorized "in the name of the hoole towne to treat, comen, conclude, and determyn with the saied Chauncelor and Counsel" the final orders and directions to be taken in the matter.

By a stroke of good luck for the historian, the conflict broke out again in 1534,[50] and as a result, there is among the case papers, a copy of the indenture drawn up between the representatives of the borough on the one part and Sir Thomas More and Sir Thomas Audeley (by 1534 Lord Chancellor, but in 1528 only general attorney of the Duchy) on the other. It is drawn up on parchment and is headed: "Articles and Ordinances," ... "agreed to between Sir Thomas More, knyght, Chancellor of the kyng our soverayn lorde of hys Duchy of Lancaster and by the Counsell of the same Duchye, by the consent and agreement of James Walton and Henry Clyfton," the authorized representatives of the borough. The ordinances do not alter the basic form of elections. They deal mainly with the abuses alleged to have occurred in the election of 1527: Everyone is to give proper reverence to the Mayor and to assist him and attend upon him in all lawful precepts and proclamations, penalty 100s. No election is to be had except in the presence of the Mayor. No burgess is to make "any secrete privy labor, conspyracy or confederacy to or with any burgesses" for election, nor are any "congregations or assembles" to be held by any burgess "to thentent to advaunce hymself to be Mayr, Bayly or other officer," penalty £40. No foreigner is to meddle, whatever his estate or degree, nor cause any meetings . . . to be had, or cause any of his tenants or friends to support any particular candidate, penalty £20. "Noe meetings to trete or comen for election" of officers are to be held out of the common hall, penalty 100s. And finally, these articles and ordinances are to be read regularly each year a week before election day. On the day itself, the tellers are to be chosen, one by the mayor and other former officeholders, one by the burgesses at large, all with due decorum.[51]

Two points are striking about these ordinances. One is that the prohibition on soliciting votes emphasized in two of its clauses comes straight out of *Utopia*. You will remember that "The man who solicits votes to obtain any office is deprived completely of the hope of holding any office at all."[52] The other is that Sir Thomas More did not belong to the wave of the future in urging this restriction on the borough of Preston. Nor was he, as local historians seem to assume, responsible for imposing a democratic procedure in the election for mayor. In fact, it is not at all clear when and how the provision for nomination of alternative candidates by the burgesses at large and a final vote by the whole body of the burgesses had been introduced or how long it lasted. According to Clemesha, Fishwick, and Abram, all historians of the borough who have discussed the matter, the method of election which prevailed in 1500, and was confirmed in 1562 by a charter of Elizabeth, was indirect. On election day, the mayor was to appoint one man, the twenty-four Chief Burgesses another. These two were to choose twenty-four of the more "discreet burgesses" who, having foresworn office for themselves, were to choose the new mayor, the town bailiff and the town sergeant.[53] I submit that this is not at all the method of election described by Walton in his petition, nor by the defendants in their answers. But More was certainly not responsible for it. The main bearing of the case on my present thesis is simply that More and Audeley negotiated with the borough representatives a revision of the borough ordinances which was in the rational spirit of *Utopia* rather than the ebullient spirit of sixteenth-century England.

The other illustration of More as a law-maker shows him more in the role of an experienced lawyer than as a Utopian legislator. I am convinced that he was the author of the original draft for a statute of uses, the one presented to parliament in November 1529[54] and almost immediately modified by the Agreement between the King and Nobility,[55] and so thoroughly altered in later sessions of parliament that the *Act of Uses* as passed in 1536 has little resemblance to the original proposal excepting parts of the preamble which are somewhat incongruous with the main body of the statute. Only the *Statute of Enrollments*,[56] passed in the same session of 1536, retains anything of the intent and spirit of More's original draft.

Now what did this original draft provide and why do I think that More was the author? Its essential provisions are the following: 1) Entails except those of "the nobyll men of thys realme," are to be abolished, 2) Uses "hereafter to be made to any person or persons upon or for eny possescions within thys realme" are to avail only if they are recorded in "the kynges courte of the comen place," 3) In every shire there is to be kept a roll or book for such transactions so that purchasers and others may know their terms, 4) "To avoyde all untrowthe for forgyng of evidences, . . . every purchaser schall, immediately after the partie that sellyth hathe selyd and fermid the deade of geft of any londes, tenementes or other hereditamentes so sold, and poscession therapon taken with sufficient recordes, that then the sayd dede to be openly red upon a holy day next folowyng in the parische cherche or cherchis in whiche parische or parisches the sayd lond schall ly, att suche tyme as most people is present, and so red, the vicar, parishe preste, or curate to fyrme the sayd deede, to the intent that the most parte of the parische may know of the sayde sale and possession so made and gevyn." There are a few other points, but these are the most important.

What are the reasons for believing More to be the author? First, the draft is written on paper of the size and bearing the water-mark of that most commonly used in the Duchy Chamber. It is written in a type of hand which, though probably not More's own, is frequently found in papers relating to cases where More's direct concern and attention is noted. This hand is scarcely, if at all, distinguishable from the handwriting of a contemporary letter addressed by More to Wolsey.[57] Furthermore, the draft was presented early in the first session of the parliament of 1529, just after More's opening speech advocating reforms of abuses. It is scarcely necessary to prove that More had ample knowledge both of the intricacies and abuses of conveyancing in his time. He had, as a young man, been associated with his father, the Frowyks, and other prominent lawyers as co-feoffee in many conveyances to uses. Dr. J. Duncan M. Derrett has recently shown us in an article in *Moreana* (No. 5)[58] how skilfully More attempted to preserve for his own family some worldly goods out of his personal disaster.

If More had need of a new look at conveyancing from the point of view of "right and conscience," he certainly had the opportunity in the Duchy Chamber. Two cases, in particular, illustrate the most common problems. One has to do with Thomas Hesketh's efforts to provide for his illegitimate children in the absence of children by his lawful wife.[59] He had married a rich heiress and by this marriage had become lord of estates vastly greater in extent than those held by his elder brother, Richard Hesketh. Richard died in 1520, leaving to Thomas his entire estate. But Thomas had no legitimate son to inherit. So, in September of 1520, he enfeoffed Bartholomew Hesketh and four others of all lands and tenements, to themselves and their heirs and assigns in perpetuity, to his own use for his lifetime, and after his death for the performance of his will. Before he died, in 1523, he made a will providing for his four illegitimate children. The eldest was to have the bulk of the estate and the reversion of the rest. The jurors in the inquisition post mortem[60] reported that he held no lands and tenements of the Crown, although before the grant to uses in 1520, most of the estate would have been subject to payment of relief. They also reported the terms of the will and the fact that the nearest legitimate heirs were the four sons or grandsons of Thomas Hesketh's four sisters. These four cousins promptly brought suit in the Duchy court a little over a year before More became Chancellor. But the case was finally in 1526 referred for settlement "to thaward, order and jugement of Sir Thomas More, knyght, Chauncellor of the Duchie." The records do not show what the award was, presumably because it was an arbitration, referred to More's wisdom, not to his decision as presiding officer of the court. But it is clear from the terms of Sir Robert Hesketh's will, proved in 1540,[61] that as Thomas's eldest illegitimate son, he inherited the entire estate bequeathed to him in his father's will, and that he died Lord of Rufford and a man of worship in the county. And his son, Sir Thomas Hesketh, under age at his death, ultimately became high sheriff of the county.[62]

The main problem about this case is why the court entertained it at all. Current rulings in the Chancery court of England would have given no case to the legitimate heirs. An allegation of riot put in by the executors on behalf of young Robert against the legitimate heirs may explain the court's reason for receiving the case. The first decree, in Easter 1526, uses the words that "for eschewyng and avoydyng morder, riottes, and other inconveniences whych herafter ys lykly to ensue"[63] the executors are to continue to take the profits on behalf of young Robert until the parties come to Westminster in Michaelmas term following, bringing with them all their evidences to prove title. But the main interest of the case, is that it illustrates the loss to the king through Chancery's recognition of grants to the use of the will of a testator who happened also to be a royal tenant-in-chief, and that it presents More as arbiter and peacemaker.

The Kirkby case illustrates some of the intricacies of uses from the point of view of the king's subjects.[64] Here the facts are that Richard Kirkby held the manors of Kirkby Hall and Kirkby Ireleth and lands and tenements in Lancashire comprising about 1700A of arable, pasture, meadow, and woodland. He held in tail male special and died leaving two sons, Henry and Richard. Henry entered according to the terms of the entail but, when it became apparent that he would have no issue male by his wife, Anne, a series of agreements were drawn up between Henry and one John Fleming, whereby Fleming's daughter Katherine was to marry Richard, Henry's younger brother, and in consideration of this and of large sums of money paid by John Flemyng, the entail and title of Richard were affirmed and a jointure settled on Katherine for term of her life with remainder to the petitioner and the heirs male of their two bodies. So far, so good. No problems. But Anne, Henry's childless wife (who may have been one of those "greedy and covetous" persons men-

tioned in the preamble to the Statute of 1536) prevailed on him to make a
subsequent grant of lands to Lucas Longlonde and other co-feoffees to *her*
use for her lifetime. Richard attacked this enfeoffment to the use of Anne in
Chancery before Wolsey, but on Anne's protest that the properties lay within
the County Palatine, Wolsey referred the case to More. The details of the case
are amusing but most of them not relevant to the argument of this paper.
Henry Kirkby had taken the precaution of leaving his will in a "lytyll trussing
coffer ensealed with his seal," in the keeping of the Abbot of Furness. The
Duchy Messenger, Roger Barker, was sent to the Abbot to bring the coffer to
Westminster. But, when the parties were confronted with it in court, they
chose to come to speedy agreement, and the clerk notes that "the sayed
trussing coffer was never there opened ne seen and, forasmoche as all the
sayed parties be nowe thys present terme agreed therfor by there assent and
agreement, it is ordered by thys court that the sayed Roger Barker shall re-
delyver the sayed coffer wyth evydences to the sayed abbot ensealed in lyke-
wyse as he receyved them."[65] More seems here, as in the Hesketh case, to have
acted as a peacemaker to try to prevent what might have become a serious and
protracted family quarrel.

It remains to be seen whether a more substantial and detailed picture of
More as a judge in equity can be produced by studying further the records of
the Duchy court. It is a pity that we have no *dicta* from him. But a careful
study of the decrees, in particular, for his term of office may yield something more than we yet know about him.

The evidence presented above for More as a "maker of English law" is
rather insubstantial. The ordinance for Preston did not last, and the 1529
draft for a statute of uses, if More was indeed responsible for it, did not become the basis for negotiations between the king and parliament.[66] On the
other hand, he emerges from the material studied so far as a hard-working
administrator, a peacemaker more concerned to get at the sources of violence
in the country-side than to inflict harsh penalties, a protector of the weak
against the strong, and an astute lawyer who could cut through a mass of
detail to the heart of the matter in hand.

SIR THOMAS MORE AS PUBLIC HEALTH REFORMER

Arthur S. MacNalty

This is a Chadwick lecture. Sir Edwin Chadwick has been called the Father of English Sanitation; his teaching promoted the study of hygiene, while his "sanitary idea" has been influential alike in medicine and legislation and especially in administrative reforms directed to securing wholesome environment and inculcating the gospel of cleanliness.

"There were great men before Agamemnon," and a great forerunner of Edwin Chadwick in public health reform was Thomas More. More is renowned as saint and martyr; he was an eloquent orator, a great statesman and legislator, Speaker of the House of Commons, royal ambassador and Lord Chancellor, a master of English prose and a classical scholar. These notable distinctions, these great gifts united in one man, in the very blaze of their glory have obscured Sir Thomas's teaching and work in public health and social medicine.

For two years, in a somewhat scanty leisure, it has been my pleasant task to study this somewhat neglected aspect of Sir Thomas More's career in Tudor State papers, in his own writings and letters, in those of his contemporaries, and in biographies and other books. I shall now attempt to give you the fruit of my labours.

Thomas More (1478–1535) was the only surviving son of Sir John More, afterwards a Judge of the King's Bench, and Agnes, daughter of Sir Thomas Grainger. Sir John is credited with the jest "that a man seeking a wife is like one putting his hand into a bag of snakes with one eel among them: he may light on the eel, but it is a hundred chances to one that he shall be stung with a snake." He seems to have been a gentle and upright man and his son, when Chancellor, is said to have invariably visited his father's court to ask his blessing before presiding in his own court.

Thomas went to a City school, that of St. Anthony's in Threadneedle Street. At the age of 13 he was placed in the household of Thomas Morton, Archbishop of Canterbury and Lord Chancellor, who prophesied that he would prove "a marvellous rare man." Here he took impromptu parts in plays at Christmas and collected material for his life of Richard III from Morton's lips.

The liberal education, beginning at Oxford, which Thomas More received well equipped him for his future work. For two years (1492–94) he was an undergraduate at Canterbury Hall, Oxford, which was afterwards absorbed in

A Chadwick Lecture, 1946. Reprinted by permission of the publisher, from *The Journal of the Royal Institute of Public Health* [now *Community Health*], 10 (1947), 7–23.

Christ Church. Here he fell under the influence of the Humanists, Linacre and Grocyn, who had brought the new learning from Italy. His studies were chiefly Latin, although he may have then been initiated into Greek. Greek was, however, not part of the regular curriculum and was frowned on by the Schoolmen. He also studied French, mathematics, and history and learned to play on the viol and flute. Alarmed at these exotic studies, Sir John More removed his son from the University before he had taken his degree and entered him at New Inn to read law. He became a member of Lincoln's Inn in 1496, was called to the outer bar in 1501 and was appointed reader or lecturer on law at Furnival's Inn.

Thomas had fulfilled his father's hopes by becoming proficient in jurisprudence, but he did not neglect to cultivate the humane studies which had so strongly appealed to him at Oxford and which Bishop Fisher was promoting at Cambridge. His instruction was facilitated by the fact that the Oxford teachers had come to London. William Grocyn was vicar of St. Lawrence Jewry. Thomas Linacre was tutor to Prince Arthur and a London physician, and Colet was shortly to become Dean of St. Paul's. More wrote to his friend John Holt in 1501: "You will ask me how I am getting on with my studies. Excellently; nothing could be better. I am giving up Latin and taking to Greek. Grocyn is my teacher" and he writes to Colet, his spiritual director, in 1504: "Meantime I pass my time with Grocyn who is, as you know, in your absence the guide of my life; with Linacre, the guide of my studies; and with our friend Lily, my dearest friend."

More and Lily worked together translating epigrams from the Greek anthology into Latin, though their book was not published until More was 40.

In 1499 More met the Dutch scholar, Erasmus. This was the beginning of a life-long friendship. He presented Erasmus to Prince Henry, afterwards Henry VIII, then a child of nine years of age. More presented the Prince with a poem. This is the first recorded meeting of More with his future Royal Master.

While enjoying the intellectual companionship of his friends and lecturing on law, More hesitated between Law and Holy Orders. For some four years "he gave himself to devotion and prayer in the Charterhouse of London." In the end he decided not to take the vows. This was largely on the advice of Dean Colet, although his father's wishes that he should follow the law no doubt had their weight. But to the end of his life he wore a hair-shirt, scourged himself and practised religious austerities; and he told his daughter, Margaret, in the Tower that had it not been for his wife and children he would long before have closed himself in the cell of a monk. More's religion, as we know from his writings, was the staff and stay of his life.

In 1501, at Grocyn's invitation, he lectured in the Church of St. Lawrence Jewry on St. Augustine's *de Civitate Dei.* The lectures were historical and philosophical and possibly criticised the social evils of the time. The chief and best learned men of the City of London came to hear him.

The Influence of Linacre

We know that Thomas More read Aristotle, for he speaks of attending Lin-

acre's Course on the Meteorologica.[1] This study must not only have trained
Thomas in politics, ethics, and political economy, but probably interested
him in biology and natural history. In Holbein's portrait of More and his
family, the artist has sketched in a small monkey beginning to climb up Lady
More's dress. Further evidence of More's love of animals is obtained from
Erasmus, who wrote of him:[2] "One of his great delights is to consider the
forms, the habits, and the instincts of different kinds of animals. There is
hardly a species of bird that he does not keep in his house, and rare animals,
such as monkeys, foxes, ferrets, weasels, and the like." The interest in natural
history, as often happens, was associated with an interest in medicine and
public health, and it is scarcely an assumption to say that More derived this
from his Greek tutor, Thomas Linacre, who was equally renowned as physician
and classical scholar. Thomas Linacre (1460?-1524), Fellow of All Souls, Oxford, travelled to Italy about 1485-6, in the suite of his old tutor, William de
Selling, who was Ambassador from Henry VII to the Pope. He went to Florence, where he was cordially received and given full facilities for classical
studies by Lorenzo de Medici. A year later, at Rome, the great scholar,
Hermolaus Barbarus, introduced Linacre to the study of Aristotle, Dioscorides,
Pliny, and other medical writers. He graduated as M.D. at Padua with a brilliant disputation, spent some time at Vicenza and after six years returned to
England to be incorporated M.D. at Oxford and to lecture in the University.
In 1500 or 1501 Linacre was appointed tutor to Prince Arthur, and soon after
the accession of Henry VIII became the Royal Physician. He received a num-
ber of ecclesiastical preferments and after being a Deacon was admitted to
Priest's Orders in 1520. He is, of course, famous for the large share he took
in elevating the standard of medical education and in the foundation of the
Royal College of Physicians in 1518, of which he was the first President. He
founded medical lectureships bearing his name at Oxford and Cambridge, for
which it is interesting to note that Sir Thomas More, Tunstall, Bishop of
London, and two other persons were appointed trustees. He died of the stone
and was buried in the old cathedral of St. Paul's. His skill as a physician was
high, and he numbered among his patients Cardinal Wolsey, Archbishop Warham, and Bishop Fox, besides his own friends, Colet, More, Erasmus, Lily,
and other scholars.

Linacre wrote several grammatical works and translated Galen into Latin.
Erasmus mentioned other completed works laid up in Linacre's desk, unpublished. It is not improbable that one or more of these lost works dealt with
public health, for both Linacre's pupils, Sir Thomas More and Sir Thomas
Elyot, were interested in the preventive aspect of disease and the preservation
of health. We can then, I submit, reasonably surmise that More learned much
from Linacre, and that this teaching led him to become a pioneer in public
health administration.

More's Interest in Medicine

There is an extraordinary and prevalent error that classical studies are
antagonistic to the study of science. Thus, in public schools, there are classical

and modern sides, and the intending biologist, chemist, physicist, and doctor neglects his general education in order to rush into the laboratory. But science derives from classical studies. The Greeks opened the portals of science and mankind owes them an incalculable debt for this. Hippocrates was the father of scientific medicine and Aristotle, a great comparative anatomist, urged Alexander the Great to establish a body of learned men with much of the aims of the present Medical Research Council. It was because the Renaissance embodied the principles of Greek thought and learning that Padua and Mont-pellier became such famous Universities; and that when the new learning came to England it paved the way for the discoveries of William Harvey and John Hunter, of Jenner, Pasteur, and Lister and so on towards the epoch-making triumphs of medical research and preventive medicine in our own time. All these wonders can be traced back to the Greeks, but the lesson has been for-gotten. The Oxford humanists were wiser in their own generation. Richard Fox, Bishop of Winchester, founded Corpus Christi College, Oxford, in 1516, in the interests of the new learning, with provision for a teacher of Greek and a reader in divinity. There was opposition from the Schoolmen to whom this new foundation was a challenge. More, with the King's approval, in 1518, wrote a letter to the Fathers and Proctors of the University of Oxford com-mending the value of Greek studies, and at his request Wolsey sent a royal letter commanding all students in Oxford to study Greek. That injunction was strictly obeyed for over 400 years, until the abolition of compulsory Greek in 1920.

In the sixteenth century, the study of Greek not infrequently led on to that of medicine, and Thomas More encouraged this departure in his own household. The house of Chelsea was always full of scholars and pupils. Nicholas Kratzer, Henry VIII's astronomer, was a frequent visitor, so were Erasmus and other scholars from overseas. More believed in the higher educa-tion of women and his daughters were liberally educated. Erasmus wrote to Ulrich von Hutten in the letter to which previous reference has been made: "I should rather call his house a school, or universitie of Christian religion, for there is none therein but readeth or studieth the liberall sciences; their speciall care is pietie and vertue, there is no quarrelling or intemperate words heard, none seen idle, which household that worthy gentleman doth not govern by proude and loftie words, but with all kind and courteous benevolence: every-body performeth his dutie; yet is there always alacratie; neither is sober mirth anie thing wanting."

There are at least three instances of members of More's learned household studying medicine. The first is Margaret Gigs, the foster-sister of More's daughter Margaret, who was to him "as dear as though she were a daughter." As a child she committed small faults in order to have the pleasure of a gentle reproof from More. She was a Greek scholar, fond of mathematics and studied medicine. More relates in the *Second Booke of Comfort agaynste Tribulacyon,* that "when he lay in a tercian fever," symptoms arose which baffled his two physicians, but Margaret Gigs, then a young girl, identified the condition in Galen's *de differentiis febrium.* More made Margaret Gigs his almoner for his outdoor charities, and she married John Clement, whom she had known from a child, and helped him in his medical work and classical studies. She was cast in an heroic mould. In 1535 ten Carthusian monks who refused to acknowledge Henry VIII as the head of the Church were barbarously imprisoned in Newgate. They were kept standing bolt upright, tied with iron collars fast by the necks to the posts of the prison, and great fetters fast rived on their legs with great iron bolts; so straitly tied that they could neither lie nor sit nor otherwise ease themselves, and they were left without food to die. For many days Margaret Clement fed them, having bribed the gaoler to allow her to enter the prison with food, disguised as a milkmaid. At length the terrified gaoler refused to admit her any more and all but one of these unfortunate men died. On her deathbed, in exile at Mechlin in 1570, Margaret told her husband that these monks stood about her bed and bade her come away with them.

I must refer next to one illustrious Tudor physician, perhaps the most lovable of them all. John Clement, M.D., Oxon, was brought up in the household of Sir Thomas More, who said of him: "He is so proficient in Latin and Greek that I have great hopes of his becoming an ornament to his country and to literature." That aspiration was fulfilled. In 1519 Clement settled in Corpus Christi College, Oxford, having been appointed Wolsey's rhetoric reader in the University and later Professor of Greek. More wrote to Erasmus: "My Clement lectures at Oxford to an audience larger than has ever gathered to any other lecturer. It is astonishing how universal is the approbation and love he gains. Even those to whom classical literature was almost anathema attend his lectures and gradually modify their opposition. Linacre, who, as you know never praises any one very much, admires him greatly, so that if I did not love Clement so much, I should be almost tempted to envy the praise he wins."

Clement's wife and former pupil, Margaret Gigs, was deeply read both in Greek and medicine, and helped him in his work. He became F.R.C.P. in 1528, and in the following year was one of the physicians sent by Henry VIII to Wolsey when he lay ill at Esher after his fall from power. In 1544 Clement was elected President of the College of Physicians. Constant, like More, in his attachment to the old faith, Clement retired to Louvain when Edward VI ascended the throne. He returned to England in Mary's reign, but the accession of Elizabeth drove him once more abroad. He died at Mechlin in 1572. His writings relate to classical studies and he does not seem to have given the world the benefit of his medical knowledge.

More's third medical protégé was Richard Hyrde. He was tutor to More's children, and when Margaret Roper translated Erasmus's *Treatise on the Pater Noster,* Hyrde contributed an introduction in English which justified the right of women to a scholarly education. Hyrde's study of Greek authors attracted him to medicine. As physician he accompanied Bishop Gardiner on his embassy to the Pope in 1528 and died of a chill.

Now it is clear that this study of medical authors and constant intercourse with the best physicians of the day were essential features in the development of Thomas More as an enlightened public health reformer. Edwin Chadwick, great as he was, necessarily based his legislative reform on the reports of Southwood Smith, Arnott, Kay, and other medical pioneers, and in the process acquired much medical knowledge. Later still, Sir Robert Morant was a walking encyclopædia of medical knowledge collected from many sources.

Like these great civil servants, Thomas More was no mean amateur in medicine. When his daughter, Margaret, fell so ill of the sweating sickness, probably in 1528, that "by no invention or devices she could be kept from sleep, so that both physicians and all other there despaired of her recovery and gave her over," More, on his knees in prayer, thought of a remedy which, when he told the physicians, they marvelled that they had not themselves remembered. The remedy was administered—unfortunately we are not told its nature[3]—and the patient was restored to perfect health. (Roper)

More's writings contain many illustrations and comparisons drawn from his medical knowledge. This is strikingly exemplified in his unfinished treatise, *De Quatuor Novissimis*, "The Four Last Things," written in 1522 when he had just been knighted and was Under-Treasurer. It is a meditation on death and he describes the book as "a short medicine, containing only four herbs, common and well known, that is to wit, death, doom, pain, and joy": "For what would a man give for a sure medicine that it should all his life keep him from sickness, namely, if he might by the avoiding of sickness be sure to continue his life one hundred years."

In Sir Thomas's last book, *A Dyalogue of Comfort agaynste Tribulacyon*, written in 1534 when he was imprisoned in the Tower of London, there are again many instances culled from the author's medical lore. I have dealt more fully with this subject elsewhere. In his keen observation, in his reflection and deductions and in his dislike of over-drugging, More had all the endowments of a wise physician. It is apparent that he would have been a great one if he had chosen medicine as his profession. Evidently he was intensely interested in medical studies and in the art of healing.

Commissioner of Sewers

On 3rd September, 1510, the young lawyer, Thomas More, was appointed one of the Under-Sheriffs of the City of London. His appointment was made on account of his legal knowledge, for the Under-Sheriff was the legal permanent official who advised the Sheriff in those numerous cases which came under his jurisdiction. In addition, this office gave him opportunity to advise the City Fathers on measures of sanitary reform, in which he was so much interested, and this interest was further shown by his appointment in 1514 as one of the Commissioners of Sewers along Thames Bank between East Greenwich and Lambeth. Though much of the work was riparian in character and directed towards preventing encroachments of the sea, flooding of low grounds, and maintenance of river banks, regulations were also made against trade effluents, deposits of rubbish in rivers, and pollution of rivers, streams, and wells. The larger towns were provided with a regular water-system with public standpipes, and water sometimes was laid on to the houses. London for a long time had been well supplied with water, but under the Tudors seven to eight more conduits were set up from which fresh water was hawked about the streets in barrels. The improvement of London's water supply was much in More's mind when he described the river of Anyder on which Amaurote, the chief city of Utopia, was situated. Anyder, like the Thames, is a tidal river:

> When the sea floweth in, for the length of thirtie miles it filleth all the Anyder with salte water, and driveth back the freshe water of the ryver : . . . They have also another river which indede is not verie great. But it runneth gently and pleasauntly. For it riseth even oute of the same hill that the citie standeth upon, and runneth down a slope into the middes of the citie into Anyder. And because it riseth a little withoute the citie, the Amauro-tians have inclosed the heade springe of it, with stronge fences and bul-warkes, and so have joyned it to the citie. This is done to the intente that the water should not be stopped nor turned away, or poysoned, if their enemies should chaunce to come upon them. From thence the water is derived and conveied downe in cannels of bricke divers ways into the lower partes of the citie. Where that cannot be done, by reason that the place wyll not suffer it, there they gather the raine water in great cisternes, whiche doeth them as good service.

These are the words of an enlightened public health administrator, and throughout his career More, despite the claims of high office, continued with his work for the improvement of England's water-supplies. In 1526 he was again appointed Commissioner of Sewers by the coast of Thames, from East Greenwich to Gravesend,[4] and, as Lord Chancellor, he probably initiated the important Act of Parliament (23rd Hen. VIII, C.5) which appointed Commissioners of Sewers in all parts of the Kingdom. The water of England was notoriously unsafe. Henry VII in a letter to Ferdinand and Isabella said it was undrinkable, and therefore the young princess, Katharine of Aragon, betrothed to Prince Arthur, should be accustomed to drink wine. "Water is not wholesome, sole by it selfe, for an Englysshe man," wrote Andrew Boorde. Thomas More endeavoured to improve the purity as well as the number of water-supplies.

Utopia

On 3rd May, 1515, the Court of Aldermen permitted More to occupy his office of Under Sheriff by deputy, whilst he went "on the kinges ambasset into Flaunders." His embassy was to the Archduke Charles, afterwards Charles V, and its purpose was to settle a dispute between London merchants and foreign merchants resident in London. He visited Bruges, Brussels, and Antwerp. In the latter city he became the friend of Peter Giles, to whom he dedicated *Utopia.* While abroad More wrote the second part of this work and added the introduction or first part on his return to England. The book was published in December, 1516, by Tierry Martin of Louvain. *Utopia* is "No-

Where," the imaginary Commonwealth of the Renaissance idealists. It contains many allusions to the state of England at the time, the harm done to agricultural labourers by the enclosure of arable land and pastures for sheep, the unreasonable savagery of the penal code, and advocates many desirable social reforms. But it is also a remarkable treatise on public health administration, so far-seeing indeed that its teaching has been insufficiently appreciated by even the most recent of More's biographers. Inspired by his knowledge of the principles of Greek medicine and influenced by the need for sanitary reform, which he had observed in the City of London, More applied his learning and experience to a description of public health provision in Utopia, for its citizens esteemed health as "the greatest of all pleasures."

He envisaged a well-built city with gardens and open spaces, a public water supply, drainage and cleansed streets, with public abattoirs outside. Public hospitals were provided for the treatment of rich and poor and isolation hospitals for cases of infectious disease. Other amenities included communal meals, the safe guarding of maternity with municipal nurses for infant welfare, nursery schools (or crèches) for children under five, free universal education for all children with continuation, adolescent and adult schools; religious instruction, industrial welfare, enlightened marriage laws and eugenic mating and obedience to the laws of health, including fresh air and sunlight and active occupation without undue fatigue. It is a comprehensive programme of social medicine which, written in the sixteenth century, expresses many of the aspirations of to-day.

A marvellous book written by a marvellous man. John Burns, a collector of More's writings, told me that he dated his interest in social reform and his political career from the accidental purchase of a copy of *Utopia* at a second-hand bookstall. And under John Burns, when President of the Local Government Board, began the social health services. Thus the written words of More exert their humane influence in modern times.

Interest in Care for the Sick and Infirm

Before turning to further aspects of More's work in public health administration, I would like to show you that his interest in medicine and the prevention of disease were joined with a kind and charitable heart, which was touched by all forms of human suffering. This is revealed in the words of Thomas Stapleton, whose *Life of More* appeared in 1588:

> More was used, whenever in his house or in the village he lived in there was a woman in labour, to begin praying, and so continue until news was brought him that the delivery had come happily to pass.
>
> The charity of More was without bounds, as is proved by the frequent and abundant alms he poured without distinction among all unfortunate persons. He used himself to go through the back lanes and inquire into the state of poor families; and he would relieve their distress, not by scattering a few small coins, as is the general custom, but when he ascertained a real need, by two, three or four gold pieces.

When his official position and duties prevented this personal attention, he would send some of his family to dispense his alms, especially to the sick and aged. This office, as already mentioned, was frequently performed by Margaret Gigs. "He very often invited to his table his poorer neighbours, receiving them . . . familiarly and joyously; he rarely invited the rich and scarcely ever the nobility. Not a week passed without his taking some poor sufferer into his house and having him tended. In his parish of Chelsea he hired a house, to which he gathered many infirm, poor and old people, and maintained them at his own expense. When More was away, his eldest daughter, Margaret . . . had the care of this house.

He even received into his household and supported a poor widow named Paula, who had spent all her money on a lawsuit.

The relief of the destitute and care of the sick were largely in the hands of the religious houses, and it was not until after the Dissolution of the Monasteries that the poor became a State problem, necessitating Poor Law legislation. More, in his wisdom and humanity, would have devised a sound system of poor law relief. The Poor Law legislation of Henry VIII and Edward VI put the onus of relief on the charity of local districts, and the problems of unemployment and destitution were not handled effectively until the celebrated Poor Law Act of Elizabeth in 1601.

In More's *Dialogue of Comfort against Tribulation* he speaks of the duty of providing not only for children, but for servants and other dependants in sickness or in old age, as he himself had already done as far as he was able: "Meseemeth also that if they fall sick in our service, so that they cannot do the service that we retain them for, yet may we not in any wise turn them out of doors and cast them up comfortless, while they be not able to labour and help themself. For this were a thing against all humanity."

More as a Health Administrator

There was much epidemic disease in Tudor times. Outbreaks of typhus fever appeared in Europe and began to be frequent in the towns and overcrowded gaols of this country. Typhoid, dysentery and malaria were endemic. Sir Thomas himself suffered from a tertian fever. Creighton notes an epidemic of influenza in 1510. The deadliest epidemics were plague and the "sweating sickness."

Plague had remained endemic in England since 1349, the terrible year of the "Black Death," which destroyed 2,000,000 people, half the existing population. At the beginning of the sixteenth century there was a general recrudescence of plague. After nearly depopulating China, it spread over Germany, Holland, Italy, Spain and Britain in the first decade of the century. In 1500 the plague was so severe that Henry VII retired to Calais. From 1511 to 1521 there is not a single year without some reference to the prevalence of plague in the letters of Erasmus and elsewhere.

The sweating sickness was one of those mysterious maladies, like influenza and *encephalitis lethargica* in our own time, which suddenly appear, wreak havoc and destruction for a time and then as suddenly disappear. The disease was first noted in August, 1485, and was also brought to England in the army of Henry VII, which landed at Milford Haven. (See Thomas Forrestier, M.D., British Museum, Addit. MS., No. 27,582, and Creighton's *History of Epidemics in Britain*, Vol. I, p. 237). It spread to London, where it caused great mortality. In 1502 it seems to have been prevalent in the West Country, and Prince Arthur probably succumbed to it at Ludlow, when Katherine of Aragon was attacked but recovered. In 1507 a milder outbreak occurred. There were severe epidemics in 1517, 1528 and 1551. The last epidemic was described by Dr. Caius. The disease has been identified by Dr. Creighton, the epidemiologist, and Dr. Michael Foster, with "military fever" (*schweissfriesel, suette militaire,* or "the Picardy Sweat") a malady repeatedly observed in France, Italy and South Germany, but not in the United Kingdom. It was characterized by intense sweating and an eruption of vesicles, lasted longer than sweating sickness, occurred in limited epidemics and was usually not fatal. The first epidemic was seen in 1717 and it continued to 1906 and even later. Dr. Michael Foster and Sir Henry Tidy saw cases of the disease in France during the war of 1914–18.[5]

In the summer of 1517, London was visited by a virulent outbreak of the disease, which spread by the following year all over the country and especially in the crowded towns. Colet succumbed to the infection, Wolsey had more than one attack and Andreas Ammonius, Henry VIII's Latin Secretary, died of it. More wrote to Erasmus on 19th August:

> We are in the greatest sorrow and danger. Multitudes are dying all round us; almost everyone in Oxford, Cambridge and London has been ill lately, and we have lost many of our best and most honoured friends; among them—I grieve at the grief I shall cause you in relating it—our dear Andrew Ammonius, in whose death both letters and all good men suffer a great loss. He thought himself well fortified against the contagion by moderation in diet. He attributed it to this that, whereas he met hardly anyone whose whole family had not been attacked, the evil had touched none of his household. He was boasting of this to me and many others not many hours before his death, for in this sweating sickness no one dies except on the first day of attack. I myself and my wife and children are as yet untouched and the rest of my household have recovered. I assure you there is less danger on the battlefield than in the city. Now, as I hear, the plague has begun to rage in Calais just when we are being forced to land there on our embassy, as if it was not enough to have lived in the midst of contagion, but we must follow it also. But what would you have? We must bear our lot. I have prepared myself for any event. Farewell in haste.

More noted the danger of relapse in sweating sickness. "Considering there is, as physicians say, and as we also find, double the peril in the relapse that was in the first sickness." (*The Pitiful Life of King Edward the Fifth.* Camelot edition, p. 230.)

Plague was also prevalent, and the diseases terrified King Henry, who fled from London to Windsor and thence to Abingdon. In April, 1518, both plague and sweating sickness were rife in Oxford. The King appointed More, who had returned from the embassy to Calais, to supervise the health measures to be taken in this emergency. On the 28th April Master More certified from Oxford to the King at Woodstock that three children were dead of the sickness, but none others; he had accordingly charged the Mayor and commissary in the King's name "that the inhabitants of those houses that be and shall be infected, shall keep in, put out wispes (of hay) and bear white rods, according as your Grace devised for Londoners." They were also forbidden to keep animals in their houses, and officers were required to keep the streets of the town cleansed and burn refuse.

Here we see notification and segregation used for the prevention of epidemic disease, and Thomas More controlled it by these means. The King's Council approved these measures, and on June, 1518, Pace wrote from the Court at Woodstock to Wolsey that "all are free from sickness here, but many die of it within four or five miles, as Mr. Controller is informed."

On the 18th July, More wrote: "We have daily advertisements here, other of some sweating or the great sickness from places very near unto us; and as for surfeits and drunkenness we have enough at home."

In the severe outbreak of 1528, More's daughter, Margaret, as already related, nearly succumbed to the sweating sickness. Anne Boleyn was attacked by it and her royal lover hastily left her for several weeks.

More's excellent sanitary regulations, no doubt, helped to prevent more widespread infection and to diminish the virulence of these pestilences. The first plague order was issued in the thirty-fifth year of Henry VIII in 1543, and, as Creighton remarked, contains the germs of all subsequent preventive practice. More had then been dead for eight years, but the order codified his previous regulations and instructions. Instead of wisps of hay the sign of the cross is to be set on every house which should be afflicted with the plague, and there continue for 40 days. Segregation, disinfection—chiefly by burning straw pallets, etc.—and scouring and the bearing of white rods by plague contacts are enforced, and this additional humane regulation breathes the spirit of Thomas More: "That no housekeeper should put any person diseased out of his house unless they provided housing for them in some other house."

The more one delves into State papers of the time of Henry VIII, the more one reads Sir Thomas More's books, treatises and letters and studies the account of his work in the letters of Erasmus and other contemporaries, the more one marvels at his wisdom and his outlook upon hygiene and public health.

Hospital Reform

This admiration for More is further enhanced when we examine his views on hospitals. He was a protagonist of hospital reform. In *Utopia* he set forth a hospital scheme in these words:

For in the circuite of the citie, a little without the walls, they have iiii

hospitalles, so bigge, so wyde, so ample and so large, that they may seme
iiii little townes, which were devised of that bignes partely to thintent the
sycke, be they never so many in numbre, should not lye to thronge or
strayte, and therefore uneasely and incommodiously; and partely that they
which were taken and holden with contagious diseases, suche as be wonte
by infection to crepe from one to another, myght be layde apart farre
from the company of the residue. These hospitalles be so wel appointed,
and with al thinges necessary to health so furnished, and more over so
diligent attendaunce through the continual presence of cunning phisitians
is geven, that though no man be sent thether against his will, yet notwith-
standinge there is no sicke persone in al the citie, that had not rather lye
there then at home in his owne house.

Sir Thomas More, when he wrote on theological or religious subjects, was
often prolix, but in this account of the best form of hospital, its amenities,
and advantages he is wonderfully concise. Yet all the points are there, situation,
provision for all sick persons, proper furnishing and equipment, medical
specialists in regular attendance, everything indeed that we are now endeavour-
ing to obtain for the sick in the middle of the twentieth century. Oh, great Sir
Thomas More!

Throughout the greater part of More's life, the sick were nursed in the
hospitals maintained by the religious houses. We know from a Chadwick Lecture, delivered in 1933 by Mr. Percy Flemming, that these hospitals were built
with reasonable regard to hygiene and sanitation. In London the five priories
of Austin Canons: Holy Trinity or Christ Church just within Aldgate, St.
Bartholomew's in West Smithfield, St. Mary Overies, St. Mary Spital and St.
Mary's Elsing Spital had maintained hospitals for the sick and infirm. They
were St. Mary Spital, St. Mary's Elsing Spital, St. Bartholomew's and St.
Thomas's in Southwark. St. Mary of Bethlehem (Bethlem, Bedlam) for insane
patients was outside Bishopsgate on the site now occupied by Liverpool Street
Station.

In 1529 Sir Thomas More succeeded Wolsey as Lord Chancellor. It was an
anxious time, for Henry was pressing on with his plans for divorcing Queen
Katherine and marrying Anne Boleyn, and More made no secret of his disapproval. He accepted office on the understanding that the King would grant
him liberty of conscience and not employ him in the divorce proceedings. This
promise Henry eventually broke. More's appointment was a popular one. The
Imperial Ambassador, Eustace Chapuys, wrote to the Emperor Charles V:
"The Chancellor's Seal has remained in the hands of the Duke of Norfolk till
this morning, when it was transferred to Sir Thomas More. Everyone is
delighted at this promotion, because he is an upright and learned man, and
a good servant of the Queen."

There was not only the affair of the divorce to trouble the new Chancellor,
but it was clear, as the French Ambassador wrote, that after the fall of Wolsey,
the King and nobles meant to attack and plunder the Church. This was fore-
shadowed before More became Chancellor in a scurrilous pamphlet called the
Supplication of the Beggars by one Simon Fish, a lawyer of Gray's Inn and a

friend of Tyndale's. It was sent to Anne Boleyn, who gave it to the King. It advocated and recommended the wholesale confiscation of Church property and endowments and included the abolition of the hospitals maintained by the monks for the benefit of the sick poor. Fish had the effrontery to pretend that this would be for the benefit of the poor. Henry apparently referred the pamphlet to More, who in 1529 published a counter-blast to it, entitled a *Supplication of Souls in Purgatory*. This pamphlet is written supposedly by holy souls in protest against Fish's denial of purgatory, and pleads for continued prayers on their behalf. More demonstrates the folly of abolishing the hospitals in the following words:

> Then cometh he at the last unto the device of some remedy for the poor beggars. Wherein he would in no wise have none hospitals made, because he saith that therein the profit goeth to the priests. What remedy then for the poor beggars? He deviseth and desireth nothing to be given them, nor none other alms or help requireth for them, but only that the king's highness would first take from the whole clergy all their whole living, and then set them abroad in the world to get wives, and to get their living with the labour of their hands and in the sweat of their faces ... and finally to tie them to the carts to be whipped about every market town till they fall to labour.
>
> He showeth himself that he nothing else intendeth but openly to destroy the clergy first, and after that covertly, as many as have aught above the state of beggars. What remedy findeth the proctor for them? He will allow them no hospital ... They must not be given money, nay not a groat; for the priests would get hold of that. What other thing then? Nothing in the world will serve but this ... that everything should be taken from the clergy ... Is not this a goodly mischief for a remedy? Is not this a royal feast to leave the beggars meatless and then send more beggars to feast with them.

More alludes to the benefits conferred by the hospitals in diminishing the amount of sickness among the destitute. He admits and laments he has no statistics to quote, but neither, he observes, has Fish: "If we should tell you what number there was of poor sick folk in days passed long before your time: ye were at liberty not to believe us. Howbeitt he cannot yet on the other side for his part neither, bring you forth a bederoll of their names; wherefore we must for both our parts be fain to remit you to your own time and yet not from your childhood (whereof many things men forget when they come to far greater age) but unto the dates of your good remembrance."

Here we can remark More's appreciation of the value of case records and of vital statistics, which were lacking in the case under consideration.

He considers that the number of the sick through hospitals are less than in times past, though he will not quarrel with those who have a contrary impression, "for sorry sights stick in the memory." But he cites the French pox: "And then of the french pockes thirty years ago went there about sick five against one that beggeth with them now ... As for other sickness the incidence is not greater than in times past."

Fish did not think the monastic alms were sufficient to prevent the

necessitous from being famished, and becoming sick and dying from hunger:
"We verily and truly think he shall seek far and find very few, if he find any at
all, for albeit the poor householders have these dear years made right hard
shift for corn; yet our lord be thanked men have not been so far from pity
as to suffer poor impotent persons die at their doors for hunger."

In his cupidity and want of humanity for his necessitous subjects, Henry
ignored More's wise counsel. By 1539 the total number of suppressed religious
establishments was 655 monasteries, 90 colleges, 2,374 chantries and free
chapels and 110 hospitals.

The Corporation of London foresaw the evil that would result and, in
1536, Sir Richard Gresham, the Lord Mayor, asked that the three remaining
hospitals, St. Mary Spital, St. Bartholomew's and St. Thomas's and, also, the
Abbey of Tower Hill, might be placed with their revenues at the disposal of
the Mayor and Aldermen so that "all impotent persons not able to labour
might be relieved." Nothing was done until 1544, when Henry refounded St.
Bartholomew's Hospital, though he afterwards resumed possession of it.
Henry's physicians said the only way of getting the King to listen to reason
was to have him fall ill. This was exemplified on his death-bed in 1547, when
he made the comprehensive agreement with the citizens, which led to his
posthumous, if unmerited, distinction as first founder of the "Royal
Hospitals." At last the citizens obtained their hospitals.

The blow struck at the treatment of the sick in the provinces by the suppression of the hospitals was more deadly. A few of the old hospitals were
refounded, but 23 of the principal English counties had no hospital until the
eighteenth century. It is a deplorable story, for Henry VIII wilfully sinned
against the light when he paid no attention to More's plea for retention of
the hospitals.

The Martyrdom

Sir Thomas More was Lord Chancellor of England for only two years and
seven months. As Miss Routh observes: "Neither time nor occasion was his to
carry out the great reforms; from the first he realized how precarious was his
position; how warily he must balance himself to maintain it."

He cleared off the arrears of work left by Wolsey, which may have included
certain measures of sanitary reform and he preserved Christ Church for Oxford.
Disagreeing with Henry's policy of disestablishing the papacy in England and
making himself supreme head of the Church, More resigned his office on 16th
May, 1532, and retired to Chelsea to engage in religious controversy. This
further annoyed Henry, as did also More's refusal to attend his marriage with
Anne Boleyn. In 1534 Sir Thomas More was committed to the Tower for
refusing to take any oath that should impugn the Pope's authority or assume
the justice of the divorce. Cranmer advised he should be allowed to take a
modified oath of fealty, but Cromwell and Anne Boleyn made the King
adamant. More aged during his 15 months' imprisonment; he wrote in the
Tower his "Dialogue of Comfort against Tribulation" which, as we have

seen, contains many medical similes, and treatises on Christ's passion.

On 1st July, 1535, he was indicted for high treason at Westminster Hall, found guilty on the perjured evidence of Rich, the Solicitor-General, and executed on Tower Hill on 6th July.

In the shadow of death, More did not lose his sense of humour. "I pray thee see me safely up," he said to the lieutenant at the scaffold, "and for my coming down let me shift for myself." He put aside his beard from the block, saying that "it had never committed treason."

More's execution shocked Christendom. Charles V declared then or previously that he would have preferred to lose his best city than have lost such a worthy counsellor. Sir Thomas was beatified on 9th December, 1886, by Pope Leo XIII.

More's Personal Appearance

We have two accounts of More's appearance. The first, written by Erasmus[6] in 1519:

> To begin, then, with what is least known to you, in stature he is not tall, though not remarkably short. His limbs are formed with such perfect symmetry as to leave nothing to be desired. His complexion is white, his face fair rather than pale, and though by no means ruddy, a faint flush of pink appears beneath the whiteness of his skin. His hair is dark brown or brownish black. The eyes are greyish blue, with some spots, a kind which betokens singular talent, and among the English is considered attractive ... His countenance is in harmony with his character, being always expressive of an amiable joyousness, and even an incipient laughter and, to speak candidly, it is better framed for gladness than for gravity and dignity, though without any approach to folly or buffoonery. The right shoulder is a little higher than the left, especially when he walks. This is not a defect of birth, but the result of habit, such as we often contract. In the rest of his person there is nothing to offend. His hands are the least refined part of his body.

The second account I take from Lord Campbell.[7] It describes More's appearance on his last days: "On the morning of the trial, More was led on foot in a coarse, woollen gown through the most frequented streets from the Tower to Westminster Hall. The colour of his hair, which had become gray since he last appeared in public; his face, which, though still cheerful, was pale and emaciated; his bent posture and his feeble steps, which he was obliged to support with his staff, show the rigour of his confinement and excited the sympathy of the people instead of impressing them, as was intended, with dread of the royal authority."

As the curtain falls on the tragic closing scene on Tower Hill, when we consider the splendour of Sir Thomas More's talents, the greatness of his acquirements and the innocence of his life, with Lord Campbell, "we must still regard his murder as the blackest crime ever perpetrated in England under the form of law."

Comparison Between More and Chadwick

There are certain remarkable points of comparison in the careers of Sir Thomas More and Sir Edwin Chadwick as public health reformers. They both derived their interest in social reform from philosophers. More from Linacre and Chadwick from Jeremy Bentham. Both men had a broad outlook on the problems of health and disease. "Chadwick," says Sir Benjamin Ward Richardson, "treated all professions with equal freedom, when any subject connected with his own pursuits were under discussion; so that they who listened often wondered, when they were not intimate with him, what his own profession might be."

Sir Thomas More, as we have seen from *Utopia,* devised a most complete system of health and social reform, which was greatly in advance of his time and in some respects in advance of our own time. His fame as public health reformer, therefore, rests more on planning and prophesy than on achievement. He was, however, a great administrator, and reference has been made to his practical measures as Commissioner of Sewers in regard to water supplies and to his distinction in initiating the control of epidemic disease and plague. Had England then been ruled by an enlightened monarch, interested in the welfare of his subjects, public health reform would have been inaugurated on wise lines in the sixteenth century, for Sir Thomas had the root of the matter in him. Henry VIII was well educated, something of a scholar, and knew he had a loyal servant and talented minister in Sir Thomas. Tyranny, greed and opportunism made the King shut his ears to wise counsel. Henry's disregard of More's advice to retain the hospitals is a glaring instance of his callous indifference to suffering. Previously, in order to build a royal manor and to make a park for hunting, he had seized a leper hospital and evicted the inmates. Such was the origin of St. James's Palace and Park.

Chadwick was more fortunate than More in that he succeeded in bringing about enduring measures of sanitary and social reform. His zeal in this matter outran his discretion, and for the latter years of his long life he had to stand aside and to see others reap the rewards of his labours. In retirement he wrote assiduously, as did More; pamphlets, presidential and other addresses, reviews and critiques came from his pen at frequent intervals. But unlike More he had an unattractive prose style and was no orator.

Edwin Chadwick learned much medicine and public health from Dr. Southwood Smith and Dr. Arnott. He was, however, too optimistic in anticipating that environmental hygiene would soon bring about a golden age in which doctors, "those necessary evils," were not very likely to last and would neither be able to live—nor die! Sir Thomas More had a higher opinion of the work and value of doctors in preventive medicine.

Both these public health reformers were advocates of liberty and the right of free speech. It was Sir Thomas, when Speaker of the House of Commons, who petitioned the King, in 1523, for freedom of speech by Members of Parliament and secured a large measure of success for this request. Chadwick was regarded as an autocrat, but he said he advocated centralization for the protection of liberty. He held that "Liberty is a right with a corresponding obligation to respect it. Liberty consists of the power of doing anything which does not hurt another." Edwin Chadwick in many ways rekindled the torch of public health reform, which had fallen from the lifeless hands of Thomas More and lay smouldering for some three centuries.

Sir Thomas More's activity in public health and the prevention of disease, which we have considered, was only one aspect of a full and busy life devoted to God and the King. Witness his last words: "I die the King's servant, but God's first."

This interest was sanctified by his religion and his love of humanity. I cannot end better than by quoting the words of Dr. Maynard Smith[8] concerning Sir Thomas More: "He was a man of infinite charm, a loving father and a chivalrous friend. He was an enthusiast for learning and an enthusiast for justice. He was a friend to the poor and a champion for the oppressed. He loved this world and all that was in it, but he gladly died for something of more value, for what he believed to be the cause of God and truth."

THE RECUSANT REPUTATION OF THOMAS MORE

James K. McConica, CSB

There can be few here today who will not recognize the judgement that with the beheading of More and Fisher, "all learning felt the blow and shrank." This comment of Professor Chambers, whatever its deeper merits, at least serves to illuminate a long-neglected truth: that the death of Thomas More was not simply a religious and political event, but a momentous challenge to the English scholarly community. It divided it as the doctrines of Luther never really did. It exacted from every scholar, whether he was confronted with the Oath of Supremacy or not, a decision on the rightness of the King's policies. And it left both those who followed Henry and those who turned away with a need to justify to posterity the stand that they had taken. The attitude adopted by the vast majority of those who might be termed "English loyalists" is perhaps sufficiently well-known to need no further discussion. It is with the other group of "Roman loyalists" that we are concerned here.

Almost thirty years ago the Belgian scholar, Mme Marie Delcourt, asserted in two articles which have found a fairly wide—if often unacknowledged—acceptance, that the recusant heirs of More distorted the facts of his life to meet the needs of their propaganda, and that this distortion had exercised undue influence on English scholarly opinion about More. At the same time she pointed to another "continental" tradition, stemming from the Basel edition of his works, the *Lucubrationes* of 1563, in which More was presented simply as a humanist and reformer. The main point of contention between these two traditions, she asserted, was More's relationship with Erasmus, that devious knight-errant of Reformation humanism, who at the height of Tridentine reaction was placed on the Roman Index, judged a heretic *primae classis.* Here then is a challenge worth examining, but I do not propose simply to consider Mme Delcourt's assertions. Behind these lies the more fundamental problem of the nature of the community which guarded the inheritance of Thomas More, of its learning and integrity, and of the degree to which we can rely upon its testimony about these momentous events at the very outset of the English Renaissance.

Traditionally, the study of "recusant history" begins in 1558. It is the wrong date, although it is easy to see why it is chosen. Recusant history

This paper was read to the annual meeting of the Canadian Catholic Historical Association in Quebec City, 9 June 1963. It is reprinted here, by permission of author and the publisher and with authorial revisions, from *Reports of the Canada Catholic Historical Association,* 30 (June 1964), 47–61.

actually begins with the death of the first martyrs, who were the first to refuse the Royal Supremacy. And the first phase of English recusant tradition is the work of the contemporaries of More and Fisher who went into exile under Edward, as their more celebrated successors did under Elizabeth. I propose to spend most of my time discussing this first group, who were responsible for preserving almost everything we know of More, since some grasp of their history is essential if we are to understand both More's own position and the later development of recusant tradition.

To begin with, it is extremely doubtful that any of More's family or circle of friends really understood his attitude at the time of his trial and death, as the correspondence of More himself indicates. Certainly the apparent failure of his daughter Margaret to grasp his stand is more eloquent than any other testimony. No one else so fully shared More's confidence, yet her recorded opinions are closer to her mother's views than they are to More's. She took the oath her father refused, and at a later date, she tried to hire the distinguished Protestant humanist, Roger Ascham, as tutor for her children.

At the same time, the sheer loyalty of the family to More's memory cannot be called in question. Margaret Roper gathered More's relics and letters with the same courageous obstinacy that drove Margaret Giggs to the relief of the imprisoned Carthusians. It is to this family resolve that we owe most of what we know about More. As the consequences of Henry's policies became more clear, we seem to see comprehension dawning among his descendants. Within a decade of his martyrdom, the family makes a conspicuous declaration of faith by its part in the "Plot of the Prebendaries" against Cranmer. Cranmer stood for the threat posed by the Royal Supremacy to the traditional Catholic doctrines of the church in England, and in 1544 More's son John, his surviving sons-in-law William Daunce and William Roper, along with such close associates of the Chelsea family circle as John Heywood, John Larke (the parish priest) and John Ireland, a family chaplain, were indicted for denying the Supremacy. In the same trial were Stephen Gardiner's nephew, evidently the moving spirit of the plot, and the Oxford Greek scholar, John Bekinsaw.

The appearance of John Bekinsaw deserves comment, since it draws attention to an important segment of the scholarly community which in the later years of Henry's reign showed signs of serious discontent. We can do little more here than record names, but the list represents impressive scholarly weight. There was Richard Smith, DD, first Regius Professor of Divinity at Oxford, who fled to France in 1549 and became first Chancellor of Douay. There was John Harpsfield, brother of More's biographer, like so many recusant scholars a product of Winchester and New College, and who seems to have been lecturing in Greek on the King's foundation at Oxford as early as 1541. Another was George Etherige, who succeeded Harpsfield, it appears, when the King's College was refounded as Christ Church in 1546. He was eminent in many fields of study, including mathematics, Hebrew, Greek and medicine, and after being deprived in 1550, he was restored to his chair by Mary.

Cambridge, too, supplies such names from the very Colleges where the new learning flourished most. Among these, John Seton, DD, of St. John's College, chaplain to John Fisher, was the author of a standard work on logic and perhaps holds first place in later public reputation. He was an associate at St. John's of Thomas Watson, who held similar views on religion and was described by Ascham as "one of the best scholars that ever St. John's College bred." Watson was also an intimate of Cheke, Redman and Thomas Smith, and became a conspicuous Catholic controversialist, described by Pollard as "perhaps, after Tunstall and Pole, the greatest of Queen Mary's bishops." Another St. John's man, John Christopherson, was a fellow of Trinity College by the King's foundation charter in 1546, and "one of the first revivers" of the study of Greek in the University. The college itself supported his exile under Edward VI, and in return received the dedication of his translation into Latin of Philo Judæus, done at Louvain. He too became a Marian bishop, and so did Ralph Baynes, who might be taken to round out this picture of Cambridge recusant scholars. Baynes was famous as a public opponent of Latimer, and during his exile under Edward his learning was recognized with an appointment as Reader in Hebrew in the University of Paris. Finally, the greatest of them all, of course, was John Clements, the only Englishman who could wear the mantle of Linacre, the dean and inspiration of the entire Catholic scholarly community in exile.

Further pursuit of this subject would lead us far afield, although more names could be added to this list. Enough has been said, however, to make clear a first point, that this original recusant community recruited its members from the top rank of the English intelligentsia. They were men fortified with scholarship and common loyalty to the greatest man and scholar they had known, Thomas More. Unlike the later generation of recusant scholars, which includes the names of Nicholas Sander, Thomas Stapleton, of Edmund Campion and Robert Parsons, they were all in their productive years under Henry's rule, and in the first period of Catholic exile under Edward VI they established the precedent and, to a large degree, the tradition of recusant learning and apologetic.

What was their version of the matter? The possible sources of information about this include accounts of More's death known to have issued from this group, biographies, and the great monument of their common enterprise, the Marian edition of More's *English Works*. Only the second and third of these can give us certain evidence. We are still much in the dark about the first accounts of More's martyrdom, and Professor de Vocht's complicated and highly conjectural reconstruction of the history of the *Expositio* and of its first cousin, the *Ordo Condemnationis*, seems to raise as many questions as it answers.[1] We are on safer ground with the *English Works* and the two biographies written while the great edition was in preparation, those of Roper and Nicholas Harpsfield. The materials gathered in the *Works* seem to have been collected by the entire group and preserved principally by the final editor, William Rastell. His career in England, it should be recalled, flourished—as did that of John Clements—in the later years of Henry's rule. It is not difficult to imagine the growing concern of the group for this little archive. It was the bond of their common identity and the pledge of their loyalty to More, as they moved from initial bewilderment to a growing sense of unease and finally into exile in protest against the implications of the Royal Supremacy. Under Mary they had their opportunity to publish, and they prepared an astonishingly compendious edition of those works which could most quickly be grasped by their fellow countrymen, those written in the vernacular. The edition of Latin works, aimed at the international world of learning, came later in less happy circumstances.

Rastell's Preface to Queen Mary would serve as the common preface to all recusant accounts of More. He is commended for his eloquence, great learning, moral virtue, and his "trewe doctryne of Christes catholyke fayth." Naturally, the editors were chiefly interested in More the martyr, the confuter of that very movement of heresy which by now had convulsed Europe and shattered Christendom. Did this lead them to distortion?

So far as is known, they omitted none of More's English works. In including even his occasional pieces, they provided one of his recreations, an ironic poem on the dangers of a "pedlar" meddling in theology which is remarkably in tune with the weary comment made by Erasmus concerning More's imprisonment, that he wished More had left theology to the theologians.[2] By confining the edition to English works Rastell had escaped the obligation of publishing most of More's non-apologetic and non-religious writing, scheduled for the later edition of Latin works. The English collection by itself was a natural and legitimate answer to the vernacular propaganda of the government. The *Life* of Pico della Mirandola is thus the one interesting clue to More's earlier preoccupations with humanism and reform, in a work where the image of More is predominantly one of great and militant orthodoxy based on profound piety and on humanism.

It is in the correspondence of this edition that we find first evidence of direct distortion. Almost all of the English letters of More that survive were in this collection, but there were significant omissions. John Palsgrave's letter, attributed to 1529, in which he appealed to More for assistance in the education of the Duke of Richmond against "our schavyn folk [who] wold in no wyse he schoulde be lernyd," is the first of these.[3] As it is now among the State Papers, separate from the rest of the collection, it is conceivable that it was unknown to Rastell, and no certain importance can be attached to the omission.

More certain is Rastell's intent with two letters concerning the Nun of Kent, both omitted from the *English Works*. The first of these[4] is More's letter to Elizabeth Barton herself, in which he made clear his refusal to hear anything of princes or of "the state of the realme," reminded her of the part played by a Carthusian (alleged to have prophetical powers) in the treason of the Duke of Buckingham, and of the scandal so brought on religion, and exhorted her "onelye to common and talke with eny person highe and low, of suche maner thinges as maye to the soule be profitable for you to shew and for them to know."

The second letter,[5] from the same collection[6] in which the first is found, was written to Cromwell by More. Burnet's accusation that Rastell suppressed it was almost certainly correct. Here More stated in explicit terms his distaste for "the lewde Nonne of Caunterburye" after the recent revelations about her career. He gave a characteristically judicious account of his relations with her, in which he quoted the previously-mentioned letter, explained his generally favourable impression, and congratulated Cromwell for exposing her deceit: "Wherin you have done, in my mynde, to your greate laude and prayse, a verye meritorious deed in bringinge forthe to lighte suche detestable ypocrisie, wherebye everye other wretche maye take warninge, and be ferde to sett forthe theire owne devilshe dissimuled falshed, under the maner and color of the wonderfull worke of God ..."

Two other English letters are known which were not included by Rastell. The first of these, unknown until the 18th century, is a moving appeal by Lady More to Cromwell in May of 1535 for financial aid.[7] The second, which is found in the same manuscript collection in which the others used by Rastell are gathered is her appeal a few months earlier to the King himself.[8] Like the appeal to Cromwell, this letter to the King seems now to add to the pathos of the family's situation once More had been imprisoned. If Rastell suppressed it, it must presumably have been through desire to avoid publishing the heart of her plea for her husband's pardon: "his offence ys growen not of eny malice or obstinate mynde, but of suche a longe contynued and depe rooted scrupple, as passethe his power to avoyde and put awey ..."[9]

Although in absence of direct proof that Rastell knew of these letters we can only conjecture about their omission, there is at least a strong probability that he wished to avoid any suggestion that would show disharmony of opinion within the Catholic camp. This conjecture is confirmed by editorial changes which are susceptible of proof.

More's letter of March 5th, 1534 to Henry VIII, in which he protested his innocence in the affair of the Nun, was altered to replace his phrase, "the wykked woman of Canterbery" with "Nunne of Canterbury."[10] Even more extensively altered was the letter which he wrote to Cromwell on the same day,[11] which is so invaluable for the history of his religious opinions. Once again his phrase, "wykked woman" was replaced by "the nonne." But the most striking distortion is the omission of a long and, for the Catholics, embarrassing passage on Anne Boleyn. More has been protesting his incompetence to decide the grave matter of the King's marital status, and continues: "... so am I he that among other his Gracis faithfull subgiettis, his Highnes being in possession of his mariage and this noble woman really anoynted Quene, neither murmure at it, nor dispute uppon it, nor neuer did nor will, but with owt eny other maner medlyng of the mater among his other faithfull subgiettis faithfully pray to God for his Grace and hers both, long to lyve and well and theyr noble issue to, in such wise as may be to the pleasure of God, honor and surety to theym selfe, reste, peace, welth and profit unto this noble realme."[12] Rastell's version of the same passage is as follows: "... so am I he, that among other his graces faithful subiectes, his highnes being in possession of his mariage, wil most hartely pray for the prosperous estate of his grace, longe to continue to the pleasure of God." At the time of More's writing, in March of 1534, Queen Catherine was of course still alive, and the Louvain group clearly found intolerable the apparent condoning of the second marriage, especially since Catherine of Aragon's daughter, now Queen, was patroness of the edition they were preparing.

Finally, Rastell made a rather inconclusive attempt to explain away the important letter of More to Margaret Roper from the Tower. In this letter[13] More refers unmistakeably to the pain which her attempts to dissuade him from his stand on the Supremacy had caused him. Rastell added a preface explaining that her letter was secretly intended to ingratiate her with Cromwell, "that she might the rather gett libertie to haue free resorte vnto her father . . ." Margaret Roper's letter to Alice Alington,[14] however, indicates that her opinions went deeper than Rastell's editorial comment suggested. Whether More or Margaret wrote this letter, it is clearly an eloquent testimony to the literary achievement of the whole More circle, and may have been intended to circulate in manuscript, exploring for the benefit of that group all the doubts which troubled them. Margaret Roper is represented in earnest and sorrowful disagreement with her father, and the dialogue dwells at length on the objections which could be brought against More's views. The result is an eloquent apology in which More urges the right—and duty—of each to follow the dictates of his own conscience. He also hints at recent changes in the opinions of some he had formerly counted as supporters of his views, and for the last time, he refuses to divulge the exact reasons for his stand: "But Margaret, for what causes I refuse the othe, the thinge (as I haue often tolde you) I will neuer shewe you, neither you nor no body elles, excepte the Kynges Highnes shoulde like to commaunde me."[15] Few documents even from the life of Thomas More can rival this for drama, when the confrontation of the two is presented with such skill, and More, who teasingly refers to his daughter as "mother Eve," learns from her that she had herself taken the oath which he refuses.

The fact that this letter was left intact, and the general faithfulness of the collection in Rastell's edition must be taken into account. There was no attempt to misrepresent More's general position; such partiality as can be detected seems intended to emphasize the solidarity of the group as a whole. Palsgrave's letter may have been suppressed to prevent an impression that More's support could be sought against the conservative clergy, and it is clear that they wished to exclude the evidence that he strongly disapproved of Elizabeth Barton's later activities and fully endorsed her arrest. But above all, it seems that they did not want it known that More's most intimate associates in the family circle itself could not understand his views on the Royal Supremacy.

Apart from this, Marian publication suggests that the repudiation of Erasmus and the attempt to dissociate More from him was a product primarily of the second exile and not of the period of revived Catholic power in England. Of the two biographies which complement the *English Works*, that of Roper is so brief that we can overlook the omissions from More's early career. Harpsfield's work is more important, and although in his own account of More's education and marriage he makes no direct mention of More's literary work or of his relationship with Erasmus, he adds to Roper principally from the correspondence of the two men. After an outline of More's career the friendship is introduced, if only briefly, in connection with More's writings. The epigrams and the Brixius affair are also mentioned, because More is "herein slaundered" by some Protestants, and the *Utopia* is said to bear "the pricke and price of all his other latine bookes of wittie invention." It is something, but it is not a great deal, although Harpsfield does say plainly, when speaking of More's classical scholarship, that "the saide Erasmus of all men in the world [most] delighted in the companye of Sir Thomas More, whose helpe and frendshipp he muche used when he had any affaires with king Henrye the eight."[16]

The best evidence that Harpsfield was not personally anti-Erasmian sheds light on the recusant tradition itself. His *Historia Ecclesiastica Anglicana*, written in the 1570's but not published until about fifty years later at Douay, was purged, apparently at publication, of an extended passage dealing with the friendship of Warham and Erasmus.[17] In the course of a most complimentary account of Erasmus and his many friends and patrons in England, Harpsfield had mentioned by name, among others: Reginald Pole, Cuthbert Tunstall, John Fisher, William Mountjoy, and Thomas More himself, all men who for various reasons were heroes of the recusant tradition. The source of Harpsfield's account was evidently Warham's *Register* combined with published correspondence of Erasmus, and although his assertions were widely known to be true, they seemingly proved to be too much for the sensibilities of the Douay editors.

The most troublesome matter in Harpsfield's account[18] is his claim that More counselled Erasmus to retract some of his early radical opinions, and to this we shall return shortly, since it becomes a firm conviction of the recusant tradition about More. In general Harpsfield's account of More the reformer, if perfunctory, is at least sufficiently honest not to detract too seriously from the high standard of the rest of his work. It is a distortion, but it is a distortion which reflects the shift in emphasis experienced by More himself under the impact of the reformation controversies. Harpsfield says of his hero: "He was the first of any whatsoever laye man in Inglande that dyed a martyr for the defence and preservation of the unitie of the Catholike Churche. And that is his speciall peerelesse prerogative."[19] It could not be better put. What is really striking about the first recusant testimony emerging under Mary is not its evident bias, but its substantial integrity. Harpsfield is even candid about the secret divisions in the camp: he promises his treatise on the divorce to explain More's stand more fully, "because the Protestantes thinke it a great folye for him that he stoode in the matter ... and many of the Catholikes doubt, for lacke of knowledge of the whole matter, and being somewhat abused with englishe bookes made for the defence of the newe mariage ..."[20] Harpsfield's temperate voice is that of More's own generation. Later recusants would be more strident.

To the second period of exile under Elizabeth we must now turn. The core of testimony produced by these writers is to be found in the Louvain edition of More's Latin works, the *Opera Omnia*, the biographies of "Ro: Ba:" and of Stapleton, and less centrally, in the writings of such Elizabethan controversialists as Nicholas Sander, Parsons and Campion.

The *Latina Opera* of More, first published in Louvain in 1565, bridges the two eras of recusant activity. The collection seems to come from the same common archive which supplies the *English Works*. William Rastell died, once more in exile, while the work was at the printers, and Professor Reed suggested[21] that the collection, especially the first printing of the Latin Richard III and pieces written by More in the Tower, was substantially his work also. At any rate, it came two years after a similar production, a collection of More's Latin works entitled simply *Lucubrationes,* which emerged from the press of Episcopius at Basel. The Louvain *Opera* claimed to represent all the Latin works known to its editors.[22] The *Lucubrationes* claimed to purge such works as it included from many errors in previous printings. The two books make a striking contrast.

Both editions printed the *Utopia* (with related correspondence), More's *Epigrams,* and the translations from Lucian. The *Opera Omnia* included beside these the Latin text of the Richard III, More's reply to Luther under the name of Rossaeus; other controversial work against Luther; the *Expositio Passionis Domini,* and the two accompanying Latin works written in prison—the "Quod pro fide mors fugienda non est" and the "Precatio ex Psalmis Collecta"—like the Richard III both appearing for the first time. The *Lucubrationes* contained none of this last material, but included sixteen important letters, mostly of More and Erasmus.

The purpose of the *Lucubrationes* is obvious: it is to present the Erasmian, humanistic More. Everything it prints is printed accurately, with standards befitting Erasmus' publishers. This is most immediately apparent in comparing the *Epigrammata* here with the version in the *Latina Opera* from Louvain. Apart from questions of editorial bias, the Basel version is simply more accurate and sophisticated. Combined with the *Utopia* and with the Lucian translations, the Epigrams of More fully proclaim his early humanistic, reforming temper, and this is all of More that the reader of the *Lucubrationes* would have in the way of major pieces. To supplement them and drive home the point there are the sixteen letters tracing the relations between More and Erasmus. They make amply clear their close agreement on matters of religious and political reform, their shared love for salutary satire of contemporary decadence, More's hearty approval of the now-deplored New Testament, and their love of the Fathers. Above all, the collection includes the last two letters of More to Erasmus which challenge the recusant version of their relationship in the years after Luther. Before dealing with this important problem we should give a general account of the Louvain *Opera*.

Here the hand of the censor can be discovered at work as it was in the *English Works*. The text of the *Utopia* was purged of a famous and very characteristic anecdote concerning an ignorant friar at the table of Cardinal Morton. The epigrams were taken from the first and unrevised edition of

1518, and were also censored slightly. Although the recent editors of the epigrams[23] concluded that the sponsors of the Louvain *Opera* were unaware of the 1520 edition, their purging cannot be explained simply on that supposition. From the 1518 text four "sexually indelicate" epigrams were omitted, as were three poems praising Erasmus' edition of the New Testament. However, it was by no means bowdlerized. The Louvain printing included the six complimentary poems addressed by More to Henry VIII at the time of his coronation, and retained some fairly trenchant material attacking superstitious religious practice and ignorant, scandalous clergy. Similarly, More's prefatory letter to the translations from Lucian, printed intact by both the Louvain and Basel editions, is a prime source for his approach to religious reform through sound scholarship and Lucianic satire.

The Louvain *Opera*, then, if slightly pruned, is hardly the propaganda vehicle it has been represented to be.[24] The recusants, like the Basel editors, made their most telling points by discreet silence. For the former, it was silence about More's Erasmianism; for the latter, silence about his deep piety and vigorous defence of Catholic orthodoxy. One particular charge made against the Louvain *Opera* by Mme. Delcourt must receive our attention. Mme. Delcourt asserted that the editors separated More and Erasmus by suppressing evidence of their early common activity, representing the period to 1520 only by the *Utopia,* the *Epigrammata,* and the translations of Lucian. It is difficult to see what else could have been included, apart from correspondence. Moreover, apart from the rather minor deletions we have already noticed, these classic utterances of More's evangelical and reforming humanism were published intact. Mme. Delcourt however wished to hold the editors of the *Opera Omnia* to the letter of their word. She therefore insisted that they should have included More's Latin correspondence. She also asserted that in the Latin epitaph composed by More for himself, which the editors used to open the volume, she had evidence that they had deliberately suppressed important material proving that More's support of Erasmus continued to their final years.

This accusation is worth examination, since it involves a matter we have touched on already: the recusant tradition that More reproved Erasmus for his earlier extravagances, a charge which first appears in Harpsfield, and was first published by Stapleton in the *Tres Thomae,* where Stapleton additionally implies that Erasmus destroyed the letter in question.

The case presented by Mme. Delcourt is as follows. The Epitaph, she claimed, was taken from a letter by More to Erasmus written in 1532, in which More went out of his way to praise Erasmus' astonishing energy in the cause of a reformed and revitalized Christianity and said that he should disregard the criticism of the ignorant. If Erasmus had foreseen the troubles of the age, More asserts, he would no doubt have said the same things with more moderation. However, anyone objecting to his vigorous spirit will also find it difficult to justify the holiest doctors of the early Church, who themselves, like the Apostles and even Our Saviour, have been misinterpreted in the light of present difficulties.

Mme. Delcourt comments: "The editor, careful to efface everything which could recall the detested name [of Erasmus], printed the epitaph but not the letter, which was the more embarrassing to him in that it contained unreserved praise of Erasmus' works, and was written in 1532."[25] It was, therefore, "une véritable fraude par omission." In her own phrase, "Que disent les textes?"

In the first place, the curious assumption that the editors of the Louvain *Opera* could have had no other conceivable access to the text of the famous Epitaph in Chelsea church deserves a passing comment. It is beyond belief that no member of the family in exile had private record of it. More important is the fact that the epitaph by itself forms an eminently suitable introduction to the edition, which the letter as a whole would not have done.

Mme. Delcourt, however, was apparently misled by the Leiden edition of Erasmus' works, the standard Clericus edition of 1703-6, in which the epitaph is indeed printed—but incorrectly—after the letter mentioned.[26] This letter of 1532 (later numbered 2659 in volume X of the Allen edition) contains nothing in the text referring to the Epitaph or to More's intention to send it. However the Epitaph is plainly explained in a letter belonging to the following year, 1533 (a letter numbered by Allen 2831). This is where Allen placed the Epitaph, following the indications of the text and the 16th century editions of More's letters. In this later letter of June, 1533, More discusses the Epitaph, but says nothing to Erasmus about his reform work or reputation. It is worth noticing, however, that in the Froben *Lucubrationes* which attracted Mme. Delcourt's admiration for its editorial accuracy, this matter also was handled correctly. Of this particular charge of editorial connivance, then, the Louvain editors can be cleared.

The more important problem remains. What were the relations of More and Erasmus in the years after 1520? The letter discussed by Mme. Delcourt is indeed a highly significant document, and suggests strongly that after the vexed and preoccupied years of More's battle against heresy and of his Chancellorship, he went out of his way to write his old friend a virtual testimonial to assist him in the severe attacks which were rained upon him from the conservative Catholic camp, as well as from the Protestant party. The ostensible occasion for writing it had been to reassure Erasmus about the circumstances surrounding More's resignation of the office of Chancellor. In the later letter of 1533, More observes that there are fresh rumours that he had been forced to resign. Alluding to a letter from Erasmus which has since been lost, More tells him[27] that Erasmus should not hesitate to publish More's earlier letter[28] with its correct account of the affair. At the same time, of course, Erasmus would be printing More's careful and generous commendation of Erasmus' whole achievement on behalf of scholarship and reform. The long inscription More wrote for his tomb, concluded by his Epitaph, is mentioned in connection with the same matter of the Chancellorship, since he explains that he wrote the Epitaph at this time to make a permanent and public statement of the true reasons for his having surrendered his high office.[29]

These two letters, the last we have from More to Erasmus, are the more interesting coming after the perfunctory exchanges between them after 1520.

What is the reason for the abrupt change? No doubt in part it was simply
More's sudden release from the many worries which had consumed so much
of his time and energy in those years; he was disposed to resume a valued link
which suffered from neglect. It is not easy to avoid the feeling that the sparse
correspondence of that period may also reveal a real estrangement between
the two men who were reacting so differently to the challenge of the times.
But probably the most important explanation is that noticed by Professor de
Vocht in the *Acta Thomae Mori:* in a time of dangerous controversy, when
every letter was prey to pirated publication, More and Erasmus and others in
their circle were exchanging the important news verbally by those messengers
whose reliability and responsibilities for verbal communication they so carefully note to one another.

All of this tends to reinforce the suggestion that More's sudden return to
the easy and fulsome communication of the earlier and happier days was
intended to provide Erasmus with a public vindication from a most distinguished friend who was also known throughout Europe as a champion of
Catholic orthodoxy.

What then, of the recusant tradition, common to Harpsfield and Stapleton,
that More reproved Erasmus for his early indiscretions? Some additional light
is shed by More's famous remarks about his friend Erasmus written in 1532
(in the same year of the letter we have been considering) in *The Confutacion
of Tyndales Aunswere.* More replies here to Tyndale's charge of partiality
towards Erasmus "his derlyng," in that More had attacked Tyndale for substituting "congregation" for "church" in his translation of the New Testament,
while he had been content to let Erasmus change *ecclesia* to *congregatio.*
More's reply is worth considering in some detail. "I haue not contended wyth
Erasmus my derlynge, bycause I found no suche malycyous entent wyth
Erasmus my derlynge, as I fynde with Tyndale. For had I fownde wyth
Erasmus my derlynge the shrewde entent and purpose that I fynde in Tyndale:
Erasmus my derlynge sholde be no more my derlynge. But I fynde in Erasmus
my derlynge that he detesteth and abhorreth the errours and heresyes that
Tyndale playnely techeth and abydeth by and therfore Erasmus my derlynge
shall be my dere derlyng styll."[30]

More then goes on to elaborate, touching on his own Erasmian writings,
but especially considering the *Praise of Folly,* which he explains was to
reprove faults and follies of people of every state, lay and spiritual. He denies
that he, personally, ever intended to hold saints' images and relics as such
"out of reverence." The *Praise of Folly,* and like writings by implication,
from the pens of both More and Erasmus, jest only at abuses of these practices. There follows then a very significant remark: More regrets that the
growth of heresy has been such, "that men can not almost now speke of such
thynges in so mych as a play, but that such euyll herers wax a grete dele the
worse . . ."[31] And he concludes that he would himself burn his *Utopia,* or such
like works, if there were any prospect of these now being translated into
English, "rather then folke sholde (though thorow theyr owne faulte) take
any harme of them, seyng that I se them lykely in these dayes so to do . . ."[32]

The general spirit of this passage was entirely in harmony with Epistle 2659 in which he endorsed all of Erasmus' work, with a caution about prudence in altered conditions. But More's reply to Tyndale added valuable information about his attitude to his own work, and elaborated his views about the changes which the appearance of Protestant heresy had wrought in the prevailing mood of Europe.

Now there was perhaps nothing here or in his letter to Erasmus which is strictly incompatible with the recusant tradition. In that same crucial letter of 1532 he referred to Erasmus' open admission that he had handled some points with too little restraint, and indicated that Erasmus should defer to the sensibilities of critics who are sincere and learned, but who are scandalized by his freedom.

On the positive side, however, there is no evidence for the tradition except the general integrity of Harpsfield and Stapleton, themselves. Their presumptive common source was John Harris, More's secretary, who might be expected to have known if such a letter had once existed. It was Stapleton, the last voice of the More circle, who gave the most detail.[33] He said that More urged Erasmus to follow the example of Saint Augustine in his *Retractationes,* and correct and explain his earlier views. When one thinks of the scale of effort required, it is not surprising that Erasmus ignored such advice, if it were ever given. Stapleton then went on to say that Erasmus, who was as remote from the humility of Saint Augustine as he was from his doctrine, did not wish to do so, and would not permit the letter to survive.[34]

For the present at least, the evidence ends here. Stapleton's account of More was in general an impressive achievement, and his candour and lack of bitterness suggest a temperament above partisan bias. However, he was not above suppressing unpleasant truth. In his account of More's trial, for example, he omitted More's admission that he had never placed the authority of the Pope above that of a General Council.[35] Similarly, Stapleton's handling of More's reply to Tyndale concerning the episode of "Erasmus his derlyng" (which begins the above account of the estrangement of the two men) does not inspire confidence. Stapleton simplified to the point of serious distortion, saying that where More could not excuse the fact of Erasmus' translation, he excused it because of its intent.[36]

The truth is that by the time Stapleton was writing, the atmosphere was much more dogmatic. Stapleton was remarkably moderate beside the young men who were the shock troops of Counter-Reformation training. Toughened by the rigours of Elizabethan persecution, and armed by Trent with dogmatic certainties of which More and his contemporaries had no inkling, they rode roughshod through the tentative opinions and honest confusions of an earlier generation, confident that More's final stand had made him a martyr of Trent by anticipation. Thus, according to Nicholas Sander, More found the Nun of Kent without "any trace" of the fanaticism alleged against her.[37] Robert Parsons, S.J., berated Erasmus with a severity which made impossible any accurate appraisal of More's career before 1520: "Whersoever Erasmus did but point with his fingar, Luther rushed upon yt, where Erasmus did but

doubt, Luther affirmed. So as upon Erasmus dubitations, Luther framed
assertions and asseverations; And not only Luther and Lutherans, but all the
pestilent sect of new Arrians in our dayes, began upon certayne doubtfull
questions and interpretations of Erasmus, whether such, or such places of
scriptures used against them by the auncient Fathers, were well applyed, or
no?"[38]

Parsons here proclaimed the standard post-Tridentine attitude to Erasmus,
not heard before in England even under Mary. His colleague Edmund Campion
aired similar views in his *Narratio Divortii Henrici VIII*. And here, I believe,
we have reached the most serious deficiency in the recusant tradition about
Thomas More.

The men and women whose task it was to preserve the memory and
records of More's life were a remarkable group. They reflected the scholarship and devotion of their martyr hero, and were recruited from the most
distinguished members of England's humanist community. The most striking
quality of their achievement is the distinction of the biographies, and the
invaluable and even heroic service to later generations represented by the
English Works and the Louvain *Opera Omnia*.

Like historians in any age, they had their characteristic preoccupations.
We cannot blame them for that, but we cannot ignore it either. What interested
them was More the martyr-statesman, the great humanist who became the
most widely-respected Englishman of his day and died for the tie with Rome,
as proto-martyr of the English laity. In More the reformer they were less
interested, and as the tide of Tridentine reaction swelled, they were tempted to
ignore his early evangelical commitments almost entirely.

The charges of direct distortion which have been brought against them are
not ultimately very serious, as we have seen. They were most guilty in trying
to preserve the fiction of the retrospective unity of the group, especially where
the Nun of Kent was involved. The mild pruning of the Latin *Opera Omnia*
seems now more pathetic than culpable, and the general charge of editorial
distortion is without foundation.

Their great failing—the distinctive failing, perhaps, of all sectarian scholarship—was *suppressio veri*. We may not be too concerned at their failure to
include More's Latin correspondence in the *Opera Omnia,* although it certainly
belied the strict claim of their title: "Omnia, quae hucusque ad manus nostras
pervenerunt, Latina Opera." No one interested could fail to know of contemporary collections of humanistic correspondence—including those of Erasmus
and the *Lucubrationes* of 1563—where the Latin letters of More could be
found. The biographers, however, did a real disservice in separating More from
Erasmus. The separation is not complete, and one might disagree with Mme.
Delcourt that all More's biographers were "radically anti-Erasmian." No final
judgement can be made as yet about their claim that More urged Erasmus to
make public emendation of his earlier and more impudent writings. But it is
clear that they deliberately ignored what they must have known: that More
and Erasmus before Luther were closely united in a common enterprise of
evangelical reform based on humanism and Lucianic satire, that More never in

his life retracted this commitment, however much he may have regretted some of its unforeseen consequences, and that in the final years of his life, he issued a striking endorsement of all that Erasmus had done. The whole meaning of his reply to Tyndale on this subject is that Erasmianism did not necessarily lead to heresy, and that in itself it was a highly salutary, if tragically unsuccessful attempt to awaken the Church to urgent reform.

Protestant commentators did no better. With their simple belief that humanism led inevitably to Protestant reform, they were committed to the view that More was either inconsistent or a fanatical hypocrite or both. The Basel editors of the *Lucubrationes* stand as the only witnesses in that age for a truth about More and Erasmus as important as the Louvain assertion of More's indomitable orthodoxy, but it was a truth which was imperilled by the doctrinaire controversies of both Protestant and Catholic apologists. In both camps, men were inclined now to reinterpret the pre-Reformation reform movements to favour their own interest in those events, and to read into the debates before Luther the issues of their own day. For the recusants, it meant that More the reforming satirist was to be masked by More the champion of doctrinal purity, who gave salutary but futile warnings to his erstwhile friend, and died an isolated witness for Rome. At best it was only part of the truth, and in losing the rest, they lost much of the true greatness of More.

THOMAS MORE, GRAMMARIAN AND ORATOR

William Nelson

The humanist, Jacob Burckhardt declares, was indispensable to the Italian popes, princes, and republics for two reasons: "namely, the official correspondence of the State, and the making of speeches on public and solemn occasions."[1] So far as Italy is concerned, Burckhardt's proposition requires little proof. It is sufficient to point to the list of scholars who made up the papal secretariat, to the rich rewards heaped upon rhetoricians by the city-states. What was true in Italy became in the course of time not less true of the countries beyond the Alps. France made ambassadors of scholars like Budé and Gaguin; England employed Italian humanists to do its diplomatic business.[2] Neo-classical Latin developed into the fashionable medium of international intercourse, and the turn of an oration, the patness of an epistle, came to be accepted as the indices of a nation's culture. The rulers of Europe, therefore, gathered about them staffs of scholars who could compose speeches and diplomatic letters in the current fashion. Quite as naturally, those who desired political preferment devoted themselves to the study of grammar and rhetoric through which disciplines they hoped to achieve correctness and eloquence. Their expression having been made correct and eloquent, they might expect to be advanced in the government service as secretaries, orators, and ambassadors. Of course, patrons supported humanist scholarship for other reasons besides its value in political affairs, and not every student of grammar had his eye on a secretaryship. Nevertheless, there is abundant evidence to show that the demand for accomplished correspondents and speakers constituted an important stimulus to the study of eloquence, not only in Italy, but in France and England.

It is as a member of this new class of humanist civil servants that Thomas More will be considered in the present discussion. When modern scholars speak of More as a humanist, they usually mean that he had read widely in the classics and had been deeply impressed by them; when these scholars discuss his rise in government service, they attribute it to his legal talents and to his

Reprinted by permission of the author and the publisher from *Publications of the Modern Language Association*, 58 (1943), 337–52. A version of this essay was read before the Renaissance Group of the Modern Language Association at its meeting in Boston, December, 1940. It is here reprinted as it appeared in *PMLA*, 58 (1943), 337–352, except for the correction of some errors, omission of an outdated first paragraph, and tempering of my enthusiasm for the identification of the Thomas More who was granted the degree of Master of Grammar in 1513 with More of the *Utopia*. Added or amended notes have been set between square brackets.

qualities of character. Unquestionably, More loved the ancient writings and learned much from them; he was certainly an excellent lawyer and a man of exceptional intelligence, humor, and probity. But there is another side to More's learning and to his political success. He was a humanist, not only because he had been impressed by the classics, but also because he had acquired from them the art of expression; and he found favor at court both because of his legal ability and because he could read, write, speak, and understand the new, difficult language which Renaissance scholars had contrived in imitation of Ciceronian Latin. It may be shown, I think, first, that More was a student of grammar and rhetoric, an intimate friend of professional grammarians, and himself a teacher of the subject; and, second, that it was his training in grammar and rhetoric that opened to him the career at court which was capped by his chancellorship.

What is known of More's formal education may be summarized briefly. His contemporaries tell us that he attended St. Anthony's School in London under the tutelage of Nicholas Holt, and that after serving as page in Archbishop Morton's palace at Lambeth he was sent to Oxford, where, for something less than two years (years which must fall between 1492 and 1496), he avidly studied the humanities. From this happy Oxford existence More's father untimely ripped him and set him to the law at the London inns of court.[3] Law and London did not, however deter More from humanistic studies. In 1501 he wrote a letter to an Oxford friend, John Holt. He says nothing of law books. "You will ask me how I am getting on with my studies. Excellently; nothing could be better. I am giving up Latin, and taking to Greek. Grocyn is my teacher."[4] And an early biographer declares, "notwithstanding [his translation from Oxford to London] did he cutt off from the studie of the lawe muche time, which he employed to his former studies that he vsed in Oxforde...."[5]

In London, More wrote and lectured in a manner proper to a teacher of grammar and rhetoric. In friendly competition with the grammarian William Lily, he translated into Latin a number of epigrams from the Greek Anthology. The way in which the work was published makes it evident that the primary purpose of the exercise was, not to spread knowledge of the beauties of Greek literature, but rather to display the translators' proficiency in the classical languages. First the Greek epigram is given, and then the rival versions of More and Lily, between which the reader is invited to judge.[6] More and Erasmus competed in similar fashion in translations from Lucian. They did not, as in the previous case, translate the same pieces, but they both wrote original declamatory responses in Latin to Lucian's *Tyrannicide,* and these parallel declamations were included in the book.[7] Here, the intent to display oratorical virtuosity is transparently clear, for the subject matter of the *Tyrannicide* is completely devoid of either practical or philosophical interest.[8] In a prefatory letter, Erasmus explains why he undertook the writing of a reply to Lucian. More strongly urged the task, he says:

> And I have done this so much the more willingly because I greatly desire
> this kind of exercise, to which no other is equally profitable, some day to

be resumed in our schools. For I think that nothing else [but the lack of such exercises] is responsible for the fact that in these times, when they are so many who study the most eloquent writers, there are nevertheless so few who do not appear altogether incapable of speech whenever the situation demands an orator. For if we were driven from childhood to follow diligently the authority of Cicero and Fabius, and the ancient example in declamations of this sort, there would not be, I think, such poverty of speech, such deplorable lack of eloquence, such shameful stammering, even among those who publicly profess oratorical learning.[9]

That More was activated by the same motive is made evident by the fact that he set his children and the pupils of his "academy" to work on just such exercises, both in Latin and in English. In his early writings, therefore, More appears a typical humanist grammarian, devoted to the study and the teaching of eloquence.

It is clear, too, that despite the assertion in his letter to Holt, More did not altogether "give up Latin and take to Greek" when he left Oxford. It must have been soon after this letter was written that he began to deliver a course of lectures to a London audience on the historical and philosophical aspects of St. Augustine's *City of God*.[10] Had he been teaching at one of the universities instead of at Grocyn's London church, he would have lectured as a member of the faculty of grammar. Classical history fell in neatly with the grammatical discipline, for it provided apposite instances with which to ornament letters and orations. Indeed, as a prerequisite for the graduate degree in grammar, the University of Oxford required several candidates to deliver free lectures on the works of the historian Sallust.[11]

A list of More's early friends corroborates the impression that however assiduously he followed the law his heart remained with the grammarians. In fact, it is difficult to find one among his friends who did not either teach grammar or foster its teaching. Grocyn gave instruction in Greek. The grammar school of St. Paul's was founded by Colet; both Erasmus and Linacre prepared text-books to be used by its students; Lily, whom More called "my dearest friend," became its first headmaster. Another of More's friends, indeed, the earliest of whom there is any record, was the John Holt mentioned above, a teacher at the famous grammar school of Magdalen College, Oxford. Concerning Holt little has been discovered, but even less is generally known.[12] It will not be amiss, therefore, to bring together the scraps of information which throw light upon the career of this friend of More and upon their relationship.

John Holt may have been related to the Nicholas Holt who was More's master at St. Anthony's School, though there is no evidence for the conjecture beyond the identity of surname and the common connection with More. In 1490, he became a fellow of Magdalen College, Oxford.[13] Among the Magdalen archives is a letter which Holt wrote to the college president, Richard Mayhew.[14] In typically humanist fashion, it very elegantly says nothing whatever. Holt is occupied chiefly with protesting the inadequacy of his uncultured language for the most learned ears of his correspondent. No year appears in the letter, but since Holt describes himself as "puer imberbis," it must be supposed that it was written before he became fellow. The letter is addressed "ex Lamhitha," and it is worthy of note that Holt's one extant work, *Milk for Children,* was dedicated to Morton, Archbishop of Canterbury and master of Lambeth Palace. About the same time as Holt's epistle must have been composed, Thomas More, similarly beardless, was serving as page to Morton at Lambeth. It may have been during this period that More and Holt first became friends. But they had other opportunities for contact. In 1494 or earlier, Holt became usher of Magdalen Grammar School, an office which he retained until 1495.[15] More's two years at Oxford must be included in the period 1492–96. The first clear proof of the association of Holt and More occurs in 1497. In or about that year Holt's elementary Latin grammar, *Milk for Children,* was published with a dedication to Morton and commendatory epigrams fore and aft written by the "disertus adolescentulus," Thomas More.[16] Holt died before July, 1504.[17] However shadowy his figure may be, he is nevertheless the earliest friend of More whom the records disclose. For More's association with him must have begun by 1497, the date of *Milk for Children,* and may reach back to as early a time as that in which More waited upon Morton's table or studied at St. Anthony's School. It was therefore at an impressionable age that More came under Holt's influence. How important that influence may have been in shaping More's career is suggested by Anthony Wood's characterization of the work of the Magdalen grammarian: "[Holt] carried on the profession of pedagogy so zealous, that by his admirable way of teaching the faculty of grammar, many from his school were transplanted to several colleges and halls in this university, that were afterwards eminent in the nation. Since which time, and that of king Henry VII, hath been a singular care of royal authority, and of worthy learned men to lay a solid foundation of all kind of learning, by producing a right grammar institution."

The epigrams which More wrote for *Milk for Children* and the letter which he addressed to Holt in 1501 have received scant attention from the biographers. The epigrams are more interesting than the commendatory poems usually appended to humanist publications.[18] The "learned youngling" More is the only contributor, and his rather elaborate poems are designed primarily, not as puffs for the author, but as supplementary guides for the reader. More praises Holt for having compressed the substance of the great grammarians into a treatise suitably simple for the elementary student. He then urges the reader to begin eagerly the study of grammar which will open to him immeasurable riches. Previously, a youth who wished to enter the castle of grammatical learning had to pound heavily at a reluctant door, but *Milk for Children* is a gate which opens at the touch of an infant's hand. It is noteworthy that More speaks of the book, not as "Holt's gate to grammar," but as "our gate" (*Janua nostra*), as though he had been concerned in its preparation. The poem at the end of *Milk for Children* even more clearly betrays the professional grammarian. More congratulates the student upon having finished his first course, but he warns that after so light a breakfast it is necessary to seek meatier sustenance. For this more solid food he suggests a number of grammarians, but advises particularly Sulpitius: the choice, More declares, is not only Holt's but also his own. In these advanced studies, says More, the student will learn about heteroclites, supines, and the rules of versification.[19]

More's letter to Holt is little better known than his epigrams in *Milk for Children*.[20] Like the epigrams, it was omitted from the collected editions of his Latin works which were published in the sixteenth and seventeenth centuries. The original copy is found in a manuscript which consists chiefly of text-book and exercise material for the study of Latin grammar, compiled, I believe, for the Magdalen School.[21] It occurs in that manuscript as one of a collection of Latin epistles written by Magdalen scholars and their friends, a collection which probably served to provide the schoolboys with models of epistolary eloquence. Besides the report on the progress of More's studies under Grocyn's tutelage, the letter mentions a certain "comedy of Solomon" to the writing of which More says that he has contributed: "Misimus ad te que volebas omnia praeter eas partes quas in comediam illam que de salamone est adiecimus illas ad te non potui mittere quippe que apud me non sunt." It is surprising that modern scholars have made so little of this statement, particularly since More's connection with early Tudor drama has received much emphasis of recent years. Holt's desire for a copy of the comedy admits of ready explanation. The drama, and especially the comedy, was a favorite device for the teaching of colloquial expression, and applicants for the degree in Grammar at Oxford were sometimes required to write comedies as a test of their "grammatical" ability.[22]

In his early years, therefore, More was a grammarian, not only in the general sense of "lover of letters" but also in the restricted sense of "professor of language." That he continued to consider himself a grammarian in the latter sense even after he had established himself as a successful lawyer and achieved a valuable connection with the merchants of the City of London is suggested by a document which appears in the archives of the University of Oxford. In 1513, the University granted "Thomas More" the right to inform in grammar, a privilege conceded in view of the fact that he had studied and taught the discipline for fourteen years. The condition was set that More deliver lectures on one book of Sallust and compose an epigram to be attached to the doors of the church of St. Mary the Virgin.[23]

The identification of this Thomas More with More the Utopian can never, I fear, be completely demonstrated, since neither "More" nor "Thomas" was an uncommon name. But such evidence as there is points in that direction. No other Thomas More is to be found in the Oxford register from the beginning of the record until 1542. Whatever is said about the grammarian Thomas More in the register fits the "true" More. We know that he was interested in grammar and that he was associated with professional grammarians. We know that about fourteen years before the action of the University, he had contributed commendatory poems to Holt's *Milk for Children*, poems which sound like the work of a professional teacher. During the intervening period, he had both studied and taught humane letters. The fact that the More of the Oxford document was required to write an epigram is an argument in favor of the identification. By 1513, More had established himself as the foremost English writer in the genre. Furthermore, no contemporary candidate for the degree in grammar at Oxford was asked to write an epigram—the task usually set was a poem of a hundred verses or a comedy. Quite as appropriate to More as the task of composing an epigram was the assignment of a book of Sallust as a lecture topic. More's lectures on Augustine's *City of God* had already gained him fame as a teacher of history. Says Stapleton, "He did not treat this great work from the theological point of view, but from the standpoint of history and philosophy...."[24] Elsewhere, Stapleton asserts that More "studied with avidity all the historical works he could find."[25] Among the historians, St. Augustine and Sallust seem to have been More's especial favorites, for in a letter to William Gunnell, tutor to his children, More suggests that they study Augustine "in addition to their lesson in Sallust."[26] The young Mores, therefore, were to be taught both St. Augustine, whose writings their father had expounded publicly at Grocyn's church during the reign of Henry VII, and Sallust, whom Thomas More of the Oxford register was asked to read in 1513. Significant, too, is the fact that More's Latin life of Richard III is expressly said by its first editor to have been written "circiter 1513."[27] As has often been pointed out, *Richard III* is one of the earliest attempts by an Englishman to imitate the classical historians. There is a close parallel between More's invention of a deathbed speech of Edward IV in which the king begs his counselors to subdue their private feuds and ambitions to the care of his children and the good of the kingdom, and Sallust's report of Micipsa's dying oration to his foster son Jugurtha, which carries precisely the same burden. In both cases, the fears of the king are later justified by the treachery of the chief counselor. I am inclined to think that the clipped, objective, and impartial quality of More's character sketches derives from Sallust. But whether or not it was Sallust who was the primary inspiration for *Richard III*, clearly More was busy imitating the ancient historians at the very time that his Oxford namesake was set the task of lecturing upon one of them. Everything we know about the grammarian of the register, therefore, is appropriate to Thomas More. Both were Oxford men, both professed the grammatical discipline, both wrote epigrams, both studied Sallust. It is tempting to conclude that the two were the same.

If it is really the humanist More who appears in the Oxford register, it becomes necessary to suggest an explanation for his seeking of the degree. During his early years, More had considered a number of professions but committed himself to none. He had studied law, thought of entering a monastery, experimented with politics, and lectured on St. Augustine. But he disliked his legal studies and continued them only at his father's insistence. His marriage signified that he had given up the idea of a monastic career. According to the traditional story, his political ambitions were cut short by Henry VII because of an indiscreet speech he made as member of Parliament. It is true that, as will be shown later, More became increasingly useful to the London merchants from 1509 on, a connection which, many years after, led to his employment at court. But, in 1513, humanism was beginning to boil over in the English universities. More's closest friends were involved in the new movement: his friend Erasmus was lecturing at Cambridge; his friend Lily was teaching at St. Paul's, the school which his friend Colet had founded. Is it not possible that More, too, thought of following an academic career? It seems reasonable to suppose that he would have been tempted by an opportunity to continue his beloved studies and to impart his passion for letters to young Englishmen. But if he wished to teach at Oxford or at Cambridge as he had taught in Grocyn's church, it would have been necessary for him to secure university permission, that is, a university degree. Such permission is precisely what the governing body of Oxford granted "Thomas More" in 1513.

In 1518, More wrote a letter to Oxford urging the University to foster humanistic studies and to prevent jealous grammarians of an older school from suppressing the new enthusiasm for Greek.[28] But the letter derives its authority, not so much from More's reputation as a scholar, as from his position at the court of Henry VIII. For More's career turned out to be, not an academic, but a political one. Various diplomatic services which he performed for the government led to a knighthood and membership in the royal council in 1521. How he achieved his position at the court has always been something of a mystery. His biographers are unanimous in declaring that he never sought advancement, that, in fact, he was much averse to court service. Nevertheless, in 1509, the year Henry VIII ascended the throne, More joined the crowd of eager flatterers who sought place and wage under the new king, dedicating to him a volume of epigrams beautifully (and expensively) inscribed in a vellum manuscript illuminated with white and red roses and the pomegranates of Queen Katherine.[29] It may be that More presented the book for no motive of personal gain but as a token of the jubilation in which all humanists joined at the coronation of a promising youth devoted to learning. (The same reason, however, cannot be alleged for the fact that More was regularly the first to appear at Wolsey's levées.[30]) If More's gift to the king had a less disinterested purpose, the seed either was sterile or bore fruit only after long germination, for his first official service for King Henry was not performed until 1515, in which year he was sent to the Low Countries as a member of a government economic mission, and he did not find a place at court for several years after. To ask whether More desired that place or whether it was forced upon him is futile. Very likely, he was not himself of one mind. The value of a scholar's services to his country is debated at length in the first book of *Utopia*. Hythlodaye concludes that he can contribute nothing, but if More had wholly agreed, why did he allow that treatise on government to be published?

For the present purpose, the problem is, not why More entered government service, but why government service claimed More. According to Roper and his followers, it was More's legal talent that made him indispensable. From the evidence which I shall now present, it must be concluded, I believe, that More rose to power at court, not only because he was an excellent lawyer, but also because he was a skilled Latinist and an eloquent orator.

Years before his embassy to the Low Countries in 1515, More had filled an important diplomatic function, not for the king, indeed, but for the merchants of the City of London. The records of the Mercers' Company for the Renaissance period bring to light this significant episode in his early career.[31]

On the twenty-first of March, 1509, Master Thomas More, gentleman, was admitted to the fellowship of Mercers "frank and free."[32] It was a particularly valuable privilege to be a member of this company, for the Mercers were the richest and most powerful of the London merchant guilds, and the guilds governed the city. Noblemen, gentlemen, and merchants not resident in London were therefore willing to pay large sums of money in order to join the fellowship. Besides these, "there were numerous officials and 'friends at Court' whom the Company found it expedient to admit free."[33] From the terms of his "frank and free" admission in 1509, Thomas More, gentleman, might be expected to render the company valuable service. He did not disappoint his sponsors.

For some time before 1509, the English merchants and the city of Antwerp had been engaged in a dispute which had resulted in a serious disruption of trade. The merchants, dissatisfied with the taxes imposed upon them and the quarters allotted to them, had refused to establish a staple in any of the towns of the Low Countries and had moved from one town to another, thus retaining their power to bargain for the privileges they desired. In 1508, Margaret, Duchess of Savoy, moved to arrange a conference, and in the following year, Jacob de Wocht, the "pensionary" (that is, legal adviser or orator) of Antwerp,[34] arrived in England for the negotiations.

What follows makes entirely clear the reason why More had been given a free membership in the Mercer's guild. After the Antwerp pensionary had presented his credentials, the Mercers' Company, acting under More's advice, decided to call a general session of the Merchant Adventurers (the exporters' guild).[35] "And than at the same Courte the said Pensonary to com and be herde. And for as muche as the same Pensonary can not speke Englisshe, the Compeny haue desired the forsaid Thomas More to be here & aunsware hym in Laten." When the court assembled and Jacob de Wocht was brought in,

> Maister Thomas More, gentilman, sytting uppon the high benches ende
> next the wyndowe spake unto the said Pensonary in Laten, desyryng hym
> to Couer his hedd, and aftir that the same Maister More began and tolde a
> longe and goodly proposicion in Laten, shewyng howe that he was welcom
> and that the Compeny had sene and understoude by the forsaid lettre
> whiche he had brought from the said towne of Andwerp, that Credens was
> to be geven unto hym in suche thynges as he had for to declare unto us on
> theire behalf. . . . Than began he [that is, De Wocht] and tolde his tale in
> Latyne and first he commended Maister More greatly for makyng of his
> Oracion. . . .

There were several sessions during which More acted as interpreter, and, finally, an agreement having been reached, More and De Wocht saluted each other in outbursts of polite Latin oratory.[36]

The old biographies of More say nothing of this association with the guild of Mercers. But they do provide an interesting parallel. According to Roper, it was the affair of the Pope's ship which finally clinched King Henry's determination to number More among his servants.[37] For some reason, the government claimed the right to confiscate the vessel which had arrived at Southampton. "... the Popes Embassadour, by suite vnto his grace, obteyned that he might for his master the Pope haue Councell learned in the lawes of this realme.... Att which tyme there could none of our lawe be found so meete to be of councell with this embassador as Sir Thomas Moore, who could reporte to the Embassador in Latyne all the resons and argumentes by the learned Councell on both sides alleaged."[38] Roper hastens to add that More not only served as interpreter but also argued so well and so learnedly that the Pope won his case. In this instance, then, as in the De Wocht matter, More's advancement was served both by his legal and by his humanistic training.

That More's services as interpreter, orator, and lawyer were appreciated by the London merchants is made evident by the promotions which he received immediately after the conclusion of the negotiations with Antwerp. In December, 1509, Thomas More, Mercer, was elected burgess for the City in the coming Parliament.[39] The year following, he became Under-sheriff. In 1515, at the request of the merchants of London, King Henry made him a member of the commercial mission to Bruges. Shortly after, he resigned his City offices and entered the court career which led to his chancellorship and to his beheading.

King Henry employed More primarily, not as a lawyer, but as a secretary and orator—the two functions which, according to Burckhardt, made the humanist indispensable to the Renaissance state. When the Venetian ambassador, Giustiniani, arrived in London in 1516, it was More's duty to welcome the distinguished visitor with a set Latin oration.[40] The same task devolved upon him in the year following, upon the appearance of the papal legate, Cardinal Campeggio.[41] The privy council chose More to soothe and persuade the angry mob of rioters on Evil May Day, 1517. Besides performing numerous embassies, More acted as royal secretary, delivered important speeches, and assisted in literary matters. He wrote dozens of the King's letters, both in Latin and in English. In 1525 and 1526, he was required to reply to the orations of a new Venetian ambassador, Lorenzo Orio.[42] He spoke in the King's name to the House of Commons. When Henry made his progress to Oxford or to Cambridge, "where he was receaved with very eloquent orations, his grace wold alwaies assigne him [More], as one that was prompte and ready therein, ex tempore to make awnswer therevnto."[43] He helped the King with his book against Luther: in this work he was, by his own account, "a sorter out and placer of the principal matters."[44] In later years, when heretical notions had gained powerful adherents, the Bishop of Durham offered More a considerable sum of money to attack the Lutheran dragon with his weapon of rhetoric. More tilted, but like a proper knight and unlike a Renaissance rhetorician, he refused the reward.[45] From these examples, and from many others that might have been cited, it is clear that, as Bridgett says, "More was the Latin orator, who had to do honour to the court of Henry...."[46]

When More entered the service of King Henry VIII, he was not forced to wander, a lonely humanist, among alien corn. Erasmus, in fact, consoled himself for his friend's loss to literature by reflecting that "under such a King, and with so many learned colleagues, it seems rather a university than a court."[47] And again, "Many learned men are now [in 1518] in the English court: Linacre, the king's physician; Tunstall, master of rolls; More, privy councillor; Pace, secretary; Mountjoy, chamberlain; Colet, preacher; Stokesley, confessor."[48] Indeed, there were other humanists at court whom Erasmus might have mentioned: the Italian scholars, Carmeliano and Ammonio; John Clerk and Dr. Thomas Savage, speechmakers and ambassadors both; John Skelton, English satirist and guide of the king's early studies; and, most important of all, the teacher at Magdalen's grammar school who became, under the king, the ruler of England: Thomas Wolsey. Many of these had other interests besides the study of grammar: Linacre was a physician, Colet a divine, Tunstall a mathematician, More a lawyer, Carmeliano a lutanist. But each was a rhetorician, and served the king as ambassador, secretary, or orator.

When Thomas More's career is understood as conforming to the pattern established by the typical humanist-diplomat of Renaissance times, it gains a unity and a meaning which, I believe, it otherwise lacks. He is then no longer a succession of rather dimly related Mores: an amateur humanist and lover of good letters; a lawyer unhappy in his profession; an under-sheriff of the city of London; a diplomat, secretary, and orator in the service of the king; a writer of voluminous anti-Lutheran tracts. His career is rooted, not in amateur, but in professional humanism, and from that root stem most of the activities of his life. As a teacher of the discipline of grammar he lectured on historical subjects, wrote commendations for elementary text-books for Latin students, in collaboration with Erasmus published a translation of Lucian which was much used in the schools, and, if the identification of the Thomas More of the Oxford register be accepted, sought the right to instruct in the humanities at the English universities. His humanistic training, in addition to his legal services, made him valuable as interpreter and orator to the merchants of London. The English government claimed him because he could make speeches, write letters, and discharge diplomatic functions. Finally, he turned his rhetorical talents to the service of his conscience.

If I have tried to show that More's was a humanist's career, I have not meant to imply that More was a typical humanist. Roper, Bridgett, and Chambers have sufficiently demonstrated the depth of his intelligence, the grace of his humor, and the strength and beauty of his character. More was certainly not, as many humanists were, underhanded, venal, bitter and abusive in language,[49] boastful, aggressively ambitious, disloyal to friends and ideals. Nor do I wish to suggest that More's humanism is of itself a sufficient explanation for all of the circumstances of his life. So great a man cannot be studied from any single frame of reference. But I have tried to demonstrate, first, that a devotion to the discipline of rhetoric marks More's activities from the earliest to the latest, and second, that that devotion was no mere extrinsic phenomenon but a functional determinant of his vocations and of his rise to political power.

ST. THOMAS MORE AND LINCOLN'S INN

Richard O'Sullivan

On his recall from Oxford where Thomas More had been sent at the instance of Cardinal Morton to study divinity, his father John More entered the boy, now aged eighteen, at one of the Inns of Chancery in London called New Inn. There were at that time some ten Inns of Chancery where young students were given instruction in the liberal arts and the outlines of law and jurisprudence before they sought admission to one or other of the four great Inns of the Court: Gray's Inn, Lincoln's Inn, Middle Temple and Inner Temple. These four Inns were, so to say, four Colleges of one legal University which, in a fine phrase, Professor Lévy-Ullmann has called "the University and Church Militant of the Common law."[1]

The Inns of Court and the lesser Inns of Chancery were situated in the open space between the City of London and the City of Westminster, where Magna Carta had directed that the Court of Common Pleas should have its permanent seat.

In his celebrated work *On the Praise of the Laws of England,* Sir John Fortescue gives a sketch of life in the Inns of Court as he knew it in the fifteenth century:

> In these greater Inns, and also in the lesser, there is besides a school of law, a kind of academy of all the manners that the nobles learn. There they learn to sing and to exercise themselves in every kind of harmony; they practise dancing and all games proper for nobles, as those brought up in the king's household are accustomed to do. In the vacations most of them apply themselves to the study of legal science, and at Church Festivals to the reading, after the Divine Office, of sacred and profane literature. There is a cultivation of all virtue and the discouragement of vice, so that barons, magnates and nobles of the realm often place their children in those Inns, although they may not desire them to be trained in the science or the practice of the law, but to form their manners and keep them from the contagion of vice. The only way they have of punishing delinquents is by expulsion from the Society, a penalty they feel more than criminals do imprisonment and chains.[2]

Fortescue elsewhere explains that the laws of the land are taught in three languages—English, French and Latin—and cases are pleaded and argued and

Reprinted, by permission of the publisher and the author's heirs, from *The Catholic Lawyer,* 3 (1957), 71–80.

decided in the royal courts (and reported also) in law-French, so that English law could not be conveniently taught or studied in the Universities of Oxford or Cambridge where the teaching was only in Latin. A man who was called to the Bar by one of the Inns of Court was immediately entitled to lecture and to teach, as Thomas More proceeded at once to do at a dependent Inn of Chancery namely Furnivall's Inn. In fact the Inns of Court were institutions where the older practitioners in the law undertook the instruction of students and "apprentices"—men newly called and not so newly called—and for several centuries the highest office and honour in each Inn was to be appointed Reader, Autumn Reader and, after an interval of four or five years, Lent Reader, who was Head of the Inn as a teaching institution. It was only after the educational character of the Inns had been shaken by the Reformation and brought to an end by the Civil War in the seventeenth century (when all lectures and disputations ceased for a couple of centuries) that the spiritual office of Reader declined and the temporal office of Treasurer attained its present pre-eminence.

Of the Inns of Court Professor Maitland wrote: "No English institutions are more distinctively English than the Inns of Court—unchartered, unprivileged, unendowed, without remembered founders, these groups of lawyers formed themselves and in the course of time evolved a scheme of legal education: an academic scheme of the medieval sort, oral and disputatious. For good and ill that was a big achievement; a big achievement in the history of some undiscovered continents."[3]

Elsewhere he speaks of the practitioners before the Courts at Westminster Hall:

> We see at Westminster a cluster of men which deserves more attention than it receives from our unsympathetic because legally uneducated historians. No, the clergy were not the only learned men in England, the only cultivated men, the only men of ideas; vigorous intellectual effort was to be found outside the monasteries and Universities. These lawyers are worldly men, not men of sterile caste; they marry and found families, some of which become as noble as any in the land; but they are in their way learned, cultivated men: linguists, logicians, tenacious disputants, true lovers of the nice case and the moot point. They are gregarious, clubable men, grouping themselves in hospices which become schools of law, multiplying manuscripts, arguing, learning and teaching, the great mediators between life and logic; a reasoning, reasonable element in the English nation."[4]

In the light of these words one can understand the language Erasmus used apropos his friend Thomas More in a letter he wrote to one Faber: "He was born in London, their most celebrated city, to be born and educated in which is esteemed by the English to be no small part of nobility (*nonnulla nobilitatis pars*)."[5] One can also understand the language of Sir Thomas Smith, in his inaugural address as Professor of Roman Civil Law at Cambridge in the reign of Queen Elizabeth I, as he exclaimed upon the skill in disputation of the students and apprentices of the Inns of Court, his admiration being excited by the way in which they were apt to handle the dispute when a point of philosophy or theology is brought into question. Again Sir Henry Finch, in his seventeenth century *Description of the Common Law*, explains that the rules of reason are of two sorts: some taken from foreign (*i.e.,* other than legal) learning, both divine and human; the rest proper to law itself. Of the first sort are the principles and sound conclusions of foreign learning: "Out of the best and very bowels of Divinity, Grammar, Logic, also from Philosophy, natural, political, economic, moral, though in our Reports and Year Books they come not under the same terms, yet the things which you find there are the same; for the sparks of all the sciences in the world are raked up in the ashes of the law."[6]

The Inns of Court were thus throughout the Middle Ages one of the chief dynamic centres of English life and thought. Each Inn had its chapel, though the two Temples shared the famous Church which was consecrated for the Knights Templars (*co-militiones Christi et Templi Jerusalemmi*) by Heraclius, the Patriarch of Jerusalem in the year 1185—at the moment when Hubert Walter was writing down the first Treatise on the Common Law, the book which is called *Glanvill*. The Chapel of Lincoln's Inn was dedicated to Our Lady and to St. Richard, one of the Bishops of Chichester, who owned the land on which the lawyers of Lincoln's Inn established their *hospice*. The other buildings of the Inn included a dining and a lecture hall, and a library which was rich in manuscripts including copies of Bracton and Britton and Fortescue and the Year Books. There was also a group of office buildings used for professional and residential purposes.

Lincoln's Inn stood in the angle between what is now the great highway of Holborn and our modern Chancery (or Chancellor's) Lane and was bounded on the west by what are now Lincoln's Inn Fields, and on the south by an open space known as Fickett's Field. The northeast corner of the Inn (the modern Stone Buildings) was taken over from the Black Friars at the end of the thirteenth century; and it is here that St. Thomas Aquinas is reputed to have attended a *studium generale* of the Dominican Order towards the end of his life.

A new Hall (now the Old Hall) of Lincoln's Inn was built in 1489, seven years before young More was admitted as a student of the Inn. The fine Tudor Gatehouse (for the building of which Thomas More lent money to the Inn) was begun in 1518 and completed in 1521.

At the turn of the fifteenth-sixteenth century Thomas More was called to the Bar at Lincoln's Inn and, while he was occupied as a lecturer in law at Furnivall's Inn, he went to live without vow at the Charterhouse, a Carthusian monastery. While living there, he gave at the Church of St. Lawrence Jewry his celebrated lectures on the *City of God* of St. Augustine, which were attended by all the learned men of London. Apart from his Augustinian learning it is clear on the testimony of Stapleton and on the evidence to be found in his speeches and writings, for instance in the long letter to Dorpius and in the *Dialogue of Comfort*, that Thomas More was deeply versed in the philosophy of Aristotle and Aquinas and in Christian theology, as indeed were Sir

John Fortescue and Christopher St. Germain and Edmund Plowden, and *teste* the autographed copy of his Library Catalogue lately published by Princeton— Sir Edward Coke.

After his call to the Bar the records of Lincoln's Inn and of the City of London and of certain of the City Companies enable us to follow the career of "young More" within his Inn, and as a legal practitioner in the world outside. It is not without interest that the first reference in the records of the Inn to "the keeper of the Black Book"[7] has relation to Thomas More. In 1507 he became Pensioner, a kind of financial secretary; and we read that as Pensioner he seized the goods of a certain Thomas Thwaites deceased, for unpaid dues and amercements. After being Pensioner, he served as Butler of the Inn as his father John More had done before him.

More was now married and living with his wife Jane Colt at Bucklersbury, where his children Margaret, Elizabeth and Cecily had been born. In 1509 his only son John was born, who, like his father and his grandfather, and his brother-in-law William Roper, would in due course become a member of Lincoln's Inn.

The Acts of Court of the Company[8] tell us that on March 21, 1509 "Thomas More Gentleman" was admitted to the freedom of the Mercers' Company "which was granted to him by the whole Company to have it frank and free." In the beginning of 1510 he is reputed to have been chosen (in the place of one Yarford, a mercer, who resigned on becoming Alderman) to represent the City of London in Parliament. In the autumn of the same year, in succession to Richard Brook (author of the Abridgement) who had been appointed Recorder of London, Thomas More was promoted to the minor judicial office of Under Sheriff in the City. In the Michaelmas Term of 1510, Thomas More was elected Marshal of the Inn; and nominated Autumn Reader for 1511. An entry in the Black Book dated February 4, 1511 records that: ". . . [I]t is agreed by the Rulers and others of the Bench, for that Thomas More was two several times appointed to be Marshal and lettid (prevented) by divers casualties, and for other causes then moving them, the said Thomas shall pay a certain sum to the Company and therefor to be discharged of the keeping of the Black Book and also of the Marshalship for ever; the which sum he paid to the Treasurer in the presence of the said Rulers." The "divers casualties" are not otherwise defined—it was the year in which his little wife (*cara uxorcula*) Jane Colt died. In Michaelmas Term of 1511, Thomas More, being excused from service as Treasurer on payment of a fine of 20/−, was elected one of the four Governors of the Inn. One may perhaps assume that he was one of the "hoolle bynche" who dealt with the case of Roger Hawkins, Butler, who (according to the Black Book entry dated October 29, 1512) was put out of office for "keeping of women in his Chamber contrary to the good and laudable rules of the house" and was now remitted to his office "soo that he the same Roger do make a Taper of wex, weyng two pounds and to be set up before Our Lady in the Chapel agaynst the Sunday next after Alhalowes Day next comynge." One may wonder whether Thomas More may not also have been one of those who on July 29,

1513 ordered that "from henceforth no gentleman of Ireland shall be admitted to this Company without the assent of a Bencher, and he shall be at the Masters' Commons at his first entry, unless he be pardoned thereof by the Governors and Benchers."

On the Feast of All Saints in 1514, Thomas More, being present as one of the Governors, was elected in regular turn as Lent Reader for the year 1515. Soon afterwards, on December 3, 1514, Thomas More was admitted to the Society of Advocates, which at a later time came to be known as Doctors Commons. At the date of his election, Tunstall, Colet, Grocyn and Bonner were members of the Society which seems to have been used as a kind of Club.

As Lent Reader for 1515, Thomas More achieved the office of highest responsibility and honour that Lincoln's Inn could offer. He would expound to the whole Inn in the Old Hall over a series of days or weeks the meaning of some Statute, old or new, or the significance of some leading principle of the common law. Of his Reading there is, so far as one is aware, no note or record, unless indeed Professor Thorne of Harvard, who is occupied in preparing for the Selden Society a second volume of Readings in the Inns of Court, may have unearthed for us some precious scroll.

A Black Book entry states that soon after his Reading in 1515: "... [A]t the suit and instance of the English merchants Thomas More was by the king's consent appointed as a member of an embassy to Flanders that had to do with certain great causes between the English merchants and the merchants of the Steel Yard."

The City Records for May 8, 1515 contain an entry: "Yt ys agreed that Thomas More Gentleman, oon of (the) undersheryfes of London which shall go on the kinges ambasset in to Flanders shall occupie his Rowme & office by his sufficient depute un tyll his cummyng home agayn."

While he was away in Flanders, Thomas More wrote Book Two of the *Utopia*. (Book One of the *Utopia* was written in the following year, after his coming home again.) In the covering letter to Peter Giles which is a kind of introduction to the *Utopia* there is a passage which describes his daily round during his busy years at the Bar:

> While I do daily bestow my time about law matters: some to plead, some to hear, some as an arbitrator with my award to determine, some as an umpire or a Judge, with my sentence finally to discuss. While I go one way to see and visit my friend: another way about my own private affairs. . . . When I come home, I must commune with my wife, chat with my children, and talk with my servants. All the which things I reckon and account among business, forasmuch as they must of necessity be done: and done must they needs be, unless a man will be a stranger in his own house. And in any wise a man must so fashion and order his conditions, and so appoint and dispose himself, that he be merry, jocund and pleasant among them, whom either nature hath provided, or chance hath made, or he himself hath chosen to be the fellows and companions of his life: so that with too

much gentle behaviour and familiarity he do not mar them, and by too much sufferance of his servants, make them his masters. Among these thing now rehearsed, stealeth away the day, the month, the year. When do I write then? And all this while have I spoken no word of sleep, neither yet of meat which among a great number, doth waste no less time than doth sleep, wherein almost half the life time of man creepeth away. I therefore do win and get only that time which I steal from sleep and meat.[9]

Soon after Thomas More completed *Utopia* he was forced to enter the service of the King, and we no longer meet him in the Black Book or the record of Lincoln's Inn. There are however two last entries in the Black Book that throw light on the character of Thomas More. On February 24, 1515 we read that at the instance of Thomas More, then Reader, one Thomas Rysshton, one of the Pre-Notaries of the Sheriff's Court of London, was admitted (on special terms) as a member of the Inn and pardoned four vacations. Rysshton had a distinguished career and in the course of years became a Serjeant-at-Law. The other entry is dated June 24, 1520, after More had resigned his office of Under Sheriff and had become a member of the King's Council. On this occasion, again "at the instance of Mr. Thomas More of the King's Council, and of George Treheyron, the Reader, one Richard Stafferton, a Pre-Notary of the Sheriff's Court of London, was admitted" (again on special terms) as a member of the Inn and pardoned four vacations. The event was clearly a source of great joy to Richard Stafferton who "gave to the Inn a hogshead of claret wine." The entry of June 24, 1520 touching the admission of Richard Stafferton is actually the last entry in the Black Book concerning Thomas More, who was now a member of the King's Council and no longer active in the domestic life of the Inn or in practice at the Bar. There is no entry relating to his appointment as Lord Chancellor in 1529 or his resignation of the office in 1532, or his arrest and imprisonment in the Tower in 1534; though we read with interest and not without surprise that in Hilary Term, 1535, William Roper, the son-in-law of Sir Thomas More, was called to the Bench at Lincoln's Inn. (No meeting of the Council of the Inn appears to have been held between June 24, 1535 and November 11, 1535, between which dates the trial and execution of Thomas More took place.) On November 11, 1535 it was decreed that a Council of the Inn should be held on the following Sunday, November 14: "... [W]hen it shall be agreed when the principal week shall be kept, what day shall be in the stead of Hallowmas (*i.e.,* All Saints) Day; forasmuch as because of death in London, Michaelmas Term was adjourned till *crastino animarum* (the morrow of All Souls), and so no Hallowmas kept this year in this House."

At the meeting of the Council on November 14, 1535 (when Thomas Rysshton, the protégé of Thomas More, was elected Treasurer) the Council decided that "this week shall be the principal week for this Term and that because of the death and many other considerations no solemn Christmas shall be kept." The election of William Roper as a Bencher early in 1535 and the election of Thomas Rysshton as Treasurer indicate that the mind of the Rulers of Lincoln's Inn was not unfriendly to the memory of Sir Thomas

More. Research into the medical history of London has shown that there was in fact a sporadic outbreak of plague in London in the autumn of 1535, though no exceptional measures appear to have been taken at the Inner Temple less than a quarter of a mile away from Lincoln's Inn. "Because of the death and many other considerations, no solemn Christmas shall be kept this year." Was the death of their most distinguished member one of the considerations that the Benchers of Lincoln's Inn had in mind? Could it possibly have been out of their minds? Out of the minds of Rysshton and of Roper? It is, one imagines, a fair inference that the death of Thomas More on July 6, 1535, was one of the matters which moved the authorities of Lincoln's Inn to abandon the solemn Christmas of that year.

In fact throughout the penal times that followed, Lincoln's Inn and its neighborhood continued to be one of the places in central London that were haunted by Catholic recusants. The records of the Inn during the Tudor and the Stuart time contain many entries which show among barristers and students the constant presence (notwithstanding sustained or sporadic persecution) of adherents of the ancient faith. After the Revolution of 1689, at the opening of what we are told was the Age of Toleration, a statute of 7 William III forbade the Inns of Court any longer to call Catholics to the Bar of England. For a whole century until the Relief Act of 1791 Catholic men of law, no longer able to be called *to* the Bar, with the good will of the profession continued to practise in Chambers as conveyancers and special pleaders *under* the Bar. The link with the older times was a certain Nathaniel Pigot who had been called to the Bar before the Disabling Act of William III and who, conforming to the temper of the times, abstained from advocacy in Court and confined himself to practice in Chambers. He was a draftsman "of consummate skill and conciseness."[10] In the early part of the eighteenth century he was succeeded by another recusant lawyer, James Booth, who has been styled "the patriarch of the modern school of conveyancers."[11] For a quarter of a century Booth "gave the law" to the profession of which he was the recognized head. Among those who read in his Chambers was William Murray, afterwards Lord Mansfield and Lord Chief Justice, a member of Lincoln's Inn, who openly discountenanced prosecutions of Catholics under the penal laws and, taking a leaf out of the book of Edmund Plowden ("no priest, no Mass") at the trial of James Webb in 1768 for unlawfully saying Mass, directed the jury to dismiss the proceeding for lack of evidence of the actual ordination as a Roman priest of the man against whom the charge was made.

In succession to James Booth two other recusants named Maire and Duane dominated the profession during the latter part of the eighteenth century, and in the language of *The Conveyancer* represent "landmarks in the history of conveyancing."[12] Duane was the master in law not only of John Scott, afterwards Lord Eldon, but also of Charles Butler, editor of the standard edition of *Coke on Littleton,* who had been in practice as a conveyancer *under* the Bar and who was the first Catholic after the Relief Act of 1791 to be called to the Bar by Lincoln's Inn. Within a little time he was joined in the Old Hall by Daniel O'Connell, the Liberator.

After Catholic emancipation in 1829, the name and fame of Sir Thomas More were honourably served and amply vindicated by members of Lincoln's Inn like Sir James Mackintosh, who wrote what R. W. Chambers has called an "exquisite little biography"[13] of More, and Lord Campbell, who, in his *Lives of the Lord Chancellors,* "could feel only indignation and disgust at an apology for Henry VIII."[14]

It was from the Sardinia Chapel in Lincoln's Inn Fields that in the person of Cardinal Wiseman the Catholic voice was heard again in England by a listening audience which included Brougham and his friends and beyond by the English people. And soon after the Courts had moved in 1882 from Westminster Hall to their new home in the Strand just south of Lincoln's Inn, a statue was erected over a building in Carey Street, Lincoln's Inn, just opposite the barristers' and judges' entrances to the new Court. On a slab beneath the statue is the inscription:

> Sir Thomas More, Knight,
> Some time Lord High Chancellor
> of England;
> Martyred 6th July, 1535.
> The Faithful Servant
> Both of God and the King.

It was a courteous gesture on the part of the Benchers (who afterwards purchased the building, with the statue) to allow a through passage from Carey Street to New Square, Lincoln's Inn, which is in daily use and called *More's Passage.*

Towards the end of the nineteenth century a member of Lincoln's Inn, Charles Russell of Killowen, became the first Catholic Lord Chief Justice of England since the Reformation. It was his son Frank, Baron Russell of Killowen, one of the Lords of Appeal in Ordinary who presided in the Old Hall of Lincoln's Inn in 1936, immediately after the Canonization, at a celebrated lecture on "The Place of Thomas More in English History and Literature," given by Professor R. W. Chambers in the presence of Cardinal Hinsley and the Treasurer and Masters of the Bench of Lincoln's Inn. On that occasion a vote of thanks to Professor Chambers was offered by Sir Frederick Pollock, a great jurist and a correspondent of Justice Holmes of the United States Supreme Court; it was seconded by Mr. T. S. Eliot, our greatest literary figure.

In these last years through the courtesy of a series of Rulers of Lincoln's Inn a memorial Mass has been said in the Old Hall early in July of each year in honour of St. Thomas More.

MORE'S FRIENDSHIP WITH FISHER

Edward Surtz, S.J.

Par nobile fratrum—it is thus that More and Fisher at the scaffold stand together in the eyes of their friends.[1] Seeing the two martyrs united in death, they cannot picture them as separated in life. They can find substantiation for their opinion in More's statements at his trial on July 1, 1535. One of the letters burnt by Fisher, according to More, contained "but certaine familier talke and recommendacions, such as was seemely and agreable to our longe and olde acquaintance" ("de choses famillieres comme requeroit nostre ancienne amytie"—"de nostris priuatis negotiis, pro vetere nostra amicitia ac familiaritate").[2] Fisher's and More's common description of the Act of Treasons as "a two edged sworde," More insists, was due, not to collusion, but to "the correspondence and conformitie of our wittes, learning and studie" ("la conformite de nostre entendement et doctrine"—"ex ingeniorum ac doctrinae similitudine").[3]

Harpsfield early set the fashion in his *Treatise on the Pretended Divorce between Henry VIII. and Catharine of Aragon.* In summarizing Fisher's un-published answer to the Latin book (1530) giving and supporting the opinions of the universities against the validity of the royal marriage, he declares: "Now when you hear the said bishop (Fisher) speak, suppose that you hear Sir Thomas More also . . . for the oneness and conformity of mind that both were in touching this matter."[4]

Yet, according to the concession of even Harpsfield, it was not with Bishop Fisher that More held conference on the divorce: "Neither did Sir Thomas Moore commune with any man so much and so often of this matter as with Doctor Wilson . . . they were in every point of an opinion."[5]

The clues to the precise degree of familiarity between More and Fisher actually lie in More's declarations at his trial. Even though Harpsfield's account is based upon the Paris News Letter and the *Expositio fidelis,* he significantly uses the single English word *acquaintance* rather than *friendship* to translate the French *amytie* and the Latin *amicitia ac familiaritas.* The Latin tongue must resort to various circumlocutions to express sharply the English distinction between *friend* and *acquaintance.* Harpsfield employs *acquaintance* because that must have been the nature of More's relationship with Fisher as far as he could determine from their writings and from the persons who had had dealings with them during life. If they had been close

Reprinted, by permission of the publisher and the author's executor, from *Moreana,* 15–16 (1967), 115–33.

friends, their partisans would have capitalized upon the fact after their
martyrdoms and made every effort to preserve the evidence of letters and
anecdotes.

More and Fisher, in a word, were old acquaintances of long standing. They
were perhaps on more than mere speaking terms, but the basis of their relationship was reciprocal respect. Before their imprisonment there is no evidence
that they sought opportunities for frequent converse or welcomed each other's
company with pleasure because of mutual personal interest and deep affection
and love. In fine, More did not treat and trust Fisher as he did Erasmus or
Tunstal or Colet or Bonvisi. Signs point also to a greater closeness of Fisher
to Erasmus than to More.

More's other statement about Fisher at his trial makes greater precision
possible: their mutual esteem sprang from conformity of minds and views.
Intellectual and scholarly kinship rather than emotional involvement distinguishes their personal intercourse. What is lacking is a kind of equality
(*amicitia aequales accipit aut facit*), made manifest in perfect freedom of
speech, genuine intimacy, shared secrets, multiple visits, and special devotion.

The reasons for the failure of More's acquaintance with Fisher to ripen
into friendship cannot be assigned. The disparity between clergy and laity,
between bishop and lawyer, is hardly sufficient as an explanation. More was
close to Colet, the Dean of St. Paul's, and to Tunstal, the Bishop of London
(later, Durham)—although one might object that the friendships were formed
prior to their promotion to ecclesiastical posts. An appeal to distance, that
between London and Rochester, is also weak. The two cities are only about
thirty miles apart—which, of course, could be a considerable distance for busy
men. Yet London must have seen Fisher rather frequently on diocesan business
or on his way to Cambridge. Besides, far greater distances did not dampen
More's devotion to Giles in Antwerp or to Erasmus in Basel. The ultimate
solution can be only the mystery and the mysteriousness of friendship itself.

The extant evidence cautions us not to assume lightly that Fisher's and
More's union in death is but a final testimonial to their close friendship
during life. Their writings witness to a certain conformity of mind on such
crucial issues as the divorce and the spiritual supremacy of Henry VIII, on
such educational problems as Scholasticism and the Greek language and
literature, and on such theological questions as the authority of tradition and
the Fathers.[6] More immediately significant is their common admiration for
Reuchlin, the champion of Hebrew, and for Erasmus, the champion of Greek.
Most important of all is their relationship to Erasmus, who serves as a catalyst
or, better, as a point of contact between them.

The earliest connection between Erasmus and John Fisher is possibly
through Robert Fisher, whom Allen identifies as "a kinsman of John Fisher"
and whom Erasmus was tutoring in Paris in 1497.[7] There is no evidence for a
meeting with John Fisher during Erasmus' first trip to England in 1499–1500.
In fact, the oft-quoted letter of December 5, 1499, which extols the civility
and learning of Colet, Grocyn, Linacre, and More, does not even mention
John Fisher in spite of being addressed to Robert Fisher.[8] It is difficult, how-

ever, to imagine that the paths of John Fisher and Erasmus did not cross in London or Cambridge during Erasmus' second English sojourn in 1505–1506. It was at Fisher's University of Cambridge that Erasmus had originally intended to take his doctorate in theology. According to Dr. Caius, Erasmus was present at Fisher's richly rewarded address to Henry VII in late April 1506.[9] When in London he might possibly have lodged at Rochester House.[10] At any rate, during his third sojourn in England (1509–1514), Erasmus lectured at Cambridge from 1511 to 1514, when his communications with Fisher by letter or in person needed to be many.[11]

It is impossible to think that Erasmus did not speak about Fisher to More (and about More to Fisher) during his periods of residence in England or that he did not introduce them to each other in the unlikely possibility that they had not met before. Hence it is not surprising to find the first pertinent extant evidence of their acquaintance in Erasmus' letters and not in official records. After January 25, 1512, that is, at least five years before More's entrance into the royal service, Fisher ceased to attend the royal councils.[12] One cannot preclude, of course, encounters between More and Fisher at the royal court whither More's business on behalf of the City took him. On his part, Fisher complains about his inability to look to his episcopal duties because of "attending after tryumphes, receiving of ambassadors, haunting of princes courtes and such lyke."[13] Nevertheless, it is significant that the first indisputable proof for their acquaintance is associated with their common friend Erasmus. When the latter stopped with Fisher in Rochester for about ten days in the latter part of August 1516, More came thither from London for a final farewell to his friend because of his fear that he might not see him again for a long time.[14]

One result of More's trip to Rochester was one more job for an already busy man! Erasmus involved More in the business of securing for Fisher a tutor in Greek. Erasmus and More had their eye on William Latimer, who, however, successfully evaded spending a month or two with Fisher. At first, Latimer pleaded a prior commitment at Oxford, but later he objected that the mastery of Greek took years, not months.[15] Stopping at Rochester for a short time at the end of April 1517, Erasmus apparently gave Fisher a few more hints about Greek. Finally, in view of Latimer's intransigence, he sent the Bishop of Rochester in September his Latin translation of the second book of Theodore of Gaza's grammar.[16]

Just as Erasmus had enlisted More's aid in the search for a Greek tutor for Fisher, so also he employed More to convey letters and books to Fisher. Under date of March 1, 1517, it was in care of More that he sent Fisher a one-volume collection of all the publications issuing from the Reuchlin affair, as well as a Latin translation of *Augenspiegel* (*Speculum oculare*). In June or July 1517, Fisher wrote to Erasmus about the copy of *De arte cabalistica* (March 1517) with which his "adored" Reuchlin had presented him: "Your friend More has sent the letter, but still detains the book in his old way; as he did before with the *Oculare Speculum*."[17]

Erasmus continues to remain at the center in the relations between Fisher and More. For example, on January 1, 1519, Erasmus gave More a copy of his letter to Fisher in the great to-do over Edward Lee's annotations to the New Testament.[18] More's own letter to Lee under date of May 1, 1519, alludes twice to Fisher's role as arbiter and conciliator.[19] In his Letter to a Monk (1519–20), More places Fisher first on the roll of his countrymen who feel gratitude for Erasmus' New Testament: "In my list the place of honor goes to the Reverend Father in Christ, John, Bishop of Rochester, distinguished for virtue as well as learning, qualities in which he has no superior among living men."[20]

Fortunately for our investigation, evidence appears for a more personal link between More and Fisher just at this time. In a congratulatory epistle, connected by E. F. Rogers and E. E. Reynolds with Fisher's polemic (1519) against Lefèvre's position on Mary Magdalene, More comments: "Your lordship writes in a style that might well be that of Erasmus. As for the subject matter, ten Erasmuses could not be more convincing." Yet the conclusion hardly indicates an unmistakable and marked degree of intimacy: "Farewell, my lord bishop, most highly esteemed for virtue and learning."[21]

More's somewhat earlier reply, however, to what might have been a congratulatory epistle from Fisher is more typically Morean: "Much against my will did I come to Court (as everyone knows, and as the King himself in joke sometimes likes to reproach me). So far I keep my place there as precariously as an unaccustomed rider in his saddle." In proportion to Henry's growth in virtue and learning, to be sure, "the less burdensome do I feel this life of the Court."[22] More denies enjoying the special favor of the king, but the succession of honors and offices conferred upon More must have encouraged Fisher to appeal to the newly knighted More on behalf of the University of Cambridge in general and of a theological student in particular.[23] In his reply (if reply it be to this special request), More graciously states: "Whatever influence I have with the King (it is certainly very little) but such as it is, is as freely available to your Paternity and all your scholars as his own house to any man." His parting is the most friendly that is extant: "Farewell, best and most learned of Bishops, and continue your affection for me (me, vt soles, complectere)." Even here, apparently mindful of Fisher's position as bishop and chancellor, More uses the Latin term complector 'embrace.' An embrace, instead of the modern handshake, was the ordinary and correct usage in greeting and farewell in the England of the day.[24]

In addition to these letters, there were historical events in which More and Fisher might have met on familiar terms. Such was the Field of the Cloth of Gold (June 1520), where Fisher was in the company of Queen Catherine and of which he left a striking description in the first of his Two fruytfull Sermons (delivered in 1520, printed in 1532).[25] In attendance as royal councilor, More took the opportunity to meet Erasmus in July at Calais, where his friend held additional interviews—certainly with Henry VIII, Cardinal Wolsey, and Bishop Longland,[26] and conceivably with Bishop Fisher.

The following year might have seen More among the many dignitaries of church and state present at St. Paul's to hear Fisher's historic sermon against

Martin Luther in May 1521.[27] The likelihood of More's assistance at his close
friend Tunstal's episcopal consecration by Wolsey, Warham, and Fisher on
October 19, 1522, and his installation in St. Paul's on October 22, is even
greater.[28] In 1523 both More and Fisher made history in a minor way. In
Parliament, Thomas More as Speaker delivered an address which Philip Laundy
views as "something of a parliamentary milestone." More "did not claim that
the privilege of free speech belonged to the Commons as of right, but he
certainly argued that debate could not be properly conducted without it."[29]
Noteworthy, too, was his highly diplomatic handling of the situation when
Wolsey in all his splendor appeared in person to overawe the Commons into
submission to his original demands. As a servant of the Crown, however, More
finally succeeded in obtaining for Wolsey the greater part of his request. As
for Fisher, in Convocation in 1523 he distinguished himself, with Bishop Foxe
of Winchester and Rowland Philips vicar of Croydon, among the many opponents of the high tax on clerical income asked by Wolsey, who mostly had his
way here too.[30]

   Two years earlier, certainly More, and probably Fisher, collaborated in the
composition of *Assertio septem sacramentorum,* a treatise which might best
be labeled as fundamentally and substantially Henry VIII's. There exists no
record of the precise contribution made by Fisher, conjectured by some persons to be the real author. The editor who placed the *Assertio* at the beginning
of Fisher's *Opera* (1597) used the cautious heading: "Assertio ... ab Henrico
VIII Angliae rege, Roffensis tamen nostri hortatu & studio edita."[31] But More's
part is manifest: he was, "after it was finished, by his graces apointment and
consent of the *makers* (italics added) of the same, only a sorter out and placer
of the principall matters therin contayned." Ironically, Henry's refusal to omit
or to soften his pronouncements on papal primacy caused More to study its
divine institution more deeply.[32]

   The two writers who upheld Henry's cause against Luther's counterattack
(*Contra Henricum regem Angliae,* 1522) were, not surprisingly, two of his
original cooperators—More and Fisher. Their separate publications give the
impression that the authors had agreed on a division of labor: More as
Baravellus or Rosseus was to quote Luther's work verbatim and to return abuse
for abuse, whereas Fisher, conformably with an explicit statement in his conclusion, would omit Luther's insults and concentrate on every important
theological question, particularly the primacy of the papacy, the interpretation
of scripture, the sacramentality of orders and matrimony, and, most thoroughly and extensively, the Eucharist as sacrament and sacrifice. More as Rosseus
makes reference to Fisher's *Assertionis Lutheranae confutatio.* His praise has
two significant features: first, his characterization is general and impersonal,
for the Bishop of Rochester is "a man illustrious not only by the vastness of
his erudition, but much more so by the purity of his life (*vir eruditionis
vbertate clarus, & vitae puritate clarissimus*)"; and, second, the article singled
out is that on the papal primacy, with its proofs from the Gospels, the Acts,
the Old Testament, the Fathers, and the Council of Florence.[33] When More
wrote Cromwell in March 1534 that he had been convinced about the divine

institution of the primacy first by the king's book and later by the Fathers and the councils during research conducted "these x yere synnys,"[34] we are carried back approximately to Article 25 in Fisher's *Confutatio* (pub. 1523), which More had commended in superlative terms in his own book against Luther. Consequently Fisher's strong defense was a decisive factor in the crystallization of More's personal convictions on the papacy. An almost amusing aftermath to More's and Fisher's replies to Luther's offensive against Henry VIII is furnished in the *Hyperaspistes* (1526) of the sensitive Erasmus, who feels hurt because Luther has singled out for attack his own temperate *Diatribe* rather than such virulent assaults as those by *Rosseus* and *Roffensis*.[35] As late as 1531, these same two are considered by Cochlaeus to be the polemist most capable of handling Melanchthon according to his deserts: "Vtinam Rosseus vester aut . . . Roffensis hunc Rhetorem digne pro meritis excipiat."[36]

In 1525 two events, the one temporary and the other permanent, could have brought More and Fisher together. The first was the English visit of the redoubtable Johann Eck to consult Henry VIII and the Bishop of Rochester. This visit, recorded by both Eck and Fisher, is commemorated also by Eck's brief letter to More in his *Enchiridion* (3rd ed., 1526) and by a reference in Eck's commentary on Haggai the Prophet (1538).[37] The second event was More's permanent appointment as High Steward of Fisher's University of Cambridge. According to Chambers, More in this office tried persons accused of crimes, engaged in academic disputations, and on royal visits answered extempore on the king's behalf the orator of the university.[38]

Because of Fisher's and More's high offices by the mid twenties, it was inevitable that not only students and scholars but also artists should resort to them for patronage and recommendation. Under date of December 18, 1526, More had promised Erasmus to find work for the visiting Hans Holbein.[39] At this time, according to Chambers' conjecture, Holbein executed a lost portrait of Fisher of which three sketches survive.[40] The investigator is again frustrated, by lack of evidence in Holbein's activity, as to More's precise relationship to Fisher here.

But of their common cause in religion there can be no doubt. Their orthodox offensive against heresy took an open form on January 26–27, 1526, when Sir Thomas More ransacked the Steelyard for heterodox books and took into custody four merchants, who with Robert Barnes abjured their heresy at a public ceremony on February 11, 1526, in St. Paul's. In his sermon on the occasion, Fisher praises, among other anti-Lutheran writings, "the boke of maister More."[41] More is lauded again in Fisher's volume against Oecolampadius published in early 1527: "Thomas Morus, eques auratus, moribus & ingenio candidissimus, neque minori praestans eruditione." This time a slightly more personal note is injected because More is described as having taken up his pen "tametsi negotiis regis & regni grauissimis, occupatissimus sit."[42]

In fact, after a five-year period of literary idleness, More seemed to pick up the pen being laid down by his erstwhile polemical associate, Bishop Fisher, with the publication of *De veritate corporis et sanguinis Christi in eucharistia* after eight extraordinarily productive years. (Fisher, of course, was soon to start his series of divorce tracts.) More began his most prolific years with Tunstal's permission to read heretical books (March 1528) and with the publication of *A dyaloge of ... dyuers maters* (June 1529). In this work he approves wholeheartedly of the use, if necessary, of force against heretics as had been recommended by Fisher. But, leaving him unnamed, he refers simply and impersonally to "an honorable prelate of thys realme in his moste erudite booke."[43] In *The confutacyon of Tyndales answere* (1532), More in his Preface mentions, as one of the examiners of Thomas Hitton, "the reuerende father the bishop of Rochester."[44] He refers twice to Fisher's citation of Origen as a witness to unwritten traditions. In the first reference, More has Origen himself characterize Fisher as "a right honorable manne very cunnyng and yet more vertuous, the good bishop of Rochester." The second allusion is simply to "my lord of Rochester" without describing his personality or his work: "my lord of Rochester hath gathered diuers (undoubted holy menne since Origen) together, and rehersed (them) ... in his boke agaynst Luther."[45] In his *Apologye* (1533), More arraigns heretics for constant and universal railing: "And some they call nought by name, whose specyall goodnesse, shall haue recorde and wytnesse of all good folke that knowe theym"—among whom would undoubtedly be Bishop Fisher, one object of Tyndale's violent attack.[46]

A person perhaps might object with some reason that controversial works are hardly the place to look for expressions of friendship. Yet adversaries are ready to capitalize even upon friendship to gain a point. Such is Tyndale's tactic against More in calling Erasmus his "darling." Compelled to spring to the defense of his friend, More has to explain: "I have not contended with Erasmus my derling, because I found no suche malicious entente with Erasmus my derling, as I fynde with Tyndall."[47] But no opponent seems to have taken such advantage of a special friendship between More and Fisher, presumably because none existed. For example, John Frith on three different occasions in *A disputacion of Purgatorye* (1533?) maintains that More and Fisher disagree on three points about purgatory—and yet he fails to allude to any close bond of affection between the two men. Their discrepancy arises in spite of More's extensive borrowing from Fisher: "How be it the chefest of his scryptures hath master More pervsed & hath in a maner nothinge but that was before wryten by my lord of Rochestre." Even when Frith builds up the reputation of his two adversaries in *An other boke against Rastel* ("no .ii. lyke myght in all this londe be founde"), he utters no word about any special tie between them.[48]

Neither can any close friendship be inferred from their evident unanimity on the validity of Henry and Catherine's marriage. In fact, More was far from being as intimately involved in the divorce, at least if one is to judge from his extant writings, as were Fisher, Cranmer, Pole, and Tyndale. More, it is true, was in Wolsey's entourage when the cardinal broached the king's "great matter" to Fisher in early July 1527, but since Fisher was pledged to secrecy, he could not have conferred with More at this time.[49] When first asked for his opinion, More advised Henry to consult the Bishops of Durham (Tunstal) and Bath (Clerk), with no mention of the Bishop of Rochester (the committed Fisher).[50] After later study, of course, he gave Henry an adverse personal judgment, as had Fisher. More and Fisher were the two most important figures who did not sign the petition of prelates and nobles (July 1530), addressed to Clement VII, for a decision favorable to Henry.[51] In the whole affair, More seems to have remained cautious, yet, according to Chapuys, his dismissal was almost occasioned in 1531 by his espousal of Catherine's cause.[52] After his resignation and especially after the parliamentary statute, More "did keepe his conscience to himselfe, and would not open his opinion in that matter, ... eyther to the Bisshopp of Rochester demaunding his iudgement, eyther to doctour Wilson requiring it at his hande": they were advised to settle their own conscience.[53]

What had immediately caused More's resignation of the chancellorship was not the question of the divorce but the submission of the clergy on May 15, 1532. Here the same attitude marks Fisher and More. To the bishops sent to persuade him to take the oath, Fisher in prison is reputed to have said: "The fort is betraied even of them that shoulde have defended yt." In his *Expositio Passionis,* More declares: "Haec similitudo dormientium Apostolorum ... valde competit in hos Episcopos, qui dum virtus & fides veniunt in discrimen, dormiunt"; or, in Mary Basset's translation: "This similitude of Apostles thus sleeping, may aptely be applied vnto those Bishoppes, which lye carelesly and sleepe full sounde, while vertue and true religion are like to ronne to ruine."[54]

The paths of More and Fisher, which had been running roughly parallel for many years, now began to converge—on the Tower. Both were implicated in the affair of the Holy Maid of Kent. More was able to extricate himself, but Fisher was indicted, convicted, and fined a year's revenue. When in April 1534 both were imprisoned for refusing the oath, they were lodged in widely separated rooms in the Tower, almost as if in token of their individuality and their independence. More asserted his freedom of conscience to the extent of telling his daughter Margaret that he would not take the oath— "not though I shoulde see my Lorde of Rochester say the same, and swere the oth hymselfe before me too." Yet he praises Fisher as *sans pareil:* "I haue hym in that reuerent estimacion, that I reken in this realme no one man, in wisdome, learning and long approued vertue together, mete to be matched and compared with hym." But More is fixed in his resolution: "I neuer entend ... to pynne my soule at a nother mans backe, not euen the best man that I know this day liuing; for I knowe not whither he may happe to cary it."[55] Consequently, when Fisher by letter inquired after the nature and manner of his answer on the oath, More replied only that Fisher should resolve his own conscience.[56] This answer, which sounds very much like an impertinent rebuff, actually was a measure of safety for both of them: if either decided later to take the oath, he would not need to inform on the other. Fisher himself declared on June 12, 1535, that in their burnt correspondence "ther is nothing else but exhortation either of other to take patience in their adversity, and to call God for grace, and praying for their enemies."[57]

In his examination, More admitted to letters, "containing for the most part nothing but comfortable words and thanks for meat and drink sent by one to the other."[58] Besides, a particularly touching bit of testimony reveals that "More, or his servant, sent him [Fisher] an image of St. John and apples and oranges after the snow that fell last winter. On New Year's Day, More sent a paper with writing, £2,000 in gold, and an image of the Epiphany."[59]

The similarity between the two men persists in the Tower. Both prisoners produce spiritual treatises. Even two titles are similar: *A dialoge of comfort against tribulacion* by More and *A spirituall consolation* by Fisher. But there are differences, too. More writes a treatise on Christ's passion, but Fisher concentrates on *The wayes to perfect Religion*, namely, ten considerations whereby to gain Christ's love.

Ironically, even the immediate causes for their condemnation were different: Thomas More was sentenced because of the perjury of Sir Richard Rich; but Fisher, because of the trick of the king's messenger who promised him no harm if he stated his true opinion on the supremacy.[60] Consequently, More denied the royal supremacy after his condemnation; but Fisher, before his condemnation—*quia hoc conveniebat Personae, quam gerebat, Episcopi,* according to Cardinal Pole's declaration.[61]

The intimacy which More and Fisher were apparently unable to effect during life was achieved in death. Their bodies, without their heads, were buried at "the belfry end of the chapel of St. Peter ad Vincula within the Tower."[62] Certainly as far as the memory of man is concerned, their names since their executions have been united indissolubly—and ever will be—for both their enemies and their friends. The division began immediately. The two were attacked—not to mention many others—by Simon Matthew in his sermon of June 27, 1535; by Richard Morison in his *Apomaxis* (1537); and by George Joye in his *Present consolacion* (1544). By November 1535, Christopher of Stadion, Bishop of Augsburg, was predicting martyrs' crowns for Fisher and More. In 1536 and 1538 Cochlaeus published his defense of Fisher and More against Sampson and Morison respectively.[63]

A retrospective survey of their lives creates the impression of two passengers in separate coaches, now slow and now fast, on parallel tracks. They may catch glimpses of each other, they may talk to each other, they may even strain to clasp hands. Yet, though their sentiments are "truly parallel," they "can never meet." They often come close to each other: in their sharing of friends, such as Erasmus and Tunstall;[64] in their zeal for learning, especially Greek literature, pagan and Christian; in their defense of orthodoxy against Luther and other Reformers; in their espousal of Queen Catherine's cause; and in their denial of royal supremacy in favor of papal primacy. What binds them together, then, is evidently "the conjunction of the mind."

What separates them is the "opposition of the stars." The stars as the symbol of fate—or providence—created those accidents of fortune which could have been crucial in preventing any special intimacy. More was nine years younger than Fisher. More was born a Londoner at the center of national life; Fisher, in Beverley in the far provincial north. They went to different universities: More to Oxford, Fisher to Cambridge. More's permanent residence was always London; Fisher's, first Beverley, then Cambridge, and lastly Rochester. More was a twice-married lawyer and royal servant;[65] Fisher, a celibate churchman and educator. But the greatest of fate's "iron wedges"[66] must have been the strong personality of the two men: each possessed marked individuality and resolute independence. Dissonant elements in their nature, impossible to pinpoint or to enumerate, prevented them from becoming friends in the way that More and Erasmus, or More and Tunstall, were friends. Consequently Fisher simply cannot be said to belong to the More Circle as such. To maintain otherwise would be falsehood or self-deception or arrant nonsense. In fact, it is difficult to conceive of Fisher as belonging to or moving in any circle; and really the same is ultimately true of More, especially at the end of his life: "euery body went forthe with all saue onely the blynde Bisshopp and he."[67]

One might perhaps ask the prying and embarrassing question: could and did Fisher show friendship or affection for anyone? There was one woman in his life whom he seems not only to have admired but to have loved—the Lady Margaret. There were two men to whom he appears more than usually attached: a much older Oxonian, Richard Foxe (1448?–1528), Bishop of Winchester, and an earlier Cantabrigian, Nicholas West (1461–1533), Bishop of Ely. Otherwise Fisher's allegiances look "institutionalized": to his University of Cambridge, to his diocese of Rochester, and to his Church Catholic. But what probing reveals is that he really loves in each of these a person— Christ. Fisher's statutes make clear that he wishes to bring the fellows and scholars of Christ's College and St. John's College to "the worship of God, the increase of the faith, and probity of morals."[68] He stresses preaching, by himself and others, because he longs to make Christ's gospel clear to the people. He knows, loves, and defends the Church Catholic as the Spouse of Christ and as the Mystical Body of Christ. This personal devotion to Christ becomes especially evident, first, in his zeal for the Real Presence in the great volume against Oecolampadius and, second, in his emphasis on the love of Christ in what might be his very last writing, *The wayes to perfect Religion*; for, in essence, *perfect* religion is nothing else than the love and friendship of Christ and His brethren.

This analysis does not mean to imply that Thomas More loved God less than John Fisher. More, too, made the supreme sacrifice of love and friendship, for, in his own words: "A greater loue no manne hath, than to geue his lyfe for his frendes."[69] One's first impression is that More laid down much more than Fisher: not only his life but also his wife, children, home, and possessions. But upon reflection one realizes that Fisher had sacrificed all these earlier: "He who is unmarried is concerned about the things of the Lord, how he may please God" (1 Cor. 7:32). Consequently Fisher was "concerned about the things of the Lord," particularly His young ones and His people and His true Church, by *special profession—quia hoc conveniebat Personae, quam gerebat, Episcopi.*

To get back to our original problem and to state our reasoned conclusion. More and Fisher can be labeled as friends, but only in a broad sense, even if in a true sense: they were on good, familiar, and respectful terms, but without constantly seeking each other's company out of deep and unreserved affection. In this regard, More's making a special trip of thirty miles to Rochester to say farewell again to Erasmus (August 1516) is at once manifestative and symbolical of their friendship. To define More's relationship to Fisher better, one might need to have recourse to the awkward designation *brothers*. For such they were and are—*brothers in Christ*. And this remark carries us back to our opening characterization of More and Fisher, but now with an addendum: *par nobile fratrum in Christo*.

RICHARD PACE'S SKETCH OF THOMAS MORE

Edward Surtz, S.J.

The mental attitude of Thomas More at the time of the composition of *Utopia* is a vexing problem—and an important one for the light that its solution could throw upon his outlook before the Protestant Reformation and upon the interpretation of his *Utopia*. Erasmus' biographical portrait of More, addressed to Ulrich von Hutten and dated July 23, 1519, is invaluable but perhaps a bit later than desirable.[1] There does exist a character sketch of More which was published almost two years earlier; and in view of the fact that its author, Richard Pace, had left England in October, 1515, two years before its publication, it should give one a glimpse of More just before the composition of *Utopia*. Interestingly enough, Pace met More on the Calais highway on October 25, 1515, as he was going on the King's business to Switzerland and as More was returning from his Utopian embassy in Flanders. Pace was in such a hurry that the two had scarcely time to exchange greetings.[2] They had not seen each other since May, the month in which More traveled from London to Bruges. The latter had composed the second book of *Utopia* during his enforced leisure in the Low Countries and was to write the first after his return to England.[3]

The character sketch occurs in a book published by John Froben at Basel in October, 1517: *De Fructu Qui ex Doctrina Percipitur Liber* [*A Book on the Benefits of Learning*]. The author, according to J. S. Brewer, is "reckoned by some as scarce inferior to Wolsey himself in ability or in the favour of Henry": Richard Pace (1482?–1536).[4]

After probably studying at Oxford, Pace went abroad to attend the leading Italian universities. As early as September, 1508, Erasmus was writing to Lord Mountjoy that Pace was "a young man endowed with such knowledge of both languages [Latin and Greek] that he alone could do honor to all England by his genius and with such modesty and uprightness in his moral life that he is most worthy of your favor and that of others."[5] In December of the same year, Erasmus deposited for safekeeping with Pace at Ferrara certain works, including the incomplete *Antibarbari,* the return of which was the subject of correspondence between them for more than a decade.[6] Five years later, Erasmus revealed his pleasure at Andrew Ammonius' friendship with Pace: the latter is "the most loving and most upright of men."[7] The next year (1515), Pace was evidently accorded some official position of importance. From Basel,

Reprinted, with permission of the publisher and the author's executor, from *The Journal of English and Germanic Philology,* 57 (1958), 36–50.

Erasmus expressed his hope that, in view of Pace's sincere character, his promotion would make no difference in their friendship. At the same time, he begs him either personally to safeguard his manuscripts (of *Antibarbari*, etc.) in case of their arrival or, preferably, to deposit them with Thomas More.[8]

The Benefits of Learning was published in October, 1517. On December 6, 1517, Erasmus told Beatus Rhenanus that Pace in a letter had boasted that Beatus had bestowed praise upon the work (*jactat libellum de Fructu Studiorum abs te laudatum*).[9] Later in the same month, Erasmus rejoiced that Marcus Laurinus found pleasure in the company of More and Pace, who had met on official business in the Low Countries: they "would be a source of pleasure to me even if they were Scythians," i.e., barbarians.[10] The very same day, he sent through Pace his greetings to More.[11] As yet, Erasmus appears not to have seen *The Benefits of Learning*.

On February 22, 1518, however, Erasmus wrote an extremely unfavorable review to More. An analysis of the letter reveals that he objects to the book on three counts: (1) the publication of the book reveals an hitherto unsuspected lack of judgment in Pace; (2) England had expected an altogether different and superior specimen of genius from her son; and (3) the constant references to Erasmus, although made in the spirit of a friend, would harm him (Erasmus) more than any enemy could. The transmission of the name of friend to the world and to posterity is sacred, but Pace has bandied the term about and has reckoned the cost only in terms of ink, paper, and lamp oil. To what purpose all that nonsense about the roll of Erasmus' theological errors, about heresies, about his poverty? Does Pace think the chatter of pettifoggers in their cups worthy of being put into print for the world? Erasmus begs More in view of his familiar intercourse with Pace (*pro tua cum illo familiaritate*) to advise him privately against any similar abuse of literature in the future. If Pace translates Greek, at least he will rely upon the judgment of another and will have to concern himself only with style! A month later, Erasmus repeats the same charges against *The Benefits of Learning* in a letter to Paolo Bombace. He further observes, however, that, as far as it is a literary work, it succeeds in being neither serious nor humorous, and it lacks unity and coherence—like the dreams of a sick man (in Horace's *Art of Poetry*).[12]

What stuck in Erasmus' craw more than anything else was Pace's picture of him as complaining about his poverty: he was afraid that this might offend his generous patrons and throw him into disfavor with them. Thus, in March, 1518, he wrote to Lord Mountjoy: "Richard Pace in his little volume has depicted me as poor and needy, whereas I seem to myself almost a Midas. This ill report in a way touches you also. But consider his statement as said in joke, provided that in earnest I may escape the shame."[13]

In the same month, Erasmus finally wrote to Pace himself. His letter opens abruptly: "You have not disported yourself handsomely in your little book, most learned Pace, nor have you ingratiated yourself much more with the theologians than I with my *Praise of Folly*. You have made me absolutely notorious with the ill report of my poverty, although I seemed to myself

almost a Midas. But this note of disgrace in a way touches my Maecenases. ...."
Erasmus then urges Pace to help in dispelling the libel on his poverty by appeals
for aid to the Maecenases with whom his influence is great![14] A week later, he
told Beatus Rhenanus of his feelings of shame and regret for Pace's "most lifeless [or trivial] little book" (*frigidissimo libello*), sure to disappoint the expectations of all his learned friends: they would think the same of it as he.[15]

But on October 22, 1518, Erasmus reported to Pace that *The Benefits of
Learning* was "being read avidly among the Germans." It offended, however,
some citizens of Constance by seeming to make them out as illiterate and
tipplers.[16] In 1519, Erasmus and Pace were still exchanging friendly letters,
the former calling the latter "my Pace, the most learned of friends and the
most friendly of the learned."[17] Pace's reputation for learning seems to have
suffered little harm from the publication of his book. In a letter to Thomas
More, November 13, 1518, John Froben, whose press had issued *The Benefits
of Learning,* commended himself to "those great heroes of letters: John Colet,
Linacre, Grocyn, Latimer, Tunstal, Pace, Croke, and Sixtin."[18] In 1519 or
1520, More himself includes Pace among the great men who can never receive
sufficient praise and who bear witness to Erasmus' adherence to the true faith:
Colet, Fisher, Warham, Mountjoy, Tunstal, Pace, and Grocyn.[19]

It has been necessary to describe the reception of *The Benefits of Learning*
at this length in order to establish the degree of its credibility and trustworthi-
ness. Erasmus' objections can be reduced to one: lack of judgment or prudence
in Pace. The latter's dramatization of Erasmus' religious position might further
antagonize the Scholastic theologians and his report of Erasmus' complaint
about poverty might offend Erasmus' patrons. Erasmus finds the passages
dealing with himself too much like the tavern chatter of petty people. Erasmus'
criticism does not touch the heart or substance of *The Benefits of Learning:*
it does discredit the crude method and lifeless style of the book. Erasmus had
hidden behind the mask of Folly: More, behind that of Hythloday. Pace's use
of real persons, such as Erasmus, under circumstances altered or created for
literary effect, could only produce embarrassment, misunderstanding, and
trouble. The mingling of the real and the fictitious was unfortunate. Pace,
however, had been confirmed in his error of judgment by Paolo Bombace, his
former teacher, who had read and approved the serious matter, the jests, and
the sallies of wit.[20]

The portrait of Erasmus in *The Benefits of Learning* may be described as
substantially accurate but crudely executed. Must the same be said of the
sketch of Thomas More? Before answering this question, it is necessary to
determine Pace's knowledge of the author of *Utopia*. Certainly by February,
1518, More was so intimate with the author of *The Benefits of Learning* that
Erasmus could appeal to his confidential friendship with Pace to dissuade him
from like literary efforts.[21] In December, 1517, the two met to do official
business together in the Low Countries,[22] but this was two months after the
publication of *The Benefits of Learning.* No letters that may have passed
between More and Pace appear in E. F. Rogers' edition of More's correspondence. Toward the end of the Utopian embassy, when he feared further

involvement in more royal negotiations abroad, More wrote Pace, among others, to request him to use his influence with Wolsey for his recall to England.[23]

In Pace's eyes, their relationship was that of friendship, for he speaks of "More, his very close friend" (*Morum amicissimum suum*). There is no reason to doubt his veracity. On the contrary. In a letter to the absent Erasmus, variously dated February or June, 1516, More longs for Pace's return and graciously continues: "I seem to lack the one half of me during his absence, the other half during your absence" (*Ego interim videor mihi dimidio mei carere dum abest ille; altero dimidio dum tu*).[24] There had been much time and occasion for the two to meet. Pace had returned to England, perhaps in 1514, to enter Wolsey's or the King's service with the recommendation of Leo X. Pace's reputation as a scholar, the friendship of Erasmus and other Humanists, and More's business taking him to court[25] would bring the two together. Pace would therefore have the opportunity to observe More at first hand and to make a literary sketch of him.

One has a check upon Pace's account in the biography of More written in 1519 by Erasmus. The two should not differ on substantials, however much they might disagree in accidentals. In addition, what is important in Pace's sketch is not merely the delineation of More's character but even more the impression More's personality created on a Humanist of reputation and ability. The latter should give a person more than an ordinary glimpse into More's attitude and position at the time of the composition of *Utopia*.

Pace does not speak in his own person: he puts his eulogy into the mouth of Grammar. But the disguise is so thin and the device is so patent, that it is just as well to attribute the encomium to Pace directly.

He begins his sketch with an expression of wonder at More's ability in languages, especially in Greek. "No man has ever existed," he says, "who did not gather the significance of every sentence from its words, except one person, our Thomas More; for he, on the contrary, gathers the significance of words from sentences, and especially in understanding and translating Greek. Moreover, this procedure is not altogether at variance with grammar, but is a little higher than grammar, namely, the method of innate discernment." One infers from this statement that in the study of a language More did not pursue the usual method, described later by Pace, of learning letters first, then syllables, then words and phrases, and then complete sentences. Instead, More employed the inductive method: divining, fixing, and defining the meaning of words from their context.[26] He could do so because he was "the possessor of a talent more than human" (*ingenium plusquam humanum*). This tribute is sounded so often in contemporary writings that it seems superfluous to quote Erasmus, who tells Hutten of More's "happy genius" (*felix ingenium*) and his "genius, effective and swift at every point" (*Ingenium praesens et vbique praeuolans*). He repeats Colet's assertion that, "although this island flourishes with so many distinguished men of talent, Britain has only a single genius" (*Britanniae non nisi vnicum esse ingenium*), namely, Thomas More.[27]

This "talent more than human" shows itself in manifold ways. Its first manifestation, according to Pace, is in More's learning: it is "not only extraordinary but also many-sided, so that wherever you turn he appears to be ignorant of nothing." In the letter addressed to Budé and descriptive of More's family life, Erasmus terms More "most learned" (*doctissimus*).[28] In particular, Pace calls attention to the extent of his knowledge of Greek, as witnessed by the Latin translation of Lucian's *Philopseudes seu Incredulus*,[29] on which Paolo Bombace, the teacher of Pace, lavishes great praise. Erasmus' letter to Hutten, of course, mentions More's predilection for Lucian (*Luciano cum primis est delectatus*) and his youthful study of Greek (*Iuuenis ad Graecas literas ... sese applicuit*).[30]

Further, Pace finds More's fluency to be incomparable, and not only incomparable but also twofold, first in his native tongue and then in a foreign language, to wit, Latin. Erasmus makes clear to Hutten that this fluency is the result of much practice, first in verse, and then in prose. In order to make the latter more graceful, More had exercised himself in every form of writing, especially in declamations on such heterodox topics as the defense of Plato's communism, even of the communism of wives. More is also extraordinarily felicitous as an extempore speaker. Pace, too, it must be noted, does not limit More's facility to written work, but makes a general statement so that one can form a conclusion as to his command of both the written and the spoken word.[31]

As he continues his sketch, Pace fastens upon a single characteristic of More's universal eloquence: he possesses no common degree of humor and suavity (*non uulgariter facetus ... & urbanus*). In fact, one might conclude that Charm itself (*leporem ipsum*) was his father and Humor (*facetiam*) his mother. For his part, Erasmus agrees with Hutten that the writings of More are unexcelled in learning and in merriness (*nihil esse potest neque doctius neque festiuius*). He finds that More's countenance corresponds with his interior disposition and always displays a charming and friendly merriness (*gratam et amicam festiuitatem*). But the term which fixes More's most prominent trait for Erasmus is "sweetness" (*suauitas*), with all its connotations of lovableness, freshness, and agreeableness. In another place in the letter to Hutten, Erasmus praises More's "rare courtesy and sweetness of manner" (*rara comitas ac morum suauitas*), so that he can cheer up the most gloomy persons. In his letter to Budé, Erasmus again speaks of More's union of great prudence "with great sweetness of manner" (*cum tanta morum suauitate*).[32]

It is difficult to find an English term which defines More's type of humor in a completely satisfactory manner. Always tempered with courtesy and charity, his humor is far from buffoonery, horseplay, or boisterous hilarity. Thomas More himself and his contemporaries use what may be probably the best word: *merriment*. The latter, however, must carry with it all the connotations of the sixteenth century: not only the lively enjoyment of festivity or play but also a certain agreeableness, pleasantness, and even happiness. Thus, William Roper reports that More before his death said to console

Master Pope: "I trust that we shall, once in heaven, see ech other full merily.
...." Even more revelatory of his *festivitas* is the remark of the Messenger to
More in *A Dialogue Concerning Heresies:* "ye vse ... to loke so sadly whan ye
mene merely [merrily], that many times men doubte whyther ye speke in
sporte, whan ye mene good ernest."[33]

But More is not always the personification of sweetness and light. Pace
continues: "Sometimes, that is to say, when the occasion demands, he imitates excellent chefs and sprinkles everything with the sharp vinegar of wit."
Whenever he wishes to exploit it, he reveals a keen nose for satire which places
him among the very masters of the art. Moreover, he employs it so artfully
that not a muscle or line of his countenance betrays his satirical purpose.
More had later to reassure Richard Croke that he need not fear his wit or
satire as a brutal or overwhelming force: he had no wish to be so exceedingly
witty as to excite dread. Erasmus, like Pace, highlights More's delight in
penetrating shafts of wit. This love of wit, even when directed against himself,
had manifested itself in his younger days in the composition of epigrams and
in partiality for Lucian. Erasmus declares, moreover, that More seems born to
indulge in jests, but never in those of the buffoonish or the stinging type. He
enjoys the cleverness of the learned, the folly of the ignorant and stupid, and
the tricks of the motley fool. Toward women, and his own wife in particular,
he always behaves playfully and jokingly. In fact, he gets more obedience and
service out of his wife by compliments and jests than other husbands by
severity and browbeating.[34]

At first sight, Pace seems to turn abruptly from More's wit and humor to
his philosophy. But he really does so only in order to revert to his Lucianic
wit and satire. In the science of philosophy, More gives every school a qualified approval and admires each according to the doctrines in which it excels.
In a word, he is an eclectic. Erasmus tells Hutten that More had early applied
himself to the study of philosophy and had had at least a taste of Scholastic
discipline in the university before devoting himself to the pursuit of law.
Many years later, he described More to Bishop Faber of Vienna as a "nature
wholly philosophical" (*ingenio plane philosophico*), which could manifest
itself in such a detail as absolute candor about his social rank and birth.[35]

In spite of the fact that his system is generally eclectic, More has attached
himself to one particular school—"as almost all people do," Pace adds slyly.
This is the school of the Greek philosopher, Democritus (460?–357? B.C.).
It was not the atomistic theories of Democritus that appealed to More, but
his traditional attitude toward life: "he had a laugh for all things human."
In Pace's eyes, More not only imitates the "Laughing Philosopher" most
assiduously but even surpasses him "by one syllable" (*una syllaba*), namely,
the prefix *de-* in Latin. Democritus regarded all human affairs as the proper
object of laughter (*ridenda*), but More views them as the fitting target for
ridicule (*deridenda*).[36] In consequence, the sketch continues, "Richard Pace
is accustomed, by way of jest, to call his very close friend Thomas More the
son or the successor of Democritus." Erasmus describes More's countenance
as pleasantly and amicably merry and somewhat set in the guise of a person

smiling or laughing (*ad ridentis habitum compositus*). He, too, does not hesitate to apply the name of the Laughing Philosopher to More. In the dedicatory preface of *The Praise of Folly* (1511), moreover, he had reminded his English friend that the latter constantly enjoys jests that unite learning and liveliness and that amid the common life of mortals he acts wholly the part of a Democritus (*omnino in communi mortalium vita Democritum quendam agere*). In the letter to Hutten (1519), he repeats that, in view of the pleasure that he derives from all sorts of people, one would label More as "another Democritus" (*alterum quendam . . . Democritum*). Erasmus then adds what he believes a better comparison: More is like the Pythagorean philosopher who, free in mind, strolls through the market place and contemplates the uproar of buyers and sellers. In view of More's connections with the London merchants, Erasmus' comparison is unwittingly ironical![37]

As a final point, Pace mentions the great war which More has declared against the ignominious people whose words are neither true, nor probable, nor befitting their characters. (More himself, as Erasmus later told Bishop Faber, was of such a philosophical and hence truthful disposition that he never pretended to or boasted about distinguished birth.) In this regard, More possesses the trait which had appealed to him and Erasmus in Lucian, namely, the latter's hatred of and animosity toward all superstition and hypocrisy in the spiritual life and all sham and superciliousness in the intellectual life.[38] To illustrate his point, Pace tells the story of More's encounter with two Scotistic theologians—of the reputedly graver sort, he adds, who monopolize the lecture platform and who had launched an ignorant and impious attack on Colet's attitude toward war.[39] These two geniuses, in all seriousness, were mutually supporting each other's affirmation that King Arthur[40] had made a toga for himself from the beards of giants whom he had slain in battle.[41] Thomas More, who apparently was still in his teens, asked how this could be done. The older theologian put on a very grave expression and said: "The reason, my lad, is manifest and the cause evident, namely, the skin of a dead man stretches wonderfully." The younger not only set his seal of approval on this reason but applauded it as subtle and Scotistic. On his part, More played the role of "lad" well: he confessed his total ignorance of the hitherto unknown phenomenon, and added: "This, nevertheless, is extremely well-known: one of you milks a he-goat and the other holds a sieve under to catch the milk" (*alterum ex uobis hircum mulgere, alterum cribrum subijcere*). Seeing that they did not understand his comment on the impossibility of their solution and the foolishness of their mutual admiration, he took his departure, "laughing to himself and ridiculing them" (*ridens sibi, & eos deridens*).[42]

What credence should be given to this anecdote? There is no reason to doubt its substantial truth. Pace could easily have obtained it from More himself and would probably not have risked More's displeasure by foisting a fictitious story upon him. Erasmus relates in 1519 how, when Henry VIII wished to relax his mind with pleasant tales, he could not find a merrier raconteur as his companion than More. The prudence of Pace in retelling and publicizing a story perhaps intended only for private circulation is another matter. More himself hesitated to include the far less ridiculous story of the friar theologian in Book I of *Utopia* and did so only on the advice of literary friends.[43]

Pace brings his sketch to a close with a lament. One misfortune dogs the footsteps of his More. As often as he falls into most learned and most acute discussion "among those 'white-capped' Fathers of yours" (*inter uestros leucomitratos patres*),[44] presumably Scotistic philosophers and theologians, in their own science of philosophy and theology in which he too is expert, they invariably censure him and call all his statements "juvenile" (*puerilia*). The reason is not that they really judge him a target deserving of censure or that they hear a juvenile word drop from his lips. "Rather," Pace concludes, "they envy him his extraordinary genius, and the sciences of which they are ignorant, and the fact that the 'lad' [*puer*], as they term him, far surpasses their graybeards in wisdom." In a word, More can hold his own with the Scholastic theologians and even beat them at their own subtle game of dialectics. As Erasmus was to tell Hutten: "You cannot conceive anyone more acute in disputations, so that he often gives trouble even to the best theologians, contending in their own field."[45]

What value is the scholar or the biographer to attach to Pace's sketch of 1517? It would hardly be fair to compare it in every detail with Erasmus' account given to Hutten in 1519. Erasmus' letter was composed expressly and exclusively as a biography. Consequently, it is careful, full, and balanced. Pace's sketch, on the other hand, is given in passing in a work devoted to the praise of learning. Therefore, it possesses brevity and fixes upon the outstanding features of its subject. Erasmus' portrait is priceless and indispensable, but Pace's sketch, nevertheless, is valuable and interesting.

Nor is this all. Pace's sketch verges on a caricature in the better sense of the term, i.e., it tends to exaggerate one characteristic over others. Pace pays due tribute to More's universal knowledge, his mastery of languages, his powers of expression, and his skill in disputation. But what receives most prominence and space is More's merriness. He has an unextinguishable love for jests, for wit, and for satire. In spite of More's philosophical eclecticism, Pace labels him another Democritus, another Laughing Philosopher, who laughs down all shams and follies, especially in the intellectual life. Here his favorite target may be the friar theologians. Erasmus, too, lays emphasis on More's predilection for humor and wit, but he is far more careful to stress the moderating influences: More's courtesy, sweetness, and charity. His jokes and satire are never scurrilous or mordacious. In March, 1518, Beatus Rhenanus, too, signalizes the goodnatured quality of More's humor.[46]

In the beginning of this essay, the statement was made that Pace's sketch is the account of More's character and attitude closest to the time of the composition of *Utopia*. Can the sketch contribute anything to the explanation of *Utopia*? If Newman can label literature as "the personal use or exercise of language," and if Buffon can speak of style as "the man himself," *Utopia* may have to be interpreted much more than hitherto in the spirit of humor and wit. When the occasion demanded seriousness, no one, says Erasmus, could be more prudent in deliberation than Thomas More. What struck his friends and the early readers of *Utopia*, however, was not only his learning, but especially his merriness—in his writings no less than in his life.[47]

This merriness does not contradict or invalidate the fundamental serious-ness of More's purpose in the *Utopia*. If it is "characteristic of More," as Chambers rightly observes, "to see the humorous side of martyrdom,"[48] it is no less characteristic of him to adopt a playful tone and a pleasant fiction in setting forth the ideas dearest to him. Truth, to use a homely comparison of More himself, may lawfully be smeared with the honey of fiction or imagina-tion to make it more palatable.[49] All literary flavor in the *Utopia* is a means to the end: the insinuation of ideas into the minds of readers. There is urgent need, consequently, for a study of the literary "tone" of More's *Utopia*, as a whole and in its parts. This study must needs be delicate, balanced, and thorough. It would help to determine More's complex underlying attitude: toward the world portrayed in Utopia and toward radical and universal reform in Europe.

ROPER'S *LIFE OF MORE*

R. S. SYLVESTER

The main biographical dimensions of Thomas More's career have been superbly covered in a recent volume, *St. Thomas More: Action and Contemplation.*[1] Because the contributors to this volume have done their work so well, I feel considerably less guilty with regard to the limitations that I have imposed on my three lectures. I shall not be concerned with the complex, and often very debatable, details of More's legal career; nor do I intend to deal, except for an occasional digression, with the literary works which he produced after his retirement from the chancellorship in 1532. My gratitude to other More scholars is deepened by our mutual realization that no one can write well about every aspect of More's complex life and literary career; the study of his life and works, like the editing of his writings, is a cooperative, almost a communal, affair. My own point of focus centers on More's literary personality, on the various roles which, as author, he assigns to himself and to others in producing his voluminous works. I would merely hope that this kind of interest in the "Man For All Seasons" will encourage other perspectives. Thomas More was, for John Colet and for Erasmus, "England's only genius";[2] if we are to comprehend that genius in its manifold dimensions then we must keep ourselves open to every possible approach which may throw light upon it.

I begin then, with William Roper's *Life of More,* the first vernacular biography and the basic source for all of the future lives. In assigning this primacy to Roper, I do not mean to neglect Erasmus' sustained character sketch of 1519 (the letter to Hutten) nor to discount the many more or less shrewd comments on More delivered by his contemporaries. These notices are valuable, but, even when taken together, they do not add up to a fully developed view of More's personality. Roper, writing of his father-in-law in the 1550s with intimate affection, claims that "no man living" understood so much of More "and of his doings" as himself.[3] It is a proud claim, one which, for many later critics, is scarcely borne out by Roper's spare narrative. Historians have been quick to pounce on Roper's errors of fact. They have often questioned either the basis or the details of several of his anecdotes. At his best, so runs the argument, Roper offers a series of valuable notes; he provides only a *memoir,*[4] and a very limited one at that, telling us nothing

Reprinted from *Moreana,* 36 (1972), 47–59, by permission of the author and the publisher. This is the first of a sequence of three lectures which were delivered at Yale University on April 6, 10 and 13, 1972. In the text presented here, a few revisions have been made.

about More's international fame and almost completely neglecting More's
writings—not even, in fact, mentioning *Utopia* at all.

Whatever justice there may be in views like these, they are singularly un-
helpful in that they tend, as negative criticism, to lead readers away from
Roper's *Life* instead of attempting to understand his method and to evaluate
his very real achievement. We ought rather to ask just what Roper's own
"understanding" of More entails, trying then to see how this knowledge can
serve to guide us when we come to consider other aspects of More's career
which Roper himself does not mention. I am convinced, for my own part,
that most of Roper's omissions are quite deliberate. He eschews a full and
detailed biography because, for his purposes, it is not necessary. Besides, he
had already enlisted the services of, as it were, a top-notch rewrite man,
Nicholas Harpsfield, who was to produce, within a year or two, precisely the
kind of lengthy narrative that he himself had so scrupulously refrained from
writing.[5]

Roper feels, in other words, that a massive agglomeration of facts about
More's life will not contribute that much to the essential understanding of
his subject. For him, though he preserves a rough chronological progression
in his narrative, it is not so much the sequence or the fullness of events that
matters, but rather the symbolic value that any given event may have, both
in itself and in its relation to other anecdotes which precede or follow it. For
the most part, Roper will not analyze, and he will not supply transitions. He
tells three little stories to illustrate More's "innocency and clearness" of
conscience in refusing to accept bribes; but, instead of continuing in this vein,
he asks his readers "by these few . . . with their own judgements wisely to
weigh and consider the same" (p. 64). Such a method is essentially dramatic.
It asks us to participate in the action as we endeavor to understand—and it
indicates, as I shall try to show later, that the influence of Thomas More on
William Roper was not merely moral and paternal but profoundly literary as
well.

Roper thus writes out of the fullness of knowledge, but he concentrates
his understanding to the utmost, recreating Thomas More for us in a series of
scenes that can easily, as Robert Bolt and others have realized, be transferred
directly to the stage. It is not difficult, as my dear friend and teacher, Davis
P. Harding, used to remark, to underestimate Roper in this biography. In fact,
he almost wilfully compounds our difficulties for us by dramatizing himself,
"son Roper", as a naïve misunderstander of many of More's actions. When
More, sitting sadly in his boat during his last trip down the Thames from
Chelsea to Lambeth, suddenly turns and says, "Son Roper, I thank our Lord
the field is won," Roper can only reply "Sir, I am thereof very glad," loath to
seem ignorant though "I wist not what he meant thereby" (p. 73).

A scene like this one (and there are many such in the *Life*) enables us to
pinpoint one central aspect of Roper's method. By dramatizing his own misunderstanding of More in the past, he provides us with a device through which
we can come to comprehend something of the mysterious greatness embodied
in a man who seldom failed to understand himself and his surroundings.

Roper's seeming lack of control over his story—his hesitancy in analyzing and
the insufficiency of his analyses when they are directly offered—is essential to
the part which he plays in his narrative. To play a part like this, to cast oneself
in such a role, becomes, dramatically, a way of understanding the play itself.

If we are alert to these dramatic values in Roper's biography, then we shall
be much less inclined to criticize him for incompleteness. He knows, as author,
far more than he understands as character, and this knowledge emerges not only
in his creation of his persona but in the structure and placing of his anecdotes.
It is true that Roper does not set More's life on an international stage, but the
first sentence and the final scene of his *Life* provide a framework which is as
universal as sixteenth-century Europe could desire. He starts with a quotation
from Erasmus, the most renowned scholar of his day: More was, in Erasmus'
words, "more pure and white than the whitest snow, and of such an angelical
wit that England never had the like before, nor never shall again" (p. 3). He
ends, one hundred pages later, with the judgement of Charles V, delivered, it
is said—and here Roper adjusts history to his purposes—when the emperor
received the news of More's death: "We say, that if we had been master of
such a servant, of whose doings ourself have had these many years no small
experience, we would rather have lost the best city of our dominions than to
have lost such a worthy councillor" (p. 104). These two testimonies frame
Roper's narrative for us; sanctioned by the witness of the most learned and
the most powerful voices in Europe, he can confidently tell his tale of this
"man of singular virtue and of a clear, unspotted conscience." We have been
reminded, and the reminder is sufficient, of what "the general council of
Christendom" thought of the Thomas More who died for its corporate ideals
rather than "conform his conscience to the council of one realm" (p. 95).

Roper's concluding anecdote of the ruler who could value a councillor
more than a city is carefully linked to an early episode in the *Life* where
More, after patiently suffering through Roper's congratulations on Henry VIII's
ardent affection for him, remarks: "Howbeit, son Roper, I may tell thee I
have no cause to be proud thereof, for if my head could win him a castle in
France, it should not fail to go" (p. 21). More's prophetic words both anticipate and are echoed by Charles' final reflection; the early anecdote lives on in
and is enlarged by the later one. Roper's method is brilliantly illustrated by
this kind of relationship which he manages to effect between his seemingly
self-contained episodes. Many of his scenes appear to be little gems, perfect in
their isolation; but the light which they emit is heightened and intensified by
similar, yet contrasting, episodes that precede or follow them in the narrative.

Nowhere is this clearer than in the two scenes which Roper employs to
show us More at the beginning and at the end of his life. Here is More, aged
about fourteen, at the house of Chancellor Morton, where

> though he was young of years, yet would he at Christmastide suddenly
> step in among the players, and never studying for the matter, make a part
> of his own there presently among them, which made the lookers-on more
> sport than all the players beside. In whose wit and towardness the Cardinal

much delighting, would often say of him unto the nobles that divers times
dined with him, "This child here waiting at the table, whosoever shall live
to see it, will prove a marvellous man." (p. 5)

More's life, for Roper, begins with its hero on the stage—and it ends with another stage scene:

And so was he by Master Lieutenant brought out of the Tower, and from
thence led towards the place of execution. Where, going up the scaffold,
which was so weak that it was ready to fall, he said merrily to master
Lieutenant: "I pray you, master Lieutenant, see me safe up, and for my
coming down let me shift for my self."

Then desired he all the people thereabout to pray for him, and to bear
witness with him that he should now there suffer death in and for the faith
of the holy catholic church. Which done, he kneeled down, and after his
prayers said, turned to the executioner, and with a cheerful countenance
spake thus to him: "Pluck up thy spirits, man, and be not afraid to do
thine office; my neck is very short; take heed therefore thou strike not
awry, for saving of thine honesty."

So passed Sir Thomas More out of this world to God, upon the very
same day in which himself had most desired. (pp. 102–03)

Roper tells us, immediately before this final scene, that Henry had requested More to "use few words" at his execution, an ironic request indeed
after More had already been convicted for his silence in the king's great matter. But Henry wants no scaffold speeches—he wishes to deny More the
opportunity "to make a part of his own," adding words to the prescribed text,
as he had done, with Morton's blessing, so many years before at Lambeth
Palace. More seems to comply with Henry's request, even though, as he tells
Master Pope, he "had purposed at that time somewhat to have spoken"
(p. 101). Yet, in his final scene, just as surely as in his first youthful role,
More manages to control the action on the stage. This is a shaky, unsound
scaffold, quite unlike the festive boards at Lambeth. One's improvisations are
limited, but there is no place for bad acting. 'Play your part well' ("do thine
office"), More instructs his fellow actor. 'Your honesty and mine depend
upon our acceptance of our roles' (p. 103). Even the exact date of this last
performance (July 6, the eve of the feast of Becket and the octave of St.
Peter) is arranged in accordance with More's wishes—though not, Roper lets
us know,[6] without a bit of providential contrivance.

Thus Roper ties together the opening and the closing scenes of his *Life*,
presenting us with his portrait of this man of many parts. The first anecdote
is light-hearted, merry, as More performs to the delight of both himself and
his audience. Yet even here, for all the twelfth-night gaiety, all the forecast of
brilliant accomplishment, the Cardinal's words ("who shall live to see it") cast
a momentary shadow of death over the platform. At Tower Hill, on the other
hand, the scene is grimly earnest, the audience tearfully sorrowing. But somehow a note of supreme merriment plays about the scaffold. More's wit in the

face of death, his confident composure in a performance under pressure, lead us back to the early scene, as we wonder, perhaps, if the truly marvellous side of this man's life is only now about to begin.

More's words to Master Lieutenant ("I pray you, see me safe up, and for my coming down let me shift for myself") can in fact be read as reflecting, in little, the pattern of his whole life. Others—his father, his teachers, friends at court, Wolsey, the king himself—have "seen him safe up", providing roles for him which he did not so much seek as accept when offered. While Roper may overemphasize More's reluctance to become a royal councillor,[7] it remains true that, up to and during the time of his chancellorship, More appears, in the *Life,* as a man who had greatness thrust upon him. As office after office is given to him, he must struggle to preserve a sense of his own identity, even, at one point (p. 12), deliberately "dissembling his nature", playing the part of the boor, so that the king would not require his attendance at court so frequently. More is not without wit in the first half of the *Life,* but, paradoxically, he is much more serious during his rise than he is after his fall. It is here, fairly early in the *Life,* that Roper tells us of his hair-shirt and of his private flagellation (pp. 48–49). Most of More's ominous, prophetic statements are uttered while he is in the midst of prosperity and it is then, not later, that he advises his children concerning the wiles of the devil and reminds them that they can't expect to go to heaven on featherbeds (pp. 26–27).

I spoke above of More's "fall", but the term is not apt. In the matter of his "coming down" More is not the victim of fortune, but rather its master. He now "shifts for himself", resigning the chancellorship of his own accord, and, in Roper's words, "pretending, for certain infirmities of his body" (p. 51), that he was unable any longer to serve. In the second half of the *Life,* his spirits mount as his prosperity wanes. The word "merry" echoes in scene after scene, as More tells his wife and family that, "if they would encourage him [as they will not] to die in a good cause," he would "for very joy thereof, 'merrily' run to death" (p. 56). He speaks "merrily" to the bishops who come to invite him to Anne Boleyn's coronation (pp. 57–59) and he puzzles Roper —again—with his "merriness" after his first encounter with the king's commissioners (p. 69). He plays the fool "merrily" with his wife, Dame Alice, when she visits him in the Tower (pp. 82–84), and his last words at his trial form a prayer for his judges that "we may yet hereafter in heaven 'merrily' all meet together" (p. 96).

There is one beautifully-situated scene in Roper (pp. 52–54) which seems to sum up the principles through which More exercized his masterly control of his situation. It comes immediately after he has given up the great seal. His family assembles together, all of them worried about their circumstances, for More would now no longer be able to pay all their expenses as he had previously done. More asks for their advice, but no one offers to help. He then assumes the role of speaker himself, "showing his poor mind unto them." "I have been brought up", he says, summarizing his whole career, "at Oxford, at an Inn of Chancery, at Lincoln's Inn, and also in the King's Court ... from the lowest degree to the highest. Yet I have now little above 100 £ a year left to me. If we are to continue together, all must become contributories; but, by my counsel, it shall not be best for us to fall to the lowest fare first." More then suggests a gradual descent, first to Lincoln's Inn fare, then to New Inn fare, and so forth, remarking as he goes how one can be well content at each level. Finally, if even Oxford fare fails, "then may we yet, with bags and wallets, go a begging together, and hoping that for pity some good folk will give us their charity, at every man's door to sing *Salve Regina,* and so still keep company and be merry together."

This is shifting for oneself with a vengeance! But More's own composure here is never in doubt. Each downward step is as completely foreseen, as carefully rehearsed and as fully controlled, as those last sad steps to the scaffold. Whatever the role, whatever the part assigned, let us play it to the best of our abilities, "merrily" indeed, even if it means becoming the most devotedly happy beggars in Christendom. For the man who has so completely triumphed over himself—and I think this is one thing which Roper means by his constant references to More's "unspotted conscience"—the assumption of such roles is managed with an innocent simplicity. And yet, beneath this calm surface, this easy flexibility, what a sense of struggle and poignant agony! For "conscience", as Roper uses the term to describe More, indicates not only a profound moral integrity; conscience is also, etymologically, and in sixteenth-century usage, a "knowing with", a full and special awareness of both oneself and the world about one. Playing one's part conscientiously entails playing it with full consciousness of the other actors in the drama. The role More felt called upon to play was not, ultimately, one which he could share with his family. In that lay the human tragedy of his death, but in that too lay the grounds of his glory.

If we look back now to consider briefly the genre out of which Roper's biography grows, that of the medieval saint's life, we can, I think, marvel at the transformation he has wrought in it. More's "saintliness" (Roper himself never calls it that) is not of the conventional order. He works no miracles, has no halo around his cradle, never hears voices from heaven, never receives, as did the Nun of Kent,[8] divine revelations of Henry VIII's wickedness. The trial which Roper describes is not a combat with the devil, but an all-too-human story of a perjured witness and coerced judges. More's virtues are those of the layman, not of the priest, but so too are his trials and sufferings—a fact which he wistfully realizes as, through his window in the Tower, he watches the first band of London Carthusians going "cheerfully to their deaths as bridegrooms to their marriage" (p. 80). The marriages of priests are made in heaven; More's own, as Dame Alice never tired of reminding him, was much more earthly.

More's comments on the execution of the Carthusians take us back, like so many of Roper's later anecdotes, to an earlier scene in the *Life.* We recall how More, while still studying law, had lived for four years in the house of these very same monks, playing the part then of the committed man of religion, testing, trying out the cowl, and finding, in the end, that it did not quite fit. He can sympathize with the painful scene before him now, because he had, in a sense, acted in it earlier; but this recollection scarcely lessens the anguish which he feels at not being able to share their lot. In contrast, he says, to their "strait, hard, penitential and painful life", his own career has been "consumed in pleasure and ease licentiously." But we know, thanks to Roper's telling scenes, that More, even here, is again playing a part, presenting himself as an abject sinner, "a most wicked caitiff", a role that in real life he hardly indulged in, but one which he must assume now as he throws himself on God's mercy.

I do not mean to suggest for a minute that More is being insincere in this moment of self-accusation. He is simply, once again, testing himself, trying out a part, and finding, this time, that it may well suit him perfectly. He is never unaware of the ambiguities posed by the great traditional metaphor of "All the world's a stage", a *topos* which reached back at least to his beloved Lucian and which had recently inspired one of the most eloquent passages in Pico della Mirandola's *Oration on the Dignity of Man.*[9] The image, as it came down to More, was double-edged: if reality was but a passing show, then human life, in itself, was transitory and had no essential value. One could join, in near despair, the throng of unreflecting fools on the stage; or one could, like the Carthusians, turn away from the theater itself and live only for a transcendent future. But the image, as Pico proclaimed it, could offer a contrary perspective. The playing of different parts by "Protean man"[10] might, if consciously elected, be an educative process. By becoming someone else, man could extend his capacities and perhaps come to understand himself more fully. As Pico had noted, such transformations could be dangerous, for man the actor, if he were not careful, could play parts beneath himself, debasing his capacities instead of enlarging them. Yet the prospect was exciting, dramatically exhilarating, and it did much to shape the aspirations of many a Renaissance man.

More's own employment of the stage *topos,* both in his life and in his art, constantly endeavors to do justice to the several aspects of the image. His supreme ability to play a part is always being checked and balanced, in Roper's biography, by his reluctance to accept a role which he has not chosen for himself. He refuses, again and again, to separate the moral implications of role-playing from the aesthetic satisfactions which it offers. Long before he went to the Tower, he had dwelt, in his meditation on the *Four Last Things* (1522), on the image of life not as a stage, but as a prison, where "the king, by whose high sentence we be condemned to die, would not of this death pardon his own son."[11] But this devout medieval insight did not prevent him, in 1534, from turning his real prison into a stage, telling an uncomprehending Dame Alice that he was quite content in his "gay house" (p. 83) and reminding Master Lieutenant that, if he proved to be an ungrateful guest, he could always be "thrust out of the door" (p. 77).

The comic element in scenes like this, as in the final scene on the scaffold, puzzled many of More's contemporaries, and it has often been slighted or ignored by later critics. The chronicler Edward Hall could not approve of More's jokes in the face of death and he ended his account by remarking that "I cannot tell whether to call him a foolish wiseman or a wise foolish man."[12] But More knew exactly what he was doing. Since "the field was won" before the battle began, then the battle itself could be treated mock-heroically. The king's good servant would never serve (or die) more truly than when he did not serve at all. Nor would More, on the other hand, deliberately seek the alternative role open to him,[13] the martyrdom which he could have chosen by explicitly denying the royal supremacy. He would, perforce, play the martyr's part at the end, but not until he, drawing upon all the resources which his legal training had given him, had used every possible human means "to avoid that indictment" (p. 86).

More's trial at Westminster Hall, as Roper dramatizes it for us, seems almost to take on a kind of sublime absurdity. The conclusion is forgone, the script is rigidly prescribed; the actors, all but one, must play the part which is set down for them. Grim as the farce was, More must have relished the moment when he told the court that he was, as all just men knew, miscast for the role of traitor which had "so wrongfully been imagined" (p. 91) against him. And he must have smiled to himself as he watched Lord Audley, More's successor as Lord Chancellor, try to shrug off the burden of judgement by appealing to Fitz-James, the Lord Chief Justice, for a technical opinion which would validate the proceedings. Fitz-James did himself proud, ignoring every moral issue in the case, ridiculously prefacing his opinion with an oath to St. Julian (the patron saint of hospitality), as he said: "My lords, I must needs confess that if the act of parliament be not unlawful, then is not the indictment in my conscience insufficient" (p. 95). Technically, as Professor Elton has recently shown,[14] Fitz-James was absolutely correct; but the "conscience" upon which he relies here is, like his syntax, a crippling, negative, puny thing, far different from the conscience, and the consciousness, of the man whose story Roper tells.

More could not, one feels, have staged it any better himself. He had, after all, been ever given to the "putting of cases," a habit instilled in him from his years as a law student when, after spending their mornings observing real cases in the courts, the young lawyers would devote their afternoons to moot trials in the mock courts at the Inns. But the hypothetical case, the imagined situation, had now been turned into a matter of life and death. As if to tighten the ironies even further, Roper makes the case for the crown hinge on the "putting of cases," or discussion of hypothetical possibilities, which had occurred during the interview between More and Richard Rich in the Tower (pp. 84–86). More maintains at his trial that, even if he had spoken the words Rich attributed to him (which he denies), this would not in itself be treasonable, for the conversation "affirmed nothing and was only the putting of cases." But More's crucial distinction between a direct statement, which involves a full personal commitment, and the detached, imaginary entertainment of an idea is lost in a court like this. If one can no longer understand the distinction between the role that a man might elect to play before others and the role which he believed, in his inmost being, to be truly his own, then one must inevitably misunderstand Thomas More. The verdict is "guilty as charged."

I hope to deal elsewhere, in further detail, with More's penchant for "the putting of cases."[15] With him, this was never a merely legal activity, but rather a kind of simultaneous exercise of the moral and literary imagination. His poetic and dramatic ability, which he passed on in no small measure to William Roper, cannot be separated from his deepest spiritual instincts. His witty roleplaying, even in the shadow of death, infuses his Christian virtue with a genial comic spirit. For More, every trial was a spiritual exercise; but, and with equal force, each of his religious insights is enriched by the play of his creative fancy. During his stay in the Tower, More turned, like any good Christian might, to the consolation of the Psalms and to meditation on Christ's passion. His annotated Psalter, now in the Beinecke Library at Yale,[16] shows us how he applied the words of the suffering David to his own, equally isolated, situation. His last literary work, the *Expositio Passionis,* is a piercing dramatization of Christ's agony in the garden in which the Savior himself is made to speak in the accents of Thomas More: "Pluck up thy courage, faint heart, and despair never a deal," or, to the sleeping Peter, "What, Simon, here playest thou not the part of Cephas, for why shouldst thou any more be called Cephas, that is to wit, a stone, which name I gave thee heretofore to have thee steadfast and strong?"[17]

To play the part of Christ in this way and at this hour was far from easy for More. He might, he knew, seem to arrogate too much to himself by taking on such a role. But then, if it were done tentatively, as a kind of literary experiment, it might go somewhat better than the putting of cases to Richard Rich. There was leisure enough now for the trial, and More could even amuse himself by turning again, as he had not done for at least twenty years, to the making of English verses. Two stanzas were preserved by William Rastell in the *English Works* of 1557 and one of these is also given by Roper. Rastell calls them "two short ballettes"; but More, always creating characters for himself, entitles the first "Lewis the Lost Lover":

> Aye flattering Fortune, look thou never so fair,
> Nor never so pleasantly begin to smile,
> As though thou wouldst my ruin all repair,
> During my life thou shalt not me beguile!
> Trust I shall God to enter in a while
> His haven of Heaven, sure and uniform:
> Ever after thy calm, look I for a storm.

After Lewis, comes "Davy the Dicer," and with him I conclude for this evening:

> Long was I, lady luck, your serving man,
> And now have lost again all that I gat,
> Wherefore when I think on you now and then,
> And in my mind remember this and that,
> Ye may not blame me, though I beshrew your cat;
> But, in faith, I bless you again a thousand times,
> For lending me now some leisure to make rhymes.[18]

APOLOGY FOR AN EXECUTION

W. Gordon Zeeveld

"Truly, sir, I am a poor fellow that would live," says Pompey in Shakespeare's *Measure for Measure,* by way of excuse for serving as helper to a hangman, and his wit comes near to exonerating the hanging profession. The moral predicament from which Pompey so blandly extricates himself is not wholly unlike that which confronted Richard Morison, a destitute scholar in the household of Reginald Pole in Padua until Thomas Cromwell recognized his potential talents as a propagandist and put him to work in defense of the government position at just the moment when the execution of Fisher and More gave him the opportunity to display his powers. The result was *Apomaxis,* which though it was not published until 1538, nevertheless remains the first official answer to that criticism to be printed. Thus the closing off of one career had opened the way to another. Morison had found his profession in the exigency of the divorce of Catherine of Aragon. Fifteen years thereafter, still basking in the bright sunshine of court favor, he would experience the satisfaction—not without its ironies—of appointment to the post of ambassador at the court of her nephew, Charles V. There is a beguiling picture of his sudden preferment in *The Letters and Papers of Henry VIII* as he joined with Queen Jane in the fashionable card game, *sent,* as the royal barge drifted idly on the Thames. On such an occasion, he might well have reflected that the cards had fallen right for him, and that at the critical moment following the executions, his skill had been a major factor in parrying the attack.

The executions of Fisher and More were of course deliberate acts, in conformity to the Act of Royal Supremacy and the Act of Succession, the reaction to which, both at home and abroad, had been calculated before the axe fell. Henry's action on the divorce had been extremely circumspect, and his decision in June of 1535 to pursue that policy by the legal means available could not have been made without due consideration of the already demonstrated acquiescence of the English people, particularly in the case of Elizabeth Barton and the Carthusian monks. But was this a true test of the public temper? It could be argued that London alone, not the country at large, was witness to the day by day events, that the victims were after all obscure figures, and this in an age when torture and execution were no novelty. The proceedings could therefore hardly be expected to arouse public opinion in

Reprinted from *Moreana,* 15-16 (1967), 353-71, by permission of the author and publisher.

any degree comparable to the same courses against Fisher and especially
More, whose reputation extended far beyond national boundaries. It was still
too early to measure foreign reaction, but it had certainly been far from bel-
licose at the rejection of papal supremacy in the previous year. The two
monarchs most directly involved, Charles and Francis, were presently standing
each other off in Italy and elsewhere, and earthly considerations could be
expected to outweigh idealistic appeals to the unity of Christendom. And
since Charles had hitherto refrained from an active role for Catherine, his aunt,
it was safe to say he would not do so to vindicate either an English bishop or
Henry's chancellor, however creditable in the world's eye. It could be assumed
that Francis in the present case would be even less likely to take up the pope's
cause in England. In the event, their failure to act proved this calculation to be
correct.

The truth is that in spite of the religious tremor which ran across the continent at the news out of England, the political impact abroad was negligible;
and in England, the effect of the executions was to be quite the opposite—an
immediate wave of patriotic sentiment which not only confirmed and solidi-
fied the present stance taken by the government but in fact continued to
energize English policy throughout the Tudor period in spite of Mary's efforts
to reverse it. But who, when the decision was made to execute Fisher and More,
was to know this? A broad defensive strategy not excluding the possibility of
invasion and/or insurrection must be adopted. Here the normal channels of
diplomacy could again be supplemented by the printing press, which had already proved its effectiveness as a weapon in the king's great matter, and
Cromwell, as director of the government program, was too good a politician
not to have mobilized whatever literary talents were immediately at his disposal to respond to the expected attack. His most available resource was the
pulpit.

On June 27th, five days after the execution of Fisher, Simon Matthew,
prebendary of St. Paul's,[1] preached a sermon in the cathedral church. On
July 30th, twenty-four days after the execution of More, it was issued from
the press of Thomas Berthelet *cum privilegio*. Matthew was one of the signa-
tories answering the king's request from the University of Cambridge in 1529
for an opinion on the divorce.[2] We cannot doubt John Strype who called him
a gentle and learned man; that he was a man of moderation the sermon itself
gives adequate proof. The theme of conformity with which he begins his discourse is reminiscent of Tyndale's *Obedience of a Christian Man*. Addressing
those who "under the pretexte of Christianitie ... thynke them selfe at liberte
to disobey their superiors," he advises "euery one to do his duetie to them,
although they were infidels and tyrauntis" (Aiii^v). In studied deference to the
Act of Succession, he asks prayers for "the catholic church of Christendom,
in especial this church of England, our souereign lord the king supreme head
under God of this church, our gracious queen, Queen Anne, my lady Elizabeth, princess and lawful heir to them both." With diplomatic expertise he
corrects the impression created by the sermon preached from the same pulpit
on the previous Sunday (two days before the execution of Fisher): "All

though the laste sonday the preacher could not fynde in his conscience to pray for the soules departed, saying, that he thought his prayer should nothynge auayle them: yet I wyll desyre you to praye for them. . . I have proved from the fathers that we shulde so do: for they are in such case, that they maye be reliued by our prayer."[3]

His ecumenism is seemingly unbounded: "The diuersitie of regions and countreys maketh not the diuersitie of churches but the unitie of feyth maketh all regions one churche, all thoughe the same regions were unknowen to vs and we to them."[4] But this is by way of saying that "manye thousandes are saued, whiche neuer harde of Peter, nor yet of the bishop of Rome" ([Aviii[v]]). His stress is on unity ("Let there be no schism among you": *Corinthians,* xiv; *Ephesians,* iv); but that unity must be fixed steadfastly in God, "not in any mortal creature, as many have thought necessary," and coming near to the essential point of difference, he denies "that if a man shuld be of the churche of Christe, he must be of the holy church of Rome and take the holy father thereof for the supreme head, and for the vicar of Christ, yea for Christ himself." He is equally emphatic in denying that to be divided from the pope would be to be divided from Christ. Out of ignorance, "such damnable teachings . . . have caused men to leave the commandments of God undone for the human traditions." The conclusion is obvious: Let us reform traditions, and not be ashamed to profess truth. "Next unto God the prince ought to be honored . . . The bishop of Rome hath no more power by the laws of God in this realm than any other foreign bishop" (Bii–[Bii[v]]).

How many in Matthew's audience knew that these were the very grounds of the statute, that they were the king's interrogatories to which More "could make no answer"?[5] One thing is certain. No one of them was not thinking of the two men now condemned to die. Condemned? Those are damned indeed who "contemning truth shall study to procure their own death, and so cause other to fall in like damnable error with them" ([Bv[v]]). Matthew descends to the particulars of which they were all wondering spectators:

> As of late you have had experience of some, whom neither friends or kinsfolks, neither the judgment of both universities, Cambridge and Oxford, nor the universal consent of all the clergy of this realm, nor the laws of parliament, nor their most natural and loving prince, could by any gentle ways, revoke from their disobedience, but would needs persist therein, giving pernicious occasion to the multitude to murmer and grudge at the king's laws: seeing that they were men of estimation, and would be seen wiser than all the realm, and of better conscience then other, justifying themselves, and condemning all the realm beside: which being condemned, and the king's prisoners, yet ceased not to conceive ill of our sovereign, refusing his laws, but also in prison [to] write to their mutual comfort in their damnable opinions, I mean doctor Fisher and Sir Thomas More, whom I am as sorry to name as any man here is to hear them named. Sorry, for that they being sometime men of worship and honor, men of famous learning, and many excellent gracis, and so tenderly sometime

beloved of their prince, should thus unkindly, unnaturally, and traitorously use themselves, our lord give them grace to be repentant.[6]

He exhorts his hearers not to be moved by either the fame, learning, or honor of Fisher and More to be anything but loving subjects to their prince, even if the bishop of Rome threaten them with interdictions or excommunications, or other persons with war ([Cviii[V]]). All must practice moderation: the clergy should not "speak of stomach"; "defenders of the king's matters" should not rage, rail, nor scold, "as many are thought to do," calling the pope the harlot of Babylon or the beast of Rome, "for a wise auditory will rather judge such preachers (and I have heard some say so) to be meeter to preach at Paul's wharf then at Paul's cross." (Di–[Di[V]]).

Matthew's sermon offers extremely valuable evidence of the state of the public mind at the precise moment of the executions and of the sensitivity of the crown in response to it. That there were murmurings and grudgings at the king's laws when the decision to condemn became public is clear. That Matthew, a trusted royal servant and no firebrand, was chosen to counteract the preacher of the previous Sunday at St. Paul's (Was it Hugh Latimer?) whose conscience would not allow him supplication for souls (More's cry in 1529) three days after Fisher was condemned,[7] and that he wrote the sermon while both Fisher and More were still alive ("our lord give them grace to be repentant") and More not yet publicly condemned,[8] argues Cromwell's anxiety over the popular reaction to the executions even while they were being carried out. Matthew may not have known, though Cromwell certainly did, that far from being seen "wiser than all the realm," More had professed: "I cannot in everything think the same way that some other men of more wisdom and deeper learning do."[9] In any case, caution while the public mind was being tested is plainly Matthew's (and Cromwell's) intent, and this is further confirmed by its immediate issuance from the king's press. Matthew could be expected to denounce "the damnable opinions" of Fisher and More; it is his equally sharp disapproval of the over-zealous fulminations of "the king's defenders" that reveals the nervous tension of the government. Plainly, Cromwell was very well aware that the quiet wisdom of two "men of estimation" who had responded to argument with silence was exerting a powerful influence on the London public and St. Paul's was the most available rostrum from which to measure dissent and restrain it. Meanwhile, in anticipation of foreign protest, the government case for the royal supremacy could be formally briefed.

Even then, however, the time was shorter than Cromwell knew. On July 26th, a little over a month after the execution of Fisher, and apparently before the news of More's death had reached Italy, Paul III wrote to Ferdinand of Hungary and Francis I requesting their help in implementing the papal displeasure. Remembering, he wrote to Francis, "what your ancestors formerly did for the Holy Roman Church, and with what strength of arms they avenged her injuries, you will when the time comes, and when you are requested of us, enforce justice against the said Henry."[10] Francis, having purposes on earth as well as in heaven, took time to assess the political advantages so fortuitously placed in his hands. Perhaps, as a good son of Holy Church, he should have girded on the whole armor of God ready to strike against Henry at the papal command. That he did nothing of the sort did not make any the less necessary—and indeed suggested—that a government white paper of unquestionable authority be directed across the channel as an immediate essential. For that purpose, there could be no doubt that Cromwell would call on Archbishop Cranmer, architect of the recent policy changes; but more especially Gardiner, whose level legal mind had already proved useful in the king's cause. Not only would Gardiner's talents be pitted against those of More, the most eminent lawyer in the realm, but since currently he was sequestered in his see for his known opposition to the ecclesiastical changes, and in fact was at that moment readying his exculpation, *De vera obedientia,* for the king's press, this new assignment could be urged as a further test of his compliance. Whatever Cromwell's reasons, Gardiner was making no secret of his assiduity in proclaiming the king's cause at a time when he had "as gret cause as any man to desire rest and quiet ... and to absteyne from bookes and wryting ... I seme to be here in otio, and I was never more buysied."[11] But Cromwell was a hard taskmaster, and by late September, Gardiner had produced a draft of an answer to the papal brief. He apologized that he had had no time to polish it with the same care he had devoted to his *Oration;* in fact, he was sending his only copy, which was scarcely legible. Had he been given another day and night, he was sure that he could have "put it *in mundum,*" adding a good portion to the end that was not yet written, "as I divised with my Lord of Cauntourbury to doo."[12]

Gardiner's *De vera obedientia* was put in mundum by Berthelet that same year; yet despite Cromwell's urgency, the answer to the brief remained in manuscript. In fact, Gardiner's holograph together with a fair copy and an English translation reposed unpublished in the Public Record Office until Janelle edited it in 1930.[13] It may be, as Muller suggests, that since the answer to the papal letter was for diplomatic rather than popular use, it was not intended for publication.[14] If so this was probably not the only reason. Cromwell was a pragmatist, and it is difficult to believe that he would have applied such pressures on Gardiner and Cranmer only to bury in diplomatic correspondence what was obviously intended as a major statement of policy. It could be equally useful at home. The English people too needed a reason, and the existence of a translation suggests that the defense was intended for the shop of Berthelet, the king's printer,—that is, for domestic use. Janelle casts doubt on the sincerity of "some at least of Gardiner's assertions" (p. xiv) but he does not elaborate, and of course Cranmer was also involved. In any case, the suggestion of duplicity is irrelevant to the political importance of the document, and that is the main concern here.

At stake, and central to Gardiner's argument, was sovereignty, which Fisher had plainly infringed. Moreover, in resisting his prince he had resisted the ordinance of God (p. 47). One might in good conscience act in accordance with a higher law than man's, but God's law as represented in the Scriptures has been variously interpreted and even misunderstood; and therefore if it comes to a difference of interpretation in the conduct of human affairs, obedience to constituted human law cannot be a sin. As Shakespeare's Henry V was to say, "Every subject's duty is the King's; but every subject's soul is his own." Likewise, the king's duty is to God without an intermediary. It follows that the public responsibilities of the king are none the less inseparable from his sovereignty, and sovereignty by its very nature is unlimited in terrestrial affairs. Henry is God's deputy-elect, but he neither has nor claims any sacerdotal functions; at the same time, he must see to it that in ecclesiastical as well as secular matters, his sovereignty is not violated. And since credally he does not pretend to anything but orthodoxy, his function can hardly be other than protective. His whole duty as God's deputy is "the mayntenance of the comen wealth in his estate" (p. 27), and that estate may not be encroached upon. It is true that he was once obedient to Rome, but those were the years of ignorance. Now England is as it once was, a realm, no longer tributary to the Roman see from which it is separated, we hope forever (pp. 37-39, 41). As for separation from the church universal, "we know none," and we hope that we are contained in it (pp. 37, 65); but we reject papal jurisdiction in secular affairs. Since Fisher's offense was within the area of human law, he was properly judged a traitor and imprisoned therefore. It is to be noted that then and not until then the pope felt him worthy to be a cardinal. He had an open trial; he was found guilty and openly executed. Even supposing Rome had authority to give sanctuary and immunity to all its cardinals, does it extend to those made cardinals for that reason? (pp. 47, 51, 55-57) To Gardiner and Cranmer, Paul's letter was only further evidence of papal interference in internal affairs and a clear violation of English sovereignty.

The reply to Paul was quite obviously official, and considering the advantages of publication, the question still remains why it was not published. The answer may be a matter of tactics. Paul's protest shows no evidence that he knew of the execution of More, and the apologia follows this delimitation very possibly by design, since the charge of traitor against Fisher could be more easily sustained. It certainly weighed against his account that in 1533 he had held secret conferences with Chapuis, Charles's ambassador—conferences that give every appearance of conspiracy.[15] No such charge could be leveled against More, and it was presently apparent that the case against Fisher would not be serviceable against both men. To Simon Matthew's English auditory on the eve of More's execution, the charge was mainly intransigence with a hope of repentance, not treason; but for listeners on the continent, alive to the rumor that More's execution would soon follow Fisher's, the collective offense must be understood unequivocally as directed against the English people. Thus while the answer to Paul had apparently taken pains not to implicate More, government strategy after his death became less precise. When Francis undertook to admonish Henry on the severity of the punishment, he was informed by the newly-appointed ambassador to France, Sir John Wallop, of "their treasons, conspiracies and practices secretly practised, as well within the realm as without, to move and stir dissension, and to sow sedition within the realm, intending thereby not only the destruction of the king, but also the whole subversion of his highness' realm."[16] And though Cromwell very well knew that during the course of the interrogation, Fisher had made particular inquiry whether the word "maliciously" was in the statute [26 Henry VIII, cap. 13], and that "yf it were so, that he thought therby, that a man, speking nothing of malice, did not offende the statute,"[17] he found it expedient to make no exemption of Fisher and More from the others executed as "having such malice rooted in their hearts against their prince and sovereign, and the total destruction of the commonweal of this realm, [that they] were well worthy, if they had had a thousand lives, to have suffered ten times a more terrible death and execution than any of them did suffer."[18] This stance had in fact been adopted in advance of the execution of More. On June 25th, Henry sent orders to all justices of the peace to declare at their sessions "the treasons traitorously committed against us and our laws by the late Bp. of Rochester and Sir Thomas More, Kt. who therby, and by divers secret practices of their malicious mind against us, intended to seminate, engender, and breed among our people and subjects a most mischievous and seditious opinion ... who lately have condignely suffered execution according to their demerits."[19] Such are the politer tergiversations of diplomacy and official pronouncements.

There were other responses on a more informal level where no holds were barred. That fashion was set in the following year with the appearance of Johannes Cochlaeus's *Defensio Clarissimorum Virorum Joannis Fyscheri Episcopi Roffensis et Thomae Mori, adversus Richardum Sampsonem Anglum.* Cochlaeus (Johann Dobneck) was a German controversialist with a penchant for the neo-Ciceronian oratorical style. He had already attacked the divorce in a tract addressed to Pope Paul. In this, his second comment on English affairs, he makes no serious effort to confront the real issue of papal sovereignty. As the title indicates, he prefers to carry the argument to the man. Undoubtedly, he intended to put the condemnation of Fisher and More in the historical context of the divorce, but the *Defensio* slips frequently and more congenially into personal invective. In highly vituperative language he castigates the king's advisors, particularly Richard Sampson, whose *Oratio de dignitate et potestate regis* (1534) had hitherto represented the official position on the divorce. To place the blame for instigating the executions on Sampson was of course supererogatory since the now Bishop of Chichester had not written against Fisher and More at all. Nevertheless Sampson becomes the scapegoat for their deaths, translated into an image of Abner who had not kept watch over King Saul but betrayed him to wicked flatterers.[20] Ultimately he directs his aim at the king himself. Henry has repudiated a holy marriage of thirty years and defamed the child by it; he has killed those who did not approve of it; he has married his mistress; and what is most detestable, he has obtained separation from the Roman Church, a crime all the greater because it has brought eternal death to the whole kingdom, which had hitherto flourished in the Christian faith ([Xiiii^v]-[Yii^v]). It is to the glory of Fisher and More that they have opposed these iniquities and accepted the death penalty in preference to acknowledging the king as supreme head or abrogating—"as you do"—the power of the pope (Ziii). Consequently, he has only scorn for those who ornament the king with his titles. They are Gnathos and evil flatterers, acting impudently and malevolently in a cause which others reject. "How," he asks Sampson with vitriolic sarcasm, "can you presume to teach men so learned and clever, you who cannot even be compared in erudition with them,—you, most obscure man, who until this your nefarious book appeared were unknown in the world?" How can you show "one little letter of divine law" which would justify this perfidious and impious withdrawal of allegiance from the Roman pontiff? By his subtle argument Sampson has blasphemed these men, martyrs of Christ, because they would not obey either pagans or heretic Europeans or a king who gives a name to paganism and heresy. Let Sampson show, if he is able, that Fisher and More would have been disobedient to any lawful and honest command of the king, and he will come off victor over all ([Aa^V]-Aaii). So excellent are they that their deaths can only be regarded as happy. Indeed one might venture the opinion that Henry VIII's martyrs can be compared with Henry II's (Aaiii–Aaiiii). After 400 years, one gathers from Cochlaeus, Rochester had challenged Canterbury in sanctity.

For Cromwell, the question now was whether England could supply a challenge to Cochlaeus in kind. Formal reason was hardly required. The highest episcopal authority had already spoken in the polished accents of Cranmer and Gardiner. Cromwell could of course have commanded their services to defend the action against More as they had already done against Fisher. There is no evidence that he did so. If diatribe was to be answered, it must hop forty paces through the public street and still breathe forth power; it must display eloquence, but occasionally the brash eloquence of London Billingsgate. Cromwell's sound instinct chose for that task Richard Morison. We wish we knew more of that itinerant and indigent scholar who had so confidently advertized his scholarly abilities to Cromwell while accepting harborage in the household of Reginald Pole in Padua. Cromwell had been sufficiently impressed to finance his passage, and from that time on, fortune was merry. A matter of months after the publication of Cochlaeus's *Defensio*, Morison had been assigned to write a reply. He seized the opportunity with avidity, Berthelet setting it in type as fast as the copy rolled from his exuberant pen. Nor was his enthusiasm in the least dampened when shortly thereafter his erstwhile patron, Pole, chose to reveal his carefully concealed opposition to Henry's divorce in an intemperate outburst, *Pro ecclesiasticae unitatis defensione.* It took Morison and the other former members of Pole's household in Padua by surprise, but Morison hastily assured his new master where his loyalties lay: "I am a graft of your Lordship's own setting, and will stand in no other's ground... Other men have but tickled the Pope, I have so pricked him that men shall say I know how to anger popes. Would it were the answer to Mr. Traitor Pole's book; if I thought he would be so mad as to put forth his, I would stop mine and 'turn Cochleus in Polum'."[21]

In this hour of high exhilaration, *Apomaxis* was indeed stopped,—not to turn Cochlaeus into Pole, but to face a national emergency. The news of the October rising in the North, now known as the Pilgrimage of Grace, had reached London, and the king's press and the elated propagandist who was feeding it copy were both diverted to the new front. How much of *Apomaxis* was at that time in print we cannot say. Certainly some, certainly not all.[22] Berthelet's colophon bears the date 1537, though the dedication to Cromwell is a separate signature dated July 12, 1538, over two years after Morison had begun to write it. Confirmatory evidence lies in the text itself, and in the helter-skelter form which Cochlaeus criticized in his consciously tidy answer, *Scopa in araneas,* published in the same year. It is a mere historical accident that *Apomaxis* was not the only attempt of the government to win public support for the executions by means of the press. Nor was it the earliest. But there can be no question of its unique historical value as the official posture adopted by the government for popular consumption. Furthermore, it has bibliographical value as a piece of first-hand reportage put to the use of propaganda. The Ciceronian tricks of debate are all there, scorn mingled with scurrility, exhortation with lamentation, all overlaid with a novel patriotic fervor born in the dust and sweat of the battle, a battle the sounds of which have not been muted by time.

Morison introduces his rebuttal of the calumnies and insults of Cochlaeus's attack on the reputation and deeds of Henry with a Sapphic ode on the *veritas vincit* theme. The magniloquent dedication to Cromwell, written when *Apomaxis* was complete, is an accolade to his administrative ability, particularly in the establishment of "the restored religion" ([Aii^V]), and hopes that the present work will compensate his many benefits, including rescue from his former life. In defending the cause of religion, he is not battling Cochlaeus alone but the whole papal mob—battle line, cohort, and army. Throughout the tract, his enjoyment of the campaign is evident, his zeal boundless. In the heat of the struggle, he flays about him, oftenest at Cochlaeus, sometimes at the pope, in a glorious disarray of vituperation, yet always with a watchful eye to the defense of the king's actions from the attack on Luther to the establishment of an Englished sacred text. Toward Fisher and More, he is deliberately restrained. Not so toward Cochlaeus who has attacked a king who restored religion. Morison's only glory will be love of country and ardor for the faith. The pope once nominated Henry *Defensor Fidei;* that he still is, but in the new light of truth.

Apomaxis answers three charges against Henry: his divorce of Catherine, his assumption of royal supremacy, and his execution of the "pope's defenders." The divorce was no sin, it was rather a too long postponed righting of a wrong, Henry had long lived with Catherine "in place of a wife,"—an evil thing, tolerated because of ignorance [Aiiii^V]. But over and above the pope's dispensation, conscience, operating within the older law of nature, eventually came to his aid ([Biiii]–C). The validity of the marriage must therefore depend on the relative authority of pope and king. Divine law should mediate, but since the appeal to sacred scriptures has always been subject to varying interpretations, Henry's case will in the end be determined by earthly judgments, and the papal record will hardly instil confidence in pronouncements from Rome. The pope has too often acted more like a quaestor of the

treasury than a tribune of the people [Ciiii], more like a priest of Mars or
Bellona than an imitator of the prince of peace ([Ciiii^V]). Allow that the pope
is the sole vicar of Christ on earth. Has he performed the offices of Christ's
vicar? The papal record gives Morison plenteous answer. Clement VII was
vexed that the king had withdrawn from incest, i.e., divorced, thinking, doubtless, that both for a king most worthy of heaven and for Catherine, by far the
most excellent woman of all her estate ("if you overlook her error"), it was a
lesser evil to endanger their salvation than for himself to be reduced in importance or for the limits of his authority, once imposed by Christ, to be re-
established ([Fii^V]). If the pope is indeed a god, as Cochlaeus on the authority
of Pope Nicholas would have him, he must look at himself without the mask
of sanctity and see if it is likely that he should be called even a vicar of God
([Fiiii^V]). Christ did not say, "Feed your sheep", but "my sheep."

Morison strengthens his ridicule of papal authority with putative personal
observation. I who have been in Italy, who have seen the ways of the pontiffs,
who have seen from whom popes spring, with how much impiety they are
elected, what great dissoluteness disgraces their entire life, how they dishonor
God, how they transgress the law when they boast of the law,—I am ashamed
that there is anyone so dull and stupid that he thinks this man is God's vicar
([Iii^V]). Let the pope and his puppet cardinals perish; the church will not
perish. Do you wish the servants of the church to be the church? Is not the
church the bride of Christ? Then wouldn't you laugh if Christ married the
pope, if he solicited the cardinals, if he gave them presents, if he wrote love
letters, and if he would now sing the song of songs for them? ([Iiiii])

What then of the royal supremacy? Morison sees it as a patriotic issue.
When Cochlaeus claims that the pope cannot be thrown out of England without loss of our salvation he causes us no fear. If God is for us, who can be
against us? The king is subject to no one but God himself, and the laws of
God; hence he has power over all those who are established within the boundaries of his kingdom—common people, nobles, priests, and bishops. It need
not be maintained that the king can compel whoever he wishes to whatever
duties he wishes; nevertheless the king has been granted absolute power over
all the inhabitants of his kingdom ([Iiiii^V]). Morison's proof is Samuel's words
to King Saul, "Behold, the Lord has anointed you as head over his inheritance".
The clergy are a part of God's inheritance which in Morison's view he has
turned over to the king. If the king is heir, if there are no bequests, no trusts,
why do these "sons of Belial" wish to be outside the inheritance?

The question so put makes an ally of divine law and thus opens an approach
to the subject of Fisher and More in secular terms. Both men refused the
authority of the king ([Ki^V]). They are unwilling for the prince of the whole
British people to be head of the British church, that is, of the Britons (Gardiner's argument from identity). They concede that he is head of barons and
dukes, but not of friars and monks. Morison is just as ready as Gardiner to
admit that the king should not administer sacred things; but it is the king's
duty to reward a faithful ministry and to punish with fetters, lashes, exile,
and even death those whose obstinacy incites the people to sedition, conditions

them for impiety, and encourages them to oppose the king's honorable actions (Kii). Is it permissible that he wage war against men but not undertake war against sins? ([Kii^v]) In not fearing the papal bulls, England has been an example to other nations, and they too will some day learn to have a little self interest. Some day some king will say "I shall place a ring in your nose and lead you back the way you came. I shall lead you back to your old stable, to your law of yesterday, to black bread, that you might finally understand that you are what you are, not by the will of God, but by the overly-long patience of kings."[23] In the matter of the divorce Henry moved with great patience. For ten years he did not appeal the judgment of the pope ([Mii^v]). But when he did, almost all the universities of Europe supported his cause. We have read Paul's letter to Ferdinand and everyone knows that he recently presented the king of Scotland with the sword and made him Defender of the Faith in the vain hope that he would attack us while we were in civil strife. Is this the proper conduct of a good shepherd toward his sheep? ([Piiii]–[Piiii^v]). By contrast with such threats, Henry is plainly superior to the pope in pastoral care.

So grounded, Morison reviews Cochlaeus's charges with regard to the immediate events leading to the executions. What are "lies" to Morison, of course, were the result of distance as much as bias; and so far as they were phrased in the florid and tasteless fashion of contemporary controversy, there is little to choose between Cochlaeus and Morison. Yet in spite of the brick-bats, what Morison's account lacks in factual value it makes up for as a statement of official policy. According to Cochlaeus, nuns, barons, and doctors have been executed; according to Morison, no nuns were executed, and Elizabeth Barton was condemned not as a nun but for her prophecies of the king's death. Morison reports the words heard while she was in her trances, and the admiration of all those who heard them (they stood dumb struck, as if in the presence of some divinity) ([Tiii^v]–[Tiiii]). They were not all simple Kentishmen; Fisher and More both visited her rather often [*saepius*] ([Tiiii]). And this made it seem as if all that was done there was done by the power of God, Fisher being considered too holy not to be able to discern a hypocrite from a saint, More too clever for a nun to befoul his tongue, and both of them more loyal than to cover up a plot against the king's life ([Tiiii]). It is possible that they were too credulous and that they honestly believed that she spoke the truth. At any rate, when the king heard of the prediction his kingdom would be taken away, the "vestal" was sent for, but nothing serious was established against her, even though she was questioned by men of known wisdom and learning. She would only say that the questioners must be pure and free from guilt ([Vi^v]). At last, before the Duke of Norfolk, she confessed that she had been suborned by the monks. Did she not deserve to perish, and some of her monks with her? The question remains: how could men of such learning have been so deluded? ([Vi^v]).

As Morison sees it, the answer poses the other question crucial in the government's case: whose authority is being applied, the pope's or the king's? He regrets that two minds of such genius should have been turned from the interest of England to the profit of the Roman pontiff, though he finds the bishop's course easily explained. Fisher's studies for by far the greater part of his life were exclusively in those authors devoted to establishing papal authority. On the other hand, while More was drawn to this opinion, there is much, particularly in the "great dialogues written in English," to indicate that he had not always been so persuaded. On the basis of the two texts "Thou art Peter, and upon this rock I shall build my church" and "I have prayed that thy faith shall not fail", More had concluded that the faith of Peter did indeed fail, but never the church, and therefore that the foundation of the church was not Peter but Christ alone ([Vii^V]).[24] Morison also reports More as often saying that the pope should thank Heaven twice over: first, because Luther had married a nun and thus alienated the hearts of the people, and second, because the king of England had undertaken a defense of the papal cause and thus freed the nobility from the authority of the king; otherwise, More had held, the poorly-shored up authority of the popes would collapse. Yet in the end, intellectual pride was their downfall. Who could be more stubborn than Fisher and More to match their opinion against the learning of all the theologians and all the lawyers of England? Could the Bishop of Rochester be compared with Thomas Cranmer, Archbishop of Canterbury, with Hugh Latimer, Bishop of Worcester, with Stephen Gardiner, Bishop of Winchester, Edward Fox, Bishop of Hereford or Cuthbert Tunstall, Bishop of London, than whom More himself testifies the world today has hardly anyone more erudite? ([Viii–Xi^V]).

Typically, Morison justifies the executions on the grounds of civil order. He agrees with Plato that while ordinary minds cannot greatly benefit nor harm the commonwealth, great geniuses must be greatly feared, for they can build up states and tear them down when they wish ([Xiiii^V]). For years, Fisher and More have defended papal authority; it would have been no less than a thing of genius to draw them away from it now. There was nothing in the scriptures or the doctors which could be stolen, drawn out, or twisted, that they did not have ready for use. And More, at every third word, even in serious matters, answered with some well-mannered evasion [scommate]. Morison describes with the eye of an observer the frustrations of "the very important men endowed with great learning" who attempted to dispute with him about the law prescribing the death penalty for those who held that the pope had any power over the English: "They hoped that they would either draw him away from his opinion or ... would willingly lay aside his cause. Now listen, I ask you, to what this great Thales replied: 'For a long time now ... I have thought of nothing but the death of Christ. Let us suffer what has been sent.'"[25] Morison assumes an air of mock perplexity: who would be so stupid unless, as Cochlaeus has suggested, More was unwilling to struggle in vain with those whom he thought he would not persuade at all? With elaborate sarcasm, Morison measures the grave danger to More's salvation against squandering a few words so that those by whose decisions he saw all things being done in England should be recalled from error, if not to do them a favor, at least to save his country from a law which, though passed with everyone's approval, was harmful to

the commonwealth ([Xiiii^V]-Y). Both men, Morison continues with droll
mockery, preferred the peril of pertinacity to the disgrace of disavowing their
own writings defending the pope. Besides, Rochester was an old man and
sickly, his hope of immortality close at hand; and More, who had already
filled all public offices and suffered from a dangerous disease of the chest,
was more desirous of glory than was fitting. Cochlaeus was right: what More
wished he came to be. O, a little glory, how powerful you are—even in minds
properly fortified. More was unwilling that his little books, the vessel of his
genius, his hope of immortality, should be lost ([Yi^V]). Our ancestors accepted
the papal supremacy for truth, and hence Fisher and More were able to err
without loss of their integrity—almost. It is no disgrace to err when conscience
forces the error. But now when the sacred writings have come to light and
been disseminated, would they not distinguish apostate from apostle, imposter
from pastor? ([Yiiii^V]).

It is a grim word play, but Morison makes capital of it. If Fisher and More
rightly sought their glory, should not the king move against the robbers of
his? For a long time the king's clemency prevented their deaths. They were
cast into prison, but no fetters were imposed on them, no force applied; their
friends had free access to them in the hope that clemency would overcome
obstinacy. The king dearly loved More's genius and wit, and wished to save
him by persuasion. They forced themselves to die rather than that they were
condemned. So Simon Matthew had said in St. Paul's before More's death. Considered in retrospect, what should the king have done? Spare these defenders
of the pope, and what would the papal phalanxes not dare with these men as
their leaders? They have offended divine as well as royal majesty when they
defend papal right. In all truth, the king has taken violent action against no
one; it is the law which has punished those men. If you wish to contend that
anything was done wrongfully by us, show that by divine right the Roman
bishop has power over the English. Show that the king has been subjected to
him, that the pope could command in all things.

Morison descends to Cochlaeus's incidental charges. Cochlaeus: More's
head was softened by long boiling before being placed on a spear. The answer:
The English customarily wash the head and limbs of traitors with hot water
as a health measure for citizens in the neighborhood ([aiiii]). Cochlaeus:
There were many criticisms of the trial. The answer: No trial was ever held in
which the confession was more noble, the judges more upright. All were more
noble than More. Cochlaeus: Letters were sent preferring to be subject to the
pope rather than the king. The answer: No one in England is permitted to
defend the tyranny of the pope, either in writing or by word of mouth (aiii^V).

It is a relief when Morison turns in the end from this heavy-handed invective to the main point of contention: Fisher and More were executed because
they preferred to be subject to the pontiff rather than to the king. Certainly
up to that time, there was no decree that those who supported the marriage
with Catherine should be given the supreme penalty; the penalty was imprisonment until either longer life had changed their opinion or death had put an
end to their obstinacy. The fundamental issue was rather the impugning of
royal sovereignty.

Henry VIII did not wish to be told whether he would reign. For he did not think it concerned his affairs very much that there had once been a king of his own name [Henry II] who handed over to his posterity the shame of servitude. He felt that it would be an eternal glory to him if he would be the one who handed over to his heirs a free English kingdom—that is, a *kingdom*. He thought that he would be the first to cast out this monstrous tyranny.[26]

On this basis, More was executed. He was not the "baron" that Cochlaeus made him, though the king held him in high estimation as a man of letters, and in the hope that he would be a stimulus to us in the pursuit of virtue bestowed on him everything which a citizen more learned than he could or should wish for from a liberal and learned prince (bi). It was true that the king divorced a wife whom he had known as his own for twenty years, and More has found this unacceptable; but the marriage was immoral, and what is immoral today will not cease to be immoral tomorrow. Mary, the king's daughter, having confessed her error "in following you and your kind," is now deservedly in greatest favor with the king.[27] In brief, says Morison, turning to his opponent, you have not proved the king culpable because he retracted a mistake. If you wish to accuse either the king or Sampson, show that those things which they are writing now conflict with the truth, not that they conflict with what they previously wrote.

The case closed, Morison insults and exults over his foe: "You wage war with me, Cochlaeus. Fight with arguments, and you will have those who will dispute with you; fight with insults, and you will be alone in the arena. Go ahead, vulgar man, with excessive bile and intolerable pride. You have someone against whom you can hurl the filth, corruption, and venom of your tongue. You have him. Enjoy him."[28]

Less than a year after he had written his flatulent dedication of *Apomaxis*, Cromwell was concluding an appraisal of affairs in the realm and added a personal recommendation:

> Amonges other, for Your Graces Parliament, I have appointed Your Majesties servaunt, Mr Morisson, to be oon of them; no doubte he shalbe redy to answer, and take up such as wold crake or face with literature of lernyng, or by indirected wayes, if any such shalbe, as I think there shalbe fewe, or noon; for asmoch as I, and other your dedicate Conseillers, be aboutes to bring all thinges so to passe, that Your Majestie had neuer more tractable Parliament. I have thought the said Morisson very mete to serve Your Grace therein; wherefore I besech the same to haue hym in your good favour, as ye have had hitherto. I knowe his hert so good, that he is worthy favour in dede.[29]

Morison had plainly found a career open to his talents. One would like to think that Henry, in accepting Cromwell's recommendation of a loyal servant, might have remembered that the final words of praise could have been spoken equally of that other servant of the king and God whom he had executed.

PART II: *UTOPIA*

CLAVIS MOREANA: THE YALE EDITION OF THOMAS MORE

Arthur E. Barker

It should not seem unseemly for an entirely somnolent advisory partner to observe that the two volumes of the Yale *More* so far published[1] must sustain confidence in the erudition being devoted to the project, set the editors of subsequent volumes a high standard and some tricky problems, and provide students of the man and his times with abundance of material for the further agitation of the interpretative problems through which More has always contributed *ad animi libertatem cultumque.* Some others of our large-scale editorial projects of late have seemed symptomatic of humanist unease in an inclination to conceive their function less in instrumental than in absolute terms (*aeternum duratura*), as requiring not only the provision of tools and the opening of doors for such as come after, but rather, the decisive resolution of all problems through the weight of authoritative scholarship buttressing declarative finalities from the editorial chair. It is a fitting tribute to More's lively and learned humanism—whatever adjective one or another may wish to attach to that substantive—that the erudition of these volumes, especially in their glosses, serves to order, consolidate, and enlarge our grasp of More's materials and to highlight the stimulating problems presented by his invigorating manipulations.

In both cases the matter of text was of course of prime importance, though the frustrated *English Works* of the early thirties had done a good deal better by *Richard* than Lupton by *Utopia.* The precise efficiency of the Yale editors provides us with substantively critical texts that should relieve us of most of our basic uncertainties. Thus we are much indebted to Sylvester for his collation of Rastell's English *Richard* of 1557 (with the often considerable variants in Grafton's two Hardyngs of 1543 and two Halles of 1548 and 1550) and the Latin of the Louvain *Opera* of 1565 (and, keyed in therewith, of MS Arundel 43, known generally hitherto only in selected readings and a relief to have entire at long last from the College of Arms). The collation certainly demonstrates that some fantastic ghosts were indeed well laid by the editors of the *English Works.* It is difficult to see how anyone could complain of Sylvester's carefully reconstructed stemma; but the hand of time has left it so bare and ruined that most students will agree with him that "further speculation seems fruitless"—at any rate as to the transmission of More's text (276). Yet his introduction's account of the texts and of sources and models, and

Reprinted from *The Journal of English and Germanic Philology*, 65 (1966), 318–330, by permission of the author and the publisher.

the wealth of material in his explanatory notes, should induce a good deal of profitable literary reflection.

Though the disembodied wraith of a *Richard* by Morton lingers in the shadows of some incidental observations and notes, and though some notes suggest a simply translative relation, Sylvester makes it clear that More's English and Latin versions were from the beginning at once closely related yet independent, and that their developments diverged increasingly in style and many details of arrangement, phrasing, and even "fact." The most admiring attention is due to the textual and critical analysis (chiefly in terms of intended audience and decorum) which supports the editor's conclusion that what is involved is a virtually unique, unprecedented (and unimitated) exercise in double composition in two languages (lvi).

As the editor says, the Grafton texts, especially in their handling of introductory material and of the main characters and their relations, must reflect an early English version of More's. But to what extent and how (as to tone and theme) would partly depend on one's reading, by comparison, of Grafton's handling of his other chronicles. This is a topic beyond the scope of this volume, along, regrettably, with the treatment of More's history by later, undramatic chroniclers. Sylvester rightly concentrates attention, in his introduction, less on the tangled problem of the historical facts of the case than on the literary background of More's history. The authorities for the facts—if they are "facts": virtually all the details of More's account are clearly labeled "some-say"—are indicated, especially in the notes, for any who want to go into the problem. In relation to contemporary accounts, it is said that More's history "reflects an image which his age bequeathed him" or "a climate of opinion" (lxvi, lxxiv). But the question arises as to the extent and manner of his "weighing possible interpretations of events against each other" (lxx), and with this such literary speculations as are aroused by the limited suggestion that he echoes the chronicle style for effects of simple tragic irony (lxxiv). Since the opaque shadow of Bishop White Kennett and his authors, with their simplified view of history, falls heavily across all our reflections on such matters, it would have been useful to have from such editorial authority some comment on the mangling later transmission of More's text. And this might have helped to put into some perspective Grafton's earlier treatment of it. Appraisal of the peculiar angle of reflection in More's English piece would seem to require fuller appraisal of its peculiar relation, especially in its handling of characters and moralizing of events, not only to its Latin version but to the English chronicle and even *Mirror* traditions—an appraisal at least as extensive as the introduction's review of the classical and Latin humanist tradition of history.

Such questions are rendered all the more interesting by the complex relations and differences in style, arrangement, detail, clearly indicated by the textual and the elaborate explanatory notes, between the Arundel Latin (which is closer to the English), the apparently somewhat later but now lost Latin version from which Rastell translated some passages for 1557, the yet later Latin of *Opera*, 1565, and the post-Grafton English printed by Rastell.

These relations involve not only variations in fact and of emphasis in characterization but also in the echoing of classical historians (as to which the English
is, surprisingly, often more interesting than the Latin) and in shades of irony.
The editor sometimes finds the Latin more witty or ironic than the English
(e.g., 35/19, 48/17, 55/18, 64/25-27, 80/28-29) and sometimes less (e.g.,
7/20-21, 79/1-2, 29-27). A curious instance is provided by the reminiscence
of the Lucianic stage, where the English deserved some comment despite the
simplification in the Latin (81/1 ff. and cf. 258). Such variations should suggest
to students the profit to be gained by further discriminations of developing
tone and intention, beyond those possible in a general introduction chiefly
concerned, of necessity, with the character of More's *Richard* rather than of
his *Richards.* In this connection, it must be regretted that the editor has so
very little to say of the possibility of editorial revision between 1565 and the
earlier Latins, despite a 1565 observation (6/14; cf. 164) about the absolute
power of the English prince which it is difficult to imagine More writing at
any time in his career—whatever the divines and the English at Louvain
thought thirty years later (cf. xlviii-l). In view of the monkeying of the
Louvain editors with the text of *Utopia* at one ridiculous and notorious point
(cf. *Utopia,* 82/3-84/20), this matter is bound to "haunt" the discussion
(xlvi). It would seem to have some bearing on the question of the relation of
the lost Latin from which Rastell translated several passages to Arundel on
the one hand and Louvain on the other. But this must of course remain largely
a matter of pure critical speculation.

As the editor says (xxxiii), the Louvain text was "patently designed for an
international audience" with, it might be added, humanist predilections. And
his detailed review and extension of what has been said of the relation of
More's history to the classical Latin historians and their humanist imitators
must at once establish itself as authoritative. Some may feel that the controlling influence of Tacitus, supported by Suetonius, is somewhat over-
weighted; some that the *Jugurtha* of Sallust gets relatively less weight than it
deserves; and a few may feel that Sylvester's predecessors have established the
pervasive, if vaguely suffused, influence of Lucian, with his peculiar notions
about how history ought to be written, more firmly than the introduction
suggests despite its references to notable authorities (lxxxii). But the review
admirably overcomes, with the support of the notes, the difficulty of pinpointing the various classical influences (lxxxv), characterizing the humanist
elements in More's history, and illustrating his manipulation of classical
techniques of characterization, set speeches, crucially dramatic scenes, and so
forth (lxxxv-xcix), while demonstrating that "More used the classics just as
eclectically as he did his historical sources" (lxxxiii).

For the principles governing More's eclecticism, apart from the dramatic
or realistic, the introduction chiefly indicates the Erasmian humanist contrast
between the tyrant and the good prince which most commentators favor, or
even the classical contrast between the good old days and the corrupt present.
But it should induce deeper pondering on other than classical influences
(lxxxv). The rather brief account of St. Augustine may provoke reflection:

when the early biographers report that More's lectures on *The City of God*
were rather historical and philosophical than theological, they can hardly
mean that he took there (or anywhere else) a principally Tacitean or
Suetonean or Sallustean view of history. It may be regretted, and not simply
out of personal sentiment but with reference to the continuity of English
chronicling and mirroring, that Chambers' notion of the comment on Hastings—"the vain sureti of mans mind so nere his deth"—as stating the principal
theme is not recollected, even to be rejected in the notes as subclassical
moralizing (cf. 224, 51/13; 225, 52/9–13). And the scholarship of the introduction, with the very large body of new fifteenth- and sixteenth-century
material in the notes, while it makes plain "the remarkably accurate way" in
which More renders the Tudor view (lxxviii) and issues in some provocative
and prophetic comments on his relations with and opinions of his own princes
(or tyrants), also makes desirable some consideration of the ironic (perhaps
satiric) relation between the development of this "history" and the development, with the revolution in government and the assistance of humanists, of
the Tudor propaganda machine. Though the fatal daughter of time has left
us little of the underscaffolding of the text, it has left us enough to sustain,
with the help of this authoritative edition, yet further decanal (or at least
subdecanal) investigations of literary problems in More's *Richard III*, not
least of the representational virtuosity through which were expressed the
meditations on historical and last things that More entertained as he watched
the eighth Henry make his realm obey and sometimes counsel take.

For *Utopia* Father Surtz provides a much needed tool by his careful
collation of the first four editions. With its textual notes, the edition clears
the air, though it is possible to regard as unduly modest the observation that
"few really important variants appear in the critical apparatus" (cxciii). In
this case more than in most, the weighing of variants depends not only on
interpretation but on deductions from the evidence about transmission
briefly reviewed in the introduction (clxxiii–cxciii) and touched on in several
notes.

It was natural to take Froben's edition of March 1518 as the copy text, on
the ground that it is more correctly printed than its two predecessors and on
the supposition that it is the last in which More can be thought to have been
concerned, the Froben edition of November being a corrective resetting of
March. Yet some of Father Surtz's decisions are rightly influenced by the
recognition that the Paris text of 1517, by Gourmont, carries considerable
authorial weight and was not, as used to be said, put through the press by
Lupset without More's approval or knowledge (clvxxv and esp. 569, 248/2).
The text of 1517 was indubitably set from a corrected copy of the first edition, by Martens of Louvain in 1516.

But the evidence provided by Father Surtz's textual notes indicates that
the relations between these three texts are by no means as straightforward as
has been assumed or as one might like to suppose out of a preference for
good printing, nor the authority of the 1518 printing as unquestionable. Not
much can be said for 1516 alone: it was rather badly printed, from copy

prepared by Erasmus and under the care of Giles; and it is not surprising that
Erasmus, with his reputation involved, was already proposing a new edition
some two months after Martens' publication. As Erasmus was quick to point
out when he received a copy after several months of unexplained delay
(clxxxv), 1517 was also badly printed by Gourmont under Lupset's care: it
reproduces in general the peculiarities of the 1516 spelling and, apart from its
own errors and as Father Surtz remarks, agrees in many (indeed most)
respects, however minor, with 1516 against 1518 (clxxxvii). In some substantive cases of such agreement and where 1517 supplies a correction or addition
which 1518 does not reproduce, it is certainly right (if one is constructing an
ideal text) to follow 1517 as the Yale text does in a number of cases (112/29,
136/11, 210/16, 218/23, 29, 220/13, 236/17, 244/9) since the evidence for
believing that More had any hand at all in the Froben text of 1518 is in fact
very weak.

The assumption depends on the deduction, from various remarks in letters
printed by Erasmus later, of implications which, for all their apparently
rational likelihood as contributory to a simple explanation, are patient, if one
has the patience, of other interpretations. The only documentary support for
the deduction of these implications and the assumption of authorial weight in
the 1518 text is an incidental remark in Pace's *De fructu,* published by Froben
in October 1517 (something like a month after the Paris edition of *Utopia* but
many months before Erasmus, according to his own testimony, had seen the
Paris edition, and five or six months before the appearance of Froben's March
printing of *Utopia*), that More had deleted *i* and substituted *y* in *considero,*
according to a preference of his in such words, in a copy of *Utopia* corrected
by his own hand (clxxxvii, cxciii), and with this the fact that Froben's printing,
unlike 1516 and 1517, does spell such words with a *y,* as Father Surtz's textual notes illustrate. From this it has seemed rational to assume that March
1518 was set from a copy thus corrected by More and sent by Erasmus to
Froben and Rhenanus, who had the care of the printing. Since Froben's compositors, having set this passage in Pace's book, may have been instructed to
change *i* to *y* in appropriate places in setting *Utopia,* and since the changes
from *i* to *y* may have been made in the copy by Rhenanus or anybody else
who had read Pace's book and thought the point for one reason or another of
moment, it hardly provides, without the support of other evidence, a sure
basis for the assumption that the Froben compositors worked from a copy
(or "the copy") corrected by More. There is no other evidence of any kind that
they did so, save a request from Erasmus to More of 1 March 1517, repeated
on 8 March, some two months after the appearance of Martens' edition, for
a corrected copy, with the observation that it might be sent to Basel or, if
More preferred, to Paris (clxxxv, clxxxvii). There is no evidence in any observation by Erasmus, Rhenanus, Froben, More, or anyone else, that a corrected
copy was ever sent to Erasmus. Froben's printing nowhere makes any claim
to having been set from such a copy. Erasmus had sent a corrected copy to
Froben by 30 May 1517 (clxxxv); but there is no evidence that it contained
any corrections but his own. However much one may admire the elegant

scholarship of its copyreader and editor or believe that the excellence of Froben's printing must please the learned world, there is thus no convincing collateral evidence for regarding the 1518 text as having any special authorial, as distinct from editorial, weight. And there appears to be no textual evidence whatever that must induce one to think it has.

Froben's basic copy for March 1518 was undoubtedly a copy of the 1516 printing. This is demonstrated, as Father Surtz notes in the commentary (347, 82/32), by the 1518 response to a tipped period of 1516. To this, in case one erroneous question mark should not be thought to make an affirmation, ought to have been added, for instance, a 1518 reproduction of a 1516 & where 1517 (followed by Father Surtz) substitutes a required *ut* (220/13). As Father Surtz notes (clxxxv), all the readings which appear (with slight differences) in 1518 but not in 1516 are already in the 1517 text. At some stage, undeterminable through the available evidence, though (if the uncertain evidence provided by a letter of Erasmus is to be trusted) very late (clxxxvii–clxxxviii), 1518 picked up (and corrected the spelling of) the additions made to 1516 by 1517, substituting a more elegant phrase for a crude word in one and missing another (138/11, 210/16). There is nothing to suggest that 1518 derived these additions from any other source apart from 1517. The 1518 text "classicized" the spelling common to 1516 and 1517 throughout, and changed *i* to *y*. In one instance Froben's compositors and editors faulted, compositors and editors being, like authors, what they have always been: it rendered the title of the Utopian magistrate *philarchus* instead of *phylarchus* (*sic*) as in 1516 and 1517 (114/7; cf. 389). This is a matter of no import, in which Father Surtz no doubt rightly follows 1517 (the 1518 compositor probably having become momentarily confused about the whys and wherefores), though his explanatory note on the implications of the alternative roots may ironically attract the attention of those who, like, say, J. D. Mackie, think Utopian government much inclined to totalitarianism, or such as may wish to argue that the inconsistent substitution in the copy text provides yet another tooth in a satire already by no means toothless. Of course 1518 frequently corrects mistakes made in 1516 and left uncorrected by 1517, and mistakes made in 1517, while making a few independently. The web of relations is highly complex; but there appears to be no reading in 1518 which could not have derived from editorial (rather than authorial) revision and correction of 1516 and 1517 (cf. clxxxv).

Of course it by no means follows that 1517 carries substantially greater authorial weight. In the case of *Utopia* it is impossible to simplify the textual problem by appealing to the authority of one text against the other. It seems quite probable, as Father Surtz observes (clxxxv and 569, 248/2), that Lupset was provided with a corrected copy of 1516 by More, as the additions made in 1517 would indicate. But the Paris printing was entirely beyond More's control. Nobody could deny the truth of the observation by Erasmus that 1517 is full of errors. Gourmont's compositors in general reproduced the spelling of their 1516 copy, but they also reproduced many of the Giles-Martens errors (including the Greek) which can hardly have had any justification in the manuscript edited for Louvain by Erasmus; and they committed many errors of their own, catching only a small proportion in the *errata.* If, as must be supposed, a copy of 1516 corrected by More lies behind the corrected and augmented claims of the 1517 title page, either it recorded no preference for *y* or Lupset and Gourmont ignored the preference. But if 1517 is editorially and compositorially inferior to 1518, it carries at the very least as much authorial weight, since Lupset evidently acted, however inefficiently (and perhaps self-regardingly), as More's agent, whereas there is no evidence at all of authorized agency for 1518.

It would seem desirable to recognize that between More and the printed versions of his *libello* stood Erasmus and Giles, Lupset, and Erasmus and Rhenanus; and consequently that between us and More's original intentions and corrections stand the printers and these editors; and hence that a modern editor is inevitably at least three times removed from the ideal authorial text. Under the circumstances, an editor has no recourse but to settle for the editorial authority of one of the editorial parties, but he cannot at any point ignore the claims of the others (as Father Surtz's textual notes and occasional readings of course do not). It may be no more than a matter of scholarly humanistic preference to regard the Erasmus-Rhenanus-Froben spellings as more "correct" and less old-fashioned than those of the other two printings; yet Father Surtz deserves our gratitude for providing a record of the latter in his notes so that we may judge in some degree for ourselves. But every significant substantive decision, where 1516 and 1517 agree against 1518 and where 1517 disagrees with 1516 and 1518, must rest not on textual evidence but on interpretative editorial opinion.

Thus Father Surtz is to be stoutly defended for rejecting his copy text in favor of 1517 in the instances noted above. But there are other instances in which the response of readers may vary. For example, when More's introductory letter to Giles declares in 1516 and 1517 that he will follow the advice of his friends, not least of Giles, as to the question of publishing his book, provided this is done according to the pleasure (*voluptate*) of the (imaginary) Hythloday, it is a question whether the 1518 reading—with the consent or in accordance with the will of (*voluntate*)—is really preferable (44/23–24). As an explanatory quotation from humanist authority indicates (294), what is involved is a studied distinction; and it is quite possible to conclude from the material usefully provided in a number of notes of this kind that More indeed had a sense of Latin as a living language, as Father Surtz insists (579), and further that he had a sense of the ironies of living usage, despite (or perhaps because of) the experience of law-Latin which Erasmus declares, along with all More's other business, makes it a wonder that he had any time at all for books (and presumably justifies the editorial hand in its more elegant revisions). Since *voluptas* is, even on the simplest reading, used pejoratively at least twice in the text (369, 94/31; 561, 240/6; cf. cxxiii, n. 1), the distinction may raise for some readers the question as to whether the Utopian scale of meaning for *voluptas* can be regarded as essentially simple and unambiguous, especially in view of Utopian fumbling over *voluntas* (whether divine or human). And since Hythloday is imaginary, others may wonder whether More is alluding ironically to the *voluptas* of some actual friend, of which it would be wise to take account.

Similarly, when More declares himself in the texts of 1516 and 1517 to be *in magnum ... dubium* and 1518 represents him as being *in magnum ... dubitationem,* the refinement of the substitution must be admitted. But it may be difficult to suppress the reflection that the original word appears in its usage to carry, more than the substitute, the implication of vacillating or swinging from side to side connected with the root. The preceding sentence alludes, with an echo of Scriptural leaves of grass or good corn, to the putting forth of green shoots in Greek and Latin letters, and the next to More's preference for an objective falsehood to an intentional lie as to anything *in ambiguo.* Fancifully close reading may thence prefer a degree of vacillation to simplified doubt, especially since what is under discussion is the length of a bridge (with Roman associations) over a waterless river which is nevertheless tidal, in an imaginary island whose seas are reminiscent of the tides of Euripus (if only in the *Adages* of Erasmus) and whose experience may, if the reader is not preoccupied by an elegant and static ideality, suggest that there are tides even in the affairs of imaginary antipodeans.

In the matter of Utopian names students will be grateful for the leads provided by Father Surtz's classically philological notes: the jokes need explaining in detail. But surely the unique 1516 reading of *Mentirano* for *Amaurotico* (146/25) deserved an explanatory note, especially in view of Lupton's inadequate and fanciful comment. This inconsistent naming of "the city of shadows" (or, as Father Surtz remarks, "even Mirage") might of course come from *mens* (cf. menticulture) or be reminiscent of the friend to whose care Ulysses left the education of Telemachus; but its more probable association would seem to be with lie, deceit, fallacy, sophism, invention, feigning, misrepresentation, counterfeiting, or, if one can imagine something like a Sidneian poetic already being involved, figuring forth. However that may be, its existence in 1516 demands explanation. It can hardly be a compositorial error and must result from an authorial or editorial slip in the removal of vestiges in the copy Erasmus sent to Giles. It must indicate the original name for the city, for which Amaurotico was substituted. By whom, and when? No doubt when the Moronic name for the country, *Nusquama,* was changed to *Utopia* with its ambiguously sounded Greek prefix. But as to that, our only evidence shows that the change was made after the manuscript left More and allows us to suspect that More had some cause for the irritation he expressed over Brixius and his sneer about incorrect titular Greek, since that sneer might perhaps have been more justly directed elsewhere (cf. 274, 10/1-2).

Thus the problems involved in the choice of readings are by no means always merely stylistic. It may be that the substitution in 1518 of *ubique* for the double negative, *nusquam ... non,* in an observation that nowhere in the imaginary island are the harbors undefended by nature or human art, renders the sentence more elegant and effortless (111/27-28). But, *hinc et ubique,* the bearing of the sentence is at least worth contemplation. Similarly, when

Tunstal's copy at Yale indicates marginally in 1516 what it thinks a better reading and 1517 produces this (232/12; cf. clxxxiv), it is a question whether the Erasmus-Giles and Erasmus-Rhenanus reading is to be preferred. They say each islander is left to conceive of the deity *e summa religione;* Tunstal and 1517 say *e sua religione.* The textual crux is of course related to the Utopian problem of religious conscience, about which they carry on the same debates as our authorities still do in council.

A comparable instance is provided by a quite barbarously framed sentence about the belief of the islanders that the good dead concern themselves directly with the welfare of the living (224/5–10)—a sentence whose contorted syntax threw 1516, 1518, and every subsequent editor. It is not easy to see why Father Surtz tentatively suggests here yet another emendation against the 1517 reading his text accepts, though most readers will be influenced by the modern English translation (by G. C. Richards, revised for this edition) printed opposite. The modern translation tells us that this belief is sustained by the conjecture of the Utopians that freedom (of movement), like all other good things, must be increased for good men after death. The Tudor translator, Raphe Robynson, managed, though clumsily, rather better: though he broke up the sentence, he allowed himself to be guided in sense by its syntax and, without seriously sacrificing its *libertate,* arrived at the conclusion that the good dead are moved by *mutuus amor charitasque,* "whych in good men after theyre deathe they cownte to be rather encreased then dymynyshede." The 1517 version supports Robynson against Richards, though his antecedent is perhaps still somewhat unnecessarily uncertain; for 1517 clearly implies that it is *charitas* which is increased in the good dead, and the rest follows from that. As Father Surtz's quotations in an explanatory note indicate (531), this is not a doctrinal crux. There is no need to wait upon Erasmus, Luther, or seventeenth-century English Protestantism to sharpen the doctrine of Christian liberty: even Aristotle had the hang of the matter. But it would be quite possible to argue that the syntax, which may seem uncertain if one does not have the hang of the matter, results from More's intentional representation of the Utopian exploration, through natural religion and conjecture, of notions he supposed otherwise confirmed for Christendom. Such difficult passages as this might yet further illuminate the implications of the fiction's comment on the relation between the natural and the revealed, on which both editors significantly comment—Hexter at lxvii–lxviii and lxxv–lxxvii, and Father Surtz in various notes such as 160/24, 166/3–5, 178/11, 12, 216/7, 27, 33, though unhappily with little reference to the analysis of the matter by Chambers and by Father Surtz elsewhere.

Such passages as this may induce the hope that Robynson's translation may be preserved from oblivion in cheap texts, despite its clumsinesses and because of its influence on so many centuries of English writing. A modern translation may, through aiming at "closer conformity with the Latin text" (cxciv), often fail to recreate the original effect of the Latin by extending the inclination of 1518 to render syntax and phrasing more elegant and meaning clear and distinct and as unambiguous as treaties and manifestoes produced by propaganda machines pretend to be. The usefulness of the revised translation in an age of less Latin and no Greek is obvious; but comparison with Robynson is likely to prove illuminating at any crucial point. It is to be regretted that his version contributes so little to the explanatory notes: on the two occasions when he does appear he provides interesting implications (291, 40/17; 313, 58/16). Though his Tudor method of translation adopts devices for rendering possible implications in the Latin that modern literal clarity finds clumsy and confusing, it at least has good precedent in More's use of such devices in similar cases in which literal clarity evidently seemed to him inadequate. As Sylvester points out, More as translator "often rendered a single word in his Latin original by two or more equivalent expressions in his translation" (*Richard*, lvi), a practice through which, as Sylvester remarks, "a translator, consciously or unconsciously, affirmed his descent from the medieval glossators." Though Robynson is not mentioned among Sylvester's examples, his innumerable doublets for Utopian words put him in the tradition with More, however inelegant and unhumanistic they may seem. And what Sylvester says elsewhere of More's apparent notion of true imitation of the classics is applicable to translation: "at least it would retain the aura of associations surrounding, in the original, the phrase that is being adapted" (lxxiv). In some such terms, despite his simplicity of mind, Robynson attempted to render what More (in a Latin phrase only a self-conceited simplicity could take literally) described as "his none too witty little book."

Thus all students must be greatly indebted to Father Surtz for the textual machinery he provides. If there remains room for differences of opinion, the evidence is indicated by his textual notes, and any further investigations must respect their implications. It is not clear that more than one copy of each edition was used in the collation. Sylvester used three copies of 1557 and two of 1565, and reports that, while there were a few minor press variants, he found no variants of any significance (civ, n. 3). It would of course be Utopian to wish for, let alone hope after, a time when the electronic scanning devices available to other disciplines might be joined with the collating machine; but in the case of a text whose transmission remains as uncertain as *Utopia*'s, it would at least be interesting to know what the textual facts are in full detail. Yet such detail would only lead us back to the various editorial desks and thence, since the early editors cannot be said to have handled their duties as efficiently or even as respectfully as the Yale editors, to problems of interpretation involving our appraisals of the tone and intention of the piece.

Here the Yale edition makes a double contribution through its two introductions, one sociological and biographical by J. H. Hexter, the other literary and textual by Father Surtz. A prefatory statement must evoke admiration: "The editors have worked in harmonious collaboration throughout the six years during which this volume has been in preparation, but they have made no attempt to disguise, in the Introduction, where they have differed from each other in interpreting the *Utopia*" (vii). Indeed the Yale editors have so sought to the best of their power to handle matters tactfully that differences of opinion between the two introductions remain unspecified. They agree in regarding *Utopia* as essentially Erasmian in principle, as induced by the distaste for European corruptions More shared with Erasmus, and as using fictional and satiric realism as the vehicle for communicating a conception of the best state of a commonwealth and its proper institutions derived from Erasmus, if somewhat extended.

Mr. Hexter's introduction is a determined, and occasionally rather truculent, version of the rationally sociological and evangelically enthusiastic Christian-humanist interpretation we have inherited, with variations, from Seebohm, Sir Sidney Lee, Karl Kautsky, and Fritz Caspari. It represents *Utopia* as evoked by the frightful social and political conditions of Europe in the quiet time before Luther began hammering things about (xxiv), seeing the Utopian ideal, especially in its basic communism (c ff.), as the product at once of exceptional poetic and prophetic afflatus (xxvi–xxvii) and a degree of realistic social and in-stitutional sense not possessed by Erasmus (lxxxiv). But the ideal Utopian institutions are for Hexter instrumental to Erasmian humanistic piety, with its moral sense and its contempt for dogma and medievalism (lxxi, xcii). The young More was, he thinks, not at all influenced by anything medieval. His experience induced a contempt not only for princes and chivalry but for English law and the English gentry (lv), and Chambers' notion that the under-sheriff of London had any sympathy with the medieval theory of corporations, secular or ecclesiastical, rests on misreadings and misconceptions (xlv). As for the later More, there is (as Lee and Kautsky and Caspari argued, though nobody is cited) a radical discontinuity, "a drastic reordering of the structure of religious priorities" (xxv, lviii), which makes the later writings useless as glosses on *Utopia.* What concerns the early More, for Hexter, is the personal problem of counsel created by his Erasmian ideals, his circumstances, and Henry, pointed up by the geological stratifications of the text revealed by the techniques of the higher criticism and now connected with what has been termed "the humanist dilemma," here associated with "the duel . . . that goes on between Erasmus' hopes for the princes of his day and the nasty cruel facts about those princes as they forced themselves on a mind not wholly immune to the impact of reality" (lxxxii). From this point of view, *Utopia* is expressive of the early More's vision of the way in which this dilemma must be resolved by the insistence of humanists on the establishment of humane and (soundly) com-munist social institutions, administered by humanists, whence, as in Utopia and as Hythloday insists, all pride, sin, and evil may be purged away, *aeternum duratura.*

In general Father Surtz's introduction would seem to be in harmonious accord with this. Though he has little to say of the humanist dilemma or its Erasmian manifestations, he agrees that "the hell in More's piece is western Christendom; the paradise is Utopia" (cxxxviii), and that for both the hell and the ideal the writings of Erasmus "are the chief source and the finest com-mentary" (cxxv–cxxvi). But he also thinks that "a simple moralism" prevails in Utopia, scholastic intellectualism ("at least in its decadent form") having been rejected, and that More's concentration on the classics achieves a simpli-fication at the cost of a rejection "which spells retrogression and loss in philosophical and scientific areas" (clxiii, clxiv). His sense in this connection of the element of Christian primitivism in the Erasmian ideal, when put together with his observation that the primitivistic strain in the literary background of *Utopia* might repay investigation, is worth pondering, especially with the eighteenth century's convenient post-Erasmus marriage of primitivism and perfectibilitarianism behind us in our humanist background. And his review of the sources behind the book must be of interest to students not only for its account of the classical Erasmian items but for its comments on extra-Erasmian influences. He very rightly observes that "a study of the influence of *The City of God* upon *Utopia* is much to be desired" (clxvi). (Such a study might begin with XVI, x, on the absurdity of the notion that antipodeans exist.) And he finds it "difficult to believe that no influence at all was exerted by the medieval treatises of John of Salisbury, Giraldus de Barri, Thomas Aquinas, Aegidius Romanus, and Vincent of Beauvais" (clxvii). He himself briefly reviews the possible influence of Mandeville and Occleve (who might have served to suggest that most of Hythloday's complaints about the hell of Christendom are medieval commonplaces) and, happily, of Fortescue (through whom law and the Inns of Court and even the medieval theory of corporate bodies might have been reintroduced into the picture).

Though Father Surtz says introductorily of Aristotle's *Politics* only that it "may be the ultimate, though remote, source" for some miscellaneous items, and though he has little to say introductorily of the later More, save that his view of the comic evidently did not change radically (cxlix), his notably learned and full notes in the commentary must be of very considerable interest and use. These not only supply innumerable "parallels" from the works of Erasmus and other humanists (chiefly post-Utopian), but a great many highly relevant, if sometimes perplexing, passages from More's later controversial and devotional works. If it is sometimes not clear what the relation is and whether More is agreeing or disagreeing with himself or Hythloday or the Utopians (as at 240/27, for instance), if little is provided to illustrate the later More's opinions about hanging matters, and if his realistic though charitable opinions about the best treatment of poverty cause a not-unusual uneasiness (66/21), these illustrations must prove illuminating—especially when taken along with the number of citations from Aristotle and Aquinas and their tendency to cluster around the objections raised by the "More" of the Utopian dialogue to what he thinks "very absurdly established" in Utopia as Hythloday describes it.

However, the objections of the "More" of the piece are not, in the opinion of either editor, to be taken as More's. Though Hexter dismisses the problem of "More" in an early footnote (xix, n. 2), Father Surtz's more literary approach enables him to argue that both "More" and Hythloday (and poor Peter, Tunstal, Morton, Henry VIII, Francis I, and the Flemish as well as the Anemolian ambassadors?) are "characters" in a dramatic fiction (cxxvi; cf. cxl, clxxx) whose circumstantial realism and touches of comedy serve simply, whether in the dialogue or the account of Utopia, to sugarcoat the ideally ideological and institutional pill. Hence "More's" objections may in general be dismissed as satirically ironic or perfunctory jokes (cxxxiii; cf. 566, 244/17, and 569, 246/2) while in general what Hythloday says and reports is to be treated with high seriousness.

Of course, as even the simplest reviewer is taught by experience and as the later More sadly implies with reference to *Moriae Encomium* and *Utopia* (in troubled passages to which there seems, strangely, to be no reference in this edition), irony is a tricky and double-edged device, even when directed, as through the mouth of Folly, against obvious vices that all men of good will must at all times condemn and that even the vicious condemn when it suits their book or the pinch is on the other foot. Perhaps harmony is best sustained by thinking the irony of *Utopia* simply directed against such abuses, or at most at the futility and indeed hypocrisy of the unhumanistic efforts of those in power in the sixteenth century to do something about them or rather to take advantage of them. Even so, Father Surtz, like Sylvester, appears to think the influence of Lucian's "extravagant fantasy and robust humor" somewhat overemphasized by previous commentators and present only "in a touch here and there" (clxii), and he can say of More's "playfulness" (if it is playfulness and not something sharper) that, "like a joke explained in detail," it "defeats its purpose" (570, 250/17). A reviewer, on the other hand, cannot avoid recalling the later More's comments on the comic tendency of human nature which leads one to ignore the bag of faults on one's own back and focus attention on those carried by others.

Yet simplification carries with it its own ironic risks. For instance, the observation (498-99, 200/7) that "More's failure to work out the implications" of the problem and principles of "just" war, especially against tyrants and with reference to ownership, has provided some justification for those who think *Utopia* "a very revolutionary document," must induce the reflection that it is not More or "More" who should here be accused of not working out implications but the Utopians, and perhaps after them the narrator, and after him at least the collection of humanists cited in explanation of Utopian views in the explanatory notes. If we are to deem More deficient, it would be just to indicate against what datum his failure is to be measured—against the opinions of Erasmus (early or late?), or of Calvin, or, not to mention the good recently dead, those good among the living who debate the principle of nuclear deterrence in our secular and ecclesiastical assemblies? The author of *The History of King Richard III* can hardly be supposed to have been unaware of the levels of irony, from the absurd and ridiculous to the terrible and tragic, involved in the problem of tyranny and the question of resistance and just war, or in the various other such questions presented to us by *Utopia.*

Problems of this kind should send students through the bibliography to further studies, and by no means least to those of Father Surtz himself, which are, surprisingly, not listed there and to which, whatever the claims of editorial modesty, it must be said that there are shockingly few references anywhere in the volume. Utopian literature is of course vast, and the more comprehensive bibliography in the *Richard* was an easier task. But it is a pity Marc'hadour's *L'Univers de Thomas More* could not be drawn on; and Kautsky and A. L. Morton should have been included, if only as company for

Alexéev in the note on clxxii. Indeed, it would have been proper to explain how a sense of proportion and of irony, if nothing else, should prevent the ideally sociological interpretation of the European hell and the Utopian paradise from being dialectically extended toward materialism and how they might keep More's *libello* in the context of the universe in which it was written, as a representation, to echo words of a recent visitor to the New World, of a stage in the development of mankind in its pilgrimage through time.

MORE'S *UTOPIA* IN ENGLISH: A NOTE ON TRANSLATION

James Binder

The portraitist wants to duplicate men, the translator wants to duplicate writings. Neither succeeds if he adds or removes or changes, for he becomes one who makes or destroys, not one who reproduces. Reasonable men assume that no portraitist or translator will ever succeed completely.

Saint Thomas More's *Utopia* was translated in 1551 by Ralph Robinson, a needy scholar become clerk to Wm. Cecil. His important labor deserves looking at because the *Utopia* did and still does reach the English-speaking public mainly via the Robinson detour.

A company of writers[1] has conned and appraised the seachange which during the Renaissance overtook non-English works on their being introduced into the mother-tongue. These writers say proper things, and well enough has been written on the subject. Translators are dangerous persons, however, and issuance of whilom warnings to that effect can be salutary. Not that readers of translations are not equally dangerous, because they are—in letting down their guard too soon.

One peculiarity of the English *Utopia* illustrates pretty well how a translator can go wrong through insufficient conscious realization of the meanings with which his text happens to be saturated.

Everyone is interested in what Plato does with poets in the *Republic.* His treatment of them engulfs him in the same radical conflict between the body and the soul, between the esthetic-sensuous and intellectual-spiritual awareness of experience that still plagues Western men. Readers at present who turn the pages of *Utopia,* having this ordinary interest (of course besides many others) are curious to learn how its Modern English Catholic Humanist author has dealt with the eternal dilemma, and how the position he takes is given embodiment in what he conjured up for the lessoning of a naughty Christian Europe—a laudable kind of imaginary commonwealth, good certainly, whether perfect or not, in essence Greco-Roman-Christian, officially and superficially exotic-heathen. They want to know in both abstract and concrete terms what it was, the good kind of life English Catholic-Christian Humanism, through More, held out for the captivation of the sixteenth and all centuries.

For theory, there is first of all the long and familiar passage, put into Hythlodaye's mouth, describing the life-ideal of the Utopians, *voluptas,* of

Reprinted, by permission of the publisher, The Johns Hopkins University Press, from *Modern Language Notes,* 62 (1947), 370–76.

which there are two sorts. The first and higher, spiritual pleasure, is recognizable as ἔρως, a striving after union with The Divine. The subordinate second one, freely recommended, is corporal pleasure, described positively as delight through the senses, and feelings of healthy well-being, negatively as pleasure "whereof cummeth no harme" ("ex quo nihil sequatur incommodi"). The possibility of excess in pursuit of the first is not mentioned, but indulgence in the next, as just noted, is explicitly bounded. The Utopian may enjoy within measure the gratifications of earthly life while he is alive (σωφροσύνη), but he believes in God and immortality and knows the life of the spirit to be paramount.

Unfortunately for the searcher into the ways of More's thinking, he did not write in a vacuum. Behind the Utopian isle looms sixteenth-century Europe. This, as well as their greater importance, helps to explain why the *animi voluptates* are fulsomely dwelt on while the corporal ones are given only a lick and a promise. Europe was putting the emphasis the other way. It may explain too why description of the external culture of Utopia is so sketchy, at times only half-conscious and indifferent. As a protester, More had what he disapproved of more on his mind than what he liked. If anybody wants to discover the exact nature of external culture in Utopia, he must scratch around.

On the subject of decorativeness and decorative art, as well as on art itself, More is obscure. He does not say whether any artists exist in Utopia. Enumerating the occupations of the people in time of peace, exclusive of holy men, scholars, and officials, Hythlodaye says: "Besides husbandry, which (as I sayde) is common to them all, euery one of them learneth one or other seuerall and particuler science, as hys own proper crafte. That is most commonly other clotheworkinge in wolle or flaxe, or masonrie, or the smythes crafte, or the carpenters scyence. For there is none other occupacyon that anye numbre to speke of doth vse there (139–40)."[2] Is the artist hidden in the craftsman, or in the last sentence of the above quotation? Is More thinking of him, or a certain type of him, when Hythlodaye refers to "vayne and superfluous occupations . . . for ryotous superfluyte and vnhonest pleasure" "where money beareth all ye swing (146)"? Regarding the result of the artist's activity, has he it or a certain type of it in mind when a little later it is stated that products of work should be "requysyte other for necessytye, or for commodytye; yea, or for pleasure, so that the same pleasure be trewe and naturall (147)"? Who knows? To relieve bafflement, all one can do is recall the direct attacks on finery, of which there are enough. There is an extended onslaught against gold and silver, jewels, fine stuffs, and color in the long passage leading up to and including the account of the Anemolian ambassadors' visit (173–83), as well as a general declaration of principle earlier: "Certeynly, in all kyndes of lyuynge creatures, other fere of lacke doth cause couetousnes and rauyne, or in man only pryde; whiche counteth it a gloryouse thynge to passe and excell other in the superfluous and vayne ostentacion of thynges. The whyche kynde of vice amonge the Vtopians can haue no place (157)." Or without getting much satisfaction, he can look around Utopia itself. Music there is, "No supper is passed without musicke (166)" (but where does it come from?), and it is in the churches too, "they sing prayses vnto God, whiche they intermixt with instrumentes of musick (295)"; but poetry, painting, sculpture, or dancing will be looked for in vain. Architecture of a sort and municipal design there had to be, because there were buildings and towns, but it is discouraging to be told merely that "As for their Cyties, he that knoweth one of them knoweth them all (126)," and that "they be all set and situate a lyke [eadem ubique], as farfurth as the place or plotte suffereth (119)." For the rest, he must be contented with such abstract attributives as "spatiosas omnes ac magnificas (119)" (applied to the cities), "egregia" and "operosa modo (289)" (to the churches), "descriptae commode (130)" (to the streets), "nec ad oculum indecora (140)" (to clothing).

There are a few references, provokingly offhand and equivocal, to an ordinary esthetic-sensuous appreciation of everyday life. Over-fastidiousness is scorned. More has only contempt for the well-off men in his own England "of so nyce and soo delycate a mynde (149)" that they disdain perfectly good houses that do not quite suit them. But there is also normal disgust for filth and menial work with filth. The most repellent work is delegated to criminals. (Inconsistently, the market-place in Amaurote is flushed for a practical reason only, "least the ayre, by the stenche thereof infected and corrupte, shoulde cause pestilente diseases (158).") Between these two extremes of over-fastidiousness and hyper-insensibility there is middle ground. The Utopians are not puritanical, they have wine and mead besides "cleane" water, and, of course, their backyard gardens, from which they derive, besides pleasure, profit and personal pride. More does not, it will be noticed, subsume this particular pride under "vayne ostentacion," and there is no mistaking an enthusiastic tone, even more in the Latin than in the English, when gardening is mentioned: "Hos hortos magnifaciunt. in his uineas, fructus, herbas, flores, habent, tanto nitore cultuque, ut nihil fructuosius usquam uiderim, nihil elegantius (131)." There is and is not uniformity of clothing. All wear the same, but in some way, one does not know exactly how, the sexes and married and unmarried persons are distinguished. At least no opportunity is given for pleasure in the wearing of garments various in color and design. Esthetically they are only "nec ad oculum indecora." They are plain and uniform, of wool without dye. Only their cleanliness is esteemed, and the fineness of thread, as in all cloth, goes ignored. But here again, in that most odd way almost reminiscent of the small boy at the cookie-jar, hungry but apprehensive of consequences, there are the minute concessions: work-clothing is not worn in public except under a cloak, and the whiteness of linen, it appears, "ys regardede (151)." In another place, during the attack on gold and silver, when decorative objects made from them are objected to (because men, delighting in them, are reluctant to melt them down for use as tender), household ware of the Utopians is mentioned in contrast, but scarcely as a pure-utilitarian alternative: "in fictilibus e terra uitroque, *elegantissimis*[3] ... edant bibantque (175)." The interiors of the churches are "subobscura (290)" and contain no eikons

(291), and the congregations dress in sober white, all in the same way, but the priests, for no given reason, are vested in parti-colored robes, interwoven with the feathers of birds (294).

What does Robinson do in the face of this delicately poised revelation of More's approach to human living? This much. He throws it off balance. By licence of translation at key points he changes the Utopian *civic architecture* from what it is, a dim, vague, abstractified, unattended reflection of Tudor London, fetched out of the penumbra of More's consciousness, and renders it up as, remembering everything else, one knows More would never have had it, gothically elaborate and splendiferous. All with a few words.

The range of distortion extends from down-toning to extravagant coloring. "Insula ciuitates habet quatuor et quinquaginta, spatiosas omnes ac *magnificas*" is made "There be in the Ilande .liiii. large and *faire* cities or shiere townes (119)," the only instance of downtoning. There is naturally no attempt to fancy up the farmsteads, which, "commode dispositas," are in English "wel appointed and furnyshed (120)." He beautifies, however, with no justification at all, the tower which stands at the mouth of the bay. "turrim" in the text becomes "*a faire and a strong towre* (117)." As much heightening is added in another place: "The stretes be appoynted and set forth *verye commodious and handsome*, both for carriage and also agaynst the wyndes" is got from "Plateae cum ad uecturam, tum aduersus uentos, *descriptae commode* (129–30)"; but these are tame. Real exuberance is shown when the following: "Nam totam hanc urbis figuram, iam inde ab initio descriptam ab ipso Vtopo ferunt. Sed *ornatum, caeterumque cultum ...*" is put beside this: "For they say that king Vtopus himself, euen at the first begenning, appointed and drew furth the platte fourme of the city into his fasion and figure that it hath nowe; but *the gallaunt garnishing, and the bewtiful setting furth of it ...* (131-2)."

Robinson's favorite extravagantising word is *gorgeous*. There are ten instances of it. The dress of the Anemolian ambassadors is so described three times in the English. "At Anemolii ... decreuerunt *apparatus elegantia* deos quosdam repraesentare, et miserorum oculos Vtopiensum *ornatus sui splendore praestringere*" is turned to "But the Anemolianes ... determined in the gorgiousnes of their apparel to represent very goddes, and *wyth the bright shynynge and glisteringe of their gaye clothinge to dasell* the eyes of the silie poore vtopians (178)"; "totus ille *splendor* apparatus" is turned to "al that gorgeousnes of apparrel (179)"; "omnem illum *cultum*" is turned to "all that *gorgyouse arraye* (181)." The word is used three times miscellaneously. "mundi huius *uisendam* machinam" emerges as "the *maruelous and gorgious* frame of the worlde (218)," "suis explicatis opibus" as "by *gorgiously* setting furthe her [Pride's] riches (306)," and "in templo diuae Mariae, quod et *opere pulcherrimum*, et ..." as "in our ladies churche, whyche is *the fayrest, the moste gorgious and curyous* churche of buyldynge in all the cytye ... (25)." These uses are innocuous, they merely heighten what is represented as truly splendid, but they serve to prepare for four uses of the word in connection with Amaurote's *décor:*

1. "Vrbs aduersae fluminis ripae ... *egregie* arcuato ponte, commissa est" becomes "There goeth a brydge ouer the ryuer ... with *gorgious and substanciall archeis* (128)";

2. "aedificia *neutiquam sordida*" becomes "The houses *be of fayre and gorgious buyldyng* (130)";

3. "At nunc omnis domus *uisenda forma* tabulatorum trium" becomes "But nowe the houses be *curiously builded, after a gorgiouse and gallaunt sort,* with .iii. storries one ouer another (132)";

4. "Delubra *uisuntur egregia ... operosa modo*" becomes "Their churches *be very gorgyous ... of fyne and curious workemanship* (289–90)."

This, when the essence of the Utopian life is its bareness, its simplicity, its austerity. Utopians live almost according to a *regula,* and indeed if it were not for explicit mitigating features, their community might almost be described without qualification as a sort of mammoth lay monastery relieved of the obligation to mortify. By taking liberties, Robinson disturbs the purity of this conception.

His behavior invites imaginative questioning. What does it mean that so many of his alterations are alike? Did he make them knowingly, half-knowingly, or unknowingly? What is their τέλος? The answer to the first question is perhaps easy. What he did looks like a rebellion against undecoratedness, plainness, homeliness even. The second is more difficult. When there is room for doubt, who will venture, today of all days, to distinguish confidently between the workings of the conscious and the unconscious? Resolution of the third, of course, bristles with even more peril. His individual taste may have been the cause, a taste that may have been awakened or fanned by exposure to the high coloring of prose romances. Then too, he was a poor man, and the poor do not yearn after austere paradises, whether celestial or mundane. Bemused with Amaurote, and finding it a little dull, he may have wanted to brighten it up a bit. Or he may have in London developed an admiration for courtly splendor. More obviously hated it, because of what it symbolized, but that does not mean his translator had to, even while he was translating diatribes against it. There is no evidence that he was a careful student of More's ideas, and the implications of all that More had to say may very well have escaped him. He was also an Englishman of the sixteenth century. Perhaps again, as must be recognized possible, his pen moved in response to the eddying of a time-spirit which need not here be further specified.

What can be said certainly? At least this: that to use the word *gorgeous* in describing anything Utopian is to violate fundamentally the whole tenor of a great man's mind.

MEDIEVALISM OF MORE'S *UTOPIA*

P. Albert Duhamel

Scholarly concentration almost exclusively on the political content of More's *Utopia* as an anticipation of modern liberal thinking has resulted in the unexpected paradox that probably the most medieval of More's works is commonly interpreted as the most Renaissance. Although most of the explicit content of the *Utopia* is concerned with contemporary Renaissance political and economic problems, the implicit heuristic method which determined this content is medieval. Just as some knowledge of the simplified medieval cosmic setting implied by Shakespeare throughout his works is of greater importance to an understanding of his plays than the recognition of any specific historical event which may be alluded to in a particular play, so the explicit content of *Utopia* can be better understood in terms of the Scholastic method which, though only implicit in the work, More employed in the construction of *Utopia* to make his criticism of the world created by an abuse of that method all the more ironical. The failure to recognize how the method controlled the content has been the greatest single obstacle to an understanding of the *Utopia* in its proper context and to its reconciliation with More's life and English works. In a somewhat similar paradoxical fashion, the *Treatise on the Passion* and the *Dialogue of Comfort Against Tribulation,* which are commonly considered as representative of More's lingering medieval dogmatism, might be better understood as the humanistic documents they are, if their controlling method were generally recognized as similar to that developed by Erasmus and other Renaissance humanists.

The method employed by an author in "inventing" and constructing his work is certainly as significant in placing that work in its historical context as the ideas which the author discusses in that same work. The method will determine what the author discovers and how he arranges what he has discovered. The attempt to define a document as "medieval" or "Renaissance" in terms of a set of ideas which are considered as specifically definitive of the Middle Ages or the Renaissance is based on the dangerous assumption that each of these historical periods had an integrating principle or set of ideas peculiarly its own.[1] Modern scholarship, in its continuing survey of the boundary line which separates Renaissance from medieval, testifies to the dangers, or at least the difficulties, of defining an age in terms of its supposedly specific subject-matter.[2] Few, if any, ideas rummaged out of the belfries of St. Gall

Reprinted, by permission of the author and publisher, from *Studies in Philology,* 52 (1955), 99–126.

and Monte Cassino were overlooked by the Middle Ages to become the peculiar property of a later age.[3] Even if Poggio Bracciolini and Filelfo had dusted off any number of forgotten classical texts, these texts would have had little or no effect on prevailing ways of living and thinking if they had been read and examined in the same old way. The best fate they could have expected would have been a niche in some latter-day *Summa* as new adversaries to be levelled in an extra "ad primum" in the refutation.

The Renaissance can be distinguished, to a large extent, from the Middle Ages in terms of its reorganization of the trivium or the formal arts. From Abelard to Petrarch, logic was the architectonic discipline to which grammar and rhetoric were subordinated. From Lorenzo Valla on, the three arts were oriented according to the needs of grammar, whose methods now controlled the investigation and interpretation of texts.[4] The significance of this change can be better understood in the light of an old Scholastic maxim which stressed that whatever is known is known, not according to its own nature, but according to the nature of the knower.[5] In late Scholastic philosophy this became the very familiar, "Quicquid recipitur, recipitur secundum modum recipientis," and as such was accepted by the Renaissance humanists. John Colet employs the principle in his Oxford lectures on St. Paul's epistles in the form which may be translated, "Everything is such as the receiver."[6] Since it is the function of the formal arts of the trivium to form or discipline the faculties of the reader, to create the proper reader, a change in the orientation of these disciplines will change the reading habits of the proper reader. "But, to change the manner of reading Aristotle, Vergil, Moses and Paul is to change one's conception of God, nature, man, morals, and religion."[7]

Peter Abelard was as radical an innovator in the twelfth century as Erasmus was in the sixteenth. Abelard turned Scholastic philosophy into a literature of questions by collecting some 1,800 texts from the early Church Fathers and sorting them out under 158 controversial "quaestiones," or seeming contradictions, in the *Sic et Non*. He attempted to resolve the resulting theological problems by the application of logical rules such as those governing the comprehension and extension of terms.[8] He was consequently charged with rationalism by William of Thierry and Bernard of Clairvaux for making the rules of logic the determinants of faith, and his *De Unitate et Trinitate Divina* was condemned at Soissons in 1121.[9] The followers of Abelard continued the development of his logical methodology and concerned themselves with the integration of Biblical statements into a systematic whole. Rarely, if ever, did they feel the need of examining original texts in an attempt to resolve contradictions by a closer study of the sources. They were satisfied with the second-hand knowledge of the Bible and the Fathers garnered in little snippets from the *Glossa Ordinaria* of Walafrid Strabo or the *Decretals* of Gratian.[10]

Erasmus, on the other hand, devoted his life to the re-editing of original sources. He edited the Greek New Testament, Jerome, Cyprian, Arnobius, Irenaeus, Ambrose, Augustine, Aristotle, Seneca, Demosthenes, Quintus Curtius, Suetonius, Pliny the Elder, Livy, Terence, tracts of Lactantius, Chrysostom, Cicero, Plutarch, Galen, and Xenophon. Death found him working on Origen. Thus he reoriented the study of theology to a careful study and grammatical explication of the original texts.[11] Erasmus was forever insisting upon a return to the sources, "ad fontes," because an examination of the correct text frequently resolved the "quaestiunculae" of the Schools, and a close attention to the historical context removed further difficulties. Erasmus read his texts as a grammarian to discover what was taught and he was little concerned with the construction of *Summae* or integrated speculative systems.[12] For him, knowledge of languages, of the precise meaning of words, became the most important part of erudition, and he belittled the knowledge of Barbara, Celarent, and Bocardo.[13] Erasmus and the Renaissance humanists sought a total understanding of a text; Abelard and some of the other Scholastics limited themselves to an analysis of those aspects of a text subject to logical paraphrase. The Schoolmen willingly limited themselves, through the method they employed, to an investigation of those problems of the universe which were demonstrable by reason alone.[14]

The explicit content of More's *Utopia* is the result of the application of that method of investigation employed by the Scholastics in establishing and solving their "quaestiones." This Scholastic Method is not dependent upon the use of such set phrases as "Respondeo dicendum," "E contrario dicitur," "at dicit aliquis," for these are only pedagogical devices, parts of the *Lehrmethode*, developed in the Schools for greater clarity in teaching.[15] The arrangement of material under various propositions introduced by "Utrum," followed by several commonly accepted solutions, then the constructive proof, and finally the replies to the rejected opinions—an arrangement familiar to all who have but glanced at some medieval *Summa*—is not essential to the method and is not found in the works of the true father of the Scholastic Method, St. Anselm of Canterbury.[16] Anselm's motto of "Fides quaerens intellectum" roughly summarizes the essence of the method, for it was fundamentally an attempt to reach an understanding of the truths of revelation, or, in other words, to achieve a rational insight into the content of faith. Investigations conducted according to this method started by accepting some statement as true because it was revealed, and then developed by searching for some way in which reason alone might approximate, if not achieve, the same conclusion.[17] For Anselm, faith provided the goal and the impulse to investigate; the revealed truth served as the hypothesis and reason sought to make its content not more certain but merely more intelligible. For More, the Christian community made available to European man by revelation provided the hypothetical ideal, and he sought to demonstrate how closely it might have been approximated through the use of reason alone.

Anselm explains his method with some diffidence at the opening of his *Monologium*. He is writing these meditations, not because he has any conviction about his own ability to reason about these truths, but because he must fulfill the injunction, contained in the first Epistle of Peter (3:15), of first sanctifying the "Lord Christ in your hearts," and then of being "always ready to satisfy everyone that asketh you a reason of that hope which is in you." Anselm, therefore, attempts to show that "nothing in Scripture should be urged on the authority of Scripture itself but that whatever the conclusion of independent investigation should declare to be true, should, in an unadorned style, wtih common proofs and with a simple argument, be briefly enforced by the cogency of reason, and plainly expounded in the light of truth."[18] He then examines the question of how many of the divine attributes known through revelation might be demonstrated by reason alone. He even attempts, in chapter 78, a rational proof of the nature of the Trinity, but the spirit and purpose of Anselm's work is usually much more restrained.[19]

As the use of this method spread throughout all the schools during the University Period, it became increasingly clear that skill in the use of the method depended almost exclusively upon a skill in the use of the canons of logic. The ability to infer and deduce from a few commonly accepted principles, and to do this in the jargon of the Schools, came to be identified with the ability to philosophize and theologize.[20] The Scholastics of the thirteenth and fourteenth centuries moved further and further away from any concern with the Biblical content they originally sought to investigate, and mingled so much of the water of philosophy with the wine of Sacred Scripture that they only succeeded in working the worst of all miracles, changing the wine into water.[21] By the end of the fifteeenth century, the humble spirit and original purpose of Anselm and Hugh of St. Victor had been forgotten, and the Scholastics were concerned with validating and defending opposed systems of thought and extrapolating increasingly trivial points from their own philosophical premises.[22] So-called "divinity lectures" were really on the *Summae* of Scotus or the *Quaestiones Quodlibetales* of other medieval commentators. When John Colet actually lectured on the Epistles of St. Paul at Oxford, in the Michaelmas Term of 1496, he made a radical break with many of the then accepted traditions.[23] The world of the early sixteenth century was still dependent in its law, philosophy, theology, ethics, and politics upon the resources of the Scholastic Method, and it was this method that More employed to construct a work which demonstrated the inadequacies of the world the method had produced.

In his *Utopia,* More attempted to define the kind of society which reason alone, but properly directed,[24] might achieve, and how closely this purely rational society might approximate the ideal of the Christian state in theory, and even surpass contemporary Christian Europe in practice. Although the distinction between reason and revelation had become part of the Christian heritage, More employed the distinction as the Scholastics had, keeping the conclusions of reason separate from those of revelation. Thus the hypothetical Christian state, which would have involved revealed truth in its definition as in the *De Civitate Dei,* is only implied, and the explicit content of Utopia is to be understood as the result of demonstration conducted by unaided human reason. The learned reader of More's day understood that More was actually demonstrating the limits of reason in its attempts to define an ideal state, and that he was not actually defining an ideal which, for him certainly, would have required the consideration of the material available through revelation. In his letter to Lupset, prefaced to the 1517 edition of *Utopia,* William Budé points out that Christ "left among His followers a Pythagorean communion and love."[25]

The establishment of this principle of love should have abolished, "at least among His followers," all the quibbling over rights according to civil and canon law. Justice in Europe and Utopia is defined according to the express dictates of civil law. No matter how logical and impartial this justice may be, it is still inferior to the law of the New Testament; and the state founded only upon natural law has accepted only one of the avenues open to it for the ordering of its polity. If men were agreed to use all the sources of truth at their disposal, which include "the simple gospel," the "dullest would understand, and the most senseless admit . . . that in the decrees of the canonists, the divine law differs as much from the human; and, in our civil laws and royal enactments, true equity differs as much from law, as the principles laid down by Christ, the founder of human society, and the usages of His disciples, differ from the decrees and enactments of those who think the *summum bonum* and perfection of happiness to lie in the money-bags of a Croesus or of a Midas."[26]

Budé does not define the nature of the true equity of which he speaks, but presumably he would have referred to the Epistle of St. Paul to the Corinthians (I Cor. 13:1–8) on charity, as a supplement to the strict justice of the law of reason. More never defines the ideal state which he would have envisioned in the light of both reason and revelation. Presumably his daily reading of the Bible and the lectures he gave on the *De Civitate Dei* while studying law at Lincoln's Inn and residing in the London Charterhouse would have furnished some of his ideas. Nicholas Harpsfield, while commenting on these lectures given in the church of St. Lawrence in Jewry in 1501, stresses the difficulty of a text like Augustine's, which requires both divine and profane knowledge to be well understood. The *De Civitate Dei,* he says, is a book "very hard for a well-learned man to understand, and [it] cannot be profoundly and exactly understood, and especially cannot be with commendation openly read, of any man that is not well and substantially furnished as well with divinity as profane knowledge."[27] The *Utopia* can be read, as it has always been read, by anyone familiar with only "profane" learning. Its full significance, however, cannot be grasped without some knowledge of the implied "divine" knowledge.

The third term in More's elaborate equation is the Europe of his day. More's criticism of his England is not direct but is rather implied in the other two terms. If the completely rational state of Utopia surpasses Europe in its integrity and administration of justice, *a fortiori,* how much further would the ideal Christian state surpass this same early sixteenth-century Europe? As Swift employed *le mythe animal,* in the voyage to the Houyhnhnms, to show the irrationality of human conduct, so More used the fiction of the imaginary state to show that Christians without charity are worse than good pagans guided by reason alone. The natural reason of the Utopians, unaided by grace, is superior to the uncharitable Christianity of the Europeans, as the natural reason of the Houyhnhnms is superior to the warped reason of the Europeans. Thus *Utopia* and *Gulliver's Travels* can both be read as meditations upon the foolish pride of European man.[28]

Professor Hexter is undoubtedly correct in his reconstruction of the order of composition of *Utopia* when he points out that the published version falls into two parts which represent two different and separate sets of intentions. The first part of the work was finished by More during his stay in Antwerp and consisted of an introduction and the discourse of Book II. Upon his return to England, More added some prefatory lines and the entire dialogue of the first book on conditions in England, and added a few concluding pages. It is thus clear that two-thirds of the entire work consists of a theoretical description of a purely rational state, and it is this second book, the original *Utopia*, which provides the clearest illustration of More's method of composition.[29]

Book II of *Utopia* can be analyzed either logically or descriptively. A descriptive analysis would involve an orderly *explication de texte* which would consider the various details of social, domestic, and political life. More's treatment of the elements of society follows—very roughly, for he was working from memory in Antwerp—the order of chapters 4–12 of Book VII of Aristotle's *Politics*.[30] He begins with a description of the advantages of the location of the island, its cities, and natural resources; proceeds to a discussion of its inhabitants and their occupations, and only then, as in the *Politics* (chapters 13–15), does he analyze the theoretical bases of Utopia. The explicit content of Book II could also be analyzed under the six elements which Aristotle considered necessary for the existence of a state—farmers, artisans, warriors, wealth, priests, judges—and these elements are very heavily stressed in More's probable source, the *Commentary on the Politics* by Aquinas.[31] Such a continuing descriptive analysis would bog down in a multitude of details and is far more appropriate to an edition of the *Utopia*. Finally, it is possible to analyze the second book of *Utopia* in terms of a logical structure which seems to grow out of two principles which are the basis of the entire work. The first principle, the definition of the end of man and consequently of the state, is based on Aristotle's *Politics*.[32] The second principle, the definition of the norm of morality, is derived from the discussion of pleasure in Book IX of Plato's *Republic*.[33]

In their definition of the just state, the Utopians were completely dependent upon a traditional use of reason which they had perfected to the point where in "music, logic, arithmetic, and geometry they have found out in a manner all that our ancient philosophers have taught."[34] Their system of logic had not been refined to such a point that it frustrated the natural movements of the mind in its search for truth, as More thought had happened with logic in the later Scholasticism.[35] Thus the Utopians faced the problem of discovering the just state in the same fashion as the Greeks, whom, More is careful to stress, they most closely resemble. What they lacked of Aristotle and Plato, obviously a hint to the reader, traveller Hythloday was able to supply.[36] Their resources in attacking an intellectual problem would also be similar to those available to the medieval philosopher who set aside the proofs from revelation to answer the gentile who asked the reason "for the hope that was in him." More's method of solving the problem of the just state to be created by reason alone can be described by paraphrasing from chapter 9 of the first book of the

Summa contra Gentiles. Aquinas says that he will first try to explain the truth which proceeds from faith but which reason can investigate, giving the demonstrative and probable reasons taken from the philosophers and the saints by means of which the truth is confirmed. More cannot, because of the terms of his problem, take Aquinas' second step, which involves the exploration of that truth which surpasses reason and the solution of various objections by supplementing the probable arguments of reason with the certain arguments provided by faith.[37]

Since More limits his arguments to rational ones which, in some matters, can only reach probable conclusions, his Utopians must tolerate certain practices which would be unacceptable to revealed religion. More pictures the Utopians as tolerating mercy killing, divorce, and diversity of religions, practices to which he certainly did not subscribe, and which were outlawed throughout Christian Europe. More thought that, without the Decalogue and its express prohibition "Thou shalt not kill," reason alone would conclude that a man who is suffering from an incurable disease and continuous pain, unable "to do any duty of life, and [who] by overliving his own death is noisome and irksome to others, and grievous to himself" would be wiser to consent to his own death.[38] Although More's Utopians are careful to limit the conditions under which suicide is permitted, they still concede to man an authority over his own life which Christianity would consider an invasion of Divine rights.[39] The Utopians also had a high opinion of the matrimonial bond, but adultery or "intolerable wayward manners" did give either party to the contract the right to seek a license from the council to take another partner.[40] Aquinas argued that the indissolubility of the marriage bond was a natural quality which had not been recognized until after the promulgation of the New Law. There was a right of repudiation under the Old Law which was not finally abandoned until it became obvious that "it was against the nature of the sacrament."[41] So More was squarely within the common teaching of his day in maintaining that reason alone could not have arrived at the idea of the indissolubility of the marriage contract.

The knowledge of God which More attributes to the Utopians is very similar to that which Aquinas maintained in the *Contra Gentiles* was availbale through reason. Of the Utopians "the most and wisest part believe that there is a certain Godly power [*Contra Gentiles,* I, cap. xii–xiii] unknown, incomprehensible, inexplicable, far above the capacity and reach of man's wit [I, cap. xiv], dispersed throughout all the world [I, cap. xliii], not in bigness [I, cap. lxxvi] but in virtue and power [II, cap. xxii]. To Him alone they attribute the beginnings, the increasings, the proceedings, the changes, and the ends of all things [II, cap. xv–xxii]."[42] The Utopians had achieved by reason alone a clearer conception of Being and its attributes than the Greeks had. Using the statements of Scripture as hypotheses, the Scholastics constructed proofs of these Divine attributes. The Utopians, without revelation to suggest goals for the flights of reason, have surpassed the Greeks and equalled the Schoolmen. In its 1760 years of continuous development, Utopian philosophy has reached a point which,[43] as a matter of actual recorded history, Western philosophy never achieved without the suggestions of Hebraic and Christian belief. Thus the ideal republic of Utopia is "Nowhere" in two dimensions: Nowhere in space and, more important still, Nowhere in time.

The Utopians consider Christianity an obvious supplement to their own thinking and are thus much readier to accept it than the historical gentile. "But after they heard us speak of the name of Christ, of His doctrine, laws, miracles, and of the no less wonderful constancy of so many martyrs, whose blood willingly shed brought a great number of nations throughout all parts of the world into their sect, you will not believe with how glad minds they agreed."

More is aware of the theological implications of this acceptance and, in a seemingly off-hand phrase, at once preserves the concept of faith as a gift and also protects it from the charge of being a blind assent. He refuses to decide "whether it were by the secret inspiration of God, or else for that they thought it next unto that opinion which among them is counted the chiefest" that the Utopians accepted Christianity.[44]

Medieval speculation on the problem of the salvation of the heathen also determined the presentation of the alternative explanations of the Utopians' ready acceptance of Christianity. The Schoolmen, as well as the earlier Fathers, were preoccupied with the eventual fate of those good pagans who died before the Church could reach them. On the one hand, the Fathers always taught that an act of faith and the remission of original sin through baptism were necessary for salvation. On the other hand, the Fathers also taught that "God wills the salvation of all men, and that no adult is damned but by his own fault."[45] Hugh of St. Victor and Bernard of Clairvaux argued that the minimum of belief necessary for salvation was an explicit belief in God's existence and in His providence, which the Utopians certainly had, and an implicit belief in some mediator between God and man.[46] Aquinas advanced what came to be accepted as the classic solution of the problem in the *De Veritate*. There he argued that, although it is not in our power to know by ourselves alone those things which are proper to faith, yet "if we do as much as in our power lies, that is to say, if we follow the directions of natural reason, God will not permit us to go without what is necessary to us."[47] Further, he thought that it must be held as most certain, "certissime est tenendum," that if anyone followed the dictates of natural reason in seeking good and avoiding evil, God would "either reveal to them by internal inspiration those things which must be believed or send them some preacher of the faith as he sent Peter to Cornelius."[48] Hythloday can thus be called a prophet to the Utopians, and the Rev. Rowland Phillips, Canon of St. Paul's, who was most anxious to go to Utopia to "further and increase" the religion "which is already there begun," may be considered their apostle.[49] More, like Langland, however, is concerned with the adequacy of the knowledge of the natural law and not with the possible appearance of an apostle.

Ac trewth that trespassed neuere ne transuersed ageines his lawe,
But lyueth as his lawe techeth and leueth there be no bettere,

And if there weren he wolde amende and in such wille deyeth,
Ne wolde neuere trewe god but treuth were allowed . . .[50]

More's quick summary of years of speculation in a seemingly offhand remark
illustrates the difficulty of identifying the sources of his thought. Working
with or without books before him, he concentrated on the principle, overlooked the details, and elaborated the argument to suit his needs.

Throughout his discussion of questions which the Scholastics would have
considered proper to natural theology, More is careful to maintain that the
Utopians are limited to merely probable conclusions. Without revelation they
may only think or believe certain theological propositions are true, but they
cannot be certain. Therefore the decree of King Utopus, "that it should be
lawful for every man to favor and follow what religion he would, and that he
might do the best he could to bring others to his opinion," is a logical consequence of the degree of certitude available in theological matters. Utopus
made this decree because he did not dare to "define and determine . . . unadvisedly [temere]; as doubting whether God, desiring manifold and diverse
sorts of honour, would inspire sundry men with sundry kinds of religion.
And this surely he thought a very unmeet and foolish thing, and a point of
arrogant presumption, to compel all other by violence and threatening to
agree to the same that thou believest to be true."[51] Obviously this was neither
the attitude of More, who died the "King's good servant but God's first," nor
of Catholic Europe, which then professed its faith in the One True Church
and silenced the unbeliever at home and abroad.

In religious matters the complete rational man, King Utopus, "gave to
every man free liberty and choice to believe what he would" with but two
reservations. He charged all men to refrain from entertaining "so vile and
base an opinion of the dignity of man's nature, as to think that the souls do
die and perish with the body; or that the world runs at all adventures,
governed by no divine providence."[52] These principles were considered either
immediately apparent or certainly demonstrable, and they could not be
denied except through ill will. Further, these two principles are the logical
basis of the just state, and to deny them is to deny the very assumptions
upon which Utopia was founded.

The Utopians and More reached their conception of the ideal state by
following the same order of investigation as Aristotle and Aquinas. They first
define the final end of man and from this argue to the purpose of the ideal
state. Aquinas, in his commentary on the opening of Book VII of the *Politics,*
argues that the rationale of any civil order is determined by the end it is to
implement. Since the end of the ideal state is the ensuring of the achievement
of the highest end of man, it follows that the final end of man must first be
known before the form of the ideal society can be ascertained.[53] For Aquinas,
More, and the Utopians, the solution of the ethical problem of what constitutes the good life must therefore precede the solution of the political problem, what constitutes the best form of society.[54] It is precisely in "that part
of philosophy which treats of manners and virtues," ethics, that the reasons

and opinions of the Utopians most agree with those of the sixteenth-century
Europeans. The Utopians reason of virtue and pleasure, the problems of ethics
and morality, "but the chief and principal question is in what thing, be it one
or more, the felicity of man consists."[55]

Yet the Utopians do not conduct their investigation of what constitutes
the felicity of man entirely within the limits of ethics as a practical science.
"For they never dispute of felicity or blessedness, but they join to the reasons
of philosophy certain principles taken out of religion, without the which to
the investigation of true felicity, they think reason of itself weak and imperfect." There are two principles which must be imported from natural theology
into the discussion of ethics. They are "that the soul is immortal," and "that
to our virtues and good deeds rewards be appointed after this life and to our
evil deeds punishments."[56] These are the same two principles which men were
required to believe by edict of King Utopus: that the soul lives on after death
and that divine providence orders the world morally as well as physically. The
Utopians believed that these principles were necessary not only to demonstrate
man's end but also to secure order in the state. Remove these fundamental
beliefs and "then without any delay they pronounce no man to be so foolish,
which would not do all his diligence and endeavor to obtain pleasure by right
or wrong."[57]

To define the happiness which is the end of man, More adapts Book IX of
Plato's *Republic* as an illustration of the best argumentation available to
natural reason on this particular problem. For the Utopians, as for Plato, the
end of man and the principle for evaluating whether or not an action is con-
ducive to that end is pleasure. "In this point they seem almost too much given
and enclined to the opinion of them which defend pleasure; wherein they
determine either all or the chiefest parts of man's felicity to rest."[58] More was
aware that most of his contemporaries would instinctively recoil from this
opinion as proper to Epicureanism as it was then understood. More, therefore,
went to show that pleasure, when properly defined, can be the norm of
morality and the end of man. "But now, sir, they think not felicity to rest in
all pleasure, but only in that pleasure that is good and honest; and that, hereto,
as to perfect blessedness, our nature is allured and drawn even of virtue."
True pleasure thus depends on a recognition of a hierarchy in the human
faculties. "Pleasure they call every motion and state of the body and mind,
wherein man had a natural delectation. Appetite they join to nature, and that
not without good cause. For like as not only the senses, but also right reason
covets whatever is naturally pleasant, so that it may be gotten without wrong
or injury, not letting or debarring a greater pleasure, nor causing painful
labor . . ."[59] True pleasure is, therefore, also natural and prefers the higher
good to the lower. Thus the Utopian, like Plato's "man of understanding,"
will regulate "his bodily habit and training, and so far will he be from yielding to brutal and irrational pleasures, that he will regard even health as quite
a secondary matter; his first object will be not that he may be fair or strong
or well, unless he is likely thereby to gain temperance, but he will always
desire so to attemper the body as to preserve the harmony of the soul."[60]

The soul, following the principles established by reason, leads a natural life which is also a virtuous life; "for they define virtue to be a life ordered according to nature; and that we be hereunto ordained by God; and that He doth follow the course of nature, which in desiring and refusing things is ruled by reason." Thus the Utopians can conclude that "even very nature prescribes to us a joyful life, that is to say, pleasure, as the end of all our operations."[61]

The Utopians think the greatest of these pleasures "comes from the exercise of virtue, and conscience of good life." More states, however, that this view of felicity need be accepted only under one condition: "unless any godlier be inspired into man from heaven."[62] More does not discuss whether the Utopians "believe well or not," for he has only undertaken "to show and declare their laws and ordinances, and not to defend them." Yet the illogic of ascetic practices in Utopia is his way of indicating the inadequacies of this view. The only logical attitude for anyone who has accepted natural pleasure as the end of man is to consider any neglect of bodily beauty, fasting, and other customs which "do injury to health, and reject the other pleasant motions of nature" as points of extreme madness, and a "token of man's being cruelly minded towards himself and unkind toward nature."[63] In a long parenthetical clause More indicates that ascetical practices, after the promulgation of Christian revelation, would not be reprehensible but even meritorious. Man might neglect natural pleasures "whiles he doth with a fervent zeal procure the wealth of other benefits, or the common profit, for the which pleasures forborn he is in hope of a greater pleasure of God."[64] The acceptance of fasts and prayers, scourgings and hair shirts as virtuous practices would require a complete revision of the conception of felicity entertained by the Utopians to one wherein the beatitude of spiritual union with God was the goal of life.[65]

In defining the end of man by importing two principles from natural theology, More was imitating Aristotle's procedure in the *Politics*. Where More adapted the ethics of Plato to solve his problem, Aristotle borrowed from his own *Ethics*. "We maintain, and have said in the *Ethics*, if the arguments there adduced are of any value, that happiness is the realization and perfect exercise of virtue, and this not conditional, but absolute."[66] Aristotle's conclusion is surprisingly similar to that of the Utopians, though their dialectical processes in reaching the conclusion have been different. More now moves ahead with Aristotle. "Since the end of individuals and of states is the same, the end of the best man and of the best constitution must also be the same; it is therefore evident that there ought to exist in both of them the virtues of leisure; for peace, as has been often repeated, is the end of war, and leisure of toil."[67] More's conception of the purpose of the Utopian society is stated in terms very close to Aristotle's: "In the institution of that weal public this end is only and chiefly pretended and minded that what time may possibly be spared from the necessary occupations and affairs of the commonwealth, all that the citizens should withdraw from the bodily service to the free liberty of the mind and garnishing of the same. For herein they suppose the felicity of this life to consist."[68]

Nothing is so frequently stressed throughout *Utopia* as the obligations of the state to provide the leisure necessary for intellectual development. The chief functions of the Syphograunts are to insure that no one "sit idle and yet that no one work continually like laboring and toiling beasts."[69] Production quotas are determined to provide sufficiency and not superfluity.[70] The resulting freedom of the citizens is to be devoted to some good science. The scheme of values in this ideal state is therefore based on the principle of whether or not a certain practice promotes or curtails the citizens' leisure.

The abolition of private property is not a major point in the logical structure of *Utopia* but an obvious inference from basic principle. The Utopians believe that private ownership is the basis of avarice and the desire for superfluity of goods, which disquiet the mind and destroy private and public peace. Remove the right of private ownership, which is not a natural right according to the Utopians, provide man with a sufficiency, and the entire society is liberated from unnecessary toil and freed to pursue the pleasures of the mind.[71] Again this is not More's real attitude but a logical consequence of the principles to which he has committed his ideal society. It should be pointed out, however, that most of the Church Fathers, and some of the later Scholastics, would have agreed with More that communal ownership of goods was superior to private ownership, and that, in the words of St. Ambrose, "things were made by the creator to be held in common and private ownership is contrary to nature."[72] For St. Chrysostom, the more perfect the nature of the individual, the less the need for those "chilling words 'mine' and 'thine.' "[73] Duns Scotus was even of the opinion that one of the consequences of the Fall of Man was the abrogation of the precept of the natural law forbidding the private ownership of goods. Alexander of Hales and St. Bonaventure believed that in a state of innocence all things would have been held in common and nothing would have been restrained within the limits of private ownership.[74] In the *Dialogue of Comfort* More argues very strongly against the common ownership of property because of the present historical state of man, fallen and redeemed but still unable to control his passions through his reason. The Utopian commonwealth must wait, for its realization, upon the perfect rationalist or the perfect Christian, the man without pride.[75] The Utopian attitudes towards war, treaties, the use of mercenaries, and the treatment of natural slaves are also immediate inferences from the Utopian conception of the state as a means of guaranteeing the leisure which is the natural end of man.

Using only reason and the methods of a medieval rationalism, More attempted to demonstrate the failings of contemporary Christian society which was the product of those same forces. More would never have been at home in the Utopian world of universal grays and humorless men vaguely reminiscent of the lands visited by Lemuel Gulliver. More and Swift fought the same enemy, for both believed that "the respect of every man's private commodity, or else the authority of our saviour Christ . . . would have brought all the world long ago into the laws of this weal public, if it were not that one and only beast, the prince and mother of all mischief, pride, doth withstand it."[76]

It is impossible in this short space to do more than suggest how many of the social, domestic, and liturgical customs of *Utopia* could also have been arrived at by an extension of this Scholastic Method in a very practical way. For Thomas More, the ideal daily life of a Christian community, living according to the counsels of revelation as well as the dictates of reason, might well have been found in the *Regula Monachorum* of St. Benedict or the Carthusian *Consuetudines* of Guigo under which More himself lived for some four years in the London Charterhouse. More attributed to his Utopians as many of the details of monastic life as he thought could have been perceived by reason alone. The simple dress of the Utopians, made out of undyed wool, suggests the old Carthusian dress or habit.[77] The regulations observed by the Utopians while on a journey, their system for founding new communities, their meetings in hall to discuss and vote upon matters of common importance—all reflect the customs of the cloister.[78] The reading and controlled conversations during meals are also echoes of monastic practices.[79] The atmosphere of the Utopian churches and their restrained use of ornamentation in their liturgy and architecture closely resemble the practices of the Carthusians.[80] The careful apportioning of the various crafts, like the monastic "obediences," among the various members of the community, the performance of manual labor by all members of the society, and the practice of ordering each hour of the day, stem directly from the Benedictine Rule.[81] More's *Utopia* is an imaginative diagram of the contemplative life which all rational men should prefer to the active life which was yearly replacing it as an ideal.

The argument for reading *Utopia* in the context of medieval thought can be further strengthened by considering how different More's method was in the composition of some of his other works. While a prisoner in the Tower, More wrote a *Treatise on the Passion* in the construction of which he was guided by the methods of the Renaissance grammarian or humanist. More shared in the spirit of Christian humanism which animated the Brethren of the Common Life and the *Imitation of Christ,* and which was chiefly concerned with the disciplining of the will and the emotions. More, like Colet and Erasmus, was intent upon knowing compunction, not as a theoretical virtue, but as an enkindling affection motivating true Christian charity.[82] More and Colet approached the Epistles of St. Paul, not, like Abelard, to discover propositions which could be employed as heuristic hypotheses or integrated into a complex dogmatic system, but as men seeking to know the message of the Epistles and how it could be applied to the improvement of their daily lives. They read the various Epistles as grammarians, to grasp their literal meaning and to assess the force of the various counsels, admonitions, and commandments. Erasmus studied the texts of scripture and his beloved St. Jerome in the same fashion. The Scholastics refused to consider Erasmus a theologian because his methods were so far different from theirs. Erasmus pointed out that there were other methods of studying theology than those which had ruled the universities since the time of Abelard, and he defended his own methods as descended from the Fathers of the early Church.[83] The methods of St. Jerome were an outgrowth of the grammatical method of his own teacher, Donatus. The methods of the classical grammarian were also the basis of the methods of Lorenzo Valla, who first systematized the grammatical method of Renaissance humanism.

More's *Treatise on the Passion* was based on the *Monatesseron* of John Gerson, a synthesis of the four Gospel accounts of the passion of Christ. The mood and purpose of the work is to pause "and with entire devotion consider" the events of the passion, searching for the practical significance of the words and actions, so that each man might thereby improve his life.[84] More explores the connotations of words, Jewish antiquities and customs, astronomical calculations, and even some of the stylistic peculiarities of Aramaic. These are the interests of Valla in his examination of the authenticity of the Donation of Constantine and an application of the methods of studying scripture outlined by Erasmus in his *Paraclesis*. More traces the significance of the feast of the Unleavened Bread through the *Dies Azymorum* of the Greeks, and, with the help of St. Jerome, through the *Pascha* of the Hebrews to its ultimate meaning of "immolation."[85] He shows how Eusebius and Chrysostom were correct in their dating of Easter, and how the later Greeks confused their calculations.[86] In a manner which would have delighted William Budé, he discusses the value of the coins Judas received for his betrayal of Christ and concludes that they were worth ten shillings.[87] Words and their fine shades of meaning also occupy him. What is the significance of the two names given to Peter in Mark 14:27, "And he saith to Peter: Simon sleepest thou?" More thinks that "it was a private check given unto him that he called him not by the name of Peter or Cephas," for the name of "Simon" in Christ's day meant "hearing and obedient," and this is the very opposite of what Peter was then doing. More again decides in favor of an ironical interpretation of Christ's words in Mark 4:41, "And he cometh the third time and saith to them: Sleep ye now and take your rest." Only after considering the commentary of St. Augustine on the passage, he concludes that Christ meant the very opposite of what he said, and his decision is based on the vigor of the figurative language.[88] Again, More is puzzled by the precise meaning of "until" (*donec*). Does it mean until Christ's Ascension or is it employed in a completely final sense?[89] He explains the "with desire I have desired" (*desiderio desideravi*) of the Vulgate by reference to the common stylistic practice of the Hebrew of doubling a word to secure emphasis.

More's meditations on the Passion are similar to a continuous series of notes of the kind to be found in Erasmus' *Novum Instrumentum*. In his note to Acts 17:34 Erasmus can not forbear resurrecting the entire discussion of the authenticity of the writings of the pseudo-Dionysius and the brilliant exposure of their falsity by Lorenzo Valla.[90] The note on Matthew 23:2 brings out the famous diatribe against those bishops who neither preach as frequently as they should nor live a Christian life. Erasmus' vehemence is not the main concern here, but rather his habit of reading the Bible as a source of practical counsel. His note on Mark 6:9 produces a long discussion of what the Roman sandal and tunic were like, and the description of the clothes of Christ carries us through the works of Horace, Plato, and Pliny the Younger.[91] The note on Matthew 16:18-19, "Thou art Peter and on this rock I shall build my Church," calls up a learned discussion of Greek and Latin particles which would have delighted Browning's grammarian.[92] The controversy over Luke 2:14, "Gloria in altissimis Deo et in terra pax hominibus bonae voluntatis" (according to the Vulgate) is familiar to everyone. Erasmus decides, on purely grammatical grounds, that the reading should be "Glory to God in the highest and on earth the peace of good will to men" because "it is clear that 'good will' does not refer to men but to peace. Further the conjunction 'and' is used and the preposition 'in' which is not present in the Vulgate of the Latin codices has been added. For the codex which we examined at the College of Constance had that preposition added in an old hand."[93] Grammar, in the larger sense of the word, thus came to replace the methods of the Scholastic in the solution of theological problems.

All this learned baggage of the *Novum Instrumentum* and the *Treatise on the Passion* is only instrumental. It is only a means of acquiring the true Christian philosophy, the philosophy or humanism of Christ as expressed in the Bible. But this Christian wisdom is described, in the *Paraclesis,* as so excellent "that it turns all of the wisdom of the world to folly."[94] This may be the reason why the eminent rationalist, the traveler Hythloday, is given a name which in Greek means "nonsense." The real Christian must leave behind him the impious curiosities, the incomplete folly, of an excessively rationalistic Scholasticism, and, employing the science of the Christian humanist, seek that knowledge of Christ which results in His imitation.[95] It is this search for the concrete, practical meaning of Scripture which brought about a change in the method of reading Scripture, and the change in the way of living which followed hard upon it.

The style of the *Utopia* is also similar to that of the medieval Scholastics. Almost any passage, selected at random, reveals the similarity of the vocabulary to the vocabulary of the Schools. It would be unfair to cite any of the argumentative passages of the *Utopia* already referred to because the subject matter might be advanced as an explanation of the choice of vocabulary. Here, however, is a passage explaining the only condition under which the Utopians go to war: "Nam eam iustissimam belli causam ducunt, quum populus, quispiam eius soli, quo ipse non utitur, sed velut inane ac vacuum possidet, aliis tamen qui ex naturae praescripto inde nutriri debeant, usum ac possessionem interdicat."[96] Descriptive passages are no less intricately organized and they are also without any of More's characteristic use of imaginative language: "Omne prandium coenamque ab aliqua lectione auspicantur, quae ad mores faciat; sed brevi tamen, ne fastidio sit. Ab hac seniores honestos sermones, sed neque tristes ac infacetos ingerunt."[97] Several other descriptive passages would show the same tightly packed sequence of detail and colorless language. Narrative passages are also lacking in More's usually vigorous and imaginative language. The famous passage describing the advent of the ambassadors from the Anemolians, who were unaware that the Utopians did not value gold or ornaments, relies upon an accumulation of facts told in general terms for its effect: "Itaque ingressi sunt legati tres, cum comitibus centum, omnes vestitu versicolori, plerique serico, legati ipsi (nam domi nobiles erant) amictu aureo, magnis torquibus et inauribus aureis, ad haec anulis aureis in manibus, monilibus insuper appensis in pileo, quae margaritis ac gemmis affulgebant: omnibus postremo rebus ornati, quae apud Utopienses aut servorum supplicia, aut infamium dedecora, aut puerorum nugamenta fuere.''[99] More's Latin style was usually more forceful and vigorous, as in the following passage from his little-known *Rossei:* "Cum his mandatis dimittit consilium, illi igitur abeunt, aliis alio, quo quemque tulit animus: et se per omnia plaustra, vehicula, cymbas, thermas, ganea, tonstrinas, tabernas, lustra, pistrina, latrinas, lupanaria diffundunt: illic observant sedulo, atque in tabellas referant, quicquid aut auriga sordide, aut servus verniliter, aut portitor improbe, aut parasitus scurriliter, aut meretrix petulanter, aut leno turpiter, aut balneator spurce, aut cacator obscoene loquutus sit.''[99]

If it is objected that the difference in style between the last passage and the preceding is the result of differences in purpose, we must reply that that is precisely the point. The style of the *Utopia* is appropriate to its method and purpose, which are logical and medieval. One sentence from the *Dialogue of Comfort* may be dismissed as not proving much, but it can illustrate how More wrote when he did not deliberately shut himself off from some of his intellectual resources. When More wrote with the full weight of the creative mind, he frequently mounted a metaphorical meaning upon an underlying rational statement. The following sentence summarizes much of the central content of the *Utopia* in a brilliant metaphor, and, it might be argued, is a good example of a unified, not a "dis-integrated," sensibility.

> Some good drugs have they the philosophers of Greece in their shops, for which they may be suffered to dwell among our apothecaries, if their medicines be made not of their own brain, but after the bills made by the great physician God, prescribing the medicines Himself, and correcting the faults of their erroneous receipts. For without this way taken with them, they shall not fail to do as many bold, blind apothecaries do, which either for lucre or a foolish pride, give such folk medicines of their own devising, and therewith kill up in corners many such simple folk, as they find so foolish to put their lives in such lewd and inlearned, blind bayard hands. We shall therefore neither fully receive these philosophers' reasons in this matter, nor yet utterly refuse them.[100]

The last sentence might be paraphrased: we shall therefore neither fully accept the philosophers in political theory, nor utterly reject them, but correct their theories according to the prescriptions of revelation.

In word choice, sentence structure, sentence movement paralleling the natural movements of the mind, the *Dialogue of Comfort* is a brilliant piece of humanistic prose addressed to the whole man. The *Utopia* is thoroughly Scholastic in its method of construction and largely medieval in its style and content. *Utopia* comes into true focus when it is viewed as the product of the Scholastic Method, revealing the limitations of that method and of the society for which it was largely responsible. The seeming paradoxes which have worried scholars as they tried to reconcile this or that practice in *Utopia* with

More's own personal life disappear when it is realized that *Utopia* is only a small part of More's beliefs. It is not necessary to call in More's sense of humor, or a reactionary old age, to account for the Utopian toleration of divorce and religious difference. Utopia is all of a piece, marking the end of the Middle Ages and their methods, and the beginning of a Renaissance which was to rely on entirely different methods of investigation and interpretation.

MORE'S *UTOPIA* AS A PARADIGM

Hubertus Schulte Herbrüggen

"The idea of a perfect and immortal commonwealth will always be found as chimerical as that of a perfect and immortal man." David Hume, 1761.

The name of Sir Thomas More is one of the most distinguished in the history of English humanism. Born the son of a shrewd London lawyer, More made the early acquaintance of the scholars Linacre, Grocyn, and Colet in his student days in Oxford and London. With many of the great and virtuous men of his age he formed lasting friendships, above all with Erasmus of Rotterdam who wrote his *Encomium Moriae* under More's roof. His friends admired his keen wit, his shrewd mind, his incorruptible judgement, his persuasive powers, the conciliation of his humor. The rare combination of such gifts raised him from a backbencher in the Commons and a rather unimportant junior member on foreign embassies to the highest position of the realm, when, in 1529, he succeeded the almost omnipotent Cardinal Wolsey. Those gifts also brought him into the special favor of Henry VIII until, eventually, the very integrity of his character got him into trouble with his royal master and made him resign from his office in 1532. His uncompromising steadfastness in "the King's Great Matter," Henry's matrimonial affairs, made him lose his freedom; and his refusal to swear the oath of royal supremacy in ecclesiastical affairs cost him his head—*indignatio principis mors est,* as the Duke of Norfolk put it. Soon after his death on July 6, 1535 he was regarded by many throughout Europe as a martyr; he was canonized in 1935.

His *Epigrams* were much admired by his contemporaries, and his Latin translations from the Greek were widely read. For centuries they seemed buried in oblivion like many of his English works, especially the controversial writings, to which he had devoted countless hours of restless nights during the twenties and early thirties of the century. It was none of these writings that secured for More a permanent place in world literature, but a slim quarto volume with the splendid Renaissance title: "Libellus vere aureus nec minvs salvtaris qvam festiuus de optimo reip. statu, deque noua Insula Vtopia authore clarissimo viro Thoma Moro inclytae ciuitatis Londinensis ciue & vicecomite cura M. Petri Aegidii Antuerpiensis, & arte Theodorici Martini Alustensis, Typographi almae Louaniensium Academiae nunc primum accuratissime editus.:. Cum gratia & priuilegio."[1] It was published at Louvain towards the

Reprinted, by permission of the author and publisher, from *Utopie und Anti-Utopie* (Bochum-Langendreer, 1960), pp. 16–37. Translated and revised by the author.

end of 1516, i.e., in a period of his life when he was closely connected with
Erasmus of Rotterdam; their mutual friend, Peter Gilles, town-clerk of
Antwerp, saw the first edition through the press. Among the many editions
on the continent, the finest, with woodcuts by the brothers Ambrose and
Hans Holbein, was printed by Johann Froben at Basel in March and, again,
in November 1518.

The first German translation—it significantly contained only the "utopian"
second book—by the humanist lawyer Claudius Cantiuncula (Claude Chanson-
nette) of Metz, was printed by Johann Bebel at Basel in 1524. The first
Italian translation, by (H)Ortensio Lando, appeared in Venice in 1548, printed
by Aurelio Pincio; the first French translation, by Jehan le Blond d'Evreux,
dated from 1550, printed by Charles l'Angelier. It is well worth noting that it
was four years after Henry VIII's death before the first English translation,
by Ralph Robynson, was published.[2] Thus neither the original Latin nor any
English version was published in England during More's lifetime. An annotated scholarly edition of the *Utopia,* printing the March 1518 Basel Latin
text and a revised version of the English translation by G. C. Richards on
facing pages, appeared as volume 4 of the *Yale Edition of the Complete Works
of St. Thomas More* in 1965, edited by Edward Surtz, S.J., and J. H. Hexter.
Quotations are from this edition.

Elementary Features

More wrote his *Utopia* in Latin, the *lingua franca* of the western civilized
world. He deliberately chose the scholars' language since he did not want to
have his book misunderstood by those half-educated "semi-scholars" able to
read English only.[3] Evidently not satisfied with that language barrier alone,
he coined himself a number of words from the Greek, which, as we shall see,
function as key-words for the understanding of the whole.

The background story of *Utopia* was taken by More from contemporary
English history as well as from Amerigo Vespucci's *Quattuor navigationes.*[4]
The inner form of the little book corresponds to its external structure.[5] It is
a framed tale where, roughly speaking, the division into two books separates
the frame from the tale proper. The frame of Book I serves to create a distinct
political and social atmosphere which then controls the form of the inner
utopian story as told in Book II, although the narrative quality of the latter
contrasts sharply with that of the frame. The frame also introduces characters
and problems which are then developed, in Book II, into the predominant
theme, "the best state of the public weale" (Robynson's title).

There is hardly any action or plot in the *Utopia.* Not even the employment
of travel stories (one of the most ancient plots in world literature) can deceive
us in that. The utter lack of any eventful plot causes the author to make
double use of the motif of the returning protagonist. In the first place it is
Morus who gives an account of his journey to Flanders (pp. 46 ff.); in the
second, a few pages later (pp. 50 ff.), it is Raphael Hythloday who relates his
voyages to the new world. In both instances, it should be noted, it is neither

on the travel nor on the traveller that the reader's interest is focussed (as would be the case in a proper traveller's tale). Both times the journey serves as a motivation for telling an otherwise plotless tale of description. Since it cannot be the plot which organizes this work, might it then be the characters?

In Book I More mentions a number of names known from contemporary history (Peter Gilles, Cardinal Morton, John Clement, his own name, etc.) whereas the fictitious Hythloday introduces quite a different literary species: that of "tell-tale names" (Hythlodaeus, King Utopus, the Macarians, the Polylerites, etc.). The historical names serve here as concrete "evidence"; they fortify the "scientific" make-believe, as it were, of the work. Here Morus and Gilles stand security as trustworthy and well-known "witnesses" for the tale. The punning names,[6] on the other hand, begin seemingly by following suit, being apparent "eye-witnesses" for the story told. Soon, however, they bring an augur's smile onto the face of any reader whom knowledge of Greek provides with the precise bearings of the happy but unreal island by explaining to him: *that* island is not of this world.

Significantly, there are no individuals named besides old King Utopus, who is mentioned only at the beginning of the report and hardly ever emerges from the mists of a remote past. Whenever characters occur in the utopian tale proper, and such occasions are rare, they appear in the articled plural and as mere functionaries, "the Phylarchs," "the physicians," "the prisoners of war," "the family fathers," "the mothers." The citizens of Utopia come before the reader's eye neither as rounded individual characters nor as traditional literary types, but as mute roles on the Utopian stage.

Since neither plot nor characters are thus strong enough to shoulder the literary superstructure of the *Utopia,* it remains now to be seen if the setting will serve here as the structural backbone of the work. In More's work the accent rests without doubt on the description of political and social conditions which runs through both books and gives them unity. Contrasting with travel tales proper, the voyages of Hythloday are no end in themselves, but serve as a vehicle first for his social criticism and then for his utopian narrative: "What he said he saw in each place would be a long tale to unfold and is not the purpose of this work ... Now I intend to relate merely what he told us of the manners and customs of the Utopians ..." (pp. 53, 55). The first utopian feature occurs when Raphael contrasts the ideal domestic policy and penal system of the *Polylerites* ("the people of much nonsense") with the rather gloomy English reality (pp. 74 ff.). Shortly afterwards a similar note is struck when, under the veil of the *Achorians* ("people without land"), he urges France to abstain from any Machiavellian form of foreign policy and to adopt instead the course of social reform at home (pp. 88 ff.). It is struck for a third time when the widespread though dubious political practice of relying on the advice of corrupt courtiers is contrasted with the ideal but modest financial policy of the *Macarians* ("the fortunate men," pp. 96 ff.). Raphael regards private property as *the* main evil in all existing states and tries to put them to shame by the common ownership of—the *Utopians* (pp. 98 ff.). Here is the cue! Book I closes with Raphael's promise to give a detailed report of that wonderful country.

Book II, with its chapters arranged under subject headings, is devoted almost entirely to displaying the characteristic setting of the ideal Utopian world. The perfect Utopian order is founded on the principle of reason, for which a mathematical and geometrical outline of their dwellings is an eloquent expression. Each of the 54 cities of the island, all designed after an equal quadratic ground-plan, have 6000 families of 10 to 16 members each, thus making a total of some 60–to 96,000 heads per city. The urban character of the Utopian state becomes more evident when one realizes that in More's England only London had as many inhabitants. Every thirty families choose annually a *phylarch,* every ten phylarchs one *proto-phylarch,* every 200 proto-phylarchs then, by secret ballot, appoint out of four candidates named by the people their governor for life (p. 122). Only scholars are chosen to official posts (p. 132). To discuss political issues outside the senate is regarded as a capital crime (p. 124). The island state's foreign policy corresponds to its splendid isolation. The Utopians know of no necessity to enter into firm treaties (pp. 196 ff.). Those of their neighbors who receive their governors from the Utopians they regard as allies, the others as friends (p. 196). War is abhorred (pp. 198 ff.). Only the defense of their own country or of that of their friends is a *casus belli,* as is the redress of injustice or the liberation of a people from tyranny (ibid.). They are well-versed in stratagems (p. 202). They prefer to send foreign mercenaries or to offer financial subsidies rather than sacrifice their own soldiers in action (pp. 148 ff., 204 ff.).

Utopia's social order is characterized by a nation-wide duty to work for six hours daily (p. 126), from which only the most educated are excepted (pp. 130 ff.). Freedom of movement is restricted by a system of visa endorsements, lest anybody dodge his work (pp. 144 ff.). Hard labor is done by volunteers, by convicted criminals, or by foreign bondsmen who "voluntarily choose slavery in Utopia" (p. 184). Just as every citizen contributes to the common weal, so all the yield of the fertile land is common to all. The whole society is like one big family. The head of the family orders from the local market all the necessary goods—and no more!—for his family. Out of the abundance all goods are available gratis (pp. 136 ff.). Any luxury in dress or manner of living is prohibited (pp. 132 ff., 152). Gold is used only for fetters and for chamber-pots (p. 152).

Children, girls included, are given a sound education. Before daybreak they start with public lectures on music, logic, arithmetic, geometry and astronomy (p. 128). The quest for true happiness is their key problem in moral philosophy (p. 160). They find it not in vulgar amusements but in the good conscience of a life spent according to common sense, i.e., respecting the very nature of all things (pp. 160 ff., 174 ff.). In religion the Utopians are tolerant (p. 220). They admit, however, no one to the civil service who does not believe in divine providence, the immortality of the soul and eternal retribution; indeed, those who deny these tenets they do not regard as human (p. 220). Their integrity directs them to practice justice and charity. The sick are nursed in public hospitals, treated by highly skilled doctors (p. 184 ff.). In choosing a husband they let themselves be guided by eugenic principles (pp. 186 ff.). Adultery is severely punished (p. 186).

Ideas

The structure of the whole work centers around the idea of Utopian ideality which is materialized here above all in the field of politics. Utopian man is hardly ever seen as an individual, but rather as a *zoon politikon* who finds perfection only in the society of the state and who does not seem to carry it within himself. The Utopian ideality takes shape in the various fields of politics. Above all, the Utopian state is a *societas perfecta,* that is to say its people form by descent, history, culture, and solidarity one nation; its territory is coherent, has natural boundaries, and is big enough for the nation. The executive power is both legal and sovereign, and it restricts itself to the indispensable. It is a functional means and not an end in itself. It is regarded as a tool for social order and not as an oppression. The static ideality of the Utopian state finds its correspondence in the dynamic ideality of its policy. In the social sphere: the fundamental institution of the macro-family; in economics: their communism at home; in foreign trade: the principle of autarky and absolute surplus of exports; in foreign policy: their splendid isolation.

As to the causes of Utopian ideality, the opinion of scholars is at variance. R. W. Chambers regards religion as the primary cause.[7] We beg to differ for two reasons. First, because there is not one but many religions in Utopia, differing profoundly from each other; secondly, because they coincide only in a rather faint deism and in the belief in eternal justice (p. 216 ff.). This sort of lowest possible common denominator is insufficient to serve as the foundation of their ideality. In fact, their concord, political prudence and fraternal communism are neither the result of their worshipping the sun, the moon, or other celestial bodies, nor of the prayers and hymns of their services which theologically are rather vague.[8] We find, rather, that Utopian ideality is founded not in their religion but in the *ethics* of their citizens. For it is not the sphere of religious and metaphysical ties between man and the godhead, but the sphere of *natural* ethical behavior of the Utopians founded on reason which prompts their actions and serves as a foundation of their thriving public institutions.[9] This form of natural ethics is common to all Utopians. When we try to concretize the concept of Utopian ethics, we find that their baser appetites are subject to reason.[10] Now, this very *rationi optemperare,* this "obeying the dictates of reason," is what medieval theology called "integrity," i.e., to be free from concupiscence and pride.[11] As has been shown before, integrity is a fundamental constituent of the Utopian world. Raphael himself may be called in as a witness: "man's regard for his own interest ... would long ago have brought the whole world to adopt the laws of the Utopian commonwealth, had not one single monster, the chief and progenitor of all plagues, striven against it—I mean, *Pride*."[12] Pride, then, prevents ideality in our real world as it is, since it prevents our behaving according to reason: "(it) acts like the suckfish in preventing and hindering them from entering on a better way of life" (p. 245). Since the Utopians behave according to reason, they also "at home . . . have extirpated the roots of ambition and factionalism along with all the other vices" (p. 245). And indeed, they have uprooted all the other familiar vices: knowing of neither money nor private property, there is no room for *avarice;* their ascetic modesty forbids any *luxury;* having all things in common, they know no *envy;* educative lectures and strict discipline at table allow for no *gluttony;* their stoic attitude controls any outbursts of *wrath;* and, finally, in a land where all citizens have to work and where leisure time is devoted to intellectual pleasures, there is no room for *sloth.*

Only where all vices are extirpated, may concord and thriving institutions (p. 244) take roots and flourish. Only then can the fundamental institutions of their communism prosper.[13] It is not their thriving institutions that are the cause of their good qualities; rather their behavior founded on their moral integrity forms the basis of their sound social, political and economical order, or, as Morus puts it, "it is impossible that all should be well unless all men were good" (p. 101). No doubt, thriving institutions, a sound way of life and a good social order will have their repercussions on men's attitudes: "all greed for money was entirely removed with the use of money. What a mass of troubles was then cut away!" (pp. 241, 243). Thus results a sort of reciproca-tion between integrity and thriving institutions, between entity and action. The Utopians' behavior according to reason coincides with natural, ethical and useful behaving. How much the integrity serves as the basis of Utopian life may be seen from the fact that the Utopians do not regard the strictly practised *raison d'état* as totalitarianism. Following reason, they comply naturally with the state's norms which, accordingly, do not have to be enforced. In Utopia a few laws suffice to insure conformity (p. 194), even in cases where it does not come naturally.

When viewed from this angle, a much debated and often misunderstood feature of the Utopian state becomes plain enough, namely, what has been called their intolerant, even brutal attitude towards their differently minded neighbours.[14] A state governed by ideally perfect reason and integrity must needs assert the total claim of absoluteness. Where reason prevails at home, the state can afford to be tolerant; where unreasonableness obtains abroad it has to be intolerant. If, as we have seen, the unifying central idea of the work is Utopian ideality relying on integrity and thriving institutions, what, then, is the *ethos* (Koskimies) of *Utopia?* A subtle question like this cannot be answered in a single sentence. Even to put the question means to enter into the controversies and clashes of the work's critics and interpreters.

Any utterance of one of the *dramatis personae* must not be construed as the author's point of view, although such notions are popular enough among the critics.[15] Some of them make *Utopia* a fighting-treatise for socialism[16] or a source for communist ideas,[17] or they take More for a herald of liberalism.[18] Others recognize in the booklet a blueprint for Christian policy,[19] or they take its utopian social statements as if they were written with the encyclical letters *Rerum novarum* and *Quadragesimo anno* in mind.[20] Others again seem to espy in it the *cant* of one whom they believe to be a pharisaical imperialist of a typically British brand;[21] others take him for an ideologist of the English insular welfare-state who is possessed by the demoniacism of power and whose methods, translated into practical policy, would not be distinguishable from the imperialism of modern empires.[22] Still others see in him a propagandist for modern technical warfare.[23] A bewildering diversity of views. What, then, is the ethos of *Utopia?*

Instead of misreading More's little book, sparkling as it is with brilliant ideas, by taking it for a political program, and instead of introducing one's own preconceived opinions into the work, we should rather let the text of More's *Utopia* speak for itself.

Towards the end of Book I for the third time Raphael makes the ideal state of things in unreachably distant kingdoms a rule by which to measure contemporary politics. Both worlds being unreconcilable, he rejects Morus' invitation to serve as a counsellor, because he would find only deaf hearers (p. 97). Thereupon Morus calls Raphael's solitary idealizing "academic scholasticism," which believed anything would fit indiscriminately everywhere. "In the private conversation of close friends this academic philosophy is not without its charm" (p. 99). Whereas, he continues, "in the council of kings, where great matters are debated with great authority, there is no room for these notions" (p. 99). Here, in the sphere of practical politics, the game is played according to the rules of a quite different philosophy:

> But there is another philosophy, more practical for statesmen, which knows its stage, adapts itself to the play in hand, and performs its role neatly and appropriately. This is the philosophy which you must employ. Otherwise we have the situation in which a comedy of Plautus is being performed and the household slaves are making trivial jokes at one another and then you come on the stage in a philosopher's attire and recite the passage from the *Octavia* where Seneca is disputing with Nero. Would it not have been preferable to take a part without words than by reciting something inappropriate to make a hodgepodge of comedy and tragedy? You would have spoilt and upset the actual play by bringing in irrelevant matter—even if your contribution would have been superior in itself. Whatever play is being performed, perform it as best you can, and do not upset it all simply because you think of another which has more interest (p. 99).

Raphael, however, continues to rave about his distant dream-kingdom and contrasts the ideal communism "out there" with the real troubles prevailing over here. For, "there is no hope, however, of a cure and return to a healthy condition as long as each individual is master of his own property" (p. 105). Morus contradicts these views by raising fundamental objections: Life could not be satisfactory where all things are common; there would never be sufficient supply of goods; since relying on the industry of others fosters sloth, there would be no motive of gain, for not even the danger of approaching dearth would incite man to work, since he could not legally keep as his own what he had gained, nor could he save it. Fear and fright would be the consequence; respect for the authority of the state would surely dwindle, leaving a political vacuum behind (p. 106).

It is significant that Raphael does not attempt to refute the *Real-politik* criticisms of Morus'. "His only reply is indirectly to appeal to the principle that no line of argumentation is valid against an actual fact (*contra factum non valet illatio*). What is Hythloday's fact? Nothing else than the island of Utopia."[24] "But you should have been with me in Utopia and personally seen their manners and customs as I did" (p. 107). His "fact," however, exists only in the "experience" of a Raphael surnamed Hythloday ("expert in non-sense"), as does his ideal picture of a reason-controlled communist state: "In that case you unabashedly would admit that you had never seen a well-ordered people anywhere but there" (p. 107). Never anywhere but there! Here lies the key to understanding the whole work. Morus here clearly distinguishes between two different spheres. He places Raphael's ideal politics into the realm of reasoning *scholastica philosophia,* which he contrasts with the *philosophia civilior* of realistic politics. To the former belongs the sphere of ideality and pure theory, to the latter reality and practice. The former has its place in learned debate amongst friends,[25] the latter in real politics, being "the Art of the Possible."[26] Ideals may be discussed, they can never, alas, be made real. At long last Morus and Raphael agree that the ideal is "politically impossible," i.e., it cannot be materialized. After stating that *Pride* prevents the effectuation of ideality in *our* world, "For this reason, the fact that this form of a commonwealth—which I should gladly desire for all—has been the good fortune of the Utopians at least, fills me with joy" (p. 245), to which Morus adds his 'Amen': "But I readily admit that there are very many features in the Utopian commonwealth which it is easier for me to wish for in our countries than to have any hope of seeing realized (p. 247)." There remains no doubt: *that* kingdom is not of this world.[27]

Now, what are the consequences for our attempted inquiry after the ethos of *Utopia?* First of all, it does show how much the ethos is an integral part of the overall structure of the work as a whole, of the homogeneous correlation of *both* books, of the alternation between historical reality and timeless ideal, of earnest social ideas and satirical ambiguity, of the dialogue-form running to and fro between Morus and Hythloday. That integration also shows that the ethos, the meaning of *Utopia* cannot be derived only from Book II, solely from Raphael's words, as if Book I and the persona Morus did not exist. Any such attempt would not only mean a distortion of the work as a complex artifact presented as a complete whole; it would mean, above all, a falsification of the author's intentions, who, although he had written Book II in 1515, did *not* publish it in that form, but waited until he had added, in 1516, Book I, which provides the key for the whole.

The often heard query—which of the two characters, Morus or Hythloday, presents the author's own viewpoint?—is wrongly put. One should rather ask, what were the author's intentions in presenting the reader with the masterly concerted inter-play of the *two* voices? The editor of the Yale edition of the *Utopia* comes to the conclusion: "Hythloday represents More's ideal views;

he himself [Morus] voices his practical judgement in his own person."[28] In other words, under the mere philosophical aspect of a *philosophia scholastica* the author presents Utopian communism as something ideal; if, however, humanity as it really is taken into account, viz. as a fallen creation, then, under the more practical aspect of a *philosophia civilior,* the Utopian ideal is politically impossible. In this connection it should be noted that even Raphael, who always draws such enthusiastic pictures of his ideal commonwealths, refuses steadfastly to employ his knowledge in the service of practical policy just as if he were aware that the colorful and attractive soap-bubbles of his ideals must needs burst when confronted with tough reality.

The ethos of the *Utopia,* then, is not the Utopian ideality nor the model of an ideal communist state, nor a ready-made program to show princes how to govern (Kautsky). Extant historical documents of the age give us no indication whatever which might lead us to assume that More ever tried, at any time, not even when he was Lord Chancellor of England, to put that so-called 'practical program' into effect, nor that he had ever tried to explain to his royal master how to govern according to his *Utopia.* He never even tried to give his work any influence by having it published in England or in English. All the more surprising to find how many interpreters of the *Utopia* take Hythloday's, the "nonsense-dealer's," words at face value, thereby clandestinely removing More's carefully placed boundary-stones from the absolute nowhere to a near-at-hand somewhere.

The ethos of the *Utopia* is, on the contrary, the *irreality* of the Utopian ideality and the impossibleness in reality of the depicted communist ideal. It is not, as has been claimed, anything like an exemplary model of the ideality or a conception as a practical political program; it is rather the contrastive character of the Utopian state, depicted by the author in order to reveal, as in a mirror, the shortcomings and downright abuses of the present world.[29] More's *Utopia* is rather an example by which the reader should contemplate truth. In a letter dated December 4, 1516, More tells his friend Erasmus that he himself, in a dream, had been made King of Utopia; the dawn of day, alas!, had divested him of all his sovereign power. However, he had found consolation in the fact that all earthly power lasts not much longer.[30] The author's own words thus underline the dreamworld character of the Utopian realm, which he would "optare verius quam sperare." The author's guidance towards a contemplation of truth arises here directly from the Utopian picture. The ideality of Utopia lies in the Nowhere, and men, try however hard they may, will never reach it.[31]

And yet, More's world remains valid: "for man is to try and fail—and with God be the rest." The literary means by which the author intends his reader to contemplate truth is the use of satire. By throwing the picture of a gloomy state of affairs in late 15th century England (Book I) into sharp relief against the Utopian ideality (Book II), reality is measured by the rule of the ideal, thereby exposing contemporary or timeless human foibles to derision. Beyond that, More's punning names (Utopia, Hythloday, Amaurotum . . .), as well as his narrative arguing, direct the spearhead of satire against his own work, suspending thus, in a way akin to 'romantic irony,' the literary world of his own creation through the absolute liberty of the artist over his artifact. Even that which had arrested the reader's particular interest, the Utopian ideality, is hereby revealed in its very frailty, nay, its absolute irreality.

The *Utopia,* however, is no *propaganda novel* of direct social moralizing. The ethos emerges only through the narrative. It is so completely integrated into the wholeness of the work of art that some critics become perplexed and lose the track.[32] *Utopia* moralizes by narration, complying thus with the classical maxims for literature, viz. to be both *dulce et utile, prodesse et delectare.* It is, in More's own words, *nec minus salutaris quam festiuus; festiuus* by opening a vista out of this troubled and often miserable world into an ideally golden realm, *salutaris* by driving home that this our earthly world is no *civitas aurea* and never will be, but rather a *civitas permixta* in which any feeble resemblance to a golden age can be materialized only through hard work and by "crossing against the wind" (p. 98).

Thus the *Utopia* enters into the field of Christian anthropology and theology by taking the position that there is no final perfection in this world; there remains, however, the completion of world history by the grace and in the judgement of God.[33] When seen in this light, More the man becomes visible behind his work. This man had translated the life of Pico della Mirandola (who had died in monastic habit); he had adopted the Florentine's "despysynge of worldly vanyte" and "desyrynge of heuenly felycite" as a model for his own life. The austerity of the Charterhouse was a vivid feature of this life, and he himself wrote a number of devotional tracts and moving prayers. Finally, it was this man More whose life and death bore witness to his creed, and whom Jonathan Swift once called "a person of the greatest virtue this kingdom has ever produced."[34]

Principles of Literary Structure

The inner affinity of the *Utopia* to the narrative genre is already evident at the beginning of Book I where, at Peter's turf seat, we find the very prototype of narrative literature: a narrator tells his story to an audience. Fittingly enough, we find in both books a basically epic way of revealing the major topics of the tale. The epic world takes shape by way of narration and description, whereas the epic preterite provides the necessary distance between the narrator and his story which is characteristic of the genre.[35] As has been shown above, neither plot nor characters are strong enough to support the fundamental structure of the whole. The dominating element of the work is its political and social setting. The imaginary social ideality, composed here by mosaic-like addition, is the unifying *leit-motif* of the whole.

Three formal principles may clearly be distinguished as characteristic of the Utopian setting. First, the *isolation* of the Utopian realm is wellnigh perfect.[36] It is effectuated by a number of features. Geographically: its insular position; politically: its being a coherent sovereign national state; in foreign politics: its independence from any *ententes;* economically: its autarky; in foreign trade: its absolute export surplus; military: its superiority and unassailability; demographically: the possibility of making colonies when required. Only seemingly is the Utopian isolation dented by the latter items. Wherever expansion becomes necessary the newly acquired country is radically subjected to the ideal absoluteness of the Utopians ("ipsorum legibus," p. 136). The Utopian requirement of isolation from reality may be seen also from the narrative form. Here the author employs the familiar traveller's report—akin to the messenger's report in drama—to make known to the reader "what cannot be shown on stage." In this function the traveller's report broadens the gap between the reader and the narrated setting.

Secondly, a *selection* takes place. Out of the perplex variety of dynamic forces in real life, two main groups are chosen, which jointly control the whole structure of the Utopian setting: the reasonable integrity of the citizens and the thriving institutions of their social and economic communism.

These two principles seem to result in a third, the *Utopian* ideality. This "result," however, is only apparent. For within perfection there is no development ("non modo felicissime, verum etiam . . . aeternum duratura"). The seeming appearance is caused by the apparent "reality" of the Utopian realm, which is being presented here *as if* it were part of the historic world. By a coincidence of opposites the Utopian ideal world makes use of the means of the "other," the real world, by employing familiar historical, biographical, and local detail. Truly the Utopian ideality is not a resulting but a preestablished harmony. It is *utopian,* i.e., it cannot be established empirically. All attempts to prove the contrary resemble, in their eagerness, their frequency, as in their results, the attempts at inventing a perpetuum mobile. It is typically utopian that the narrated world here may not be any optional world but must needs be a quite distinctive one, viz. the public world of the state, and of an ideal state at that. Beyond that, More's *Utopia* does not show merely the ideal state, but the *idea* of such a state, its X-ray picture as it were. What is made visible before the reader's eyes is a skeleton of its structural ideas, its principles, its inner form. All else remains rather shadowy and vague: the territory and provinces, its citizens, their every-day life. More does not deal with any such historicity, he is concerned with timeless structural principles. His Utopian world is, to the last detail, ideal and abstract. Its cities lack any local color, "lingua, moribus, institutis, legibus prorsus ijsdem, idem situs omnium, eadem ubique quatenus per locum licet, rerum facies" (p. 112). "Who knows one of the cities will know them all, since they are exactly alike" (p. 117). Just like the cities, the citizens, too, all look alike. For More is not interested here in individual features but in what is general and typical. His ideal commonwealth is conceived from the idea and not from any detailed objectivity. This, after all, un-epic, even a-literary tendency reveals the inner affinity of *Utopia* with philosophy, from which the ultimate origin of that whole literary species eventually stems.

Looking back, we realize how much the structure and form of the *Utopia* are one complete, almost perfect whole. The dialogue serves the function of elaborating the *leitmotif* of Utopian opposition to contemporary reality, and

Raphael's report displays an apparent panorama of the Utopian counter-picture before our eyes until, at long last, the threads between picture and counter-picture are knotted once again. This contrast dominates the whole work: the presentation of a defective contemporary world is meaningful only when seen against the contrasting ideal island. *Vice versa*, the ideality of that realm finds its meaning only in its *vis-à-vis* position to reality. And that means its clear and distinct demarcation as irreality.

DENYING THE CONTRARY: MORE'S USE OF LITOTES IN THE *UTOPIA*

Elizabeth McCutcheon

Thomas More's talk of a "neglectam simplicitatem" of language and style in his "libellum," his little book,[1] says a great deal about the apparently impromptu and effortless effect he wanted, and implies what it seems to deny: a rhetorical sophistication we are exploring in increasing detail. Two articles, in particular, have surveyed major areas of More's Latin style. In the one, R. Monsuez looks at the language and grammar of the *Utopia* in relationship to classical Latin texts and the ideals of the humanists. In the second, Father Surtz, drawing specifically upon Erasmus' *De copia*, studies More from the point of view of Renaissance rhetoric, and finds a style shaped as a whole by More's awareness of his audience, other Christian humanists, and his form, a dialogue.[2] Because of these studies it is now both possible and necessary to look still more closely at the foreground of More's text. By isolating a single rhetorical turn of thought and phrase—in this instance, litotes, "in which a thing is affirmed by stating the negative of its opposite,"[3]—and fine variations in its use, we can catch hold of what is in fact a far more intricate and subtle verbal structure and a denser, more distinctively literary texture, than the narrator of the *Utopia* was always willing to admit, except by indirection.

The most immediate and obvious fact about litotes in the *Utopia* is how often More uses it; I count over one hundred and forty examples in the one hundred Latin pages of the Yale text.[4] It is hard, at first, to know how much to make of this. Litotes was a common figure in the Renaissance, and the Tudor rhetorician, sensitive to the state of his own language, and anxious to enrich it, tended at times to dismiss it rather casually. As Hoskins says, "But why should I give examples of the most usual phrases in the English tongue? As, we say *not the wisest man that ever I saw,* for *a man of small wisdom.*"[5] From this point of view, then, perhaps all we can surely say is that More is concerned with a functional and idiomatic, even colloquial, prose, rather than an ornate one; litotes, whether in Latin or English, is not, usually, the showiest of figures.[6]

A closer look at More's text, however, suggests that these litotes cannot be seen simply in the light of a period style at its most ordinary or habitual, that they are, rather, a major element in the fine brushwork of the *Utopia*. The repetition, which allows us to think of litotes as part of More's technique and

Reprinted, by permission of the author and publisher, from *Moreana,* 31-32 (1971), 107-21.

style to begin with, is too various, too purposeful. There is, to mention isolated grammatical features of the figure first, a striking variation in the forms
of negation which introduce the litotes. More commonly uses *non*—there are
over sixty instances of this. In addition, *haud,* an emphatic particle, and *nec*
and *neque* are used at least twenty-eight times. Still other words of negation
include *haudquaquam, minus, ne, nemo, neuter, neutiquam, nihil, nihilo,*
forms of *nullus, nunquam, nusquam,* and *tantum non.* The construction as a
whole is more varied still. Litotes based on adjectives and adverbs are certainly
common, and More does occasionally repeat such adjectives as *exiguus,
insuavis, magnus* and *paucus,* and a few adverbs, such as *dubie, facile, minus*
(the most important single example of repetition), *saepe, temere,* and *unquam.*
He likes an elegant construction the classical writers also liked—a negative followed by the negative form of an adjective, as in "non dissimiles" (128/18-
19), "non imperiti" (52/18), "non indoctus" (48/32), "non inhonesti"
(146/20-21), and so on. Yet litotic constructions based on nouns or verbs or
both, so that a complete idea is twice negated, as when Raphael underscores
the absurdity of punishing a thief and a murderer alike by concluding . . .
"nemo est, opinor, qui nesciat" (74/4), ["There is no one," I suppose, "who
does not know"], are not infrequent.[7] There is rather little, then, even grammatically, that indicates a formula, and a great deal that indicates not only a
concern for variety as such but a fine awareness of effect and a lively alertness
to the idea played upon, so that we begin to see why litotes is the not so
simple rhetorical equivalent of what the Renaissance logician knew as ob-
version or equipollence—"expressing a thought by denying its contradictory."[8]

Even more striking than the grammatical variety is the tremendous range
and variety of effect which More achieves. There is the apparently casual
simplicity of conversational remarks, as in persona More's granting of points
to Raphael: "Profecto non ualde pronis inquam." (90/22), ["'To be sure, not
a very favorable one,' I granted." (91/31)] ; or "Surdissimis inquam, haud
dubie." (96/31-32), ["'Deaf indeed, without doubt,' I agreed" (97/39)]. By
contrast there are such intricate sentences as the one which immediately
precedes our introduction to Utopia: "Nam Scyllas & Celenos rapaces, &
Lestrigonas populiuoros, atque eiuscemodi immania portenta, nusquam fere
non inuenias, at sane ac sapienter institutos ciues haud reperias ubilibet"
(52/31-54/1). This sentence, with its double negations of thought, carefully
though asymmetrically balanced and suspended, is perhaps the best single bit
of evidence of the sophisticated and extraordinarily complex effect More can
accomplish with litotes. Understatement, emphasis, irony, a rapid movement
of the mind from one extreme to the other, a kind of double vision: all are
present in this cunning juxtaposition of all sorts of horrid monsters, in fact
both fallacious and imaginary, yet so "real" they even have names, and the
idealized abstraction of "well and wisely trained citizens" (53/39), who are
imaginary for quite other reasons (which the *Utopia* will reveal). More turns
different levels of reality upside down as he contrasts the former, which (translating the negatives literally) you almost never don't find, with the latter,
whom by no means can you find wheresoever you please. Crucial here are

the contrary perspectives and inverse directions built into the denials; the first moves towards *always* from *never,* the second towards *never,* not quite from *always,* but from the place you'd like to think there would be some. But since the first do not really exist, where will we find the second? In Utopia, Noplace, in terms of the story. It does indeed seem that this sentence is the natural climax to the section originally written as the introduction to Book II, following Hexter's outline of the sequence in which More worked on the actual *Utopia* (xv–xxiii).

As More uses litotes again and again, continuously affirming something by denying its opposite, the figure becomes, ultimately, a paradigm of the structure and method of the book as a whole, echoing, often in the briefest of syntactical units, the larger, paradoxical and double vision which will discover the best state of the commonwealth in an island called Noplace. The more immediate purpose and effect of litotes can rarely be apprehended in a single term, however. Few of More's are as simple as the "haud dubie" already cited, which, although admittedly somewhat formulaic, is not quite as simple as it seems, either. Inevitably one rhetorical effect merges more or less imperceptibly with another, sometimes changing before our eyes, because litotes is not a static figure. The understatement and the mental movement inherent in a process of negation allow for a multiple effect which it becomes exceedingly difficult to generalize about, even though we can start where the sixteenth century did.

The Renaissance, in particular, often thought of litotes as a kind of modesty figure, a way to avoid boasting and to ingratiate oneself by way of understatement. Hence Sidney's famous comment near the beginning of his *Apologie for Poetrie:* ". . . I wil giue you a neerer example of my selfe, who (I knowe not by what mischance) in these my not old yeres and idelest times, hauing slipt into the title of a Poet . . ."[9] Erasmus uses it no less wittily; Folly's first words in her encomium include an elegant and especially paradoxical variation of a common litotes, as she, Foolishness, explains that she is not ignorant of the world's opinion of her: "Utcumque de me vulgo mortales loquuntur, neque enim sum nescia . . ."[10] These are, in fact, simply the most explicit form of what Henry Peacham and other rhetoricians saw as its most common usage: "This form of speech tendeth most usually to praise or dispraise, and that in a modest forme and manner,"[11] a definition which clearly reflects the Renaissance tendency to think of all literature in terms of a rhetorical formula O. B. Hardison calls "the theory of praise."[12]

Praise is an oddly general word to twentieth century ears; we will need more precise terms. But many of the litotes in the *Utopia* can, of course, be read this way, just as the *Utopia* itself can be read both as a praise "de optimo reipvblicae statv" and a dispraise or satire of men and societies as they exist. A clear, and one of the few examples of a modesty figure as such, is spoken, significantly, by persona More early in Book I, as he is about to meet Raphael: "Ergo inquam non pessime coniectaui" (48/28), [" 'Well then,' said I, 'my guess was not a bad one' " (49/34)]. Its presence here seems, primarily, to enlarge our dramatic sense of this fictional More and his courtesy, yet it also, usefully, calls attention to his inference about Raphael's occupation as "nauclerum" (48/29), an

inference which is immediately qualified by Giles, who thereby transforms a
realistic detail into something more symbolic: Raphael has sailed in search of
truth. There are many instances of praise, though some are more straightforward than others. Among the simpler are sailors who are "non imperiti" [not
unskilled] in sea and weather (52/18); Cardinal Morton, in company "non
difficilis" [not hard to please] (58/23–24); a fool who occasionally said things
which were "non absurda" [not absurd] (80/27); Plato, who "bene haud
dubie" [without doubt well] foresaw the behavior of kings (86/16); an academic philosophy which is "non insuauis" ["not without its charm" (99/6–
7)] among friends (98/6). So, too, many elements of Utopian society are
singled out for praise by subtle variations of litotic understatement which
emphasize the less tangible. Their food, for instance, includes a supply of
licorice "haud exiguam" [not at all meagre] (116/5); their buildings are
"neutiquam sordida" [in no way mean] (120/4); their clothes are "nec ad
oculum indecora" [not unbecoming to the eye] (126/5). But their language
is "neque uerborum inops, nec insuauis auditu, nec ulla fidelior animi inter-
pres est" [not lacking words, not without charm to the ear, nor is there a
more faithful expounder of thought] (158/13–14), while their music, by its
harmony of feeling, sound, and sense, which "wonderfully affects, penetrates,
and inflames the souls of the hearers" (237/8–9) allows the Utopians "haud
dubie" to far surpass us in this respect (236/3).

A conspicuous and humorous example of dispraise, using the word in its
simplest sense, is ascribed to Cardinal Morton as he interrupts the verbose
lawyer in Book I, neatly inverting the lawyer's tedious claim to make all clear
"paucis" ["in a few words" (71/25)]. "Tace inquit Cardinalis: nam haud
responsurus paucis uideris qui sic incipias" (70/22–24); "'Hold your peace,'
interrupted the Cardinal, 'for you hardly seem about to reply in a few words
if you begin thus'" (71/30–32). More devastating in its patent understatement is Raphael's final attack on the commonwealth, which heaps gifts on
so-called gentlemen and bankers, and other lazy men, but provides "nihil
benigne" (240/10) [not at all generously] for "farmers, colliers, common
laborers, carters, and carpenters without whom there would be no commonwealth at all" (241/12–14). Yet a third example of litotic dispraise, the subtly
understated "haud pauca" (244/14) of the fictional More's final statement
belongs here, though it is subsumed in still more complex effects, for now the
grounds of dispraise, expressed with conventional litotic irony, become the
unconventional grounds of praise.[13] What results is as powerful and sophisticated in its way as the much briefer sentence on the Scyllas, the Celaenos,
and other terrifying monsters in Book I. At first, persona More seems to
temper his objections to the customs and laws of the Utopians, and speaks as
the well-intentioned, and certainly the well-mannered gentleman he is, who
finds "haud pauca" [not a few things] which bother him about the Utopian
society. But his list of objections is really a reductio ad absurdum. As he singles out for special reproach "their common life and subsistence," (245/22–
23) because it eliminates the "exchange of money" (245/23) and with it the
nobility, splendor, and so on which are "in the estimation of the common

people, the true glories and ornaments of the commonwealth" (245/25-26), his whole argument is undercut. So the internal convention of dispraise, while itself ironic in its initial understatement, is ironically and dramatically reversed.

More's "haud pauca," with all that follows it, magnifies and dramatizes effects which led Puttenham to call this figure "the Moderator." In his words, ". . . we temper our sence with wordes of such moderation, as in appearaunce it abateth it but not in deede, and is by the figure *Liptote,* which therefore I call the *Moderator,* and becomes vs many times better to speake in that sort quallified, than if we spake it by more forcible termes, and neuertheles is equipolent in sence . . ."[14] What Puttenham, and a host of other Renaissance rhetoricians are sensitive to, in part, is the emphasis which litotes somewhat paradoxically achieves by seeming to understate, moderate, or diminish its case by negating its contrary. Indeed, as Hoskins points out, "these figures are but counterfeits of amplification"; in Thomas Blount's words, litotes (called diminution in this connection) "descends by the same steps that *Amplification* ascends, and differs no more then up Hill and down Dale . . ."[15] If we press Blount's analogy a bit, we can see one reason for litotes' appeal to writers like More or Sidney, for whom *ars celare artem* was a literary ideal. It allows for the apparently relaxed and easy descent, rather than the laborious climb. Understated instead of hyperbolic, it often seems to turn attention away from itself, like its cousin, paralipsis, which emphasizes something by pretending to ignore it,[16] and it can disarm potential opponents and avoid controversy; yet it emphasizes whatever it touches.

Emphasis through litotes is too ubiquitous in the *Utopia* to need many more examples. We may not be altogether conscious of it each time that it underscores a concrete detail, but it becomes extremely noticeable, because of its order in the sentence, its construction, or its frequency—or all three— as More builds towards crucial points. Thus the actual narrative virtually starts with a litotes. Most translations obscure this; the Yale translation talks of "certain weighty matters" (47/10) which it places towards the latter part of a clause turned into a sentence. By contrast, More's own words, almost at the very beginning of what is an exceptionally long sentence, "Qvvm non exigvi momenti negocia quaedam" (46/8), are a key to the tone of much of the subsequent work by their diminution and an understatement which is played against regal superlatives: "inuictissimus" (46/8-9), "ornatissimus," and "serenissimo" (46/10). So too More ends his introductory sentence to the occupations of the Utopians with an emphatic litotes which brings home, without seeming to do so, the place of agriculture in Utopia; agriculture is the one art "cuius nemo est expers" (124/21-22), [which no one does not share in]. And More's last remarks include not only the dramatic "haud pauca" (244/14) but the emphatic and ironic "non satis" (244/25), in reference to those men who are afraid they may not be thought wise enough unless they criticize the discoveries of others.

By clustering litotes like these, More can achieve some very brilliant effects indeed. There are, for example, thirteen litotes in just over the first four pages of the *Utopia*—all leading up to and preparing us for our first introduc-

tion to the customs and institutions of the Utopians. The practices of Utopia
and other newly discovered countries are cunningly underscored by this sort
of repeated understatement, subsequently embellished by marginal references,
apparently added by Peter Giles and Erasmus.[17] Raphael's account of the
Polylerites is a case in point. He tells us, in the space of a few lines, that this
people, whose penal system distinguishes between the value of life and money,
being therefore everything England's is not, is "neque exiguum, neque imprudenter institutum" (74/21-22); that they are "nulla in re maligne" content
with the fruits of their land (74/25); that not often do they visit other countries, or are they visited ["neque adeunt alios saepe, neque adeuntur." (74/26)];
nor do they care to push their frontiers ["neques fines prorogare student"
(74/27)]; that they live "haud perinde splendide, atque commode" (74/29-
30); that even by name they are not "satis noti" (76/1) [enough known] except to their closest neighbors. As these litotes follow several others on the
same page, the reader is barraged by all sorts of negatives negated and confronted with a massive decoding process. So much that is in fact desirable is
described in terms of the undesirable it is not—the Polylerites are not a small
country; they are not unwisely governed; they are not eager for more land, or
fame, or fortune; they live by no means as splendidly as comfortably—that
here, and everywhere, we have to reckon with irony as well as emphasis by
diminution.

Irony of some sort is, of course, inseparable from the understatement and
process of denied denial in litotes. As Hoskins explains, ". . . the former
fashion of diminution sometimes in ironious sort goes for amplification; as,
speaking of a great person, *no mean man*, etc." He adds that "this is an ordinary figure for all sorts of speeches,"[18] and indeed litotic irony, although it
says one thing and means another, is often thought to be mild. Rosemond
Tuve, for example, calls it "slight" because, she explains, "We simply intend
to be taken as saying a mere modicum of what we mean."[19] Read this way, a
litotes which describes the Polylerites as "populum neque exiguum, neque
imprudenter institutum" (74/21-22) would be ironic because they are, at
least, "a nation that is large and well-governed" (75/27-28). So when, in
Book II, we are told that "sunt tamen, hijque haud sane pauci" (224/20-21)
["There are persons, however, and these not so very few" (225/26-27)] who
give up all learning and leisure to perform good works for others at the cost
of pleasure in this life, we would notice the apparently simple irony of
diminution and denial. More than a very few (few? some? many? a great
many?) do this. More, however, obtains far more powerful and ironic effects,
though perhaps nowhere so dramatically as in the concluding "haud pauca"
passage, because of the radical contrast between two value systems, one concerned with well-being, the other with power, which stands behind so many
of these litotes.[20] When, then, Raphael compares the justice (so-called) of
other nations with that of the Utopians, and asks how it can possibly be just
that the nobleman, the banker, or anyone whose work "non sit Reipublicae
magnopere necessarium" (238/24-25) [is "not very essential to the commonwealth" (239/32)] lives in magnificence, while the common man lives

less well than the beasts of burden, the ironic understatement is painfully intensive. Again we hear a living voice.

Irony is itself sometimes subsumed in a more complex effect which is satiric in force, a result of the alternatives which litotes as a figure requires. The denied negations do, in fact, frequently comment indirectly, but nevertheless pointedly, on aspects of life elsewhere. We have, on the most microscopic scale, examples of what A. R. Heiserman, citing Erasmus' definition of satire generally, calls the *via diversa*.[21] While, then, the speaker seems to be looking at some new world when he says, for instance, that the Polylerites are not unwisely governed, the words he denies come closer to home. Again, the virtuous and loving behavior of those "haud sane pauci" (224/20–21) in Utopia who pursue hard work for the well-being of others obliquely points to the very few in the known world who would dream of doing such a thing. Thus that general and ironic "awareness of contradiction between the two worlds" which Father Surtz speaks of in his introduction to the *Utopia* (clii) is made much more precise by way of litotic contrasts like these.

Sometimes More uses litotic combinations of irony and satire, which are also of necessity emphatic—however understated they pretend to be—to lightly hit and run. Early in Book I, for example, we are told that Raphael found towns and cities and "very populous commonwealths" (53/1) "non pessime institutas" (52/1) [with not bad institutions]. At the bottom of the same page we learn that persona More and his friends did not ask for information about monsters, "quibus nihil est minus nouum" (52/31) [than which there is nothing less new], a palpable hit at the taste for tall traveller's tales which, simultaneously, calls attention to the newness of Utopia. The Polylerites feed their prisoners "haud duriter" (76/13) [by no means harshly], while the Utopians elect the tranibors annually but change them "haud temere" (122/21) ["not ... without good reason" (123/22–23)] and "never claim payment of most of the money" (149/29) they receive for the goods they trade, because they think it "haud aequum" (148/26) [not at all fair] to take away something they don't need when others do. Again, the Utopians go to war "non temere" (200/4–5) ["not lightly" (201/4–5)]; their priests wear vestments of a material "non perinde preciosa" (234/17–18) [not equally costly], for though the design and pattern are wonderful, no gold or precious stones are used. In each instance, of course, the litotes as a whole is an especially effective form of praise, the understatement making it less incredible. At the same time, the alternative to be denied is an oblique attack on the real world, its cruelty to prisoners, its political corruption, its greed and usury, its love of war, the corruption of its church.

At times More develops the satiric implications of litotes like these by making more explicit the contrasts between the Utopian world and Christendom. A superb instance of this occurs when Raphael's discourse turns to the Utopian attitude towards gold and silver. Those metals "quae caeterae gentes non minus fere dolenter ac uiscera sua distrahi patiuntur, apud Vtopienses, si semel omnia res postularet efferri, nemo sibi iacturam unius fecisse assis uideretur" (152/15–18). Here Raphael, through More, actually talks of other

nations, and underscores their greed by a powerful and painful litotic analogy
("non minus fere dolenter") between the loss of their entrails and the loss of
their gold. In absolute contrast is the state of mind in Utopia, where, though
all the gold was carried away, "no one would feel that he were losing as much
as a penny" (153/20).

Subsequent litotes in this same passage are exploited, delightfully, for their
possibilities as figures of satiric diminution. When Utopian children see no one
but children ["non nisi pueros" (152/23)] using gems, they put them aside.
And still another litotic contrast glances at our practices: "non aliter ac nostri
pueri, quum grandescunt nuces, bullas, & pupas abijciunt" (152/25-26). The
"non aliter ac," [not otherwise than], which allows More to be explicit without being too obvious, also forces us to weigh, in our own minds, gold and our
attitude towards it against the worthless trifles, the lockets and the dolls of
our childhood. With greater subtlety, it satirically diminishes gold to a mere
nothing, a "bulla" or even a bubble, if More is half-punning here. It is this
analogy, of course, which leads directly to the splendidly absurd procession of
the Anemolian ambassadors, loaded down with gold and gems, expecting
applause, but mistaken for slaves (which they are, of a sort), a sight Raphael
tells us, in yet another litotes, he found "non minus erat uoluptatis
consyderare" (154/18) ["no less delightful to notice" (155/20)] than their
misplaced pride in their fine clothing. Further litotes crowd the page as the
temporary comedy of the procession is followed by a more vehement attack
on the way of the world. There are the ambassadors, who were to discover
that gold there was held "nec in minore contumelia quam apud se honore"
(156/4-5) [not in less contempt there than in honor among themselves], so
that we have another contrast between Utopia and another nation (itself, however, fictional) which again ironically diminishes the value of gold. There are
the Utopians, who wonder why anyone can possibly think he is more noble
because the texture of his woolen clothing is finer, since ... "ouis olim
gestauit, nec aliud tamen interim, quam ouis fuit" (156/17-18) ["a sheep
once wore the wool and yet all the time he was not other than a sheep"
(157/18-19)]. This litotes is both funny and satirically diminishing; in more
serious vein is a litotic reference to the blockhead, "nec minus etiam improbus
quam stultus" (156/22-23) [no less dishonest than foolish], who enslaves
many wise and good men but will be enslaved in turn, when he loses his
"great heap of gold coins" (157/27) because of chance or a legal trick that no
less than chance ["nihil minus ac fortuna" (156/26) can "confound high and
low" (157/29-30). Or, most shocking litotes of all, because the apparent
diminution intensifies the horror of a value system which virtually makes
gold its god, there is the madness (as the Utopians see it) of those who pay all
but divine honors ["tantum non diuinos" (156/34)] to those who are rich.
In passages like this one, then, litotes becomes an extremely powerful weapon
with which More can attack the misguided values of the known world while
praising Utopian customs.

Still other effects are inherent in litotes, as More uses them. Ambiguity is
one, for reasons both logical and psychological. The Renaissance was well

aware of the logical complications and ambiguities which result when something is affirmed by negating the contrary. Litotes and ten other figures (an important group in the *Utopia,* including antithesis, irony, paradox and paralipsis) can be specifically related to that topic of invention called opposites, of which there were thought to be four sorts in all: contraries, relatives, privatives, and contradictories. To affirm one contradictory is to deny the other, but litotes based on the first three categories may well be ambiguous. Though immediate contraries (faith/unbelief, for example) have no species between, so that "one or the other must be affirmed,"[22] mediate contraries do have a mediate or middle ground between the two extremes. "Not white" is the seemingly inevitable text-book example; as Thomas Wilson says, "if a cloth be not white, it is no reason to call it blacke. For it may bee blewe, greene, redd, russett ..."[23] Relatives (Isidore cites "few" and "many") and privatives (sight and blindness, for example, for which a mediate could be an eye inflammation, according to Isidore)[24] can also be ambiguous. On these grounds such common litotes as "non pessime" (48/28, 52/1, 80/16), "non exigvi" (46/8, 214/22), "haud pauca" (54/2, 244/14), "haud pauci" (218/9, 224/20-21), "nec pauci" (222/14), "haud multi" (158/5), "haud saepe" (188/25), "non saepe" (184/29), or "haud semel" (212/6) are logically ambiguous. We may, at first, think of their opposites, just as we do with white-black, yet all have one or more species between. "Non pessime," for instance, has to move from *worst* through *rather bad* and *bad* even before it can move towards *good, quite good,* or *the best,* if it does; "haud pauci" may mean *more than a few, some,* or *many,* and "haud semel" [not once] is even more open ended.

A second kind of ambiguity arises from the psychological peculiarity of negating a negation.[25] As Jespersen has observed, "... it should be noted that the double negative always modifies the idea, for the result of the whole expression is somewhat different from the simple idea expressed positively." He calls attention to the same phenomenon which led Puttenham to call litotes the "Moderator," though he interprets it differently, when he adds that *"not uncommon* is weaker than *common, ...* the psychological reason being that the *detour* through the two mutually destroying negatives weakens the mental energy of the hearer and implies on the part of the speaker a certain hesitation absent from the blunt, outspoken *common ...*"[26] In fact, since litotes as a rhetorical and literary technique not only moderates but intensifies, so that, as John Smith points out, "... *sometimes a word is put down with a sign of negation, when as much is signified as if we had spoken affirmatively, if not more,"*[27] it may be either stronger or weaker. But it is ambiguous. We can and must depend upon the context, of course, but even so we do have to hesitate and decide to what extent a particular litotes is moderating, to what extent emphasizing, or better, attempt to hold two apparently contradictory but equally real effects in our minds at the same time. I do not think, pace Jespersen, that this necessarily "weakens the mental energy of the hearer." More probably it arouses it,[28] requiring us to linger over the construction and its context—hence its particular effectiveness as a figure of emphasis. But we are required to undergo a complex mental action; if something is, for example, *not uncommon,* to pursue Jespersen's example, we move from a *common* which isn't quite stated to the *uncommon* which is, and then, because that is denied, back towards *common* again. But we do not usually know quite where to stop, a process we can visualize this way:

It is just this sort of ambiguous area which a recent cartoon exploits.[29] A husband and wife are standing in front of what should be a welcome mat. But this mat reads, "not unwelcome," to the chagrin of the wife, who says, " *'See what I mean? You're never sure just where you stand with them'.*"

In a larger sense we're never quite sure where we stand in the *Utopia,* either. It is, of course, a commonplace to talk about ambiguity in the *Utopia.* But on the smallest syntactical level ambiguity does exist of a sort which can never be altogether resolved, and probably was not meant to be. For this ambiguity vivifies the text, arouses its readers, and agitates its points, however casually they appear to be made, so that they neither evaporate nor solidify. We are constantly, though obliquely, teased by the many litotes already cited, not least those institutions "non pessime" (52/1) which Raphael found in the new world, or persona More's "haud pauca" (244/14) in his concluding speech. Curiously, perhaps consciously, this last "haud pauca" contradicts the implications of another "haud pauca" early in Book I (54/2), which More uses in apparent and ironic antithesis to the positive "multa" (54/1) earlier in the sentence. Here More observes that Raphael did, of course, find many ["multa"] customs which were ill-advised in those new countries, "so he rehearsed not a few points from which our own cities, nations, races, and kingdoms may take example for the correction of their errors" (55/2-4).

We can sense inherent ambiguities and the potential spread of meaning in a given litotes from still another point of view by looking at various translations of the "non exigvi momenti negocia" (46/8) of More's first sentence. Ralph Robinson, thinking of litotes as an emphatic and intensifying device, doubles the idea in a positive sense; it becomes "weightye matters, and of greate importaunce." Gilbert Burnet, however, preserves the litotic implications, though slightly modifying the meaning, when he renders the litotes as "some Differences of no small Consequence." Closer to our period, H. V. S. Ogden, who chiefly hears the moderating possibilities, turns the phrase into "some differences." In an attempt to reconcile the moderating impulse and the emphatic one, Paul Turner writes of "a rather serious difference of opinion."[30] The Yale translation settles for simple emphasis: "certain weighty matters" (47/10). Burnet alone has left some of the ambiguities unresolved; all the other translators have, in a sense, made our minds up for us. But what we gain in clarity we lose elsewhere. The alternatives, and therefore any pos-

sible irony, disappear, as does the ambiguity, and with that, the tension and
movement of mind, so that nuances of meaning are also dissolved. In short,
this litotes becomes far less significant, both in what it says and the way it
says it, as an anticipation of the *Utopia* to come. For the phrase More writes
certainly calls attention, however obliquely, to the kind of issue being argued
about in the known world. He does not, admittedly, spell out the details of
what was a massive commercial problem,[31] but he certainly says enough to
reinforce our sense of the power and splendor and pride which activates almost all states (except, as we shall discover, Utopia). Indeed, "negocia" itself
has commercial overtones which are very unlike the word Raphael will later
use for what he thinks of as the public welfare: "salutem publicam" (104/8).
By beginning, then, with "non exigvi momenti negocia" More is able to raise,
for just a moment, a question to which much of the subsequent discussion
returns: what sorts of state matters are trifling? And what sorts are not? But,
whatever else it does, this first "non" foreshadows the processes of negation
and opposites which typify so much of the *Utopia.*

Like all other negatives, only more so, because now the negative is itself
negated, litotes speak of a habit of mind, a tendency to see more than one
side to a question.[32] Intellectual, judicial, and persuasive, they ask us to weigh
and consider alternatives which the writer has himself considered. So each
litotes does, then, link writer with reader, who tries to repeat, as best he can,
the mental and judicial processes the figure so economically and often ambiguously encloses. As Puttenham says, litotes is a "sensable figure," one which
"alter[s] and affect[s] the minde by alteration of sense."[33] The persuasive
bias of Renaissance rhetoric is implicit here. Where a modern writer in the
ironic mode, like Herman Melville or Henry James, will use this sort of negation to reveal hesitations, qualifications, uncertainties and ambiguous complications in the consciousness of the narrator or a major character in his fiction,
More's fiction, though no less ironic, uses litotes, primarily, to affect and
alter *our* minds. Yet it is also true that the alternatives were More's to begin
with, so that litotes makes us simultaneously much more aware of his mind in
action and certain divisions in it; it reinforces our sense of More himself as one
who, indeed, saw more than one side of a question.[34]

From this point of view, even such a seemingly conventional litotes as "haud
dubie" (62/25, 86/16, 96/32, 236/3) or a more emphatic "Neque dubium est"
(216/27–28) or a "non dubito" (242/16) implies a process of mental assessment
on the part of the speaker. It suggests, as "to be sure" or "certainly" cannot,
that someone has weighed the possibilities and reached a decision—hence its
usefulness as a persuasive figure. The same effect is multiplied in one of More's
favorite litotic constructions, which, unlike most, does spell out (but qualify)
its alternatives: some combination of a negative with *minus* or *minus quam.*
Like the "nec minus salutaris quam festiuus" of the title page, or the several
non minus . . . quam litotes in the passage describing the Utopian way with
gold, these constructions seem to ask us to weigh or try to balance different
ideas or values, almost as if we were asked to find the balance point on a moving see-saw. The ideas are grammatically "equal,"[35] yet, often, the figure is

weighted on one side; there is, in other words, a kind of dynamic emphasis which requires that we hold the two elements both together and apart. It can startle, or it can result in ironic or satiric incongruities: things which shouldn't be "equal" are, but things which should be, too often aren't. Raphael's description of the robber, who is in no less danger "if merely condemned for theft" than "if he were convicted of murder as well" (75/8-9) is an instance of the first sort; his description of the Utopian way of providing for its citizens, an instance of the second: "Then take into account the fact that there is no less provision for those who are now helpless but once worked than for those who are still working" (239/22-25). But most litotes in *Utopia* do not, in fact, spell out the alternatives in this way. With litotes like "non pessime" or "haud pauca" it is almost as if we saw one side of a metaphysical see-saw. So the mind is stimulated or teased into the sort of action described earlier, having, often, to construct the opposite which is denied and hold on to contraries which it weighs, each against the other. And once again, though in a more oblique way, we discover a weighting, a persuasive action which often favors Utopian attitudes, however negatively they may appear to be described. As More says, in a fine piece of understatement, which also reveals an awareness of just how complex this sort of question is, Raphael found nations "non pessime institutas" (52/1). But with this we come back, full circle, to Peacham's point; litotes does, indeed, "praise or dispraise, and that in a modeste forme and manner."[36] In the *Utopia*, more precisely, it praises and dispraises, often almost simultaneously, since to deny something about Utopia is to affirm it, indirectly, of the world as we know it.

More ended his book with a famous wish. My own present hope is a more modest one—that somehow litotes be more systematically retained in translations of *Utopia*, which have, usually, made at best tepid attempts to preserve it, often converting a litotic construction to a simple positive. Obviously, syntactical patterns are difficult to turn from one language to another, and negatives are trickier still. But when, for example, More's final "haud pauca" (244/14) becomes "many" (245/17), or the frequent litotic descriptions of the Polylerites and the Utopians, which comment *via diversa* on the way of this world, are transformed into straightforward descriptions, we lose the emphasis and the understatement, the irony and possible satire, and the ambiguity of the original. The complicated action of More's mind is coarsened, his meaning blurred, the energy and tension of a muscular prose relaxed. On a larger scale, we lose the cumulative effect of a device much repeated, and we have, too often, only one side of what is at least a two-sided vision inherent in every denial of the contrary. In More's hands, litotes was, in fact, a superlative tool for both the exceedingly polite gentleman, the fictional More, and the passionate visionary who had seen Utopia. Avoiding controversy, it constantly calls attention, without seeming to do so, to the purpose and values behind the countless delightful details with which More created both dialogue and discourse; it truly is a figure of and for the mind. Intensive yet understated, emphatic, often drily ironic, sometimes humorous or wry, concealing tremendous energy in its apparent ease and frequent brevity, litotes is not the least of the rhetorical figures in the vision and satire we call *Utopia*.

MORE, PLUTARCH, AND KING AGIS: SPARTAN HISTORY AND THE MEANING OF *UTOPIA*

R. J. Schoeck

I

"The great principle on which the life of the Utopians is based," wrote Lupton in his valuable introduction to More's *Utopia*, "is community of goods. There is no private property; no use of money, except as a means of commercial intercourse with other nations. In this, More seems to have taken his idea from what he had read of Solon or Lycurgus." There are, to be sure, numerous indications of indebtedness to Plato's *Republic,* but we must remember that Plato adopted many things from the institutions of the Spartans: their public meals, their discarding the use of the precious metals for money, the garrison life for males and the gymnastic training for women, severe discipline of the children, and others.[1] Lycurgus and the Spartan culture, then, lie athwart the dominant organizing principle of Utopian life.

But I do not think that it has previously been suggested that there is one period in Spartan history which offers startling correspondences not only with Book II (which portrays the commonwealth of Utopia), but also with Book I (which gives a picture of contemporary England): Sparta in the middle of the third century B.C. Like Europe at the end of the fifteenth and at the beginning of the sixteenth centuries, the third-century Mediterranean world was torn by war: and in Greece itself we find bitter social discontent, even the threat of social revolution in class struggle of poor against rich, much like the English situation that More so graphically and so tellingly describes in Book I. (Though all of this was generally known in More's time, we now see the lines of struggle and the long-range implications of many of the forces at work far more clearly from our vantage point in history.) The story of one of the kings of this period in particular, Agis IV of Sparta, is a startling one, and it was read by More and his contemporaries in Plutarch's *Lives*, a work familiar to all.

II

In Plutarch's *Life of Agis* we are introduced to the biography of this remarkable Spartan king through the framework of a discussion of "the true condition of men in public life, who, to gain the vain title of being the people's

Reprinted, by permission of the publisher and author, from *Philological Quarterly,* 35 (1956), 366–75.

275

leaders and governors, are content to make themselves the slaves and followers of all the people's humors and caprices"; and there is emphasis upon the degree of madness in men of large power and authority: "now they no more think what is good, glorious, but will have those actions only esteemed good that are glorious. . . ."[2] This, Plutarch relates, was the period when Sparta fell away from almost all of her former virtue and repute because of the love of gold and silver—avarice and baseness of spirit in the pursuit of it, and luxury, effeminacy, and prodigality in the use of it. (Here one recognizes many of the specific charges in More's indictment of his own England, both in Book I of *Utopia* and, obliquely, in many of the Epigrams.)

In the year 244 B.C. Agis became king and proposed "that every one should be free from their debts; all the lands to be divided into equal portions." The people were transported with admiration, for "at last there had appeared a king worthy of Sparta." But Agis was opposed by his colleague Leonidas and put to death by the ephors.[3] There is an ironic coda to this story: Cleomenes tried to institute the social reforms of Agis, including the redistribution of land, but failed; he fled to Alexandria and there later committed suicide. His wife (the widow of Agis) and his children were killed by Ptolemy's command: thus, like Utopus and Lycurgus, Agis left no successor.

For Sparta the situation in 244 B.C. was no less desperate than the situation in England when More finished his book in 1516.[4] Hythlodaye, like Agis, saw the remedy for the social-economic problem in the radical idea of redistributing the land. But the irony confronts us of a Tudor reading of the story told by Plutarch: neither Henry VII nor his equally wealth-demanding son would have favored the radical solution of Agis—and increasingly after 1516 one might well wonder about the prudence of such a proposal.

The importance of Plutarch in the early Renaissance must be recalled. Plutarch's influence upon the later figures of Montaigne and Shakespeare is well known; what is less generally remembered is that Plutarch's impact upon the late fifteenth and early sixteenth centuries was enormous.[5] The high valuation of Plutarch is perhaps best summed up in Erasmus' Preface to the *Apophthegmata,* dedicated to young Prince William: "For neuer hath there been among the Greke writers (especially as touchyng matters of vertue and good behauour) any one more holy than *Plutarchus,* or better worthie of all men to bee reade." Such respect was doubtless shared by Richard Pace, Sir Thomas Elyot, and the other Tudors who also translated Plutarch, and by all of those who studied him with care. That others saw parallels between Greek times and the Tudor period may be seen in the very interesting *Life of Agesilaus,* dedicated to Cromwell, which includes a parallel between Agesilaus and Henry VIII. More, we may be certain, knew his Plutarch well. In what has been called his list of Great Books[6] (in chapter vi of the Second Book of *Utopia,* where Hythlodaye itemizes and describes his 'pretye fardell of bookes'), Hythlodaye says rather cryptically, "They sett great stoore by Plutarches bookes." And in the *Epigrams* there are many ideas and sentiments which seem to echo rather closely many of the concepts to be found in the *Lives* and the *Moralia.*

III

There is one reinforcement of this parallel between third-century Sparta and sixteenth-century England that seems too specific to be mere coincidence. More speaks of the history of Utopia going back 1760 years:[7] that is, to 244 B.C., figuring from 1516 (the year of publication). And 244 B.C., as we have seen, was the year Agis became king.

Though I do not know of a Tudor chronology that dates Agis' reign precisely, the practice of dating B.C. was common enough. There was at least one chronicle that covered the third century and the form of which would have permitted any reader to work through Plutarch's dating of Cleomenes and to arrive at a computation of Agis' reign as beginning in 244 B.C.;[8] and another, the *Eusebii Caesariensis Chronicon,*[9] that dated the accession of Ptolemy Euergetes at *anno mundi* 4953, with the means of easily translating this to 246 B.C. (giving on f.175[r] the equivalence of *anno mundi* 6711 for 1512 A.D.), which More would have known was two years before the kingship of Agis. This, we may recall, was a history-hungry age, a period when the universal *Polychronicon* of Higden was reprinted, after the Caxton edition of 1482, in 1495 and again in 1527; a period that saw Bede's *Ecclesiastical History* published in 1475, his *De Temporum Ratione* in 1507, and his *Chronicon* in 1505 and 1507.

From one point of view, this is a kind of date-game that is much like the elaborate word-play that More and his times were so fond of: Utopia and Eutopia, the river with no water, and his playing upon his own name.[10] The use of the precise figure of 1760 derives from More's Tudor habit of mind; Erasmus' punning title, *Encomium Moriae,* is known to everyone, and Camden discusses many more, though less familiar, examples in his end-of-the-century work, *Remaines.* With all this might be placed the still-conventional enterprise of etymologizing, and much to the point is the curiously coincidental example of Peloponnesus.[11]

But from another point of view we might regard More's use of the figure 1760 as an important clue to the meaning of his *Utopia.* And that clue should be even more important for our times than for More's, as a guide to the intended meaning of this work. The 1760 and all that should enable us to see what should have been apparent without it, that More is not writing a tract to proclaim a revolution. We might here echo the sound comment of the distinguished scholar of Greek social and economic history, M. Rostovtzeff, on the applicability of such a notion to Greek history (and suggest the relevance of his comment to Tudor history):

> It is inappropriate to talk of the existence of socialism in Greece. Socialism as a theory is a creation of modern times. But social discontent was rife in Greece in the fourth and third centuries, and the poor in their struggle with the rich were fighting not so much for political rights as to get the lands of the rich divided among themselves and debts abolished. Behind this demand for γῆς ἀναδασμός and χρεῶν ἀποκοπή [redistribution of land and aboli-

tion of debts] there was no elaborate social programme based on a special economic and social theory.[12]

Rather, I should think, readers might find common ground in the extraordinary (to us) blending of *joculatio* and high seriousness in *Utopia,* and there is in More's use of such a figure as 1760 the valuable hint (and this apart from the merits of the interpretation here advanced) of the way his mind worked. Stapleton has told us that More's lectures on St. Augustine's *De Civitate Dei* (itself a theological work grounded upon a definite theory and sense of history) were political-historical, not theological, and such a parallel as the one here advanced confirms one's impression of More's as an historically sensitive mind. And in a work like *Utopia* that mind operated within a strong sense of Christian order, but through the complex system of prisms and mirrors of his irony; in *Utopia* we rarely catch sight of that mind in a direct light as we certainly do in the earlier life of Pico and again in the later works. We have not yet succeeded in exploring with very much success the areas suggested many years ago by Sir James Mackintosh, when he wrote that More regarded the views presented "with almost every possible degree of approbation and shade of assent." This is not to say that there were no parts of *Utopia* that presented More's ideas and beliefs with unequivocal conviction, but too much has been done in recent years to rigidify those ideas; too much commentary has attempted "to crystallize what More purposely left in a state of solution."[13] But we must first isolate and analyze all of the constituents of the solution before we can state with acceptable certitude what holds More's *Utopia* together. We cannot make a sixteenth-century socialist out of More, for he would doubtless have expected that any latter-day Agis would be put to death. Instead (and on this crucial point both Chambers and Hexter are in agreement), he put the emphasis on the sin of pride. Of this much we may be sure: More's ranging mind and fertile imagination would have seized upon this parallel between Sparta and England, between Agis and Henry VIII and Utopus, for it reinforced his view of the corrupting disease of contemporary England.[14] That such a suggestive parallel was ready at hand for More in Plutarch's *Life of Agis,* a work everywhere read and highly valued, we must consider.

IV

This line of inquiry interprets More's view of the world in general and of England in particular in the year 1516 as deeply serious without being pessimistic. During the year that he was engaged in writing and rewriting his *Utopia*—a year which ended in September 1516 with his sending the finished manuscript to his friend Erasmus, who saw to its publication—More was troubled by drifts of thought and belief which few others sensed, as we may judge from the testimony of Roper on several occasions. Unlike Skelton he had no great "bias in favour of monarchy": one may readily see this in the *Epigrams* written during the years prior to the finishing of *Utopia;* there are twenty-three epigrams on kings and government, a new emphasis among epigrammatists.[15]

> His favorite concern is for the difference between a good king and a tyrant; but it is evident from a reading of this group of epigrams that, whereas the existence of good kings is a theoretical possibility, the existence of tyrants is a present danger. The attack on the policies of Henry VII, so sharply expressed in the long poem on the coronation of Henry VIII (Ep. I), throws light upon the origin of some of More's thoughts about tyrants; and the opinions of Hythlodaye in the first book of *Utopia*, written seven years later, show that there had been no significant change in his attitude. Ep. 62, on death as a tyrannicide and avenger of the tyrant's suffering subjects, is expressed with such bitter and sardonic hatred as to leave no doubt that here More is giving vent to his own emotions. . . .[16]

But we must heed two cautions against attempting to apply too rigidly the ideas found in the *Epigrams* to those expressed in the *Utopia:* first, the *Epigrams* were doubtless composed over a spread of years, and therefore do not represent the same single-mindedness as *Utopia*, which, though no doubt it has roots at least as early as his lectures on Augustine's *De Civitate Dei*, seems to have been composed within a small stretch of time; further, although he selected the poems for translation, More's *Epigrams* are limited by the fact that about a fourth of them are translations, and translations of a highly stylized genre. Finally, we must beware equally of identifying Hythlodaye's ideas with More's as we must of assuming that the voice of the *Epigrams* is completely More's and only More's, though his is the hand of the translator.

The years between More's Augustine lectures of about 1502 and 1515, the birth of the Utopia idea, are also the years whose ferment produced (though in another land, yet under the same cultural horizon) the revolutionary ideas of Machiavelli which were the last stage of a long-developing concept of the prince.[17] And as Machiavelli was deeply concerned with Roman history as a parallel to his Florence, so was More equally concerned with Sparta as another kind of parallel with Renaissance England. The converging lines of More's interest in history as a man of affairs, and in the classics as a humanist, would have met in startling focus in Plutarch; there in the *Life of Agis* More could find the *speculum* to hold up to his own age. To Greek history, then, More was impelled—perhaps as a result of his hard experience with Henry VII (which apparently led him to contemplate extended exile), perhaps as a development of deep-seated convictions; and Plutarch's *Life of Agis* would have been meaningful indeed for More after 1509 (after the false promise of the new young king who came to the throne in 1509 and was greeted with such enthusiasm at first) and especially in that *annus mirabilis* 1516.[18] And we have in the great product of that year, the *libellus Utopia*, not a program for social revolution but first of all an imaginative work obviously intended to profit its readers by its teaching and at the same time to amuse them; for the prevalent critical thinking (as later with Sidney)[19] was that the end of poetry is to teach and delight, and the *dulce* is not to be

subordinated to the *utile*. Then, following the argument of Father Edward
Surtz, we may see *Utopia* as a pre-Reformation work that has

> an eye to the reform of all phases and departments of the Christian state.
> If an ideal pagan state like Utopia which is based solely upon Nature and
> philosophy can attain such glory and triumph, what a paradise upon earth
> could not a Christian nation create, which has, besides the finest products
> of reason and antiquity, the surpassing treasures of revelation and grace to
> aid and sustain it![20]

The implied framework of values in *Utopia,* we must agree with Father Surtz
and the late R. W. Chambers, and must again insist, is an ordered sense of the
concepts and ideals of Christian faith; yet it is only implied, and the bond of
understanding between written work and reader is as nebulous but as strong
as this linkage with a commonly accepted framework. Within this implied
framework More felt completely free to try on "points of view without any
responsibility for rejection or adoption"; he regarded the views presented
"with almost every possible degree of approbation and shade of assent." But
there is a conceptualized distinction between the real and the fanciful, and
one of the functions of some of the playful names is to call attention to their
imaginary quality as much as it is to suggest their fundamentally real essence.
And I would suggest that the dating of Utopia's history at precisely 1760
years is an ironic signal that there was once a king who had made so radical
a proposal as the redistribution of land and the cancellation of debts, and for
this proposal (so pertinent to the urgent conditions More saw about him in
1516, but so obviously more radical than any actual proposals), that Spartan
king had been put to death. To such complex problems there can be no simple
answers, More would seem to be saying; and to the irony of this extraordinarily
clear-eyed view that subsumed Agis and Hythlodaye and Cardinal Morton and
Henry VIII, we must conjoin a More beheaded two decades later: it would
seem, as Eliot softly reminds us, that human kind cannot bear much reality.

'A NURSERY OF CORRECT AND USEFUL INSTITUTIONS': ON READING MORE'S *UTOPIA* AS DIALOGUE

R. J. Schoeck

Like Shakespeare's *Hamlet,* Thomas More's *Utopia* is a work on which all men have firmly established, expert opinions, and consequently disagree. The interpretation of More's *Utopia* covers a wide spectrum ranging from that of a Kautsky or a Chambers to that of C. S. Lewis.[1] That is to say, while all critics and readers are agreed that it is a great book, we have on the one hand those who see it as a program or manifesto, and on the other, those who urge that the 'mistake lies with those readers who take the book *au grand sérieux,*' as Lewis does not.[2] The fault, I suggest, lies rather with those who fail to see what the book says before leaping to argue what it means, with those who ask us to choose only between black and white alternatives, and with those who argue that the *Utopia* was written by 'More the translator of Lucian and friend of Erasmus, not More the chancellor or the ascetic.'[3] The Thomas More of 1515–1516 was one man, a person who was still an ascetic (wearing his hair-shirt and continuing the devotional habits of the Charterhouse), and very much the king's good servant, spending five months on a single embassy for the king at the time he began to write the *Utopia,* and at the very same time also a man of letters and a friend of Erasmus, among others: let us not divide the man for all seasons into several men for different seasons. But fragmentation of More exists, and it would be heuristic to inquire into the diverse academic courses in which his *Utopia* is taught, and into the diverse ways by which it is taught (as I have sketchily done for the Canadian scene[4]), but that is not my concern here. I shall urge that we consider and accept the book as having a serious purpose but argued through an ironic structure. The writer had a strong sense of *Angst,* as we would now say, but his work was full of *festivitas,* as his friends did then say.[5]

In a letter which is first prefaced to the 1517 Paris edition of the *Utopia,* Guillaume Budé—a humanistic scholar second only to Erasmus in the European world of letters and called by Hexter "the shrewdest and most perceptive commentator on the book at the time of its publication"[6]—writing to More's young friend Lupset had this to say: "Now I pay him [More] the highest possible love and veneration for his island in the new world, Utopia. The reason is that our age and succeeding ages will hold his account as a nursery of correct and useful institutions from which every man will introduce and adapt transplanted customs to his own city." (p. 15) Not a joke, mark, not yet a program,

Reprinted, by permission of the author and publisher, from *Moreana,* 22 (1969), 19–32.

but a *seminarium*—translated as 'a nursery' in the Yale Edition, but perhaps better, less ambiguously, rendered as 'a seed-bed'—and doubtless used by Budé with full and deliberate evocation of the Ciceronian phrase *seminarium rei publicae.*[7] I want to hold this Budé passage as a guide for our reading, but first I wish to begin at the beginning, by turning to consider More at the time of his writing the *Utopia*.

A Glance at the Author and the Times

Thomas More was above all else a busy man with one foot in the business world and another in the legal, one arm working for the king and the other able only in the early hours of the morning to do his part-time scholarship. Another of the prefatory letters to the first edition of the *Utopia* is from Thomas More to Peter Giles, an historical person who figures in Book I; in it More apologizes for taking nearly a year to finish up his book since his visit to Antwerp in 1515; and it tells us much about More the private man:

> Yet even to carry through this trifling task, my other tasks left me practically no leisure at all. I am constantly engaged in legal business, either pleading or hearing, either giving an award as arbiter or deciding a case as judge. I pay a visit of courtesy to one man and go on business to another. I devote almost the whole day in public to other men's affairs and the remainder to my own. I leave to myself, that is to learning, nothing at all.
>
> When I have returned home, I must talk with my wife, chat with my children, and confer with my servants. All this activity I count as business when it must be done—and it must be unless you want to be a stranger in your own home. Besides, one must take care to be as agreeable as possible to those whom nature has supplied, or chance has made, or you yourself have chosen, to be the companions of your life, provided you do not spoil them by kindness, or through indulgence make masters out of your servants.[8] (p. 40–1)

As a preliminary document to an actual reading of the book, More's letter gets across the point that he was a man of many activities, and this does add to the verisimilitude of the work. By this time, let us note, More was pushing 40; he had put out a number of things: his life of Pico, his manuscript *Richard III*, the Lucianic translations and epigrams, and some lost dramatic pieces; and in addition he had given his early lectures on Augustine at St. Lawrence Jewry, and presented more recently his two legal readings, or lectures, at Lincoln's Inn (unhappily, neither of the last two seems to have survived).

In May 1515 More had been appointed by Henry VIII as one of a team charged with negotiating an agreement on trade between England and the Netherlands. For several weeks the talks went on at Bruges, seemingly as ineffective as the current peace talks in Paris; by July it was seen[9] that the negotiators, especially those speaking for Prince Charles of Netherlands, had to return for consultation with higher authorities; and so the negotiations were recessed, and the English emissaries in Bruges, or More at least, were left with very little to do. Although More worried, no doubt, about his family at home and about his finances (for not only did he suffer the loss of the usual lawyer's fees but he had to pay his expenses out of his own pocket), he did have the precious commodity of an enforced leisure, and he seems to have used it to spend time to meet and visit with the two humanists, both friends of Erasmus. About Jerome Busleyden (a great figure in the story of northern humanism, a member of the high court of justice for the Netherlands, and a leading figure in the new *mos gallicus* of jurisprudential scholarship[10]) and Busleyden's fine house in Mechlin, More wrote an epigram and described the house in a letter to Erasmus, being as impressed by his host's well-stocked mind as by his well-stocked library. With Peter Giles, town clerk of Antwerp and another humanistic jurisprudent, it would seem that he spent more time and hit it off at once; for as he wrote to Erasmus, ". . . the most pleasant experience of my entire trip was my personal relationship with your host, Peter Giles of Antwerp; his learning, his wit, his modesty, his genuine friendliness are such that, bless my soul, I would be happy to pay a good part of my wealth to purchase the companionship of that one man . . ."[11] One can only conjecture, of course, about the conversation of More and Giles, but some of it is projected into Book One of the *Utopia:* talk about recent discoveries in the New World and no doubt the problems of the Old one; about the rôle of humanists like themselves in giving counsel, and the hopes of achieving the dreamed-of humanistic millenium of a well-ordered commonwealth.[12] Perhaps too they talked about the Fifth Lateran Council, then in progress in Rome—begun in 1512, it would be finished in April 1517, three or four months after publication of the *Utopia*, six months before the publication of Luther's theses. The Fifth Lateran Council had addressed itself to the theme of reform, having been so exhorted in a powerfully moving, and widely read, sermon by Giles of Viterbo at the opening session, in which the Master General of the Augustinians cried out on the need for reform. More or Giles might well have punned on the coincidence of the two Giles. But surely for all thoughtful men, the problems of reform were in the air, and they were discussed more fully on the continent than in England; surely More and Giles would have agreed, in 1515, on the great urgencies and have decried the failure of the Council to achieve reform: three years of council meetings had gone by, and there were too many ominous signs, stirrings of discontent and rebellion.[13] For More, the affair of Richard Hunne in London had produced a great confrontation just before he left in early 1515: Parliament, the hierarchy, King and council, all were deeply involved in this conflict of canon and common law, and only a typically English compromise solution had gained time but without solving the problem.[14] Economically, things were far from well; nearly everywhere the laws needed reform as badly as the Church. It was a year which generated in nearly all and carried nearly everywhere a sense of great urgency, of crisis. *If only we humanists would think about the problems and speak out, especially those of us who are councillors to kings and princes and city-states. If only Reason could be the master . . .*

Before leaving the Low Countries, More wrote a long letter to Martin Dorp, a new theologian who had attacked Erasmus—the letter takes up 56 pages in the *Selected Letters*—and it is important for giving us a sense of the mode, the emphases and controls of More's thinking during the period when the *Utopia* was taking shape. We can see his thinking about the problem of persuading other men, and of doing this by reason and not by authority—More always was on the side of the angels here: "A conviction that is first handed on by stupid teachers and then strengthened in the course of years is extremely capable of perverting the judgment of even sound minds."[15] Even in the domain of logic, More could write that a certain syllogism "is not a syllogism for the reason that it is properly constructed in accordance with the precepts of dialectics and fashioned as a BARBARA syllogism, but because reason, which made such a rule for that very purpose, tells us that the conclusion follows the premises . . ."[16]

Authority alone could not make men change, More recognized, and it would not compel them to use reason to reflect upon their problems. As a Renaissance humanist, More had a high regard for rhetoric, and he would have been familiar with the rich resources of rhetoric for persuasion. (One letter alone, if time permitted, would support this assertion, his letter to Oxford University.[17]) Among traditional resources was the *declamatio*,[18] much beloved of those classical authors whom he and Erasmus studied, discussed and translated. *Declamatio* might do the job of getting men to see an old thing with new eyes, as Erasmus had done in his *Praise of Folly,* with his mock encomium that is also a declamation.[19]

Now the basic theme of Book II of the *Utopia* is that the Utopians have a working economy and society, and that all things work by the light of reason. Reason, that is, can achieve such a nearly-ideal commonwealth; and More's extended *declamatio* spins out this idea to the degree required to win readers to accept the notion that the Utopian commonweal does work, that all things might be made to work by reason.[20] By humanistic definition, this useful aspect should best be presented with a sense of pleasure—the *utile et dulce* of Horace.[21] And so it is pleasurable: at the level of verbal play, first (for More loved puns, especially multi-lingual puns, as much as James Joyce: 'city with no people,' 'river with no water,' Hythloday, the 'speaker of nonsense' whose first name was *Raphael,* which meant 'God hath healed' and who was a divine messenger, and all that); second, at the level of dramatic satire (the uses of gold, with the Utopians using gold for their chamber-pots and the European ambassadors foolishly bearing chains of gold), and so on. But perhaps not least of all as play, in the *declamatio* proper, the spinning out in a Renaissance game of the initiating *questio:* suppose there *were* a commonwealth based entirely on reason—could it work, and how could it work? Part of the fun at this level would be the exploration of the limits to which reason can lead a man—like the Utopian practice of bride and groom being seen naked before marriage: the play of reason might lead a man to this notion, but how un-reasonable a thing to propose!

A Bifocal Book

The original title, it is well to recall, was not simply *Utopia*. It was *De Optimo Reipublicae Statu deque nova insula Utopia libellus vere aureus...* but let me give it in full in English: 'The Best State of a Commonwealth and the New Island of Utopia, A Truly Golden Handbook, No Less Beneficial than Entertaining, by the Distinguished and Eloquent Author, Thomas More, Citizen and Sheriff of the famous City of London.' Sylvester recently suggested that More's book had a double focus: "... it concerns the 'best state of a Commonwealth' *and,* at the same time, it concerns 'a new island called Utopia.' We tend, naturally enough, to fuse the two halves of the title into one unit, to identify, that is, Utopia as the land in which the best state of a commonwealth obtains."[22] If we speak of a double focus in the book, we can also state it as: 1—*problem;* 2—*on solving the problem*—for the two-book structure works in more than one way. Indeed, it has occurred to me, in thinking of differing approaches that representatives from several disciplines bring to a reading of *Utopia,* that many of More's generation would still have had the *habitus,* the habit of mind we would say, to look at all inquiry in terms of the Aristotelian four causes. In these terms, then, the matter of More's handbook is the Utopian commonwealth; the form, the dialogue; the mover, Hythloday; and 'that for the sake of which,' the creation of a model or mirror, for an end which I shall make more specific shortly.[23]

Sylvester's most challenging essay, " 'Si Hythlodaeo Credimus',"—i.e., if we believe, or believe in, Hythloday—takes us into the work by focusing on the aspect of vision and revision with Hythloday as the central concern; it is sound and valuable criticism. He concludes that "we must believe Hythlodaeus, if only for a time; for without having entertained beliefs such as his, our disbelief becomes bankrupt ..."[24] Surely, More expected his contemporary readers to believe Hythloday—else the entire structure of the book would collapse—and I agree that we must, for he is the mover of the complex act of presenting the Utopian commonwealth to us and involving us in a total act of response.

But we must also, as I believe, press more firmly on the nature of the form, on the formal cause as the neoscholastics would have it. *How does the dialogue work?* is the question we must ask in reading such a literary construct, and *how far does it work?*

About Book I there is a firm core of agreement; nearly all would agree with Edward Surtz that "several speakers conduct a dialogue that offers various solutions to the social and political problems besetting Western Europe," though some would want to extend this, in ways that I shall return to develop. It is Book II that causes strains of disagreement, for some, like the Yale editor again, would refer to it as monologue, and deplore "the relinquishment of the form of dialogue."[25] But this is surely to think too rigidly of the dialogue form, in too limitingly a literary way, and to think too little of the metaphysicians' formal cause.

For there are several kinds and levels of dialogue at work in Book I, and we must take pains to indicate them.

(1) There is of course the obvious 'literary' or dramatic dialogue of several persons engaged in conversation—of More and Giles and Hythloday, and also the reported dialogue which had taken place nearly twenty years earlier in England.

(2) But there is also the widening of this kind of dialogue into the public and very much open dialogue of the introductory letters, where are given the impression (and is it altogether false?) that Budé and Busleyden and Erasmus and the others are continuing the dialogue, with one another and with More, and, even more significantly, within their own national and cultural communities. The dialogue goes on, and all of these humanists will have counsel to offer their princes and political institutions.

(3) Yet there is still a third aspect of dialogue. For the Europe of 1500, I think it can be said, there were no political or cultural models other than the Platonic communities of the past and their like. Europe was then an extraordinarily closed society, and it would have taken a moving outside their society to look at it from outside. Does not More's *Utopia* do just that? Does it not give another model—one operating within a totally different historical context, on fundamentally different religious principles, from the European experience? One has to think of the impact of Tacitus' *Germania* for a comparable effect, where we have the picturing of a primitive society that implied a judgment on the Roman *dolce vita*.[26] Once published, the *Utopia* offered such an external model, for like any Renaissance poem it imitates, represents, and figures forth. To indicate that it was so read in More's own century, we have Sidney's citation of the 'speaking picture' of *Utopia* for being so effective and delightful a teacher: "But even in the most excellent determination of goodness, what philosopher's counsel can so readily direct a prince [which is the question debated in Book I], as the feigned Cyrus in Xenophon; or a virtuous man in all fortunes, as Aeneas in Virgil; or a whole commonwealth, as the way of Sir Thomas More's *Utopia?*"[27]

Christendom Listening to the World

Or, to turn from literary to theological contexts, may we not ask whether More did not prophetically anticipate Schillebeeckx's notion of the relation of the Church to the world as not simply one of a 'teaching Church' to a listening world, but "an exchange, a dialogue, where contributions are made from both sides and both sides listen to each other, even in the authoritative proclamation of the Church's unique message."[28] One of the prefatory verses of the first edition, by the now-forgotten humanist Schrijver, catches this note when it asks the reader: "Do you want to see new marvels now that a new world has been discovered not long ago? Do you want to learn ways of living different in nature from our own?" (p. 31)

Dialogue has been made possible between the European Christians and the non-Christian Utopians, and the Utopians at once profited from this potentiality by adopting the Christian religion. For the travel to no place (or good place) More draws not only upon a tradition of political philosophy, as he did in Book I, Sylvester writes, but also on "the new literature of exploration, particularly on the narrative of Vespucci, which had seen several editions before 1515."[29] Yet what More further succeeds in doing is to lift that new travel literature to the higher plane of the mind: just as Hythlodaeus is introduced to us as one whose sailing "has not been like that of Palinurus [Aeneas' pilot who fell asleep and plunged into the sea] but that of Ulysses or, rather, of Plato," (p. 49), so the reach of the reader's reaction is to countries of the mind; we all become voyagers, risking the journey away from home and the fixed points of the past, moving out of eye-sight of the old landfalls. By the time we are well into Book II, then, the operation of the work is intended to involve the reader, to lead him in his own way to extend the full dramatic of I and the one-sided dialogue of II. (I call it one-sided dialogue, for even in a purely literary sense, "it is not fair to speak of Hythlodaeus' description as monologue"—Surtz writes—[30] "for the answers to supposed objections, the antagonism of the invisible rich, the imperatives and exclamations, the consciousness of an audience, even though ill-defined, all help to give Hythlodaeus' discourse on Utopia the effect of *one-sided dialogue*.")

This then is the reading of the *Utopia* I would bring forward. Viewed philosophically, More has created as his matter the 'speaking picture' of the Utopian commonwealth: the maker of Utopia is not subject to nature as given (history), and yet goes hand in hand with nature, not abstracting from her (as in moral philosophy). That matter is presented in the form of a dialogue, by one angelic speaker of nonsense, to the end of creating a model by reference to which reforms might be achieved. Viewed rhetorically, More has presented an extended *declamatio*, that rhetorical form which posits an imagined situation and attempts by every device and means available to persuade the audience of its actuality, or potentiality. As the verse by Geldenhauer (or Noviomagus, another forgotten Dutch humanist) expresses it: "Reader, do you like what is pleasant? In this book is everything that is pleasant. Do you hunt what is profitable? You can read nothing more profitable. If you wish both the pleasant and the profitable, this island abounds in both." (p. 31)

There is no conflict between the *jeu d'esprit* and the sense of urgency, provided that we do not exaggerate either or insist on the one to the exclusion of the other. For the sense of urgency was there, in 1516; the sense of crisis in book I is unmistakable. But that does not prevent More from having his fun, from allowing his rich sense of *festivitas* its full play: "reader, if you like what is pleasant and profitable, both are here." And that is indeed the essence of the spirit of the book: that one finds a fusion of the *dulce* and the *utile*—just as three generations later, another English humanist will indulge in a parallel play of wit and *sprezzatura* in his quite serious *Defence of Poetry*. The plea is never made too blatantly; we are not offended by one who thrusts his hands into our pockets; but the undercurrent of seriousness is not to be missed. There is of course the danger that such irony may be misread. We know that some have misread that celebrated medieval treatise on Courtly Love, the *De*

Arte Honeste Amandi of Capellanus: in the twelfth century men were tried
by the code of courtly love, and some in the twentieth century take it as
seriously—yet in 1290 one Drouart la Vache laughed hard and long over it.[31]
We know that Erasmus' *Praise of Folly* was taken *ad litteram* by many contemporaries (like Dorp, who asked that Erasmus write a *Praise of Wisdom* to
show his good faith!).[32] In the case of More's ironic work, there was the contemporary priest—usually identified as the Vicar of Croydon—who wanted to
go to Utopia to become bishop of that splendid place (p. 292).

But for those who do not see all things as black and white (and there are
those who are familiar enough with the black and white fallacy in formal
logic, yet still want to force the interpretation of a work of art as complex as
the *Utopia* into one or the other, play or program), there are the rich and
rewarding pleasures of comprehending both *dulce et utile* in their reading of
the Utopia. "Do you want to see new marvels now that a new world has been
discovered not long ago? [a nice ambiguity that embraces both Utopia and
the geographical new world]. Do you want to learn ways of living different
in nature from our own?" (p. 31) For readers then and now addressed by
Schrijver, and for those who want to "continue successfully to devise, execute,
and perfect ever fresh benefits for the commonwealth" (as Busleyden wrote
to More, p. 37), there is the ever-challenging book, the ever-green world, of
Utopia.[33]

Small wonder that Budé felt that "our age and succeeding ages will hold
[More's] account as a nursery of correct and useful institutions from which
every man may introduce and adapt transplanted customs to his own city." I
pause to note that the original Latin for Budé's 'introduce and adapt' is
'importent & accommodent.' Surtz glosses *accommodent* only, and as follows:
"This is an important word. Utopian institutions, when introduced, are to be
adapted to national customs and religious belief . . . The idea of adapting is a
qualification or limitation." (ed. *Utopia*, p. 276). So it is. But we should add
that *importent & accommodent* suggest the ordinary Roman importing of
grain—ordinary but vital—and this carries forward the seed metaphor of
seminarium. The point is that living things must grow; one does not impose
patterns.

Utopia is as close to us, as valuable for us, as that, *if* we engage ourselves in
such a dialogue, *if* we insure that our response be both creative (or co-creative)
and critical, *if* we detach ourselves from too limiting a view of our own problems because we have never been simultaneously both engaged and detached,
as Sylvester exhorts. And we must, as Sylvester goes on to conclude, be willing
"to appreciate how nowhere can be somewhere. We must believe Hythlodaeus,
if only for a time; for without having entertained beliefs such as his, our disbelief becomes bankrupt and we find ourselves with no riches left to
squander."[34] Further, we must be willing to carry on such dialogue: dialogue,
first, with the traditions of the past, for is this not the role, the responsibility,
ultimately, of the humanist critic? And at the same time we must be willing
to continue and to extend dialogue with other models from cultures and
societies not our own. One must reflect that we are far richer in this second

dimension of dialogue than was More, at the same time that we must recognize that we are so immeasurably poorer than he and his fellow humanists were in reflecting upon and drawing from models of the past. Above all we must never stop trying to bring home to our own age, and to succeeding ages, understanding of the "good life" as did Hythloday for More's generation when, as Budé wrote to Lupset (p. 13), he borrowed from the Utopians "and brought home to us the pattern [*argumentum*] of the good life."[35]

"SI HYTHLODAEO CREDIMUS": VISION AND REVISION IN THOMAS MORE'S *UTOPIA*

R. S. Sylvester

The *Utopia* of Sir Thomas More is a book which has meant many different things to many different men. Like other great books, its literary excellence has generated a host of varying interpretations. On the one hand, to simplify a complex story, the "radical" interpretation of *Utopia* takes Utopian communism very seriously indeed, viewing the second book of More's work as a blueprint for the ideal society;[1] on the other hand, what might be called the "conservative" school of opinion sees the work as a delightful trifle that should be valued primarily for its witty satire on Western Europe, but which is by no means to be viewed as offering a concrete program for social reform.[2] Between these two poles of interpretation the critics—political scientists, Tudor historians, social philosophers—range freely and, it should also be noted, so do the literary artists. For *Utopia,* however ambiguous it may be in itself, is a book which seems to demand imitation. When Thomas More wrote it in 1515-1516 he created not only a masterpiece, but also a whole new genre of literature. In the last four centuries, we have had almost as many fresh utopias as we have had interpretations of the first *Utopia.*[3] Both these aspects of the work's influence (we might call them the "creative" and the "critical") provide ample testimony to the dynamic power of the original book. In what follows, I shall not be primarily concerned with the later fortunes of *Utopia,* but I do hope to offer, through an analysis of the text, some insight into the literary factors that structure its seminal greatness.

Even a brief review of the circumstances surrounding the composition of *Utopia* indicates something of the paradoxical nature of the work. In the first place, More and his humanist friends, when discussing the book before its publication in December, 1516, do not refer to it as "*Utopia*" but rather as "Nusquama." The change from Latin to Greek, which must have occurred shortly before More released his manuscript,[4] may seem of little moment for us—"Nowhere" is nowhere in any language; but for a group of men who habitually wrote and spoke Latin, the effect of More's shift to Greek was to distance the entire concept of his new country that did not, as its name insisted, really exist. In addition, the substitution of "Utopia" for "Nusquama" is related to the decided preference which More's narrator, the fabulous Raphael Hythlodaeus, manifests for Greek culture and learning. With the

Reprinted from *Soundings* (formerly *The Christian Scholar*), 51 (1968), 272-89 by permission of the author and publisher.

transition goes an increased isolation, an emphasis on the esoteric. "Nus-quama" was a joke, but "Utopia," and all the other paradoxical Greek names which More employs, is a very learned joke indeed.[5] When More, in a post-script letter to his friend Peter Giles, stops to explain what he is up to, he seems to be denying, with deliberate irony, that his narrative has any literal dimension whatsoever: "Thus, if I had done nothing else than impose names on ruler, city, and island such as might suggest to the more learned that the island was nowhere, the city a phantom, the river without water, and the ruler without a people, it would not have been hard to do and would have been much wittier than what I actually did. Unless the faithfulness of an historian had been binding on me, I am not so stupid as to have preferred to use those barbarous and meaningless names, Utopia, Anydrus, Amaurotum, and Ademus." (251)[6] But More did, of course, prefer those "barbarous" names, names which deny as they affirm; and we must constantly recall, as we read his work, that when we use the word "utopia" lightly to mean an ideally perfect society, we are contradicting the avowed etymology of the word as it was first invented and employed and that we may also be contra-dicting the unavowed intention of its author in writing his book.

Nor, for that matter, is *Utopia* itself the true title of More's work. All of the early editions bear a somewhat cumbersome legend, which can be literally translated as follows: "Concerning the best state of a commonwealth, and concerning the new island, Utopia; a truly golden little book, no less beneficial than entertaining, by the distinguished and eloquent author Thomas More, citizen and sheriff of the famous city of London." When we, like More's contemporaries, shorten all this to *"Utopia,"* we are not acting merely for convenience's sake, but are also paying tribute to the fact that the most salient feature of the volume is its second part, the description of the island itself and of its inhabitants. This new world entrances us, our disbelief is conveniently suspended; we know that Utopia must be somewhere. The book which describes the new country is in our hands; must not the society itself be within our grasp? As Peter Giles reminded his friend, Jerome Busleyden, in a prefatory letter to the first edition, it is not really so incredible that Utopia should have escaped discovery in the past: "Don't we, nowadays," he says (thinking of Columbus and Vespucci), "find very many lands cropping up which were unknown to the ancient cosmographers?" (25). Certainly many a sixteenth-century reader must have reacted to Utopia in this way and it is quite remarkable that three of the early vernacular translations (the German, Italian, and Spanish) omit More's first book entirely and are content with the new island of Book II alone.[7]

Yet the full title of the work, like the word "Utopia" itself, carefully sets up a tight dichotomy. More's book, so the title affirms, has a double focus: it concerns the "best state of a Commonwealth" *and,* at the same time, it con-cerns "a new island called Utopia." We tend, naturally enough, to fuse the two halves of the title into one unit, to identify, that is, Utopia as the land in which the best state of a commonwealth obtains. But we do so at a certain risk, for the double title can be otherwise interpreted. The first half calls attention to those numerous discussions of ideal governments which, from Plato on, had occupied the minds of many philosophical writers.[8] More himself had written several thoughtful epigrams on precisely this subject.[9] As stated, the first part of the title leaves the whole question open; it signals the subject matter (the best way to counsel princes), if not also the mood and tone, of the first book of *Utopia,* where several speakers conduct a dialogue that offers various solutions to the social and political problems besetting Western Europe.

The second half of the title points directly to Book II, which is not a dialogue at all but a fervently eulogistic monologue in which the new island is described. Here More draws not on a tradition of political philosophy, as he did in Book I, but on the new literature of exploration, particularly on the narrative of Vespucci, which had seen several editions before 1515. Yet we are also asked to remember, both directly in the preliminary letters of More and his friends, and indirectly in Hythlodaeus' narrative itself, that Utopia has no concrete, geographical existence. Because someone coughed too loudly, Peter Giles tells us, everyone missed Hythlodaeus' words giving the latitude of the new land; Hythlodaeus himself never tells us precisely how he got to Utopia,[10] nor do we know exactly what happened to him after he delivered his discourse at Antwerp. Giles thinks he may have returned to Utopia (25), but More tells us that he was heard of in Portugal on last March 1 (253).

I shall return to Hythlodaeus and his unchartable wanderings a bit later. Perhaps enough has been said already to indicate that More wants us to consider the whole world of travel literature as a kind of metaphor for the new type of mental exploration which his book will introduce.[11] To reflect on the best state of the commonwealth, so his double title affirms, involves the creation of a new model. But should the model itself—in this case the island of Utopia—be viewed as a substitute for reality, a best of all possible worlds where rationality reigns supreme? Or, to leave the question open, must not the mind return from its fanciful excursion to the bleak contemporaneity of Book I where the stresses and strains of human existence are all too evident? Certainly Book II ends on this latter note, as More, who has faithfully listened to Hythlodaeus' impassioned account, leads his guest out of the garden where their conversation took place and back into the house, remarking as they go, that there are "very many features of the Utopian commonwealth which it is easier for me to wish for in our countries than to have any hope of seeing realized" (247).

Thus we will do best, I believe, if we view the title-page of *Utopia* as posing a question rather than offering a solution to an age-old problem. Is the best state of a commonwealth, More seems to ask, to be identified with a totally new society? To answer that question, the reader must ponder the book itself very carefully. He will have to ask whether or not the apparently negative view of the contemporary world that emerges from the scathing satire of Book I is counterbalanced by the apparently positive view of Utopia itself that is advanced in Book II; and he will have to decide how each of these views is affected by the literary form in which it is presented, the dialogue, that is, of Book I, and the monologue of Book II. The relationship between the two books is further complicated by our knowledge, thanks to a remark made by Erasmus in a letter of 1519, that More wrote Book II before he wrote Book I.[12] Thus the order in which we read the work, which represents More's final intention, reverses the order in which he conceived it; the genetics of composition have been displaced by a measured rethinking and reassessment; what was once an autonomous monologue has been set in a dialogic framework. Perhaps our own interpretations of the work as a whole should be modelled on this process. *Utopia*, as we have it, begs us to continue the discussion, to confront Hythlodaeus for ourselves so that, as Thomas More puts it at the end of Book II, we may have another chance "to think about these matters more deeply and to talk them over with him more fully" (245).

If we adopt such an attitude toward *Utopia*, we shall be imitating the way in which the circle of More's humanist friends received the book when it was first published. Their comments on the book, some of which I have already quoted, have been rather unjustly neglected. Most editions of *Utopia* either omit the prefatory letters completely, or give only More's first letter to Peter Giles which serves as an immediate introduction to Book I. Yet these *parerga*, to give them a convenient short title, are far more than mere advertising blurbs.[13] More himself deliberately solicited comments from his friends and they responded handsomely. The 1516 Louvain edition began with the famous map of Utopia and the Utopian alphabet, followed by some verses praising the island that are assigned to the Utopian poet-laureate. Peter Giles's letter to Jerome Busleyden followed; then came a letter by John Desmarais and verses by him and two other humanists. Busleyden himself next produced a letter to More, preceding More's own first letter to Giles. In the 1517 Paris edition, a letter from the famous French scholar Guillaume Budé to Thomas Lupset was added and a second letter from More to Giles was appended to the second book. Finally, in the two Basel editions of 1518, Erasmus himself recommended the work to the reader, but he also dropped some of the other *parerga* which had appeared in the first two editions. All later editions of the *Utopia* follow one of the early issues and it is, consequently, somewhat ironic that before the Yale edition of 1965 appeared no printing of *Utopia* preserved all of this introductory and supplementary material.

Now the writers of these prefatory poems and addresses are not merely enthusiastic in their praise for the new volume. As their comments pile up in the first three editions they both echo and modify each other's opinions, reshaping the book to their own image and likeness, but never offering a completely comprehensive interpretation of it. The subtler spirits among them, especially Budé and Peter Giles, ironically imitate More's own evasions on the question of whether or not the country Utopia actually exists; but all of the writers enter wholeheartedly into the fiction itself, praising More's commonwealth as a rival of Plato's *Republic*, or even as going beyond Plato. Most of them too, when they praise More himself, single out for special mention the remarkable fact that a man so involved in public affairs could manage to find time to pen such a fine work. Somehow, they feel, he has reconciled his

private interests with the public welfare. More himself, in his first letter to
Giles, is not so sure about this. He speaks at length (39-41) of the way his legal
business and his family responsibilities impinge on his literary pursuits—but he
never denies that each sphere of activity has its just claims and that he must
remain true to both of them. Thus the large problem of the work as a whole—
how the public welfare and the welfare of the private citizen are related to
each other—is transposed here, in the *parerga*, to the personal level of More's
own everyday life and we are gently conditioned for the broader treatment of
the subject which follows in Book I.

Nor is that all that the writers of the *parerga* do for us. Accepting the fiction of Utopia's existence, they are moved immediately to contrast its harmonious society with the injustice prevalent in Europe itself. And the critical
process thus initiated does not end with the prefatory materials but continues
throughout the volume in the form of apt marginal glosses which call attention
to the way Utopian practices differ from those of contemporary society. Peter
Giles and Erasmus seem to have been responsible for these marginalia, but they
were approved by More, who revised his text slightly for the second and third
editions and did not, in so doing, delete or add to the marginal glosses. Many
of the marginalia are acidly satiric, particularly in the second book, where, for
example, they contrast the lack of lawyers in Utopia with "the useless horde"
of them in Europe (195) or, in a note dear to academics, praise Utopian intellectual achievements by remarking that in their own world, nowadays, "block-
heads and loggerheads devote themselves to scholarship, whereas the best
endowed talent is being ruined by pleasures" (181).

Yet for all of their commitment to the Utopian game, the shrewdest of the
humanists do not fail to see that Utopia is really nowhere. Even if the Utopian
poet-laureate (whose name, Anemolius, means "windiness") suggests that a
better name for the country would be "Eutopia" or the "Happy-Land (21),"
Budé, in his letter to Lupset, says that he hears Utopia is also called "Udepotia,"
or "Never-Land," not only, that is, a country which has no geographical reality,
but a society which will never come into existence in the future, no matter how
firmly men may believe in the desirability of its birth. For Budé, who has temporarily interrupted the building of his country estate in order to read More's
work, *Utopia* is a "nursery of institutions" (15), a kind of fictional seedbed
"from which everyman may introduce and adapt transplanted customs to his
own city." Moreover, both Budé and Peter Giles are very cautious about the
reliability of Hythlodaeus himself. Twice Budé hedges his praise for Utopian
institutions with the words "if we may believe Hythlodaeus" (*si Hythlodaeo
credimus*) or "if we may believe the story" (11-13); and he distinguishes carefully between Hythlodaeus, whom he calls "the real builder of the Utopian
city," and Thomas More, who, as author, has adorned Hythlodaeus' account
with style and eloquence. Giles goes even further. As a character in the book
itself he has a special interest in such problems. Yes, he says (23), Hythlodaeus
did have "a special skill of his own in unfolding his narrative"; but "when I
contemplate the same picture as painted by More's brush, I am as affected as
if I were sometimes actually living in Utopia itself. By heaven, I am even dis-

posed to believe that in all the five years which Raphael spent on the island, he did not see as much as one may perceive in More's description."

The words of Peter Giles, echoed and modified by Budé, can serve to lead us out of the prefatory matter to *Utopia* and into the book itself. His distinction between what Hythlodaeus sees in the new land and what More's narrative reveals to us about both the ideal country and Hythlodaeus' view of it is crucial. "If we believe Hythlodaeus," says Budé. Much depends, in both Book I and Book II, on whether or not we believe him, so much, indeed, that each book of the *Utopia*, in the early editions, has the full subtitle: "The speech (or discourse) which the extraordinary character Raphael Hythlodaeus delivered concerning the best state of the commonwealth—as reported by Thomas More, citizen of London etc." Not only is almost all of Book II presented, without direct comment, as Hythlodaeus' speech, but he is also the driving force behind and the monopolizer of the conversation in Book I. Nor should we shrink from facing the fact that, if we say we believe him, we are not simply saying that Utopia ought to exist; to believe Hythlodaeus is to accept what he stands for as true, and it is also to identify his views with those of Thomas More himself, whose fictional creation Raphael Hythlodaeus most certainly is.

That we as readers should be placed in this tentative position, "if we believe Hythlodaeus," is to a certain extent Thomas More's own fault. When More created Hythlodaeus, he also recreated himself, so to speak, by introducing a character with his own name into his book. This fictional "Thomas More" is indeed very much like the historical Thomas More, the author of *Utopia*, and it might well seem that the presence of such a character, a first person narrator at that, who argues with Hythlodaeus in Book I, would serve to warn us against identifying More's deepest beliefs, as the author, with those views which Hythlodaeus presents. Yet in actual fact, as any reader knows, the effect is just the opposite. The fictional "Thomas More" grants the truth of many of Hythlodaeus' arguments. Neither of them believes that the brutal English penal system should be maintained; both of them sympathize wholeheartedly with the poor and downtrodden; each admits that it is a very difficult thing to offer wise advice to kings who are bent on self-aggrandizement and selfish exploitation of their subjects. In the narrative, to put the matter briefly, More and Hythlodaeus agree about ends. Men should find, if they can, the best state of the commonwealth.

Yet they disagree sharply on the question of means. Where Hythlodaeus advocates a complete demolition job on the hierarchical society of Western Europe, with communism taking its place, More is unwilling to advocate such a tremendous upheaval. He doubts Hythlodaeus' wisdom here, just as, at the end of Book II, he has many doubts about the validity of Utopian practices in war, religion, and social organization. The fictional Thomas More is a doubting Thomas indeed,[14] but his skepticism hardly counts for much in the face of the revelations which Hythlodaeus brings. The weight of Raphael's arguments is so great that More is rather easily overwhelmed by them even as he tries to maintain that he is unconvinced. If we identify the character "Thomas More" with the author Thomas More, then we are bound to feel that the latter has put his best words and his deepest beliefs not into his own mouth, but into the mouth of his "extraordinary character," Raphael Hythlodaeus.

But this is surely too simple. More had read Chaucer, and there, if nowhere else,[15] he would have found ample justification for a literary *persona* whose naive views were by no means a direct reflection of a poet's deepest creed. The "Thomas More" who debates with Raphael is not the real man but a kind of temporary representation of him, a figure who, while serving on a temporary mission for his king, entertains a strange visitor in his temporary lodgings at Antwerp. But it is this strange visitor himself who concerns us most deeply. Is his character consistently developed? Does what he says really probe to the heart of things? What is his attitude toward the new country which he has discovered? What kind of values emerge from an analysis of his passionate rhetoric? If we give a positive answer to queries like these, then we shall have to say that, yes, we do believe Hythlodaeus.

And it is, to be sure, very hard not to believe him; perhaps, I am inclined to think, he has become easier to believe since More first published his book. Hythlodaeus presents himself as a grand humanitarian, one who has the fullest interests of the common man constantly before his eyes. His doctrines of social utility often make him sound like a distant ancestor of Jeremy Bentham, and his insistence on the greatest good for the greatest number, plus his program, "From each according to his talents, to each according to his needs," should endear him to the hearts of the most sincere Marxists. Moreover, his analysis of the early sixteenth-century political and economic world, as he presents it in Book I, is cogently convincing. He is not the ordinary traveler, Peter Giles tells More as Book I opens (49–51), who comes back, like Ulysses, with wild tales of monsters; nor is he a mere sailor like Palinurus, who traverses everything in a sleepy dream. He has traveled, Giles says, like Plato, through a mental landscape. Hythlodaeus is a man of ideas, passionately committed to what he believes in, and his emotional force draws us to him, just as his claim to have seen more than has been revealed to other mortals intrigues our curiosity and makes us willing to hear him.

Yet his name, when Giles mentions it to More, should give us pause. "Raphael," first of all, is an angelic appellation. Its Hebrew etymology offers the meaning "healer of God," and the angel Raphael's role in the Book of Tobit (5:14) suggests that More's traveler should be understood as a kind of divine messenger who comes to bring comfort and solace to the poor and distressed. But the other half of Raphael's name turns these connotations inside out. "Hythlodaeus" is a Greek compound which means "well-learned in nonsense." Immediately, we confront our old paradox: How can a messenger of heavenly salvation be, at the same time, a teller of trifling, if well-learned tales? How can Utopia be both somewhere and nowhere?

Other features of Hythlodaeus' character, as they emerge in Book I, tend to enlarge the kind of contradictions which his name suggests. I had one student recently who told me that Raphael was one of the first hippies; if we recall his beard, his sunburn, his careless dress, plus the fact that he has decidedly "opted out" of society, then the remark shows a certain aptness. But Hythlodaeus' various "trips" should not be confused with those that are often taken by today's Bohemians. He needs no external stimuli to prompt him into vision; possessed by a fiery spirit, he forces himself upon his audience like an Old Testament prophet. Once started, his flow of words cannot be checked. Thomas More tells us at the end of Book II that he would have asked Raphael some questions about the Utopian commonwealth, but he refrained from doing so because "I was not quite certain that he could brook any opposition to his views, particularly when I recalled his censure of others who feared that they might not appear to be wise enough unless they found some fault to criticize in other men's discoveries" (245, adapted).

Hythlodaeus, then, is a man obsessed with his own insights. His past history reveals that, unlike the Thomas More who tried to remain true to both public and private obligations, he has deliberately severed himself from the world that gave him birth. "Nunc sic vivo ut volo," he proudly announces, "I now live as I please" (57). Having bought off his family by settling a trust fund upon them, he feels that they "ought to be satisfied" (55). Despite his learning and his experience, he will not serve either his court or his country.[16] Paradoxically enough, this great humanitarian is disgusted with the manifestations of human nature that he encounters in Western Europe—and this includes not only corrupt kings and conniving courtiers, but also his own family. Even more significantly, he does not believe that Western society contains within itself enough energy or enough resources to throw off the disease which besets it (105). The solution of its problems can come only from new institutions, vigorously established and maintained, that will eradicate the vices—especially pride and avarice—to which mere humanity is all too prone.

Hythlodaeus is thus both uprooted himself and an uprooter of others. His most urgent pleas for reform bristle with metaphors of deracination and eradication. Like King Utopus, whom he will describe in Book II, he believes that man must cut himself away from the mainland of his present and past existence, must start from scratch, building a new society according to a prearranged plan. So far we may well follow him, believe in him even, all the more so if, as one of the dedicatory poems in the *parerga* puts it, we have seen into "the great emptiness lying concealed at the heart of things" (31). But we may also wonder whether the price which Hythlodaeus asks us to pay is too high—not so much the cost involved in losing all that has been bequeathed to us, but rather the loss in terms of human personality itself. Given Hythlodaeus' isolation from the rest of humanity, can we really trust him to lead us into the promised land?

In literary terms, our answer to this last question must depend on the way in which we respond to Hythlodaeus' critique of Western society as he offers it in Book I. One of the most interesting aspects of his argument is the way in which it increasingly tends, as the book proceeds, to seek a solution to current problems in terms of a new model. There are three main moments to the progress of the debate in Book I, each of them marked out with a story told by

Hythlodaeus to prove a point. The first is historical, his account of his visit to the household of Cardinal Morton in the summer of 1497 (59 f.).[17] The second episode is hypothetical, yet it is tied to history by being set in France. "Suppose," says Hythlodaeus, "I were at the court of the French king" (87). The third and final situation is totally imaginary, offered without reference to locality or to time: "Picture the councillors of some king or other . . . suppose I were to rise and maintain" (91, 95). Hythlodaeus' argument, in other words, moves from a firm grasp on a past historical situation, to a hypothetical revision of contemporary history, and, finally, to a totally aloof fabrication. He develops all of his anecdotes to illustrate the way in which his wisdom would be spurned in the courts of princes, but each story works against him as well as for him. If we read too quickly, we fail to see that the most elaborate of his stories, the one concerning his experience in Morton's household, where More himself was trained as a boy, illustrates precisely the opposite of what Hythlodaeus claims it to show. For the fact is that Morton, far from turning a deaf ear to Hythlodaeus' proposals regarding the punishment of malefactors, says that it would be a good thing try this system! In the one real-life anecdote which Raphael tells, he stands convicted, by his own words, of a kind of blindness.

Moreover, in each of his three anecdotes he offers, to clinch his argument, not so much a rational analysis as an alien example. Before Cardinal Morton, he describes the realm of the Polylerites, whose name means "a people of much nonsense." Dwelling far away in the confines of Persia (75), they are still, as it were, on the map. In his fictive advice to the French king, Hythlodaeus rests his case on the example of the Achorians, a "people without a country," who live "on the mainland to the south-southeast of the island of Utopia" (89). We still have some geography, but it is merely directional. Finally, in his last anecdote, Raphael points to the Macarians, the "blessed or happy men," who dwell "not very far distant from Utopia" (97). Thus with each of the three countries, and in each of the three episodes, we draw farther and farther away from the known world. The names of these strange lands chart the mental course upon which we are sailing. Beginning with "much nonsense" (Hythlodaeus' own name and his misreading of his own story), we progress to a countryless people (the middle, indeterminate stage, where Utopia still has only a negative meaning), and then to the blessed land itself, or at least to a country quite close to it, where the radiant power of the Utopian ideal commonwealth begins to be manifested.

In Book II, so carefully set up by the three phases of Book I, we get our first full look at Utopia itself. We see it, however, not as if we were watching a documentary film, nor as if we were reading a dispassionate prose narrative: we see it through Hythlodaeus' eyes from the perspective which he has reached at the end of Book I, where the scales were already heavily loaded in favor of all things Utopian. "Hythlodaeus," Budé had told us, "is the real creator of Utopia," and it is his creative activity which shapes a new world for us. We do not go wrong if we see Book II as an extended image of Hythlodaeus' own personality: Utopia enshrines his ideals and virtues, but it also—and he himself is completely unaware of this—hints at the defects in his thinking and at the moral flaws in his character. Utopia is made, like all famous creations, in the image and likeness of its creator. If we accept the country, we accept its founder.

In a sense, More took a considerable risk when he cast Book II in the form of an unabated monologue. Many a reader has been so swept away by the speaker's voice and by his wonderful ability to image forth a new picture of reality that he has almost lost his awareness of the man behind the dream. Yet Book I has shown us the character of the speaker, and in Book II he reveals himself indirectly on many occasions. The questions we should ask ourselves as we read Book II might run as follows: What is Hythlodaeus' attitude towards the people and customs he is describing? How do we determine this attitude, or, more significantly, what are we to make of those passages where he seems to express no opinion but where the subject-matter clearly demands some comment? We can grant at once that Hythlodaeus is tremendously enthusiastic about his new island—and this in spite of his claim that "We have taken upon ourselves only to describe their principles, and not also to defend them" (179). In this very sentence, coming at the middle of Book II, Hythlodaeus lapses into the plural, not merely an editorial "we" but a clear affirmation of his kinship with the Utopians. And he goes on in the next sentence to say, patently contradicting himself, that "nowhere (*nusquam*) in the world is there a more excellent people nor a happier commonwealth." So too, in the other rare instances where he seems to be criticizing Utopian customs, we find that he quickly rights himself and launches into a vigorous defense of the very thing he had just cast doubt on. Utopian pre-marital inspection, for example, which "seemed to us very foolish and ridiculous" (189), is wittily rationalized in the next paragraph so that it seems suddenly to be the only sensible procedure.

There are not many passages like this where Hythlodaeus doubts Utopian values, but one other key instance should be noted. As he describes at great length (161–179) the Utopians' philosophy of pleasure, the rationale, as it were, which informs their mental and moral life, he finds it "astonishing" that "they seek a defense for this soft doctrine from their religion, which is serious and strict, almost solemn and hard" (161). As Father Surtz remarks in his note to the Yale edition (444), "Hythlodaeus here dissociates himself subtly from the conceptual base of the ethical theory dominant in Utopia." But one might also add that, as he does so, he fails to perceive the inner logic of his own vision. Of course Utopian manners and morals draw support from their religion; if religion did not support their eminent pragmatism, we can be sure that the Utopians would ruthlessly do away with it. Hythlodaeus' hesitation here is nothing compared to the bland tone in which he describes the empty negatives of Utopian religion itself at the end of Book II. By then, however, his own argument has so overwhelmed him that he is never tempted to criticize, much less to attack.[18]

It should not be necessary here to enlarge upon the matter of the defects in the Utopian system as Hythlodaeus describes it. Most of these are no longer escaping notice, perhaps because so many of them have become grim reality in our own century. To praise the Utopians when they brutally take over neighboring territory to accommodate their expanding population is to speak the language of *Mein Kampf* and *Lebensraum*. Here as elsewhere Hythlodaeus makes no criticisms. Once one accepts, as Hythlodaeus does, the principle that institutions are more important than individual personalities, then every social and political energy, no matter what the consequences, must be devoted to maintaining the static stability of life for its own sake. Hence flow that look of pharisaical self-satisfaction on every identical Utopian face, their consciousness of their own well-being, their Machiavellian tactics in time of war.

We may see these defects, but Hythlodaeus himself fails to notice them. As his narrative develops in Book II he becomes less and less concerned with possible alternatives to Utopian practices. In the early portions of the book his account is orderly enough: a detailed rendering, in fairly objective terms, of Utopian topography is followed by an account of the cities and the system of local government;[19] next come agriculture and trade, then social relations. But with the long section called "Utopian Travel," which runs for forty pages (145–185), Raphael begins to lose control of his tale. Earlier he had stopped several times to contrast Utopia with Europe, always, of course, to the latter's detriment; now he ranges erratically, making a wide excursion into Utopian philosophy and then juxtaposing (185–189), with unconscious irony, an account of slavery with an account of marriage. The last two sections of Book II, those on Military Affairs and Religion, find him singing the praises of all that is worst in Utopia. The two chapters balance each other, illustrating the way in which the life-worshiping Utopians will suffer any hardship, even complete annihilation in war (211), yet manage to hold as a fundamental principle that no man, under any circumstances, should suffer for his religion (219). Hythlodaeus' final word, before he launches into his feverish peroration, aptly illustrates More's point: On holydays, after church, "they pass the rest of the day [which is the best part of the day] in games and in exercises of military training" (237).

At the end of Book II, More praises Hythlodaeus' speech and then, *taking him by the hand,* leads him in to supper. How is one to interpret this final gesture? Should we think of a father watching over his child, a sage protecting and yet drawing on his disciple? Certainly the gesture is very warm, human and open, a last affirmation of the bond that ties More and Hythlodaeus together now, as it did in the dialogue of Book I. But More is perhaps also indicating that Hythlodaeus, once so proudly independent, so all-knowing and so all-seeing, now needs a helping hand quite desperately. Blinded by his absorption in his own vision, cut off from his auditors by being hypnotized with himself, he can no longer find his own way back to reality. Yet for all that, Hythlodaeus is not to be scorned. He has, after all, created the model, even if he has exhausted himself in the process. He is not, in the last analysis, a Utopian, for the one thing that a utopian citizen can never imagine is a world better than his own. And if human ideals are always defective, then this does not mean that we should shrink from them any more than it means that we should embrace them without reservation.

More's great book, then, is a plea for both engagement and detachment, both dialogue and monologue, in matters that concern the best state of a commonwealth. To use the terms with which I began, our response must be both creative *and* critical. Without such a disciplined control of both positive and negative factors in life, one can never discern, to use the words of Peter Giles, "the sources from which all evils actually arise in the commonwealth or from which all blessings could possibly flow" (23). If the structure of More's *Utopia* suggests nothing else, it does affirm that the source of the evils may well become the source of the blessings. But in order to realize this fully we must be willing, at least temporarily, to appreciate how nowhere can be some-where. We must believe Hythlodaeus, if only for a time; for without having entertained beliefs such as his, our disbelief becomes bankrupt and we find ourselves with no riches left to squander.

SIR THOMAS MORE IN NEW SPAIN

Silvio Zavala

When we study the relations between English and Spanish humanism in the sixteenth century our attention is at once caught by the attraction which the life and work of Sir Thomas More had for the Spanish-speaking peoples.

One tribute, born of the religious and political controversies of the time, is the *Cisma de Inglaterra* (1588), in which the Jesuit Ribadeneyra extols the memory of More as a martyr to Christian faith and liberty. Another is the life of Thomas More written by Fernando de Herrera (Sevilla, 1592; Madrid, 1617). *Tomás Moro* he calls his book, according to the well-established Castilian usage, and it shows not only a veneration for a religious hero but a sincere appreciation of More's qualities as a man—his modesty, his gentle manners, his integrity, his moderate way of life, and his gay yet gracious disposition. Herrera praises, moreover, More's reconciliation of philosophy with government, inasmuch, he writes, that 'it seemed as though, with him, there entered into England that felicity promised to kingdoms by the ancients, when princes and rulers loved learning and promoted the sciences which enlighten men and temper their passions.'[1]

Again, in 1637, there appeared in Córdoba, with certain significant omissions and annotations, *La Utopia de Tomás Moro, Gran Canciller de Inglaterra, Vizconde y Ciudadano de Londres. Traducida del Latín al Castellano por don Gerónimo Antonio de Medinilla y Porres.* It may be remembered that some passages in the *Utopia,* which lent themselves to free interpretation, had led to the inclusion of this work in the Portuguese index of 1581 and in the Spanish one of 1583, prepared by the Archbishop of Toledo. Although it was recognised that the author was a pious man and a Catholic, permission could only be given to read his book in an expurgated version. That is why, in the version produced in Córdoba, care was taken to emphasize that: 'If at any time there was a need for expurgation in other editions of it, in the present one there is none.' The Cordoban publication has an elegant introduction written by Francisco de Quevedo. A copy was found not long ago in the National Library of Madrid, in the Louvain edition of 1548. It belonged to Quevedo himself and included annotations of his own which reveal scant toleration for the traces of Erasmus which are to be found on several pages of More's work.[2] Later echoes of Hispanic interest in More's book may be observed in the

Reprinted, by permission of the author and publisher, from *Recuerdo de Vasco de Quiroga* (Mexico, Editorial Porrúa, 1965), pp. 101–16. An earlier version of this essay appeared in *The Huntington Library Quarterly,* 10 (1947), 337–47.

second Spanish edition of the *Utopia,* which came out in 1790, and in the third in 1805.[3]

It is, however, the influence of Sir Thomas More across the Atlantic which forms the principal subject of this lecture; and here I should mention that some years ago when I was examining the documents in the National Library in Madrid relating to the subject of the enslavement of the Indians, I came across an extensive report, written in 1535, upon the various aspects of the Spanish colonization of America (Ms 7369). The author was a judge of the royal audiencia, or high court of justice in Mexico, Vasco de Quiroga, and the report itself had been published in 1868 in volume X of the *Colección de Documentos . . . de Indias* by Torres de Mendoza. Mendoza had attributed it to the licenciado Rojas (p. 333), simply because Quiroga had appended to his report an opinion or commentary by Rojas. The index, however, correctly ascribed the authorship to Quiroga, and the manuscript itself left the question in no doubt.

Having settled this first question, I embarked upon the study of the text and realized at once the considerable extent to which, as the author himself admitted, he was influenced by More's *Utopia.* This revealing confession prompted me to search for complementary documents and to try to discover the links between the ideas of Quiroga and the Utopian thought of More. Some time afterwards, amongst the remains of the fine library of the first Bishop of Mexico, Friar Juan de Zumárraga, the friend and admirer of Quiroga, I was so fortunate as to find, with the help of Professor Carlos Castañeda, an annotated copy of More's *Utopia* in the Basel edition of 1518, which had belonged to the Mexican collector, Genaro García and which is now preserved in the library of the University of Texas. Without doubt the work had reached Mexico at an early date.

In the meantime, the distinguished French hispanist, Marcel Bataillon, engaged in a study of the influence of Erasmus upon the Spanish world, had pointed out that a branch of Erasmus' 'Christian Philosophy' had inspired the treatise, or *Doctrina,* which Zumárraga had had printed for the instruction of the Indians.[4] And from this combination of discoveries there began to emerge, in a quite unexpected manner, a network of links between the thought of the European Renaissance and Spanish colonial endeavour in the New World.

* * *

Américo Castro, in his study of Cervantes, has drawn attention to 'that mystical fervor of the Humanists who dreamed of a world sufficient unto itself, free from the ugly tarnish with which time, error, and the passions had overlaid it; as pure and as gleaming as when it first emerged from the stamp of God and Nature.'[5] This zeal turned, on the one hand, toward a chimerical past, the Golden or Saturnine Age—a theme which the Renaissance inherited from the ancient world; on the other hand, it led to an idealization of the present. Therefore, children and their games; the people, their songs and sayings; the aborigines unspoiled by civilization; and rural life, in contrast to that of the court, were all extolled.

The political fruits of this atmosphere were the Renaissance Utopias.

Thomas More opened his with this daring foreword: 'How would it be if I were to propose a government on the style of that which Plato defines in his book *De Republica,* or like that which is practised in Utopia, so different from the manner of our government which is based upon the rights of property?'

Campanella proposed nothing less in drawing up the plan for his ideal City of the Sun, where all goods were to be held in common.

Let us not forget that the discovery of America coincided with this intense agitation in European thought. As a vast continent full of unknown natural resources, peopled by men whose civilization was strange to the Occidental, it was bound to stir the imagination of the Utopians. An accident of geography offered them a material opportunity to try to fulfil their longings, not entirely satisfied either with the chimerical past of the Golden Age or with the opportunity to adapt the conventions of humanism to the spent and sophisticated atmosphere of Europe.

That humanistic vision of America still remains a vast subject for exploration.

More read the descriptions of Amerigo Vespucci, and in his *Utopia* he marvelled at the amazing discoveries.

One night in the autumn of 1532, as the Spanish humanist, Juan Maldonado, was standing high on a tower in the walls of Burgos, he abandoned himself to his dreams and evoked a newly Christianized America. The noble savages, he dreamed, had acquired within ten years the purest of orthodox faith. They were marvellously predisposed to it by their idyllic existence— blessed by Nature, free from the taint of fraud and hypocrisy. In the festivals of beauty which they held the women hid none of their charms from the judges. There was no false sense of modesty or decorum, but only of shame for morally reprehensible actions. Men and women mixed together in the games like brothers and sisters. Marriage was monogamous and the priests preserved celibacy. Plenty reigned. They understood trading and money; but the shops were so well supplied and the fairness of the prices was so well acknowledged, that the customers helped themselves. The land was fertile and the heavy agricultural labour was carried out in a very few days with the help of the entire population. Maldonado was not dismayed that in their ceremonies the Indians failed to comply to the letter with all the demands of Christian ritual; the Spaniards would teach them all that they needed to know. Meanwhile, he prayed that they might keep intact their simplicity and their purity of heart.[6]

In Mexico, Vasco de Quiroga revealed the same spiritual attitude when, in 1535, he wrote simply and aptly: 'for not in vain, but with much cause and reason is this called the New World, not because it is newly found, but because in its people and in almost everything it is like as was the first and golden age . . .'[7] Without shutting his eyes to the 'lawlessness and the savage and tyrannical way of life of these natives,' he saw in them, on the other hand, natural virtues which he describes in enthusiastic terms.

It will not come amiss to quote a passage in the characteristic style of Quiroga, in spite of the difficulty of rendering a faithful translation of it. The behaviour of the Indians towards one another in their pagan state, he wrote, re-called the Golden Age of the kingdom of Saturn, in that there seem to have been in both 'the same customs and manners, the same equality, simplicity, goodness, obedience, humility, festivities, games, pleasures, drinking, idling, pastimes, nudity and lack of any but the poorest of household goods and of any desire for better, the same clothing, footwear and food, all just as the fertility of the soil provided freely and almost without any labour, care or seeking on their part; so that it seems now, in this New World, one may see these natives, with their disregard and scorn for everything superfluous, existing in the same contentment and enjoying the same great freedom and liberty in their tranquil lives, seemingly immune from the hazards of fortune, pure and wise in their carefree simplicity, marvelling, rather, at us and our preoccupations and the worries and restlessness which dog our footsteps, as some of them have at times already remarked to one of us with great astonishment; and almost the same customs, manners and conditions of life, not only in the matter of the servants but even in the selection of the chiefs or head-men whom they elect, as well as the same habit of being content with very little, satisfied to have sufficient for the day without care for the morrow, contemptuous or oblivious of all those other things so beloved, sought after and coveted in our turbulent world—so scorned and discounted by them in this golden world of theirs—with all its greed, ambition, arrogance, ostentation, boasting, its toil and anxiety, which clearly find no place and play no part, nor are they known in the life of these natives in this new, and to my way of thinking, what is to them a golden world, but with us already one of iron and steel and worse.'[8]

This assiduous student of More was to advocate the adoption of the Utopian rule in regulating the life of the Indians, placing himself in a rarefied political atmosphere where the world of ideas became confused with reality.

* * *

It has been customary to regard the theme of the Noble Savage as one peculiarly pertaining to the eighteenth-century. But Gilbert Chinard has noted the outstanding precedent of Montaigne's essays, and once in the midst of the sixteenth and seventeenth centuries the influence of the Spaniards immediately becomes apparent. Carlos Pereyra, in a little-known article in *Escorial,* has shown the link between Montaigne and Gómara, and A. Castro and M. Bataillon (in his courses at the Collège de France) have both drawn attention to the story, which Antonio de Guevara relates and Vasco de Quiroga mentions, of the 'Villano del Danubio,' the uncivilized peasant who astonished the Roman Senate by the wisdom and natural good sense which he displayed in condemning the greed and ambition of his arrogant, corrupted and civilized conquerors. This was a theme later adapted by La Fontaine, inspired by the French translation of Guevara's essay on Marcus Aurelius, where the story is included.

No, the legend of the Noble Savage is far older than the eighteenth century. As we can see from the words of Maldonado and Quiroga, Spanish humanism, confronted with the newly discovered regions of America, displayed an interpretation of nature which identified nakedness with a lack of hypocrisy and

barefootedness with Christian humility. And so, as we shall see, the appearance
of the humble Indians is compared with that of the Apostles—an image in part
due to the influence of Christian painting. Their sexual innocence and virtue—
matters then linked with polemics over the celibacy of the clergy—are found
worthy of all praise. The property which they own and the labour which they
perform in common are contrasted with the greed and misery of the times in
Europe. And, finally, as against the toil and anxiety which distract the inhabitants of the Old World, there is set, as a welcome escape, the freedom and
the tranquility of those of the New.

*   *   *

It is unfortunate that in tracing the spiritual biography of Vasco de Quiroga
we are left in darkness about the course of his education. Both his older and
his modern biographers have failed to tell us at what university he studied,
who his teachers were, how he developed his taste in reading. According to a
recently published document, he held a degree in canonical law, but not in
theology. Where did he first feel the stirrings of humanism? Was it in Spain,
perhaps through the influence of men highly esteemed at the court of Charles
V, or in Mexico, while he enjoyed the favour of Bishop Zumárraga, whose
writings have completely established his own acquaintance with Erasmus?
Who protected Quiroga in Spain and set his feet upon the path to obtaining
the high temporal and ecclesiastical offices which he later held?

Let us leave these questions unanswered and turn to the man at the moment when his spiritual characteristics may be studied, and let us follow him
to the final flash of his humanistic zeal.

It is known that Quiroga went to New Spain (Mexico) in 1531 as one of
the judges chosen to open the second audiencia—primarily the highest judicial
body in the colonies, though it had other functions as well. To this court were
also attached as judges, Salmerón, Maldonado, and Ceynos, and, later, the
learned Don Sebastián Ramírez de Fuenleal. Some ill-informed writers believed that Quiroga was a missionary. This term refers, in fact, to the brothers
of the evangelical orders, but it would not be entirely applicable to a man who
acted as a judge of the audiencia and who was later promoted to the bishopric
of Michoacán, that is, to an office pertaining to the secular and not to the
regular clergy in an order. This does not mean that Quiroga lacked a religious
and charitable temperament, or that his activities were wanting in apostolic
fervour. But such facts do not allow us to confuse concepts and categories.
Motolinia, Gante, Betanzos, Sahagún, and many others form a well-defined
group of missionaries among whom no one in the sixteenth-century would
have placed Quiroga, who was a judge and a bishop.

When the judges reached Mexico, they found an arduous task awaiting
them. The country was not yet free from the immediate effects of the Conquest, which had taken place a decade earlier. The adjustments between the
Spanish and the aboriginal elements, between the 'two republics,' to use the
language of contemporaries, still occasioned many difficulties which had to
be smoothed out in accordance with the ideals of Christianity and of a high-
minded policy. The condition of the slaves, the organization of the *encomiendas*

(groups of Indians apportioned by the Crown to various individuals) and of the *corregimientos* or regional royal districts, the use to be made of the *tamemes*, or carrier Indians, the regulation of tributes, the status of the native chieftains, the establishment of villages and cities, government, justice, the Church, and fiscal affairs, were all matters which called for strength, prudence, and shrewdness on the part of the men in government. A new and complex society, in which the warp and woof that later would constitute the very essence of the historic entity of Mexico were beginning to be woven, must be incorporated into the Spanish monarchy—a spiritual and temporal fabric of occidental culture.

It is not our task here to probe into all the minutiae of the problem. For our purpose it is sufficient to distinguish the incipient nature of that society, which could not be governed in accordance with traditional models. The humanistic aspirations of Quiroga would soon find occasion to be made manifest.

On the 14 of August he wrote to the Council of the Indies that the life of the natives should be regulated by placing them in villages 'where by working and tilling the soil, they may maintain themselves with their labour and may be ruled by all the good rules of policy and by holy and good and Catholic ordinances; where there may be constructed a friars' house, small and not costly, for two or three or four brothers, who may not leave their task until such time as the natives may have acquired the habits of virtue and this has become a part of their nature.' He wanted to establish a village in each district. He talked hopefully of the simplicity and humility of the aborigines: men barefoot, bareheaded, and long-haired, 'as the Apostles went about.' Once the villages were established, he offered, with the help of God, 'to place and plant righteously the same kind of Christians as in the primitive Church, for God is as powerful now as He was then to do and to fulfill all that which may serve Him and which may conform to His will.'[9]

Not long after having written this letter, Quiroga expounded more extensively his humanistic programme, based upon More's *Utopia*, which, in his judgment, should serve as the Magna Carta of European civilization in the New World. *Utopia*, for Quiroga, had a realistic meaning, it was something that could be applied, not an idle dream. M. Bataillon quite rightly observed, in one of his four lectures devoted to Quiroga, in the 1949–50 course at the Collège de France, that *Utopia* did not enter here as a gratuitous fantasy, to materialize a fair dream of an artist dealing with a particularly favourable human substance, but as the only possible cure for a tragic situation.

The Crown ordered the second audiencia to send a detailed description of the provinces and villages of New Spain. Such a geographical and statistical study would serve the central government as a basis for the general division of the *encomiendas* among the Spaniards in perpetuity. This prize had been offered before this time, but the Emperor, wary of the strength that would thus be given the conquistadors by such perpetual manorial grants, maintained them as temporary. Hence the constant and urgent petitions of the conquistadors and the Spanish settlers, which were frequently supported by the religious

and juridical groups. The description now asked for was to be accompanied
by the opinion of each judge regarding the organization which he believed
suitable to the new kingdom.

On the 5 of July, 1532, the members of the audiencia informed the Empress
that they were sending the description and account of the land and the personnel of the conquistadors and the settlers. New Spain, they thought, should
be divided into four provinces. They had discussed with the prelates and the
clergy the system which the Emperor should set up in order that the land
might be settled and maintained, and they enclosed the collective and individual opinions of the judges and the clergy with the rest of the papers.[10] A letter
from the audiencia, dated 17 September of the same year,[11] states that the
vessel in which the descriptions were sent sailed from San Juan de Ulua at the
end of July, but returned to port at the beginning of September because it was
leaking—an ill-omen, perhaps, for Quiroga's Utopian hopes. On the next sailing,
however, the description would be sent in duplicate, as His Majesty wished.
President Ramírez de Fuenleal finally wrote, on the third of November,[12] that
the ex-judges Matienzo and Delgadillo were sailing for Spain, carrying the documents with them.

The Queen replied to the audiencia from Barcelona on 20 April, 1533: 'A
wooden case in which you sent the depositions which you took from Nuño de
Guzmán and the licenciados Matienzo and Delgadillo and other private persons
was received in council, and the description of that land as well, and also the
several opinions, yours and those of certain religious persons and of other
people of that land dealing with the said description, excepting only that of
the licenciado Salmerón who came here, and because my lord the Emperor
will be in these kingdoms during all the month of April at the latest . . . His
Majesty will be given a long and particular account, and he will order to be
provided whatever may be proper.'[13]

Consequently, the individual opinion of Vasco de Quiroga must have reached
Spain in the wooden case received in Council. The opinions of Ramírez de
Fuenleal and of Ceynos have been found and published, but, so far as I know,
the whereabouts of Quiroga's manuscript is still unknown.

To a certain extent the omission is not irreparable, thanks to the data which
Don Vasco set forth in the legal brief of 1535, already mentioned. He explains
that the particular opinion concerning the description was drawn up as a 'pattern' from the very good republic proposed by Thomas More—'an illustrious
and ingenious man, more than human.' Quiroga stressed in his manuscript that,
the Indians being scattered singly through the countryside, they were suffering
privations and were lacking the necessities of life; and he proposed to bring
them together in order by cities: 'for one alone may be but ill secure and the
man who has neither a craft nor a trade may be very bad for himself, if not for
others.'[14]

He invited the Royal Council to lay down laws and ordinances suited to
the quality, manners, and condition of the land and its people, who were simple
and docile. To this end, he suggested the laws which his reading of More's
Utopia had inspired. He believed that the Spanish government would be justi-

fied in introducing such beneficial reforms, and he pointed out the object which might be attained by organizing the cities: 'that the natives may have enough for themselves and for those whom they must support; that they may be sufficiently well kept and that they may be properly converted, as they should be'; that is, he was aiming at economic well-being, a rational political system, and Christian faith. The republic he contemplated was to be the product of the art of mixed polity, because, by that, both the temporal and the spiritual aspects of man would be satisfied; once political order and humane relations were established, the roots of all discord, luxury, covetousness and sloth would be cut out; and peace, justice and equity would reign. Quiroga, like other inspired politicians of the Renaissance, not only gave due weight to the problems of property and labour, but he also made the enjoyment of spiritual values rest upon a satisfactory solution of them.

In the Indian Utopia, the magistrates would be perfect. A city of six thousand families—each family composed of from ten to sixteen couples—would be ruled, regulated and governed as though it were a single family. The father and mother would control the families. Each magistrate would take care of thirty families. Each governor would preside over four magistrates. In addition, there would be two ordinary mayors and a *tacatecle*.[15] The magistrates would be chosen according to a method copied from the *Utopia*. At the head of the whole organization would be a mayor-in-chief, or a Spanish corregidor, appointed by the audiencia, which would be the supreme temporal tribunal. The religious orders, in these cities, would instruct as many of the people as possible.

Quiroga complained that this opinion may have been disregarded, or at least forgotten, by those who must have examined it in Spain.

* * *

After writing his opinion of 1532, Vasco de Quiroga did not give up the ideas which he had conceived regarding the life of the Indians. On the contrary, he resumed his humanistic readings and sent the Court, on the 24 of July, 1535, his full legal opinion.[16] This was prompted by the issue in Toledo of a royal decree, on 20 February, 1534, which permitted the enslavement of the Indians. Quiroga opposed the arguments of the pro-slavery group with all the weight of his juridical knowledge. At the same time he insisted upon the desirability of adopting his forgotten Utopian opinion and reinforced it brilliantly with new arguments.

Between his first reading of the *Utopia* and the opinion of 1535, Don Vasco tells us that he came upon Lucian's account of the Saturnalia, that is, of the transcendental humanistic theme of the Golden Age: 'so often mentioned and praised by all in these our times.' He explained that never before had he seen or heard those original words of Lucian, and the circumstances in which he encountered them, taken in conjunction with More's *Utopia*, moved him to think that Providence had brought them to his attention 'perchance to seal and cap and to make finally understood this in my opinion so ill-understood matter of the lands and the people, the property and the quality of this New World.'

Lucian had been translated by Erasmus and More, so that there is no doubt
but that Quiroga knew the version rendered by the English humanist, for he
cites it literally.[17] His reading convinced him that the simple people of New
Spain would be found capable of dwelling in the state of innocence of that
Golden Age, and in accord with the virtues of a 'renascent Church.' For the
Indians, as we have seen in Quiroga's words, were good, obedient, humble,
fond of festivities and drinking, care-free and naked, like the people of the
time of the Kingdoms of Saturn. With their very great freedom of life and of
soul, they despised the superfluous. In short, such a people—so gentle, so new,
so unspoiled and so like soft wax—were ready for whatever one might care to
make of them. Europe, on the other hand—a civilization of iron—had lost much
of its simplicity. It was inaccessible to what the newly discovered Humanism
could accomplish on this earth, for, as it was repeatedly stated by the Christian
writers of the period, covetousness, pride, and sorrow abounded there. The
task of civilization in the New World should therefore consist, not in transplant-
ing the old culture among the newly discovered peoples, but in elevating them,
in all their natural simplicity, to the ideal standards of humanism and of primitive Christianity. The instrument of that elevation would be More's *Utopia*,
for its laws were the most suitable for regulating this enthusiastic task of bet-
tering mankind.

Quiroga's project is distinguished by the will to apply one of the noblest
political ideas of the Renaissance. He had observed at close hand the life of
the Indians, and he exalted the civilizing mission of Occidental man to heights
which have few parallels in the history of colonizing thought.

The Royal Council did not welcome the idea on this occasion any more
than it had accepted earlier the opinion of 1532. Quiroga, grown impatient,
founded two hospital-villages which he called Santa Fe, putting his own
resources behind them and availing himself of the help of the Indians. One
village was near Mexico City and the other in Michoacán, where he made a
beginning of his experiment with a new social life. He dispensed with the
continental plan he had drafted in the manuscript which he sent to Spain,
but he did finally transplant the programme to Mexican soil.

On the 30 of June, 1533, the enterprise had been discussed in the
municipal council of Mexico, and it was said that Judge Quiroga began the
work 'under the pretext and claim of undertaking what could be pointed out
as a *pater familias* enterprise.'[18]

The rules set forth in the opinion of 1532, drawn from More's *Utopia*,
were somewhat modified, for as yet there was no question of cities of thousands of inhabitants, but of small villages. Don Vasco converted the regulations into ordinances for the hospital-villages of Santa Fe.[19]

In his last will, he took pains to explain that he founded the two villages:
'being a judge for His Majesty . . . in the Royal Chancery, who resides in the
City of Mexico, and many years before he became a member or received any
income from the Church . . .'[20] That is, he initiated his work before he gained
the increased income which came to him as bishop of Michoacán. His election
to this ecclesiastical office took place in the year 1537. He was then able to

establish new hospitals in the diocese and to begin the teaching of crafts to the Indians.

The date when Quiroga established and put into effect the ordinances for the hospital-villages of Santa Fe is unknown. The text discovered and published by Juan José Moreno, in the eighteenth century, is incomplete at the beginning and at the end. It can only be stated that the ordinances antedated the authorized testament of 1565.

I established the parallel between More's *Utopia* and the ordinances of Quiroga in a book published some time ago,[21] and I have nothing to add to it. The conclusion is that the ordinances, according to the words of Don Vasco, set forth on various occasions, faithfully transmitted the theory of More, but translated it from the atmosphere of theoretical speculations to immediate application. Undoubtedly the Chancellor of England would have been interested to know how the Indians near Mexico City and in Michoacán were faring in their life based upon his *Utopia*. But on the 6 July, 1535, a few days before Quiroga wrote his opinion, More was beheaded.

In his villages of Santa Fe, Quiroga established the common ownership of property; the integration of large families; the systematic alternation between the urban and the rural peoples; work for women; the six-hour working day; the liberal distribution of the fruits of the common labour according to the needs of the inhabitants; the foregoing of luxury and of all offices which were not useful; and the election of the judiciary by families.

He survived the founding of the hospital-villages by about thirty years, and he was able to observe the course of his experiment. In his testament of 1565, far from contemplating the demise or abandonment of his applied idealism, he recommended carrying out the ordinances and 'not yielding at any point.'

A visitor from the little town of Santa Fe, near Mexico, the Augustine annalist, Grijalva, said, at the beginning of the seventeenth century, that 'the Indians there were, up to a certain point, imitating the monks, living together in communities and devoting themselves to prayer and the pursuit of a more perfect life.' It is not easy to follow up in detail the history of these people in later times. But the memory of the Bishop of Michoacán is preserved even to the present day in the regions where he worked with apostolic zeal.

So it was that Vasco de Quiroga, through his opinions and his establishments, gave to humanistic thought an unexpected American application, and ennobled, for a time, the relations between the Europeans and the aborigines, thanks to a doctrine which owes some of its basic features to the *Utopia* born in distant England.[22]

PART III: OTHER WORKS

LITERARY PROBLEMS IN MORE'S *RICHARD III*

Leonard F. Dean

Sir Thomas More's *History of Richard III* has been adequately studied as an historical document,[1] but not as a work of literature; and yet since the time of Ascham it has been praised chiefly and properly for its literary qualities.[2] It is the purpose of this article, therefore, to discuss some of the important literary problems presented by *Richard III*. An attempt will be made to show how closely More's narrative conforms to classical theory and to what extent it is imitative of classical histories. Of chief concern, however, will be More's use of irony. It will be evident throughout that his approach to history writing was that of a Christian humanist.

By 1513, the probable date of composition of *Richard III*,[3] More's formal education had been completed and he had served his literary apprenticeship. He had been educated in Morton's household, at Oxford and the Inns of Court; he had lectured on the philosophical and historical ideas of St. Augustine's *De civitate dei;*[4] he had composed a few poems and an English version of a life of Pico della Mirandola,[5] and with Erasmus he had translated some of Lucian's dialogues.[6] In More's home Erasmus, among other things, had finished translating two plays of Euripides, and on his return from Italy in 1509 had composed the *Encomium Moriae*. An unusual background for an historian. More had not been trained, as he would be today, in the handling of historical documents and had not been impressed with their fundamental importance. Although his education had included wide reading in the classical and Christian historians,[7] it was primarily theological, legal, and literary rather than scholarly, and his theory of history writing must have been influenced chiefly by the ancient rhetoricians, all of whom discussed history in connection with epideictic oratory.[8]

Lucian's dialogue, *Quomodo historia conscribenda sit,* is a typically conservative classical treatment of its subject, and it was no doubt fresh in More's mind when he began *Richard III.*[9] It is significant that even Lucian, who so bitterly attacked sophistic excesses, could think of history only as a branch of oratory. The historian, Lucian argues, is superior to the research worker because he composes artistically the material that the latter has merely collected. The historian is like a sculptor: his material is at hand, and his business is to superinduce upon events the charm of order, proportion, and lucidity.[10] He interprets what is known, and he is able to do this by virtue of his faculty of

Reprinted, by permission of the author and publisher, from *Publications of the Modern Language Association*, 58 (1943), 22–41.

expression and his political insight that has been gained from practical experience.[11] It is generally agreed that More worked in this fashion. He was an interpreter and a composer, not a compiler.[12]

At the same time, Lucian warns the historian that he should employ artistic or epideictic devices intelligently; they should be functional rather than decorative. Most commonly abused is ἔκφρασις, or description. God save us, says Lucian, from long descriptions of persons, arms, towns, mountains, plains, and rivers. It is ignorance of what is really essential that leads to description of things that are insignificant or fantastically theatrical. "You observe," he concludes, "how indispensable it all is to the history; without the scene, how could we have comprehended the action."[13] The ironical implication is clear: this legitimate reason for description is too often an excuse for over-indulgence. Speeches, likewise, should not be merely opportunities for display; they may be eloquent but at the same time they must suit the occasion and the character of the speaker.[14] The greatest danger, however, is the tendency to eulogize excessively. Although the historian may praise moderately, he must not misrepresent the facts. That would destroy the value of his narrative, for "should history ever repeat itself, the records of the past may give present guidance."[15] Praise and blame should be conveyed subtly, Lucian implies, and as far as possible by the actions themselves. Apparently the historian should emphasize the fifth topic of the conventional encomium, ἐπιτηδεύματα, or deeds which imply choice and therefore reveal character.[16] Every reader of *Richard III* knows that descriptions and speeches are generously employed by More, but always for a functional rather than a decorative purpose, and that he excels at subtly controlling our attitude towards his characters. These matters will be returned to in connection with More's use of irony. Another problem raised by Lucian, however, does need discussion at this point.

When one admits, as does Lucian, that the "historian's spirit should not be without a touch of the poetical,"[17] and that epideictic devices when properly used are legitimate in history-writing, the way is opened to an obvious abuse. Why not heighten the effectiveness of one's narrative by closely imitating the successful descriptions, speeches, and critical comments of earlier and greater historians? That this was the common practice in Lucian's time is indicated by his severe criticism of it. Imitations of Pericles' funeral oration draw from him, he says, tears of laughter.[18] The charge of plagiarism is the one that is oftenest lodged against early humanist historians. When Feuter, for example, labels an historian "rhetorical," this is a criticism he generally implies. More himself has been so labeled.[19] What is the evidence against him?

According to Stapleton, More "studied with avidity all the historical works he could find."[20] Judging from such evidence as references in the writings of More's friends, library catalogues, bibliographical surveys, and school curriculums, the classical historians most popular around 1513 were these, and in about this order: Livy, Sallust, Valerius Maximus, Plutarch, Xenophon, Justin, Curtius, Caesar, Florus, Arrian, Thucydides, Herodotus, Josephus,

Suetonius, and Polybius.[21] More was doubtless well acquainted with all of them. Nevertheless, a careful comparison of the sections of these histories which are at all similar in subject-matter to *Richard III* with both the English and Latin versions of More's narrative reveals no examples of what we would call plagiarism.[22] As might have been expected, a writer of More's intelligence and talent would not imitate slavishly. Instead of borrowing passages or aping mannerisms, he imitated in a truer fashion by adapting classical literary methods to his own ends.

The ironical method is the one which chiefly distinguishes *Richard III*. It was a method congenial to More's temperament,[23] but his natural bent may well have been strengthened and directed by classical theory, by his study of the practice of Tacitus and Thucydides, and particularly by his intimate knowledge of Lucian and the *Encomium Moriae*. There is some evidence that classical rhetoricians recommended the use of irony in vituperative portraits, of which *Richard III* is in part an example.[24] The most pertinent remarks are in the *Rhetorica ad Alexandrum,* a standard textbook in More's day. "In finding fault you must employ irony...." Do not simply scoff at the object of your attack, but describe his life; for the evidence is always more convincing and damaging than any comment.[25] This is More's practice; his characters condemn themselves, and we seem to form our own judgment of them. The irony in this method springs, of course, from the disparity between the characters' apparent opinion of themselves and our opinion of them. They are described as behaving in a way that can bring them only into disrepute.

Other classical discussions of irony center around verbal and Socratic irony and the ironical character. Aristotle distinguishes the ironical man from the boastful man; they are both extremes from the mean of matter-of-factness. The ironical man is characterized by excessive self-depreciation. Although this is preferable to excessive boastfulness, it is still generally a vice.[26] Theophrastus, in his character of the ironical man,[27] followed Aristotle, but further narrowed and degraded the conception so that it resembles somewhat the *eiron* of ancient Greek comedy.[28] The ironical man is one who obtains an abnormal pleasure from misleading or inconveniencing others by disguising his real feelings and intentions. *Richard III* is often ironical in this sense. The controlling principle in his life is dissimulation.[29] His foil is not the stupid, overweening *alazon*, of course, but the tragically helpless and simple people of England; yet More continually implies that here is a vice in royalty which must be corrected or replaced by Aristotle's mean of matter-of-factness or sincerity. Since, as Pollard points out,[30] there was not historical evidence for Richard's consistent dissimulation, it is possible that More constructed the tyrant's character partly on the basis of these classical descriptions of abnormal behavior. In addition, he could have found portraits in the classical historians of men who disguised their greed for power under a feigned reluctance to accept it. Such is the portrait of Tiberius in Tacitus and Suetonius, or of Pompey in Plutarch.[31] More was working as an artist and a teacher rather than as a scholar. The result was not necessarily truthful, but it was instructive and effective since everything

was organized into an intelligible and moving whole. The historical Richard
was a more complicated personality, but this picture of him is consistent, and
therefore artistically more satisfying.

Verbal and Socratic irony were the kinds most often discussed by the classical rhetoricians, just as they were in More's age.[32] Quintilian's treatment is
typical. He defines irony[33] as both a trope and a figure of thought in which
there is a discrepancy between the language or action and the intended meaning. In the trope the conflict is purely verbal; whereas in the figure, the meaning and sometimes the whole aspect of one's case conflicts with the language
or tone of voice adopted. A man's whole life may even be colored with irony
as was the case with Socrates, who for the sake of intellectual criticism assumed the rôle of an ignorant man lost in wonder at the wisdom of others.[34]
Quintilian also observes that irony is closely dependent upon *ethos,* by which
he appears to mean a kind of restrained emotion. He does not go on, however,
to develop the interesting connection between the emotional force of irony and
its artistic reticence, the idea that silences or understatements often speak
louder than words.

Verbal and Socratic irony chiefly distinguish the dialogues of Lucian. This
More himself observed. It is not without Socratic irony, he stated in his dedicatory epistle to Thomas Ruthall, that Lucian in *Philopseudes* ridicules inordi-
nate love of lying. But Lucian's irony is often tiresomely ineffective either
because it is merely verbal dexterity (in which the reader is constantly being
asked to reverse what is said), or because the Socratic interrogation leads to
cynicism rather than affirmation. More's subject-matter did not permit extended
use of Socratic irony and his devoutness safeguarded him from cynicism. Although he delighted in wordplay, he used it artistically for serious purposes.
Thus, one of the clear examples of verbal irony in *Richard III*[35] is successful
because it is placed in a context of great emotional intensity. Richard attempts
to excuse his tyrannical execution of Hastings by accusing him and Jane Shore
of treason and immoral relations. Unable to pin the charge of treason on her,
Richard ". . . laid heinously to her charge the thing that herself could not deny,
that all the world wist was true, and that nevertheless every man laughed at to
hear it then so suddenly so highly taken, that she was nought of her body. And
for this cause (as a goodly continent Prince, clean and faultless of himself,
sent out of heaven into this vicious world for the amendment of men's manners) he caused the Bishop of London to put her in open penance."[36]

The intensity results from More's ability to create in his famous description
of Shore's wife, which precedes this passage, a living character. The irony of
his comment upon her vilifier, that "goodly continent Prince," would have
been less bitterly shocking if she had not been portrayed with such vivid
sympathy. This sort of thing is largely lacking in Lucian, who works with cari-
catures and puppets. We admire his skill, but it often remains a game.

Much closer to More's irony than Lucian's is that in the *Encomium Moriae.*
Sometimes, of course, Erasmus, whose irony is many-sided, writes in Lucian's
manner. He employs, for example, what may be called irony of exclusion, or
exaggerated simplification. He takes a human situation or habit, and emphasizes

the element of folly in it to the exclusion of all else. Then he says naïvely: See, the bases of life are foolish; should not folly be praised? This is cynicism affected for satirical purposes; he professes to believe that all motives and actions are selfish or stupid in order to persuade us that some of them are. This easily becomes mere sophistry in which an argument is over-extended. A fool, for instance, is governed by passion; a wise man by reason. But to deny a man any passion is to unman him. It is then simple enough to describe, as Erasmus does, a cold, colorless, inactive creature and thus 'prove' that we would all prefer the foolish-passionate man.[37] And, indeed, in his dedicatory epistle to More, Erasmus professes to be writing only a paradox in which the worse is made to appear the better, after the manner of the classics, including Lucian's *The Fly*. But this, too, is ironical; for Erasmus' purpose was, of course, really serious.

The burden of the *Encomium Moriae* appears to be this: In a world of fools, it is folly to be wise. But Erasmus is a realist rather than a cynic. Consequently, his true theme is the arduousness of the devout and rational way of life. He says in effect: I know well enough what the world is like—here is its picture; therefore you may realize that my argument for a life of reason and faith is not merely facile. I am aware of the consequences, but this is my choice. This method is ironical in the sense that Erasmus presents the strongest possible arguments for Folly, and pretends to agree with them; yet he does this not merely to display his dexterity, but in order to establish the context for his own argument, in order, that is, to persuade us that he has chosen maturely after considering all the issues. If bishops, cardinals, popes, and kings had any true wisdom, he observes, they would lead lives of poverty and service. But now "it comes about—by my [Folly's] doing, remember— that scarcely any kind of men live more softly or less oppressed with care. ..."[38] This is that false-foolish happiness which comes from being content with Appearance and being blind to Reality. When the problem is thus presented in an ironic context, there is no answer. By arguing as Folly, Erasmus says all that can be said for folly, but in such a way that it is obviously not enough. The reader must ultimately judge by the writer's standards. Folly has imperceptibly become apathy, insensibility, the blindness of the Cave—an image that often reappears. But while Erasmus' serious purpose is to rouse us to Reality, he does not underestimate or disguise the cost.

> ... what difference is there between those who in Plato's cave look admiringly at the shadows and simulacra of various things, desiring nothing, quite well satisfied with themselves, as against the wise man who emerges from the cave and sees realities? ... there either is no difference or, if there is difference, the state of fools is to be preferred. First, their happiness costs least. It costs only a bit of illusion. And second, they enjoy it in the company of so many others. The possession of no good thing is welcome without a companion. And who has not heard of the paucity of wise men—if indeed any is to be found.[39]

It will be observed that one of the great virtues of this kind of irony, which might be called the irony of complexity, is its opposition to dogmatism.[40] By means of it Erasmus is able to examine in all its difficult complications a central human problem: the relation between comfortable conformity and the painful independence of wisdom. We are convinced, consequently, that his choice is neither that of a dreamy idealist nor of a rigid moralist. It is a kind of irony consonant with Erasmus' character and with the common quality of most forms of Renaissance humanism, namely, that attitude towards life which is comprehensive and flexible without being irresponsible.

It is this kind of irony, furthermore, which pervades *Richard III*. Proof and explanation can be nicely begun by examining a crucial passage—the image of the stage play—that appears in Lucian's *Necromantia* (one of the dialogues translated by More in 1506), in the *Encomium Moriae,* and in *Richard III.*

Lucian's *Necromantia* (Loeb translation, IV, 99-101):

> So as I [Menippus] looked at them [the dead] it seemed to me that human life is like a long pageant, and that all its trappings are supplied and distributed by Fortune, who arrays the participants in various costumes of many colours. Taking one person, it may be, she attires him royally, placing a tiarra upon his head, giving him body-guards, and encircling his brow with the diadem; but upon another she puts the costume of a slave. Again, she makes up one person so that he is handsome, but causes another to be ugly and ridiculous. I suppose that the show must needs be diversified. And often, in the very middle of the pageant, she exchanges the costumes of several players; instead of allowing them to finish the pageant in the parts that had been assigned to them, she reapparels them, forcing Croesus to assume the dress of a slave and a captive, and shifting Maeandrius, who formerly paraded among the servants, into the imperial habit of Polycrates. For a brief space she lets them use their costumes, but when the time of the pageant is over, each gives back the properties and lays off the costume along with his body, becoming what he was before birth, no different from his neighbor. Some, however, are so ungrateful that when Fortune appears to them and asks her trappings back, they are vexed and indignant, as if they were being robbed of their own property, instead of giving back what they had borrowed for a little time.
>
> I suppose you have often seen these stage-folk who act in tragedies, and according to the demands of the play become at one moment Creons, and again Priams and Agamemnons; the very one, it may be, who a short time ago assumed with great dignity the part of Cecrops, or of Erectheus soon appears as a servant at the bidding of the poet. And when at length the play comes to an end, each of them strips off his gold-bespangled robe, lays aside his mask, steps out of his buskins, and goes about in poverty and humility.... That is what human affairs are like, it seemed to me as I looked.

Encomium Moriae [*Opera Omnia* (Leyden, 1703), IV, cols. 428-429]:

> Si quis histrionibus in scena fabulam agentibus personas detrahere conetur, ac spectatoribus veras nativasque facies ostendere, nonne is fabulam omnem

perverterit, dignusque habeatur, quem omnes e theatro velut lymphatum saxis eiiciant? Exorietur autem repente nova rerum species, ut qui modo mulier, nunc vir: qui modo iuvenis, mox senex: qui paulo ante Rex, subito Dama: qui modo Deus, repente homunculus appareat. Verum eum errorem tollere, est fabulam omnem perturbare. Illud ipsum figmentum et fucus est, quod spectatorum oculos detinet. Porro mortalium vita omnis quid aliud est, quam fabulam quaepiam, in qua alii aliis obtecti personis procedunt, aguntque suas quisque partes, donec choragus educat e proscenio? Qui saepe tamen eundem diverso cultu prodire iubet, ut qui modo Regem purpuratum egerat, nunc servulum pannosum gerat. Adumbrata quidem omnia, sed haec fabula non aliter agitur. Hic si mihi sapiens aliquis coelo delapsus subito exoriatur, clamitetque hunc quem omnes ut Deum ac dominum suspiciunt, nec hominum esse, quod pecudum ritu ducatur affecti-bus, servum esse infimum, quod tam multis, tamque foedis dominis sponte serviat. Rursum alium, quid parentem exstinctum luget, ridere iubeat, quod iam demum ille vivere coeperit, cum alioqui vita haec nihil aliud sit quam mors quaedam. Porro alium stemmatis gloriantem, ignobilem ac nothum appellet, quod a virtute longe absit, quae sola nobilitatis sit fons, adque eumdem modum de caeteris omnibus loquatur, quaeso, quid is aliud egerit, nisi ut demens ac furiosus omnibus esse videatur? Ut nihil est stultius praepostera sapientia, ita perversa prudentia nihil imprudentius. Siquidem perverse facit, qui sese non accomodet rebus praesentibus, foroque nolit uti, nec saltem legis illius convivalis meminerit, ἢ πίζι, ἢ ἄπιζι, postuletque ut fabula iam non sit fabula. Contra, vere prudentis est, cum sis mortalis, nihil ultra sortem sapere velle, cumque universa hominum multitudine vel connivere libenter, vel comiter errare. At istud ipsum, inquiunt, stultitiae est. Haud equidem inficias iverim, modo fateantur illi vicissim hoc esse, vitae fabulam agere.[41]

Richard III (EW, pp. 447–448):

And in a stage play all the people know right well that he that playeth the Sultan is perhaps a souter. Yet if one should can so little good, to show out of season what acquaintance he hath with him, and call him by his own name while he standeth in his majesty, one of his tormentors might hap to break his head, and worthy, for marring of the play. And so they said that these matters [Richard's machinations] be King's games, as it were stage plays, and for the most part played upon scaffolds. In which poor men be but the lookers-on. And they that wise be will meddle no farther. For they that sometime step up and play with them, when they cannot play their parts, they disorder the play and do themselves no good.[42]

It is clear, as the editors of *Richard III* point out,[43] that More took the *tormentors* and *satellites* from the *Necromantia,* and that he therefore had Lucian's image in mind. But it is equally clear—and More's editors do not suggest this—that his application of the image is like Erasmus' rather than Lucian's. The latter implies that when life is viewed with detachment, human beings are revealed as the playthings of Fortune or Chance. We can do little more than laugh cynically at the spectacle, or at best attempt to safeguard ourselves by leading simple lives which change will but slightly disorder. In the *Encomium*, however, this image, like that of the Cave, is of central importance to the main theme and its ironical treatment. Erasmus is illustrating the complexity and difficulty of behaving as an intelligent non-conformist. He is not saying that it is impossible to act in a rational manner, that we are helpless in Fortune's grip; on the contrary, he is pointing out the arduousness as well as the worthiness of the life of reason. More, because he was writing a political history, applies the image to the narrower problem of political non-conformity, but his basic intention is the same as Erasmus'. He seems to say that matter-of-factness and honesty can have no place in state-craft, that all must be done by formal hocus-pocus, and that it is dangerously futile or forward for ignorant, sincere men to meddle in affairs which most nearly concern their heart's ease. It is a game played on *scaffolds*, and the serious pun gives the key to the tone of the whole passage. This is clearly not cynicism but rather what we have called the irony of complexity. By means of it More avoids dogmatism and unrealistic simplification; he acknowledges the difficulties of living under a tyranny at the same time that he urges his readers to act like rational men and oppose it.

Furthermore, by using irony, More follows Lucian's recommendation that the historian's generalizations, his lessons of "wisdom and wariness" in Ascham's words, should be conveyed subtly. In view of his subject-matter, it is not surprising that most of More's ironical comments or generalizations are concerned with the character of ruler and ruled and with their proper relationship. Although More does not depart from aristocratic and classical tradition to the extent of championing the masses, their simplicity by being continually contrasted with the hypocrisy of the rulers becomes something of a virtue. This is reminiscent of the last section of the *Encomium*, where Erasmus, parodying the scholastic method, 'proves' that in the Bible and the Fathers folly is recommended above knowledge. Here folly, like More's simplicity, has acquired the child-like or Christ-like quality of sincerity and faith as opposed to that knowledge which is the shrewdness of dissimulation.[44] One recalls More's engaging story of Edward sending venison to the citizens of London; so "that no one thing, in many days before, got him either more hearts or more hearty favour among the common people, which oftentimes more esteem and take for greater kindness a little courtesy than a great benefit."[45] Their childishness is granted, but people who possess only a naïve heart are not to be entirely scorned in comparison with rulers who possess only a sophisticated mind.

Kings are cruel and deceptive. More appears to say, at first reading, that this is inevitable. Edward, for example, "... was of youth greatly given to fleshly wantonness, from which health of body in great prosperity and fortune, without a special grace, hardly refraineth." He and his two brothers "... as they were great states of birth, so were they great and stately of stomach, greedy and ambitious of authority, and impatient of partners." And Richard was "... such as is in states called warlike, in other men otherwise."[46] Thus More acknowledges the truth of the commonplace that great power involves great temptations, and that we should remember this in our judgment of kings. At the same time he reminds us ironically that kings, too, are men with the power to be virtuous if they choose. By admitting the difficulties of their position, he strengthens his condemnation. This is evident in Richard's speech of acceptance at the climax of his dissimulation. For an honorable man, says Richard with mock piety, the crown is more labor and pain than pleasure; and a dishonorable man is not worthy to have it.[47]

Indeed, by translating More's ironic characterization of Richard, we are able to picture many lineaments of his ideal of royalty. Practically every utterance of Richard's is hypocritical. More has given us information which forces us to penetrate the disguise. We participate in the act of literary creation by constantly interpreting all that Richard says, and our enjoyment is consequently heightened at the same time that we are instructed.[48] We note the sharp contrast between Richard's pretended humanity in desiring playfellows for the young king and his real purpose, which is to get the princes into his power. When he abhors the queen's effort to cause dissension, we know that it is dissension which he has labored for. His request for "some honourable trusty man" to persuade the queen to release the princes, must be translated as some man who has an honorable reputation but who can be coerced into acting hypocritically for the occasion.[49] Even the discussion of sanctuary which follows is ultimately molded to More's method and purpose. Its length, which may seem to be inartistic and which may be partly the result of current controversy,[50] is offset by the ending. "Knoweth any man any place," concludes Buckingham, "wherein it is lawful one man to do another wrong?"[51] And the ironic answer is the opposite of the negative one expected. Yes, at Richard's court, where there is no law but his will. In short, from this and other ironical evidence we obtain a picture of an ideal king who rules in accordance with the laws of God and man, and who safeguards the interests of simple men of good will.

It will be observed that by consistently portraying Richard as a dissimulator More not only subtly conveys his lessons of social morality but also unifies his narrative. The achievement of unity was an important task of the historian who wished to surpass the annals of the Middle Ages. A Christian world chronicler had, in a sense, no problem; his plan, perfectly integrated and complete, was supplied by the orthodox picture of human life extending from the Creation to the return of Christ. Many simple monastic or civic annalists attempted to acquire prestige and a sort of abortive unity for their brief notations by enclosing them in bald summaries of the beginning and end of things. This was impossible for a sophisticated writer like More; nor could he conscientiously undertake a world history. The practice of the classics and the higher standards of historical scholarship in his day prevented him. Humanistic theorists who faced this problem suggested, as we have seen, that unity should be gained by a more complete and accurate explanation of causes. Now, when cause meant only personal motive, this advice amounted to suggesting that some leading figure should be consistently characterized so as to integrate all of the action while he prevailed. This is obviously More's method. He makes everything hinge on the character of Richard.

Furthermore, since Richard is a tyrant who falls from high degree, we have here the pattern of medieval tragedy. The *de casibus* example can be very dull and undramatic, as Chaucer demonstrated in the Monk's Tale, which More had probably read.[52] It is suggestive to think of *Richard III* as an intermediate stage in the history of the use of the biographical or historical example. That history is a part of the movement from allegory to realism. We find William of Malmesbury, one of the best of the medieval chroniclers, saying typically: "I shall relate such anecdotes of him [William the Conqueror], as may be a matter of incitement to the indolent, or of example to the enterprising; useful to the present age, and pleasing to posterity. But I shall spend little time in relating such things as are of service to no one, and which produce disgust in the reader, as well as ill-will to the author."[53] In 1521, John Major, an acquaintance of More's circle, believed it to be his duty to write history in such a way that James V might "learn not only the thing that was done, but also how it ought to have been done...."[54] He tells us, for instance, that William Rufus destroyed religious houses so that he might have more room for his favorite sport, hunting; but while hunting he was killed. Where "a man sins there too shall come the penalty of sin. Of the holy place he made a profane pleasance; but a great and public sin must needs be followed by a condign punishment."[55] Likewise, Lydgate's method in his *Fall of Princes,* as Professor Farnham has remarked, was "that of the impatient moralist ardently desiring, and finding, retribution for sinners here and now...." His "crude moral didacticism, using examples of tragic justice for its transparent ends, could of itself never have produced great tragedy..." since he assumes "that we may see all the meaning of adversity immediately and schematically." Therefore, he "is almost incapable of a view of tragedy which gives suffering some traceable cause in human character without making the cause a simple sin easily classified."[56]

Far removed from this is Bacon's request that historians follow Machiavelli and "write what men do and not what men ought to do."[57] We have enough examples of ideal conduct, he says sharply, but no satisfactory treatment of the psychological sources of our conduct which might guide us in approaching the ideal. Many writers have "made good and fair examplars... of Good, Virtue, Duty, Felicity;... but how to attain these excellent marks, and how to frame and subdue the will of man to become true and conformable to these pursuits, they pass it over altogether or slightly and unprofitably.... The reason of this omission I suppose to be ... that men have despised to be conversant in ordinary and common matters."[58] Their attention, in short, has been focused too closely on final causes. Just so, the medieval chronicler or poet was unprofitably concerned with only the didactic catastrophe of his *de casibus* example. All was adjusted, foreshortened, or falsified to enforce the moral conclusion. Little or no regard was paid to those "ordinary and common matters," the psychological changes in character through which the good or evil person passed to his doom.[59] In short, one may trace in history-writing, as does Professor Farnham in tragedy, the change from the use of the crudely artificial didactic example towards a more realistic interpretation of life.[60]

We have remarked that *Richard III* may be thought of as an intermediate stage in this process of change. More does not present the realistic and relatively amoral picture of political life that Bacon calls for. Although his method is unusually subtle, he is still in a sense teaching what men ought to do rather than what is simply expedient. He sometimes worked deductively and he carefully points the moral of Richard's fall. But he does attempt with some success to transfer the interest of the reader from Richard's catastrophe to the steps by which he reaches it. This is accomplished in part, as we have seen, by the fullness and consistency with which More characterizes Richard and describes the details of his dissimulation. Of equal importance is More's use of dramatic irony. This kind of irony is, of course, implicit in the *de casibus* example. As Christians who believe in the doctrine of *contemptus mundi* or as pagans who perceive the unpredictability of Fate, we recognize the irony of a person striving for a reward which is evil in itself or which may be snatched away from him. A writer may take advantage of this situation by underlining the latent irony. Every act of the ambitious person thus becomes fraught with ominous significance. Bacon's "ordinary and common matters" are charged with importance for the informed spectator, whose attention has been transferred from the conclusion to the process in the sense that he is led to foresee the conclusion in every stage of that process.[61]

Thus, at the very beginning of his narrative, More introduces the characters and tells us what the outcome is to be. Edward, in his dying speech, foresees that greed for power will be the cause of tragedy. We are explicitly informed of Richard's hypocrisy and of the forthcoming murder of the young princes, and the ultimate fall of the tyrant is clearly implied. There is constantly in our minds the thought of More's comment on the famous scene of Hastings riding to his execution, "never merrier nor never so full of good hope in his life." "But I shall rather let anything pass me than the vain surety of man's mind so near his death."[62]

The Latin versions break off directly after Richard's coronation, when he is at the height of his prosperity; but the English continues, and with it the dramatic irony. Richard's fall, which before had been implied, is now declared. "Now fell there mischiefs thick. And as the thing evil got is never well kept, through all the time of his reign never ceased there cruel death and slaughter, till his own destruction ended it."[63] After relating the murder of the princes and moralizing upon it in a less subtle fashion than usual, More briefly describes the fate of the murderers and their master, "King Richard himself, as ye shall hereafter hear" in detail.[64] Thus we begin to read the unfinished account of the conspiracy between Buckingham and Morton in the light of its conclusion. And thus, too, we see More to the very end writing history as a Christian humanist, using intelligently the methods of ancient rhetor n order to make persuasive his conception of the life of faith and reason world complicated by the presence of evil and irrationality. It was natural that he should turn next to the composition of the *Utopia*.

SOME ASPECTS OF SIR THOMAS MORE'S ENGLISH

Joseph Delcourt

If a candid Utopian, after landing in England in the present year, inquired of those he came across about the fame of Sir Thomas More and the reasons which have endeared him to his compatriots, he would certainly receive more than one answer. Some would be content with asserting that socialistic ideas have gained considerable ground within recent years and that it is fair to do homage for them to the man who first revealed their existence in the island fashioned like to the new moon. Others—more probably all—would think that whatever else Sir Thomas was, he was a man of character, and that character is the thing English people prize most. But then would not there be some in that large body who, having read the Chancellor's works, the English even more than the Latin, would point out that he was a living force in his nation by the way in which he used and enriched his native language? The writer of the present essay had better state at the outset that he has long been familiar with those various sections of More's friends—and feels particularly drawn towards the third. While understanding the admiration of the English for their hero and their saint, and sharing it to the full, he thinks that no side of the great Chancellor's activity is more attractive than his language, because he was, if anything, a maker of English.

It may be mere feeling rather than definite certainty, but the feeling exists and it is widely spread. No schoolboy can have read Shakespeare's *Richard III* in an annotated edition without knowing that some of its most popular scenes owe to More not only their matter but some of the words which have most contributed to make them famous. More advanced students, who have gone into Skeat's *Specimens,* often remember the curious passage about *nay* and *no* in which the Chancellor, while carefully drawing the line between the two, manages to follow the example of Homer caught napping and mis-states his own rule. This is hardly enough to recommend a writer as an authority on things linguistic, it is true, but then one need not go very far to discover that that is an exceptional passage and that elsewhere Sir Thomas's wording is no less safe than his teaching. His love of distinctions applies to *the* and *a,* to *the* and *that,* to *no* and *not,* and on those various points, to say nothing of others, his pen does not go wrong. Then there are his references to the grammatical vocabulary itself, the *subjectum* and the *praedicatum,* the *copulatives* and the *disjunctives* and the rest, which are sure to delight the schoolmaster, while an

Reprinted, by permission of the publisher and the author's heirs, from *Essays and Studies,* 21 (1936, for 1935), 7–31.

occasional rhyme, such as *the tail of a tale* or *the underpropper not very proper,* seems calculated to please a less learned and larger public. Would not a sentence like the following appeal to many, either learned or unlearned?

> These folke ... vttrely loue no lenton fast, nor lightlye no faste elles, sauing brekefast, and eate fast, and drinke fast, and slepe fast ... and than come furth and rayle fast.

It seems only Shakespeare, or Dickens, could beat More at the game. Last, but not least, his interest in grammar never turns into pedantry, nor does his interest in words and the amusement he takes in their unexpected associations drift into mere word-tomfoolery. He was a master of his vocabulary, not its slave. We are told that when reading ancient texts he would not, as so many others—including, we are afraid, many twentieth-century undergraduates—first ascertain their meaning and from them gather the meaning of the sentences which they compose, but inversely gather the force of the words from the sentences in which they occur; and we may quite agree with Richard Pace, the author of the remark, when he points out that this is not contrary to grammar, but above it, and an instinct of genius. A writer of an early stage of English prose, then—and a prolific one at that—not only sufficiently aware of the technical elements of his language, but keen upon its niceties, fully open to its possibilities, and at the same time justly anxious to make his phrase the handmaid to his thought, does not all that give promise of a rich and attractive contribution to the history of English?

If we consider the more external aspects of it first, it is not, of course, a maker but a witness that we must look for. The phonetic and even the morphological facts of a language are independent of a given writer, and all that can be expected from the data supplied by More in the field of early modern pronunciation to begin with is an illustration of the facts made clear to us by Professor Zachrisson, or Professor Wyld, or Professor Luick. What that state of things was we know pretty well now. The great modern shift which at one time affected the English vowels and made them so puzzling in their spoken form to those who try to learn the language from the written one was then, and to a certain extent had been for some time, an accomplished fact. The accented vowels of such words as *make, deep, soon* had thus reached the pronunciation they have at the present day or a stage very near to it, and the parallel process of diphthongization had already begun in those of *desire, house.* Of this we have direct evidence in the works of our author. Not only does he, for example, sometimes write *diepely* for *deeply* or *souner* for *sooner* in his autograph letters, but the same spellings occasionally occur in the same or similar words in the texts printed by Rastell, in spite of the tradition, even then against such spellings, which was to lead to an all but complete rejection of them. An interesting case in connexion with the vowel-shift is that of the word *danger,* which in the letters frequently, and in the printed texts once at least, occurs with the spelling *dayngeor* (or *daingeour*), apparently a proof that in late medieval times a previous *au* before *ng(e)* had become long *a* and later long *e* for which *ai, ay* are well-known spellings. Another word to which it is perhaps worth while drawing attention, though it occurs but a few times, and that in the latter texts only, is the word *berive* (or *byryue*, or *berieve* = our *bereave*), showing, it seems, a sound that was new in the word *bereave* in the sixteenth century, when the regular vowel was as certainly a long slack *e* in *bereave* as it was a long *i* in *believe*. We may also point to two short passages, equally from the printed texts, the interest of which is to offer intentionally phonetic spellings. Having occasion somewhere to quote the opinion of a German on the habit of fasting More writes: 'Fare to sould te laye men fasten, let te prester fasten,' and, wishing elsewhere to represent the language of a Northerner, he quotes it as follows: 'What good felow (quod one of the northern men) whare wonnes thou? Be not we aleuen here, and thou ne but ene la alene, and all we agreed?'

fare and *whare* for *where,* and also on the other hand *ene* and *alene* for northern *one, alone* are, we repeat, merely illustrations of well-known facts. So well, apparently, was the *e*-sound established for a Middle English long *a* that the *a*-sign is here used to represent what could not be anything but long slack *e*. The amusing thing is that Rastell (as perhaps More had done before him) renders the same sound once by *a* and in the next line by *e*. But even in his intentionally phonetic spellings consistency can hardly be expected from a sixteenth-century printer.

Can we go farther than this and draw additional information on the pronunciation of the sixteenth century from the rhymes of our author, for we have some poems written by him? The first thing that strikes us when we look up the said poems is that a certain number of the rhymes used in them would be bad to-day. *Watch* does not rhyme with *catch*, neither does *peered* rhyme with *friared* (written, it is true, *freered*), nor *devil* with *evil*, nor *fall* with *shall*, nor *blood* with *rood*. But this need not surprise us when we remember that the great vowel-shift of the late Middle Ages was followed by numerous other changes in the course of the following centuries, and that a sound common to two words four hundred years ago has often remained in one and changed in the other. The difficulty is hardly greater when neither of the two words of a pair has preserved the sound it had in the early sixteenth century, whether both have actually changed as in the case of *pass: was, bereven* (= our *bereave*): *heven, none: alone, gone: every chone* (= *every one*), or whether in one of the two words there has been, not an actual sound-change but a substitution of one sound for another as in the case of *enclose: lose*. This is nothing new to us, and Professor Wyld has taught us that the various rhymes just quoted were all good in the sixteenth century. Where the difficulty really begins is when we come across cases which are not in accordance with what we know about the pronunciation of the time, but which show, or seem to show, a pronunciation that is either behind it or in advance of it. Even those cases, however, will not detain us long.

It is certainly curious, from an objective point of view, that such pairs as *way : aye, yours : towers* may have been considered—indeed that they should be considered still—as acceptable rhymes in English poetry if the two words in each pair had not the same sound at the time considered. And still it is a

fact, and the reason why the said rhymes can pass muster is that the sound
had been the same in the two words some time before. Such rhymes 'occur in
the best poets; they are convenient. What more is necessary?' Thus Professor
Wyld. But if the venerable tradition thus appealed to, a tradition at least as
old as the age of early printed books, has its full value in the field of rhymes,
little can be inferred from it in the field of pronunciation in general. The same
applies to the coupling of syllables that bear different accents. When we find
officere rhyming with *enquere*, we may admit that the rhyme was still possible about a century after Chaucer as it had been in his day, but it does not
follow that the sound of the third syllable of *officere* was as full in our period
as it had been about a hundred and fifty years before. Though we cannot say
exactly what the degree of stress, and thence the sound, of that syllable was
in More's day, there is reason to believe that the rhyme considered gives no
clue to current pronunciation. Unless we are much mistaken, the same remark
applies to those cases in which a difference of accentuation between the final
syllables of two words is accompanied by one in the quality of their consonants, as for instance in *otherwise : promise : wise*. Here again the spelling
counts more than the actual pronunciation. Should we hesitate to admit the
fact we should find it confessed implicitly by Levins in his *Manipulus Vocabulorum,* which professes to be a rhyming dictionary, and explicitly by Puttenham in his *Arte of English Poetry*. The date of the latter work is 1589 and
that of the former 1570; the habits of poets cannot have been very different
seventy or eighty years earlier. Thus such rhymes as show a pronunciation behind that of their time have not, after all, much to teach us, and their importance is further reduced by the fact that they are not numerous.

The advanced type is more interesting but still less largely represented.
One representative of that type at least is *fryre : desyre*, in which there is no
reason why *fryre* (our *friar*) should not be pronounced with a diphthong, thus
showing a double change, one from Middle English $\bar{e}$ to $\bar{\imath}$ and one from $\bar{\imath}$ to *ei*
(also probable in *enquire, entyre,* and *bryer* which are sometimes thus written
in our printed texts). It cannot be said that *sike* (our *sick*) : *like* is another,
for the vowel of *sike* cannot be a diphthong, and only an imperfect rhyme is
here possible, between $\bar{\imath}$ and the early diphthong—a kind of rhyme which is
far from unknown in the sixteenth and even in the seventeenth century; but
what can be said is that we have here the Early Modern English *sike*, through
which the Middle English *sēke* must have passed before it became the later
sick.

To these few remarks on More's pronunciation it should be added that, in
his case as in that of others, we are not to worry too much about the acquisi-
tion of a definite knowledge which it is probable we shall never fully possess.
If, as we have seen, *beryve* is significant, the same may be said of *bereven*, and
fryre (no doubt our *friar*) should not make us forget *frere*. What can be inferred from our data is obviously that though English had at our period given
up its medieval system of sounds and reached a new one, the earlier tradition
could easily be appealed to, while the door was open to new developments, or
to influences from outside the main current.

Much more might be said about the minutiae of phonetics, and some additional curiosities in sentence-stress will be dealt with under Syntax. In the field of accidence and word-formation again more than one feature might be emphasized as distinctly modern: the genitive singular *ladies* occurs several times in our texts; half a dozen examples of the third person singular of the present indicative in *s* crop up here and there, some in the poems but some in the prose texts too; the verbs with infinitive in *ate* are by no means unknown, the compound adjectives of the type *double-edged* grow and multiply under our author's hands; a few examples of the comparative *farther* might be quoted. But though on some of those points at least we could not quote any example earlier than those found in More's *Works,* none of them really represents the introduction of a new element into the language, and it is again as a witness of the things that were rather than as a moulder of the things that were to be that our author appears in the forms, as well as in the sounds, testified in his writings. We must turn to the internal aspects of his language, beginning with his syntax, if we wish to try and discover More's personal contribution to the common stock.

Here again, however, we must proceed with some caution, for there can be no question of fathering the introduction of this idiom or that upon our author with absolute certainty. The syntax of Early Modern English has not been written in detail, and even the general treatises we possess, admirable as they are, still fail to give us the complete picture we could desire. This is not the place to enlarge upon the immense difficulties of the task, the necessity authors feel of limiting themselves some way or other, the temptation that assails them to give up the historical aspect of language for the purely psychological, and finally the practical impossibility there is of discovering the exact moment when such or such a liberty taken by a writer, or perhaps several contemporary writers, with the tradition of English succeeded in becoming part and parcel of that tradition itself. And still, whatever all those difficulties may be, it is not out of place to try and make clear some few, some very few, points on which More's syntax seems to be decidedly on the modern side.

It should be pointed out in the first place that the instrument he had to handle was still, at the beginning of the sixteenth century, a sorely imperfect one. To take as an example the question of the auxiliaries, those handy, nimble auxiliaries which now enable one to express the shades of one's thought almost *ad infinitum,* the language was still, in More's days, far from having evolved the delicate, consistent principles which have since prevailed. Our author himself combines *have* and *shall* with an infinitive: '. . . eny more distrust of my trowth and devotion toward yow than I have or shall during my life geve the cause . . . ,' he uses *to be* with verbs that denote an action rather than a state: 'they wene that they wer not far walked . . . ,' and he makes what we to-day cannot call otherwise than further confusions between *will* and *shall, would* and *may, may* and *can, had* and *was, had* and *would. . . .* It is true that by the side of those 'mistakes' he frequently offers examples of the modern distinctions: '. . . By my trouthe syr quod he & it like your grace I can not tell you what I woulde haue done, but I can tell you what I shoulde

haue done ...,' and so on in a number of places. But if it cannot be asserted
that the former sort is more largely represented than the latter, it must at least
be admitted that the coexistence of the two evinces a somewhat chaotic state
of things.

That More, nevertheless, applied his analytical mind to some points at least
in order to take full advantage of the resources of his language is shown, among
other proofs, by his remarks about the articles. Nowhere before him, so far as
we know, had the importance of the distinction between the definite *the* and
the indefinite *a* or *an* been emphasized—indeed nowhere had it been stated as
it is in the following passage:

> ... Ye shall vnderstande that the latine tonge lacketh one certain article
> that ye greke hath, and which article in parte bothe our englyshe language
> hath, & the frenche also, and diuerse other tonges, and it is in englishe thys
> worde, the. For where as we haue two articles in english, a, and the : a or
> an (for bothe is one article, the tone before a consonant the other before a
> vowell) is commen to every thinge almost. But the, sygnifieth often times
> some speciall thing, and dyuideth it from the generall. ...

That is obvious enough, and one's first impression is that it could not be
anything new, even in the days of More; but one has only to look up the verse
of St. John, referred to in the passage just quoted, to notice that the text
which had run *Eart ðu witega* in Old English, *Art thou a prophet* in Wyclif
and in Tindale, runs *Art thou the prophet* in Miles Coverdale's text, in the
Douay translation, and in the Revised Version, the Authorized Version making
the phrase still more definite by adopting the words *that prophet*.

> ... And in the latine tonge this thinge is lefte in doubte for lacke as I
> told you of an article correspondent to the greeke artycle, and to the
> englishe article the, & for y^t cause some right holy men and very well
> learned, were for lacke of the greke tonge muche troubled with that place,
> how it might be vnderstanden right. But Tyndall by the greke tonge per-
> ceiuing the article, saw well inough that he should not haue translated it
> into the englishe, art thou a prophete, but art thou ye prophet, and then
> were the matter open and playne. ...

That is not the only place where our author proves that he knows how to
avail himself of the possibilities of the modern definite article. Other specimens of his instinct in that respect are to be found in the use he makes of it,
apparently in its emphatic form, indeed in the use he seems to make of the
emphatic word in general. It is a pity the gramophone had not been invented
in the sixteenth century, and we cannot say for certain to what extent that
striking feature of modern English, the emphatic word, was or was not then
what it is at the present day. Whatever the real state of things, and whatever
the notions entertained about emphasis at a time when the word itself has
not been recorded, is not it the echo of a modern voice we seem to hear when
we read sentences like the following?—

If Tindal saye that he can so conster these texts as they shal not hurt his heresies: I deny not that he so may do, and I can to so conster them, that they shall not hurte the trouth. . . .

To say that the whole thing is inuisible, whereof he sayeth we may see euery part, is a thing aboue my pore wit, and I suppose aboue his to, to make his sayeng trew. . . .

. . . yet that the onely electes though they be a church, be ye church (which is the thing that he sholde proue) that hathe he neyther prooued. . . .

More examples might be adduced, containing such words as *we, us, them, one, very, every, alone,* or a noun, or an adverb, or a verb—auxiliary or not. But to return to the articles. Is not *the man* a particularly modern phrase in such a depreciatory context as this: '. . . I suppose, that when the man was writting this, hys witte was walking toward the holy lande,' and is it not also a modern custom we have to deal with when we come across the indefinite *a* before a noun in apposition after a clause? '. . . they might haue hadde poore men inoughe to bestowe that money vpon in reliefe necessarye, that they there spent vpon the temple, a thinge as these men cal it, voluntary. . . .'

The earliest example of *the man* in a context similar to that quoted above that is given in the *Oxford English Dictionary* is dated 1674; as to the use of *a* before a noun in apposition after a clause we take it on Mätzner's authority that the phrase is exclusively modern.

It need hardly be added that the texts quoted, and those they represent, are by no means a proof that, on the one or two points chosen so far, More's syntax is identical with that of the present day. It would not be difficult to oppose other texts to those, in which the definite article is used by More contrary to modern habits, as when he writes

. . . she knit the browes . . .
. . . For so doth the man ye wote well in the sleepe . . . ,

where we should expect possessive adjectives. But the fact remains that in the majority of cases More's practice, or at least his tendency, with regard to the words taken as specimens, is in agreement with that to which we are accustomed, viz. that compared with that of the Middle Ages it makes for individualization and greater precision.

Precision is one of the qualities of modern syntax, but concision is another. One of the means by which it reaches it is undoubtedly the use it makes of the pregnant word. Thus the conjunction, the complete omission of which is in some cases allowable, may in others represent not only its own value but the whole conjunctive phrase which it is meant to introduce. The tendency exists in More, to an exaggerated degree: '. . . in the provision of such thinges as theyre slaknes hyther to mych hath hyndered the comen affayres,' in which *as,* of course, stands for *as those in which.* The same applies to *that,* the missing words being here those which should come not after, but before, the conjunction: 'This Webbe . . . was by dyuers heretykes detected vnto me, that he had sold and vsed continually to sell many of these heretikes bokes. . . .'

Though neither kind of turn has survived within recent centuries, both

may be said to illustrate the search for brevity which, through many alternatives, has been on the whole, and remains, one of the leading characteristics of
English syntax.

A peculiar illustration of brevity, and one that does not seem to be forgotten, chiefly in familiar language, is given by More in the use he makes of
'that versatile mercurial word,' as Mr. Belloc somewhere puts it, 'our plain *and*':
'... though sometyme it hap that a man be accused or endyghted of malice,
or of some likelihod which happed him of chaunce and not his faut therin, yet
happeth it ...'

What words are to be supplied in that and similar texts we leave it to the
reader to determine, but we are in no doubt that popular feeling easily supplies what may be required in such cases. The more genteel *and he* is no less
known to More than the plain *and,* but of this we have noted only one example: '... that ther shuld be but one prince ... and he to contynue ...,' and
we are on more familiar ground when we meet the curious *and* invested with
the full dignity of *who* or *which:*

> Here seemeth a goodlye thyng and is indeed very deuelishe....

> ... as the churche of Christe is but one so there be of those a vengeable
> maynye, and be not comprehended vnder any one churche ...

where *and* is as easily intelligible as in Shakespeare's

> Here's a young maid with travel much oppress'd
> And faints for succour.

The use may be old, but we understand it is more modern still, though
recent authorities apparently fail to record it.

We will not give way to the temptation to show that More also knows the
inverse phenomenon, viz. the use of *which = and,* of which Dickens, for
instance, offers examples. We had rather draw the reader's attention to a
specially pregnant use of the conjunctive pronoun, equivalent to preposition
plus pronoun, which need not be explained exclusively by the tradition of the
old cases:

> ... and no man that heard hym left to bear vs wytnesse what he said,

> ... all hys teachyng of knowledge where some of the church be, withoute
> ye knowledge who they be ...

> ... yf God were not ... at his libertie stil in the gouernaunce and teach-
> ynge of hys churche, what he wyl have belieued and what he wyll have
> done ...

Here again, unless we are mistaken, we may have a traditional turn, but a
more modern one still.

It is not surprising that the chapter of the verb should offer particularly
striking specimens of the pregnant word. The absolute construction of a transi-
tive verb occurs four times at least in the case of *to fret* in which, as far as we
know, it is new or at least recent: '... so doth the enuious parson, fret, fume,

& burne in his owne hert . . . ,' and we are not aware that *to drink one's self drunk* has been recorded before More. But the salient point here unquestionably is the convenient—and very modern—use to which More puts his postpositions:

> . . . Tyll he dispute,
> His money cleane away . . .
>
> . . . till with her daunsynge she daunsed of Saynt Iohns head . . .

Construction of the same kind might be quoted with the verbs *to accurse out of, to bless away* (and *out*), *to call back, to drink down, to face out, to muse out,* of none of which an earlier example has been recorded. Well may we understand the compliment here paid to More by his recent French biographer, the Abbé Brémond, on that secret of English prose by which, as he says, thanks to the postposition, a new sense of the verb is formed which makes it at the same time so precise, and so full of meaning—and so untranslatable.

Having thus attempted to make it clear that some features at least of the modern English framework were not unknown to More, we can now examine the element with which he has helped to fill it—a task which the incomparable lists of words, phrases, dates, and texts put at our disposal by the *Oxford English Dictionary* will make infinitely easier than the one immediately preceding.

Perhaps some readers expect us to repeat here the usual restriction about what actually was as against what we know. Though we have already made it before touching our author's syntax, and though we are here on far safer ground than we were a few pages back, we need not hesitate to admit once more that there is a difference between being the originator of a word or phrase or only its propagator, and that for all our wealth of information we may frequently mistake the latter for the former. It is only subject to those limitations, therefore, that we shall consider More as a creator, or an importer, of words in the following pages.

Before launching into the inquiry, it is amusing to try and realize to what extent the English vocabulary had already attained its present state about the beginning of the sixteenth century. A glance at this page or that of the Folio of 1557—so incomparably more reliable for the purpose than the early word-compilations themselves—is instructive in that respect.

More seems to find it quite natural to remind us of our *breakfast,* or to warn us against eating *ratsbane,* or to conjure up the idea of a *costermonger* covering his basket, or to point out to us that the world is not a *football,* or to draw our attention to his *spectacles;* on one occasion, when wanting to encourage us to make a poor man work in our garden rather than give him alms, he tells us that by our alms the poor man would run the risk of living idle and turning a *loiterer.* No doubt the words we have italicized, and a number of similar ones, though none of them apparently was old when he wrote them, were practically as familiar then as they are now. Equally current, if not more so, at least among the better educated class, were terms of a less popular kind, particularly the law terms, which would naturally occur to More and which seem to have meant for him exactly what they mean to-day, such as *action, to arraign, indictment, oyer, suit,* and others. To return to the more general class, it is not only, of course, the words themselves but also their new acceptations and developments that are of importance; of these interesting examples are not lacking in our Folio. By the side of *scabbed* human beings, and animals, and plants, *scabbed sheep* in the figurative sense had long received the freedom of the language; a *passion* had gone through a string of successive or simultaneous senses, the chief of which had been the passion of Our Lord, martyrdom, a vehement emotion, an outburst of anger—and had reached that of a fit of anger; the verb *to desire* was no longer limited to the sense of 'to wish,' but also meant 'to express a wish'; the verb *to milk* had come to apply not only to milkmaids but to swindlers as well. The English vocabulary was undoubtedly pretty rich already four hundred years ago if we consider the crude words: after a rough calculation based upon the first hundred full sepa- rate entries listed in the great *Dictionary* under each of the letters *a, g, r, t,* taken as specimens, it represented about one-fifth of what it is now—but how much richer if we consider the uses to which the words were put!

Let us now turn to More's contribution and examine its various aspects. There is a class of words which, before all others, appeals to the lovers of English, viz. the clear-cut units, often monosyllabic, which strike the ear with their sharp consonantic distinctness. More frequently than not they belong to the Germanic stock, but it is not the stock which matters so much as the English garb, and *jest* and *musty* which are originally Romance are just as good representatives of the class as *lift* or *tub* which are not; in fact some of them, such as *hiss* or *swap,* are neither Germanic nor Romance, but merely 'root- creations.' It is no wonder that we can at least suspect More to have coined, or half-coined, a few words of that class, though in almost each individual case there is some additional restriction to be added to the general caution mentioned above. It is easy to point out that *to peddle,* or *to pule,* or *to fimble,* or *to shuffle,* or *to taunt* have not been found in any texts previous to those we are considering, but then examples of *pedlar,* which may be con- nected with *to peddle,* have been traced back to a century and a half earlier; *to pule,* which may be More's creation, may also be an imitation from the French; *to fimble* sounds like a mere grade of the series *fimble—famble— fumble,* the last two members of which have been recorded before our period; and *taunt* was also known before it, at least as an adjective meaning 'haughty.' As for *to shuffle (up),* the sense in which More employs it, viz. 'to patch up,' has not lived. It is worth while, anyway, to note here a few curious terms: *to jumper* in the sense of 'to harmonize,' *to tolter* in that of 'to move unsteadily,' also the substantive *sleight* meaning 'indifference'—the first two because More offers isolated, or almost isolated, examples of them, and the third because our text is nearly two hundred years older than the first quoted in the columns of the *Dictionary:*

> . . . let vs yet further see how his diffinicion of the churche and hys heresies, will iumper and agree together among themselfe.

... whan he catcheth once a fall, ... there lyeth he still tumblyng and toltryng in myre....

... lest his ouer bold hope may happe to stretch into presumpcion, and occasion of sleight regarding sin ...

Cannot we regret that the first two, to say nothing of the third, did not become, and remain, current?

A remarkable case is that of the verb *to scud,* not known before the sixteenth century, though of this word in particular we read that 'it may have been much older in colloquial use.' Another is that of the substantive *glade,* both in its proper and in its figurative senses; it is curious that the latter use should be the earlier of the two. We are here tempted to add the expressive *dolt,* but then it is not More's own, occurring, as it does, not in his English works but in the English translation of the part of the *Treatice vpon the passion of Chryste* (written by him in Latin) which Mrs. Basset inserted in the Folio of 1557. It is comforting, at all events, for the admirers of More's originality to think that, if he had nothing to do with the introduction of that word into English, it is at least the More School that seems responsible for it.

After the root-creations, or half-creations pure and simple, a few compounds, chiefly of the reduplicating kind, tell their own tale. We find in More's pages not only *bibble-babble, pit-pat, hucker-mucker,* the originals of which are not far to seek, but also *beetle-blind, far-fet* (*far-fetched* is somewhat later), *key-cold,* which are more likely to bear his own stamp. However much older in colloquial use these, and the words quoted before, may have been when our author wrote them, is not the use of the popular process illustrated here, in works some of which at least may lay some claim to be called literature, a proof of a deep-set instinct in agreement with the fundamental tendencies of his language? The instinct is perhaps the more noticeable as it is not the popular but the learned element that one naturally looks for at first in the writings of a scholar and a favourite child of the Renaissance.

On the French element we need not say much. Though it remained a rich storehouse of words even after the Middle Ages, and though More himself actually wrote a few good lines in French in *The Boke of the fayre Gentylwoman,* what we read in his epigrams does not make it likely at first sight that he should have felt inclined to borrow much from that source:

> ... nimirum placet,
> Verbis tribus, si quid loquatur Gallicis,
> ... Sic ergo linguam ille et Latinam Gallice,
> Et Gallice linguam sonat Britannicam ...
> Et Gallice omnem, praeter unam Gallicam.

To put it in other words, he must have been of the opinion of Ascham, namely that 'bothe wyne, ale and beere ... be all good, every one taken by hym selfe alone.' In fact, we should find it difficult to quote from his works many new words to which a French origin can be ascribed. We can indeed glean *absurdity, function, precision, to qualify, to taunt,* some of which are particularly interesting because our dates for them are earlier than those given by the *Oxford Dictionary*:

> It is not this company & congregacion of al these nacions, y^t without ... precysion from the remenant, *professe* the name and faith of christ?

> ... the conflict of the diuers qualifyed elementes tempered in our body, continually laboring ech to vanquish other,

but then we should not venture to go much farther. One word which we feel sure will endear our author to the readers of this essay far more than all the rest, to wit the word *marmalade,* is also given by the *Oxford Dictionary* as of French origin—but then for linguistic and other reasons we suspect marmalade to have come not from France but from Spain.[1]

When we referred to the learned element above, we meant, of course, the Latin—classical or medieval—vocabulary, which could not but be very familiar to an author whose writings are partly in Latin. On coming to this aspect of our subject, though we are confronted with lists longer than those we have had to deal with before, we should beware of applying the word 'learned' to all of More's borrowings. The appearance of some is no doubt pedantic and Johnsonese, and we are not surprised that common use has long rejected such words as *to allect* (and *allective*), or *to insimulate*, though it has retained such others as *to adhibit, antiphrasis, concomitance, irrefragable,* and *sorority;* but others again have unquestionably met a much-felt need, and we are not surprised either that the verbs *to anticipate, to dissipate, to exaggerate, to extenuate, to insinuate,* as well as the substantives *monopoly,* or *paradox,* or *pretext,* are fully current. It may seem strange to realize that the word *fact,* a word so simple and so frequent that it might almost have figured among the native, or quasi-native, terms mentioned above, should have to be added to the number, but then—it is a fact. '... albeit our Lorde dooeth suffer hys church to erre in the knoweledge of a facte or dede doone among men. ...'

If we now extend our view to the broader field of compound and chiefly of derived words, we obtain, of course, a far more important total. The compounds supply us with the expressive *blockhead,* the convenient *hair-breadth,* the peculiar *text-hand,* the indispensable *playfellow,* and the puzzling *grasswidow.* The derived nouns appear in denser numbers, *co-heir* and *foreknowledge* coming first under the prefixes, while under the suffixes we find names of agents: *bungler, detector, cooperant;* abstract nouns: *acceptance, connotation, obstruction, damnability, clerkliness, success,* and other nouns including *monosyllable, interrogatory,* and the word *vocabulary* itself, for which we have to thank More as for the others. The other parts of speech are even better provided and the native formation has a greater part to play in them. By the side of *incorporeal, endurable, mootable, impenitent, combustible, comprehensible, frivolous,* all of which have a more or less Romance appearance, More presented his language with the indispensable *drowsy,* and the amusing *apish,* and the exquisite *daughterly* which reminds us of charming Margaret Roper kissing her father on Tower-wharf, as *playfellow* reminded us of the little princes beguiling their anxious hours inside the Tower, and that other

delightful find *elderly* which, though it has no personal association with Sir
Thomas in his text, '. . . of olde they vsed commonly to chose wel elderly men
to be priestes . . .' reminds us of himself surrounded by his family at Chelsea.
The verbs in their turn have to offer us in the native section *to forefigure, to
misgive, to misremember, to mistranslate*—in the other one *to detest, to en-
tangle, to explain.*[2] Our lists do not claim to be exhaustive.

The creation, or the introduction, of fresh linguistic elements is sure to
entitle a writer to the gratitude of the lovers of his language, but the praise he
deserves for the use he may make of the existing material at his disposal is
hardly less. The word *metaphor* cannot, any more than the word *trope,* be
claimed as due to More, but one is often struck by the instinct with which he
coins metaphors. An *itch* is an itch in his works as everywhere else, but is also
a hankering after something, and, talking about an itch, it is perhaps a pity
that the verb *to tickle* used by him when referring to Romans vii. 5 '. . . as the
reliques of original sinne, whereby we be ticled towarde great actuall deadely
sinnes . . .' could no longer be used in the same manner. The verb *to inveigh,*
first used in the sense of 'to introduce,' takes under his pen that of 'raising a
protest,' the only one that has been current for centuries; he makes *open* refer
to a man's disposition and *faithful* to a translator's method, he employs *to
fume* of a person giving way to anger;[3] he declares that he does not intend . . .
to pin his soul at another man's back. The reader need not be reminded of the
particularly expressive character of some at least of the words just quoted; he
is not likely to disagree with us if we add that *bigly* in the sense of 'boastfully'
(older than *big* in the sense of 'boastful') or *lumpish* in the sense of 'melancholy' are not less felicitous.

Is it worth while to go farther and insist upon the way in which More avails
himself of those old resources of language so dear to the schoolmaster—
metonymy and synecdoche? We may at least quote one or two examples of
the former. The use of the adjective *clear* referring to a person, as in '. . . anye
of those articles wherein euery good christen man is clere . . .' is an excellent
metonymy—of the class that expresses the cause for the effect, and one that,
we believe, has become of pretty frequent occurrence in the language. That of
the substantive *frailty* preceded by the indefinite article, as in 'So may a man
speake very lewde . . . woordes . . . of a passion and of a frayltie . . .' is another
of the variety in which the abstract quality stands for a specimen of it, and
seems hardly less current. Other cases in point are *allegory* and *cavillation,*
meaning in each instance 'a specimen of the phenomenon,' while *conjecture*
once represents in our text a third variety, to wit 'the working of a faculty'
for the faculty itself. The principle of synecdoche More applies to the word
bush, when, taking the whole for the part, he makes it mean 'a branch of ivy
hung as a vintner's sign,' and to the word *natural* when, substituting the qualifying word for the word qualified, he employs it to describe one naturally
deficient in intellect. We might look for more illustrations of the two principles, and of other figures of speech as well; but then is it not sufficient to
point out that when coining them he is merely following the natural bent of
language? What is more remarkable is that when he has to name the process

he uses, he more than once takes care to put in an apologizing word or two so as not to be taxed with pedantry. Thus about the periphrasis: 'Lo there haue I fallen on a fayre fygure vnwar, that is I trowe called periphrasis,' and about hyperbole: '. . . he sayd it onely by a maner of speking which is amonge lerned men called *Yperbole*, for the more vehement expressing of a matter . . .'.

Modern analysis has made us familiar with a process—concatenation, if we may use the expression—which consists in adopting for a word more and more specialized, or generalized, applications on its way, with the final result that the starting-point may be entirely lost sight of. We come across such words in the pages of More at various stages of their history. The starting-point is clearly visible in the word *meeting* in its political acceptation, of which *The history of king Richard the thirde* offers the first known example, but the same cannot be said of some others. More has heard of '. . . a bed of Snakes [that] was . . . founde out & broken . . .' and he talks about errors subtly *couched*, though the former word had previously been reserved to persons—or plants, and the latter had been until his time reserved to more material connotations; he writes of some '. . . that haue engroced into their handes . . . other mennes goodes . . . ,' in which the original meaning of *to engross* (in gross) represents but part of its total sense; he describes a defendant as laying no *exception* to many a witness, in which *exception* keeps neither its etymological sense nor the intermediate sense of 'reservation' but is practically equivalent to 'objection.' Perhaps the two most characteristic examples of words that occur in a new sense under More's pen are the adjective *fain* meaning 'compelled' (after starting from the meaning 'glad' and passing through that of 'glad under the circumstances') and the almost homophonous substantive *fine* meaning 'a sum imposed as the penalty for an offence,' after going through the successive stages: 'conclusion,' 'agreement,' and 'composition-fee.'

Before we leave the words proper a final remark may be made here about the use More makes of a few adjectives. That the adjective is a particularly delicate part of speech is a well-known fact. As Earle wrote in *The Philology of the English Tongue*, 'it involves a greater chance of making a mistake, or of coming into collision with the judgment of others, than any other . . .'; from which it follows that 'there is a shyness in the utterance of adjectives,' at least of 'such as can at all carry the air of being the speaker's own . . .'. Now it seems to us that some adjectives do carry the air of being More's own. *Solemn* is not a case in point, though it is apparently one of his favourites, because the use of it is earlier. Neither is the more characteristic *peremptory,* though he actually supplies the first examples of it that are known, at least in a work meant for the general public, because, after all, it is not really a popular word. But then cannot we say that *jolly* and *pretty* in their ironical sense are both popular, and that they both belong to him? Apparently we can:

> Here shall you see Iudas play the ioylye marchaunt I trowe. . . .
> Maister Masker maketh vs a prety shorte crede nowe . . .

The last words quoted bring us back to the point from which we started, namely the popular element without which a writer can hardly expect to have a hold upon the many. If we now cast a glance at a few more uses of current words and at a certain number of set phrases the first examples of which are, as far as we know, due to More's pen, we shall perhaps have made it clear that not only could he not fail to have a hold upon the many in his time, but that he has kept it to the present day.

There is no lack of variety in the list. A short, all but worn-out word such as *like* has assumed a particularly familiar—nay, even colloquial—sense in a context like the following: 'That woord was like Eue ...'.

Then there are some collocations such as *I cannot help it, to make the best of, of a sudden,* which, though more or less abstract in their component parts, cannot fail to be associated with the everyday occurrences in people's lives:

> ... ther is none other remedi but you must let him haue it: better would I wish it, but I cannot helpe it.

> ... we shall geasse at hys mynde as nere as we canne, and make the beste of hys matter ...

> ... a sermon ... not of a sodayne brayed, but sore studied and penned ...

Others, again, are more life-like in themselves, because it is easy even to unimaginative minds to see the image that lurks behind their apparently colourless parts. Of these we can at least mention *by the way* (used long before More but not in its figurative sense of 'incidentally'), *to come short of, to lay open.*

> But yet consider one thing by the waye, that ye missetake him not ...

> ... or els I wene he wyll come short of hys whole summe, and lacke fiue of his hundred ...

> ... so that ye mai see some of the fauts of hys exposecion by them selfe, ... & hys solucions auoyded by them selfe, & the notable notes that he maketh of my notable repugnances last of al layed open to you by them-selfe ...

But by far the largest portion have that spontaneous, unmistakable, concrete ring which, when it does not rather appeal to the ear as in *to harp upon a string,* sounds like an invitation to visualize things. More talks about telling some thing *to some one's teeth,* or showing another person a thing *with a wet finger,* about *one driven to the hard wall,* or one *that cannot see the wood for the trees:*

> ... yet would he never be angry with them, though they would neither belieue y^t he told them, nor do y^t he bode them: but tel him wel and plainly to hys teth, y^t if he woulde be belieued or obayed, he shoulde haue made hys apostles wryte it.

> But and yf ye woulde cease youre persecucion once, and lette them liue in reste, ye shoulde see them flocke together so fast, y^t they should sone shew you the churche with a wete finger.

... then may euery chylde see that he is drieuen to the harde walle, and fayne to seeke a shamefull shyfte.

... And as he might tell vs, that of Poules churche we maye well see the stones, but we can not see the church. And then we may well tell him agayne, that he can not see the wood for the trees ...

The last two phrases, it is worth noticing, are given in the *Oxford Dictionary* as occurring for the first time in John Heywood's *Proverbs* in 1546. Here, as in the few other cases in which we have quoted our texts in full, we disagree with the great *Dictionary,* but if it has committed a fault at all we venture to call it a *felix culpa,* as it opens us one more vista upon the More School, where Heywood was one of the young people More loved to have about him, as Professor A. W. Reed recently reminded us. Other phrases suggest to us other associations. While every one of us is free to connect *the needle one looks* (for) *in a meadow* and *the grammar no more like to faith than an apple is to an oyster* with what experience of his life he chooses, nobody can help associating *a tale of a tub* with Jonathan Swift and the story of the three brothers, and More's opponent conveying himself *out of the frying pan into the fire* with Charles Dickens and Mr. Winkle. But we refrain. More of our author's 'new phrases' could be quoted, no doubt, but perhaps enough has been said to show his power of handling the elements of his language and making them effective.

It is not intended in the present essay to push the inquiry farther and show how the materials reviewed above—turns, words, and phrases—combine under More's pen with those his language possessed before to make up a new whole, viz. his personal style. Neither does it enter into our plan to investigate to what extent More's language may have influenced that of his contemporaries and successors, whether inside, or outside, the More School. It falls more immediately under our task, it seems to us, to point out how far the results here arrived at might be improved, and how far they may be considered as final.

One way obviously points to progress in the knowledge of More's English, to wit an analysis of Early Modern English more detailed, because more limited, than the gigantic inquiry which the Oxford University Press has put at our disposal. That such an analysis is being prepared through its medium is well known, and it is with confidence that those interested in the undertaking are looking forward to its results. But then are there not other ways of breaking new ground? When the present writer submitted, now over twenty years ago, his *Essai sur la langue de Sir Thomas More d'après ses oeuvres anglaises* to the University of Paris, he admitted on the last page that the full value of More's English could be but imperfectly estimated because the English of More's contemporaries had not yet been sufficiently reconnoitred. Why should things stand in that respect as they stood twenty years ago? Are there not in the universities of the world numerous young men and women in search of subjects for future degrees? To those who may choose to tackle the language of Tindale, or Fisher, or Elyot, to say nothing of others, an abundant harvest of interesting facts may be promised; may there be some among the lovers of

English that will take up the suggestion before long.

It does not seem likely, however, that the importance of More's contribution to his language will suffer much from a comparison between him and other Tudor writers. And the reason is not far to seek. To his instinct for the popular side of his language, to his learning and culture, which, while making for the enrichment of it, knew how to keep within tactful bounds, to his aptitude for using the traditional processes which, by his skilful handling of them, he could make fruitful of new means of expression, did not he add that sense of humour which is sure to impart life to everything it comes into contact with? It would be strange indeed if Sir Thomas turned out to have touched the English language without improving it.[4]

ST. THOMAS MORE'S TREATISE ON THE FOUR LAST THINGS AND THE GOTHICISM OF THE TRANS-ALPINE RENAISSANCE

H. W. Donner

It is to an unexpected climax that the symphony of the Middle Ages seems to rise on the very eve of the transalpine Renaissance. The intellectual synthesis of the thirteenth century had long been dissolved into a variety of emotional themes, employed as a means of enforcing a lesson rendered unimpressive by over-long reiteration. "Au XIIIᵉ siècle," says Mons. Mâle, "le symbole domine l'histoire, au XVᵉ siècle, le symbolisme, sans disparaître complètement, s'efface devant la réalité et devant l'histoire."[1] In that lack of synthesis lies, perhaps, the secret both of the intellectual weakness of the fifteenth century (even in Italy[2]) and of the chaotic impression given by that age of transition. But if that is so, it may also go some way towards explaining the real dichotomy which so puzzles scholarship and help in answering the question how seemingly irreconcilable trends of ideas could thrive side by side and find fertile soil even in one single mind. For, just as it may swing from one extreme to the other, so wherever it assumes control, emotion has a mysterious power of reconciling opposites and of merging the apparently irreconcilable. But emotion's instrument is the arts, and hence it is consistent with this view that painting, sculpture, and, above all, the woodcut, should be the chief carriers of those emotional themes which triumph north of the Alps only just before, or even after, 1500. "Die Kunst ist mächtiger geworden als der Mythos," says a German historian.[3] Nor is it altogether surprising, from this point of view, that the fine arts should manifest themselves so much more vigorously than the chiefly repetitive literature of the period.[4]

It is perhaps sufficient to instance the two all-absorbing subjects of the Apocalypse and the Dance of Death. A favourite theme of the fourteenth, the matter of the Apocalypse was further embroidered in the late fifteenth century and popularized by Vérard, with all the famous tokens of the impending Doom, the three moral and fifteen cosmic signs which Bede had attributed to the vision of St. Jerome. But it was not till 1498 that all these cataclysms were given that visible shape in Dürer's woodcuts which so dominated later designs that the artist's name became coupled with that of St. John's in as close an association as Dante's with the living image of Hell.[5] Similar was the case of the Dance of Death. First painted in the fashionable promenade of the busy

Reprinted, by permission of the publisher and author, from *English Miscellany*, 3 (1952), 25–48.

cloisters of Les Innocents in Paris in 1424, it was copied in Pardon Churchyard of St. Paul's in London about 1430, at Klingenthal convent at Kleinbasel
some ten or a dozen years later, in the Dominican cemetery at Grossbasel
about 1480, all over France, England, Switzerland, and Germany, even as far
away as Bergen in Norway and Reval in Esthonia.[6] It was spread abroad in the
woodcuts of Guyot Marchant in 1486, it was woven into tapestries, carved on
columns and choir-stalls, used in devices and ornaments.[7] It was to be given a
new lease of life by the Romantic movement, and to this day has not ceased
playing in poets' fancies.[8] But it was the genius of Holbein, assisted by Lützel-
berger, that endowed the theme of the *Danse Macabre* with eternal life, and it
was Holbein's version that was to be reissued and imitated ever after, although
his designs were quite foreign to the original conception.[9]

Now, in the same year as Dürer's woodcuts of the Apocalypse were first
published, Colet delivered at Oxford his passionate denunciation of the allegorical interpretation of the Gospels in lectures which seem to ring the knell
of the Middle Ages. By the time Holbein had completed his designs of the
Dance of Death the Holy City of Christendom had been sacked, and the artist
was on the point of departure for England, where it is thought he stayed with
More and where he certainly painted his portrait and those of his family and
friends. His *Dance of Death* was published at Lyons in 1538, three years after
the death of his English patron on the scaffold, at a time when Wyatt's work
was nearly done and the young Earl of Surrey was entering upon his career. It
is against this background that I wish to consider St. Thomas More's treatise
on the *Four Last Things,* written in, or about, 1522.

A German scholar has suggested that it was composed in imitation of Plato's
Phaedo in what he describes as a Humanist form.[10] However, it was not even
written in dialogue, either mediaeval or Platonic. Neither is there here any
quest for a philosophical solution of the problems of truth and immortality.
One of the images employed, that of life as a prison of man, is certainly common to both, and it may be derived from Plato, but it was a commonplace
which More had long made his own in his *Epigrams.* His manner of presentation is therefore important, i.e. the actual picture of life's prison given in the
Four Last Things. This is no general concept as in Plato, it is a vivid visualiza-
tion of Newgate or the Marshalsea. More certainly refers also, and in so many
words, to the subject of Plato's discussion and to "the best of old philosophers,"[11] but not as a model, only in support, on a lower plane, of the
Christian doctrine. The classical references, to Plato, Æsop, Plutarch, Pliny,
and Cicero, are balanced by others of a more general character, to legal customs, geographical distinctions, natural phenomena, ancient and contemporary history, anecdotes out of his own experience, all in the usual encyclopedic
humanist fashion; but all greatly outnumbered by the references to Holy
Scripture and the Fathers of the Church. Standing in the front rank of the
Humanists, not only in England but in all Europe, and the most brilliantly
imaginative of them all, More eminently shared the facility of transalpine
Humanism in general, and of Colet's school, including Erasmus, in particular,
of reconciling, without the extravagances of Pico and Ficino, what was ser-

viceable in Ancient philosophy with the tenets of Christianity and of making classical learning subservient to Christian teaching.

No theme could be more characteristic of the late Middle Ages than the last verse of the seventh chapter of *Ecclesiasticus:* "Memorare novissima, et in aeternum non peccabis." "Remember," says More, "thy last things, and thou shalt never sin in this world." Those *quattuor novissima* being: death, judgement, heaven, and hell, or in More's words "death, doom, pain, and joy." Even if it goes back more than three hundred years to Innocent III's anathema on the flesh in *De contemptu mundi*—as coldly repulsive a picture as ever given of life's ugliness and the horrors of decomposition in death—, it was not till the fifteenth century that the theme became universal, largely through the instrumentality of that pious and ascetic mystic, prolific writer and meddler in politics, the "Doctor extaticus" of the fifteenth century, Denis the Carthusian, whose treatise *De quattuor hominum novissimis,* with all its nauseating details of the torments of hell, was copied and imitated everywhere. We know, for instance, that it was read—somewhat lugubrious reading— at meals at the convent of Windesheim,[12] just as More's treatise was evidently meant to be read to his family and household—what he used to refer to as his school[13]—for at Bucklersbury and Chelsea, as at Colet's house, or in Utopia, the custom survived of reading at mealtime something of an elevating nature. But there is evidence that in the course of writing he forgot about his "school" and addressed himself most particularly to his daughter Margaret[14] who was at the same time writing a similar treatise in noble rivalry with her learned father and at his command. In the outstanding merit of her work family tradition sought the reason for the abandonment of his own,[15] but her work is lost and comparison impossible. Whatever the reason—and as Under-Treasurer of England he was certainly a busy man—More's treatise remained the merest fragment. He never completed as much as the first part dealing with Death and the Seven Deadly Sins, and the fragment breaks off just as he was starting on the section "Of Sloth." All that we can say of its construction is that, as far as it reaches, the treatise is well balanced, the different sections being self-contained and adapted for independent reading, yet happily held together by the recurring image of the title-verse as a potent medicine against what Shakespeare called "life's fitful fever." But the image of the deadly sins as so many "old, hard, swelling, and deadly sores" and "fierce, raging fevers" is itself traditional and derived from Denis the Carthusian.

For what worried the late Middle Ages even more than the fear of death, to which they were being inured by the permanent political broils, recurring pestilence, famine and warfare, was the fear of being taken unawares, of dying without a chance of repentance and so being condemned to eternal torments.[16] Then, says Sebastian Brant, there will be no postponing of amendment, no crying like the crow, ever present in the woodcut illustration of the *Ship of Fools:* cras, cras, cras.[17] And this is the reverse of the medal of symbolism, that having for so long represented all ideas in material likeness, the spiritual content became gradually weakened, until only the physical image remained; and all the Church could do was to heighten the colours and sharpen the outlines of the visual representation of the pains of death and the torments of Hell. The late Professor Huizinga wittily compared the second half of the fifteenth century to a patient long overdosed, requiring ever stronger medicines. Hence Death also, in the unnumerable pictures and wood-cuts, becomes ever more aggressive.

In thrusting his lesson home More brings to his aid also the Dance of Paul's, i.e. the Dance of Death painted in the cloisters of Pardon Churchyard of old St. Paul's with the verses faithfully, if somewhat verbosely, translated out of the French by Lydgate, the Monk of Bury.[18] The Dance of Death was one of the Church's strongest medicines against the sickness of the Seven Deadly Sins, and there hovers something of the spirit of Savonarola over the account of Frère Richard preaching in the cloisters of Les Innocents in 1424.[19] Lest those who could not read, however, should interpret the pictures in the spirit of the *Carmina Burana*—and "Au cimetière des Innocents," says Emile Mâle, "les filles de joie erraient sous les cloîtres et parmi les tombeaux"[20]—against such a perversion of the text the Church provided other antidotes, intended to im-press the urgency of repentance and so assuaging the fears of death—this spectre, which, in Professor Stammler's words, would no longer be laid by merely ex-ternal means, such as absolution, relics and saint-worship (the saints were be-coming all too familiar), pilgrimages and fraternities.[21] One of the prophylactics was of course exactly those treatises *De quattuor novissimis,* of which More's is one. But the many themes playing Death's tune, or, should I say, Death's horn-pipe? are so interlaced in the late fifteenth and early sixteenth centuries that it is not surprising to find another of them knocking for admission into More's text. This was the book of the *Ars moriendi,* printed again and again with its suggestive illustrations of the school of Cologne, not uninfluenced by Roger van der Weyden.[22] It is impossible here to go into its complex and interesting bibliography. Suffice it to say that in addition to the principal Latin versions there was Caxton's abridgement *Of the Arte and Craft well to dye* about 1491, the English edition of Vérard's *Art de bien vivre et de bien mourir,* 1503,[23] and a lost translation by Skelton.[24]

And it is fascinating to observe how closely More's description follows the *Ars moriendi* woodcuts. Here are the temptation of Pride and Despair, of a pompous funeral—such a one as Erasmus so entertainingly describes in the *Colloquia*—; the friends crying: "What shall I have? What shall I have?"; the devil at the bedside; but also the final consolation of the Crucifix; and, to fol-low up the pictorial reminiscences, here is also the figure of Death, as we know it from the woodcuts of Guyot Marchant's *Danse macabre,* shrunk and withered, a mummy rather than a skeleton, what the Germans call a "Haut-skelett," Shakespeare's "Hard-favoured tyrant, ugly, meagre, lean." (It is regrettable that More should not have found time to proceed to the vision of the Last Judgement. I am not sure what he would have made of it, a Jeromian as he was. Hints of cataclysms are not absent from his writings.)

More's imagination was wholly visual, and his treatise contains a wealth of imagery worthy of a poet. In this he is at one with his period, but we can see also why his medium, like that of his age, as Huizinga has shown, must be prose rather than poetry.[25] Two short sentences must serve to illustrate his visualized, graphically descriptive style. "We look upon death either so far off that we see him not at all, or but a slight and uncertain sight, as a man may see a thing so far off that he wotteth not whether it be a bush or a beast."—"The devil anon took his own unhappy daughter to wife, and upon pride begat envy; by whose enticement he set upon our first parents in paradise, and by pride supplanted them, and there gave them so great a fall by their own folly that unto this day all their posterity go crooked thereof."[26]

How mediaeval was his style appears from a rather lengthy quotation—but length, alas! was inherent in the Middle Ages: ". . . as condemned folk and remediless in this prison of the earth we drive forth a while, some bound to a post, some wandering abroad, some in the dungeon, some in the upper ward, some building them bowers and making them palaces in the prison, some weeping, some laughing, some labouring, some playing, some singing, some chiding, some fighting, no man, almost, remembering in what case he standeth, till that suddenly, nothing less looking for, young, old, poor and rich, merry and sad, prince, page, pope and poor soul priest, now one, now other, sometimes a great rabble at once, without order, without respect of age or of estate, all stripped stark naked and shifted out in a sheet, be put to death in diverse wise in some corner of the same prison, and even there thrown in an hole, and either worms eat him under ground, or crows above."[27] Here is all the classification essential to the analytical mind of the period, the tiresome enumerations which, I fear, were exciting to the audience (and More handles them with skill, always rising to a climax); the circumstantial description and rhetorical elaboration in which writers of the fifteenth and early sixteenth century excelled. But the vision is that of the Dance of Death, inviting all to join, regardless of rank. It is painted without spite and uncontaminated by that satiric malice against the friars, or even the Church itself, which detracts from the grandeur of so many late versions of the theme. Here the tragedy is universal, and Horace himself could not have been more detached.

> Golden lads and girls all must,
> As chimney-sweepers come to dust.

There is more in this picture than the mere crawling worms in the open stomachs of the putrefying corpses, known from the more lugubrious versions of the Dance of Death, and which from there invaded so many independent treatments of the subject of Death, travelling as far as the Campo Santo at Pisa, whose famous frescoes, now so tragically destroyed, in the transalpine manner represented the Petrarchan theme of the Triumph of Death, otherwise, with little regard for the text, engraved in the manner of a Roman triumph.[28] And this was a subject that More, also, had treated in his youth in a pageant of the Ages of Man and the Triumphs of Love, Death, Fame, Time, and Eternity. In the *Four Last Things*, however, with the crows pecking at the eyes of the dead—or so we may imagine them; crude cures for sensuality in a "coarse and licentious age"[29]—we remain in the world of Villon and Urs Graf.

A striking feature of the long passage quoted is the alliteration, omnipresent

in the treatise as a whole and in More's writings always. This also is derived
from the mediaeval tradition and ultimately from AElfric. More's style does
not share in the rhythmical qualities of the latter; nor does he ever fall into
the sing-song lilt of Tyndale; his prose-rhythm is always manly like that of a
father speaking to his children or a man of authority talking to his flock; but
alliteration is extensively used to bring the lesson home. In most cases it is of
the simple type of alliterative adjective and noun, like "sage saws" and "solemn
sight."[30] A little more like AElfric is the alliteration of a noun followed by its
adjuncts, like "his corpse cast out," "goods gathered together,"[31] or of a noun
or adjective and a following adverbial, like "figure for a fantasy," "present in
every place."[32] Often also co-ordinated nouns or other parts of speech are
coupled by alliteration in a manner anticipating a beloved practice of the
Elizabethans, as in "prince and page," "rolleth and reeleth."[33] Subject and
verb, verb and object, are often linked in the same way, as when "the world
wondereth,"[34] or when he "pampereth his paunch."[35] Noun and predicate
may be similarly linked, "no man is so mad";[36] auxiliary and verb, "I would
ween";[37] adverb and verb, "deadly deceive," "sunderly to send";[38] or, more
commonly, and again more like AElfric, verb and adverbial, "pour in by the
pottle";[39] adverbial and subject, "there dieth in good years great people of
gluttony";[40] adverb and object, "consider well the weight";[41] or object and
verb, "the other part we cannot perceive."[42] Means are thus plentifully provided for knitting the clauses together and for carrying on alliterative sequences beyond the immediate phrase, as in the following magnificent instance: "but carrieth his carrion corpse into the choir, and with much solemn
service burieth the body boldly at the high altar."[43]

A particularly interesting passage occurs in the paragraph on the pleasure
derived from virtue (a favourite subject for discussion in Utopia), where More
started off with the simple alliteration of the nouns: "Wonder it is that the
world is so mad," (and it is worth noting that he does not overdo it with
"wood" for "mad") "that we had liefer take sin with pain, than virtue with
pleasure."[44] But in the very next line, almost by accident as it seems, substituting "vice" for "sin," he strikes on the double alliteration: "virtue bringeth
his pleasure, and vice is not without pain." And then again a line or two further
on he cannot refrain from repeating the device in inverse order: "if virtue were
all painful, and vice all pleasant." And now that he has hit upon the trick he
goes on to "the pain of the one and the pleasure of the other." He does not
ride it to death, however, but with admirable restraint returns to the simpler
scheme in the phrase "our sin is painful and our virtue pleasant," in order to
finish up with the grandiose contrast between "eternal pain in hell" and
"eternal pleasure in heaven." Not for nothing did he learn his lesson. Immediately after this passage follows another double alliteration in the fine phrase:
"tell us worldly wretches the words of holy Writ."[45] And just before the end
he cannot refrain from playing on the letters *m* and *s* in a rather more complicated scheme: "Of the mortal sin of sloth, men make a small matter,"[46] i.e.,
m, s, s, m, m, sm, m. After such a display one is tempted to recognize an anticipation of the Baroque pattern in the very last phrase of the treatise: "even
sloth alone is able to destroy."[47]

All this is small matter, but it may serve to show on the one hand how completely absorbed More was in the English tradition, for English, like the other Germanic languages, always lent itself to alliteration and perhaps even more so in the more advanced stages with the added resources of a mixed and enlarged vocabulary; but on the other hand More's experiments show also how it was that English prose could pass so seemingly without effort from the Middle Ages into the Baroque with only the briefest possible Renaissance interlude. This phenomenon is moreover symptomatic of literature and the arts in England as well as in Germany.

More's treatise is still of the Middle Ages, as will presently appear from the application of yet another test. In pronounced opposition to the late Wilhelm Worringer's equally brilliant and deep-sounding, though, perhaps, slightly speculative analyses of style, Dr. Georg Weise had insisted on the evidence of the vocabulary.[48] More's references to classical literature and one or two classical similes prove nothing except what we knew before, i.e., that he was widely read, and it is notable that it is his vocabulary that has proved the most reliable guide to his classical reading.[49] And no more does a satirical gibe at the irascibility of women[50] establish a new connexion with the death-bed conversation of Socrates, for never was woman more satirized than during the Middle Ages, and More's little joke is entirely in the spirit of his period. More notable is the fact that his choice of words should remain equally mediaeval. There is here no "majesty," no "dignity," favourite words of the Italian Renaissance, nor the richness in vocabulary that the late Theodore Spencer noted as a feature of the thanatology of sixteenth-century English literature. Christ's passion is "painful" and "bitter," his death "piteous," in the traditional mood and the traditional vocabulary of the fifteenth century.[51] There is no word here of any victor triumphant, such as Savonarola had conceived Our Lord in his passion in the terms of a Roman emperor and as Titian handed it on to late Renaissance art.[52] More's treatise seems to belong entirely to that world of thought which conceived the *Vado Mori* poems, the *Memento Mori* verses, pictures, prints, devices, emblems, medals, jewels, rings, and rosaries —More himself, like Erasmus, possessed a Memento Mori seal[53]—the *specula hominis,* the moralities of *Everyman,* the many versions of the *Three Living and the Three Dead,* the *Ars Moriendi,* and, most formidable of all, the Dance of Death. It is the end of the Middle Ages, but it covers, with a heightened intensity, and even dominates the whole of the first half of the sixteenth century in Northern Europe. Even after that it dies but slowly, handing over, ready-made, to the Baroque its favourite ornamental skull, elaborated with cross-bones, to Bernini the symbolic caryatid skeleton of Alexander VII's monument in St. Peter's, to the Elizabethans much of the macabre apparatus of their tragedies, and to the Jacobeans lugubrious matter in plenty for their wits to play upon.[54]

A younger generation, growing up during More's life-time, could admonish defiantly, in the words of the proud Earl of Surrey:

> Contented with thine own estate,
> Ne wish for death, ne fear his might,

echoing Martial's line: "summum nec metuas diem, nec optes." And Ronsard
was to go one better. But More lived in the world of Villon and Dunbar:
"Timor mortis conturbat me."

More's treatise shares its mediaeval qualities with his contemporaries in
English literature. But there is a freshness in its homely, direct speech which
is not to be found in the imitative style of the fifteenth century. "Ah well, I
say, now ye come home, lo."[55] There are few contemporary parallels, except,
perhaps, in the sermons of St. John Fisher, of Rochester, not those preached
before the Court, but where he addresses a popular audience, and even then
he is not quite as intimate as More writing for his favourite daughter.[56] On
the other hand there are notes of bitter irony too, not found in mediaeval
literature before Villon.[57] There is a new note of cynicism in the image of the
"friends" by the bed-side of the dying man as so many "flesh-flies," (and the
image is duplicated in the "ravens about thy corpse");[58] in the "gay hearse"
and the "mourners laughing under their black hoods";[59] or the drunkard
whom More would leave "in the King's highway, that is free for every man."[60]
Altogether the stark naturalism of the description of the stinking carrions, the
dunghills, the sores, the vomits, the putrefaction in the bowels, although in
the tradition of mediaeval religious literature, possess a homely vigour which
strikes the reader as being a new element, something of which the fifteenth
century was incapable; which marks it as belonging to the beginning of the
sixteenth.

If we want to realize in what that novelty consists, we need only compare
an episode in the early fifteenth-century *Journal d'un bourgeois de Paris*[61]
with one of More's graphic descriptions, that of the Sack of Rome in his great
Dialogue concerning Heresies, written some six years after the *Four Last
Things*. The contrast is significant between the horror of the Paris burgher at
the shameless cupidity of those plunderers who would not leave as much as
the trousers of their victims, "one of the greatest cruelties," he says, "and
worst crimes against humanity that can be spoken of"; this undisguised horror
at what appears to us a comparatively minor offence, stands in relief against
More's entirely factual, grimly restrained account of the unspeakable bar-
barism and primitive cruelty of the Lance-knights, an account which leaves
nothing untold and would be impossible to read aloud in a modern lecture
room, including details from which even the most scholarly of modern
historians shrink.[62] Or, again, take a few steps in Winchester Cathedral, from
the pompous chantries of Cardinal Beaufort and William of Waynflete, who
died, the one in 1447, the other in 1486; to those of their successors in the
see, Foxe and Gardiner, deceased in 1528 and 1555, and where in the one
place the eye rests on the grand figures lying in serene state on their coffins,
it is, in the other, arrested by the miserable mummified skeleton in a low
horizontal niche in the chantry wall. The device was not as new as all that,[63]
but by 1517 or 1518 it had become so much *de rigueur* that it was imposed
even on Italian artists working in France, and one of them was forced to
adorn the rich Renaissance tomb of Louis XII and Anne of Brittany at St.
Denis with *gisants* all emaciated and withered, their empty stomachs showing

the deep slits of the embalmer's knife and the unsavoury holes made by the needle in sewing them up again.[64] If we think of the unearthly beauty and eternal youth, the serenity and bliss, of the seemingly transfigured images on the French tombs of the thirteenth century,[65] what a change is here!

Or contrast once more the sharply outlined, wrinkled and distorted faces of suffering humanity in German art of about 1500 with the idealization of the High Renaissance in Italy, and the distinction drawn by Wölfflin is vividly brought home.[66] It is possible to follow the heightening of the realism of the portraits of Jan van Eyck and the miniaturists employed by the Duc de Berry into the increasing naturalism of the later fifteenth century in Flanders, from Hugo van der Goes and Geertgen to Sint Jans to Quentin Matsys on the one hand and the Gothic fantasies of Hieronymus Bosch on the other; from the prints of Martin Schongauer in Germany to the drawings of Dürer and Holbein and the paintings of Mathias Grünewald and Niklaus Manuel Deutsch. The Gothic love of naturalistic over-emphasis on detail expresses itself clearly in the carvings of the so-called "Gotische Barock." The same mediaeval spirit is reflected in the preference for the macabre and the increasing prevalence of corpses, skulls, and snake-lined skeletons in the works of Hans Sebald Beham, Hans Burgkmair, Hans Baldung, and Urs Graf. The naturalistic portraiture, bordering on caricature, enters into the Tournay tapestries of the first decade of the sixteenth century. Nor was naturalism confined to the fine arts only. The spectators of the seasonal pageants, Passion plays, and Mysteries delighted in the undisguised naturalism of the performance of scenes of torture and execution.[67] Indulgence preachers depicted the torments of the poor souls in Purgatory in as lurid colours as possible, in order to extract money from their relatives.[68]

There is little difference of opinion concerning the origin of this naturalism in the works of the mystics, of St. Bernard, St. Bridget, Tauler, and others. Dame Julian of Norwich is an English example. It was given a medium in the vernacular when the friars had the supervision of the nunneries thrust upon them.[69] What was expected from an English preacher may be seen in the widely read *Summa Praedicantium* of Bromyard. There was now a public also, ready to listen to the friars outside the monasteries, in the prosperous burgher civilization of the later Middle Ages. But I think it is an exaggeration when German historians would explain the spread of the Macabre, and of naturalism as a whole, exclusively by reference to social conditions.[70]

One or two individual case-histories may, I think, more satisfactorily reveal some more deep-lying causes. Late in life Dürer regretfully owned himself guilty of producing in his youth "bunte und formenreiche Mahlereien ... und missgestaltete, bizarre Figuren."[71] But it was in the attempt to master the Renaissance conception of the whole that he overcame the chaos of Gothic detail in a balanced design that made those very features even more effective. He became, in Worringer's words, the martyr "dieses Zusammenpralls zweier im Grunde unverträglicher künstlerischer Ausdruckswelten," Gothic and Renaissance.[72] The conflict between these two worlds is possibly even more striking in the works of Niklaus Manuel Deutsch, the Germanic world of

devils, witches, and death, of torture and massacre, and the gay worldly finery
of the Italian Renaissance. It is a contrast, inherited from the Middle Ages and
present also in nearly all transalpine art of the period, between the cruel, ugly,
evil-looking, caricatured Christ-baiters and the patient Man of Sorrows, the
pious saints, and faithful Christians. And it is not without relevance to the solution of our problem that Mathias Grünewald should have been under the influence of the Mystics.[73] The frightful ulcers of the so-called Demon of
Leprosy, the horrible wounds everywhere covering the body of our very
Saviour in the Isenheimer Altar, the strong pathos of the attending figures, the
crowded panels: these are purely Gothic features. But whether Grünewald
himself visited Italy or not, the physical beauty of that lacerated body belongs
to the Renaissance.

   Dr. H. A. Schmid, of Bâle, has, I think, found the key to the mystery, when
in his great work on Holbein he draws attention to the fact that, deep and lasting as the Renaissance influence was on Holbein's art, it did not become effective at once. On the contrary, so far from ennobling and idealizing his forms,
his view of man became coarser after his visit to Italy. He indulges in the drawing of boorish faces and manners, knock-kneed legs like those of Urs Graf, full
forms, impossible proportions, and faulty perspectives.[74] The effect of the
direct influence of the Renaissance and of the mastery of Italian technique
was in the first instance a heightening of his Gothicism.

   The secret of Dürer's, Holbein's, Grünewald's art, which Worringer discovered in the marriage of Gothic and Renaissance and the tension produced
by that uneasy marriage, seems to me to contain the secret also of their
naturalism, and not theirs alone, but also that of Niklaus Deutsch, Urs Graf,
Albrecht Altdorfer, Hans Baldung, and the rest. In the sensuous women of
Baldung and the frivolous ones of Deutsch the Renaissance receives its full
transalpine expression, but in the greedy, grinning, mouldering skeletons,
eager to devour them, the Gothic tradition of the Dance of Death reasserts
itself. The importance of the Renaissance influence will be more easily gauged
if we remember that the only skeleton in any mural of the Dance of Death
that is at all correctly drawn is that of the Doctor at Grossbasel, and this was
entirely repainted in 1578, after Vesalius had arrived from Padua to print at
Bâle his great anatomical work *De humani corporis fabrica* with its skeletons
as life-like and as pathetic as those of Signorelli at Orvieto.[75] It was only the
progress of Renaissance science that gradually revealed the right anatomy of
the human body and so enabled the artists of Northern Europe to indulge in
fresh orgies of Gothic naturalism. Transalpine art achieves now more powerful
effects than ever before, thanks to Italian technique and the mastery of classical perfection of form.

   To return to More and the *Four Last Things,* it is not without significance
that at the end of a most repulsive description of the physical effects of gluttony he finishes with a simile drawn from "the great moral philosopher
Plutarch."[76] He relies on classical illustration to enforce his Gothic lesson,
and part of his matter was borrowed from the classics. Neither must we forget that he was the close friend of the greatest of all Humanist medical

scholars, Thomas Linacre. It was, moreover, during years of Latin authorship that More became aware of the problems of form and style, and however much in the English tradition, More's prose is enriched by the study of the classics. Erasmus tells us that in his early poetical practice in Latin More was so successful "ut prosam orationem redderet molliorem, per omne scripti genus stilum exercens."[77] Expressing himself in his own language he brought to it a new sense of form and control, acquired in the mastery of the Classics, though in later years sometimes forgotten in the heat of mediaeval argument in religious controversy.

If we look at the contemporary English authors who share in something of the same naturalism of expression, they are all in varying degrees masters of classical learning: Fisher of Rochester, Dunbar, Skelton, Lyndsay. We may trace the prelude to this eruption in the dying confessions of that seemingly Machiavellian statesman Dudley, dwelling on purely Gothic themes while lying in the Tower waiting for his execution. We may watch the preparations in the increasing taste for homely detail and neighbourly reference, a greater circumstantialism as compared with the fifteenth century, of Alexander Barclay and William Nevill. It may be pursued in the occasional successes of the early sixteenth-century satirists. But with them all classical learning is only so much added to their store of knowledge; their Humanism is a matter of taste and an approach to form; it did not change them. Persius remains their model as in the Middle Ages, not Horace as during the Renaissance proper. It is still the Gothic temper that inspires the form, and here it may not be out of place to recall Comparetti's observation how much more vivid and realistic and alive the same writer, even such a giant as Dante, could be when writing, not in Latin, but in the vernacular.[78]

Hence we do not find any naturalism in the Latin productions of the period, where the Ciceronian form was a matter of course. Erasmus has none of it. Even when he came to treat of the subject of death, as in "Charon" in the *Colloquia*, he is altogether classical,[79] with only the barest suggestion of Brant's *Narrenschiff*. Neither did the contemporary achievement of the visual arts mean anything to Erasmus, and we have his dismissal of them early, in the *Enchiridion Militis Christiani:* "No Apelles ever sketched the form and figure of a human body in such a perfect way as to compare with the mental image formed in prayer."[80] That was Erasmus's answer to what Bishop Creighton called "the heresy of the Renaissance."

More also draws such a comparison in the *Four Last Things* when he says that the Dance of Paul's "is not half so grisly as the deep conceived fantasy of death in his nature, by the lively imagination graven in thine own heart."[81] And in More's description there is that which brands it as belonging to the early sixteenth century. For whereas the Dance of Paul's, then nearly one hundred years old, still represented the universal symbol, Death had, during the intervening century, stepped out of the cloister wall and assumed individuality. By 1500, as he appears in the prints, he was a highly enterprising character, playing tricks on the living everywhere, interrupting their carousals, pushing them off their stools, cutting the leash of the blind man's dog so as to make him fall into the pit, hurling another on his back and strangling him; disguising himself in the various professions of the living, as in Holbein, and running the knight through with his lance. More's description is abreast with contemporary art.

Just at that moment, then, both art and literature, by means of the new Renaissance technique, achieve the full realization of the Gothic themes of the late Middle Ages. But if that is so, it would be legitimate to ask why it is that this comprehensive naturalist movement has not yet found its historian. The answer, or part of the answer, would be that it is only one out of the many disparate tendencies of a highly complex period. It is a tendency which appears, not in opposition to, but in conjunction, and only in conjunction with the classical influence. It is strictly tied to certain defined subject matters and is never all-embracing in its application. It is moreover the manifestation of a fleeting moment only, often of the crisis in an artist's life when Gothic and Renaissance influences are contending for his soul, and not one of them is consistently naturalistic. It is the manifestation, also, of a fleeting moment in history, before the Reformation in Germany—the real protest against "the heresy of the Renaissance"—turned men's minds away from art and learning; and, elsewhere, before the Gothic spirit succumbed to classical discipline. It is, in addition, a national manifestation—how national, a comparison between the tamed animal devils of Lucas van Leyden with the aggressive monsters of Niklaus Manuel Deutsch will show—and thus geographically limited. It might have become universal if the Reformation had not irrevocably split the unity of Christendom. Yet something remained even of this incoherent, episodic, and spasmodic movement, the language of emblems and ornament that seems as if made to order for the Baroque,[82] the subject matter for its play of wit in prose and poetry; the strong pathos and dramatic tension of which the Counter-Reformation was to avail itself; the transcendentalism which was to come to the fore so vigorously in the seventeenth century. Has not Grünewald been called the prophet of the Baroque?[83]

What applies to the fine arts during this period applies also to literature. Only a small part of More's work is naturalistic, in the contemplation of the *Four Last Things;* fragments only of Bishop Fisher's, where he turns to the mediaeval themes of death and corruption, of the Crucifixion and the bleeding wounds of Christ. Even pronouncedly national poets, like Dunbar and Sir David Lyndsay, and that most Joycian of all literary figures before Joyce, John Skelton,[84] turn naturalistic only when touched by pity for Christ's passion, or in their occasional Breughelesque attitudes. Skelton also, like John Heywood and one or two of the satirists, only in their Rabelaisian moods. But, here again, if what survived of this Gothic naturalism in painting reached its peak in Bosch and Breughel, François Rabelais is its literary executor.

The early sixteenth century is the hey-day of such manifestations. But if the above analysis is correct, it cannot be mistaken to look for similar phenomena wherever Gothic clashed with Classical, in the poetry of the Vagantes, the Carmina Burana, in the productions of what Lenient called the "opposition" ever active in the feudal state, mediaeval satire, burlesque and fabliau.[85] Would it be too bold to see something of this conflict and synthesis in the works of Boccaccio and Chaucer, Ariosto and Marguerite de Navarre, in the facetiae, "flyting" and jest-books of the sixteenth century? It is not wholly absent even from the Quattrocento. But its prime mover was undoubtedly that interest in the ugly which the late J. J. Tikkanen recognized as in a manner a protest of the Germanic sense of art against the Classicism that steadily penetrated northwards from Italy.[86]

THE EARLIER ENGLISH WORKS OF SIR THOMAS MORE

W. A. G. Doyle-Davidson

Sir Thomas More has always been dear to Englishmen. Ever since his death
he has been, despite a changed faith, a popular favourite, beloved of all for his
sweetness and nobility of character—from the Elizabethan play of *Sir Thomas
More,* in which he is celebrated as a London hero,[1] to the charming Victorian
Household of Sir Thomas More of Miss Manning. And there has been a constant
stream of biographies of More from the sixteenth century to the present day.
Not, however, that the story of his fame has been altogether simple and straightforward—for when on 6 July 1535 he died it was as a traitor on the scaffold,
and ugly stories were circulated about his cruelties to heretics. For he died in
the fiercest of all struggles, a religious quarrel—in which no quarter is given.
Lives of More were written by his friends and disciples in exile abroad: by his
son-in-law William Roper, who set down briefly his own personal reminiscences,
as material for the use of Nicholas Harpsfield, whom he commissioned to write
the first full-length biography of More; by his nephew William Rastell; and in
Latin by Thomas Stapleton. But these were Catholic Lives claiming More as a
martyr for the Faith, and could not be printed in Protestant England—with the
happy exception of Roper's short sketch which, first printed abroad, eventually
won in England a popularity which it has retained in edition after edition till
to-day. Later composite Catholic Lives, based on Roper, Harpsfield and Stapleton—one by an author who has left us only his initials, "Ro. Ba.," and another
by More's great-grandson, Cresacre More—were published, it is true, during the
eighteenth and nineteenth centuries, but the original contemporary Lives have
remained in manuscript until recently, while Rastell's *Life,* probably the fullest
of all, is lost. And the fate of More's own writings has been similar. Universally
known and admired as scholar, lawyer and statesman, More is to-day almost
entirely forgotten as a writer—except, of course, of the Latin *Utopia.* But he
wrote a good deal, principally, too, in English. The bulk of his work, however,
is Catholic controversy—undertaken against his inclination, be it remembered,
at the command of Henry VIII, and continuing the work begun by the King
himself in the book which, ironically enough, gained for him the title of Sacrae
Fidei Defensor—and this also could not be reprinted in a Protestant England.
During More's lifetime his books were nearly all printed by his nephew, William Rastell, who on his uncle's death preserved them carefully through dangerous times, taking them with him eventually into exile. The brief reign of
Mary gave him the opportunity of realising his life's ambition, and in 1557 he

Reprinted, by permission of the publisher, from *English Studies,* 17 (1935), 49–70.

published, in one of the best edited and best printed volumes of the sixteenth century, a collected edition of More's English Works, a magnificent folio which, as a memorial raised by the loving devotion of his disciples to one of the greatest of Englishmen, can be paralleled only by the First Folio of Shakespeare. And although with the death of Mary in the following year the opportunity had gone of printing either the early Lives or anything further of More's, Rastell's splendid volume sufficed to enable the discerning, from Ascham to Hallam at the beginning of the nineteenth century, to estimate justly More's importance in the history of English literature, and his reputation as a writer of English prose was high.

With the nineteenth century, however, and the spread of education, we reach a new stage in the history of More's fame. History and literature became the interest now, not of the few, but of the many—with the result that the demand for books far exceeded the supply. Copies of the few old editions of early Lives were no longer sufficiently numerous to go round, and new 'popular' Lives of More were written, in ever increasing numbers. It was a pleasant and grateful task, indeed, to retell the story of the wise and witty Chancellor whose personal charm endeared him to all with whom he came into contact, and to describe his relations with his friends all over England and the continent and with his happy household at Chelsea. But then came the difficulty of the final stage of More's career, and in their interpretation of this the biographers took their lead from the historians. Now the official historians of Protestant England, in the nineteenth century as in Elizabethan days, saw Henry VIII as a champion of religious liberty, justification of whom involved the condemnation of More. Repeating the charges of persecution, they regarded More as in later life a narrow-minded and intolerant bigot whose obstinate perversity brought down on himself the troubles which overwhelmed him; while even to the most sympathetic biographer More's death, heroic though that was, became an unfortunate mistake, to be passed over as unobtrusively as possible. Thus arose a view, prevalent to our own day, of More's career as one opening in full promise but ending in tragic failure. Side by side with this, however, from the time when the news of More's execution shocked all Europe, has persisted the Catholic view, which regards his death, not as a failure, but as a heroic and triumphant climax to a blameless life, and this claim, voiced in England by a small but steadily growing band, was recognised at long last in 1886, when More, together with his friend and companion in death, John Fisher, Bishop of Rochester, was beatified.

This is not the occasion on which to discuss the validity of the principles for which More died. That is a question which involves the whole issue between Protestant and Catholic, and, since this has not yet been settled, opinions must remain partisan: it is *aut* Henry *aut* More—one cannot be on both sides. But there is another question of a different kind, one, moreover, of interest to all admirers of More: the problem, namely, of his personal character. There are many who, while believing More a merciless bigot, are quite prepared to ignore this and to concentrate their admiration on his early promise. But such an attitude is eminently unsatisfactory. For if the charges

of persecution against More are true, then he is no hero at all, but a black-
guard and a liar, for he himself denied them. If these blemishes on his character exist, then they are serious and cannot be slurred over lightly. Happily this
is a matter not of mere subjective opinion but of objective demonstration.
For it has been the work of the twentieth century—once and for all, it is to be
hoped—to clear More's character, and to prove that the stories of persecution
and cruelty were in origin mere malicious slanders which have remained in
currency mainly owing to the fact that the genuine tradition as given by the
contemporary Lives was not known nor More's own writings generally accessible. It is evidence, too, that this is no mere partisan judgment, that it is
principally non-Catholic scholarship which has finally vindicated More and
removed the blemishes from his fair name. One likes to know, after all, that
even an adversary was an honest man. And it is cause for rejoicing, indeed, to
all Englishmen, a matter of national pride, that in May, exactly four hundred
years after his death, Blessed Thomas More is to be raised to the highest
honours of the altar, and his name, together with that of Blessed John Fisher,
to be added to the long roll of the canonised saints of the Church.

It may be of some interest, before proceeding to the discussion of some of
More's works which is the chief concern of this article, to give a summary
sketch of recent work on More and to indicate briefly his place in English
literature. For the present century, especially since the War, has seen a great
revival of interest in More, and he seems at last to be coming into his own. A
great deal has already been done, for the number of workers on More is large,
among whom, however, none have done more distinguished work than Pro-
fessors R. W. Chambers and A. W. Reed. In 1925 Prof. Reed in a notable
essay[2] emphasised More's consistency of mind, while in the following year, in
a paper read before the British Academy,[3] Prof. Chambers thoroughly investigated the whole question and completely vindicated More's character against
the historians, showing that the neglected Tudor biographies, which he calls
the 'Saga,' give us a true picture of More, the modern accounts representing a
mere Myth which is utterly contradicted by all the documentary evidence.
Prof. Chambers has also given an excellent account,[4] very inadequately sum-
marised above, of the way in which the Myth grew up. For More's biography
a first necessity has been to make accessible the early Lives. Of Roper's *Life* a
good edition has existed since 1817,[5] but a full critical edition up to modern
requirements is in preparation by Dr. Elsie V. Hitchcock, who has already published from MSS. for the first time a magnificent edition of Harpsfield's *Life,*[6]
together with the few extant fragments, relating to Fisher, of Rastell's lost
Life of More;[7] while Stapleton's *Life* has been published for the first time in
England in a translation by Mgr. P. E. Hallett.[8] The 'Saga' is thus now available.
There is, of course, no lack of modern biographies, among which the standard
Victorian biography,[9] the first to be based not only on the early Lives but also
on the official records preserved among the State Papers, is still one of the best.
Among other Catholic Lives may be mentioned those by Henry Brémond,[10]
Daniel Sargent,[11] Christopher Hollis,[11] and Joseph Clayton;[12] by non-Catholics
those of the Rev. W. H. Hutton,[13] G. R. Potter,[14] and Miss E. M. G. Routh,[15]

this last utilising the results of all the latest work on More; while a full Life by Prof. Chambers has been announced for publication[16] at Easter.

As for More's own writings—apart from their literary interest hardly less important than the early Lives for the illustration of More's consistency—the collected edition of 1557 had by the nineteenth century become scarce and its black letter difficult and tiring to the eyes of readers accustomed now to comfortable modern reprints. Yet almost alone among his contemporaries More has remained unreprinted, with the result that he has at last dropped out of English literature altogether, for in what are still our standard literary histories to-day he is ignored as a writer of English. The *Cambridge History of English Literature,* for example, says: "His fame rests chiefly on his Latin epigrams and *Utopia;* but his other work requires to be mentioned,"[17] and contents itself with a mere list of titles; Saintsbury has it that "his place in the strict History of English literature is very small, and not extraordinarily high";[18] while in anthologies of English prose he is usually represented by someone else's translation of *Utopia.* Yet More's English writings fill nearly 1500 double-column folio pages. They fall into three main groups: the earlier works; the controversial treatises, forming the greater part of his writing (over a thousand pages); and the books written in the Tower, including his last letters. Of the shorter, non-controversial pieces there were some late nineteenth-century editions, of the *Life of Picus* by J. M. Rigg[19] and of the *History of Richard III* by J. R. Lumby;[20] while of Bridgett's anthology, *The Wit and Wisdom of Sir Thomas More,* and *The Four Last Things,* edited by D. O'Connor[21] (long out of print but recently reissued) the circulation was practically restricted to Catholic circles. It may be mentioned that the best edition of *Utopia* is still that of J. H. Lupton.[22] In 1924 Prof. P. S. and Mrs. Allen published an admirable little book of Selections drawn from the whole range of More's English writings,[23] and editions of complete texts have followed, so that already all More's most important books are once more easily accessible. A complete edition of More's English Works, in the form of a facsimile of the 1557 edition accompanied by a modernised version and full critical apparatus, is in course of publication,[24] under the editorship of Mr. W. E. Campbell and Prof. A. W. Reed, and two volumes have already appeared, Vol. I (1931) containing the Earlier Works (*Poems, Life of Picus, History of Richard III,* and *Four Last Things*), Vol. II (1927) containing the *Dialogue concerning Tyndale.* The *Apology* has been very ably edited by Prof. A. I. Taft,[25] while the fine *Dialogue of Comfort against Tribulation* is available in a popular reprint in the Everyman Library.[26] A penetrating study of More's language and style has been made by Prof. J. Delcourt,[27] while the best general accounts of More's writings are to be found in Bridgett's biography and in Prof. G. P. Krapp's *Rise of English Literary Prose.*[28] At last, though must still remains to be done, we are in a position to estimate More's contribution to English literature and to appreciate his literary and linguistic importance.

It has always been difficult to explain the sudden brilliance of Elizabethan prose and drama: they seemed to have sprung from nowhere, for they could not be traced back on the one hand to such known writers as Pecock, Malory or Berners, each highly individual and of limited range, nor on the other hand, in certain important respects, directly to the mediaeval miracles and moralities. But when More is restored to his place all becomes clear: he is seen not only to fill the gap himself in a remarkable manner as the centre of an important group of writers who are restored with him, but also to bridge it, enabling the lineage of English prose to be traced beyond him into the mediaeval period. Coming at the opening of the modern period, a hundred years after Chaucer and some fifty before Shakespeare, he is an essential link between mediaeval and modern. And in his English writings there is a richness and variety of matter and style that makes the 1557 volume a worthy precursor of all the glories of the seventeenth century. More and his circle, indeed, dominate the early sixteenth century. It has recently been emphasised, for example, how great was the influence of More, an influence hitherto entirely unsuspected, on the development of the drama. For Prof. Reed has shown[29] how in early Tudor times a new imaginative drama grew up in that very household in which as a youth, as Roper tells us, More was noted for his impromptu acting, beginning with Cardinal Morton's chaplain, Henry Medwall, and continued by the Rastells and the Heywoods, close friends of More; and, while none of the *Comœdiae iuveniles* attributed to More by Pitseus are extant,[30] Prof. Reed sees his direct influence in certain of the plays of the young John Heywood, *discipulus suus familiarissimus.* And Prof. Chambers has pointed out how it is to More's own lively dialogues and 'merry tales' that we must look for the prototype of the prose dialogue of Shakespeare. Not that this is entirely More's invention, any more than it was Shakespeare's—individual originality must not be pressed too far: the important point is that, as has of late years been shown from legal records, especially the verbatim reports of witnesses, theirs was an exceptionally dramatic age, and More the lawyer, no less than Shakespeare, was in close touch with the natural drama of the life around him and had the genius to record it in permanent form. From the life of the people came the realistic prose dialogue of Shakespearean comedy and tragedy, and More anticipated it, as did also, to a smaller extent, as Dr. Owst has shown, many a mediaeval preacher. Now it is More's further importance, beyond his own literary achievement, that he makes it for the first time abundantly clear that it is in this mediaeval religious prose (and not in the prose of history, law or fiction, which, interrupted completely by the Norman Conquest, had to start all over again) that the tradition of native English prose continued unbroken—and it goes right back, in fact, to its fountain-head in the Anglo-Saxon prose of AElfric, Alfred, and the *Chronicle.* And this native prose, continuing through the *Ancren Riwle* via the fourteenth-century mystics to More, is a thoroughly workmanlike vehicle of expression, simple and clear, and without any artificial literary adornments that would limit its usefulness: it is, in a word, the easy, natural prose that is represented later by Dryden and Bunyan, Swift and Addison and Steele. All which necessitates in our histories of literature an important new chapter, on the Age of More—a chapter that has already, indeed, been written most eloquently by Prof. Chambers.[31]

The great 1557 volume of More's Works opens, not with prose, but with

four poems written by More "in his youth for his pastime" and by a happy
thought included by Rastell at the last minute, after the rest of the book had
been set up. The first, *A Merry Jest how a Sergeant would learn to play the
Friar,* composed probably, as Prof. Reed suggests, for the Sergeants' Feast of
November 1503 at which his father was elected one of the Sergeants-at-law—
when, that is, he was twenty-five—introduces us at once to that lively sense of
good-natured fun that characterised More all his life, from the time when, as
a boy of thirteen or fourteen in Cardinal Morton's house, he would, as Roper
says, "at Christmastide suddenly sometimes step in among the players and,
never studying for the matter, make a part of his own there present amongst
them, which made the lookers-on more sport than all the players beside,"
till on the scaffold he uttered his last jests; while, again characteristic of More,
the simple 'moral'—that men should stick to their own business—is serious:

> When a hatter
> Will go smatter
>   In philosophy,
> Or a pedlar
> Wax a meddler
>   In theology:
> All that ensue
> Such craftès new
>   They drive so far a cast
> That evermore
> They do therefor
>   Beshrew themselves at last.

The poem tells of the unsuccessful attempt of a law-officer (the Tudor
policeman) to arrest a debtor by entering his house disguised as a friar. It begins with an introductory section in which is stated the 'moral' to be illustrated, and then follows a lively picture of the young spendthrift who, having
run through his patrimony, has got into debt and to avoid arrest is reduced to
lying low at a friend's house, shamming sickness. The action proper does not
begin till nearly halfway through the poem, with plans for the debtor's arrest.
An officer, called in by one of the creditors, promises to capture him and, in
order to effect this, exchanges clothes with a friar and practises his part. Then
the "fained friar" calls on the debtor and, convincing the servant who opens
the door, is shown upstairs. Greetings are exchanged and then, as soon as the
maid has retired, the officer throws off his disguise and proclaims his errand.
The catastrophe is swift—and unexpected: for the debtor shows fight and
lays about him lustily till both are struggling on the floor, when "the maid
and wife," hearing the clamour, come up and join in, and together they throw
the sergeant, "well nigh slain," headlong down the stairs, with a parting shot
of "Commend us to the Mayor!" A brief epilogue, repeating the moral, ends
with a welcome to the feast. Though only a light piece of fooling, mere knock-
about comedy, this little poem shows already More's gift of vivid storytelling,
his easy fluency, and his admirable sense of form.

Many have noted the striking contrasts in More's character, his hearty interest in the world side by side with a constant preoccupation with the spiritual, the rival attractions of learning and faith, law and philosophy, matrimony and the cloister all finely balanced in the man of the world who was also a saint. And this contrast we find in him from his earliest years—even at his merriest he is always serious. This essential seriousness of More's nature is fully brought out in the three remaining poems, the common theme of which is the vanity of earthly things. The first of these is a set of verses for a "goodly hanging of fine painted cloths" he had "in his youth devised in his father's house." There were nine "pageants" or scenes: Childhood, Manhood, Venus and Cupid (or Love), Age, Death, Fame, and Eternity, each in turn being overcome by its successor and the poet finally pointing the moral in twelve Latin elegiacs. Here is Childhood:

> I am called Childhood, in play is all my mind,
> To cast a quoit, a cock-steel or a ball;
> A top can I set, and drive it in his kind—
> But would to God these hateful bookès all
> Were in a fire burnt to powder small!
> Then might I lead my life always in play,
> Which life God send me to my ending day

a vignette which may well be placed with the schoolboys of Shakespeare and Blake.

The third poem, perhaps More's best, is a moving Elegy on the death in 1503 of Elizabeth of York, Henry VII's Queen, of great historical interest for its references to Henry's recent rebuilding of the palace at Richmond and to the newly begun Henry VII Chapel at Westminster—to which and to her husband, her children, and her people in turn the dead Queen is represented as saying farewell, each stanza ending with the touching refrain "For lo, now here I lie"—

> O ye that put your trust and confidence
> In worldly joy and frail prosperity,
> That so live here as ye should never hence:
> Remember death and look here upon me.

The last poem consists of "certain metres" written to be prefixed to the *Book of Fortune,* an ingenious and amusing fortune-telling book so popular that no copy earlier than 1618 has survived the constant handling to which it was subjected. Here the best part is that in which More warns "them that trust in Fortune," especially the passage beginning with the fine stanza:

> And first upon thee lovely shall she smile
> And friendly on thee cast her wandering eyes,
> Embrace thee in her arms and for a while
> Put thee and keep thee in a fool's paradise;
> And forthwithal, whatso thou list devise[32]

> She will thee grant it liberally perhaps—
> But for all that beware of afterclaps.

The *Merry Jest* is in the energetic short-lined rhyming doggerel[33] of the sort that one associates most readily with the name of Skelton, but the others are all in More's favourite rhyme-royal stanza.[34] Now when we consider the parlous state of English metre in More's day, in the unsettled interval between Chaucer and the Elizabethans, and remember that even in the following generation, with Wyatt and Surrey, the metre is still often halting and uncertain, More's verse, though at times awkward and hesitating, frequently, as in the stanza just quoted, moves surprisingly surely and smoothly.

However, noteworthy both for their matter and metre as these poems are, they possess the further interest of forming part of the literary apprenticeship of a prose-writer. Verse is an excellent discipline, its regular rhythms serving as a good introduction to the more varied rhythms of prose. Thus it is from verse that More learns the rhythmical value of the word-pair and the balance given by what we may call the adjective-and-noun pair, both illustrated in the already-quoted opening lines of the Elegy:

> O ye that put your *trust and confidence*
> In *worldly joy and frail prosperity,*

and of frequent occurrence throughout the poems; while verse also gave More practice in confining the expression of a complete thought symmetrically within the compass of a single line or couplet. Hence his tendency to concise, epigrammatic expression and to the proverbial which we shall find to be a feature of his prose. So, for example, Fortune's

> Without good hap there may no wit suffice:
> Better is to be fortunate than wise

and, in More's answer to her,

> The head that late lay easily and full soft
> Instead of pillows lieth after on the block

and

> None falleth far but he that climbeth high.

We meet already here, too, another feature that becomes more striking later in his prose, what Prof. Reed calls the "quality of quantity of content,"[35] seen in his fondness for agglomerations that indicate a richly stocked imagination, as, for example, in the opening stanza of Fortune's tempting words "to the people":

> Mine high *estate, power and authority*
> If ye ne knew, ensearch and ye shall spy
> That *riches, worship,*[36] *wealth and dignity,*
> *Joy, rest and peace,* and all things finally
> That any pleasure or profit may come by

To man's *comfort, aid and sustenance,*
Is all at my device and ordinance

where we may note also, besides the word-pairs, the use of the triplet. Most striking, however, as illustrating this richness of More's mind is the stanza quoted by Prof. Reed in which are pictured the grim companions of Lady Fortune:

Fast by her side doth weary Labour stand,
Pale Fear also, and Sorrow all bewept,
Disdain and Hatred on that other hand,
Eke restless Watch with sleep from travail kept,
His eyes drowsy and looking as he slept;
Before her standeth Danger and Envy,
Flattery, Deceit, Mischief and Tyranny

a stanza which, as Bridgett says, "might have been written by Spenser or by Gray."[37]

Erasmus tells us of More: "His first years were given to poetry. Then for a long while he exerted himself to acquire a flexible prose style, making experiments in every kind,"[38] and we may therefore regard his apprenticeship in writing as being further continued in the next three items in the 1557 volume, even though the last of these is dated 1522, when More was forty-four, for he commenced author comparatively late, the great bulk of his writings belonging to the six crowded years of his fifties.

His first prose work is the *Life of John Picus, Earl of Mirandula,* the remarkable young Italian humanist whom, as a layman who put devotion before learning, More when a young man took for a pattern in life. The *Life* is translated closely, except for a few appropriate and well-managed omissions[39] and for two characteristic additions, from the Latin of Pico's nephew, and is followed by translations of three of Pico's letters and his 'Interpretation' of Psalm xv and by expanded verse-renderings of certain short prose apophthegms: the Twelve Rules of Spiritual Warfare, the Twelve Weapons of a Christian Soldier, and the Twelve Conditions of a Lover—the whole forming an attractive little book of semi-devotional reading which More dedicated to Joyce Leigh (or Lee), Minoress at Aldgate and a childhood friend.

The verses, which we may consider first, form the last third of the book, and are for the most part original poems by More on the themes suggested by Pico's aphorisms, More developing the subjects in his own way. There are some fine single lines:

To the most odious and vile death of a tree ...

To vile carrion and wretched wormès meat ...

But only faithful heart and loving mind

and, of life:

But fast it runneth on and passen shall
As doth a dream or shadow on the wall[40]

while the proverbial sounds in:

> For he that loveth peril shall perish therein.
> Perilous is the canker that catcheth the bone.
> Nothing impossible is that hath been done.

The Third Rule of Spiritual Warfare More versifies as follows:

> Consider well that folly it is and vain
> To look for heaven with pleasure and delight:
> Since Christ, our Lord and sovereign captain
> Ascended never but by manly fight
> And bitter passion—then were it no right
> That any servant, ye will yourself record,
> Should stand in better condition than his lord.

Other striking stanzas are that on the peace of a good mind, with its eighteenth-century final couplet:

> Why lovest thou so this brittle worldès joy?
> Take all the mirth, take all the fantasies,
> Take every game, take every wanton toy,
> Take every sport that men can thee devise—
> And among them all, on warrantise,
> *Thou shalt no pleasure comparable find*
> *To th'inward gladness of a virtuous mind.*

and, apart, for modern ears, from the last word of the first line, the moving:

> When thou in flame of the temptation friest
> Think on the very lamentable pain,
> Think on the piteous cross of woeful Christ,
> Think on His blood beat out at every vein,
> Think on His precious heart carvèd in twain,
> Think how for *thy* redemption all was wrought:
> Let Him not lose thee that He so dear hath bought.

More translates Pico's Twelve Conditions of a Lover and then expands them in a poem throughout which, giving two stanzas to each 'property,' he contrasts human with divine love. These are the opening lines:

> The first point is to love but one alone
> And for that one all others to forsake,
> *For whoso loveth many loveth none . . .*

again neat and epigrammatic; while the best stanza is perhaps the following:

> Diversely passioned is the lover's heart:
> Now pleasant hope, now dread and grievous fear,
> Now perfect bliss, now bitter sorrow smart;
> And whether his love be with him or elsewhere
> Oft from his eyes there falleth many a tear—

> For very joy, when they together be;
> When they be sundered, for adversity.

The book closes with a twelve-stanza Prayer of Pico's that once again is more More's than his model's. It is a fine poem, eloquent and dignified, expressing well More's own sincere piety:

> O holy God of dreadful majesty,
> Verily one in three and three in one,
> Whom angels serve, Whose work all creatures be,
> Which heaven and earth directest all alone:
> We Thee beseech, good Lord, with woeful moan,
> Spare us wretches and wash away our guilt
> That we be not by Thy just anger spilt.
>
> In strait balance of rigorous judgment
> If Thou shouldst our sin ponder and weigh,
> Who able were to bear Thy punishment?
> The whole engine of all this world, I say,
> The engine that enduren shall for ay,
> With such examination might not stand
> *Space of a moment in Thine angry hand.*

However, though his poems, as these quotations show, are by no means lacking in power and inspiration, More realised that his true medium was prose, and he wrote no more verse till, his work finished and his troubles nearly over, he composed two short 'ballads,' as Rastell says, "for his pastime while he was prisoner in the Tower."

To return to the *Life,* when he set out 'to acquire a flexible style,' More wisely began with translation, and this earliest prose of his has all the technical interest of a conscious stylistic exercise. Here we can see how his own naturally simple and straightforward English gains from the balance and antithesis of the Latin and added dignity and grace, though it is nowhere over-Latinised. Mostly he translates literally, and the fine balance, for example, of "a deadly wound to the soul and a mortal poison to charity" results directly from *letale vulnus animæ venenumque charitatis mortiferum.* The word-pair[41] occurs already in the Latin, and More adopts it readily, rendering *odisse ... et detestari* by "hated and abhorred," *officia et dignitates* by "offices and dignities"; though he does not hesitate, when the rhythm gains by it, to render single Latin words by English word-pairs, translating *petitas* by "picked and sought out," *contueri* by "behold and consider," *dogmata* by "lessons and instruction," *aculeos* by "twitches and pangs," and *dominandi curis* by "the charge and business of rule or lordship," while, with the addition of adjectives, *benignitas et gratia* becomes "the great benignity and singular courtesy," *viribus aut fortunis* "strength of body or goods of fortune," and *immensa dei bonitate* "the especial provision and singular goodness of almighty God"; though, *vice versa,* he is also for the same reason ready at times to suppress one of two Latin words, rendering *turmatim ac coacervatim* simply "by heaps," *voluptate et illecebris* by "pleasure," *eliminandis explodendisque* by "extermination."

The translation is marked especially by one of More's most striking gifts, that of felicitous phrasing: he always has the right word, just as difficult to find in translation as in original writing. Thus many of the most vivid and picturesque phrases are translated direct from the Latin: "in the chief city of the world" representing *in prima orbis urbe*, "the crooked hills of delicious pleasure" *devios mollitudinis voluptariae anfractus*, "converted to the way of justice from the crooked and ragged path of voluptuous living" *converso ad justitiae semitas ex distorto et obliquo libidinum calle*, and "somewhat besprent with the freckle of negligence" *incuriositatis naevo macularetur*; though the effect is often secured by judicious and usually slight changes and additions: small alterations are "in rest and peace" for *in alta pace* and "travail and watch" for *vigiliae reconditae*, while somewhat more considerable changes are "the voluptuous broad way *that leadeth to hell*" for *mollem illam et spatiosam* multorum *viam*, and the finely balanced "more meet for secret communication of learned men than for open hearing of common people" for *non passim vulganda triviis sed secreto congressu inter doctos et paucos disputanda*.

More is also fond of alliteration, which occurs frequently in his verse, and which in the prose of the *Picus* he manages to achieve in both its simple and cross forms with a minimum departure from strict literal translation. Thus *ad captandam vulgi auram atque imperitorum applausum* he neatly renders by "to win the *f*avour of the *c*ommon people and the *c*ommendation of *f*ools" (f c c f), while with a trifling addition *captiunculas cavillaque sophistarum* becomes "*c*aptious *s*ubtleties and *c*avillations of *s*ophistry" (c s c s). A more complex example of cross or chain alliteration occurs in the translation of Pico's Interpretation of Psalm xv: "many *v*oluptuous *p*leasures, many *v*ain *d*esires, many *d*iverse *p*assions" (v p, v d, d p), from which it may be seen how More uses alliteration, not only for emphasis, but also as a link, to carry a sentence forward and at the same time hold its parts together.

It is in the *Picus* that we find More's first original prose—in the Dedication; in a notable and characteristic passage on honour and ancestry which he works in at the beginning of the *Life*,[42] and in one or two other small additions, including three short paragraphs introductory to the Letters. From the Dedication, which is in the same careful and balanced style as the rest of the translation, may be illustrated most of the rhythmical elements of this formal, studied prose:

> It is, and of long time hath been, my well-beloved sister, a custom in the beginning of the New Year, friends to send between presents or gifts, as the witnesses of their love and friendship, and also signifying that they desire to each other that year a good continuance and prosperous end of that lucky beginning. But commonly all those presents that are used customably all in this manner between friends to be sent, be such things as pertain only unto the body, either to be fed or to be clad or some other wise delighted—by which it seemeth that their friendship is but fleshly and stretcheth in manner to the body only. But forasmuch as the love and amity of Christian folk

should be rather ghostly friendship than bodily, since that all faithful people are rather spiritual than carnal (for as the apostle saith: "We be not now in flesh, but in spirit, if Christ abide in us"), I therefore, mine heartily beloved sister, in good luck of this New Year have sent you such a present as may bear witness of my tender love and zeal to the happy continuance and gracious increase of virtue in your soul; and whereas the gifts of other folk declare that they wish their friends to be worldly fortunate, mine testifieth that I desire to have you godly prosperous. These works, more profitable than large, were made in Latin by one John Picus, Earl of Mirandula, a lordship in Italy, of whose cunning[43] and virtue we need here nothing to speak, forasmuch as hereafter we peruse the course of his whole life, rather after our little power slenderly than after his merits sufficiently. The works are such that truly, good sister, I suppose of the quantity there cometh none in your hand more profitable, neither to the achieving of temperance in prosperity, nor to the purchasing of patience in adversity, nor to the despising of worldly vanity, nor to the desiring of heavenly felicity—which works I would require you gladly to receive, ne were it[44] that they be such that for the goodly matter (howsoever they be translated) may delight and please any person that hath any mean[45] desire and love to God, and that yourself is such one as for your virtue and fervent zeal to God cannot but joyously receive anything that meanly[45] soundeth either to the reproach of vice, commendation of virtue, or honour and laud of God—Who preserve you.

Here occur the word-pair, whether of synonyms or of words similar in meaning ("presents or gifts," "love and friendship," "love and amity," "love and zeal," "delight and please," "desire and love," "honour and laud"); larger rhythmical units such as the adjective-and-noun pair ("good continuance and prosperous end," "happy continuance and gracious increase") and the triplet phrase ("either to the reproach of vice, commendation of virtue, or honour and laud of God"); while balance and antithesis combine in "whereas the gifts of other folk declare that they wish their friends to be *worldly fortunate,* mine testifieth that I desire to have you *godly prosperous*" and "rather after our little power slenderly than after his merits sufficiently"; and finally, balance on an extended scale is attained in "neither to the achieving of temperance in *p*rosperity nor to the *p*urchasing of *p*atience in adversity, nor to the *d*espising of worldly vanity nor to the *d*esiring of heavenly felicity," which consists of two differently built pairs of three-beat phrases, each pair being further linked by unobtrusive alliteration and all four phrases ending with a word in -*ity* at a sufficient distance from the others to avoid an unpleasant jingle.

More's second prose book is the *History of King Richard the Third,* the only one of his English writings that has long been accessible and thus the best known, and yet by an irony of fate—on a late and trifling doubt and against the strongest contemporary evidence, as has lately been conclusively shown by Prof. Chambers[46]—nowadays generally denied him. Justly celebrated from Ascham down to modern times, it is the first great piece of modern English historical writing. After More's execution it found its way, at first anonymously, into the current histories, where, even in a garbled version[47] standing out vivid and dramatic among the dull, mechanical compilations in which it was embedded, it arrested, it will be remembered, the attention of Shakespeare. Saintsbury, however, will have it that the *Richard III,* whether it be More's or not, has been "much overpraised,"[48] but when one remembers that the tradition of English historical prose was completely interrupted by the Norman Conquest, being replaced by Latin, and when it started again in the fifteenth century did so with an inferiority-complex about the poverty of the English language, *Richard III,* compared with the contemporary chronicles, mere collections of facts stilted and pretentious in style, remains an achievement sufficiently notable to arouse wonder. It is "a deliberately designed and carefully finished whole,"[49] and in its interpretation of events in the light of human character, its method is essentially modern.

It opens with the death of Edward IV, and a fine character sketch of that king gives the clue to the political situation at the end of his reign. Then, says More, speaking of Richard, then Duke of York: "But forasmuch as this Duke's demeanour ministreth in effect all the whole matter whereof this book shall entreat, it is therefore convenient somewhat to show you ere we farther go, what manner of man this was that could find in his heart so much mischief to conceive," and there follows a masterly, though partisan, portrait of the man on whom the whole action hinges. For More's tale is the story of the plotting and treachery that led up to Richard's crowning and the murder of the little Princes, and, though unfinished, the catastrophe is powerfully sketched. After the introductory character sketches More relates how Richard, taking advantage of the "long-continued grudge and heartburning between the Queen's kindred and the King's blood" whom in a moving deathbed speech Edward IV made a last vain attempt to reconcile, under cover of this animosity makes his first two moves in the five-act drama. The young Prince being on his father's death in Wales, with the Earls Rivers and Grey, relations of the Queen, Richard with every show of loyalty persuades the Queen to have him brought to London immediately "with a sober[50] company," and his first act is to meet the Prince on the way and, arresting Rivers and Grey (which suits the King's party well enough), thus to obtain custody of the young heir to the throne. Whereupon the Queen, in great dismay, takes sanctuary at Westminster with her younger son. With the further support of the King's party, especially of Lord Hastings and the Duke of Buckingham, Richard, as the children's uncle, is made Protector, and, realising that until he has both the Princes in his power he cannot prosecute his own plans, he next, with the same show of loyalty, persuades the Council "that it was a heinous deed of the Queen, and proceeding of great malice towards the King's Counseliors, that she should keep in sanctuary the King's brother from him, whose special pleasure and comfort it were to have his brother with him—and that by her done to none other intent than to bring all the lords in obloquy and murmur of the people," adding that if the Queen resists there can be no objection to taking the Prince away, as he stands in no need of sanctuary (the privileges of which anyhow, says Buckingham, are much abused). An embassy, led by the Archbishop of Canterbury, is sent to the Queen, who, though she understands the Protector's designs well enough, realises that she cannot prevent him from taking her son and so surrenders him to the care of the Archbishop. Successful so far, Richard has now to proceed warily. He takes Buckingham into his confidence and gets his full support, and then, fearing Hastings' loyalty, picks a sudden quarrel with him and has him summarily executed on Tower Green. To justify his action he issues a Proclamation charging Hastings with treason, which does not succeed, however, in completely allaying suspicion. More then passes on to the Protector's treatment of Jane Shore, Edward IV's mistress, of whom he gives a very sympathetic account, which leads easily to a discussion of King Edward's marriage. For Richard's next step is to arrange for a sermon to be preached at Paul's Cross alleging the illegitimacy of the Princes and proclaiming himself the true heir to the throne. This being unfavourably received, for suspicion is now rife, the arguments are repeated by Buckingham to a 'packed' meeting at the Guildhall, and on the following day a deputation offers the crown to Richard, who has to be 'persuaded' to accept it. He is crowned, and his coronation opens the final act: as More says, "Now fell there mischiefs thick." For there follows the murder of the Princes in the Tower, after which Richard "never had quiet in his mind" but went about haunted and suspicious, till two years later he fell at Bosworth against Henry Richmond. More relates how he quarrelled with Buckingham, whom Cardinal Morton urged to rise against the tyrant, and in the middle of a conversation between the two his account breaks off.

More's is a dramatic story, full of colour and movement, in which what is most remarkable is the variety of treatment. Besides the character sketches (of Edward IV, Richard, Hastings, Morton, etc., and the unforgettable portrait of the unfortunate Jane Shore), there is the main narrative, a series of vivid pictures (Richard's treachery at Stony Stratford and the Queen's midnight flight into sanctuary; the great scene of Richard's quarrel with Hastings and the latter's execution; Edward IV's marriage; and the murder of the Princes), diversified by eloquent set speeches (that of Edward IV on his deathbed; Buckingham's discourse on sanctuaries and the Queen's reply to the Protector's embassy—both good pieces of argument; Shaw's sermon and Buckingham's Guildhall oration) and brisk dialogue (the Richard-Hastings quarrel, Buckingham and Morton), this especially in the many little incidental details—anecdotes and illustrations—that give weight and reality to a narrative and whose dramatic value Shakespeare fully appreciated (Pottyer's midnight visitor on the death of Edward IV; the story of the Bishop of Ely's strawberries; Lord Stanley's dream; Hastings' meetings with the priest and the pursuivant; the schoolmaster's comment on the Proclamation; the Recorder of London; Richard's page; etc.); while through it all, in touches of humour and irony,[51] and especially in its moralising tone (as particularly, for example, in the account of Hastings' premonitions and in the comments on the misfortunes of Jane Shore), sounds More's own voice, for he makes this indeed, as Prof. Chambers has said, almost a sermon against ambition.

More began, in the *Picus*, with translation from Latin, and it is interesting to watch his progression here, for of the *Richard III* he wrote both an English and a Latin version. The Latin text, from which Rastell translated three short passages to fill gaps in the MS. of the English, was published at Louvain in 1565, the year of Rastell's death, in an edition of More's Latin Works probably prepared by him for the press.[52] The Latin version is shorter than the English, ending with Richard's coronation. It is difficult to say which was written first, though the internal evidence would seem to indicate that More was working on both versions simultaneously, writing here a passage first in Latin, here one first in English. Each version, in fact, in spite of their closeness, reads like an original, and there is an interesting series of small differences. To quote what I have written elsewhere: "It is easy to see why More should make some changes. He was writing the English for his own countrymen, but the Latin would be addressed to the wider public of the Continent, among whom he had many friends. This in itself is sufficient to account for a certain difference in method. The English is more detailed and particular, while the Latin, shorn of some of the accidents of time and place, is more general. For example, in the English dates and local names are given, and other details, as of costume, besides illustrations and anecdotes. In the Latin these are omitted—for the names of outlying villages unknown to the foreigner is substituted merely their distance from London;[53] and other instances of a like nature might be cited. On the other hand, also for the benefit of strangers, the Latin has explanatory comments on English institutions,[54] besides other small additions[55] and expansions—in all more or less equalling in bulk the passages contained only in the English. Again, as would be expected, there is practically no direct speech in the Latin, passages in which it occurs in the English usually being omitted entirely. It would be dangerous to attempt to assign a reason for every variation, but many would be quite sufficiently accounted for by the writer occasionally letting his pen run on in one of the versions according as a particular topic was easier to develop in that tongue."[56] The *Richard III*, in its two versions, represents a unique and attractive experiment.

The careful, balanced style of the *Picus* is in the more ambitious *Richard III*, as befits its high theme, expanded into a stately historical style rising at times to the grand manner and varied by More's simple, direct *English* style, often admirably compact and concise.[57] More makes here full use of all the devices to which attention has already been called in the Verses and the *Picus*. So the word-pair, often alliterative, in all its variations,[58] and the less frequent triplet,[59] are employed to secure balance in long sounding sentences and massive paragraphs, and there is much alliteration, both simple and cross, used with excellent effect for emphasis and to link clause with clause.[60] The epigrammatic and proverbial abound,[61] and there are some similes[62] and a single pun.[63] Here, in fact, are all the elements of Euphuism, though it is important to stress the fact that though when collected together the list of these literary devices is a formidable one, with More they never become mere mechanical artifices, repeated *ad nauseam*. He uses them, not, like Lyly later, for their own sake and to excess, but restrainedly, to vary and colour his prose, and so successfully, indeed, does he conceal the stylistic process that it is possible for a critic who has read More carefully to say: "But even in his more literary moments, he is not manneristic. All such tricks of style as alliteration, the use of doublets ... he consistently avoids"[64]—which, though not literally exact, is certainly true in so far as More never lets them become mere tricks.

From *Richard III*, written about 1513, when More was Under-Sheriff of London, we pass to the *Four Last Things*, written in 1522, when More was forty-four. Six years previously, in 1516, on the eve of reluctantly entering the King's service, he had published, in a form half jest, half earnest (as was ever his wont), his protest against the new statesmanship and new economics of the day: the *Utopia;* and now, amid the splendours of the Court, to which, as Erasmus says, he had been dragged, he wrote, for himself and his family, a meditation on the text *Memorare novissima et in æternum non peccabis.*

"What would a man give," says More, "for a sure medicine that were of such strength that it should all his life keep him from sickness?"—yet here to hand, he says, is "a short medicine containing only four herbs, common and well known, that is to wit, Death, Doom, Pain and Joy, ... able to keep us all our life from sin" and preserve our soul to everlasting health. And if it be said that this 'medicine' is "bitter and painful to receive," that is not so, for, though even if it were so it would still be worth it, actually these four things are not so unpleasant as they might seem. We are asked, after all, he says, not to take them, but only to remember them, and yet have "the joy of heaven therewith to temper them withal." And to the objection that "the bare remembrance of death alone ... were able to bereave a man of all the pleasure of his life" and that much more painful, then, must be "the deep imagination of the dreadful doom of God and bitter pains of purgatory or hell, of which every one passeth and exceedeth many deaths," he replies that these are but the arguments of those who have not tried it. For in the "operation and working" of this medicine the pleasure of life is not lost but marvellously increased, indeed—for there is a spiritual pleasure beside which all earthly delight is "but a false counterfeit image." But our appreciation of this is hindered by our infected taste: "our soul can have no place for the good corn of spiritual pleasure as long as it is overgrown with the barren weeds of carnal delectation. For the pulling out of which weeds by the root there is not a more meet instrument than the remembrance of the four last things." And in support of his claim that even in this present life there is in spiritual exercise "very sweetness, comfort, pleasure and gladness," he invokes the testimony of saints and martyrs to the joy to be found even in suffering and pain.

After this introduction More passes to the "remembrance of death"—its pains[65] and accompanying troubles[66] and temptations;[67] and then, noting that though while we are well we cannot easily be brought to a full realisation of the imminence of death (no stranger but a "nigh neighbour")—for "so is there none old man so old but that, as Tully[68] saith, he trusteth to live one year yet"—yet "commonly when we be sick then begin we to know ourselves" and therefore the quintessence of all philosophy is to be "such when we be whole as we think we will be when we be sick," he draws a picture of "all our whole life" as "a sickness never curable," for meat and drink are but medicines

and sleep a swoon, "the very image of death." Then he proceeds to the contemplation of death as a help against the deadly sins, of which he treats five,
Pride, Envy, Wrath, Covetousness and Gluttony, and just begins the sixth,
Sloth, there breaking off, for he did not get beyond the first part of his subject, the meditation of death.

Although a mere sketch, unfinished and unrevised, the *Four Last Things*
is the most intimate and powerful of More's writings. Death is a favourite subject with the preachers of all ages, but this little treatise stands apart as the
work of a layman. Intent on bringing home to his fellow man-in-the-street
that it is no mere academic question he is treating but a problem of the utmost
urgency to each and every one of us, he relies not so much on argument to
convince as on illustration, and his essay is a succession of vivid pictures,
startling in their realism. He was never so grim as in this treatise, and his descriptions of the deathbed scene and of "gorbellied gluttony,"[69] for example,
are almost revolting in their detail. But he is not morbid, for there is throughout the leaven of his humour and a mordant irony reminiscent at times of
Swift or Donne. No cloistered spirit, but a man of the world playing his own
part in the great pageant of life, he draws examples from actual occurrences.
Already in his early Verses he had sounded warnings of the treachery of Fortune, and in *Richard III* he had lingered, in the story of Hastings, on the
irony of fate and "the vain surety of man's mind so near his death," and also
on the pathos of the death of the little Princes; and here, in the sketch of "the
fall of a great Duke,"[70] he refers with topical and impressive appropriateness
to the execution in the previous year of the Duke of Buckingham, which had
much affected him. Other illustrations, for his method is above all practical,
are from everyday life, "homely examples"—that of the thief at Newgate
"that cut a purse at the bar when he should be hanged on the morrow; and
when he was asked why he did so, knowing that he should die so shortly, the
desperate wretch said that it did his heart good to be lord of that purse one
night yet"; and especially the extended comparison in which More likens the
world to a prison and all men to prisoners condemned to death and "already
in the cart, carrying forward."

In the *Four Last Things* More is in deep earnest, fully preoccupied with
his subject, and his style is accordingly, as Prof. Reed says, "homely, direct,
almost brutally frank." He gains his effect, not from the neatness and precision of balanced phrases, but from the sheer overpowering piling up of detail
upon detail, in those "agglomerated passages" which, occurring occasionally
in the *Richard III*—in the accounts of the Queen's flight into sanctuary,[71] of
the murder of the little Princes,[72] and of Richard's last years[73]—are here the
rule.[74]

The *Four Last Things* marks the end of More's apprentice period and completes the group of what may be called his Earlier Works. Writing in an age
which saw a rebirth of English prose and the first attempts at the cultivation
of a literary style, we see More here consciously experimenting in the technique
of writing. In the *Picus* and the *Richard III* we see the invaluable lessons he
learnt from Latin for the shaping of his English style, and can appreciate his

sanity of judgment and strength of will in refusing to be led astray by the attractions, fatal for so many a later writer, of the various literary figures and devices of which he showed here his easy mastery. For he realised that English is not Latin, and his feeling for the rhythms and sentence-forms of the vernacular reveals itself in the rapid, nervous English of the *Four Last Things*, which he was to develop into the easy, straightforward, idiomatic style that distinguishes his later books. Attention has been centred here chiefly on the technical aspects of his earlier pieces, though their interest even from this point of view has by no means been exhausted. Apart from style one may note already in these four items, comprising verse, biography, history and homily, More's wide range of subject. On another occasion it may be possible to discuss the great books of his prime.

THE DRAMATIC STRUCTURE OF SIR THOMAS MORE'S
HISTORY OF KING RICHARD III

Arthur Noel Kincaid

Despite the growing acceptance and appreciation in this century of More's *History of King Richard III* as a literary work, and More as an author of great stylistic brilliance, the dramatic aspect of his writings has been all but ignored and never carefully and systematically studied. In *The History of King Richard III*, More's use of the dramatic approach in his writings reaches its culmination. The structure of this work is essentially founded upon a dramatic conceit, and it is subtly through this dramatic structure that More makes clear the moral intention of the *History*. So closely woven together and so completely inter-dependent are all the various aspects of the work that without an understanding of its dramatic nature, neither its literary structure nor its moral purpose can be properly comprehended. Failure to view the *History* from this angle has led to centuries of misinterpretation and to insufficient appreciation of its value as a work of art.

Although of all the Tudor histories, Sir Thomas More's *History of King Richard III* is the only one which can claim a place in the front rank of literary masterpieces, it has for some inexplicable reason found limited renown in this capacity. What fame it has found has sprung rather from the failure or refusal of scholars to comprehend its literary nature and their consequent acceptance of it as the main historical source for the period it covers. However, the literary techniques and intentions of the work are so prevalent as considerably to over-shadow any historical value it may have and should disqualify it as much from unquestioned acceptance as a historical source as the dramatic medium dis-qualifies Shakespeare's play. It is one of those brilliant character studies of which C. V. Wedgwood says: "To ask whether they are true accounts of the people whose names they carry is irrelevant. The poetic truth is too effective to be challenged by mere historical truth."[1]

Despite the praise which important critics in every century have accorded its literary merits, as R. W. Chambers points out in his numerous works on More,[2] it is an extraordinary fact that the literary quality of this work has been all but ignored. In this century there have been a few analyses of More's literary style, both English and Latin, in the *History*,[3] prompted partly by the doubt regarding its authorship, and partly in recognition of More's unique position as a linguistically adept author who stands at the transitional point

Reprinted, by permission of the author and publisher, from *Studies in English Literature*, 12 (1972), 223–42.

between medieval and modern prose, and whose genius in manipulating a rapidly developing language looks forward to Shakespeare's complete realization of this language's potential. More's is an ingenious, inventive, and hence individual style, which makes the most of the resources available in the language it inherits.

But linguistic facility is not the only area in which More's brilliance is particularly evident. Beginning in the last century, the dramatic quality of the piece occasionally came in for a small share of praise. James Mackintosh remarked on the artistry of characterization in the speeches, and their almost invariable suitability to character and situation.[4] E. E. Reynolds makes the same point, observing More's increased facility and clarity in his dramatic passages: "The narrative moves easily but an occasional unevenness comes when a long involved sentence is used in explaining policy or the significance of events. It soon becomes clear that More is happiest when he is recording action or writing dialogue, when, that is, he is writing dramatically."[5] A. F. Pollard lists the dramatic aspects of the work which would tend to classify it as literature rather than as history: the introduction of *dramatis personae* in the opening pages; numerous speeches and dialogues; avoidance of dates and constitutional and social details; the development of Richard as a villain figure.[6]

Although its most neglected aspect, the dramatic nature of the *History* is certainly its most important. It is the aspect which brings it closest to Shakespeare's play. Lily B. Campbell notes how the physical description of characters and the tracing of motivations, schemes, and causes behind actions, notably Richard's action of usurping the crown, made the history lend itself to Shakespeare's dramatic portrayal, a transformation facilitated by More's frequent use of speeches and dialogues.[7] R. W. Chambers sees an even deeper relationship between the history and the play: Shakespeare, he says, takes from More "something of the tragic idea in which Shakespeare's *Richard III* reminds us of Greek drama—the feeling of Nemesis: the fate hanging over blind men who can see what is happening to others, but are unconscious of the sword over their heads."[8]

In addition to its importance as a link with Shakespeare's play, the dramatic quality of the work has an essential structural function, with which the major portion of this paper will concern itself.

Throughout his life, More was particularly drawn to the theatrical mode of expression. He was related by marriage to the dramatist John Heywood. His brother-in-law John Rastell had his own stage at his estate. More's son-in-law, William Roper, tells us that as a child in the household of John Morton, More impressed the Archbishop, as he was then, by his impromptu performances: "thoughe he was younge of yeares, yeat wold he at Christmas sodenly sometimes steppe in among the players, *and* neuer studyeng for the matter, make a parte of his owne there presently among them, which made the lookers on more sporte then all the plaiers beside."[9] In fact, A. W. Reed credits this talent of More's for improvization within a play with indirectly originating a type of Elizabethan subplot, through the writing of Henry

Medwall, who was Morton's chaplain during More's residence in that household, and who, in his interlude "Fulgens and Lucrece," shows two pages
intervening in the action.[10]

Erasmus mentions that in his youth More wrote plays and acted in them,[11]
though none of these plays survives. And certainly More seems to have been
known among his family and friends for his dramatic propensities, for the
dramatic metaphor comes naturally to Erasmus's mind in describing him.[12]

More's theatrical leanings, combined with his legal experience and his classical studies, led him to employ with considerable skill the dialogue form in
his writings. So strong was his sense of justice that he was inclined to give the
most careful consideration to opposing views. Roper reports that his father-
in-law once said to him, "I assure thee on my faith, that if the parties will at
my hand*es* call for iustice, al were it my father stood on the one side, and the
Divill on the tother, his cause being good, the Divill should haue right."[13]

In his controversial works, More employs considerable particularity of
detail in creating *personae* to represent all sides of his argument, and he sees
to it that the adversary gives the "More *persona*" strenuous and able competition. A confutation through cogent argument was far more effective than a
mere diatribe, the confutation being strongest when the adversary's arguments
were strong, but only a dramatic genius, a man possessed of great "negative
capability," could have employed this method with such notable success. In
Utopia, More has been so skillful at "giving the devil his due" that no one has
yet been able satisfactorily to untangle More's own beliefs from the arguments
and accounts presented by the three *personae,* More, Giles, and Hythloday. In
fact he has so minutely arranged his circumstantial details that the book was
originally received in many quarters as a true account.

For More the theater had the profoundest significance, bound up, as it was
to be for Shakespeare, with his whole view of life. Over and over again the
image of the theater appears in his works. He employs it in literary criticism
when he says of Erasmus's *Encomium Moriae* "that boke of *Moria* dothe in
dede but iest vpoon the abuses of such thinges, after the maner of the disours
parte in a playe. . . ."[14] In his devotional treatise *The Four Last Things,* he
twice employs the theatrical image to illustrate the superficial and transitory
nature of life. This is one of these two examples:

> If thou sholdest perceue that one wer ernestly proud of the wering of a gay
> golden gowne, while the lorel playth the lord in a stage playe, woldest thou
> not laugh at his foly, considering that thou art very sure, that whan the
> play is done, he shal go walke a knaue in his old cote? Now thou thinkest
> thy selfe wyse ynough whyle thou art proude in thy players garment, &
> forgettest that whan thy play is done, thou shalt go forth as pore as he.
> Nor thou remembrest not that thy pageant may happen to be done as sone
> as hys.[15]

In *Utopia* More uses the theater image in considering a moral problem which
became increasingly urgent to him as he was drawn more and more into government, and which ultimately brought about his death: the extent to which a

philosopher should intervene in politics. He wonders whether, by expressing his opinions too boldly, such a man might not risk ruining the "play" by interpolating into it something incongruous.[16]

More's ability to see all sides of a question with equal clarity and his profound sense of the theater have enabled him to create in Richard III a character of many dimensions, a character of such vividness, detail, complexity, and unity that it has remained with us, sharing the stage only with Milton's Satan, as the prime villain of literature. More, not Shakespeare, was the originator of this portrait, and although Shakespeare heightens it by adding lines and shadings, most of his notable additions to More's portrait are at least inspired by More's implicit suggestions.

The picture emerges as much more than a mere stereotype of evil. It is notable that in writing about an evil character, More prefers the complex process of development and detailed accumulation of evidence to the easier technique of pure vituperation. He gives us first a description of Richard's appearance and personal qualities, and then contrasts Richard in these respects with other characters. This is followed by a narration of his former actions, a continuing analysis of his motives and machinations, and a developing view of the effect he has upon others.

The character is wholly consistent. Every aspect of characterization points him on a determined pursuit of his ambition through the means of dissimulation. This dissimulation, only hinted at in previous "historical" treatments of Richard III, More makes the focal point for his character. Since More was aiming at bringing literary consistency to a character based on historical tradition, this approach was inescapable. It was necessitated by the curious and irreconcilable discrepancies occasionally apparent in the portrait of Richard III—discrepancies resulting from the superimposing of Tudor propaganda on the historical facts of Richard's character and career. To give the character consistency, it was necessary for More to portray him as an actor, a central feature which Shakespeare adopts in his portrayal.

The unity and prominence of this character and his dominating trait of dissimulation give a unity to the whole work which is unique in Tudor histories. Leonard F. Dean explains how and why More's *History* surpasses its contemporaries:

Many simple monastic or civic annalists attempted to acquire prestige and a sort of abortive unity for their brief notations by enclosing them in bald summaries of the beginning and end of things. This was impossible for a sophisticated writer like More, nor could he conscientiously undertake a world history. The practice of the classics and higher standards of historical scholarship in his day prevented him. Humanistic theorists who faced this problem suggested ... that unity should be gained by a more complete and accurate explanation of causes. Now, when cause meant only personal motive, this advice amounted to suggesting that some leading figure should be consistently characterized so as to integrate all of the action while he prevailed. This is obviously More's method. He makes everything hinge on the character of Richard.[17]

Most writers on the literary nature of More's *History of King Richard III* have alleged that its structure is based upon Richard's determined progress toward the throne, and derives its unity from the central character's manipulation of all the events in the story. To an extent this is true. Richard is introduced very near the opening of the work, and More informs the reader that this character is to be its moving force: "this Dukes demeanoure ministreth in effecte all the whole matter whereof this booke shall entreate."[18]

The *History*'s most recent editor, Richard S. Sylvester, plausibly conjectures[19] that an earlier draft of More's actually opened with the immediate introduction of Richard rather than with the description of Edward IV. It is in this form that the *History* appears in Grafton's continuation of Hardyng and in Hall. Although the English version continues on to include conjecture concerning the death of the Princes and to introduce Buckingham's rebellion, the Latin version of the *History* concludes with Richard's attainment of his end, his coronation. We may thus perhaps suggest that a structure formed by Richard's manipulation of events as he strives toward the crown, from the inception of his ambition to its fulfillment, represented an earlier plan of More's.

But what we have in the Rastell edition of the English version is somewhat different. Here the work opens with a picture of order and harmony, at the end of Edward IV's reign, which Richard, when he enters, destroys. Toward the conclusion of the history we have a description of Richard's punishment in life through guilt and rebellion, and of his ignominious death. In the final pages before the work breaks off, we are led to see, through the introduction of Morton, the triumph of the rational mind over the confusions and alienations created by Richard's selfish pursuit of ambition.[20]

Thus throughout the work we have not merely the single driving movement of Richard's progress toward the throne, but another movement as well, which becomes more obvious when we consider the opening and closing of the *History* as they are given in the Rastell edition: the beginning praising Edward IV's peaceful and ideal government, and the ending with the introduction of the rational man's incipient moral victory over the tyrant's minion. This other movement defines the work as an *exemplum,* and those who persist in seeing Richard's progress toward and ultimate achievement of the crown as the sole theme or even the major theme are ignoring the essentially exemplary nature of the work.

This other movement is outlined in the gradual reaction against Richard, which points toward a reestablishment of the state of natural order postulated at the beginning in the ideal reign of Edward IV. Richard's success is only apparent and only temporary. Almost from the beginning, certain characters are able to see through him, and gradually the distrust becomes more and more general. His schemes begin to fail. His greatest crime, the princes' murder, proves to be his greatest failure: he loses his peace of mind, but his victims win the reward of heaven. I think we are justified in calling this movement the primary structure, since it frames the narrative and establishes its moral, then works as an undercurrent, as it pulls against the more obvious but only temporary dominance of Richard in his progression toward the crown, and gradually reemerges toward a reassertion as the *History* breaks off.

The metaphor of the stage is the most important element of this structure, since it defines Richard's position relative to the reader and also to the populace. It is through these relationships that More makes clear his moral purpose. The *History* is similar to a morality play, using an *exemplum* to show how the violation of natural order, particularly on the part of a monarch, whose function should be to uphold and protect order, brings consternation and woe upon the land, and God's punishment on the offender. Like a morality play, it depends for its effect upon the relations between the actor and audience. These take place on two levels. On one level, the reader is the audience, viewing the "history" of the tyrant, observing the tragic struggle for material gain, and, beholding it from the point of view of the *contemptus mundi* tradition, seeing the intrinsic worthlessness of the object of ambition.[21] The irony inherent in this dramatic relationship deflates Richard's apparent success.

On the other level, Richard is an actor watched by an audience *within* the play in which he is leading performer—an audience composed of the other characters and of the general public. He performs for them a series of scenes, to which they react. The subtle shifts of this audience's attitude toward Richard define his gradual downfall. The extent to which the responses of the internal audience (the populace) and the external audience (the reader) combine or diverge adds a further dimension to the work and can be manipulated for mood and emphasis.

More is intentionally placing his readers in the position of a theater audience, for the techniques which he uses to bring the narrative into vivid focus are dramatic in nature: characterization, dialogue, oration, and action. The first few pages introduce *dramatis personae:* Edward IV, the good king at the end of a peaceful and prosperous reign, just, merciful, beloved by his people; Clarence, "a goodly noble Prince" (p. 7); and Richard, inferior in strength and stature, deformed and ugly, "malicious, wrathfull, enuious" (p. 7).

Direct discourse, which dominates over a third of the work, More skillfully manipulates by leading into it through indirect discourse, from which he shifts unobtrusively. He presents a vivid description of Elizabeth Woodville's receiving, near midnight, news of Rivers and Grey's arrest, and her ensuing consternation and distress as she hastily prepares to enter sanctuary. Then there is a rapid shift to a simultaneously occurring scene at the residence of the Archbishop of York: "Nowe came there one in likewise not longe after myddenighte, fro the Lorde Chaumberlayn vnto the arch bishoppe of Yorke . . . to his place not farre from Westminster" (p. 21).

With the word "nowe," our attention is quickly directed to the new scene, and in that brief passage the set has been altered by the introduction of time, place, and characters. Action ensues: the messenger persuades the servants that this errant is urgent, the servants awaken the Archbishop, who admits the messenger. Then follows a passage in direct discourse, summarizing the effect of the message, and shifting almost imperceptibly into dialogue, bringing the scene into immediate dramatic focus. The Archbishop grants audience to the messenger,

Of whome hee hard, that these dukes were gone backe with the Kynges grace from Stonye Stratforde vnto Northampton. Notwithstanding sir quod hee, my Lorde sendeth youre Lordeshippe woorde, that there is no feare. For hee assureth you that all shall bee well. I assure him quod the Archebishoppe bee it as well as it will, it will neuer bee so well as wee have seene it. (p. 21).

When the messenger departs, we are returned to the original scene, where the Archbishop now comes to the Queen as she prepares to enter sanctuary.

The dialogues and orations are used for developing character just as much as for expounding messages which the author wishes to convey. At no point is the message permitted to interfere with the characterization. More skillfully manipulates style in dialogue to show both character and change of mood. This is particularly well demonstrated in the scene between Elizabeth Wood-ville and the Cardinal, who comes to take away the Duke of York. The Queen's obstinacy and anger express themselves first in a series of defiant rhetorical questions, which she answers herself: "Wherby should I truste that (quod the Quene) In that I am giltlesse? As though they were gilty. In y^t I am with their enemies better beloued than thei? When they hate them for my sake.... For I assure you, for that I se some men so gredye withowte any sub-staunciall cause to haue him, this maketh me much the more farder to deliuer him." (p. 37).

Her rage ultimately rises to sputtering hysteria, as she mocks Richard's words, first with inverted syntax and rapid alterations of subject, then with insistent parallel construction: "But the childe cannot require the priuelege, who tolde hym so? he shal here him aske it and he will. Howbeit this is a gay matter: Suppose he could not aske it, suppose he woulde not aske it, suppose he woulde aske to goe owte, if I say hee shall not, if I aske the priuilege but for my selfe, I say he that agaynst my wyll taketh out him, breaketh the sanctuary." (p. 38).

The humor of the Queen's willful rage and the Cardinal's indignation at her behaving as if "all other ... saue herselfe, lacked either wit or trouth" (p. 40) serves two purposes in the drama: comic relief for the tension we have had to experience in watching the trap close on its innocent victims, and also an ironic purpose of pointing up through contrast with the humor of the Queen's apparent extravagance of behavior, the genuine terror of the situation in which she and her son stand. Exhausted, chagrined, and reduced to helpless tears at the end of the scene, the Queen parts from her son with words and movements which carry pathos in their simplicity: "And therewithall she said vnto the child: farewel my own swete sonne, god send you good keping, let me kis you ones yet ere you goe, for God knoweth when we shal kis togither agayne. And therewith she kissed him, & blessed him turned her back and wept and went her way, leauing the childe weping as fast." (p. 42).

The numerous orations are all models of persuasive construction. At the same time they reflect character and situation by use of particular stylistic devices. Edward IV's deathbed oration builds to a desperately emphatic climax in a series of phrases in parallel construction: "I exhort you and require you al, for ye loue you haue euer borne to me, for the loue y^t I haue euer born to you, for the loue that our lord beareth to vs all, from this time for-warde, all grieues forgotten, eche of you loue other" (p. 13).

Richard's speech to the council in regard to the Duke of York's release from sanctuary is given a pseudo-rational quality through use of long, well-modulated sentences: "The prosperytye whereof standeth ... not all in keep-ynge from enemyes or yll vyande, but partelye also in recreation and mod-erate pleasure: which he cannot in this tender youthe take in the coumpanye of auncient parsons, but in the famylier conuersacyon of those that bee neyther farre vnder, nor farre aboue his age." (p. 26). The Cardinal's reply is more rhetorical, deriving emphasis from repetition and alliteration. The build-up of detail which enforces the inviolability of sanctuary leads to a crescendo in the lengthening of the periods. The climax comes in the emphatic repeti-tion and internal rhyme: "there was neuer so vndeuowte a Kinge, that durst that sacred place violate, or so holye a Bishoppe that durste it presume to consecrate" (p. 28).

Buckingham's reply is scornful and cleverly ironic in contrast. Alliteration falls upon the consonants "w" and "f" throughout: "Womannishe feare, naye womannishe frowardenesse...." The word "fear" is brought into utter con-tempt by a tenfold repetition of it in the course of the speech. Buckingham exhibits a colloquial touch: "yea and ryche menne runne thither with poore mennes goodes ... and bidde their creditours gooe whistle them" (p. 31). This is reinforced by his shrewd sense of ironical humor: "all the worlde woulde saye that wee wer a wyse sorte of counsaylers about a kynge, that lette his brother bee caste awaye vnder oure noses" (p. 29). He even indulges in playful rhyme: "sithe the priuileges of that place ... haue been of long continued, I am not he that woulde bee aboute to breake them. And in good faith if they were nowe to begynne, I woulde not bee he that shoulde bee aboute to make them" (p. 30). A similar style is reproduced for Buckingham later in his oration to the people in favor of Richard's assuming the crown.

More occasionally assumed the customary habit of the morality actor in stepping downstage to the audience to comment on the characters and action, and to state moral messages, in order to be sure that the instructions which the drama conveys are kept constantly in mind. After the death of Hastings, More steps forward to draw our sympathy to him by giving a brief eulogy, and then he presents a moral message for which the episode of Hastings's downfall has served as an *exemplum:* "O good god, the blindnes of our mortall nature, when he most feared, he was in good surety: when he rekened him self surest, he lost his life, & that w^{t}in two howres after" (p. 52).

In the episode of Jane Shore's penance, More, conscious of the difficulty of winning sympathy for a harlot, instead of giving an objective description, addresses the reader directly and makes him share in estimating her beauty: "nothing in her body y^t you wold haue changed, but if you would haue wished her somewhat higher" (p. 54). In connection with Mistress Shore, More preaches a lesson in charity, telling us that now she is poor and friendless she is much more worthy of remembrance.

More uses irony to enforce the moral view, often undercutting Richard's pretenses with an ironic comment. This type of irony becomes more frequent and more bitter as the work progresses and Richard's actions become more deeply sinful. More mocks Richard's protestations of piety: he cannot dine until Hastings is executed "for sauing of his othe" (p. 49). He punishes Jane Shore's adultery as if he were "a goodly continent prince clene & fautles of himself, sent oute of heauen into this vicious world for the amendement of mens maners . . ." (p. 54). After the murder of the Princes the irony becomes less playful and more bitter. More points up Richard's desire to have the Princes buried in a better place with the remark: "Loe the honourable corage of a kynge" (p. 86).

These are among the many methods More uses to present a dramatic effect to the reader, putting him in the place of an audience at a play. But if we go into the work itself, we find in effect an actor-audience relationship on another level of reality, as if we are watching a play within a play. Here the audience is the London populace observing the shows staged by Richard, the actor-producer, hypocrite in the original as well as in the modern sense of the word. Ultimately the success or failure of Richard's schemes depends upon the audience's response to them, and we see this response withdrawing from him increasingly as the work progresses, thus outlining the moral structure in theatrical terms.

After Edward IV's death, Richard's feigned regard for the new young king has managed to deceive the public, and the motives for his actions go unquestioned until he stages his first dramatic scene, the arrest of Rivers and Grey. He prepares for this act by first setting a scene: he positions his men along the road and locks the door. Then he stages a quarrel with Rivers upon false grounds, and answers his denials with arrest. Immediately thereafter he stages another quarrel with Grey, again on grounds which he knows to be false. The distrust into which Richard falls as a result of this action is very short-lived, as if the people could not be sure whether the action were genuine or staged. He recovers his popularity and is named protector.

After this, however, there is nothing Richard does which does not bring suspicion upon him from some quarter. As his movements become more defined in his efforts to obtain possession of the Duke of York, the general fear and distrust become more acute. Elizabeth Woodville clearly sees Richard's "painted processe" (p. 38), and his actions caused "not comen people only that waue with the winde, but wise men also & some lordes, yeke to marke the mater and muse theron" (p. 45). The seeds of distrust have been planted, but have not yet come to the surface.

The Tower council comes at the center of the book and represents the climax of Richard's dissimulation. Richard has carefully planned this culminating scene, and he acts it with perfect timing and aplomb. He enters late and disarms the council by "saluting them curtesly" (p. 47). More then moves the scene into dramatic focus by turning to direct discourse, as Richard asks Morton for strawberries. Richard enters "saieng merely that he had bene a slepe that day. And after a little talking w^t them, he sayd vnto ye Bishop of

Elye: my lord you haue very good strawberies at your gardayne in Holberne
..." (p. 47). From this point on, the scene is played in dialogue. Richard goes
out, returning some time later with altered countenance, and after a dramatic
silence to heighten the uncertainty of the assembly, he accuses Elizabeth
Woodville and Mistress Shore of witchcraft in withering his arm. When
Hastings, relying on what he believed was a mutual love between him and the
protector, attempts to mitigate his wrath, Richard pretends to take exception
at the word "if," accuses Hastings of taking part in the conspiracy, and gives
the cue for the elaborate and carefully timed stage machinery, which he had
placed in readiness beforehand, to be set in motion: "And therew^t as in a
great anger, he clapped his fist vpon ye borde a great rappe. At which token
giuen, one cried treason without the cambre. Therwith a dore clapped, and in
come there rushing men in harneys as many as ye chambre might hold" (p. 48).

Despite Richard's technical skill in executing this scene, those who are
present at its performance cease before the end to be taken in. They realize
that "this matter was but a quarel" (p. 48), since they know that Elizabeth
Woodville would never join in a plot with her late husband's mistress. They
are also aware that Richard's accusation of witchcraft is false, since they know
that Richard's arm had been deformed from birth. Nor is the populace deceived. As the story of Hastings's death spread over the city, how little it was
credited is indicated in the words of the schoolmaster, natural spokesman for
the people's reason, who comments on the discrepancy between the length of
the proclamation and the brevity of the time between Hastings's execution
and its publication. Indeed, says More, "eueri child might wel perceiue, that it
was prepared before" (p. 54).

The public reaction becomes more clearly defined during the episode of
Jane Shore's penance. Before, it had been a shadowy, secret thing which those
who felt it could not verbalize, even to themselves. Then with the schoolmaster's comment one person voiced what all were silently thinking. Now
there is outright laughter at Richard's suddenly charging Jane Shore with the
adultery which had been common and accepted knowledge for many years
past.

Richard takes advantage of the confusion into which the minds of the
populace have been thrown to make his decisive move, commissioning a sermon
to publicize the illegitimacy of Edward IV's children and his own right to the
crown. Again he carefully blocks out a scene, but this time it does not go according to plan. Richard is supposed to enter on the preacher's cue so that he
will appear to have been chosen by God. But God refuses to take part in Richard's play. When the protector fails to appear on cue, the preacher, not so
expert an actor as Richard himself, bungles the scene and makes a fool of himself by repeating, word for word, a considerable portion of the speech leading
up to the cue. This is the worst possible way of covering a delayed entrance,
as every actor knows, and as More, the child improviser on Morton's stage,
would have been well aware. Instead of merely reporting the preacher's repetition, More actually reproduces it in his text, thus making it possible for the
reader to be drawn into the internal play by identifying with the audience

within it. He may experience the situation at first hand and share in the embarrassment and levity at the preacher's helplessness. The audience reaction in this case goes completely awry. The scene was calculated to draw audience participation at a certain point, but by the time this point arrives, the audience's willingness to believe in the play has been lost: "the people wer so farre fro crying king Richard, y^t thei stode as thei had bene turned into stones, for wonder of this shamefull sermon" (p. 68). Before this, the distrust of Richard's schemes, though invariably present, had been little more than whispered. Now it has become general and overt.

Buckingham's subsequent oration to the people falls under a similar cloud. A brilliant example of persuasive oratory, it fails because the public reaction is not in tune. When his speech arouses no response, Buckingham places himself in a foolish position, like the preacher, by repeating it, and then having the recorder repeat it once again. By means of these repetitions, More depicts the lack of spontaneity and the very careful plotting behind the whole affair. After the second repetition, the only reaction is a general buzzing whisper. Against this background, some "prentices and laddes" and servants of Buckingham "began sodainelye at mennes backes to crye owte as lowde as their throtes would gyue: king Rycharde kinge Rycharde, and threwe vp their cappes in token of ioye" (p. 76). The contrast between the depressed and doubting populace and the sudden noisily enthusiastic shout from a few throats provokes the reader's laughter. But the people are oppressed with sadness. Buckingham thanks them for their unanimous assent. They are caught in a trap. In this instance an effect is achieved in the discrepancy between the reader's and the internal audience's response: the contrast of the reader's laughter with the helplessness of the people's situation makes it seem all the more horrible.

Immediately thereafter, Richard, by prearrangement with Buckingham, stages another show, at Baynard's Castle. He pretends to be surprised by the visit of Buckingham and the city officials, "as though he doubted and partly dystrusted the commyng of suche noumbre vnto him so sodainelye, withoute anye warnyng or knowledge, whyther they came for good or harme" (p. 77). Richard first feigns reluctance to assume the crown, out of loyalty to the young king and fear for his own reputation, but at last he is "forced" to accept it. The people are perfectly well aware that these proceedings represent a previously contrived act, but they excuse it on the grounds of formality.

Before his coronation, Richard plays one more scene in an attempt to disarm the people by pardoning all offenders. In token of this he performs the ritual of taking one of his enemies by the hand, "Whiche thyng the common people reioysed at and praised, but wise men tooke it for a vanitye" (p. 82).

Richard's succession of dramatic scenes succeed or fail for precisely the same reasons as do the plays we see in the theater. The Tower scene is perfect in its technical execution. But the audience, which up to a point have been convinced by it, find a flaw in the argument and at that point realize that it is only fiction. The sermon scene fails because the timing goes wrong. The discomforts of a flustered, inexperienced actor, and the absurd discrepancies produced by the delayed entrance give rise to humor. Buckingham's address fails because, although the acting is good, the audience is not sympathetic with the theme. Like any theater audience of which participation is required, they are reluctant to make fools of themselves by entering into the performance, and coaching makes them balk all the more. When all else fails, men "planted" in the audience attempt to lead the way. The performer then thanks the audience for its helpful participation, but the hypocrisy of the situation makes the majority feel sick and depressed, because, of course, they know that there has been no genuine participation, and the play has proceeded on false grounds. The show whose purpose was ostensibly to entertain them has only exploited them. The final scene, at Baynard's Castle, is smoothly and correctly executed. The audience accept it because it is stylized by nature, but because it is insincere and obviously contrived, they fail to find it appealing.

The *History*'s dramatic images culminate in a passage which overtly expresses the significance inherent in all the scenes leading up to it. In terms of the *History*, the "play within a play," this speech explicitly makes the identification, of which we have been conscious all along, of the populace as audience and the King as leading actor. It stands as a culmination of all the elaborate arrangements of pseudo-theatrical scenes, effects, and posturings which More has had his characters perform throughout the work, and its aptness takes the reader's breath away. But the speech has relevance as well in terms of More's own relations with his audience of readers. He is speaking directly to them here, as the actor in the morality play would address his audience in order to express the play's moral message. He is commenting, on the basis of his own experience and of his premonitions about his own future, on the place of the wise man in government, a dilemma which was troubling his mind at the time of writing the *History*. The speech in even more general terms is a lesson on the frailty, uncertainty, and transience of human life:

> And in a stage play all the people know right wel, that he that playeth the sowdayne is percase a sowter. Yet if one should can so lyttle good, to shewe out of seasonne what acquaintance he hath with him, and calle him by his owne name whyle he standeth in his magestie, one of his tormentors might hap to breake his head, and worthy for marring of the play. And so they said that these matters bee Kynges games, as it were stage playes, and for the more part plaied vpon scaffoldes. In which pore men be but ye lokers on. And thei y^t wise be, wil medle no farther. For they that sometyme step vp and playe w^t them, when they cannot play their partes, they disorder the play & do themself no good. (pp. 80–81).

It took a man of considerable experience and insight into all phases of the theater to probe and describe so minutely such a variety of audience reactions. We see in More the talents of the boy page who in his patron's house stepped in among the players and performed parts extempore; the young man who wrote plays and interludes; the lawyer who was so far capable of seeing both sides of the question with sympathy that he was willing to give justice to the devil; and the religious controversialist who created *personae* to represent opposing doctrines and put formidably plausible speeches in the mouth of the opponent.

In *The History of King Richard III,* More's dramatic vision has informed the whole of the work in all of its aspects, creating its structure and, by means of this structure, setting forth its moral message. And in this method lies another facet of More's originality. Instead of overtly moralistic preaching with which the annalists presented their series of *exempla*, More adopts a new approach toward his readers to convey in a method far more subtle and hence more effective his moral view of history. He makes of his readers an audience and presents before them a group of characters playing out a moral tragedy.

THOMAS MORE

C. S. Lewis

We must now turn to those two less courteous, but far greater figures, the opposed martyrs Thomas More and William Tyndale; and though they were deeply divided by temper as well as by doctrine, it is important to realize at the outset that they also had a great deal in common. They must not, except in theology, be contrasted as the representatives respectively of an old and a new order. Intellectually they both belonged to the new: both were Grecians (Tyndale a Hebraist as well) and both were arrogantly, perhaps ignorantly, contemptuous of the Middle Ages. And if the view be accepted (it is said to be very doubtful) that a feudal world was at this time being replaced by something harsher in the social and economic sphere, then More and Tyndale both belonged to the old. Both inveighed against enclosure and sheep-farming and demanded that the desires of the 'economic man' should be completely subordinated to traditional Christian ethics. Both disapproved of the annulment of the king's marriage. To the men themselves what they had in common doubtless seemed a mere 'highest common factor': but it was enough, had the world followed that only, to have altered the whole course of our history. Nor is it, perhaps, irrelevant to add that they were alike in their fate; even curiously alike, since both risked death by torture and both were mercifully disappointed, for More was only beheaded (not disembowelled alive) and they strangled Tyndale at the stake before they lit the fire.

Thomas More, who held his place in our older critical tradition on the precarious tenure of one Latin work, has in recent years been restored to his rightful place as a major English author. Of his poems I have spoken already.[1] His remaining works fall into three classes; first those of 'pure' or comparatively 'pure' literature, secondly the controversies, and thirdly the moral and devotional treatises.

His Latin prose, with the exception of the *Utopia,* may be ignored in a history of English literature, the more so because its chief glory, the *Historia Ricardi Tertii,* can be read in his own unfinished English version. It is an ambitious undertaking modelled on the ancient historians, and in it the long set speeches dear to Thucydides and Livy claim the lion's share. Although their dramatic function is not neglected the author is more interested in them as rhetoric, and Queen Elizabeth pleading for her child's right to sanctuary is not really much less 'facundious' and forensic than Buckingham addressing

Reprinted, by permission of the publisher, from *English Literature in the Sixteenth Century Excluding Drama* (Oxford: Clarendon Press, 1954), pp. 164–181, 191–92.

388

the citizens in the Guildhall. More, who had been so purely medieval in his poetry, is here medieval and humanistic at once; he writes for an audience in whom the medieval love of fine talk had been slightly redirected and heavily reinforced by classical example. He expects us to share the enjoyment of the citizens when Buckingham 'rehersed them the same matter again in other order and other wordes, so wel and ornately and natheles so euidently and plaine, with voice, gesture and countenance so cumly and so conuenient, that every man much meruailed that herd him.' More is also a lawyer writing for an audience whose education had for the most part a legal twist, and law is the worst influence on his style. He sets out for a whole column the proclamation of Hastings's treasons and probably regards its conveyancing prolixity as an ornament rather than a blemish to his page. The character sketches, pithy and sententious and much indebted to the ancient models, will be more congenial to a modern taste. The portrait of Hastings would not disgrace Tacitus, and that of Jane Shore is a beautiful example of the author's mingled charity and severity. The book now pleases best in those passages which are most intimate —Hastings chatting with his namesake, Richard calling for the mess of strawberries, Richard with his eyes 'whirling' and his hand on his dagger 'like one always ready to strike again,' or the lively picture of a queen moving house with 'heavinesse, rumble, haste and businesse . . . chestes, coffers, packes, fardelles, trusses . . . some lading, some going, some discharging, some coming for more.' It is not an economical style, but it lives. We must not, however, represent a sixteenth-century book as a modern one by over-emphasizing merits which are really subordinate. More is not an early Strachey nor even an early Macaulay. The *Historia* in its entirety will succeed only with readers who can enjoy the classical sort of history—history as a grave and lofty Kind, the prose sister of epic, rhetorical in expression and moral in purpose. If read in the right spirit, More's performance will seem remarkable. He brings to his work a great knowledge of affairs, a sufficient measure of impartiality, a sense of tragedy, and a sense of humour. He makes an attempt, something more than half-hearted, to sift fact from tradition; and to his dramatic moulding of the story Shakespeare's close discipleship is sufficient testimony. He produces a much more interesting example of the new kind of history than Boece.

In 1516 came the *Utopia* which, though it was written in Latin, is so good and has given rise to so many controversies that I should hardly be forgiven if I passed it over in silence. All seem to be agreed that it is a great book, but hardly any two agree as to its real significance: we approach it through a cloud of contradictory eulogies. In such a state of affairs a good, though not a certain, clue is the opinion of those who lived nearer the author's time than we. Our starting-point is that Erasmus speaks of it as if it were primarily a comic book; Tyndale despises it as 'poetry'; for Harpsfield it is a 'iollye inuention,' 'pleasantly' set forth; More himself in later life classes it and the *Praise of Folly* together as books fitter to be burned than translated in an age prone to misconstruction; Thomas Wilson, fifty years later, mentions it for praise among 'feined narrations and wittie invented matters (as though they were true indeed).' This is not the language in which friend or enemy or author (when the author is so honest a man as More) refer to a serious philosophical treatise. It all sounds as if we had to do with a book whose real place is not in the history of political thought so much as in that of fiction and satire. It is, of course, possible that More's sixteenth-century readers, and More himself, were mistaken. But it is at least equally possible that the mistake lies with those modern readers who take the book *au grand sérieux.* There is a cause specially predisposing them to error in such a matter. They live in a revolutionary age, an age in which modern weapons and the modern revolutionary technique have made it only too easy to produce in the real world states recognizably like those we invent on paper: writing Utopias is now a serious matter. In More's time, or Campanella's, or Bacon's, there was no real hope or fear that the paper states could be 'drawn into practice': the man engaged in blowing such bubbles did not need to talk as if he were on his oath. And here we have to do with one who, as the Messenger told him in the *Dialogue,* 'used to look so sadly' when he jested that many were deceived.

The *Utopia* has its serious, even its tragic, elements. It is, as its translator Robinson says, 'fruteful and profitable.' But it is not a consistently serious philosophical treatise, and all attempts to treat it as such break down sooner or later. The interpretation which breaks down soonest is the 'liberal' interpretation. There is nothing in the book on which the later More, the heretic-hunter, need have turned his back. There is no freedom of speech in Utopia. There is nothing liberal in Utopia. From it, as from all other imaginary states, liberty is more successfully banished than the real world, even at its worst, allows. The very charm of these paper citizens is that they cannot in any way resist their author: every man is a dictator in his own book. It is not love of liberty that makes men write Utopias. Nor does the *Utopia* give any colour to Tyndale's view that More 'knew the truth' of Protestantism and forsook it: the religious orders of the Utopians and their very temples are modelled on the old religion. On the other hand, it is not a defence of that old order against current criticisms; it supports those criticisms by choosing an abbot as its specimen of the bad landlord and making a friar its most contemptible character. R. W. Chambers, with whom died so much that was sweetest and strongest in English scholarship, advanced a much more plausible view. According to him the Utopians represent the natural virtues working at their ideal best in isolation from the theological; it will be remembered that they hold their Natural Religion only provisionally 'onles any godlier be inspired into man from heuen.' Yet even this leaves some features unaccounted for. It is doubtful whether More would have regarded euthanasia for incurables and the assassination of hostile princes as things contained in the Law of Nature. And it is very strange that he should make Hedonism the philosophy of the Utopians. Epicurus was not regarded by most Christians as the highest example of the natural light. The truth surely is that as long as we take the *Utopia* for a philosophical treatise it will 'give' wherever we lean our weight. It is, to begin with, a dialogue: and we cannot be certain which of the speakers, if any, represents More's considered opinion. When Hythloday explains why his philosophy would be useless in the courts of kings More replies that there is 'another philosophy more ciuil' and expounds this less intransigent wisdom so sympathetically that we think we have caught the very More at last; but when I have read Hythloday's retort I am all at sea again. It is even very doubtful what More thought of communism as a practical proposal. We have already had to remind ourselves, when considering Colet, that the traditional admission of communism as the law of uncorrupted Nature need carry with it no consequences in the world of practical sociology. It is certain that in the *Confutation* (1532) More had come to include communism among the 'horrible heresies' of the Anabaptists and in the *Dialogue of Comfort* he defends private riches. Those who think of More as a 'lost leader' may discount these later utterances. Yet even at the end of the *Utopia* he rejects the Utopian economics as a thing 'founded of no good reason.' The magnificent rebuke of all existing societies which precedes this may suggest that the rejection is ironical. On the other hand, it may mean that the whole book is only a satiric glass to reveal our own avarice by contrast and is not meant to give us directly practical advice.

These puzzles may give the impression that the *Utopia* is a confused book: and if it were intended as a serious treatise it would be very confused indeed. On my view, however, it appears confused only so long as we are trying to get out of it what it never intended to give. It becomes intelligible and delightful as soon as we take it for what it is—a holiday work, a spontaneous overflow of intellectual high spirits, a revel of debate, paradox, comedy and (above all) of invention, which starts many hares and kills none. It is written by More the translator of Lucian and friend of Erasmus, not More the chancellor or the ascetic. Its place on our shelves is close to *Gulliver* and *Erewhon,* within reasonable distance of Rabelais, a long way from the *Republic* or *New Worlds for Old.* The invention (the 'poetry' of which More was accused) is quite as important as the merits of the polity described, and different parts of that polity are on very different levels of seriousness.

Not to recognize this is to do More grave injustice. Thus the suggestion that the acquisitive impulse should be mortified by using gold for purposes of dishonour is infantile if we take it as a practical proposal. If gold in Utopia were plentiful enough to be so used, gold in Utopia would not be a precious metal. But if it is taken simply as satiric invention leading up to the story of the child and the ambassadors, it is delicious. The slow beginning of the tale, luring us on from London to Bruges, from Bruges to Antwerp, and thence by reported speech to fabulous lands beyond the line, has no place in the history of political philosophy: in the history of prose fiction it has a very high place indeed. Hythloday himself, as we first see him, has something of the arresting quality of the Ancient Mariner. The dialogue is admirably managed. Mere conversation holds us contented for the first book and includes that analysis of the contemporary English situation which is the most serious and the most truly political part of the *Utopia.* In the second book More gives his imagination free rein. There is a thread of serious thought running through it, an abundance of daring suggestions, several back-handed blows at European institutions, and, finally, the magnificent peroration. But he does not keep our

noses to the grindstone. He says many things for the fun of them, surrender-
ing himself to the sheer pleasure of imagined geography, imagined language,
and imagined institutions. That is what readers whose interests are rigidly
political do not understand: but everyone who has ever made an imaginary
map responds at once.

Tyndale's belief that More 'knew the truth and forsook it' is a crude form
of the error which finds in the *Utopia* a liberalism inconsistent with More's
later career. There is no inconsistency. More was from the first a very orthodox
Papist, even an ascetic with a hankering for the monastic life. At the same time
it is true that the *Utopia* stands apart from all his other works. Religiously and
politically he was consistent: but this is not to say that he did not undergo a
gradual and honourable change very like that which overtook Burke and Wordsworth and other friends of liberty as the Revolutionary age began to show its
true features. The times altered; and things that would once have seemed to
him permissible or even salutary audacities came to seem to him dangerous.
That was why he would not then wish to see the *Utopia* translated. In the
same way any of us might now make criticisms of democracy which we would
not repeat in the hour of its danger. And from the literary point of view there
is an even greater gulf between the *Utopia* and the works which followed. It is,
to speak simply, beyond comparison better than they.

It is idle to expect that More's polemical writings, to which I now turn,
should be as good in their own kind as the *Utopia* is in its. In the first place
they are commissioned works, undertaken at the instance of the Bishop of
London and conscientiously carried out not because More wants to write them
but because, on his view, they must be written by someone. There is no evidence that he ever felt a literary and intellectual, as distinct from a religious,
vocation to this kind of work. His weariness, until the task has become a
habit, is apparent. 'Would God,' he says in the *Confutation,* 'after all my
laboure done, so that the remembrance of their pestilent errours were araced
out of Englishe mennes heartes and their abominable bookes burned up,
myne owne were walked with them, and the name of these matters vtterly
putte in oblivion.' In the second place More was limited by the very terms of
his commission to write for the vulgar, *simplicibus et idiotis hominibus.* He
was not allowed to fly very high in theology: how high he could have flown
if free, I am not qualified to judge. Hooker, writing many years later, gave it
as his opinion (*Sermon on Justification*) that More, though a very learned
man, had not fully understood the position that his own church was defending against the Lutherans.

One work in this group, the *Dialogue* of 1528, stands apart from the rest.
It is the first and the iron has not yet entered into More's soul. The plan of it
is good. More feigns a series of visits from a mysterious Messenger who puts
forward the Lutheran positions with a disinterested air, disclaiming all belief
in them but sometimes betraying it. Considerable dramatic humour results
from this device. The discussion is brought to life in true Platonic style by
notes of time and place, by interruptions, and by references to Lady More.
Passages of hard dialectic are relieved by 'merry tales' and by lengthier speeches

which aim at eloquence. As controversy it does not rank very high and perhaps in the circumstances could not: the main questions at issue hardly admit
of so popular a treatment. It is easy to put the case for justification by faith
as it appears to a text-hunting and ignorant fanatic, and easy to reply in terms
of commonplace good sense and morality. But the real problem, set by the
very nature of Christian experience, remains where it was. On saints' miracles
More does better, and the marvellous story of the young couple of Walbrook
is at once a piece of excellent comedy and an effective argument; but too
many pages are wasted on that facile interchange of anecdotal credulity and
anecdotal incredulity which you may hear in any casual conversation about
spiritualism or flying saucers. A lawyer, we feel, ought to have had something
more pertinent to say about the whole nature of evidence. But if this book
is not great theology, it is great Platonic dialogue: perhaps the best specimen
of that form ever produced in English. Berkeley is urbane and graceful and
more profound, but his Hylas and Philonous are mere men of straw beside
More and the Messenger. The latter is perhaps too stupidly obstinate and
repeats himself too often. No doubt this is so because More wishes to depict
the patience of the Papists, but he has not foreseen how severely he would
also exercise the patience of his readers. But for the most part the thing is
admirably alive. We watch with delight the slow, inevitable progress of the
Messenger into snare after snare; and this, together with the richness of its
colloquialisms and the wholly excellent humour of its funny stories, will always make the *Dialogue* worth reading.

One more work is worth separate mention before we reach the real slough.
The *Supplication of Souls* (1529) is a defence of the doctrine of purgatory
and More has chosen to put it into the mouth of the souls whom purgatory
now contains. The first book, which is almost entirely factual and statistical,
contains some of More's best and most muscular prose—for More is happiest
when he is not trying to be eloquent. The second book, which has a peculiar
literary merit of its own, illustrates a further stage in the degradation of the
idea of purgatory. In Fisher the pain has been separated from any spiritual
purification, but the torments had at least been inflicted by angels. In More
this last link with heaven is severed. The attendants (if that is the right word)
are now devils. 'Our keepers,' say the imprisoned souls, 'are such as God kepe
you from, cruell damned spirites, odious enemies and despitefull tormentours,
and theyr companye more horrible and grieuous to vs than is the payn itself
and the intollerable tourmente that they doo vs, wherewith from top to toe
they cease not to teare vs.' The length of the sentence has thus become the
sole difference between purgatory and hell. Purgatory is a department of hell.
And More's humour, continued even here, somehow increases the horror.
Instead of the psalms and litanies which resounded on the sunlit terraces of
Dante's mountain from souls 'contented in the flame,' out of the black fire
which More has imagined, mixed with the howls of unambiguous physical
torture, come pearls of harsh laughter. All is black, salt, macabre. I make the
point not to disgrace a man before whom the best of us must stand uncovered,
but because the age we are studying cannot be understood without it. This

sort of thing, among others, was what the old religion had come to mean in
the popular imagination during the reign of Henry VIII: this was one of the
things a man left behind in becoming a Protestant. Nor, I think, is that its
only relevance for the history of taste. Has not the wildness of the 'eldritch'
poetry in Scotland a secret affinity with it? The thing cannot be proved: but
I feel that the burlesque heaven of *Kynd Kittok* springs from the same mood
as the serious, yet dreadfully comic, purgatory of the *Supplication.*

Although we have now skimmed more than four hundred columns of the
1557 folio, the greater part of More's controversial writings remains—the
Confutation of Tyndale's Answer (1532 and 1533), the *Letter* (against Frith)
(1532-3), the *Apology* (1533), the *Debellation of Salem and Byzance* (1533),
and the *Answer to the Poisoned Book* (1533). The earliest criticism ever made
on these works is recorded by More himself ('The brethren cannot beare that
my writing is so long') and it cannot be seriously questioned. There are indeed differences between them. The *Confutation* is the longest, the harshest,
and the dullest. The *Letter* is exceptional not only for its brevity but for its
charitable and almost fatherly tone. In the *Apology* we see More being drawn,
as all controversialists are drawn, away from the main issue into self-defence.
In the *Debellation* what was first undertaken as a duty is only too plainly becoming a habit. More is at pains to excuse himself for answering what in his
own judgement needed no answer, and tells us the illuminating fact that this
huge treatise was composed in a few days, A not unwelcome air of senility is
perceptible in the rambling pages with which it opens and there is a charm in
the passage where the old lawyer pictures himself once more a young man at
a moot. In the *Answer to the Poisoned Book* this loss of grip becomes even
more noticeable and we repeatedly escape from the matter in hand into digressions—on gluttony, on the Arian heresy, on the Annunciation, on Free Will, on
Judas Iscariot. This twilight is welcome after the heat of such a day.

But in spite of these differences the controversial works, after the *Dialogue,*
may well be criticized in the lump. Pure literature they do not aspire to be;
and theologically More's commission confines him to stating the 'stock' case
for orthodoxy in an entirely popular form. It only remains, therefore, to judge
them as specimens of the art of controversy. That this art can produce masterpieces which outlive their occasion, no one who remembers Plato, Hooker,
Burke, or Newman will deny. But More's controversies are not on that level.
Apart from the deficiencies of his style (a point we must return to) he is
hampered by two self-imposed principles which are fatal to the highest kind
of success. In the first place he has decided that his case against the heretics
should be in his books as the soul is in the body—*tota in toto et tota in
qualibet parte;* that the reader, whatever page he lights upon, should find
there all that he needs for refutation of the enemy. He is monotonously anxious to conquer and to conquer equally, at every moment: to show in every
chapter that every heretical books is wrong about everything—wrong in history,
in logic, in rhetoric, and in English grammar as well as in theology. And secondly his method of attacking a book is to go through it page by page like a schoolmaster correcting an exercise, so that the order and emphasis of the discussion

are in fact dictated by his opponent. How to throw the grand arguments into bold relief and to condense the lesser, how to decline small points and to answer others while seeming to decline them, where to refresh the reader with some eloquent assault over the ruins of a lately demolished fortification—of all this More has no notion.

Yet even in these books his real talent sometimes appears. Wherever he allows himself to use the weapon of low comedy he is at once excellent. Even the faintest hint of it—as in the last book of the *Confutation* where he transfers the case against Barnes to two imaginary old women—is sufficient to refresh us; and the fully developed 'merry tales' will bear comparison with anything of the same kind in Chaucer or Shakespeare. It is true that the best of them all, the story of Richard Hunne, comes in the *Dialogue:* but even in the later works we have the good-wife of Culham, *Te igitur clementissime pater,* the lady who stopped her husband's lecture on astronomy, and the woman who talked in church. About these there can be only one opinion; but More has other devices bordering on the comic which do not seem to me so successful. He has the Arnoldian trick of catching up some phrase used by the enemy and ridiculing it by repetition. No instance of this is as good as 'Wragg is in custody,' but it can be effective enough when the pilloried phrase has the rhythmic qualities that go to make a good refrain; like 'the great, brode, bottomless ocean sea of euils' in the *Supplication.* But at times it may descend to a kind of nagging or snarling which is unattractive—'I have not contended with Erasmus my derling because I founde no such malicious entente with Erasmus my derling as I fynde with Tyndall. For hadde I founde with Erasmus my derling the shrewde entente and purpose that I fynde in Tyndall, Erasmus my derling should be no more my derling,' &c. What is this but the rhetoric of the preparatory school?

The mention of More's humour brings us to the question of his scurrility. From the moral point of view no very serious charge can be made; More is not much more scurrilous, only more amusingly scurrilous, than many of our older controversialists. Even if we judged his scurrility to be a fault it would be hard to wish away a fault so intertwined (or even identical) with what is the chief and often the only merit of these works: that is, the gusto of their hard-hitting, racy, street-corner abuse. It was More's business to appeal to the vulgar, to play to the gallery, and it suited one side of him extremely well. He is our first great cockney humorist, the literary ancestor of Martin Marprelate and Nashe. It would be a loss to his polemical writings if they were purged of their references to heretics who 'haue as much shame in their face as a shotten herring hath shrimps in her tail,' to 'lowsy Luther' and his disciples' 'long babelary,' to 'hammer-heads meete to make horse-shoon in helle.' If he would talk a little less about faggots and Smithfield and about Luther's 'abominable bichery,' a theme that almost obsesses him, I for one should have no quarrel with his comic abuse. It is when he is being serious that his abusiveness becomes a literary fault. To rebuke magnificently is one of the duties of a great polemical writer. More often attempts it but he always fails. He loses himself in a wilderness of opprobrious adjectives. He cannot denounce like a prophet; he can only scold and grumble like a father in an old fashioned comedy.

As we read these controversies we become aware that More the author was scarcely less a martyr to his religion than More the man. In obedience to his conscience he spent what might have been the best years of his literary life on work which demanded talents that he lacked and gave very limited scope to those he had. It may well have been no easy sacrifice.

I turn with relief to his devotional works. One of these, the meditation *De IV Novissimis* was early work and might on that account have been treated at the very beginning. I have preferred to place it here, side by side with the *Dialogue of Comfort,* in order to bring out the almost laughable, wholly beautiful, contrast between them. The late work written under the shadow of the scaffold, is full of comfort, courage, and humour; the early meditation is a piece of unrelieved gloom. Thus some men's religion fails at the pinch: that of others does not appear to pluck up heart until the pinch comes. The *De IV Novissimis* is, for its darkness, a pendant to the *Supplication.* It may justly be called a religious 'exercise' provided that we do not associate with that word any idea of insincerity. That is to say, it is not an outpouring of individual experience. The theme comes first and is selected for its intrinsic and objective importance; the business of the writer is to find reflections suitable to it. Self-improvement, not self-expression, is the purpose. More's scheme consisted in applying each of the four last things to each of the seven deadly sins in turn, and he gave it up in the middle of applying the first *Novissimum* (death) to the sixth sin (sloth), having thus completed five of the twenty-eight panels or niches intended. Of its value as a devotional work who dares consider himself a judge? If most of it now seems helpless either to encourage or to alarm, the fault may be ours: but not, I think, all ours. Almost everywhere it tries to prove too much. Gross exaggeration of the part played by gluttony in our diseases leaves the conscience undisturbed. The passage in which all life is compared to an illness shows some inability to distinguish between a conceit and an argument. The colours are too dark. In the true late medieval manner More forgets that to paint all black is much the same as not to paint at all. What was intended to be a rebuke of sin degenerates almost into a libel upon life and we are forced into incredulity. It is true that More once assures us that even in the natural order 'virtue bringeth his pleasure and vice is not without pain' but this little taper does not cast its beam very far in the general gloom. The real merits of the book are incidental. The medieval homiletic tradition wisely admitted the grotesque and the comic and where More avails himself of this licence he writes well. The picture of the glutton 'with his belly standing a strote like a taber and his noll totty with drink' is as good as that in the *Ancren Riwle.* We are reminded of Falstaff's death when we read of the dying man 'thy nose sharping, thy legges cooling, thy fingers fimbling.' Few pictures of the deathbed are more vivid than the following:

> Haue ye not ere this in a sore sickness felt in very grieuous to haue folk babble to you, and namely such thynges as ye sholde make aunswere to, whan it was a pain to speake? Thinke ye not now that it wil be a gentle

pleasure whan we lye dying, al our body in pain, al our mind in trouble, our soul in sorow, our hearte al in drede, while our life walketh awaiward, while our death draweth toward, while the deuil is busy about vs, while we lack stomak and strength to beare any one of so manifold heynous troubles, wil it not be as I was about to say, a pleasaunt thing to see before thine eyen and heare at thine eare a rable of fleshly frendes, or rather of flesh flies, skipping about thy bed and thy sicke body (now almost carreyn) crying to thee on euery side, What shal I haue, what shall I haue.... Than shall thyne executours ask for the kayes....

But I have done the author a little more than justice by making one omission and by stopping where I did. More sows from the sack, not from the hand.

The *Dialogue of Comfort against Tribulation* (1534) is the noblest of all his vernacular writings. It was written in the Tower while More waited for death (for all he knew, death by torture, hanging, cutting down alive, and disembowelling). Its form is an imaginary conversation between two Hungarian gentlemen who foresee the possibility of martyrdom if the Turk comes much nearer. It is thus a fairly close parallel to Boethius' *De Consolatione* and the difference between them is interesting. In Boethius the thought that would be uppermost in any modern mind—that of physical pain—is hardly present at all; in More it is ubiquitous. We feel that we are reading the work of a man with nerves like our own, even of a man sensitive in such matters beyond the norm of his own coarse and courageous century. He discusses at length whether a man should envisage such horrors beforehand. To do so may clearly lead either to false confidence (reckoning with pain's image, not pain) or to despair (reckoning without the grace which will not perhaps be given before the need). His reply is that there is no choice. When once the matter has been raised we cannot refuse to think about it, and to advise us otherwise is 'as much reason as the medicine that I haue heard for the toothache, to go thrice about a churchyard and never think on a fox tayle.' He would therefore have everyone, of whatever sex or age, 'often to thinke thereupon.' We must do the best we can, meditating much on the Passion of Christ, never 'full out of feare of fallynge' but 'in good hope and full purpose' to stand. There is no attempt to disguise the situation; 'whan we remember the terrour of shameful and painefull death, that poynt sodaynly putteth us in obliuion of all that shold be our comfort.' There is here a precision unusual in More. 'Whan we remember'—the mind is numb for hours even in a condemned cell, and then the terror rushes back: and 'sodaynly.' Worse even than this is the haunting fear that the pain itself might force a man 'to forsake our Saviour even in the myddes, and dye there with his synne, and so be damned foreuer.' Yet when all's said, a man must 'stand to his tackling' and any Christian would be very glad today to have so suffered yesterday.

The theme is almost the gravest that the human mind can entertain, but it must not be supposed that the book is a gloomy one. The *Dialogue of Comfort* justifies its title; it overflows with kindliness and humour and the beautiful self-mockery of old age aware of its own garrulity and its own limitations. The 'merry tales' are here in abundance, the old medieval jokes about women, so stale in themselves yet, after all, so amusingly handled, and so touching when we remember the hard road which they are now helping the author to travel. In a slightly different vein the longer story of a false alarm in war (ii. 12) is admirably told. But I would not quote much from this book: it is (or was) accessible in a cheap reprint and should be on everyone's shelves.

Of the *Treatise on the Passion* in its English form, we have only part from More's own hand; the rest, translated from his Latin by Margaret Roper's daughter. Those who turn to it expecting to find the beauties of the dialogue continued will be disappointed. It is as much exegetical as devotional and takes the form of a commentary on Gerson's *Monatesseron* (a gospel concordance made on a rather clumsy plan). As a Biblical commentator More is wholly medieval. Long ago in the *Supplication* he had used as a proof of the existence of purgatory the fact that Hezekiah wept when told that he must die; here he allegorizes in the old fashion on Our Lord's repetition of the word *Father,* on the name Simon, and on Malchus. From the literary point of view the most unfortunate feature of the book is the indiscretion with which More puts words into the mouth of Christ. It can be done successfully; witness the *Imitation.* But More seems wholly unaware of the dangers involved: it is indeed remarkable how one who had been, as a man, so attentive to the spirit of the Dominical utterances, could have remained, as a critic, so deaf to their style. Already in the *Answer to the Poisoned Book* this insensibility had led him to grotesque results ('For I am, as I dyuers times now haue told you, the very bread of life'); here it leads to the following:

> Thys is the shorte whyle that is graunted yee and the libertie geuen vnto darknesse, that now ye maye in the night, which till this howre ye could neuer be suffered to bring to passe in the daye, like monstruous raueninge fowles, like skriche owles and hegges, like backes, howlettes, nighte crowes and byrdes of the hellye lake, goe aboute with your billes, your tallentes, your teeth and your shyrle shrychinge, outrageouslye, but all in vayne, thus in the darke to flee uppon me.

All this (and there is much more than I have quoted) is a gloss on the words 'This is your hour and the power of darkness'; and More cannot see that he is weakening them. It is true that the words quoted are his granddaughter's translation: but those who know More's English best will not say that the style is much inferior to his own, and those who look at the Latin will not find its *bubones striges* and *nycticoraces* much of an improvement on their vernacular equivalents. Yet these errors (of which there are plenty in the *Treatise*) are balanced by passages of exquisite pathos and insight. The following, also put into the mouth of Our Lord and explaining the final cause of the agony in the garden, is noteworthy—though more, I confess, for the matter than for the style.

> Plucke up thy courage, faint heart, and dispaire never a deale. What though ye be fearefull, sory, and weary, and standest in great dread of most

painful tormentry that is like to falle uppon thee, be of good comfort for all that. For I myself have vanquished the whole worlde, and yet felt I far more feare, sorowe, wearinesse, and much more inward anguish too, whan I considered my most bitter, painful passion to presse so fast uppon me. He that is strong harted may finde a thousand gloryous valiant martyrs whose ensample he may right joyfully follow. But thou, now, o temerous and weke sely shepe, thynke it sufficient for thee onely to walke after me.

Great claims have in modern times been made for More's English prose; I can accept them only with serious reservations. To compare it with that of the *Scale of Perfection* or the *Revelations* of Lady Julian will, in my opinion, only reveal its inferiority to them. The man who sits down and reads fairly through fifty pages of More will find many phrases to admire; but he will also find an invertebrate length of sentence, a fumbling multiplication of epithets, and an almost complete lack of rhythmical vitality. The length of sentence in More is quite different from the fullness of impassioned writers like Cicero or Burke or Ruskin, or from that of close thinkers like Hooker or Coleridge. It is not even the winning garrulity of Montaigne, or not often. Its chief cause is the fact that More never really rose from a legal to a literary conception of clarity and completeness. He multiplies words in a vain endeavour to stop up all possible chinks, where a better artist forces his conceptions on us by the light and heat of intellect and emotion in which they burn. He thus loses the advantages both of full writing and of concise writing. There are no lightning thrusts: and, on the other hand, no swelling tide of thought and feeling. The style is stodgy and dough-like. As for the good phrases, the reader will already have divined their nature. They come when More is in his homeliest vein: their race and pith and mere Englishry are the great redeeming feature of his prose. They ring in our ears like echoes of the London lanes and Kentish villages; 'whispered in huker-moker,' 'damn us all to Dymmingesdale,' 'the goose was ouer the moon,' 'every finger shall be a thumb,' 'fume, fret, frot, and foam,' 'sauing for the worshipfull name of wine ichad as leue a drunken water.' They belong to the same world as his merry tales. Nearly all that is best in More is comic or close to comedy.

We think of More, and rightly, as a humanist and a saintly man. On the one hand, he is the writer of the *Utopia*, the friend of Erasmus, the man whose house became a sort of academy. On the other, he is the man who wanted to be a Carthusian, who used a log of wood for his bolster and wore the hair, the martyr who by high example refused the wine offered him on his way to execution. The literary tragedy is that neither of these sides to his character found nearly such perfect expression in his writings as they deserved. The *Utopia* ought to have been only a beginning: his fertility of mind, his humour, and his genius for dialogue ought to have been embodied in some great work, some *colloquies* meatier than those of Erasmus, some satiric invention more gravely droll than Rabelais. As for his sanctity, to live and die like a saint is no doubt a better thing than to write like one, but it is not the same thing; and More does not write like a saint. 'Unction' (in the good sense of that word) is noticeably lacking in his work: the beauty of holiness, the fragrance of the

Imitation or of St. François de Sales or of Herbert. What is actually expressed in most of his work is a third More, out of whom both the saint and the humanist have been made and with whom (that is both his glory and his limitation) they never lose touch—the Tudor Londoner of the citizen class. However high he rises he remains unmistakably rooted in a world of fat, burgher laughter, contentedly acclaiming well-seasoned jokes about shrewish wives or knavish servants, contemptuous of airs and graces and of what it thinks unnecessary subtleties; a world not lacking in shrewdness, courage, kindness, or honesty, but without fineness. No man even half so wise and good as Thomas More ever showed so little trace of the *cuor gentil.* There is nothing at all in him which, if further developed, could possibly lead on to the graces of Elizabethan and Jacobean literature. It might have led to things which some would prefer, but very different things. . . .

As a writer, Tyndale is almost inevitably compared with More. In one quality he is obviously inferior to his great antagonist: that is, in humour. He ventures on an occasional pun ('Nicholas de Lyra *delirat*'), and he has contemptuous coinages—*chopological* for *tropological* is the best. Nor would he be a man of his age if he could not sometimes fling out a happy violence, as when he speaks of a sickly stomach 'longing after slibbersauce and swash.' Only once does he venture on to More's own territory and then with a joke (to my thinking) so good that, however he detested the application, the Chancellor's lips must have twitched when he read it. Tyndale has been attacking the doctrine that we can profit by the superfluous merits of the religious orders; and ends with the advice 'If thy wife geue thee nine wordes for three, go to the Charterhouse and bye of their silence.' But it is only one flash against More's recurrent summer lightning. In scurrility they are about equals; except that hard words sound less unlovely from the hunted than from the hunter. Digressions are a fault in both, not always from the same causes. Tyndale's is the digressiveness of a stretched mind, full of its theme and overflowing all bounds in its impetuous and happy prodigality: More's, sometimes, the rambling of a brooding, leisurely mind—a man talking, with the whole evening before him and the world full of interesting things. Where Tyndale is most continuously and obviously superior to More is in style. He is, beyond comparison, lighter, swifter, more economical. He is very unadorned (an occasional alliteration, some rhetorical repetitions, some asyndeton) but not at all jejune. The rhythm is excellent, the sort of rhythm which is always underlining the argument. In its sharpness of edge, its lucidity, and its power of driving the reader on, it has certain affinities (allowing for the difference of period) with the prose of Mr. Shaw's prefaces. What we miss in Tyndale is the manysidedness, the elbow-room of More's mind; what we miss in More is the joyous, lyric quality of Tyndale. The sentences that stick to the mind from Tyndale's works are half way to poetry—'Who taught the Egles to spy out their pray? euen so the children of God spy out their father'—'that they might see Loue and loue againe'—'where the Spirit is, there it is always summer' (though that last, we must confess, is borrowed from Luther). In More we feel all the 'smoke and stir' of London; the very plodding of his sentences is like horse traffic in the streets. In Tyndale we breathe mountain air. Amid all More's jokes I feel a melancholy in the background; amid all Tyndale's severities there is something like laughter, that laughter which he speaks of as coming 'from the low bottom of the heart.' But they should not be set up as rivals, their wars are over. Any sensible man will want both: they almost represent the two poles between which, here in England, the human mind exists—complementary as Johnson and Shelley or as Cobbett and Blake.

THOMAS MORE AND THE EARLY CHURCH FATHERS

R. C. Marius

Thomas More, humanist, statesman, and martyr, was one of the most prolific apologists for the Catholic Church in the early years of the Reformation. In numerous polemical and apologetic works he ranged widely over the issues raised by the controversy.[1] But if his scope was large, he possessed one sure foundation to which all his arguments inevitably returned. This was the faith of the early Church Fathers, those men who interpreted the life and faith of the Church from the time of the Apostles to the end of the pontificate of Pope Gregory I in 604.

When we attempt to examine More's use of the Fathers, we find ourselves wandering in an immense landscape. More read the Fathers all his life, and no single paper can do justice to their influence upon him. But there are some promontories of his thought regarding the Fathers which we can examine briefly. On the one hand we can see more clearly what it meant for a northern, Catholic humanist to go back to the sources. For More these sources were both Scripture and the Fathers, and it was almost impossible for him to separate them. On the other hand we are brought directly into one of the most vital fields of recent Reformation research—the question of the relation of the Reformation to the tradition of the Church. As we shall see, this became for More the question whether history possessed any meaning at all.

The Fathers as Interpreters of the Bible

Throughout his religious works More used the Fathers as interpreters of Scripture. The Fathers had established certain lines of interpretation, and without these the difficulties of Scripture would be overwhelming. In this we see how great was the gulf fixed between More and many Protestants. For Martin Luther, Scripture was a clear light needing only to be allowed to shine for the mists of a dark age to be burned away. There were obscurities. Luther would admit that. But their source lay in ignorance of the vocabulary and the grammar of the sacred text. If a few places were dark, there were many others which were perfectly clear. No objective authority beyond itself was needed to interpret Scripture. The exegete had only to use the bright places to illuminate the obscure.[2] But in More's mind, Scripture was wracked with difficulty. Hardly a text could stand without its interpretative gloss.[3] There was always a sense

Reprinted, by permission of the author and publisher, from *Traditio,* 24 (1968), 379–407.

in More that Scripture was a repository of mystery whose meaning was revealed to the Church only when it pleased God so to do. This thought was in line with a penchant for the esoteric which we find in More's theology, and it helped him justify the development of Catholic tradition.[4] Left to private judgment regarding Scripture, the arrogant or the ignorant or even the pious and learned could easily lose the way. The example of the Reformers with their innumerable schisms was proof enough to More of the dangers of reliance on Scripture alone.[5]

The authority of the Fathers as interpreters of the Bible had several pillars. Obviously they were better than the 'newe men'—the Reformers. As More said, the Fathers were as intelligent, their diligence as great, their erudition greater, their study fervent, their devotion hotter, their number far greater, and most importantly, the interpretations made by the Fathers had been certified by the Catholic Church through many ages. It was apparent to More that with regard to Scripture, God has 'opened theyr eyen and suffered and caused them to see the trouth.'[6]

Throughout his works More fell back onto the patristic interpretations as a guide to his own use of Scripture. Quite often it seems that his very reference to the Scriptural text is really to the text *as it was interpreted* by some Father. This may be demonstrated in the Scriptural glosses which appear as sidenotes in the early editions of the polemical works. Usually the meaning of these glosses is rather clear. But at times they appear, at least to this student, to be meaningless without reference to some patristic commentary on the Scripture being cited.

For example, in the fourth book of the *Confutation of Tyndale's Answer* there is a passage in which More is arguing that Christians can fall from grace into mortal sin. This was in opposition to what More understood to be the Reformers' doctrine of predestination. He says:

> For all crysten people excepte a few heretykes, both now byleue and all thys .xv. hundred yere before euer haue byleued, that good men & chyldren of god maye fall in to dedely synne, and become chyldern of the deuyll/and yet aryse by grace thorowe penaunce, and be made the chyldern of god agayne. Many textes also of holy scrypture playnely proue, that good folke maye falle & peryssche. And the scrypture is full of good counsayle/aduysynge all good men to stande faste alway and euer lyue in fere of fallynge/but yf any specyall reuelacyon be geuen to some certayne man besyde the comen ordinary course.[7]

A number of glosses appear in the margin by this passage. Most are clear. The gloss to Romans 11 must refer to Paul's word about the branches (the unbelieving Jews) who were cut out of God's stock.[8] Elsewhere More directly applies this passage to heretics who rebel and are cut off from God and cast into hell. But if heretics repent, they may be grafted onto the tree again and so redeemed.[9] The gloss to 1 Corinthians 10 undoubtedly refers to the thirteenth verse of that chapter, one of More's favorite passages. He used it constantly to prove that sin could be resisted. The implication was that if men failed to

resist, they would fall from grace.[10] The reference to 1 Corinthians 16 is
probably to the thirteenth verse, 'Vigilate, state in fide, viriliter agite, et con-
fortamini.' But what of the gloss which points to Psalms 32 and 33? Here we
confront Biblical texts which in themselves give no clue to what More meant.
Psalm 32 (Vulgate) is a hymn of praise for the watchfulness of God over his
people. Psalm 33 is a song of jubilation for deliverance. Nothing in either
Psalm speaks overtly of the possibility of falling from God's grace.

Making any positive claims for the sources of any Biblical exegesis in this
period is hazardous business. But in understanding More's use of the Bible, we
are often aided by consulting the *Glossa ordinaria,* the great commentary on
the Bible compiled from the Fathers, probably in the ninth century.

In looking at the glosses for Psalm 32 (Vulgate), our eyes fall upon the
entry for what we call verse 17. Here the A.V. reads, 'An horse is a vain thing
for safety.' The Vulgate is more emphatic: 'Fallax equus ad salutem.' Now
the horse was a symbol which the patristic commentator could not ignore, and
the *Glossa ordinaria* here compresses the comments of many of the Fathers. It
notes that St. Augustine wrote concerning the horse: 'Animal, in cujus velo-
citate vel virtute confiditur, figurate quaelibet amplitudo saeculi unde superbi-
tur: sed quanto in eo altius erigeris, tanto gravius cadis.'[11] This is a considerable
paraphrase of Augustine's *Enarratio* for Psalm 32. It does not adequately
reproduce the spirit of Augustine's original except that the sin of pride is condemned. But this was the very sin for which More reproached the Reformers
for their conviction of the certainty of their salvation. Later in his argument
in the *Confutation* More makes Tyndale to be one of those heretics 'as wolde
make us wene yᵗ some were goddes wanton cokneys in such a speciall wyse,
yᵗ what so euer they do no thyng could displease hym.'[12] And a little earlier
in his argument he says,

> it is euydent & playne by clere and open textes of scrypture, full & plen-
> tuouse in euery part therof, that there is no man here (excepte some spe-
> cyall reuelacyon therof) so sure of his owne fynall saluacyon, nor of his
> own present estate neyther, but that he hath good cause to fere & temper
> hys hope of goddys mercy with the drede of his iustyce, lest his ouer bolde
> hope may happe to stretche in to presumpcion & occasyon of sleyght re-
> gardyng synne.[13]

Professor Heiko A. Oberman has demonstrated with regard to Gabriel Biel
that this was a common thought in late medieval theology. The most basic
Christian virtue is humility, says Oberman. This, he says paraphrasing Biel,
'can be acquired when we consider our insufficiencies and the abyss of God's
judgment which does not allow us to know our present state or future destiny.'[14]
One may have only a 'fiducial certainty' of his salvation.[15] That is to say that
we know God will judge us justly by the rules He has set down and that if we
do our very best (facere quod in se est), we may confidently expect God's love
and not His wrath.[16]

All this might be summarized in the admonition concerning pride, 'sed
quanto in eo altius erigeris, tanto gravius cadis.' Hence it would seem possible

and even probable that More's gloss against his own text is really a reference to the patristic commentary on Psalm 32.17 as noted in the *Glossa ordinaria*.

A similar hypothesis may be made for the reference to Psalm 33 at this point in the *Confutation*. Throughout this Psalm there are many admonitions to goodness. There is also the promise of verse 18, 'Clamaverunt iusti, et Dominus exaudivit eos: et ex omnibus tribulationibus eorum liberavit eos.' This thought is quite like that of 1 Cor. 10.13, already cited as one of More's favorite passages. Perhaps we need look no further for an explanation for the gloss here.

Yet at Psalm 33.6 we find an interesting congruence between the *Glossa ordinaria* and one of More's most important theological positions. Here the Vulgate reads, 'Accedite ad eum, et illuminamini.' To this the *Glossa ordinaria* appends a note from Augustine: 'Accedite fide inhaerendo, et duobus pedibus geminae charitatis currendo.'[17] On turning to Augustine's full commentary on this passage we find that he interprets it to apply to the people who come to Christ. Again we find the original to be somewhat different from the abbreviated citation of the *Glossa ordinaria*. Augustine wrote: 'Unde accedunt Gentes? Fide sectando, corde inhiando, charitate currendo. Pedes tui, charitas tua est. Duos pedes habeto, noli esse claudus. Qui sunt duo pedes? Duo praecepta dilectionis, Dei et proximi. Istis pedibus curre ad Deum, accede ad illum. . . .'[18] But in either version the comment is in line with More's persistent emphasis on love or charity in the process of salvation. Like so many others, when he heard the Reformers speak of justification by faith, he heard them in an antinomian sense. That is, he understood them to say that one could commit any sin without fear of damnation so long as the propositions of the faith were received. To counter this supposed libertinism, More always maintained that faith had to be joined or 'formed' with love before it could be sufficient for salvation.[19] This was a part of his attack on what he considered to be the proud certainty of the Reformers of their salvation. The Scriptural corollary was James 2.19–20:

> Tu credis quoniam unus est Deus:
> Bene facis: et daemones credunt, et contremiscunt.
> Vis autem scire o homo inanis, quoniam fides
> sine operibus mortua est?

Nothing in this was new. It was all worked out in Aquinas, to mention only one of the scholastics.[20] More was more thoroughly immersed in late medieval Catholic theology than some scholars have been willing to admit. He was simply using an old and well worn weapon against the heretics. Their sola-fideism called up this kind of response from him again and again. Hence it is not at all unlikely that the gloss to Psalm 33 at this point might be derived from the reference to Psalm 33.6 in the *Glossa ordinaria* with its appended Augustinian comment.

More obvious is the gloss to '1 Timoth.1.' at a place where More is defending persecution of heretics.[21] This is certainly 1 Tim. 1.18–20: 'Hoc praeceptum commendo tibi fili Timothee, secundum praecedentes in te prophetias ut milites in illis bonam militiam, habens fidem, et bonam conscientiam, quam quidam repellentes, circa fidem naufragaverunt: ex quibus est Humenaeus, et Alexander: quos tradidi Satanae, ut discant non blasphemare.' These cryptic words More applies to 'good chrysten p128prynces & other vertuouse people' who in the beginning were tolerant towards heretics. But the heretics were so malicious and seditious that it was necessary 'to folow thensample of saynte Poule/and as he betoke some of them to the deuyll, to the punysshement of theyr bodyes in helpe of theyr soules or ceacynge of theyr synfull blasphemy: so by temporall lawes & bodyly punyshement, to fynysh y^t infynyte malyce & intolerable trouble of those heretykes, for the sauegarde of good people in peace & tranquyllite.'[22] This was one of the cardinal texts used by Augustine to justify persecution against the Donatists.[23] It should be noticed that both of Augustine's reasons for persecution are present here in More. On the one hand, persecution aids the soul of the heretic by making him cease piling up blasphemies for which he will be punished. And on the other, persecution aids Christians by leaving them in tranquility.[24] Thus at this passage, though the name of Augustine is not immediately mentioned, the Scriptural gloss offers a clue to the source of More's argument. It was, of course, a frequent argument among Catholics, and later in the *Confutation* More cites Augustine specifically.[25]

At this point two conclusions are to be noted. First, More used the *Glossa ordinaria* frequently as a commentary on the Scriptures, and it is probable that the work became a kind of index to the Fathers for him. I would surmise that he often used its references without checking them out in the editions of the Fathers themselves.[26] Since the *Glossa ordinaria* was often printed in the margins of the Bible, it would be difficult to imagine how More could have avoided its use, and indeed he mentions the work at least once in the *Confutation*.[27] Second, More seems to have done the glossing himself of the editions of his works published during his lifetime. The glosses often carry us to Scriptural passages related only in a roundabout way to his arguments. Consultation of the patristic commentaries in many cases leads to enlightenment. I doubt that the casual glossator would have made these connections.

At times More's reliance on the Fathers for his interpretation of Scripture is so great that he adopts their readings of the sacred text in preference to the text of the Vulgate. There is, for example, the case of a favorite phrase of his which he glosses frequently as Psalm 67.[28] More's reading of this text is usually simply the phrase, 'qui facit unanimes in domo.' Often he renders it in English by 'maketh all of one mynde in that house.'[29] Always for him the 'house' is the Church, and he uses the verse to extol the unity which always prevails there.

Ultimately this reading was derived from one of the old Latin versions of the Bible, that is, one of the versions in use before Jerome's Vulgate. The reading, with the interpretation of 'domus' as the Church, turns up occasionally in the works of Augustine, who, as he acknowledges, relies here on Cyprian.[30] Cyprian made much of the reading and the ecclesiastical interpretation in his tractate, *De unitate ecclesiae*.[31] This work turns up from time to time in More's

Confutation,[32] and in a list of More's favorite ancient authorities Cyprian would have to rank second only to Augustine.

Jerome took another reading of the text. 'Deus qui inhabitare facit unius moris in domo.' I have examined a number of incunabula of the Bible in Yale's Beinecke Library, and this is the text of all of them, so that I think it might be presumed to be the text of any edition of the Vulgate which More might have used. Of course the meaning is not substantially different from Cyprian's reading, and like Cyprian Jerome interprets the 'house' to be the Church, for he writes: 'In ecclesia, in qua fideliter consistentibus spiritum charitatis infundit qui unius moris sunt, et non mutantur.'[33] Augustine in his commentary on this psalm gives yet another version: 'Deus qui inhabitare facit unius modi in domo.' This probably reflects the use of yet another old Latin version of the Bible.[34] He was, however, aware of the reading taken by Jerome, for in his discussion of the Psalm he mentions it in a parallelism with his own.[35]

There were difficulties with the passage as might appear from the variant readings we have noted. In his comments on the psalm Jerome had noted that the Hebrew text differed here from the accepted Latin versions. 'In Hebraeo autem habet: Dominus inhabitare facit monachos in domo.'[36] This is the sense of the edition of the Vulgate done by the Benedictine monks of St. Maur who gave the reading, 'Deus habitare facit solitarios in domo.'[37] It is also the sense of the Septuagint's ὁ Θεὸς χατοιχίζει μονοτρόπους ἐν οἴχῳ, and it is like the A.V. reading, 'God setteth the solitary in families.' The accepted Hebrew text is in line with all this: אלהם מושיב יחידים ביתה Luther adopted this reading without any special comment in his German exegis of the Psalms done in 1521. 'Er ist der gott, der do macht eynnmütige woner ym hauss.'[38] So it is clear that More was going against common traditions regarding this text when he adopted the reading which he did. He was probably simply not concerned with the textual problem, and if he noticed the variation between his usage and the Vulgate he made nothing of it. Cyprian's (or Augustine's) reading made an impression on him, and he used it as Holy Scripture. He glossed it as such. We can assume that some readers, checking the gloss by their fireside edition of the Vulgate, must have experienced that peculiar mystification, common to scholars of all times before the doubtful footnote.[39]

A similar instance is to be found in More's reading of Isaiah 7.9, a text which occurs frequently throughout the *Confutation*. More's rendering is always, 'But yf ye beleue, ye shall not vnderstond.'[40] Once again we have a reading which is not from the Vulgate, for here Jerome has, 'si non credideritis, non permanebitis.' The Hebrew text here, אב לֹא תאמינופי לֹא תאמנו. agrees with Jerome. Ultimately the origin of More's reading was the Septuagint's ἐὰν μὴ πιστεύσητε, οὐδὲ μὴ συνῆτε, and this was also the sense of an old Latin version (itself largely a translation from the Septuagint) where we find, 'Et si non credideritis, neque intelligetis.'

But we do not have to explain More's rendition by a supposition of the use of the Septuagint or the Old Latin. Both Jerome and Augustine recognized the discrepancy here between the Septuagint and the better Latin texts of the Old

Testament. But both found great meaning in the Septuagint version and expounded upon it.[41] Indeed it was, as Beryl Smalley notes, the habit of the Fathers to make double commentaries on two diverse readings of a text without choosing between them.[42] Something of this attitude is to be found clearly expressed in More in those days when he gave himself so unreservedly to a defence of his friend Erasmus. To an obstreperous monk who thought there should be only one edition of the Bible, the Vulgate, More wrote:

> Supposing there would be several editions; what harm would result? What you fear, Saint Augustine considers extremely useful; while they could not all be of equal value, still one has a more suitable translation of one passage, another of another passage. But, you object, such a situation will raise doubts in the reader's mind as to which one of the many editions he should trust most of all; that is a valid objection, if the reader is such an absolute blockhead as to lack both brains and judgment. If, on the other hand, he has intelligence, it will be all the easier for him, as Augustine says, to choose from the various versions the accurate rendering. Now tell me, why do you fear that a great risk is involved in a variety of versions even at variance with one another, since you take no offense at all in reading the manifold explanations of the commentators, who, in commenting on the identical text, come to no agreement at all on the meaning of the text, and very often those discrepancies have a value in that they provide an opportunity for scholars to think and judge for themselves? To conclude this point, at least, the Psalms with their different versions and variant readings offer clear evidence of the value of having a variety of editions and also of the fact that no confusion results in the Church.[43]

So it would be altogether natural for More to accept a reading from the Fathers and to quote it as Scripture without worrying too much about the textual problems involved. He was a world away from that attitude of some Protestants, particularly of the English variety, which held that the beginning of Christian wisdom lay in the discovery of the precise Scriptural text and its exact grammatical sense. It is my impression that More's attitude towards matters of Biblical text differed significantly from that of his friend Erasmus, but this issue is too complicated to treat here.

It would not be accurate to say that the Scripture and the Fathers are the same thing in More's thought. But in doctrinal matters at least, the distinction between the two is a little like the distinction in Aristotle between form and matter. Scripture without its patristic interpreters could not have any meaningful existence for the Church. And if the Fathers presented a reading of the Scripture which appealed to More's theological needs, that usage alone was sufficient authority to allow him to adopt it.

More's dependence upon the Fathers also led him to mistake the arguments of his opponents, especially in their interpretations of Scripture. 'Among many other things, the Reformation was a crisis of Christian vocabulary': so Gordon Rupp has observed in one of those trenchant epigrams of his.[44] More frequently misunderstood the vocabulary of the Reformers. Partly, the cause may have been a deliberate polemical instinct, the desire to make their opinions appear as noxious as possible. But another reason was that he kept expecting heresies the Fathers had faced in their days to rise again in his own in all the ghostly perfection of Samuel summoned by the Witch of Endor.

This fact is particularly evident in relation to the interpretation of one of the most perplexing texts of the New Testament, Hebrews 6.4–6. In the *Confutation* More translates this entire passage no fewer than three times and refers to it many times more.[45] In the Authorized Version it reads: 'For it is impossible for those who were once enlightened and have tasted of the heavenly gift, and were made partakers of the Holy Ghost, and have tasted the good word of God, and the powers of the world to come, if they shall fall away, to renew them again unto repentance, seeing they crucify to themselves the Son of God afresh, and put him to an open shame.' This text was important to More because his antagonist William Tyndale made it so.

Tyndale's interpretation is interesting because of the light it throws on his theology. One of his beliefs was that the intellect of man was superior to his will. To Tyndale this meant that the will of man would follow his reason. Salvation for him, at least in his *An Answere unto Sir Thomas Mores dialoge,* was brought about by God's revelation of himself to the elect. The rational perception of this revelation by the elect is the agent which causes the elect to respond willingly to the laws of God. Or, as Tyndale said, 'And then when we see his mercie/we loue him agayne and chose him and submitte our selues vn to his lawes to walke in them. For when we erre not in witt/reason and iudgement of thinges/we can not erre in will and choyse of thynges. The choyse of a mans will doeth naturally and of hir awne accorde folowe the iudgement of a mans reason/whether he iudge righte or wronge. So that in teaching only resteth the pith of a mans liuinge.'[46]

I take this to mean that salvation for Tyndale involved a kind of purification of the intellect through an immense, divine enlightenment and that it entailed a process of sanctification for the Christian man. The more a man penetrated the meaning of his faith, the more he possessed the good will to be a more perfect Christian. This was not merely the belief that knowledge of propositions was all that was required to make a man Christian. More often accused Tyndale of this version of antinomianism while at the same time ridiculing Tyndale's attempt to avoid antinomianism by means of the distinction between 'historical' and 'feeling' faith.[47] Tyndale's 'knowledge' was not simply factual or propositional. It was an overwhelming act of divine revelation. He described it as the kind of knowledge one would gain from being in a city sacked by the Turks. This direct experience conferred a far different knowledge than that which one might hear from another that such and such a city had been taken by the Turks on the dim frontiers of Europe. 'Historical faith' is the faith a child has that his mother is telling the truth when she tells him that fire will burn. 'Feeling faith' is the knowledge one gets from putting his finger into the fire.[48] As this 'knowledge' grew with continual experience, the will was strengthened, and men received the power to observe the law of God. I would suggest that here we have one of the ways in which a humanist impulse may be carried over into Protestantism and transformed into Puritanism. It is a case of rationality feeding a tradition of legalism.[49]

Whence then did sin arise? Certainly not from mere ignorance. Tyndale was no Greek philosopher in Christian guise. But neither was sin a defect in the will as More believed, following Augustine.[50] Rather Tyndale had discovered (or rediscovered) a more profoundly Pauline explanation of sin. This was that the 'flesh' represented a daemonic power in man, capable at times of carrying the Christian off into abysmal evil in spite of the resistance of both Will and Intellect. Paul wrote, 'For the good that I would I do not; but the evil which I would not, that I do.'[51] And Tyndale wrote of the Christian who fell down into trances and did horrible deeds only to rise again from his sin at the voice of reproof.[52] It was an unfortunate image, and More ridiculed it.[53] But Tyndale's intent was not to minimize sin, as More thought. Rather it was to console the Christian in dubious battle against evil with the assurance that God's electing grace would not let him go.

Yet Tyndale's discussion was murky, and laced through it were grim comments about an unpardonable sin. For him this was the sin rooted in deliberate malice, in the cold, calculating decision of the Will to do evil. In his commentary on the First Epistle of St. John as well as in his preface to the book of Hebrews in his New Testament, he employed Heb. 6.4–6 as a prooftext for this position.[54] It is nowhere clear just who it was that he expected to commit this malicious sin. I suspect that it was in some way a barb thrown against his Catholic opponents, perhaps a consolation to himself that they ultimately would be consigned to hell for their malicious rejection of his pure Gospel. We must point out that his view of the unpardonable sin differed in no substantial way from a suggestion of St. Thomas Aquinas that the sin against the Holy Spirit was a sin 'ex certa malitia, id est ex ipsa electione mali.'[55]

Hebrews 6.4–6 had been one of the favorite prooftexts of the Novatians, that rigorous group which arose in the Church after the Decian persecution of A.D. 250. They interpreted the passage to mean that any sin committed after Baptism damned the soul irrevocably to hell. Evidently latter-day Novatians kept cropping up for years because the Fathers wrote against them for several centuries. More took his understanding of this text from the Fathers and insisted that Tyndale was a Novatian come to venomous life in the sixteenth century.[56]

In the second book of the *Confutation* More takes up this question in some detail. What does Hebrews 6.4–6 mean? Paul writes 'impossible' here when he means 'extremely difficult,' says More. It is almost impossible if one commits a deadly sin after Baptism to return to that pure state which Baptism confers. For if the Christian should die on ascending from the waters of Baptism, he would continue his ascent to Paradise without passing through Purgatory. Baptism cannot be repeated. But Penance is provided for those sins which are committed after Baptism, and no matter how great the sin we must 'neuer exclude the specyall pryuylege of goddys absolute mercy. For by hys myghty mercy the thynge that is impossyble to man is not impossyble to god.'[57]

In part More's interpretation may be taken from Nicholas of Lyra whose gloss was, like the *Glossa ordinaria,* a feature of many printed Bibles in More's time. Nicholas held that impossible here means difficult, as when we say that a lame man cannot walk. Repentance is not absolutely impossible as long as a man lives.[58] But the substance of More's interpretation is probably sketched from that which Ambrose gives to Hebrew 6.4–6 in his *De poenitentia,* in part directed against the Novatians. Here Hebrews 6.6 is taken up and treated in the light of the nature of Baptism. That which is impossible for man is affirmed as possible for God. It is impossible to receive the purification of Baptism by being baptized again, but it is entirely possible to trust in God's grace through penance for the remission of sin.[59] The unpardonable sin was viewed by Ambrose as a persistence in wrong faith until death, but no sin seemed so great that a man could not repent of it if he willed to do so.[60] This was the belief of St. Augustine,[61] and it became common in the Catholic tradition. More calls upon the authority of both these men along with that of Cyprian, Jerome, and Gregory the Great in denouncing Tyndale as a Novatian.[62]

Not surprisingly More uses Hebrews 6.4–6 to prove that the tradition of the Church is necessary to understand Scripture aright. He calls this passage 'the darke and hard wordes of saynt Poule. Whych places of them selfe all olde holy doctours confesse for dyffuse and almost unexplycable.'[63] Without the tradition of the Church the passage could not be understood at all beside the rest of the Christian faith.[64] But the point to be made here is that the Fathers helped More misunderstand Tyndale. By using Hebrews 6.4–6 in an essentially speculative way, Tyndale became a Novatian reincarnate. More was thus placed in the incongruous position of accusing Tyndale of rigorism in some places and libertinism and license in others.

Throughout all the polemical works More repeats his constant thesis that Scripture cannot stand alone. Scripture was a precious treasure of the Church, though not the most valuable. For the most valuable possession of the Church was the Spirit of God. It was that Spirit which made Scripture meaningful, and if anyone had ever possessed that Spirit it was the saintly Fathers of the patristic age.

The Fathers as Validators of Catholicism

But if More made pragmatic use of the Fathers to interpret the Bible, his more fundamental appeal to their authority lay on a different plane. The testimony of the Fathers vindicated the Catholic Church of the sixteenth century. For More this was to say that the meaning of history was so intertwined with the Catholic Church that if the Church were false, history made no sense at all.

In this regard it is significant that More's great text in defence of the Church was not Matthew 16 with the promise of Christ to give to Peter the keys of the Kingdom. He rarely employs this text in any way, and he never uses it in the sense of the extreme papalists. His great texts are rather Matthew 28.20 and John 16.13. On the one hand there is the promise of Christ to be with his followers always, even to the end of the world. And on the other, is the promise of Christ not to leave his disciples alone but to send them the Comforter who would lead them into all truth. More took these texts to mean that God's own promise validated the teaching of the Catholic Church through all the ages. God had made the promise in Christ. God would violate His own honor if He allowed the Church of Christ to fall into error.[65]

But the Reformers believed that at some point in history the Catholic Church had indeed fallen. The exact nature of this 'fall' was, like nearly everything else, a matter of disagreement among Protestants of the Reformation era, and it is still a question about which Protestant theologians frequently exercise themselves.[66] Luther's conception seems to have been that the Church had been more perverted in some eras than in others, but he did not seem to believe that there was one moment when the Church fell irrevocably into apostasy.[67] William Tyndale kept saying that the Catholic Church had been corrupt for eight hundred years. More could never understand what he meant by that figure.[68] But the sense of the charge was clear enough: the Catholic Church of the sixteenth century was *essentially* different from the Church of early Christianity. It was fallen, apostate. Among other things this meant that the Reformers could appeal to the Fathers to justify their own opinions and their assault on the Catholic Church.

More's appeal to the Fathers could serve two purposes. On the one hand he could establish that their idea of the Catholic Church was not substantially different from that Church which the Reformers were attacking as the bastion of Antichrist. On the other he could take considerable polemical or rhetorical advantage from the very respect with which the Reformers held the Fathers. For if it were so that the venerated Fathers would have rejected the Reformers, then the citations of the Fathers by Luther and the others would have seemed quite hollow. Beyond all this, the proof that the Fathers would have rejected Luther would isolate the Reformers more profoundly in history. To a man possessed of More's sense of the past, this would be proof enough of their error.

Consequently More summoned the Fathers to witness to a great many beliefs and practices which the Reformers rejected. Many examples could be cited. Perhaps basic to all the rest was More's belief in the relation of Scripture to tradition. He was one of that large number of Catholics in the sixteenth century who believed in the existence of an 'oral tradition' emanating from the Apostles and passed along through the history of the Church. The problem is extraordinarily complex. It has been taken up by a number of scholars recently, and we cannot hope to treat all of its ramifications here.[69] More clearly believed that this extrascriptural tradition contained doctrines which were not in Scripture but which were still authoritative for Christians. It does not seem that he believed the tradition was still unwritten in the sixteenth century since all the things he attributes to it were written about often enough by that time.[70] What More called 'oral tradition' seems no different from that which the Council of Trent would later call simply 'Tradition.' His point was that Scripture was not the only thing bequeathed by the Apostles to the Church.

To support this position he appealed to the testimony of the Fathers. He maintained that they had not been strict Biblicists; that they had, on the contrary, given their allegiance to an extrascriptural tradition. Using a list compiled by John Fisher, Bishop of Rochester, More quoted passages from the works of Origen, John of Damascus, 'Dionysius,'[71] Cyprian, Hilary, Theophilactus, Jerome, Leo the Great, Augustine, and Cassian.[72] All of these supported his thesis. Interestingly enough, More nowhere mentions Clement of Alexandria in this connection, though Clement's belief in the esoteric nature of the oral tradition was very much like his own.[73] But the substance of his argument was to dispute the *sola scriptura* principle of the Reformers by proving that this had not been the belief of the Fathers.[74]

Other things at issue made More call upon the Fathers. The Reformers rejected Purgatory. They could not locate the doctrine in Scripture, and the idea of an intermediate state where merit might be gained after death conflicted with their theologies of grace and predestination. In response More called on the witness of Augustine who prayed for his mother Monica at Masses after her death.[75] He also recalled that John Chrysostom had advised prayers and Masses to be said for the dead.[76] From this he thought that the Fathers had had a notion of Purgatory, and it is difficult to deny his point. The Reformers were also given to condemning much of the ceremonial piety of the Catholic Church, especially those forms which did not have some clear meaning. This was especially true of William Tyndale who in this as in so many other things stands as a harbinger of Puritanism. Tyndale spoke of the sign of the cross made by the bishop as the wagging of two fingers. To this More retorted with a story from Gregory Nazianzen. Gregory told of Julian the Apostate who, on consulting the necromancers, was so startled by their summoned apparitions that he blessed himself with the sign of the cross and so dispelled them.[77] And elsewhere, in a general way, More refers to the 'good holy doctours and of ye eldest' to substantiate that essentially Catholic proposition that material working can have an effect on the soul.[78] For the mixing of wine and water in the Mass, which Luther vehemently rejected, he found a witness in St. Cyprian.[79] For the perpetual virginity of Mary he employs the authority of Jerome as well as that of Augustine.[80] This was an important issue to More precisely because the Reformers did not dispute it. Since there was nothing of Mary's perpetual virginity in the Scriptures, the Reformers must admit, he thought, that they were accepting an extrascriptural Catholic tradition. More's question, then, was why should they accept part of this tradition without accepting it all? What was their authority for discrimination?

Certainly, too, More's acquaintance with the Fathers must have reinforced his condemnation of sexual sins. With Luther's marriage to the nun, Katherine von Bora, ever before his horrified eyes, he could view the whole Reformation as a kind of bawdy show. If God were to make such a revelation against His Catholic Church, More was certain that He would not send a 'frere out of a nonnes bedde to preache yt.'[81] He drew his authority for this view from all the Catholic tradition but especially from the Fathers. And it is difficult to imagine a more constant asceticism with regard to sex than that which prevailed among the Fathers. Ostensibly it was not that proper sexual relations between husband and wife were sinful. More was married twice. Yet sins related to sex were regarded with especial loathing in the patristic age, and the worst loathing of all was reserved for those who made and broke vows of chastity.[82] Marriage in the shadow of such a broken vow was the filthiest of lusts, a clear choice of the flesh over God. On occasion More called on 1 Tim. 5.3–16 for support. Here the implication was that widows who break vows are damned.[83] More's interpretation was that of the Church since the Fathers, that the passage had a wider meaning, that any broken vow of continence, whether by virgin or by widow, was reprehensible.[84] It was with some confidence that More could call upon an imaginary council of the Church, drawn from all its history, to judge Luther and 'Cate.' Suppose, he said, that Luther would represent to such a council that

> who so maketh any suche vowe, wenynge that he haue the gyfte bycause he feleth no contrary grudge at that tyme/yet whan so euer he feleth after any flesshely mocyon in hys frayle membres, he maye thanne perceyue well and be very sure, that he hath not the gyfte/and that therfore he was deceyued by the deuyll, whan he made hymself a frere. And that he maye now therfore ronne out of his relygyon, and folow the flesshe. And whan he fyndeth a nonne that feleth the lyke, and that eche of theym fele other, and lyke well eche other for theyr felynge fayth/than maye they bothe be sure that they maye boldely breke both theyr vowes and wedde theym selfe to gyther.[85]

This sarcastic passage is something of a parody of Luther's attitude towards vows, but like most parodies it embodies much of the true nature of the position which is attacked.[86] With all confidence More could assume that his imagined general council of historical Christianity would condemn such an opinion, excommunicate Luther and the rest, and witness to their damnation.[87] As if anticipating such a judgment by Catholics, Luther had dismissed the opinions of the Fathers regarding vows. The Fathers were simply wrong. The Scripture was clear, and, citing Paul as a witness, he declared that he would accept no authority beside Scripture, not even that of an angel from heaven.[88] It was an attitude expressed more than once by Luther,[89] and it goaded More to the summit of almost inexpressible fury.[90]

Yet More never claimed that the Fathers were infallible. Indeed he pointed out a number of their mistakes. He knew that Origen had taught the eventual redemption of all creatures, including the Devil himself.[91] On the basis of a pseudonymous text he believed that Cyprian had taken the washing of feet to be a divine command still binding on the Church.[92] He points out that almost all the Fathers had erred regarding the immaculate conception of the Virgin.[93] He knew that Augustine had once thought demons to be corporeal in nature.[94] In regard to this error of his favorite saint he made a statement which summarizes his whole attitude towards the Fathers: 'Homo erat, errare potuit. Credo ei quantum cui plurima, sed nemini vni omnia.'[95]

The same thought was later to be expressed against William Tyndale: 'Here must Tyndale understand, that we neuer bynde hym to any thynge of necessyte upon the saynge of any one doctoure be he olde or yonge/but eyther by

the comen faste fayth of the whole catholyke chyrch, growe*n* as yt euer doth
by the spyryte of god, that maketh men of one mynde in his chyrche, or by
the determynacyon of the chyrche assembled for such causes in the generall
counsayles.'[96] Here was the crux of the matter. The Fathers had varied, but
they had submitted their wills to the Church over which God's Spirit presided
according to the promise of Christ. Here the dimension of time is crucial. For
in time God, acting according to His own pleasure which always for More lay
beyond man's capacity to understand, worked out a consensus of belief within the Church. Said More, speaking of Tyndale with relation to the Fathers:

> If he wyll saye that sometyme the doctours whyche we call holy sayntes
> haue not all agreed in one/but some one hath sometyme thought in some
> one thyng otherwyse then other haue done: I saye that thys his sayenge is
> nothynge to purpose. For god doth reuele hys trouthes not alwayes in one
> manner/but sometyme he sheweth yt out at onys as he wyll haue yt
> knowen and men bounden forthwyth to byleue yt/as he shewed Moyses
> what he wolde haue Pharao do. Sometyme he sheweth yt leysourly, suf-
> fryng his flokke to comen & dyspute theruppon/and in theyr treatynge of
> the mater, suffreth them wyth good mynde & scrypture and naturall wise-
> dome, with inuocacyon of his spirituall helpe, to serche and seke for the
> treuth, and to vary for the whyle in theyr opynions, tyll that he rewarde
> theyr vertuouse dylygence wyth ledyng them secretely in to the consent
> and concorde and bylyef of the trouth by his holy spirite *qui facit vnanimes
> in domo,* whyche maketh his flokke of one mynde in his house, that is to
> wyt his chyrche. So y^t in the meane whyle the varyaunce is wythoute
> synne, and maketh nothyng agaynst the credence of the chyrch.[97]

So, though the Fathers had varied, in the midst of their variance they had remained faithful to the Catholic Church. None of the 'holy doctours helde
obstynatly, the contrarye of that thynge whyche the hole catholyque chyrch
had in his tyme determyned for an artycle of ye fayth.'[98] Explicit in this statement is the idea that times change, and that in the unfolding of history God
settles the disputes which arise among His people. Implicit is an essentially
positive evaluation of history itself as the realm in which God progressively
reveals Himself.

What More did was to make the passion for ecclesiastical unity the most
important single element in patristic theology. But how did he define this
unity? Or, to put the question as he put it, what was this Church to which the
Fathers were devoted? To discuss this question in any detail would lead us far
afield, but it must have brief mention. Otherwise More's foundation of belief
regarding the Fathers would be ignored and his arguments subject to misunderstanding.

For More the Church was the whole body of professing Christians. 'The hole
chyrch is the hole crysten people/and therfore they call it the catholyke
chyrche that is unyversall.'[99] It contains both good and bad, faithful and
hypocrites, men who now stand in a state of saving grace but who will be lost
because of future sins and men who will persevere to the end and so come to

the eternal Kingdom of God.[100] The Church cannot err. This does not mean
that popes cannot err, for the pope is not the whole Church any more than the
Bishop of London is the whole Church of London or the Archbishop of Canterbury the whole Church of his province.[101] The pope, while vicar and head
of the Church,[102] was not the highest authority in the Church, for he could be
deposed by the General Council, and indeed popes had been deposed by such
councils.[103] Though at the end of life More professed his personal belief in the
divine establishment of the papacy,[104] he was earlier willing to grant that the
Church might conceivably abolish the office altogether and instead be ruled
by 'prouyncyall patryarches, arbysshoppes [sic], or metropolytanes.'[105] Admittedly many problems would be raised by such an action, but it was within
the realm of possibility, and, for that reason, said More, 'I purposely forbare
to put in the pope as parte of the dyffynycyon of the chyrche, as a thynge
that neded not/syth yf he be the necessary hed, he is included in the name of
the hole body. And whyther he be or not/yf it be brought in questyon, were
a mater to be treated and dysputed besyde.'[106] In so far as any institution
within the Church was concerned, the General Council did enjoy supreme
authority as long as it was 'assembled lawfully'—a condition which More never
defined.[107] One council might change the decision of an earlier council with
regard to some ecclesiastical practice because different times brought different
practical necessities. 'For,' as More said, 'in dyuerse tymes, dyuerse thynges
may be conuenyent and dyuerse maners of doynge.'[108] Matters of faith enjoyed a different status. Wrote More, 'But in maters of bylyefe & fayth,
whyche be trouehes [sic] reueled & declared by god unto man/though that in
dyuerse times there may be more thinges farther and farther reueled, and other
then were desclosed at the fyrst: yet can there neuer any thynge be by god
reueled after, that can be contrary to any thynge reueled by hym selfe by-
fore.'[109] Real authority within the Church rested in the whole congregation of
Christian men, and the council received its power because it was representative
of the whole Church.[110] The council was not required to confirm every point
of doctrine, for that which the whole body of Christians believed had the
force of dogma whether it had been certified by a council or not.[111]

All this represents a certain flexibility in More's ecclesiology. Room was
left for variation and change, and the exact institutional structure of the
Church was left open to honest debate. Implicit in his idea of progressive revelation was the notion that the Church of the sixteenth century might well vary
considerably from the Church of the Fathers. As we have seen, this meant that
some of the Fathers had frankly erred in their expression of particular doctrines.
But the consensus of the Fathers was always that there was one Church known
to be Catholic and Apostolic and that it might be readily determined who belonged to that Church and who belonged to some sect among the heretics.

It appears that the essence of More's ecclesiology is this: the Catholic Church
is known. He is endlessly given to using such terms as 'the comen catholyke
fayth' or 'the knowen catholyque chyrch' or 'the comen knowen catholique
chyrch.'[112] Augustine, said More, believed 'the holy catholyque chyrche of the
ryght bylyefe, to be y[e] comen one unyuersall knowen chyrch dystyncte and

dyuyded from all the knowen chyrches of heretyques.'[113] In part this emphasis on the fact that the Church is known is a reaction to the doctrine of the
'invisible church' which he believed to be the hallmark of the ecclesiology of
the Reformers.[114] But on a more profound level his appeal was to what he
conceived to be historical common sense. From the time of the earliest Church
to the sixteenth century a historical entity had existed which had been called
the Catholic Church. No rival to that Church had ever possessed any historical
continuity. If William Tyndale were right, if the Church had been fallen for
eight hundred years, he could still point to no other known Church which had
enjoyed any continuity since that time.[115] That would mean that eight hundred
years before, God had suddenly, mysteriously, and without informing his people
changed His way of working in the world. Religiously More could not accept
such an argument, and historically he found that it conflicted with 'the consent of all the olde holy doctours and sayntes of euery age synnys chrysten-
dome fyrste began.'[116] For all his prolixity of argument in *defending* the Church,
More was never really to go far beyond that *definition* which held that the
Church was that body which was known as the Church in history. The Church
in its history might become infected with 'dede flesshe . . . in the syke and sore
partes of the same.'[117]

The Church might well become a minority of those professing Christians.
This latter notion seemed to possess More in 1533—the year that Henry VIII
sundered the last fragile links which tied him to Catholic Christendom. More
did not comment directly on the turbulent events of that fatal year, but he
brooded over them, and the brooding left its imprint in the *Confutation,* part
two of which came from the press in 1533. If a man or a country fell from the
Church, 'they be controlled, noted, and reproued by the hole body & soone
knowen from the body.'[118] And in another place he wrote, 'And yf any person
departe from the fayth of thys chyrch, or that any pertyculare chyrche fall fro
the doctryne of the whole catholyke chyrche, and so departe therfro: yet re-
mayneth the remanaunt styll the very full catholyke chyrch.'[119] Though the
Church be diminished until it become a 'small flocke' in comparison to heretics,
yet still it will be the Church, 'the pylar & the fote or grounde/that is to say
the sure strengthe or fastenynge of the trouthe . . . that knowen catholique
chyrche.'[120] No matter what came, in England or elsewhere, the Church would
be known. The Fathers had known it in their time; More knew it in his.

Conclusion

This Catholic interpretation of the relation of the Fathers to the Church of
the sixteenth century has never gone unchallenged by Protestants. More's
claim was always that the Fathers and the Church stood or fell together and
that to reject the Catholic Church required rejection of the Fathers.[121] Obviously the Reformers did not accept this choice. With their preoccupation
with the power of divine grace, they especially reveled in a part of the work of
Augustine of Hippo, More's favorite saint and Father. Luther cited him frequently, and a recent scholar has assembled a hefty volume which is simply an

index to the use of Augustine by John Calvin.[122] Still more recently yet another scholar has made an extraordinarily impressive study of the relationship
of the Fathers to the thought of Philip Melanchthon.[123]

The Protestant use of the Fathers was necessarily selective. More's arguments which we have examined in this paper are enough to prove that. But as
we have also seen, there was a great deal of selectivity to More's use of patristic
authority. He emphasized their commitment to the Catholic Church. Any
Protestant reading this paper would be sure to notice that there is nothing in
it regarding an attitude of More to Augustine's doctrine of grace and predestination. This is not accidental, for More largely ignored these difficult texts
from his beloved saint and instead wrote incessantly of Augustine's ecclesiastical
devotion. Naturally enough the Protestants felt justified in emphasizing those
abundant expressions of the Fathers seemingly consonant with their own
theology.

Who was more correct? Such a question still finds different answers according to the religious conceptions of the people undertaking to respond to it.
Professor Jaroslav Pelikan, as a Protestant theologian of history, has summarized the 'Protestant Principle' of the Reformation in a recent book with the
intriguing title *Obedient Rebels*.[124] Mr. Pelikan finds that the chief objection
of Luther and Melanchthon to Catholic ecclesiology was to the Catholic faith
that a historical institution could be infallible. 'History is the conditioned
bearer of the activity of God.'[125] This means that any historical institution can
err because it is conditioned by its existence in a world permeated with sin.
'Lutheran theology [Mr. Pelikan says] does not discard its regard for the
historical church. . . . It devotes itself to the study of patristic theology not
with authoritarian reverence, nor yet with supercilious contempt, but with a
deep regard and a healthy suspicion.'[126] Mr. Pelikan rather accurately presents
the general attitude of the Protestants towards the Fathers. He would not, I
presume, then object if I argue that this attitude is itself an admission that
More and Catholics like him were correct in their assessment of the Fathers.
For More usually came down to present the patristic argument in something
like the following: if Cyprian, Origen, Cassian, Gregory, Jerome, Augustine
and all the rest were alive today, would they accept or reject Luther, Tyndale,
and the others? For More the answer was obvious.[127]

In a day like our own, when the literary critic is given to finding elaborate
patterns of symbolism in novels never dreamed of by their authors, More's
argument is probably not compelling. Augustine in the flesh, miraculously
propelled through time to the sixteenth century, would have regarded Luther
with horror and loathing. So what? There is still much in Augustine's works
which Luther might validly use. Since men of our age are weaned in the air
of doubt and uncertainty, any claim to historical infallibility enjoys among
the masses the status of the fairy tale or perhaps the Emerald City of Oz.

More lived at a different time. The Fathers were to him giants in the earth,
the greatest men besides the Apostles who had ever lived. Their moral example
radiates throughout all his works. Even in the *Utopia* there may be some reflection of his feelings towards them in the Utopian conviction that the spirits

of the dead hover ever about on earth to encourage the living.[128] All these men were resolutely committed to the Catholic Church. But if the Reformers were correct, all of them had been in error. For More the error was not some mere peccadillo, something which could be glossed over in the name of something called the 'Gospel.' The error was fundamental to their whole understanding of themselves, of the universe, and of God. In More's mind saintly men could not have been *so* wrong. 'I laye you also that if it had bene otherwise and that they had therin damnably bene deceiued, than liuyng & dying in damnable error they could not haue bene saintes.'[129] I do not believe we exaggerate if we say that ultimately More's defence of the Catholic Church, built as he conceived it on the foundation of the Fathers, was a defence of the cosmic value of goodness.

In large measure too More's defence of the Catholic Church was a defence of the idea that God was constantly active in creation. This was the more profound theological principle behind More's incessant emphasis upon the importance of the miraculous. God moved in the world in ways that were unmistakable. The Fathers possessed holiness of life and a plentitude of grace, and God had 'opened theyr eyen and suffered and caused them to see the trouth.'[130] He had confirmed their teaching 'by many a thousand myracle both in their liues & after their deathes.'[131] But if the Reformers were correct, the Fathers had fallen into catastrophic error, and God had remained silent for centuries until the advent of Luther. In phraseology this thought usually was embedded in the argument that if Tyndale and Luther were correct, 'then hath Chryste broken all hys promyses by whyche he promysed to be wyth his chyrche all days to the worldes ende.'[132] This is a rhetorical expression of an attitude which could not understand how God as Christians conceived Him could remain quiescent while so much error was abroad among people who lived saintly lives and believed they knew God's will. The implication was that if Luther's protest were allowed, the conception men had of God would be so changed as to become unrecognizable.

In summation of More's view of the Fathers, I think we are brought back to a fundamental trait of his personality—his sober, melancholy awareness of the coming of death. Perhaps next to the publication of More's works themselves, this has been the greatest contribution of the current 'More renaissance' —this laying bare of this side of the man, the dark image standing behind the light cast by the witty, urbane, and talkative gentleman whom Henry VIII delighted to have at his dinner table. This was the More who partook of the late medieval dread of death, the dread illustrated by the macabre fifteenth-century funerary monuments preserved in the Louvre, by the dance-of-death motif in art, and by innumerable solemn treatises on the 'Four Last Things.'[133] This More is the somber man of Holbein's famous portrait, the More who could translate Pico's verses on death with such feeling:

> Consider well that euer night and daye
> While that we besily prouide and care
> For our disport reuill myrth and playe,
> For pleasaunt melody and daintie fare,

> Death stealeth on full slily and unware.
> He lieth at hande, and shall us enterprise,
> We wote not howe soone, nor in what manerwise.[134]

Or again:

> This wretched life, the trust and confidence
> Of whole continuance maketh us bolde to synne,
> Thou perceiuest well by experience,
> Sith that houre, in which it did beginne,
> It holdeth on the course, and will not linne,
> But fast it runneth on, and passen shall
> As dothe a dreame or shadow on the wall.[135]

Before this dread, and in a time when a swell of change rolled disturbingly beneath the old certainties, it is not surprising that men sought to cling to some sure authority. After all, this was a ground of Luther's Reformation. And though Luther turned from devotion to an infallible historical church, he found a kind of infallibility in the 'Gospel.' But More was too deeply impressed by the existence of the Church through centuries of history to be able to cast it off in the name of some trans-historical faith resting upon nothing more, as he thought, than the rhetoric of a vagabond monk. Like his fellow martyr, John Fisher, More could have asked, 'For what is the doctryne of the churche/ but the doctryne of the fathers?'[136] These saintly men so possessed his imagination that he could not let them go, and since he equated their being with the being of the Church that meant that he could not relinquish his hold upon that Church in his own time.

We must take account of this passion. It figures in the most rational summation we can make of the man. He was one of those people who are able to look beyond the edge of the immediate and to see the darkness of mystery crouching beyond the firelight cast by history. It was a strange and troubling darkness to More. He recoiled from it and stood the more closely to the witness of the Fathers. These godly men had lived in the world of death in the conviction that God had spoken a word of life to His Church, that the true light had shone in darkness and that the darkness could never extinguish it. More's work was an extension of their labors. His death was a defence of their life.

THE MAKING OF SIR THOMAS MORE'S *RICHARD III*

A. F. Pollard

Were this volume exclusively, as it is essentially, mediaeval in content, it would imply some neglect of services rendered by a mediaevalist to post-mediaeval studies; and an essay dealing with a problem of Renaissance historiography will not appear out of place at the end of a tribute to labours which included *Lancashire Quarter-Sessions, Taxation in Salford Hundred,* 1524–1802, and a score of notable articles in the *Dictionary of National Biography* on such outstanding Yorkist and Tudor figures as Warwick the kingmaker; Buckingham of the rebellion; the Stanley who married the first Tudor's mother and placed the crown on his head at Bosworth; the other Stanley who turned that field into a Tudor victory and ten years later lost his own head on a Tudor scaffold; the grim and effective bishop who made the Marches of Wales safe for Henry VIII; and Burghley's immediate predecessor, *ortus e salice, non ex quercu,* who was lord high treasurer to Edward VI, to Mary, and to Elizabeth.

The most revolutionary year in this Yorkist-Tudor period, the only year in English history since the Conquest in which there have been three English kings—including incidentally the whole Yorkist dynasty—is also the theme of the first "history" in English that has any claim to be English literature. The problems relating to More's *Richard III* are manifold—its authorship, its authority, its sources, the date of its composition, the circumstances of its publication, the relation of the English to the Latin versions, the absence of any original autograph, the variations in the printed texts, the motive of its conception, and the reasons for its unfinished state and abrupt termination. More's authorship has commonly been accepted, without being proved, by historians: it was not till 1596 that Cardinal Morton appears in gossip as a rival parent; and that story was obviously the offspring of More's known connexion with Morton, his apparent derivation of knowledge from that source, and a sentence in the earliest printed text in which "I myselfe that wrote this pamphlet" claims that he "truly knewe" the facts about Edward IV's last illness.[1] This would rule out More, who was barely six years old, at most, when Edward died. But Morton also is ruled out by the various references in the text to events long after Morton's death; and the case for More's authorship—subject to possible interpolations by translators, transcribers, editors or printers—has been pretty conclusively proved. Morton neither wrote nor

Reprinted with permission from *Historical Essays in Honour of James Tait,* ed. J. G. Edwards, V. H. Galbraith, and E. F. Jacob (Manchester, for Subscribers only, 1933), pp. 223–38.

dictated either the English or the Latin text; More was responsible for the substance of both.

Nor is there much doubt about the date of composition. The statement of More's nephew and editor, William Rastell, that *Richard III* was written "about the year 1513" by More "then one of the undersheriffs of London" is confirmed by internal evidence, though the reference on the first page to Thomas Howard "after Earl of Surrey" points to a year between 1513 and 1524;[2] and, if it was written while More was undersheriff, it must have been written before 23 July 1518 when, on More's resignation, John Pakington was elected his successor.[3] In all probability it was written before 8 May 1515, when More, on his appointment to his mission to Flanders, was licensed by the city to exercise his office by a sufficient deputy.[4] What leisure that mission left him was spent on the *Utopia;* and, whatever the cause of the abrupt termination of *Richard III,* it is improbable that More ever gave it a thought thereafter, either by way of continuation or revision. The spaces for names and dates, which More originally left to be filled in, were still blank when, forty years later, Rastell printed his text from both More's English and his Latin autographs: the "after earl of Surrey" stands,[5] though Surrey succeeded his father as duke of Norfolk in 1524; "for yet she liveth" remains after Catherine, countess of Devonshire, though she died in 1527, and the same remark is still appended to Jane Shore, who died in 18 Henry VIII.[6]

When we come to the sources whence More derived his information, we are driven into the more doubtful realms of conjecture. Apart from a few boyish recollections, More can have had no personal knowledge of what took place when he was six years old. The lack was supplied, according to common assumption, by fragments of Morton's conversation overheard by More while a page in Morton's household between 1486 and 1492.[7] The fallibility of recollections as materials for history and biography is strikingly illustrated by Roper's life of More himself. Roper married More's eldest daughter on 2 July 1521: for sixteen years, before and after that, he was, he tells us, "continually resident" in More's house. Yet he says that "while Sir Thomas More was chancellor of the Duchy [of Lancaster, *i.e.,* 1525–9], the see of Rome chanced to be void," and proceeds to give an account of Adrian VI's election and Wolsey's failure in 1522.[8] He also makes More succeed Sir Richard Weston as under-treasurer, though More was appointed in 1521, and Weston, who was not appointed till 1528, held the post until his death in 1541.[9] More's recollection in 1514 of what he had heard Morton say more than twenty years before is therefore a somewhat slight foundation for the superstructure of his *Richard III.* Nor, in point of fact, does More ever mention Morton as his authority for anything. His references are all with one exception anonymous; but, with that exception, they are always in the plural[10] and relate to different and specific points, and not to a general comprehensive source; and that exceptional reference is not to Morton but to More's father.

It is, however, incredible that More should have learnt no more from his father, who was living when More wrote, about Richard III than that one detail; and it is unreasonable to limit his oral informants to Morton who had been dead fourteen years, while excluding others who had participated in public affairs while Richard reigned and were not only alive when More was writing, but were his friends, acquaintances, or neighbours. Did More learn nothing, for instance, from his bishop, Richard Fitzjames who had been chaplain to Edward IV, treasurer of St. Paul's almost throughout Richard's reign,[11] almoner to Henry VII, and was bishop of London from 1506 to 1522; from the bishop's nephew John Fitzjames, the chief-justice, who occurs on Richard's patent rolls, was M.P. and apparently recorder of Bristol in 1492,[12] and helped William Roper in making out his quarterly reports of the king's wards; or from William's father John Roper, Richard III's commissioner of array for Kent and Fitzjames's successor as attorney-general?[13] Some of these living witnesses had a common friend in Erasmus whose correspondence testifies to their acquaintance with More. Bishop Fox of Winchester was one of them, and he had been in exile with Henry Tudor representing his interests at the French court and being debarred on that account by Richard from institution to the vicarage of St. Dunstan's, Stepney.[14] Morton's successor Warham, with whom More was, according to Erasmus, in daily communication in November 1511, was less involved than Fox; but, as master of the rolls from 1494 to 1502 and then lord-chancellor, he must have known a good deal about Richard III. Christopher Urswick, another friend of Erasmus and More, had been initiated into the schemes of Margaret Beaufort and Morton in the early autumn of 1483, escaped abroad to Henry, and became his chaplain, confessor, and almoner. He was frequently employed on embassies after 1485, was registrar of the Garter, and an executor of Margaret Beaufort's will. He lived in his later years near More at Hackney, of which he was rector and where he was buried in 1521.[15] Nor does the fact that Polydore Vergil's history was not published till 1534 preclude the possibility that he had given More oral information in 1514: he had been seeking materials for his history from Henry VII, James IV, and lesser folk as early as 1505; he was given a prebend in St. Paul's in 1513, lived mainly in London and was acquainted with More and was (at times) a friend of Erasmus.[16] Bishop William Smith, who died in 1514, is a less likely informant though he had knowledge enough, having been brought up by Margaret Beaufort and the Stanleys and having been appointed clerk of the hanaper within a month of Bosworth field. He succeeded Morton as chancellor of Oxford University, took an active part in the judicial work of the king's council when More was practising, was victimized by Empson and Dudley, and was an executor of Henry VII's will; but his intellectual affinities and official duties kept him as a rule at a distance from London and More's circle.

Smith's successor as clerk of the hanaper, Roger Lupton, is a more probable source, as is also Lupton's successor in that office, Sir John Heron, whose son Giles subsequently married More's daughter Cicely. Lupton had, on 15 September 1484, succeeded to the living of Harlton, vacant by the death of the notorious Dr. Ralph Shaa,[17] who, says More, "by his sermon [declaring bastards the princes in the Tower] lost his honesty and soon after his life." Lupton became provost of Eton and founder of Sedbergh school, and was succeeded by Heron as clerk of the hanaper on 30 September 1514;[18] and Heron introduces a number of family and financial connexions which may have added to More's historical information, and certainly helped him into the under-treasurership under Norfolk. Heron had been an adherent of Henry Tudor during Richard III's reign, and from the beginning of Henry VII's assisted Sir Thomas Lovell in financial administration; about August 1492 he became treasurer of the chamber, an office he did much to develop, and he held it till his death on 10 June 1522. He had named Christopher Urswick "parson of Hackney" one of his executors,[19] while his cousin, another John Heron[20] who died in 1515, dilates in his will on his friendship with Sir John Cutte, under-treasurer, and with Sir John Daunce (or Dauntsy) the general surveyor. More succeeded Cutte as under-treasurer, and Daunce's son William married More's third daughter, Elizabeth. Cutte could have given More no little information about Richard III: he was that king's servant and receiver of crown lands in half a dozen counties, executor of Sir Reginald Bray, and third husband of Warwick the kingmaker's niece, Lucy Neville.[21]

All these men had been bound in one way or another to Sir Thomas Lovell, who had been attainted in Richard III's only parliament, was Speaker in Henry VII's first parliament, and was in 1514 treasurer of Henry VIII's household; his will contains a reference to More.[22] The head of this financial hierarchy was, however, Norfolk, the lord treasurer, who was succeeded in 1524 both in his office and in his dukedom by his son the earl of Surrey; and who, if not Norfolk (then Sir Thomas Howard),[23] can have told More what Hastings said to him on 13 June 1483 as Howard accompanied the lord chamberlain to the fatal council at the Tower? To these survivors of Richard III's usurpation—abettors and victims, critics and partisans—their recollections of revolution and of "the happy union of the two illustrious houses" must have been a constant topic of conversation and of congratulation on the milder auspices under which they lived in the early days of Henry VIII. More's *Richard III* is a résumé and result of such conversations: it is concerned, as Lord Acton hoped of the last projected volumes of the *Cambridge Modern History,* with "secrets" that could not "be learned from books, but from men."[24]

More, indeed, could learn little of Richard III from books in 1514. The Croyland continuator had, it is true, written his brief but excellent summary of the period in 1486; but More certainly never saw the MS., and it was not printed till 1684.[25] His City connexion may have enabled him to see the Cotton MS., Vitellius A xvi,[26] and the MS. of Fabyan's similar chronicle, which was not published till 1516; and there remain such possible sources as the MS. "Cronica Cronicorum," which Edward Hall used, possessed, and bequeathed "to lye in the counsell chamber" of the City,[27] and the *Great Chronicle of London,* which still remains in private hands and from which only a few isolated extracts have appeared in print.[28] But the wholesale way in which Grafton, in his two editions of Hardyng (1543), and Hall in his own chronicle (bequeathed for publication to Grafton by Hall's will, proved 25 May 1547), incorporated More's *Richard III* indicates the superior attraction of More's work to any other MS. material at their disposal. Stow was apparently the first to recover from the fascination, and the form of his *Annales* led him at least to temper More's dramatic art with extracts from the *Great Chronicle.* As history, More's book stands or falls by the value of its oral information.

There are obvious drawbacks as well as advantages in writing secrets learnt from men and not from books, particularly when the men are the historian's friends or colleagues burdened with a past which, while it gives them a *locus standi* in the court, does not always make their testimony exact or encourage its publication. Norfolk, for instance, may have told More that he, as Sir Thomas Howard, had been sent by Richard III to fetch Hastings to the Tower, and then to ransack the unfortunate Jane Shore's house. But these were not details for undisguised publication, or even committing to paper, by a friend in 1514. So "Sir Thomas Howard" appears in More's *Richard III* simply as "a knight" and "this knight," or is omitted altogether, as when we are told that "the Protector sent into the house of Shore's wife . . . and spoiled her of all that ever she had."[29] More, too, must have learnt that Norfolk's father was—next to Buckingham—Richard III's principal support. Yet the first duke is never mentioned in More's text, and the second duke is never mentioned by name; the third duke, only ten years old in 1483, was, however, innocent enough to be politely introduced by name on More's first page as the husband to whom Edward IV's third daughter Anne was "honourably" married in Westminster Abbey on 4 February 1495. So far as More's *Richard III* is concerned, the Howards might not have existed. So, too, Bourchier is always "the Cardinal," but is never named nor even called archbishop of Canterbury, and the Stanleys fade away after Richard's *coup d'état* on 13 June: the facts that Thomas remained steward of Richard III's household, officiated (with his wife Margaret Beaufort) at his coronation, and profited more than anyone else, except Norfolk and Northumberland, from his bounty, have to be gathered from less considerate sources. Naturally Northumberland, who also officiated at the coronation and was granted Buckingham's office of great chamberlain of England four months later, is also absent from More's pages: his son was in favour and repute in the early years of Henry VIII till Wolsey fell foul of him in 1516. Indeed, the difficulty of giving any detailed description of Richard III's coronation without reviving memories, decaying and distasteful in 1514, probably accounts for its dismissal by More in two lines[30] and may have contributed to the discontinuance of More's whole narrative. Only the dead or the degraded figure as accomplices in More's indictment; and his *Richard III* is not free from the bias which attaches to history written or inspired by the victors.

Such are some of the defects in history composed by men who have to consider their position and that of those upon whom they depend for information. But it may be questioned in what sense, if any, More regarded himself as writing history. He does not appear to have been responsible for any of the various titles under which his book has appeared. Assuredly the title given to the official text, edited from More's autograph by his nephew William Rastell, is Rastell's and not More's composition. But, supposing More did call it a

history, need we call him a historian any more than Shakespeare, who also
wrote certain famous "histories" of kings, including Richard III? Moreover,
does not More, in his prefatory letter to Peter Giles, call his *Utopia* a "history"?
Does he not further, in that same epistle to Peter Giles, contrast "olde rustie
antiquities" with "the flower and grace of the noveltie" of *Utopia*?[31] Novelty
in flower and grace has also been claimed for *Richard III;* but is there any evidence that More ever suffered from the modern disorder of historical research,
or that he was deeply versed in history at all? *Richard III* was the outcome of
what he had heard, not what he had read. He was, we are told, "a very good
hater"[32]: but a good hater and a good historian are not synonymous terms;
and if, as Ascham said, More's *Richard III* "doth content all men,"[33] its appeal
was to the old Adam, rather than to the new science, in man.

That More could tell a "story," and tell it supremely well, is not in doubt;
he welded the stories he heard about Richard III into a piece of magnificent
English prose. That he had a highly-developed dramatic sense is also beyond
dispute: he attracted Morton's attention by his youthful and Yule-tide
dramatic sallies which, Roper tells us, "made the lookers-on more sport than
all the players beside." About 1514 his brother-in-law, John Rastell, was busy
with projects which played no small part in the early Tudor drama,[34] and the
most learned authority on More in our own days has written about "The
Chelsea academy of dramatic art."[35] Was not *Richard III* More's contribution
to its common stock? It has all the requisite stage-properties: it begins with
the *dramatis personae,* and a third of the text consists of their speeches; dates
are almost as rare in More as they are impertinent to any legitimate drama,
and his Richard III possesses all the qualities for a villain of the piece. All other
elements except the dramatic are eschewed. Harpsfield puts elegance and eloquence side by side as the prime qualities of *Richard III;*[36] and Tudor drama,
if not always as elegant as More, was greatly given to eloquence. Foreign relations, social conditions, constitutional problems are passed over in silence;
there is not a word about Edward V's one general election or Richard's super-
session of that parliament; and More, as dramatist, could not even pander to
his legal instincts so far as to use the year-book for Edward V's one and only
term and tell us the legal reason why all the judges and serjeants, being present
in Chancery on the day that Richard usurped the throne, decided "que le roy
ne poet estre dit un qui fist tort."[37]

And, if More's *Richard III* is primarily dramatic, the question of its fidelity
to historical fact hardly arises. History may be dramatic, but the more dramatic
it is, the less attention it pays to the canons of historical evidence, historical
criticism, and historical circumspection. Even Froude, who thought *Macbeth*
would be "perfect history," qualifies it with the proviso "were it literally
true," and admits that the dramatist "is not bound, when it is inconvenient,
to what may be called the accidents of facts."[38] Dramatic art involves, indeed,
an economy of historical truth and a liberal use of poetic imagination; and the
accidents of facts in *Richard III* are rather serious. There is the astonishing
statement in its first sentence that Edward IV "lived fifty and three years,
seven months, and six days," whereas he really lived but forty years, eleven

months, and twelve days.[39] This allegation would put back Edward's birth to
3 September 1429, make havoc of Yorkist family history and of Edward's
biography, and might well, if true, have justified Richard III's slander about
his brother's legitimacy; the error seems original in More.[40] Another, equally
illogical, is the substitution of Elizabeth Lucy for Eleanor Butler (*née* Talbot)
as the lady whose alleged precontract with Edward IV would have made his
sons by Queen Elizabeth Wydeville illegitimate. This again is a self-destructive
error; for the allegation would also have made Elizabeth Lucy's son by Edward IV (viz.: Arthur Plantagenet, created Viscount Lisle on 25 April 1523)
legitimate and therefore king *de jure* on Edward IV's death:[41] he ought by
rights, it would seem, to have preceded the spurious princes to their Tower-
tomb.

A third legend is the story that Warwick the kingmaker "was sent over in
embassy . . . unto Spain to intreat and conclude a marriage between King
Edward and the King's daughter of Spain." This appears to be a confusion
partly with the project for a marriage with Bona of Savoy and partly with the
fact that a proposal was suggested from Spain for a marriage with Isabella of
Castile.[42] But More, abstaining as usual from dates, skips six years, 1464–9,
and makes Warwick, on hearing of Edward's secret marriage (1 May 1464)
with Elizabeth Wydeville, "assemble a great puissance against the King" (1470),
and drive him out of his kingdom, "where he remained for the space of two
years," instead of five months and eleven days."[43] Minor lapses are More's
placing of Richard III's coronation in June instead of July 1483; his putting
the Queen's surrender of her second son to Richard before, instead of after,
the *coup d'état* of 13 June; his attribution of chief-justice Markham's dismissal to his connexion with Thomas Burdett's case in 1477 instead of with
the case of alderman Sir Thomas Cook in 1468; his error with regard to the
date of the execution at Pontefract of Earl Rivers, Lord Richard Grey, and
Sir Thomas Vaughan; his representation of Sir James Tyrrell as a stranger to
Richard III and knighted by him after the murder of the princes in the Tower,
when Tyrrell had been knighted by Edward IV after the battle of Tewkesbury
on 3 May 1471, and had been further created a knight banneret by Richard
himself for his services in the Scotch campaign on 24 July 1482; the confusion
between the archbishops of Canterbury and York;[44] and the mistakes about
Buckingham's, Lord Hastings', and Dr. Shaa's Christian names.[45]

Such errors were inevitable in a work derived almost exclusively from oral
tradition dating from nearly thirty years before; and it must be remembered
that More, if ever he intended *Richard III* to be published (apart from being
performed), never revised it or intended it to be published as he left it. One
does not intend to publish sentences like his statement that Elizabeth (afterwards Edward IV's queen) "was maried unto one   Gray a squier whom
King Henry made knight upon the field that he had on   at   against
King Edward" or this: "When he [Richard III] had begun his reign the
day of June, after this mockish election, then was he crowned the   day of
the same month"; or systematically leave unfilled the blanks in one's MS. But
More's text was holy writ and his omissions sacrosanct to Rastell's more than

filial piety: the numerous corrections and additions made by Grafton and Hall are simply so much "corruption" of More's text. From an editorial point of view Rastell was right; but he need not have assumed that the function of these chroniclers was, like his own, that of editing More's works, and not that of writing English history. There is ample room on better ground for criticism of these chroniclers. Hall, the best of them, makes some sad bungles in his use of More's *Richard III*. Thus, having given, under the last year of Edward IV, one dying speech to that king, he gives a very different one, taken from More, in the beginning of Edward V.[46] It need hardly be said that More's is the finer effort, both in matter and in style, though even Hall's is probably a more finished composition than anything Edward could achieve *in articulo mortis*. The dramatic (or pious) convention of set orations on the death-bed was itself doomed soon to disappear from the sober page of history. Cavendish followed More's example in Wolsey's case; but neither Hall nor Foxe nor any later historian gave Henry VIII, Edward VI, Mary, Elizabeth, Oliver Cromwell, Charles II, or William Pitt anything more elaborate than a few broken words as their last message to the world. The scaffold, of course, was a different setting, though even there More spoke far fewer words than he puts into the palsied mouth of Edward IV: the fewer the dying words, the clearer the stamp of gospel-truth.

  More's dramatic genius plays most freely round his principal characters. It is far easier to substantiate from records his more scanty details about the smaller fry. There is, for instance, a sinister but confirmatory coincidence in the appearance on Richard III's patent roll,[47] immediately above the record of Dr. Ralph Shaa's death, of an annuity granted to "Joan Forrest, widow, late wife to the king's servant Miles Forrest," one of the murderers of the princes in the Tower; and the fact that she was a widow before 9 September 1484 may be some foundation for More's gruesome embroidery that "Forest at St. Martin's piecemeal rotted away." His colleague in crime, John Dighton, appears six months earlier in the same rolls with a grant for life of the bailiwick of Ayton, Staffordshire.[48] Much is found there and elsewhere about Richard's less criminal agent John Nesfield;[49] and even Richard's obscurer friend, "one Pottier," who prophesied, More says on "credible information," on the night of Edward IV's death that Richard would be king, may perhaps be identified with the Richard Potyer who was one of the commissioners appointed[50] on 13 November 1483 to arrest and imprison all rebels in the counties of Somerset and Dorset. More knows, too, that Dr. Shaa died "for very shame" not long after his notorious sermon; that his colleague in subservience, Dr. Penketh, was more shameless and did not;[51] that Fitzwilliam, the Recorder of London, was on 24 June 1483 "so new come into that office that he had never spoken to the people before"; he had in fact been elected only five days earlier.[52] Nor is there much reason to doubt that "one Mistlebrook" who brought the news of Edward's demise was the king's servant who was appointed by Richard III and reappointed by Henry VII as auditor of numerous crown lands, and died before 29 March 1513.[53] It is clear that much of More's information is authentic, and there is historical truth in his *Richard III* as there is in Shakespeare's historical plays. The historian's criticism relates to the poetic licence which ignores the qualities commending Richard III to a fairly respectable bench of bishops and inspiring the city of York to lament (after his death), the king "late mercifully reigning upon us"; and paints Richard as "black as pitch," foreseeing Edward IV's death at the age of forty and scheming almost from his 'teens for a crown which could never have been his had Clarence not been murdered or had Edward lived fifty-three years and left sons as old as they would have been by then to succeed him. For, without a royal minority and a Protector's stepping-stone, there could have been for Richard no accession to the throne.[54]

It is true that More himself admits this scheming as hypothesis, and relegates the positive accusations to speeches put into the mouths of Richard's dupes. That is legitimate drama, but illegitimate history. The dramatist does not pretend to be a reporter, but the historian does; and statements in the speeches in More's *Richard III* have been commonly taken as true on More's authority, although phrases in them are illogically cited, irrespective of the speakers, as evidence of More's literary style. Yet More is not reporting Edward IV or Richard III, their mother or Elizabeth Wydeville, Buckingham or Bourchier any more than Shakespeare is reporting Mark Antony, Hamlet, or King Lear; and the bare possibility that he is reporting Morton is the nearest approach to evidence that he is doing so. There is no real doubt that the whole of these speeches are More's own composition, aided perhaps by the oral tradition of fragmentary remarks. Buckingham's lengthy discourse on the abuse of sanctuary contains all the points from a scholastic treatise on the subject which is less likely to have been read by Buckingham than by More.[55] The right of sanctuary was a burning political question when More wrote, and his personal experience was not without its effect upon the text of *Richard III:* in view of his comparatively extended reference on his first page to Edward IV's daughter Catherine and her "very prosperous estate," it is pleasant to learn from the statute-book that "Thomas More, gentleman," was one of the arbitrators charged with some details of the settlement.[56]

If not a speech, the report of a lengthy conversation provides us with a clue, not to More's motive in writing *Richard III,* but to the reason for its abrupt termination and its lack of revision or publication until after More's death. That he intended, when he wrote it, at least to revise it is clear from the names and dates he left to fill in. Yet he neither revised *Richard III* nor began the "Henry VII" or "Perkin Warbeck" he half promises therein:[57] *Richard III* remained his sole historical effort, and that he did not finish. Why? More's was a comprehensive, receptive mind, and it passed through various phases of expression. Deeply religious always, it was sometimes passionately so: at others, political, legal, literary, social, or controversial interests supervened. Was the historical interest just a mood which passed? The idea that he was diverted simply by pressure of business is not convincing: he was under-sheriff of London while writing *Richard III* and busy with other things

which he details in his preface to *Utopia;* he turned from *Richard III* to
Utopia—perhaps with relief—and was quite as busy with other things when he
wrote that famous work.

He broke off when and where he did because the last sentence he wrote in
Richard III brought him back, with a shock, from dramatic art to real politics.
He is constructing[58] or re-constructing the famous conversation between
Buckingham, hitherto Richard's chief supporter, and Morton, the duke's
prisoner at Brecknock Castle, in September 1483. Each interlocutor is trying
to probe the other's feelings towards the usurper, and Morton has got so far
as tentatively to remark that "for the weal of this realm whereof his Grace
[Richard III] hath now the governance, and whereof I am myself one poor
member, I was about to wish that to those good abilities whereof he hath already right many, little needing my praise, it might yet have pleased God for
the better store, to have given him some of such other excellent virtues meet
for the rule of a realm, as our Lord hath planted in the person of your Grace."
There More stops with this plain hint of Morton's to Buckingham to put forward his own claims to the throne. As More says, Morton "craftily sought the
ways to prick him forward," and his "wisdom abused his [the Duke's] pride
to his own deliverance [Morton escaped] and the Duke's destruction." More
stopped because he remembered that history—as distinct from the writing of
it—"never does stop short."[59] Incitement to treason was no safer in 1514 than
in 1483; there was a third duke of Buckingham in the field when More was
writing, just as ready to be incited and with the same claims to the throne as
the second duke of Buckingham whose temptation he was depicting. More
was so conscious of this third duke of Buckingham that he inadvertently gives
his christian name Edward to his father Henry.[60] He may not have known
that, some six years before Henry VII's death, high officials at Calais had discussed what would happen in that event, "and some of them spake of my
lorde of Buckyngham, saying that he was a noble man and wold be a ryall
ruler";[61] that Ferdinand of Aragon in the spring of 1509 offered the young
Henry VIII an armed force in case his succession were disputed;[62] and that in
August 1509 Lord Darcy was reporting to Fox, the lord privy seal, a plot in
the north to make Buckingham Protector[63] (he was six months older than
Richard III when he became Protector, and Henry VIII was still legally a
minor when he came to the throne).[64] But More cannot have been unaware
of the attention drawn to Buckingham's position by the fact that in 1514
Henry VIII was still, after five years' reign and marriage, without either son
or daughter to succeed him. On 20 February 1514 Buckingham himself remarked to his future son-in-law, Ralph earl of Westmoreland, that "there be
two new dukes created in England,[65] but that if anything but good should
happen to the king, he, the duke of Buckingham, was next in succession to
the crown of England."[66]

Was this the time to think of re-furbishing—let alone publishing—persuasions used by the foster-father of the Tudor dynasty to "prick forward"
another duke of Buckingham on a similar errand to the scaffold or the throne?

Two years later we find More begging Erasmus not to be hasty to publish, and carefully to avoid all occasions of giving offence.[67] He had followed his own precept so far as *Richard III* was concerned, dropped his pen on Morton's plot, and never wrote another word of history.[68]

SIR THOMAS MORE'S VERSE RHYTHMS

Fitzroy Pyle

Scanty though it is, the poetry of Sir Thomas More deserves to be held in esteem, if it were only for the interest of its rhythms. This is an aspect of his verse to which little consideration has as yet been given, largely, no doubt, because of the uncertainty of the metrics of his day. Here it will be sufficient simply to state that while work in sustained Chaucerian heroics was not unknown in the first decade of the sixteenth century (when all the poems to be examined were written), the prevailing mould of conventional "literary" verse was a mixture in Troilus stanza-form of four- and five-accent (mainly heroic) lines—with sometimes a few of six accents as well—assembled almost invariably without regard for rhythmical effect.

In two of his pieces, the "Nyne pageauntes" and the "Ruful lamentacion," that, in a restrained form, is certainly More's medium. The first occurs only as one of the "Fowre thinges" added at the last moment to William Rastell's edition (1557) of More's works—likely enough from a single manuscript source; and, as the other three of the "Thinges," as gathered by Rastell, had suffered "improvement" agreeably with the rhythmical taste of the age, the text of the "Pageauntes" is necessarily suspect. Even so, as many as ten of its fifty-seven English verses are probably four-stress, and only one stanza is consistently heroic in movement. As for the "Lamentacion," while in Hill's copy (MS. Ball. 354) there are fifty-two syllabically normal heroics and fourteen equivalenced heroics—such figures will, of course, be received with due reserve —at least ten of the remaining eighteen lines are four-accent. In another poem, the "Twelue rules of John Picus," More fails to keep to the metre in which he starts: in the first nine stanzas only one line is of four accents, but gradually such verses intrude more and more, so that in the second half of the poem there are six consecutive stanzas where they predominate. On the other hand, all the lines of the other three Pico translations—and they total 350—are intelligible as heroics, and in the verses prefatory to the "Boke of Fortune" (259 ll.) there may be as few as four of four stresses.

On the whole, then, More has a far greater measure of metrical consistency than the majority of his contemporaries of the early sixteenth century. And in one respect he stands head and shoulders above all of them but Skelton. It is in the management of his rhythms, in which he repeatedly displays unquestionable artistic feeling. This is most obvious, perhaps, in the "Mery jest." Look at the vigour of this, for instance:

Reprinted with permission from *The Times Literary Supplement,* January 30, 1937, p. 76.

> They rente and tere
> Eche other here/and clave togyder fast
> Tyll with luggynge
> Halynge & tugynge/they fell doune both at last
> Than on the grounde
> Togyder rounde/with many a sadde stroke
> The[y] roll and rumble
> They tourne & tumble/lyke pygges in a poke.

Then consider the variations (as given by Hill) of the refrain-line in the "Ruful lamentacion":

> Your quene but late loo her I lye
> hath me for sake ‖ loo here I lye
> he hath me somond ‖ loo here I lye
> the yere yet lastyth & lo now here I lye
> More wo than welth & lo here I lye
> My place bilded ys | for lo here I lye
> the moders parte also | lo wher I lye
> fro you departe I fyrst | lo here I lye
> prey for my sowle for now lo here I lye
> thy moder never know | for lo here I lye
> ffarewell & prey for me for lo here I lye
> shew to thi seruantes now for lo here I lye.

These verses are not written with underlying metrical uniformity, for if in the opening stanzas we accentuate *loó, hére,* making five-stress lines, the same accentuation makes the concluding refrain-lines six-stress. Yet obviously the variations have been designed with artistic intent; and their cumulative rhythmical effect is remarkably impressive. Again, from the "Boke of Fortune" metres a number of interesting variations might be cited, *e.g.* "And over that, may forther and encreace / *an hole regyon, in ióye rést and peace*" and—a vigorous example of trisyllabic substitution—"Bycause he lept & lept, & coulde not come bý them (: defý them)." In this piece we have orderly heroic verse, relieved, however, by types of variation which may be regarded as ordered by artistic sense out of the chaotic rhythms of tradition.

The same is true—truer even—of the last three of the Pico translations. But I must pass over the many telling variations that we meet with there—the broken-backed "For our dispórt réuill myrth and playe / whyle other pláye, réuil, sing, and daunce" and the headless "whóm héll, eárth, and all the heauen obaise," for example—for it is the endings of these poems I want to dwell on. The vigorous "Twelue weapons of spirituall battayle" concludes with quite a riot of trisyllabic substitution:

> Sinne to withstande saye not thou lackest myght,
> Suche allegacions foly it is to vse,
> The witnes of sainctes and martirs constaunt sight,
> Shall thee of slouthfull cowardise accuse,

> God will thee helpe, if thou do not refuse,
> If other haue stande or this : thou maist eftsone,
> Nothing impossible is that hath bene done.

And as there are only four other such lines in the rest of the poem we have strong grounds for believing that their presence here is due to artistic feeling seeking for a forceful rhythmical climax. Most readers will agree that such a climax has been splendidly achieved in those last two lines. The final stanza of "The twelue properties or condicions of a louer" is, I think, very neatly managed too:

> Serue God for loue then, not for hope of meede,
> what seruice maie so desirable bee,
> As where all turneth to thyne owne [owën] spede :
> who is so good, so louelye eke as hee,
> who hath all readye done so muche for thee,
> As hee that firste thee made : and on the roode,
> Efte thee redemed with his precious bloode.

Here the appeal is tender, as contrasted with the militant close of "The twelue weapons," and once more the rhythm is admirably adapted to the matter. Lastly we come to the lovely "Praier of Picus Mirandula vnto God." Its conclusion rises by successive enjambment (even from stanza to stanza, which More uses elsewhere only in the "Mery jest") up to a magnificent crescendo, and then dies away with a beautiful headless line:

> Graunte I thee praie, suche heat into mine heart,
> That to this loue of thine may be egal :
> Graunt me fro Sathanas seruice to astart,
> with whom me rueth so long to haue be thrall.
> Graunt me good lorde : and creatour of all,
> The flame to quenche of all sinnefull desire,
> And in thy loue sette all mine heart a fire.

> That whan the iorney of this deadly life
> My sely goost hath finished, and thence
> Departen must, without his fleshly wife
> Alone into his lordes high presence
> He may thee finde : O well of indulgence,
> In thy lordeship not as a lorde : but rather
> As a very tender louing father.

When we remember that there are no other headless lines in this piece and that More normally betrays no tendency to use syllabic variations wantonly and often employs them very artistically, there can be no doubt at all that the rhythm of this passage (which, surely, is worthy of a place among the loveliest there are) is the direct result of the fusion of emotion with a feeling for artistic fitness.

That More was not unaffected by the forces making for chaos is shown by the drift into four-accent verse in the "Twelue rules." That he was not always consciously concerned about metrical uniformity we see, for instance, from the refrain-lines of the "Ruful lamentacion." But proofs of his being possessed of a fine feeling for rhythm are to be found in every one of his poems; and in spite of, and because of, his not coming to metre intellectually, he composed rhythms incomparably superior to those of the more "regular" versifiers of the next generation. More's verse is the measure of what a man with a sensitive ear could do even though he was not always particular about rhythmical correspondence. The reaction against fifteenth-century disregard of metrical uniformity had to take the line of scrupulous intellectual insistence upon such uniformity, even to the point of blindness to the possibility— and necessity—of diversity in uniformity. More's line of approach was not that of intellect but of artistic intuition, and though this was fortunate for the quality of his own verse, it meant that—even if he had written more—he could not be recognized as a metrical prophet. The times needed something cut and dried, and that an artist could not give.

WILLIAM RASTELL AND MORE'S ENGLISH WORKS

A. W. Reed

On the last day of April 1557, William Rastell, Sergeant-at-Law, completed his great edition of the *English Works* of Sir Thomas More, dedicating it to Queen Mary in an Epistle that closes with the prayer that it may be "joyously embraced and had in estimation of all true English hearts." Diligently, he tells us, he had collected all the books, letters and other English writings of More that he could come by, whether printed or unprinted; he had guarded them and kept them securely in his own hands through the dangerous years between; and now, "that they might be preserved for the profit of posterity," he had brought them together in a single volume. We are in danger of under-estimating Rastell's difficulties. More's possessions had been seized, his library and papers confiscated. Any expression of sympathy for More, Fisher or the Carthusian Fathers had been considered an open challenge to the king, and an act of treason; and this danger increased rather than diminished until Mary's accession. To collect and save More's works in the face of such difficulties was a very remarkable achievement.

Acts of piety such as these are not common even when unattended by danger. It was such an act that Shakespeare's fellows, John Hemming and Henry Condell, performed when they gathered his plays and published them in the famous *First Folio*. "*We have*, (they said,) *but collected them and done an office to the dead ... only to keep the memory of so worthy a friend and fellow alive.*" The More and Shakespeare Folios are separated by less than seventy years; and it is significant not only that the two greatest Englishmen of the Renaissance have like memorials, but also that they *owe* them to the loyalty of old colleagues or disciples. These two memorial volumes stand apart in the history of English literature; it is not easy to name a third that can be placed in their company. More himself, however, had been greatly influenced in the days of his early manhood by a similar book, *The Life and Works of Pico della Mirandula*, edited and published in 1496 by Pico's nephew. "When he determined to marry," we are told, "More propounded to himself for a pattern in life a singular layman, John Picus ... whose life he translated and set out, as also many of his most worthy letters." When in his turn, therefore, William Rastell determined to save and publish his uncle's works he had a

Reprinted from *The English Works of Sir Thomas More*, vol. 1 (London, Eyre and Spottiswoode, 1931), pp. 1–12, by permission.

model and precedent in the memorial volume prepared by the nephew of Pico; and it was with More's *Pico* that the 1458 pages of Rastell's volume opened.

The More and Shakespeare volumes differ from the Pico in having no biographical introduction. What a world of debate would have been prevented if his two fellows had left us a Life of William Shakespeare! In More's case the Life was ready to hand, if it had been in Rastell's mind to print it. For while he was seeing the *English Works* through the press, a Life of More was being prepared for William Roper by Nicholas Harpsfield, which shows that the two works were in the making at the same time: "We trust," Harpsfield says, "shortly to have all the English Works (of More) . . . wherein Master Sergeant Rastell doth diligently travail." The truth is that Rastell himself had it in mind, after his task of saving More's *Works* was completed, to prepare an elaborate work on More and his times; but of this we shall have occasion to speak in its proper place in the following account of William Rastell's life.

II

The Rastells were a Warwickshire family closely associated with Coventry during the fifteenth century, when the capital of the Midlands was at the height of its prosperity, and the Earl of Warwick dominated the fortunes of Yorkists and Lancastrians. William Rastell's father, John, a lawyer of astonishing activity, versatility and enterprise, was the last member of the family to hold office in Coventry. He had been a member of the Middle Temple while Thomas More was a law student at Lincoln's Inn; and already at that time Rastell was intimate with the Mores. In 1499 his name appears with those of John More and his son Thomas as securities for repayment to the Treasury of a considerable obligation, which in the following year they duly met. Before 1504 he had married More's sister, Elizabeth, and returned to Coventry, where he succeeded his father in the legal office of the Coronership. There he and his wife were visited by More, as More himself tells us in an amusing account of an adventure with an old Franciscan friar; and there, in Coventry, the three Rastell children were born. The eldest child was Joan, afterwards the wife of John Heywood the dramatist, one of the closest of More's younger friends; the second, John, inherited his father's enterprising and restless disposition; the third, William, was born in 1508 shortly before Rastell came to London.

The accession of Henry VIII in 1509 seemed to young men of ardour like More and Rastell to be the dawn of a day of new things. Humanism, invention and adventure were in the air, and John Rastell conceived the idea of playing his part in this new world by setting up a printing-press for his own use and profit. Amongst his first publications were More's *Life of Pico,* a Latin Grammar which Linacre submitted to Colet for adoption in his new school, and a play, *Fulgens and Lucres,* by Henry Medwall, chaplain in the household of Cardinal Morton when More was a boy there. It was as a printer of law-books, however, that he was most distinguished. To realise the energy with which Rastell set to work one must examine the *Liber Assisarum* and read its Preface, or turn over the pages of the massive folio volume of Fitzherbert's *Grand Abridgement*, or consult the *Table of the Grand Abridgement*, Rastell's third great law-book in folio. The labour of preparing for the press and printing these three works must have been enormous; and it should not be overlooked that of two of these works Rastell was himself the compiler.

The completion of John Rastell's first great printing period coincided approximately with the publication of More's *Utopia*; and in the following year, 1517, he took a leading part in organising an expedition that set out to reach the New Found Lands. The expedition failed, for the mariners mutinied and refused to go further than Ireland, but the story of the adventure may be read[1] in the depositions of witnesses in Rastell's lawsuit against the leaders of the mutiny, and interesting references to it occur in a play, the *Four Elements*, which Rastell himself wrote. The voyage had been intended to bring the new lands and their unexplored wealth under the influence of England.

In 1520 this busy man was engaged in designing the roofs of the great banqueting hall for the Field of the Cloth of Gold; and a year later he designed a pageant in Cheapside for the visit to London of the Emperor Charles V. Meanwhile in term-time at Westminster he was actively engaged as a professional lawyer. Of his other interests and enterprises one must speak briefly. He was not only a writer of plays, but had his own stage in the grounds of his house at Moorfields. He served in two campaigns and seems to have had some reputation as a sapper; he produced the first Tudor Jest-book, the *Hundred Merry Tales*, and he wrote and printed an English Chronicle which is distinguished by the boldness and interest of its woodcuts. When More replied in his *Supplication of Souls* to the attack made by Simon Fish on the Catholic doctrine of Purgatory, Rastell supported his brother-in-law by compiling his very original *Book of Purgatory*. He was a keen and entertaining controversialist, but he had always been temperamentally unorthodox, and in the process of his disputations with the brilliant young Lutheran, John Frith, he was won over to the party of Tyndale's followers. For the last five years of his life he was actively engaged in the service of Thomas Cromwell, and apparently was convinced that he was a pioneer in great social reforms. It was John Rastell, not More, who was the Utopian dreamer; but the masters he was serving were prosecuting not Rastell's schemes but their own ends. He attempted to convert the imprisoned Carthusians, but they are reported to have been amused by this ardent apostle of "natural reason and good philosophy." Finally, he embarked on a dangerous crusade, arguing that the clergy should relinquish their tithes and offerings, endowments and livings, and work for their bread. In this way Rastell would have relieved the indigent. Fighting this question of tithes he was cast into prison, where he died, almost exactly a year after More's execution. With bitter irony he nominated as one of the executors of his will no less a person than Henry VIII himself.

III

In his son, William Rastell, were combined the enterprise and energy of his father and the orderliness and inflexible loyalty of the Mores. Born in 1508, he was of the same age as his cousins, More's four children, Margaret the eldest being two years his senior, and John the youngest two years his junior. During William Rastell's boyhood the two families lived within reach of one another in the City, and he was probably educated with the More children in More's house, The Barge, in Walbrook. The earliest reference to him, however, occurs in a will drawn up by his father and signed by the younger Rastell as the "scriptor huius testamenti." It was the will, dated 1st April, 1525, of Richard Leigh of St. Stephen's, Walbrook, the eldest brother of Joyce Leigh, to whom More had dedicated his *Life of Pico*. At the age of seventeen, therefore, William Rastell was assisting his father in legal practice. Two years later he was helping him at Greenwich in the preparation of an elaborate pageant in which Hans Holbein collaborated. For this service we learn from the State Papers that he received a fee of eightpence a day for a period of forty-four days. In these years he also learnt the mystery of printing and made his activity felt in his father's printing-house, for in the years 1527 to 1529 John Rastell's press was more active than it had been since his first great burst of law-printing. It is said by Antony à Wood that William Rastell went into residence at Oxford but took no degree. His Oxford life, like More's, must have been a short one, seeing that he was working for his father in 1525 and 1527. It was, however, the academy or school of More that was the *Alma Mater* of William Rastell; it was there that he formed his most enduring friendships.

When William Rastell came of age in 1529 he set up his own printing-press in St. Bride's Churchyard. There were now two Rastell presses, the father's and the son's, working independently; and with the new press More was closely associated. He was now engaged on the task of refuting the heretical writers, and there are good grounds for looking upon the establishment of his nephew's press as a project inspired by More's need of a printer with whom he could collaborate with confidence and understanding. This association of More with Rastell's printing calls for emphasis. From the summer of 1529, when he began to print More's *Supplication of Souls*, until 1534, when More went to the Tower, William Rastell was engaged on More's work. This included a second edition of the *Dialogue concerning Tyndale* (1530), the *Confutation of Tyndale*, Part I (1532), the *Confutation of Tyndale*, Part II, the *Apology*, the *Debellacion* and the *Letter against Frith* (1533), the *Answer to Tyndale* and the *Answer to the Poisoned Book* (1534). The first of these works was published shortly before More became Lord Chancellor; the last shortly before his imprisonment. Indeed, the question of the dating of the *Answer to the Poisoned Book* marks the beginning of the attack on More. There had recently been published by the King's printer a book of *Articles devised by the Whole Consent of the King's Council;* and suspecting that More's *Answer to the Poisoned Book* was an attack on the *Articles,* Cromwell summoned William Rastell to appear before him. A letter from More to Cromwell explained that though Rastell had dated the book 1534, the printing had been completed before Christmas and before the publication of the *Articles.* The printer had advanced the date and treated the New Year as beginning on the 1st January. In February More was accused of holding communication with the Nun of Kent, and though he was proven to be innocent in this, more serious attacks were developing. He was examined by Royal Commission at Lambeth on 13th April, and four days later was sent to the Tower, where he remained a prisoner until his execution on 6th July, 1535.

IV

With More's imprisonment Rastell's printing ceased. He had been More's own printer, and the press had served its purpose. It had had a life of less than five years, during the whole of which time More was feeding it. Rastell's printing has great distinction. His careful press work and his new types, particularly the beautiful secretary letter, gave to More's writings an added dignity that must have been pleasing to him. The two worked together. To have his own printer, and what was in effect his own private press, must have greatly facilitated More's labours in the very busy days of his Chancellorship. Even when Rastell was not printing for More, one recognises in his work the same kind of personal relationship or motive: thus, of the five plays he printed, four were for his brother-in-law, John Heywood, part of whose house in St. Bride's Churchyard may have been occupied as printing-premises; the fifth play, Medwall's *Nature,* reminds us on the title-page that Medwall had been chaplain to Cardinal Morton—a link with More's boyhood. The handsome edition of Fabyan's Chronicle was done for the Fabyan family, whose arms are represented in a full-page wood-cut. John Fabyan, a wealthy physician of literary tastes, like John Clement, a member of the Royal College of Physicians, lived near the Law Courts. Rastell's edition of *Prester John* is explained by the fact that it was the work of young John More; nor is it surprising that he printed two sermons by Fisher. His law-books also explain themselves: they were of his own compiling. In no other printer of this period are such close relationships found between author and printer. Some of his father's work, it is true, bears the same kind of investigation, but in this respect the two Rastell presses are peculiar.

There are indications that when More resigned the Chancellorship in 1532 he and William Rastell began to look to the younger man's future. In September Rastell was specially admitted at More's own Inn, Lincoln's Inn; and though the year 1533, More's first and last year of freedom, was much the most productive year in Rastell's career as a printer, its close, as we have seen, witnessed the beginning of More's troubles. Rastell was joined at Lincoln's Inn on 25th July, 1534, by John Heywood's brother Richard, who was present as a law-clerk at More's trial a year later, and is mentioned by Roper as one of his authorities for the account he gives of the proceedings. Roper and Richard Heywood were close friends and lifelong associates. They became legal partners as Prothonotaries of the King's Bench, and shared quarters in Lincoln's Inn. It was in this year (1534) that John Heywood cheered the seventeen-year-old daughter of the superseded Queen Katharine by addressing to her a ballad, *"Give place, ye Ladies,"* which may be read in Tottel's *Miscel-*

lany. There, however, the following verses are omitted as being inappropriate
when Mary had become queen:

> This worthye ladye too beewraye
> A kinges doughter was shee
> Of whom John Heywoode lyste to saye
> In such worthye degree,
>
> And Marye was her name weete yee
> With these graces Indude
> At eightene yeares so flourisht shee
> So doth his meane conclude.

V

For eighteen months after his admission at Lincoln's Inn Rastell combined
his studies with his printing, and as during the year 1533 his press was particularly busy, little time can have been left for law. He nevertheless met the
situation ingeniously by preparing and printing under the title *Natura Brevium*
a collection of the twelve principal text-books of instruction in legal practice,
dedicating it to his fellows, the gentlemen-students of the law. This admirable
little book is of a convenient size for the pocket, but is printed in a type necessarily, but painfully, small. "Thus have you," says the editor at the conclusion
of his address to the aforesaid gentlemen-students, "these twelve small books
(but containing very great learning) compact in one volume right studiously
corrected." He might have added that he had completed the collection by compiling for it a full and careful index.

Four years after More's death, in the Trinity Term 1539, William Rastell
was called to the Bar. Troubles again beset the More family. Cicely More's husband, Giles Heron, was sent to the Tower in July 1539, charged with treason
on information laid before Thomas Cromwell by a tenant whom Heron had
put out of a farm. An appeal by his young sons Thomas and John, written in
Latin, French and English, was of no avail; their father was executed at Tyburn
on 4th August, 1540. Cromwell himself had suffered the same fate a week
earlier on Tower Hill, but not before the attainder of Giles Heron had been
secured. Three years later John More, William Roper and John Heywood became involved with Germain Gardiner and others in an attempt to convict
Cranmer of heresy. In this they imagined that they were supported by the
plain terms of the Statute of the Six Articles. More's old parish priest John
Lark was executed along with Gardiner, and John Heywood narrowly escaped
the same fate. At Christmas in this year, 1544, as though broken by this renewal of anxiety, Margaret Roper died at the age of thirty-eight.

In these troubles neither William Rastell nor the Clements were involved.
Clement, the most distinguished English member of the medical profession of
his time, devoted himself to his practice; Rastell applied himself to his legal
work and soon was marked out for promotion as an important member of his

profession and Inn. He is mentioned in the Black Books of Lincoln's Inn in 1541 as having clerks under him; in 1545 he was Pensioner of the Inn, and in 1546 was elected Autumn Reader. In 1547 he was nominated to inquire into misdemeanours that had occurred at the Sergeants' Feast, and to levy fines. He had already acquired a property of over a hundred acres at North Mimms, where he had John Heywood as a neighbour, and in 1544, when Heywood was in trouble, he bought from him lands and houses in Tottenham. It was in this year that Doctor Clement was elected president of the Royal College of Physicians and William Rastell married his seventeen-year-old daughter Winifred. The Rastells took an important house in the Vintry, Skales Inn in Whittington College, not far from More's old house in Walbrook where the Clements now lived. Rastell proceeded rapidly through the stages of promotion in the government of Lincoln's Inn. In 1547 he was one of the representatives of the Inn at the coronation of Edward VI. In 1548 he became Keeper of the Black Book, from which most of these facts are gathered; and in 1549 he became Treasurer of the Inn. Then occurs a startling entry in the Black Book: *"Rastell the Treasurer fined ten pounds, because he went to foreign parts without leave of the Governors."*

Until the third year of the reign of Edward VI the loyal Catholics of London had been able, under the sympathetic protection of Bishop Bonner, to maintain their religious practices; but on 9th June, 1549, the use of the First Prayer Book was enjoined under an Act of Uniformity. Dr. Clement, "for his concience' sake," left the country in July, More's old friend Antonio Bonvyse left in September, Margaret Clement in October, and William Rastell and his wife Winifred joined them in December in Louvain.

By their flight the exiles forfeited their possessions to the Crown, and inquisitions were held to take evidence and report upon the confiscated goods and estates. From these we learn in considerable detail what Bonvyse left behind him at Crosby Hall, the Rastells at Skales Inn, and the Clements at The Barge.

We have pointed out that neither Rastell nor the Clements were involved in the troubles of the More family between 1540 and 1544. Now, under the rigours of Edward's reign, it was the Rastells and Clements who took flight. These facts must be borne in mind when we read in the Dedicatory Epistle to the *English Works* how William Rastell had not only diligently collected More's writings, but had kept them in his hands very surely and safely, *certain years in the evil world passed.* He had saved them in Henry's reign by avoiding occasions of conflict. In Edward's reign, when conflict became inevitable, he saved them by flight. For Rastell carried his precious collection with him to Louvain.

VI

During his three and a half years of exile Rastell was engaged not only in the preparation of More's English works for the press, but also in the compilation of the two great law-books afterwards printed for him by Tottel, well known as *Rastell's Statutes* and *Rastell's Entries.* Edward VI died on 6th July, 1553, but eleven days later a very cruel blow fell upon the exiles. Winifred Rastell died of fever in Louvain at the age of twenty-six, and was buried in St. Peter's Church. Her epitaph, which may be read in Pitseus, closes with the words, "Latinae linguae non imperita, Graecam vero eximie callens. . . . Cui, pie lector, Deum quaeso, deprecare propitium." Her parents and the Bonvyses returned with William Rastell to England, and in November Richard Tottel printed for him More's *Comfort against Tribulation,* a work of serene courage, written in the Tower during the first year of the imprisonment.

Nothing that More wrote in the Tower had hitherto been printed, and the circumstances that led Rastell to publish this work separately before the others have a peculiar personal interest. More's *Comfort against Tribulation* is a work of singular cheerfulness, abounding in reminiscences and references that must have awakened many memories in those who had been brought up under him. It is not surprising that to More's most familiar friends it was a precious book. Twenty years later (1573) when the saintly and beautiful Jane Dormer, Duchess of Feria, lost her devoted husband, a young English exile, John Fowler, printed and dedicated to her at Antwerp a second separate edition.

Our first record of Rastell after his publication of this book is found once again in the Black Book of Lincoln's Inn, where on Ascension-day 1554 it was recorded that he had restored the altar of the chapel, furnishing it with a great picture of the Descent from the Cross, and that the Governors unanimously allowed his request that prayers should be said at every mass for the soul of Winifred Rastell, her kinsfolk and friends.

VII

During the short reign of Queen Mary Rastell was a busy man, and he more than recovered his material prosperity. He became a Sergeant-at-Law, and on 25th October, 1558, was raised to the Bench. But his legal preoccupations had not diverted him from fulfilling the task of publishing More's *English Works.* His Dedicatory Epistle is dated 30th April, 1557. Few books in the English language have been edited with greater care. Like everything that William Rastell did, it was a completed achievement; yet he had a brilliant idea at the last moment. When the 1458 pages that begin with the life of Pico were already in type, and the Dedicatory Epistle, Table of Contents and Index had been set up, he added to them fourteen pages of verse, written by Master Thomas More in his youth *"for his pastime."* The great volume opens, therefore, with *A Merry Jest How a Sergeant would learn to play the Friar.* This argues in Sergeant Rastell a sense of fun; but the addition had another appropriateness: it takes us back to the days of More's youth, and helps us in the very necessary duty of seeing him, as he really was, unchanged at heart whatever his fortunes, always the same witty, grave and humorous figure, facing, clear-sighted, the facts and fun of life. Even in the Tower he wrote verses *"for his pastime"* that might have been written in his youth—on *Lewis the Lost Lover* and *Davy the Dicer.*

Less than a month after Rastell became a judge, Queen Mary died, and four years later he and the Clements again fled—from Gravesend—to Louvain on 3rd January, 1562–3. John Heywood and his wife followed on 20th July, 1564, and none of them returned. William Rastell did not long survive his second flight. He died of a fever on 27th August, 1565, and was buried beside his wife. It is characteristic of him that his affairs were left in perfect order. On 8th August, 1564, he had filed an autograph duplicate copy of his will with the registrar at Antwerp; probate was granted to Doctor Clement and Ellis Heywood on 5th October, 1565. He had, moreover, purchased from the city of Antwerp a perpetual annuity of seven hundred and eighty florins which he left partly to Ellis Heywood, partly to Bartholomew More, and partly to the Ursulines and Poor Clares of Louvain. His gold locket with the portrait of More he left to Ellis Heywood, to whom also he left his printed books. What became of his papers is not known; amongst them there must have been the Life of More to which we have already referred. Some damaged fragments of this Life remain in the British Museum, extracts dealing with the trial and death of Bishop Fisher. It appears from these to have been a work of considerable dimensions, the portions extracted being taken from the fifty-fifth and fifty-eighth chapters of Book III. These fragments will shortly be made accessible in an appendix to the edition of Harpsfield's *Life of More* in preparation for the Early English Text Society by Dr. E. V. Hitchcock and Professor R. W. Chambers. There are indications that the Life was in Rastell's possession abroad during his second exile. Neither Roper nor Harpsfield betrays any knowledge of it, nor does Stapleton refer to it in 1588, though he mentions William Rastell in the preface to his *Tres Thomae*. Cresacre More, a great-grandson, is silent about it in the Life of More that he compiled in the reign of Charles I; yet it appears to have been known to a fellow-exile of Stapleton's, Nicholas Sander, in whose posthumous history of the Anglican schism there is at one point a marginal note: *Haec narrantur a Gulielmo Rastello iudice, in vita Thomae Mori.* The recovery of this lost work would be an event of the first importance.

VIII

Of the little band of exiles, members of the More family, Dr. Clement and his wife were dead by 1572 and Rastell's sister, Joan Heywood, by 1573. After William Rastell's death, Ellis Heywood had become a Jesuit, and in 1573 was living in the Jesuit house at Antwerp, where it is said his knowledge of many languages made him useful. His father, now a widower, was living at Malines, where Ellis used to visit him regularly, but as that interfered with his duties, the General of the Order gave quarters to the old man within the college. In 1578 troubles broke out at Antwerp and the Jesuits sent John Heywood, now eighty-one, to Cologne, under the care of one of the fathers; but on arriving at the gates they were refused admission, and had to return. The college was sacked and John, Ellis and all the fathers were sent by water as prisoners to Malines. They narrowly escaped assassination at the hands of the Orange party, but through the intervention of the Catholic governor, they reached the safe stronghold of Louvain on 26th May, 1578. Ellis, the most devoted of sons, died on 2nd October following. Old John Heywood, still famous for his merry wit, outlived them all, but as John Clement's daughter, Margaret, was prioress of the Ursuline convent in Louvain, and her sister Dorothy was also in Louvain, a Poor Clare, the old man was not friendless.

IX

In reproducing for the first time since 1557 William Rastell's edition of More's *English Works* it is appropriate that there should be given to him a place of honour. His edition of the *English Works* was the fulfilment of a duty which he felt he owed to More, his religion and his country. Everything that William Rastell undertook to do he carried through. At the age of twenty-six he had not only produced finely printed editions of More's controversial writings, but had established himself as probably the best English printer of his day. The careful workmanship, for example, and good paper of his edition of Cicero's *Friendship* make it worthy of its place in the volume of Caxton's in which it may be read in the British Museum; whilst its secretary type is quite in keeping with Caxton's bolder work, and even shows something of the same form and inspiration. To students of law his legal books are well known. The last of them, his *Collection of Entries,* familiarly known as *Rastell's Entries,* for long a leading work of reference, is a remarkable example of scrupulous editorial care and honesty, completed during his second exile, a year before his death. The following passage taken from his Preface to this book throws light on William Rastell's conception of editorial responsibility:

> And understand this, Good Reader, that all the notes and referments, and all that is in French in this book, and all the words in the margin, be mine and of my study. But none of the declarations, pleadings, matters, entries, &c. that be in Latin in this book be of my making or compiling. For all of them (except a few which I gathered while I was a prentice of the law, sergeant and justice) have I taken and gathered out of four several books of good precedents: *first,* the old printed book of Entries; *the second* a book of Precedents of matters of the Common Pleas diligently gathered together and written by Master Edward Stubbs that was one of the Prothonotaries of the Common Pleas; *the third,* a book of good Precedents of matters of the King's Bench written and gathered by John Lucas, secondary to Master William Roper, Prothonotary of the King's Bench; *the fourth,* a book of good Precedents which was my grandfather's, Sir John More, sometime one of the Justices of the King's Bench (but not of his collection). And all the Precedents that be in all these four books have I collected into this book ... which (with such copies as I had, being out of England, and lacking conference with learned men) to the furtherance and practice of the law I have finished the eight and twenty day of March in the year of our Lord God a thousand five hundred three score and four.

Nothing in the story of the More circle is more impressive than the loyalty to his memory of the young people who had been brought up under him.

John Clement, who accompanied him to the Low Countries when More met
Peter Giles and his *Utopia* was designed; the witty and learned foster-sister of
Margaret Roper, Margaret Giggs, Clement's wife; "merry John Heywood,"
Sewer of the Chamber under Henry VIII, Edward VI and Queen Mary, musi-
cian and dramatist; William Roper, and his colleague, Richard Heywood—to
all of these More's memory was sacred; nor must we forget his servants: Walter
Smythe, whose *Twelve Merry Jests of the Widow Edith* has a picture of the
More circle that is not generally known;[2] Richard Hyrde, who wrote a pref-
ace—which also throws light on the More household—to a little book of
Margaret Roper's; and John à Wood, who was in attendance on More in the
Tower, and played his part in saving some of More's most valuable works,
those written in imprisonment. More's last letters were probably in Margaret
Roper's keeping until her death in 1544. She had been brought before the
Privy Council and charged with retaining possession of his books and writings,
and with keeping her father's head as a sacred relic. Her answer was worthy
of him. She had saved his head from being devoured by the fishes and to bury
it; she had hardly any books and papers but what had been already published,
except a very few personal letters which she humbly begged to be allowed to
keep for her own consolation. More inspired entire confidence in his younger
people and stretched them to their best. When he invited William Rastell at
the age of twenty-one to print for him he was acting with his usual insight and
trust; and William Rastell honoured his obligations to the full. To the present
writer it seems plain that William Rastell made up his mind, when More went
to the Tower and the press closed, that one day all the works of More that
he could save should be published; and he carried out his resolution. Nor do
we owe to him More's *English Works* only; for within a few weeks of his death
at Louvain the printers of the Louvain edition of More's Latin Works (1565)
obtained their privilege of copyright. It was the first edition to contain the
Latin version of *The History of Richard III*, a copy of which Rastell is known
to have possessed. This, and the fact that the volume was printed in Louvain,
where Rastell had lived in exile and where he was buried, justify us in looking
on the Louvain edition as his. He died while it was in the hands of the printers,
and that sufficiently explains its appearance without a Dedication or Editorial
Preface.

SIR THOMAS MORE'S LETTER TO BUGENHAGEN

E. F. Rogers

Even in the first years of the Continental Reformation, much of the Lutheran pamphlet literature was brought into England. This literature harmonized with the interests of English heretics and with the survival of Wyclifite heresy. It was brought quickly, too, as we learn when a heresy case lists the books discovered and includes the most recent German publications.

Sir Thomas More's deep piety and sincere loyalty to the Catholic Church made him immediately concerned at this attack on religious creed and life. His diplomatic missions brought him opportunities of acquaintance with leading Churchmen at home and abroad, and the resulting correspondence must often have discussed the problems resulting from this attack on the Church. As early as 1521, Erasmus wrote to Pace of More's letters on the subject (not now extant) written in July of that year during his service in Bruges.[1] When Luther attacked Henry VIII for his *Assertion of the Seven Sacraments,* More wrote a long defence of the King's position, under the pseudonym of Gulielmus Rosseus. Even short tracts did not escape More's attention and their significance was keenly appreciated.

One of these short tracts was Bugenhagen's *Epistola Sanctis qui sunt in Anglia,* which was published in 1525. It was written because Bugenhagen had heard that Evangelical teaching was not accepted by many in England, and that evil reports were circulated by Luther's opponents, asserting that lax morals and variety of doctrine were true of the Lutherans. The tract was brief and simple, but it carried weight because of the personal respect in which Bugenhagen was held and because of his position as pastor of the city church in Wittenberg.

Bugenhagen was a Pomeranian by birth, educated at the University of Greifswald, and ordained to the priesthood about 1509. He was an accurate Classical scholar and under the influence of Erasmus' works began a close study of the Bible, and gave public lectures on St. Matthew, the Epistles to Timothy, and the Psalms. He was shocked by his first reading of the *Babylonian Captivity,* but on re-reading agreed with its point of view. He wrote to Luther, who replied and sent him the *Liberty of a Christian Man.* Desiring to know Luther personally, he moved to Wittenberg, matriculated in the University, and had some intercourse with Luther before he was summoned to the Diet of Worms. Again he lectured publicly on the Psalms and won the confidence and admira-

Reprinted, by permission of the publisher and author, from *The Modern Churchman,* 35 (1946), 350–60.

tion of Melanchthon. He supported Melanchthon against Carlstadt and the Zwickau prophets during Luther's absence at the Wartburg. In October 1522 he married Eva, the sister of Georg Rörer. In the following year he became pastor of the city church, unanimously elected by the Senate of the University and the Council of the city. Here he was most closely associated with Luther and Melanchthon, and was Luther's confessor and colleague.[2] Like Luther, he wished changes to be made very slowly. For these changes he had wisdom and administrative ability.

More had, then, no mean antagonist to answer. His reply to this brief tract is a pamphlet of some 12,000 words. It was evidently intended for publication, but was laid aside, perhaps because of greater interest in the later English controversies. It was published at Louvain in 1568 by John Fowler, an English exile, who printed from More's manuscript, found probably among the papers in the possession of his father-in-law, John Harris, once More's secretary.[3] The title includes Fowler's comment that More replies 'no less facetiously than piously,' and in one margin Fowler adds *facete,* lest we miss More's humour by our stupidity.

More wrote this time in Latin, as Bugenhagen had done. His sentences are often long and involved, and there are unnecessary repetitions in his argument. His method is to quote a sentence or short paragraph from Bugenhagen, and then answer it. He is scrupulously fair to his opponent in the accuracy of his quotations and in full appreciation of the force of his arguments. His style is easy and popular, and full of brilliant, sharp, sarcastic, humorous thrusts. Some passages are scurrilous, and comments on the marriages of Bugenhagen, Lambert and Luther are too bitter and scathing to quote. More used his letter to Bugenhagen as his reply to the whole Lutheran movement as far as it had then progressed.

His preparation for this task was good. The Jesuit, Stapleton, whose biography of More was published in 1588, tells us that he found More 'to have been a most diligent student of the Holy Scriptures, and to have had a considerable acquaintance with the Fathers and even with the disputes of the Schools. ... When he speaks of grace, free will, merit, faith, charity and other virtues, original sin and even predestination, he is so guarded and exact in his statements that a professional theologian could scarcely speak more accurately.'[4] He uses, for very apt quotation in his discussion with Bugenhagen, passages from Deuteronomy, Kings, Psalms, Proverbs, Ecclesiastes, the four Gospels, first Corinthians, first Thessalonians, first Timothy, James, and the Apocalypse. Of the controversial literature of this period, to date, he had read Luther's *Babylonian Captivity,* the *Address to the Christian Nobility,* his tracts on *The Holy Cross in Churches* and on *Marriage,* Erasmus' *Diatribe on Free Will,* and Luther's *Bondage of the Will.*

The question of how he received information about events in Germany is less easy to answer. The writer of the article, 'Sir Thomas More and the Reformation,' probably Seebohm, in the North British Review for 1859, says that More's correspondent was Cochlaeus. But a study of the dates shows that they were not then acquainted. The *Epistle to Bugenhagen* was not dated, but

must, from internal evidence, have been written in 1526. It was not until 25
August 1527 that Erasmus wrote to congratulate Cochlaeus[5] on gaining More's
friendship. Cochlaeus was at that time 'making advances to many English
statesmen' and was soon after writing to Erasmus to request him to write
against the Anabaptists. He made the same request to Bishop Fisher of Rochester.[6]

The late Dean Hutton considered More's correspondent to be Goclenius.[7]
The acquaintance began with Erasmus' introduction of Goclenius to More in
1520.[8] Their extant correspondence for this period, however, does not prove
the point. Whoever his correspondent was, More's visits abroad in 1520, 1521,
probably 1523,[9] would allow him to know the reports in the Netherlands. In
any case, his information is detailed, bitterly opposed to Lutheranism and
anxious as to the results of such disloyalty to the Church.

Bugenhagen's *Epistola Sanctis qui sunt in Anglia* awaited More's return
from a journey. It had been left for him by an unknown person. The editor
has identified him as William Barlow, at this time wavering between orthodoxy
and heresy, later a zealous Reformer, and finally, after persecution under Henry
VIII and again under Mary, appointed by Elizabeth to the bishopric of
Chichester.[10]

Bugenhagen began his epistle with a paraphrase of St. Paul's form of address,
rejoicing that the Gospel was heard gladly in England. More criticized him for
arrogating to himself the Apostolic style when it would have been more modest
for him to imitate the Apostolic character. He did not consider himself one of
the 'saints' to whom the letter had been addressed, since to the 'saints' nothing
was holy except the Lutheran sect. Bugenhagen's opening sentence More could
answer adequately only in several pages. A summary, given largely in words
translated from his own, will perhaps illustrate More's controversial style best.

There are very few in England, he writes Bugenhagen, who gladly hear the
'Gospel of God' as preached by the Cacangelists Luther, Carlstadt, Oecolampadius. It is not the Gospel as it has been preached in England for a thousand
years. Most people in England are too strong in the faith to accept such a
'Gospel,' because they hear of the evils resulting from its profession—the destruction in Germany wrought by the Peasants' Revolt, the setting of laity
against clergy, the arming of common folk against magistrates, the stirring of
people against princes, the causing of battles, ruins, wars and massacre, the
breaking of vows of celibacy.

Does it profit the Gospel to destroy the sacraments, to scorn the saints, to
blaspheme the Mother of Christ, to despise the Cross, to release from vows of
celibacy, to urge monks and nuns to marry?

The whole of Christian tradition, More writes, is opposed to this new sect,
the certain words of Scripture, the condemnation of the Fathers, and this in
spite of the fact that the Lutheran heretics had thought they alone knew all
things, Luther blasphemously writing that he cared not for ten Jeromes, nor
a hundred Cyprians, a thousand Augustines, nor ten thousand Chrysostoms.

Orthodox books have been preserved through the centuries, but works of
heretics have perished with them. As there was in earlier times no burning of

heretical books, this loss was plainly by the hand of God. From the works of
the holy Fathers the faithful will take an antidote for the poison of Bugenhagen's writing. There is agreement among the Fathers, but dissension among
the heretics.

More adds that Bugenhagen should not think it possible to win the English,
since even he should know what an opponent Luther has in the King. Does
Bugenhagen think he can win them by arrogating to himself the title of Bishop
of Wittenberg, by daring to teach men to break their solemn vows as he had by
his own marriage, so that he can discharge the office of Pope among the
English?[11]

More's allusions at this point need some comment. The fact that he cites
the king as defender of the Church[12] is part of the evidence for dating the letter early in 1526, for the divorce case, and its questioning of the Pope's power
to dispense, was suggested as early as September of that year.[13]

More was distressed by the breach of monastic vows, and treated the marriages of the Reformers without respect. Bugenhagen had married in 1522;
Lambert, the first French monk to marry, in 1523; Luther in 1525. There had
been some pamphleteering on the subject before any of these marriages took
place. Carlstadt had written 'Concerning Celibacy' in 1521.[14] In 1519 Luther
had published a sermon on 'Matrimony,' but had then said nothing of marriage
for the clergy. In the 1522 and 1523 editions of it he had commented on marriage in spite of previous vows, and even earlier had published the tract 'Concerning Monastic Vows.' Lambert wrote against clerical celibacy in 1524, and
in the following year Bugenhagen wrote 'Concerning the Marriage of Bishops
and Deacons.'

The reference to Luther as despising the Cross seems to come from Luther's
sermon 'Of the holy Cross in Churches,' preached and published in Wittenberg
in 1522.[15] In it Luther teaches that it is an error to dedicate churches to the
cross of wood on which Christ hung, that we should not adorn fragments of
the true cross with gold, but give the money to the poor. He would do away
with all crosses which have been objects of pilgrimage. More comes back to
this in a later passage in his letter, where he says sharply that Christ had not
taught Luther that his cross should be cast away lest it should cost gold. This
Luther learned from his brother Judas, when he said, to what purpose is this
waste?[16] It could have been sold for much and given to the poor. Luther,
More states, is deserving of more than one crucifixion for his blasphemies
against the cross.[17]

The reference to Bugenhagen as bishop or pope perhaps has its origin in
some jest of Luther's, such as his reply to the papal legate, Paul Vergerius, in
1535, acknowledging Lutheran ordinations: 'Certainly we do it, for the Pope
will consecrate and ordain none for us. And look, there sits a Bishop, whom
we have consecrated and ordained,' and he pointed to Dr. Pommer, as he
often called Bugenhagen.[18] And this jest was made a year before the Elector of
Saxony appointed Bugenhagen General Superintendent of the churches.[19] In
1526 he held no position among the Lutherans which could be seriously considered that of an overseer.

As More's letter continues, he treats of the theological questions most at issue between Roman Catholics and Lutherans. The reader feels that More makes good replies, that he does touch weak points, but that Bugenhagen could have refuted some of the statements of this pamphlet if he had replied. He did not, as a matter of fact, answer either Cochlaeus or More.

In reply to the Lutheran emphasis on the scriptural foundations of their doctrinal teaching,[20] More stressed the value of the tradition taught in the Church.

As in all controversy in the age of the Reformation, there is much discussion in this correspondence of justification by faith *alone,* or by faith *and* good works. Each controversialist might fairly claim that the other had imperfectly understood his position. More is very concerned with all antinomian tendencies in Bugenhagen's teaching on justification by faith. When Bugenhagen tries to guard against this very misunderstanding, More considers his system of thought inconsistent.

More defends Catholic doctrine by showing that the Church does not put its confidence in good works. Nothing is more inconsistent with the doctrine of the Church than that anyone should attribute anything to himself, yet in the common name of the whole Church it is permissible for Catholic Christians to glory in the fact that they alone are just, they alone are Christians. For among mortals there is none holy outside the Church, nor is anyone a Christian.[21]

As Bugenhagen had slurred monastic life, as an example of confidence in good works, More defended differences in the mode of life in various religious orders: 'I do not think it is a great evil if under one leader Christ some fight under divers others as it were Tribunes, and while all live well and according to Evangelical rule from the Evangelical precept, each spends his time in different ways and each abounds in different kinds of virtues.'[22] More admitted frankly that many failed in the monastic life, but considered that even so the purest part of the Christian people was always found among the religious. They bear the Cross above all others, he said, who selling all that they have and giving to the poor, follow Christ, while dedicating their whole life to fasting and prayer and following the Lamb in chastity, they crucify their flesh with its vices and desires. More held up to scorn the softness of the 'Evangelical' life in contrast to monastic life.[23]

The Lutherans must know, More continued, that Catholics believe and teach that good works without faith have no merit, for when they have done all, they are unprofitable servants. Even so, God rewards them, as the master of the vineyard those whom he had set to work at the eleventh hour.[24] If the Lutherans take away the fruit of good works, they make men lukewarm to doing well.[25]

As Bugenhagen, in his very anxiety to avoid antinomianism, has said that he who has faith is a good tree which must in its time bear good fruit, More chides him for inconsistency: 'For if there is such a thing as good works which faith necessarily produces: what else are you doing, disputing against good works, than blabbing out against the fruit of faith? "Faith without works is dead, which the demons also believe and shudder." '[26] And then he adds sarcastically: 'It is vain to quote to you the *Epistle of James,* for as you formerly found it inconvenient, it ceased to be apostolic to you.' Luther had called it 'an epistle of straw.' And, again, perhaps Bugenhagen will not accept the passage from *St. Matthew,* 'Lord, Lord, did we not prophesy in thy name, and in thy name cast out demons, and in thy name do many mighty works?'[27]

> It is not therefore true, Pomeranus, that faith alone suffices, and whoever has faith, necessarily produces the fruit of good works.
>
> But why should I adduce Christ to you?[28] Why not rather Luther to a Lutheran? Hear therefore what he says, whose authority with you is incontestable. "Nothing," he says, "can damn a man except incredulity. For all other things, if faith remains or returns, are absorbed by faith."

By such confidence in faith alone, More considers that Bugenhagen and Luther confirm a licence to sin and a freedom to reject the holiness of a more austere life.

More asks Bugenhagen

> whether the man who neglects good works and commits evil does not close heaven and open hell to himself. If you deny this, you leave no one in doubt ... that you are he, who provokes the whole world to sin, having offered impunity for such deeds. But if you concede the value of good works, which you must, then you can never deny that if the evil of our works plunges us to hell, the goodness of those which we do with the divine aid, helps us from hell and renders us to some degree suitable for the promised reward of heaven. It would be absurd ... if God, who is so merciful, did not reward virtue, when he punishes wickedness.[29]

Since the publication of Erasmus' *Diatribe concerning Free Will* in 1524 and Luther's *Bondage of the Human Will* in 1525, the differences between Catholics and Lutherans on this doctrine had been much discussed. More wrote to Bugenhagen:[30]

> Why should you persuade anyone to do good if there is no freedom of the will? You should merely pray God, that He should accomplish all things in me, but not urge me to try anything myself. If all things proceed from faith, if nothing is truly free for men, as you Lutherans hold with the teeth, you have assuredly left no cause, why you should move anyone to virtue, or punish any guilty one. Nor have you anything which you can object to your adversaries, if they do nothing freely, but are in everything forced by fate, unless perchance you reply, that even the things which you yourself write, you write not by your own will, but by an instinct of fate.

More accused the Lutherans of omitting all passages of Scripture which defend the freedom of the will. Nor did Luther answer the Scriptures which Erasmus quoted in his *Diatribe on the Freedom of the Will.* He has no reply to the passage 'keep my commandments'[31] by which the sacred Eloquence witnesses the freedom of the will. God would not command man to do what

He knew man could not do. This would be insane comment. Finally, to take away the freedom of the will, makes God not the avenger so much as the author of all wrongs.[32]

To interpret doctrine so narrowly seems exaggeration of its tendency to fatalism. But evidently More had in mind striking passages from the *Bondage of the Human Will,* in which Luther said that it was 'the highest step in faith to believe that He is clement, who saves so few.' And again, 'Free will can never be predicated of man, but only of God.' And finally, the most picturesque passage of all: 'The human will is like a beast of burden. If God mounts it, it wishes and goes as God wills; if Satan mounts it, it wishes and goes as Satan wills. Nor can it choose its rider, nor betake itself to him it would prefer, but it is the riders who contend for its possession.'[33]

In his discussion of the sacraments, Bugenhagen had again said that the Lutheran creed is summed up in 'Christ is our justice,' and that their beliefs are entirely based on the Scriptures. More replied by pointing out the differences between Catholics and Lutherans with regard to the sacramental system. More considered that his opponents untaught all that Christ did not expressly teach. All that Christ taught the Church through so many holy Fathers, Evangelists, Martyrs and Apostles is to be untaught, he said, unless Christ taught it expressly during His earthly life.[34] 'Who before this had ever "despised the prayers of the Church? Who disparaged decoration in churches? Who scorned the worship of the Saints? Who denied Purgatorial fire? Who did not consider the Thanksgiving of the Mass a sacrifice? Who thought that bread remained with the flesh of Christ?" '[35]

It is clear, however, that More misinterpreted the differences in Eucharistic doctrine among the Reformers, and said that Carlstadt, Zwingli and Oecolampadius had taken away completely the flesh of Christ in the Eucharist, leaving mere bread.[36] The truth of it is that Zwingli did believe in the Presence of Christ in the sacrament, and taught that His body is eaten in the Communion 'sacramentally and spiritually.'[37] Luther tolerated few differences, but said 'there is not much danger whether you believe there is or there is not bread in the Sacrament.'[38] More noted the antagonism of Luther to Carlstadt, Zwingli and Oecolampadius and said that Luther will not allow anyone else to be Heresiarch of this sect.[39]

The Epistle ends with a most earnest plea to Bugenhagen to leave the Lutheran sect and return to the Catholic Church, to give up the Episcopate which he sinfully holds, to end his unlawful union, and to do penance for the rest of his life.[40] 'If you do these things, Pomeranus (I pray God that you may) then you will at last rejoice about us and we in turn, who grieved that you should be lost, shall be glad that you are found.'[41]

More's biographers make scant comment on his *Epistle to Bugenhagen.* Although Stapleton quotes from it as an example of More's controversial style, it is without citation.[42] The epistle can have reached only a small circle in More's own day. It is curious that it is not even mentioned by Bugenhagen's biographer.

More wrote the epistle when he was already Chancellor of the Duchy of

Lancaster and a member of the King's council of twenty members, and one of those appointed to be in 'contynuall attendence' at ten and two each day.[43] He could find time for such theological study only by rising at two and studying till seven.[44]

His arguments did not avail to the conversion of Bugenhagen and Luther. He himself realized that that was not to be. In that same year he said to his son-in-law,

> 'Troth it is indeed, sonne Roper, I pray God, that some of vs, as highe as we seeme to sitt uppon the mountaynes, treading heretikes vnder our feete like antes, live not the day that we gladly wold wishe to be at a league *and* composition with them, to let them have their churches quietly to themselves, so that they wold be contente to let vs have ours quietly to ourselves.' Roper replied, 'By my troth, sir, it is very desperately spoken. . . .' More, by thes wordes perceiuinge me in a fume, said merily vnto me: 'Well, well, sonne Roper, It shall not be so, It shall not be so.'[45]

But, if the Lutherans were unconvinced, More's controversial writing won the respect of the leaders of the Church. In March 1528, Cuthbert Tunstall, Bishop of London, licensed him to own and read heretical books for the purpose of refuting them.[46] The first fruit of this license was his 'Dialogue with Tyndale,' in English, which, interestingly enough, repeats much of the argument to Bugenhagen. The Chancellorship from 1529 to 1532 interrupted his writing but not his concern. When he had resigned his office and had only a small income left to him, a gift was collected for him by the clergy in gratitude for his service, but More had written with thought only of loyalty to the Church, and refused the gift.[47]

In time, the spirit of his controversy gradually changed. The letter to John Fryth, 1 December 1532, deals gently with the young heretic, though his 'erronyouse wrytyng . . . agaynst the blessed sacrament of the aultare' touched More's religious sensitiveness far more than the debate over faith and good works. Professor Chambers noted that the *Dialogue of Comfort against Tribulation*, written during imprisonment in the Tower in 1535, is 'his farewell to controversy,' as he hoped that the Germans, caused by God 'to agree together in the defence of His name' against the Turks, may be brought 'to agree together in the truth of His faith.'[49]

To himself, More was innocent of cruelty or too great severity in his treatment of heretics. Still there is his comment in his epitaph that he was not 'odious to the nobility nor unpleasant to the people, but yet to thieves, murderers and heretics grievous.'[49] Surely even in writing his epitaph, his sense of humour did not desert him. Any good judge would hope he had been grievous to thieves and murderers, and any good theologian would hope he had been grievous to heretics.

THOMAS MORE'S *EXPOSITIO PASSIONIS*

Giovanni Santinello

I. A New Moment in History

When Erasmus debated with Colet over the meaning of Christ's sorrow in the Garden, he—although no longer very young—was just at the beginning of his long career as a New Testament "theologian," and the times were less sad than they would be later. Thirty-five years afterwards, we have the *Expositio passionis Christi* of Thomas More, *conscripta in carcere arcis Londiniensis*[1] during the long months of imprisonment while he awaited his execution. The sorrow of Christ, debated at Oxford, had spread through humanist Europe and had become the sign of new times. It was no longer the subject of an academic *conflictatiuncula,* but a conflict fought out among the people with the weapons of speech, of the press, of excommunication and condemnation, and also with swords. New men had appeared, many of whom came from the circle of Erasmian humanism: Luther and Zwingli, Ecolampadius and Capito, Henry VIII and Leo X.

If we re-read the texts of Erasmus and Colet in the light of the events which occurred in that thirty years' interval, many of their expressions and ideas have a prophetic tone. Colet was concerned that the charity of Christ should not appear to be less than that of all the martyrs who had followed him over the centuries, while Erasmus wanted to see in Christ an example not of *animositas,* but of *mansuetudo.* Christ's charity shines even in the fear that he experienced *imminente supplicio crucis,* because life is a value and death is evil. When we face the greatest pains, when our nature rebels, he does not ask of us that *alacritas* which he would not show in himself. Might it then be that martyrs are no longer necessary? How far ought the value of one's own life to be defended before that defense becomes a betrayal of truth? Erasmus had to confront the reality of this problem: he fled from Louvain to Basle to withdraw himself from Catholic intransigence; he fled from Basle to Freiburg to avoid the compromising invasion of the Protestants; he was able to die in his bed without betraying truth or his ideal of peace and toleration. His friend Thomas More, who was the first theorist of religious toleration, had encountered the same problem, but as a dilemma that forced a stark choice between two alternatives. By choosing death and martyrdom, he defended the value of life to the last, without ostentation, with serenity and gentleness.

Reprinted by permission of the author and publisher from *Studi Sull'Umanesimo Europeo* (Padua, Editrice Antenore, 1969), pp. 116–28. English translation by Dale B. Billingsley.

The dilemma could perhaps be seen, formulated in another way—like another prophecy—in the conflict between Erasmus and Colet concerning the unity of the sense of Scripture. In certain aspects, Colet's position presages the same spirit of intransigence and absolutism in understanding the Word of God which Catholic theology will oppose to that of the Protestants when they enter into conflict with each other. Erasmus' position presages that which did not then come true and which, perhaps, is being glimpsed only today. More would be the victim of a real situation that his theory repudiated, but that he accepted realistically and freely. More agreed with Erasmus, not with Colet.

The friendship between More and Erasmus goes back to Erasmus' first visit to England (1499). More was not present at the Oxford debate, but he must have been well acquainted with it, for his exposition of the Passion shows the influence of the ideas that were discussed so many years before. The same exposition also shows the influence of the annotations that Erasmus made in his Greek and Latin edition of the New Testament (1516), an edition that inspired, at the same time, both Luther and the Catholic martyr.

Erasmus' notes on the Gospel passages about the prayer in the garden of Gethsemane do not give a particular edge to his thesis of Christ's human fear of death, except for one note on the sweat of blood (Lk. 22.44), where he observes that Jerome and Hilary admitted that they did not find this episode —any more than that of the angel comforting Jesus—in many Greek and Latin codices: the passage, he conjectures, was deleted by people who feared to attribute to Christ *tam insignia humanae infirmitatis argumenta*.[2] More will agree with Erasmus on this point about the human fear of Christ. Another of Erasmus' notes (Mt. 26.45), also recalled in More, merits attention for its own significance. When Jesus goes to the disciples for the third time and again finds them asleep, he tells them to sleep and rest themselves, while the first time he had awakened and reproved them. Perhaps Christ's tone is ironical, Erasmus notes: sleep if you wish, since you shall be awakened suddenly and be made aware of what awaits us.[3] Nor is More scandalized to put *illud ironiae genus* into Scripture, and he even cites by way of confirmation many other passages that imply the use of irony. It is an annotation that reflects the common temperament of the two friends in their common love of Lucian. *The Praise of Folly* is an exaltation of the Christian vision of the world in ironic terms. And in the dedication to his translation of Lucian, More points out that John Chrysostom, *doctorum omnium christianissimus*, had inserted a good part of Lucian's *Cynicus* into a homily of his on the Gospel of St. John.[4]

Thomas More wrote his *Expositio passionis* in 1535 while in prison, where he had also written *A Dialogue of Comfort against Tribulation*. He could not finish the work because one fair day his imprisonment was made more severe and he was denied permission to write.[5] The Latin part was translated into English by his grand-daughter Mary Roper Basset. More had composed an earlier part, in English, probably before he was imprisoned.[6] The Latin *Expositio*, based on the texts of the four Gospels, begins with Christ's departure from the Last Supper and his arrival at the Garden of Gethsemane. It breaks off at the moment of his arrest. It thus covers the same Gospel passages that brought about the discussion between Erasmus and Colet, and it has a subtitle analogous to that of the Oxford debate: *De tristitia, taedio, pavore, oratione Christi ante captionem eius.*

More's composition differs in character from Erasmus'. It belongs, like his other Tower works, to what may be called "consolation literature." As in More's other works, beginning with the *Utopia* itself, and as in Erasmus' works, many references to the personal situation of the author, to contemporary events and people, are allowed to appear, sometimes implicitly, sometimes explicitly.[7]

The prayer of Christ occasions a digression on our way of praying: we are distracted, we think of useless things. Our bodily posture itself contrasts with the disposition of a true pray-er (one who prays) placing himself before God. *Insani certe nobis videremur ipsis, si capitalem causam ad hunc tractaremus modum apud mortalem principem.* And yet an earthly king can deprive us only of our bodies, while God has power over our very souls.[8] More's allusion to his own situation is evident, although much veiled. Jesus prays to the Father several times in order that, if it be possible, the cup of his passion may pass from him. He wants, as it were, to show us by his example that it is not wrong to ask God to deliver us from evil, especially in cases where *in magnum (etiam Dei causa) periculum venimus.*[9] Christ needed help and the comforting angel came. Not all martyrs can be alike, comments More. Some are courageous, and know *triumphata morte coelum violenter irrumpere.* Others are afraid, horrified by that which awaits them, facing death with fear and trembling. God does not prize their sacrifice the less on that account; the wisdom of God, which understands human feeling, knows how to temper the trials in proportion to each one's strength.[10]

Six days had not passed since Christ's triumphal entry into Jerusalem; now he would be condemned to death by the people who had sung hosannas to him. More, who had passed from the Lord Chancellorship to condemnation for treason, emphasizes this passage: *assidue se vertentem humanarum rerum vicissitudinem.*[11] Immediately thereafter, one may read an allusion to Henry VIII: those who condemn Christ are the highest order of Judea, chief priests, Pharisees, scribes, elders of the people: *quodque natura est optimum, ita quum semel coepit in diversum tendere, evadit tandem pessimum.*[12] There is no sin more hateful to God than that *si quis leges ad iniuriam propulsandam natas transferat ad inferendam.*[13]

To some it seems strange that an enlightened man like More could have chosen death for a cause that, in the light of reason, seems to be a superstition.[14] More seems to answer them when he comments on Christ's reproof to Peter after the disciple tried to defend him by striking Malchus, as if to keep him from being obedient to the Father: I have spent my life giving examples of obedience and humility. I have taught that one should obey magistrates, honor one's parents, give to Caesar what is Caesar's and to God what is God's; and now, as I am about to conclude my work, do you wish that I should rend that fabric which I have woven for so long, and that the Son of Man should not be obedient to God?[15]

More is not *animosus;* just as the *Utopia* differs from the moralistic idealism
of Erasmus by the realism and pessimism which undergird it, so his martyrdom
is a far cry from the fanaticism of the Christian neophyte, inspired by excessive zeal, whom the Utopians condemned for incitement to sedition.[16] At the
end of the *Expositio* is a long commentary on the flight of the apostles and on
the mysterious figure of the young man who, for a while, followed Christ the
prisoner, but who in his turn fled away naked when the soldiers seized him by
his shirt (Mk. 14.51-52): this final tract is a complex meditation on the legitimacy of flight. If one does not have enough courage to confront the danger,
one should flee while there is time. When it is too late, flight becomes a fault,
and it would be foolish to save one's present life at the cost of the life to come.[1]
One of the articles of faith in the natural religion of *Utopia* is the reward in an
after-life.[18] If one flees to avoid being forced to offend God, insofar as one
despairs of knowing how to resist by one's own force, even this is foolish and
evil, since it is desertion and lack of trust in divine aid. But if, as said at first,
it is possible to flee without offending God, then flight is better *quam
cunctando captum in horrendi criminis discrimen cadere.* When lawful, hasty
fleeing in due time is easy; facing the struggle is difficult and dangerous. The
youth fled because his clothes did not hinder him; he could escape naked, leaving his shirt in the hands of the persecutors. But he who is weighed down by
clothes that are too heavy, or even by a single poor garment that is too straitly
laced, will not be able to get away easily; rather than forfeit the much or the
little that he has—to which he is foolishly attached—he will end up falling into
the peril. In conclusion, More says, the example of the youth teaches us that,
when about to face grave perils from which circumstances do not permit flight,
we must be prepared, not weighed down by attachments to our things, but
ready to give them up, leaving our garments behind and fleeing naked.[19]

The long meditation on the flight seems to reflect very closely the weighty
consideration, the doubts and finally the serenity and decisiveness with which
More chose his own road, without fanaticism or ostentation.

He reveals as well the kind of faith and values for which he sacrificed his
life. The Son of Man was given into the hands of sinners. The mystical body
of Christ, the Church, *christianus videlicet populus,* then as now is threatened
by divisiveness: *partes alias truculenti Turcae Christianae ditionis invadunt,
alias intestino dissidio multiplices haereticorum sectae dilacerant.* More explicitly thereafter, his profession of faith appears by his quoting in full the
Gospel text for the primacy of Peter.[20]

There are frequent hints at the heresies of the reformers and explicit references to the discussions, within the reformers' camp, about the Real
Presence: the long quarrel, still alive, of the Bohemian utraquists, the radical
position of Zwinglians, *servantes tantum corporis sanguinisque vocabula.*[21]
More condemns the reformers, but does not even then forget his former stand
in favor of religious toleration. Concerning the utraquists, he writes: *sub
utraque specie non solum sumunt ipsi (quae res utcunque posset ferri), sed
universos damnant;* that is, they condemn those who do not do as they do;
their fault is in being intolerant. Concerning the repression of heresy on the

Catholic side, he recalls that, in the episode of Peter's striking Malchus, Christ disapproves not only of the use of the material sword, but also of the spiritual sword, *illum gravem et periculosum excommunicandi gladium,* which is to be used only when *horrenda necessitas* requires it. For the most part, it should be kept back *in clementiae vagina.*[22]

II. Christ's Human Fear

In the *Expositio,* then, More meditates upon his situation and the condition of the times, which appeared to belie the ideals of peace and toleration that had constituted so large a part of his and Erasmus' program for humanistic religious renewal.

To Erasmus he turns in the first pages of his work, which shows the direct influence of the Oxford debate that had unfolded so many years before in a very different climate of hope. The peculiarity of More's text, in comparison with the Erasmus–Colet exchange, is first of all the absence of the controversial tone: some traces of it remain (*miretur aliquis fortasse . . . ; sed hic fortassis obiicias . . .*), but these do not take on a character different from that of the whole work, which, as we have said, is an exposition of Christ's agony as an object of meditation and of comfort. In consequence, the theological and philosophical apparatus used by Erasmus, especially in the second draft of his argument, disappears. All the problems raised by Erasmus and Colet are still present, but they are now fused in a unified treatment that proceeds quickly and that, in the light of good sense, of *pietas* and of a theology—so to speak—of simplicity, dissolves all that remained of the technically theological and philosophical in Erasmus' work. More succeeds, through a single integrating vision, in resolving certain oppositions that had divided Erasmus and Colet. He thus carries out Erasmus's theological program, which was meant not as doctrine for the intellect, but rather food for the spirit and an exercise of piety in the reading of the sacred text.

What does "Cedron" signify? What does "Gethsemane" signify? Following Erasmus' notes to the *Novum Testamentum,* More relates the significance of these Hebrew words and interprets their sense allegorically. The words of the sacred books, therefore, are not to be read in one sense only, but are fertile with many mysteries.[23] It was this prejudicial question that Colet posed to Erasmus, and that Erasmus refused to debate in depth. More accepts the plurality of scriptural sense, the possibility of diverse interpretations, and makes ample use of this possibility throughout this work. Colet tied his own position to a theological affirmation, which Erasmus did not exclude in his response: the unity of the sense of Scripture depends upon divine inspiration; the multiple sense, upon the weakness of the human interpreter. Concerning the agony in the garden More says expressly: *ab uno pariter ipsius Spiritu universa dictata sunt.* But the unity of divine inspiration does not prohibit human study from struggling with interpretation and does not preclude his exploring diverse senses. On the contrary, what matters to More is the attitude of veneration before the incomprehensibility of God's judgments and his ways. His attitude contrasts with the facile approach of certain *homines novi, subito de terra progerminati theologi,* who maintain their personal interpretations and argue among themselves, conquerors or conquered as the case may be, who thus destroy the *catholicam fidem.* More stands thinking of all the great theological controversies provoked by the reformation, but he attributes the cause of controversy to an attitude that he, with Erasmus, does not share with the reformers: *omnia scire videri volunt.*[24] Evil resides in the pretense to knowledge, in the reduction of theology to science. From that evil the contests and conflicts about interpretations were born. If that attitude is dropped and if, with Colet, one distinguishes between the hidden truth which is one, and the human theological approaches to it, which can be diverse, then the conflicts too cease. Thus one comes to the position of Erasmus and More: the plurality of compatible senses within the unity of revealed and mysterious truth.

Christ in the garden is afraid. Of what? Of death, maintains Erasmus; that his death should not be a cause of the Jews' perdition, maintains Colet in opposition. Now let us read More. An immense heap of suffering crushes *tenerum piumque sanctissimi Servatoris corpus:* the betrayal of Judas, the enemies, the imprisonment, the calumnies, the blasphemies, the blows, the thorns, the nails, the cross and other tortures that will continue for terrible hours. Moreover, he is afflicted by the fear of the disciples, *perditio Judaeorum,* the death of the faithless traitor himself, the unspeakable sorrows of his beloved mother.[25] More has combined the two theses (of Erasmus and Colet); more importantly, he has put them on the same level, binding them together with a single sense of compassion—rich in human and familiar touches: the tender body of Christ at the beginning and the afflicted mother at the end—toward a sorrow and a fear which Christ feels in himself for both his own troubles and all the troubles of others. The contrast between Erasmus and Colet was striking because the sorrows and fear of Christ were placed at levels endowed with different significance: for Erasmus, they were purely human; for Colet, theological and divine. More will go on to say more: all that Christ did or suffered or prayed for in his agony happened to him *ut homine.* Thus for More, even solicitude for the fate of the Jews could be made an integral part of the human sorrows of Christ.

From this question of Christ's human fear came the long justification that Erasmus gave of his thesis. More resolves it by responding to a double interrogative: *potuit? voluit?*

Christ could fear and suffer because, although he was truly God, he was also truly human. He was subject to *humani generis affectus, qui quidem culpa careant,* and these derive *ab inferiore humanitatis suae parte*—that is, his sensible being—in which was seated, as in all men, a natural horror of death.[26] Here are recalled all the concepts that had entered the theological and anthropological fabric of Erasmus, who had leant upon Bonaventure, the Fathers, St. Paul and the stoics. The same thesis is to be found in More, but it is expressed with the intuitive simplicity of good sense, without the over-subtle distinctions that even Erasmus indulged in. More is more truly erasmian than Erasmus. This does not mean, however, that More had no explicit theology;

he had that common, clearly defined theology which he accepted without the intricacies of overly scholastic distinctions. Writing in an atmosphere of heresy, he seizes the opportunity to recall the classic heretical oppositions that assert only the human nature or only the divine nature of Christ. For him, the miracles demonstrate his divinity, the agony in the garden, his humanity.

That Christ had been able to suffer is beyond doubt. But why did he choose to? Here again we find, even in More, the objections of Colet that we already know: Christ was required to give an example of strength, for after him there would be a host of strong and courageous martyrs.

More's answer is similar to that of Erasmus, but it is filled and impregnated with the experience he himself is living through. Christ had not willed that his own should in no way *horrerent necem;* his will was that they should not be afraid to the point of fleeing from temporal to eternal death, by denying the faith. He wanted them to be *milites prudentes,* not *stupidos et amentes.* It is better to confront death, when it is impossible to avoid it, than to separate oneself from Christ through fear: *desciscimus autem, si coram mundo fidem eius abnegamus;* but he does not ask us *vim naturae facere,* nor that we should never fear in any case. Thus, when flight does not harm the cause, he agrees that one should eschew torture by fleeing. His providence willed that some martyrs should hide and, when not required to do so, should not reveal themselves as Christians; and that others, on the contrary, should accuse themselves to their persecutors and spontaneously offer themselves to martyrdom. But if anybody found himself in a situation where he must either face torture or deny God, let him not doubt that into *has angustias* he has been led by the will of God himself. He must have every reason to hope that God will either set him free or else assist him in the battle and crown him victor.[27]

Should one believe, perhaps, that martyrs felt no fear? Christ himself has given us an example of it with his fear in the garden and his courage in confronting the cross. More stresses the signs of Christ's human suffering, by noting that he had suffered not only in his body but also, with the terror which caused him to sweat blood, in his soul. Among all the motives for which Christ would not hide *hos affectus infirmitatis humanae,* pride of place goes to that for which *infirmis infirmus factus, infirmos alios sua infirmitate curaret.*[28] More's insistence on this *infirmitas* is analogous to that of Erasmus on *humanitas: Homo tum hominum causa apud homines loquens humanis verbis reformidationem humanam significavit.* Humanity, which Erasmus at the beginning of the century had loved to see in Christ, is changed in the suffering Christ to the infirm humanity of More awaiting torture.

THOMAS MORE: HUMANIST IN ACTION

R. S. Sylvester

I should like to begin with a text, a text not from Thomas More, and certainly not from the Bible—for in either case, perhaps especially so in the former, the selection might seem to imply not an essay, but a sermon. It does seem to me, however, that, given the title I have chosen, we need to begin with a definition of the term "humanist," a much-abused word that, despite the poor treatment which has been given it, is still absolutely indispensable to a discussion of early Renaissance literature.[1] Hence my text, from Paul Oskar Kristeller:

> The common elements which we find in all humanists, and in other scholars with a humanist background, include a certain familiarity with the classical languages and authors, a certain method of philological and historical criticism, and a certain ideal of literary style; moreover, a historical view that combines an unbounded admiration for classical antiquity, an often unfair contempt of the middle ages, and a belief in the recent or impending rebirth of learning and literature; and also an emphatic and genuine concern with man, and with human, that is, primarily moral, problems.[2]

What I should like to suggest is that such a definition fits the Thomas More of the period 1515–1520 like a glove. We shall find him, in the works I shall be discussing, not only upholding and defending the humanist view, but also illustrating it in the literary form, structure, and tone that he employs. Except for a few casual references, I am omitting *Utopia* deliberately, partly because it is indeed *sui generis* and deserves the whole stage to itself, and partly too because it has received and will continue to receive its share of tribute.[3]

More's other works from this period (1515–1520) have, on the whole, been sadly neglected, and this despite the fact that they are both valuable in themselves and can throw light on *Utopia's* own content and shape. *Richard III* and its relationship to *Utopia* I have dealt with elsewhere.[4] Here I should like to consider, however briefly, More's great Latin letters, most of them written in defense of Erasmus, or of the humanist position in general, or of More's own literary productions. These include the *Letter to Dorp* (1515), the *Letter to the University of Oxford* (1518), the *Letter to a Monk* (late 1519), and the *Letter to Brixius* (1520). Other letters from about this period fit into the pattern I shall try to develop, particularly More's correspondence with Edward Lee and his letters to his children concerning their education.

Reprinted from *Medieval and Renaissance Studies*, 1, ed. O. B. Hardison, Jr. (Chapel Hill, University of North Carolina Press, 1966), 125–37, by permission of the author and the publisher.

One further preliminary note: in all of his literary work composed before the polemical pieces that he was called upon to produce after 1528, More impresses me as a writer who, above all, took special pains not to repeat himself. Erasmus tells us that More tried all forms of composition in these early years and this statement is borne out by even the most cursory glance at his productions: literal translations of Lucian from Greek to Latin, both literal and paraphrastic translation into English from Latin in his *Life of Pico,* English poetry and Latin poetry, English and Latin history in *Richard III,* and of course the really new form of *Utopia* itself. More was not a man to waste his fire. Perhaps the least legal thing about him is his refusal to be unexperimental; and, when he does later write against the Protestant reformers, he constantly complains about the way in which he has to repeat the same point over and over again. Even in this long series of often dull treatises I think one can discern his making many efforts to diversify his prose style and his methods of argumentation. His letters too, even when they have a common subject, show a fine literary flexibility, a concern for tone and audience that makes them far more than merely occasional pieces.

This is especially true of the four letters I wish to treat. The *Letter to Oxford* (1518) is a public performance, an oration addressed to the university officials who were opposing the introduction of Greek into their curriculum. More speaks humbly, but confidently, reminding the university of its commitment to the liberal arts and only occasionally indulging his penchant for irony, as when he says, "Just think, too, what they are doing at Cambridge, which you have always outshone" (p. 101). The Oxford letter eloquently sums up the main humanist educational argument: secular learning trains the soul in virtue; it is the proper handmaid of theology, which, without it, degenerates into *questiunculae,* the "petty and meretricious" 'questions' of late medieval philosophy which More and Erasmus constantly campaigned against. Nothing could be more foolish, in More's eyes, than the performance of the university preacher who, at a *university* assembly, had condemned all literature—all the poets, orators, and historians—even if they were in Latin, much less in Greek!

More's strength, in this letter, stems from his quiet forcefulness, his articulate awareness of the antiquity of the tradition that he is trying to re-establish; but he also is confident of the power behind him as he speaks publicly on the royal behalf. The letter ends with a reaffirmation of its opening modesty, but not before More has unveiled his threat that, if Oxford does not reform itself, then "outsiders will be forced to take a hand in helping the good and wise among you" (p. 101). The "outsiders" were, of course, not only the Chancellor of the University, Archbishop Warham, Cardinal Wolsey, the Lord Chancellor of England, and the King (all of whom More mentions), but More himself, the humble orator, who has just demonstrated, by his literary performance in his letter, the way in which the new learning could produce a new type of man.

If the *Letter to Oxford* crystallizes and summarizes More's humanist position, then the *Letter to Dorp,* written two and one half years earlier (September, 1515), illustrates it in detail with a wonderful subtlety. Martin Dorp was, of course, no Oxford "Trojan," resolutely opposed to all literature, but a Louvain professor and a friend of Erasmus, who had moved into theological studies after a decade of humanistic teaching.[5] As he advanced in the university hierarchy he became more conservative—a tendency which can still be observed in such circles. In 1514, Dorp had written Erasmus, objecting to the satire in *The Praise of Folly*.[6] Though approving of Erasmus' plan to edit Jerome, he had advised him not to tamper with the Vulgate text of the New Testament. Although More did not as yet know Dorp personally, his whole strategy toward him in his letter is couched in personal terms. The letter, though sent, was not published until 1563; More keeps his discussion private, for he is trying to recall a sheep to the humanist fold, and among the learned such discussions should always be *entre nous*.

But this does not by any stretch mean that More is less intense in his humanist commitment here than he was to be later in the *Letter to Oxford*. The *Letter to Dorp* is perhaps the most grandly ironic of all More's writing; and the irony is not merely verbal but completely pervasive, affecting both the tone and structure of the letter on almost every page. More later called it (p. 113) a "wordy" composition and, at the end, he apologizes to Dorp for the hastiness with which it was written. But even these statements are part of the over-all strategy, deliberately designed to flatter Dorp's own literary perceptiveness at the very moment when More is illustrating the poor use to which that perceptiveness had been put. Again and again, in the course of the letter, More reminds Dorp that he couldn't *really* have meant what he said when he criticized Erasmus, or when he defended dialectic, or when he opposed the study of Greek. The pressure exerted on Dorp never lets up, and it reaches its climax when More quotes (pp. 58–59) from some of Dorp's own earlier works (which More himself has carefully studied) to prove that really, all along, Dorp must have been a humanist without knowing it. It is almost as if Dorp is being asked to wake up one morning and, like Byron later, find himself famous. He did in fact wake up within the next year, becoming a supporter of Erasmus and, despite some subsequent vacillations under academic pressure, remaining so until his death in 1525. Erasmus himself wrote his epitaph. More's letter is one of the few polemical pieces ever written which actually persuaded an opponent to change his mind, and it must have been with great relish that More could later write a happy note to Dorp congratulating him on his new attitude (p. 111).

There is hardly time here to go over the Dorp letter, which runs to fifty-five pages in the *Selected Letters*, in great detail, but a few important features must be noted. At the outset, More carefully sets up the basic point which he wishes to make: Dorp matters to him personally; it is the *man* that counts, not the system, and the humanism that More is advocating is not so much a system as a way of life, a definite intellectual and moral program that will reaffirm all that is most human. Hence More's accusation (p. 29) against the theologians: they are as far removed from true theology (based on the classics, Scripture, and the Church Fathers) as they are from the common feelings of humanity. This is true especially because they have added to an extraordinary ignorance of all subjects a perverted opinion of all sorts of knowledge, by means of which they so flatter themselves as to judge themselves alone capable of giving a ready interpretation, according to their own whims, of any piece of literature, even of Scripture, of anything they have heard on any occasion, although they have never seen the passage, have never looked into the work, and do not know in what context the passage occurs.

"The common feelings of humanity" (*communis sensus hominum*)—More's phrase has both a temporal and a spatial meaning. On the one hand it joins the new humanist position with what all wise men thought in the past, and on the other it looks around in the present for a new community of spirit and feeling that would enable men to be as charitable and as free from self-love as More would have, in this letter, Dorp himself to be. If we think such a vision Utopian, then we must recall that More set it down in writing only a few weeks after he had finished Book II of *Utopia* itself. And both *Utopia* and the Dorp letter demonstrate to the full the moral side of the humanist position—that "emphatic and genuine concern with man, and with human problems," which my opening text saw as characteristic of the whole movement.

The intellectual side of humanism is equally well demonstrated in the Dorp letter. In his attack on late scholastic dialectic, More bases himself on the premise that "Speech is surely a *common* possession" (p. 23). If it is common, then men must be able to use it to communicate with each other; but communication at the intellectual level presupposes that one knows the meaning of words, not merely the formal mental pattern that might make it possible for the dialecticians to argue endlessly over the sense in which a statement like "The whore will be a virgin" might be true. And only grammar, in the full sense of the term, can get at meaning in context—thus the study of languages and literature should be *logically prior* to, and ultimately more valuable than, the pursuit of dialectic for its own sake.

This last point cannot be too strongly emphasized, for it suggests More's own patient procedure throughout his letter. What he is really doing is to use "dialectic" against itself by redefining the term so that it will embrace a level of rational discourse available to all men and not merely to the academic schools. Dorp has misunderstood Erasmus, but rational discussion like that which More is engaging in will enable Dorp to understand: "Yet why do I mention these things to you, Dorp? I have no doubt such childish prattle [that of the dialecticians] irks you as it does me. You could change, and perhaps you will be able to, with the help of men like yourself, provided you do not decide to give in to the silliness of men who would more suitably be following *your* judgment" (p. 24). Understanding, to be sure, does not always come easily. Look at the difficulties raised by the literal sense of Scripture in many places—even for those who know Greek and Hebrew. But it is only when men rationally discuss "problems which treat of human affairs seriously, and of divine affairs reverently" (p. 40) that understanding can come at all. This is the heart

of More's assault on both the method and the content of a system which, in
his eyes, was making men intellectually impotent.

The beauty of the Dorp letter, then, stems in no small part from its very
indirectness. Delicately it sketches an ideal man, slowly edging Dorp into an
attitude of mind which he can hardly refuse to recognize as good and wholesome. More was not always so gentle and, in the other two letters we are considering, he adopts a completely different procedure in order to defend the
humanist position. The *Letter to a Monk,* published in 1520, goes over much
the same ground as the *Letter to Dorp* but, as its subtitle indicates, More's
audience, tone, and entire literary manner have shifted radically. The letter is
addressed "to a certain Monk whose ignorance was equaled by his pride," and
it refutes what the title calls "his angry and abusive charges" (p. 114). The title
sets the structure, which falls very neatly into two parts, the first demonstrating with at times almost pedantic detail the Monk's completely unmitigated
ignorance, and the second illustrating his repulsive arrogance in daring to
attack Erasmus as a heretic. We now know, thanks to the researches of Dom
David Knowles,[7] that the Monk involved was a certain John Batmanson, a
contemplative Carthusian whose works have been lost. More evidently intended that they should be, for he deliberately refuses to name his opponent,
whom he had known personally for a number of years. More says his refusal
stems from charitable motives, but he was certainly aware that such anonymity
would rhetorically heighten the insignificance of the monk's views.

In the Dorp letter More was placating and gentle, talking to one of his peers
—or at least pretending to do so. To the Monk, he is abusively scornful, indig-
nant that such a fellow, "utterly incapable of telling what style or language is,"
should presume to circulate criticisms of Erasmus. Intellectually, the Monk is
a fool, mistaking belief for knowledge, and "screaming like a baby if someone
proves that Hugh of Saint Cher made a mistake, or that Nicholas de Lyra was
delirious" (*quod delirasset Lyranus*). More has a relatively easy task as he lectures the Monk in the first part of the letter. One or two quotations from his
opponent's Latin—ungrammatical and solecistic—are almost enough, and the
Monk even thinks that the Septuagint Bible was written in Latin!

But as More's attack continues, his indignation rises. It is not just that the
Monk has detected scholarly errors in Erasmus' works where no such errors
existed; he has also said that Erasmus' only goal was "to cause discord and
bring in deception" (p. 114). This is very nearly slander and More finds such
statements completely reprehensible in one who should be spending his life in
prayer and contemplation. The Monk lacks charity and so do all his fellows
who think that "squatting in a cell" is necessarily better than being out in the
world. What the Monk called Erasmus' "vagabondage" is really Christian missionary work at its best—not even St. Paul journeyed through greater hardships
than Erasmus, and Paul did so for a similar purpose, to give men a better life.
More even tells (p. 132), becoming now almost slanderous himself, an Oliver
Twist sort of story about a prior who ran a gang of murderers and robbers
from his own cell and who opened every new plot with pious recitations of
the Hail Mary!

Another feature of the Monk letter worth remarking is the very large number of scriptural quotations which it contains. More constantly quotes the Bible against his opponent, giving him a lesson in what it means to be a practical Christian whose life is based on the words of Christ and his disciples. The Monk has abused Christianity both intellectually (through his ignorance) and morally (through his gossipy lying). More turns his method against him, showing him how Scripture should be interpreted and how a true monk should live. What More cannot stand is the Monk's "strong conviction of his own sanctity ... a most disastrous attitude in a religious" (p. 139). He has betrayed the whole idea of Christian community, even though he himself, leading the monastic life, should be one of the staunchest upholders of the communal ideal. We recall that it was early Christian communism that made Christianity so attractive to the Utopians,[8] and we may also recall More's own high admiration for the Carthusian monks, with whom, as a young man, he had spent four years in contemplation and devotion.[9] The Monk's betrayal was thus both universal and personal, and More replied in kind with a scathing attack on both Batmanson himself and on the type of mentality and morality which he represented. Perhaps the situation did not remain entirely hopeless, for among the list of Batmanson's lost works we find a *Retractatio*.

Savage satire is also the predominant manner of the last of the four great letters from this period, the *Letter to Brixius* of 1520. But here the situation is entirely different, for with Brixius More is again engaging one of his peers, as he had done in the Dorp letter. Brixius, or Germain de Brie, was a French humanist of no little ability. He had worked with Erasmus at Aldus' press in Venice as far back as 1508 and he and Erasmus remained on friendly terms. Indeed Erasmus did everything he could to prevent Brixius from publishing his *Antimorus* and to prevent More from replying to it. Although More denies the fact very cleverly in his epistle, he did actually start this quarrel with the Frenchman by writing a series of piercing epigrams in which he attacked Brixius' poem, the *Chordigerae navis conflagratio* of 1513. More's epigrams were not published until 1518, but when they were Brixius replied virulently in the *Antimorus,* accusing More of false quantities of his verse, bad grammar in the *Utopia,* and even of false devotion to Henry VIII, whose father's policies More had attacked in two of his poems.

If Dorp was, for More, a sort of lapsed humanist, then Brixius becomes for him the real heretic, the false humanist who, though apparently soaked in the new learning, was actually using his knowledge of the classics in a perverse way. The quarrel is internecine; it turns, for the most part, on purely literary issues, but it is nonetheless interesting for all that. In the Dorp letter (p. 22) More could ironically defend poetry and literature by remarking: "And so poets treat of trifles, dialecticians of serious matters. Poets use their imaginations and tell untruths; dialecticians never speak aught but the truth, even when they affirm as true: 'A dead man can celebrate Mass.' " With Brixius, however, More attacks the idea that poetic license allows a poet who selects a historical subject to indulge in every sort of contradictory fantasy. One can begin to see that there is great deal of "poetry" in More's dialectic and an almost equal amount of "dialectic" in his poetry.

Brixius' poem, which portrayed the French Commander Hervé as vanquishing almost single-handedly the English fleet, no doubt offended More's patriotic feelings; but it also offended his literary sensibility. He found it full of "frightful monstrosities, distortions and unabashed lies, absurd fantasies, and purple patches plucked from various authors and inserted, quite out of place, in Brixius' own crude woolen cloak." Only a study of Brixius' poem can illustrate the truth of More's judgment; but, for me at least, the *Conflagratio* reads like a sort of sixteenth-century *Annus Mirabilis,* full of sounding phrases, but signifying little. Bombast is one thing, however, and crude imitation of the classics is another. More's own literary principles emerge quite clearly as he castigates Brixius for lifting phrases from the classics without showing any awareness of the context from which they came. This is fake humanism, a mere verbal echoing of the best that has been thought and said. We find it everywhere in the sixteenth century, especially in the Neo-Latin verse of the period. More will have none of it, for his own view of the classics is both more respectful and more intelligent.

The *Letter to a Monk,* as we have seen, was saturated with scriptural quotations; that to Brixius is studded with allusions to Horace's *Art of Poetry,* as in the purple patch passage just quoted. Here again More is giving his opponent a lesson in the proper way to write at the same time that he is criticizing what the other fellow has written. The Horatian allusions work because More is using them, as Horace did, against poor poets and poorer poems. Brixius' contrary method can be illustrated only by quotation, but here is how More describes one of his grander passages:

> At long last, you utterly devoured men and ships in the blaze, so that not even a *deus ex machina* (as often happens in tragedies) could preserve just one individual to relate to you the details of this story; for you swept away in the flames "the stars together with the sky, and the sea along with the very fish," and not with just a brief hyperbole, but in several elaborately dull verses, done in striking imitation of Ovid; and you even outstripped Ovid, for he portrayed a world-wide conflagration caused by the Sun's steeds as they roamed, bereft of their rider, while you, in very elegant verse, reduce the heavens and the earth and the seas with the flames of your burning bark, etc.

More's lesson, for Brixius, but also for us as we study sixteenth-century works that imitate the classics, must surely run something like this: we must always ask whether or not the writer who tessellates his work with classical phrases is using them as real echoes that draw upon their original context to reinforce the new passage in which they appear.[10] To answer this question effectively, we must first read, as the best humanists did, the classics as literature, not as mere storehouses of glittering language. The Brixiuses in the Renaissance poetic tribe are legion—as More put it aptly in an epigram, they do indeed write like the ancients, for they impose senescence on everything they touch.

There are also moral implications to the *Letter to Brixius,* questions raised by the whole matter of the humanist at court—how he behaves there, what sort of advice he gives, or what kind of court poetry he writes. This is another problem and I will not go into it here. More himself explores it fully in *Utopia.* With regard to Brixius, however, we can feel sure that poetry like his was certainly not the type that More thought suitable for a king to read.

We can summarize, I think, the main points which I have been trying to make by characterizing each of the four letters as not only a defense of humanism but also an illustration of it in action. In each case, working through the epistolary form, More acts out a different role in literary terms. In the *Letter to Oxford,* he is the public orator, speaking in defense of humanism on his king's behalf. With Dorp, he reshapes the polemical letter into a semi-dialogue, putting words in Dorp's mouth and cajoling him with an ironic intimacy. The *Letter to a Monk* balances the Oxford letter: where the latter dealt with the high and mighty university illiterates, the former, through powerful diatribe, attempts to blot out one of the lesser monastic know-nothings. The strident tones of the Monk letter both recall Hythlodaeus' tirades in *Utopia* and point ahead to More's attack on Luther in 1523. Finally, the Brixius letter reveals and employs More's own literary principles in a clearer way than any other of his works. Together with some of his satiric epigrams, it forms his *Ars Poetica*— and he was always, as Erasmus was to say later, "a poet even in his prose."[11]

Through all four letters too, More's humanism shines brightly. It combines a thorough knowledge of the classics, the Bible, and the Fathers with a reverence for self-abnegating human endeavor. It is moral as well as intellectual, public as well as private. Above all, it is flexible and humane, able to reshape itself for any occasion, adjusting its stance as circumstances demand and showing More to be here, as well as in other respects, truly "a man for all seasons."

PART IV: GENERAL VIEWS

PREFACE TO *A MAN FOR ALL SEASONS*

Robert Bolt

SIR THOMAS MORE

More is a man of an angel's wit and singular learning; I know not his fellow. For where is the man of that gentleness, lowliness, and affability? And as time requireth a man of marvellous mirth and pastimes; and sometimes of as sad gravity: a man for all seasons.

Robert Whittinton

He was the person of the greatest virtue these islands ever produced.

Samuel Johnson

The bit of English History which is the background to this play is pretty well known. Henry VIII, who started with everything and squandered it all, who had the physical and mental fortitude to endure a lifetime of gratified greeds, the monstrous baby whom none dared gainsay, is one of the most popular figures in the whole procession. We recognize in him an archetype, one of the champions of our baser nature, and are in him vicariously indulged.

Against him stood the whole edifice of medieval religion, founded on piety, but by then as moneyed, elaborate, heaped high and inflexible as those abbey churches which Henry brought down with such a satisfying and disgraceful crash.

The collision came about like this: While yet a Prince, Henry did not expect to become a King for he had an elder brother, Arthur. A marriage was made between this Arthur and a Spanish Princess, Catherine, but Arthur presently died. The Royal Houses of Spain and England wished to repair the connection, and the obvious way to do it was to marry the young widow to Henry, now heir in Arthur's place. But Spain and England were Christian Monarchies and Christian law forbade a man to marry his brother's widow.

To be a Christian was to be a Churchman and there was only one Church (though plagued with many heresies) and the Pope was its head. At the request of Christian Spain and Christian England the Pope dispensed with the Christian law forbidding a man to marry his brother's widow, and when in due course Prince Henry ascended the English throne as Henry VIII, Catherine was his Queen.

Reprinted, by permission of the author and publisher from *A Man For All Seasons* (London: Heinemann, 1960), pp. v–xix.

For some years the marriage was successful; they respected and liked one another, and Henry took his pleasures elsewhere but lightly. However, at length he wished to divorce her.

The motives for such a wish are presumably as confused, inaccessible and helpless in a King as any other man, but here are three which make sense: Catherine had grown increasingly plain and intensely religious; Henry had fallen in love with Anne Boleyn; the Spanish alliance had become unpopular. None of these absolutely necessitated a divorce but there was a fourth that did. Catherine had not been able to provide Henry with a male child and was now presumed barren. There was a daughter, but competent statesmen were unanimous that a Queen on the throne of England was unthinkable. Anne and Henry were confident that between them they could produce a son; but if that son was to be Henry's heir, Anne would have to be Henry's wife.

The Pope was once again approached, this time by England only, and asked to declare the marriage with Catherine null, on the grounds that it contravened the Christian law which forbade marriage with a brother's widow. But England's insistence that the marriage had been null was now balanced by Spain's insistence that it hadn't. And at that moment Spain was well placed to influence the Pope's deliberations; Rome, where the Pope lived, had been very thoroughly sacked and occupied by Spanish troops. In addition one imagines a natural disinclination on the part of the Pope to have his powers turned on and off like a tap. At all events, after much ceremonious prevarication, while Henry waited with a rising temper, it became clear that so far as the Pope was concerned, the marriage with Catherine would stand.

To the ferment of a lover and the anxieties of a sovereign Henry now added a bad conscience; and a serious matter it was, for him and those about him.

The Bible, he found, was perfectly clear on such marriages as he had made with Catherine; they were forbidden. And the threatened penalty was exactly what had befallen him, the failure of male heirs. He was in a state of sin. He had been thrust into a state of sin by his father with the active help of the Pope. And the Pope now proposed to keep him in a state of sin. The man who would do that, it began to seem to Henry, had small claim to being the Vicar of God.

And indeed, on looking into the thing really closely, Henry found—what various voices had urged for centuries off and on—that the supposed Pope was no more than an ordinary Bishop, the Bishop of Rome. This made everything clear and everything possible. If the Pope was not a Pope at all but merely a bishop among bishops, then his special powers as Pope did not exist. In particular of course he had no power to dispense with God's rulings as revealed in Leviticus 18, but equally important, he had no power to appoint other Bishops; and here an ancient quarrel stirred.

For if the Pope had not the power to appoint bishops, then who did have, if not the King himself—King by the Grace of God? Henry's ancestors, all those other Henries, had been absolutely right; the Bishops of Rome, without a shadow of legality, had succeeded over the centuries in setting up a rival reign within the reign, a sort of long drawn usurpation. The very idea of it used to throw him into terrible rages. It should go on no longer.

He looked about for a good bishop to appoint to Canterbury, a bishop with no ambitions to modify God's ruling on deceased brothers' wives, yet sufficiently spirited to grant a divorce to his sovereign without consulting the Bishop of Rome. The man was to hand in Thomas Cranmer; Catherine was divorced, Anne married, and the Established Church of England was off on its singular way.

That, very roughly indeed, is the political, or theological, or politico-theological background to the play. But what of the social, or economic, or socio-economic, which we now think more important?

The economy was very progressive, the religion was very reactionary. We say therefore that the collision was inevitable, setting Henry aside as a colourful accident. With Henry presumably we set aside as accidents Catherine and Wolsey and Anne and More and Cranmer and Cromwell and the Lord Mayor of London and the man who cleaned his windows; setting indeed everyone aside as an accident, we say that the collision was inevitable. But that, on reflection, seems only to repeat that it happened. What is of interest is the way it happened, the way it was lived. For lived such collisions are. 'Religion' and 'economy' are abstractions which describe the way men live. Because men work we may speak of an economy, not the other way round. Because men worship we may speak of a religion, not the other way round. And when an economy collides with a religion it is living men who collide, nothing else (they collide with one another and within themselves).

Perhaps few people would disagree with that, put like that, and in theory. But in practice our theoreticians seem more and more to work the other way round, to derive the worker *from* his economy, the thinker *from* his culture, and we to derive even ourselves from our society and our location in it. When we ask ourselves 'What am I?' we may answer 'I am a Man' but are conscious that it's a silly answer because we don't know what kind of thing that might be; and feeling the answer silly we feel it's probably a silly question. We can't help asking it, however, for natural curiosity makes us ask it all the time of everyone else, and it would seem artificial to make ourselves the sole exception, would indeed envelop the mental image of our self in a unique silence and thus raise the question in a particularly disturbing way. So we answer of ourselves as we should of any other: 'This man here is a qualified surveyor, employed but with a view to partnership; this car he is driving has six cylinders and is almost new; he's doing all right; his opinions . . .' and so on, describing ourselves to ourselves in terms more appropriate to somebody seen through a window. We think of ourselves in the Third Person.

To put it another way, more briefly; we no longer have, as past societies have had, any picture of individual Man (Stoic Philosopher, Christian Religious, Rational Gentleman) by which to recognise ourselves and against which to measure ourselves; we are anything. But if anything, then nothing, and it is not everyone who can live with that, though it is our true present position. Hence our willingness to locate ourselves from something that is certainly larger than ourselves, the society that contains us.

But society can only have as much idea as we have what we are about, for it has only our brains to think with. And the individual who tries to plot his position by reference to our society finds no fixed points, but only the vaunted absence of them, 'freedom' and 'opportunity'; freedom for what, opportunity to do what, is nowhere indicated. The only positive he is given is 'get and spend' ('get and spend—if you can' from the Right, 'get and spend—you deserve it' from the Left) and he did not need society to tell him that. In other words we are thrown back by our society upon ourselves at our lowest, that is at our least satisfactory to ourselves. Which of course sends us flying back to society with all the force of rebound.

Socially, we fly from the idea of an individual to the professional describers, the classifiers, the men with the categories and a quick ear for the latest sub-division, who flourish among us like priests. Individually, we do what we can to describe and classify ourselves and to assure ourselves that from the outside at least we do have a definite outline. Both socially and individually it is with us as it is with our cities—an accelerating flight to the periphery, leaving a centre which is empty when the hours of business are over.

That is an ambitious style of thinking, and pride cometh before a fall, but it was with some such ideas in mind that I started on this play. Or else they developed as I wrote it. Or else I have developed them in defence of it now that it is written. It is not easy to know what a play is 'about' until it is finished, and by then what it is 'about' is incorporated in it irreversibly and is no more to be separated from it than the shape of a statue is to be separated from the marble. Writing a play is thinking, not thinking about thinking; more like a dream than a scheme—except that it lasts six months or more, and that one is responsible for it.

At any rate, Thomas More, as I wrote about him, became for me a man with an adamantine sense of his own self. He knew where he began and left off, what area of himself he could yield to the encroachments of his enemies, and what to the encroachments of those he loved. It was a substantial area in both cases for he had a proper sense of fear and was a busy lover. Since he was a clever man and a great lawyer he was able to retire from those areas in wonderfully good order, but at length he was asked to retreat from that final area where he located his self. And there this supple, humorous, unassuming and sophisticated person set like metal, was overtaken by an absolutely primitive rigour, and could no more be budged than a cliff.

This account of him developed as I wrote: what first attracted me was a person who could not be accused of any incapacity for life, who indeed seized life in great variety and almost greedy quantities, who nevertheless found something in himself without which life was valueless and when that was denied him was able to grasp his death. For there can be no doubt, given the circumstances, that he did it himself. If, on any day up to that of his execution, he had been willing to give public approval to Henry's marriage with Anne Boleyn, he could have gone on living. Of course the marriage was associated with other things—the attack on the abbeys, the whole Reformation policy—to which More was violently opposed, but I think he could have found his way round that; he showed every sign of doing so. Unfortunately his approval of the marriage was asked for in a form that required him to state that he believed what he didn't believe, and required him to state it on oath.

This brings me to something for which I feel the need to explain, perhaps apologise. More was a very orthodox Catholic and for him an oath was something perfectly specific; it was an invitation to God, an invitation God would not refuse, to act as a witness, and to judge; the consequence of perjury was damnation, for More another perfectly specific concept. So for More the issue was simple (though remembering the outcome it can hardly have been easy). But I am not a Catholic nor even in the meaningful sense of the word a Christian. So by what right do I appropriate a Christian Saint to my purposes? Or to put it the other way, why do I take as my hero a man who brings about his own death because he can't put his hand on an old black book and tell an ordinary lie?

For this reason: A man takes an oath only when he wants to commit himself quite exceptionally to the statement, when he wants to make an identity between the truth of it and his own virtue; he offers himself as a guarantee. And it works. There is a special kind of shrug for a perjurer; we feel that the man has no self to commit, no guarantee to offer. Of course it's much less effective now that for most of us the actual words of the oath are not much more than impressive mumbo-jumbo than it was when they made obvious sense; we would prefer most men to guarantee their statements with, say, cash rather than with themselves. We feel—we know—the self to be an equivocal commodity. There are fewer and fewer things which, as they say, we 'cannot bring ourselves' to do. We can find almost no limits for ourselves other than the physical, which being physical are not optional. Perhaps this is why we have fallen back so widely on physical torture as a means of bringing pressure to bear on one another. But though few of us have anything in ourselves like an immortal soul which we regard as absolutely inviolable, yet most of us still feel something which we should prefer, on the whole, not to violate. Most men feel when they swear an oath (the marriage vow for example) that they have invested something. And from this it's possible to guess what an oath must be to a man for whom it is not merely a time-honoured and understood ritual but also a definite contract. It may be that a clear sense of the self can *only* crystallize round something transcendental, in which case our prospects look poor, for we are rightly committed to the rational. I think the paramount gift our thinkers, artists, and for all I know, our men of science, should labour to get for us is a sense of selfhood without resort to magic. Albert Camus is a writer I admire in this connection.

Anyway, the above must serve as my explanation and apology for treating Thomas More, a Christian Saint, as a hero of selfhood.

Another thing that attracted me to this amazing man was his splendid social adjustment. So far from being one of society's sore teeth he was, like the hero of Camus' *La Chute*, almost indecently successful. He was respectably not nobly born, in the merchant class, the progressive class of the epoch, distinguished himself first as a scholar, then as a lawyer, was made an Ambassador, finally Lord Chancellor. A visitors' book at his house in Chelsea would have looked like a Sixteenth Century *Who's Who:* Holbein, Erasmus, Colet, everybody. He corresponded with the greatest minds in Europe as the representative and acknowledged champion of the New Learning in England. He was a friend of the King, who would send for More when his social appetites took a turn in that direction and once walked round the Chelsea garden with his arm round More's neck. ('If my head would win him a castle in France, it should not fail to fall,' said More.) He adored and was adored by his own large family. He parted with more than most men when he parted with his life, for he accepted and enjoyed his social context.

One sees that there is no necessary contradiction here; it is society after all which proffers an oath and with it the opportunity for perjury. But why did a man so utterly absorbed in his society, at one particular point disastrously part company from it? How indeed was it possible—unless there was some sudden aberration? But that explanation won't do, because he continued to the end to make familiar and confident use of society's weapons, tact, favour, and above all, the letter of the law.

For More again the answer to this question would be perfectly simple (though again not easy); the English Kingdom, his immediate society, was subservient to the larger society of the Church of Christ, founded by Christ, extending over Past and Future, ruled from Heaven. There are still some for whom that is perfectly simple, but for most it can only be a metaphor. I took it as a metaphor for that larger context which we all inhabit, the terrifying cosmos. Terrifying because no laws, no sanctions, no *mores* obtain there; it is either empty or occupied by God and Devil nakedly at war. The sensible man will seek to live his life without dealings with this larger environment, treating it as a fine spectacle on a clear night, or a subject for innocent curiosity. At the most he will allow himself an agreeable *frisson* when he contemplates his own relation to the cosmos, but he will not try to live in it; he will gratefully accept the shelter of his society. This was certainly More's intention.

If 'society' is the name we give to human behaviour when it is patterned and orderly, then the Law (extending from empirical traffic regulations, through the mutating laws of property, and on to the great tabus like incest and patricide) is the very pattern of society. More's trust in the law was his trust in his society; his desperate sheltering beneath the forms of the law was his determination to remain within the shelter of society. Cromwell's contemptuous shattering of the forms of law by an unconcealed act of perjury showed how fragile for any individual is that shelter. Legal or illegal had no further meaning, the social references had been removed. More was offered to be sure, the chance of slipping back into the society which had thrust him out into the warring cosmos, but even in that solitude he found himself able to repeat, or continue, the decision he had made while he still enjoyed the common shelter.

I see that I have used a lot of metaphors. I know no other way to treat this subject. In the play I used for this theme a poetic image. As a figure for the superhuman context I took the largest, most alien, least formulated thing I know, the sea and water. The references to ships, rivers, currents, tides, navigation, and so on, are all used for this purpose. Society by contrast figures as dry land. I set out with no very well formed idea of the kind of play it was to be, except that it was not to be naturalistic. The possibility of using imagery, that is of using metaphors not decoratively but with an intention, was a side effect of that. It's a very far from new idea, of course. Whether it worked I rather doubt. Certainly no-one noticed. But I comfort myself with the thought that it's the nature of imagery to work, in performance at any rate, unconsciously. But if, as I think, a play is more like a poem than a straight narration, still less a demonstration or lecture, then imagery ought to be important. It's perhaps necessary to add that by a poem I mean something tough and precise, not something dreamy. As Brecht said, beauty and form of language are a primary alienation device. I was guaranteed some beauty and form by incorporating passages from Sir Thomas More himself. For the rest my concern was to match with these as best I could so that the theft should not be too obvious.

In two previous plays, *Flowering Cherry* and *The Tiger and the Horse,* I had tried, but with fatal timidity, to handle contemporaries in a style that should make them larger than life; in the first mainly by music and mechanical effects, in the second mainly by making the characters unnaturally articulate and unnaturally aware of what they 'stood for.' Inevitably these plays looked like what they most resembled, orthodox fourth wall dramas with puzzling, uncomfortable, and, if you are uncharitable, pretentious overtones. So for this one I took a historical setting in the hope that the distance of years would give me Dutch courage, and enable me to treat my characters in a properly heroic, properly theatrical manner.

The style I eventually used was a bastardized version of the one most recently associated with Bertold Brecht. This is not the place to discuss that style at any length, but it does seem to me that the style practised by Brecht differs from the style taught by Brecht, or taught to us by his disciples. Perhaps they are more Royalist than the King. Or perhaps there was something daimonic in Brecht the artist which could not submit to Brecht the teacher. That would explain why in the *Chalk Circle,* which is to demonstrate that goodness is a terrible temptation, goodness triumphs very pleasantly. And why in *Mother Courage,* which is to demonstrate the unheroic nature of war, the climax is an act of heroism which Rider Haggard might have balked at. And why in *Galileo,* which is to demonstrate the social and objective value of scientific knowledge, Galileo, congratulated on saving his skin so as to augment that knowledge, is made to deny its value on the grounds that he defaulted at the moment when what the world needed was for one man to be true to himself. I am inclined to think that it is simply that Brecht was a very fine artist, and that life is complicated and ambivalent. At all events I agree with Eric Bentley that the proper effect of alienation is to enable the audience *reculer pour mieux sauter,* to deepen, not to terminate, their involvement in the play.

Simply to slap your audience in the face satisfies an austere and puritanical streak which runs in many of his disciples and sometimes, detrimentally I think, in Brecht himself. But it is a dangerous game to play. It has the effect of shock because it is unexpected. But it is unexpected only because it flies in the face of a thoroughly established convention. (A convention which goes far beyond naturalism; briefly, the convention that the actors are there as actors, not as themselves.) Each time it is done it is a little less unexpected, so that a bigger and bigger dosage will be needed to produce the same effect. If it were continued indefinitely it would finally not be unexpected at all. The theatrical convention would then have been entirely dissipated and we should have in the theatre a situation with one person, who used to be an actor, desperately trying to engage the attention—by rude gestures, loud noises, indecent exposure, fireworks, anything—of other persons, who used to be the audience. As this point was approached some very lively evenings might be expected, but the depth and subtlety of the notions which can be communicated by such methods may be doubted. When we use alienation methods just for kicks, we in the theatre are sawing through the branch on which we are sitting.

I tried then for a 'bold and beautiful verbal architecture,' a story rather than a plot, and overtly theatrical means of switching from one locale to another. I also used the most notorious of the alienation devices, an actor who addresses the audience and comments on the action. But I had him address the audience in character, that is from within the play.

He is intended to draw the audience into the play, not thrust them off it. In this respect he largely fails, and for a reason I had not foreseen. He is called 'The Common Man' (just as there is a character called 'The King') and the word 'common' was intended primarily to indicate 'that which is common to us all.' But he was taken instead as a portrayal of that mythical beast The Man In The Street. This in itself was not so bad; after all he was intended to be something with which everyone would be able to identify. But once he was identified as common in that sense, my character was by one party accepted as a properly belittling account of that vulgar person, and by another party bitterly resented on his behalf. (Myself I had meant him to be attractive, and his philosophy impregnable.) What both these parties had in common—if I may use the word—is that they thought of him as somebody else. Wherever he might have been, this Common Man, he was certainly not in the theatre. He is harder to find than a unicorn. But I must modify that. He was not in the Stalls, among his fashionable detractors and defenders. But in the laughter this character drew down from the Gallery, that laughter which is the most heartening sound our Theatre knows, I thought I heard once or twice a rueful note of recognition.

THE WIT OF THOMAS MORE

T. E. Bridgett

In the time of Sir Thomas More the words wit and wisdom had almost or altogether the same meaning, yet the quality that we now designate by wit was ever distinct from wisdom, though by no means opposed to it. Wisdom and wit are like heat and light. In addition to knowledge, wit supposes a play of the imagination or the fancy, a faculty of detecting hidden congruities or incongruities, and of bringing images or ideas together in such a way as to cause both surprise and pleasure to the hearer or reader. I take wit here in its generic sense, not as distinct from humour but as comprising it. To defend the use of wit would be as absurd as to defend the human intellect and the cultivation of its faculties. To apologise for the union of wit with sanctity would be as superfluous as to apologise for the use of poetic imagery, and exalted language by inspired prophets. Yet, as wit is of various kinds, it may be asked whether there is not something at least incongruous in employing jokes and laughter-moving sentences in serious religious controversy, or in exciting merriment and fun in the midst of spiritual discourses, and while treating serious or even pathetic themes. This, nevertheless, is a characteristic of the genius of Blessed Thomas More, and it seems to demand, not so much defence, as explanation, lest it should be misunderstood.

In More's time, the English prided themselves on being a merry nation, though Froissart remarks that they took their mirth sometimes *moult triste-ment.* But merriment or mirth as very clearly distinguished from levity or want of seriousness. No one could condemn levity of character more severely than did this gay and mirthful, yet most earnest-minded writer, whose character we are considering. The following passage will both state his serious view of life, and serve as a specimen of his bright and witty style of writing:

> An evil and a perilous life live they that will in this world not labour and work, but live either in idleness or in idle business, driving forth all their days in gaming[1] for their pastime, as though that else their time could never pass, but the sun would ever stand even still over their heads and never draw to night, but if they draw away the day with dancing or some such other goodly gaming. God sent men hither to wake and work; and as for sleep and gaming (if any gaming be good in this vale of misery, in this time of tears), it must serve but for a refreshing of the weary body; for rest and recreation be but as a sauce, and sauce should (ye wot well)

Reprinted, by permission of the publisher, from *The Wisdom and Wit of Thomas More* (London, Burns and Oates, 1892), pp. 11-25.

serve for a faint and weak stomach to get it the more appetite to the meat, and not increase its voluptuous pleasure in every greedy glutton, that hath in himself sauce malapert enough. And therefore, likewise as it were a fond feast that had all the table full of sauce, and so little meat therewith, that the guests should go thence as empty as they came thither; so is it surely a very mad ordered life that hath but little time bestowed in any fruitful business, and all the substance idly spent in play.[2]

It is clear from these words of Blessed Thomas that if he indulged in any merriment, or defended its use, it had no connection in his mind with that levity and frivolity against which our Divine Master uttered His anathema when He said: "Blessed are they that mourn: woe to you that now laugh." The blessedness is to those who mourn over sin, the woe to those who laugh at sin or in sin, or who make their whole life a frivolous pastime. It is not a woe pronounced against those who laugh at what is laughable in due season. Laughter is like anger: it may be good or bad, according to circumstances. We must consider both the person who laughs and the object of his laughter. Laughter does not befit the wilful enemies of God, though it may be sometimes skilfully and lawfully awakened in such to lead them to a better mind. Laughter in applause of what is wicked, vile, or impure is criminal laughter. "A fool will laugh at sin," says the Holy Ghost. Laughter at incongruous trifles which are innocent belongs by right to childhood and youth, yet it may have its season even in the life of the wisest and the saintliest; while laughter at the errors, the vices, the foolish pretences of men, may be a participation in that Divine sarcasm or irony which is attributed to God. "Why have the Gentiles raged and the people desired vain things: the kings of the earth stood up, and the princes met together against the Lord and against His Christ? He that dwelleth in heaven shall laugh at them, and the Lord shall deride them." The spectacle of worms of earth in revolt against their Creator, of earthly kings contending with the King of heaven, this spectacle is worthy of—which shall I say, laughter or tears? Of both, according as we regard it. It "makes the angels weep," said our great poet, by a bold figure. It makes God laugh, says the Psalmist, by a still bolder figure.

I do not remember that Blessed Thomas More has anywhere discussed in general the lawfulness or congruity of laughter, or the moral fitness of witty terms of expression in writing on Divine or spiritual things. In his *Dialogue of Comfort against Tribulation* he touches slightly on the subject, and if his tone is apologetical it befitted the modesty of his character, and it must be remembered that he is inquiring, not as to the lawfulness of mirth in general in our human life, but as to the expediency of turning to it for consolation when God is sending afflictions. (In the following dialogue Vincent is a young nobleman, Antony his aged, wise, and holy uncle.)

Vincent.—And first, good Uncle, ere we proceed farther, I will be bold to move you one thing more of that we talked when I was here before. For when I revolved in my mind again the things that were concluded here by you, methought ye would in nowise, that in any tribulation men should seek for comfort either in worldly thing or fleshly, which mind, Uncle, of yours, seemeth somewhat hard. For a merry tale with a friend refresheth a man much, and without any harm lighteneth his mind, and amendeth his courage; so that it seemeth but well done to take such recreation. And Solomon saith, I trow, that men should in heaviness give the sorry man wine to make him forget his sorrow.[3] And St. Thomas saith, that proper pleasant talking, which is called $εὐτραπελία$,[4] is a good virtue, serving to refresh the mind, and make it quick and lusty to labour and study again, where continual fatigation would make it dull and deadly.

Antony.—Cousin, I forgot not that point, but I longed not much to touch it. For neither might I well utterly forbid it, where the cause might hap to fall that it should not hurt; and, on the other side, if the case so should fall, methought yet it should little need to give any man counsel to it. Folk are prone enough to such fantasies of their own mind. You may see this by ourselves, which coming now together, to talk of as earnest, sad matter as men can devise, were fallen yet even at the first into wanton, idle tales. And of truth, Cousin, as you know very well, myself am of nature even half a giglot[5] and more. I would I could as easily mend my fault, as I can well know it; but scant can I refrain it, as old a fool as I am; howbeit, so partial will I not be to my fault as to praise it.

But for that you require my mind in the matter, whether men in tribulation may not lawfully seek recreation and comfort themselves with some honest mirth: first, agreed that our chief comfort must be in God, and that with Him we must begin, and with Him continue, and with Him end also: a man to take now and then some honest worldly mirth, I dare not be so sore as utterly to forbid it, since good men and well learned have in some case allowed it, specially for the diversity of divers men's minds. For else, if we were all such as would God we were, and such as natural wisdom would we should be, and is not all clean excusable that we be not in deed, I would then put no doubt, but that unto any man the most comfortable talking that could be, were to hear of heaven: whereas now, God help us! our wretchedness is such, that in talking awhile thereof, men wax almost weary, and as though to hear of heaven were a heavy burden, they must refresh themselves after with a foolish tale. Our affection towards heavenly joys waxeth wonderful cold. If dread of hell were as far gone, very few would fear God: but that yet a little sticketh in our stomachs.

Mark me, Cousin, at the sermon, and commonly towards the end, somewhat the preacher speaketh of hell and heaven. Now, while he preacheth of the pains of hell, still they stand yet and give him the hearing; but as soon as he cometh to the joys of heaven, they be busking them backward and flock-meal fall away. It is in the soul somewhat as it is in the body. Some are there of nature, or of evil custom, come to that point that a worse thing sometimes steadeth them more than a better. Some man, if he be sick, can away with no wholesome meat, nor no medicine can go down with him, but if it be tempered with some such thing for his fantasy, as maketh the meat or the medicine less wholesome than it should be. And yet while it will be no better, we must let him have it so. Cassianus, that very virtuous man, rehearseth in a certain collection of his, that a certain holy father, in making of a sermon, spake of heaven and heavenly things so celestially, that much of his audience with the sweet sound thereof, began to forget all the world, and fall asleep. Which, when the father beheld, he dissembled their sleeping, and suddenly said unto them, I shall tell you a merry tale. At which word, they lifted up their heads and harkened unto that. And after the sleep therewith broken, heard him tell on of heaven again. In what wise that good father rebuked then their untoward minds, so dull unto the thing that all our life we labour for, and so quick and lusty towards other trifles, I neither bear in mind, nor shall here need to rehearse. But thus much of the matter sufficeth for our purpose, that whereas you demand me whether in tribulation men may not sometimes refresh themselves with worldly mirth and recreation, I can no more say; but he that cannot long endure to hold up his head and hear talking of heaven, except he be now and then between (as though heaven were heaviness) refreshed with a merry, foolish tale, there is none other remedy, but you must let him have it. Better would I wish it, but I cannot help it.

Howbeit, let us by mine advice at the leastwise make those kinds of recreation as short and as seldom as we can. Let them serve us but for sauce, and make them not our meat: and let us pray unto God, and all our good friends for us, that we may feel such a savour in the delight of heaven, that in respect of the talking of the joys thereof all worldly recreation be but a grief to think on. And be sure, Cousin, that if we might once purchase the grace to come to that point, we never found of worldly recreation so much comfort in a year, as we should find in the bethinking us of heaven in less than half-an-hour.[6]

From the above quotations, it will be seen that the question of facetious writing is very much narrowed, when it is considered in relation to Sir Thomas More. In his youth he loved epigrams. It was a period when the scholars of the Renaissance were copying the obscenity no less than the wit of their heathen models. From this vice young More carefully abstained, though a few trifles have been printed against his will, which he afterwards regretted.[7] In his early manhood he translated three of Lucian's dialogues, which he especially admired for their wit as well as for their matter. He was ever fond of a joke. In 1508, when he was thirty years old, Erasmus calls him *insignis nugator,* a famous lover of fun. His humour brightens up his most serious controversial writings, and gives a flavour to his ascetic treatises which few (I think) can fail to relish.

Erasmus, who lived long in Blessed More's house, and was his dearest friend, says that his handsome face seemed always ready for mirth; but that his fun was self-contained, not noisy, and never uncharitable, never bitter, and never verged on scurrility or buffoonery. He describes him as a man who could be all to all men, whose company, whose look, whose conversation increased joy, dissipated dulness, and soothed sorrow. Such a character cannot be illustrated by relating a few *bon mots* or pleasant sayings. It is only by reading his works that any adequate conception can be formed of his deep wisdom and brilliant wit, his lively fancy, his richness of illustration, his shrewdness, his clever turns of expression, his homely, forcible words, his light banter, or his scathing sarcasm. His life as related by his contemporaries, and his writings, show throughout a strange yet beautiful mixture of joyousness and seriousness, of almost boyish fun and altogether saintly earnestness, of gentle merriment and tender pathos, of unfaltering confidence in God united with awe and adoration of His majesty and justice. We must not think of him for a moment as a jocose man, a jester, or a punster. Now and then, indeed, his wit will play upon words, but generally it is busied with deeper things than external forms. All are familiar with the quaint sayings uttered by him at the scaffold. It was these that gave occasion to Hall, a chronicler and panegyrist of the stupid pageantries in which Henry VIII so delighted, to accuse Henry's victim of buffoonery; and some dull historians have not known whether to admire his intrepidity or be shocked at his levity. They must know little of his character or of the facts of his life who speak of levity in connection with his heroic death. Such men would doubtless call the conduct of Elias levity, when, after his fast of forty days, he summoned the prophets and priests of the idol Baal to meet him on Mount Carmel, and mocked their prayers. "Cry with a louder voice; for he is a god, and perhaps he is talking, or at an inn, or on a journey, or is asleep and must be waked."[8]

Let us examine a little these levities of Blessed Thomas. During his fifteen months' imprisonment in the Tower he had prepared himself in prayer, and fasting, and hair-shirt for his death. He had had—as we know from his own testimony—many a night of agony, when he thought, not so much of his own end as of the distress and temporal ruin that his refusal of the oath was bringing on his wife and children. His meditations were on the agony of our Lord in the Garden, on which he composed a most affecting treatise. He had fought his battle and gained his victory. He had been strengthened by his angel in his weakness, and at the end all weakness had passed away. He had committed his family to God, and the summons to die was to him a glad message of release— a call of the Bridegroom to His heavenly banquet. He went towards the scaffold with a light heart. The ladder was unsteady and he was weak with long sickness and imprisonment. Turning to the lieutenant of the Tower, who accompanied him, he said: "I pray thee see me safe up, and for my coming down let me shift for myself." Levity! Say rather the elasticity of a heavenly heart, as the weary feet began to mount the ladder of heaven. His prayer on the scaffold was the psalm *Miserere,* the penitent's psalm. When it was said, and he had spoken his few words to the people, declaring his loyalty both to his king and his God, he laid his head upon the block. "Wait," he said, half to himself, half to the executioner; "let me move aside my beard before you strike, for that has at least committed no treason." Levity again! Say rather the scorn of a loyal heart at being condemned to a traitor's death. These playful sayings were neither buffooneries nor jokes, but rather fitting antiphons before and after the psalm of penitence and hope.

But let us go back from his death to his life, and see what use he had made of these special gifts, of his peculiar character or temperament. His wit taught him, in the first place, to strip the mask from the world in which he mixed, so that it neither dazzled nor seduced him; and, in the second place, it taught him to strip the mask from the deadly heresies which arose in his latter days, so that they became, under his caustic pen, as ridiculous as they were hateful to the thousands who read his books. (1) First, then, his wit—not alone, of course, but with prayer, and meditation, and the grace of God—kept his soul pure from the seductions of the world. Without any ambition he had been forced into the life of a court, and had risen from dignity to dignity. He was constantly in the company of great men and of princes, in the midst of banquets and pageantry. Wit gave him a keen insight into the essence of things, so that pomp and pageantry amused rather than dazzled him. One who lived with him, Richard Pace, the king's secretary and Dean of St. Paul's, called him a Democritus, a laughing philosopher. Diplomacy, treaties of peace and commerce, war and truce, were to him the trifling of grown-up men, not very much wiser or more serious than the games of children. His *Utopia* is full of quaint irony on these matters. His wit even helped him to make light of imprisonment. So habitually had Blessed Thomas looked on this world as God's prison-house, that when he was actually thrown into prison he could realise no change except that the bounds of his wandering were now somewhat narrower. Thus his wit, that is to say, his deep, subtle, penetrating insight into human life, his amusement at its emptiness and pretence, went along with the grace of God to keep his heart simple, steadfast, undefiled, undeceived in prosperity, undismayed in adversity. (2) Wit also helped Blessed Thomas to strip the mask from heresy. In the latter part of his life he was thrown into controversy with the first Lutheran re-formers. Some have accused him of rudeness, and bitterness, and insolence in his manner of conducting this controversy. But they forget the difference be-tween his day and ours. Protestants to us are men and women, erring indeed, yet who may be supposed to be in good faith, since they have been brought up in error, and are confirmed in it by inherited traditions. They deserve, therefore, to be treated courteously and respectfully. Blessed More had to deal with men who were formal heretics, apostates from the Church; with priests, and monks, and friars who had deserted their altars and their cloisters, and violated their sacred vows. Yet, while they indulged in every kind of licence and neglected every sacred duty, and were fighting against the Holy Ghost, and seeking by every means to destroy the work of our Lord's Precious Blood, they made sanctimonious pretences, quoted unceasingly Holy Scripture, and affected zeal for truth and the glory of God. Simple souls were often deceived by these pretences, not seeing the ravening wolf under the sheep's clothing, dazzled (to use a metaphor of Blessed More) by the peacock's tail, and not noticing his ugly feet and strident voice. Now Blessed More's shrewdness and fineness of perception not only enabled him to see the true character of this revolt against the Church, but to expose it. He ruthlessly strips off the mask, sometimes with stern indignation, sometimes with biting sarcasm, sometimes with overpowering ridicule. His wit, humour, and power of ridicule saved many an honest man who read his books from becoming a victim of heresy. And let it be said, in passing, that a little of Blessed More's sarcastic spirit is a great help to those who are obliged to mix much with unbelievers and misbelievers, and to hear or read their attacks upon the Catholic Church. It is only when a child comes to the *age of reason* that he begins to approach the tribunal of penance; when he arrives at the *age of discretion* that he is allowed to kneel at the altar. A further advance is necessary before he can safely read anti-Catholic literature, or mix with mocking heretics. He must have reached the *age of disdain*. Now the age of reason is seven or eight, that of discretion is ten or twelve; how many years must we count for the age of disdain? It is not a question of years: some never reach this age; some are always timorous, overawed by the pretences of heretics—such can never read without danger attacks on Catholic faith or institutions. The age of disdain is when we get a little of the knowledge of the world, the insight into human character, the sarcastic spirit of Blessed Thomas More. This spirit was left as a legacy to the Catholics of England by the martyr-chancellor, and can be traced through all our controversial literature, from Dr. Harding in the days of Elizabeth to Dr. Lingard in our own days.[9] It has nothing to do with pride or uncharitableness. It is consistent with perfect fairness towards an adversary. Never was there a fairer controversialist than Sir Thomas More. Above all, this lofty scorn of empty pretenders has nothing to do with hatred. Hatred of any one is inconsistent with charity and humility; scorn of falsehood and impiety is simply loyal allegiance to God.

We have seen the uses to which Blessed Thomas put his natural gifts and character. Let me mention briefly the dangers to which he was exposed by it, and how he avoided them. (*a*) The first danger of a man of keen perception and sarcastic humour is that of degenerating into a habit of scoffing and jeering at every man's foible, of suspecting every man's motives, distrusting all virtue, believing no man's word, seeing unreality in every noble sentiment or specious work, imposture in every tale of suffering. Such a temper is often found in experienced men of the world, and affected by those who would wish to appear men of the world. Its motto is *nil admirari*—"to be moved to admiration by nothing and to be surprised at nothing." It despises enthusiasm above all things. It is *good form* in English society among men, and yet it is a detestable disposition, of which not the least shadow will be found in Blessed Thomas More. He was preserved from it by two things especially: by humility, which made him think little of himself, and keep his own faults and weaknesses ever before his eyes; and by charity, which made him look out for good in others, by charity which "is not puffed up, rejoiceth not in iniquity, but rejoiceth with the truth." (*b*) The second danger to which wit is exposed is that of frivolity, of making light of everything, always seeking out the ridiculous side of things, even in the service and worship of God. There is a good deal of this in certain literature of the present day. Now, piety and reverence for Divine things do not make men affect solemnity in look or tone of voice. Sanctimoniousness, and cant, and religious jargon are offensive to true piety. Blessed Thomas More could make a playful jest about holy things without a touch of profaneness. His faith was so robust, that it had no need to prop itself up with mannerisms and phrases. And if ever there was a man who took not only religious worship, but the whole of life, as a profoundly serious matter, it was the blessed martyr. While other men, even priests and bishops, were making light of taking the oath exacted by the king, Blessed Thomas watched them "playing their pageant," as he called it; but rather than join them in this pageant, he went to prison and to death. He knew that for every idle word that a man shall speak he shall give an account at the Day of Judgment: and this man of cheerful mirth has left an everlasting example of earnestness in life, of fear of God's judgments and adoration of His holiness. Lastly, there is a word of his that explains best of all how he understood merriment. He used constantly to speak, when taking leave of his friends, of his hopes of being *merry with them with God in heaven.* Heaven to him was merriment, perfect truth, sincerity, innocence, joy in congenial society, above all joy in the source of all genuine and lasting mirth: "Enter thou into the joy of thy Lord."

MARTYR OF THE REFORMATION: THOMAS MORE

R. W. Chambers

From his own day to ours, Sir Thomas More has always appeared to the practical Anglo-Saxon mind as a paradoxical figure. When we learn, in our schooldays, of the great statesman and lawyer who would rather be decapitated than tell a lie, we are moved by feelings of respect, tempered by astonishment; like the little American girl when she read the story of the boy who stood on the burning deck, we are inclined to say, 'I think he was very good; but he wasn't very smart.'

A boy grows into a man, and a man on rare occasions into an eminent historian, into a Froude, or an Acton, or a Creighton. The respect for More remains; and though the grounds for the perplexity may have shifted, the perplexity remains also. To our great historians More is an incomprehensible riddle.

From those who adhere to the faith for which More died, he has generally received a tribute of complete and understanding sympathy. Elsewhere, however (and sometimes even among those of his own faith), More is regarded as a daring innovator, who somehow or other became one more example of 'the lost leader,' one more example of the Triumphs of the World:

> 'Behold,' she cries, 'so many rages lull'd,
> So many fiery spirits quite cool'd down.'

As to the cause of this change, historians are not agreed. Some great writers put it down to the bad influence of Henry VIII. More, they say, allowed his sentiments to be moulded by the official theology of the court, till under that sinister influence he was changed from a 'liberal' into a 'pseudo-liberal.' Creighton and Acton had their little quarrels, but upon this estimate of More they are in complete agreement. Froude also agrees, except that his respect for Henry VIII will not allow of that monarch retaining the part of More's misleader, a role which in Froude's pages has to be undertaken by the Roman Catholic Church: it was that which turned the 'genial philosopher' into the 'merciless bigot.'

Thirty years ago, the great English biographer and organizer of English biography, Sidney Lee, expressed the traditional English view of More:

> None who read the *Utopia* can deny that its author drank deep of the
> finest spirit of his age ... There is hardly a scheme of social or political

Reprinted, by permission of the publisher, from *Man's Unconquerable Mind* (London, Jonathan Cape, 1939), pp. 172–89.

reform that has been enunciated in later epochs of which there is no definite adumbration in More's pages. But he who passes hastily from the
speculations of More's *Utopia* to the record of More's subsequent life and
writings will experience a strange shock. Nowhere else is he likely to be
faced by so sharp a contrast between precept and practice, between enlightened and vivifying theory in the study, and adherence in the work-a-
day world to the unintelligent routine of bigotry and obscurantism. By the
precept and theory of his *Utopia* More cherished and added power to the
new light. By his practical conduct in life he sought to extinguish the illuminating forces to which his writing offered fuel.

The facts of the situation are not open to question ... Sir Thomas
More's career propounds a riddle which it is easier to enunciate than to
solve.[1]

Yet one thing is clear. There is no sixteenth-century Englishman as to
whom there exists more intimate information. If we wish to solve the 'riddle
of his career,' there is no one whose motives we can learn to appreciate so
fully. More's son-in-law, William Roper, 'knowing at this day no one man living, that of him and of his doings understood so much as myself,' wrote, in
Queen Mary's reign, his deeply understanding notes on More's life. Nicholas
Harpsfield, in the same reign, wrote a careful official biography. An even more
elaborate biography by More's nephew, William Rastell, has been lost, but
some priceless fragments remain. Had it not been for Rastell, much of More's
written work might have been lost also. The reminiscences of the young
people who had lived with More in the Great House at Chelsea were collected
by yet a fourth biographer, Thomas Stapleton. The family tradition did not
finally work itself out till a fifth biographer and a sixth (Cresacre More, More's
great-grandson) had told the story.

Even more important are More's own writings. In *Utopia* More expressed
the hopes and fears for the world felt by the scholarly circle surrounding
Erasmus and himself. More's defence of the things for which he most cared is
extant in his voluminous controversial and devotional writings. And, in his
letters, we can trace his thoughts (especially during his last months of imprisonment) in a way which is possible with only very few of the great men of
history.

Yet, abundant as this material is, much of it has only been made easily
accessible during the past few years, and much of it is not easily accessible
even now. The misunderstanding of More is chiefly due to neglect of what he
has himself written, and also in some degree to neglect of what his biographers
tell us.

Let us take a single paragraph from Roper's *Life,* and see what we can get
from a study of it.

As an example of the 'fruitful communication' which he 'had ofttimes with
his familiar friends,' Roper records a conversation in which More told him of
the three great wishes of his life:

So on a time, walking with me along the Thames' side at Chelsea, in talking of other things he said unto me: 'Now would to our Lord, son Roper, upon condition that three things were well established in Christendom, I were put in a sack, and here presently cast into the Thames.'

'What great things be those, Sir,' quoth I, 'that should move you so to wish?'

'Wouldst thou know what they be, son Roper?' quoth he.

'Yea, marry, with good will, sir, if it please you,' quoth I.

'In faith, son, they be these,' said he. 'The first is, that where the most part of Christian princes be at mortal war, they were all at an universal peace. The second, that where the Church of Christ is at this present sore afflicted with many errors and heresies, it were settled in a perfect uniformity of religion. The third, that where the king's matter of his marriage is now come in question, it were to the glory of God and quietness of all parties brought to a good conclusion.' Whereby, as I could gather, he judged that otherwise it would be a disturbance to a great part of Christendom.[2]

We can date this conversation pretty exactly—it must have been after the King's marriage had come in question, but before the peace of Cambrai, in which More took a big part and by which England secured the only long-continued cessation from foreign warfare which this country enjoyed during the troubled reign of Henry VIII. More, when he spoke these words, was a man of fifty, and was shortly to become Lord Chancellor. He could look back on a life of public service. The son of a Lincoln's Inn lawyer, he was taught the ways of the great whilst still a boy, by service in the household of Cardinal Morton. He was subsequently himself trained as a lawyer at Lincoln's Inn, after a short spell of education at Oxford. This was a combination which, though it may seem natural enough to us to-day, was rare in More's time—but it is typical of More's two great interests. Oxford, with its theological training, led to the secular priesthood or the cloister—a calling which throughout his life had a great attraction for More. Lincoln's Inn and the Law led to the political career which, after a period of hesitation between the Church and the Law, was to be More's vocation. Like some great modern statesmen, More came to political life after an apprenticeship in the service of his city. For nearly eight years he had been one of the two Under-Sheriffs of London. The post was then a very important one, for the Sheriffs had to perform legal duties for which, being men of business rather than lawyers, they had not usually any special qualifications, and their permanent legal officials consequently carried a considerable responsibility. Then More left the service of the city for that of Henry, and for nearly a dozen years had been rising in political life, when this conversation with his son-in-law took place.

The passion for universal peace was one which More shared with his scholar friends, and above all with Colet and Erasmus. During the twenty years of Henry's reign England had been plunged into one futile campaign after another, till the vast accumulated wealth of Henry VII had been wasted, and the resources of the country so exhausted as to make for a time any further war impossible. No danger had been averted and no advantage gained;

historians have been puzzled to find the justification or even the explanation of Henry's wars, or, as Sir Walter Ralegh described them, 'his vain enterprises abroad, wherein it is thought that he consumed more treasure than all our victorious kings did in their several conquests.' It is true that there was comparatively little fighting, and that such fighting as there was proved quite inconclusive. Continuous war in the sixteenth century had become too expensive for the resources of any government, and Henry had but few subjects compared with his rivals, Francis I or Charles V. Historians often speak as if, therefore, Henry's wars were negligible. That is not so. Taxation and the depreciation of the coinage caused terrible suffering. We are the poorer to this day for the confiscation of art treasures, treasures which the monasteries of England had created and housed during eight centuries, but which were destroyed in the vain attempt to refill Henry's exhausted treasury.

All these useless wars More detested. Yet his ideal was anything but a policy of selfish isolation for England. It is because he cares for Europe, not because he ignores Europe, that More is a lover of peace. European scholars were hoping for a Reformation by reason and argument, not by violence. If this was to be brought about, it could only be in an atmosphere of European peace. The scholars were an international body, very closely knit together. Their greatest danger lay in the rising passions of nationalism. We may take Erasmus as their great example. To Erasmus, Europe was one great State. For Holland, as the country of his birth, he had a certain love, combined with a feeling that it was rather a provincial backwater, remote from the real centres of civilization. His feeling towards his country was very much what an Englishman long resident in London, where he has grown eminent, might cherish towards a remote district of agriculturists and fishermen in which he happened to have been born and bred. Erasmus has a sentimental combination of affection and dislike for Holland, but Europe is the country which demands his allegiance.

More's feelings are much more complicated: he is a thoroughly loyal Englishman. But we can never understand More if we allow ourselves to forget the Great Turk. The threat to the whole of Christian civilization from the marauding bands of Asia was a very real thing to him. That Christian princes should be struggling one against another whilst Belgrade and Rhodes were falling, and whilst all the chivalry of Hungary perished on the field of Mohacz, till the Turk reached the gates of Vienna, seemed to More to be treachery to the common cause. There were Lutheran pacifists in More's day, who held that the Turk was a divinely appointed scourge, and that Christians should allow themselves to be enslaved and butchered without offering resistance to the Moslems, who had at least the merit of not being Papists. More disagrees, and (in language which has found an echo in later ages) he complains that these pacifists are so pugnacious. Whilst they argue that no man should withstand the Turk, but let him win all, says More, they arise up 'in great plumps' to fight against their fellow-Christians, and destroy many a good religious house. More feels that war between Christians is detestable. The wars of Christendom are, to him, civil wars. He has both an English and a European patriotism.

This balance and combination of loyalties brings More very closely into touch with problems of to-day. To More, the whole question cannot be entirely settled by allegiance to a king, or loyalty to the country in which a man happens to have been born. Yet he would have been the last to deny the binding power of these obligations.

Few in these days will censure More for his longing for peace among the states of Europe; there will in some quarters be less sympathy for his second aspiration, that whereas the Church is afflicted with many errors and heresies, it were settled in perfect uniformity. More was very frank as to his hatred of heretics. The accusation that he was himself a bitter persecutor can be refuted; but the fact remains that he believed it necessary to prohibit 'the sowing of seditious heresies'; and he believed that, in extreme cases, it was right to punish with terrible death those who defied this prohibition.

Seditious heresies. Emphasis must be laid upon the adjective. To those who were in any kind of doubt or spiritual trouble, More was always the gentlest of counsellors. His son-in-law, Roper, had in his youth a violent bout of Lutheranism. More and he lived together in the same house, and argued together constantly, but Roper records that he never knew More lose his temper; never knew him 'in a fume.' People in spiritual difficulties, troubled with 'vehement and grievous tentations of desperation,' would come to More for advice. At the time when More was Chancellor, and at the height of his controversy with the Lutherans, a distinguished Lutheran scholar, Simon Grinæus, needed to come to England to consult manuscripts of Plato and commentaries thereon, in the College libraries of Oxford. More entertained him hospitably, and gave him every possible assistance, only insisting on a promise that his guest would not spread his heresies during his stay in England. Grinæus acknowledged More's kindness by dedicating his work, when published, to More's son John. Rather naïvely, Grinæus emphasizes the enormous personal trouble More took, accompanying him everywhere, and, when that was not possible, sending as escort his secretary, a young scholar, John Harris. Grinæus would have been pained had he known that, in fact, More had very little belief in the value of any heretic's promise. We know from John Harris himself that he was instructed to see that Grinæus issued no Lutheran propaganda. If Grinæus had done so, More would have bundled him out of the kingdom unceremoniously. But, so long as he behaved properly, More showed him untiring generosity and kindness. And also, amid all the cares of office, More spent many hours in a vain attempt to bring Grinæus back into the fold, first by discussion in his home, and later by correspondence. Nor was this merely the freemasonry of scholarship. More would have been even gentler with a poor and ignorant heretic than with a learned one. 'Little rigour and much mercy should be showed,' he said, 'where simpleness appeared, and not high heart or malice.' More argued eloquently that the whole Bible might be suffered to be spread abroad in English among the laity. His sense of discipline was too strong to allow him to press this claim against the opinion of the bishops; but under episcopal supervision, at any rate, translations of the Bible in whole and in part should be issued, he thought, and even issued, where necessary, gratis. But it must be an authorized translation, made by the most responsible scholars.

At a time when civil war might break out over the interpretation of a biblical text, More denied the right of Tyndale, or any individual, to issue his translation of the Bible on his own authority. The public and deliberate defiance of authority in matters of religion was, to More, sedition; and, like other forms of sedition, might, in extreme cases, merit the death penalty.

The trial of heresy was a matter for the bishops. But the responsibility of the Church, More held, ended with the excommunication of the heretic. It was the State which, 'from fear of outrages and mischiefs to follow,' had decreed that the seditious heretic, when the Church had excommunicated him, should suffer a terrible death.

Unless we realize More's haunting fear of religious violence, we shall never understand how he came to defend the persecution to the death of 'seditious heretics.' The most noteworthy thing about More is his political foresight. He realized, as few other men did, how chaos and religious wars would follow, if the unity of the Medieval Church were shattered. 'The world once ruffled and fallen in a wildness,' he asked, 'how long would it be, and what heaps of heavy mischiefs would there fall, ere the way were found to set the world in order and peace again?' That those who disturbed the unity of Christendom by deliberate defiance of ecclesiastical authority should suffer for it, seemed to More as natural as that a rebel should suffer for deliberate defiance of civil authority. And so, in his *Dialogue against heresies* he gives 'his opinion concerning the burning of heretics, and that it is lawful, necessary, and well done.' In a later treatise he examined the case of the heretics (seven in all) who had suffered death in recent times—(actually within the past eighteen years). He maintained that they had had no wrong, under the law. (There were at least five other cases during those eighteen years of which More seems to have been unaware.) But, further, More went so far as to say that, if the bishops had 'taken as good heed in time as they should have done,' there would have been more burnt by a great many in the preceding seven years, though perhaps fewer in the end. Nothing can justify his words—we can only understand them if we realize his horror at the impending destruction of everything he loved. 'For heretics, as they be,' he says, 'the clergy doth denounce them; and, as they be well worthy, the temporalty doth burn them; and after the fire of Smithfield hell doth receive them, where the wretches burn for ever.' Not that Reformers were more merciful to each other. Lutherans burnt Anabaptists. Latimer refers to the burning of fourteen Anabaptists with no disapproval. 'We should not have disapproved of it, if we had lived then, unless we had been Anabaptists ourselves,' says Froude, very truly. If we ask why Latimer is forgiven for his intolerance, and More blamed, the answer is to hand. More, it is asserted, had shown a dozen years before, in *Utopia,* that he knew better.

More has suffered the fate of many pioneers, in that he has been interpreted in the light of those who have followed him. *Utopia* has been followed by a long series of 'Ideal Commonwealths,' often written in direct imitation. Francis Bacon in the *New Atlantis,* and William Morris in *News from Nowhere,* have drawn pictures of the world as they would like to see it. So *Utopia* has been christened an 'ideal commonwealth.' Now the citizens of Utopia are depicted as not insisting on any dogma except in the existence of God and the immortality of the soul. Therefore, it has been argued, More believed the vague deism of the Utopians more 'ideal' than the Catholic faith of his own day. And it is certainly the case with the romance of William Morris, that it represents the writer's ideal—the world as he would have it, if he could shatter it to bits and remould it nearer to the heart's desire. But if we want to understand *Utopia* or *News from Nowhere,* we must think of the first as published in 1516, and the second as published in 1890.

More's education was Medieval; and the Middle Ages recognized many kinds of law: canon law and common law, the law of God and the law of nature. In 1516 one of the most debated questions of the day was whether, apart from revelation, nature and philosophy taught that the soul was immortal. Three years before, this question had led to an important decision of the Lateran Council. By that decision teachers of philosophy were put in their place. They were instructed to point out the difference between the merely philosophical and the Christian view as to the immortality of the soul.

More's contribution to the discussion is to depict a Commonwealth based entirely upon the law of nature and on philosophy, the Commonwealth of Utopia. But the views of the Commonwealth, as to what *unaided philosophy* can teach regarding the immortality of the soul, are actually stricter than those of many Christians, and a marginal note is added drawing marked attention to this. So far is the Utopian Commonwealth from having any doubts about immortality, that the man who does not accept the immortality of the soul is not allowed to rank as a citizen, or even as a man. The Utopian cannot believe that a man who holds that the soul perishes with the body can be anything but a potential criminal, restrained from felony only by his cowardice, 'and thus he is of all sorts despised, as of an unprofitable and of a base and vile nature.' And then comes the sentence upon which are based the many laudations of the toleration of Utopia: 'Howbeit, they put him to no punishment.' No punishment, indeed! It is a mere mistranslation, as More's critics might have seen, if they would have referred back to the Latin original.

In Utopia, as in ancient Sparta, where all life was lived in common, to be sent to Coventry was a living death. What More really wrote was that the unbeliever is not put to any bodily punishment. The Utopians do not threaten him with violence, to make him dissemble his disbelief. He may, in private, with learned men, even argue in defence of it. On the same principle More, whilst silencing Simon Grinæus publicly, was willing to spend long hours in trying to convert him privately. So the Utopian disbeliever in immortality is not allowed to counter the public odium by defending himself *publicly* in argument. And nobody, in Utopia, is allowed to argue vehemently or violently about religion. If he does so, he is punished with bondage. If still recalcitrant, the bondsman is punished with death.

An inhabitant of Utopia has little liberty, as little as a warrior in the Spartan State, or an inmate of a monastery, although the Utopian has an easier life than either. Utopia is indeed modelled on the Spartan and the monastic disciplines, with the austerities of both alleviated. That God exists, and that in an after-state vice is punished and virtue rewarded, are the only Utopian religious dogmas. But there is a Utopian State religion—a kind of greatest common measure of all the different religions prevalent among the Utopians. In their dark churches an elaborate ritual is practised with music, vestments, incense, and candles. The Utopian priests are inviolate. And the Utopians believe that miracles happen among them very often. It is odd that, a year before Luther began his attack by fastening the Ninety-five theses to the church door at Wittenberg, More should have singled out so many things which the Protestants were later to impugn. More makes them part of the State religion of Utopia— a religion based upon reason, and containing nothing to which any reasonable man can object, More thinks.

More is very careful to point out that the Catholic Church has many practices to which a man would not be led by his unaided reason. From his early manhood to the day before his death, More from time to time wore a hair shirt, and followed other ascetic practices. Reason, the Utopians hold, would not lead a man to such austerities, 'unless any goodlier opinion be inspired into man from Heaven.' There are celibate ascetics in Utopia; the Utopians would ridicule them if they based their austerities on reason; but as they base them on religion, the Utopians honour them.

But what comes out most emphatically in Utopia is the prophetic fear which More, the moderate reformer, felt of the violent reformer. Any man who, in Utopia, *attacks* any established religion, even though it be idolatrous and superstitious, in the interests of his own purer and more spiritual religious outlook, is liable to be punished with bondage, and, if still recalcitrant, with death. *It is one of the weak points of Utopia, that any kind of reformation is impossible.* More has guarded his citizens so strenuously against violence, that they seem to have nothing before them but a monotonous eternity of the benevolent despotism of their patriarchal constitution. No man may use contentious rebuking or inveighing against any of the recognized religions of Utopia upon pain, first of bondage, and, if that fails, of death. But contentious rebuking and inveighing were the stock-in-trade of the Protestant Reformer. As More said of the Reformers, 'In railing standeth all their revel.' A Protestant Reformer in Utopia, who publicly derided miracles, vestments, music, incense, candles, the inviolability of the priesthood, and salvation by works, would soon have sighed for the (comparative) toleration of England in the days of Chancellor More.

More's third wish, as he walked along the Thames, side by side with Roper, was for a settlement, to the satisfaction of all parties, of the question of Henry's marriage with Catherine of Aragon, because otherwise he saw that it would be a disturbance to a great part of Christendom. Many reasons combined to make More long for this good conclusion: firstly, his sympathy and friendship with Catherine. He had hailed her with enthusiasm when, some twenty-seven years before, he watched her entering London as Prince Arthur's bride. 'There is nothing wanting in her,' he had said, 'which the most beautiful girl should have.' Since that time she had been his gracious hostess many and many a year: she and Henry had so enjoyed More's company that they had asked him, when the day's routine was done and after the Council had supped, to be merry with them. This happened so frequently that not once in a month could More get leave to go home to his wife and children.

But, apart from the personal question, the separation of Henry from Catherine meant a quarrel between England and the Emperor Charles; yet, on the friendship between those two, in More's view, rested all hopes of permanent European peace and stability. But the threat to European unity was more deadly even than that. If the Emperor opposed the divorce, and the Pope would not grant it, then Henry had his own solution. So far as England was concerned, Henry would be King, Emperor, and Pope all in one; he would be Supreme Head of the English Church, and his Archbishop of Canterbury should declare him to be still a bachelor.

Wolsey's failure to achieve any solution on less drastic lines led to his fall, and More was commanded to fill Wolsey's place as Chancellor. More tried to avoid the dangerous honour. Already the King had consulted him on the 'divorce' question, and he had been unable to accept the royal view. But when Henry had promised More that in prosecuting the matter of the divorce he would use only those whose consciences were persuaded, while those who thought otherwise he would use in other business, More had no excuse for refusing office. The judicial side of his office he transacted with a dispatch and incorruptibility which, together with his reputation as a jester, made him one of the most popular figures of sixteenth-century tradition.

Otherwise his short Chancellorship was a succession of disappointments and humiliations. The business of the divorce went on, and with it the King's claim to be Supreme Head of the Church of England. Finally, on 15 May, 1532, came the event which, if there be any one such event, must mark the beginning of modern England. The clergy of England made their submission to the King. It is here that we should make, if we make it anywhere, the division between Medieval life and our Modern life. The fact that this division cuts into the middle of a dynasty and of a reign is all to the good, because it emphasizes the fact that you can mark no deep gulf between Medieval and Modern history. The deepest is here. Within ten years all the Abbeys in England had been dissolved, and were in rapid process of conversion into gentlemen's country mansions. The epoch which had begun with the landing of St. Augustine and his monks in 597 had come to its close. In the Refectory of (shall we say) Northanger Abbey, in 1530, St. Augustine, the Venerable Bede, Thomas Becket, and Thomas More might all have felt at home. Nothing except some differences in the pronunciation of their Latin would have prevented them from understanding each other perfectly. Ten years after More's death, Northanger Abbey has just been adapted out of the old monastic remains by Master Tilney, of the Court of Augmentations. Imagine Jane Austen paying him a visit. She would soon have got used to the archaic fashions and archaic English of her host, and, as he showed her with pride the remodelled kitchens, where every invention had been adopted to facilitate the labour of the cooks, she would have remarked to him that 'his endowments of that spot alone might at any time have placed him high among the benefactors of the convent.'

On 15 May the clergy made their submission. On 16 May More resigned the Chancellorship. His public career, then, had fallen entirely within what we may call the Monastic or Medieval Period of English History. Mommsen has remarked that, when an age is passing away, Destiny seems to allot to it one last great figure, so that it may not pass without honour and dignity. More is the last great hero of Medieval England.

For a time, More was permitted to live quietly in his Chelsea home, carrying on his controversy with the heretics. But his refusal to be present at the coronation of Anne Boleyn embittered the quarrel, and an attempt was made to involve him in the matter of the 'Holy Maid of Kent.' His proved innocence saved him, but on 13 April, 1534, he was summoned before the royal commissioners at Lambeth. Roper tells us that he would not allow his wife and children to follow him, as they usually did, to the riverside, 'but pulled the wicket after him, and shut them all from him, and with a heavy heart, as by his countenance it appeared, with me and our four servants there took his boat toward Lambeth. Wherein sitting still sadly a while, at the last he suddenly rounded me in the ear, and said: "Son Roper, I thank our Lord the field is won." ' More was quite willing to swear the oath recognizing Elizabeth as heir to the throne, for that was a matter on which he considered himself bound by the decision of Parliament. But, in the form in which the oath was tendered, he could not take it without renouncing the spiritual authority of the Pope, and that he would not do, though he tried to avoid offence by not stating exactly his reasons for refusing the oath. More was not, as is frequently stated, put to death for this refusal to take the oath. Refusal was not treason, but only 'misprision of treason,' and the penalty was not death, but confiscation of all goods and imprisonment during the king's pleasure.

Like some other inmates of Tudor prisons, More found opportunity for much writing. But he no longer carried on controversy with the heretics. This was not from any motive of caution; indeed, he might have continued to dispute with the Lutherans without using any argument to which Henry would have objected. But More's writings in the Tower are for the most part devotional. The exception is his *Dialogue of Comfort,* in which he returns to that favourite form of debate which he had used with success in the first book of *Utopia,* and in the *Dialogue concerning Heresies.* But in the *Dialogue of Comfort* More is no longer defending this dogma or that; he is defending the right of the individual soul to hold any dogma at all against the command of the civil power.

The *Dialogue of Comfort* takes the form of a discussion between two Hungarian noblemen, as to how they ought to act in face of the Turkish conquest. There is no word of reflection upon Henry or his advisers; but clearly much of what is said is applicable to the case of More and his fellow sufferers. The *Dialogue of Comfort* is one of the most delightful of More's books. Whilst his own personal case grew more perilous, he saw more cause for optimism as to the future of Christendom. The Lutherans were coming to recognize that they must make common cause with their fellow-Christians, at least in resisting the Turk; and there was even talk of further reunion. So More, in the words which he puts into the mouth of the old Hungarian gentleman, sees causes for hope:

> The first is, that in some communications had of late together, hath appeared good likelihood of some good agreement to grow together in one accord of our faith.
>
> The second, that in the mean while till this may come to pass, contentions, despicions (i.e. disputations) with uncharitable behaviour is prohibited and forboden, in effect, upon all parts ...
>
> The third is, that all Germany, for all their diverse opinions, yet as they agree together in profession of Christ's name, so agree they now together in preparation of a common power, in defence of Christendom against our common enemy the Turk; and I trust ... that as God hath caused them to agree together in the defence of his name, so shall he graciously bring them to agree together in the truth of his faith. Therefore will I let God work, and leave off contention.[3]

It is unjust to remember the bitter words which More uses in his controversies with the heretics, unless we also remember the words in which he says farewell to controversy. He sees that reunion, if it is to come, will come through the common defence of those things upon which all Christians are agreed: 'Therefore will I let God work.'

So he turned to the devotional writing which occupied his last days, enduring, with contented good humour, the imprisonment which was the legal penalty of his refusing to take the oath.

Further legislation was passed, making it high treason maliciously to attempt to deprive Henry of his titles, one of which was Supreme Head of the Church of England. But More continued to take refuge in silence. He was nevertheless placed upon his trial. He claimed the liberty of silence. He said to his judges:

> Ye must understand that, in things touching conscience, every true and good subject is more bound to have respect to his said conscience and to his soul than to any other thing in all the world beside; namely [i.e. particularly] when his conscience is in such sort as mine is, that is to say, where the person giveth no occasion of slander, of tumult and sedition against his prince, as it is with me; for I assure you that I have not hitherto to this hour disclosed and opened my conscience and mind to any person living in all the world.

But the Solicitor-General, Rich, was prepared to swear that More, in conversation with him in the Tower, had said that Parliament could not make the King Supreme Head of the Church. More denied this, and there is no doubt that Rich was lying. But More was found guilty, and sentenced to death. After the verdict had been given he felt it his duty to speak out, stating that England 'might not make a particular law, disagreeable with the general law of Christ's Universal Catholic Church, no more than the City of London might make a law against an Act of Parliament to bind the whole realm.' After some friendly words to his judges, he was taken back to the Tower. On the way, his daughter Margaret, 'pressing in among the midst of the throng and company of the guard, that with halberds and bills went round about him, hastily ran to him, and there openly in the sight of them all, took him about the neck and kissed him.' On the fifth day after, he was executed on Tower Hill. A depressed Winchester man, obsessed by 'very vehement and grievous tentations of desperation,' had in old days found comfort from his advice. As More passed to execution, 'he thrust through the throng and with a loud voice said, "Mr. More, do you know me? I pray you for our Lord's sake help me: I am as ill troubled as ever I was." Saint Thomas answered, "I remember thee full well. Go thy ways in peace, and pray for me: and I will not fail to pray for thee."' He made (according to Henry's wish) only a brief speech from the scaffold, stating that he suffered 'in and for the faith of the Holy Catholic Church,' and that he died 'the faithful servant of the King, and, in the first place, of God.'

More's case is different from that of the 'seditious heretics' whose punishment he had justified, in that he had avoided any act or word which could be construed as giving occasion of slander or of tumult. (Lord Acton has indeed blamed him for the length to which he carried his submission.)

The outstanding fact about More is, that his regard for an oath was such that he cheerfully faced perpetual imprisonment rather than swear an oath which he thought false. He remained firm, though he knew that nothing less than his death would satisfy Henry. Indeed, he feared the Government might resort to torture, which was mercifully spared him. His death was compassed by deliberate perjury.

More's claims to distinction are very various. He was a member of that earliest group of Greek students, with whom English classical scholarship begins. He was High Steward of Oxford and Cambridge, an educational pioneer, particularly enthusiastic about the education of women. As a writer of English prose, his position is specially important. It was not till long after his day that anyone could rival his mastery of many different types of English: dramatic dialogue and rhetorical monologue, narrative and argument combined in a style at once scholarly and colloquial. More's *History of Richard III* remained a pattern of historical writing unequalled for a century. His death as a martyr 'for the faith of the Catholic Church' was also a stateman's protest against the claim of the civil power to dictate religious belief, and should make him the hero of all who care for religious liberty. For over twenty years he exercised important judicial functions of different kinds, and it was his promptitude and incorruptibility as a judge that most impressed his countrymen. It is as 'the best friend that the poor e'er had' that his fellow Londoners remembered him, in the old play of *Sir Thomas More*. Swift had learnt from *Utopia* many of the things which make *Gulliver's Travels* remarkable, and he repaid his teacher by giving him the magnificent testimonial of being the person 'of the greatest virtue this kingdom ever produced.'

A TURNING POINT IN HISTORY

G. K. Chesterton

Blessed Thomas More is more important at this moment than at any moment since his death, even perhaps the great moment of his dying; but he is not quite so important as he will be in about a hundred years time. He may come to be counted the greatest Englishman, or at least the greatest historical character in English history. For he was above all things historic; he represented at once a type, a turning point and an ultimate destiny. If there had not happened to be that particular man at that particular moment, the whole of history would have been different.

We might put the point shortly by saying that the best friend of the Renaissance was killed as the worst enemy of the Reformation. More was a humanist, not only in the sense in which many crabbed and pedantic scholars earned that name by their real services to Greek and Latin scholarship, but in the sense that his scholarship was really both human and humane. He had in him, at that relatively early date, all that was best in Shakespeare and Cervantes and Rabelais; he had not only humour but fantasy. He was the founder of all the Utopias; but he used Utopia as what it really is, a playground. His Utopia was partly a joke; but since his time Utopians have seldom seen the joke. He was even famous for taking things lightly; he talked, I believe, about whipping children with peacock's feathers; and there came to be a legend that he died laughing. We have to realise him as a man thus full of the Renaissance before we come with a sort of shock to the reality of his more serious side.

The great Humanist was above all a Superhumanist. He was a mystic and a martyr; and martyrdom is perhaps the one thing that deserves the cant phrase of practical mysticism. But he was not, like so many mystics of his time, one who lost his common sense in face of the mysteries. And it will remain a permanent and determining fact, a hinge of history, that he saw, in that first hour of madness, that Rome and Reason are one. He saw at the very beginning, what so many have now only begun to see at the end: that the real hopes of learning and liberty lay in preserving the Roman unity of Europe and the ancient Christian loyalty for which he died.

Reprinted from *The Fame of Blessed Thomas More, Being Addresses Delivered in his Honour in Chelsea, July 1929* (London, Sheed and Ward, 1929), pp. 63–64, by permission of the publisher.

THE FAITH OF ST. THOMAS MORE

G. G. Coulton

Professor Chambers has written a great book, which seems destined to take its place in the highest rank of British biographies.[1] It has a noble subject, studied for thirty years with scholarly care, and now developed in a style admirable not only intrinsically but especially in its adaptation to the matter. It is he who has taught us to trace the fine ancestry of English prose from the English Chronicle down to More. He is himself steeped in those same devotional writings which had inspired his hero and in that literature which More in turn helped to inspire, the dramatists and the Authorised Version of the Bible. Nothing in this book is more remarkable than those opening sections in which the author introduces us in turn to each one of More's circle whom he is about to put into the witness-box: men and women whom he knows so well that he brings them without effort into our intimacy, each with his individual character, yet all speaking with the same voice on essential points. We may think that the author's love leads him sometimes to believe too implicitly in these domestic witnesses, detail by detail. But *noscitur a socio;* we see More, like St. Bernard and St. Francis, reflected in his disciples; and the unanimity of those is not mechanical, but the living inspiration of one central ruling spirit. Margaret Roper would charm us in herself, wherever we found her; but she gains immensely by reflection from her father and the other members of that circle. More stands out in these pages as one of the greatest of Englishmen and one of the truest saints in the Roman Calendar: therefore, if I venture here to express considerable reservations, these are founded on problems less directly connected with More's character than with his environment. The greatness of a martyr cannot be estimated *in vacuo;* it must be conditioned in great part by the justice of his cause. Here, then, we are confronted with one of the thorniest of all world-controversies. It is not only from present-day Germany or Russia that we may learn the immense power of religious or antireligious motives, and the corresponding menace to concord which would exist in that field even though men had ceased to quarrel over money or women. Thus my hearty agreement with Professor Chambers on the main point, that religion and anti-religion are among the prime factors in human life and therefore in all real history, moves me all the more strongly to suggest important reconsiderations on the subject of this lamentable quarrel between the English King and the Papacy. For there, in plain words, lies the whole core

Reprinted from *The Quarterly Review,* 265 (1935), 327–43, a review article on R. W. Chambers' *Thomas More* (London, 1935).

of this tragedy. Much is written nowadays concerning the evils of a totalitarian state. More lost his head because he had the misfortune to live simultaneously in two totalitarian states, one of hoary antiquity and the other new-born in England.

As Professor Chambers repeatedly insists, we must strive to put ourselves into the mind of an average Englishman of 1530. Only thus can we fairly judge the actors. For this, however, we must begin much earlier: his story needs much more pre-history than he actually gives us. Let us take two subjects, closely allied in practice, which became mainly responsible for More's fatal entanglement between the upper and the nether millstone. These are first the marriage-laws and, secondly, the independence of the judiciary. It is too often assumed, but with no attempt at real proof, that money-worship, as a serious danger to society, first appeared soon after the Black Death. Yet, at the end of the eleventh century, Lanfranc, Gregory VII, and St. Anselm were struggling against the Irish custom of selling wives, or 'exchanging them as freely and publicly as horses or any other chattels, or quitting them causelessly at their own fancy.' One of the greatest Parisian theologians, Petrus Cantor, wrote about 1190: 'We [clergy], for money's sake, and at our own choice, join or separate whom we will,' to the scandal and disgust of decent layfolk. The still greater Ivo of Chartres (about 1110) had complained that this venality turned the sacrament of matrimony into a laughing-stock for the laity. In Chaucer's day we find two first-rate witnesses. The Dominican Bromyard describes in detail the abuses of matrimonial law, and sums up: 'Nowadays, when a wife displeases, or another woman is coveted, then a divorce is procured'— *divortium procuratur.* 'Piers Plowman' tells the same tale; Church lawyers make and unmake matrimony for money; you may get rid of your wife by giving a fur cloak to the judge. Erasmus writes emphatically on the subject of 'so many unhappy divorces'; he thinks it would be better if the State took the matter out of Church hands and guaranteed the permanence of the matrimonial bond by the same securities as are afforded for other contracts.

It will be noticed that, in spite of theological and legal distinctions drawn between the two ideas of *divorce* and *decree of nullity,* both the learned Bromyard and Erasmus frankly use the word *divortium.* This is quite characteristic; for this essential legal distinction was in practice almost negligible. That is plainly confessed by a very ardent champion of the Middle Ages, Léon Gautier, in his study of society as mirrored in the romances of chivalry. Writing of these frequent decrees of nullity he says: 'Here was a revival, under pious and canonical forms, of the ancient practice of divorce.' Side by side with this, we must take account of the venality of all law-courts, civil or clerical. John of Salisbury, bishop of Chartres (d. 1180), singles out St. Bernard and his pupil, Pope Eugenius III, for their horror of bribery, 'a continence most rare even among the clergy; ... the house of prayer' (he writes) 'has been turned into a den of thieves.' So great were the temptations of judges in the Church courts that it was rhetorically discussed whether any archdeacon could find his way to heaven. Suitors (says John) slip into the Papal palace, as Jupiter came in unto Danaë, under cover of a shower of gold.

So also with the temporal princes; no office is gratuitous, even the judges must buy themselves into the judgment seat. All this is borne out by bare business records. The account-rolls of monasteries and civil corporations teem with gifts to judges and officers of Church or State. Edmund Rich, Saint and Archbishop, cried in despair, 'unless Christians study to cure themselves of this plague [of bribery in law-courts], Christendom will be ruined before we are aware.' Yet, three centuries later, it was one of More's main claims to sanctity that on the judgment-seat he would accept no gifts.

Gascoigne, one of the most prominent of Oxford chancellors, complained in about 1450 that the Welsh clergy were habitually concubinary, and that the bishop of St. David's made enormous profits from winking at these infractions of Church discipline. More, even in the heat of his polemic against Tyndale, was not able to deny this; here is one of the points on which he most definitely quibbled in controversy.[2] Again, from the thirteenth century onwards, pious theologians had been scandalised by the sale of indulgences: the 'penny-preachers,' they said, sent thousands of souls to hell. This, again, was one of the main problems in 'Piers Plowman.' Gascoigne constantly harped on this subject. He wrote: 'sinners say "I care not how many or what evils I do in God's sight; for I can easily and quickly get plenary remission of all guilt and penalty by an absolution and indulgence granted to me by the pope, whose written grant I have bought for 4d. or 6d., or have won as a stake for a game of tennis." '

This bitter anti-Lollard goes on to inveigh like any Lollard against the notorious venality of the Roman Court, and asserts that no Pope can set his face steadily against this except at the risk of poison.[3]

Such venality was encouraged by the weltering chaos of mediaeval marriage-law. The Roman Church had striven with imperfect success to bring order into the tangle of pre-existing Roman and Teutonic law and custom. Even a very sympathetic critic confesses: 'The varying standards of what constituted a valid marriage in the early Middle Ages would almost defy enumeration.'[4] There is strong evidence for a Papal licence given to King Henry of Castile, in 1437, for two wives at a time, in order that he might have an heir to the throne. It is quite certain that the Privy Council of Castile, in 1521, appealed to this as an historical fact.[5] Again, in 1530, Clement VII secretly proposed to Henry's envoy that the King 'might be allowed to have two wives'; a proposition which is even more significant if we believe that it was made insincerely. Cranmer's appeal to the Universities of Europe may give another measure of an honest enquirer's difficulties in 1530. Decisions in Henry's favour were received from Oxford, Cambridge, and eight Universities in France and Italy, including the three greatest, Paris, Bologna, and Orléans. It is frequently pleaded—and perhaps true—that these favourable judgments were bought. But, if More believed this, it would have cast him back upon one more difficulty: is it more unhappy to live in a world where the politician gives money for the theologian's assent to sin, or in a world where the theologian is such that a cynic may count on getting good value for his money? The men who lived in that world thought of it in terms which, I must frankly confess, seem irreconcilable with the regretful picture which Professor Chambers gives in many different contexts, of an England whose disappearance we should deplore. St. John Fisher wrote, long before Luther had appeared,

> But an we take heed and call to mind how many vices reign nowadays in Christ's church, as well in the clergy as in the common people, how many also be unlike in their living unto such as were in times past; perchance we shall think that Almighty God slumbreth not only, but also that he hath slept soundly a great season. Lord ... show thy mercy on thy Church afresh ... for it is time so to do, sith our faith beginneth to fail and wax scant.[6]

A volume might be filled with similar evidence for the four or five generations before Henry VIII.

On all these points, it is true, More's England differs from ours only in degree, however great that degree may be. But in another field the difference may almost be claimed as absolute. I allude to the almost complete dethronement, in our day, of mediaeval eschatology. Not one man in a hundred—shall we say, not one in a thousand?—can now see heaven and hell as More saw them. St. Thomas Aquinas, like almost every other Schoolman who ventured upon that ground, concluded that the happiness of the blessed in heaven would be heightened by the sight of the damned writhing below in everlasting torture.[7] Not, of course, that they rejoice in the torture as such—nobody conceived anything so devilish as that—but because it bears continuous witness to them of God's justice and at the same time of His mercy to them. St. Bonaventura is even more severe; and his fellow Franciscan, St. Bernardino of Siena, writes how these 'bellowings and cries' from hell 'shall sing to Paradise with ineffable sweetness,' a greater joy than 'all the joys of this world melted into one.'[8] More himself, in his last months, thanks God for His mercy in providing Hell.[9] And this, though the Schoolmen describe infernal torments with a pitiless detail far beyond the parallel passage in Calvin's 'Institutes,' which is ignorantly mis-described by writers who can never have looked at the actual text.

It is commonly said that men did not so much believe these things, as believe that they believed them. Yet More himself emphasises the extent to which, in most men's minds, the fear of hell-fire outweighed the hopes of celestial bliss.[10] Even more significant are the words of his fellow-martyr Fisher, speaking of Henry VII's deathbed terrors.

> As touching his soul, in what agony suppose ye that he was, not for the dread of death only, but for the dread of the judgment of Almighty God; for albeit he might have great confidence, by the reason of his true conversion unto God, and by the sacraments of Christ's Church which he with full great devotion had received before, yet was not he without a dread. *Nemo novit an sit odio an amore dignus:* 'there is no man, be he never so perfect, unless he have it by revelation, that knoweth certainly whether he be in the state of grace or no'; for of another manner be the judgments of God than of men. And the holy abbot Hely said likewise. 'Three things' (said he) 'there be that I much dread; one is what time my soul shall depart

out of my body, another is when I shall be presented before my Judge, the third is what sentence he shall give, whether with me or against me.' If these holy fathers which had forsaken this world and had lived so virtuously were in this fear, no marvel though this great man which had so much worldly business, and daily occupied in the causes thereof, no marvel though he were in great fear.[11]

More himself, in his 'De Quatuor Novissimis,' reckons that not fourteen men in four thousand think on these things with deep earnest during their life-time, until at the last 'the fear of hell, the dread of the devil, and sorrow at our heart in sight of our sins, shall pass and exceed the deadly pains of our body.'[12]

And here comes in a third point, no less essential to the comprehension of More's age. Eternity of bliss or of torture depends upon nothing so much as upon a man's faith at the moment when the breath leaves his body. The doctrine *extra ecclesiam nulla salus* was applied then with a strictness for which it would be impossible to find any parallel to-day. In a society which held these beliefs, the Inquisition was a natural—we may almost say an inevitable—birth. True, the Inquisition, in the strict sense, functioned only for one moment in England before More's time. Presently, when Wyclif appeared, his doctrines spread so rapidly that an orthodox chronicler, with obvious exaggeration, complained that almost half the men one might meet on the road were Lollards. But Lollardy had been driven underground by stern measures in which King and Parliament concurred. The Act *De Haeretico Comburendo* (1401) made heretics directly amenable to the secular authorities; and in 1408 Archbishop Arundel's decree made it a burning matter to contradict or pertinaciously misinterpret the Bible or any Papal decree or decretal.

Such was the position in More's time: no State has ever been more definitely totalitarian than the Church into which he was born. As a *societas perfecta* in the philosophical sense, it claimed for its laws not only spiritual but physical sanctions. Those laws were despotic within the realm of faith and morals; and a brief inspection of any treatise on faith and morals will show that this realm is taken by the Church to embrace almost every activity of mankind. Though learning and science were spreading, there was no sign of abatement in the Church's totalitarian claims. More, it is true, kept a judicial balance between Henry and the Pope which was one of the most wonderful things in his life. But Saint John Fisher worked secretly for a foreign invasion of England, with all the horrors that this implied; a few months after his death, when Paul III declared war on Henry, he condemned to slavery all Englishmen who should fight for their country. Moreover, those totalitarian principles have not been abandoned to this moment. The present Papal Legate in Malta is Cardinal Lépicier, who published at Rome in 1910, with special Papal approbation, the doctrine that Popes had always the *right* (as distinguished from temporary *expediency*) of deposing any baptised sovereign whom they might judge to be apostate. The Maltese clergy, naturally enough, go on from this to refuse absolution to any one voting against their party at the parliamentary elections; and the constitution has had to be suspended. That, again, is at the root of the present civil war in Mexico. There, the new State constitution provides that the Roman Church—to which 95 per cent. of the population nominally belong—shall have equality with other religions and nothing more. The Pope declares that, if any State law 'violates the authority of Jesus Christ in the Roman Pontiff' then 'to resist becomes a positive duty; to obey, a crime.'[13] Thus on the one hand President Obregon was assassinated by a young man who claimed the prompting of 'Christ our Lord, in order that religion might prevail in Mexico.' On the other, the clergy publish a book called 'Blood-drenched Altars.' Mr. Hilaire Belloc puts the matter in a nutshell: 'The Catholic Church is in its root principle at issue with the civic definition both of freedom and of authority.'[14] It is as impossible for honest, thinking man to be neutral in modern Mexico as in More's and Fisher's England.[15] Their death is one of the greatest tragedies of English history; More was beheaded for being an exceptionally able, pious, and resolute man born in England; but we must recognise that, born in Italy, he might well have gone to the stake. Hundreds have been condemned on smaller excuses than an inquisitor might have found in his *Utopia*.

Professor Chambers does not attempt, as some have done in our time, to write off his book as a mere *jeu d'esprit*. He recognises its deep earnest and its far-reaching effects: but he insists (more clearly, I think, than any predecessor) on the mediaeval distinction between the 'cardinal' (or natural) virtues of Prudence, Justice, Temperance, and Fortitude, and the 'theological' virtues of Faith, Hope, and Charity. No doubt this distinction was always in More's mind, and we can follow Professor Chambers in pleading that More's main, if not his sole object, was to show how far society might advance on the basis of the four natural virtues alone. Not wholly, perhaps, since the Utopians certainly had a strong dose of Hope and Charity: at any rate of Charity in its earlier and broader sense, apart from the later mediaeval modification which tended, in its use of that word, to lay more stress on 'rightness' with God than on love for fellow-man. Even of Faith they had a strong dose, if here again we may take that word in the sense which it bears in Hebrews xi, and neglect the mediaeval habit of restricting it mainly or entirely to credence in ecclesiastical tradition. But let us for the moment accept all the emphasis which Professor Chambers lays upon this restriction of 'Utopia' to the natural virtues. Are we not thus driven, on careful consideration, to minimise the influence of orthodoxy upon the moral behaviour? Every one admits the book to be a satire on Henry VIII's England: but was it not in effect, if not to some extent in purpose, a satire upon Church as well as upon State? Is not this view implicit even in Professor Chambers's analogy of Swift and the Houyhnhnms? There, we are ashamed to see how much more decently non-human creatures might conceivably live than men and women did in Swift's own England; and so does More shame Christendom by a picture of the conceivable virtues of a heathen land.

But surely Swift would not have been deeply repentant if we told him that by his contrast he was dragging humanity through the mire; can we therefore say that More was equally reckless of bespattering the Church? Does not 'Utopia' raise in every thoughtful mind the inevitable question: If the natural virtues can blossom into a State so far superior to actual Christendom in peace-

fulness and the ordinary decencies of life, can we really maintain the immense
superiority of the theological virtues? And, especially, was Henry VIII's England justified in treating Faith as so all-important that the blackest of all
crimes is that of repudiating ecclesiastical tradition? Professor Chambers
rightly reminds us that Utopia falls far short of the modern ideal of toleration,
so that, in conceivable extreme circumstances, a man might even be judicially
executed for his faith. But there is no hint that this has actually happened;
and in general religious peace Utopia contrasts as strongly with actual Europe
as in international peace. The narrator, Hythlodaye, had five other Christians
with him. Two, it is true, died during the sojourn. But even the four did not
take their missionary opportunities very seriously (pp. 266 ff.). In the spirit of
the much-abused Cowper-Temple clause, they preached not the distinctive
doctrines of the Roman Church, but Christ's 'name, teaching, morals and
miracles,' together with that constancy of the Christian martyrs which 'has
brought such populous nations into their sect'—*in suam sectam.* This teaching
impressed the Utopians immensely, and partly because it 'seemed nearest to
that particular opinion [*haeresis*] which is most powerful' among this people
where everybody may choose what religion he will. In other words, Christianity seemed consonant with the most reasonable form of natural religion: therefore 'you will scarce believe with how glad minds they agreed thereunto,'
especially since Christ had approved of a sort of communism [*communem
victum*] and the truest Christians (i.e. the monks) still practised this. Therefore
'no small number' were baptised. But among these travellers there was no
Christian priest and no bishop to ordain one. Yet the Utopians (without any
hint of dissent from Hythlodaye and his three fellow-Catholics) contemplated
(and perhaps actually consummated) 'the choice, without any bishop sent unto them, of somebody from their own number to exert the character of the
priesthood.' And then, as if this contempt of Apostolic Succession were not
sufficiently scandalous—though in effect it amounts to that for which multi-
tudes had suffered a cruel death in Christian lands—More recounts an incident
which might almost have been chosen in deliberate contempt for the time-
honoured motto of his Church: *Extra Ecclesiam nulla salus.* One of the new
converts, 'as soon as he was baptised, began against our wills, with more
earnest affection than wisdom, to reason of Christ's religion; and began to
wax so hot in his matter, that he did not only prefer our religion before all
other, but also did utterly despise and condemn all other, calling them profane,
and the followers of them wicked and devilish, and the children of everlasting
damnation.' The Utopians bore with him a long time, but then 'condemned
him into exile, not as a despiser of religion but as a seditious person' (270).
Thus, the typical religious brawler in Utopia is the orthodox who has *trop de
zèle,* and who, among this 'naturally' virtuous folk, behaves as the orthodox
commonly behaved in More's 'theologically' virtuous England.

   In the face of this, can we safely deny that More, in his earliest maturity,
nourished germs, at least, of those ideas which are incalculably more powerful
than dynamite? Professor Chambers (I say it with all due respect) seems to
take insufficient account of this. His pages 356 ff., in which he shows how

much more conservative 'Utopia' is than we generally assume, is one of his most important contributions, and shows his mastery of detail at its best. But he seems to miss, altogether, in his synthesis of all these important points, the crucial fact that great innovators are to be judged not so much by the hundred ways in which they ran with the multitude as by the two or three, or even the single divergent path which they discovered and followed for themselves. 'Utopia,' as he says, is in many ways rather mediaeval than modern. But, even if we neglect a good many minor matters and look no farther than the two salient points—community of property, and private judgment in religion—it will still be a book which might well have convinced St. Thomas Aquinas that the writer must recant or burn. Mediaeval orthodoxy fought for private property and stamped out private religion with fire and sword. Utopia gives hitherto undreamed of freedom to private religion, but would put the impenitent public preacher of private property to banishment, or even to death in the last resort, just as it would the impenitent religious brawler. For King Utopus (whose laws it was death to oppose pertinaciously) had been led to decree complete liberty of private religion by his own experience; he saw that religious quarrels were fundamentally fatal to public peace, and indeed his own conquest of the country had been facilitated by the fact that 'the inhabitants had constantly fought with each other concerning their religions.' Two centuries earlier, Marsilius of Padua had publicly proclaimed direct Papal responsibility for all the worst wars in Europe, and More's contemporary Machiavelli said the same. Therefore, when we take account of that haunting and natural fear of the victorious advancing Turk which constantly crops up in More's writings, and the fact that he wrote 'Utopia' just when Erasmus and all the best minds in Europe were outraged by 'that trumpet of [Pope] Julius' which 'summoned all the [Christian] world to [domestic] war' we may see at once how these Utopians found not only social bliss but also defence against foreign conquerors in the abolition of all religious violence. Here again, therefore, the book forces us to ask what the theological virtues were doing in 1515: and it is difficult to believe that More can have been utterly blind to that question.

For that question is more directly relevant, and needs more emphasis when we would put ourselves in More's place, than even Henry's tyranny, which Professor Chambers seems to exaggerate beyond all due measure. When Marsilius argued, in the spirit of 'Utopia,' that Popes have no right to inflict physical violence for religion's sake, John XXII condemned him with scarcely more ceremony than Swift attributes to my Lord Peter: 'God confound you eternally if you offer to believe otherwise!' So was it, again, when twenty-five Franciscans refused to renounce their faith in Holy Communism, their conviction that neither Christ nor His apostles had possessed any private property. These twenty-five were gradually weeded down to four by imprisonment and intimidation; and those four were burned at Marseilles in 1318; men pounced to collect their bones and ashes as the relics of martyrs. For these four, as for Marsilius, the Pope had the same answer: 'It is my function to interpret the Bible; I interpret it in a sense contrary to yours; therefore, recant or burn.'[16]

Let us imagine More thus confronted with John XXII. He is (let us say) the most respected and in many ways most distinguished layman in the whole land, yet he is immovably convinced that Christ and his Apostles had been Utopian in their communism. Threats and cajolery are vain; he will not descend to the lie of the soul. By holding out alone amid an obsequious world, would he not have made John feel exactly as Henry felt, that this single conspicuous and incorruptible dissentient was the one fatal obstacle to his totalitarian policy? The denial of the Poverty of Christ was as necessary to John XXII's political position in 1318 as the denial of Papal supremacy was to Henry's in 1534. More, who warned Henry in 1523, 'the Pope is a prince as you are,' would have found, in 1313, that a Pope might be a politician no less unscrupulous and pitiless than an English king.

There is another crucial point which Professor Chambers seems to recognise imperfectly: he seems to confuse the *Reformation* with the *Reformers*. No doubt More in his later controversial years did thus confuse; but that was the weakest point of all his writings. In the face of men like Tyndale and Barnes, who were certainly in a sense brawlers, More consistently argued as though great religious innovators always had been and always would be brawlers or worse. Yet he might have known that Wyclif was the ablest English philosopher of his day, and began his antipapal career with treatises in reasoned scholastic Latin. Certainly, again, he might have found out, even if he did not know already, how Bishop Pecock, half a century later, had died in prison for the crime of attempting to confute the Lollards not with fire or sword but by argument. If the Lollards of More's time were violent, it could scarcely have been otherwise: 'one cannot parry a sword-thrust with a precept from Plato.' The Church gets such heretics and the State such rebels as they deserve. Professor Chambers regrets pathetically, again and again, 'that frustration and arrest which blights the fair promise of the early sixteenth century.' But that promise was merely superficial; for there was little sign of true inner Reformation in answer to the frequently bungling efforts of the Reformers. Those promising buds could have been saved from blight only if warmth from the sun had been added to shelter from the north wind. Something, indeed, might have been done if so fearless a soul as More's could have foreseen the future, and told Paul III that no martyrs should die in his defence against the King so long as other martyrs were constantly made from among pious and well-meaning folk who demanded from the Church those reforms upon which the greatest Churchmen had long been insisting.

For, on that point More, in his later controversial years, showed more legal acumen than philosophic candour; and Professor Chambers, by confining his social survey almost entirely to that single generation, fails to show the weakness of orthodox defenders in the face of cold, indisputable facts. In his dispute with the distinguished lawyer St. Germain, a man whose theological position seems to have been very much like that of Erasmus, More objects to the quotations from Gerson: that is, from the greatest churchman, perhaps, of the whole fifteenth century. It is not that St. Germain had exaggerated Gerson's complaints; on the contrary, he had rehearsed only five out of seventy-five, and even those in an attenuated form. More's complaint is quite different: this great Chancellor of Paris University might indeed write thus in Latin for an esoteric clerical audience, but no man had a right to translate these accusations into English for 'the lay people, both men and women,' to read. Nor does More, even now that the harm is already done and that layfolk can read something of Gerson's indictments, face them squarely and completely. After dealing sentence by sentence with his antagonist's introductory chapter, he deliberately avoids coming to hand-grips on the far more important Gerson points which follow directly after. He even permits himself to imply that clerical unpopularity was a comparatively new phenomenon, due to the recent heresies. Yet St. Germain quotes, what More must have known perfectly well, those opening words of Boniface VIII's bull *Clericis Laicos* in 1302: 'Antiquity tells us that the laity are very hostile to the clergy.'[17] When, in More's own age, Bishop FitzJames of London complained that no cleric could ever get justice in the civic courts, and when Charles V's ambassador wrote to him from London 'nearly all the people here hate the priests,' these were merely a repetition of what heretics and orthodox had said in almost every century. To read More and St. Germain side by side, in the light of known historical evidence, is less likely to provoke the reflection 'what fair promise for religion and culture was blighted by Henry with his foreign wars and his tyranny at home!' than to recall the words of Gerson, after he had grown grey and weary in the cause of peace and reform: 'The Church is as if smitten with an incurable cancer, and the very remedies do but make her worse!' Yet we must face the fact that this was the very Church for which More, who knew her as intimately as any layman of his time in England, was willing to suffer martyrdom. Here, then, I must hazard an explanation from a standpoint which differs on some important points from that of Professor Chambers.

Too much has hitherto been made of the great mediæval classics and too little of the myriad small indications that enable us to read between the lines. Aquinas's contributions to the theory of usury are rightly emphasised, but scarcely anybody notes how the Angelic Doctor's refinements failed to get into preachers' heads or to secure recognition from princes and magistrates: yet it is a stock maxim of Canon Law that 'custom is the best interpreter of the laws.' Similarly, behind the folios of the Schoolmen we must look for stray indications of those fireside talks in which men unbosomed themselves better than in the lecture-room, and from which epoch-making thoughts had probably their origin. Ideas were thus exchanged at Paris University for centuries before they came fully into the open; and, even if we had no definite evidence, we should anticipate something of the kind from that intimate group which included More, Erasmus, Colet, and so many other scholars. What was more natural than that these talks should blossom out into 'Utopia,' a book as much deeper than Erasmus's 'Praise of Folly' as More by his steadfastness in martyrdom surpassed Erasmus in personal courage? In that book More ventured into deep waters: he looked sympathetically into a fundamentally non-Catholic world; like Lord Acton who, while declaring that his religion was dearer to him than life, could yet criticise that creed with a frankness which might bring a Protestant into suspicion of bigotry. There was in him the man

who, one day, thought Papal Supremacy a mere human ordinance for convenience's sake, and the man who, after a few days' reflection, reproached himself bitterly for such an unadvised thought.[18] More had not that knowledge of
the past which enabled Marsilius to anticipate the general verdict of modern
historians;[19] but, in happier times, he might well have passed his life in suspense
on this crucial question, as he did on that of salvation for good pagans. But first
came Lutheranism, with what More felt as hopelessly bungling surgery for the
Church's cancer. Here in his righteous zeal he begins to forget his earlier self;
he rails so violently and so one-sidedly against Tyndale and Barnes, 'calling
them the children of everlasting damnation,' that he could not have escaped
banishment from his own Utopia. Then at last came war between King and
Pope, with the cruel necessity of clear-cut choice between two loyalties; and
there a man of More's character could no longer hesitate. For there he was not
faced with the subtle temptation of defending existing order with a violence
of speech which betrayed rather than covered the half-heartedness of his conviction. Here was no conflict or separation between the 'natural' and the
'theological' virtues: for his intellect shrank from a lie of any kind, and his
soul shuddered at the thought of hell. We have seen how, nineteen years earlier,
in full prosperity and apparent security, he had drawn a picture of the common deathbed where even bodily pains are overshadowed by the anticipation
of eternal torment.[20] Now his own soul was in the balance. We cannot doubt
his sincerity in describing the joys of heaven as greater than the pains of hell;
yet we must not forget St. John Fisher's words: 'If these holy Fathers, which
had forsaken this world and had lived so virtuously, were in this fear . . . !'
More went to the block not with St. Stephen's ecstatic vision but (as Professor Chambers brings out admirably) with the homely and unforced philosophic
serenity of Socrates. May we not go further, and speak of his life and death
as Utopian? The verdict of posterity would seem to point that way. During
four centuries his natural virtues have stood out in history, but it has taken all
this time to discover his supreme theological eminence. Moreover, even so, he
and Fisher are among the very few saints who have no miracles to their credit;
it is by infraction of Roman tradition that they have been exalted at last. In
this, moreover, they seem essentially English. In no great country were ecclesiastical and social life less irregular than in post-Conquest England; yet, with all
that diffused light, there were very few comets; our canonised saints are most
disproportionately rare. The Utopians might have distinguished here between
England and the Continent as they did between the two sorts of monks: 'they
counte this secte the wiser, but the other the holier.'

ENGLISH SPIRITUAL WRITERS: ST. THOMAS MORE

Bernard Fisher

"Few characters in English history have drawn to themselves such admiration and even love as Sir Thomas More. Men of all classes, non-Catholic as well as Catholic, respect and venerate him as one of the noblest, if not the noblest, Englishman who ever lived.... I have come to the conclusion, in reading through his works, that he paid special attention to the study of dogmatic theology. For when he speaks of grace, free will, merit, faith, charity and other virtues, original sin and even predestination, he is so guarded and exact in his statements that a professional theologian could scarcely speak more accurately." These are the words of Stapleton in the *Tres Thomae* of 1588.

More's modern biographers have elaborated on the theme "the noblest of Englishmen" but very little indeed has been written on St. Thomas as a theologian or as a saint. As three-quarters of More's writings are either ascetical or theological treatises, it is obvious that there is still a great gap in our understanding of the genius of More.

That More was a great saint and great contemplative is easily demonstrable. Mr. Richard O'Sullivan has pointed out a certain rhythm in the life of St. Thomas. It begins in the cell of the London Charterhouse where he was trying his vocation. He married and was then "forced" to Court. Upon his resignation of the Great Seal he returned home for a time and finished his life in a cell in the Tower. In a letter to Meg, written from the Tower, he says "that among all His great benefits heaped upon me so thick, I reckon upon my faith my prisonment, even the very chief." To the same Meg he remarked "... if it had not been for my wife and ye that be my children ... I would not have failed long ere this to have closed myself in as straight a room, and straighter too. But since I am come hither without mine own desert, I trust that God of His goodness will discharge me of my care, and with His gracious help supply my lack amoung you.... Methinketh God maketh me a wanton, and setteth me on his lap and dandleth me." The language here is, surely, the language of a mystic and of a piece with the wonderful phrase in his last letter to Meg "tomorrow long I to go to God." The passage suggests, too, that this is the happiest period of More's life. The agony in the garden, the period of doubt and fear, comes between 1528 and his confinement to the Tower. His imprisonment was, as he says, a special grace, a period in which he gathered the fruits of a life of great holiness. It is clear also that St. Thomas was conscious of the Carthusian roots of his spirituality. It is this aspect that we are concerned with here.

Reprinted, with permission of publisher and author, from *The Clergy Review*, 45 (1960), 1–10.

Chambers has shown More's great regard for liberty of conscience. The age in which he lived was a dangerous one for talkers and doubly so as the "king's matter" came to a head. In this crisis St. Thomas asserted time after time "that he would meddle with no man's conscience and asked only to be left in peace with his own." The unique circumstance of his case only deepened his extreme and habitual reticence. Thomas More is a silent man. For all his mirth and friendliness, few men have been more careful not to wear their heart upon a sleeve. This inner silence is the key to More's character and it is something he learned from the Carthusians. What is here meant by silence is best illustrated by his conduct on the scaffold. Here he had a great opportunity to deliver himself of a most telling *apologia*. Instead he merely said: "I die the King's good servant but God's first." That is, of course, a superb sentence and it deeply impressed all who were there, but it is essentially meant only for Henry. In 1516, when More entered the royal service, Henry had given him this command "that he look first to God and then to the King." More's words in 1535 are his *Nunc Dimittis*.

Again, until he entered the Tower, More was clean-shaven. The beard was an exact measure of his imprisonment. At his trial he had contended that as he was already serving life imprisonment (for refusal to take the Oath of Succession) before ever the Act of Supremacy was passed, he was, as far as that Act was concerned, dead and therefore untriable. Hence the final jest and the last words he ever spoke as ". . . he bade the executioner stay until he had removed aside his beard, saying: 'That never committed any treason'." His judges of a week before, standing now at the foot of the scaffold, would have understood.

As one would expect, this silence is greatest when it is a question of his relationship with God. None of More's ascetical works were ever intended for publication. The two great works the *History of the Passion* and the *Dialogue of Comfort against Tribulation* were written during his imprisonment in the Tower. They were written out of his experience, no doubt, and partly for his enlightenment and because he was a born writer who enjoyed the discipline and effort of composition. They are not formal and present no system of ascetical theology; they tell us practically nothing of any mystical experiences he may have had. What is obvious, of course, is the spirit and deep faith of the writer, but one could not out of these books alone build up a "way of life."

On the other hand, when dealing with More's spirituality the theological writings cannot be ignored. They are not systematic, they are works of controversy. The matter is never allowed to become a question of pure abstract theological argument. More was acutely conscious that the fight was for souls and it is his constant preoccupation to show the practical effects, morally and spiritually, of the new theological ideas. For this reason, one can find passages in the theological work which reveal his burning faith and charity far more than any passages from the ascetical works.

In the preface to the *Confutation against Tyndale*, St. Thomas says that he would that people ceased from reading either his or Tyndale's writings but read "English books as most may nourish and increase devotion, of which be Bonaventure's *Life of Christ*, Gerson on the *Following of Christ* and the devout contemplative book *Scala Perfectionis.*" The last is obviously the most important in More's own life. Chambers has shown how rooted in the writings of the early English mystics is the prose of More. So too is his spirituality, and it is with Hilton, "the most theological of these writings," that St. Thomas has most affinity. Here, again, the Carthusian influence is at work for three of the surviving MSS. of Hilton are Carthusian copies *c.* 1500–10 and two of these come from the London Charterhouse.

If we had nothing but More's works upon which to base our opinions, we could do little more than guess that Hilton was his mentor. And although he spent long hours in the chapel at Chelsea, usually behind locked doors, scarcely any prayer written by him would have been found. But the letters he sent to Meg from the Tower, and the two collections of prayers: *A Godly Meditation* (written in 1534) and *A Devout Prayer* (made during the last week of his life) were preserved by the family. The prayers were written and sent to Margaret that father and daughter might pray together for what little time remained to him. They incorporate, here and there, prayers of Margaret, but they are really both a priceless relic of a life of prayer and his last instructions to his most beloved disciple. The whole would cover a mere thirty pages of print and it seems a crime to select from such a source. But it must be done, for the only way to understand More's spirituality is to start from the prayers and to use his ascetical and theological works as a commentary, as it were, upon them.

> Give me thy grace, good Lord.
> To set the world at nought,
> To set my mind fast upon thee.
>
> *   *   *   *
>
> To be content to be solitary,
>
> *   *   *   *
>
> Gladly to be thinking of God,
> Piteously to call for his help,
> To lean unto the comfort of God,
> Busily to labour to love him.
>
> *   *   *   *
>
> To bear the cross with Christ,
>
> *   *   *   *
>
> To have continually in mind the passion that Christ
>   suffered for me,
> For his benefits uncessantly to give him thanks.
>
> *   *   *   *
>
> Of worldly substance, friends, liberty, life and all, to
> set the loss at right nought, for the winning of Christ.
>
> *   *   *   *

Almighty God, Doce me facere voluntatem tuam. Fac me currere in odore ungentorum tuorum. Apprehende manum meam dexteram, et deduc me in via recta propter inimicos meos. Trahe me post te. In chamo et freno maxillas meas constringe, quum non approximo ad te.

Good Lord, give me the grace, in all my fear and agony, to have recourse to that great fear and wonderful agony that thou, my sweet Saviour, hadst at the Mount of Olivet before thy most bitter passion, and in the meditation thereof, to conceive ghostly comfort and consolation profitable for my soul.

Give me, good Lord, a full faith, a firm hope, and a fervent charity, a love to thee good Lord incomparable above the love to myself; and that I love nothing to thy displeasure, but everything in an order to thee.

Take from me, good Lord, this lukewarm fashion, or rather key-cold manner of meditation, and this dullness in praying unto thee. And give me warmth, delight and quickness in thinking upon thee. And give me thy grace to long for thine holy sacraments, and especially to rejoice in the presence of thy very blessed body, sweet Saviour Christ, in the holy sacrament of the altar, and duly to thank thee for thy gracious visitation therewith, and at that high memorial, with tender compassion, to remember and consider thy most bitter passion.

Make us all, good Lord, virtually participant of that holy sacrament this day, and everyday make us all lively members, sweet Saviour Christ, of thine holy mystical body, thy Catholic Church.

Lord, give me patience in tribulation and grace in everything to conform my will to thine: that I may truly say: Fiat voluntas tua, sicut in coelo et in terra.

The things, good Lord, that I pray for, give me thy grace to labour for. Amen.

One is struck first, by the depth of faith, tenderness of devotion and the beauty of language of these prayers. But they are couched, too, in the careful language of a lawyer and a theologian. Luther had appeared, and these devotions are, therefore, firmly set against a background of faith and works, and the gratuity of faith has been emphasized.

In the fourth book of his *Dialogue against Tyndale,* More deals with the question of faith and works. The question has been dealt with, he says, in the time of the Pelagian heresy, and Luther, by his doctrine, is an even worse opponent of grace than Pelagius. All our sufficiency is from God. He does not need either our faith or our works, but He has appointed that these are the conditions of our salvation. One quotation must suffice to show both More's theological exactness and his burning faith.

Nor that all the laws of Moses, nor all the good works of man, were not able to save one man of themselves, nor without faith and that Christ freely redeemed us. For neither had he or ever shall have any reward of us, for the bitter pains taken in his blessed passion for us. Nor never deserved we unto him that he should so much do for us. Nor the first faith, nor the preaching thereof nor the first justification of man thereby, nor the sacrament and fruit of our baptism, was not given to the world for any good works that ever the world had wrought; but only for God's mere liberal goodness.

The remarkable theological accuracy of the prayers is the first point to be noted. The second is the obvious influence of Hilton. In the space available this latter fact cannot be adequately demonstrated, but here are some indications: "A man shall not come to ghostly light in contemplation of Christ's Godhead, unless he is come in imagination by bitterness, and by compassion and by steadfast thinking on his manhood," says the Ladder. "Imagination by bitterness," "compassion," "steadfast thinking"; all these phrases are apt descriptions of the spirit of More's *History of the Passion* and of his prayers to our Blessed Lord in His agony—"with tender compassion, to remember and consider Thy most bitter passion."

Nowhere is Hilton's influence stronger than in the prayer which is the key to More's spirituality. "Give me, good Lord, a full faith, firm hope and fervent charity, a love to thee, good Lord, incomparable above the love to myself; and that I love nothing to thy displeasure, but everything in an order to thee."

"Full faith" is Hilton's "Feeling faith." "Feeling faith" had assumed, by 1535, Lutheran overtones and could not now be used with safety. In the early days of conversion, says Hilton, a man who wishes to serve God will need to rely on his "natural wit"; he will need to study and to read and there will be little conscious devotion in his prayers. Soon, if he is faithful in his work and prayer he will be led to some "ghostly contemplation." Under the influence of the Holy Spirit his faith will deepen: he will *realize* more deeply the implications of the dogmas of faith. There are stages in this development; at one time the affections are used more than the understanding, but ultimate perfection in contemplation is both "in cognition and understanding." This "way" to perfection is implicit in More's prayers; it is obvious in the adaptations of St. Paul's phrases and in prayer which asks for a "taste of thy holy Spirit." Hilton had been careful to point out, of course, that the higher gifts of contemplation are seldom continuous, for this is not a doctrine of disguised quietism, and there will always be need of formal prayer and meditation. In More's words one must "Busily labour to love thee." Hence, too, the hair shirt, returned to Meg only on the last day of his life. This conscious belief in the process by which the soul is gradually "opened" to the influence of grace is evident everywhere in the writings of St. Thomas. On persecution, for instance, he can write:

> This manner of ours, in whose breast the great good counsel of God no better settleth nor taketh no better roots may well declare us that the thorns and briers and the brambles of our worldly substance grow so thick, and spring so high in the ground of our hearts, that they strangle, as the Gospel saith, the word of God that was sown therein. And therefore is God a very good Lord unto us, when he causeth like a good husbandman his folk to come afield (for the persecutors be his folk for this purpose) and with their hooks and stocking-irons grub up those wicked weeds and

bushes of our earthly substance, and carry them right away from us, that the word of God sown in our hearts may have room therein, *and a glade round about for the warm sun of grace to come and make it grow.*

Such a deep realization of God's providence and the power of grace demands an equally deep appreciation of Man's weakness and the limited nature of his understanding. Luther had gone so far in stressing the effects of original sin, that, as More says, he makes as if "all our works were brought forth out of us without our will . . . out of a brute beast by appetite of sensual motion." More can put the situation quite simply:

> One tribulation is it to good men, to feel in themselves the conflict of the flesh against the soul, the rebellion of sensuality against the rule and government of reason, the relic that remains in mankind of old original sin of which St. Paul so sore complaineth in his epistle to the Romans. And yet we may not pray to have this kind of tribulation taken from us. For it is left us by God's ordinance to strive against it and by *reason and grace* to master it, and use it for the matter of our merit.

So much for "full faith" to which "firm hope" is but the natural corollary. Such hope is obvious in these prayers. As an example of humility and hope what better example could there be than the answer he gave to Cromwell? ". . . I have not been a man of such holy living, as I might be bold to offer myself to death, lest God for my presumption might suffer me to fall; and therefore I put not myself forward but draw back. Howbeit, if God draw me to himself, then I trust in his great mercy, that He shall not fail to give me grace and strength."

Now the second half of the important prayer quoted above: "that I love nothing to thy displeasure but everything in an order to thee" is magnificent in its simplicity. Here is a statement of the "way of acceptation"; an affirmation of the goodness of God's creation, the way to perfection of the layman who needs must live in the world. Of this "way" Hilton had written in *The Mixed Life,* but by his example and in his writings St. Thomas goes beyond anything Hilton had written. This aspect of More's teaching is so important that it needs special treatment. His adaptation of "Poverty," "Chastity" and "Obedience" to the lay state is especially interesting and here he is well in advance of his age. One example may be given; it is rather complicated and involved, but he is feeling his way to an idea that he is half frightened to suggest.

> If there be a man such (as would God there were many) that hath unto riches no love, but having them fall abundantly upon him, taketh to his own part no great pleasure thereof, but, as though he had it not, keepeth himself in like abstinence and penance privily as he would do in case he had it not, and in such things as he doth openly bestow somewhat more liberally upon himself in his house after some manner of the world, lest he should give other folk occasion to marvel and muse and talk of his manner, and misreport him for an hypocrite, therein between God and him doth

truly protest and testify, as did the good queen Hester, that he doth it not
for any desire thereof in the satisfying of his own pleasure, but would with
as good a will or better, forbear the possession of riches, saving for the commodity that other men have by its disposing thereof, as percase in keeping
a good household in good Christian order and fashion, and in setting other
folk a work with such things as they gain their living the better by his
means, this man's riches I might (Methinketh) in merit match in a manner
with another man's forsaking of all, if there were none other circumstance
more pleasant unto God farther added unto the forsaking beside, as percase
for the more fervent contemplation by reason of the solicitude of all worldly business left off, which was the thing that made Mary Magdalene's part
the better.

The sentence is indeed involved, but the idea is fairly clear. Hilton had said
that to neglect business, wife and children in order to contemplate was like
dressing the head of Christ with a lovely diadem whilst leaving the body all in
rags. More takes the matter further and tries to work the principle out in
detail. It is also interesting in that it clearly shows why St. Thomas looked
upon his imprisonment as the greatest blessing given him by God. At last he
had "time and opportunity" for prayer. In earlier years he had had to steal
from sleep the time to pray and write his theology. After serving with Martha
he now had a few months to contemplate with Mary Magdalene.

Finally, notice the prayers to the Blessed Sacrament given above, ending
with the prayer that we may all "be lively members, sweet saviour Christ, of
thine Holy mystical Body, thy catholic Church." Again, there is evident here
the same theological exactness; for the words "virtually participant" are,
surely, a reference to the teaching of Aquinas on the Eucharist as the source
of grace. The important feature, however, is that whereas the earlier mystical
writers, and even Hilton, had *assumed* the sacramental life, More finds it necessary, because of the advent of Luther, to integrate his great devotion to the
person of our Blessed Lord, with the Mass, in a more conscious manner; but
beyond that, there is a deep awareness of the mystical Body, an awareness
somewhat rare in the sixteenth century. This aspect of More's writings needs
an article on its own. Chambers has shown how strong was More's "mediaeval
sense of unity." It is more than that. Few men have had a deeper realization
of the dogma of the mystical Body, and his passionate defence of European
unity is not the oratory of a statesman but the cry of a saint. It is this that
makes him such a "saint for today."

There is so much more that could be said. Scarcely anything has been said
on penance. No reference has been made to à Kempis or to St. Augustine, and
both of these exerted great influence on More's spirituality. Since so many
societies and groups, of lawyers, civil servants, local government officials,
politicians, writers, students and many others have taken him as their patron,
more attention should be paid to him as a teacher of a "lay spirituality." He is
intensely English and directly in the line of the English mystics. Faced with
the challenge of Luther, he recast, as it were, the essence of their teaching, in
a safe and modern framework of theology. How refreshing, too, to be bidden,
as were his children, "to serve God, and be *merry* and *rejoice* in him"!

A CONSCIENCE UNDEFLOWERED

Rudolf B. Gottfried

The Renaissance has frequently been described as the age of the complete or universal man. In that glorious time, so runs the popular conception, single minds were somehow able to realize a greater number of human possibilities than single minds have ever done before or since. Freed from the inhibitions of his medieval past, the individual is said to have spontaneously acquired new and multifarious powers; he put forth branches on all sides. Nature, as it were, became so vigorous that she exceeded herself; and the mighty figures of the period, if we consider them together in their preternaturally full-grown humanity, were like a magnificent pantheon of Hindu gods, not one of them with less than half a dozen arms.

In favor of this romantic idea one should add that it is not entirely false. Among the artists, and particularly the Italian artists, of the Renaissance it is possible to find examples of an astonishing versatility. Leon Battista Alberti, who is known primarily as an architect, was also a painter, a musician, and a moral philosopher. It is hardly necessary to cite the name of Michelangelo, who turned his hand to painting, sculpture, poetry, and architecture. And Leonardo might be called an earthworm of genius: cut him in half, the painter and the scientist would both go on squirming.

But to a large extent the artist of the Renaissance presents a special and not a typical problem. His versatility, for one thing, was often merely technical, illustrating the variety of his media rather than the variety of his human powers. At the same time, the versatility of a Michelangelo or a Leonardo depended in part on the peculiar social position to which a great painter was then compelled to adapt himself, at once a craftsman and a gentleman, a servant and a companion of princes. The case of artists, in other words, cannot be used as effective proof that the Renaissance was indeed the age of the complete or universal man.

When we turn to an assortment of representative figures, rather than to artists alone, we are in a better position to evaluate the common view; and we can see that it is based on a perception of the truth, but a perception which is falsified in its statement. The Renaissance is really characterized, not by completeness, but by complexity, and not by universality, but by division. The men who were typical of the period were not demigods, crowned with their shining powers and enjoying a new dominion over all the various provinces of

Reprinted, complete and verbatim, from the edition privately printed at the Stinehour Press (Lunenburg, Vermont, 1958), by permission of the author and publisher.

knowledge; they were only human beings who, consciously or unconsciously, faced a multitude of new, perplexing dilemmas, the result of converging and often conflicting traditions which it was almost beyond the human mind to reconcile. The problems, not the men, were titanic. Men, to be sure, constantly made their theoretical attempts at reconciliation, on the levels of philosophy, of education, and of historical study. But none of these attempts has that fatal significance for us which attaches to the work of Petrarch, the father and the representative of so much that was to follow: Petrarch, in spite of what he intended and by means of his very learning and eloquence, leaves us with an indelible impression of weakness, division, the failure to resolve the conflicts which already beset the early Renaissance. He was drawn and quartered by the forces of his time.

Not, however, that the predicament of thoughtful men was altogether, or even primarily, their loss. If Petrarch was weak, he made his weakness his subject, deriving from it the psychological finesse which carried the influence of his love poetry into every cranny of Europe. And to a coarser, more heroic thinker the intricate cleavages between classical and medieval, spirit and flesh, individual and group, active life and contemplative, Catholic and Protestant, might represent not merely a danger, but a challenge, an opportunity for judgment and conscientious choice. If the man of the Renaissance did not have that omnicompetence which has been claimed for him, he was not without competence; he could at least make his own peculiarly momentous decisions. In fact, to know your right hand from your left, as we shall see in the case of Thomas More, may be far more important than to have six arms, or even seven wings.

The lifetime of Thomas More covers the period during which the Renaissance, with all its bewildering problems, arrived in England; and his achievement consists of having faced the problems and reached certain decisive conclusions in regard to them. Such a simplification cannot, of course, pretend to cover his whole career: he was, if not a universal genius, at any rate a lawyer, a statesman, and a controversial pamphleteer, as well as a humanistic man of letters; and what with the early biographies and the material which can be gathered from official documents, not to mention his own writing, we probably have more real information about him than about any other Englishman of the sixteenth century. But the essential meaning of his life can also be read in a radical abridgment of the sources; it can even be illuminated, perhaps, if we focus our attention on three of his vital decisions.

To consider the earliest of these: More probably decided to marry in 1503, when he was twenty-five. At a first glance, indeed, nothing may seem to be more ludicrously commonplace than the decision of a private man to do what almost all his fellowmen do likewise, to tie himself up in the matrimonial knot. One hesitates to use the words, but no others will do so well: marriage is an archetypal pattern, especially in the bourgeois circles to which More belonged. And old John More, Thomas's father, who could speak with the authority of an expert since he was married four times himself, used to say that choosing a wife was perilous, as if 'ye should put your hand into a blind bag full of snakes and eels together, seven snakes for one eel.' Wisdom of this kind, one must confess, transcends the Renaissance.

But More's decision to marry was not based on a calculation of snakes and eels. We know that it was made after four years during which he had lived in the Charterhouse of the London Carthusians, sharing their religious observances as far as possible, although he took no vows. He contemplated becoming a monk; and the genuineness of his monastic bent is revealed by the various ascetic practices to which he still adhered in the days of his greatest prosperity, such practices as wearing a hair shirt. Long after 1503 he was to regret the Carthusian life which he had missed. Nevertheless, he did not become a monk. Erasmus, who knew him intimately, writes that More preferred to be a chaste husband rather than an impure cleric, and explains, 'At the appropriate age he was not averse to the love of young women, but without dishonor, so that he might enjoy it as something offered rather than sought, allured rather by an affinity of mind than by coition.' It seems clear, therefore, that when he married, More made a difficult, but an honest and intelligent choice: in spite of all the attractions of an ascetic life, the seclusion, the surrender of will, the opportunity to concentrate on spiritual matters, he recognized that by his own nature he was morally committed to the world. And this private choice was important, not only in its immediate consequences, but as a prelude to those heroic decisions which he was later to reach, as it were, in public.

The immediate consequence of his marriage with Jane Colt was that he became the father, in rapid succession, of four children; and when Jane died in 1511, he remarried within a month, obviously to ensure the youngsters of the care they needed. Thus More early developed into what we call a family man. The term 'family,' indeed, should be extended to cover the whole household in Chelsea for which he was responsible: not only his own children and his second wife, that voluble character Mistress Alice, whom he described, with a kind of rough affection, as 'nec bella nec puella,' neither a pearl nor a girl— but also several other young people who were educated under his personal supervision. If we may judge by the number and variety of his domestic contacts, he seems to have invited, and not merely accepted, human duties. It is clear that the life of his household, next to his religion, gave him his deepest pleasure.

The quality of this feeling may be studied in the letters which More addressed to his young family. One of them, a Latin poem written when the oldest of his children was perhaps only thirteen or fourteen, reminds them how lenient he is: 'You know how often I have kissed, how rarely spanked you, and then only with a peacock's tail; even that I wielded gently, with hesitation, lest it should leave a sorry welt across your tender buttocks. The man who would not weep at the tears of his child is a brute unworthy to be called a father.' Expressed in Latin and in elegiac distichs, the passage has an indefinable air of humanistic persiflage which may have eluded his children; but a few years later they were probably better able to appreciate the raillery with which he seasons his loving if didactic words, written this time in Latin prose and from the Court:

> Yesterday [he tells them] the Bristol merchant brought me your letters, which I was overjoyed to have. For nothing, however rude and uncultivated, can come from your workshop which does not give me more satisfaction than the most painstaking composition of another: so much does my fondness commend what you have written.... None of your letters failed to please me; but to tell you honestly what I think, John's, both because it was longer than the others and because he seems to have spent rather more work and care upon it, pleased me especially. [John was the youngest of the children and the only boy.] For not only has he described everything charmingly and expressed it in no more words than necessary, but he plays agreeably with me and caps my jokes without awkwardness, observing a kind of restraint which reveals that he knows he is sporting with his father, whom he should study to entertain and yet fear to offend.
>
> Now I expect a letter from each of you almost every day; nor will I accept these excuses which some of you offer ..., the want of time or the sudden departure of the postboy or the lack of something to say.... How can you possibly lack something to say when I am glad to hear about your studies and your games, and particularly pleased if, having nothing to write, you set it forth at great length, as you have no trouble in doing, especially being women and quite talkative by nature, nay, incessantly talkative? ... But I would warn you of one thing: whether you are writing of serious matters or the merest nonsense, I want all to be written with diligence and thought.

In such a passage one cannot help thinking that More reveals talents which would have been wasted in a Carthusian monastery. The dating of his letter from the Court, on the other hand, betrays that the family life which meant so much to him had already been curtailed by a less attractive occupation.

A few years earlier than this, between 1516 and 1518, when he was nearly forty, More had made the second of his important decisions: he had consented to enter the service of the king. And just as the decision to marry had not killed his regret for the monastic life, the decision to become a royal servant was immediately paid for by the hours and days during which it compelled him to be away from his family; his domestic retirement was constantly at the mercy of the royal business or, what was more painful, the royal whim. Nevertheless, from the abstract point of view which makes it so easy to deal with the lives of others, we can see a logical continuation rather than a conflict here: by marriage More had already committed himself to the narrower reaches of a world whose mainstream he now entered as a member of the government. Conflict there was, but in another way.

His decision is not, moreover, the first evidence we have of his concern with politics. When Edward IV died in 1483, More was only five years old; but at the time he overheard it reported to his father, he tells us, that the Duke of Gloucester, the future Richard III, intended to usurp the throne. The boy who remembered that momentous news later received an important part of his education in the household of Cardinal Morton, one of those magnates who were chiefly responsible for the overthrow of Richard and the establishment of Henry VII; More's London background, in any case, would predispose him to support the new Tudor dynasty. Yet his first political act, as a distinctly junior member of Parliament in 1504, was made in opposition to the king. Henry VII, who had requested a special tax of £90,000, had to be contented with about a third of that amount because young More persuaded a majority of his colleagues to resist the royal greed. The king, characteristically, took his revenge by imprisoning the offender's father and fining him £100; the offender himself held no more public offices under Henry VII and did not become a member of the government until Henry VIII had been on the throne for several years.

In the end this mishap had fortunate results for More. It meant that instead of drifting into the royal service at an early age, as a young lawyer with his exceptional gifts would otherwise have done, he developed his political philosophy outside of that service. When he finally chose to become a servant of the king's, therefore, he was able to make an independent and mature decision.

In the meantime he gained political experience from acting as the Under-Sheriff of London and representing the mercantile interests of the city in trade negotiations on the Continent. What is more important, his writing in this period reveals that he by no means laid aside the critical point of view which had led him to oppose the special tax in Parliament. A minor translation of his shows that he did not believe in the divine right of kings; and we also have his *History of Richard III*, in a literary sense the most accomplished of all his works, as evidence of his opinions. The *History* has immortalized the Tudor interpretation of Richard's character, an interpretation which assured its author of the most complete official approval; but to see the book merely as Tudor propaganda is to miss nine-tenths of its significance. In the same year that Machiavelli was setting forth his theoretical justification of the new prince, More was describing what the new prince, in the person of Richard, was actually like. He devotes all his irony and all his dramatic skill to pinpointing the royal depravity—and nowhere more effectively than in the scene where the widow of Edward IV, whose elder son, the young king, has already fallen into her uncle Richard's power, is compelled to surrender her younger son as well:

Therewithal she said unto the child, 'Farewell, my own sweet son. God send you good keeping. Let me kiss you once yet ere you go, for God knoweth when we shall kiss together again.' And therewith she kissed him and blessed him, turned her back and wept and went her way, leaving the child weeping as fast. When the lord Cardinal and these other lords with him had received this young duke, they brought him into the Star Chamber, where the

Protector [that is, Richard] took him in his arms and kissed him with these words: 'Now welcome, my lord, even with all my heart.' And he said in that of likelihood as he thought. Thereupon forthwith they brought him to the king his brother, into the bishop's palace at Paul's, and from thence through the city honorably into the Tower, out of which after that day they never came abroad.

Here it will be noted how More's tenderness in family matters reinforces his political indignation.

But the drift of his views on monarchy emerges with greater clarity in the *Utopia*, written in 1515 and 1516, on the eve of his decision to join the government of Henry VIII. This work is divided into two books, the first describing the political and social problems of contemporary England, the second offering a solution of these problems in the ideal commonwealth of Utopia. One of the most important features of Book Two has often been overlooked, understandably, since it is stated obliquely, by omission: the crucial fact that the ideal commonwealth has no king. Book One, on the other hand, attacks the misgovernment of actual kings, both directly and by implication. Not that More names Henry VIII when he attacks the policies of his régime, a course which would hardly serve the writer's purpose; but the red herrings which he uses are transparent. The well-known passage in which he elucidates the evil which results from allowing the peasants' lands to be enclosed in sheep walks, evils that lay under his eyes at the time he wrote, is deliberately dated well back into the reign of Henry VII; and when the folly of contemporary foreign policy is uncovered, the reader is asked to imagine himself at the court of the king of France.

Both the sweeping nature of More's criticism in the *Utopia* and the rather thin veil through which it is allowed to appear have an important bearing on our central problem: there can be no doubt that Henry VIII was already attempting to lure him into the royal fold but that More had not as yet made up his mind. The choice before him was as perplexing as any he ever had to face, and for his own no less than for the king's enlightenment, he laid his cards on the table and calculated all the dangers in which acceptance would involve him. One section of the book, indeed, provides an astonishing discussion of his personal quandary: he represents himself as urging Hythloday, the traveler who has visited Utopia, to enter the service of some prince whom he may benefit by his unusual experience; but Hythloday is one of those uncompromising idealists who fear all contact with the world, a kind of philosophical Carthusian. After showing how ineffectual his advice would be when it encountered the blind materialism of the men who really had the ear of the king, he concludes:

'With princes there is no place for philosophy.'
'Indeed there is [More objects], but not for that school philosophy which finds all things becoming in all circumstances. There is another, more urbane variety that knows its proper scene and adapts itself to the play in hand, preserving the decorum of its part. This is the philosophy

which you should use. . . . If bad opinions cannot be torn out by the roots
or settled faults corrected as you wish, that is no reason why you should
forsake the commonwealth; in stormy weather you must not abandon ship
merely because you are unable to control the winds. Nor ought you to
press your strange, extravagant advice on others when you know it will not
carry weight with those who take a different view. But rather you must
labor to guide affairs by indirection, so that you may handle everything as
well as you are able, and what you cannot turn to good you may at least
succeed in rendering least bad. For all things could not possibly go well unless all men were good, and that I do not expect to see as yet for some few
years.'

'The only result of this [Hythloday replies] will be that while I strive to
cure others of their madness, I myself will go mad along with them. . . . I
cannot understand what you mean when you speak of guiding affairs by
indirection so that if all things cannot be made good, they may, through
skillful handling, as far as possible be made least bad. Nay, in councils
there is no opportunity to feign or acquiesce in silence: a man must openly
support the worst decisions and sign the most pestiferous decrees.'

The *Utopia* leaves the issue suspended between the speakers, each of whom
obviously represents a side of More's own mind; and so, in a sense, he hands
the solution of his private dilemma over to the reader. But we are also aware
that his private dilemma is not merely private. The debate which goes on in
the forum of his conscience actually deals with a problem which was vital for
the Renaissance as a whole, the problem of reconciling morality with the
newly asserted powers of the king.

In the end, soon after completing the *Utopia,* More decided to become a
royal servant; his conscience accepted the challenge to make the best of what
was probably quite bad. When he had reached his decision, as he was later to
remember, Henry told him that he should 'look first unto God and after God
unto him,' that is, the king: a command which was in effect a reassurance, an
endeavor to satisfy his deep reluctance. If he was no longer free to oppose or
criticize Henry's policies in public—and from now on, More scrupulously
avoided anything which might suggest public criticism—he was enjoined to
advise his master freely, as his conscience would suggest. This, we may be sure,
meant far more to him than all the duties and honors which followed: knighthood and promotion, in rapid order, to the offices of Master of Requests,
Privy Councillor, Under-Treasurer, Speaker of the House of Commons,
Chancellor of the Duchy of Lancaster, and Lord Chancellor of England. All
the externals of success cannot have weighed very heavily with one who from
the first saw the royal service as an opportunity to guide affairs, for good ends
if possible and, if impossible, for those which were least bad. His primary function was to be performed in the secret councils of the king.

How well he succeeded at first in persuading Henry to work for the good
of his people, or at least to avoid doing what was worst for them, it is hard to
say. On one occasion, as Speaker of the House of Commons, he helped to establish the principle of freedom of speech in the deliberations of that body; and

on another he circumvented an invasion of Parliamentary privilege when
Cardinal Wolsey attempted to browbeat the House into voting a huge subsidy
—a measure, incidentally, which More himself, as a member of the government,
now felt obliged to support. But in the secret councils of the king he found,
one must suspect, that Hythloday's pessimism was largely justified. In an official letter he mentions the bravado with which Henry, who was spoiling for
a chance to display his military prowess, received a confidential report on the
weakness of the French: 'the king's Grace said that he trusted in God to be
their governor himself and that they should by this means make a way for
him as King Richard did for his father.' And More, who is writing to Wolsey,
another proponent, on occasion, of a war with France, adds his own rueful
comment: 'I pray God, if it be good for his Grace and this realm, that then it
may prove so; and else, in the stead thereof, I pray God send his Grace one
honorable and profitable peace.' Prayer, indeed, is as reasonable as any course
for a man who finds himself in the company of wolves.

'Wolf,' however, is not quite the right word to hit off Wolsey. He was rather
what is called an able administrator: he neglected no opportunity to advance
either England's or his own prestige. And if More had little effect on English
policy, there was a kind of mental compensation in understanding the folly
and hypocrisy of those who did control affairs. In a book written after both
he and Wolsey had fallen from power, More describes a dinner at the house,
as he explains, of 'a great man of the Church' in Germany, a great man whom
the biographers have agreed to identify as Wolsey:

> So happed it one day that he had in a great audience made an oration in
> a certain manner, wherein he liked himself so well that at his dinner he sat
> him thought on thorns till he might hear how they that sat with him at his
> board would commend it. And when he had sit musing awhile, devising (as
> I thought after) upon some pretty, proper way to bring it in withal, at the
> last for lack of a better (lest he should have letted the matter too long) he
> brought it even bluntly forth and asked us all that sat at his board's end
> (for at his own mess in the middest there sat but himself alone) how well
> we liked his oration that he had made that day. But in faith . . . when that
> problem was once proponed, till it was full answered, no man (I ween) ate
> one morsel of meat more, every man was fallen in so deep a study for the
> finding of some exquisite praise. For he that should have brought out but
> a vulgar and a common commendation would have thought himself shamed
> forever. Then said we our sentences by row as we sat, from the lowest unto
> the highest in good order, as it had been a great matter of the commonweal
> in a right solemn council. When it came to my part, I will not say it . . . for
> no boast, me thought, by our Lady, for my part I quit myself meetly well.

> And I liked myself the better because me thought my words, being but
> a stranger, went yet with some grace in the Almain [that is, German]
> tongue, wherein, letting my Latin alone, me listed to show my cunning.
> And I hoped to be liked the better because I saw that he that sate next me,
> and should say his sentence after me, was an unlearned priest, for he could
> speak no Latin at all. But when he came forth for his part with my lord's

commendation, the wily fox had been so well accustomed in court with the craft of flattery that he went beyond me too-too far. And then might I see by him what excellence a right mean wit may come to in one craft that in all his whole life studieth and busieth his wit about no more but that one. But I made after a solemn vow unto myself that if ever he and I were matched together at that board again, when we should fall to our flattery, I would flatter in Latin, that he should not contend with me no more. For though I could be content to be outrun of an horse, yet would I no more abide it to be outrun of an ass.

But ... here now began the game. He that sat highest and was to speak [last] was a great-beneficed man, and not a doctor only, but also somewhat learned indeed in the laws of the Church. A world it was to see how he marked every man's word that spake before him. And it seemed that every word the more proper it was, the worse he liked it, for the cumbrance that he had to study out a better to pass it. The man even sweat with the labor, so that he was fain in the while now and then to wipe his face. Howbeit in conclusion, when it came to his course, we that had spoken before him had so taken up all among us before, that we had not left him one wise word to speak after.... [But when this good ancient, honorable flatterer] saw that he could find no words of praise that would pass all that had been spoken before already, the wily fox would speak never a word, but as he that were ravished unto heavenward with the wonder of the wisdom and eloquence that my lord's Grace had uttered in that oration, he sent a long sigh with an 'Oh' from the bottom of his breast, and held up both his hands, and lift up his head, and cast his eyen into the welkin, and wept.

If More shows himself participating in this courtly exercise, he was clearly in no danger of being contaminated by the folly and hypocrisy of the great world he had decided to enter; although his sense of humor could operate only in private, it flourished and protected him. On occasion, also, his comic understanding became what it might be better to describe as tragic insight. His son-in-law, William Roper, provides us with such a serious pendent to the scene at Wolsey's dinner, in this case an unexpected visit which the king, the real wolf, paid to More at his house in Chelsea:

On a time, unlooked for, he came to dinner to him; and after dinner, in a fair garden of his, walked with him by the space of an hour, holding his arm about his neck. As soon as his Grace was gone, I, rejoicing thereat, told Sir Thomas More how happy he was, whom the king had so familiarly entertained as I never had seen him to do to any other except Cardinal Wolsey, whom I saw his Grace once walk with, arm in arm. 'I thank our Lord, son,' quoth he, 'I find his Grace my very good lord indeed, and I believe he doth as singularly favor me as any subject within this realm. Howbeit, son Roper, I may tell thee I have no cause to be proud thereof, for if my head could win him a castle in France,... it should not fail to go.'

It is worth noting that More's remark to Roper must have been made ten years before Henry was to require the payment of his servant's head. From very early More seems to have lost whatever delusions he may once have had about the king's real character; he recognized and, in the spirit of the Renaissance, he accepted the inhuman egoism of his 'very good lord,' that is, the tyrant whom God had imposed on the English people. The most that one could hope for was somehow to guide that treacherous force into the right paths. When More resigned the Lord Chancellorship, and with it the royal service, he had these sad words for Thomas Cromwell, the man of the hour:

> 'Master Cromwell,' quoth he, 'you are now entered into the service of a most noble, wise, and liberal prince. If you will follow my poor advice, you shall, in your counsel-giving unto his Grace, ever tell him what he ought to do, but never what he is able to do. So shall you show yourself a true, faithful servant and a right worthy councillor. For if a lion knew his own strength, hard were it for any man to rule him.'

This is at once a warning and a confession of failure: More is advising, not the king by now, but the king's worst adviser, and advising him not to do exactly what he intends to do.

But the word 'failure' cannot with any real justice be applied to More's whole position at the time of his retirement from office. We have seen that as Speaker he was able to support and extend the privileges of the House of Commons; as Lord Chancellor, also, he could apparently take satisfaction in the conscientious performance of important legal duties. And if we consider him as an adviser of the king, the function which he chiefly sought when he decided to enter the royal service, it is clear that he was not a failure on his own terms: from the first he did not expect that much, if any, of his good advice would ever be adopted by Henry; on the other hand, he never succumbed to the folly around him or went mad along with others, as Hythloday had feared; his very words to Cromwell, aware though they show him to be of the catastrophe which will almost inevitably come, are themselves a triumphant act of conscience. And all this experience gained from the service of the king was, in any case, the groundwork of his third and culminating choice, the decision not to take the oath of the royal Supremacy.

More decided to refuse the oath of Supremacy in 1534, two years after he had resigned the Lord Chancellorship; the roots of the oath, however, go back to the time when he was still in the royal service, and they are entangled with an even earlier matter, the conflict over Henry's divorce from Catherine of Aragon. Cromwell slipped the Supremacy, which was his baby, into the same cradle with the divorce, which was Wolsey's.

In proposing the divorce, years before, Wolsey initiated the long series of marital adventures by which Henry almost seems to qualify as one of the heroes of science, an experimental psychologist who conducted a statistical study of snakes and eels on his own person. But the divorce, or more properly the annulment, was at first intended to correct a dynastic mistake: since Henry had no living sons by Catherine of Aragon, there must have been a theological flaw in their so-called marriage, and it would be best to start over from scratch. Unluckily for Wolsey, the pope did not see it this way, and the pope's refusal arrived at a time when the king began to want, not only a son, but Anne Boleyn for his wife. As a result of these and other miscalculations, Wolsey was removed from power in 1529, and More succeeded to the Lord Chancellorship.

That he should assume the highest office under the throne in such circumstances is an anomaly: before this he had made it quite clear to Henry that on religious grounds he could not approve of the divorce. Nevertheless, he was already high in the royal service; and the king now repeated his original assurance the More should 'look first unto God and after God unto him,' in other words, that his conscience would be free. Henry probably hoped that he could persuade his new Lord Chancellor to accept the divorce in the end; in the meanwhile, since he contemplated a very unpopular action, he was glad to use the most popular and respected member of his government for a figurehead. More himself certainly knew that he was a figurehead and that as time went on, he enjoyed less and less of the royal confidence; yet his diminishing effectiveness did not relieve him from the responsibility to do what he could.

The man who really succeeded to Wolsey's influence was Cromwell, and this student of Machiavelli soon discovered the means of exploiting the situation for the benefit of the monarchy: since the pope would not grant the divorce the king wanted, the king could find it only in his own national church; as the head of such a church he could also gain a tremendous increase of power and wealth—he could, for example, confiscate the huge monastic properties. Thus Cromwell taught the lion how to know his own strength, and Henry was easily persuaded to couple his need for the divorce with his royal Supremacy. Assuming the title Supreme Head of the Church in England, he broke with Rome and began to ally himself with the English Protestants.

For two and a half years, while these great changes were in the making, More held the Lord Chancellorship. During that period he loyally refused to express his opinion of the divorce in public; as a layman, he was not yet faced with the necessity of declaring himself on the Supremacy, although the issue filled him with increasing fear and embarrassment. The government, to be sure, still adhered to its long-established view that Protestants were heretics, and More devoted himself to strengthening that position. It is uncertain whether or not he was personally responsible, while in office, for the execution of any of those whom he regarded as heretics; but there is no doubt that he redoubled his efforts to answer them in print. With a kind of dogged heroism which does not improve the literary quality of his controversial pamphlets, he hurled attack after attack against the Protestants at the very time when he knew that the king, under the influence of Cromwell and Anne Boleyn, was veering to the Protestant side. More's usefulness as a figurehead, in the circumstances, rapidly declined; and Henry accepted his resignation from the Lord Chancellorship and governmental service in 1532.

Retirement from office restored More to his family, and the prospect of living together on a reduced income filled him, for the moment, with gaiety; but he was too important to be forgotten in the march of great events. Their course may easily be studied in the royal calendar for 1533: about January 25 Henry secretly married Anne Boleyn; on May 23 Cranmer, his new Archbishop of Canterbury, granted him a divorce from Catherine of Aragon; on June 1 Anne was crowned Queen of England; and on September 7 she gave birth, not to the son whom Henry had confidently expected, but to the future Queen Elizabeth—the order and timing of these events betray their physiological concatenation. Attendance at the crowning of Anne on June 1 was obviously designed as a test of loyalty to the new order of things; and three friendly bishops, all Catholics still, invited More to accompany them to Westminster Abbey. In declining their invitation, he told them that it

> did put me in remembrance of an emperor that had ordained a law that whosoever committed a certain offence (which I now remember not), except it were a virgin, should suffer the pains of death, such a reverence had he to virginity. Now so it happened that the first committer of that offence was indeed a virgin, whereof the emperor hearing was in no small perplexity, as he that by some example fain would have had that law to have been put in execution. Whereupon when his council had sat long, solemnly debating this case, suddenly arose there up one of his council, a good plain man, among them and said, 'Why make you so much ado, my lords, about so small a matter? Let her first be deflowered, and then after may she be devoured.'—And so, though your lordships have in the matter of the matrimony hitherto kept yourselves pure virgins, yet take good heed, my lords, that you keep your virginity still.

And More added, referring to his opponents in the government, 'It lieth not in my power but that they may devour me; but God being my good Lord, I will provide that they shall never deflower me.'

Soon after this, he experienced a first attempt to devour him: he was charged with complicity in the treasonable prophecies of a demented nun. Since he had actually refused to listen to her, the charges against him had to be dropped; but the episode shows that the government had already decided to trap him or to frighten him into submission. His own reaction is also significant; with a legalistic wiliness which is sometimes disconcerting to his modern admirer, he anticipates and eludes any possible charge of treason. Two characteristics of the man are worth noting in this connection: sedition, much less rebellion, was abhorrent to More; and he was determined not to be devoured for the wrong cause.

The right cause turned up within a few weeks. Early in 1534 Parliament passed an act which fixed the succession to the crown in Henry's children by Anne Boleyn and permitted the government to require of all subjects a corporal oath to maintain 'the whole effects and contents' of the act; hereupon Cromwell shrewdly devised an oath which included not only the succession but the royal Supremacy. More, although opposed to the divorce, would have been willing to subscribe to the succession of Anne's children, which Parliament had the legal right to determine; but he was convinced that neither Parliament nor any other merely English authority had the legal right to substitute the king for the pope as the Supreme Head of the Church in England. Further-more, to require an oath maintaining such an illegal change was to do violence to the individual soul. More had always thought that it was wrong to force a man to swear that he believed what he did not believe; in Utopia even atheists were guaranteed freedom of conscience. This freedom he was ready to assert for himself and others now.

At any rate, he knew what was in store for him when he was summoned to appear at Lambeth on April 13, 1534. His departure from Chelsea is described by Roper:

> Whereas he evermore used before, at his departure from his wife and chil-dren, whom he tenderly loved, to have them bring him to his boat and there to kiss them all and bid them farewell, then [on this occasion] would he suffer none of them forth of the gate to follow him, but pulled the wicket after him and shut them all from him; and with an heavy heart, as by his countenance it appeared, with me and our four servants there took he his boat towards Lambeth. Wherein sitting still sadly awhile, at the last he suddenly rounded me in the ear, and said, 'Son Roper, I thank our Lord the field is won.' What he meant thereby I then wist not; yet loath to seem ignorant, I answered, 'Sir, I am thereof very glad.'

More's final decision almost seems to be reached in front of us; we see him subordinating love of family to claims which were at once larger and more private, and yet enhancing love of family too. He comes full circle, in a sense, back to his first decision, completing rather than reversing it.

As soon as More arrived at Lambeth, the oath of Supremacy was submitted to him by the lords appointed for that purpose, and he refused to subscribe. Then the names of all the members of Parliament who had already subscribed were shown to him; he was allowed to see a large group of happy clergymen making a festivity of their subscription; the Archbishop of Canterbury demon-strated to him the absurdity of not subscribing; and in the end he still refused to subscribe. He was one of only three, and ultimately only two, important Englishmen who found that they could not accept the Supremacy when Henry's government demanded it. Inevitably, four days later, he was committed to the Tower, out of which after that day he never came abroad except to his trial and his execution.

His imprisonment during the remaining year of his life was hard for More only insofar as it endangered his household and, in good part, separated him from them. But Margaret Roper, the member of his family in whom he found it easiest to confide, contrived to see him after a month; and he told her, 'I believe, Meg, that they that have put me here ween they have done me a high displeasure; but I assure thee on my faith, my own good daughter, if it had not been for my wife and you that be my children, whom I accompt the chief part of my charge, I would not have failed long ere this to have closed myself in as strait a room, and straiter too.'

Margaret had secured permission to visit More by hinting that she might persuade him to accept the oath; and in a long letter to a relative she writes how she debated the issue with him, never, one feels sure, expecting to succeed. When she argues that by not yielding he will lose the support of all his friends, he replies without bitterness:

> Albeit that I know mine own frailty full well and the natural faintness of mine own heart, yet if I had not trusted that God should give me strength rather to endure all things than offend Him by swearing ungodly against mine own conscience, you may be very sure I would not have come here. And sith I look in this matter but only unto God, it maketh me little matter though men call it as it pleaseth them and say it is no conscience, but a foolish scruple.

He is equally unwilling to accept her appeal to the act of Parliament:

> As for the law of the land, though every man being born and inhabiting therein is bounden to the keeping in every case upon some temporal pain, and in many cases upon pain of God's displeasure too, yet is there no man bounden to swear that every law is well made, nor bounden upon the pain of God's displeasure to perform any such point of the law as were indeed unlawful.

The act of Parliament is unlawful, More tells her, because it reverses the law which has long been accepted by the whole of Christendom and not merely by one kingdom. Furthermore, even if a man believes what the whole of Christendom finds damnable, this is 'a very good occasion to move him, and yet not to compel him, to conform his mind and conscience unto theirs.' And Margaret is finally driven to admit that he is right:

> When he saw me sit with this very sad [she tells her correspondent] ... (my heart was full heavy for the peril of his person, for in faith I fear not [for] his soul), he smiled upon me and said, 'How now, daughter Marget? What how, mother Eve? Where is your mind now? Sit [you] not musing, with some serpent in your breast, upon some new persuasion to offer father Adam the apple yet once again?' 'In good faith, Father,' quod I, 'I can no further go, but am (as I trow Cressid saith in Chaucer) comen to Dulcarnon, even to my wit's end.'

Throughout his last exchange of letters with Margaret, strong as her spirit is revealed to be, it is More who strengthens her and his whole household through her. 'Thus, mine own good daughter,' he will write,

> have me recommended to my good bedfellow and all my children, men, women, and all, with all your babes and your nurses and all the maids and all the servants, and all our kin, and all our other friends abroad. And I beseech our Lord to save them all and keep them. And I pray you all, pray for me; and I shall pray for you all. And take no thought for me whatsoever you shall hap to hear, but be merry in God.

His imprisonment seems then to have actually tightened the bond between More and his family; at the same time, however, it reminded him of the monastic life which he had sacrificed when he decided to marry. One day, while Margaret was visiting him, three humble Carthusians who had refused the oath of Supremacy were taken past his window on their way to execution; and he exclaimed,

> Lo, dost thou not see, Meg, that these blessed fathers be now as cheerfully going to their deaths as bridegrooms to their marriage? Wherefore thereby mayst thou see, mine own good daughter, what a great difference there is between such as have in effect spent all their days in a strait, hard, penitential, and painful life religiously, and such as have in the world, like worldly wretches, as thy poor father hath done, consumed all their time in pleasure and ease licentiously.

More still felt the pinch of his old decision, made thirty years before; yet he must also have been aware that by his new decision he had, in a sense, returned to the Carthusians, whom he was soon to follow to execution. And he spent much of the intervening time like a monk, in prayer, in solitary contemplation, and in writing works of a religious nature.

One of these, the *Dialogue of Comfort against Tribulation,* throws light on his immediate problem, particularly in a passage where he distinguishes between the tribulations which men must learn to bear and the troubles which they seek by their own vindictiveness. He cites the story of a shrewish wife in Budapest who was determined to have her husband kill her so that he might be hanged; finally

> as her husband (the man was a carpenter) stood hewing with his chip axe upon a piece of timber, she began after her old guise so to revile him that the man waxed wroth at last and bode her get her in, or he would lay the helm of his axe about her back, and said also that it were little sin even with that axehead to chop off that unhappy head of hers that carried such an ungracious tongue therein. At that word the Divel took his time and whetted her tongue against her teeth. And when it was well sharped, she sware to him in very fierce anger, 'By the mass, whoreson husband, I would thou wouldst: here lieth mine head, lo,' and therewith down she laid her head upon the same timber log; 'if thou smite it not off, I beshrew thine whoreson's heart.' . . . And so the good man up with his chip axe and at a chop chopped off her head indeed. There were standing other folk by [who] said they heard her tongue babble in her head and call, 'Whoreson! whoreson!' twice after the head was fro the body.

More adds that the husband was soon pardoned for her death.—This trenchant little scene, we are tempted to believe, may very well reflect his anticipation of his own beheading; but such a possibility is overshadowed by the obvious lesson, reiterated in the *Dialogue of Comfort,* that when martyrdom is sought, especially through malice or pride, it is not martyrdom at all.

While More skirted this religious pitfall, he was also avoiding another kind of trap. By construing the Act of Succession to suit themselves, the government had been able to imprison him for refusing the oath of Supremacy; but in order to execute him as a traitor, it was necessary for Parliament, early in 1535, to pass a second act which made it treason to speak 'maliciously' against the Supremacy. The government at once concluded that not only an outright attack on the Supremacy, but any explanation which a man might give for not taking the oath was maliciously spoken and therefore treasonable. Canny lawyer that he was, More had realized this danger even before the passage of the second act and had avoided all explanation of why he had refused the oath. Members of the government, among them Cromwell, who posed as his friend, frequently attempted to lure him into such an explanation, but in vain. He used his wits, not to save his life, which was clearly lost, but to avoid a legal conviction on the charge of treason, a conviction which would mean dying for the wrong cause.

In the end, when he was brought to trial in Westminster Hall on July 1, 1535, the government was able to secure a conviction on the charge of treason, but a conviction based on evidence which was obviously perjured and on the curious argument that his silence on the subject of the Supremacy was in itself treasonable. More, who after a year in prison was too weak to address the court standing up, could nevertheless defend himself so well that the verdict of guilty was a self-evident miscarriage of justice: he was really convicted, not of treason, but of refusing to take the oath. His command of the situation, morally speaking, is revealed by what happened when the jury brought in the verdict. Audeley, his successor in the Lord Chancellorship, began immediately to pass sentence; but More interrupted him, saying, 'My lord, when I was toward the law, the manner in such case was to ask the prisoner before judgment why judgment should not be given against him.' And while the Lord Chancellor, we may imagine, glowered foolishly at the prisoner, More made the full and considered explanation of his views on the Supremacy which he had so carefully avoided hitherto. Since the spiritual pre-eminence of Rome had been established by Christ and by the whole Christian tradition, he said, 'therefore am I not bounden, my lord, to conform my conscience to the council of one realm against the general council of Christendom.' More ratified his decision, as it were, in public.

After Audeley had pronounced the inevitable sentence of death, the condemned man was taken back to the Tower, with the edge of the symbolic axe turned towards him. Roper tells us how Margaret waited for More on Tower Wharf:

> She, hasting towards him and, without consideration or care of herself, pressing in among the middest of the throng and company of the guard that with halberds and bills went round about him, hastily ran to him and there openly, in the sight of them all, imbraced him, took him about the neck, and kissed him. Who, well liking her most natural and dear daughterly affection towards him, gave her his fatherly blessing and many godly words of comfort besides. From whom after she was departed, she, not satisfied with the former sight of him, and like one that had forgotten herself, being all ravished with the entire love of her dear father, having respect neither to herself nor to the press of the people and multitude that were there about

him, suddenly turned back again, ran to him as before, took him about the neck, and divers times together most lovingly kissed him; and at last, with a full heavy heart, was fain to depart from him.

Four days later, anticipating his execution on the day which would follow, More wrote to her for the last time. After asking her to give his blessing to all their family and friends, he adds:

I encumber you, good Margaret, much; but I would be sorry if it should be any longer than tomorrow, for it is St. Thomas's Even . . . , and therefore tomorrow long I to go to God. It were a day very meet and convenient for me. I never liked your manner toward me better than when you kissed me last, for I love when daughterly love and dear charity hath no leisure to look to worldly courtesy.

Farewell, my dear child, and pray for me, and I shall for you and all your friends, that we may merrily meet in Heaven.

More's desire to die on the eve of St. Thomas, that is, on the day before the feast of St. Thomas à Becket, was fulfilled; and it is not hard to understand the pleasure he received from a date so very meet and convenient for him in a religious sense. But the coincidence will also serve the broader purposes of definition.

The lives of Becket and More, separated though they are by nearly four centuries, present us with some remarkable parallels: not only were both of them named Thomas, but both were sons of the London middle class, both became Lord Chancellors, both were martyred at the behest of kings named Henry, and both are now saints. These similarities, however, really underline the basic dissimilarities between the two men, not only as individuals considered by themselves but, what is more important for us, as individuals living in very different periods of history.

It is a temptation to describe the character of Becket in all its brilliant, proud, unloving harshness, the character of the irate archbishop who brandished his cross like a sword at Northampton, the overbearing exile who rode through France at the head of three hundred followers, or the bold victim who angered his murderers beyond endurance by shouting, 'Pander!' But Becket's relation to his time is better illustrated by the crucial choice of his career, the decision to place the interests of the Church, as he saw them, above those of the crown.

This decision is curiously unlike those which we have already examined in the case of More. It is not a natural consequence of Becket's life before he became Archbishop of Canterbury; and he probably had not yet reached it, in the sense of realizing what it implied, even at the time when he was consecrated. For all his willfulness, there is something indecisive about his character too: after first opposing Henry II, he gave in to him at Woodstock and again at Clarendon. Furthermore, the value of his decision, when it grew firm at last, is largely qualified by its historical context: for nearly a century the prestige and authority of the pope had been expanding throughout Western Europe, and when Becket defied the royal power, he was riding the crest of a wave; he could count on the support not only of the Church itself but of the king of France and of Christian opinion everywhere. In the end, realizing the strength of his position, he deliberately courted death by his relentless excommunication of the bishops who had aided Henry II and by his open attempts to rally popular opinion against the king. When Henry's folly had been provoked into sending the four knights to Canterbury, Becket insisted that they should slay him in the church itself: 'If you wish to kill me, kill me here.' The contemporary accounts make it plain, beyond the shadow of a doubt, that he sought martyrdom, and sought it under the most dramatic circumstances.

How well he understood his medieval world is revealed by the consequences of his death. Miracles were witnessed at once, and the common people had already acclaimed him as a saint when he was canonized only two years later. The pope and many of the temporal rulers of Europe put such pressure on Henry that he immediately humbled himself and endeavored to establish his innocence; in the upshot, however, he found it worth his while to do penance by prostrating himself before the monks of Canterbury and receiving three hundred strokes on his bare shoulders. In time Canterbury Cathedral, which before that had been dedicated merely to Christ, became the Church of St. Thomas and one of the leading shrines of Christendom. For three and a half centuries it was visited and enriched by kings as well as thousands of ordinary pilgrims who did honor to the martyr's relics. And when Henry VIII—More's Henry—having established his Supremacy, decided to enjoy it, we are told that the storerooms of St. Thomas yielded him two chests of jewels, each so heavy that six or eight men were needed to carry it, and twenty-four wagonloads of other treasures.

The very completeness of Becket's victory, therefore, betrays that his decision, however brave and resourceful he was in implementing it, depended as much on the general drift of his period as on his inner choice; and when the medieval system had disappeared, the consequences of his decision vanished too. But the Renaissance which superseded Becket's world provided the matter for decisions of a rather different order. Not only was the boot now on the other foot in the conflict between papal and royal authority, but the basis of all authority was shaken. Thoughtful men found themselves, not borne along on one great stream, but caught in a welter of dangerous crosscurrents; they had their painful choices to make between conflicting traditions which had nearly equal claims upon them; they were on their own, and the moral stress of that new experience gave a certain inner and personal weight to their decisions.

Of this inner stress which differentiates the thoughtful man of the Renaissance from Becket and his time, there is no finer representative than More. His strong inclination toward the medieval past only sharpened his perception of the conflicts before him; his appeal to the Council of all Christendom served only to emphasize his isolation from his countrymen; yet the peculiar difficulty which he felt in reaching his decisions only increased their cumulative meaning. At first he rejected the monastic life for that of the world; then he accepted the public as well as the private responsibilities of the world; in the end he rejected the supernatural pretensions of the world in favor of the supernatural itself. The theme of his decision was even recapitulated on the scaffold: he faced the executioner, not shouting 'Whoreson!' or 'Pander!' or 'Kill me here,' but protesting 'that he died the king's good servant, but God's first.'

When he entered the royal service, we may remember, the same crucial distinction had assured him of his inner freedom of choice; and his whole career, futile or even tragic as its outcome may sometimes now appear to be, asserts that not yet quite forgotten scale of values. More still illuminates the life of the conscience which was fostered by the Renaissance.

A NAME FOR ALL SEASONS

Germain Marc'hadour

If this disquisition were a pastiche of More's own exhaustive fashion—in the Lucianic declamations of his youth no less than in his later polemics—half a dozen reasons could easily be lined up to justify and magnify a historico-philological analysis of his name. One reason is the great fun with words and especially with etymology which he shared with his age—or should one say with all ages? Another is provided by the double rebus in his coat of arms. Significant, too, is the multiple punning which the syllable *Mor-* lends itself to in Greek and Latin as well as in English, while the very banality of "Thomas More" (or "Thomas Moore," which is the same from our standpoint) has misled historians into identifying our More with an assortment of his namesakes, thus further crowding his already eventful career, and all but crediting him with multilocation.

The many subtitles emulate the marginal glosses which served as guides into the treatises on "various matters" published by Erasmus and More, enabling the busy reader to select congenial items from the crowded menu.

This essay—an Erasmian *meletê* without Erasmus' genius—reproduces the substance of "Les arcanes d'un nom," which appeared in three instalments, in *Moreana* no. 2 (55–70), no. 3 (71–80), no. 5 (73–88) and of three postscripts from various readers published in no. 6 (109–10), no. 7 (116) and no. 8 (102). The pages on More's Christian name are based on "Thomas More's Biblical Namesake," in Part IV of my *The Bible in the Works of St. Thomas More* (Nieuwkoop, 1971), 13–18.

Since the first installment (February 1964), the bibliography of More and Erasmus has increased beyond the highest expectations. The footnotes have been keyed to the critical editions done by the Yale University Press and by North-Holland, as well as to the Collected Works of Erasmus in English, headquartered in Toronto.

The light this rambling chase throws on the age of More, especially into the undergrowth of past mentalities and sensibilities, has encouraged me not to shorten the original version. I have left out one or two points that were geared specifically to a French language public, and compensated for the loss by the addition of a few remarks. I have also come to terms with the facts of modern culture by dropping all use of the Greek alphabet, even where the quotation of Greek words was essential to the matter in hand.

Reprinted, by permission of the author and publisher, from *Moreana* 2 (1964), 55–70, *3* (1964), 71–80, and 5 (1965), 73–88. Translated and revised by the author.

Nomen Omen

Like many giants of antiquity, such as Plato, Cicero, St. Augustine, and like
the majority of great writers after him, from Rabelais through Shakespeare
and Victor Hugo to James Joyce, More was a zestful player with words, not
excluding people's names. Even in controversy over "matters of religion," he
was apt to pun on his opponent's patronym. In the *Responsio ad Lutherum,*
he seems to resist for a while the urge to capitalize on the variant Ludher/
Luder, which the Saxon monk had employed in signing his early letters. Johann Eck had seized on this chance of guffawing at Luder's ludicrous theology. The shift, "imminent" in More's refusal to take Luther seriously,[1] becomes explicit in Book II, chapter 19. Once he had taken the ludic plunge,
More kept at the game through the remaining nine chapters and fifty pages.
Ludens herus, a mock etymology parodying those of the Golden Legend,[2]
might be englished as "Master Mock," a title which George Joye was later to
bestow on More himself. The allusion is rubbed in every now and then by the
repetition of the verb: "Dominus Luderus illudit apostolum" (586/9), "pergit
pater Luderus ludere" (586/12).[3] The name itself, in its ludic form, occurs
more than thirty times. This is not uncontrolled nagging: the game is suspended
through chapter 20, presumably in reverence to the Blessed Sacrament, and
not carried into the peroration, which belongs to a nobler level of rhetoric.

The game would be unfair, and its yield polemically irrelevant, if no intrinsic
correspondence existed between names and realities, if as Aristotle held,[4] all
names were arbitrary labels; but Aristotle being Luther's *bête noire,* a subtle
irony justifies More's recourse to the nobler alternative, Plato, whose *Cratylus*
is devoted to exploring the mysterious pregnancy of names, as God's own
marks declaring the identity of each person.[5] If our age refuses to be amused,
let alone swayed, by such trifles, More's first readers must have responded
warmly to them. The most sophisticated (and least gamesome) of them, Guillaume Budé, in a letter urging Erasmus to accept the French king's offer of a
readership in Paris, used the two titles, *Francus* and *Franciscus,* as a double
omen betokening frankness, and guaranteeing mighty deeds.[6]

In his English controversy, More repeatedly called the Wittenberg heresiarch
"lewd Luther," the nearest English could come to "Luderus." A more gruesome pun occurs in the *Supplication* when a survey of Lollard anticlerical
maneuvers in the parliaments of Henry V leads to an obscure contemporary
of Jan Hus whose name, John Goose, corresponded exactly to that of the Prague
theologian. Predictably, Goose's name dictates the metaphoric coloration of
the story: "And yet longe after thys was there one Iohn Goose rosted at the
towre hyll. And thereupon forthwith some other Iohn Goose . . . made some
gagling a while . . . And now because som heretiques haue ben of late abiured,
this goseling therefore gaggleth again vpon the same matter" (*EW*, p. 302 H).
The gosling thus exposed to gaggle his way to the roasting pyre was Simon
Fish. Had More known his name, he might have played with *goose* and *fish,* as
Fisher, for the rebus of his episcopal coat-of-arms, had chosen the inevitable
dolphin for "fish," only adding three ears of corn to represent the second syllable of his surname.

Nor could the reformers poohpooh the notion that names are fraught with ontological significance, since it receives abundant support in the Bible, from naming-day in Eden to the heavenly bestowal of a new name on each elect in the Apocalypse.[7] Christian exegesis did not extenuate the scriptural scenes in which names are explained, or providentially imposed, or prophetically modified, from Adam and Eve, through Abram/Abraham and Sara/Sarai and Jacob/Israel, to Jesus himself and his precursor John, both of whom received their names from the Lord's angel before they were conceived: "Iohan," as John Fisher reminds his audience, "by interpretacyon is to saye the grace of god."[8] It is in the light of this interpretation that Erasmus, featuring Dean Colet as his fellow-pilgrim to Becket's shrine, changed his Christian name John to *Gratianus.* Colet he latinized into *Pullus,* from the word used a dozen times in the Vulgate to designate the donkey's colt Jesus mounted for his entry into Jerusalem. The pun throws some light upon the contemporary pronunciation of Colet—apparently a monosyllable, it was equated with the fairly current surname of Colt, borne by the father of More's first wife: he too had a colt in his arms, and this may have been the source of Erasmus' etymology.[9]

A number of specific incentives fed and fostered early Tudor England's preoccupation, not to say fascination, with names. For one thing, settled patronyms were a relatively recent phenomenon, by no means universal yet: so their nickname value was still vividly perceived. The coats-of-arms granted by the Crown to make up for the decimation of the nobility during the Wars of the Roses (also to purchase the service of the learned, the money of the prosperous burgher, and the loyalty of both) faced many a new gentleman or knight with the problem of deciphering his name. The professional herald would at times be assisted by a scholar-friend in the choice of a "speaking" design to grace a brandnew shield. The result was a wealth, almost a riot, of onomastic punning.

Devotion to the Holy Name of Jesus, fostered already by St. Bernard, was fanned by the Franciscan friars until it became a leitmotiv in the preaching of St. Bernardine and bore its full fruit in the institution of a special feast. Like all good movements, it had its lunatic fringe.[10] That perfect image of the Saviour, in a book like *The Image of Love,* was offered to the meditation of the christian elite as an adequate substitute for all carved or painted representations. More disagreed for all his love of words and names, and inserted a careful refutation of that thesis into the second edition of his *Dialogue Concerning Heresies:* a name, he there argues, is "onely an ymage representynge to you the ymagynacyon of my mynde." In their written form (which printing had begun to endow with a new prestige), names are one further remove from the real objects. They "be no naturall sygnes or ymages but onely made by consent and agrement of men." Thus the "wordes Christus crucifixus/do not so lyuely represent vs the remembraunce of his bytter passyon/as doeth a blessyd ymage of the crucyfyx."[11]

With secular escutcheons, there was no such danger of pictorial evacuation. As John More's coat-of-arms had been granted by Edward IV, young Tom, though a commoner, received his heraldic initiation under his father's own roof. He got more of the pageantry in the house of Archbishop Morton, whose emblem was a mulberry-tree (or *more*) issuing from a barrel (or *ton*). A likelier etymology, of course, was a town (or village) in or near a moor or heath, but the tree and barrel, if somewhat far-fetched, lent themselves better to pictorial stylization.[12]

An *esquire* by right of birth, Thomas More did not have to wait until 1521 (when he was knighted, rising from *armiger* to *miles*) before he was entitled to an escutcheon. How did he feel about his "armes parlantes"? The very diversity of the allusions his short surname prompted from his erudite friends at home and abroad would have been enough to demystify it, if need were, in his own eyes and ears. The game was played least at home: the English humanists never suffered from that infatuation with surnames which led their continental counterparts, in Germany particularly, to coin for themselves or to impose upon each other Latin or Greek *cognomina*.[13] The sesquipedalian Oecolampadius seems to have told on More's nerves.[14] He used it toward the end of his *Supplication*, but then apparently made a point of employing a kind of Dutch-sounding form of the German original: the 1532–1533 edition of the *Confutation* writes it Husken, Huskyn, Huyskyn, sometimes spelt Huiskyn, or Huyskyne. An -s is occasionally added, making it Huskens, or Huyskyns. In Book VI (*CW 8*, 652/27), "saynt Huyskyns" immediately follows "saynte Huchyns," which probably betrays an intention to bring the two names as close to each other as possible in order to make Tyndale, alias Huchyns, share the odium which attaches to Oecolampadius, *né* Huyskyns, for denying the reality of the Blessed Sacrament. The purpose of the association becomes explicit toward the close of Book VI: why has Tyndale deserted Luther (on the real presence) to adopt the Basel heresy? Maybe "he fauored frere Huskyn, bycause his own name was Huchyn" (661/32). *Nomen omen:* not for shortness' sake alone is More partial to the German diminutive Huyskin against the majestic Grecian nom-de-plume.[15]

More is not hostile to the principle of Hellenizing vernacular names: he uses *Capnio* respectfully in referring to Reuchlin, and *Cochleus* almost affectionately in addressing Johann Dobneck, although the latter was not quite happy about the form of this pseudonym. Nor was Erasmus satisfied with the name he had chosen: when it was too late to modify it, he at least took care to have the adjectival form *Erasmius* used for his godson, Froben's son. More had no qualms about putting the two jarring forms side by side, when he exclaimed in a famous letter of 1517: *Erasme mi erasmiotate!*[16] The superlative must have touched his friend, whose initial purpose, somewhat clumsily attained because he knew too little Greek then, had been to emphasize the love root *eran* in his name, and his warmest friends attuned their expressions to this "accent."

Holy Writ, as we have seen, forbade any Christian to treat proper names indiscriminately as empty, merely conventional tags.[17] More, in his Tower meditation, pauses to enucleate the mystery of such Hebrew words as *Cedron, Gethsemani, Malchus.*[18] But his usual common sense strikes a balance between wholesale worship and utter contempt. When Juliet, distraught and desperate, asked "What's in a name," she still needed Romeo's name in the very act of urging him to "doff his name"; "gentle Romeo" and "fair Montague" are indispensable tools for her wooing and pleading, because, as she is discovering, a name clings to its bearer in a way no garb can: "Art thou not Romeo, and a Montague?"[19] The unpossessive Thomas More, the constant advocate of detachment from the unessential, causes some of the "silly souls" in his purgatory to confess and deplore their vain pride in their worshipful name. Instead of studying how we "might die penitent and in good christen plight," they say, we made provisions to "haue gay and goodly funerales," with full display of our helmets and coat-armors: "Then deuised we some doctor to make a sermon at our masse in our monthes mind, & there preache to our prayse with some fond fantasy deuised of our name."[20] More was to have no funeral but, both in his lifetime and after his death, an orgy of "fond fantasy" has been devised on his name in the various languages reached by his fame.

Erasmus may well have initiated the game: it certainly was irrevocable, once he had linked it with the very title and the preface of his best-selling book. Erasmus punned chiefly on names which their holders should learn to ponder, that is the Roman pontiffs, key-figures in Providence's salvific plan for mankind. After the pagan, hawkish names of Alexander and Julius, Leo X must prove a true lion, a meek user of his regal strength, while his Medici surname calls him to remedy the disease of Christ's mystical Body. The second Medici pope has chosen the name of Clement: may the augur prove true. His successor, baptized Alexander, rules as Paul III: Paulus betokens humility, modesty, littleness, to which Greek *paula* adds a pledge of calm and peace.[21]

Three Moorcocks and a Moor's Head

In England, as E. E. Reynolds wrote to me in 1963, "far more names come from places and trades than from nicknames." *More,* therefore, regardless of its (unsettled) spelling, "may have derived from early holders living near a moor or heath." Without pressing the point as if it were a proof, one might notice that More's father married Agnes Graunger in the parish of St. Giles outside the Cripplegate: now this gate, which guarded the North wall of London, led out into a vast marshy tract of land. How much "moor" there was about London is recorded in words such as Moorfields, Moorgate, Moreditch, Moorlane, not to mention the fen in *Fins*bury.[22] In the under-populated England of the middle ages, those reedy heaths were allowed to lie waste, which no doubt enabled a Richard Rolle to extend the word to the arid wildernesses of Palestine: "He brake the stane in the more" is his rendering of "interrupit petram in heremo."[23] The marshes across the Channel, some of them already reclaimed as polders for the needs of a dense population, were also called much as in English, despite the spelling *moer:* the Latinized forms *mora, morus* can be found in Flemish deeds and cartularies. A moer was overseen by a *moermeister.*[24]

If the English moors were wasteland for agriculture, they were a paradise for the red grouse, which was popularly called moorfowl. Hence, of course, the three moorcocks in More's escutcheon, the sable of their plumage relieved by the gules of their comb. Harmonizing with the black cocks is a Moor's head at the crest of the shield: a neat Negro profile, with the white teeth setting off the blackness of the skin.

The moorcock, despite the Latin transliterations we have encountered, was hardly meaningful outside of the vernacular. The blackamoor, on the other hand, spoke to all christendom: Maurus, or its popular variant Morus, was to all purposes a synonym of Niger, or Aethiops. In a letter of 1528 to Vives, when England was heading toward the divorce crisis, Erasmus conceals the identity of More by calling him *Niger:* "Nigro commiseram epistolam," he writes; "I had entrusted *the Moor* with my letter to Queen Catherine."[25]

More may have used the pun as early as July 16, 1517, when he comforted Erasmus over the attacks on the *Moria* of a certain Jean Briselot. The man was a former Carmelite, or White-friar, who had become a Benedictine, or black-monk. This mixture of white and black seems to call forth the buffoon's motley and to explain the sentence beginning "Niger ille Carmelita": "How can that black White-friar possibly attack *Folly,* being himself wholly compact of folly?"[26]

Given Erasmus' way with epithets, and his love of subtle paradox, he no doubt relished the piquancy of antiphrasis when, in 1519, he dwelt on the glowing whiteness of More's skin: "cute corporis candida; facies magis ad candorem vergit quam ad pallorem."[27] He may have had the beloved name in mind again when, in August 1535, wounded by the news of More's death, he praised the snow-white purity of his soul: "cui pectus erat omni nive candidius."[28]

Maurus

The ironic association of blackness with the fair-skinned and snow-white-souled Thomas More, adequately based on the ripe fruit of the common mulberry-tree, sometimes called "more berry," was supported and com-pounded, as we have seen, by the popular rendering of *Maurus* as *Morus,* in both spelling and pronunciation. "Vulgo Maurum vocant Morum" is one of G. Lister's first glosses to the *Moria.*[29] For English examples, we need not look outside of More's circle: his son John, when translating Damian a Gois' *The Legacy of Prester John* (1533), rendered "incredulorum Maurorum" by "mysbeleuyng Moers" or "myscreant Moers."[30] The French dispatches re-ferring to Charles V's North-African campaign of 1535 likewise speak repeatedly of "Turcs et autres Mores," etc. The literary form, showing aware-ness of the Latin model, retained the diphthong: thus Barthélemy Aneau, in his 1559 French edition of the *Utopia,* calls the author "Thomas Maure" (Gibson no. 20), a spelling one encounters fairly seldom because the original *Morus* prevailed on the Continent until this century. The -o- form predominated the more easily in family names because these, at least in French, are usually diminutives: Moreau, Morel, Moret, Morellet, Morin, Morot, Morois, Morillon, Moureau, Morant, Morisot, etc. Awareness of the stem was kept vivid by the nickname value of the word: thus an archbishop of Tours in the days of

Louis XI, called Jean Bernard, was referred to as "Moreau" simply because of his black hair and dark complexion.[31] A Moor's head, as black as the one in More's arms, figures in the printer's device not only of M. Lenoir,[32] but also of Martin Morin (Rouen): today the word *more* is hardly used to connote darkness, though it is still widely understood.

Maurus as African is a meaning which gave its Roman name—Mauretania— to much of North-Africa, and gives its present-name to the little Islamic Repub- lic of Mauritania, South of Morocco. The same toponym survives as Mortagne, Maurienne or some other French dress, in places either reached by the advanc- ing Moors after their conquest of Spain,[33] or else occupied by an African regi- ment of the Roman occupation army. A similar origin is ascribed to the fairly frequent place-name La Morinière, or Maurinière.

Maurus was also the name of a popular saint, the favorite disciple of St. Benedict, who sent him to Gaul. The story told by St. Gregory, in his im- mensely influential *Dialogues* (book 2), of how young Maurus at Subiaco miraculously saved his fellow-monk Placidus from drowning in the lake, con- tributed to Maurus' prestige. In France, where he settled and died, his name is stamped on the map with over twenty places called Saint-Maur, and another fifteen or so called Sainte-Maure. Guillaume Budé's *rus* or *pagus,* his equivalent to More's Chelsea, was Saint-Maur-des-Fossés, a few miles from Paris. It must have been pronounced something like "Sammor," judging from the way he writes it in Latin and in Greek.[34] In English, the duly de-nasalized result was Seymour, which Camden, no doubt correctly, derives from French Saint-Maur.

Partly because Glanfeuil, in the Loire valley,[35] where Maurus made his main foundation, was in Plantagenet territory, the Angevin kings fostered devotion to him in England. His feast-day on January 15 was a kind of land- mark in the calendar. "Maur" and "Benet" were rightly felt to belong together, as they do in Chaucer's Prologue to the *Canterbury Tales* (line 173): "The reule of seint Maure or of seint Benet." The saint's standing in medieval Flanders needs no other yardstick than Memling's featuring him with St. Christopher and St. Giles in his famous painting (Bruges, 1484).

A saint's name, then, further increased the spread of the polysemic syllable *Mor-* throughout Europe. Its Italian form won lasting fame through the Quat- trocento monk Fra Mauro, known to his age by a world-map (1459), and to ours by the lunar plain named for him. *Moro,* whatever its stem, has long been a banal name in Italy. The Duke of Milan, Lodovico Sforza, who died in France (1510) a prisoner of Louis XII, was nicknamed *Il Moro,* not, it would seem, because of his complexion, but because his model and emblem was the wary "moro," the mulberry-tree. A famous Alpine pass is called Monte Moro, and holidaying friends have sent me postcards of it: does it claim any Moorish connection? Or do its grey rocks look dark against the perennial snow of the surrounding summits?

Domenico Regi, in his very influential *Vita di Tommaso Moro* (1675),[36] makes his hero a "More of Venice." More's father, he claims, was a Venetian nobleman who sailed to London on business, and took an English wife. Through him, our More descended from Cristoforo Moro, the doge who in

1464 joined Pius II in Ancona with a fleet to check the pride of the Ottoman (Preface to the reader). Regi's book includes two parerga punning on the name of *Moro:* in the first, *mori* means "to die"; in the second, it is the genitive of *morus,* for mulberry.[37] The extreme currency of *Moro* as a surname in Italy— Aldo Moro has been the country's premier at least three times since 1960— would suffice to account for the naturalization of Thomas More's name as *Moro.* Sicily, at least in earlier days, perhaps because it lies closest to Africa, was most exposed to Moors in the geographical sense—Othello's sense. A younger contemporary of More—he died in 1589—is venerated as St. Benedict the Moor (il Moro): he was born in Sicily of African slaves. Another Sicilian of the period, who kept the French King's popinjays at Amboise, is called "Jérome le More" or "Jérome le Nigre" in court accounts.

Spanish, like its fellow Latin tongues, uses *moro* for "darkie": some Malay tribes in the Philippines were dubbed Moros on account of their skin, while the image of Our Lady of Guadalupe (which entered Mexican devotion as early as 1531) owed the epithet of Morena to its copperbrown Indian complexion. The Moorish occupation of Spain, however, and the crusading spirit of the Reconquista, gave prominence to the religious connotation of the word. The doughtiest knight was ready to sport as a *matamoro,* and the term was bound eventually to designate a species of the "Miles Gloriosus." This practical equating of *Moor* and *Muslim* is what gives point to Lope de Vega's epitaph for Thomas More (in *Rimas,* 1623): "Aquí yace un Moro Santo." The eight lines, with their luxuriance of verbal conceits, are quoted and analyzed in *Moreana,* 5 (February 1965), 36–37, by Francisco López Estrada, who then produces an allusive reference to the martyr as "un moro cristiano" from the *Criticón* of that other Siglo de oro Spaniard, Baltazar Gracián.

The Latin *Maurus* does not seem to convey this religious meaning to even a Counter-Reformation theologian such as Stapleton. A brief poem he composed on More's name reads as follows:

> More, nec es Maurus, quod vox sonat Anglica Mori,
>   Nec fatuus, quod vox Attica, *môros,* habet.
> Scilicet infausti correxit nominis omen
>   Et vigor & candor maximus ingenij.

Clearly, as the vigor of More's genius gives the lie to Greek *moron,* its *candor,* or fairness, contradicts the black in English *moor* (Latin *Maurus*).[38]

The More Tree

A visit to More's mulberry-tree was a regular treat for each pilgrim to the site of his Chelsea house as long as the Adoration Réparatrice sisters had their convent there. The tree claims to have been planted by Sir Thomas' own hand. But why a mulberry? The more-tree in Morton's heraldic rebus gives one answer. Another lies in the biblical and classical associations of "morus." Erasmus borrows from Pliny's *Natural History* a remark about the irony of the name: *môrus* means foolish, and yet no plant is shrewder. Its flower blossoms late, so it is less exposed to deadly frosts; and then, to make up for the tardy start, the sprouting takes place within one night, so fast that you can hear the burst: rightly then is it hailed as the wisest of trees.[39] Its wisdom became proverbial. Alciati has an emblem on it. In Cesaro Ripa Perugino's *Iconologia* (Rome 1603), the helmet of Wisdom is garlanded with "foglie del moro," "il tardo moro" as the caption calls it. In French, *mûre* also designates the berry of another species, the wild blackberry, which grows, on bushes called brambles, all over the European countryside. The black mulberry—*morus nigra*—was common in Pliny's Italy (XXI: 21), and the Peloponnesus owed the nickname of *Morea*—a Greek form of the word—to being overgrown with it.

This marvellous berry, says Pliny, looks younger as it grows older, because age, which makes the rest of us hoary, blackens it (LXXIX: 2).[40] Blackness, however, has its "darker" symbolism, which can involve the Prince of Darkness himself.[41] In late Latin the words *Maurus* and *morus* tended to coalesce under the simpler spelling; thus two converging etymologies made *moro* a synonym of *nigro*.

The habit of sitting "sub moro" for learned confabulation added to the humanist appeal of the mulberry,[42] but the Plinian encomia suffice to its Morean relevance; the seventeenth-century exegete Cornelius à Lapide, commenting on Luke 17: 6, after quoting Pliny's tribute to the wisest of plants, turned to the plant's namesake and said: "Likewise, Thomas More, England's Chancellor, was the wisest of men."

The trees called in Greek *sykaminos* and *sykomoros,* beside sharing the syllable whereby they belong with the fig-tree, share the distinction of appearing in the Gospel of Luke, and not far apart either: in 17: 6 and 19: 4. The Vulgate translates them respectively as *arbor morus* (hence Wiclif's "more tree" at 17: 6) and *sycomorus*. Erasmus, in his *Annotations* on the New Testament,[43] examines their botanical identity more than their allegorical significance. He adds a third word, Celsus' *morosykos,* or "foolish fig-tree." Despite the short -o- of *moros* in these compounds, he advocates linking those trees with the mulberry, whose foliage has affinities with theirs. Now, in Greek *môra, môrea,* there is an *omega,* and the root-vowel of the Latin equivalent *môrus* is also long, as appears from the scansion in Ovid and Palladius (the fourth-century agriculturist). Thus the Lucan trees are eligible too for "silly" symbolism.

As if to atone for the tedious indecorous punning of Brixius, another Canon of Notre Dame, Ludovicus Rumetius, of Abbeville, dedicated to More one of the sixty groves in his "Orchard of Holy Writ," or *Scripturae Sacrae Viridarium.*[44] To match the biblical figure of Jezebel, heresy has provided another royal harlot who has splashed herself with the blood not of the mulberry but of Thomas More: "non mori sanguine, sed Thomae Mori."[45] The More *arboretum* (no. 16) ends with a couplet which has a twofold pun, *mori* (of the more-tree) and *mori* (to die): see the text in *Gibson,* no. 492. Francisco López Estrada, in an article "Sobre las ediciones del *Tomás Moro, de Fernando de Herrera,"*[46] wonders whether the Neo-Latin poet is here indebted to Gongora's sonnet addressed to Don Christoval de Mora, which also plays with "noble berries" and "blood."

A post-Plinian addition to the accomplishments of the mulberry was its service to the silkworm. This too was in due time extended to More. Domenico Regi ends his *Vita di Tomaso Moro* (1675) with these Latin words: "Mori folia utilia & dulces fructus," "the *more's* foliage is useful, and sweet are its fruits." The sericultural mulberry-tree is *morus alba,* the white variety.

Only a few years later, at Graz, Austria, Stapleton's *Vita Mori* was published as a companion to More's *Opera Omnia Latina* (1689). An engraving of More occupies in the frontispiece a medallion garlanded with mulberry-leaves on which silkworms are feeding. Below, in a flowery cartouche, four lines play on *morus* and *Morus* (plus *moribus*), inviting the young reader[47] to spin a moral coccoon of wisdom and virtue from More's examples, to be "the bombyx of *this* mulberry-tree."[48]

The Chelsea Convent was host in 1929 to a large scale Thomas More Exhibition with a set of lectures on *The Fame of Blessed Thomas More,* the shortest of which—Chesterton's—is included in this book. That event may have prompted the *Southwark Record* of April 1929 to publish a poem "by the late Father Bampfield" on "The Mulberry Tree of Blessed Thomas More," which provides some warm strains to wind up this section.

> In pleasant mockery of his lowly self,
> One of God's fools, far wiser than the wise . . .
> Planted a mulberry tree, on his own name
> Ringing the changes . . .
> A tree which readily pours forth its blood,
> Bearing unstinted berries, and each fruit
> Opening its veins for every one who plucks
>   . . . and with its leaves
> Feeding the worm that clothes high queens in silk.[49]

Morian = Men of Inde = Negro

Morian, in present-day English, like *morien* in French, can hardly mean anything else than "belonging to Thomas More." But in the days of his flesh, Morian was synonymous with Blackamore, Blackmoor, or man of Inde. The best spots for studying these terms in an age of biblical translations are the verses where the land of Cush is mentioned: Num. 12: 1 (with its double mention of Moses' Cushite wife), 2 Kings 19: 9, Psalms 68: 31 and 87: 4. The Vulgate equivalent is Aethiopia, which in popular etymology came from a Greek word meaning "burnt-facedom"—the land where a torrid sun scorches men's complexions into an indelible black, in addition to frizzling their hair and swelling their lips.

Luther's word—"Morenland, dem Moren, eine Morinne zum Weibe"—may have contributed to the prevalence of the same root in the earliest Anglican versions: his "dem Könige der Moren" seems to have inspired Tyndale's "King of the black mores" (in the Matthew Bible), which Coverdale changed to "the Morians" (2 Kings 19: 9). The Prayer-Book version of the Psalms (1549) retains "the Morians" both in Ps. 68: 31 and 87: 4. Later versions of the Bible—

Geneva, Douai, King James—returned to the time-honored *Ethiopia,* used by both Vulgate and classical Latin to designate the land of unchangeably dark skins. This region lay south of Egypt, along the upper reaches of the Nile; it corresponded to North Sudan (Roman Nubia), not modern Abyssinia. Jeremiah (13: 23) alludes to the negroid complexion of the Cushites, who, in Egyptian art too, appear as Negroes.[50]

More never uses the word Morian in his references to negritude. When he says "man of Inde," he means black, as is clear from the following remark: "For no man is so mad that will recken that thing for pleasant, that hath with litle plesure much pain. For so might we call a man of Inde white, because of his whit teeth."[51] The equivalence between Inde and Ethiopia was not new, or peculiar to English: Erasmus, in an Adage, renders by *Aethiopem* the word *Indicon* found in a Lucianic epigram.[52] Tyndale, who describes Tirhakha's subjects as "black mores" in 2 Kings, calls Moses' Midianite bedfellow "his wife of Inde . . . one of India," in his rendering of Numbers. The equivalence, though received, was not obvious: hence the gloss to "the black Ethiopian" in Grafton's *Chronicle* (ed. 1569, p. 559): "That is a man of Inde, commonly called a black Moryan." The sophisticated *Ethiopian* is clearly asserting itself, and relegating the alternatives to the margin. The native Midian of Moses' wife is called Ethiopia, says a note in the Geneva Bible, because it borders on Ethiopia and is included in the definition: given that congenital vagueness, the term did practical duty for all of Black Africa, indeed for all of Negrodom. We shall soon find More calling Thomas the Apostle "St. Thomas of Inde": the impact of the geographic discoveries had not yet been such that one could distinguish, at least in popular literature, between the Dravidians of the Malabar Coast and the Sudanese of biblical Cush or imperial Nubia. The term proved elastic enough to be used of the Amerindians, when transatlantic discovery added their brick- or copper-like complexion to the other varieties of non-white skins: their being outside the spiritual pale of Western Christendom was one trait that likened them to the populations scattered in the Arab lands and in the unknown beyond, faraway to the South and the East.

Master Moron?

The Greek word which has survived in our *moron* (for very low IQ) has begotten the deservedly most famous pun on More's name. It owes much of its success to the genius of Erasmus, and to the uninterrupted popularity of his *Encomium Moriae.* The little book was dashed off under More's roof at Bucklersbury in the gleeful summer of 1509,—the first of Henry VIII, who had just turned eighteen. It was published in Paris in 1511. All languages of culture, including Hebrew and Japanese, boast one or more translations of it. The pun on More's name, especially when the work is referred to as just *Moria,*[53] is clear enough in the title, and made quite explicit in the dedicatory letter to More. Riding northward from Italy, Erasmus says, and looking forward to England, and especially to you, dear More, I began to muse on your surname, "which is as near to the Greek word for folly, *moria,* as you are far from it in fact."[54] The whole page bears reading over and over again; it contains, among other gems, the phrase *omnium horarum hominem* which has won such fame in its early Tudor garb as "a man for all seasons."[55] Within the book itself, "Folly" refers to More when she tells of one whose name is akin to hers, and, at a deeper level, may have the young hair-shirted lawyer in mind when, having donned the lionskin to hide the long ears and hush the little bells of her fools-cap, she tells us "another story" and praises a higher "kind of madness and folly," the lifestyle ("at full odds with commonsense") of a man "wholly possessed by the ardor of Christian piety."[56]

It seems, from other hints, that early in life More impressed Erasmus as someone determined to play the full Gospel game of loss-and-gain. The public read the pun at a lower and simpler level, as suggested by the preface: the teasing incongruity between the brilliant mind and the moronic patronym. Erasmus himself repeats his pun in a letter to More of June 1516, when in Pauline fashion he begs leave to talk nonsense: "With Master Moron," he writes, "I shouldn't fear to mouth ineptitudes."[57]

In a letter of 1518, Guillaume Budé expressed his embarrassment at having to address as *Morus,* that is "Mr. Blunt," the sharpest and shrewdest of his pen-friends. Let me, he said, double the name into Oxymorus, and he did end his letter with *Vale, mi Oxymore:* "Farewell, bright Mr. Moron" (or "my sharp Blunt"), adding in Greek *mallon de morosophe:* "or rather foolish sage."[58] The Paris hellenist, a nice weigher of words, could not be unaware that *môro-sophos* had been used in a derogatory sense by Lucian, and by Erasmus, both in the *Moria* (Garnier, p. 14) and in the *De Copia* (I: 9): the definition here of the "morosopher" as a fool who thinks himself wise may have paved the way to More's coining of "foolosophy" in his 1532 letter answering Frith: "thys yong mannes vayn childysh folosophy" (*Rogers,* p. 462/810). By using the term against such odds, Budé raises the compliment to the heights of thought or vision from the rhetorical level of the pointed phrase called oxymoron. More is not only a clever manipulator of the language, but a profound and inspired wizard; a year earlier, Budé, prefacing the Paris edition of the *Utopia,* had stressed the "seminal" quality of the wisdom hidden under the fanciful, at times absurd crust of Hythlodaeus' prating.

A startling pun in the final section of Erasmus' *Moria* scandalized some morose readers of his day, and escapes most readers of our day because they are unfamiliar with the Vulgate. After depicting the "preposterous" ways of true christians—those crazy lovers—Folly says: "Haec est *Moriae pars, quae non aufertur* . . . ," a clear echo of Jesus' saying: *"Maria optimam partem* eligit, *quae non auferetur* ab ea" (Luke 10: 42). It may be that the pun was "made in England," where long *a* has always tended to a dark *o*-like quality. Now the Catholic homiletic tradition, encouraged by liturgical usage, had extended to the Virgin Mary herself the praise bestowed by Christ on Martha's sister: both had chosen the best part (in defiance of common sense) by preferring contemplation to action, "idle sitting" to efficient house-keeping. More in his turn was to side repeatedly with the mad excesses of Mary-Magdalen against the sober ethics of the Reformers.[59]

Although he was a church-man, Germain de Brie, a prebendary of Notre-Dame in Paris, ignored not only the mystical connotations in Erasmus' *Moria,* but the very gist of his basic antiphrasis. Rather foolishly, as even his friends agreed, he took *môros* in its literal sense throughout the pamphlet *Antimôrus* (1519), taxing More with real stupidity and crass ignorance. More's crime had been a few epigrams ridiculing Brixius' chauvinistic *Chordigera,* but the French humanist launched a wholesale attack on his Latin poems, including the 1509 Ode on Henry VIII's coronation. Deeply stung and galled, More retorted with a pen dipped in gall; Erasmus prevailed on him not to publish the letter, which was already in print, however, and has therefore come down to us. I have earlier quoted his taunt about wanton puns from surnames, such as making the Venetian scholar Barbaro a barbarian. "Your *Antimôros* is actually a *môros* through its genuine folly . . . Far worse, because its furious tone, its shrill invectives breathe a maniacal spirit."[60]

The breeze of Anglo-French reconciliation helped More and de Brie bury the war-hatchet. They both attended on their respective sovereigns at the June 1520 encounter of the Cloth of Gold, and rather liked each other (More was truly "born for friendship"). Budé, too, was present and met More in the flesh. Hence the extra touch of affection in his next letter, of May 23, 1521. Here he leaves out the artificiality of a modified name, but the philologist in him remains haunted and disturbed by the standing lie of *Morus:* "with that candid irony of yours, and festive urbanity, spiced with innocent tropes . . . you are anything but what you are called."[61] My rendering hugs the Latin on purpose, retaining the words on which the sentence hinges: *candida,* applied to the white salt of More's humor, denies the blackness portended by *Maurus,* while *urbanitas festiua* gives the lie to the morose and boorish obtuseness which *Môrus* can also connote.

A few years later, it was Vives' turn to join the friendly game: writing to Francis Cranevelt in 1525, when relations were tense between More's England and their own Flanders, he concealed More's name under a protracted Greek circumlocution: "the man most like a fool in name, but most unlike one in deed."[62] This letter was not meant for More to read, and he probably never knew of it. But he must have enjoyed, beyond such affectionate playing with his name, the challenge, if not the omen, inherent in it. When I visited Canon de Vocht at his Louvain-house, in 1954, he showed me the autograph of More's short letter thanking the young priest and scholar Conrad von Gockelen for the dedication of a work translated from Lucian. "Do you," he said, "notice the accent on Morùs? He may have been alluding to the Greek *môròs,* which does bear the accent on the second syllable. And well he might, because the letter accompanied a cup full of gold coins, a real folly about which he cannot have consulted his sensible wife."[63]

Many an extravagant gesture of this kind, and his habit (recorded by Erasmus) of giving money away even when he was in debt, prepared Thomas More for the ordeal which demanded the folly of the cross. The remarks of his triumphant enemies when he is in disgrace or in prison, and even those of his dismayed family and friends, are almost verbatim repetitions of the Roman governor's angry shout at St. Paul: "you're raving. All this study is driving you mad" (Acts 26: 24). Unable, like the apostle, to prove his sober truth, More could only proclaim his loyal troth. The accusation of folly is exposed in a beautiful letter, in which Margaret Roper purports to relate to her stepsister Alice Alyngton her last visit to their father in the Tower. Alice had been the recipient of an earlier letter, from no less a person than Thomas Audley, More's successor as Lord Chancellor: there a transparent fable of Aesop put More in the role of the man who retired to his cave while all the remnant were having their brains washed away by a mad rain: the wise loner proved the worst fool of them all, because the crowd of lunies—*nodies* is More's word[64]—refused to be ruled by his wisdom. The prisoner won't recognize himself in the odd sage, but he humbly—perhaps with humble pride?—acknowledges his folly:

> How be it doughter Roper, whome my Lorde taketh here for the wyse men and whome he meaneth to be fooles, I cannot very well gesse, I can not reade such riddles. For as Dauus saith in Terence (Non sum Oedipus) I may say you wot well (Non sum Oedipus, sed Morus) which name of mine what it signifieth in Greke, I nede not tel you. But I trust my Lorde rekeneth me amonge the foles, and so reken I my selfe, as my name is in Greke. And I finde, I thanke God, causes not a fewe, wherfore I so shoulde in very dede. (Rogers, p. 519/183f)

Another fable in Audley's message likened More to "the folish scrupelous asse," that had a sore conscience "for taking of a strawe for hungar out of his maisters shoo" (p. 520/224). No offence was meant in these clumsy attempts to save the prisoner, and More took no offence. His mention of "My lord Cardinal" (p. 518) makes it probable that he remembered the scene when, all alone of the King's council, he had opposed Wolsey's ambition to be appointed High Constable. When the Cardinal rebuked the foolish Councillor who dared "dissent from so many noble and prudent men," More replied: "God must be highly thanked that the King's Highness has but one fool in his supreme Council."[65]

A fool he remained even unto death. Edward Hall, who knew of the merry mocking spirit of a man he had watched since at least as early as 1523 when More was Speaker of the Commons, records in his *Chronicle* the special problem put to him by More's jesting at the scaffold: "I cannot tell," he writes, "whether I should call him a foolish wise man or a wise foolish man." Fifty years later Stapleton published a Greek distich answering the chronicler's jibe. The words *morosophos* and *sophomoros* give the epigram a pointedness which is lacking in the Latin couplet, and in P. E. Hallett's rendering:

> To thee, fond Hall, seems More both fool and wise:
> A fool to men may wise be in God's eyes.[66]

Hall's formula crystalized, if not public opinion, at least the sentiment of the solemn, humorless Tudor burghers who found their prophets in Tyndale and Joye, and then Fox. George Joye had enough Greek to know that *môros,* a key-term in the New Testament (and hardly less ambivalent there than in Erasmus' *Moria*), meant *fool;* he informed his public of the fact on the very title page of his *Subversion of More's Foundation* (1534): "Moros in Greke is stultus in Latyn/a fool in Englysshe."

One French scholar abused More in the heyday of his favor; another French scholar reviled him on the morrow of his death—and used the same well-tried tool—the pun on *môros*. Nicolas Bourbon, a parasite under the protection of Anne Boleyn, stigmatized the martyr to "please the party who were dominant."[67] A better poet than that sycophantic versifier, and one attuned in soul to Thomas More, Francis Thompson will provide our parting lines on the theme of More's folly, even though he need not have been thinking of the far-reaching pun:

> Ah! happy Fool of Christ, unawed
> By familiar sanctities . . .
> You served your Lord at holy ease!
> Dear Jester in the courts of God—
> In whose spirit, enchanting yet,
> Wisdom and love, together met,
> Laughed on each other for content![68]

Morosus?

We have encountered several puns by Plautus on *morus* and various realizations of the root *mos/moris*, which is represented in English by *mores* for "manners" or folkways, by *moral*, and even by *morose:* moroseness being the peevish wilful condition of one who follows his *morem*, his every mood, instead of tempering his humors with reason and charity. The opposite to this vice, then, is a sense of humor, which controls these fickle humors which mar life in society.

Moroseness was a mortal sin against the humanist ideal, and Erasmus often warns the young against it. Of course there was not the least touch of it about More, hence the possibility of friendly punning, as used by Budé in 1519: "No letter this year?" he asks. "Has sweet *Morus* changed for me to *morosus?*"[69] In an Ode published in April of the same year, Whittinton used *morosus* as a foil to *moriger,* in praise of More's engaging affability. The following "hexastichon" of the London grammarian launches into a cascade of verbal *concetti,* four puns within the six lines of verse: on *morus* the tree, *mores, mora* the delay, and *amor.*[70] The apheresis whereby More's name was found in the ablative *amore* was an accepted game, and posed no serious linguistic problem, since *mo* bears the stress (and the length); least so in Tudor English, which often left out the first syllable in words like apostle, apprentice. Even Old English offers the kind of variants which survive in such pairs as bide/abide, rise/arise, round/around. So Whittinton has more support than just Plautus' *Trinummus* to justify his last and boldest pun. Nor did Caspar Cunradus the Silesian need any one model to write his distich beginning *Morus Amoris Amor* (1615).[71] One might therefore wonder whether More, or some of his readers, did not hear the ring of his name when they created or discovered Amaurotum: *amauros* is but the

longer twin of *mauros* (*maurus*), both betokening the same smoky or smoggy
swarthiness.

The *mores/Morus* pun is so plain that it was bound to multiply. It certainly
constitutes the point of Fowler's caption under the engraving of More in the
1568 *Epistola* ("*moral* portrait not so easy to achieve"); it may flavor Sagun-
dino's 1521 letter to Musuro describing More as "vere optimorum morum
insigne exemplar,"[72] and John Constable's 1520 poem "ad Thomam Morum."[73]
Through the mediation of the proverb *Honores mutant mores,* or "Honors
change manners," it produced a merry exchange between Sir Thomas More and
Sir Thomas Manners, which has come down to us along various channels, notably
John Hoddesdon (1652, Gibson, nos. 104–105). Franklin B. Williams has found
it in *Joe Miller's Jests: or, The Wits Vade-Mecum,* of 1739.[74] Authentic or not,
the anecdote does not lack felicity: the proverb had wide currency, even in
Latin, as is proved by the two lines in the scurrilous pamphlet *Rede me and be
not wroth* (Strasbourg 1528),

> I perceive well now that honores,
> As it is spoken, mutant mores,

perhaps a sly attack on More, too popular in 1528 for an open attack. As Manners and More were together in the king's service, especially on occasions like
the Field of the Cloth of Gold, they may have been familiar enough for
reciprocal teasing.

Erasmus' longest "Memento Mori" has little to do with death; it fills chapter
32 of the first part of his *De duplici copia: verborum et rerum* with 200 stylistic variations on the theme: "My dear More is never absent from my mind."
The words *memor* and *memoria* are usually placed close enough to More's
name to constitute an alliterative cluster: "Mori memoria" (22, 56, 116, 195),
"Mori mei memoria" (98), "Morica memoria" (85, 131), "mea memoria
Morus" (170), "Mori immemor erit" (45). Death does appear in item 162,
which might serve by way of sample: "Clavis adamantinis nostrae memoriae
infixus est Morus, quos non nisi una mors valeat abrumpere: More is fastened
to our memory by adamantine nails, which nothing but death alone is able to
break." Had it not been a rhetorical exercise, he would have said, "not even
death."[75]

One last pun, a paltry one, occurs toward the end of *The Supper of the
Lord,* a work written probably by George Joye, to refute "M. Moris letter
agenst Johan Frythe." More quotes and dismisses the taunt in the *Answer to
the Poisoned Book* (*EW,* 1037 D) as follows: '"Maister mocke whom the
veriti most offendeth, and doth but mocke it out when he can not soile it, he
knoweth me well inoughe." Thys sadde and sage ernest man that mocking at
myne name, calleth me master Mocke, doth in these wise woordes nothynge
but mocke the readers of hys booke.'

Memento Mori

Thomas More was a zealous devotee of that highest philosophy which

Socrates defined as meditating upon death, and an eager disciple of Qoheleth, who said: "Remember thy last ends, and thou shalt never sin."[76] Pages on death are scattered throughout his writings, in English and Latin, from the "pageants" he penned in his father's house to the "godly meditations" of his prison days. The words "memento mori" were his motto if ever they were anybody's. It may be their very pun value that kept them out of More's comments on death: should the warning be divested of its starkness, and the mind thus distracted from the *unum necessarium*? The qualms of the disciplined ascetic might have been compounded by the fastidiousness of the artist, reluctant to practise the phonetic legerdemain which turns the *mŏri* of dying into the *Mōri* of his name? With Luther's name, remember, he did not have to play any such trick: the forms *Luderus, Ludherus* had been used by Luther and his friends. There is the posthumous story of More's greeting one of his debtors with the words: "Memento Mori." To dodge the reminder, the debtor replied with "Memento morieris," which he thought proof against any interpretation other than "remember thou shalt die." But ruthless More retorted: "Memento Mori aeris," "remember More's money." No problem to the eye, but orally it meant altering the stress or the length of two syllables. The debtor, if he existed, must have been a consummate Latinist to get the message through the ear.

Anyway, the initial pun was inevitable, so it keeps reappearing. In the elegant dialogue of *IL MORO*, which Ellis Heywood published in 1556, when he was only thirty, a certain Paul shows the rest of the party "a ring on his finger, which bears the inscription Memento Mori." Lawrence the merchant would not mind wearing that golden ring, but he is allergic to its message. I will wear it, he says, "provided it be understood to put me in mind, not of death, but of you, Mr. More: non della morte, ma di voi, Signor Moro."[77]

A similar pun occurs in Thomas Linaeus' epitaph for Erasmus: "Moro ne careat, non fugit ipse mori," in Alan Cope's distich on More's death: "Quis Moro nolit sic moriente mori?" and in a terse line by John Fowler: "Te fecit vere vivere, More, mori."[78]

French, in its present phonetic stage, makes no perceptible difference between *More, Maure,* and *mort,*[79] which can create embarrassing puns in spoken treatments of More's death, as it also prompts deliberate punning. I remember a harassed confrère sighing from the thorny bush of his entanglements with tramps and lunies and other social cases: "Thomas More is lucky, he is dead!" The rueful humor came through in English, but French adds the grace, however prosaic, of a sturdy rhyme: "Thomas More a de la chance—il est mort!" The Sioux cemetery entered in the maps of Missouri as *Butte de More* was originally "de mort" or "des morts." Henry Brabant has discovered an actual pilgrimage to "Saint Mort" at Haillot, near Huy on the River Meuse (Flemish Maas); he adds that this saint was often confused with St. Maur.[80]

Moratory

Latin *mora*, with a short -o-, means a space of time, and survives as *more* in the parlance of musicians, the root vowel having grown somewhat longer to compensate for the loss of the end vowel. A similar lengthening was current in the speech of early imperial Rome. The verb *moror/morari,* which meant to pause, to delay, to beat time, eventually to waste time, would be made, when pronounced with a long -o-, to connect with Greek *môros,* and to connote foolish behavior. The Hellenomania prevailing in society made this a fashionable game, and Erasmus in *De Copia* (I, 9), quoting Suetonius (no. 33 of his *Twelve Caesars*), tells how Nero loved to say that his predecessor Claudius had ceased *"mōrari"* (that is "to play the fool") on earth, instead of saying "to abide" among men: *mŏrari.*

This classic precedent underlies the Latin quatrain More composed upon his name a few years before his death, and which was first published by John Fowler along with More's *Responsio ad Pomeranum* (Louvain 1568).[81] The circumflex accents help the reader scan the lines, where the long -o- for stupidity (in *mōraris, mōrari, mōrus*) alternates with the short -o- for staying on earth (*mŏrandi, mŏrari*), More's own name providing the hinge and the refrain.[82]

More loved Suetonius, he also loved Plautus, whose comedy reflects the language of the Roman streets and shops. The Greek ingredient here was due, of course, to the high percentage of slaves and other recent immigrants in the lower strata of the population. When they hurled at each other the *môros* of abuse, or its Latin replica *môrus,* the older citizens could understand it as easily as New Yorkers guess at the meaning of *tonto* in an Italian neighborhood, or of *loco* among Mexicans or Puerto-Ricans. As one should expect, the funny drawl occurs on stage between characters with Greek names: thus the "Morus es! You fool!" thrown by Periplectomenes at Pleusicles in *Miles Gloriosus* (III, i, 78). The game becomes more sophisticated in *Trinummus* (III, ii, 43), where a cascade of long o's creates a sense of woe. Says, or sighs, Lysiteles: "Ita est amor ... Atque is mores hominum moros et morosos efficit."[83] A crude literal paraphrase might yield something like: "These amours will mar men's morals and morale, making all mortals as morose as morons." Much as if Puck exclaimed: "What morons these mortals be!"[84] If we return to *Miles Gloriosus,* we find a Philocomasia as clever as Nero at the *moror* double entendre: "Ego stulta moror multum/quae cum hoc insano fabuler" (II, iv, 17). Given the double epithet *stulta* and *insano,* she clearly does not mean just "I am spending lots of time ... ," but "it's sheer nonsense of me to waste so much time chatting with this idiot," or "The fool that I am is proving real mad indeed, thus chatting with an idiot."[85]

These rather cheap histrionic effects, quite acceptable on the comic stage, would be out of place in more decorous genres. *Moror,* in its normal Latin sense of remaining—preserved in French *demeurer*—was nobly used in Horace's famous Ode to Mecaenas: "If a hasty fate wrenches thee away, who art one half of my soul, why do I, the other half, linger behind: *quid moror altera?*" (II, Od. 17.5). More must have had these lines in mind when, in his *Carmen Gratulatorium* for the wedding and coronation of Henry VIII and Catherine of Aragon, he evokes the "many years" which the Infanta stayed alone in England after the untimely death of Prince Arthur: "Solā tui longā mansit amōre mōrā." The prosodic alternation is so delicately poised! And the bride's long wait is turned into an amorous mooring in the uncertain roadsteads of hope (*B. & L.*, p. 21).

The suckfish Pride retarding the advance of the fair vessel Progress puts another measure of the same unobtrusive music in *Utopia:* "velut remora retrahit ac remoratur" (*CW 4,* 244/1). If the fish, as Pliny says, owes its name to its hindering ways (*ibid.*, p. 565), the word-play involves a plain repetition, to which More never objects. He could have exploited the *mor-* syllable more fully, by substituting "remorae more" or "remorae ad morem" for "velut remora," but it suited his purpose, or his ear, better to emphasize the prefix— *re-* for resistance!

We have encountered the diminutive Morillon among the many patronyms stemming from *Maurus/Morus* (the blackamoor).[86] A Burgundian friend of Erasmus went by that name: this Guy Morillon, "vice-secretary of Utopia" as he once termed himself, held a real secretarial position in Charles V's administration, which meant a prolonged stay in Spain (1525–1531). When a letter took a year to reach him, Erasmus accused the mail, and excused the sender, "although his surname apparently derives from *moror* (delay): licet a morando cognomen videatur sortitum."[87]

"More and More"

The simplest and crudest pun is afforded by the English comparative *more.* In the sixteenth-century, and even in Shakespeare and the King James Version of the Bible, its main use was as adjective, meaning *greater*. The line "More is Thy mercy far than all our sin," in More's rendering of Pico's prayer (stanza 4) represents that usage. The *Supplication* has a "merry tale" of a young gallant asking an austere barefoot friar why he took such pain: "And he aunswered that it was very little payn, if a man would remember hel. Ye frere quod the galant, but what and there be none hell? than art thou a great foole. Ye master quod the frere, but what and there be hell? than is youre maistershyppe a muche more foole."[88] More's domestic fool, Harry Pattenson, once said flatteringly: "A king cannot make a Sir Thomas More." "He can," the master retorted. "The King can make me Chancellor of the realm, then he will make Sir Thomas *more.*"

All modern biographers of More—at least since Lord Campbell's *Lives of the Chancellors* (1845)—have repeated the nostalgic quatrain born of More's legendary dispatch as head of the judiciary:

> When More some time had Chancellor been
> No more suits did remain.
> The same shall nevermore be seen
> Till More be there again.

The success of Robert Bolt's *A Man For All Seasons* prompted more than one journalist to adopt or adapt the simple cry in Oliver Twist: "Oliver wants more! All the people want MORE." They keep up a tradition well-established in the Elizabethan play *The Book of Sir Thomas More:* thus Randall there, disguised in his master's apparel, complete with the gold chain, says to Erasmus "I am neither more nor less than merry Sir Thomas always." The ruffian Falkner further in that scene (III, i) seems to be also punning on More and Moreditch, and Sir Thomas himself may be doing so here and there.

We still say "the more is the pity," but they used to say Cato the More, and St. James the More (for "the Elder," that is "the greater"), and pilgrims would describe Santa Maria Maggiore basilica as Mary-the-More. The Northern form was Mair, the name of the Sorbonne professor in Erasmus' day who signed his books "Joannes Major." The same root in the various Celtic languages accounts for such place-names as Kilmore, Baltimore and Brynmawr, or as Lanmeur and Coëtmeur (in Brittany).

Although the word, then, means *great* or *greater,* and did not become a (weakened) function-word until the modern period, it was already so common that one should limit the spotting of allusions to the cases when it bears a stress. The game has continued to our day: in a delightful pastiche of Love-lace's "To Lucasta," Eric L. Mascall inscribes "To a dignitary who spoke contemptuously of a saint" a twelve-line poem ending:

> "I could not love thee, Dean, so much
> Loved I not Thomas More."[89]

A Chime of Rhymes

In a Skeltonic poem written in 1961, at the Thomas More Project, by the late Davis Harding, *More,* thus spelt, rhymes with *lure, Fleur, cure, whoor* (sic), *Gower, boor,* and . . . *Marc'hadour!* Not even excluding *Gower,* as long as it is made to rhyme with Mower—a frequent (and perhaps etymologic) variant of More, documents from Tudor days prove the poet right in every instance. In the English of Southern Britain, he could have added *maw,* but in Tudor times the -r- was still firmly sounded, hence the dissyllable of a genitive like "Moris" (More's) in our quote from G. Joye. A dark -u- sound is suggested by the spelling *Moure* in the French dispatches of Jean du Bellay and of Chapuys, whether they speak of Thomas More or of Wolsey's castle and by "Tomas *Mur*" in the Spanish *Cronica de Enrique VIII.* Remember that Shakespeare's characters could still pun on *Rome* and *room;* that Roper, Pole, are often written Rooper, Poole, while Paul in early editions of More is usually spelt Powle, or Poule. The glide which appears in John More's *Prester John,* with the spelling *moers,* broadens in the next generation into *Moare.* This variant, without extinguishing the rhyme with *lure* (though many speakers link it with the written form *moor*), is reflected in spellings such as *Moa,* to transliterate the Japanese interpretation of *More.*[90]

Thomas

If More's surname—whether spelt thus, or Mor, Moor, Moore mattered not at all—was fairly common in early Tudor England, his christian name, Thomas, was second only to John as a boy's given name. No doubt because John the Baptist, as well as John the Evangelist, are exceptionally appealing figures in the New Testament and therefore great favorites of popular piety through liturgy, homily and iconography, the name of John was an easy winner in all the provinces and languages of christendom. Ivan and Ivanowicz, Ian and Hans, Hansen and Hanson, testify to its vogue as eloquently as John and Jack or Jones, Johnson, Jackson, Jenkins and Johnston. The typical Englishman was ready to be called and to call himself John Bull because his language had used *john* and *jack* in literally scores of everyday derivations, from *jackass* to *Union Jack*. Where English differs from all other "christian" languages is that "Jack-of-all-trades" has a twin, namely "Tom-of-all-trades." Both are, on an almost equal footing, names of all seasons. Likewise, "Jack-Tar," the Navy's everyman, has a counterpart in the Army private, Tommy Atkins.

That England alone witnessed this proliferation of Thomases is obviously due to the immense prestige of St. Thomas Becket, "the holy blissful martyr" to whose shrine in Canterbury long processions of pilgrims walked or rode or drove "from every shire's end." London in particular prided itself on the saint born in its commercial heart, at Cheapside. Despite the fame of the Norman Conqueror, and a number of Williams in the annals of the middle ages (such as Ockham) and in More's close acquaintances (his son-in-law Roper, Warham, Grocin, Latimer, Mountjoy), this name was less typically English than Thomas. The cosmopolitan Erasmus found some William at every turn of his life since the age of ten, as he says to one of them, Budé, in 1517.[91] Becket's hallowed name gathered further momentum when another Chancellor of England, Bishop Thomas of Hereford (d. 1282) was canonized. Its vogue seems to have culminated precisely in Thomas More's days. One requires no special interest in names to be struck by the Henrician pleiad of Thomases: Wolsey, and Audley who respectively preceded and succeeded More as holders of the Great Seal; Norfolk, Cromwell and Cranmer, who, sometimes together, conducted his examination in the Tower. Four of the twelve jurymen on whose verdict his life depended went by the name of Thomas: this percentage seems close enough to the national average.

A child's name used to be chosen by the sponsor at baptism, who was often one of the grandparents. With Thomas Graunger and Thomas More for his grandfathers, our More was almost bound to be christened Thomas. His own son would accordingly be named John after old Sir John, while his first grandsons, Meg Roper's first boy and John More's heir, would in turn carry on the name of Thomas. The More family tree has at least one Thomas at each ramification among the direct heirs alone. The secular priest (Cresacre's eldest brother) who died in Rome in 1625 was Thomas More IV.

No wonder, then, if the great English clerk in the first instalment of Rabelais' Giants' saga was named Thaumaste: the Greek word *Thaumastos* means "marvellous," but to the popular audience Thaumaste must have suggested plain Thomas, the stage designation of the Englishman.[92] By 1533, the date of *Pantagruel*, Becket's vilification was under way: Tyndale had branded him as a traitor; "reforming" calendars, under the name of "Saint Thomas the martyr," featured Thomas Hitton, a priest recently burnt at the stake. Henry

VIII's destruction of the Canterbury shrine dealt a severe blow to the saint's cult. The language, however, being the nation's memory, has continued to attest the past ascendancy of the name, not only through a wealth of patronyms—Thomason, Thomson, Tomlin, etc.—and such proverbial uses as Tommy Atkins or Tom Thumb, but by a lot of familiar words like tomboy, tomcat, tomtit, or tomfool. The last one is doubly telling as a quasi-synonym of jackass: thus *Thomas* and *John* compete afresh for the lowest rung on the semantic scale. Until Nick took over, *Tom* could even designate the devil, worse, the pet fiend of a witch. Unlike John, Thomas had no exalted biblical station to protect him against the vagaries of fashion. Only in wild legends did "Didymos, the Twin" rank as Jesus' twin. In traditional exegesis, his name suggested duplicity (as etymology would have it), a wavering spirit, and lack of singlemindedness. His readiness to die with the Master (John 11:16) could easily be construed as a rash, desperate mood. Of greater relief, of course, was his reluctance to believe in the Lord's resurrection (John 20:24–25), whereby "doubting Thomas" became a proverbial type in christendom: More, for his part, evokes the apostle's "diffidence and distrust," and "hardness of belief" at least five times in his English controversial works.[93]

More always designates his apostolic namesake as "Saint Thomas of Inde," on account of the well-attested tradition which makes him the planter of the Christian faith in Southern India. Rather more startlingly, Becket, even in London, was called "Saint Thomas of Acon," because his sister had endowed a pious foundation under his patronage in that Palestinian harbor, then a major headquarters garrison for the Crusaders.

Erasmus loved to view More as his twin, that is his "Thomas" if he had cared to exploit More's Hebrew nomen in the way he capitalized on his *cognomen*. But he was hardly attracted by any Thomas in the calendar: Didymos' glory was dimmed by the stock image of slowness to belief; Becket's rigid stand and the enthusiasm his relics inspired were both uncongenial to his temperament, while Thomas Aquinas, even though by far the greatest of the schoolmen, was too systematic, too much of a philosopher, to hold any profound appeal for the Dutch humanist. As Thomas Vogler of Obernai cherished the trilingual appellation of Thomas Didymus Aucuparius (Vogler is Fowler), Erasmus humored him by using the Greek vocative *Didyme;* yet even here, he tried no pun on the word.[94]

"Thomas" is so familiar in England that its currency outweighs the stock epithets of unbelief; that is why More's "good Tom Treuth" can without any soupçon of irony or paradox stand for the over-trusty innocent who, when accused, neglects to bring a witness along or to sort his evidence. Hence also the perfect naturalness of the Messenger's choice when he refers to a certain parish priest as "haltynge Syr Thomas" in his irreverent "merry tale" of Walsingham.[95]

More owned and wore a relic of St. Thomas the Apostle, which is still to be seen, with its Greek caption, at Stonyhurst College in Lancashire, encased in a handsome cross of gold. It would be like him to treat the apostle as his foremost patron-saint, even if he could hardly warm up to him as he did to such New Testament heroes as Peter and Paul, Magdalen and Stephen. From his last, unfinished, prison letter, we also know how much the martyrdom of Becket meant to him. It was quite befitting, then, for a Thomas Stapleton to combine his biography of More with shorter accounts of Thomas—Didymos and of the Archbishop, in his *Tres Thomae.*

The octave linking those red-letter days: the feast of St. Thomas the Apostle (December 21) and that of St. Thomas of Canterbury (December 29), with Christmas half-way, constituted a goodness week in "merrie England," when poor housewives were allowed to go "a-Thomasing" for flour toward their Christmas pudding.

The apostle's name is often cited today in connection with the apocryphal "Gospel of Thomas": More never heard of this Coptic document, which did not enter the stream of Western scholarship until after World War Two.

The biggest bell in the Oxford of More's adolescence was called *Great Tom.* A "mad" song of c. 1620 was entitled "Tom o'Bedlam," and Shakespeare's Edgar becomes "Poor Tom" when "the foul fiend haunts" him "in the voice of a nightingale."[96]

The position of Thomas as John's competitor and runner up is illustrated in the history of beatifications and canonizations. The last two English saints to enter the calendar before the Reformation were a contemporary of Thomas Aquinas: the bishop and Lord Chancellor Thomas of Hereford, and a contemporary of John Wiclif: John of Bridlington. Out of fifty men martyred under the Tudors and beatified in 1886, more than half were named either John (sixteen) or Thomas (ten). The two of them singled out for canonization in 1935, John Fisher and Thomas More, again represented the two names. Obviously both names were eligible in Tudor times to stand for "Everyman": when More in the *Debellation* chose to call his unnamed opponent "Sir John Some-say," he might as well have said "Sir Thomas Some-say," except for reasons of euphony. Lots of "Sir Johns" and "Sir Thomases" walked the streets of London in the 1520s, hundreds of them among the clergy alone.[97]

More's own fame, almost equal to Becket's in Catholic Europe, further contributed to associating *Thomas* with England. Each branch of his descendants, as we have seen, vied with the others to retain the name in the family. The martyr's last heir male, Father Thomas More (1722–95), English provincial of the Jesuits at the suppression of the Society (1773), owned his ancestor's relic of St. Thomas the Apostle. The direct representative of the saint today is Thomas More Eyston, of East Hendred in Oxfordshire, whose manor is rich in Morean relics. He is descended through the Metcalfes from Bridget More, a sister of the eighteenth-century Jesuit. The name was expected, almost assumed by strangers, as appears from the parish register recording the burial of Cresacre More, and calling him "Thomas More," "a slip easy enough for a man who was the son of Thomas and the father of Thomas."[98]

Nomen Omnium Horarum

As Becket's enormous prestige multiplied the name of Thomas, so More's fame is reflected in a certain (at times strange) ubiquity of his name: unidentified portraits of very different people have been captioned "Thomas More" in European museums; unsigned and unassigned "bons mots" have been pegged onto him. "The wise old dog of a Dutch household is called Morus, while the cat completes the name with Thomas."[99] Objects and faces which would otherwise belong to Nowhere are placed in his safe-keeping: "Aut Morus, aut nullus" said the old anecdote; one might add: "aut Mori, aut nullius." Since the canonization, too, thousands of boys have been christened Thomas More; others have chosen his name at their confirmation, or (nuns included) at their religious profession. One feels it to be a quality label. Why, asked Kenelm Digby in 1826, do I entitle my book *MORUS?* The name "at once designates the object and commemorates the boast of learning as well as the glory of our nation." The same kind of feeling prompted Robert Southey, three years later, to choose *Sir Thomas More* as a title for his "Colloquies on the Progress and Prospects of Society."

While *More* in itself, even without "Sir Thomas" or "Saint Thomas," has come, for better and for worse, to designate our "man for all seasons," the spelling he used (inherited perhaps from his father) has become a relative rarity in surnames; the form *Moor(e)* has gained a huge statistical advantage, and rightly so since it better evokes the two origins More himself embodied in the moorcock and the Moor's head. This predominance, however, should not obscure the fact that, in the early days of fluid orthography, the name of More, and such combinations as John More and Thomas More, were quite frequent. Henry VIII's household in 1540 included one John More, "page of thoffice," and two Thomas Mores, a yeoman of the cellar and a groom of the scullery. One martyr of Queen Mary's reign, burnt at Leicester on June 2, 1556, was a merchant's servant named Thomas More.[100] Archives yield so many that great caution is needed before the mind should jump to any connection with the Chancellor. Identities are made safe only by peculiar first names such as Christopher Cresacre (the Chancellor's greatgrandson), or even his grandson Austin More. That very currency may explain why both More and his father were called "Master More" ("old Master More," "young Master More"), the legal title limiting the chances of confusion more efficiently than the banal Christian names.[101] Even after his knighting, even as Chancellor, More is often referred to, especially among his peers and colleagues, as "Master More." "Sir Thomas"[102] was to take over as the legend, or the myth, took over from the man in the flesh of daily life and business.

CONSCIENCE THE ULTIMATE COURT OF APPEAL

André Prévost

1534: "For and Against"

The hardly veiled historical allusions in the *Dialogue of Comfort* enable us to situate the work in the texture of contemporary events. The years 1534 and 1535 remain among the most critical of all for the conscience of the English people.

Every subject of both sexes having reaching legal age was required to take an oath to the "Act of Succession." To recognize the validity of the marriage of Henry VIII with Anne Boleyn was implicitly to deny the Pope's jurisdiction. Nor did the denial remain just implicit: people were to sign the documents, printed in hundreds of copies for that purpose, which recognized the king as "Supreme Head of the Church of England." In London, a commission composed of Cranmer, Archbishop of Canterbury, Lord Chancellor Audley, and the Duke of Suffolk, sat in Lambeth Palace to administer the oath. One by one laypeople and clergymen filed past and they all swore, except the Bishop John Fisher and Thomas More. Both were imprisoned.[1]

The Northern and the Southern Convocations of the Clergy declared that the Bishop of Rome ... "had no more jurisdiction over this kingdom than any other foreign bishop." The Universities of Cambridge and Oxford expressed the same opinion.

Commissions travelled the North and the South of England to tender the oath to the clergy, and they encountered but little opposition. Two monks undertook to secure the oath from the monasteries. On 21 June 1534, one of them wrote: "So far no religious has completely rejected the oath of obedience." The few who did resist were promptly dispersed and imprisoned.

By the end of 1534, no spiritual authority of the kingdom, except for that of John Fisher, had remained independent and loyal to the universal church. "Bishops, canons, parish priests, religious men and women, dons, the personnel in hospitals and charitable institutions, all had recognized the king as the only spiritual head."[2]

The Final Spiritual Preparations

To us nothing is more precious than to retrace the thoughts which led the great humanist Thomas More to the supreme sacrifice. His was a lucid prepa-

Reprinted, by permission of the author and publisher, from *Thomas More et la crise de la pensée européenne* (Paris, 1969), pp. 343–54. Translated by the author.

ration. He deemed it beneficial to anticipate martyrdom, and to tell oneself one would die rather than commit perjury. Most authors, he grants, advise you not to linger on what you would do in time of persecution; in their opinion, you run the risk of sinning either out of presumption, by prejudging victory, or out of weakness, by abjuring in thought beforehand. But, as More sees it, the faithful should assert to themselves that they would rather die than abjure. Is this a mere attempt at self-delusion? Or is it just an exercise in self-control? By no means—it stems from a desire to prepare oneself for impending developments. Admittedly, Saint Peter incurred the Lord's rebuke for his presumption; but it was not Peter's determination to face any trial in order to follow his master that was blamed, it was the self-conceit whereby he based his resolution on his own strength.

To More, who trusted in God's strength, the will to face death for the faith was good and meritorious. He wished Christians "from their very childhood to accustom them dulcely and pleasantly in the meditation thereof, whereby the goodness of God shall not fail so to aspire the grace of His Holy Spirit into their hearts in reward of that virtuous diligence that, through such actual meditation, He shall confirm them in such a sure habit of spiritual faithful strength."[3]

More was to need "spiritual strength" during his fifteen months' imprisonment. The treasured seventeen *Letters from Prison* fortunately enable us to discover the secret of this lucid strength.[4]

Mysticism and Lucidity

The fortitude of the martyr is far from being a blind fanaticism. True, a taste for the picturesque and the extraordinary has led some hagiographers to emphasize the lyrical enthusiasm of Saint Polycarp or the Stoic virtue of Saint Lawrence. But, the example set by Thomas More, his serenity and humour before death, are nonetheless full of lessons for us. It is not so much the last hour that counts as the hours that have prepared for it. Those who have quipped that, had he not been a martyr, More would be no saint, have read neither his *Dialogue of Comfort* nor his last letters. They have no idea of the serene heroism that reveals itself on each page: "Pray for me, and I shall for you and all your friends, that we may merrily meet in heaven," he wrote to his daughter Margaret in his last letter;[5] and, in the meditation on the agony of Christ in the garden, his last Tower work, he pauses to consider the example of the Saviour who, after lying prostrate at the thought of death, "suddenly rises like a giant and rushes towards it filled with elation and exulting joy."[6]

Is this exaltation, is the transformation of the humblest human experiences —poverty and pain—into "triumphal values,"[7] still Christian humanism, or is it genuine mysticism?[8]

The question is worth pondering for a while. If the word "mystical" conjures up something extraordinary and cut off from the common, if "mysticism" implies an intrusion of supernatural forces into the human, or an ecstasy of man out of this world, one catches no glimpse of it in More. Although he is familiar with both the vocabulary and the literature of mysticism,[9] the author of the *Dialogue of Comfort* and of the *Tower Letters* never borrows words or images from sources other than those pertaining to rational, ordinary human behaviour.

And yet, at the top of its spiritual ascent, More's soul shows an inner balance of such nobility that the mere interplay of human reasons cannot possibly account for such sublimity. His serenity, his self-control in the face of contradiction, his bliss in the midst of pain illumine his last works, and make the reader feel in communion with the mystery of the world above.

But it is precisely the simplicity of More's soul that is extraordinary. The supernatural did not have to force its way into the thick of human reasons. It emerged gradually and developed without any discontinuity from starting-points commonly taken for granted. Now, this very ease in perfection radically excludes the ruptures, crises and paroxysms inherent in mysticism. It is therefore because of its very perfection, and by no means on account of any incapacity, that More's soul and work have remained free from every trace of the extraordinary.

If sanctity sometimes takes on the features of Joan of Arc or John of the Cross, it is no less genuine when it combines with a serene and lucid humanism. The comparison with Joan of Arc is quite suggestive. On both sides, an ignominious trial conducted by the representatives of spiritual authority, confusion in the minds and consciences; on both sides, a witness of loyalty even unto death. But whereas Joan was guided by supernatural beings, and in her last words on the stake re-asserted that her voices had not deceived her, More's only comfort was the lucidity of his mind and faith; his only tower of strength was the inalienable rights of his conscience which, in spite of all the difficulties, remained his only point of reference.

Loyalty to Conscience

Since More had an opportunity to define what this conscience meant to him, we should be unfaithful to his thought and humanism if we failed to stress the part it plays, according to him, in each person's destiny.

But first of all, was his conscience that of an obstinate man? Some historians claim that it was. They consider More, in his last years, as an "ultramontane," a fanatic,[10] the persecutor of heretics, a reactionary who reverted to inquisitorial practices. Constant and others have answered these charges in detail.[11] Besides, the mere reading of the *Letters* and other works written in jail is enough to make us realize that one cannot find the faintest resemblance between this caricature and the true portrait.

A fanatic would have condemned the king as an unjust tyrant; he would have hurled fiery imprecations at the bishops; unwaveringly he would have offered himself as a martyr to the blows of injustice. Nothing of the sort is to be found in More. To the last day, he retained the same reverence and loyalty, the same courtesy he had always shown to Henry VIII. His conception of the nature and necessity of authority was too high for him to voice a single criticism of the king and his action: when, he says, I realized that "therein do his Grace service to his pleasure I could not, and in anything meddle against his pleasure I would not, I determined utterly with myself to discharge my mind of any further studying or musing of the matter."[12] No subject could submit with more conspicuous proofs of his loyalty. Before his judges, More was able to assert that he had never uttered the slightest seditious word. At the moment of his death, and although he had prepared a speech which would probably have contained a protestation of his loyalty to the Catholic Church, he obeyed the king's desire that he should not speak and by so doing he was obedient unto heroism.[13]

More did not judge the king and neither did he condemn those whose opinions differed from his. In the divorce matter, he left everyone to their conscience. In a letter to Margaret Roper, he states that he "will not . . . dispute" with anyone about the king's marriage, so as "to meddle with . . . no man's conscience."[14]

Therefore, his appeal to his own conscience rings with richer undertones. Conscience for him is an absolute, his own and no one else's concern; no man has a right to exert any pressure whatsoever on it; so highly does he value it that he will offer his life in order to remain true to it.[15] Individual conscience stands above all opinions. It knows no other rule than itself, God and God's will: "But as concerning mine own self, for thy comfort shall I say, daughter, to thee, that mine own conscience in this matter (I damn none other man's) is such as may well stand with mine own salvation; thereof am I, Meg, as sure as that is God is in heaven."[16]

This testimony is the final judgement More passed on his whole personal life. Conscience is a self-sufficient absolute, which each individual can rest upon. So nobody but oneself has a claim to control it or listen to it. In the interview narrated by Margaret Roper to Alice Alington, he says to Meg:

Verily, daughter, I never intend (God being my good Lord) to pin my soul at an other man's back, not even the best man that I know this day living, for I know not whither he may hap to carry it. There is no man living of whom, while he liveth, I may make myself sure. Some may do for favour, and some may do for fear, and so might they carry my soul a wrong way. And some might hap to frame himself a conscience and think that while he did it for fear God would forgive it. And some may peradventure think that they will repent and be shriven thereof, and that so God shall remit it them. And some may be peradventure of that mind that, if they say one thing and think the while the contrary, God more regardeth their heart than their tongue, and that therefore their oath goeth upon that they think, and not upon that they say, as a woman reasoned once (I trow, daughter, you were by). But in good faith, Marget, I can use no such ways in so great a matter: but like as if mine own conscience served me, I would not let to do it, though other men refused, so though other refuse it not, I dare not do it, mine own conscience standing against it.[17]

Conscience and Objectivity

However, the inalienability of conscience does not mean that its dictates must be followed blindly. Everybody "is bounden if he see peril, to examine his conscience surely by learning and by good counsel, and be sure that his conscience be such as it may stand with his salvation, or else reform it."[18]

Although conscience represents an outstanding value which cannot be "made captive," it is nonetheless dependent upon *objective reality*. Therefore such conscience is not the fixed idea of an obstinate man who will not listen to reason. Before coming to a conclusion which imposed itself to his conscience, More submitted himself to a tremendous amount of homework.[19] And even after forming his conscience, he still acknowledged two authorities that could prevail against his own conclusions: the decrees of a General Council, or the unequivocal expression of the "common faith" of the universal church,[20] which, in his opinion, have received from God the power of expressing revealed truth.

Any other human authority is powerless before an upright and assured conscience. The number and quality of the opponents might provide some ground for re-assessing the issue, but they could not force your conscience and make it change its decision.[21]

Supreme Value of Conscience

The leading principle in this respect remains unchanged: "I can see none that lawfully may command and compel any man to change his own opinion and to translate his own conscience from the tone side to the tother ... I have myself a respect to mine own soul."[22]

How cogent all this account is![23] How sound is the thought which, while it looks the difficulties in the face, allows itself to be disturbed by none! No "sturdy stubbornness" here[24] but a total confidence in the reliability of human reason and in the everlastingness[25] of the pledge a man takes when he follows his conscience.[26]

Against the false accusations and the false witnesses, against the "powers that be," against his king, against the wavering or resigned bishops—who, after entrusting him with the defence of the old faith and its traditional expressions, and making him the champion of the independence of the spiritual power, were the first to approve of the new Caesaro-papism of Henry VIII and to swear him fidelity,—against the depravation of moral sense "where white is called black and right is called wrong," man's conscience will resist and, eventually, assert itself, if only beyond death.[27]

Reading the last pages written by More makes one feel more of a man. The conscientious objection which he raised, in full lucidity, alone against all established authorities, comes to full fruit in sanctity.

Such is Thomas More's strong personality as we discover it in his last letters and works. They disclose the thoughts which stirred his spirit when in the utter misery of his imprisonment, he fed it with all that could establish it in serenity and certitude. His winsome, and sometimes baffling character opens up to our intelligence, and provides reasons for acting. More's soul, after revealing the diaphanous light which pervades it and the nature of the gentle quiet joy which brightens its gaze and shines through its innermost being, casts a subtle spell on the beholders, its liberating charm unveiling the mystery enclosed in everyone.

The Man of the Eternal

On the morning of July 6, 1535, More signed with his blood his double testimony: on one hand, his death bore witness to the visible Church he had defended with pen and tongue, a church at once universal and national, incarnate in a sinful flesh, constituting the Mystical Body of Christ in the world; on the other hand, it attested his humanism, which, out of absolute loyalty to his conscience, has reached the level of pure love and the most self-effacing sanctity, without sacrificing anything that is valuable in Man.

This loyalty to Saint Thomas of Canterbury and to Saint Peter, to the Church of England and to the Church of Rome, along with a delicate longing to embody Christ's charity in the most human gestures, are expressed in his last letter, written "with a coal" on the eve of his death: "I cumber you, good Margaret, much, but I would be sorry if it should be any longer than to morrow. For it is Saint Thomas even and the Utas of Saint Peter,[28] and therefore to morrow long I to go to God. It were a day very meet and convenient for me." Hinting at the mark of affection of his daughter who, on 1 July, had twice elbowed her way through the crowd and jostled the guards in order to kiss and embrace her father protractedly, More adds: "I never liked your manner toward me better than when you kissed me last: for I love when daughterly love and dear charity hath no leisure to look to worldly courtesy."[29]

Loyalty to the church he had chosen to serve, loyalty to all the human realities he never ceased to love, such is the supreme image Saint Thomas More has left of himself: it makes him one of the most beautiful illustrations of the English genius, one of the men who best honour sanctity, a witness of achievements to be found where religion combines with humanism.

SIR THOMAS MORE, HUMANIST AND LAWYER

R. J. Schoeck

Thanks to Erasmus, we are still being asked to accept a picture of Thomas More as a humanist who was a reluctant prisoner at law, chained to the study and practice of a barbaric mystery, first by parental discipline and then by other pressures. Erasmus writes of More's father, Sir John More, that being himself skilled in English law

> he almost disowned his son, because he seemed to be deserting his father's profession. The study of English law is as far removed as can be from true learning, but in England those who succeed in it are highly thought of. And there is no better way to eminence there; for the nobility are mostly recruited from the law. And no man is considered an expert unless he has laboured at it for a great many years. Although More's mind, fitted for better things, naturally dreaded these studies, still, after making trial of the schools, he became so skilled in the law that no one of those who concentrated entirely on it had a better practice.[1]

Erasmus' antipathy to English law we can well understand, for this description of More and English law is written not long after Erasmus' experience with English custom-house officials, who confiscated all but £2 of the money which Erasmus had with him—despite the misguided assurance of More and Mountjoy that all would be well, provided the money were not in English currency. Besides, English law was written and conducted in Law-French, not Latin. However, we must leave Erasmus' confiscated £18, along with the fascinating story of his horse.

But Erasmus' view of More and English law has been adopted by later historians and biographers of More. Chambers pretty much follows the Erasmian view, and more recently Hexter has developed that view into a thesis: that More was "dragooned into the legal profession by his father" and showed a "revulsion against the practice of law" in the *Utopia*.[2] Erasmus' view, then, has had a widening rather than diminishing development and influence. It is time, I think, to question it.

Outside of More's career and writings there are several reasons to question the Erasmus-Hexter theory—to give a short title to the conventional view that I have been sketching. There were many humanists on the Continent who were lawyers, and, to turn this humanist-lawyer coin about, More was not

Reprinted from *University of Toronto Quarterly,* 26 (1964), 1–14, by permission of the author and University of Toronto Press.

unique in being an English lawyer of distinction who had broad and deep humanistic interests. We can profitably begin by examining what I shall call the tradition of learning in the Tudor Inns of Court. This tradition begins in Chaucer's time and carries through the sixteenth century (often called the golden age of the Inns of Court) and well into the seventeenth, the age of Spelman, Dugdale, and Selden.

We cannot attempt a survey of the earlier traditions of learning in the Inns of Court and among the judges, but, focusing on the second half of the fifteenth century, we can accept it as part of a continuity of early English legal learning and literature. It was the age of Littleton and Fortescue, as Hazeltine has aptly summarized: "Sir Thomas Littleton was judge of the court of common pleas; Sir John Fortescue was chief justice of the king's bench. Although the judgments of these great lawyers contributed materially to the growth of the common law of England, the fame of each of them rests not so much upon the part he played in moulding the law by the exercise of his judical power as upon the wealth of learning and the enlightenment of the constructive thought which he embodied in his writings."[3] Littleton, we might point out, came from a Worcestershire family, was at the Inner Temple, and died in 1481. Fortescue, who was from Devon and attended Exeter College, Oxford, was a member of Lincoln's Inn and died some time after 1476. It is on Fortescue that I wish to focus.

Perhaps less of the professional lawyer than his contemporary Littleton, "at any rate inferior in his contribution to the study of substantive law," Arthur B. Ferguson has written, "he became a pioneer in the investigation of comparative law and was unique in his awareness of the close relationship between law and the society it served."[4] He was mediaeval in seeking the cause of social evils in man's moral nature—and on the point that the root of evil in the *Utopia* is pride, such diverse critics as Chambers and Hexter are agreed—and he drew from that great mediaeval font of politico-historical thought, the *City of God* of Augustine. Yet while Fortescue had an awareness of social development, up to a point, like most English lawyers of the fifteenth and early sixteenth centuries, he "assumed that the custom upon which the common law rested was of immemorial antiquity."[5] In the words of Ferguson's conclusion, "Fortescue was never quite able to appreciate the dynamic implications of Renaissance society":[6] certainly More, as we shall see, had this appreciation to an extraordinary degree.

Fortescue, we do well to recall, was long involved in the affairs of Lincoln's Inn (the Inn of John and Thomas More), and his readings would have contributed strongly to the Lincoln's Inn tradition—a connection which I do not think has been observed by More scholars. As a student in this Inn in the 1490's, More is likely to have felt the force of Fortescue's influence among the Readers and barristers of that Inn. His own father was admitted to Lincoln's Inn in 1474, well before Fortescue's death, and is likely to have known him. But legal historians have much to do in this unplowed field: how much did each Inn have its own intellectual and professional traditions, its own climate of opinion? Enough has been done—chiefly by Professor Samuel

Thorne of Harvard, in a Gray's Inn lecture published five years ago, and most recently by Sir Ronald Roxburgh on the origins of Lincoln's Inn[7]—to indicate that there was great weight to family traditions, and that within each Inn there were important personal relationships and a good deal of institutional tradition.

Another important figure at Lincoln's Inn at this time was Sir Robert Rede, a distinguished lawyer and a benefactor of the humanities. Grandson of a Serjeant-at-law—so much ran in families—Robert was educated at Cambridge and became a fellow of King's Hall. After his years of study in Lincoln's Inn he became a Reader in 1480 and again in 1486, being called at about this time to become Serjeant-at-law himself. In 1495 he was made a judge of the King's Bench, and in 1506 Chief Justice of the Common Pleas.

All of this, and the rest of his distinguished legal career—he continued as Chief Justice of the Common Pleas under Henry VIII, until his death in 1519—sounds not too unlike the careers of others who reached the top in early Tudor law. And some of his other activities can doubtless be duplicated. But what is striking is that this common lawyer established a fellowship at Jesus College and three public lectures in Cambridge (which in the nineteenth century were consolidated into the one Rede Lecture, under whose auspices Maitland appropriately gave his brilliant lecture on "English Law and the Renaissance"). And we may now turn to Maitland for the observation on the fact that "had it not been for his last will and testament, we should hardly have known Sir Robert except as an English lawyer who throve so well in his profession that he became Chief Justice of the Common Bench." Yet, that pious founder of the lectures which now bear his name did have a care for more than the law which he taught and had for so many years practised and administered, a care "for the humanities, for logic and for philosophy natural and moral [that] was a memorable sign of the times."[8]

We can take time to look forward as well as backward, to the continuing tradition of learning in Thomas Elyot and Edmund Plowden, in Lambarde, Coke, and Bacon, and later in Spelman and Selden. And I use the word *tradition* deliberately, for (as I have elsewhere written) the bulk of early Anglo-Saxon scholarship is the work of common lawyers, and more than two-thirds of the forty-plus members of the Elizabethan Society of Antiquaries were members of the Inns of Court.[9] All traditions have roots, and the roots of the tradition of learning of which I have been speaking are in the late fifteenth- and early sixteenth-century Inns of Court. The fruits of that tradition are to be found in the teaching of the distinguished lawyers, in the early English legal literature of which Plucknett has recently written so cogently, and in wider activities. An unsummoned witness to their learning is the lawyer's library, a preliminary study of which has appeared in *Manuscripta,* starting from the challenge of a generalization by Sears Jayne that "there were apart from the clergy only two groups of people who as a class owned books in any numbers; these were physicians and University scholars." In "The Libraries of Common Lawyers in Renaissance England" I have gathered evidence that collections of books by common lawyers begin in the fifteenth century and that the libraries of common lawyers will bear comparison with those of any other learned group.[10]

Let us now return to the year 1519, the year of Sir Robert Rede's death and that of John Colet, the much loved Dean of St. Paul's (and therefore a date of some significance as well as convenience), and let us turn to Maitland's splendid rhetoric:

> Is it beneath the historic muse to notice that young Mr. More, the judge's son, had lately lectured at Lincoln's Inn? [Young Thomas More had been making his mark in the affairs of the City, and three years earlier he had published his *Utopia*.] Perhaps so. At all events for a while we will speak of more resonant exploits. We could hardly (so I learn at second-hand) fix a better date than Rede's death for the second new birth of Roman law. More's friend Erasmus had turned his back on England and was by this time in correspondence with two accomplished jurists, the Italian Andrea Alciato and the German Ulrich Zasi. They and the French scholar Guillaume Budé [I shall speak later of Budé's comments on the legal importance of *Utopia*] were publishing books which mark the beginning of a new era. Humanism was renovating Roman law. The medieval commentators, the Balduses and Bartoluses, the people whom Hutten and Rabelais could deride, were in like case with Peter Lombard, Duns Scotus and other men of the night. Back to the texts! was the cry, and let the light of literature and history play upon them.[11]

We have since Maitland had the scholarship of Guido Kisch on Erasmus and jurisprudence, and other works, to stress the importance of the Basel school of jurisprudence, and there is important work on the impact of Roman law on political thought and, more recently, on humanism and jurisprudence, by Myron Gilmore.[12] The point that is important here is that Erasmus and Budé were among More's friends, and he would have been as enthusiastic as they in these pursuits.

In the first volume of *Studies in the Renaissance,* ten years ago, Linton C. Stevens called our attention to the contribution by French jurists to Renaissance humanism: there were, he pointed out, more distinguished humanists to be found among the legal profession than in any other group. "An examination of the biographies of some thirty of these leading jurists," Stevens concluded, "convinces me that most of them were capable of reading Greek and were widely read in Latin literature. Their critical and philological treatment of juridical sources not only led them to a more profound acquaintance with the ancient world, but persuaded them to formulate a new philosophical conception of the relationship of legal principles to the moral status of the individual in relation to society."[13] And this is the thrust of Budé's letter to Lupset in the Paris edition (November 1517) of *Utopia,* as Allen has recently reemphasized.

There are other parallels which one would wish to explore: between law-reporting in France and England (on which Professor Frank Pegues of Ohio State University has been engaged), and the astonishing parallel between the

Parisian Basoche and the London Inns of Court, each with its own dramatic traditions—a parallel which no one, to my knowledge, has explored. But here I want simply to indicate that a high degree of learning and cultural activity among lawyers was demonstrably viable across the Channel.

More had many connections with Continental humanist-lawyers, and these can only be listed. Erasmus must come first, and through him More would have had access to the Basel school of jurisprudence. Through Cuthbert Tunstal, who was with More on the 1515 mission to Brussels and had received an LL.D. at Padua (and was Master of the Rolls in England), More surely would have been introduced to jurisprudents at the courts and cities visited during that mission. Peter Gilles figures importantly in the first edition of *Utopia,* and Busleiden almost as much: both were significant humanist-jurisprudents. Gilles' now neglected publication in 1517 of *Summae ... legum diversorum imperatorum,* a study of the sources of the Justinian code, was an important contribution to legal studies: here, too, we may be sure that More showed interest, and that Gilles would have made introductions. Vives, who had lived in the More household, had close ties with the study of law in Spain and, as Gilmore has noted, "his legal writings, notes on Cicero's *De legibus* and the *Aedes legum,* have been little noticed." Finally, there was Guillaume Budé, whose *Annotationes* of 1508 was a landmark in the humanistic approach to Roman law; his letter in the second edition of *Utopia* is important in itself and for lending Budé's legal prestige on the Continent to More's great publication. More than any other of the parerga of *Utopia,* Budé's letter helped to point contemporary readers towards a reading of *Utopia* in the light of its underlying philosophical principles. Above all, let us recall More's habit of disputing in foreign universities whenever he happened to be on the Continent, for this habit would have kept him in touch with currents of legal thought.[14]

But the major part of More's life was spent in London, and the Inns of Court must be our chief concern. We know lamentably little about education in the Tudor Inns of Court. To be sure, the major emphasis was technical, and we shall want to glance at the Tudor legal education. "During the law-terms," as Professor Hastings has authoritatively pictured the late fifteenth-century custom,

> Inn activities were confined to afternoons and evenings, the mornings presumably being devoted to attendance at Westminster or other courts. The afternoons were spent in argument and discussion and the evenings in the more formally conducted arguments of mootings. During the "learning vacations" readings replaced the court sessions in the morning, and the rest of the day was continued as in term time. During mesne or dead vacations no program was prescribed for the morning; otherwise study continued as during the law terms and the learning vacations, although attendance was not required.[15]

The readings may be compared with the lectures of Oxford and Cambridge, and the moots and bolts with the disputations; as at the universities, the maintenance of the educational system at the Inns depended "upon the resi-

dence of the members of the Inns in term time and in the learning vacations,"
and depended also upon the drawing of Readers and teaching barristers from
practitioners of the legal profession. In several important aspects, then, the
parallelling of Serjeants of the law with academic doctors has point, and there
is little doubt that the rigorous educational and intellectual discipline of the
Inns at this time is the chief cause of the pre-eminence of the Renaissance in
the long history of the Inns of Court.[16] Let us recall that More was associated
with Lincoln's Inn for more than a quarter of a century, and that he was twice
Reader there, which "is as often as ordinarily any Judge of the lawe doth
reade."[17] We do not have manuscripts of More's readings, nor is any reference
to them known to me. Yet inasmuch as the custom in the Inns was for each
Reader to follow the exposition of the statute under study, usually a chapter
at a time, it may be possible by a kind of extrapolation to arrive at the statute
and chapter on which More's readings were based.

These technical aspects of education in the Inns lead us to Maitland's words
about it being difficult to "conceive any scheme better suited to harden and
toughen a traditional body of law, than one which, while books were still uncommon [or relatively so], compelled every lawyer to take part in legal education and every distinguished lawyer to read public lectures." One would know
nothing of this from Erasmus' testimony, except the fact that More's fees were
handsome. But another sixteenth-century witness, Dr. Thomas Smith, in his
inaugural lecture as the first Regius Professor of Civil Law at Cambridge, exclaimed with a *Deus bone* at the eloquence and skill in disputation shown by
the students of the Inns of Court: "Even when some point of philosophy or
theology comes in question, how aptly and clearly they handle it, with what
ease and fullness, with what attractiveness and grace they reinforce their own
argument or repel their opponent. In sooth, there is not lacking in them the
force of logic or the splendour of eloquence."[18] From Roper's biography we
learn that More continued to attend readings at Lincoln's Inn even during his
Chancellorship.[19]

And there is more to life in the Tudor Inns of Court than the professional,
for there was both social life and intellectual activity in England's third university. There was dancing (and much of Thomas Elyot's high regard for dancing in *The Governour* doubtless developed during his days in the Middle
Temple), and along with dancing, drama was part of the ancient and elaborate
but largely unrecorded ritual of the Revels. As to the intellectual, it will for
now suffice to declare that more translators and poets came out of the Inns
than out of either Oxford or Cambridge during the sixteenth century.[20]

Thomas More, as we have seen, continued in the life and activities of
Lincoln's Inn: not merely attending the readings, but serving as Governor and
Lent Reader in 1514–15, and, as I have elsewhere given account, being named
as alternate Master of the Revels in 1528–29. One might be surprised that so
important a man as More should have been elected (even as alternate) to such
an office, for the winter of 1528–29 saw More, already knighted and a Privy
Councillor, high in the favour of Henry.[21] But one cannot assume that the
office of Master of the Revels was regarded by early Tudor lawyers as childish

amusement, any more than one can assume with Norfolk that More should have thought singing in choir with a surplice on his back beneath the dignity of the Lord Chancellor.[22] The fines for refusing the office of Master of the Revels were not light, and it clearly was a tradition in the More family to serve: John More, the judge, had done so when he was nearly forty and not far from the assumption of the Serjeant's coif, and others would do so after Thomas More. What is clear is that Thomas More continued as an active member of Lincoln's Inn long after the increasing pressure of public offices and his rise to royal favour: this is not the way of one who hated the legal profession.

In the space remaining I want to suggest lines for future investigation of More the lawyer, and points for development of the relationship of the lawyer to the humanist.

We do not know any books that were in More's library, but we can say what books would likely have been in that library—beginning with the tools of an early Tudor lawyer: Littleton's *Tenures*, Statham's *Abridgment of Cases*, Fitzherbert's *Abridgment* (*La Graunde Abridgment* was printed in three volumes, by More's brother-in-law, John Rastell), *Book of the Justice of the Peace*, and the *Doctor and Student*. Then there would certainly have been some Statutes and Year Books; and surely More would have had other books printed by his brother-in-law, perhaps the *Liber assisarum* (1513), or the *Exposiciones terminorum legum anglorum* (1525). We know of a book of precedents which belonged to Sir John More and came down to William Rastell; perhaps it passed through Thomas More's library on the way.

Nearly all of these would have been standard in the library of any common lawyer; others would have been included in the library of Serjeants and judges, such as: *Natura Brevium, Novae narrationes, Diuersite de courtz et lour iurisdictions, Modus tenendi curiam baronis,* and *Modus tenendi unum hundredum*. Surely there would have been something of Fortescue: *De Laudibus Legum Angliæ*, the *Governance of England*, and perhaps *De natura legis*. There were likely some books of canon and civil law, though it is still too early to identify More's working books in this area. Doubtless he had access to Lyndwood's *Provinciale*; but he also worked from one or more *summae*, and he mentions Gratian's *Decretum* and various collections of *decretales*. Almost certainly he had some legal manuscripts.

From the library of More's nephew William Rastell, whom we know to have been intimately connected with More in the 1520's and especially during the years of controversial writing from 1532 to 1534 (when he printed More's books)—from this library we can learn much of the range of interests and quality of reading of one common lawyer. At a time when he was Justice of the Queen's Bench, Rastell fled England on January 3, 1562–63, and a special commission sat at the Guildhall to take an inventory of the belongings of this Justice who had left England without licence. Among the furniture, robes, highly priced maps, and the like left behind in his chambers in Serjeants' Inn, were some forty books, of which only half are law books. The rest, Reed writes, "include a Euclid, a Eusebius, a St. Augustine, an (Erasmus) New Testament in Latin and Greek, a Horace with commentary, a Psalter in Greek,

Eliot's Dictionary, an *Aeneid* in French, a Greek Dictionary, a Cicero *de Oratore,* a French Testament, Gardiner's book against Bucer, Euripides in Latin and Greek, an *Illucidarius Poeticus, Adrianus de modo Latinae loquendae,* a Bible in parchment, Lucian's *Dialogues* in Greek, and a Theodore Gasius."[23] It is idle, though fascinating, to speculate on which of these books might have come from the More library; but we can say that this library—even though we are judging only from the books left behind—accords with what we know of Rastell himself, other lawyers' libraries, and the state of learning among lawyers, though doubtless there is rather more of Greek learning than would be usual.[24]

We shall want to study more closely these working tools and humanistic readings of the Tudor lawyers for a number of reasons; from such study (together with the records of his work as Chancellor of the Duchy of Lancaster and as Lord Chancellor, indicated below) we shall be prepared to analyse More's legal thought and methods and to appraise his debt to legal traditions. Such questions as More's reading in rhetoric, one of the liberal arts but one directly contributory to the practice of the law, and one in whose development during the sixteenth century common lawyers played a very large role, have scarcely been asked. And equally fruitful, I have suggested, is the question of what concepts or attitudes he might have drawn from the vast sea of canon law literature, particularly in the areas of political thought and of concepts of jurisprudence and equity.[25]

The question of More's readings was mentioned above; there is the still unworked quarry of More's career as lawyer and judge, and also as arbitrator. Untapped, I believe, is More's work as Chancellor of the Duchy of Lancaster.[26] This, together with what has been made known of More's career in the Privy Council and with the documents of his work as Lord Chancellor,[27] provides a very large body of material. At the moment, however, we simply do not know enough about him as a lawyer; there has been nearly as much mouthing of legal platitudes as there has been of the pious and devotional: More the lawyer is perhaps even less studied than More the saint and More the student of the sacred sciences. One legal anecdote will serve to sum up the point that much further study of More's legal expertise is needed, the widely repeated but little understood story of *withernam.*

In the anecdote recounted by Stapleton, there is a microcosmic fusion of More's humanistic irony and his technical knowledge of the law—but until recently the technical aspects have kept modern students from understanding this legal practical joke.

> While [More] was at Brussels on an embassy to the Emperor Charles V, it chanced that some braggart in that illustrious Court affixed to the wall a paper in which he issued a challenge to all and sundry. He professed himself ready to answer any questions or dispute upon any point in law or literature. Seeing the man's vanity, Thomas More proposed the following question in English law, 'Whether cattle taken in withernam be irrepliviable?' [*Utrum animalia* (or *averia*) *carucae* (*capta*) *in Withernamia sint irre-*

plegibilia. In non-technical language, can cattle that have been seized by due process of law in reprisal for the owner-defendant's having driven over the border the cattle which he had seized in distraint for a debt he claimed was owed to him by the plaintiff, be recovered by the process of replevin while the cattle originally taken by him have still not been delivered to the plaintiff and the withernam discharged?]—adding that one of the suite of the English ambassador desired to dispute upon that subject. The braggart could of course make no answer to a question of which he did not even understand the terms, and was forced to acknowledge his vanity in thus issuing a general challenge, becoming the laughing-stock of the whole Imperial Court.[28]

But the point of the question was not to show "that a jurist who did not understand English law was a fool to issue such a challenge (as Stapleton thought) and as Dr. Derrett has admirably shown, withernam was no strange thing to the jurists of the region in which More was. More's question asks, in effect, whether withernam was contrary to natural and divine law—a question fit for a civilian—and, if this was so, what was the status of this customary and widespread practice? The foreign jurist could scarcely debate the question without raising the question of the right of the Emperor; and thus, Derrett concludes,

> when the jurist refused to discuss this subject with More it was because he was clever enough to realise that the question, seeming an innocent question in a customary law, was in fact a trap. Silence was the best part of discretion. To get into difficulties on a subject of international and municipal law at the court of the Emperor in disputation with a member of a foreign embassy would not help his career. Some people may indeed have laughed at his discomfiture, but they would not have been lawyers, and he would be unlikely to enlighten all and sundry as to the nature of the trap which More had set for him.[29]

In such works as the epigrams and the *Richard III* there is need for a study of the ideas concerning the law and especially their sources: how much of the political thought is in the tradition of Bracton, and how much, if anything, is owed directly to Fortescue? In these works—chiefly in Latin, with *Richard III* being written both in Latin and in English—More manifests a deep concern for the dignity of man, for the privileges and responsibilities and abuses of authority and power (with the rights and duties of the individual generally); and in the *Utopia* above all we have a full expression of his preoccupation with the ethical basis of human society. Certainly a close reading of Budé's letter to Lupset will confirm such a reading of the *Utopia;* few readers of 1516 or 1518, we might put it, would have thought it overstatement or oversimplification to say simply that natural law was the subject of *Utopia.*[30]

There is the important question of More's interest and competence in canon law, and there has been some doubting of that competence. More than ten years ago I asked, "Was Sir Thomas More a 'Roman Lawyer'?" wanting to point out the stiff requirements for admission to Doctors' Commons (the "club" of ecclesiastical lawyers and civilians in London), which More did not at that time meet, and to strike a cautionary note by indicating that there were other Thomas Mores in the legal profession at that time. I am now convinced that More had expert knowledge of canon and Roman law, and have recently marshalled evidence to that point.[31] Just before his imprisonment in the Tower, More was involved in a controversy with Christopher St. German, a common lawyer with knowledge and some experience in civil and ecclesiastical law (in the common law courts and in equity). But it does not appear that More knew his opponent—for he chaffs at the anonymity of *Salem and Bizance* —and he does not seem to connect the thought of his opponent in the controversies of 1532–33 with the ideas of the anonymously published *Doctor and Student,* which had engaged St. German's energies from 1528 to 1531–32 (and may have been first published as early as 1523).

Few writers are so important in early English legal literature as St. German, who very nearly deserves the epithet of "that most erudite of early Tudor lawyers"; and his *Doctor and Student,* as Holdsworth writes, "has exercised as great an influence upon the development of modern equity as Bracton's treatise has exercised upon the development of the common law. From both books many generations of lawyers drew the root principles underlying the many technical rules to which a continuous development gave rise."[32] The range of his authorities is impressive: not only the usual common law references (Bracton, the Yearbooks, Statutes, Fortescue, and so on), but also Scripture, Augustine, Aquinas, Dionysius, St. Bridget of Sweden, and Gregory; with great consistency and frequency he uses John Gerson, and he is indebted to such compilations as *Summa Angelica* and *Summa Rosella,* Raymond, and Badus de Perusia. Two concepts stand out in all of St. German's writings, and both are implicit as early as *Doctor and Student.* The first is the concept of parliamentary supremacy, and the second the concept of a spirituality (that is, of a clergy and hierarchy) with greatly reduced responsibilities and powers; perhaps both ultimately Marsilian in inspiration, both were new ideas in 1528, and both concepts St. German tried to fit under his view of natural law.

The pivotal issue between St. German and More was a conflict between two views of natural law, the one choosing to ground his arguments on traditions of common law and the other on church law. The particular issue that is controverted in More's *Debellation* is the *ex officio* question, the oath in ecclesiastical courts that could compel witnesses to answer all questions put to them; that *ex officio* question is again debated by Cosin and Morice at the end of the sixteenth century. The controversy between More and St. German was most significant—in all of English legal history it may well be the only such controversy—and in St. German More had an opponent as worthy of his expertise in law and jurisprudence as Tyndale was in other matters.

Have we lost sight of our original point of question? We began by challenging the Erasmus-Hexter theory that More detested the legal profession, with its built-in corollary that there must therefore be a split between humanism and the law, between the humanist and the lawyer. I have tried to show that the legal strands of More's thought run steadily through his life, down to the final years before the imprisonment in the Tower, if not to within the Tower itself, and certainly to More's masterful defence of himself at his trial. To change the figure: in the flowering tree of More's thought, the legal roots are so intermingled with the humanistic that we could not cut the one kind away without killing the other. This is as true of the pre-*Utopia* as of the post-*Utopia* More.

And I have tried to show that More was by no means unique, either as a lawyer with humanistic concerns or as a humanist with legal interests. In the Tudor Inns of Court there would have been an atmosphere that fostered some, at least, of the emphases of humanism—rhetoric especially, for out of the Inns were to come those fountain-heads of Elizabethan literary energy, the *Mirror for Magistrates* and *Gorboduc,* as well as that first of scholarly societies, the Society of Antiquaries.

The burden of my concern has been that we should think of and study Sir Thomas More, not as a humanist in spite of his being a lawyer, but rather as a humanist *and* lawyer. This, I have been arguing, is the Thomas More known to his friends in England and on the Continent.

NOTES

NOTES

ANDEREGG, "The Tradition of Early More Biography"

1. The More biographies are cited from the following editions: William Roper, *The Lyfe of Sir Thomas Moore*, ed. E. V. Hitchcock (London: Early English Text Society, 1935); Nicholas Harpsfield, *The Life and Death of Sir Thomas Moore, Knight*, ed. E. V. Hitchcock and R. W. Chambers (London: Early English Text Society, 1932); Thomas Stapleton, *The Life . . . of Sir Thomas More*, tr. Philip E. Hallett, 1928; ed. E. E. Reynolds (London: Burns & Oates, 1966); Ro. Ba., *The Lyfe of Syr Thomas More*, ed. E. V. Hitchcock et al. (London: Early English Text Society, 1950).

2. Roper, p. 3. Hereafter cited by page number in my text.

3. Briefer first-hand accounts of More include the famous biographical letter Erasmus sent to Ulrich von Hutten (see *Opus Epistolarum Des. Erasmi Roterodami*, ed. P. S. Allen, H. M. Allen, et al, 12 vols. [Oxford: Clarendon Press, 1906–1958], Vol. 4, ep. 999), the fragment of Rastell's projected *Life of More* (Harpsfield, pp. 219–52), and (for More's trial) the "Paris Newsletter" (Harpsfield, pp. 258–266).

4. For evidence that Roper may have used some of More's letters, see the article by John Maguire, "William Roper's *Life of More*: The Working Methods of a Tudor Biographer," *Moreana*, No. 23 (1969), pp. 59–65.

5. See R. S. Sylvester, "Roper's *Life of More*," *Moreana*, No. 36 (December, 1972), pp. 47–59.

6. *English Literature of the Sixteenth Century, excluding drama* (Oxford: the University Press, 1954), p. 287.

7. For a view of the historical Duke of Norfolk that somewhat modifies Roper's portrayal, see M. J. Tucker, "The More-Norfolk Connection," *Moreana*, No. 33 (1972), pp. 5–13.

8. The relationship between this play and the early biographies of More is discussed by Marie Schütt, "Die Quellen des 'Book of Sir Thomas More,'" *Englische Studien*, 68 (1933), 209–226.

9. Harpsfield, p. 6.

10. Harpsfield, p. xlv. Hereafter cited by page number in my text.

11. *English Literature of the Sixteenth Century*, p. 286.

12. For a recent study of Stapleton's career, see Marvin R. O'Connell, *Thomas Stapleton and the Counter Reformation* (New Haven: Yale University Press, 1964).

13. Stapleton, p. 204. Hereafter cited by page number in my text.

14. When Christ, facing danger, decides to go into Judea to raise Lazarus from the dead, it is Thomas who says "Let us also go, that we may die with him" (John, 11:16).

15. "Recherches sur Thomas More: la tradition continentale et la tradition anglaise," *BHR*, 3 (1936), p. 29. Delcourt's thesis that Thomas More's early biographers were unsympathetic towards his humanist achievements as well as hostile to Erasmus has recently been re-argued by James J. Greene, "Utopia and Early More Biography," *Moreana*, No. 31–32 (November, 1971), pp. 199–207. I dispute some of Greene's points in "*Utopia* and Early More Biography: Another View," *Moreana*, No. 33 (February, 1972), pp. 23–29.

16. The question of More's relationship with Erasmus is discussed by James K. McConica in *English Humanists and Reformation Politics* (Oxford: Clarendon Press, 1965), pp. 285–294.

17. Ro. Ba., p. 41. Hereafter cited by page number in my text.

18. See above, pp. 4–5.

19. Ro. Ba. may have read this story in Sir John Harington's *A New Discourse of a Stale Subject, Called the Metamorphosis of Ajax* (1596), ed. Elizabeth Story Donno (New York: Columbia University Press, 1962), p. 101.

20. *Thomas More* (London: Jonathan Cape, 1935), p. 40.

21. The title page of the first printed edition reads: *D.O.M.S. / THE LIFE AND DEATH OF / SIR THOMAS / MOORE / Lord high Chancellour of / England. / WRITTEN BY / M.T.M. and dedicated to the Queens / most gracious Maiestie.* No date or place of publication is given, but it seems clear that the book was printed on the continent, perhaps at Douai, sometime after May 1, 1625, the date on which Henrietta Maria was married to Charles I. All signature references to the *Life of More* in my text are to this edition. Cresacre More's *Life* is also extant in at least five manuscripts.

22. *Sir Thomas More* (London: Methuen & Co., 1895), p. viii.

23. *The Life of Erasmus* (London: John White, 1808), I, 163.

24. *BHR, 3* (1936), 22–42; p. 53, n. 1.

25. Of the early biographies of Thomas More written in English, only Roper and Cresacre More were published and available in print in the seventeenth and eighteenth centuries. Ro. Ba.'s *Life* was first printed in 1810 by Christopher Wordsworth in his *Ecclesiastical Biography* and Harpsfield's *Life* was not printed until 1932. Stapleton's Latin *Vita Mori*, first published in 1588, was not translated into English until 1928.

26. For the history of the More family before Thomas More II, see especially Margaret Hastings, "The Ancestry of Sir Thomas More," *The Guildhall Miscellany, 2* (1961), 47–62, and A. W. Reed's appendix to the *EETS* edition of Ro. Ba., "From Thomas More to Cresacre More," pp. 311–14. For Thomas More II, I am heavily indebted to a series of articles by Monsignor D. Shanahan on "The Family of St. Thomas More in Essex: 1581–1640," which have appeared in *Essex Recusant (1* [1959], 62–74; 95–104; *2* [1960], 44–45; 76–85; 109–113; *3* [1961], 71–80; *4* [1962], 1–5). See also the "Note on Mr. Thomas Moare, Owner of the Emmanuel Harpsfield," in Harpsfield, pp. 294–96.

27. For an explanation of the term "recusant," and a brief discussion of Elizabethan recusant laws, see the introduction to *Catholic Record Society* (cited hereafter as *CRS*), vol. 57, *Recusant Roll No. 2* (1593–1594), ed. Dom Hugh Bowler (London, 1965). Some idea of what Thomas II had to suffer may be gathered from "A Yorkshire Recusant's Relation" (c. 1586) in *The Troubles of Our Catholic Forefathers,* Third Series, ed. John Morris (London: Burns and Oates, 1877).

28. Much of what follows has been gathered from a biographical study by Francis G. Murray, "The Contribution of the More Family to the Counter-Reformation, II: Thomas More IV, Henry More, Thomas Moore V, S. J.," in *Venerabile, 25* (1970), 113–23, and several studies by D. Shanahan: "The Death of Thomas More, Secular Priest, Great-Grandson of St. Thomas More," *Recusant History, 7* (1963), 23–32, and "Thomas More IV, Secular Priest: 1565–1625," *Essex R., 7,* 88–91, 105–14.

29. See the *Epistle Dedicatory* to Cresacre's *Life of More.*

30. Portions of the will are printed by Shanahan, *Essex R., 7* (1965), 105–109. Two copies are extant in the Westminster Archives.

31. The accounts of Thomas IV and Cresacre More given by Anthony à Wood (*Athenae Oxonienses,* ed. Philip Bliss, 4 vols. [London, 1813], Vol. 1, col. 79 ff.) are hopelessly confused, primarily because Wood depended on Cresacre's "Preface" while believing that it was written by Thomas IV. Joseph Gillow, depending partly on Hunter, gives brief and generally accurate notices of both men in his *Literary and Biographical History . . . of the English Catholics,* 5 vols. (1885–1902; rpt. New York: Burt Franklin, n.d.). For recent biographical information on Cresacre, see D. Shanahan in *Essex Recusant (4* [1962], 55–

64; 103–106; 5 [1963], 49–57) and P. R. P. Knell, "The Descendants of St. Thomas More in Hertfordshire: 1617–1693," *Essex R., 6* (1964), 1–12. Some interesting contemporary observations on Cresacre and his family can be found in Augustine Baker's *Life* of Dame Gertrude More (revised and ed. by Benedict Weld-Blundell, 2 vols. [London: R. T. Washbourne, 1910]), cited hereafter as "Baker."

32. Cresacre had planned at one time to write a life of his father but, presumably, this ambition was never fulfilled (*Life of More*, sig. ZZ$_1$v).

33. So Augustine Baker tells us, p. 3.

34. For the relevant documents, see *Essex R., 4* (1962), 60–63, P. R. P. Knell, "John Grove and Cresacre More," *Essex R., 12* (1970), 56–61, and Alan Davidson, "Persecution or Protection?" *Essex R., 11* (1969), 43. See also the entry in *Historical Manuscripts Commission Reports* [cited as *HMC*], *Salisbury [Cecil] Manuscripts,* vol. 19 [1965], dated January 24, 1606: "Grant to Edward Carpenter, gent., of the benefit of the recusancy of ... Cresacre Moore, late of Leyton, Essex, gent., standing convicted."

35. *CRS*, vol. 9, *Miscellanea,* VII (London, 1911), p. 365.

36. See Baker, pp. 5–6.

37. *Utopia* (1624), sigs. A$_2$–A$_2$v.

38. Cresacre witnessed an official document at Douai on September 14, 1625 (*CRS*, vol. 10, *Douay Diaries: 1598–1654,* Vol. 1, p. 246). On October 30, 1625, he obtained probate at Antwerp on his brother's will (Shanahan, *Recusant History,* 7 [1963], p. 31, no. 12).

39. Hunter's air-tight argument that George Cavendish wrote the *Life of Wolsey,* on the other hand, has been generally accepted. See Hunter's *Who Wrote Cavendish's Life of Wolsey?* (London: Richard Rees, 1814).

40. See, for example, E. E. Reynolds, *The Trial of St. Thomas More* (New York: P. J. Kenedy & Sons, 1964), p. 32; D. Shanahan, "Thomas More IV Secular Priest: 1565–1625, "*Essex Recusant,* 7 (1965), 105–114, p. 113; and Germain Marc'hadour in *Moreana,* No. 13 (1967), p. 88.

41. *The Life of Sir Thomas More, by his Great-Grandson Cresacre More,* ed. Joseph Hunter (London: William Pickering, 1828), pp. xxii–xxiv.

42. Joseph Hunter's good friend, Benjamin H. Bright, suggested, in a letter to Hunter dated August 11, 1826, that Cresacre's purpose might have been to repay his older brother for the inheritance (the letter is in Hunter's correspondence in the British Museum, *Add. Ms. 25, 676*).

43. *Signatures:* 4 to. ✠ , A–Z, Aa–Zz, Aaa–Hhh^4; *collation:* title [✠ ^{1}, verso blank;$_1$ (Epistle dedicatory to) ... MARIE HENRIETTE, 6 pp. unnumbered; A^1, The Preface to the Reader, p. numbered 1–10; B^2, text.

44. Roper's *Life of More* was published in 1626, but it is not possible to determine whether the publication of Cresacre's *Life* occurred before or after that of Roper's.

45. Roper, p. 35.

46. *English Works* (1557), sig. ZZ$_5$v.

47. Cf. the comment by Elsie Vaughan Hitchcock (Roper, p. xliv): "Cresacre's supernatural embroidery is well-known ..."

48. After William Roper's death, Cresacre tells us, and "whilst his bodie lay vnburied for three or foure daies there was heard once a day for the space of a quarter of an hower the sweetest musike that could be imagined, not of anie voices of men, but angelicall harmonie, as a token how gratious that soule was to Almightie God, and to the quires of Angells" (sigs. X$_1$–X$_1$v). We are also told that after More's death one of his teeth parted in two (sigs. Ccc$_2$v–Ccc$_3$).

49. *English Biography Before 1700* (Cambridge, Mass.: Harvard University Press, 1930), p. 5.

50. "For a vivid and clearly accentuated portrait as bequeathed to us by history, we substitute an ideal figure who is the personification of an abstraction: in place of the individual, the people know only the type" (H. Delehaye, *The Legend of the Saints*, tr. V. M. Crawford, ed. R. J. Schoeck [Notre Dame: University of Notre Dame Press, 1961], pp. 23-24).

AVELING, "The More Family and Yorkshire"
    The following abbreviations are used in the notes:
        B.I.—Borthwick Institute of Historical Research, York.
        C.R.S.—Catholic Record Society, Record Series.
        H.M.C.—Historical Manuscripts Commission.
        P.R.O.—Public Record Office.
    1. *Visitations of Yorkshire, 1584/5 and 1612*, ed. Joseph Foster, 1875; *Dugdale's Visitation of Yorkshire, 1665/6*, ed. J. C. Clay, 1912.
    2. *Studies in Tudor and Stuart Politics and Government*, vol. I, G. R. Elton, 1974, p. 138; P. R. O. Lord Treasurer's Remembrancer, Memoranda Rolls; E. 368/526; J. C. Clay, op. cit., I, pp. 89-91.
    3. *The Life of Syr Thomas More by Ro:Ba:* ed. A. W. Reed, 1950, Early English Text Society, pp. 311-4, notes.
    4. *Complete Peerage*, G. E. Cockayne, 1912 ff. Scrope; Monumental inscriptions, Hambleden church, Bucks., and parish registers; *Victoria County History, Yorkshire, the North Riding*, 1, pp. 257 ff.; *Alumni Cantabrigienses*, ed. J. Venn, 'Roper Scrope.'
    5. *English Humanists and Reformation Politics under Henry VIII and Edward VI*, J. K. McConica, 1965, passim; A. W. Reed, op. cit.
    6. Barnborough church register, Sept. 4, 1557; *Record Series*, Yorkshire Archaeological & Topographical Society, 111 (i), p. 219, 309; *Victoria County History*, op. cit.
    7. *The Buildings of England: Yorkshire, the West Riding*, N. Pevsner, 1958; *A History of Barnburgh*, J. S. Large, 1952.
    8. *Recusant History*, vol. 6, no. 5, April, 1962, *St. Thomas More's Family Circle and Yorkshire*, H. Aveling, pp. 238-44; C. R. S., *Catholic Recusancy in York, 1558-1791*, J. C. H. Aveling, 1970, pp. 294-306.
    9. *John Parkyn, Fellow of Trinity College, Cambridge*, A. G. Dickens, Proceedings of the Cambridge Antiquarian Society, vol. XLIII, 1950, pp. 21-9; *South Yorkshire Letters, 1555*, A. G. Dickens, Hunter Archaeological Society, vol. VI (vi), pp. 278-84; *Yorkshire Clerical Documents, 1554-6*, A. G. Dickens, Bodleian Library Record, vol. 3, no. 29, Jan. 1950, pp. 34-40; *Robert Parkyn's MS Books*, A. G. Dickens, Notes and Queries, 19 Feb. 1949, pp. 73-4; *Robert Parkyn's Life of Christ*, A. G. Dickens, Bodleian Library Record, vol. 4, no. 2, Aug. 1952; *Aspects of Intellectual Transition amongst the Parish Clergy of the Reformation Period: a Regional Example*, A. G. Dickens, Archiv für Reformationsgeschichte, 1952, Freiburg im Breisgau, pp. 51-70.
    10. Barnborough church register, Sept. 4, 1557; *Oeconomia Rokebiorum*, British Museum, Add. MS 24470, fols. 294-333; Aveling, op. cit., pp. 294-5; B. I., Dean and Chapter Wills, f. 67v.
    11. *Northern Catholics: the Catholic Recusants of the North Riding of Yorkshire, 1558-1790*, H. Aveling, 1965, passim; *Calendar of Patent Rolls, 1560-3*, pp. 187-8; *Dictionary of National Biography*, 'William Rastell'; *Matricule de l'Université de Louvain*, ed. A. Schillings, 1950, vol. IV, Feb. 1528–Feb. 1569; *Catholic Recusancy in York*, op. cit., p. 299.
    12. *Recusant History*, op. cit.; *Northern Catholics*, op. cit.
    13. *The Catholic Recusants of the West Riding of Yorkshire, 1558-1790*, H. Aveling, Proceedings of the Leeds Philosophical & Literary Society, vol. X (vi), pp. 190-306.

14. A considerable number of conservative, 'old priests' were arrested in Yorkshire in these years. They were charged and convicted of every sort of 'ritual' disobedience, but exceedingly rarely of saying a Latin Mass. Self-made lay 'new Catholics' tended to have great difficulty in finding any Latin Mass or sacraments over wide areas (e.g., the case of Anthony Travers of Preston, Lancashire, B.I., Cause Papers, R. VII/G. 897.) I have identified over 100 'vagrant' old priests in Yorkshire in 1559–72. The evidence of their actions is copious; 3 or 4 were sheltered in the Doncaster deanery. But there is no evidence of one at Barnborough.

15. B.I., R. VI/A. 1–3a.; *Journal of the Yorkshire Archaeological Society,* vol. 2, pp. 34 ff.; B.I., R. VI/A. 2, f. 53.

16. J. C. Clay, op. cit. 'West of Aston and Aughton'; B.I., Wills, vol. 19, f. 388.

17. *Life of Sir Thomas More,* cit.; *The Family of St. Thomas More in Essex, 1581–1640,* D. Shanahan, The Essex Recusant, vol. 3, 1961, no. 3, pp. 118–123; ibid. no. 4, pp. 1–5; Henry Maire's Pedigree Book, Lawson MSS, Brough Hall, Yorkshire.

18. *Calendar of Patent Rolls, 1558–60,* p. 245.

19. B.I., High Commission, 1564–8, ff. 94, 99v., 108; 1566–8 (sic), f. 31; Cause Papers, R. VII/G. 1290; R. As. 20. 54.

20. B.I., Wills, vol. 19, f. 388.

21. Aveling, *Northern Catholics,* op. cit., and *Catholic Recusancy in the West Riding,* op. cit.; B.I., High Commission, 1569–71, f. 233v.; 1571–4, f. 45, 72; 1572–4, f. 40; 1574–6, f. 169v.; P.R.O., S.P. 12/74.32; *History of Hallamshire,* J. Hunter, 1881, p. 82; P.R.O., S.P. 12/187.12.

22. P.R.O., E. 137/133.1. (Rebels pardoned); *Memorials of the Rebellion of 1569,* C. Sharp, 1841, passim. The Francis More listed in C.R.S. 13, p. 118 and note has no place in surviving northern papers of the rebellion.

23. B.I., High Commission, 1568–70, ff. 175 ff., f. 226v.

24. *Northern Catholics,* op. cit.; B.I., High Commission, 1571–2, f. 103, f. 170; 1572–4, f. 36v.; *North Riding Quarter Sessions,* ed. J. C. Atkinson, 1902, ii, p. 217.

25. P.R.O., S.P. 15/21.3. (The income qualification is "those able to spend £100 a year or far more.")

26. C.R.S., 22, pp. 3 ff. (Most of them 'corrupted by D. Cumberford.')

27. Shanahan, op. cit.; *Pedigrees of Yorkshire Families,* Joseph Foster, 1905, 'More of Barnbrough.'

28. *Register of the University of Oxford, 1571–1622,* ii, pp. 48 ff., Oxford Historical Society; *Oxford and Cambridge in Transition, 1558–1642,* M. H. Curtis, 1959; *Reformation and Reaction in Tudor Cambridge,* H. C. Porter, 1958; *Early Collegiate Life,* J. Venn, 1913; British Museum, Lansdowne MS 33; *The First and Second Diaries of the English College, Douay,* T. F. Knox, 1878. John More was badly equipped for Oxford, or a slow learner. He and Raynolde Lawson esq. of Yorkshire were put to a *Grammar* tutor on entry into Trinity College.

29. Mrs. Garford in later life appears in recusancy presentments in Essex with the Mores. A John Garford of Heck was presented for recusancy in 1590–5 (*Recusancy in the West Riding,* op. cit.)

30. Ibid., p. 215. Some south Yorkshire Catholic gentry had properties in north Lincolnshire outside the jurisdiction of the York High Commission and Council of the North, and went there for refuge.

31. B.I., Chancery Book 1574–9, f. 129.

32. B.I., High Commission, 1580–5, f. 27v. ff.

33. Ibid., ff. 64, 64v. Reresby was buried at Barnborough in 1613 (church register).

34. B.I., R. H/5; ibid. High Commission 1580–5, f. 84v.; ibid. R. VI/A.6, f. 250; J. Foster, op. cit., Thomas More de Barneburgh, in prisona, recusans. There are only two

other similar entries in the list: Christofer Rokeby de Mortham ar., mortuus, filius in prisona religionis ergo; Roger Mennel de Hawnby ar. in prisona.

35. *Edmund Campion*, Richard Simpson, 1896, pp. 187 ff.; *Letters and Memorials of Robert Persons*, ed. L. Hicks, Catholic Record Society, vol. 39; *History of Hallamshire*, op. cit., p. 479; Yorkshire Archaeological Society, Record Series, 5, p. 130; *Calendar of State Papers, Domestic, 1581–90*, p. 87. It is by no means certain that Campion passed through the West Riding.

36. Barnborough church register, May 2, 1620. Mr. Everard More buryed (sic); Somerset House, P.C.C. 67 Stafforde; B.I., High Commission, 1591–5, f. 63 ff.; C.R.S. 8, p. 40. Who was the Edward More who daringly, as a jest, in 1594, wrote to Robert Cecil, offering him £1000 for the Presidency of the Court of Wards (H.M.C., *Salisbury MSS*, 4, p. 494)?

38. Thomas More II was arrested at Greenstreet, near London (site of Robert Persons' secret press) in 1582, was in gaol in the Marshalsea, London, April 1582 to June 1586 and was regularly presented as a recusant at the Essex Quarter Sessions (as of Low Leyton) 1586 to his death 1606. (Information from D. Shanahan.) H.M.C., *Salisbury MSS*, 4, p. 273.

38. B.I., R. VI/B. 2; R. VI/A. 26.

39. George More esq. of Allerton; Edward More of Cowley. For the Mores of Angram and Loftus, see *Northern Catholics*, op. cit., passim. Compare the claims of the More family of St. Inigoes, Maryland (emigrants from England to St. Mary's county, 1667), set out in *Maryland Catholicism on the Frontier*, T. J. O'Rourke, 1974.

40. P.R.O., E. 368/526; *Acts of the Privy Council*, ed. J. R. Dasent, 1619; *Recusancy in the West Riding*, op. cit., p. 293; *Calendar of the Committee for Compounding*, IV, 2243 (Nov. 24, 1652).

41. *The Jesuits and the Independents: 1647*, Thomas H. Clancy S. J., Archivum Historicum Societatis Iesu, vol. XL, 1971; C.R.S. 34, p. 151; J. Foster, op. cit., 'More of Barnbrough.' In the 1630s–1650s the Mores seem to have been living in Herefordshire (*Historical Collections*, J. Rushworth, 1721, ii, 824; *Aubrey's Brief Lives*, ed. O. L. Dick, 1972, p. 376).

42. Bar Convent Archives, York, *Notices of Chaplains*, V, 38; Leeds City Library Archives Dept., Gascoigne MSS, G.C./F. 8.1; ibid., Mexborough MSS, Reresby Letters, File 14, 83; *Complete Collection of State Trials*, ed. F. Hargrave, 1776, vol. 3, p. 1 ff.; Clerk of Peace Office, Wakefield, Quarter Sessions, Indictment Book, 1678–9; B.I., St. Mary's, Castlegate church register.

43. Quarter Sessions cit., Sessions Rolls, 1680; Reresby Letters cit., File 15, 84, 17, 19, 31; File 21, 13.

44. Bodleian Library, Oxford, Rawlinson MSS. A. 139a., ff. 274 ff.; *Catholic Recusancy in York, 1558–1791*, J. C. H. Aveling, C.R.S., 1970, p. 104.

45. B.I., R. VI/A.34, A.35; E/2a; Quarter Sessions cit., Rolls, 1691; Barnborough church register.

46. J. Foster, op. cit.; Will of William More (Lawson MSS, Brough Hall, Yorkshire, papers of Sir John Lawson).

47. B.I., R. VI/B.6; E/66; Quarter Sessions cit., Registrations of Papists' Estates; Barnborough church register (1721, Mrs. Elizabeth More married to Mr. Hodgshon of Southwell, July 18th); J. Foster, op. cit.

48. Henry Maire's Pedigree Book, Lawson MSS cit.; *The Chronicles of an Ancient Yorkshire Family: the Ullathornes;* B. L. Kentish (privately printed, 1963), pp. 68 ff.; C.R.S. 32, p. 227; *Northern Catholics*, op. cit.; C.R.S. 13, p. 185 (James Pole *alias* Foxe S. J. 'at Mrs. Bincks in Richmond, Yorksh.'); York City Archives, Quarter Sessions 1744–56.

49. C.R.S. 25, p. 112; B.I., R. Bp.b. 1764: Barnborough 72 householders: 353 inhabitants: about 60 (Anglican) communicants: 40 at Easter: no Dissenters: one papist. The maximum number of papists there was the 16 of 1706: 11 in 1735: 1780 one. (*Recusancy in the West Riding*, op. cit., p. 293.) But Burghwallis-Frickley had 1735: 42; 1767: about 44; 1780: 49; Stubbs Walden 1706: 24; 1735: 14; 1780: 29; Walton 1706: 37; 1735: 20; 1767: 13.

50. Woodward MS, St. Joseph's Presbytery, Pontefract (puts the More marriage in 1732).

51. *Recusancy in York*, op. cit., pp. 273, 389.

52. Ibid. passim; Bar Convent, York archives, Procuratrix's Accounts.

53. *Recusancy in York*, op. cit., pp. 157–8, 389.

54. *The Chronicles of an Ancient Yorkshire Family*, op. cit., p. 70. Mrs. Bridget Dalton's son, William Dalton, was educated at the Jesuit Academy at Liège, 1773–82 and, appropriately, a schoolfellow of a son of Simon Scrope of Danby. (C.R.S., 13, pp. 205, 210.) Her son 'Thomas More' (Metcalfe) was there 1774–6 (ibid., p. 208).

DERRETT, "Thomas More and the Legislation of the Corporation of London"

1. For More's associations with the City see R. W. Chambers, *Thomas More* (London, 1935), p. 103 and references there cited.

2. J. D. M. Derrett, "Neglected Versions of the Contemporary Account of the Trial of Sir Thomas More," *Bull. Inst. Hist. Res.*, XXXIII, 1960, 202ff, at 221 (§12).

3. 26 H.VIII, c. 13.

4. 26 H.VIII, c. 1.

5. The affair of Friar Standish (later Bishop of St. Asaph), 1518, concluded at Baynard's Castle. R. Keilwey, *Relationes Quorundam Casuum* (London, 1602), fos. 180v–185v. The report is translated by A. Ogle in *The Tragedy of the Lollard's Tower...* (Oxford, 1949). Pollard, *Wolsey*, 43–9; Pickthorn, *Henry VIII*, 114–8.

6. W. Roper, *The Lyfe of Sir Thomas Moore, Knighte*, ed. E. V. Hitchcock (London, Early English Text Society, No. 197, 1935, repr. 1958), p. 93.

7. *Ibid.*, Introd., p. xlv.

8. W. Blackstone, *Commentaries on the Laws of England*, I, 475f.

9. On the legislative power of Common Council see A. Pulling, *Laws, Customs, Usages and Regulations of the City and Port of London*, 2nd edn. (London, 1854), pp. 43f. This is the most helpful source on the point, citing, as it does, numerous decided cases relating to Acts of Common Council. The information given in Sir Edward Coke, 2 *Inst.* 20–1, 126, 327, 675; 4 *Inst.* 249 is somewhat summary.

10. Pulling, p. 10.

11. *Ibid.*, citing Magna Charta; Rot. Parl. 1 Ric. II, c. 11; 1 Ed. III, st. 2, c. 9; 14 Ed. III, st. 1, c. 1; 1 Hen. IV, c. 1. See also n. 19 below.

12. The charter of 3 June, 15 Ed. III, enabled the city to ordain remedies for defective customs, 'so that the same were agreeable to good faith, and reason, for the common advantage of the citizens, and other liege subjects sojourning with them [i.e., the citizens], and useful to king and people.' A by-law contrary to reason and the welfare of the realm might thus be declared void by the king's courts. Yet an Act of Parliament, 3 H.VIII, c. 9, was thought necessary to render void an ordinance of London on the ground of the damage likely to result from it.

13. Hil. 14 & 15 Car. II. B.M., Hargrave MSS. 56, fos. 22–57.

14. *Ibid.*, fo. 27.

15. *Ibid.*, fo. 51r.

16. W. Bohun, *Privilegia Londini: or the Laws, Customs, and Priviledges of the City...* (London, 1702), p. 131, an allusion to a case in the Common Pleas of 28 Eliz. I.

17. Pulling, p. 185. See, for the scope of Common Council's legislation, "A Code of Laws Published by Common Council" (Guildhall Library, MS. 267(2)); and *A List of the By-Laws of the City of London, Unrepealed* (printed by Henry Kent, London, 1769). Item 83, p. 18 of the latter is interesting. It is a 'declaration' of the custom that citizens' widows shall have but a third part (of the movables) if there be children—an illustration of an Act to clarify or remedy ancient custom. On the inconveniences due to the conflicts between City custom and the common law see the provisions of an Act of 19 Ed. III given in the first-named 'Code' above at p. 50.

18. Pulling, 49.

19. The Attorney-General's 'replication' alleged that the charge against the City was "for makeing an illegall Law for Levying Severall Summes of money of his Maj^ties Subjects and Liege People as well free as not free of the Citty in Subversion of the good rule and Government of the Citty and the great Oppression and Impoverishing of the subjects the manifest disheriting of the King and contrary to the confidence reposed in a Body Politick by him and the Laws of this Realme." The City thought this odd in view of the precedents and the statutes of Ed. V, H.VII, H.VIII and others recognising the City's legislative power. See *Certaine Questions of Fact which the Counsell for the Citty in the Quo Warranto proposed to be satisfied in the better to guide theire Opinions in delivering theire Judgm^ts upon the Citties Rejoinder* (Guildhall Library MS. 94, fos. 123r–191r). The printed material on the case is voluminous. See *Case of the Quo Warranto* (1690); *Replication to "the City of London's Plea..."* (1682); *City of London, Rejoinder to Mr. Attorney General's Replication* (1682); *Surrejoinder of Mr. Attorney General* (1682); *Pleadings and Arguments and other Proceedings in the Court of Kings-Bench upon the Quo Warranto* (1690); *Reflections on the City-Charter...* (1682); T. Hunt, *Defence of the Charter...* (1682); R. L'Estrange, *Lawyer Outlaw'd...* (1683); *Case of the Charter of London stated...* (1683).

20. 33 H.VIII, c. 27.

21. Sir Orlando Bridgman's judgment in *Hutchins' case*, fo. 53r. Pulling, p. 2 n. (e). S. E. Thorne, ed., *Discourse upon the Exposicion and Understandinge of Statutes* [*c.* 1557] (San Marino, 1942), index, 'London.' T. F. T. Plucknett, *Statutes and their Interpretation* (Cambridge, 1922), p. 64. G. O. Sayles, *Select Cases in the Court of King's Bench*, III (London, 1939), p. xxxix (the mortmain case). Y.B.19 Hen. VI, fo. 64–5 (Pasch. no. 1) *per* Fortescue.

22. Plucknett, *op. cit.*, also *Concise History of the Common Law* (London, 1956), p. 318 n. 3.

23. See n. 21 above. It is noteworthy that London was exempted from the statute 27 H.VIII c. 16, whence it followed that a bargain and sale of land was still valid according to the custom of London, though it was oral—an inconvenient custom if ever there was one. W. Sheppard, *Touch-stone of Common Assurances*, 6th edn., 1791, p. 222.

24. fo. 53r.

25. Plucknett, *Statutes;* also *Concise History*, pp. 336–7. Bacon, *Maximes*, Reg. xix.

26. Derrett, *op. cit.*, 220–1, where the reference to the Great Charters is obscure. Roper, at pp. 93–4, makes the reference explicit.

27. fo. 53v, Bohun, *Privilegia*, p. 155: we note that foreigners (i.e., non-citizens) as well as freemen might devise lands in mortmain—for the rule affects the land, not its devisor.

28. Mich. 32 & 33 Eliz. I, referred to by Bridgman, C. J., at fo. 53v.

29. Upon this were based the statutes of Praemunire and Provisors, which ultimately served as a foundation for the Reformation statutes. It is impossible to discuss these, here, but see M. McKisack, *The Fourteenth Century* (Oxford, 1959), ch. x, particularly pp. 280–3.

30. The customs of London determined how tenements in London (in most boroughs called 'burgages') were transferred, inherited, and devised. Hustings for Pleas of Land and Assize of Buildings were the relevant courts. An Enquiry of 14 Ed. I determined the question, when it was doubted whether an owner of a tenement in the City, not a freeman, could devise his tenement. The City was not bound by the general inability, until the statutes 27 H.VIII, c. 10 and 32 H.VIII, c. 1, to devise more than a term of years. Custom of the City determined how land in the City passed on intestacy and custom determined what legacies, and in particular what devises, were valid. *The City Law or the Course and Practice in all Manner of Juridicall Proceedings in the Hustings in Guild-Hall, London* (London, 1647), pp. 3–4. Wills had to be enrolled in the Hustings. See R. R. Sharpe, *Calendar of Wills Proved and Enrolled . . .*, I, (London, 1889), pp. xxiv, xxxv, xxxvi, xxxvii, xxxviiif. Bohun, *Privilegia*, pp. 148–9, pp. 156f. Instances of defective testaments are given in H. T. Riley, *Liber Albus . . .* (London, 1861), pp. 594f. While all tenements in the City were bound by custom wherever the owner lived (*Note:* he might be disfranchised for non-residence, but that would not affect his tenure), chattels, including chattels real, passed subject to the City customs of orphan's portion, widow's dower, etc., provided the deceased was a freeman. On these customs see works cited above.

31. There is evidence, e.g., Chapuys' protest before the Council in 1534, and the Hansa merchants' counsel's case at the negotiations at Bruges in 1520, that continental jurists believed that fundamental laws inhibited a king's legislation (and therefore Parliament's). A statute to amend or protect a general custom, in the interest of the whole realm, might it seems, be accepted as valid at international law, provided it did not conflict with reason. The subject is too complex for discussion here.

32. See instance cited in n. 12 above.

33. Derrett, *op. cit.*, p. 220 (¶ 10). E. F. Rogers, *Correspondence of Sir Thomas More* (Princeton, 1947), pp. 499, 506.

34. Whether they might be binding *spiritually* might well be doubted, and it seems that even Lord Audley doubted it as late as 1547 (J. A. Muller, *Letters of Stephen Gardiner*, Cambridge, 1933, pp. 369–70).

35. Compare its behaviour in the first year of Queen Mary.

DERRETT, "The Trial of Sir Thomas More"

1. Shown clearly in Derrett, 'More's conveyance of his lands and the law of "fraud,"' *Moreana* 5 (1965), 19–26.

2. E. E. Reynolds, *The Field is Won* (London, 1968).

3. N. Harpsfield, *The Life and Death of Sr. Thomas More . . .*, ed. E. V. Hitchcock and R. W. Chambers (London, E.E.T.S. no. 186, 1932), pp. 268, 269–76. Public Records Office, *Baga de Secretis*, K.B. 8/7/3, m.7.M.3, with verdict and sentence, is another copy. *Letters and Papers of the Reign of Henry VIII* (hereafter cited as *L. & P.*), viii, no. 974, pp. 384–6. *Third Report of the Dep. Keeper of the Public Records* (1842), App. ii, 240–1. *Canonizationis beatorum martyrum Iobannis Card. Fisher . . . et Thomae More . . . informatio* (Typis Vaticanis, 1944). Citations of the indictment below are from the first work above, referred to as 'Harpsfield.' For the abstract used in preparing the indictment see p. 56, n. 18 *inf*. An old treatment: *Archaeologia*, xxvii (1838), 361–74. G. de C. Parmiter's 'The indictment of Saint Thomas More,' *Downside Review*, lxxv (1957), 149–66 is useful.

4. *The Lyfe of Sir Thomas Moore . . .*, ed. E. V. Hitchcock (London, E.E.T.S. no. 197, 1935). For his mistakes see pp. xlvi–xlvii.

5. *Ibid.*, p. 96. Sir Anthony St. Leger, Richard Heywood, John Webbe. The first two were members of the Bar.

6. *Cit. sup.* at pp. 183–97; also pp. 254–76, 362–8. The rephrasing of FitzJames's answer (see below) suggests that different versions were current.

7. Derrett, 'Neglected versions of the contemporary account of the trial of Sir Thomas More,' B [ull.] I[nst.] H[ist.] R[es.], xxxiii (1960), 202 ff., at 206.

8. *Dict. Nat. Biog.*, liii. 333; E. Foss, *Judges of England*, v (1857), 234.

9. *Life and Raigne* (1649), 393.

10. *History of the Reformation*, ed. N. Pocock, i (1865), 556–7.

11. B. M. Ms. Harg. 388, f. 98v, 'Corone 32.' The reports of Spelman (Spilman) are being edited for the Selden Society by Dr. J. H. Baker.

12. H. de Vocht, *Acta Thomae Mori* (Louvain, 1947), justly suspected by E. E. Reynolds, *Saint Thomas More* (London, 1953), pp. 376–7, is not now to be followed.

13. Derrett, *cit. sup.*

14. R. Pole, *Ad Henricum Octavum . . . pro Ecclesiasticae Unitatis Defensione Libri Quatuor* (1536), bk. iii, fos. 89r–90r.

15. *R.* which corresponds to the conjectured original manuscript* X is printed parallel with the P.N.L. in B.I.H.R. xxxiii, at pp. 214–23.

16. Pole, *cit. sup.* at fo. 93; the *Expositio*; the *Ordo Condemnationis* (published in de Vocht's *Acta*); pseudo-Chauncy; and Harpsfield, *op. cit.* p. 213: the picture is of 'Christi martyr.'

17. *Vita Thomae Mori* in *Tres Thomae . . .* (Douai, 1588). P. E. Hallett, trans., T. Stapleton, *The Life and Illustrious Martyrdom of Sir Thomas More*, ed. E. E. Reynolds (London, Catholic Book Club, 1966), ch. 18.

18. Excepting answers by Fisher: *L. & P.* viii, nos. 814, 856, 858. E. E. Reynolds, at *Moreana* 1 (1963), pp. 12–17, gives a version of the abstract of More's talk with Rich from P.R.O., S.P. Hen. viii, 2, Folio R., fos. 21–2, *i.e.*, no. 814, 2 (ii). A reexamination of the document is at Derrett, 'The "new" document on Thomas More's trial,' *Moreana* 3 (1964), 5–22. Reynolds' handling is to be seen in his *The Field is Won* (cited above). The conversation is printed there at pp. 385–6.

19. Margaret had died some years before. He himself says, 'as farre as my poore wit and memory wold serve me' (p. 97).

20. See below, n. 35.

21. B.I.H.R., xxxiii, 211, n. 2.

22. It is essential to realize that the attitude of the archbishops and convocation was part of a reforming, and to that extent revolutionary, movement. The details of the canon law position are reserved for treatment elsewhere.

23. The authenticity and source of these reports, in particular this item, has been greatly clarified by A. W. B. Simpson, 'Keilwey's Reports . . . ,' *Law Quarterly Review* 73 (1957), pp. 89 ff. The item, R. Keilwey, *Relationes Quorundam Casuum* (London, 1602; *Reports d'ascuns Cases*, London, 1688), fos. 180ᵛ–185ᵛ, is our only source on the incidents and bears a marginal note of uncertain age, *Lou supreme jurisdic' preteign' al Roy ou al Pape.*

24. The main point was that the ordinary 'did not know what to do with them,' since crime alone gave the ecclesiastical judge no jurisdiction over them. L. Gabel, *Benefit of clergy in England in the later Middle Ages* (Smith Coll. Studies in History, xiv, 1929). A. Ogle, *Tragedy of the Lollard's Tower* (Oxford, 1949). P. Heath, *The English Parish Clergy on the Eve of the Reformation* (London & Toronto, 1969).

25. *Op. cit.* p. 86, ll. 6–9, 17–19. Pole was better informed, it seems: *op. cit.*, fo. 89ᵛ.

26. For the Act, 26 H.8, c. 13 (*Statutes of the Realm*, iii. 508–9), see I. D. Thornley, 'The treason legislation of Henry VIII (1531–1534), *Trans. Roy. Hist. Soc.* (3rd ser.), xi (1917), 88–104. See also the same, 'Treason by words . . . ,' *ante*, xxxii (1917), 556 ff.

27. The original commission (not 'writ') is *Baga de Secr.* Pouch 7, Bundle 3, m. 10.

28. Of the judges only FitzWilliam absented himself; of the others, Lord Montague. The judicial element was strong, including Sir Anthony FitzHerbert, a celebrated legal

author who was a scrupulous friend of the old religion (J. Pits, *Relationum Hist.*, i (Paris, 1619), p. 707). Coke, no lover of tyranny, calls these men 'reverend sages of the law' in his *Reports.*

29. T. More, *Dialogue concerning Tyndale* (1528), ed. Campbell and Reed (London, 1927), bk. iii, chaps. 1–7 (Bilney's affair), esp. at pp. 189 ff.; the same, *Apology,* ed. Taft, pp. 149–54. C. St. German, *Doctor and Student,* ii, chap. 48 (edn. of 1787, pp. 259–62).

30. Harpsfield, *op. cit.* pp. 349–50. For a possible attempt to influence the jury see Henry's order, 25 June 1535, in *L. & P.* viii, nos. 876 (p. 348), 921.

31. *Year Book 9,* Ed. 4, Pasch., pl. 4. Coke, 3 *Inst.* 29.

32. The word does not appear in the indictment.

33. For the right to demur when a statute is misapplied to the case, see, e.g. [J. March] *Brook's New Cases* (1651), tit. *Demurer* (32 H. 8).

34. Harpsfield, p. 270, l. 3.

35. Op. cit. fo. 89^V: '*ad hoc vero . . . non uteretur.*'

36. '*Ex quo ego in custodia sum detentus. . . .*'

37. The indictment merely says *in terra,* but the meaning is much the same. But see T. More, *Correspondence,* ed. E. F. Rogers (Princeton, 1947), p. 552, l. 35.

38. Harpsfield, p. 270, l. 22–271, l. 14.

39. He was engaged on the *Treatise on the Passion. Corr.* p. 552, ll. 61–68; p. 536, ll. 96–101. B. Foord, ed., Sir Thomas More, *Conscience Decides* (London, Chapman, 1972).

40. St. Thomas Aquinas, *Summa Theol.,* Ia IIae q. 71, a. 5. *Hales* v. *Petit* (1563), Plow. 253, 259a; Hale, I *Pleas of the Crown,* 434.

41. Coke, 3 *Inst.* 12–14, 137; Hale, I P.C. 108; Foster, *Crown Cases,* 220; Blackstone, 4 *Comm.* 79, 86. E. Wingate, *Maximes of Reason . . .* (London, 1658), p. 107.

42. For the meaning of this word see its use in *Corr.* p. 495, l. 105; p. 500, l. 297, 300; p. 516, l. 66–71; p. 537, l. 333 and *passim.* St. German, *op. cit.* i. chap. xv (Latin text).

43. Eight items, one of which appears in Latin in the plural. The Spanish translation is correct.

44. This is not sarcasm. Fisher could not remember any noteworthy matter in the principal letter: *L. & P.* viii, no. 858, p. 331.

45. For the allusion, and explanation see *B.I.H.R.* xxxiii, at pp. 211, n. 1, 212. For a comparable mistake see *L. & P.* viii, no. 856, item 41, p. 330.

46. *State Trials* (n.s.), p. 463; Wingate, *op. cit.,* p. 110.

47. Interrogatories and recorded depositions enabled two and two to be put together. John a' Wood seems not to have been illiterate: he knew too much.

48. Fisher's statement on 12 June: 'four or thereabouts from either to other' (*L. & P.* viii, no. 858, p. 331; E. E. Reynolds, *Fisher,* p. 268). At least three were burnt: *L. & P., ibid.* no. 856. More was cautious about his letters (cf. *Corr.* p. 538, ll. 190–2), but that does not imply treason.

49. More's own report, *Corr.* p. 552, ll. 38–49, agrees both with *R* and John a' Wood's evidence; his deposition (*L. & P.* viii, no. 867, item 3) relates more, namely a discussion of 'maliciously.' This was not treasonable.

50. *L. & P.* ix, no. 213 (1), p. 70 made use of them.

51. As appears from the indictment, it was a pure conjecture. The allusion is probably to Sir. xxi. 3.

52. *Corr.* p. 557, l. 62–558, l. 105. *Cf.* (for Cromwell's part) *Corr.* p. 552, ll. 50–52; p. 553, ll. 73–76.

53. On More's refusal to swear see Derrett, '*Juramenta in Legem:* St Thomas More's crisis of conscience and the "good Roman,"' *Downside Rev.* 91, No. 303 (1973), 111–116.

54. Tyndale echoes Henry himself: *Obedience of a Christen Man* (1535), fo. 29b, 33a. *Gladium portat princeps:* Wilkins, *Concilia,* iii. 763. Fox, *Opus Eximium* (1534), fo. 56^V ('*gladium gladio copulemus*'). Gardiner to Somerset (1547) in J. A. Muller, *Letters of Stephen Gardiner* (Cambridge, 1933), p. 406.

55. *L. & P.* viii, no. 814, 2 (i).

56. On the oath see More himself, *Apologye,* pp. 146–52.

57. *Cf. Corr.* pp. 557–8.

58. It is sufficient to cite the *Discourse upon the Exposicion and Understanding of Statutes* (c. 1557), ed. S. E. Thorne (San Marino, 1942), p. 162.

59. 28 H. 8, c. 7, sec. 12 (1536).

60. *Corr.* pp. 490, l. 70–491, l. 90.

61. *Cf.* Roper, pp. 85–86, and Harpsfield, pp. 274, l. 17–276, l. 2. The abstract, evidently originating from Rich, supports (where the ms. is legible) the indictment based upon it, but Rich further represented that he had said in parting '... I see your mynd wyll not change which I fear will be very daungerous to yow ...' (see Reynolds, *op. cit.,* p. 15). More could well have used this, *had he heard it.*

62. The indictment: Harpsfield, pp. 275–6. Parliament's power to regulate the succession was exercised in 1536 and later in the reign. Sir Roger Twysden, *Considerations upon the Government* (London, 1849), p. 78. 13 Eliz. 1, c. 1, sec. 4.

63. So the abstract (Reynolds, cited *supra,* n. 18).

64. *Corr.* no. 199, 5 March 1534.

65. Here follows the conversation in Roper's abridged version.

66. 'Company,' 'society,' as in the A.V. It is the antecedent of 'who.'

67. Otherwise Roper (who knew) was wasting his time setting out More's submissions on the evidence. Note Francis Bacon's speech to Mr. Justice Hutton (1617): '... you should be a light to jurors to open their eyes, but not a guide to lead them by the noses.'

68. 5 & 6 Ed. 6, c. 11, sec. 12.

69. Cromwell's 'remembrances,' nos 424, 494, cited by Chambers in Roper, *op. cit.,* pp. 119. The man, More's son-in-law Giles Heron, had in the end to be attainted by statute.

70. Put down by some to Rich's stink: T. More, *Life of More* (1726), 240.

71. Holbein's portrait of Southwell speaks volumes: his refusal to testify would hardly be attributed to scruples of conscience or lack of intellectual conviction; but that stupid face would be consistent with superstitious fears.

72. *Op. cit.,* pp. 91–92.

73. 1 John 1:8. Citation of scriptural texts in a common law argument was normal. The technical discussion of *malitia* (cf. *Summa Theol.* Ia IIae qq. 18–21; IIa IIae q. 60 a. 2) in interpretation of statutes was still open.

74. 8 Hen. 6, c. 9. A. FitzHerbert (see above, n. 28), *New Natura Brevium,* trans. (London, 1652), pp. 616–8; [J. March], *cit. sup.* tit. *Action upon the Statute;* Coke, 1 *Inst.* 257.

75. There is general agreement here with More's letter to Cromwell: *Corr.* no. 199 (5 Mar. 1534).

76. On the debate see *L. & P.* viii, no. 856; Reynolds, *Fisher,* pp. 256, 267.

77. The historical and current scope of 'maliciously' is too involved for treatment here. The common law was not confined to philosophical (*e.g.,* Thomist) or canon-law usages. In criminal pleading the word was taken seriously. 'Malice' was and is a distinct ingredient of certain crimes and torts. For instances see Foster's *Crown Cases,* p. 256; *Queen* v. *Pembliton* (1874) 2 C.C.R. 119 (and refs.); *Reg.* v. *Cunningham* [1957] 2 Q. B. 396; and *Sairle* v. *Roberts* (Trin. 9 Will. 3) 1 Lord Raym. 374 (and refs.); *Hargrave* v. *Le Breton* (1769) 4 Burr. 2422; *Pitt* v. *Donovan* (1813) 1.M.&.S. 639. Bacon, *Maximes of the Law,*

reg. vii. For the meaning, 'without just cause or excuse,' see *Jones* v. *Givinn* (1713) Gilb., p. 185, *per curiam* at p. 193. *R.* v. *Solanke* [1969] 3 All E.R. 1383 (C.A.).

78. Above, n. 74.

79. Rastell in Harpsfield, *op. cit.*, p. 230.

80. *R.* v. *Donovan* (1928) 21 Cr. App. Rep. 20, 21.

81. The law, not the *bona fides* of the court, was in doubt.

82. See the arguments of Chapuys, himself a jurist, before the council, bishops, and judges on 19 May 1534: P. de Gayangos, ed., *Calendar of Letters . . . between England and Spain*, v, pt. 1 (Henry VIII, 1534-5), (London, 1886) no. 58, pp. 156-7.

83. *Vindicatio Henrici VIII . . . a Calumniis Lutheri* (London, 1523, under the pseud. G. Rosseus), quoted in Reynolds, *Fisher*, pp. 104-5. *Corr.* no. 199, p. 498.

84. Henry's letter to convocation (1533), in Wilkins, *Concilia*, iii. 762 f. S. Gardiner, *De Vera Obedientia*, p. 117. More had a precedent (did he use it?) in a dictum of Frowicke, C. J., *Year Book* 21, H. 7, pl. 1 (pp. 2-4) cited and discussed by McIlwain, *High Court of Parliament*, pp. 277 f. Lyndwood, *Provinciale* (1679), pp. 129-30 (and refs.).

85. Was More intellectually egoistic?—a point put to him by the abbot of Westminster in 1534; *Corr.* p. 506. The same point was urged against Gardiner by Cranmer and his colleagues when he relied upon 34 & 35 H. 8, c. 1.

86. *Corr.* no. 199, p. 499. Stephen Gardiner (More's contemporary), though pliant under Henry VIII, became equally stubborn later: *cf.* Gardiner, *Letters*, pp. 291-2, 313, *et passim* 1547-9. Both he and Edmund Bonner proceeded on the basis that no Christian had the right to profess an unapproved faith.

87. For Chapuys's speech, see n. 82 above. More: *Corr.* no. 200, pp. 505-6, esp. ll. 114-6. A debate between More and German civilians (1520) as to parliament's legislative capacity appears at *Hanserecesse* iii, vol. 7 (ed. D. Schäfer, 1905) pp. 583-611.

88. A comment on the Act, not the Parliament. Chambers, Harpsfield, *op. cit.*, pp. 350 f., was misled by the mistranslation.

89. *Cf. Corr.* no. 206, p. 528, ll. 521-3.

90. *Cf. Corr.* no. 206, p. 528, ll. 527 f. (obviously the source of the words chosen— where Roper deviates we can be sure there was good reason). It cannot be said that the saints are not witnesses: see Heb. xii. 1.

91. *Cal. of Letters . . . between England and Spain*, v, 1, p. 157, *ad fin.*

92. R. Moryson, *Apomaxis Calumniarum* (London, 1537-8), fo. 79b.

93. *L. & P.* viii, nos. 876, p. 346; 909, p. 358.

94. Coke, 2 *Inst.* proem., pp. (2, 4), 2, 3. Wilkins, *Concilia*, iii. 555. The statute figured against Wolsey: Gardiner, *Letters*, p. 391; and the relevant sections were used (*e.g.*, Fox, *Opus Eximium*, fo. 53) as guarantees against *foreign* interference.

95. 1 Cor. 4, 14-5.

96. More's point is answered by Gardiner, *De Vera Obed.*, 161 f. An untrue oath, like a bigamous marriage, is not to be kept.

97. In the *Assertio Septem Sacramentorum*. *Corr.* no. 199, p. 498, ll. 204-6.

98. *Cf. Corr.* no. 199, p. 498-9.

99. The peculiar position of London, having a legislature of its own, founded upon customary law which was partially protected from parliamentary infringement, is discussed in Derrett, 'Thomas More and the legislation of the Corporation of London,' *Guildhall Miscellany*, 1963, ii, no. 5 (Oct. 1963).

100. See the trials of the Carthusians and Reynolds in M. Chancaeus, *Historia aliquot Martyrum* (Monstrol, 1888), the most convenient ed.) and that of Fisher in Rastell, *ubi cit. sup.* (but note discrepancies noticed by Constant, *Reformation in England*, i. 219).

101. Pole, *ubi cit.* fo. 89^V. '. . . *omnes haerere, aestuare omnes coeperunt.*' The informa-

tion is hooked on the wrong stage of the trial, as suggested by *R*. The embarrassing pause became a part of tradition, and was inserted by 'Ro: Ba:' (who otherwise adheres to Harpsfield): *Lyfe of Syr Thomas More*, ed. E. V. Hitchcock and P. E. Hallett (London, E.E.T.S. no. 222, 1950), p. 246, ll. 13–14.

102. Henry's letter to convocation, at pp. 763, 764. *The Bishops' Book*, pp. 120–1. Gardiner, *De Vera Obed.*, and more briefly in letter no. 53 in Muller. St. German, the reformation statutes, and the apologists, *e.g.*, Moryson, Fox, were in perfect agreement. St. German's reservations (*Doctor and Student*, 1787 edn. pp. 294–5) are beyond our present scope.

103. Acts, vii. 58.

104. St. German, *An Answere to a Letter*, sig. B. 5a. So, apparently Gardiner: P. Janelle, *Obedience in Church and State* (Cambridge, 1930), p. lxiii—note his conduct at Ratisbon (1540), *ibid.* pp. xlii–xliii, xliii, no. 2.

105. The classic instance is Henry's triumphant pointing to biblical texts (were they Lev. xviii. 24–8 read with xviii. 3–5?) by which the law of *nature* prohibited his marriage: More, *Corr.* no. 199, p. 493, l. 60–62; p. 494, l. 76–96. 25 H. 8, c. 4 effectuates the law of God; human laws only are repealable: 25 H. 8, c. 14 and 25 H. 8, c. 21. Wiclif, *De Civ. Dom.*, p. 400. Tyndale, *Practyse of Prelates* (Marburg, 1530), fos. 64–5. So even Gardiner, *Letters*, pp. 280, 300; *De Ver. Obed.*, pp. 91, 99; *Bishops' Book*, 121; *King's Book*, p. 316; later R. Hooker, *Laws of Eccl. Pol.* I, iii. 2. So Coke, 7 *Rep.* 1, 13b: 8 *Rep.* 107, 118a (Bonham's case and refs.). The Latin version of St. German is explicit, particularly the text corresponding to *Doct. & Stud.*, English version (1787 edn.), pp. 5, 11, 15–16, in which there were excisions.

106. F. Le Van Baumer in *Am. Hist. Rev.* xlii (1937), 637 ff., 644. G. R. Elton, *Reform and Renewal. Thomas Cromwell and the Common Weal* (Cambridge, University Press, 1973), 74–6, 129.

107. *Salem and Bizance* (London, 1533), fo. 73.

108. *Second Dialogue* (1530), chap. 55 (pp. 281 ff. in the 1787 edn.).

109. The question of stat. 45 Ed. 3 (*Sylva caedua*), and the provincial constitution of Archb. Winchelsey. St. German shows what the Church should have done (pp. 293–4): they should have worked for legislation on their lines.

110. *Apologye* (original edn., fo. 159); repeated in *Debellacyon of Salem and Bizance* (London, 1533), fo. 127b–129a. For 'unlawful laws' see *Corr.* p. 524, l. 393; p. 542. It is curious that even Audley, in conversation with Henry, reported by Gardiner (*Letters,* 369–70), admitted that parliament's Acts on spiritual matters might be vulnerable.

111. This conforms to More's behaviour regarding the Acts of Succession and Supremacy. Pole at *Epistolarum Reginaldi Poli . . .* , ed. Quirini, iv (Brescia, 1752), pp. 79–80 is, as often, out of focus.

ELTON, "Sir Thomas More and the Opposition to Henry VIII"

1. Chambers, *More*, 236, is right to say: 'More knew quite well what was coming.'

2. T. E. Bridgett, *Life and Writings of Sir Thomas More* (1891), 225.

3. Chambers, *More*, 236.

4. *St Thomas More: Selected Letters*, ed. E. F. Rogers (New Haven, 1961), 209.

5. Roper, 224.

6. Nicholas Harpsfield, *The Life and Death of Sir Thomas More*, ed. E. V. Hitchcock and R. W. Chambers (E.E.T.S., 1932), 51. Roper (p. 219) mentions only More's formal disabling speech, after the appointment was in effect settled.

7. 'The Rastell Fragments' (printed in Harpsfield), 222. The material in the fragments was collected for a life of Fisher and deals only incidentally with More.

8. Allen, viii. 294: 'Ego me rebus accommodo. . . .'

9. Hall, *Chronicle*, 761.

10. Allen, x. 136, 180.

11. E.g., A. Cecil, *A Portrait of Thomas More, Scholar, Statesman, Saint* (1937), 201.

12. J. K. McConica, *English Humanists and Reformation Politics* (Oxford, 1965), ch. 5.

13. C. Hollis, *Sir Thomas More* (1934), 157.

14. Chambers, *More*, 236.

15. *LP* iv. 6026.

16. Allen, viii. 294.

17. E.g., Chambers, *More*, 274 ff.

18. More's attack on Wolsey (Hall, *Chronicle*, 764) included references to 'new enormities' among the people for which no law had been made, a conventional term of the time for divagations in religion.

19. Allen, x. 138.

20. Hall, *Chronicle*, 771.

21. Allen, x. 33-4.

22. Harpsfield, *More*, 223.

23. Chambers, *More*, 279 ff.; Allen, x. 138.

24. 'Quum habeat ius occidendi,' said Erasmus; but More had no such right.

25. Allen, x. 116, 135, 180.

26. *LP* v. 982.

27. *LP* vi. 573.

28. PRO, SP 1/78/246-7: cf., J. A. Froude, *History of England from the Fall of Wolsey to the Defeat of the Spanish Armada* (12 vols., 1872), i. 556-9. Froude's transcript contains his usual quota of unimportant errors.

29. Ms: of.

30. Both *LP* and A. I. Taft, in his edition of the *Apologye of Syr Thomas More Knyght* (E.E.T.S., 1930), 328 ff., identify this John Field with one who petitioned Cromwell in Nov. 1536 (or a later year) for his release (*LP* xi. 1164). But even if the two Fields are the same man, the later imprisonment cannot be linked with the former. Field then spoke of having spent nearly three years in the Counter: i.e., at some point he must have been newly jailed, and in a different prison, since on the earlier occasion he was certainly free for a year from Oct. 1532. The second petition deals manifestly with some non-religious offence; the first, despite Taft's unconvincing doubts, concerned a point of the faith since Field's books were investigated. The tone of the second petition, acknowledging that 'such grievous complaint is made against me that they to whom God has given authority to punish offences may no less do of justice than keep me in prison until the time of judgment,' is very different from that of the first. If only one John Field (a common enough name) is involved in these two cases he may be thought accident-prone, but his later troubles are quite clearly distinct from his earlier and cannot be used, as Taft tries to do, to explain them away.

31. Bridgett, *More*, 270; Chambers, *More*, 277.

32. *The Workes of Sir Thomas More, Knyght ... written by him in the Englysh tonge* (London, 1557), 905-6. The danger of suicide was the greater because a cousin of Phillips's called Holy John had drowned himself in a well when accused of heresy!

33. Hall, *Chronicle*, 827. Taft, who discussed Phillips's case in his edition of the *Apologye* (pp. 320 ff.), missed this revealing point.

34. E.g., the defence of orthodoxy by an attack on heretical books had to wait until the king's policy had begun to turn against Rome (*Tudor Royal Proclamations*, i, 193 ff. The correct date of ibid. no. 122 is also 1530). Or cf. the Commons' reaction in 1529 to Fisher's charges of heresy (Hall, *Chronicle*, 766).

35. Chambers, *More*, 242.

36. McConica, *English Humanists,* 107.

37. Chapuys (*LP* v. 171) and Hall (*Chronicle,* 775 ff.) report in very similar terms.

38. Roper, 225.

39. *LP* v. 112.

40. It seems to have been sincere—at least at first. As is well-known, More did not sign the appeal from the nobility to the pope which Henry VIII arranged in 1530. But this was not a courageous refusal, as Chambers (p. 249) in probable reliance on Rastell's dubious notes (Harpsfield, *More,* 223) supposed. Chapuys knew that More, together with Catherine's supporters among the bishops, was not called to the meeting which prepared that document (*Calendar of State Papers Spanish,* iv. I. 599), and while he ascribed the selection to suspicion it looks like a concession to the sort of promise that Henry had made to More.

41. Hall, *Chronicle,* 785.

42. J. Gairdner, *The English Church in the Sixteenth Century from the Accession of Henry VIII to the Death of Mary* (1903), 116-17.

43. Hall, *Chronicle,* 788. Harpsfield's note in his *Pretended Divorce between Henry VIII and Catharine of Aragon,* ed. N. Pocock (Camden Soc., 1878), 197 is clearly taken straight from Hall. The editor of *Cal. S.P. Spanish,* iv. II. 994 confused Temse's intervention with the motion of a member for the city of London reported by Chapuys a year later, which in any case was quite different (cf. *LP* vi. 324).

44. Merriman, i. 427 ff. Also printed in *StP,* vii. 633 ff.

45. The only historian to use it was, inevitably, Froude (ii. 283-6); he quoted it in a mock-Tudor translation of his own which is at times excessively free, though it does not pervert the essential sense.

46. 'Et ubi publicum Regni concilium (quod parliamentum uocant) pro Regni quiete stabilienda, ut ad certa tempora haberetur, indictum foret, ceperunt undecunque sollicita cum sedulitate clanculum exquirere, qua de re tractari, quidque in hoc parliamento, ut expediens rei publicae agi oporteret, quicquid uero aliorum delatu ex re praeterita rerum usu, uel coniectura usque collegissent id statim communibus consiliis trutinabant, omnia secus interpretantes que Regni quies ac utilitas exposcebat.'

47. Cf. D. Knowles, *The Religious Orders in England* (Cambridge, 1948-59), iii. 201; H. Maynard Smith, *Henry VIII and the Reformation* (1948), 442.

48. *LP* v. 171. Charles's letter has now been printed by H. Schulte Herbrüggen, *Sir Thomas More: Neue Briefe* (Münster, 1966), 97.

49. *LP* v. 120. Earlier, Chapuys had heard that More's frequent defence of Catherine had put him in danger of dismissal (*Cal. S.P. Spanish,* iv. I. 727).

50. *LP* v. 187.

51. PRO, SP 1/125/247-41; cf., *LP* xii. II. 552. His account contains some dating problems: writing up to eight years after the event, he was liable to telescope several parliamentary sessions. In re-telling the story I have adopted the most likely way out of several confusions.

52. E.g., Temse could have been a client, as suggested above, p. 85.

53. Throckmorton says it happened shortly after the Parliament opened and when he had been arguing to the Act of Appeals (1533): both cannot be correct. Since he speaks of More as chancellor, I prefer the earlier date.

54. Harpsfield, *More,* 59-62. Continental reformers, too, spoke of More as 'iure depositum' (Allen, x. 116).

55. E.g., Roper, 225; Harpsfield, *More,* 58-9 is curiously condensed on the whole of More's chancellorship on which, quite contrary to his usual practice, he does not quote Roper.

56. As he explained to Erasmus (Allen, x. 31-2).

57. Ibid. 124: 'fortasse metuebat invidiam repudii, quod semper dissuasit.'

58. G. R. Elton, 'The Commons' Supplication of 1532,' *English Historical Review*, 66 (1951), 507–34; J. P. Cooper, 'The Supplication against the Ordinaries reconsidered,' *EHR* 72 (1957), 616 ff.; M. J. Kelly, 'The Submission of the Clergy,' *TRHS* (1965), 97 ff.

59. *LP* v. 1013.

60. Kelly, *TRHS* (1965), 105.

61. Had More in his younger days experienced doubt about catholic orthodoxy?

62. *More: Selected Letters*, 217.

63. Cf. G. R. Elton, 'King or Minister? The Man Behind the Henrician Reformation,' *History*, N.S. 39 (1954), 216–32.

64. Quoted by Chambers, *More*, 287.

65. In More's ultimate troubles, Cromwell's considerate treatment and his regret at More's 'obstinacy' became very plain (e.g., *More: Selected Letters*, 222, 236). It looks almost as though Cromwell would have left More alone if it had not been for the king.

HASTINGS, "The Ancestry of Sir Thomas More"

1. More's *English Works*, 1557, edited with a modern version by W. E. Campbell, London, 1931, pp. 1419–21. The translation is by the editor, More's nephew, William Rastell, later Judge Rastell.

2. *Comfort against Tribulation*, Bk. III, cap. 9. This reference was brought to my attention by Professor A. W. Reed, who has generously given me both advice and help from his vast resources of knowledge of the period and the More family.

3. *Erasmi Epistolae*, X, p. 136, No. 2750, *see* Appendix A.

4. To quote a letter of 9 Sept., 1952, from Professor Reed, "It is worth noting that the references that More's sixteenth century biographers make to the status of the Mores are not original but are adapted from More's Epitaph, a copy of which he sent to Erasmus when he retired from the Chancellorship in 1532 and from a letter sent by Erasmus to John Faber, Bishop of Vienna, later in the same year correcting reports that More had been dismissed. With this letter Erasmus enclosed a copy of the epitaph." See Appendix A for the words of the original letter in Latin.

5. R. W. Chambers, "Historical Notes," in Harpsfield's *The Life and Death of Sir Thomas Moore*, edited by E. V. Hitchcock and R. W. Chambers, Oxford, 1932, pp. 298–303.

6. P. C. C. Jankyn (24). See Appendix B.

7. "Young More," in *Under God and the Law*, edited by R. O'Sullivan, Blackwell, Oxford, 1949, p. 2, n. 1.

8. In the registers at Somerset House and at Guildhall Library for the dates 1400 to 1550, I found wills of twenty-four John Mores, thirteen Williams, and eight Thomases. In this tabulation, I did not count such variant spellings as *Mower*, although it is clear that in more than one family it was used interchangeably with *More*. Among the seventy-five or so Mores whose wills are in the registers for the period, a few distinct families emerge, even on rather superficial examination. There is a Bristol family, perhaps that of William More, "scrivener," a Norwich family, an Oxfordshire family, a Cambridge family, a Yorkshire family (with some sort of cousinly connection between the last two), and of course there are the Mores of Losely, Surrey, to whom Christoper More, one of Sir John More's executors belonged. He was brother to Alice More, later Alice Clerke, whom John married as the last of his four wives. She survived Sir John by many years and kept Sir Thomas out of part of his inheritance in the period of his "honourable poverty." (R. W. Chambers, *Thomas More*, London, Jonathan Cape, 1935, pp. 54–5.) In London the Mores were many and well-distributed among the parishes and the crafts, professions, and ranks of society. In the roll of the drapers' company alone, there are at least six

Mores listed between 1406 and 1533 (Percival Boyd, *Roll of Drapers Co.*, Croydon 1934, p. 129). A John More, citizen and goldsmith, died in 1521 leaving a widow, two children and a child in the womb (P. C. C., 22 Maynwaring, 1521). And a John Moore, esq., died in 1529, leaving a wife, Johanna, and two sons called William, an elder and a younger (P. C. C., 10 Jankyn). Some of the country Mores sound like prosperous gentlefolk; others are obviously more humble folk like Richard More, "husbandman," who died in 1511, leaving various legacies of sheep.

9. Corporation of London Records Office, Husting Roll 200, Item 3, 1 March, 1470, and Item 7, 10 Sept., 1470. The second of the charters mentions not only the messuage in Breadstreet ward but also property in the parish of St. Sepulchre extra Newgate in Faringdon Without Ward, "namely two tenements in Knyghtryderstrete opposite the church of St. Sepulchre between the tenement of Agnes Brown, widow, and the tenement called the Cardinalshatte on the east, the house of the earl of Worcester which John, lord Dudley holds in the right of his wife, on the west, Knyghtriderstrete on the north and the parcel of the earl's house and the said cedda on the south," and two other tenements on the lane called "le lyttyl wayly" also in the parish of St. Sepulchre. But these properties are not mentioned in the documents relating to the common recovery in 1499.

10. This is a typical family entail intended to guarantee the property against alienation from the right heirs of the original donor.

11. Corporation of London Records Office, Husting Roll 226, Items 5, 6, 7, and 8.

12. *Ibid.*, Pleas of Land, 171 (18).

13. Chambers, *op. cit.*, pp. 52 and 68.

14. Husting Roll 207, Item 11, 8 Sept. 1477.

15. C 54/305, 33 Henry VI, 2 June 1455, m. 11d. An essential line mentioning Johanna, wife of William More, is omitted in the transcript of this document which is printed in the Calendar, *C.C.R. 1454-1461*, p. 68.

16. *Home Counties Magazine*, edited by W. J. Hardy, F.S.A., IV, 1902, p. 125, referred to in *V.C.H.* II, pp. 256-7.

17. Inquisitions post mortem, 21 Ric. II, C 136/99/30. A John More, mercer, was condemned to death with other supporters of John of Northampton in 1384. The sentence was later commuted to imprisonment and then banishment from the vicinity of London. In 1391 (evidently at the instance of John of Gaunt), John of Northampton, John More, and Richard Norbury were pardoned and restored to their estates. And in January, 1395, they were restored to the liberties of the City. *Calendar of Letter Books* H (London, 190 1907), pp. 42, 64, 176, 178, 198, 210, 211, 218, 248, 265, 266n., 281-2, 304, 305-6, 307, 315, 317, 370, 428-9.

18. Cf. Charles Sisson. "Sir Thomas More and North Mimms," in *Review of English Studies*, V (1929), pp. 54-5, for later history of the More property in North Mimms.

19. Commissary Court of London, Sharpe, Guildhall Library, MS. 9171/5, 169.

20. Commissary Court of London, Wilde, Guildhall Library, MS. 9171/6, 13.

21. Edward Foss, *Judges of England*, V, pp. 193-198.

22. "Saint Thomas More and the Law," in *Dublin Review*, CXCVII (1935), pp. 53-72.

23. *Records of the Society of Lincolns Inn*, Admissions, I, pp. 18 and 19. Foss overlooks the second of these entries. He says (p. 198) that there is no record of the admission of the younger John More.

24. *Records of the Society of Lincolns Inn*, Black Books, I, pp. 39, 50, 51.

25. See Chambers *Historical Notes* in Harpsfield's life referred to above, note 5.

26. Bridge accts. annual, 1484-1509 (Corporation of London R.O.), from fol. 35b to 274 *passim* and Bridge rentals, 1509-1525, 166b, a note that John Pakenron replaced him in 1517. He was paid 13s. 4d. as his regular fee, but presumably there were, as in other legal jobs, additional fees and perquisites.

27. I hope to write an article which will show more fully how Sir John More got his start in the legal profession and built up the family fortunes. Sir John was, according to his son, less than extravagant in providing for his son's expenses at Oxford and elsewhere during his early years, but that may have been a matter of principle rather than necessity (Cf. Chambers, *op. cit.,* p. 65, and Stapleton, I p. 156).

28. A. R. Wagner, *Heralds and Heraldry in the Middle Ages,* London, 1939, p. 19 and pp. 90-1, for the grant of arms in Edward IV's reign. Cf. *Archaeologia,* LXIX, p. 74, for the heralds' rolls of Henry VIII's time. I have confirmation of this information about John More's arms in a letter from Mr. Wagner, Richmond Herald, dated 10 Sept. 1951.

29. Appendices C–H in the original article are not reprinted here.

HASTINGS, "Sir Thomas More: Maker of English Law?"

1. Published by the Cambridge University Press, 1938, pp. 98–9.

2. Mr. Guy presented a paper entitled *The Early-Tudor Star Chamber* to the Legal History Conference at Ave-ystwyth, 18–21 July 1972. The paper is now published in *Legal History Studies,* edited by Daffyd Jenkins (Cardiff, 1975).

3. C1/706/34.

4. D.L.5/5, fols. 298-393.

5. Chapuys, 21 Feb. 1531 in *Letters and Papers, Foreign and Domestic of the Reign of Henry VIII,* 1509-1545, vol. V edited by James Gairdner, p. 112; *The Lyfe of Sir Thomas Moore, Knight,* written by William Roper, Esquire, ed. by E. V. Hitchcock, p. 51.

6. Robert Somerville, *History of the Duchy of Lancaster,* 1265-1603, vol. 1 (London, 1953), p. 325.

7. Thirteen of seventeen who held the office from 1399 to 1525 were laymen. Somerville, pp. 388-393.

8. Somerville, pp. 392-393. Sir Henry Marny was a soldier who fought for Henry VII at Stoke and Blackheath. Sir Richard Wingfield fought in France in 1523, and in 1525 was in Spain, where he died. He may have studied law at Gray's Inn.

9. G. R. Elton, *The Tudor Constitution* (Cambridge, 1960), p. 94.

10. See, for example, D.L.5/5/179v.

11. D.L.1/5/G2.

12. D.L.5/5/355.

13. D.L.1/18/R4/29.

14. D.L.3/14/B3.

15. D.L.5/5/302v.

16. D.L.5/5/306.

17. D.L.5/5/337 and 347.

18. D.L.5/5/350v.

19. D.L.5/5/324.

20. D.L.5/5/354v.

21. D.L.3/14/G1/qq-vv.

22. D.L.1/4/R8/13.

23. D.L.1/21/M3/54.

24. W. J. Jones, *The Elizabethan Court of Chancery* (Oxford, 1967).

25. Some entries note that a privy seal was sent to several persons jointly. It does not seem profitable to make a detailed count.

26. D.L.5/5/308v.

27. D.L.5/5/301.

28. Again it seems well nigh impossible to establish an exact count, particularly of each category as given below, because riot cases, for example, often arise from a dispute about rights of common or of inheritance.

29. D.L.5/5/303. Cf. also the statement by a witness on the 7th of June 1526 in his

deposition "afore the Michaelmas terme at London that was not kept at that tyme but was prorogued" (D.L.3/17/B3c) and a similar statement in D.L.3/17/B3e.

30. The draft decrees are in two bundles as they were presumably left by William Heydon, clerk of the court in More's term of office.

31. D.L.5/5/304v, 316v, 335v.

32. D.L.5/5/324 and 334v, 367v, 378, 381.

33. D.L.3/18/R2.

34. R. W. Chambers, *Thomas More,* The Bedford Historical Series (London, 1938), p. 274.

35. D.L.5/5/353.

36. D.L.1/5/G5.

37. D.L.3/14/G1; D.L.3/7/B5; D.L.3/17/B3.

38. D.L.3/18/E2; D.L.1/21/M3; D.L.5/5/333, 337v, 341v.

39. D.L.1/6/R4; D.L.1/6/T5; D.L.1/4/T2; D.L.1/6/W3; D.L.5/5/333v and 350.

40. D.L.3/14/G1qq through vv. Cf. above n. 21.

41. D.L.1/21/M3.

42. D.L.5/5/331v.

43. D.L.3/19/T3; D.L.5/5/312v, 315.

44. D.L.5/5/312v.

45. D.L.5/5/315.

46. D.L.5/5/337v.

47. D.L.3/19/T3h.

48. *The Yale Edition of the Complete Works of Thomas More,* vol. 4, (*Utopia*) edited by Edward Surtz and J. H. Hexter (New Haven, 1965), 195.

49. D.L.1/6/W9; D.L.1/19/B1 and H3; D.L.3/19/W2; D.L.3/18/F1; D.L.3/19/W2.

50. D.L.1/6/W11.

51. D.L.1/6/W11a.

52. Surtz and Hexter, *Complete Works,* vol. 4, 193-195.

53. W. A. Abrams, *Memorials of the Preston Guilds* (Preston, 1882), pp. 24-26; H. M. Clemesha, *A History of Preston in Amounderness* (Manchester, 1912), pp. 107-108; Henry Fishwick, *The History of the Parish of Preston in Amounderness in the County of Lancaster* (London, 1900), pp. 260-264.

54. *State Papers* 1/56, fols. 36-39; *Letters and Papers,* vol. IV, 6043(6).

55. Cotton MSS/Titus B IV.

56. 27 Henry VIII, c. 16.

57. Cotton MS, Galba B v., fol. 134.

58. "More's Conveyance of his Lands and the Law of 'Fraud.'"

59. The controversy over the will of Thomas Hesketh began in 1524 with a petition of Richard Agton to Wingfield, then Chancellor of the Duchy, against Bartholomew Hesketh and the other executors (D.L.1/3/A2). In a second petition to Wingfield, Henry and Rowland Kyghtley and Roger Nowell, cousins of Thomas Hesketh, join with Richard Agton in claiming Rufford manor and advowson and chantry in the chapel there and a long list of other manors in Lancashire, Westmoreland, and Yorkshire as co-heirs to Thomas Hesketh (D.L.3/15/K2). They also complain that the executors withhold certain evidences relating to the land. In More's time, in Michaelmas term 1525, Robert Hesketh brought in a complaint of riot against Richard Agton and others.

60. The Inquisitions Post Mortem are dated 16 September 1523 and 6 September 1523 respectively for the Lancashire lands and those in Yorkshire. D.L.7/5/16 and C20/29.

61. British Museum Additional MS. 32104, fols. 6, 6b, 7.

62. College of Arms, Norf. 27, 5.

63. D.L.5/5/309.

64. The original complaint was addressed to Wolsey and appears in Early Chancery Proceedings (C1/531/54). It was transferred to the Duchy Court by a petition addressed to Wingfield in Michaelmas 1524. (D.L.3/15/K1, K3, and K4).

65. D.L.5/5/335v.

66. For a full and detailed discussion of the genesis of the Statute of Uses, see the article by Dr. E. W. Ives in the *English Historical Review*, LXXXII, 1967, pp. 673–697. Dr. Ives thinks that the 1529 draft was a "well-intentioned but inexperienced proposal emanating from a private individual with a grievance about concealed titles."

MAC NALTY, "Sir Thomas More as Public Health Reformer"

1. Ad Dorpium, *Lucubrationes*, 1563, p. 417.

2. Letter to Ulrich von Hutten, 23rd July, 1519.

3. The remedy was a clyster, or enema [eds.].

4. *Letters and Papers* (Henry VIII), IV, No. 2758.

5. *Brit. Med. Journ.* II, 1945, 63, 196.

6. Letter to Ulrich von Hutten.

7. *Lives of the Lord Chancellors*, 1856, Chap. XXX, *Life of Sir Thomas More*.

8. *H. Maynard Smith: Pre-Reformation England.* Macmillan & Co., Ltd., London, 1938, Ch. VI, 484.

MC CONICA, "The Recusant Reputation of Thomas More"

1. The matter is discussed in a work which was in press when this paper was written: E. E. Reynolds *The Trial of St Thomas More* (New York [1964]).

2. Ep. 3048 to Barthomeus Latomus, 24 August 1535, ll. 59–60; see P. S. Allen *Erasmi epistolae* XI (Oxford 1947), p. 216.

3. E. F. Rogers *The Correspondence of Sir Thomas More* (Princeton 1947), p. 404 (Ep. 168, ll. 30–1).

4. Rogers, *op. cit.* Ep. 192, ll. 41–3.

5. Rogers, *op. cit.* Ep. 197, ll. 211–16.

6. British Library MS Royal 17 D xiv, folios 380 and 376 respectively.

7. Rogers, Ep. 215.

8. Rogers, Ep. 212; see note 7; c. Christmas 1534.

9. ll. 36–9.

10. Ep. 198, ll. 27–8; cf. *The Workes of Sir Thomas More Knyght* (London 1557), p. 1423G.

11. Ep. 199.

12. ll. 191–9; cf. *The Workes*, p. 1427G.

13. Rogers, Ep. 202, May? 1534; *The Workes*, p. 1431C.

14. Rogers, Ep. 206 [August 1534].

15. ll. 470–3; in connection with the present conjecture about the real purpose of this letter, notice that More, in a circular letter at the time of his imprisonment, told his friends he was forbidden to see anyone but his daughter Margaret, and referred them to her for information about his needs; Rogers, Ep. 204.

16. Nicholas Harpsfield, *The life and death of Sr Thomas Moore, knight* ... edited by E. V. Hitchcock. EETS, os, 186 (London 1932, for 1931), pp. 101–2, 136.

17. British Library Arundel MS 73 folios 96^v–7; cf. *Historia anglicana ecclesiastica ... auctore Nicolao Harpsfeldio archidiacono cantuariensi* (Duaci 1622), p. 632, l. 44 f. The alteration was first detected by Lord Acton; cf. Hitchcock, ed. *Harpsfield's Life of More*, introduction, cxciv, cxcix–cc.

18. Ed. E. V. Hitchcock, p. 109.

19. Loc. cit.

20. Ibid., p. 213.

21. Introduction to *The English Works of Sir Thomas More*, vol. I (1931), pp. 8 f.

22. *Omnia, quae hucusque ad manus nostras pervenerunt, Latina opera.*

23. L. Bradner and C. A. Lynch, eds., *The Latin Epigrams of Thomas More* (Chicago, 1953), p. xvii.

24. Notably by Mme Marie Delcourt: "L'amitié d'Erasme et de More entre 1520 et 1535," *Bulletin de l'Association Guillaume Budé* (January 1936), 7–29 and "Recherches sur Thomas More: la tradition continentale et la tradition anglaise," *Humanisme et Renaissance,* III (1936), pp. 22–42.

25. Delcourt, "L'amitié," p. 10.

26. J. Leclerc, ed., *Desiderii Erasmi Roterodami opera omnia,* vol. IIIb, 1439F–1442D.

27. *Erasmi epistolae,* ed., P. S. Allen, vol. X, p. 259; Ep. 2831, ll. 29–31.

28. Ibid., Ep. 2659.

29. The text, which follows the letter, is printed by Allen at the end of Ep. 2831, ll. 73–131.

30. *The Yale Edition of The Complete Works of St Thomas More,* vol. 8: *The Confutation of Tyndale's Answer,* Part I, The Text, Books I–IV (New Haven, 1973), p. 177, ll. 15–23.

31. Yale Edition, p. 178, ll. 29–30.

32. Yale Edition, p. 179, ll. 15–17.

33. T. Stapleton, *Vita Thomae Mori* in *Tres Thomae . . .* Coloniae Aggripinae, 1612, pp. 192–3.

34. "Sed Erasmus qui ab humilitate Augustiniana tam multum abfuit quam ab doctrina, nec id facere voluit, nec has Mori literas superesse passus est, ut Farragini cum caeteris insererentur," p. 193.

35. Rogers, Ep. 199, ll. 260–2 and note.

36. Stapleton, *Vita,* p. 193.

37. N. Sander, *De origine ac progressu schismatis Anglicani* (Cologne 1585), I, c.xv.

38. *A Treatise of Three Conversions of England* [St Omer], Pt. III, 1604, pp. 307–08.

NELSON, "Thomas More, Grammarian and Orator"

1. *The Civilization of the Renaissance in Italy,* translated by S. G. C. Middlemore (New York, 1935), p. 236.

2. See my *John Skelton, Laureate* (Columbia University Press, 1939), pp. 29–31.

3. R. W. Chambers, *Thomas More* (New York, 1936), pp. 56–66.

4. Translated, *ibid.,* p. 81, from MS Arundel 249, fol. 85.

5. *Harpsfield's Life of More,* EETS, Or. Ser. 186 (1932), p. 13. [But see Richard J. Schoeck, "Sir Thomas More, Humanist and Lawyer," *University of Toronto Quarterly,* 34 (1964), 1–14.]

6. *Progymnasmata,* published with More's *Epigrammata* (Basle, 1518). Though not published until 1518, the work was certainly completed much earlier. See Chambers, *More,* p. 89. [Professor James Hutton suggests that More and Lily may have done these translations as a model for schoolboys (*The Latin Epigrams of Thomas More,* ed. Leicester Bradner and Charles Arthur Lynch, University of Chicago Press, Chicago, 1953, p. 239).]

7. *Luciani opuscula* (Paris, 1506).

8. A man kills a tyrant's son, and the tyrant thereupon kills himself. Is the assassin entitled to the money which, in this hypothetical republic, is legally the reward of tyrannicides? Lucian argues the affirmative; More and Erasmus maintain the negative. See C. R. Thompson, *The Translations of Lucian by Erasmus and St. Thomas More* (Ithaca, N.Y., 1940), pp. 29–44.

9. The Latin of this dedication is quoted by Thompson, *op. cit.*, p. 40.

10. Stapleton, *Vita Thomae Mori*, translated by P. E. Hallett (London 1928), p. 9.

11. *Register of the University of Oxford*, edited by C. W. Boase (Oxford, 1885), vol. I, p. 299 (Smyth, More).

12. [A. W. Reed provides information about Holt in his essay "Young More" in *Under God and the Law*, ed. Richard O'Sullivan, Blackwell, Oxford, 1949, pp. 6–11. See also A. B. Emden, *A Biographical Register of the University of Oxford to 1500*, Oxford, 1957–1959.]

13. W. D. Macray, *A Register of the Members of St. Mary Magdalen*, I, 120.

14. MS Magdalen College, No. 168, fol. 36.

15. R. S. Stanier, *Magdalen School* (Oxford, 1940), pp. 36, 57, 59. [Holt served as master to Archbishop Morton's boys *c.* 1496 and later as master of the Chichester prebendal school. In 1502 he succeeded the poet John Skelton as tutor to Prince Henry.]

16. Anthony à Wood, *Athenae Oxonienses* (1813), I, Col. 15. The three extant editions are all of later date, but the dedication of the book to Morton, who died in 1500, makes Wood's statement altogether probable.

17. Bale, *Scriptorum Catalogus* (Basel, 1559 [?]), Cent. undec. no. 89, says that Holt "claruit anno Domini 1510." [But see Emden, *A Biographical Register.*]

18. [The texts of these epigrams, originally printed as part of this essay, are here omitted since they are included in *The Latin Epigrams of Thomas More*, ed. Bradner and Lynch, pp. 117–119. See *ibid.*, pp. 119–120, for More's epigram introducing Linacre's *Progymnasmata grammatices vulgaria* (*c.* 1512).]

19. It is noteworthy that every one on More's list of recommended grammarians: Sulpitius, Phocas, Perottus, and Diomedes, appears also on a similar list prepared by that most prolific grammar master of the Magdalen School, Robert Whittinton (*The Vulgaria of John Stanbridge and the Vulgaria of Robert Whittinton*, edited by Beatrice White, EETS, Or. Ser. 187 [1932], p. 34). This fact, read together with More's early friendship with such Magdalen scholars as Holt, Lily, and Grocyn, suggests that whatever his formal Oxford residence, More may have studied at the Magdalen Grammar School, one of the earliest and most influential centers of humanism at the English universities. The supposition is rendered more likely by the fact that, by direction of its founder, instruction at the Magdalen School was free to all who sought it (R. S. Stanier, *Magdalen School* [Oxford, 1940], pp. 19–20). If More were a member of Canterbury Hall or St. Mary's Hall, therefore, he would have been permitted to attend Magdalen lectures.

20. MS Arundel 249, fol. 85^V. [The letter has been printed in *The Correspondence of Sir Thomas More*, ed. Elizabeth Frances Rogers, Princeton University Press, Princeton, 1947, pp. 3–5.]

21. [See my edition of part of this manuscript, *A Fifteenth Century School Book*, Clarendon Press, Oxford, 1956.]

22. *Register of the University of Oxford*, edited by C. W. Boase (Oxford, 1885), I, 298 (Watson).

23. University Archives, Register G, fol. 183: "Eodem die [June 13, 1513] sup*plicat* [a letter, perhaps a "d" for "*dominus*," has been lined through by the scribe] thomas more quate*nus* studium quod ha*b*uit 14 annis informa*ndo* scolares gram*m*aticam possit sibi suffic*ere* vt admitta*tur* ad informa*ndum* in grammatica h*e*c est *conc*ess*a* sic q*u*od legat unu*m* libru*m* salustij et compona*t* ephegra*m*ma appon*endum* vallibus e*cc*lesie beate marie virginis."

24. Stapleton, *Vita Thomae Mori*, translated by P. E. Hallett (London, 1928), p. 9.

25. *Ibid.*, p. 15.

26. *Ibid.*, pp. 103–104.

27. *Thomae Mori Omnia Latina Opera* (Louvain, 1566), p. 44.

28. T. E. Bridgett, *The Life and Writings of Sir Thomas More* (1891), pp. 172-176.

29. MS Cotton Titus D IV.

30. Allen, *Opus epistolarum Erasmi*, II, No. 389.

31. *Acts of Court of the Mercers' Company*, edited by L. Lyell and F. D. Watney (Cambridge, 1936). My attention was first drawn to these records by Professor C. J. Sisson. They are mentioned in a brief and unindexed "additional note" in Chambers' *More*, p. 405. [See A. W. Reed, "Young More," in *Under God and the Law*, pp. 18-19.]

32. *Acts of Court*, p. 320. Chambers, depending upon Watney, *Hospital of St. Thomas of Acon* (1906), gives the date as March 21, 1508. *Acts of Court* makes it clear that the date is 1508/9.

33. *Ibid.*, p. xiii.

34. A "pensionary" of Bruges was the humanist Francis of Cranevelt who became a friend of More and carried on a lengthy correspondence with him (see *Literae ad Franciscum Craneveldium*, edited by Henry de Vocht [Louvain, 1928]).

35. Although in theory the Adventurers were composed of all the guilds which sent their products into foreign trade, in practice it was almost always a mercer that presided over the Adventurers, and the records and accounts of the exporters were kept by the Mercers' clerk and preserved in the Mercers' books.

36. *Acts of Court*, pp. 329-345. In the *Journal of the Common Council of the City of London* (Guildhall Record Office, Journal 11, fol. 181^V), under the date March 23, 1513, one Thomas More, mercer, is said to be "defunct." This entry has been alleged against the identification of the Thomas More, Mercer, who was elected burgess in Parliament in January, 1509, with the great St. Thomas (Chambers, *More*, p. 405). It might, with equal strength, be referred to the More who was involved in the conversations with Antwerp. But on March 5, 1518, five years after the death of "Thomas More, mercer," the Master of St. Thomas of Acon brought before the court of Mercers the books of ordinances and statutes proposed for a new foundation "whiche quayres before alle the said parsones were redd in Inglysshe, and uppon euery article theryn conteyned amonge theym they had Communycacion, and agreed that the said quayre shulde be shewed unto Maister Thomas More and to have his advise and Counseyll theryn ..." (*Acts of Court*, pp. 452-453). I do not think it can be doubted that the Master More who was called upon to advise the Mercers in 1518 was the man who aided the company during the negotiations of 1509.

37. No one has as yet been able to track down the case in court records.

38. *The Life of Sir Thomas Moore*, edited by E. V. Hitchcock (Early English Text Society, Original Series 197 [1935]), p. 10.

39. Chambers, *More*, p. 405. See above, Note 36.

40. Allen, *Opus epistolarum*, II, No. 461.

41. Bridgett, *op. cit.*, p. 177.

42. *Ibid.*, pp. 177-178.

43. Roper, *The Life of Sir Thomas Moore*, EETS, Or. Ser. 197, p. 22.

44. Chambers, *More*, p. 193.

45. Chambers, p. 255.

46. *Op. cit.*, p. 178. [G. R. Elton, who is convinced that More actively sought membership in the royal council, describes his role at court bluntly: "More was to be Henry's tame humanist." See "Thomas More, Councillor," in *St. Thomas More: Action and Contemplation*, ed. Richard Sylvester, Yale University Press, New Haven, 1972, p. 109.]

47. Allen, *op. cit.*, III, No. 832.

48. Abridged from Erasmus' letter by Bridgett, *op. cit.*, p. 167. See Allen, *Opus epistolarum*, III, No. 855.

49. Humanist atrabiliousness may be detected in More's epigrams on Brixius and in his

anti-Lutheran tracts. But in neither case was More fighting a personal battle. Brixius had attacked England, and the Lutherans had declared war on true religion.

O'SULLIVAN, "St. Thomas More and Lincoln's Inn"

1. Levy-Ullmann, *The English Legal Tradition*, 87 (Mitchell transl. 1935).

2. Fortescue, *De Laudibus Legum Angliae*, 172 (Selden ed. 1775).

3. Maitland, "English Law and the Renaissance," in 1 *Essays in Anglo-American Legal History*, 199 (1908).

4. Maitland, *Christian Philosophy and the Common Law*, 13.

5. Harpsfield, *Life of More*, 303 (1932).

6. Finch, *Description of the Common Law*, 6 (1627).

7. The Black Book contains the records of Lincoln's Inn. References in the text to this work are from the multi-volume 1897 edition entitled *The Records of the Honourable Society of Lincoln's Inn.*

8. The Acts of Court of the Company deals with the doings of the Mercers' Company, one of the London companies.

9. More, *Utopia*, 8 (Everyman ed. 1918).

10. Butler, *2 Reminiscences*, 274 (1827).

11. *Ibid.*

12. 17 *The Conveyancer*, 142 (1932).

13. Chambers, *Thomas More*, 353 (1935).

14. Campbell, *2 Lives of the Lord Chancellors*, 53 (7th ed. 1885).

SURTZ, "More's Friendship with Fisher"

1. See G. Constant, *The Reformation in England,* trans. R. E. Scantlebury, I (London: Sheed & Ward, 1934), 200. Horace applies the phrase ironically to the sons of Quintus Arrius, "nequitia et nugis, pravorum et amore gemellum" (*Satires* II. iii. 243–244).

2. N. Harpsfield, *Life and death of Sr Thomas Moore . . .*, ed. E. V. Hitchcock (London: E.E.T.S., 1932), pp. 186–187; Paris News Letter, *ibid.*, p. 261; and "Expositio fidelis," *Opus epistolarum Des. Erasmi Roterodami*, ed. P. S. Allen *et al.* (Oxford: Clarendon Press, 1906–58), XI, 371.

3. Harpsfield, *Moore*, p. 188; Paris News Letter, *ibid.,* p. 262; and "Expositio fidelis," Erasmus, *Ep.*, XI, 371.

4. Edited by N. Pocock (London: Camden Society, 1878), p. 28. The "conformity of mind" is evidenced even by the possibility of ascribing a prayer first to More and later to Fisher, as by A. G. Dickens: see "A New Prayer of Sir Thomas More," *Church Quarterly Review*, CCXLVII (1937), 231–236, and *Tudor Treatises* (Wakefield: Yorkshire Archaeological Society, 1959), p. 19.

5. Harpsfield, *Divorce*, p. 28.

6. Theologically significant, for example, is More's reference to the *partim-partim* source of revelation as allegedly found in Pseudo-Dionysius' *Ecclesiastical Hierarchy:* "the leaders and maisters of the christen fayth . . . deliuered vs many thynges to bee kepte, partly by writyng and partly by theyr institucions vnwriten" ("Confutation of Tyndale," *Workes* [London: Cawood *et al.*, 1557], p. 515). Cf. Fisher, "Assert. Luth. confut." prooem., veritas 9, *Opera* (Wirceburgi: Fleischmann, 1597), col. 294.

7. Erasmus, *Ep.*, I, 174, 188, introd.

8. *Ibid.*, I, 273–274.

9. *Ibid.*, I, 590–593, Appendix VI, "Erasmus at Cambridge in 1506." Fisher's address is printed in J. Lewis, *Life of Dr. John Fisher . . .* ed. T. H. Turner (London, 1855), Coll. No. *VIII, II, 263–272.

10. Erasmus, *Ep.*, I, 415. The other possibilities are the London residences of

Fisher's friends: Lambeth Palace of Archbishop Warham or Winchester House of Bishop Foxe.

11. See the detailed account in D. F. S. Thomson and H. C. Porter, *Erasmus and Cambridge* (Toronto: University of Toronto Press, 1963), Introd., pp. 1–103.

12. W. H. Dunham, "The Members of Henry VIII's Whole Council, 1509–1527," *English Historical Review*, LIX (1944), 198, n. 1; and Table II, p. 208. Thomas More first sat on the council on October 27, 1519 (*ibid.*, pp. 194, 210).

13. Speech to Synod, "Jean Fisher," ed. F. van Ortroy, *Analecta Bollandiana*, X (1891), 258.

14. Erasmus, *Ep.*, II, 320.

15. *Ibid.*, II, 347, 371, 485–487; More, *Selected Letters*, ed. E. F. Rogers (New Haven: Yale University Press, 1961), pp. 77–78. Studying Greek at this same time, Colet was using "the solicited help of my boy Clement" (More, *Selected Letters*, p. 77, and Erasmus, *Ep.*, II, 347).

16. Erasmus, *Ep.*, II, 553, introd., II, 598, and III, 75, 237. There was no Trojan war at Cambridge as at Oxford, as Erasmus tells Peter Mosellanus in April 1519, "quod eius scholae princeps sit R. P. Ioannes Phischerius, episcopus Roffensis, non eruditione tantum sed et vita theologica" (*Ep.*, III, 546).

17. *Ibid.*, II, 494, 496, 598, trans. F. M. Nichols, *The Epistles of Erasmus* . . . (New York: Russell and Russell, 1962), II, 569. It was actually Colet who held up the delivery of the book, for Erasmus had permitted More to show it to Colet before giving it to Fisher (*Ep.*, III, 75). On September 29, 1516, Erasmus had written to Reuchlin: "Adorat te propemodum Episcopus Roffensis" (*ibid.*, II, 350).

18. Erasmus, *Ep.*, III, 464.

19. *The Correspondence of Sir Thomas More*, ed. E. F. Rogers (Princeton: Princeton University Press, 1947), pp. 139–140, 148–149.

20. More, *Correspondence*, pp. 191–192, trans. *Selected Letters*, p. 125. This same letter makes reference to Erasmus' long sojourn with Fisher as well as with other Englishmen (*Correspondence*, p. 169). Fisher's praise of the Novum Instrumentum is to be found in Erasmus, *Ep.*, II, 268.

21. More, *Correspondence*, pp. 136–137, trans. E. E. Reynolds, *Saint John Fisher* (London: Burns & Oates, 1955), p. 79. In view of More's unexpected reference to his "delight . . . for the sake of our country," it is likely that he is alluding rather to Fisher's defense of his king (*Defensio regie assertionis*, wr. 1522–23, pub. 1525).

22. More, *Correspondence*, p. 111, trans. *Selected Letters*, p. 94.

23. More, *Correspondence*, p. 253.

24. *Ibid.*, pp. 253–254, trans. *Selected Letters*, p. 147. At his first visit to England, Erasmus was struck by the universality and frequency of kissing in social intercourse (*Ep.*, I, 239).

25. Sigg. A3–B4.

26. Erasmus, *Ep.*, IV, 296, introd.

27. Reynolds bases the probability upon More's reference in *The confutacyon of Tyndales answere* (1532) to Fisher's use of Origen in a sermon against Luther and Tyndale (*More*, pp. 214, 244). But More specifies the date as "about the tyme of the burnyng of Tyndals euill translated testament . . . not much aboue .vii. yere since" (*Workes*, p. 410), a designation which more feasibly carries us back to Fisher's sermon at Robert Barnes's abjuration in February 1526 and even later.

28. G. Marc'hadour, *L'Univers de Thomas More* (Paris: Vrin, 1963), p. 324.

29. *The Office of Speaker* (London: Cassell, [1964]), p. 156. On More as Speaker, see *ibid.*, pp. 156–159; R. W. Chambers, *Thomas More* (London: Jonathan Cape, 1935),

pp. 200-208, following J. E. Neale, "Free Speech in Parliament," in *Tudor Studies*, ed. R. W. Seton Watson; and Reynolds, *More*, pp. 176-181.

30. Polydore Vergil, *Anglica Historia ... A.D. 1485-1537*, tr. D. Hay (London: Royal Historical Society, 1950), pp. 306-307; Reynolds, *Fisher*, pp. 98-100. Naming Fisher with More, Tunstal, Lee, Warham, and others, Vergil had bestowed superlative praise on the Bishop of Rochester in the dedication of his *Adagia sacra* (1519) to Richard Pace: see D. Hay, "The Life of Polydore Vergil of Urbino," *Journal of the Warburg and Courtauld Institutes*, XII (1949), 150-151.

31. *Opera*, p. 6.

32. W. Roper, *The Lyfe of Sir Thomas Moore, knighte*, ed. E. V. Hitchcock (London: E.E.T.S., 1935), pp. 67-68; and Letter to Cromwell, *Correspondence*, p. 498. In 1536, Cochlaeus declared that all the scholars in England could never refute the arguments for papal primacy erstwhile expounded by Henry VIII, More, and Fisher ("Defensio ... Roffensis & ... Mori," in *Epistola Nicolai ...* [Leipzig, 1536], sig. Z3)!

33. More, *Omnia ... Latina opera* (Louvain, 1565), fol. 68^V, trans. T. E. Bridgett, *Blessed John Fisher* (London: Burns & Oates, 1888), p. 138; and Fisher, "Assert. Luth. confut." art. 25, *Opera*, cols. 530-580.

34. *Correspondence*, p. 498.

35. *Hyperaspistes diatribae aduersus seruum arbitrium Martini Lutheri* (Basel, 1526), sig. A3.

36. Cochlaeus to More, June 29, 1531, in More, *Neue Briefe*, ed. H. Schulte Herbrüggen (Münster: Aschendorff, 1966), p. 104.

37. Eck, *Enchiridion locorum communium* (Landesutae, May 1526), sig. A2; Eck, *De sacrificio missae* (October 1526), sig. A4^V; Eck, *Super Aggaeo Propheta* (Salingiaci, 1538), fol. 58, quoted in More, *Neue Briefe*, ed. Schulte Herbrüggen, p. 53, n. 15; and Fisher, "Ver. Corp." 1.prooem., *Opera*, p. 748.

38. Chambers, *More*, p. 215.

39. Erasmus, *Ep.*, VI, 443.

40. *More*, p. 222. Reynolds favors Holbein's second sojourn in England (1532-43) rather than the first (1526-28) (*Fisher*, p. vii).

41. *A sermon ... concernynge certayne heretickes / whiche than were abiured ...* (London, [1526]), sig. E1.

42. "Ver.corp." 1.prooem., *Opera*, pp. 748-749.

43. More, *Workes*, p. 285; cf. Fisher, "Assert. Luth. confut." art. 33, *Opera*, cols. 633-634. There may be an allusion to Fisher and St. John's College (as well as to Foxe's and Wolsey's colleges) in *The supplycacyon of soulys* (1529), where More maintains that the only great foundations made in his time are to be seen in the universities: "the substance of [these foundations] be not al founden vpon temporall landes, newe taken out of temporal handes into the church, but of such as the churche hadde long afore, and now the same translated from one place vnto an other" (*Workes*, p. 333). The revenue for St. John's College came partially from the suppression of hospitals in Cambridge and Ospringe and nunneries at Bromhall and Higham.

44. *Workes*, p. 345.

45. *Ibid.*, pp. 410, 515.

46. *Ibid.*, p. 866. Cf. Tyndale, "The Obedience of a Christian Man," *Doctrinal Treatises ...*, ed. H. Walter (Cambridge, 1848), pp. 213-215, 220-223.

47. *Workes*, p. 422.

48. *A disputacion of Purgatorye* (1533?), sigg. A5^V-6, G4^V-5, K3, L2^V-5, and *An other boke against Rastel* (1533?), sig. A3^V. The reference is to Fisher, "Assert. Luth. confut." art. 18, *Opera*, cols. 496-502.

49. Chambers, *More*, p. 229.

50. Roper, *Moore*, pp. 32–33. Roper is depending upon his memory, for Tunstal was not transferred from London to Durham until 1530, three years afterward.

51. T. Rymer, *Foedera* ... (London, 1727-35), XIV, 405-407.

52. Chambers, *More*, p. 250.

53. Harpsfield, *Moore*, p. 151, and Notes, p. 343; cf. Harpsfield, *Divorce*, pp. 222-223.

54. "Jean Fisher," ed. F. van Ortroy, *Analecta Bollandiana*, XII (1893), 157-159; More, *Opera*, fol. 124, and *Workes*, p. 1371. More spoke to his daughter Meg about "a weake Cleargie lackinge grace constantly to stand to their learninge" (Roper, *Moore*, p. 78; cf. Harpsfield, *Moore*, Notes, p. 359). In his second sermon on Vulg. Ps. 101, Fisher thirty years before had pictured "almyghty god to be in maner in a deed slepe" because He suffers "many vyces [to] reygne now a dayes in crystes chyrche, as well in the clergy as in the comyn people" (*English Works*, ed. J. E. B. Mayor [London: E.E.T.S., 1876], p. 170).

55. More, *Correspondence*, pp. 520-521. Chambers surmises that More was "nettled by the suggestion that his obstinacy was due to Fisher's example" (*More*, p. 309). For his part, Fisher persisted even when he had been falsely informed that More had taken the oath ("Jean Fisher," ed. Ortroy, *Analecta Bollandiana*, XII, 152-153).

56. "Expositio fidelis," Erasmus, *Ep.*, XI, 370-371.

57. Reynolds, *Fisher*, p. 270.

58. *Ibid.*, p. 275.

59. Reynolds, *More*, p. 323. Reynolds conjectures: "The £2,000 'in gold' must have been one of More's bits of fun; perhaps the sum in figures, or a drawing of money bags, was on the scrap of paper" (*ibid.*).

60. See the elaborate note in Harpsfield, *Moore*, pp. 363-368. On the whole vexing question, see E. E. Reynolds, "An Unnoticed Document," *Moreana*, No. 1 (1963), 12-17; G. Marc'hadour, Review of *The Trial of Saint Thomas More*, by E. E. Reynolds (London: Burns Oates, 1964), *Moreana*, No. 2 (1964), 90-96; J. D. M. Derrett, "The 'New' Document on Thomas More's Trial," *Moreana*, No. 3 (1964), 5-19, with note by E. E. Reynolds, 20-22; J. D. M. Derrett, "The Trial of Sir Thomas More," *English Historical Review*, LXXIX (1964), 449-477; and B. Byron, "The Fourth Count of the indictment of St. Thomas More," *Moreana*, No. 10 (1966), 33-46.

61. *Venetian Calendar*, V, no. 531, p. 224, referring to *Epist. Poli*, ed. Brescia, 1752, IV, 73-81.

62. Reynolds, *Fisher*, p. 286.

63. Matthew, *A sermon made in the cathedrall churche of Saynt Paule* ... (London, 1535), sig. C7ᵛ-8; Morison, *Apomaxis calumniarum* ... (London, 1537), foll. 44ᵛ, 53, 61ᵛ, 76-99; Joye, *A present consolacion for the sufferers of persecucion for ryghtwysenes* (1544), sigg. F8ᵛ-G1ᵛ; Stadion, in Erasmus, *Ep.*, XI, 255; and Cochlaeus, "Defensio ... Roffensis & ... Mori, aduersus Richardum samsonem," in *Epistola Nicolai* ..., sig. Z3, and *Scopa* ... *in araneas Ricardi Morysini* (Leipzig, 1538), sigg. B3ᵛ-D1. For a more detailed treatment of the fame and significance of Fisher and More, see "Jean Fisher," ed. Ortroy, *Analecta Bollandiana*, XII, 215-232; Bridgett, *Fisher*, Chapters XIX-XX; Reynolds, *Fisher*, Chapter XXX; Chambers, *More*, Epilogue, pp. 351-400; and Reynolds, *More*, Chapter XXIX.

64. Tunstal, to whom Fisher had submitted the manuscripts, approved heartily of the publication of Fisher's *Assertionis Lutheranae confutatio* (1523) and *Sacri sacerdotii defensio* (1525). See the dedicatory epistle to the latter work, ed. H. K. Schmeink (Münster: Aschendorff, 1925), p. 4.

65. The Carthusian, John Bouge, who had married More to his second wife (1511),

was Fisher's fellow student at Cambridge (Letter to Dame Katherine Man or Manne, *English Historical Review*, VII [1892], 713-715).

66. This and previous quotations are taken from "The Definition of Love" by Andrew Marvell, *Poems and Letters*, ed. H. M. Margoliouth (Oxford, Clarendon Press, 1963), I, 37.

67. Remark of Sir Thomas Audley, in the Letter of Alice Alington to Margaret Roper, *Correspondence*, p. 512.

68. *Early Statutes of Christ's College, Cambridge ...*, ed. H. Rackham (Cambridge: Fabb & Tyler, 1927), pp. 86-87; and *Early Statutes of the College of St. John the Evangelist in the University of Cambridge*, ed. J. E. B. Mayor (Cambridge, 1859), pp. 88, 309, 373.

69. *Workes*, p. 1036; cf. *ibid.*, p. 1314, and Fisher, *English Works*, pp. 138-139, 408. These references to John 15:13 are due to the kindness of Father Marc'hadour.

SURTZ, "Richard Pace's Sketch of Thomas More"

1. Ep. 999, *Opus Epistolarum Des. Erasmi Roterodami*, ed. P. S. Allen, *et al.* (Oxonii, 1906-47), IV, 12-23. This edition will be designated as *Eras. Ep.*

2. Ep. 388: 104-106, *Eras. Ep.*, II, 196; *Letters and Papers ... of the Reign of Henry VIII* (London, 1862-1932), II, No. 1067, p. 282. See the present writer's "St. Thomas More and His Utopian Embassy of 1515," *Catholic Historical Review*, XXXIX (1953), 272-97.

3. Ep. 999: 259-60, *Eras. Ep.*, IV, 21. For an excellent history of the composition of *Utopia*, see J. H. Hexter, *More's Utopia: The Biography of an Idea* (Princeton, 1952), esp. pp. 21-30.

4. *The Reign of Henry VIII* (London, 1884), I, 112. Pace's volume is now available in the edition and translation of R. S. Sylvester and F. Manley (New York, Renaissance Society of America, 1967).

5. Ep. 211: 43-46, *Eras. Ep.*, I, 445.

6. Ep. 30: 16 n., *Eras. Ep.*, I, 121.

7. Ep. 283: 136-37, *Eras. Ep.*, I, 546.

8. Ep. 350: 1-5, *Eras. Ep.*, II, 139. The nature of Pace's new position is not clear. His biographer, Jervis Wegg, *Richard Pace: A Tudor Diplomatist* (London, 1932), speaks simply of his entrance into Wolsey's service (p. 67) and of his later appointment as the King's principal secretary in reward for his negotiations with the Swiss, 1515-17 (p. 98). As a matter of fact, in a letter to Erasmus dated about June 21, 1516, More speaks of him as secretary to the King: *illum a secretis esse Regi nostro* (Ep. 424: 77-79, *Eras. Ep.*, II, 261).

9. Ep. 732: 52-53, *Eras. Ep.*, III, 162. F. M. Nichols suggests as probable the emendation *ab eo laudatum*, i.e., by Bombace, for *abs te laudatum*, i.e., by Beatus (*Epistles of Erasmus* [London, 1901-18], III, 470 n.). This may not be necessary since Beatus, being in Basel, would have seen the book immediately upon its publication by Froben.

10. Ep. 740: 6-7, *Eras. Ep.*, III, 170.

11. Ep. 741: 10-11, *Eras. Ep.*, III, 171.

12. Ep. 776: 1-25, *Eras. Ep.*, III, 218-19; Ep. 800: 24-35, *ibid.*, III, 254-55; *De Arte Poetica*, 6-9: "credite, Pisones, isti tabulae fore librum / persimilem, cuius, velut aegri somnia, vanae / fingentur species, ut nec pes nec caput uni / reddatur formae."

13. Ep. 783: 17-20, *Eras. Ep.*, III, 235-36.

14. Ep. 787: 1-8. *Eras. Ep.*, III, 242.

15. Ep. 796: 1-4, *Eras. Ep.*, III, 251.

16. Ep. 887: 5-7, *Eras. Ep.*, III, 425.

17. Ep. 962: 37–38, *Eras. Ep.*, III, 577; Ep. 937, *Eras. Ep.*, III, 525–26. In a letter dated March 2, 1518, Richard Sampson spoke to Erasmus of Pace's "outstanding erudition" (Ep. 780: 40, *Eras. Ep.*, III, 232).

18. Ep. 67: 25–27, *The Correspondence of Sir Thomas More*, ed. E. F. Rogers (Princeton, 1947), p. 133.

19. Ep. 83: 140–49, *Correspondence of More*, p. 169.

20. "Ricardus Paceus omnibus omnium scientiarum professoribus," *De Fructu*, p. 6.

21. Ep. 776: 16–18, *Eras. Ep.*, III, 219.

22. Ep. 623: 20 n., *Eras. Ep.*, III, 47.

23. Ep. 388: 99–104, *Eras. Ep.*, II, 196.

24. Ep. 388: 8–13, *Eras. Ep.*, II, 193.

25. See Appendices C and D in Russell Ames, *Citizen Thomas More and His Utopia* (Princeton, 1949), pp. 184–90.

26. *De Fructu*, pp. 82, 84–85. In his letter to Dorp, More declares that in grammar it suffices to learn those observances by which one can "speak Latin oneself and understand the Latin writings of others without apprehensively hunting down innumerable rules and growing gray among letters and syllables" (*Correspondence*, p. 37). Here, as elsewhere, More manifests the great influence of Erasmus, who insists upon learning a language by analysis and imitation of classical authors, while studying as few rules as possible. By way of John Colet and William Lily, the Erasmian attitude and method became traditional in the grammar schools of England. See the extended treatment of the first half of the sixteenth century in T. W. Baldwin, *William Shakspere's Small Latine & Lesse Greeke* (Urbana, 1944), I, 75–256. The opposing school of thought, represented by Robert Whittinton, emphasized memorized rules and precepts (*ibid.*, I, 127, 697) and finally lost out to Lily (*ibid.*, II, 690–91).

27. *De Fructu*, p. 82; Ep. 999: 262–63, 267–70, *Eras. Ep.*, IV, 21.

28. *De Fructu*, p. 82; Ep. 1233: 49, *Eras. Ep.*, IV, 577.

29. *Luciani ... Compluria Opuscula ... ab Erasmo Roterodamo et Thoma Moro ... in Latinorum Linguam Traducta* (Parisiis, 1506).

30. *De Fructu*, p. 82; Ep. 999: 119, 141–42, *Eras. Ep.*, IV, 16–17.

31. *De Fructu*, p. 82; Ep. 999: 246–65, *Eras. Ep.*, IV, 21. On More's voice, see Ep. 999: 75–79, *ibid.*, 15.

32. *De Fructu*, p. 82; Ep. 999: 1–3, 44–46, 111–12, 301, *Eras. Ep.*, IV, 13–14, 16, 22; Ep. 1233: 95–96, *ibid.*, 578. On March 2, 1518, Richard Sampson praised More's erudition and merriment (*festiuitate*) as evidenced by his *Utopia* and other lucubrations and by his very humorous conversations (Ep. 780: 44–49, *Eras. Ep.*, III, 232–33). The translation of Latin terms characterizing More's wit and humor was very difficult at times, even after consultation with Latinists. For a masterly disquisition on a similar problem involving the meaning of *facetus* and *lepor*, see T. W. Baldwin, *Shakspere's Five-Act Structure* (Urbana, 1947), pp. 805–809.

33. *The Workes of Sir Thomas More* (London, 1557), p. 127; William Roper, *The Lyfe of Sir Thomas Moore, Knighte*, ed. Elsie Vaughan Hitchcock (London, 1935), pp. 101–102.

34. *De Fructu*, p. 82; Ep. 81: 18–22, *Correspondence of More*, p. 163; Ep. 999: 113–19, 122–26, 181–82, *Eras. Ep.*, IV, 16, 19. The clause "omnia acri perfundit aceto" is an echo of Horace, *Sat.* i.7.32: "At Graecus postquam est Italo perfusus aceto / Persius exclamat," quoted in Erasmus, *Adagiorum Opus* (Lugduni, 1539), 1252 (*Acetum habet in pectore*), col. 563. In the *Utopia* (ed. J. H. Lupton [Oxford, 1895], p. 75), More speaks of the friar as "tali perfusus aceto" translated by Robinson freely and picturesquely as "thus towchyd one the quicke, and hit on the gawl." The reference to the letter to Croke reads: "Non est ... quod meum nasum velut elephantis promuscidem reformides,"

where More plays upon the word *nasus* "nose" as an organ used to express scorn or ridicule, the term *promuscis* being a corrupt form of *proboscis* "trunk."

35. *De Fructu*, p. 82; Ep. 999: 141-42, 153, *Eras. Ep.*, IV, 17; Ep. 2750: 66-69, *ibid.*, X, 136.

36. The same play upon a single syllable added to a word occurs in More's *Utopia*, p. 36: "Bona uerba, inquit Petrus; mihi uisum est non ut seruias regibus, sed ut inseruias. Hoc est, inquit ille [Hythlodaeus], una syllaba plus quam seruias."

37. *De Fructu*, pp. 82-83; Ep. 222: 14-18, *Eras. Ep.*, I, 460; Ep. 999: 44-46, 126-28, *ibid.*, IV, 14, 16. According to Diogenes Laertius, *Lives of Eminent Philosophers*, tr. R. D. Hicks (London, 1925), II, 327, 329, Pythagoras "compared life to the Great Games, where some went to compete for the prize and others went with wares to sell, but the best as spectators; for similarly, in life, some grow up with servile natures, greedy for fame and gain, but the philosopher seeks for truth." Robert Burton, *The Anatomy of Melancholy* (London, 1923), I, 13, writes that Democritus betook himself to a private life, "saving that sometimes he would walk down to the haven, and laugh heartily at such variety of ridiculous objects, which there he saw." The reference given for this quotation is "Hip. Ep. Damag.," viz., the alleged epistles of Hippocrates of Cos to Damagetus (*Hippocratis Opera Omnia* [Genevae, 1657], II, 1276-77, 1279-83), which helped to establish Democritus' reputation as the Laughing Philosopher.

38. See Ep. 5: 38-83, *Correspondence of More*, pp. 12-13, and Ep. 193: 26-61, *Eras. Ep.*, I, 425-26.

39. The reference is probably to Colet's sermon on war in 1512 and to the subsequent events, in which two Franciscans, Birkhead and Standish, spearheaded the opposition to Colet. See Ep. 1211: 557-75 (cf. 576-616), *Eras. Ep.*, IV, 524-26. Erasmus' version of Colet's stand, "pacem iniquam praeferendam bello aequissimo" (*Eras. Ep.*, IV, 524) is far more debatable and challenging than Pace's version, "salutarem pacem pernicioso bello longe esse praeferendam" (*De Fructu*, p. 83). See J. H. Lupton, *A Life of John Colet* (London, 1887), pp. 188-93. Lupton (p. 189, n. 1) calls attention to Cicero's sentiment (*Epp. ad Div.* vi.6): "Quum vel iniquissimam pacem justissimo bello anteferrem."

40. Pace uses the form *Arcturus* which Erasmus employs in "Moria," *Opera Omnia* (Lugduni Batavorum, 1703-1706), IV, 447. This confirms H. H. Hudson's contention that the British king and not the star Arcturus is meant (*The Praise of Folly* [Princeton, 1941], p. 147). Pace declares that some deny even Arthur's birth, whereas others affirm that he never died but disappeared somewhere or other (*De Fructu*, p. 83).

41. One anecdote as given by Geoffrey of Monmouth, Book X, tells how Arthur won the beard of the giant Ritho and the latter's garment woven of the beards of kings slain by Ritho. See Jacob Hammer, ed., *Historia Regum Britanniae* (Cambridge, Mass., 1951), pp. 172, 242.

42. *De Fructu*, p. 83; Ep. 2750: 67-69, *Eras. Ep.*, X, 136. In the explanation of the adage *Mulgere hircum*, Erasmus relates a strikingly similar anecdote from Lucian's *Demonax*. See Erasmus, *Opera Omnia*, II, 132, and *Luciani Samosatensis Opera Graece et Latine ad Editionem Tiberii Hemsterhusii et Ioannis Frederici Reitzii Accurate Expressa* (Biponti, 1789-93); V, 244-45. One reason for More's objection to these two theologians is the same as that for his attitude toward the theologian in Hythloday's humorous anecdote in *Utopia*, pp. 75-78, namely, a lack of agreement between profession and conduct. Just as the two theologians in *De Fructu* spoke words totally unbefitting their professed pursuit of truth and wisdom (*a personis suis alienissima* [*De Fructu*, p. 83]), so at Cardinal Morton's table the theologian who was grave even to the point of moroseness (*prope ad toruitatem grauis* [*Utopia*, p. 75]) began to jest foolishly with the result that he made himself soon appear a fool in the contention with the foolish parasite.

43. *Utopia*, pp. 75–78; Ep. 999: 224–25, *Eras. Ep.*, IV, 20; Ep. 1087: 323–27, *ibid.*, 224.

44. *Lit.* "white-mitered," "white-headdressed," or "white-girdled." The term "leu-comitratus" does not appear in the Latin and Greek lexicons available to the author. From the context it appears that Pace intends the phrase to be taken metaphorically and translated simply as "gray-haired" or "white-headed." The adjective λευκός "light, clear, white, pale, fair, gay" may also be translated "gray," e.g., in reference to hair. Hence it is possible to translate the phrase as "gray-cowled," in which case it would refer to the Grayfriars or Franciscans who were Scotists.

45. *De Fructu*, pp. 83–84, Ep. 999: 265–67, *Eras. Ep.*, IV, 21. The English "puerile" would appear to be too contemptuous a term to translate the play upon *puerilia* and *puer*.

46. Prefatory Letter to Willibald Pirckheimer, *The Latin Epigrams of Thomas More*, eds. Leicester Bradner and Charles Arthur Lynch (Chicago, 1953), pp. 4, 126. In the 1520 edition of the epigrams, More suppressed the following statement of Beatus: "Just as Syrus in the play by Terence neatly praises Demea by saying 'You are every inch pure wisdom,' so it will be proper to say of More 'He is every inch pure jest'" (*loc. cit.*). Professor Bradner, who was so kind as to point out this change, observes: "Evidently More did not think this exclusive emphasis on his jocular side a very fitting comment on a man who was now a member of the king's council" (p. xvi).

47. Ep. 999: 1–3, 223–24, *Eras. Ep.*, IV, 13, 20; Newman, "Literature," *The Idea of a University* (London, 1923), p. 275.

48. R. W. Chambers, *Thomas More* (London, 1935), p. 347.

49. *Correspondence of More*, p. 91.

SYLVESTER, "Roper's *Life of More*"

1. New Haven, Yale University Press, 1972. Cited hereafter as *Action and Contemplation*. Included are four essays by, respectively, R. J. Schoeck ("Common Law and Canon Law in their Relation to Thomas More"), L. L. Martz ("Thomas More: The Tower Works"), G. R. Elton ("Thomas More, Councillor, 1517–1529"), and G. Marc'hadour ("Thomas More's Spirituality").

2. *Opus Epistolarum Des. Erasmi Roterodami*, ed. P. S. Allen et al. (Oxford, 1906–1958), *4*, 21. Erasmus here repeats the remark of John Colet, "a man of sharp and precise judgement."

3. William Roper, *The Lyfe of Sir Thomas More, knighte*, ed. E. V. Hitchcock, London, 1935, p. 3. Page numbers in the text refer to this edition; I have modernized spelling and punctuation in my quotations from early texts.

4. See the review of *Two Early Tudor Lives*, ed. D. P. Harding and R. S. Sylvester (New Haven, 1962), in *The Times Literary Supplement*, March 15, 1963, p. 188.

5. Nicholas Harpsfield, *The Life and Death of Sir Thomas Moore*, ed. R. W. Chambers and E. V. Hitchcock, London, 1932.

6. Note his words (p. 100), "according as he in his letter the day before had wished." Providence, in this case at least, accommodates More's desire.

7. Elton emphasizes this point. See *Action and Contemplation*, pp. 88–91.

8. For this lady, see J. Duncan M. Derrett, "Sir Thomas More and the Nun of Kent," *Moreana*, 15–16 (1967), 267–84.

9. For More's translation of Lucian's *Menippus*, see CW 3, Part I (New Haven, 1974), and Craig R. Thompson, *The Translations of Lucian by Erasmus and St. Thomas More* (Ithaca, N.Y., 1940). Pico's *Oratio* is available in the translation of Elizabeth Forbes, *The Renaissance Philosophy of Man*, ed. E. Cassirer, P. K. Kristeller and J. H. Randall (Chicago, 1948). For a discussion of the play metaphor, see my "A part of his own:

More's Literary Personality in his Early Works," *Moreana, 15-16* (1967), 29-42.

10. Proteus' role in the Renaissance is ably studied by A. B. Giamatti, "Proteus Unbound: Some Versions of the Sea God in the Renaissance," in *The Disciplines of Criticism: Essays ... Honoring René Wellek*, New Haven, 1968, pp. 437-75.

11. *English Works*, 1557, sig fg2r.

12. *The Union of the two noble and illustre families etc.* (London, 1548), sig. PPP4V.

13. Cf. Professor Clarence Miller's suggestive remarks on this subject, summarized in *Action and Contemplation*, p. 7.

14. *Action and Contemplation*, p. 5.

15. This subject was taken up in a small way in the second and third lectures of the series, "The Utopian Years (1513-1520)," and "Thomas More, Polemicist (1523-33)."

16. See *Thomas More's Prayer Book*, ed. L. L. Martz and R. S. Sylvester, New Haven, Yale University Press, 1969, for a facsimile and transcription.

17. *St. Thomas More's History of the Passion*, ed. P. E. Hallett (London, 1941), pp. 22 and 33.

18. *English Works*, sigs. XX8v-YY1. Roper (p. 82) gives only the first of these stanzas.

ZEEVELD, "Apology for an Execution"

1. John Strype, *Ecclesiastical Memorials* (1822), I, 265.

2. Gilbert Burnet, *The History of the Reformation of the Church of England*, ed. Pocock, VI, 30.

3. [Av^v]-[Avi].

4. [Avii^v].

5. *State Papers, Henry VIII*, I, 436: Would he obey the king's highness as supreme head on earth, immediately after Christ, of the Church of England, according to the statute? Would he consent and approve the king's marriage with Anne to be good and lawful, and the marriage with Lady Catherine pretensed, unjust, and unlawful?

6. [Cvii^v]-[Cviii^v].

7. Germain Marc'hadour, *L'Univers de Thomas More* (1963), p. 506.

8. July 1 (Marc'hadour, p. 507).

9. John Strype, *Ecclesiastical Memorials* (1882), I (part ii), 203.

10. *Obedience in Church and State: Three Political Tracts by Stephen Gardiner*, ed. Pierre Janelle (1930), pp. 17-19.

11. *State Papers, Henry VIII*, I, 430.

12. *The Letters of Stephen Gardiner*, ed. Muller (1933), p. 68.

13. As "Si sedes illa" in *Obedience in Church and State*. Calendared in *Letters and Papers of Henry VIII*, VIII, no. 1118.

14. James A. Muller, *Stephen Gardiner and the Tudor Reaction* (1926), p. 350 n26.

15. A. G. Dickens, *Thomas Cromwell and the English Reformation* (1959), pp. 62-63.

16. Burnet, VI, 117: Cromwell's instructions, August, 1535.

17. *State Papers, Henry VIII*, I, 434.

18. Burnet, VI, 118.

19. John Strype, *Ecclesiastical Memorials*, I, ii, 211.

20. [Xiiii]-[Xiiii^v]. Citations are taken from a collection of works cited by Cochlaeus, "Ex officina M. Lottheri: Lipsiae, 1536."

21. *L & P*, XI, no. 1481.

22. England's praise of Henry for saving her from the perils of the Pilgrimage was written some months after the danger was past (Riii), but when the rising under Sir Francis Bigod in January was still recent (Si).

23. ([Liii^v]-[Liiii]).

24. *Dialogue Concerning Tyndale* (ed. Campbell), p. 68: Question: When Christ said

to St. Peter, "Sathanas hath desired to sift thee as men sift corn, but I have prayed for thee that thy faith shall not fail" [Luke 22: 31, 32], said he this as a promise of the faith to be kept and preserved in St. Peter only, or else in the whole church? Answer: Sometimes Christ referred to Peter particularly, sometimes to all. If to him alone, it would be hard to hold, for his faith did fail. But since God made him "universal vicar and under him head of his church" he showed him "that his faith, that is to wit the faith by him confessed, should never fail in his church, nor never did it, notwithstanding his denying."

25. Cf. More's answer to interrogations in *State Papers, Henry VIII*, I, 434: "My lorde, I am determyned to medle of nothing, but only to geve my mynde upon Godd, and the summe of my hole studie shalbe to thinke upon the Passion of Christe, and my passage out of this worlde, with the dependences therupon."

26. [aiiii^V].

27. [bi^V]-bii. Mary's confession, June 10, 1536, is in *State Papers, Henry VIII*, I, 455-9.

28. ciii.

29. *State Papers, Henry VIII*, I, 603-4.

BARKER, "*Clavis Moreana:* The Yale Edition of Thomas More"

1. The Complete Works of St. Thomas More. Vol. 2: *The History of King Richard III*. Edited by Richard S. Sylvester. New Haven and London: Yale University Press, 1963. Pp. cvi + 312. $12.50. Vol. 4: *Utopia*. Edited by Edward Surtz, S.J., and J. H. Hexter. New Haven and London: Yale University Press, 1965. Pp. cxciv + 629. $15.

BINDER, "More's *Utopia* in English: A Note on Translation"

1. In addition to the *Tudor Translations* prefacers, Charles Whibley again, *CHEL*, iv, Ch. i; F. O. Matthiessen, *Translation: an Elizabethan Art* (Cambridge, Mass., 1931); and latterly Douglas Bush, *English Literature in the Earlier Seventeenth Century* (Oxford, 1946), Ch. ii.

2. Nos. in parentheses refer to pages in J. H. Lupton, *The Utopia of Sir Thomas More* (Oxford, 1895).

3. Italics mine throughout.

DUHAMEL, "Medievalism of More's *Utopia*"

1. Cf. Richard P. McKeon, "Renaissance and Method in Philosophy," *Studies in the History of Ideas III* (New York, 1935), pp. 40-41.

2. Cf. W. K. Ferguson, *The Renaissance in Historical Thought* (Boston, 1948) for a detailed survey of definitions of the Renaissance.

3. Cf. Pearl Kibré, "Intellectual Interests in Fourteenth and Fifteenth Century Libraries," *Journal of the History of Ideas,* VII (1946), 259, 279, 280; J. S. Beddie, "Ancient Classics in Medieval Libraries," *Speculum,* V (1930), 3-20.

4. Cf. McKeon, *op. cit.,* p. 87.

5. Boethius, *Consolation of Philosophy,* V, Prose 5 and 6. Cf. the discussion by Thomas Aquinas, *Commentum super Lib. Boetii De Consolatu Philosophico* (New York, 1930), XXIV, 140-41, 144. All references to Aquinas are to this photographic reproduction of the Parma 1852-1873 edition.

6. John Colet, *Enarratio in Epistolam Pauli ad Romanos,* ed. J. H. Lupton (London, 1873), p. 164; John Colet, *Enarratio in Primam Epistolam Pauli ad Corinthios,* ed. J. H. Lupton (London, 1874), pp. 13, 167.

7. McKeon, *op. cit.,* p. 47.

8. Cf. *ibid.,* pp. 67-69; also G. Paré, A. Brunet, R. Tremblay, *La Renaissance du XIIe Siècle* (Ottawa, 1933), pp. 289-91; Peter Abelard, *Sic et Non,* in Migne, *Patrologia Latina,*

vol. 178, cols. 1339-49. All later references to the *Patrologia* will be made with the usual MPL followed by volume number, and then column number. Cf. also Abelard, *Expositio in Epist. Pauli ad Romanos*, MPL 178, col. 866 ff.

9. Paré, Brunet, Tremblay, *op. cit.*, p. 289; Bernard, MPL 182, col. 1055; William of Thierry, MPL 180, cols. 249-82.

10. Cf. Martin Grabmann, *Die Geschichte der Scholastischen Methode* (Freiburg, 1909-1911), II, 387.

11. Cf. Thomas More, "Letter to Martin Dorp," in *The Correspondence of Sir Thomas More*, ed. Elizabeth F. Rogers (Princeton, 1947), pp. 45-72; Urban Regius, "Letter to Erasmus," in *Opus Epistolarum Des. Erasmi*, ed. H. S. Allen and H. M. Allen (Oxford, 1906-1947), V, 2.

12. Desiderius Erasmus, "Paraclesis," in *Opera Omnia* (Leyden, 1702-5), V, 141; cf. also "Ratio seu methodus compendio ad veram theologiam," in *Opera Omnia*, V, 77.

13. Cf. Christian Dolfen, *Die Stellung des Erasmus von Rotterdam zur scholastischen Methode* (Osnabruck, 1936), pp. 64-82 for many illustrations of the logical method as applied by the Scholastics, from Duns Scotus to Gabriel Biel, to various questions which Erasmus attempted to solve by grammatical exegeses.

14. Cf. Dom John Chapman, *The Spiritual Letters*, ed. Roger Hudlestone (Fordham, 1935), pp. 195-96.

15. Cf. Grabmann, *Methode*, II, 517.

16. Cf. *ibid.*, I, 32.

17. Cf. *ibid.*, II, 85 and 91.

18. Anselm, *Monologium*, trans. by S. N. Deane (Chicago, 1935), p. 35.

19. Anselm, *Proslogium, ibid.*, p. 7. Cf. with the attitude of Hugh of St. Victor, *Summa Sententiarum*, MPL 136, cols. 41-42, and the rationalism of Abelard in *Introductio ad Theologiam*, MPL 178, col. 1039.

20. D. Erasmi, *Opuscula*, ed. Wallace K. Ferguson (The Hague, 1933), pp. 178 ff.

21. St. Bonaventure, *Collatio, Hexaemeron*, in *Opera Omnia* (Quarrachi, 1882-1902), V, 421.

22. Cf. Karl Werner, *Die Scholastik des späteren Mittelalters* (Vienna, 1887), IV, *passim*. Ernest V. Moody, *The Logic of William of Ockham* (New York, 1935), chap. 1.

23. D. Erasmus, *Lives of Jehan Vitrier and John Colet*, ed. J. H. Lupton (London, 1883), pp. 23-24; cf. also P. A. Duhamel, "Oxford Lectures of John Colet," *Journal of the History of Ideas*, XIV (1953), 493-510.

24. Cf. Edward L. Surtz, "Logic in Utopia," *Philological Quarterly*, XXIX (1950), 389-401; also P. Boehner, *Medieval Logic* (Chicago, 1952), pp. 1-5.

25. Thomas More, *Utopia*, ed. J. H. Lupton (Oxford, 1895), pp. lxxxvi-lxxxvii. All later references are to this edition and the translation of Robinson has occasionally been modernized in spelling and phrasing.

26. *Ibid.*, pp. lxxxiv-lxxxv.

27. Nicholas Harpsfield, *Life and Death of Sir Thomas More*, ed. E. V. Hitchcock for EETS 186 (London, 1932), p. 13.

28. Ricardo Quintana, *The Mind and Art of Jonathan Swift* (London, 1953), p. 71; cf. J. H. Hexter, *More's Utopia* (Princeton, 1952), p. 76.

29. Hexter, *op. cit.*, pp. 26-29. In Lupton's edition the original *Utopia* consists of pp. 24-34, 115-307; and the sections written later in London of pp. 21-24, 34-114, 307-9.

30. More could have used the *editio princeps* of Aristotle by Aldus Manutius (Venice, 1495-98) or the very free translation of the *Politics* (c. 1435) by Leonardo Bruni Aretino, originally dedicated to Humphrey, Duke of Gloucester. He could have derived little from the French translation (1371) of the *Politics* made by Nicholas d'Oresme (cf. F. Ueberweg, *Geschichte der Philosophie* [Berlin, 1928], II, 595, 599, 784) from the

Latin of William of Moerbeke. This translation, completed about 1260 (cf. M. Grabmann, *Guylielmo di Moerbeke: il traduttore delle opere di Aristotele* [Rome, 1946], p. 112) at the request of Aquinas, usually accompanied the latter's commentary on the *Politics*, and it is most likely in this form that More knew the work.

31. Aquinas develops *Politics*, 1328b 5–15 throughout the entire sixth Lectio of Book VII of his commentary (*Comm. in Politicorum*, XXI, 654–56) clarifying the six requirements without which a state cannot exist. More's reading of Aquinas can be argued from his descriptions of the site of Amaurot (cf. *Utopia*, p. 126, with Aquinas, *op. cit.*, p. 650) and the discussion of the necessity of city walls (cf. *Utopia*, p. 129, with Aquinas, *op. cit.*, p. 666).

32. More's elaboration on this principle is also similar to Aquinas' commentary on *Politics* 1278b 15–25. Cf. Aquinas, *op. cit.*, XXI, 463.

33. The *editio princeps* of Plato was that of Aldus Manutius (Venice, 1513) but the translation of Ficino was completed by 1477 and printed in 1484. The translation of the *Republic* begun by Chrysoloras and concluded by Pier Candido Decembrio in 1439 included only the first five books. Plato is only the possible ultimate source, for since More worked from a principle, and not the particular statement of the principle, he may have known the discussion through Cicero *De finibus* v. 7–8, or elsewhere.

34. *Utopia*, p. 184.

35. Cf. Surtz, "Logic in *Utopia*," pp. 400–1.

36. *Utopia*, pp. 214–15.

37. Aquinas, *Summa Contra Gentiles*, I, 9; *op. cit.*, V, 6. "Modo ergo posito procedere intendentes, premium nitemur ad manifestationem illius veritatis, quam fides profitetur et ratio investigat; inducendo rationes demonstrativas et probabiles, quarum quasdam ex libris philosophorum et sanctorum collegemus, per quas veritas confirmetur et adversarius convincatur. Deinde, ut a manifestioribus nobis ad minus manifesta fiat processus, ad illius veritatis manifestationem procedemus, quae excedit solventes rationes adversariorum; et rationibus probabilibus et auctoritatibus (quantum Deus dederit) veritatem fidei declarantes."

38. *Utopia*, pp. 223–24.

39. Aquinas, *Summa Theologica*, I–II, cf. 100, 8, ad. 3.

40. *Utopia*, p. 227.

41. Aquinas, *Summa Theologica*, I–II, cf. 102, 5, ad. 3, II–II, 154, 2.

42. *Utopia*, pp. 266–67.

43. *Ibid.*, p. 132.

44. *Ibid.*, pp. 268–69.

45. T. P. Dunning, "Langland and the Salvation of the Heathen," *Medium Aevum*, XII (1943), 47.

46. *Ibid.*, p. 48; cf. Hugh of St. Victor, *De Sacramentis*, MPL 176, cols. 339 ff. Bernard, *Tractatus de Baptismo*, MPL 182, cols. 1038 ff.

47. Aquinas, *De Veritate*, cf. XIV, a. xi, ad. 2m. (incorrectly cited in Dunning).

48. *Ibid.*, A. xi, ad. 1m. Aquinas has "per internam inspirationem," *Utopia*, "secretius inspirante Deo" which would lend some color to the possibility that More carries some traces of what E. Gilson has called "l'Augustinisme avicennisant."

49. Cf. *Utopia*, p. 7.

50. *Piers Plowman*, B xii, 284–88.

51. *Utopia*, p. 272.

52. *Ibid.*, p. 274.

53. Cf. Aquinas, *Comm. in Pol.*, Book VII, Lectio 1; *op. cit.*, XXI, 633.

54. Aristotle, *Politics*, 1323a 14–19.

55. *Utopia*, p. 187.

56. *Ibid.*, p. 188.

57. *Ibid.*, p. 189.

58. *Ibid.*, p. 188.

59. *Ibid.*, p. 194.

60. Plato, *Republic*, 591 C-D.

61. *Utopia*, pp. 190 and 192.

62. *Ibid.*, pp. 207 and 211.

63. *Ibid.*, p. 210.

64. *Loc. cit.* Cf. entire discussion in Edward L. Surtz' "Epicurus in Utopia," *English Literary History*, XVI (1949), 89–103; and also by the same author, "Defense of Pleasure in More's Utopia," *Studies in Philology*, XLVI (1949), 99–112.

65. Aquinas, *Summa Theologica*, II-II, q. 44, i. c.

66. Aristotle, *Politics*, 1332a 9–10. Cf. Aquinas, *Comm. in Pol.*, Book VII, Lectio X, *op. cit.*, XXI, 670.

67. Aristotle, *Politics*, 1334a 11–16. Cf. Aquinas, *Comm. in Pol.*, Book VII, Lectio XI, *op. cit.*, XXI, 679, who adds very significantly that a virtuous life frees man from attachment to external things.

68. *Utopia*, p. 152.

69. *Ibid.*, p. 141.

70. *Ibid.*, pp. 143 and 146.

71. Here More parts company with Aquinas on the much vexed question of whether or not private property was defensible according to natural law. Cf. Aquinas, *Summa Theol.*, I, 21, a. 1, ad. 3 and Heinrich A. Rommen, *The Natural Law* (St. Louis, 1947), p. 233, who maintains that the right of private property is not one of the immediately apparent dictates of the natural law.

72. William J. MacDonald, "Communism in Eden?," *New Scholasticism*, XX (1946), 101.

73. *Ibid.*, p. 114.

74. *Ibid.*, pp. 115 and 116.

75. Cf. Edward L. Surtz, "Thomas More and Communism," *PMLA*, LXIV (1949), 549–64.

76. *Utopia*, pp. 305–6.

77. *Ibid.*, pp. 150–51; cf. Guigo, *Consuetudines*, MPL 153, cols. 685–86.

78. *Utopia*, pp. 155, 167; cf. Guigo, *op. cit.*, cols. 651–52.

79. *Utopia*, pp. 161–65; cf. Guigo, *op. cit.*, cols. 661–62.

80. *Utopia*, pp. 290, 291, 299; cf. Guigo, *op. cit.*, cols. 705–8, 717–18.

81. *Utopia*, pp. 139–40; cf. St. Benedict, *Regula Monachorum*, MPL 66, cols. 485–86.

82. Richard Whitford, trs., *The Imitation of Christ*, ed. E. J. Klein (New York, 1941), pp. 3–4.

83. Erasmus, *Opuscula*, pp. 178, 180.

84. Thomas More, *The Workes of Sir Thomas More* (London, 1557), p. 1270c.

85. *Ibid.*, p. 1294d.

86. *Ibid.*, p. 1307c–1309f.

87. *Ibid.*, p. 1304b–c.

88. *Ibid.*, p. 1320d.

89. *Ibid.*, 1322f, 1321g.

90. Erasmus, *Opera Omnia*, VI, 503.

91. *Ibid.*, VI, 117, 172–73.

92. *Ibid.*, VI, 88.

93. *Ibid.*, VI, 232.

94. *Ibid.*, V, 139–40.

95. *Ibid.*, V, 77.

96. *Utopia*, p. 155. "For they count this the most just cause of war, when any people holds a piece of ground void and vacant to no good nor profitable use, keeping others from the use and possession of it, which notwithstanding by the law of nature ought thereof to be nourished and relieved."

97. *Ibid.*, p. 165. "They begin every dinner and supper by reading something that pertains to good manners and virtue. But it is short, because no man should be grieved by it. Hereof the elders take occasion for honest communication, but neither sad nor unpleasant."

98. *Ibid.*, pp. 178-79. "So there came in three ambassadors with one hundred servants all apparelled in changeable colors: most of them in silks, the ambassadors themselves (for at home in their country they were noble men) in cloth of gold, with great chains of gold, with gold hanging at their ears, with gold rings upon their fingers, with broaches and aglets of gold upon their caps, which glistened full of pearls and precious stones, to be short, trimmed and adorned with all those things, which among the Utopians were either the punishment of bondmen, or the reproach of infamous persons, or else trifles for young children to play with."

99. Thomas More, "Rossei," in *Opera Omnia* (Frankfort and Leipzig, 1689), p. 38. "When these things had been decided, he [Luther] dismissed his councilors and they therefore went off, different ones to different places, wherever and by whatever means they were inclined, and they dispersed by every wagon, carriage, even boat throughout the public baths, eating houses, barber shops, taverns, gambling houses, bakeries, privies, and brothels and there they carefully observed and brought back on tablets whatever was said sordidly by any groom, fawningly by any servant, improperly by any carrier, scurrilously by any parasite, wantonly by any prostitute, vilely by any pimp, filthily by any bath keeper or obscenely by any defecator." A demonstration of the stylistic differences between the *Utopia* and More's other Latin works would require a much more detailed study but the above sentence is obviously Ciceronian in parataxes and periodicity. Where are these sentences in the *Utopia*? A sampling of the vocabulary of the *Utopia* will show its great similarity to that of Aquinas as defined in the *Lexicon* compiled by DeFerrari.

100. Thomas More, *A Dialogue of Comfort against Tribulation* (London, 1937), p. 131.

HERBRÜGGEN, "More's *Utopia* as a Paradigm"

1. Louvain, 1516; available in reprint (Scolar Press), 1966, 1971. R. W. Gibson, *St. T. More: A Preliminary Bibliography to the Year 1750*, New Haven, 1961, lists 22 Latin editions before that year.

2. London (Abraham Vele), 1551; second corrected edition 1556. Gibson, *op. cit.*, lists 9 English editions before 1750. E. Arber, *English Reprints*, 1869, and J. H. Lupton's edition of the *Utopia*, 1895, print the text of the second English translation by Robynson.

3. Cf. his concern expressed later in his *Confutation of Tyndale's Answer*, Book II: "I saye therefore in these dayes in whyche men by theyr owne defaute mysseconstre and take harme of the very scrypture of god, vntyll menne better amende, yf any man wolde now translate *Moria* in to Englyshe, or some workes eyther that I haue my selfe wryten ere this, all be yt there be no harme therin / folke yet beynge (as they be) geuen to take harme of that that is good / I wolde not onely my derlynges bokes but myne owne also, helpe to burne them both wyth myne owne handes, rather then folke sholde (though thorow theyr own faute) take any harme of them, seynge that I se them lykely in these dayes so to do." Yale Edition, *CW 8*, 179.

4. St. Dié, 1507, introd. by Martin Waldseemüller. Facsimile ed. C. C. Herbermann (U.S. Cath. Hist. Soc., IV), New York, 1907.

5. The sumptuous Renaissance outfitting of the book with letters, epigrams and other accessories must be left aside here, highly significant and revealing though it is.

6. More, in his second (1517) letter to Peter Gilles (*CW 4*, 248–52), explains the meaning of these Greek words.

7. "Utopia is founded on religious enthusiasm," "... based on religion," "... but religion is the basis of all," *Thomas More* (London, 1935), p. 137.

8. The lack of religious foundations in Utopia was already noted by More's contemporaries, as may be seen from most of the accompanying letters that embellish the original edition. Cf. Yale Edition, *passim*.

9. It is not the three *divine virtues* (Faith, Hope, Charity) after which the Utopians are modelled, but the "heathen" *cardinal virtues* (Prudence, Justice, Courage, Temperance), as already Jerome Busleyden observed in his letter to More of 1516.

10. "The Utopians define virtue as living according to nature since to this end we were created by God. That individual, they say, is following the guidance of nature who, in desiring one thing and avoiding another, obeys the dictates of reason" (p. 163). "Where Erasmus in the *Praise of Folly* had portrayed the rule of unreason, More replaced the negative signs by positive ones, turned the picture around and depicted the rule of reason," F. Caspari, *Humanism and the Social Order in Tudor England,* Chicago, 1954, p. 50.

11. Cf. St. Thomas Aquinas, *S. Th.,* 1, 2, q. 77, a. 5.

12. Pride, "the very hed and rote of al sines ... the mischieuous mother of al maner vice," as More calls her in his *Four Last Things* (*Workes*, 1557, p. 82), where he dedicates a whole chapter to her. In medieval theology she occupied the supreme position among the seven *capital sins,* thus being opposite to the chief virtue, Prudence.

13. For the views of More and his contemporary humanist friends on communism see E. Surtz, "T. More and Communism," *PMLA,* 64 (1949), 552 ff., and Caspari, *op. cit.,* pp. 51 ff.

14. E. Schaper, *T. More und die Geschichte,* phil. diss. Münster i. W., 1950, follows views current among senior German historians between the two World Wars, e.g., H. Oncken, *Die Utopia des T. Morus und das Machtproblem in der Staatslehre* (Sitz.-Ber., Phil.-Hist. Kl., XIII), Heidelberg, 1922, and *Nation und Geschichte,* Berlin, 1935; Gerhard Ritter, *Machtstaat und Utopia: Vom Streit um die Dämonie der Macht seit Machiavelli und Morus,* München & Berlin 1940, 6th rev. ed. as *Die Dämonie der Macht,* München, 1948; F. Brie, *Imperialistische Strömungen in der englischen Literatur,* 2nd ed. 1928, and also in his "Machtpolitik und Krieg in der Utopia des T. Morus," *Historisches Jahrbuch,* 61 (1941).

15. Generally speaking, the Catholic interpretation tends towards a conservative view of More's social ideas, as expressed in the *Utopia by Morus.* Cp. e.g., G. Möbus, *Die Politik des Heiligen: Geist und Gesetz der Utopia des T. Morus,* Berlin, 1953; also Belloc, Chesterton, and W. E. Campbell, *More's Utopia and his Social Teaching,* London, 1930. Alternatively, whoever takes More to be a reformer will stress *Raphael's* statements and make him the author's mouthpiece. Cf. J. W. Allen, *Political Thought in the 16th Century,* 1928; Karl Kautsky, H. Oncken, and others; see F. L. Baumann, "Sir T. More," *JMH,* IV (1934), 610 ff.

16. Kautsky, *More and His Utopia,* 7th ed., 1947, *passim;* More's *Utopia,* ed. Michels-Ziegler (Lateinische Literaturdenkmäler des XV. und XVI. Jahrhunderts, 11), Berlin, 1895, introduction, p. xxxv; R. Ames, *Citizen More and His Utopia,* New York, 1949, *passim.*

17. W. P. Wolgin, *Campanellas kommunistische Utopie,* Berlin, 1955, p. 5.

18. K. Sternberg, "Über die 'Utopia' des T. Morus," *Archiv für Rechts- und Wirtschaftsphilosophie,* 26 (1932), 27 (1934), 240, 491.

19. Möbus, *op. cit.*, p. 7.

20. Cf. J. H. Hexter, *More's Utopia: the Biography of an Idea*, Princeton, 1952, p. 33; Campbell, *op. cit.*, *passim*.

21. H. Oncken in his introduction, *passim*, to G. Ritter's German translation of More's *Utopia* (Klassiker der Politic, 1), Berlin, 1922, and in his above mentioned article in Heidelberger *Sitzungsberichte*, XIII (1922), p. 20; H. Freyer, *Politische Insel* (Meyers Kleine Handbücher, 2), Leipzig, 1936, pp. 101 ff.; similarly G. Ritter, K. Fischer, E. Troeltsch and others. *Versus* Oncken: O. Bendemann, *Studie zur Staats- und Sozialauffassung des T. Morus*, phil. diss., Berlin, 1928, *passim*.

22. G. Ritter, *Dämonie der Macht*, ⁶1948, pp. 53 ff.; F. Brie, *Imperialistische Strömungen*, ²1928, pp. 8 ff.

23. M. Freund, "Zur Deutung der Utopie des T. Morus," *Historische Zeitschrift*, 142 (1930), 273.

24. Surtz, "T. More and Communism," 1949, p. 558.

25. That is, the very situation in which the present dialogue between Morus, Hythloday and Gilles takes place.

26. Oncken, too, regards this place as the decisive starting point for the understanding of the whole *Utopia*, although, in a complete reversal of positions, he does *not* recognize it as being part of the *philosophia scholastica* but, having been revised after More's return to London, as "die politische Programmschrift eines Mannes, der jeden Tag englischer Minister werden konnte," introduction to *Utopia*, 1922, pp. 23 ff.

27. The same view of the *irreality* of the communist ideality is shared by the other humanists (Budé, Erasmus, Lister). Cf. also the marginal note in More's *Responsio ad Lutherum*, CW 5, 118.

28. Surtz, "More and Communism," *op. cit.*, p. 558, n. 45. E. Schaper comes to a similar conclusion: "In beiden Gestalten des Dialogs lebt ein Stück von Thomas Mores eigenem Selbst, die Überzeugung nämlich, dass sich der reine Gedanke nicht loslösen darf vom Boden der Realisierbarkeit, dass sich aber dennoch der politisch Handelnde am Ideal des zeitlos Gültigen orientieren soll," *op. cit.*, p. 123.

29. "Utopiam ad hoc consilio aedidit, ut indicaret, quibus rebus fiat, ut minus commode habeant respublicae," Erasmus to Hutten, *Opus Epistolarum Des. Erasmi*, ed. Allen, vol. IV, no. 999, ll. 256 ff. Cf. Bridgett, *op. cit.*, p. 104: he "extols the natural piety of his Utopians so as to put Christians to the blush."

30. Ed. Allen, vol. II, no. 499, ll. 40 ff.

31. Nowhere is not merely 'for the time being a Nowhere,' as Oncken supposes in his introduction to *Utopia*, p. 13. It is principally a Nowhere; it is *U*-topia, not *Me*-topia as we have seen. Ever since the Vicar of Croydon in More's own day (cf. More's letter to Peter Gilles, ed. Rogers, no. 25, ll. 64 ff.), there have been readers and critics who claimed that "Nowhere was Somewhere"; thus A. E. Morgan's book-title (Chapel Hill, 1946) in which he points out "that More's book in the main is not a fictitious story, but a record of a trip to Peru and what was observed there" (p. 34). H. S. Jevons's "Contemporary Models of Sir T. More: Utopia and the Socialized Inca Empire," *TLS*, 34 (1935), p. 692, later in *Tribune*, 13. Feb. 1948, placed Utopia in Peru; H. Brockhaus, *Die Utopia-Schrift des T. Morus* (Beiträge zur Kulturgeschichte des Mittelalters und der Renaissance, 37), Leipzig & Berlin, 1929, in the Athos monastery Hagionoros; G. C. Richards, *Utopia*, 1923, introduction, in Japan. Cf. G. B. Parks, "More's Utopia and Geography," *JEGP*, 37 (1938), 226.

32. E.g., Hexter, *op. cit.*, p. 11; C. S. Lewis, *English Literature in the Sixteenth Century*, Oxford, 1954, p. 169.

33. Cf. Möbus, *Politik*, p. 82. Even the well-nigh perfect Utopians are prepared to sacrifice their religion of reason in favour of revealed religion as the higher truth (p. 218).

"Nicht einmal in Utopien reicht die Vernunft zur letzten menschlichen Erfüllung aus: wieviel weniger als in der wirklichen Menschheit, die in ihrer menschlichen Bedingtheit noch nicht einmal annähernd zu utopischer Tugendhaftigkeit gelangt!" Schaper, *op. cit.*, p. 169. J. Kühn observes a "restraint eschatologism" in the *Utopia*, where an eschatological state of society is contrasted with a historical one ("T. Morus und Rousseau," *Historische Vierteljahrschrift*, 23, Dresden, 1926, p. 162).

34. *Prose Works*, ed. Temple Scott, 1897-1908, vol. III, p. 301.

35. Even where, as in direct speech and in report, we find the present tense, it is in fact the preterite of the 'historic present.'

36. Although Oncken (*Die Utopia . . .*, p. 12) traces the feature of isolation from Plato 'to Campanella and the most recent,' he does not recognize it as a formal characteristic of the literary genre, but takes it for a real historical phenomenon 'more akin, by nature, to the political thinking of the English rather than to the European continental.'

McCUTCHEON, "Denying the Contrary: More's Use of Litotes in the *Utopia*"

1. See More's prefatory letter to Peter Giles in *Utopia, The Complete Works of St. Thomas More,* eds. Edward Surtz and J. H. Hexter, IV (New Haven: Yale Univ. Press, 1965), 38/13 and 38/3. Subsequent citations from the *Utopia* are from this, the Yale edition, unless otherwise specified.

2. R. Monsuez, 'Le Latin de Thomas More dans "Utopia",' *Annales publiées par la Faculté des Lettres et Sciences Humaines de Toulouse,* Nouvelle Série, Tome II, Fasc. I (Janvier, 1966), *Caliban 3,* 35-78; Edward Surtz, "Aspects of More's Latin Style in *Utopia,*" *Studies in the Renaissance,* 14 (1967), 93-109. As Father Surtz writes, "Detailed and painstaking studies need to be made of every element of style . . .", p. 107.

3. I have deliberately used a common handbook definition here; see William Flint Thrall and Addison Hibbard, *A Handbook to Literature,* rev. and enlarged C. Hugh Holman (New York: The Odyssey Press, 1960), "Litotes," p. 263. Richard A Lanham, *A Handlist of Rhetorical Terms: A Guide for Students of English Literature* (Berkeley: Univ. of California Press, 1968) is also useful. *The Encyclopedia of Poetry and Poetics,* ed. Alex Preminger et al. (Princeton, N.J.: Princeton University Press, 1965), includes a working bibliography.

4. R. Monsuez, 'Le Latin de Thomas More dans "Utopia",' also comments on its frequency in a brief discussion of litotes, p. 48. In my own count I have included such apparently conventional formulas as "haud dubie" and cases where the use of litotes might seem at first less rhetorical than logical. In either case the negation of the negative has an incremental effect, and it is, in practice, impossible to draw a clear line of division between rhetorical and logical uses of a figure in what is a fictional work.

5. John Hoskins, *Directions for Speech and Style,* ed. Hoyt Hudson (Princeton: Princeton Univ. Press, 1935), p. 35. See too Thomas Blount, *The Academie of Eloquence* (London, 1654), p. 31. For a brief selection of litotes in English writings of the Renaissance, see Veré L. Rubel, *Poetic Diction in the English Renaissance from Skelton through Spenser* (New York: MLA, 1941), passim.

6. Obviously it is a characteristic mark of certain styles in literature, though. For two discussions of litotes as a period style, see Frederick Bracher, "Understatement in Old English Poetry," *PMLA,* 52 (December, 1937), 915-934, and Lee M. Hollander, "Litotes in Old Norse," *PMLA,* 53 (March, 1938), 1-33. In spite of studies like these, litotes has been a kind of Cinderella figure in twentieth century rhetorical criticism.

7. Whenever the Yale translation suggests the original litotic construction, I have used it. In other cases, as here, where the litotes is rendered . . . "surely everyone knows . . ." (75/5), I have translated or paraphrased the Latin text so as to preserve the negative features of the construction.

8. Sister Miriam Joseph, *Rhetoric in Shakespeare's Time: Literary Theory of Renaissance Europe* (1947; rpt. New York: Harcourt, 1962), p. 323. Because litotes does involve logic, I found this study, which stresses the relationships the Renaissance saw between rhetoric and logic, particularly helpful.

9. Sir Philip Sidney, *An Apologie for Poetrie*, in *Elizabethan Critical Essays*, ed. G. Gregory Smith (1904; rpt. London: Oxford Univ. Press, 1964), I, 150.

10. *Desiderii Erasmi Opera Omnia*, IV (1703; rpt. Hildesheim: Georg Olms Verlagsbuchhandlung, 1962), 405. This example reveals more about Erasmus' understanding of litotes than his terse comments in his *De copia*, where he treats it as a kind of diminution; see *Opera Omnia*, I, 22 [Lib. I, Cap. XXIX]. But see also his comments on negation, 39–40 [Lib. I, Cap. LI].

11. Henry Peacham, *The Garden of Eloqvence* (London, 1593), p. 151; see also Sister Miriam Joseph, *Rhetoric in Shakespeare's Time*, p. 323.

12. O. B. Hardison, Jr., *The Enduring Monument: A Study of the Idea of Praise in Renaissance Literary Theory and Practice* (Chapel Hill: Univ. of North Carolina Press, 1962), p. 26.

13. For a slightly different approach to the irony of this passage see Father Surtz, "*Utopia* as a Work of Literary Art," Yale *Utopia*, clii.

14. George Puttenham, *The Arte of English Poesie* (1589; rpt. Menston, Eng.: The Scolar Press, 1968), p. 153.

15. Hoskins, *Directions for Speech and Style*, p. 36; Blount, *The Academie of Eloquence*, p. 31.

16. Father Surtz discusses paralipsis (preterition) in the *Utopia*, briefly; see his "Aspects of More's Latin Style in *Utopia*," p. 104.

17. Edward Surtz, "Editions of *Utopia*," and n. 22/21, 280–281.

18. Hoskins, *Directions for Speech and Style*, p. 36; see also Peacham, *The Garden of Eloqvence*, pp. 150–151.

19. Rosemond Tuve, *Elizabethan and Metaphysical Imagery: Renaissance Poetic and Twentieth-Century Critics* (1947; rpt. Phoenix ed., Chicago, Illinois: Univ. of Chicago Press, 1961), p. 205. See too Heinrich Lausberg, *Handbuch der literarischen Rhetorik*, I (München: Max Hueber Verlag, 1960), 304–305.

20. I owe the term "radical" to J. H. Hexter, of course; see, in particular, his "A Window to the Future: The Radicalism of *Utopia*," cv–cxxiv in the Yale *Utopia*.

21. A. R. Heiserman, "Satire in the *Utopia*," *PMLA*, 78 (1963), 164.

22. Sister Miriam Joseph, *Rhetoric in Shakespeare's Time*, p. 322.

23. Thomas Wilson, *The Rule of Reason; Conteining the Art of Logike* [1551] (London, 1567), fol. 52ᵛ, as cited in Sister Miriam Joseph, *Rhetoric in Shakespeare's Time*, p. 322.

24. Isidorus, *Etymologiarum*, in *Patrologiae cursus completus ... Series latina*, ed. Jacques Paul Migne (Paris, 1844–1864), LXXXII, 153–154 [Book II, ch. 31: "De oppositis"].

25. Litotic constructions should, logically, be part of Empson's seventh type of ambiguity, but he does not discuss double negations, although he does comment usefully on negatives in general; see William Empson, *Seven Types of Ambiguity*, 3rd ed. (London: Chatto and Windus, 1956), pp. 205–214.

26. Otto Jespersen, *Negation in English and Other Languages*, in *Selected Writings of Otto Jespersen* (1917; rpt. London: George Allen & Unwin Ltd., n.d.), p. 63. Cf. Ch. 24 in his *The Philosophy of Grammar* (1924; rpt. Allen & Unwin, 1948).

27. John Smith, *The Mystery of Rhetorick Unveil'd* (London, 1688), sig. *a*4.

28. See also Lee M. Hollander, "Litotes in Old Norse," p. 1.

29. *The New Yorker*, February 6, 1971, p. 36.

30. Ralph Robynson, trans. (1551) in *The Utopia of Sir Thomas More,* ed. J. H. Lupton (Oxford: Clarendon Press, 1895), p. 21; Gilbert Burnet, trans., *Utopia: Written in Latin by Sir Thomas More, Chancellor of England: Translated into English* (London, 1684), p. 1; H. V. S. Ogden, ed. and trans., *Utopia,* by Sir Thomas More (New York: Appleton-Century-Crofts, 1949), p. 1; Paul Turner, trans., *Utopia,* by Thomas More (Harmondsworth, Middlesex, Eng.: Penguin Books Ltd., 1965), p. 37.

31. In this connection see the note to 46/8, 295 in the Yale *Utopia.*

32. More's use of negatives in general, though beyond the scope of this study, is an important element in his style (and his thought) and needs more investigation. In thinking about negatives, I found some terse comments by Ian Watt on the negative in Henry James illuminating; he talks of what he calls "the right judicial frame of mind." See Ian Watt, "The First Paragraph of *The Ambassadors:* An Explication," *Essays in Criticism,* X (July, 1960), 250–74; rpt. in *Rhetorical Analyses of Literary Works,* ed. Edward P. J. Corbett (New York: Oxford Univ. Press, 1969), pp. 184–203; the words I cite are on p. 190.

33. Puttenham, *The Arte of English Poesie,* p. 148.

34. An intensive example of a reading on these lines is David Bevington, "The Dialogue in *Utopia:* Two Sides to the Question," *S.P.,* 58 (1961), 496–509. Compare and contrast with this J. H. Hexter, *More's Utopia: The Biography of an Idea* (1952; rpt. Torchbook ed., New York: Harper, 1965).

35. Jespersen, *Negation in English and Other Languages,* discusses *non minus quam* briefly, pp. 83–84.

36. Peacham, *The Garden of Eloqvence,* p. 151.

SCHOECK, "More, Plutarch, and King Agis: Spartan History and the Meaning of *Utopia*"

1. J. H. Lupton, ed., *The Utopia of Sir Thomas More* (Clarendon Press, 1895), Introduction, pp. xlv, lii–liii.

2. I shall use Dryden's clear and readily accessible English translation, for it is only a very general view of Sparta, as Plutarch presents it, that I wish to convey.

3. I have here compressed Plutarch's presentation. *The Cambridge Ancient History* notes that "Phylarchus, whose *Histories* covered the period 272–220 B.C., gave a lively account of the attempts at reform in Sparta by Agis and Cleomenes. As an ardent supporter of Cleomenes, he is denounced by Polybius, who favoured Aratus, and even Plutarch admits his bias and love of theatrical devices, but at least he managed to make his hero stand out sharp and clear against the background of his time" (VII [1928], 259). I do not know whether More was familiar with Phylarchus and Aratus, but it is curious that Budé comments upon Aratus in his letter to Lupset: Hic enim muero periculum esse quispiam autumarit, ne forte Aratus et poetae prisci opinione falsi fuerint. (This, together with Budé's play upon Hagnopolis and Udepotia, are discussed briefly in *N & Q,* n.s., I [1954], 512–3.)

Cf. the list of historians in Book II of *Utopia* (Lupton, p. 216), where Plutarch is coupled with Lucian.

4. The picture is sharply and succinctly drawn by E. M. G. Routh: an impoverished countryside, a nobility that had suffered from the civil wars, increasing unemployment with crime that "became terribly prevalent and was punished savagely" (*Sir Thomas More and His Friends* [Oxford, 1934], pp. 70 ff.); cf. Chambers, *More,* pp. 131 ff.

5. This influence is touched at only a few points by Gilbert Highet in his *Classical Tradition* (Oxford, 1949). Still the best general survey is the unpublished dissertation of Rudd Fleming, *Plutarch in the English Renaissance* (Cornell, 1935), though there are such special studies as Wegehaupt's *Plutarchstudien in Italienischen Bibliotheken* (Cuxhaven, 1906), which needs to be brought up to date. I am indebted to Fleming's

dissertation first for its survey of Italian translations, and second for the summary of Erasmus' deep interest in Plutarch. It is relevant to point out that in 1511, in his *De Ratione Studii*, Erasmus recommended a study of Plutarch in the schools; in 1512 Erasmus named Plutarch as the principal source for *sentences* or *exempla*. The translation of *De Discrimine Adulatoris et Amici* was dedicated to Henry VIII and presented to him in manuscript; Erasmus had spoken of translating it in a letter of November 1512, but the work was presented to the king in 1517. In 1513 the *De Tuenda Bona Valetudine* was dedicated to Dr. John Young; and in January 1514 appeared the *Quomodo Utilitas Capiatur ex Inimicis*, with its dedicatory epistle to Wolsey. Clearly Erasmus was deeply engaged in working with Plutarch during the years just preceding More's writing of *Utopia*, as well as during the year 1515-6 itself, and from their letters we know how closely More and Erasmus shared their intellectual discoveries and activities.

6. Of More's as a list of Great Books, Surtz has written that "Thomas More's program of Greek studies is an important document in the history of the early Renaissance in England"; he maintains that More is largely following Erasmus' Plan of Study of 1511, the *De Ratione Studii*; see Edward L. Surtz, S.J., "Thomas More and the Great Books," *PQ*, XXXII, 43-57. No doubt the outline of More's general ideas on Greek studies accords with the list of books here being discussed, but we should be careful not to argue that the list of books in *Utopia* gives us More's exact program and his total program.

7. Lupton, *op. cit.*, pp. xliii and 132.

8. I refer to *Fasciculus Temporum Omnes Antiquorum Cronicas Succincte Complectens*... (Paris, 1518); and I acknowledge the kindness of Prof. C. W. Jones in lending me his copy. In this work the date is ruled across the page, the *anno mundi* usually on the left-hand page, and the *anno ante christi nativitatem* on the right-hand page upside down. Although the dates in such a chronicle as this are of necessity only roughly indicated, still through Plutarch's dating of the death of Cleomenes under Ptolemy IV, Philopator, the dates of Cleomenes' reign (and thus those of Agis) could be computed fairly closely.

And although this *Fasciculus Temporum* is to be sure two years later than More's *Utopia*, it indicates a practice of dating events B.C. in a readily accessible form; it seems reasonable to conjecture that More was familiar with, or had available, a chronicle similar in form, like that described in footnote 9.

9. The *Eusebius Caesariensis. Chronicon, quod Hieronymus presbyter divino eius ingenio Latinum facere curavit*... was widely known and used, and it may well be closer to More's source. The edition I have consulted in the Cornell University Library is the Estienne (Paris, 1518), but others would have been available to More, of course. This work presents historical dates in a much more direct tabular form, and on F.72v, e.g., at anno mundi 4953, the accession of Ptolemy, Euergetes is given: "Aegypti.3. Ptolemaus Euergetes. an.26." (In view of More's geographical interests, we may note that under the date of 1509 there is an account of the arrival at Rouen of several natives of Oran, with descriptions of their appearance; under 1500, references to the Voyages of Cadamosto.)

10. Cf. "Levels of Word-Play and Figurative Signification in More's *Utopia*," *N & Q*, n.s., I, 512-3, and *ibid.*, CXCVI, 313, and *ibid.*, n.s., I, 193-4.

11. The name Peloponnesus, or Isle of Pelops, proves that the whole territory was considered an island. "Ancient geographers knew about its peculiar shape, comparing it to the leaf of a plane-tree; the medieval name Morea is said to have been taken from the mulberry" (*Oxford Classical Dictionary*). I have briefly discussed the likelihood of More's interest in the Morea-mulberry name in "Levels of Word-Play" cited above.

12. *The Social and Economic History of the Hellenistic World* (Oxford, 1941), III, 1367.

13. Lupton, *op. cit.*, p. xli.

14. As Prof. Mackie has noted, "More's Latin poem on the accession of Henry VIII denounces the rapacity and delation which had marked the reign of Henry VII" (*Earlier Tudors, 1485-1558* [Clarendon Press, 1952], p. 216 n. Book I of *Utopia* goes further and deeper to discover the "sicknesses of sixteenth century society": see J. H. Hexter, *More's Utopia* (Princeton, 1952), p. 65.

The riots of 1514 were to culminate in the evil May Day riot of 1517, which More alone seems to have had the power and wisdom to quell; see K. Pickthorn, *Early Tudor Government, Henry VIII* (Cambridge Univ. Press, 1934), pp. 37 ff., and cf. Tawney and Power, *Tudor Economic Documents* (1924), III, 17.

15. See L. Bradner and C. A. Lynch, *The Latin Epigrams of Thomas More* (Univ. of Chicago Press, 1953), p. xxvii.

16. *Ibid.*, p. xxviii. Cf. Mackie, *op. cit.*, pp. 216 ff.

17. "More cannot have read *Il Principe* in print, for it was not published until 1532; but it was written, or at least begun, in 1513 and it must have circulated to some extent in manuscript, for it was plagiarized soon afterwards. In any case, *The Prince* was only a fixation—perhaps even a criticism—of the amoral doctrine of politics which was current in Italy at the beginning of the sixteenth century, and to these doctrines the *Utopia* was certainly a reply." J. D. Mackie, *op. cit.*, pp. 264–5.

This view of *Utopia* as a reaction against the ideas of Machiavelli in *Il Principe* was first put forth by Hermann Oncken in his lecture on *Utopia* in *Sitzungsberichte der Heidelberger Akademie, Phil.-Hist. Klasse*, II (1922), 12, and is supported by R. W. Chambers in his *Thomas More* (1935), p. 132.

18. Cf. Chambers' section on 1516, 'the wonderful year of Erasmian reform' (pp. 121 ff.)—so called because in this year Erasmus brought forth his Greek *New Testament*, the *Institutio Principis Christiani* (which, like More's *Utopia*, is in part to be read as a reaction against Machiavellian ideas), and the first part of his edition of Jerome.

19. G. G. Smith, *Elizabethan Critical Essays* (Oxford, 1904), I, xxv. This point has been made before in my survey, "Towards Understanding St. Thomas More," *The Month*, n.s., II, 45.

20. Edward L. Surtz, S.J., "Interpretations of *Utopia*," *Cath. Hist. Rev.*, XXXVIII, 156–74; cf. "Towards Understanding St. Thomas More," *loc. cit.*, p. 46.

SCHOECK, " 'A Nursery of Correct and Useful Institutions': On Reading More's *Utopia* as Dialogue"

1. For C. S. Lewis, pp. 167-9 in *English Literature in the Sixteenth Century, Excluding Drama* (Oxford: the Clarendon Press, 1954—Oxford History of English Literature, III). For Kautsky, *Thomas More und seine Utopia* (Stuttgart, 1890); for Chambers, *Thomas More* (London, 1935). For a recent pointing of the problem of varying interpretations, see R. S. Sylvester, " 'Si Hythlodaeo Credimus': Vision and Revision in Thomas More's *Utopia*," *Soundings* (1968), 272–289.

2. Lewis, *op. cit.*, p. 167.

3. *Ibid.*, p. 169.

4. In "The Place of Sir Thomas More," *Revue de l'Université d'Ottawa*, xxxiv (1964), 176–90.

5. For a conflation of two points of view that proceed from different cultural contexts in discussing More, see my "Pilgrim and Peregrine—Thomas More in Chelsea," *Thought*, xxxviii (1963), p. 558.

6. In introduction to Yale Edition of The Complete Works of St. Thomas More: vol. 4, *Utopia* (New Haven: 1965), p. xlviii, hereafter cited as *Utopia*. Cf. p. lv.

7. Cf. Cicero, *De Off.*, I, 17, 54. The word was ambivalent, even in classical Latin; in Livy, the Bacchanalia are termed a *seminarium scelerum omnium* (39 epist.), and Valla used the phrase 'seminary of heresies.'

Classical and Renaissance Latin *seminarium* becomes both modern *seminary* and also *seminar:* see my note 'Towards a Definition of Terms for Group Scholarship,' to appear in the annual volume of the Editorial Conference at Toronto, to be edited by W. J. Howard, 1969.

8. On More's legal career, see "Sir Thomas More, Humanist and Lawyer," *University of Toronto Quarterly*, xxiv (1964), 1-14.

9. See Hexter, Introduction to *Utopia*, pp. xxix ff., and Appendix A, 'More's Visit to Antwerp in 1515'; also Edward Surtz, "Sir Thomas More and his Utopian Embassy of 1515," *Catholic Historical Review*, xxxix (1953), 272-98.

10. *Ibid.*, p. xxx: cf. Elizabeth F. Rogers, *St. Thomas More: Selected Letters* (New Haven: Yale, 1961), p. 71—hereafter cited as *Selected Letters.*

On the schools of jurisprudence in the sixteenth century, see M. P. Gilmore, "The Jurisprudence of Humanism," *Traditio*, xvii (1961), and my survey-article in *Renaissance Quarterly*, xx (1967), 279-91.

11. *Selected Letters*, p. 71.

12. I have in mind such works as Patrizi's *De regno et regis institutione.* See *Utopia*, p. 349.

13. For a useful survey of the reform problem at this time, see John W. O'Malley, "Historical Thought and the Reform Crisis of the Early Sixteenth Century," *Theological Studies*, xxviii (1967), 531-48.

In stressing the cracks in the institutional structures, I do not wish to ignore the genuine and creative movements towards *renovatio:* see, among other studies, Surtz, '*Utopia* and the Christian Revival' in *Utopia*, pp. xcii ff., and the posthumously published work of H. Outram Evennett, *The Spirit of the Counter-Reformation* (Cambridge: University Press, 1968).

14. I have recently summarized the conflict of canon and common law, and More's views of the case of Richard Hunne, in a paper to appear in *Proceedings of the Congress of Medieval Canon Law* (Strasbourg, 1968).

15. *Selected Letters*, p. 20.

16. *Ibid.*, p. 23. As promised on p. 585 of the *Utopia*, I intend to treat More and formal logic in a future study.

17. *Ibid.*, pp. 94-103. For a recent discussion, see my 'On the Letters of Thomas More' in *Moreana*, xv-xvi (1967), 193-203.

18. In classical rhetoric there were two main sorts of *declamatio:* 1) *suasoria*, in which some eminent character is imagined to deliberate with himself or to have advice tendered to him at a political or strategic crisis: and 2) *controversia*, handling a fictitious case in imitation of actual pleadings in court—thus the *Oxford Classical Dictionary;* for further examples, see C. S. Baldwin, *Ancient Rhetoric and Poetic* (New York: 1924), pp. 87 ff., and the same author's *Medieval Rhetoric and Poetic* (New York: 1928), pp. 82 ff., for the medieval continuations, especially in the schools of Gaul, and p. 92 for the development of *declamatio* in the long-popular textbook of Martianus Capella. Quintilian of course treats *declamatio* in Book II, chapter 10, of *De Institutione Oratoria*, and this would be a prime source down through the centuries.

On More and the Lucianic *declamatio*, see further Craig R. Thompson, *The Translations of Lucian by Erasmus and St. Thomas More* (Ithaca: 1940), pp. 12 ff.

It is to be noted that both Erasmus and More translated the *Tyrannicida* of Lucian, and both wrote replies to it (Thompson, p. 29). Further, we have the testimony of Erasmus that More was fond of making declamations (Thompson, p. 38), and we know that he encouraged the pupils in his school to write declamations: "His brilliant daughter Margaret composed a *declamatio* of the same kind as her father's" (Thompson, p. 40).

19. The Greek of Erasmus' own title became in Latinized Greek *Moriae Encomium;* the work is a mock encomium, "a eulogy or panegyric, a species of the genus oration," as Hudson writes in his introduction to *The Praise of Folly* (Princeton: 1941), p. xv, but the strong Lucianic tone in the work, and the fictitious or imagined situation, make it indeed something of a *declamatio.*

20. For a brief sketch of this notion, see note above, and the article on *Utopia* in the *New Catholic Encyclopedia.*

21. See the full discussion by Geoffrey Shepherd in his recent edition of the *Apology for Poetry* (London: 1965), pp. 66–9.

22. Sylvester, " 'Si Hythlodaeo Credimus'," p. 275.

23. But cf. pages 27 and 35 in *Utopia.*

24. Sylvester, p. 289.

25. *Utopia*, p. cxxxix.

26. On More and Tacitus, see Sylvester's introduction to the Yale edition of *Richard III* (1963), pp. lxxxix–xcvii.

I have of course excessively telescoped a most complex problem, and in another context I should want to begin by discussing and bringing to bear on our reading of the *Utopia* C. S. Lewis's provocative essays in *The Discarded Image* (Cambridge, 1964), particularly 'The Medieval Situation' (pp. 1–12), and 'The Human Past' (pp. 174–85). But even this would be only a beginning; yet I do not want to open these boxes of Pandora beyond the point of indicating the following studies as valuable for initiating further exploration: Lynn Thorndike, 'Mediaeval Interest in Intellectual History,' *Speculum*, xxv (1950), 94–99; R. J. Schoeck, 'Mathematics and the Languages of Literary Criticism' [for ideas about models and metaphors], in *Journal of Aesthetics and Art Criticism*, xxvi (1968), 367–76; and E. H. Kantorowicz, 'The Sovereignty of the Artist: A Note on Legal Maxims and Renaissance Theories of Art,' rptd. in *Selected Studies* by E. H. Kantorowicz (Locust Valley, N.Y.: J. J. Augustin, 1965), pp. 352–65.

27. Shepherd edition of Sidney's *Apology*, p. 108/19–23.

28. Thus E. Schillebeeckx, O.P., 'The Magisterium and the World of Politics,' in *Concilium*, xxxvi (1968), p. 23. Cf. his 'De Kerk als sacrament van de dialoog,' *Tijdschrift voor Theologie*, vii (1967), n. 4.

29. *Art. cit.*, p. 275.

30. *Utopia*, p. cxxxix.

31. J. J. Parry, ed., *The Art of Courtly Love* (New York: 1941), p. 22.

32. *Selected Letters*, p. 10.

33. Cf. Harry Berger, Jr., "The Renaissance Imagination: Second World and Green World," *Centennial Review*, ix (1965), 36–77, and Sylvester, *art. cit.*, p. 276 *n.*

Erasmus stresses the necessity to make fictitious narratives probable, and he writes as follows in *De Copia:* "Now fictitious narratives of events, if they are presented as true for the sake of persuasion, ought to be composed with the highest possible degree of plausibility" (Erasmus, *On Copia of Words and Ideas*, ed. by Donald B. King and H. David Rix [Marquette University Press, 1963], p. 86).

34. Sylvester, *art. cit.*, p. 289.

35. Like so much of the language of his letter, this phrase of Budé's evokes much of the ethical strain of humanism, and the phrase *beatae vitae* (12/15) re-establishes a fusion between Christian and stoic concepts of the good life: and it must be urged that 'pattern' is probably much too limiting and too static an equivalent for the Latin

'argumentum,' which could mean not only the subject-matter of a poem but even, by metonymy, the poem itself, and there was in Cicero (*Cael.* 27) the figurative signification of 'intrinsic worth' or 'truth.'

SYLVESTER, " 'Si Hythlodaeo Credimus': Vision and Revision in Thomas More's *Utopia*"

1. The classic Marxist interpretation of *Utopia* remains that of Karl Kautsky, *Thomas More und seine Utopie* (Stuttgart, 1888). See the English translation by H. J. Stenning (London and New York, 1927), Russell Ames, *Citizen Thomas More and His Utopia* (Princeton, 1949), and the discussion by R. W. Chambers (*Thomas More* [London, 1935], pp. 372-374).

2. One of the ablest defenders of this interpretation is C. S. Lewis (*English Literature in the Sixteenth Century* [Oxford, 1954]), who finds *Utopia* to be "a holiday work, a spontaneous overflow of intellectual high spirits, a revel of debate, paradox, comedy and (above all) invention, which starts many hares and kills none" (p. 169).

3. The best succinct treatment of Utopian interpretation and imitation is contained in R. W. Gibson and J. Max Patrick, *St. Thomas More: A Preliminary Bibliography to 1750* (New Haven, 1961), pp. 291-412. The utopian genre is described and analyzed in Hubertus Schulte Herbrüggen, *Utopie und Anti-Utopie* (Bochum-Langendreer, 1960). See also the convenient anthology, *The Quest For Utopia*, ed. G. Negley and J. Max Patrick, Anchor Books (New York, 1962).

4. It is just possible that all the names in *Utopia* were originally Latin. See the excellent discussion by Arthur E. Barker in "Clavis Moreana: The Yale Edition of Thomas More," *Journal of English and Germanic Philology*, LXV (1966), 318-330, especially p. 325.

5. What the literary effect of the Utopian names might have been—if More had *not* finally rejected *Nusquama* as a title for his book—can be observed in the irrelevant flippancy of Paul Turner's recent translation (Penguin Books, 1965), where every Greek word is given a direct (and occasional incorrect) English equivalent. Thus Hythlodaeus becomes "Nonsenso" and Anemolius' poem on Utopia is rendered as "Mr. Windbag's" lines describing "Noplacia" (p. 27).

6. The Yale Edition of the Works of St. Thomas More, volume 4, *Utopia*, edited by E. Surtz and J. H. Hexter (New Haven, 1965). All page references in the text are to this edition.

7. For these vernacular versions, see Gibson and Patrick, *A Preliminary Bibliography*, nos. 34, 37, and 44. One cannot completely account for the absence of Book I from these translations by remarking that fear of ecclesiastical censorship caused publishers to delete it. More's attack on corruption in the Western Church is if anything much stronger in Book II. Even More himself could feel the creative power of his vision of the Utopian world. See his letter to Erasmus of December, 1516, where he imagines himself, wistfully, as the ruler of "a distinguished retinue of Amaurotians" (*St. Thomas More: Selected Letters*, ed. E. F. Rogers [New Haven, 1961], p. 85).

8. For Plato and other sources employed by More, see Surtz's extended discussion in the Yale Edition, pp. cliii ff.

9. *The Latin Epigrams of Thomas More*, ed. L. Bradner and C. A. Lynch (Chicago, 1953), pp. xxvii-xxviii.

10. More manages this business very deftly (pp. 51-55). Hythlodaeus' wanderings after he had been left behind by Vespucci are vaguely, but alluringly, described as he travels from Ceylon to Calcutta and then into a realm which contains many (unnamed) "new nations."

11. Much of the interpretation which follows originated years ago in conversations

with my friend and former colleague, Professor Harry Berger, Jr., of the University of California at Santa Cruz. He has since developed his views in "The Renaissance Imagination: Second World and Green World," *The Centennial Review,* IX (1965), 36–77, an article to which I am greatly indebted. For further criticism of utopian ideals, see the Spring, 1965 (vol. XCIV) issue of *Daedalus.*

12. *Opus Epistolarum Des. Erasmi Roterodami,* ed. P. S. Allen et al., 12 vols. (Oxford, 1906-58), IV, 21: "Secundum librum prius scripserat per ocium, mox per occasionem primum adiecit ex tempore." See J. H. Hexter, *More's "Utopia": The Biography of an Idea* (Princeton, 1952) and the same author's discussion in the Yale edition, pp. xv f.

13. For biographical data on the writers of the *parerga,* see the commentary to the Yale edition and P. R. Allen, "*Utopia* and European Humanism: The Function of the Prefatory Letters and Verses," *Studies in the Renaissance,* X (1963), 91–107.

14. I owe this phrase to Father Surtz, whose introduction to the paperback edition of *Utopia* (English translation only, New Haven, 1964) is an invaluable summary of conflicting interpretations.

15. The classics, especially Lucian and Horace, offer other obvious precedents. See A. R. Heiserman, "Satire in the *Utopia,*" *Publications of the Modern Language Association,* LXXVIII (1963), 163–174; Robert C. Elliott, "The Shape of Utopia," *English Literary History,* XXX (1963), 317–334; and T. S. Dorsch, "Sir Thomas More and Lucian: An Interpretation of *Utopia,*" *Archiv für das Studium der Neueren Sprachen,* CCIII (1966), 345–363. The last article is particularly interesting. Dorsch refuses to accept any interpretation which argues "that More intended his Utopia to be regarded as a desirable, if scarcely attainable ideal" (361); but he bases his case mainly on the historical fact that More, in later life, strongly opposed many Utopian practices (divorce and remarriage, euthanasia, religious toleration, etc.). As Hexter has demonstrated (Yale edition, pp. xxvi-xxvii), there is nothing to keep a man, especially a complex writer like More, from changing his mind on such matters. If Dorsch's conclusion is to stand, then it must be supported through a close literary analysis of the text of *Utopia* as we have it. In addition, although Lucian's influence on More is highly probable, it too must be demonstrated through detailed criticism and not merely claimed as a most likely possibility.

16. It is important to note here that Raphael "wrested permission" ("extorsit," 50/8) from Vespucci so that he could be left behind in the fort at Cape Frio during the fourth voyage. In the original account used by More, there is no indication whatsoever that any of the twenty-four sailors *wanted* to be stationed there. Hythlodaeus' exile is completely self-willed and More's deliberate variation from his source emphasizes this point.

17. For a suggestive analysis of the episode in Morton's household, see David M. Bevington, "The Dialogue in *Utopia:* Two Sides to the Question," *Studies in Philology,* LVIII (1961), 496–509.

18. Even the famous anecdote of the Utopian chickens, which comes very early in Book II (p. 115), is far more than a mere *jeu d'esprit* on Hythlodaeus' part. The chicks, because they were hatched in manmade incubators, follow human beings rather than hens after they are born. So too the new country of *Utopia,* now being hatched by Hythlodaeus, will artificially follow the design which his own imagination imposes on it.

19. It should be noted, however, that the realistic details in these sections are not without their own ironies. For example, as Berger has observed ("The Renaissance Imagination," pp. 66–67), the shifting landmarks in the utopian harbor are an admirable forecast of their cunning procedures in wartime.

ZAVALA, "Sir Thomas More in New Spain"

1. See the excellent comparison drawn between the works of Ribadeneyra and Herrera,

by R. O. Jones, "El 'Tomás Moro' de Fernando de Herrera," *Boletín de la Real Academia Española*, xxx (Sept.–Dec., 1950), 423–438.

2. This discovery is due to R. O. Jones, 'Some Notes on More's 'Utopia' in Spain,' *The Modern Language Review*, xiv, No. 4 (Oct., 1950), 478–82.

3. A typical late Spanish quotation in *Clave Historial con que se abre la puerta a la historia eclesiástica y política* ..., segunda edición, corregida y limada por su autor, el P. M. Fr. Henrique Florez, del orden de S. Agustín ... En Madrid, por Antonio Marín, año de 1749, p. 315: "Thomàs Moro, Chanchillèr de Inglaterra, à quien cortò la cabeza Henrique VIII, por no querer condescender con sus errores."

4. See his final conclusions in *Erasmo y España* (México, 1950), II, 435, 448–454.

5. A. Castro, *El Pensamiento de Cervantes* (Madrid, 1925), pp. 177–78.

6. *Somnium* in *Joannis Maldonati quaedam opuscula nunc primum in lucem edita*, Burgos, 1541, fols. g 4° r° ss., studied by M. Bataillon in his *Erasmo y España*, ii, pp. 251–252, and in his 1949–50 course at the Collège de France. See also, Edición Nacional de las Obras Completas de Menéndez Pelayo, *Bibliografía Hispano-Latina Clásica*, III, Consejo Superior de Investigaciones Científicas, Santander, Aldus, 1950, pp. 164–177.

7. *Colección de Documentos Inéditos del Archivo de Indias* (hereafter referred to as *D.I.I.*) (Madrid, 1864–89), x, 363.

8. *D.I.I.*, x, 482–483.

9. *D.I.I.*, xiii, 420.

10. *Epistolario de Nueva España* (México, 1939), ii, 180–82.

11. *Ibid.*, 197–201.

12. *D.I.I.*, xiii, 250.

13. Vasco de Puga, *Cedulario* (México, 1563), fol. 83v (2d ed., México, 1878–79, i, 291–92).

14. *D.I.I.*, x, 376. And *Don Vasco de Quiroga* (México, Editorial Polis, 1940), p. 303.

15. This refers to an office in the indigenous, pre-Hispanic administration.

16. MS. in Biblioteca Nacional, Madrid, No. 7369. *D.I.I.*, x, 333–513. *Don Vasco de Quiroga*, pp. 291–406.

17. There is in existence a Venetian edition of 1516, reprinted in Paris in 1529. [La primera edición es: Luciani Dialogi ... compluria opuscula longe festivissima ab Erasmo Roterodamo et Thoma Moro interpretibus optimis in latinorum lingua traducta, Paris, 1506. Otra edición: Luciani Opuscula Erasmo Roterodamo interprete, impressum Florentiae per haeredes Philippi Juntae, anno MDXIX y en apéndice los opúsculos traducidos por T. More.]

18. *Actas de Cabildo de México* (México, 1862–89), iii, 41.

19. *Reglas y Ordenanzas para el gobierno de los hospitales de Santa Fe de México y Michoacán* (México, Talleres Gráficos de la Nación, 1940), xviii, 38 pp.

20. N. León, *D. Vasco de Quiroga* (México, 1903), pp. 75–103.

21. S. Zavala, *La Utopia de Tomás Moro en la Nueva España* (México, 1937). Second edition in the *Memoria de El Colegio Nacional*, México, 1950.

22. See also the following: Juan José Moreno, *Fragmentos de la Vida y Virtudes del V. Ilmo. y Rmo. Sr. Dr. D. Vasco de Quiroga* (México. En la Imprenta del Real y más antiguo Colegio de San Ildefonso, 1766). Silvio Zavala, *Ideario de Vasco de Quiroga* (México, El Colegio de México, 1941); 'Letras de Utopia. Carta a don Alfonso Reyes,' in *Cuadernos Americanos*, Vol. II, No. 2 (México, March-April, 1942), pp. 146–52.

DEAN, "Literary Problems in More's *Richard III*"

1. By A. F. Pollard, "The Making of Sir Thomas More's *Richard III*," *Historical Essays in Honour of James Tate* (Manchester, 1933), pp. 223–238.

2. Ascham, *Works*, ed. J. A. Giles (London, 1864), III, 5–6: a letter to John Astley,

1552. Ascham predicates that a history should be a true, orderly account of events and their causes, that the historian should comment upon the merits of motives, counsels, and actions, should note general lessons "of wisdom and wariness," and should stress "the inward disposition of the mind" as did Thucydides, Homer, and especially Chaucer. More's *Richard III*, concludes Ascham, "doth in most part, I believe, of all these points so content all men, as, if the rest of our story of England were so done, we might well compare with France, or Italy, or Germany, in that behalf." One notices the presence of Homer and Chaucer among historians, and wonders also whether Ascham was thinking of the similarity between More's and Chaucer's use of irony in character portrayal.

Even Pollard (*op. cit.*, pp. 230–231) admits that since More's purpose was to write dramatically, criticism of his factual errors is sometimes irrelevant. Yet he comments sarcastically, for instance, upon the improbability of More's dramatic version of Edward's dying speech.

3. This is the date given by Rastell for the Latin version. Internal evidence indicates that neither the Latin nor the English version could have been begun before 1509, and that they may have been worked on as late as 1517. Cf. R. W. Chambers, "The Authorship of the 'History of Richard III'," More's *English Works* (London, 1931), I, 34 and 37.

4. In 1501. Stapleton states that "he did not treat this great work from the theological point of view, but from the standpoint of history and philosophy; and indeed the earlier books ... deal with these two subjects almost exclusively...." *The Life and Illustrious Martyrdom of Sir Thomas More*, tr. P. E. Hallett (London, 1928), p. 9.

Augustine's greatly influential statement of the providential theory of history is interesting in connection with More's treatment of the *de casibus* example.

5. In 1505? More's purpose, according to Stapleton (*op. cit.*, pp. 9–10), was chiefly self-guidance. He had just decided against becoming a priest, and Pico appealed to him as a man who successfully combined "encyclopedic knowledge and ... sanctity." The preoccupation with the task of harmonizing the Christian and classical attitudes is evident in *Richard III*.

6. In 1505–06. More contributed translations of *Cynicus, Menippus* or *Necromantia, Philopseudes*, and *Tyrannicida*, with an original declamation in answer. Between 1503 and 1517 Erasmus translated thirty-six of Lucian's writings. Cf. Craig Thompson, *The Translations of Lucian by Erasmus and St. Thomas More* (Ithaca, New York, 1940).

7. For history in the schools, see especially Foster Watson, *Vives: On Education* (Cambridge, 1913); W. H. Woodward, *Erasmus Concerning the Aim and Method of Education* (Cambridge, 1904), and *Vittorino da Feltre and other Humanist Educators* (Cambridge, 1905); and J. A. Gee, *The Life and Works of Thomas Lupset* (Yale Univ. Press, 1928), pp. 88–89.

8. Cf. T. C. Burgess, "Epideictic Literature," *Univ. of Chicago Studies in Classical Philology*, III (1902), 195–213. For the continuation of the tradition among the early Italian humanists, many of whose writings were known in England in More's time, see Remigio Sabbadini, *Il metodo degli umanisti* (Firenze, 1922), Cap. VIII: "Storiografia." The tradition was carried to England in person by Polydore Vergil, who began his *Anglica historia* shortly after 1501 and published it in 1534. A satisfactory comparison of Polydore's theory and method of history-writing with More's must await the appearance of a critical edition of the *Historia*, which has been promised. The important Vatican MS. is a first draft in Polydore's own hand, which was written in 1512–13 and ends in 1513. Cf. Denis Hay, "The Manuscript of Polydore Vergil's 'Anglica Historia'," *EHR*, LIV (1939), 240–252.

9. Although not translated by More or Erasmus, it was in the edition of Lucian which they used. The story of Diogenes at the opening of *Utopia* may be from it. It was trans-

lated into Latin by Pirckheimer (Nuremberg, 1515), to whom More had dedicated his *Epigrammata*.

10. *The Works of Lucian of Samosata*, tr. H. W. and F. G. Fowler (Oxford, 1905), II, 118, 131-133.

11. *Ibid.*, pp. 126-127.

12. The traditional distinction between the historian and the compiler was well established. Bacon observed, a century after More, that a great inconvenience in historical composition in his time was the lack of adequate chronicles or catalogues of brute facts upon which the historian could exercise his powers of interpretation and synthesis.— Preface to *Henry VII, Works*, ed. Spedding, Ellis, and Heath (Boston, 1860-64), XI, 35.
This distinction is also important in the controversy over the authorship of *Richard III*. There has never been any reasonable doubt that the extant versions are More's, but it has been suggested that his source was written and fairly elaborate, and that, in short, he may have done little more than reproduce a composition by Morton or someone else. Cf. W. G. Zeeveld, "A Tudor Defense of Richard III," *PMLA*, LV (1940), 946-957. This cannot be settled without further external evidence, but certainly it was considered proper in More's time for an historian to use a previous chronicle as the basis for his literary and interpretative treatment. It should be clear from the present discussion that a great merit of *Richard III* is its literary excellence, and that probably More alone was responsible for that excellence.

13. *Works*, tr. Fowler, pp. 119-120, 123. Cf. T. C. Burgess, *op. cit.*, pp. 200-201.

14. Tr. Fowler, p. 134.

15. *Ibid.*, pp. 113-116, 120, 121, 124, 125, 129-130.

16. Cf. T. C. Burgess, *op. cit.*, p. 124.

17. Tr. Fowler, p. 130.

18. *Ibid.*, p. 122.

19. Eduard Feuter, *Histoire de l'historiographie moderne*, tr. Émile Jeanmaire (Paris, 1914), pp. 20, 21, 27, 198-199. Cf. Emilio Santini, "Leonardo Bruni Aretini e i suoi 'Historiarum Florentini populi libri XII'," *Annali della R. Scuola Normale Superiore di Pisa*, XXII (1910), 47-48, 114-116.

20. *Op. cit.*, p. 15. He tells us also (p. 104) that Sallust was used as a textbook in More's household.

21. The historical reading of a mature scholar would differ, of course, from that prescribed for a schoolboy, and there is some evidence that Tacitus, and especially Thucydides, would be ranked higher by More's humanist contemporaries than this list indicates. This is important in connection with More's use of irony; consequently their histories as well as those listed above have been compared with *Richard III*. There is, for example, the item "Cornelius Tacitus" in the catalogue of Grocyn's library made in 1520 by William Linacre (*Collectanea*, Oxf. Hist. Soc., sec. ser., pt. v, 1890). This was probably the Tacitus purchased in 1521 for Corpus Christi. See J. R. Liddell, "The Library of Corpus Christi College, Oxford, in the Sixteenth Century," *The Library*, n. s., XVIII (1938), 385-416. Dorne, in 1520, records (no. 1811) "Cornelius Tacitus nouus magnus in quaternis." See "Day-Book of John Dorne," ed. F. Madden, *Collectanea*, Oxf. Hist. Soc., first ser., 1885. Corpus Christi had two copies of Thucydides by 1538 (Liddell, *op. cit.*); one copy is listed in Linacre's will (1534) according to J. N. Johnson, *The Life of Thomas Linacre* (London, 1835), p. 344; and John Clement, More's protégé, owned three copies before 1549 as shown in A. W. Reed, "John Clement and his Books," *The Library*, VI (1925-26), 329-339. Thucydides was one of the Aldine Greek historians prized by the Utopians (Bk. II, chap. vi).

22. Two passages in Sallust have the closest parallels in *Richard III*. The first, some-

what of a stereotype, is a characterization of Jugurtha at the climax of his bloody career, after he has murdered Bomilcar and other former confederates.

But from that time forward Jugurtha never passed a quiet day or night; he put little trust in any place, person, or time; feared his countrymen and the enemy alike; was always on the watch, started at every sound; and spent his nights in different places, many of which were ill suited to the dignity of a king. Sometimes on being roused from sleep he would utter outcries and seize his arms; he was hounded by a fear that was all but madness. [Tr. J. C. Rolfe (Loeb Classical Library, London, 1921), pp. 287-289.]

Richard suffers in a similar fashion after he has climaxed his crimes with the murder of the young princes.

... after this abominable deed done, he never had quiet in his mind, he never thought himself sure: where he went abroad, his eyes whirled about, his body privily fenced, his hand ever on his dagger, his countenance and manner like one always ready to strike again; he took ill rest o' nights, lay long waking and musing, fore wearied with care and watch, rather slumbered than slept, troubled with fearful dreams, suddenly sometime started up, leaped out of his bed and ran about the chamber, so was his restless heart continually tossed and tumbled with the tedious impression and stormy remembrance of his abominable deed. See *English Works*, I, 451-452. Cited hereafter as *EW*. It is impossible to compare the Latin since both Latin versions of *Richard III* (Louvain 1565 and MS. Arundel 43) break off before this.

More states that he has this information about Richard's condition "by credible report, of such as were secret with his chamberers"; but it is possible that his treatment was influenced by Sallust, whom he must, indeed, have had by heart.

The second parallel is that between the dying speeches of Edward and Micipsa. (*EW*, 403-405; Sallust, *op. cit.*, pp. 147-151. There are no verbal similarities between the Latin versions.) The passages, which are too long for quotation, contain these similarities. In both instances a dying king is leaving the royal power to minors and therefore pleads with the nobles to preserve harmony and lawful order by being loyal to kin and country. And in both instances the nobles reply ironically, pretending to accede when they are really plotting to rebel. Edward's speech is, as Pollard observes, a "more finished composition than [he] could achieve *in articulo mortis*" (*Op. cit.*, p. 234). Judged as an epideictic device, however, it conforms to Lucian's precepts, because it is suitable to the speaker and the occasion, because it heightens the emotional effect, and because, as we shall see, it performs an integral function in the structure of the history as a whole.

23. Cf. R. W. Chambers, *Thomas More*, pp. 18-19, and Stapleton, *op. cit.*, pp. 132-139.

24. Cf. T. C. Burgess, *op. cit.*, p. 110. Evidence is scanty because classical rhetoricians generally contented themselves with saying that the principles of the vituperative portrait were simply the counterpart of those of the encomium.

25. *Works of Aristotle*, ed. W. D. Ross (Oxford, 1924), XI, 1441b.

Ironical invective was of course employed by Christian writers and preachers, including More's favorite Father, St. Augustine. Cf. Sister M. Inviolata Barry, *St. Augustine, the Orator* (Washington, D.C., 1924), p. 126: "This figure [irony] is admirably adapted for reproving sin and error, consequently Augustine makes a liberal use of it."

26. *Nicomachean Ethics*, IV.7; see also II.7, IV.3, and *Eudemian Ethics*, III.7.

27. *Characters*, ed. with translation and notes by R. C. Jebb, rev. by J. E. Sandys (London, 1909), 51-53; see especially note 1, p. 51.

This character was in the *editio princeps* published with a Latin translation by More's friend Pirckheimer at Nuremberg in 1527 from a MS. given him in 1515 by Pico della Mirandola. More may well have seen a MS. of Theophrastus before writing *Richard III.*

28. Cf. J. A. K. Thomson, *Irony* (Harvard Univ. Press, 1927), p. 3 ff.

29. The ironical man "will praise to their faces those whom he attacked behind their backs, and will sympathize with them in their defeats." (*Characters*, p. 53.) Cf. More's description of Richard: "He was close and secret, a deep dissimulator, lowly of countenance, arrogant of heart, outwardly compinable where he inwardly hated, not letting to kiss whom he thought to kill...." (*EW*, p. 402).

Richard is unlike Theophrastus' character in that his deception is not always 'motiveless'; he is "dispiteous and cruel, not for evil will always, but ofter for ambition, and either for the surety or increase of his estate" (*EW*, p. 402). He is also sometimes unduly brutal, as in his toying with Hastings before the latter's execution. There he continues to act a part after the deception has become obvious, and he goes out of his way to bring in the strawberries in order to equate them with the value of Hastings' life. (*EW*, pp. 426-427.)

30. *Op. cit.*, p. 235.

31. See especially the scenes in which they 'bow to the will of the people.' North's Plutarch (London, 1895-96), IV, 238; Philemon Holland's Suetonius (London, 1899), I, 191; and Tacitus, *Annals* XII, v-vii. Cf. *EW*, pp. 445-447. J. B. Bury has remarked that in Tacitus the picture of Tiberius has been "psychologically reconstructed ... on the assumption that the mainspring of his character is dissimulation; he simply reveals the man in this light, interprets his actions and words in this sense, and uses all the devices of innuendo, of which he was so subtle a master, to bring it out...."—*The Ancient Greek Historians* (New York, 1909), p. 231.

Of interest here, also, is the kind of rhetorical exercise employed by More in his answer to *Tyrannicida* or by Lucian in *Phalaris I.* A. M. Harmon remarks of the latter: "To put yourself in another man's shoes and say what he would have said was a regular exercise of the schools, but to laugh in your sleeve as you said it was not the way of the ordinary rhetorician." (*Lucian*, Loeb Classical Library [London, 1913], I, 1; cf. I, 5-6 and *EW*, p. 440 ff.) More's interest in these matters is well known. Cf. Stapleton, *op. cit.*, p. 116 ff., and W. G. Crane, *Wit and Rhetoric in the Renaissance* (Columbia Univ. Press, 1937), pp. 18-20.

32. Cf. Wynken de Worde (1502): "Yronye of grammar" occurs when "a man sayth one & gyveth to understande the contrarye." (Quoted in *NED, s.v.* "Irony.")

Puttenham in the *Arte of English Poesie* (1589) mentions irony under the heading of figures which are characterized by a "certaine doubleness, whereby our talke is the more guileful & abusing." Irony he calls the "merry skoffe" or the "Drie Mock," and distinguishes it from sarcasm, the "bitter taunt." (Ed. G. D. Wilcock and A. Walker [Cambridge, 1936], III, 18.)

The conventional epithet *dry* points to the relation between the ironical character and the system of bodily humours. Ironical speech or action might be expected from the melancholy man, who was dry and cold, and especially from the choleric man, who was dry and hot. A typical description is Thomas Newton's in *The Touchstone of Complexions* (1565): "... the Cholerike are bitter taunters, dry bobbers nypping gybers, and skornefull mockers of others...." Quoted by Lily B. Campbell, *Shakespeare's Tragic Heroes* (Cambridge, 1930), p. 59. See W. C. Curry, *Chaucer and the Mediaeval Sciences* (Oxford, 1926), p. 71 ff., for an account of medieval treatises on the subject, which More probably knew, and which illustrate those characters in Chaucer who are "choleric ... and, therefore, cunning and crafty," as well as proud and cruel.

33. *Institutio oratoria* VI. 2, 3, 54; IX. 1, 2. The *Institutio* was a textbook in More's household.

34. For other similar classical definitions, see Cicero, *De oratore* II. 66–67; the *Rhetorica ad Herennium,* as summarized by A. S. Wilkins in his edition of the *De oratore* (Oxford, 1888), p. 63; and the passages previously cited from Aristotle and the *Rhetorica ad Alexandrum.* Aristotle adds the suggestion that the ironical man jokes to amuse himself, the buffoon to amuse others.

35. For other examples of verbal irony, see *EW,* pp. 423, 432, 433, 434, 437, 438, 440, 449, 451. More is particularly skilful in making the evil Richard mouth the conventional sayings of virtue. "Ah, whom shall a man trust?" Richard asks when Sir Robert Bracken-bury refuses to murder the princes. But this is more properly a part of Richard's dissimula-tion rather than a comment by the author expressed in the form of verbal irony.

36. *EW,* 431.

37. *The Praise of Folly,* tr. Hoyt H. Hudson (Princeton University Press, 1941), pp. 39–40.

38. *Ibid.,* p. 99.

39. *Ibid.,* pp. 64–65.

40. This kind or use of irony is often encountered (as in Chaucer), but it has not been satisfactorily studied. It is related to the subtler forms of verbal irony. When Chaucer, for example, pretends to agree with the Monk's rationalizing ("I seyde his opinion was good"), he is not only ironically condemning his victim, but he is also acknowledging the difficulty of deciding how the world shall be served. If the Monk were sincere, his arguments would have some cogency. Cf. William Empson, *Some Versions of Pastoral* (London, 1935), p. 56: "An irony has no point unless it is true, in some degree, in both senses. . . ." A rather rare example in Lucian is his statement about historical description quoted above.

Its relation to Socratic irony has been suggested by J. H. Robinson, *The Mind in the Making* (New York, 1939), pp. 107–108: "Plato's indecision and urbane fair-minded-ness is called irony. Now irony is seriousness without solemnity. It assumes that man is a serio-comic animal, and that no treatment of his affairs can be appropriate which gives him a consistency and dignity which he does not possess. . . . Human thought and conduct can only be treated broadly and truly in a mood of tolerant irony. It belies the logical precision of the long-faced, humorless writer on politics and ethics." Emphasis on the dual nature of man is, of course, a characteristic of More and other humanists. Cf. Douglas Bush, *The Renaissance and English Humanism* (Univ. of Toronto Press, 1939), pp. 54–56.

I. A. Richards and T. S. Eliot and their followers also have some suggestive remarks in this connection. See the summary of their position by Cleanth Brooks in *Modern Poetry and the Tradition* (Univ. of North Carolina Press, 1939), pp. 29–37: ". . . nearly all mature attitudes represent some sort of mingling of the approbative and satirical. Frequently the more complex attitudes are expressed, and necessarily expressed, in varying degrees of irony . . . The sentimentalist takes a short cut to intensity by removing all the elements of the experience which might conceivably militate against the intensity . . . Sincerity as irony, on the other hand, reveals itself as an unwillingness to ignore the complexity of experience."

41. Tr. Hudson, pp. 37–38: If a person were to try stripping the disguises from actors while they play a scene upon the stage, showing to the audience their real looks and the faces they were born with, would not such a one spoil the whole play? And would not the spectators think he deserved to be driven out of the theater with brickbats, as a drunken disturber? For at once a new order of things would be apparent. The actor who played a woman would now be seen a man; he who a moment ago appeared young, is old; he who but now was a king, is suddenly an hostler; and he who played the god is a sorry little scrub. Destroy the illusion and any play is ruined. It is the paint and trappings that take the eyes of spectators. Now what else is the whole life of mortals but a sort of comedy,

in which the various actors, disguised by various costumes and masks, walk on and play each one his part, until the manager waves them off the stage? Moreover, this manager frequently bids the same actor go back in a different costume, so that he who has but lately played the king in scarlet now acts the flunkey in patched clothes. Thus all things are presented by shadows; yet this play is put on in no other way.

But suppose, right here, some wise man who has dropped down from the sky should suddenly confront me and cry out that the person whom the world has accepted as a god and a master is not even a man, because he is driven sheeplike by his passions; that he is the lowest slave, because he willingly serves so many and such base masters. Or again, suppose the visitor should command some one mourning his father's death to laugh, because now his father has really begun to live—for in a sense our earthly life is but a kind of death. Suppose him to address another who is glorying in his ancestry, and to call him low and base-born because he is so far from virtue, the only true fount of nobility. Suppose him to speak of others in like vein. I ask you, what would he get by it, except to be considered by everyone as insane and raving? As nothing is more foolish than wisdom out of place, so nothing is more imprudent than unseasonable prudence. And he is unseasonable who does not accommodate himself to things as they are, who is "unwilling to follow the market," who does not keep in mind at least that rule of conviviality, "Either drink or get out"; who demands, in short, that the play should no longer be a play. The part of a truly prudent man, on the contrary, is (since we are mortal) not to aspire to wisdom beyond his station, and either, along with the rest of the crowd, pretend not to notice anything, or affably and companionably be deceived. But that, they tell us, is folly. Indeed, I shall not deny it; only let them, on their side, allow that it is also to play out the comedy of life."

42. Louvain, 1565: "Jam eum qui Imperatoris personam agit in tragoedia, populus non ignorat forsitan esse cerdonem. Tamen tantae inscitiae est illic scire quae scias, ut si quis eum vocet qui vere est, non qui falso fingitur, veniat in periculum, ne ab personatis satellitibus malo joco bene vapulet et id quidem merito totam fabulam sit aggressus intempestiva veritate turbare."

43. *EW*, p. 210.

44. Tr. Hudson, p. 118. Erasmus concludes: "The Christian religion on the whole seems to have a kinship with some sort of folly, while it has no alliance whatever with wisdom."

45. *EW*, p. 400.

46. *EW*, pp. 400, 402.—Innuendo of a similar kind is to be found in Tacitus. When Italicus was sent as king to the Cerusci, his "admirers flocked around a prince who practised occasionally the inoffensive foibles of courtesy and restraint, but more frequently the drunkenness and incontinence dear to barbarians." (*Annals* XI. xvi, Loeb translation.) Nero's affair with Acte was countenanced because "there was always the risk that, if he were checked in this passion, his instincts would break out at the expense of women of rank." (*Ibid.*, XIII. xii.) Compare Edward's "wantonness," which "fault not greatly grieved the people, for neither could any one man's pleasure stretch and extend to the displeasure of very many...." (*EW*, p. 400.)

47. *EW*, p. 446. Cf. Erasmus' treatment of the same problem. "I say that if the prince weighed these things [royal hardships], and many more like them, within himself—and he would do so were he wise—I am afraid he could neither sleep nor eat in any joy. But as it is, with my assistance, kings leave all these concerns to the gods, [and] take care of themselves nicely...." (Tr. Hudson, p. 94.)

The subtlety of More's approach is emphasized by comparison with that of Commynes, a chronicler of great native shrewdness, but of little learning or literary sophistication. In his *Mémoires*, published about ten years after the completion of *Richard III*, he decides that for each nation God has set up another in opposition to it in order to keep both within the bounds of fear and humility. God is forced to make this arrangement because only He is powerful enough to chastise princes, and because without this check, princes, who are even more wicked than ordinary men, would be unbearable. (Ed. Joseph Calmette [Paris, 1924], II, xviii–xx.)

48. The subject of the reader's participation in ironic writing is well developed by David Worcester, *The Art of Satire* (Harvard University Press, 1940), pp. 31–32.

49. *EW*, pp. 412–413.

50. Cf. N. M. Trenholme, "The Right of Sanctuary in England," *Univ. of Missouri Studies*, I, 5 (1903), *passim*.

51. *EW*, p. 416.

52. If not Lydgate's *Fall of Princes.*

53. *De gestis regum Anglorum; Historiae novellae*, ed. William Stubbs, Rolls Series (London, 1887–1889), II, 283–284. The translation is by J. A. Giles, *The Chronicles of the Kings of England* (London, 1847).

54. *A History of Greater Britain* (1521), tr. and ed. by Archibald Constable, Scottish Hist. Soc., first series, X (Edinburgh, 1892), p. cxxxv.

55. *Ibid.*, pp. 129–130. Major is often more realistic and detailed than in this passage where he is following medieval models, but it is significant that neither he nor Polydore Vergil felt it necessary to exclude such artificial examples. In this respect they are less advanced than More.

56. Willard Farnham, *The Medieval Heritage of Elizabethan Tragedy* (Univ. of California Press, 1936), pp. 162–163, 168.

57. *Advancement of Learning, Works*, VI, 327.

58. *Ibid.*, VI, 309–310. For a fuller treatment of Bacon's discussion and use of the exemplary method, see the writer's article, "Sir Francis Bacon's Theory of Civil History-Writing," *ELH*, VIII (1941), 161–183.

59. This distinction between medieval chronicle or theatrical humanist history and a narrative like More's resembles that between melodrama and tragedy. A melodrama administers shocks by piling up horrors which are insufficiently motivated because they are dependent upon coincidence or acts of God. In a tragedy "the excess of tragic feeling is removed from the actual catastrophe and transferred to apparently insignificant events." This is done by exposition of causes and dramatic irony. (Cf. David Worcester, *op. cit.*, pp. 138–139.) Just so, in the chronicles, saints, devils, miracles, sudden conversions, and rivers red with blood, like sinister mustachios and the arrival of the marines, supply the deficiencies of the author. Cf. Eleanor P. Hammond, *English Verse between Chaucer and Surrey* (Duke Univ. Press, 1927), p. 28: "the notion of bringing the figure closer to the eye ... is outside the comprehension of most medieval narrators. Was a narrative to be more impressive or more heroic, it had more tortures and more combats added to it." More's account is better narrative, if not more truthful history, because, as in tragedy, causation and dramatic irony are stressed.

60. Much of the material used as evidence by Farnham was familiar to More—Boccaccio, Chaucer, and the moralities, especially those produced by Henry Medwall at Morton's. Cf. Farnham, *op. cit.*, pp. 94–97, 201–221; R. W. Chambers, *Thomas More*, pp. 61–62; and A. W. Reed, *Early Tudor Drama* (London, 1926), p. 154, where we are told that in 1538 John More was left "Chauseer of Talles and Boocas" by Walter Smyth, who had been Sir Thomas' servant from 1520 to 1529.

61. It is perhaps pertinent to recall that this is also the method of Thucydides, since his history was studied in More's circle. Thucydides, like More, was writing a history and not a drama, but beneath the multiplicity of skirmishes runs the ironic undertone: the tragic ruin of a people whose democratic ideals were perverted by the brutality of war. Pericles' funeral oration is the expression of those ideals. Thereafter, Thucydides is careful to point the irony. Hard upon the oration comes the statement that "on neither side were there

any mean thoughts ...; they had never seen war, and were therefore very willing to take up arms." [Tr. B. Jowett (Oxford, 1900), I, 107.] At the death of Pericles we are given a preview of the inevitable disaster when the people shall have departed from his counsel. (I, 148). For "war, which takes away the comfortable provision of life, is a hard master and tends to assimilate men's characters to their conditions." (I, 242) How the character of the Athenians has been corrupted is shown us in the cynical dialogue with the Melians before the wanton destruction of Melos. This kind of preparation so heightens the tragedy in Sicily that one is inclined, like Professor Thomson, to read more irony than was perhaps intended into the quiet conclusion: "Thus ended the Sicilian expedition." (Cf. J. A. K. Thomson, *Irony*, pp. 139–162.) More guides the reader in a similar manner.

62. *EW*, p. 428.

63. *Ibid.*, p. 448.

64. *Ibid.*, p. 451.

DELCOURT, "Some Aspects of Sir Thomas More's English"

1. In spite of our efforts we have not yet been able to discover what brought marmalade into use in England about 1520. It is amusing in any case to compare with the following text from *Utopia* (1516): ... *mulieres grauidae picem & seuum corrupto gustu melle mellitius arbitrātur,* the following one from *De quatuor nouissimis* (1522): ... *some women with child haue such fond lust that thei had leuer eate terre than tryacle, & rather pitch than marmelade.* ...

2. To put it more exactly: *to detest* and *to explain* are new verbs belonging to roots already imported in English. The substantive *detestation* is known as far back as 1432, and *explanation* as far back as 1386.

3. The example occurs in the *De quatuor nouissimis* (1522). The first example of the substantive *fume* in the sense of 'anger' in *O.E.D.* bears the same date.

4. The foregoing study is a summary of a few chapters of the *Essai* mentioned on p. 341, revised in the light of recent investigation; special use has, of course, been made of the last volumes of the *Oxford English Dictionary* (including its *Supplement*), which were not available in 1914. To save space the texts quoted, most of which are taken from *The workes of Sir Thomas More* (1557), are given without references; should the latter be required the reader will find at least the greater part of them in the pages of the *Essai*. The spelling and punctuation of the original have been scrupulously respected.

DONNER, "St. Thomas More's Treatise on the Four Last Things and the Gothicism of the Transalpine Renaissance"

1. Émile Mâle, *L'art religieux de la fin du moyen âge en France*, 2nd ed., Paris, 1931, p. iv.

2. H. W. Garrod, *Scholarship. Its Meaning and Value*, The Gray Lectures, Cambridge, 1946, p. 27.

3. Hubert Schrade, *Über Symbol und Realismus in der Spätgotik*, "Deutsche Vierteljahrschrift für Litteraturwissenschaft und Geistesgeschichte," V, 1927, p. 93.

4. J. Huizinga, *The Waning of the Middle Ages*, Eng. transl., London, 1924, chap. XX–XXI.

5. Mâle, *op. cit.*, pp. 440-1.

6. See chiefly James M. Clark, *The Dance of Death in the Middle Ages and the Renaissance*, Glasgow, 1950. The Reval Dance of Death was copied in the church of St. Nicholas at Ingå in southern Finland (L. Wennervirta, *Suomen Keskiaikainen Kirkkomaalaus*, Borgå, 1937, p. 133 seqq.).

7. See chiefly Francis Douce, *The Dance of Death*, 2nd ed., London, 1833; F. P.

Weber, *Aspects of Death and Correlated Aspects of Life in Art, Epigram and Poetry,* London, 1922; and Clark, *op. cit.,* p. 13.

8. See chiefly Leonard P. Kurtz, *The Dance of Death and the Macabre Spirit in European Literature,* Publications of the Institute of French Studies, Columbia University, New York, 1934.

9. *The Dance of Death by Hans Holbein,* ed. with an Introduction and Notes by James M. Clark, Phaidon Press, London, 1947, p. 27.

10. Paul Meissner, *Mittelalterliches Lebensgefühl in der englischen Renaissance,* "Deutsche Vierteljahrschrift," etc., XV, 1937, p. 447.

11. *English Works,* 1557, pp. 73 C, 77 B.

12. Huizinga, *op. cit.,* p. 198.

13. *The English Works of Sir Thomas More,* ed. W. E. Campbell, with Introduction and Philological Notes by A. W. Reed, London, 1931, Introduction, pp. 22–3.

14. "Thou" replaces the earlier "ye," *English Works,* p. 98 F.

15. Cresacre More, *Life and Death of Sir Thomas More,* 1626, p. 184. Cf. however Stapleton, *Tres Thomae,* chap. XI; English translation by Monsignor Philip E. Hallett, London, 1928, p. 113.

16. Mâle, *op. cit.,* p. 185.

17. *The Ship of Fools,* ed. 1874, p. 163.

18. The Dance of Paul's was unfortunately destroyed in 1549, when the Protector Somerset had the cloisters pulled down in order to use the stone for the building of the original Somerset House (Clark, *op. cit.,* p. 11). Lydgate's verses are printed with the French original and informative notes in Eleanor P. Hammond, *English Verse between Chaucer and Surrey,* London, 1927, pp. 124–42 and 418–35.

19. Kurtz, *op. cit.,* p. 75.

20. *Op. cit.,* p. 380.

21. Wolfgang Stammler, *Von der Mystik zum Barock,* 1400–1600, Stuttgart, 1927, p. 278.

22. Facsimile reprint, ed. W. H. Rylands, Introduction by G. Bullen, London, 1881, p. 8.

23. *Ibid.*

24. H. L. R. Edwards, *Skelton,* London, 1949, p. 58.

25. *Op. cit.,* p. 262.

26. *English Works,* pp. 79 E, 85 C; modernized version, Campbell, I, pp. 471, 481.

27. *English Works,* p. 84 E–F; Campbell, p. 480.

28. See e.g., Weber, *op. cit.,* pp. 123–30. Cf. Bembo's Epitaph on Poliziano.

29. The phrase is Thomas Wright's, *A History of the Caricature and the Grotesque,* London, 1875, p. 325.

30. *English Works,* ed. Campbell, I, pp. 460, 479. Other instances are "blessed body" (468), "daily dulness" (496), "delicate dainties" (472), "dreadful day" (498), "false forswearing" (498), "feigned figure" (493), "fleshly filth" (494), "forbidden fruit" (493), "gay gear" (472), "gay golden gown" (479), "gorbellied gluttony" (493), "great glutton" (494), "headstrong horse" (493), "holy head" (468), "lewd lad" (479), "painful peril" (492), "painful plight" (492), "poor men's purses" (493), "proud prisoner" (480), "solemn service" (497), "strait stocks" (494), "intolerable torment" (496), "diverse viands" (496), "worldly worship" (479). Similarly: "Lady Lechery" (472).

31. Pp. 497, 492. Cfr. "the corruption of our custom" (495), "the dazing of death" (498), "all manner mischief" (494), "in the midst of his matters" (494), "the way of the wicked" (495).

32. P. 480. Cf. "higher in their hearts" (480), "too merry for this matter" (479).

33. Pp. 479, 485. Cf. "bush or beast" (471), "the cup and the kitchen" (497), "pernicious and pestilent" (494), "conserve and keep" (496), "hate and abhor" (493), "laid and left" (498), "gorge upon gorge and grief upon grief" (496).

34. P. 497. Cf. "his heart heavily harkeneth" (497), "they should relieve us therewith when the remnant were bereft us" (493).

35. P. 494. Cf. "balk up his brews" (494), "bear the burden of his own belly" (494), "carrieth his carrion corpse" (497), "cast covetousness" (492), "make them more moderate" (498), "master the meat" (496), "withdraw the wind" (479).

36. P. 496. Cf. "her paths are peaceable" (495), "sour seemeth us sweet" (495), "the lorel playeth the lord" (479).

37. P. 498. Cf. "compelled to cast" (496), "would not, ween ye" (479), "they would, I ween" (492).

38. Pp. 498, 496. Cf. "greedily to gather" (492), "they may well wit" (496), "willingly wink" (492).

39. P. 498. Cf. "borne to bed" (495), "borne in a bier" (495), "frame and form in the fantasy by foul imaginations" (493), "labour less for what we shall so lose" (493), "made in manner a goddess" (493), "puffeth us up in pride" (479), "running to ruin" (494), "ye wot well" (498), "would well and advisedly remember" (498).

40. P. 497.

41. P. 498.

42. P. 495.

43. P. 497. Cf. "their feasts make them fall into foolish talking and blasphemy" (494); "eating the forbidden fruit, fell from the felicity of paradise" (493): "greedily to gather together that other men shall merrily soon after scatter abroad" (492); "Then care we little for our gay gear, then desire we no delicate dainties: and as for Lady Lechery, then abhor we to think on" (472); "carrieth it forth like a headstrong horse, till he have cast his master in the mire" (493 sq.); "no man is so mad that will reckon that thing for pleasant that hath with little pleasure much pain" (496); "so the soul is so stifled in such a stuffed body" (494); "maketh the sourness very sweet, and the very pain pleasant" (463); "And we shall be wearied, shall the wretches say, in the way of wickedness; we have walked in hard and cumbrous ways; and the wise man saith" (495); "willingly wink and list not to look" (492).

44. P. 495.

45. *Ibid.*

46. P. 498.

47. P. 499. R. W. Chambers detected the balance and cross-alliteration of *Euphues* in More's *Richard III* (*Fame of Blessed Thomas More*, 1929, p. 255).

48. *Vom Menschenideal und von den Modewörtern der Gotik und der Renaissance,* "Deutsche Vierteljahrschrift," etc., XIV, 1936, pp. 171-222. Cf. Theodore Spencer, *Death and Elizabethan Tragedy,* Cambridge, Mass., 1936, with its probings into the enriched vocabulary of the sixteenth as compared with the fifteenth century.

49. Thomas More, *L'Utopie ou le traité de la meilleure forme de gouvernement.* Texte latin édité par Marie Delcourt, Paris, 1936, pp. 213-16. For the classical simile of sleep as death's image, see *English Works,* p. 80 F; Campbell, I, p. 473; cf. *Macbeth,* II, iii, 76, "death's counterfeit."

50. *English Works,* p. 88 C; Campbell, I, p. 486.

51. Spencer, *op. cit.,* More, *English Works,* p. 77 H; Campbell, I, p. 468.

52. Mâle, *op. cit.,* p. 280 sq.

53. F. P. Weber, *op. cit.,* p. 136. A present-day reminder of the once universal occurrence of *Memento mori* devices is the hour-glass design seen on the window shutters of seventeenth century houses everywhere in Holland.

54. Spencer, *op. cit.*, pp. 182-209; Mario Praz, *The Romantic Agony,* 2nd ed., Oxford, 1951, p. 3; J. B. Leishman, *The Monarch of Wit.* An Analytical and Comparative Study of the Poetry of John Donne. London, 1951, pp. 39, 115, 239.

55. *English Works,* p. 92 F; Campbell, I, p. 490.

56. *English Works of John Fisher,* ed. J. E. B. Mayor, E.E.T.S., Extra Series, XXXVII, 1876, repr. 1933, p. 408.

57. *English Works,* pp. 79 B, 85 C; Campbell, I, pp. 470, 481.

58. *Ibid.,* pp. 78 D; 469.

59. *Ibid.,* pp. 79 B; 470.

60. *Ibid.,* pp. 97 D-E; 495. Cf. also pp. 84 H; 478, where the praise of men is compared to "a blast of wind of their mouths."

61. Ed. A. Tuetey, Publications de la Soc. de l'histoire de Paris, III, 1881; quoted Huizinga, *op. cit.*

62. *English Works,* pp. 258 F-259 A; Campbell, II, p. 274 sq.; cf. the account and contemporary records given by J. S. Brewer, *Letters and Papers Foreign and Domestic of the Reign of Henry VIII,* IV, 1875, pp. clxii-clxxv.

63. The first tomb of the kind seems to be that of the famous physician to Charles VI, Guillaume de Harcigny, who died in 1393; the second the monument of Cardinal Lagrange at Avignon, dead 1402 (Mâle, *op. cit.*, p. 348). The earliest in England is that of Archbishop Chichele at Canterbury, dead 1443 (Weber, *op. cit.*, pp. 106-22). It is of interest in the present connexion that More's and Erasmus's friend and patron, the great Dean of St. Paul's, John Colet, had a similar monument executed for himself in old St. Paul's, the portrait bust above and a skeleton on the coffin-lid below.

64. J. F. Noël et P. Jehan, *Les Gisants,* Paris, 1949, pl. XIX. Catherine de Medicis ordered Girolamo della Robbia to execute an image of what would be left of her after death, *ibid.,* pl. XXIII.

65. Mâle, *op. cit.*, p. 342 sq.

66. Cf. Dagobert Frey, *Gotik und Renaissance als Grundlagen der modernen Weltanschauung,* Augsburg, 1929, pp. 116-117 and pl. 45; see also Georg Weise, *Der doppelte Begriff der Renaissance,* "Deutsche Vierteljahrschrift," etc., XI, 1933, p. 517.

67. Stammler, *op. cit.*, p. 11.

68. Margaret Mann Phillips, *Erasmus and the Northern Renaissance,* London, 1949, p. 158.

69. James M. Clark, *The Great German Mystics,* Oxford, 1949, p. 4 sq.

70. Wilhelm Fehse, *Der Ursprung der Totentänze,* Halle, 1907; E. Döring-Hirsch, *Tod und Jenseits im Spätmittelalter,* Berlin, 1927; Wolfgang Stammler, *Die Totentänze,* Leipzig, 1922, *Totentänze des Mittelalters,* Munich, 1922, and *Der Totentanz. Entstehung und Deutung,* Munich, 1948.

71. Georg Weise, *Der doppelte Begriff der Renaissance,* p. 515.

72. *Formprobleme der Gotik,* Munich, 1920, p. 78 sq.

73. G. Bebermeyer, *Die deutsche Dicht- und Bildkunst im Spätmittelalter,* "Deutsche Vierteljahrschrift," etc., 1929, p. 326; Worringer, *op. cit.*, p. 78.

74. H. A. Schmid, *Hans Holbein der Jüngere,* vol. I, Basel, 1948, pp. 86-94.

75. Clark, *The Dance of Death,* p. 63. The attribution of the illustrations to Titian's pupil John Stephan of Calcar has been questioned by C. Singer and C. Rabin, *A Prelude to Modern Science,* Cambridge, 1947.

76. *English Works,* pp. 99-100.

77. Allen, IV, No. 999, p. 21.

78. *Vergil in the Middle Ages,* transl. E. F. Benecke, London, 1895, p. 192.

79. Cf. Horace: "Pallida mors aequo pulsat pede pauperum tabernas / Regumque turres" (*Odes,* I, 4, 13).

80. Louvain, 1518, col. 37. I quote Cardinal Gasquet's translation in *The Eve of the Reformation*, London, 1905, p. 381.

81. *English Works*, p. 77 E; Campbell, I, p. 468.

82. In writing his article on "Death and the Baroque" ("Horizon," XIX, 112, April 1949), Mr. Aldous Huxley seems to have forgotten his own better informed description of the waning Middle Ages in *Beyond the Mexique Bay*, 1934, p. 55: "The fifteenth century, for example, was a time when corpses, skulls and skeletons were extravagantly popular. Painted, sculptured, written about and dramatically represented, the Danse Macabre was everywhere. To the fifteenth century artist a good death-appeal was as sure a key to popularity as a good sex-appeal is at the present time." The worst orgies, however, only break loose at the beginning of the sixteenth century.

83. Erwin Panowsky, *Albrecht Dürer*, 2 vols., Princeton, 1935, I, p. 146.

84. Joycian in his preference for the humorously obscene and often nonsensical rhyming and in his inability to restrain his own verbosity.

85. C. Lenient, *La Satire en France au moyen âge*, Paris, 1859, p. 14. Cf. Huizinga, *op. cit.*, chap. XX, p. 2.

86. *Konsthistoria*, Helsingfors, 1925, p. 161.

DOYLE-DAVIDSON, "The Earlier English Works of Sir Thomas More"

1. And in which Shakespeare had a hand, leaving us incidentally three precious pages of his autograph.

2. "Sir Thomas More," in *The Social and Political Ideas of Some Great Thinkers of the Renaissance and the Reformation*, ed. Prof. F. J. C. Hearnshaw (Harrap, 1925).

3. *The Saga and the Myth of Sir Thomas More*, Literary History Lecture, 5 Nov. 1926.

4. "Sir Thomas More's Fame among his Countrymen," Introductory Essay in *The Fame of Blessed Thomas More* (Sheed & Ward, 1929).

5. Ed. S. W. Singer, second improved edition 1822.

6. *The Life and Death of Sir Thomas More* by Nicholas Harpsfield, ed. E. V. Hitchcock, with an Introduction by R. W. Chambers, E. E. T. S. No. 186 (Oxford, 1932)—see *English Studies* XV, pp. 28-31.

7. Previously ed. by Fr. van Ortroy, *Vie du bienheureux martyr Jean Fisher*, in *Analecta Bollandiana* X and XII, 1891/3 (issued separately Bruxelles 1893, pp. 396-418).

8. *The Life and Illustrious Martyrdom of Sir Thomas More* by Thomas Stapleton, trans. P. E. Hallett (Burns, Oates & Washbourne, 1928).

9. *The Life and Writings of Sir Thomas More*, by the Rev. T. E. Bridgett, C. SS. R. (Burns & Oates, 1891).

10. Trans. Harold Child (London, 1904).

11. Both published by Sheed & Ward, 1934.

12. Burns, Oates & Washbourne, 1933.

13. Methuen, 1895.

14. Roadmaker Series, Parsons, 1925.

15. *Sir Thomas More and his Friends* (Oxford, 1934).

16. By Jonathan Cape.

17. Vol. III, p. 16.

18. *Short History of English Literature* (Macmillan, 1919), p. 212.

19. Tudor Library (David Nutt, 1890).

20. Pitt Press Series (Cambridge, 1883, still in print).

21. Paternoster Books (Art & Book Co., 1903).

22. *The Utopia of Sir Thomas More*, Latin text of 1518 and Ralph Robinson's trans.

of 1551 (Oxford, 1895). A very convenient edition of Robinson's translation (1556 edition, with the Latin text of 1516 in an appendix) is that of G. Sampson and A. Guthkelch (Bohn's Standard Library, Bell, 1910), which contains also a critical edition of Roper's *Life* and More's Last Letters, and includes a useful bibliography.

23. Clarendon Series (Oxford).

24. By Eyre & Spottiswoode. The edition is to be completed in five further volumes, as follows: III. *The Supplication of Souls* and *Confutation of Tyndale*, Part I; IV. *The Second Part of the Confutation of Tyndale*; V. *The Letter to Frith, The Apology*, and *The Debellation of Salem and Bizance*; VI. *The Answer to the Poisoned Book* and *The Dialogue of Comfort against Tribulation*; VII. *Treatise on the Blessed Sacrament, Treatise on the Passion, Devotions* and *Letters*. [No further volumes were published after the two mentioned in the text.]

25. E. E. T. S. No. 180 (Oxford, 1930).

26. Together with *Utopia* (Dent. 1910).

27. *Essai sur la langue de Sir Thomas More, d'après ses oeuvres anglaises* (Paris, Didier, 1914), containing also an edition of More's autograph letters, a very useful bibliography of MSS. and early editions, and an excellent biographical sketch.

28. Oxford, 1915, esp. pp. 80–102.

29. *The Beginnings of the English Secular and Romantic Drama*, read before the Shakespeare Association, 29 Feb. 1920 (Oxford, 1922); see also *Early Tudor Drama* (Methuen, 1926).

30. Mentioned also by Erasmus: *Adolescens comoediolas et scripsit et egit*, Letter to Ulrich Hutten, 23 July 1519.

31. *The Continuity of English Prose from Alfred to More and his School*, forming pp. xlv to clxxiv of the Introduction to Harpsfield's *Life of More* (E. E. T. S. No. 186, Oxford, 1932) and also issued separately—see *English Studies* XIV pp. 203–4 and XV pp. 28–31.

32. I.e., whatever you like to think of.

33. A six-lined stanza rhyming *aabccb*, the couplets in two-beat, ll. 3 and 6 in three-beat lines.

34. Or Chaucerian stanza, seven five-beat lines rhyming *ababbcc*. I wonder whether it is only an accident that in the latter part of the Elegy, in five stanzas out of a total of twelve, the last line is lengthened to six beats, thus more than faintly suggesting the slowing movement, particularly appropriate in a lament, of the Spenserian stanza.

35. "If I were asked what was the most unmistakable mark of More's workmanship, I should say that it was the loading and piling up of matter in what one may call agglomerated passages ... This quality of superabundance is something very much more than style. It is the inimitable quality of quantity of content, a quality that gives to only the great writers their unassailable pre-eminence," *English Works of More*, Vol. I, 1931, Philological Notes, pp. 192–3.

36. I.e., honour.

37. P. 15.

38. *Primam aetatem carmine potissimum exercuit. Mox diu luctatus est, ut prosam orationem redderet molliorem, per omne scripti genus stilum exercens*, Letter to Ulrich Hutten, 23 July 1519.

39. Of which the most considerable is a long four-page account of Pico's writings: More is for the occasion more interested in Pico's holiness than his scholarship.

40. Cp. also the definition of Time in the second poem (stanza on Eternity):

> Thou mortal Time, every man can tell,
> Art nothing else but the mobility
> Of sun and moon changing in every degree.

41. The history of the word-pair has not yet been worked out, but it has been noted as of wide occurrence in most of the older literatures (e.g., Latin, Old French, Old Icelandic) and seems, in translation (e.g., in the Old English Bede and the English Prayer Book) as well as in original writing, to be due often, not so much to a desire for emphasis or for clarity, as to a feeling for sentence rhythm. The fact that the words of a pair are not always synonyms is a further indication of the rhetorical nature of the device.

42. This addition (beginning with the second sentence here quoted) runs as follows:
"But we shall let his [Pico's] ancestors pass, to whom (though they were right excellent) he gave again as much honour as he received, and we shall speak of himself, rehearsing in part his learning and his virtue. For these be the things which we may account for our own, of which every man is more properly to be commended than of the nobleness of his ancestors, whose honour maketh us not honourable. For either they were themselves virtuous, or not; if not, then had they none honour themselves, had they never so great possessions: for honour is the reward of virtue. And how may they claim the reward that properly belongeth to virtue, if they lack the virtue that the reward belongeth to? Then, if themselves had none honour, how might they leave to their heirs that thing which they had not themselves? On the other side, if they be virtuous and so, consequently, honourable, yet may they not leave their honour to us as inheritants, no more than the virtue that themselves were honourable for. For never the more noble be we for their nobleness, if ourselves lack those things for which they were noble; but rather, the more worshipful that our ancestors were, the more vile and shameful be we if we decline from the steps of their worshipful living, the clear beauty of whose virtue maketh the dark spot of our vice the more evidently to appear and to be the more marked."

43. I.e., learning.

44. I.e., were it only.

45. I.e., moderate(ly).

46. "More's 'History of Richard III'," *Modern Language Review* XXIII, Oct. 1928, pp. 405-23, reprinted as "The Authorship of the 'History of Richard III'" in *The English Works of Sir Thomas More*, Vol. I, 1931, pp. 24-41.

47. Still to be found, strangely enough, instead of More's own text, in a modern reprint, edited (with *Utopia*) by Maurice Adams, Camelot Series (Walter Scott, [1890]).

48. Saintsbury continues: "The eulogies of critics like Hallam were probably determined by the fact that it is an early and not unhappy example of the rather colourless "classical" prose, of which a little later we shall find the chief exponents to be Ascham and his friends at Cambridge. It is, of course, a good deal better than Capgrave, and it is free from Pecock's harshness and crudity of phrase. But as it cannot on the one hand compare for richness, colour, and representative effect with the style of Berners, one of the two best writers of prose nearly contemporary with More, so it is not to be mentioned with that of Fisher, the other, for nice rhetorical artifice and intelligent employment of craftsman-like methods of work. But it is much more "eighteenth century" than either; and this commended it to Hallam" (*Short History of English Literature*, 1919, p. 212). Now Saintsbury was a great critic who did yeoman service, especially in directing attention to undeservedly neglected writers, and this estimate is quoted only because it is a good instance of a dangerous tendency of his to exalt the lesser known at the expanse of those of established fame, interest in what is little known being aroused by the neat but rather unscrupulous method of bringing it into favourable comparison with the better-known. So here the well-known *Richard III* is used as a sort of stepping-stone for Berners and Fisher. It is the emphasis that is chiefly at fault, for while it might well be claimed that *in certain respects* (mainly rhetorical) Berners and Fisher have the advantage of More, on the whole neither of them has anything like More's range (even in the *Richard III*) of

matter and style. And as for Saintsbury's curiously disparaging application to *Richard III* of the term "eighteenth century," if we remember what, just in prose, were the achievements of this century, we shall regard it as in reality a compliment—and a comparison that, and still more in More's later prose, gets very near the mark.

49. *Cambridge History of English Literature*, Vol. III, p. 335.

50. I.e., moderate, small.

51. So, e.g., on his putting Jane Shore to public penance, Richard is described as acting "as a goodly continent prince, clean and faultless of himself, sent out of heaven into this vicious world for the amendment of men's manners"; and later, on Buckingham urging him to accept the crown: "These words much moved the Protector, which else, as every man may wit, would never of likelihood have inclined thereunto"; etc. Neither of these examples occurs in the printed Latin text (see following paragraph), though the former does appear in MS. Arundel 43.

52. There is also an interesting MS. of the Latin (Arundel 43, at the College of Heralds) which, containing a number of passages not in the printed Latin text, is intermediate between this and the English and, though not in More's autograph, may represent an early draft of the Latin version.

53. So, e.g., "at Hornsey" is represented by *quatuor ab urbe milibus*, "at his palace of Westminster" by *in palatio ... quod est apud Benedictorum coenobium, ad occidentem solem circiter mille passus Londino distans*.

54. So to "by authority of Parliament" is added *cuius apud Anglos summa atque absoluta potestas est;* of the Prince (who is described as *Rege designato*) being in Wales it is explained *nam ea deinceps primogenitis regum, vivis adhuc parentibus, propria ditio est;* of the title of "Chamberlain" is added *quod est apud Anglos perquam honorificum;* to the mention of Jane Shore's "going before the cross in procession upon a Sunday with a taper in her hand" is added *qui mos est illic agentium publicam poenitentiam;* and of the London Recorder is added *qui praefecti assessor est eruditus patriis legibus, ne quid in reddendis iudiciis imperitia peccetur.*

55. Including the important biographical passage, referring to the conversation between Mistlebrook and Pottyer: *quem ego sermonem ab eo memini, qui colloquentes audiverat, iam tum patri meo renuntiatum, cum adhuc nulla proditionis eius suspicio haberetur.*

56. "The Textual Problems of the 'History of Richard III'," *English Works of More*, Vol. I, 1931, pp. 42–53, in which further details are given and the textual history of *Richard III* also discussed. See also Oscar Hübschmann, *Textkritische Untersuchungen zu Mores "Geschichte Richards III"* (Halle, 1910, and reprinted in *Anglia* XXXIII–IV, 1910–11), and A. F. Pollard, "The Making of Sir Thomas More's *Richard III*," in *Historical Essays in honour of James Tait*, ed. J. G. Edwards, etc. (Manchester, 1933), pp. 223–38.

57. Prof. Reed has remarked that the style of the English version is balanced and formal up to the point at which the Latin breaks off and that after this it hurries on more direct and vigorous: I should prefer to say that throughout the *History* the Latinised style is reserved for the more formal parts—the character sketches, set speeches, and moralising—while in the narrative, rapid dialogue, and anecdotes the English is brisk and idiomatic. Thus the account of the Queen's flight into sanctuary is 'English,' the conversation between Buckingham and Morton 'Latin.'

58. E.g., "professed and observed" (*professa et ... ducente*), "favour and affection" (*charitatem desideriumque*), "sharp and fierce" (*acer et ferox*); "friendly and ... familiar" (*magnifico ac sumptuoso*), "robbers and reivers" (*improbis hominibus, latrociniis*); "bold and hardy" (*promptus*), "stretch and extend" (*diffundere*), "division and dissension" (*divisio*); and note also "benignity" (*pietate beneficentiaque*), "heaviness" (*dolore lachrymisque*), "good" (*boni atque egregii*), etc.; "a marvellous fortress and sure armour"

(*mirum firmamentum*), "piteously bewailed and sorrowfully repented" (*misere deplora-vit*).

59. E.g., "cruelty, mischief and trouble," "forlaboured, forwearied and weaked" (*fatigata*), "fully, plain and directly"; and "evil company, sinister procuring and un-gracious example," "many a meeting, much wooing and many great promises."

60. E.g., "in which many princes, by a long-continued sovereignty, decline into a proud port from debonair behaviour of their beginning" (d p p d b b; *quum plerosque principes diu confirmata potentia vertat in superbiam*); "not letting to kiss whom he thought to kill" (*nec eorum abstinens complexibus quos destinabat occidere*); "rather by pleasant advice to win themselves favour than by profitable advertisement to do the children good" (*placitura magis omnes quam profutura*); flattery shall have more place than plain and faithful advice" (f p p f—and note the vowels); "*well* to prosper in *wealth-ful peace*" (w p w p); "so great a change marvellously misliked" (*tam magnam ... mutationem magnopere admirabatur*); "lest your causeless fear might cause you further to convey him" (c f f c); many folks' malice and more folks' folly" (m f m, m f f); "those that have not letted to put them in duress without colour will let as little to procure their destruction without cause" (d c d c, or, taking account of the 'undertones': l, p D C, l l, p D C); and finally, as a link: "these innocent tender children, born of most royal blood, brought up in great wealth, likely long to live to reign and rule in the realm, by traitorous tyranny taken, deprived of their estate, shortly shut up in prison, and privily slain and murdered" (b b, b, l l l r r r, t t t, , sh sh pr, pr).

61. E.g., "Whoso divineth upon conjectures may as well shoot too far as too short," "as women commonly, not of malice but of nature, hate them whom their husbands love," "as opportunity and likelihood of speed [= success] putteth a man in courage of that he never intended," "ever at length evil drifts drive to naught and good plain ways prosper," "Such a pestilent serpent is ambition and desire of vainglory and sovereignty," "None of us, I believe, is so unwise oversoon to trust a new friend made of an old foe," "sometimes without small things greater cannot stand," "evil words walk far," "the de-sire of a kingdom knoweth no kindred," "For what wise merchant adventureth all his goods in one ship?," "as friends fail fleers," "For men use, if they have an evil turn, to write it in marble; and whoso doth us a good turn, we write it in dust," "For small plea-sure taketh a man of all that ever he hath beside, if he be wived against his appetite"; "common people ... that wave with the wind," "experience, the very mother and mistress of wisdom"; etc.

62. More is especially fond, as Prof. Reed has pointed out, of comparisons with precious stones and, as one would expect, "stage plays."

63. This is the Queen's bitter retort to Richard's embassy: "Troweth the Protector (I pray God he may prove a protector), troweth he that I perceive not whereunto his painted process draweth?"—which reminds one of Shakespeare's use of the pun in serious con-texts.

64. G. P. Krapp, *Rise of English Literary Prose*, 1915, p. 100.

65. "thou seest (if thou fantasy thine own death, for so art thou by this counsel ad-vised), thou seest I say, thyself, if thou die no worse death, yet at the least wise lying in thy bed, thy head shooting, thy back aching, thy veins beating, thine heart panting, thy throat rattling, thy flesh trembling, thy mouth gaping, thy nose sharping, thy legs cool-ing, thy fingers fumbling, thy breath shortening, all thy strength fainting, thy life vanish-ing, and thy death drawing on."

66. "Have ye not ere this, in a sore sickness, felt it very grievous to have folk babble to you, and namely [= especially] such things as ye should make answer to when it was a pain to speak? Think ye not now that it will be a gentle pleasure, when we lie dying, all our body in pain, all our mind in trouble, our soul in sorrow, our heart all in dread, while

our life walketh awayward, while our death draweth toward, while the devil is busy about us, while we lack stomach and strength to bear any one of so manifold heinous troubles, will it not be, as I was about to say, a pleasant thing to see before thine eyes and hear at thine ear a rabble of fleshly friends, or rather of flesh flies, skipping about thy bed and thy sick body, like ravens about thy corpse, now almost carrion, crying to thee on every side, "What shall I have? What shall I have?" ? Then shall come thy children and cry for their parts; then shall come thy sweet wife, and where in thine health haply she spake thee not one sweet word in six weeks, now shall she call thee sweet husband and weep with much work and ask thee what shall she have; then shall thine executors ask for the keys, and ask what money is owing thee, ask what substance thou hast, and ask where thy money lieth. And while thou liest in that case, their words shall be so tedious that thou wilt wish all that they ask for upon a red fire, so that thou mightst lie one half-hour in rest."

67. E.g., "And instead of sorrow for our sins and care of heaven, he [=the devil] putteth us in mind of provision for some honourable burying—so many torches, so many tapers, so many black gowns, so many merry mourners laughing under hoods, and a gay hearse, with the delight of goodly and honourable funerals: in which the foolish sick man is sometimes occupied as though he thought that he should stand in a window and see how worshipfully he shall be brought to church."

68. I.e., Cicero.

69. "If God would never punish gluttony, yet bringeth it punishment enough with itself: it disfigureth the face, discoloureth the skin, and disfashioneth the body; it maketh the skin tawny, the body fat and fobby [= flabby], the face drowsy, the nose dripping, the mouth spitting, the eyes bleared, the teeth rotten, the breath stinking, the hands trembling, the head hanging, and the feet tottering, and finally no part left in right course and frame." Note also the covetous man: "But look if ye see not some wretch that scant can creep for age, his head hanging in his bosom and his body crooked, walk pit-pat upon a pair of patens, with the staff in the one hand and the paternoster in the other hand, the one foot almost in the grave already, and yet never the more haste to part with anything nor to restore that he hath evil gotten, but as greedy to get a groat by the beguiling of his neighbour as if he had of certainty seven score years to live," in which, as Prof. Chambers has remarked, More has in the balanced sentences caught the rhythm of the old alliterative verse.

70. "If it so were that thou knewest a great Duke, keeping so great estate and princely port in his house that thou, being a right mean [= poor] man, hadst in thine heart a great envy thereat, and specially at some special day in which he keepeth for the marriage of his child a great honourable court above other times; if thou being thereat, and at the sight of the royalty and honour shown him of all the country about resorting to him, while they kneel and crouch to him and at every word barehead begrace him, if thou shouldst suddenly be surely advertised that for secret treason lately detected to the King he should undoubtedly be taken the morrow, his court all broken up, his goods seized, his wife put out, his children disinherited, himself cast into prison, brought forth and arraigned, the matter out of question [= doubt], and he should be condemned, his coat-armour reversed, his gilt spurs hewn off his heels, himself hanged, drawn and quartered: how thinkest thou, by thy faith, amid thine envy shouldst thou not suddenly change into pity?"

71. "And thereupon by-and-by after the messenger departed, he [= the Archbishop of York] caused in all the haste all his servants to be called up, and so, with his own household about him and every man weaponed, he took the Great Seal with him and came yet before day unto the Queen—about whom he found much heaviness, rumble, haste and business, carriage and conveyance of her stuff into sanctuary, chests, coffers, packs, fardels, trusses, all on men's backs, no man unoccupied, some lading, some going, some

discharging, some coming for more, some breaking down the walls to bring in the next
[= nearest] way, and some yet drew to them that helped to carry a wrong way. The Queen
herself sat alone alow on the rushes, all desolate and dismayed, whom the Archbishop
comforted in the best manner he could, showing her that he trusted the matter was nothing so sore as she took it for."

72. Quoted above, note 60.

73. "For I have heard by credible report of such as were secret with his chamberers,
that after this abominable deed done he never had quiet in his mind, he never thought
himself sure [= safe]. Where he went abroad his eyes whirled about, his body privily
fenced, his hand ever on his dagger, his countenance and manner like one always ready to
strike again; he took ill rest o'nights, lay long waking and musing, sore wearied with care
and watch, rather slumbered than slept, troubled with fearful dreams, suddenly sometimes started up, leapt out of his bed and ran about the chamber, so was his restless heart
continually tossed and tumbled with the tedious impression and stormy remembrance of
his abominable deed."

74. Only extended quotation, impossible in a short article, could do adequate justice to
either the *Four Last Things* or the *Richard III*, but both these pieces are easily accessible
in inexpensive reprints—shilling editions, of *Richard III* published by Gowans & Gray, of
the *Four Last Things* by Burns, Oates & Washbourne.

KINCAID, "The Dramatic Structure of Sir Thomas More's *History of King Richard III*"

1. C. V. Wedgwood, *Truth and Opinion* (London, 1960), p. 99.

2. R. W. Chambers's fullest treatment of More's style in the *History* is his essay "The
Continuity of English Prose," in Nicholas Harpsfield, *The Life and death of Sr Thomas
Moore*, ed. Elsie Vaughan Hitchcock, Early English Text Society, original series no. 186
(London, 1932), p. cxli-clxxiv.

3. Chambers, pp. cxli-clxxiv; also W. A. G. Doyle-Davidson, "The Earlier English
Works of Sir Thomas More," *English Studies*, XVII (1935), 49-70; J. Delcourt, "Some
Aspects of Sir Thomas More's English," *Essays and Studies*, XXI (1935); and Richard S.
Sylvester's introduction to his edition of More's *History of King Richard III* (New Haven,
1963). Sylvester's article, "A Part of His Own: Thomas More's Literary Personality in His
Early Works," *Moreana*, no. 15 (1967), pp. 29-42, which appeared after this study was
completed, says little about the *History* but applies to several of the early works a type of
analysis similar to that employed in this paper in its observation of some of the dramatic
techniques.

4. James Mackintosh, "Sir Thomas More" in *The Cabinet Cyclopaedia*, ed. Dionysius
Lardner, Vol. I: *Eminent British Statesmen* (London, 1831), p. 417.

5. E. E. Reynolds, *Sir Thomas More* (London, 1965), p. 13.

6. A. F. Pollard, "The Making of Sir Thomas More's *Richard III*," in *Historical Essays
in Honour of James Tait*, ed. J. G. Edwards (Manchester, 1933), p. 230.

7. Lily B. Campbell, *Shakespeare's "Histories," Mirrors of Elizabethan Policy* (San
Marino, 1947), pp. 66-67.

8. Chambers, pp. clxv-clxvi. This passage is repeated in revised form in Chambers, *Sir
Thomas More* (London, 1935), p. 117.

9. William Roper, *The Lyfe of Sir Thomas Moore, knighte*, ed. Elsie Vaughan Hitchcock, EETS orig. ser. no. 197 (London, 1935), p. 5. This account is repeated in Harpsfield, p. 102.

10. A. W. Reed, *Early Tudor Drama* (London, 1926), p. 101.

11. Desiderius Erasmus, *Opvs Epistolarvm Des. Erasmi Roterodami*, ed. P. S. Allen
(Oxford, 1904-1958), Vol. IV, p. 16, letter of 23 July 1519 to Ulrich Hutten.

12. Erasmus, Vol. I, p. 460, letter to More of 9 June 1511 (dedication of *Moriae*

Encomium): "et omnino in communi mortalium vita Democritum quendam agere."

13. Roper, p. 42.

14. Thomas More, *The Confutacion of Tyndales Avnswere*, in *Workes* (London, 1557), p. 422.

15. More, *A Treatyce . . . vppon these wordes of holye Scripture . . . Remember the last thynges, and thou shalt neuer synne*, ed. W. E. Campbell (London, 1931), p. 34. I have expanded abbreviations. The second passage employing this image occurs on p. 85.

16. More, *Utopia* (New Haven, 1965), Book I, p. 98.

17. Leonard F. Dean, "Literary Problems of More's *Richard III*," *PMLA*, LVIII (March, 1943), 28.

18. More, *History*, ed. Sylvester, p. 6. All subsequent quotations are from this edition, and page numbers will henceforth be given in the text.

19. Sylvester, pp. xxvi–xxviii.

20. This interpretation of the Morton Sequence is given by H. Glunz in *Shakespeare und Morus* (Bochum Langendreer, 1938), pp. 71–72.

21. This suggestion of the *Contempus mundi* approach is made by Dean, p. 40.

LEWIS, "Thomas More"

1. Early in his history (p. 133), Lewis had written as follows: "All Barclay's works are outweighed in value by the few poems which Thomas More wrote in his youth. These are quite free from traces of humanism. The 'Merry Jest' about a sergeant disguised as a friar is written correctly enough in a jerky dimeter and begins in true medieval fashion with nine successive variations on the proverb *ex sutore medicus*. It is a dull trifle and has none of that superb mastery of comic anecdote which More was later to reveal in his prose. But the lamentation on the death of Queen Elizabeth (1503) is of real value, and the next piece, the verses for the *Book of Fortune*, is perhaps better. Here, on a characteristically medieval theme, and in firmer metre, we have something like an anticipation of Spenser's court of Philotime in the underworld, and allegorical figures which are not much below Sackville's. Few things even about More are more impressive than the merit of these two poems. They are quite off his own beat: they owe nothing to his humour or to his classical scholarship; they succeed not by anticipating any new conception of poetry but by momentarily restoring the medieval kind to something of its former value."

MARIUS, "Thomas More and the Early Church Fathers"

1. The following abbreviations to More's works will be used in the footnotes of this paper. Complete bibliographical information on the original editions may be found in R. W. Gibson, *St. Thomas More: A Preliminary Bibliography of His Works and of Moreana*, with a Bibliography of Utopiana Compiled by R. W. Gibson and J. Max Patrick (Yale University Press, 1961).

> 1532—*The confutacyon of Tyndales answere made by syr Thomas More Knyght lorde chauncellour of Englonde*, Prentyd at London By wyllyam Rastell, 1532.

> 1533—*The second parte of the confutacion of Tyndals answere . . .* Prentyd at London By wyllyam Rastell, 1533.

> EW —The workes of Sir Thomas More Knyght, sometyme Lorde Chauncellour of England, wrytten by him in the Englysh tonge. Printed at London . . . [by William Rastell] . . . 1557.

> 'Heresies'—'A dialogue concernygne heresyes & matters of religion,' EW, sigs. h1–t4^V.

> *Selected Letters—St. Thomas More: Selected Letters*, edited by Elizabeth Frances Rogers (Yale University Press, 1961).

> *Correspondence—The Correspondence of Sir Thomas More*, edited by Elizabeth Frances Rogers (Princeton University Press, 1947).

Other special abbreviations:

WA—D. *Martin Luthers Werke: Kritische Gesamtausgabe* (Weimar 1883).

Answere—William Tyndale, *An answere unto Sir Thomas Mores dialoge* (Antwerp, S. Cock, 1531).

2. See Luther's statement in *De servo arbitrio*, WA 18, 606: 'Hoc sane fateor, esse multa loca in scripturis obscura et abstrusa, non ob maiestatem rerum, sed ob ignorantiam vocabulorum et grammaticae, sed quae nihil impediant scientiam omnium rerum in scripturis. Quid enim potest in scripturis augustius latere reliquum, postquam fractis signaculis et voluto ab hostio sepulchri lapide, illud summum mysterium proditum est, Christum filium Dei factum hominem, Esse Deum trinum et unum, . . . Tolle Christum e scripturis, quid amplius in illis invenies? Res igitur in scripturis contentae omnes sunt proditae, licet quaedam loca adhuc verbis incognitis obscura sint. Stultum est vero et impium, scire, res scripturae esse omnes in luce positas clarissima, et propter pauca verba obscura, res obscuras dictare, Si uno loco obscura sunt verba, at alio sunt clara. . . .'

3. 'Heresies,' EW, sig. m1.

4. 1532, sig. O 3^v.

5. 'For in Saxony firste and among al the Lutherans there be as many heades as many wittes. And all as wise as wilde geese. And as late as thei began, yet bee there not onely as many sectes almoste as men, but also the maisters them selfe chaunge theyr mindes and theyr oppynions euery daye and wote nere where to holde them. Boheme is also in ye same case. One faith in the towne, another in the fielde. One in Prage, another in the next towne. And yet in Prage it self one faith in one strete, another in ye next. So that if ye assigne it in Boheme, ye must tell in what town. And, if ye name a towne, yet muste ye tel in what strete.' 'Heresies,' EW, sig. m6.

6. *Ibid.*, sig. m2.

7. 1533, sig. f3^v. More was quite clearly in that late medieval tradition which placed a moral value on the uncertainty of salvation. The idea has been examined by Heiko A. Oberman, *The Harvest of Medieval Theology* (Harvard University Press 1963), 185–248. More's position seems very much like that of John Gerson as noted in Oberman's work, 231 note 126.

8. Romans 11.13–23.

9. 'Heresies,' EW, sig. 14^v.

10. 'Tentatio vos non apprehendat nisi humana: fidelis autem Deus est, qui non patietur vos tentari supra id, quod potestis, sed faciet etiam cum tentatione proventum ut possitis sustinere.' 1 Cor. 10.13. For More's use see 1533, sigs. h3, s1^v, t3, et passim in all the English works.

11. PL 113.890.

12. 1533, sig. g1^v.

13. 1533, sig. e1^v.

14. Oberman, *op. cit.*, 222.

15. *Ibid.*, 223.

16. *Ibid.*, 224–227. This requirement of a 'middle way' between presumption and fear did not originate with Gabriel Biel or even in the late Middle Ages. The writer of the little tractate *De vera et falsa poenitentia* (falsely attributed to St. Augustine) made it basic to his theology. See PL 40.1118. More knew this work and used it, thinking it was genuinely that of St. Augustine: 1533, sigs. A4 and Oo2. It really dates from about the eleventh century.

17. PL 113.891.

18. PL 36.313.

19. Thomas More, *The Answere to the fyrst parte of the poysened booke, whych a*

namelesse heretyke hath named the souper of the lorde, London, W. Rastell, 1534, folio
31. 'Heresies,' EW, sigs. s1–s4^v, 1533, sigs. a5^v–a6^v, t1.

20. Aquinas, *Summa Theologiae* 2.2.a.4.q.4.

21. 1533, sig. m1^v.

22. *Ibid.*

23. PL 33.325.

24. PL 33.322–323.

25. 1533, sig. CC3.

26. If my assumption regarding the gloss to Psalm 32 is correct, it would seem that More is more likely to have taken his interpretation regarding verse 17 from the *Glossa ordinaria* than from the *Enarratio* itself. For here is one of the places in which Augustine's stress on the unmitigated power of grace would have been more congenial to the interpretations of the Reformers than to More's. It is clear that Augustine here castigates the pride of trusting in anything but the free grace of God. Especially forbidding, from More's point of view, would be the sentence, 'Si enim Deus voluerit, liberaberis: si Deus noluerit, cadente equo altius cades' (PL 36.297). This is not far removed from Luther's dreadful word, 'Sic humana voluntas in medio posita est, ceu iumentum, si insederit Deus, vult et vadit quo vult Deus, ut Psalmus dicit: Factus sum sicut iumentum et ego semper tecum. Si insederit Satan, vult et vadit, quo vult Satan, nec in eius arbitrio ad utrum sessorem currere aut eum quaerere, sed ipsi sessores certant ob ipsum obtinendum et possidendum.' WA 18.635.

27. In the eighth book of the *Confutation* More mentions 'the ordynary glose.' Here he uses it as an authority for the interpretation of Isa. 55.11. He mentions also the 'interlynyare glose,' which indicates that he was using a Bible such as that printed by Froben and Petri in six volumes in Basel in 1498. See 1533, sig. Pp4^v. Both the interlinear gloss and the *Glossa ordinaria* as well as the commentary by Nicholas of Lyra are mentioned by More in *Correspondence* 182.

28. Psalm 67.7, Vulgate; 68.6, A.V.

29. For the Latin see *Correspondence* 329; 1532, sig. D1 et passim. For the English see 1533, sig. G2 et passim.

30. Augustine, citing Cyprian, uses it in his tractate, *De baptismo,* CSEL 369–370. A slight paraphrase appears in the Confessions, PL 32.770.

31. Caro Christi et sanctum Domini ejici foras non potest, nec alia ulla credentibus praeter unam Ecclesiam domus est. Hanc domum hoc unanimitatis hospitium designat et denuntiat Spiritus Sanctus in Psalmis dicens: Deus qui inhabitare facit unanimes in domo: PL 4.522.

32. 1533, sigs. D4, M2–M2^v, M3. In these passages the title of Cyprian's *De unitate ecclesiae* is, oddly enough, not mentioned, though More does name Cyprian himself, and his argument follows closely that of Cyprian, even to the use of illustrations which Cyprian uses.

33. PL 26.1074. This citation is from the *Breviarium in Psalmos,* a work attributed to Jerome throughout the Middle Ages. In modern times doubts have been thrown upon its authenticity, for it seemed to be a collection of comments from numerous patristic authorities. See 'Admonitio,' PL 26.849–850. But according to the latest scholarship it seems that the homily on Psalm 67 is indeed from Jerome, perhaps by way of a student's notebook. See *The Homilies of St. Jerome,* tr. Sister Maria Lignari Ewald (Catholic University of America Press), xxi–xxx.

34. PL 37.815.

35. PL 37.816. 'Sed locus sanctus ejus sunt quos, habitare facit unius modi, vel unius moris in domo.'

36. PL 26.1074.

37. PL 28.1239.

38. WA 8.8.

39. When this paper was presented as a lecture after the annual luncheon of the St. Thomas More Project at Yale University in December, 1966, Professor Roland H. Bainton made an interesting observation regarding this point. He spoke of the problems of the Biblical text in the sixteenth century. They were immense. Manuscript copies of ancient texts were being sought with persistent vigor, but they were still quite hard to come by. He mentioned the difficulties of Erasmus in assembling manuscripts of his Greek New Testament in 1516. Thus the Scriptural citations by the Fathers might well antedate any available manuscripts. Thus More was not necessarily exhibiting a slovenly attitude towards the text when he took a reading from any of the Fathers. In the absence of more scientific canons of textual criticism, he was simply choosing among various authorities available to him.

40. 1532, sig. I3, 1533 sig. M2 *et al.* The 'but if' is the sixteenth-century idiom for 'unless.'

41. See Jerome's commentary on Isaiah, PL 24.104–105, Augustine's letter no. 120, PL 33.453, and his *De doctrina christiana*, PL 34.43.

42. Beryl Smalley, *The Study of the Bible in the Middle Ages* (2nd ed. University of Notre Dame Press, 1964), 13.

43. *Selected Letters*, 116.

44. Gordon Rupp, *The Righteousness of God* (London, 1953), 81.

45. For the translations see 1532, sigs. x1^v, T3, and 1533, sig. e4^v.

46. *Answere*, sig. C4.

47. 'Historical faith' for Tyndale was a mere knowledge of the propositions of Christianity. 'Feeling faith' was knowledge of salvation which came through direct experience with God. More says in one place (1533, sig. V4) that Tyndale took this distinction from Philip Melanchthon. Melanchthon does speak of the distinction, though in 1521 in the *Loci Communes* he commented that 'historical faith' hardly deserved the name of faith at all. See *Melanchthons Werke*, herausgegeben von Hans Engelland (Gütersloh, 1952), 2.1 p. 92. More delivers a lengthy attack on what he understands to be Tyndale's position, 1533, sigs. V3^v–Cc2^v.

48. *Answere*, sig. D5^v.

49. Something of this has been seen in Tyndale by William A. Clebsch in his book, *England's Earliest Protestants, 1520–1535* (Yale University Press, 1964), 163–168. But Professor Clebsch has not seen fit to emphasize the relation of will and intellect in Tyndale's theology, and he has not considered Tyndale's humanism to be a source of his legalism. I have commented elsewhere on this book and these issues. See *Moreana* No. 6 (May, 1965), 69–73.

50. More argued that it is the will of man which must take responsibility for its choices. See 1533, sigs. o3–p1^v. With relation to reason More taught that reward is greater for men who believe something by revelation which goes contrary to reason than it is to believe something evident to reason. See 1533, sig. p2. But if someone do some wrong unwillingly, More said it was not sin. See 1532, sig. x3. No man commits any deadly sin against his will. See 1533, sig. h2^v.

51. Romans 7.19.

52. *Answere*, sigs. C4^v–C5^v.

53. 1533, sigs. n1–n4^v.

54. 'The Fyrste Epistle of Seynt Jhon,' *English Reformers*, edited by T. H. L. Parker (Philadelphia, 1966), 111; *The New Testament*, translated by William Tyndale, 1534, edited by N. Hardy Wallis (Cambridge, 1938), 500.

55. *Summa theologiae* 2.2.a.14.q.1c.

56. 1533, sig. e2^v.

57. 'Here sheweth thys blessed apostle Poule that the dedely synne commytted after baptysme/putteth a man in that case, that it shall be very harde (for so is impossyble somtyme taken in scrypture) by penaunce to be renewed agayne/that is to wyt to come agayne to baptysme or to the state of baptysme, in whyche we be so fully renewed, and the olde synne so fully forgyuen, that we be forthwyth in suche wyse innocentes, that yf we dyed forthwyth, there were neyther eternall payne nor temporall payne appointed for us, that is to wyt neyther helle nor purgatory. But that dedely synne commytted after baptysme/is very harde by the sacrament of penaunce, confessyon, contrycyon, and greate payne taken to, to brynge vs agayne in the case, that the temporall payne dew therfore in purgatory, shall be worne all out by our penaunce done here. In all whyche thynges we neuer exclude the specyall pryuyledge of goddys absolute mercy. For by hys myghty mercy the thynge that is impossyble to man, is not impossyble to god/as our sauyour sayth in the gospell of Mathewe': 1532, sigs. x1^v–x2.

58. *Biblia Latina* (Basel, Johann Froben and Johann Petri, December 1498), vol. 6, sig. x3^v.

59. PL 16.520.

60. PL 16.522–528. See esp. note 3, cols. 522–524.

61. PL 38.465.

62. 1533, sig. e2^v.

63. *Ibid.*

64. 1532, sigs. T3–T3^v.

65. 'Heresies,' EW, sig. 1 4^v et passim.

66. See, for example, the chapter entitled 'Church and Church History' in Jaroslav Pelikan, *Obedient Rebels* (London, 1964), 27–41. In essence this is a theological defence of the Reformation confessions of faith which attacked the Catholic Church for its faith in its own history. No real effort is made to give a sympathetic interpretation of the Catholic position as it was seen by Catholics of the time. Eck and Cochlaeus, perhaps not the best spokesmen for their faith, are called up only to be slapped down. The Catholic position emerges without any of its subtleties and complexities, almost a caricature of itself.

67. John M. Headley, *Luther's View of Church History* (Yale University Press, 1963), 216–223.

68. Tyndale probably arrived at his eight hundred years by confusing the Boniface who was missionary to the Germans with Pope Boniface III who occupied the papal throne for a few months in the year 607. Boniface III was on good terms with the usurping Byzantine Emperor Phocas. Phocas recognized him as *caput omnium ecclesiarum.* Tyndale refers to this event in his vitriolic little booklet, *The practyse of prelates,* 1530, sig. B7^v. He thought it was one of the major steps in the corruption of the Church, which corruption he thought came from the Church's submission to the papacy. But Tyndale also says Boniface extended his power then over all the bishops of Germany. But in 607 there were no relations to speak of between the papacy and the Germans. In fact the Germans east of the Rhine Valley were still mostly pagan, and those Germans who were Christians were grouped in a *Landeskirche* arrangement, for all practical purposes completely independent from Rome. In 722 Pope Gregory II gave to the English missionary Winfred the name Boniface and made him something of a papal emissary for the conversion of the Germans. If Tyndale confused Pope Boniface III with Boniface the missionary and took the date 722 or thereabouts as crucial, we would have his eight hundred years almost to the year of his publication of the English New Testament in 1525. For a brief note on the confusion of the two Bonifaces, see William Tyndale, 'The Practice of Prelates,' edited for the Parker Society by Henry Walter, in *Doctrinal Treatises* (Parker Society 42; 1849), 258–259. Mr. Walter did

not relate the confusion of the two men to Tyndale's concept of the Church's fall.

69. See George H. Tavard, *Holy Writ and Holy Church* (London, 1959). Tavard maintains that the idea that Scripture and Tradition are separate and possibly contradictory entities is a late medieval development. He discusses the English scene, including the *Assertio* of Henry VIII. He does not discuss Thomas More. A shorter discussion of the issue, with a critique of Tavard's work, appears in Oberman, *op. cit.* (n.7 *supra*), 361-422.

70. For instance, the perpetual virginity of Mary, 1532, sig. P2^v, the Assumption of Mary, 1532, sig. H3^v, putting water into the wine at the Mass, 1532, sig. M3, the Lenten fast, worship on Sunday rather than Saturday, veneration of images, 1532, sig. S1^v, as well as the abrogation of certain practices commanded by Scripture—such as circumcision, 1532, sig. T3^v, the washing of feet, 1532, sig. T2, etc.

71. This is the only place in all of More's works where I have found the *Celestial Hierarchies* of Pseudo-Dionysius quoted as authority.

72. 1532, sigs. S2-S4.

73. For an expression of this esoteric view, see 1532, sig. I2.

74. We cannot here go into the complex problem of how the Reformers themselves conceived of their relationship to Christian tradition. More understood them to claim that they rejected everything but Scripture. In fact, as is well known, Protestants suffered many divisions over what to reject of tradition and what to keep.

75. 1532, sig. S4.

76. 1532, sig. T1, 1533, sig. Q1^v.

77. 1532, sigs. I1-I1^v.

78. 1532, sig. h2^v.

79. 1533, sig. k4^v.

80. 1532, sigs. H3^v, R2 et passim.

81. 1532, sig. O3^v.

82. 1533, sig. b3^v et passim.

83. 1533, sig. b3^v, c3^v, H4^v, I3, et passim.

84. For a characteristic patristic treatment of 1 Tim. 5 with relation to vows of chastity, see Augustine, *De bono viduitatis*, PL 40.437-438.

85. 1533, sig. Xx1^v.

86. Luther's attitude on this subject was most vehemently expressed in his diatribe, *De votis monasticis* of 1521. For Luther, to vow celibacy for the sake of gaining merit before God was blasphemy. Salvation came only by faith, and to place confidence in monastic vows was to follow a delusion of the Devil. Such vows for the sake of merit were clear proof of a lack of faith and hence were damnable. It became a work of faith to break such a vow (WA 8.602-603). He did not believe that the vow in itself was necessarily wrong. If Christians chose to make vows, knowing there was no merit of salvation in the practice, then they were free to do so. But such vows were not irrevocable. In describing the kind of vow he would accept, Luther wrote: 'Votum castitatis et totius monasticae, si pium est, debet necessario secum involvere libertatem rursus omittendi et in hanc ferme sententiam interpretari: Voveo tibi obedientiam, castitatem, paupertatem servandam cum tota regula S. Augustini usque ad mortem libere, hoc est, ut mutare possim, quando visum fuerit. Si aliter interpreteris aut intellexeris, cernis ex praedictis, peccari adversus libertatem divinam nobis mandatam, nec posse fieri ut deus aliter acceptet, nisi revocet libertatem, id est, nisi neget seipsum' (WA 8.614). It will be seen that in spite of More's fierce anger, he rather accurately represents Luther's position.

87. 1533, sig. Xx1^v.

88. WA 8.614.

89. See, for example, his response to Henry VIII, WA 10.2.215.

90. *Correspondence* 329 et passim.

91. 'Heresies,' EW sig. 12.
92. 1532, sig. T2.
93. *Correspondence* 172.
94. *Ibid.,* 52.
95. *Ibid.*
96. 1533, sig. R3.
97. 1532, sig. D1.
98. *Ibid.*
99. 1532, sig. P2.
100. 1533, sigs. Tt3, Tt3^V, Tt4, Tt4^V, Vv3 et passim.
101. 1533, sig. Tt2^V.
102. 'Heresies,' EW, sig. m6, 1533, sig. A1^V.
103. 1533, sig. B3, *Correspondence* 499.
104. *Correspondence* 498.
105. 1533, sig. A2.
106. *Ibid.*
107. *Correspondence* 498–499.
108. 1533, sig. Vv4.
109. 1533, sigs. Vv4–Vv4^V.
110. 1533, sigs. AA3, AA4^V.
111. 1533, sig. AA4^V.
112. All these descriptions happen to appear 1533, sig. Tt3, but they are also scattered throughout the polemical works.
113. 1533, sig. FF3^V.
114. In fact More continually exaggerated the extent to which the major Reformers felt the Church to be 'invisible.'
115. 1533, sig. N2^V.
116. 1533, sig. L1^V. The reference is to Luther in this particular passage, but the thought applies to any idea of a 'fall' of the Catholic Church.
117. 1533, sig. M2^V.
118. 1533, sig. b1.
119. 1533, sig. Nn1.
120. 1533, sig. F1. This thought had patristic authority. In 1533, sig. V3, More calls upon the witness of Augustine in his *Contra epistolam Parmeniani* to establish the necessity of the Church's being clearly known. There one finds the sentiment of the Father: 'Nulla est igitur securitas unitatis, nisi ex promissis Dei Ecclesia declarata, quae super montem, ut dictum est, constituta abscondi non potest: et ideo necesse est, ut omnium terrarum partibus nota sit.' PL 43.104.
121. *Correspondence* 338–339.
122. Luchesius Smits, *Saint Augustin dans l'oeuvre de Jean Calvin* (Louvain, 1958), vol. II.
123. Peter Fraenkel, *Testimonia Patrum* (Geneva, 1961).
124. *Op. cit.* (n. 66).
125. *Ibid.,* 40.
126. *Ibid.,* 40–41. Mr. Pelikan is here quoting himself from an earlier essay.
127. This idea of the personal rejection of the Reformers by the Fathers crops up again and again throughout the polemical works. It is most lengthily expressed in More's account of a great mythological general council of the whole Church from all history which appears in *The second parte* (1533), sigs. Xx1–BB1.
128. Thomas More, *Utopia,* ed. J. H. Hexter and Edward Surtz (Yale University Press, 1965), 224–225.
129. 'Heresies,' EW, sig. m2.

130. *Ibid.*

131. *Ibid.*

132. 1533, sig. N2^v.

133. One of which was done by More himself. See 'A Treatyce (unfynyshed) upon these woordes of holye Scrypture, Memorare nouissima & in eternum non peccabis,' EW, sigs. e5^v–f8. The best general study of this morbid sentiment of the later Middle Ages and the Renaissance remains that of Alberto Tenenti, *Il senso della morte e l'amore della vita nel Rinascimento* (Giulio Einaudi Editore, 1957).

134. EW, sig. b5^v.

135. *Ibid.*

136. John Fisher, *A Sermon had at Paulis* (London, T. Berthelet, 1525), sig. F1^v.

POLLARD, "THE MAKING OF SIR THOMAS MORE'S *RICHARD III*"

1. Professor Chambers (*More's English Works*, i. (1931), 39) charitably ascribes this to a "corrupt text," but there is something worse than a corrupt text here: some one is pretending to a knowledge or an authorship that was not his.

2. He was created earl of Surrey on 1 Feb. 1513/14, at the same time that his father became duke of Norfolk and Charles Brandon duke of Suffolk. In More's enumeration of Edward IV's children he only specifies Catherine as being still alive. If this implies that the others were all dead, it would add to our obituary knowledge of some of the daughers.

3. City records, *Journal* II, f. 118b; *Letter Book M*, f. 177 (per Miss Winifred Jay). More's retainer as king's counsel was £100 a year, the regular fee which had been raised from 100 marks in 1516. It ran from 21 June, 1518 (*Letters and Papers*, ii. 4247; the undated list, *ibid.*, ii. 2736, in which More's appointment also appears, contains appointments of various dates, some of them later than 1516, under which year it is placed in the calendar). Like his predecessors in the under-shrievalty of London and in the Speakership—Edmund Dudley and Sir Thomas Neville (*Letters and Papers*, i. (1920), 3107 [42])—More resigned the former office on becoming king's counsel. The *D.N.B.* remarks that More "accepted a pension of £100 a year for life" without reference to the counsel's duties attached thereto.

4. Miss Winifred Jay in Harpsfield's *Life of More*, Early English Text Soc., p. 313. It is possible but not probable that More's counsellorship dates from his embassy to Flanders in 1515, and that this appointment of a "sufficient deputy" removed the incompatibility between the under-shrievalty and the counsellorship. It is in April 1518 that Erasmus refers to More's translation from letters to the court (*Epistolae*, ed. Allen, iii. 295).

5. Hall (p. 345) adds "and duke of Norfolk" after "earl of Surrey."

6. *Ibid.*, p. 363.

7. He is not likely to have been a page in Morton's household before Morton became chancellor in 1486; and 1492 is the traditional date of More's going to Oxford.

8. Adrian died in 1523 and Wolsey failed again, but there was no further vacancy till 1534; Roper is vaguely remembering the rumour of Clement VII's death in Jan. 1529.

9. There are similar anachronisms in Cavendish's *Wolsey*. Neither Roper nor Cavendish, I think, ever gives a specific date, and neither thought of doing so. More, on the other hand, did intend to supply specific dates for his *Richard III*, but it was almost impossible in those days for biographers without access to records to date events in the lives of persons recently deceased.

10. There are, for instance, on a single page (*Works*, i. 402) half a dozen references like "it is for truth reported," "as men constantly say," "some wise men also ween," and so forth.

11. He was appointed on 18 Sept. 1483 (*Le Neve*, ii. 355).

12. *Bulletin, Institute of Hist. Research*, iii. 170. Under Richard Fitzjames the *D.N.B.*

says first that John was his nephew, and then (*bis*) that he was his brother, with a cross-reference to the article on John where he is called his nephew.

13. *Cal. Pat. Rolls*, 1467–77, pp. 302, 389; 1476–85, pp. 398, 490. The fact that John Roper was attorney-general is not mentioned in the *D.N.B.*, and his appointment is erroneously dated Feb. 1522 in the list of attorneys-general in Steele's *Proclamations* (vol. i, p. ccvii), instead of 3 July, 1521 (*Letters and Papers of Henry VIII*, iii. 1389).

14. Thomas Fowler, in his life of Fox in the *D.N.B.*, cites a letter from Richard III, said to be preserved in Stow's *Survey*. The letter is not in Kingsford's edition, but is to be found in Harleian MS. 433 (fol. 206), a volume said to have belonged to Burghley and to have been purchased by Harley from John Strype, who printed the letter in his edition of Stow's *Survey* (1720), vol. II., App. ii. pp. 94–5; it is dated 22 Jan. 1484/5.

15. See my article on Urswick in *D.N.B.* and authorities there cited; also *Cal. Pat. Rolls*, 1467–77, p. 451.

16. *D.N.B.* and *Erasmi Epistolae*, ed. P. S. Allen, ii. 469.

17. *Cal. Patent Rolls*, 1476–85, p. 473.

18. *Letters and Papers of Henry VIII*, i. (ed. 1920), 3324 [44].

19. Chancery proceedings (P.R.O.), C.1 bundle 703/37–8, s.v. "Giles Heron."

20. Professor A. P. Newton in *Engl. Hist. Rev.* 1917, p. 371.

21. *Cal. Pat. Rolls*, 1476–85, p. 505; Nicolas, *Testamenta Vetusta*, p. 447; *Letters and Papers of Hen. VIII* (1920), i. *passim*, ii. 2736; my *Henry VII*, i. 240, 246.

22. *Letters and Papers*, iv. p. 155.

23. John, baron Howard, was created duke of Norfolk, and his son, Sir Thomas Howard, earl of Surrey, on 28 June 1483, two days after Richard's reign began. Both were attainted after Bosworth, but Surrey was restored as earl in 1489 and duke in 1514: it was his son Thomas who married Edward IV's daughter, became earl of Surrey in 1514, and succeeded as duke in 1524. More's reference to the second duke as (before 28 June 1483) "a meane man at that time, and now of gret auctoryte" has been misinterpreted by his latest editors (i. 206): "mean" is obviously equivalent to "mesne" (of which "meane" may even be a misprint), and simply contrasts his moderate status as a knight on 13 June 1483 with his dukedom and lord high treasurership in 1514.

24. Privately circulated to contributors in 1900 and published as Appendix I to his *Lectures on Modern History*, 1906.

25. Ed. W. Fulman in vol. iii. of T. Gale's *Scriptores*, Clarendon Press, 1684.

26. Ed. Kingsford in *Chronicles of London*, 1905.

27. *Bulletin, Inst. of Hist. Research*, ix. 177.

28. Cf. Isobel D. Thornley, *England under the Yorkists*, pp. xix, 32–3, 116–18, 134–5, 169.

29. Neither More nor Hall mentions Jane's imprisonment in Ludgate at Richard's command and proposed marriage with Thomas Lynam, Richard III's solicitor-general. That story is told, again in a letter of Richard III (*Harleian MS.* 433, f. 340*b*; printed in Halliwell's *Letters of Kings*, i. 161, and in Gairdner, *Richard III*, pp. 71–2) to the lord chancellor, bishop Russell of Lincoln. Lynam was pardoned by Henry VII, held various offices under him and Henry VIII, and survived till 1518 (*Cal. Pat. Rolls*, 1476–1509, *passim*; *Letters and Papers of Henry VIII*, vols. i. and ii.).

30. And those lines do not occur in the English, but only in the Latin, version of *Richard III*.

31. More is expressing his reluctance, "florem illi gratiamque novitatis historiae suae praecipere." Ralph Robinson's "old rustie antiquities," is a free translation of More's Latin a few lines lower down (ed. Arber), p. 25.

32. *Works*, vol. i. (1931), p. 40.

33. *Ibid.*, p. 29.

34. *Ibid.*, p. 3.

35. Harpsfield's *Life of More*, Early English Text Soc., 1932, pp. clvii–clxvii.

36. *Ibid.*, p. 102.

37. Tottel, *Year-book, Edward V* (ed. 1580), fol. viii.

38. *Short Studies*, ii. 486.

39. The only doubt about Edward's birth was whether he was born on the 27th or the 28th of April 1442; see Gairdner, *Richard III* (1898), p. 4, and Scofield, *Edward IV* (1923), i. 1–2. There is a strange contradiction on the point in the *D.N.B.*: under "Edward IV" Dr. Gairdner gives the correct date; under his father "Richard, Duke of York," he says (or is made to say) "the eldest child of their large family, Edward (afterwards Edward IV), was born in August 1439." I suspect an editorial abbreviation; the eldest child was not Edward, but Anne, who was born in August 1439.

40. The *Croyland Continuator,* the Vitellius MS., and Fabyan refrain from any statement of Edward's age; the earlier William of Worcester has it correctly except for one day; other unprinted authorities have it correctly (Scofield, *loc. cit.*).

41. Lisle was sent to the Tower in 1540, charged with complicity in an alleged plot to deliver Calais to Cardinal Pole; his name was included in a bill of attainder introduced in the House of Lords on 17 July, but was taken out of it on the 21st (*Lords' Journals*, i. 158–9), and he was subsequently pardoned. Nothing would have conduced more to his imprisonment than a suggestion that his mother was lawful wife of Edward IV. More's story was first printed in 1543 in Grafton's edition of Hardyng, but his *Richard III* was current in MS. at least as early as 1538 (*Letters and Papers of Henry VIII*, 1538, ii. 828). Dr. Gairdner's description of Elizabeth Lucy as "a courtesan of obscure birth" (*Richard III*, p. 92) is, however, hardly justified: the naming of her son "Arthur Plantagenet" in 1510 (*Statutes of the Realm*, iii. 41) and his ultimate promotion implies a recognized liaison with Edward IV; both More and Hall call her "Dame Elizabeth Lucy," and the Louvain version of More adds "erat Elizabetha quaedam gentilicio nomine Lucia, puella nec ignobilis et egregia forma" (More, *Works*, 1931, i. 300*b*). The lady is not easy to identify. In 1514 "Dame Elizabeth Lucy" was the wife of Sir Thomas Lucy (*d.* 1525); she was the daughter of the notorious Sir Richard Empson and married George son of William Catesby, the "cat" of Collingbourne's rhyme; in the pardon roll of 1 Henry VIII (*L.P.* i. p. 221) she is described as of Ashby St. Leger, widow and executrix of George Catesby; and on 12 Sept. 1514, being described as "Elizabeth Catesby, the King's kinswoman," she was granted an annuity of 40 marks for her services to Elizabeth, late Queen of England, and to Mary [Tudor] the French queen (*ibid.*, i. 3324 [12], 3582 [22], ii. 643). She had apparently married Lucy by Michaelmas term 1514 (*ib.* Addenda, i. 562), but in 1527 was wife of Richard Verney. Her long life and many marriages, as well as her Empson parentage, can be traced by numerous references, chiefly under her husbands' names, in the *Letters and Papers of Henry VIII*, vols. i.–xii. (*e.g.*, i. 190 [31]; ii. pp. 1459, 1467; iii. 327–8, 513, 577, 1550, 2391 (the king's "right dere and welbilovede"); iv. 1227, 1930 (Ashby St. Legers), 4228, 5870 [ix.–xi.], App. 52–3; v. *passim, s.v.* "Verney"; vi. 919 (Sir T. Empson, R. Verney, and Lady Lucy); vii. 923 [iii., xliv]; viii. 1119 (Ric. Catesby). She died early in 1536 (*ibid.*, x. 871, Cromwell's reference to her executors); Charlecote reverted to Sir Thomas Lucy's son William, while Ashby St. Legers descended to Lady Lucy's son by George Catesby (*ibid.*, XII. i. 795 [25]; *Early Chanc. Proc.*, C1 bundle 586, Nos. 65–8). But this lady cannot have contracted a marriage with Edward IV before 1 May 1464, the date of his marriage with Elizabeth Wydville, and More's story probably arose out of the recognition of Arthur Plantagenet and his mother's existence, which must have become fairly well known when, in 1511, he married the notorious Edmund Dudley's widow, even if, as Edward IV's mistress, Empson's daughter, and Catesby's daughter-in-law, she was not notorious before. The

confusion appears most likely from More's statements that Edward IV had a child by his alleged wife, Dame Elizabeth Lucy, which is not alleged of Jane Shore or any other mistress, and that, of the three mistresses whom More describes, two were—unlike Jane—"somewhat greater personages, and nevertheless of their humility content to be nameless and to forbear the praise of those properties." Empson appears as attorney-general to the duchy of Lancaster in 1480, about the time that Arthur Plantagenet was born (*Cal. Pat. Rolls*, 1476–85, p. 214; *D.N.B.*, *s.v.* "Plantagenet, Arthur"). But Buckingham could never have called this lady (as More makes him do) Edward IV's "very wife, dame Elizabeth Lucy," on 24 June 1483.

42. The story appears almost in More's words (except that "syster" is written instead of "daughter" of Spain) in a note in "a contemporary hand" to Brit. Museum Cotton MS. Nero, C. xi., the second part of Fabyan's "Chronicle" (ed. Ellis, p. 654 *n.*; Ellis there simply calls it "the British Museum MS., but in his preface, p. xvii, he is a little more definite, saying Cotton MS. C. xi.; "Nero" should be interpolated). It seems impossible to determine whether More got the story from this Fabyan MS. or Fabyan's annotator got it from a More MS. Hall, who remarks (p. 262) that "many men have said and few or none have written" this tale, and denies flatly Warwick's embassy to Spain, concludes (p. 263) that "although it be not unpossible, yet for the causes aforesaid, it semeth not alitle unlikely." For the grain of truth in it (which does not include Warwick's alleged mission), see Ellis, *Original Letters*, II. i. 152, and Miss Scofield in *Engl. Hist. Review*, 1906, pp. 732-5, and *Edward IV*, i. 329). The story, introduced with the words "sum there be that afferme" and concluding with an even more emphatic denial than Hall's, also appears in the "Fragment of an old English Chronicle" appended by Hearne (p. 292) to his edition of Sprott.

43. Edward IV sailed from Lynn on 3 Oct. 1470 and landed again at Ravenspur on 14 March 1471 (Ramsay, *Lancaster and York*, ii. 257, 365).

44. *Works*, i. (1931), pp. 48*b*, 402, where More has "archbishop of York" and Hall corrects to "Archbishop of Canterbury." The Louvain edition, which is not so scrupulous as Rastell about correcting More, has "Cardinalis" (*i.e.* Bourchier, archbishop of Canterbury), which Rotherham, archbishop of York was not (*ibid.*, p. 294). Rotherham had already been placed in confinement on 13 June.

45. Shaa's name is given as John by More and Holinshed, and alternatively as John or Ralph in the *D.N.B.* (*s.v.* "Shaw or Shaa, Sir Edmund"). Fabyan, Polydore Vergil, and Hall have Ralph, and their correctness is proved by the record of Ralph Shaa's death in 1484 (*Cal. Pat. Rolls*, 1476-85, p. 473).

46. Hall, *Chronicle*, pp. 339-41, 334-5. It almost looks as though Hall had written his account of the period before he came across More's book, and then hastily substituted or superimposed it on his own. We know that he cancelled his account of Sir John Oldcastle after he had read Bale's account of him published in 1544 (see *Bulletin, Institute of Historical Research*, ix. 173).

47. *Cal. Pat. Rolls*, 1476-85, p. 473 (cf. *Harleian MS.* 433, f. 187); Forrest's son Edward and grandson Myles fared better than the other criminals' progeny (see indexes to vols. i.-iv. of the *Letters and Papers of Henry VIII*).

48. *Ibid.*, p. 436.

49. *Ibid.*, 1467-76, and 1477-85, *passim; Harleian MS.* 433, ff. 38*b*, 47*b*, 74*b*; *Croyland Cont.*, pp. 567, 571.

50. *Cal. Pat. Rolls*, 1476-85, p. 371. In *Harleian MS.* 433, f. 10*b*, is a note of the appointment of "Richard Pattyere" as attorney of the duchy of Lancaster; this would be to succeed Richard Empson, who is described as "late attorney of the duchy" in Earl Rivers' will, dated 23 June 1483 (Bentley, *Excerpta Hist.* pp. 246, 248). The "credible information" is particularized, in the Louvain edition, as More's own recollection of the

report made of the conversation to his father at the time (*Works*, i. pp. 35, 291; the collation, *ibid.*, p. 304, does not show whether it occurs in Arundel MS. 43 as well as in the Louvain edition).

51. In More's text the name appears as "Penker," in the index as "Penter"; "Penketh" is the form in the *Cal. Patent Rolls*, 1476-85, p. 543, and *Harleian MS.* 433, f. 97, recording the grant to him on 22 March 1485 of an annuity of £10. He is there described as "of the order of St. Augustine, professor of theology," which sufficiently identifies him with More's "provincial of the Augustine friars, doctor of divinity."

52. R. R. Sharpe, *Cal. Letter-books of the City of London*, Letter-book L, p. 209 *n*.

53. *Cal. Pat. Rolls*, 1476-85, pp. 438, 474, 529; 1485-94, pp. 6, 219; *Letters etc. of Henry VIII*, i. 1804 [6]; *Harleian MS.* 433, ff. 80 (*bis*), 92.

54. Davies, *York Records*, p. 218; Gairdner, *Richard III* (1898), pp. 33-8, etc.; Oman in *Political History*, iv. 475.

55. Isobel D. Thornley in *Tudor Studies* (1925), pp. 186 *n.*, 195 *n.*

56. *Statutes of the Realm*, iii. 56-7; *Rot. Parl.*, Suppl. p. vb; among his fellow-arbitrators were Warham, Foxe, and chief-justice Fineux. More refers to his arbitrations in the prefatory epistle to *Utopia:* "Whiles I doe dayelie bestowe my time aboute lawe matters; some to pleade, some to heare, some as an arbitratoure with myne awarde to determine, some as an vmpier or a judge, with my sentence finallye to discusse" (trs. R. Robinson, Arber's reprint, p. 22). The city records also contain references to More's arbitrations (Harpsfield's *Life*, E.E.T.S., pp. 312-13). This identification seems clear, though More has been wrongly identified with the Thomas More, mercer, common councillor, and M.P. for London in the parliament of 1510; with the other Sir Thomas More whose name actually appears in a chancery petition addressed to his namesake when lord chancellor (*ibid.* and *Early Chancery Proc.*, C1 bundle 636, Nos. 3-4); and with the Thomas More of Sherfield-upon-Lodden, Hants, J.P. for that county from 1502 to 1518.

57. *Works*, i. (1931), 67, 449.

58. The argument that Morton must have repeated this conversation to More is no stronger than an argument that either Edward IV or his mother must have repeated to him the two pages of conversation between them which More also puts into their mouths in 1464. On this assumption it could probably be shown that not only Morton, but Edward IV, the duchess of York, and Buckingham anticipated some of that original mastery of English prose attributed to More.

59. Lord Morley (*Notes on History and Politics*, p. 72) quotes this from Sorel.

60. On 7 Dec. 1512 More had, with his father, been appointed by the City on a committee to speak with Buckingham about the bill (4 Henry VIII, C. 3) concerning juries and sheriffs in London (Harpsfield, *loc. cit.*). There are no journals for that session, but More's father was concerned with the same bill in the previous session in March; he was also concerned with the bill of one John Burdett, a grandson, I think, of the Burdett who figures in *Richard III* (*Harleian MS.* 158, f. 135, *apud* Nicolas, *Barony of L'Isle*, p. 420).

61. *Letters and Papers of Henry VII* (Rolls Ser.), i. 233, 239.

62. *Cal. Spanish State Papers*, 1509-25, p. 9.

63. Printed verbatim in P. S. Allen, *Letters of Richard Fox* (1929), pp. 43-4, and almost verbatim in *Letters and Papers of Henry VIII*, i. (1920), 157; cf. Fuensalida to Ferdinand, March 1509, "the kingdom is in danger with only one heir" (my *Henry VII*, i. 322).

64. Henry VIII is almost invariably said to have been eighteen when he succeeded to the throne; but, born on 28 June 1491, he was still on 21 April 1509 two months short of completing his eighteenth year. Eighteen was the usual age for royal majorities, but the precedents in English history (Henry III, Edward III, Richard II, Henry VI) threw no clear light on the question.

65. Norfolk and Suffolk, created on 1 Feb. 1514.

66. *Letters and Papers*, iii. p. 491. This only comes from Buckingham's indictment in 1521, but there seems no reason to doubt its truth. It was a perfectly natural remark to make, and there was nothing treasonable about it. Buckingham was naturally annoyed that, having been the only duke in England (except the king himself) since Jasper Tudor's death in 1495, he should now find himself flanked, if not outflanked, by Norfolk and Suffolk.

67. *Erasmi Epistolae*, ed. Allen, ii. 371; *Letters and Papers*, ii. 2492.

68. By a curious coincidence, in the month (April, 1557) in which Rastell dedicated the volume containing *Richard III* to Queen Mary, this last Buckingham's grandson, Thomas Stafford, seized Scarborough, and proclaimed himself Protector and next heir, after Mary, to the throne. He obtained short shrift, was seized on 2 May, and hanged and quartered at Tyburn on the 28th. The poison in Morton's counsel was working out, though late in Elizabeth's reign suspicions of treason cast their shadow over yet three more members of the clan (see my articles in the *D.N.B.* on Stafford, Sir Edward; Thomas (1531?-1557); and William (1554-1612).

REED, "William Rastell and More's English Works"

1. *Early Tudor Drama* (Methuen), pp. 187-201.

2. *Early Tudor Drama*, pp. 148-159.

ROGERS, "Sir Thomas More's Letter to Bugenhagen"

1. Allen IV, Ep. 1218, i, 46; and Vives to Erasmus of 13 November 1524. Allen V, 1513, i, 15f.

2. Karl Vogt, *Johannes Bugenhagen Pomeranus*; Bugenhagen's *Briefwechsel*, ed. O. Vogt; Kawerau's article in Herzog-Hauck, *Realencyclopädie*.

3. Bridgett, *Blessed Thomas More*, p. 218n.; De Vocht, *Epistolae ad Franciscum Craneveldium*, Ep. 115, introd.

4. Stapleton, cap. 4 (tr., Hallett).

5. Allen VII, Ep. 1863, xi, 3-4, and note.

6. Allen VII, Ep. 1928.

7. Hutton, *Sir Thomas More*, p. 200.

8. Allen IV, Ep. 1220.

9. De Vocht, *op. cit.*, p. 231.

10. Identification in marginal note. For Barlow, *cf.* D.N.B. article.

11. *Epistle to Bugenhagen*, f. 1-11^r.

12. *Ibid.*, f. 9^v(B^v).

13. A. F. Pollard, *Wolsey*, p. 151.

14. Herzog-Hauck, art. *Karlstadt*; Hermann Barge, *Andreas Bodenstein von Karlstadt*, 2 vols., 1905.

15. *Vom hailigen Creutz in den Kirchen*; *Epistle to Bugenhagen*, f. 10.

16. *Mark* xiv, 4.

17. *Epistle*, f. 10^v.

18. Vogt, *op. cit.*, p. 364.

19. *Ibid.*

20. *Cf.* quotation from Bugenhagen, in *Epistle*, f. 16.

21. Cyprian, Ep. 73, xxi; *Epistle to Bugenhagen*, f. 21^v-22.

22. *Ibid.*, f. 24^v.

23. *Ibid.*, f. 24^v-25^v.

24. *Matt.* xx, 10.

25. *Epistle*, f. 25^v-f. 27.

26. *Ibid.*, f. 28^v-f., 30; *James* ii, 19.

27. *Epistle*, f. 30; *Matt.* vii, 22, 23.

28. *Epistle*, f. 30ᵛ–f. 31ᵛ.

29. *Epistle*, f. 37–37ᵛ.

30. *Ibid.*, f. 43–43ᵛ.

31. *Matt.* xix, 17.

32. *Epistle*, f. 43ᵛ–45.

33. Quoted by Preserved Smith, *Erasmus*, c. xii; *cf.* also Herzog-Hauck, art. *Luther*, by Köstlin.

34. *Epistle*, f. 50.

35. *Ibid.*, f. 50–50ᵛ.

36. *Ibid.*, f. 50ᵛ.

37. Walther Köhler, *Zwingli und Luther: Ihr Streit über das Abendmahl, passim*, especially p. 49; G. Mehnert, *Luthers und Zwinglis Streit über das Abendmahls-Dogma*; Barclay, *The Protestant Doctrine of the Lord's Supper*, pp. 41–106.

38. *Address to the Christian Nobility*, 24.

39. *Epistle*, f. 51ᵛ.

40. *Ibid.*, f. 55.

41. *Ibid.*, f. 55ᵛ.

42. The quotations have been identified by Monsignor Hallett in his excellent translation of Stapleton.

43. Harpsfield, *Life of More*, ed. Hitchcock, pp. 107, 318–319.

44. Stapleton, *Tres Thomae*, 1588, p. 43.

45. Roper, *Life of More*, ed. Hitchcock, pp. 34–35.

46. Tunstall, *Register*, f. 138; Wilkins, *Concilia*, III, p. 711.

47. Harpsfield, *op. cit.*, pp. 111–113.

48. R. W. Chambers, *The Place of St. Thomas More in English Literature and History*, pp. 52–54; quotation from *English Workes*, p. 1153.

49. Harpsfield, *op. cit.*, p. 280. The translation is Rastell's.

SANTINELLO, "Thomas More's *Expositio Passionis*"

1. Cited in this essay is the text of the Latin version ("*EP*") from Thomae Mori, *Opera omnia latina* (Francofurti-Lipsiae, 1689; rpt. Frankfurt, 1963), pp. 147–78.

2. *Nov. Testamentum*, in *Opera*, VI, 322E.

3. *Nov. Tes.*, 136E: Verum, salvo aliorum iudicio, potest sermo Christi habere nonnullam ironiam: *hactenus non potui a vobis impetrare, ut paulisper mecum vigiletis, nunc ipsa res excitabit vos, cum videritis meum supplicium et vestrum periculum.* Cf. *EP*, p. 162 a–b.

4. *Dialogi Lucianei*, in *Opera*, p. 258a. For a discussion of theology and irony, especially in *The Praise of Folly* (which the two friends had discussed with the theologian Martin Dorp), see P. Mesnard, "Humanisme et théologie dans la controverse entre Erasme et Dorpius," *Filosofia*, XIV (1963), 885–900.

5. See the editor's note on p. 178 of the *EP*: "Thomas Morus in hoc opere ulterius progressus non est, hactenus enim cum esset perventum, omni negato scribendi instrumento, multo arctius quam antea in carcere detentus; non ita multo post prope turrim Londinensem loco consueto securi percussus est."

6. E. E. Reynolds, *Thomas More and Erasmus* (London, 1965), p. 232.

7. *The Dialogue of Comfort*, too, is an attempt by More to comfort his own family while he strengthens himself. The fictional setting, Hungary during the Turkish invasion of 1529, when all were preparing to be persecuted, is allegorical and alludes to Henry's persecution of the Catholics. See L. Miles, "Introduction," in St. Thomas More, *A Dialogue of Comfort against Tribulation* (Bloomington and London, 1965), pp. xvi, xxii–xxiii.

8. *EP,* 153b.

9. *EP,* 158a.

10. *EP,* 159b.

11. *EP,* 166a.

12. *EP,* 166b. This may recall Plato, *Republic,* VI, 491e.

13. *EP,* 168a.

14. Reynolds, p. 243, quoting Sir Sidney Lee, in his *Great Englishmen of the Sixteenth Century* (1904).

15. *EP,* 172b.

16. *Utopia,* ed. E. Surtz and J. H. Hexter, *The Complete Works of St Thomas More,* IV (New Haven and London, 1965), 218: "Talia diu concionantem comprehendunt, ac reum non spretae religionis, sed excitati in populo tumultus agunt." On what is called "realism by negation" in More's utopian thought, see R. Mucchielli, "L'utopie de Thomas Morus," in *Les utopies à la Renaissance* (Bruxelles: Presses Universitaires, 1963), pp. 99–106.

17. *EP,* 177b: "Verum si nos sentimus animo parum firmos, tunc hactenus eorum illam fugam omnes imitemur: quatenus sceleris admittendi periculum fugere sine scelere possumus. Alioqui enim, si quis tunc aufugiat, quum aut suae salutis causa, aut suorum, quorum curam sibi commissam videt, Deus eum stare iubet et confidere: hic (nisi forte propter praesentem vitam facit, imo si propter praesentem vitam facit) facit omnino stolide. Quid enim stolidius, quam breve tempus et miserum aeternae felicitati praeferre?"

18. *Utopia,* p. 220: "Atque ideo post hanc vitam supplicia vitiis decreta, virtuti praemia constituta condunt."

19. *EP,* 177b–178a. In another of the Tower works, *Quod pro fide mors fugienda non sit* (*Opera,* p. 180), More begins thus: "Vita per offensam Dei servata, erit ei qui sic se servaverit odibilis. Nam qui sic vitam tuam servaveris, tute postridie vitam tuam odio habebis, et dolebis vehementer mortem te non pertulisse pridie. Nam restare tibi mortem recordaberis, quae, qualis futura sit, nescis, neque quam cito ventura."

20. *EP,* 165a, 172a.

21. *EP,* 167b.

22. *EP,* 167b, 172a.

23. *EP,* 149a: "Sed ut sunt sanctorum verba voluminum non ad unum sensum, sed pluribus foecunda mysteriis . . ."

24. *EP,* 170a.

25. *EP,* 150a. "Tenerum piumque corpus" is a literal rendering of a phrase in the *Dialogue of Comfort,* p. 233: "Consider the many sore bloody strokes that the cruel tormentors with rods and whips gave Him upon every part of His holy tender body."

26. *EP,* 150a, 156b.

27. *EP,* 150b–151a.

28. *EP,* 153b.

SYLVESTER, "Thomas More: Humanist in Action"

1. This essay was also read, in a somewhat different form, at the Catholic University of the West, Angers, in April, 1965. Of the letters discussed here, those to Dorp and to Oxford and the latter half of the *Letter to a Monk* are translated in *St. Thomas More: Selected Letters,* ed. Elizabeth F. Rogers (Yale University Press, 1961). Complete Latin texts of all four letters are available in *The Correspondence of Sir Thomas More,* ed. E. F. Rogers (Princeton University Press, 1947). Except for the *Letter to Oxford,* which has been translated by Professor T. S. K. Scott-Craig, the translations are those of the Reverend Marcus A. Haworth, S.J., of St. Louis University. Page references in the text are to the *Selected Letters.*

2. *Studies in the Renaissance,* IX (1962), 17.

3. See, for example, the Introduction by J. H. Hexter and Edward Surtz, S.J., to

Utopia ("Yale Edition of the Complete Works of St. Thomas More," Vol. IV [Yale University Press, 1965]).

4. R. S. Sylvester, ed., *The History of King Richard III* ("Yale Edition of the Complete Works," Vol. II [Yale University Press, 1963]), pp. lxxxii, lxxxv–lxxxvi, xcix–ciii.

5. For a convenient summary of Dorp's career, in addition to the introductory material supplied by Rogers, see Sister M. Scholastica Cooper, "More and the Letter to Martin Dorp," *Moreana*, No. 6 (1965), 37–44.

6. P. S. Allen, *Erasmi Epistolae*, 11 vols. (Oxford, 1906–1958), Vol. II, No. 304.

7. *The Religious Orders in England*, 3 vols. (Cambridge, 1959), III, 469.

8. *Utopia*, p. 218.

9. See the story as told by More's son-in-law, William Roper, in *The Lyfe of Sir Thomas Moore, knighte*, ed. E. V. Hitchcock (Oxford: Early English Text Society, 1935), p. 6.

10. For examples of this approach, see Davis P. Harding, *The Club of Hercules: Studies in the Classical Background of Paradise Lost* (Urbana, 1962), and Leo Spitzer, "The Problem of Latin Renaissance Poetry," *Studies in the Renaissance*, II (1955), 118–38.

11. *Ciceronianus*, trans. Izora Scott, in *Controversies Over the Imitation of Cicero* (New York, 1910), p. 104.

BRIDGETT, "The Wit of Thomas More"

1. By the context it appears that gaming here means games or amusements in general.

2. *Answer to Masker*, Works, 1047.

3. Proverbs xxxi. 6.

4. Summa. 2, 2_{ae}, q. 168, a. 2.

5. A giddy fellow, always ready to laugh.

6. *Dialogue of Comfort*, Works, 1171.

7. "You know," he says in a letter to Erasmus, "that when my epigrams were being printed, I did all I could to suppress those that might be personal, as well as a few that did not seem to me serious enough: quod quaedam mihi non satis severa videbantur, etiamsi procul absint ab ea obscoenitate, qua ferme sola quorumdam epigrammata video commendari." (*T. Mori Lucubrationes*, p. 435. Ed. 1563.)

8. 3 Kings xviii. 27.

9. I allude not to his history, but to his tracts, which are very clever and very pungent.

CHAMBERS, "Martyr of the Reformation: Thomas More"

1. *Great Englishmen of the Sixteenth Century*, 1904, pp. 32, 33, 61.

2. *The Lyfe of Sir Thomas Moore*, by William Roper, ed. by E. V. Hitchcock, 1935, pp. 24, 25.

3. *Works*, 1557, p. 1153.

COULTON, "The Faith of St. Thomas More"

1. In this article I give no references for statements which I have printed elsewhere, often more than once, with the support of documentary evidence and without (so far as I know) contradiction by other documents.

2. 'English Works,' pp. 231, 485, 619. This is also one of the biographer's weakest points. An episcopal visitation of Hereford diocese (A.D. 1397) shows that clerics were presented for incontinence in 18 per cent. of the parishes: a Swiss visitation of a few years later gives 30 per cent.

3. 'Loci e Libro Veritatum,' pp. 72, 147, 153, cf. 35.

4. A. L. Smith, 'Church and State in the Middle Ages,' p. 60. Compare p. 95 for the author's protest against that harsher verdict of Pollock and Maitland: 'the incalculable harm done by a marriage-law which was a maze of flighty fancies and misapplied logic.'

5. 'Calendar of State Papers (Spanish),' vol. II, p. 396; A. F. Pollard, 'Henry VIII,' 1905, p. 207.

6. Fisher, 'English Works' (E.E.T.S. Extra Series, 1876), pp. 170, 183.

7. 'Sum. Theol.,' App. q. xciv. When I published this once in 'The Daily Telegraph,' it seemed so incredible and aroused such contradiction that I met my critics by printing the whole section in a leaflet, from the authorised translation by the Dominican Fathers. Copies are still at the service of any reader who cares to send a stamped and addressed envelope to me at St. John's College, Cambridge.

8. 'Quadragesimale,' Serm. XII and XIII.

9. 'English Works,' p. 1257.

10. 'English Works,' p. 1258.

11. 'Fisher's English Works' (E.E.T.S. Extra Series, 1876), p. 277. Abbot Elias's words are in 'Lives of the Fathers' (Migne Pat. Lat., vol. 73, col. 861).

12. 'English Works,' pp. 73, 78.

13. Encyclical of Leo XIII, 'Sapientiae Christianae' (Jan. 1890).

14. Hilaire Belloc, 'The Contrast,' p. 182.

15. See pp. 674 ff. of 'International Affairs' for Sept.–Oct. 1935; and especially 'The Basic Facts in the Mexican Problem,' an open letter by a distinguished American lawyer, Mr. C. C. Marshall, author of 'The Roman Catholic Church in the Modern State.'

16. I have given further details in a recent booklet, 'A Critic and a Convert,' pp. 48–9. See H. C. Lea, 'History of the Inquisition in the Middle Ages,' III, p. 66 ff.

17. More's 'Apology' (E.E.T.S. Extra Series, 1930), pp. 51, 60, 68, 74–5, 108–9, 212 ff. This volume, which contains the whole of St. Germain's treatise in its Appendix, is admirably edited from the textual and philological point of view; but the eighty pages of historico-theological introduction are untrustworthy; and it would seem a pity that the Society should in this way step beyond its natural limits.

18. 'Chambers,' p. 196.

19. He falls twice (for instance) into the exact blunder for which Freeman used to gird against Froude *ad nauseam*, writing 'Albericus bishop of Hostiens' and 'the byshoppe of Carnotenses' (811 b, f.). Moreover, it is practically certain that he seriously misinforms us about pre-Wycliffite English Bibles: see M. Deanesly, 'The Lollard Bible,' ch. I.

20. 'English Works,' p. 78.

MARC'HADOUR, "A Name for all Seasons"

1. J. Headley's epithet in note on p. 584/15 of *Responsio* (*CW 5*, p. 965). This paragraph owes much to his commentary.

2. The marginal gloss on p. 584/16 apparently refers to the "legend" of St. Hippolytus.

3. These quotations all come from chapter 19. The game continues all the way to chapter 26. See *CW 5*, 603/30, 632/18, 662/14, 668/27.

4. More quotes Aristotle's maxim as *Nomina sunt ad placitum* (*CW 5*, 584/11). To counter Brixius' hostile punning on *Môros*, More wrote that by the same rule Ermolao Barbaro was a barbarian (*Rogers*, p. 228/553).

5. Had More fully espoused the Platonic view, he could, in embarrassing instances of incongruity, have concocted etymologies *e contrario*; no problem even with Holy Writ, since he never put it past the apostles or even the Lord to use irony: see his exegesis of Mark 14:41 and 2 Cor. 12:13 in *De Tristitia Christi* (fol. 72r, 73, 74).

6. "nomine ... ut augurari licet, ad res magnas ominoso" (February 5, 1517, Allen *2*, 446).

7. In Revelation 2:18, the Spirit, says More, promises the winner "a white suffrage, and in his suffrage a new name written" (*EW*, p. 1259 E). Exodus 3:14, he says, shows the word *AM* as "the name by which Our Lord would ... be named unto Pharao" (*EW*, p. 146 F).

8. *The English Works of John Fisher,* ed. J. E. B. Mayor, EETS (no. 27), reprint 1935, p. 50.

9. For *pullus,* see Mat. 21:2, 5, 7; Mk. 11:2-7; Lk. 19:30-35, Jn. 12:15, and *Erasmi Opera Omnia,* 1/3: "Colloquia" (Amsterdam 1972), p. 488. C. R. Thompson takes for granted Colet's identification with Gratianus Pullus: *The Colloquies of Erasmus* (Chicago 1965), p. 286. In a letter to Lupset, Erasmus suggests a "numinous" intention in Colet's nearness to *Coheleth,* "which is Hebrew for preacher" (Allen, *4,* 569/12). In Tudor English, "colet" also meant "acolyte."

10. Dame Folly features an English sermon enucleating "the mystery of the name of Jesus": the medial letter *s,* says the preacher, represents its counterpart *syn* in the Hebrew alphabet, because Jesus "takes away the sin of the world" (*Encomium Moriae, LB* 4, 476 B).

11. *A Dialogue Concerning Heresies,* in the spelling of the second edition (1531) which first handles *The Image of Love* (*EW,* p. 117 FG).

12. William Camden's *Remains* (1605), under "Morton," endorses the Cardinal's more and tun "canting," although it links "More" with moorland.

13. With the consonant clusters of German names, one understands the temptation: Wolphangus Capito simplifies two such clusters in Wolfgang Köpfel. From Erasmus' spelling *Latamerus* for the name of William Latimer (*LB 1,* 1012 F et alibi) it seems that he was not aware the name derived from *Latin-er* and betokened an ability to read and write Latin.

14. Willibald Pirckheimer, the Nuremberg bourgeois so like More in a number of ways, also disliked that name, and coined satirical variants such as Caecolampadius (blind man's lamp), using it in the title of an open letter to Luther (see Allen, *7,* 216, n. 51).

15. Neither in the *Supplication* (*EW,* p. 330 G, 331 D) nor in the *Confutation* (where he names him a good sixty times, from Book I to Book IX), does More drop the German form. In the *Apology,* ch. 8, his annoyance extends to "Phylyp Swarterthe (whych lyke as frere Huskyn hath named hym selfe Ecolampadius, hath made hys name now Melanchthon)" (EETS edition, p. 42).

16. Allen, *3,* 104/13; October 7, 1517.

17. See my *Thomas More et la Bible* (Paris, 1968), pp. 474-77. Rabelais' Epistemon, after invoking "le Cratyle du divin Platon," points "en quelle observance et religion ... estoient les noms propres avec leurs significations" to the Hebrews and their inspired authors (*Le Quart Livre,* ch. 37). His own name, of course, means "the one who knows."

18. More plays on the equation "God" = "God's name" (compare for instance his two renderings of Is. 42:8 in *EW,* p. 139 D and 191 E), but, unlike most of his contemporaries, he never treats Hebrew as a sacrosanct language. The meanings of Cedron (gloomy), Gethsemani (oil-press), Malchus (King) are prophetic by God's appointment, not by any virtue of the Hebrew tongue.

19. *Romeo and Juliet,* II, ii, 45-64.

20. *Supplication,* toward end of Book II (*EW,* p. 335 EF). This "fond" habit of English preachers is ridiculed by Erasmus in a page he added to *Moria* (after the sermon on *Jesus* quoted in ftn. 10).

21. Especially in his congratulatory letters, for instance to Leo on May 21, 1515, Allen, *2,* 80 f., with allusions to the honey in the lion's mouth (83/131) and "Medici ... debemus remedium" (83/137); to Paul III on Jan. 23, 1535, Allen, *11,* 61-62. *Julius Exclusus* also capitalizes on that pope's warlike name.

22. As author of an *Introduction to Heraldry* (London 1940), E. E. Reynolds has been confronted with no end of punning arms. For the Castle of the More, Hertfordshire, a favorite haunt of Wolsey's, he suggests the same derivation. The definite article makes the meaning "the greater" also possible, but does not rule out a marshy land. Indeed "at

the moor" gave the name "atte More" which may have been that of our More's ancestors (*Moreana*, 23, p. 23, in E. E. Reynolds, "The Mores and Hatfield").

23. Rolle adds: "in the more ... that is as a desert forsaken of god" (*The Psalter of David*, ed. H. R. Bramley. Oxford. 1884, p. 279).

24. *Mora* is defined as "muccosa et humida planities"; *morosus* is used as a synonym of *paludosus*. The Latin name of *Morini* for Picardy is commonly linked with Flemish *moer*. English *morass* certainly derives from Dutch *moeras*.

25. Allen, 7, 471, letter of September 2, 1528. Though he guesses from the context that this "Mr. Black" must be More, Allen fails to see the pun.

26. "Sed in Moriam quod inuehitur, id vero vix credi potest, homo totus ex Moria conflatus" (Allen, *3*, 11/19).

27. Letter of July 23 to U. von Hutten, Allen, *4*, 14/37.

28. Preface to *Ecclesiastes*, Allen, *11*, 192/102, a sentence quoted by Roper in the opening lines of his *Life of More*.

29. And Morus, he adds, "is Greek for foolish" (*LB, 4,* 401–402, n.6). In his view, *Maurus* is the "normal," the etymologic form of More's name, *Morus* is a popular reduction of it.

30. *Moreana*, 14 (May 1967), 55/7, 57/1, 12. No other spelling than *moers* is found in this text.

31. Was H. G. Wells alluding to More's name when he subtitled *A Modern Utopia* (1896) "The Island of Doctor Moreau"?

32. The homonymy perhaps prompted this Lenoir to print *Epistole Francisci Nigri* (an undated incunabulum).

33. The Moroccan ancestry of the Moslem dynasties that ruled in Spain accounts for the misnomer *Moorish* as applied to the Arabs of the Iberic peninsula, says Mahmoud Manzalaoui: *Moreana, 3* (June 1964), 93.

34. See for instance Allen, *2*, 528/12, 13.

35. Both abbey and hamlet are still called Saint-Maur. The spelling Saint-Mor is already found in Froissart's account of the capture of Glanfeuil by the English (1369–70).

36. For some editions of **Regi** over the next 120 years, see *Moreana*, 47–48 (Nov. 1975), 4, 72.

37. Respectively on p. 328 and p. 334 of the 1681 edition.

38. Appendix to *Vita Thomae Mori*, Frankfurt 1689, p. 77.

39. "ob id dicta sapientissima arborum" (*Hist. Natur.* XVI, 41:4), quoted in Erasmus' *Similia* (*LB, 1,* 618 B).

40. Pliny has a predilection for the *morus:* other praises by him will be found in *Moreana, 3,* 79–80.

41. Martial's phrase "cadente moro nigrior" (I, 75) shows its blackness to have been proverbial. See R. J. Schoeck, "More, Erasmus and the Devil" (*Notes and Queries, 196*, July 21, 1951, 313). For the (pseudo) Rabanus Maurus, despite his own name, "morus est diabolus" (*Allegoriae in Sacram Scripturam*, on Lk. 17:6). Love "strong as death" is also symbolized by the dark mulberry, which wears black to mourn the double suicide of Pyramus and Thisbe, after being dyed in their dying blood (Ovid, *Metam.* 4. 55 f.).

42. Even the austere John Fisher would thus converse with friends, according to *The Tablet* (Sept. 11 and 25, 1954).

43. *LB, 4,* 300 E, 306 DEF.

44. ... *Viridarium in tres libros et sexaginta arboreta digestum*, Paris (Jean Foüet), 1626 (*Gibson*, no. 492).

45. The first words may echo 1 Mac. 6:34: "sanguinem uvae et mori."

46. *Revista de Bibliografía Nacional*, Madrid, VII (1946), 5–6.

47. The edition is dedicated to Baron Zollner, a physics bachelor at the Jesuit College of Graz.

48. Text and portrait in Stanley Morison, *The Likeness of Thomas More*, London (1963), pp. 68–69.

49. For a different (and longer) excerpt, see F. and M. P. Sullivan, *Moreana-Bibliography*, Los Angeles, *1* (1964), 46. The berry, which admits of treatment as gules or sable, is frequent in the blason of families like Moret, Morin, Mourrain, etc. The dictionaries of most European languages are rich in (semi-)scientific derivatives from *mora/maura*, with the notion of black as dominant: *morula, moraceous, morello, morel* (the black nightshade).

50. *Egypt,* says More, "signifieth by interpretation darkness," and symbolizes "the dark devilish worldly and fleshly subjection" (*EW,* p. 1196 FG).

51. *Four Last Things, EW,* p. 98 H. Pleonasms or synonyms abound in Tudor English. G. Joy's *Psalter* of 1530 has "the Mooris of yinde" (fol. 140 v). *The Pilgrimage of Perfection* (1526) alternates "blacke moryan" with "man of ynde," and uses both to mean "miscreant" as well as "non-white." In old French, "Moriaines" (from Latin *Moriani*) are "les crestiens du pais du prestre Jan."

52. *Adagiorum Chiliades,* I, ix, 38 in *LB, 2,* 947 B, complete with a description of the Negro: "nigrore vultus, intortis capillis, labris tumentibus, dentium candore."

53. In his famous defense of Erasmus' good "intent," More calls the book "Moria, whyche worde in greke sygnyfyeth foly" (*CW 8,* 178/5). He repeats the title a half-dozen times (pp. 177/14 to 179/11) without ever translating it.

54. Betty Radice's translation in *The Praise of Folly,* Penguin edition (1973).

55. *CWE, 2,* 162/23.

56. "Quos christianae pietatis ardor semel totos arripuit" (*LB, 4,* 500 AB).

57. "Apud Morum non verear vel ineptire," Allen, *2,* 242/26.

58. Epistle of Sept. 9, 1528, Rogers, p. 126/9–14 and p. 132/228.

59. Four quotations spread over the years 1519 to 1534 will be found in my *The Bible in the Works of St. Thomas More,* II, 110, under Luke 11:38–42, to which one may add a fifth from Pico (*EW,* p. 14 D).

60. "Antimoron tuam, non Moriam modo, sed Maniam quoque spirare," Rogers, p. 236/872. *Mania,* also in Erasmus, designated a somber folly, hell-inspired and havoc-working.

61. "Tua autem ista siue ironia ... candida, siue vrbanitas festiua, et figuris innocuis condita ... nihil vt minus esse te in iis doceas quam quod ... vocaris," Rogers, p. 251/19 f.

62. H. De Vocht, ed. *Literae virorum eruditorum ad Franciscum Craneveldium: 1522–1528,* Louvain 1928, no. 160.

63. Goclenius' dedication is Rogers, no. 112. More's answer is Rogers no. 113, included in *SL,* pp. 153–54. The signature is among the samples on the frontispiece page of Gibson.

64. Rogers, p. 518/169; *noddies* in modern English.

65. Stapleton: "unicum tantum stultum" uses the regular Latin equivalent of *môros* (*Thomae Mori Vita,* ch. 13, 1689 edition, p. 47).

66. *Ibid.,* p. 48, for the Greek and Latin, also quoted in *Moreana, 3,* 77–8. I have quoted Hallett's rendering, from Th. Stapleton, *The Life of Sir Thomas More,* London 1966, p. 28. A closer translation might read as follows: "Am I wise-foolish, you ask, or foolish-wise? A fool to this world, I'm wise in God's eyes."

67. See two pages in Philomorus (J. H. Marsden), *Notes on the Latin Poems of Sir Thomas More,* London 1878, pp. 260–62. Even friends of Bourbon's seem to find this in bad taste: neither G. Carré in *De Vita et scriptis Nicolai Borbonii* (Paris 1888), nor V. L. Saulnier in *Les Bagatelles de Nicolas Bourbon* (Paris 1945) so much as allude to these poems.

68. *The Poems of Sir Francis Thompson,* Oxford University Press, 1938, "To the English Martyrs," p. 284.

69. "Morositatem in primis effuge," says Erasmus in a model letter ("De conscribendis epistolis") in *Opera Omnia* 1, 2 (1971), 491/19. "Vitiat enim omnem vitae jucunditatem morositas," he adds in his *Guide to Christian marriage* (LB, 5, 673 C). Budé's pun of August 12, 1519 is beautifully supported by long vowels: "pro More suauissimo morosus" (Rogers, p. 162/59).

70. The two poems have been edited and translated by R. S. Sylvester, *Huntington Library Quarterly*, 26 (February 1963), 147–154.

71. The couplet is quoted in M. P. Sullivan, *Moreana-Bibliography, 1* (1964), 235. The motto "Magnes Amoris Amor" (Love is Love's Magnet) on the title-page of Dame Gertrude More's *Confessiones Amantis* (Paris, 1658) probably alludes to her name.

72. See context in G. Marc'hadour, *L'Univers de Thomas More* (Paris 1963), p. 247.

73. Lines 7–8 of the first of "John Constable's Poems to Thomas More," edited and translated by R. S. Sylvester, *Philological Quarterly*, 42 (October 1963), 525–31. The allusion is more doubtful in line 8 of the second poem.

74. See his "Joe Miller on Thomas More" in *Moreana, 38* (May 1972), 59–61.

75. LB, 1, 26 C to 29 E. My longer quotation occurs at 29 A.

76. *The Four Last Things* has this verse (Ecclesiastes 7:40) in its very title (*EW*, p. 72 A).

77. *IL MORO*, ed. by R. L. Deakins, Cambridge, Mass. (1972), p. 62. The rendering is mine.

78. Cope's couplet is followed, in the Appendix to Stapleton's *Vita Mori*, by a quatrain of Cope's, playing on *mores* as well as *mors*. Fowler's line heads his 1568 dedication to Philip II of the *Epistola* (Gibson, 61).

79. Hence the startling quality of *Le Maur ... vivant* (1959), for the biography of a Capuchin, Frère Maur, in whose papers was found a prayer to become, through mortification, "un Maur ... mort."

80. *Maladies et médecins d'une cité mosane à l'époque de la Renaissance: Huy 1490–1630* (Bruxelles, 1968), p. 145.

81. Verso of the title-page.

82. The text is reproduced in Harpsfield's *Life of More*, EETS, p. 181, as well as in B. & L., where the translation (p. 243) needs revision.

83. Two more puns from Plautus, quoted in *Moreana, 5, 78–9*, involve the ablative *môre* (from *mos*) and the adjective *môrus*, both to laugh at some of society's "more moronic mores."

84. *A Midsummer Night's Dream*, III, ii, 115.

85. The textual variant "stulta et mora" substitutes a flat repetition for a pointed ambivalence.

86. Even in Breton, *morillon* designates a Negro (or Negro-looking) child.

87. Letter of August 21, 1531 (Allen, *9*, 323/61).

88. *EW*, p. 329 H. We still say "the more fool you ..."; the hurdle in More's tale is the repeated use of *and* in the sense of *if*.

89. The entire poem is in *Moreana, 21*, 21. Students of *Titus Andronicus* have sensed puns on *Moor/more* in Tamora's "Ah! my sweet More, sweeter to me than life" eliciting from Aaron the answer: "No more, great empress." (II, iii, 50–51.)

90. In *Julius Caesar* (I, ii, 156), "Now is it Rome indeed, and room enough," the hinge words are perfect anagrams of *More* and *moor*. Thomas More II (John's son and Cresacre's father) is designated as *Moare* in the 1582 document of his arrest as a recusant (Harpsfield's *Life of More*, EETS, p. xiii, and 294–96).

91. Allen, *2*, 478–79. Erasmus names three Guglielmus in his native Holland, three in Paris, one in Basel, and four in England. In the French *Mystère de Saint Louis*, England is represented by Johan, Thomelin and Vuilam. Out of some 75 Mores whose wills she studied, Margaret Hastings found 24 Johns, 13 Williams, only 8 Thomases.

92. *Pantagruel*, ch. XVIII-XII (vol. 1 in *Oeuvres de Rabelais*, Paris 1837, pp. 227 f.). Some critics have seen an allusion to More here, but the "grandissime clerc" who cuts a somewhat ridiculous figure in the debate with Panurge better fits a professional scholar like Linacre, whose works were actually printed in Paris. *Thomas Anglicus* is a headache in medieval bibliography; it can designate Thomas of Sutton, Thomas Walleys, Thomas Wilton, even Thomas Pinchet the Paduan Augustinian, and no doubt other authors.

93. *Supplication*, Book II, *EW*, p. 325 D; *Confutation*, *CW 8*, 533/29. For other references see my *The Bible in ... More*, II, 200-01.

94. *The Poems of Desiderius Erasmus Roterodamus*, ed. C. Reedijk (Leiden 1956), p. 315. In a 1506 letter, Erasmus says Whitford used to find him and More as like as "vllos gemellos" (Allen, *1*, 423/31).

95. *Dialogue Concerning Heresies*, 1, 15, *EW*, p. 136 H.

96. *King Lear III*, v passim, and III, vi: "poor mad Tom," "madman and beggar too."

97. The Nun's Priest in Chaucer is another "Sir John." The Monk is "daun Piers," but the Host, until he knows his name, is tempted to try "daun John/Or daun Thomas" (*Canterbury Tales*, lines 3119 f.).

98. Daniel Shanahan, "The Descendants of St. Thomas More in Herefordshire," *Essex Recusant*, 15, 3 (Dec. 1973), p. 104.

99. P.S. Allen, *Sir Thomas More: Selections from his English Works*, Oxford 1924, p. 1.

100. *The Manuscript of William Dunche*, ed. A. G. W. Murray and E. F. Bosanquet, Exeter, 1914, *passim*.

101. E. E. Reynolds, "Which Thomas More? A Retractation," *Moreana*, 13, pp. 79-82, restores to Hampshire born lawyer Sir Thomas More several Commissions for the Peace he had bestowed on our More. The other More, a J. P. for Hampshire 1502-18, was also Lent Reader in 1511, which added to the risk of confusion. Within More's family itself, duplication was rank. While John More's wife (Thomas' mother) was Agnes, John's first cousin, also John More, married another Agnes. John's fourth wife was née Alice More, like his own sister; with Thomas' second wife and his stepdaughter, there were four Alices around. The Jesuit Thomas More (1586-1623) was the martyr's descendant on the distaff side: his father was an Edward More of Oxfordshire, his mother Mary More was a daughter of Thomas More II, a sister of Cresacre and of Thomas More IV (the secular priest).

102. "Sir Thomas" was a title which the accused of July 1, 1535, shared with two men of the jury, Palmer and Peirt, both knights, as also with the man who, five days later, brought him the official notice of his impending execution. But the prisoner addressed him as "Mr. Pope," just as he himself was called "Mr. More" by everybody: by his wife, by the obsequious Rich, by Cranmer writing to Cromwell on his behalf (April 17, 1534), by the men sent to question John Fisher (June 12, 1535). In contrast to Roper's consistently speaking of his father-in-law as "Sir Thomas More," the dialogues in the memoir illustrate the constant use of "Mr. More" (EETS, pp. 83/13, 85/1, 100/12, 101/5, 12, 14 et alibi).

PRÉVOST, "Conscience the Ultimate Court of Appeal"

1. On 17 April 1534, an imprisonment which was to last fifteen months.

2. G. Constant, *La Réforme en Angleterre*, Paris, 1930, I, Le Schisme Anglican, pp. 68-72; cf. A. F. Pollard, *Henry VIII*, London, 1951, pp. 229-241.

3. *A Dialogue of Comfort*, Book I, ch. 16 (London, 1969), pp. 184-187.

4. More's serenity and fortitude must not screen from our sight the dramatic inner struggle he had to fight. Unwillingly, as it were, he utters words which betray the pangs of this superhuman struggle: "... things not a few terrible toward me ...." The struggle

includes agony of the heart: "your lamentable letter had not a little abashed me . . . a deadly grief unto me . . . ," and agony of the faith: "I beseech him [Our Lord] . . . give me grace and you both in all our agonies and troubles devoutly to resort prostrate unto the remembrance of that bitter agony which our Saviour suffered before his passion at the Mount." St. Thomas More, *Selected Letters*, ed. E. F. Rogers, New Haven, 1961, pp. 224–5.

5. Letter to Margaret Roper, "written with a coal," *Selected Letters*, p. 258.

6. "O salutifer Christe, tu, nuper tam timidus, qui te prosternens in faciem tam lacrymabili modo cum sudore sanguineo precabaris Patrem ut calicem passionis auferret: nunc vice versa tam subite velut gigas ad currendam viam exilis et exultas et te quaerentibus ad passionem alacer occurris obvius!" *Opera Latina*, Francfort, 1689, p. 168 b.

7. "This same short and momentary tribulation of ours, that is this present time, worketh within us the weight of glory above measure on high." *Dialogue of Comfort*, p. 291.

8. To clarify the often ambiguous ideas conjured up by the word "mysticism," one might reread the analysis by E. Boutroux of the main stages in mystical development: "an aspiration to the absolute (Sehnsucht), an effort of purification, an ascetic life . . . a re-shuffling of one's anterior life, a reorientation of one's judgement and conduct, and a reali-zation—either individual or social—of the perfect life." André Lalande, *Vocabulaire de la Philosophie*, Paris, 1938, I, p. 497.

9. More had translated Giovanni Pico della Mirandola's letter to his nephew, where one can find the familiar words of mystical literature: light, darkness, inexplicable. "When I stir thee to prayer, I stir thee not to the prayer that standeth in many words but to that prayer which in the secret chamber of the mind, in the privy closet of the soul with very affection speaketh to God, and in the most *lightsome darkness of contemplation* (italics added) not only presenteth the mind to the Father but also uniteth it with him by un-speakable ways, which only they know that have essayed." *The English Works of Sir Thomas More*, ed. W. E. Campbell, London, 1927, I, p. 367.

In the last chapter of the *Dialogue of Comfort* (pp. 293–301), one can perceive how vibrant and burning is More's passionate tender yearning for Christ. The text is reminiscent of the Middle Ages, so familiar with the Saviour incarnate, and worthy of St. Bernard.

10. J. A. Froude, *History of England from the Fall of Wolsey to the Spanish Armada*, London, 1856. See especially I, pp. 344–345, II, pp. 73–74 and 227.

11. G. Constant, *La Réforme en Angleterre*, I. Le Schisme Anglican, pp. 68–72.

12. Letter to Nicolas Wilson, *Selected Letters*, p. 231.

13. Was there not also heroism in the touching fidelity of the martyr praying for his persecutor: "Whose [God's] high goodness I most humbly beseech to incline the noble heart of the king's highness to the tender favor of you all and to favour me no better than God and myself know that my faithful heart toward him and my daily prayer for him do deserve . . ." Answer to a letter from Margaret Roper, *Selected Letters*, p. 225.

14. *Rogers*, pp. 527, 528; *Selected Letters*, pp. 232–33. Conscientious objection can be defined as follows: the absolute refusal, in the name of one's personal private conscience, to obey a specific injunction of an authority whose legitimacy is otherwise acknowledged.

15. ". . . leaving every other man to their own conscience, myself will with God's grace follow mine. For against mine own to swear were peril of my damnation." Letter to Nicolas Wilson, *Selected Letters*, pp. 227–28. We read "God's grace" (with *E.W.* p. 1443 D), not "good grace."

16. *Rogers*, p. 528. The reading "as sure as that God is in heaven" (apparatus to line 550) is less clumsy.

17. Letter of Margaret Roper to Alice Alington, *Rogers*, p. 521.

18. *Selected Letters*, p. 242.

19. More enumerates "the laws and councils, and the words of St. Austin *de Civitate Dei*, and the epistle of St. Ambrose *Ad paternum*, and the epistle of St. Basil translated out of the Greek, and the writing of St. Gregory ... and the places of Scripture," to Nicolas Wilson, his fellow-prisoner in the Tower of London, *Rogers*, p. 535, and *Selected Letters*, p. 230. Compare his words to Margaret Roper: "I forget not in this matter the counsel of Christ in the Gospel, that ere I should begin to build this castle for the safe-guard of mine own soul, I should sit and reckon what the charge would be. I counted, Margaret, full surely many a restless night ... what peril was possible for to fall to me, so far forth that I am sure there can come none above ... I never thought to change, though the very uttermost should hap me that my fear ran upon." *Rogers*, p. 530.

20. *Rogers*, p. 524.

21. The number and quality of witnesses "is of very truth a very good occasion to move him and yet not to compel him to conform his mind and conscience unto theirs." *Rogers*, p. 526.

22. *Rogers*, pp. 525, 524. Cf. *Utopia*, Basel, Nov. 1518, p. 145.

23. More sacrificed his own life in perfect serenity: "I do nobody no harm, I say none harm, I think none harm, but wish everybody good. And if this be not enough to keep a man alive, in good faith I long not to live." Letter of 2 or 3 May, 1535, to Margaret Roper, *Selected Letters*, pp. 247–8.

24. "... all sturdy stubborness whereof obstinacy groweth was very far from my mind ... It is none obstinacy to leave the causes undeclared while I could not declare them without peril." *Selected Letters*, p. 236.

25. "But I am very sure that if I died for such a law, I should die for that point innocent afore God" (*Selected Letters*, p. 237). To the same effect, More adds that his conscience and his salvation agree perfectly: "Whereto I said that I was very sure that mine own conscience, so informed as it is by such diligence as I have so long taken therein, may stand with mine own salvation" (*Selected Letters*, p. 253).

26. "Here is a high comfort lo for them that are in the case. And in this case their conscience can shew it them, and so may fulfil their hearts with spiritual joy, that the pleasure may far surmount the heaviness and the grief of all their temporal trouble." *Dialogue of Comfort*, Book I, ch. 10, p. 31.

27. "... surely if a man may, as indeed he may, have great comfort in the clearness of his conscience, that hath a false crime put upon him and by false witness proved upon him, and be falsily punished and put to worldly shame and pain therefore, an hundred times more comfort may he have in his heart, that where white is called black and right is called wrong, abideth by the truth and is persecuted for justice." *Dialogue of Comfort*, I, 10, p. 31.

28. The translation of the relics of Saint Thomas of Canterbury was commemorated on 7 July. The Octave day of St. Peter's feast (29 June) was on 6 July.

29. *Selected Letters*, p. 257.

SCHOECK, "Sir Thomas More, Humanist and Lawyer"

1. *Opus Epistolarum Des. Erasmi Roterodami*, ed. P. S. Allen, IV, 1519–21, no. 999, 17. I quote from the translation in R. W. Chambers, *Thomas More* (1935), 85.

2. J. H. Hexter, *More's Utopia: The Biography of an Idea* (Princeton, 1952), 108.

3. In the General Preface ("The Age of Littleton and Fortescue: its significance in the history of English law and its literature") to S. B. Chrimes's edition of *Sir John Fortescue, De Laudibus Legum Anglie* (Cambridge, 1942), xii.

4. See "Fortescue and the Renaissance: a Study in Transition," *Studies in the Renaissance*, VI (1959), 175–94. I have touched on Fortescue's knowledge of canon law in

"Canon Law in England on the Eve of the Reformation," *Mediaeval Studies*, XXV (1963), 132.

5. *Ibid.*, 189. See my discussion of common lawyers' attitude towards antiquity in "Early Anglo-Saxon Studies and Legal Scholarship in the Renaissance," *Studies in the Renaissance*, V (1958), 102-10.

6. *Ibid.*, 190.

Younger than Fortescue but about fifteen years older than More, Edmund Dudley carried forward Fortescue's appraisal of society, although still in the mediaeval framework of the allegory of the commonwealth as a tree. Like Fortescue's *The Governaunce of England*, a manual written for the education of an English prince, Dudley's *Tree of Commonwealth*—written while imprisoned in the Tower in 1509-10—suggests the concern of common lawyers with the welfare of their society and with the role of the common law within it.

7. Samuel E. Thorne in "The Early History of the Inns of Court with Special Reference to Gray's Inn," *Graya*, no. 50 (Michaelmas Term, 1959), 79-97; Sir Ronald Roxburgh, *The Origins of Lincoln's Inn* (Cambridge, 1963)—for discussion of which see my forthcoming review in *Speculum*.

8. *English Law and the Renaissance*, the Rede Lecture for 1901 (Cambridge, 1901); reprinted in *Selected Historical Essays of F. W. Maitland*, ed. Helen M. Cam (Cambridge, 1957), 135.

9. See "The Elizabethan Society of Antiquaries and Men of Law," *Notes & Queries*, n.s. I (1954), 417-21, and "Early Anglo-Saxon Studies and Legal Scholarship."

10. In *Manuscripta*, VI (1962), 155-67; see also "Early English Legal Literature," *Natural Law Forum*, IV (1959), 182-9.

11. Maitland, *Selected Historical Essays*, 136-7.

12. See Guido Kisch, *Humanismus und Jurisprudenz: Der Kampf zwischen mos italicus und mos gallicus an der Universität Basel* (Basel, 1955), and *Bartolus und Basel* (Basel, 1960). The work of Kisch is fully discussed by Myron P. Gilmore in "The Jurisprudence of Humanism," *Traditio*, XVII (1961), 493-501, and by myself (more briefly) in "Canon Law in England," 136. Unfortunately, M. P. Gilmore's important study *Humanists and Jurists* (Harvard, 1963), was not available to me.

13. In "The Contribution of French Jurists to the Humanism of the Renaissance," *Studies in the Renaissance*, I (1954), 92-105.

14. J. D. M. Derrett, "Withernam: A Legal Practical Joke of Sir Thomas More," *Catholic Lawyer*, VII (1961), 211 ff., citing *Harpsfield's Life* (EETS ed.), 140-2; see also Peter R. Allen, "*Utopia* and European Humanism: the Function of the Prefatory Letters and Verses," *Studies in the Renaissance*, X (1963), 91-107; and "Canon Law in England," 132 ff., 136.

15. Margaret Hastings, *The Court of Common Pleas in Fifteenth-Century England* (Ithaca, N.Y., 1947), 66.

16. I am here drawing from "Rhetoric and Law in Sixteenth-Century England," *SP*, L (1953), 113.

17. See "Sir Thomas More and Lincoln's Inn Revels," *PQ*, XXIX (1950), 428.

18. See "Rhetoric and Law," 118. Maitland has noted that Smith was a civilian and that this is the higher praise coming from a civilian: see Maitland, *Selected Historical Essays*, 138-9, 145-6.

The range and profundity of legal learning can be seen in Plowden, most recently and most excitingly studied by the late E. H. Kantorowicz in *The King's Two Bodies* (Princeton, 1957).

19. See "More and Lincoln's Inn Revels," 429.

20. All of this is to be described and discussed in a forthcoming study of the Inns of

Court, but some documentation and discussion has already appeared in my "Rhetoric and Law in Sixteenth-Century England," in "More and Lincoln's Inn Revels," and in "Canon Law in England," cited above. See also "A Legal Reading of Chaucer's *Hous of Fame*," *UTQ*, XXIII (1954), 185–92.

21. "More and Lincoln's Inn Revels," 429.

22. The incident is described by Chambers, *More*, 29.

23. A. W. Reed, *Early Tudor Drama* (London, 1926), 90–91; cf. *Inquisitiones Post Mortem* for London (Index Library), XV, 108–110, and Duff, *Century of English Book Trade*, 130. Reed goes on to comment on the pricing of these books: "The prices named vary from 4s. for a book of Statutes from Henry III to Henry VIII, to 4d. for the *Olde Abridgment* of the Statutes. The MS. Bible on parchment was valued at 2s.; Eliot's Dictionary, the Euripides and the French Virgil were priced at 1s. each. The *Grand Abridgment*, which John Rastell priced new at 42s."

24. See my "Libraries of Common Lawyers," and "William Rastell and the Prothonotaries," *N&Q*, 197 (Sept. 13, 1952), 398–9, which owes much to Reed's treatment in *Early Tudor Drama*, ch. 3.

25. As an example of method (and of the fruitfulness of such studies) see A. E. Malloch, "John Donne and the Casuists," *SEL, 1500–1900* II (1962), 57–76, even though this is only a partial statement; see further "Canon Law in England," "Rhetoric and Law in Sixteenth-Century England," and the studies cited in note 30, below.

26. It is good to be able to report that Margaret Hastings is at work on these materials.

27. The 4000-odd documents in the P.R.O. are being studied by Hubertus Schulte Herbrüggen of Münster.

28. See Derrett, "Withernam," *Catholic Lawyer*, VII (1961), 211 ff.

29. *Ibid.*, 222. Derrett adds: "The joke would have been appreciated by Rastell and Roper, who both wrote about More." He then argues, less convincingly: "Since Roper does not mention the story we can be sure that More did not tell him the key to it. If he did not tell his son-in-law and close confidant he did not tell anybody." But surely, we might observe, the reason is that Roper in general omits any aspects of More's legal career: he is telling a saint's life.

30. See Edward Surtz, *The Praise of Pleasure* (Cambridge, Mass., 1957), 98 ff., and *The Praise of Wisdom* (Chicago, 1957), 9, for suggestive introductory notes; and see Allen, "*Utopia* and European Humanism," 102 ff., on the importance of the letters of Busleiden and Budé in pointing towards the natural law. See also "The Intellectual Milieu of More's *Utopia:* Some Notes," *Moreana-Bulletin Thomas More*, no. 1 (1963), 40–46.

31. In "Canon Law in England," cited above.

32. See *History of English Law*, v (3rd ed., 1945), 269. On the immediate impact of St. German, see "The Date of the *Replication*" [seen as a reply to *Doctor and Student*], *Law Quarterly Review*, LXXVI (1960), 500–503. An edition of *Doctor and Student*, and a full study of St. German, are still great needs. Professor T. F. T. Plucknett is at work upon the first, and I hope to bring forth a monograph on St. German's career and thought, building upon the work of Baumer and others (see "Canon Law in England," 132–3).